# Dynamic HTML
*The Definitive Reference*

SECOND EDITION

# Dynamic HTML
*The Definitive Reference*

*Danny Goodman*

O'REILLY®

Beijing · Cambridge · Farnham · Köln · Paris · Sebastopol · Taipei · Tokyo

**Dynamic HTML: The Definitive Reference, Second Edition**
by Danny Goodman

Published by O'Reilly & Associates, Inc., 1005 Gravenstein Highway North, Sebastopol, CA 95472.

O'Reilly & Associates books may be purchased for educational, business, or sales promotional use. Online editions are also available for most titles (*safari.oreilly.com*). For more information contact our corporate/institutional sales department: (800) 998-9938 or *corporate@oreilly.com*.

| | |
|---|---|
| **Editor:** | Paula Ferguson |
| **Production Editor:** | Colleen Gorman |
| **Cover Designer:** | Edie Freedman |
| **Interior Designer:** | Melanie Wang |

**Printing History:**

| | |
|---|---|
| July 1998: | First Edition. |
| September 2002: | Second Edition. |

ISBN: 0-596-00316-1
[M]

# Table of Contents

**Preface** . . . . . . . . . . . . . . . . . . . . . . . . . . . . . . . . . . . . . . . . . . . . . . . . . . . . . . . . . . **ix**

**Part I.    Applying Dynamic HTML**

**1.  The State of the Art** . . . . . . . . . . . . . . . . . . . . . . . . . . . . . . . . . . . . . . . . . . . . **3**
   The Standards Alphabet Soup                                              4
   Version Headaches                                                        4
   HTML                                                                     5
   XHTML                                                                    7
   Style Sheets                                                            9
   Document Object Model                                                   11
   Web Accessibility Initiative (WAI)                                      17
   ECMAScript                                                              18
   A Fragmenting World                                                     19

**2.  Cross-Platform Compromises** . . . . . . . . . . . . . . . . . . . . . . . . . . . . . . . . . . . **21**
   What Is a Platform?                                                     21
   Navigator 4 DHTML—Fading Fast                                           22
   Internet Explorer DHTML                                                 23
   Netscape 6 (Mozilla) DHTML                                             28
   Other Browsers                                                          32
   Cross-Platform Strategies                                               32
   Cross-Platform Expectations                                             41

**3.  Adding Style Sheets to Documents** . . . . . . . . . . . . . . . . . . . . . . . . . . . . . . **42**
   Observing HTML Structures                                               42
   Understanding Block-Level Elements                                      45

Two Types of Containment 47
The CSS Platform 49
Of Style Sheets, Elements, Attributes, and Values 49
Embedding Style Sheets 51
Common Subgroup Selectors 56
Advanced Subgroup Selectors 63
Cascade Precedence Rules 66
Cross-Platform Style Differences 69

4. **Adding Dynamic Positioning to Documents** .......................... **70**
Creating Positionable Elements 71
Positioning Attributes 77
Changing Attribute Values via Scripting 82
Cross-Platform Position Scripting 85
Common Positioning Tasks 94

5. **Making Content Dynamic** ....................................... **101**
Writing Variable Content 101
Writing to Other Frames and Windows 103
Links to Multiple Frames 107
Image Swapping 108
Changing Tag Attribute Values 111
Changing Applied Style Values 112
Changing Content 117
Dynamic Tables 129
Client-Side Includes 133
Working with Text Ranges 140
Combining Forces: A Custom Newsletter 142

6. **Scripting Events** ............................................. **150**
Event Types 150
Event Objects 153
Binding Event Handlers to Elements 156
Preventing Default Event Actions 162
Event Propagation 165
Understanding Keyboard Event Data 169
Dragging Elements 173
Event Futures 178

**7. Standardization Trends** ................................ **179**
W3C Modularization 180
XHTML Modularization (XHTML Basic and 1.1) 181
CSS Modularization (CSS3) 183
DOM Modularization (DOM2 and DOM3) 184
What Is Conformance? 186

## Part II.   Dynamic HTML Reference

**8. HTML and XHTML Reference** ........................... **189**
Attribute Value Types 190
Shared HTML Element Attributes 195
Alphabetical Tag Reference 204

**9. Document Object Model Reference** ................... **469**
Property Value Types 471
About client- and offset- Properties 472
Default Property Values 476
Event Handler Properties 476
Shared Object Properties, Methods, and Events 477
Alphabetical Object Reference 532

**10. Event Reference** ...................................... **1015**
Alphabetical Event Reference 1016

**11. Style Sheet Attribute Reference** ................... **1037**
Attribute Value Types 1037
Pseudo-Elements and Pseudo-Classes 1040
At-Rules 1042
Conventions 1043
Alphabetical Attribute Reference 1044

**12. JavaScript Core Language Reference** ............... **1123**
Internet Explorer JScript Versions 1123
About Static Objects 1124
Mozilla Get and Set Methods 1125
ECMAScript Reserved Keywords 1126
Core Objects 1126
Operators 1191

Control Statements ........................................................... 1204

Miscellaneous Statements .................................................. 1211

Special (Escaped) String Characters ..................................... 1213

## Part III.   Cross References

13.   **HTML/XHTML Attribute Index** ....................................... 1217

14.   **DOM Property Index** ................................................. 1221

15.   **DOM Method Index** ................................................... 1243

16.   **DOM Event Handlers Index** ......................................... 1257

## Part IV.   Appendixes

A.   **Color Names and RGB Values** ........................................ 1267

B.   **HTML Character Entities** ............................................ 1272

C.   **Keyboard Event Character Values** .................................. 1279

D.   **Internet Explorer Commands** ....................................... 1283

E.   **HTML/XHTML DTD Support** .......................................... 1287

**Glossary** .................................................................... 1337

**Index** ....................................................................... 1345

# Preface

I am going to admit a selfish motive for writing this book and, more recently, updating it to the second edition: I needed the finished product for my own consulting and development work. After struggling in the early Version 4 browser days with tangled online references and monstrous printed versions of Netscape, Microsoft, and World Wide Web Consortium (W3C) documentation for Dynamic HTML (DHTML) features, I had had enough. My human brain could no longer store the parallels and discrepancies of the hundreds of terms for HTML attributes, style sheets, and scriptable object models. And no browser maker was about to tell me how compatible a particular feature might be in another browser. It was clearly time to roll my own reference.

At first, I thought the project would be a relatively straightforward blending of content from available sources, with a pinch of my development experience thrown in for flavoring. But the more I examined the existing documents, the worse the situation became. Developer documentation from the browser makers, and even the W3C, contained inconsistencies and incomplete (if at times erroneous) information. From the very beginning, it was clear that I could not trust everything I read, but instead had to try as much as I could on as many browsers and browser versions as I could. Multiply all that code testing by the hundreds of HTML attributes, CSS attributes, object properties, object methods, and event handlers for the first edition … before I knew it, many extra months of day-and-night coding and writing were history.

Creating the second edition was no less harrowing. The W3C DOM had come on the scene, bringing entirely new concepts about object models. Reconciling the ideals of the W3C specifications against the development work on the Mozilla browser meant many hours combing through the browser's source code and bug reports for clues about what was broken, about-to-be-fixed, or put on hold for the future. Combining those developments with an ever-growing vocabulary in the proprietary Internet Explorer world, the amount of information had grown to unimaginable proportions: more than 15,000 unique instances of properties, methods, and event handlers supported by numerous document objects.

That's all the more reason that I'm thrilled to produce this second edition, so that I have a DHTML reference that is always within arm's reach at my workstation. I even have the duct tape ready for the day when the cover surrenders to too many twists and turns.

I would be the last person on the planet to promise that this book is perfect in every way. While the predictability and reliability of DHTML scripting has increased significantly since the days of the first edition, I still find many discrepancies between vendor or standards documentation and observable reality in mainstream browsers. In such cases, I document the reality. In doing so, I recall my high school physics teacher who would shout to the class, "Seeing is believing!" and then promptly demonstrate an optical illusion. I hope that my long experience in this field has helped me see through the illusions, so that I may relate the *true* reality.

## What You Should Already Know

Because this is a reference book, it has been written with the assumption that you have at least dabbled in Dynamic HTML. You should already be HTML-literate and know the basics of client-side scripting in JavaScript. You need not be a DHTML expert, but even the instructional chapters of Part I are very much crash courses, intended for readers who are already comfortable with hand-coding web pages (or at least modifying the HTML generated by WYSIWYG authoring tools).

## Contents of This Book

This book is divided into four parts:

Part I, *Applying Dynamic HTML*
> After making sense of the alphabet soup of industry standards surrounding DHMTL, the chapters in this part demonstrate the use of cascading style sheets, element positioning, dynamic content, and scripting events. These chapters reveal not only how each browser implements the various DHTML technologies, but also how to deploy as much as possible in a form that works on both Internet Explorer and Netscape Navigator.

Part II, *Dynamic HTML Reference*
> The chapters of Part II provide at-a-glance references for the tags, attributes, objects, properties, methods, and event handlers of HTML, XHTML, CSS, DOM, and core JavaScript. These are the chapters I use all the time to look up the attributes of an HTML element or to see whether a particular object property is available in the desired browser brands and versions. Every effort has been expended to present this information in a condensed yet meaningful format.

Part III, *Cross References*

The chapters in Part III slice through the information of Part II along different angles. Perhaps you recall the name of an attribute you found useful some time ago, but don't recall which elements provide that attribute. Here you can look up that attribute (or object property, method, or event handler) to find all the items that recognize it.

Part IV, *Appendixes*

Several appendixes provide quick lookup for a variety of values useful in HTML authoring and scripting. New in this edition is Appendix E, *HTML/XHTML DTD Support*, which provides a quick view of element and attribute support in five popular HTML and XHTML DTDs. A glossary also gives you quick explanations of some of the new and potentially confusing terminology of DHTML.

# Conventions Used in This Book

*Italic* is used for:

- Pathnames, filenames, program names, email addresses, and web sites
- New terms where they are defined

**Bold** is used for:

- Keys
- GUI menu items and buttons

`Constant Width` is used for:

- Any HTML, CSS, or scripting term, including HTML tags, attribute names, object names, properties, methods, and event handlers
- All HTML and script code listings

`Constant Width Italic` is used for:

- Method and function parameters or assigned value placeholders that indicate an item is to be replaced by a real value in actual use

Throughout Part II, compatibility tables accompany most entries. A number shown for an item indicates the version of the designated browser or web standard in which the term was first introduced. If an item premiere predates Navigator 2, Internet Explorer 3, or HTML 3.2, it is assigned the value "all". If an item is not supported by a browser or standard as the book went to press, it is assigned the value "n/a". If an item has been removed from a browser, a less-than symbol precedes the version that no longer supports the item (e.g., <6). And if an item is available in only one browser version, the number is surrounded by vertical bars (e.g., |4|).

# Request for Comments

Please address comments and questions concerning this book to the publisher:

O'Reilly & Associates, Inc.
1005 Gravenstein Highway North
Sebastopol, CA 95472
(800) 998-9938 (in the United States or Canada)
(707) 829-0515 (international/local)
(707) 829-0104 (fax)

Your feedback on the quality of this book is important to us. If you discover any errors, bugs, typos, explanations that you cannot grok, or platform-specific issues not covered here, please let us know. You can email your bug reports and comments to us at:

bookquestions@oreilly.com

Also be sure to check the web page for this book, which lists errata, examples, or any additional information. You can access this page at:

http://www.oreilly.com/catalog/dhtmlref2

Previously reported errors and corrections are available for public view and further comment.

For more information about books, conferences, Resource Centers, and the O'Reilly Network, see the O'Reilly web site at:

http://www.oreilly.com

# Acknowledgments

Despite the ever-increasing heft of the books I have written in the last several years, you'll have to take my word for it: I do not delight in making forests tremble with each added word. It's just that the subject matter has grown to outsized proportions. No matter how succinct one tries to be, the pages add up quickly.

A book of this scale and design complexity places enormous burdens on a great many people who turn my mere bytes into gorgeous pages and chapters. Thanks to Tim O'Reilly for continuing to be true to his author-friendly roots, while building a technology powerhouse whose reputation for quality is awe-inspiring. His editorial and production staffs consistently work miracles under extreme deadline pressures. My favorite miracle worker is the editor for both editions of this title, Paula Ferguson. She not only groks the technology, but she instinctively knows what's best for readers and sees to it that the book delivers on the promise.

I also appreciated having someone else who knows this subject look over my shoulder, to make sure I didn't fall asleep at the keyboard while describing the 700th object property. For this massive second edition, my friend Rob Hoexter—a first-rate user interface designer and DHTML coder from the trenches—sacrificed what should have been a well-deserved multi-week vacation to test my code, find gaffes, and recommend improvements that I incorporated into the text. For reading this reference book from cover to cover while offering insightful comments *and* maintaining his sanity, Rob deserves a medal.

Although my words have appeared in print for nearly 25 years, no writing of mine has produced as much fan mail (make that email) as the first edition of this book. My true reward, though, comes from having helped you unlock your own talent to create great solutions. Your encouragement has inspired me to do what I hope is an even better job this second time around to guide you through the newest advances in client-side scripting and web development. To new readers, I bid you welcome. Let's all have some fun exploring the power and promise of Dynamic HTML.

# PART I

# Applying Dynamic HTML

This part of the book, Chapters 1 through 7, tries to make sense of the alphabet soup of industry standards surrounding DHTML and demonstrates the use of cascading style sheets, element positioning, dynamic content, and scripting events. These chapters explain how Microsoft Internet Explorer and Netscape Navigator implement the various DHTML technologies, and they discuss how to develop cross-browser web applications.

Chapter 1, *The State of the Art*

Chapter 2, *Cross-Platform Compromises*

Chapter 3, *Adding Style Sheets to Documents*

Chapter 4, *Adding Dynamic Positioning to Documents*

Chapter 5, *Making Content Dynamic*

Chapter 6, *Scripting Events*

Chapter 7, *Standardization Trends*

# The State of the Art

An invisible, gravity-like force continues to draw the computing world to the World Wide Web. The ubiquity of the web browser in desktop, laptop, and even handheld computers opens a magic gateway for people and organizations to communicate ideas and carry on daily business. The Web isn't merely a place to publish a personal fanzine or sell thing-a-ma-jigs through e-commerce. Institutions are converting massive corporate software applications to the Web, so that employees, vendors, and customers can interact directly with huge databases through the usually free browser that comes preloaded on every computer.

The allure—in theory anyway—is that publishers and application developers can rely on well-known standards that facilitate the rendering of data and user interface elements. Freed from details of painting dots on monitor screens, managing memory, and controlling internal data flows on dozens of operating systems, publishers and developers can focus on their content and server-side data handling. Browsers do all the operating-system–specific dirty work by interpreting Hypertext Markup Language (HTML) directives embedded in the content.

Publishing content in today's videogame-charged e-atmosphere, however, creates enormous challenges to attract an audience and keep it entertained, even if all you offer is simple text and image content. Application developers face related challenges to minimize delays between user actions and program responses: every second waiting for a page refresh is lost productivity.

The industry, which includes standards bodies and commercial interests that provide input to those bodies, has risen to the challenge. In particular, browser-oriented standards have expanded rapidly to embrace the notion of *dynamic* content—pages that can "think and do" on their own, without much help from the server once they have been loaded in the browser. Additionally, some browser makers support features that are frequently very useful, but are available on only one brand of browser or on just one operating system.

Although dynamic web pages are implemented under the umbrella of Dynamic HTML (DHTML), successful deployment requires knowledge of several technologies and standards that exist outside the charter of the original HTML Working Group. In this chapter, I'll discuss the applicable standardization efforts. As disparate as this collection may appear at first, they all magically come together as a system to let creative designers implement engaging DHTML content.

## The Standards Alphabet Soup

There is no such thing as a single Dynamic HTML standard. DHTML is an amalgam of specifications that stem from multiple standards efforts and proprietary technologies built into current versions of the two most popular DHTML-capable browsers, Microsoft Internet Explorer 4 or later and Netscape Navigator 6 or later (a product based on an open-source browser engine created by The Mozilla Organization), as well as numerous less-popular, but no less feature-rich browsers. Browsers prior to Netscape 6 and Internet Explorer 4 employed either very few DHTML capabilities or techniques that today's browsers no longer support.

Efforts by various standards bodies and working groups within those bodies are as fluid and fast moving as any Internet-related technology. As a savvy web content author these days, you must know the acronyms of all relevant standards, such as HTML, XHTML, CSS, DOM, and ECMA for starters. You also have to keep track of the current release of each standard, in addition to the release that is incorporated into each version of each browser that you are developing for. Unfortunately for the authoring community, it is not practical for the various standards bodies and the browser makers to operate synchronously with each other. Market pressures force browser makers to release new versions independent of the schedules of the standards bodies.

## Version Headaches

As a further complication, there are the inevitable prerelease versions of browsers and standards. Browser prereleases are sometimes called "preview editions" or "beta" versions. While not officially released, these versions give you a chance to see what new functionality will be available for content display in the next-generation browsers. Authors who follow browser releases closely sometimes worry when certain aspects of their current pages fail to work properly in prerelease versions. The fear is that the new version of the browser is going to break a carefully crafted masterpiece that runs flawlessly in released versions of the browser.

Prerelease browsers are valuable resources for content developers. On the one hand, testing existing content on a preview release allows you to uncover bugs in the browser before the browser is released. Report those bugs! Wherever possible, provide a simple test case (or link to a test case) that proves the bug so that the browser engineers can see exactly what you mean and test their fixes against real code. On the other hand, testing may allow you to learn about the rare case in which a feature you rely on is removed or changed (usually to meet a standard definition). While browsers tend to be backward compatible with previous versions, many developers were caught unaware when Netscape 6, in its effort to adopt industry standards, completely dropped support for a couple of features implemented in the previous version (Netscape 4). Developers who tested preview versions of the browser would have learned of this important change early in the process, and planned for the new deployment ahead of time.

Avoid the urge, however, to modify your public HTML or scripting code to accommodate what may be a temporary bug in a prerelease version of a browser. Any page visitor who uses a prerelease browser does so at his own risk. If your pages are breaking on that browser, they're probably not the only ones on the Web that are breaking. A user of a prerelease browser must understand that using such a browser for mission-critical web work is as dangerous as entrusting one's life work to a beta version of a word processing program.

On the standards side, working groups usually publish prerelease (draft) versions of their standards. These documents are very important to the people who build browsers and authoring tools. The intent of publishing a working draft is not much different from making a prerelease browser version public. The goal is to get as many concerned netizens as possible looking over the material to find flaws or shortcomings before the standard is published.

Speaking of standards, it is important to recognize that the final releases of these documents from standards bodies are called not "standards" but "recommendations." You will also find details within a recommendation that are optional, thus allowing a browser maker to claim full compliance, even when not every feature is implemented.

No law or contract forces browser makers to implement the recommendations. Fortunately, from a marketing angle, it plays well to the web audience that a company's browser adheres to the "standards." Eventually—after enough release cycles of both standards and browsers allow everyone to catch up with each other—our lives as content creators should become easier.

In the meantime, the following sections provide a snapshot of the various standards, and their implementation in browsers, as they relate to the technologies that affect DHTML.

# HTML

While the World Wide Web Consortium (W3C) continues to refer to its document content markup effort (*http://www.w3.org/DF/*) as HTML, Version 4.01 of HTML (published in December 1999) may mark the end of a venerable sequence of recommendations to go by that four-letter acronym. Subsequent versions will likely be released as part of the XHTML effort (described in the next section). In the evolution of HTML and content delivery on the Web, however, the Version 4 family played a critical transitional role in the way authors regarded their content.

Many of the features that were new to HTML 4 were designed for browsers that make the graphical user interface of a web page more accessible to users who cannot see a monitor or use a keyboard (see "Web Accessibility Initiative (WAI)," later in this chapter). The new tags and attributes also acknowledge that a key component of the name World Wide Web is World. Users of all different written and spoken languages need equal access to the content of the Web. Thus, HTML 4 included support for the alphabets of most languages and provided the ability to specify that a page be rendered from right to left, rather than left to right, to accommodate languages that are written that way.

Perhaps the most important long-term impact of HTML 4, however, was distancing a web page's content from its formatting. Strictly speaking, the purpose of HTML is to provide structural meaning to the content of pages. That's what each tag does: this blurb of text is a paragraph, another segment is labeled internally as an acronym, and a block over there is reserved for data loaded in from an external multimedia file. HTML 4 sought to wean authors from the familiar tags that make text larger, bold, and red, for example. That kind of information is formatting information, and it belongs to a separate standardization effort related to content style.

In the HTML 4 world, a content author indicates that a chunk of text in a paragraph is to receive emphasis. The HTML standard, however, does not dictate whether the browser conveys emphasis through a bold or italic or green font. Instead, a separate style definition controls the formatting for an emphasized string of text. This separation of content and style allows the same content to be rendered differently for a variety of output devices. When the text is viewed in a browser on a video monitor, the color may be green and the style italic, but when the same page is viewed through a projection system, it may be a different shade of green, to compensate for the different ambient lighting conditions, and bold, so it is more readable at a distance. And when the content is being read aloud electronically for a blind user, the synthesized voice speaks the tagged words with more emphasis. The key point here is that the content—the words in this case—is written and tagged once. Style definitions, either in the same document or maintained in separate files that are linked into the document, can be modified and enhanced independently of the content.

HTML 4 was also the first version of HTML to account for the role that client-side scripting was playing in the real world. Not only were <script> and <noscript> tags part of the specification, but most elements that get rendered on the page had a basic set of scripting event handler attributes explicitly defined for them (onclick, onmouseover, onkeypress, and the like). If nothing else, these acknowledgments validated the idea of client-side processing instructions delivered as part of the document. It also allowed HTML-validating programs to accept attributes that link elements to script actions.

Internet Explorer 4 (for all operating-system platforms) was the first browser to provide a reasonably complete implementation of the HTML 4.0 recommendation. The depth of support improved significantly in IE 5, with Microsoft's IE 6 promotional information proclaiming complete HTML 4 compatibility. On the Netscape side, Navigator 4 included limited support for HTML 4 (the browser preceded the standard chronologically), whereas the new browser engine in Netscape 6 (and especially Netscape 6.2 and later) goes to great lengths to support the required elements and attributes.

## XHTML

The industry-wide drive to embrace the Extensible Markup Language (XML) way of describing electronic information had a big impact on the W3C HTML Working Group. For example, while HTML has a rigid set of elements and attributes, XML supports the creation of new elements and attributes that accommodate a new or specialized (discipline-specific) kind of data. If an HTML document can exist in an open, XML-flavored world, a content author can wrap content inside a custom contextual tag that might be used in conjunction with a style sheet to create a special appearance for that kind of element. If such a document were linked to an external Document Type Definition (DTD), the document would pass XML validation, yet in all other respects, the document would behave like an HTML document.

To demonstrate how traditional web page content can (some might say should) course its way across the Net as XML data, the W3C reconfigured the HTML 4 standard so that it also adhered to fundamental XML tagging practices. The result is an XMLized HTML recommendation, or XHTML for short. Version 1.0 of the XHTML recommendation is a very thin document because it encompasses all HTML 4.01 elements and attributes. Most of the XML-oriented features of XHTML govern how authors should format source code and structure elements and attributes in a document.

In concert with the trend of many W3C recommendations, XHTML evolved to embrace the idea of modularity. In place of one giant XHTML recommendation, the group divided the elements into 20 modules of related elements. The version of the standard that embraces this modularization is known as XHTML 1.1. The rationale behind modularization is to allow specialized devices to support subsets of the XHTML standard that make the most sense for the content they intend to convey or the rendering facilities of the device. For example, an HTML-rendering engine embedded into a cellular telephone might not need to support the loading of external code objects. Such a phone-based "browser" could support all XHTML modules except for the Object Module, which contains the object and param HTML elements. For more details about XHTML 1.1 modules, see Chapter 7.

It is important to bear in mind that as of XHTML 1.1, no new elements or attributes were added to what had been in the HTML 4.01 recommendation. Some long-standing items are deprecated, however (as detailed in Chapter 8). With only a few exceptions, the source code structure and formatting requirements of XHTML coincide with many coders' existing styles. In any case, the requirements impose a more rigorous style in order to pass XML source code validation. The key requirements are:

- HTML tag and attribute names must be spelled only in lowercase characters
- All attribute values must be quoted
- All elements that can contain other elements require an end tag
- All empty elements, such as img and hr, require either an end tag or must include a forward slash immediately before the right angle bracket (as in <hr/>)
- All attributes must be stated as name-value pairs, including those that had previously been defined as one-word, minimalized attributes (e.g., checked="checked")
- The name attribute is deprecated in favor of the id attribute
- The target attribute (of the a and form elements, for instance) is not permitted in Strict validation

Moreover, in recognition of compatibility issues with HTML code that must also run on non-XHTML–aware browsers, the XHTML 1.0 recommendation includes provisions for backward compatibility. For example, because older browsers may become confused by an end tag for an empty element (a </br> tag, for example), you can use the XML internalized slash technique, but with an extra space before the end slash, as in <br /> or <hr />, which older browsers accommodate. In the case of forms, where an older browser needs the name attribute to convey the form or form control's identifier with a submission, you can assign the same identifier to the name and id attributes of a form element or form control.

Neither IE 6 nor Netscape 6 or later requires that HTML content follow the XHTML format. In fact, because these browsers (and many more versions to come) must be compatible with a web full of HTML content in the real world, the decision to follow the XHTML recommendation is up to each content developer. If you take comfort in having your source code successfully pass XHTML validation, you can specify the XHTML document type at the top of your documents. Be aware, however, that such validation will reject proprietary attributes (such as IE-specific event handler attributes) unless they are labeled with XML namespaces. But even if you are not overly concerned with following the XHTML recommendation, you should nevertheless gravitate toward its formatting requirements; they will become the norm as automated authoring tools begin generating code to meet that standard.

Example listings throughout this book focus more on the scripting than the tagging. Therefore, HTML code examples in the present edition of this book follow a middle ground in the HTML/XHTML discussion. They adhere to XHTML formatting for tags and attributes, but they follow HTML 4 end tag rules. Except where intended for full backward compatibility, examples try to avoid elements and attributes deprecated in HTML 4 to instill good practice as authors move toward XHTML. Also, for the sake of demonstration clarity and brevity, tags occasionally include event handlers and other attributes that go beyond the limited set that validate under XHTML-

Strict. Unless otherwise specified, however, all listings assume a browser's default document type. If you are an experienced XHTML author, you won't have to go far to adapt these listings to XHTML document types if you so desire.

# Style Sheets

A style sheet contains definitions of how content should be rendered on the page. The link between a style sheet and the content it influences is either the tag name of the HTML element that holds the content or an identifier associated with the element by way of an attribute (such as the id or class attribute). When a style sheet defines a border, the style definition doesn't know (or care) whether the border will be wrapped around a paragraph of text, an image, or an arbitrary group of elements. All the style knows is that it specifies a border of a particular thickness, color, and type for whatever element or identifier is associated with the style. That's how the separation of style from content works: the content is ignorant of the style and the style is ignorant of the content.

A W3C working group undertook the task of creating a supplementary markup syntax that allowed styles to be associated with HTML content (*http://www.w3c.org/Style/*). The technology, called Cascading Style Sheets (CSS), matured relatively quickly during a time when mainstream browser versions had difficulty keeping up with the latest standards. The W3C document that contains the most detailed information about CSS is the second version of the recommendation, called CSS2. This version includes the original CSS1 standard, special features for element positioning (initially released separately as CSS-P), and a large number of features that are new with CSS2.

Just as the current XHTML effort embraces modularization, so does CSS. The recommendation known as CSS3 is a modularized version of CSS2. Given the enormous size and range of style attributes in CSS2, modularization provides browsers an opportunity to claim support for well-defined subsets of the CSS2 recommendation, without supporting features that don't apply to the devices they support. For example, CSS2 contains many attributes that control how content should sound when delivered on a client device employing synthesized speech. One attribute defines whether the sequence of numerals "123" should be spoken as "One two three" or "One hundred twenty-three." This kind of style attribute is meaningless for a browser designed to render on a video display for sighted users. See Chapter 7 for more information about CSS3 modules. Chapter 11 provides a complete reference for CSS style attributes.

## CSS Rationale

The Cascading Style Sheets recommendation lets authors define style rules that are applied to HTML elements. A rule may apply to a single element, a related group of elements, or all elements of a particular type (such as all p elements). Style rules influence the rendering of elements, including their color, alignment, border, margins, and padding between borders and the content. Style rules can also control specialty items, such as whether an ol element uses letters or roman numerals as item markers. CSS defines a full syntax for assigning style attributes to rules.

Theoretically, CSS frees you from the anarchy behind the arbitrary way that each browser measures fonts and other values. Font sizes can be specified in real pixel or point sizes, instead of the absurd 1-through-7 relative scale of HTML. If you want a paragraph or a picture indented from the left margin, you can do so with the precision of ems or picas, instead of relying on hokey arrangements of tables and transparent images. (Of course, in practice, a browser's default style sheet and user preference settings can still prevent text styles from appearing identical everywhere. We're still a long way from replicating the precision of print publishing on pages viewed through a web browser.)

Many of the style specifications that go into CSS rules derive their inspiration from now-deprecated (that is, soon-to-be-deleted) HTML tag attributes that used to be the only way to control visual aspects of elements. Visual properties, such as element alignment, belong in style sheet rules, rather than align or valign attributes inside an element tag. In some cases, style sheet rules even supplant entire HTML elements. For example, in the world of CSS, you do not direct font changes for a string of text within a paragraph by way of <font> tags. Instead, you define the font characteristics for that special text in a style sheet rule and then associate the rule with a structural HTML element that surrounds the affected content.

On their own, style sheets are not dynamic. They simply set rules that guide the browser in rendering content as a page loads. But scripts can change style rules after a page has loaded. Of course, the browser must be constructed to allow such on-the-fly changes. I'll have more to say about that in the section on the document object model.

The earliest browsers to support a substantial amount of CSS1 were Netscape Navigator 4 and Internet Explorer 4 (IE 3 implemented a smaller set of CSS1 attributes). These early implementations exhibit numerous quirks in the ways the more complex style features work. This is especially true in Navigator 4 with respect to form controls and tables (inheritance rules frequently fail) and in all browsers in the area of CSS-produced element borders. You find much more thorough support for CSS1 and a healthy selection of CSS2 attributes starting in IE 5 for the Macintosh, IE 5.5 for Windows, and Netscape 6 (for all operating-system platforms). With such broad support among installed browsers, basic style sheet control of content formatting is deployed very commonly around the Web.

## Element Positioning and Layering

Begun as a separate working group effort, Cascading Style Sheets-Positioning offers script authors much more in the way of interactivity on a page: more of the D in DHTML. Its inclusion into the CSS2 recommendation validates the techniques and user interface possibilities that positioning offers.

> ## Speaking of "Quirks"
>
> The convergence of W3C standards and releases of the Version 6 browsers from Microsoft and Netscape have given the browser makers a chance to atone for their most egregious past implementation sins. But the browsers must also walk a fine line between supporting the terabytes of legacy HTML currently published on the Web and promoting the "right" way of marking up text according to present-day standards. To that end, both IE 6 and Netscape 6 let your documents dictate whether the browsers should behave the old, quirky way (so that your old code—but not the NN 4 layer element—continues to work the same way in the new browsers), or the new, standards-compatible way. The switch that toggles the browser between modes is the content of the `<!DOCTYPE>` element, which must be the very first line of your HTML file. Chapter 8 covers this element in detail, but the impact of your choice also affects numerous CSS characteristics, as described throughout Chapter 11.

The basic notion of positioning is that an element or group of elements can be placed in its own plane above the main document. The element lives in its own transparent layer, so it can be hidden, shown, precisely positioned, and moved around the page without disturbing the other content or the layout of the document. It was CSS-based positioning that first allowed overlapping of HTML elements.

As remarkable as these features sound, the syntax for turning an element into a positioned element is no more difficult than making an element's text appear in a color or bold font weight. A handful of CSS attributes, described in Chapter 4, follow the same syntax conventions as other CSS attributes.

By controlling position-related properties of an element, a script can make elements fly around the page or it can allow the user to drag elements around the page. Content can pop up out of nowhere or expand to let the viewer see more content—all without reloading the page or contacting the server. Scripted positioning with nearly identical cross-browser syntax is possible starting with IE 5 and Netscape 6.

# Document Object Model

When an HTML page loads into a scriptable browser, the browser creates a hidden, internal roadmap of all the elements it recognizes as scriptable objects. This roadmap is hierarchical in nature, with the most "global" object—the browser window or frame—containing a document, which, in turn, contains, say, a form, which, in turn, contains form elements. For a script to communicate with one of these objects, it must be able to reference the object in order to call one of the object's methods or set one of its property values. Document objects are the "things" that scripts work with.

## The Netscape 4 Layer—R.I.P.

Prior to the release of the CSS-P recommendation, Netscape had been lobbying the W3C to adopt a different technique for handling content positioning, involving both a new HTML tag and a scriptable object. Navigator 4 implemented the `<layer>` tag (and a corresponding scriptable `layer` object). A Netscape layer is conceptually the same as a CSS-P layer, except that Netscape wanted to make it a part of the HTML syntax as well.

Unfortunately for Netscape and Navigator 4, the W3C did not adopt the `<layer>` tag for HTML 4.0, preferring to make layering a part of CSS. In the effort to make the next browser generation as standards-compliant as possible, the group responsible for future development of the Netscape browser (the Mozilla group) made the difficult but correct decision to abandon the `<layer>` tag. Thus, the element and the way scripts reference that element, work only in Navigator 4. The need to support this syntax diminishes each day, as Navigator 4 browsers retire from the installed base in favor of Mozilla-based browsers, IE, or other modern browsers.

Without question, the most difficult challenges facing scripters throughout the short history of scriptable browsers has been how each browser builds its internal roadmap of objects. This roadmap is called a *document object model* (DOM). When one browser implements an object as scriptable but the other doesn't, it drives scripters and page authors to distraction. Pioneering scripters felt the sting of this problem when they implemented image-swapping mouse rollovers in Navigator 3, only to discover that images were not scriptable objects in Internet Explorer 3. As a result, their IE 3 users were getting script errors when visiting the sites and moving their mice across the hot images. The situation only worsened when Microsoft developed its DOM for IE 4 in one direction, while Netscape took a different path for Navigator 4.

In an effort to standardize this area, a separate working group of the W3C is charged with setting recommendations for a Document Object Model (*http://ww.w3c.org/DOM/*). The foundation for the W3C DOM is the Core DOM module, which defines fundamental building blocks (objects, properties, and methods) that apply to any document-oriented web content (whether pure XML or HTML and its descendants). The Core module includes definitions for basic objects, such as the document, an element, element text content, and an element's attributes. Beyond those generic building blocks of the Core, specialized modules define the objects that apply to particular kinds of documents or entities within documents. For example, the working group patterned an HTML module of the W3C DOM after the elements defined for the W3C HTML 4 specification. Every HTML 4 element is represented in the HTML DOM module as a DOM object. Thus, the HTML DOM includes objects for the p element, the form element, and so on down the line. HTML 4 element attributes, in turn, become properties of HTML DOM element objects. This is how a script can read the value assigned to an attribute in the source code and perhaps modify the value in response to user activity.

A primary goal of this effort is to create a recognized common denominator among browsers (or any document engine). By the time the first round of W3C DOM standards came into being, however, Netscape and Microsoft had already deployed two or more versions of their own rapidly diverging DOMs. With companies that held sometimes radically different philosophies participating in the W3C DOM process, finding a common ground was not easy.

The resulting recommendation, as best described in the modularized DOM Level 2, created a DOM that in many ways resembled none of the existing models. While the recommendation maintains backward compatibility with early object models (as implemented in Navigator 3 and IE 3), and it exposes all HTML elements as objects just as the IE 4 model does, the W3C DOM created an entirely new framework for pieces of a document. Perhaps the greatest impact on DOM coding practices at the time was in the way scripts reference elements.

## DOM Level 0

The first object model, which the W3C specification calls DOM Level 0 (but in truth predates the W3C DOM), was restricted to only a handful of element objects. Inside a window, the document object is the master container of all content. After a document loaded into the browser, its content was largely static with the exception of forms and form controls (text fields, buttons, and select lists). References to element objects (plus a couple of abstract objects, such as location and history) entailed a hierarchical name, starting with the document object. To refer to a form control, the reference "walked" through an element hierarchy that matched the nested tag hierarchy in the document—at least to the extent that elements were recognized as objects. Thus, a reference to a form control included the document, the form, and the control itself:

```
document.formName.controlName
```

These models also treated multiple instances of elements as arrays of those elements. Using JavaScript array syntax, you could reference the element by way of numeric or named array indexes, as in:

```
document.forms[0].elements[0]
```

or:

```
document.forms["formName"].elements["controlName"]
```

or any combination of reference types:

```
document.forms[0].controlName
```

Given the initial purpose of scriptable browsers—primarily for client-side form validation and dynamic navigation—the limited object model was sufficient. Despite its limitations, DOM Level 0 from Navigator 2, Navigator 3, and IE 3 was intriguing enough to attract a wide audience hungry for more flexibility.

## Microsoft IE 4 DOM

In advance of the W3C's DOM activity, Microsoft boosted the powers of IE 4 to allow scripts to modify any piece of a document's content after the page had loaded. The key to this feature was automatic reflow of the page to accommodate changes in an element's dimensions due to the scripted change.

With the luxury of being able to render any modified content, it was meaningful to expose all HTML elements as scriptable objects for the IE 4 DOM. What scripters needed, however, was a quick way to reference those elements without having to take the structure of the document into account. A property of the document object (or any other container object for that matter) flattened the hierarchy of nested elements so that as long as the script had the id of the desired element, the document.all array (collection) offered instant access to the element in multiple syntax approaches, such as:

```
document.all.elementID
document.all("elementID")
document.all["elementID"]
```

In addition to this referencing syntax, the IE 4 DOM empowered all elements with properties and methods that facilitated the reading and writing of plain text and HTML content on the fly. You could, for example, insert some HTML inside an element by first assembling a string of HTML tags, attributes, and content, and then assigning that string to the innerHTML property of an existing element. The inserted content got rendered instantly, as the page reflowed to adjust for the inserted HTML. If the content contained no tags, you could assign the string to the element's innerText property.

The nested structure of HTML elements also played a role in the IE4 DOM. The notion of parent and child elements followed traditional paths. An element's container was its parent element; an element nested inside another was a child of the outer element. The element was king, and an element contained either just plain text or additional HTML elements.

## W3C DOM Architecture

The W3C DOM working group based its architecture on an object type that is more granular than the element: the *node*. The concept behind this is that a document and its contents can be diagrammed, in a sense, as a hierarchy of items—nodes—of different types. Some nodes are containers (branches from which other nodes hang), while others are self-contained (leaves at the ends of branches).

The root node of a document is the *document node*—the master container of all content. In an HTML document, an item denoted in the source code by a tag is an *element node*. Text content between a matched start and end tag pair is a *text node*. Other types of nodes also occur in a document, such as *attribute nodes, comment*

---

*nodes*, and *document-type nodes*. To visualize the basic node arrangement, consider the following HTML for a simple document:

```
<!DOCTYPE ... >
<html>
<head>
</head>
<body>
<p>A simple paragraph.</p>
</body>
</html>
```

Figure 1-1 shows a diagrammed version of the node hierarchy of this document.

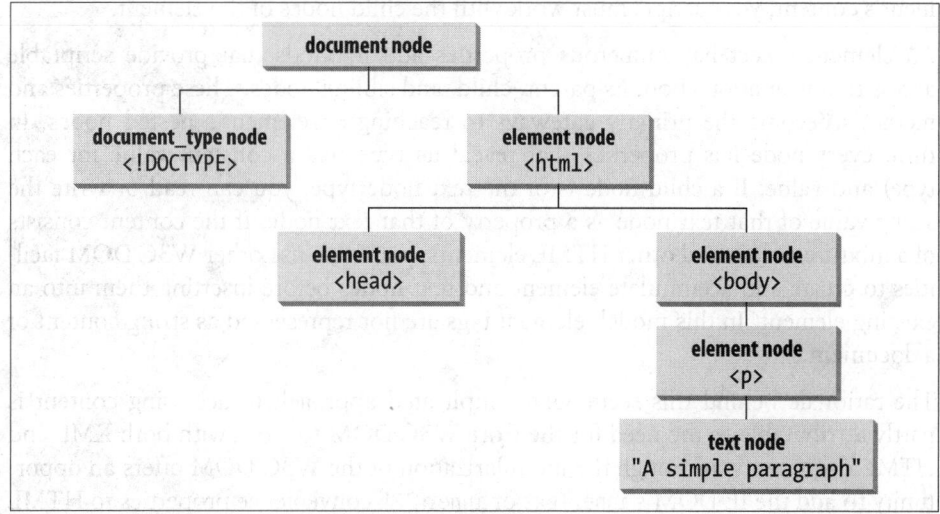

*Figure 1-1. A simple document's node structure*

The tree structure shown in Figure 1-1 lends itself to describing relationships among elements in parent-child terms. For example, the document node in the illustration has two child nodes, the DOCTYPE and html elements. These two child nodes are siblings to each other. The html element node is, itself, also a parent to the head and body nodes. (Note that some W3C DOM clients, such as Netscape 6, also treat line breaks in HTML source code as separate text nodes. Examples later in this book take this behavior into account.)

As you can see, the parent-child relationships are not conceptually different from the containment hierarchy that well-formed HTML documents exhibit. In fact, the IE 4 DOM, at least at the element level, treats relationships the same way. But when it comes to using the W3C DOM to reference elements and what you see in the source code as text content, the approach is different from any DOM that came before it.

In place of the IE 4 document.all collection, the W3C DOM implements a root document object method, document.getElementById( ), that dives through the entire document in search of an `id` attribute value matching the parameter of the method. For example, if a paragraph element's `id` attribute is `myP`, a script can reference the paragraph as follows:

```
document.getElementById("myP")
```

The method returns a reference to the element, whose properties and methods may be invoked as needed. Unlike the IE 4 DOM, however, a W3C DOM element object has no direct knowledge of its child nodes, other than the fact that they exist. For example, the text content of a W3C DOM p element is not a property of the p element object. In other words, W3C DOM Level 2 provides no analog to the `innerText` or `innerHTML` properties of the IE 4 DOM. To read or modify the content of an element's content, your scripts must work with the child nodes of the element.

An element object has numerous properties and methods that provide scriptable access to information about its parent, child, and sibling nodes. These properties and methods become the primary gateways to reaching an element's nested nodes. In turn, every node has properties that reveal its type (via a constant value for each type) and value. If a child node is of the text node type, you can read or write the string value of that text node as a property of that text node. If the content consists of a mixture of text and other HTML elements, you must use other W3C DOM facilities to create and accumulate element and text nodes before inserting them into an existing element. In this model, element tags are not represented as string content of a document.

The rationale behind this seemingly complicated approach to accessing content is partly attributable to the need for the Core W3C DOM to work with both XML and HTML documents. Although the modularization of the W3C DOM offers an opportunity to add the IE DOM's `innerText` or `innerHTML` convenience properties to HTML element objects, this has not occurred in the HTML module for Level 2 (which remains unfinished as of this writing). Recognizing the significant scripting convenience of reading and writing an element's content as a string, however, the Mozilla engine (in Netscape 6 and later) implements the `innerHTML` property for all element objects. You can, of course, use the `innerHTML` property to put plain text into an element as well, so this one property handles all situations nicely.

Netscape 6 implements a substantial portion of the W3C DOM Level 2 specification. Support in IE was sketchy in IE 5, but IE has gradually embraced more—but certainly not all—of the specification through Version 6. In other words, IE 5 and later support both the Microsoft proprietary DOM (from IE 4) and significant portions of the W3C DOM. As of IE 6, however, Microsoft has not implemented the W3C DOM modules governing events and text ranges. Chapter 5 and Chapter 6 cover the current W3C and IE DOM implementations, while Chapter 9 provides a complete cross-DOM reference.

## An Object-Oriented Model

The parent-child relationship between nodes in a document depends solely on the nesting and source code order of the tags and related content. This kind of containment hierarchy, however, does not necessarily imply inheritance of properties from parent to child. If you assign a value to the id attribute or property of a table element, nested rows do not inherit the parent element's ID. The closest that inheritance touches HTML elements is in the style sheet area, where most style attributes are inherited by an element's child elements (but CSS inheritance is governed by rules that have nothing to do with object orientation).

The W3C DOM, however, is built upon an abstract model that looks very object oriented. The abstract model defines what constitutes a node, an element, and so on. All content-related objects are derived from the Node object, defined in the Core module. This fundamental building block comes with nearly three dozen constants, properties, and methods that define what a Node is and what it can do. More specific kinds of nodes, such as the Document, Element, Attr[ibute], and Text nodes, inherit all of the Node object's constants, properties, and methods, adding properties or methods that are appropriate for whatever kind of node it is. Carrying this inheritance further to the DOM's HTML module, the HTMLElement inherits from the generic Element object, and each tag-specific element (such as HTMLBodyElement or HTMLInputElement) inherits from the HTMLElement object.

You can also find places in the W3C DOM abstract model where object "classes" act as interfaces to other objects. For example, in the Events module, an important object is called the EventTarget. As you'll see in more detail in Chapter 6, any node can be a target of an event. Thus, the DOM specification implies that all node objects should implement the EventTarget interface.

None of this abstract model construction impacts the way your scripts reference objects within a document. But it does help explain why all HTML element objects share such a large number of properties and methods, as shown in the beginning of Chapter 9.

# Web Accessibility Initiative (WAI)

An important W3C activity that frequently escapes the notice of content developers addresses accessibility of web content by users with a variety of disabilities. The Web Accessibility Initiative (*http://www.w3.org/WAI*) publishes recommendations for both technology producers and content authors. Because overuse of DHTML techniques can render a site's content unavailable to users with mobility, vision, hearing, or reading disabilities, authors should be aware of the guidelines while a site or application is still in the design stage. In truth, many of the existing HTML, CSS, and DOM standards include features aimed at improving accessibility. Unfortunately, mainstream browsers tend to assign low priority to implementing them. Do not, however, consider that a license to abuse DHTML at the expense of a sizable potential audience for your content. In some countries, web sites representing organizations of legislated minimum sizes may be legally obligated to assure they are accessible to all visitors.

# ECMAScript

When Navigator 2 made its debut, it provided built-in client-side scripting with a new language called JavaScript. Despite what its name might imply, the language was developed at Netscape, originally under the name LiveScript. It was a marketing alliance between Netscape and Sun Microsystems that put the "Java" into the JavaScript name. Yes, there are some striking similarities between the syntax of JavaScript and Java, but those existed even before the name changed.

Internet Explorer 3 introduced client-side scripting for that browser. Microsoft provided language interpreters for two languages: VBScript, with its syntax based on Microsoft's Visual Basic language, and JScript, which, from a compatibility point of view, was virtually 100% compatible with JavaScript in Navigator 2. The name variation had more to do with licensing and corporate politics than it did with programming syntax.

It is important to distinguish a programming language, such as JavaScript, from the document object model that it scripts. It is too easy to forget that document objects are not part of the JavaScript language, but are rather the "things" that programmers script with JavaScript (or VBScript). The JavaScript language is actually more mundane in its scope. It provides the nuts and bolts that are needed for any programming language: data types, variables, control structures, and so on. This is the *core* JavaScript language.

From the beginning, JavaScript was designed as a general-purpose language that could be applied to any object model, and this has proven useful. Adobe Systems, for example, uses JavaScript as the core scripting language for Acrobat Forms scripting. The same core language you use in HTML documents is applied to a completely different object model in Acrobat Forms.

To head off potentially disastrous incompatibilities between the implementations of core JavaScript in different browsers, several concerned parties (including Netscape and Microsoft) worked with a European computer standards group now known only by its acronym: ECMA. The first published standard, ECMA-262 (*http://www.ecma.ch/stand/ecma-262.htm*), also known as the politically neutral ECMAScript, is essentially the version of JavaScript found in Navigator 3. A second edition of the standard repaired small errors in the first edition. But the third edition added some new language features that had already been implemented in cross-browser compatible fashion. That version of ECMAScript has essentially been a part of Navigator and IE since the Version 4 browsers. More recent browsers implement features of the core language that will find their way into future versions of the standard. Microsoft and

Netscape (the latter by way of the Mozilla group) display a high degree of cross-browser compatibility with respect to the core ECMA-based scripting language.

After the dissonance in the object model arena, it is comforting for web authors to see so much harmony in the core language implementation. For the objects in the core JavaScript language, see Chapter 12.

# A Fragmenting World

As you will see throughout this book, implementing Dynamic HTML applications that work equally well in Internet Explorer, Netscape Navigator, and other modern browsers can be a challenge unto itself. Understanding and using the common-denominator functionality among the various pieces of DHTML will lead you to greater success than plowing ahead with a design for one browser and crossing your fingers that things will work in the others.

It is equally hazardous to use the W3C and ECMA standards as your sole guides to implementing DHTML features in your applications. Actual implementation of the standards is far from complete, even more so if visitors to your pages use browsers even one generation old. As if that weren't scary enough, the same browser brand and version may not behave identically across different operating systems. While Netscape 6 exhibits very predictable compatibility across operating systems as diverse as Solaris and the Mac OS, the same can't be said for Internet Explorer. Microsoft readily admits that some features (detailed in later chapters) are guaranteed to work only on Win32 operating systems (Windows 95 through XP). But even features that are supported in both IE/Windows and IE/Mac do not always behave or render the same way on both operating-system platforms. Web sites that present DHTML content to the public at large need to take the legions of Mac users into account in developing and testing.

If the inexorable flow of new browser versions, standards, and authoring features teaches us anything, it is that each new generation only serves to fragment further the installed base of browsers in use throughout the world. While I'm sure that every reader of this book has the latest subversion of at least one browser installed, the imperative to upgrade rarely trickles down to all the users of yesterday's browsers. If you are designing web applications for public consumption, coming up with a strategy for handling the ever-growing variety of browser versions should be a top priority. It's one thing to build a DHTML-based, context-sensitive pop-up menu system into your pages for IE 6/Windows users when that's the browser you use. But what happens to users who visit with IE 5/Mac, Netscape 6, Navigator 4, or Opera 5, or a pocket computer mini-browser, or Lynx?

There is no quick and easy answer to this question. So much depends on your content, the image you want to project via your application, and your intended audience. If you set your sights too high, you may leave many visitors behind; if you set them too low, your competition may win over visitors with more engaging content and interactivity. On the other hand, you could find yourself in the ideal situation, designing applications aimed at a single, organization-wide browser version.

It should be clear from the sheer size of the reference section in this book that those good old days of flourishing with only a few dozen HTML tags in your head are gone forever. As much as I'd like to tell you that you can master DHTML with one hand tied behind your back, I would only be deceiving you. Using Dynamic HTML effectively is a multidisciplinary endeavor. Perhaps it's for the best that content, formatting, and scripting have become separate enough to allow specialists in each area to contribute to a major project. I've been the scripter on many such projects, while other people handled the content and design. This is a model that works, and it is likely that it will become more prevalent, especially as each new browser version and standards release fattens the following pages in the years to come.

# CHAPTER 2

# Cross-Platform Compromises

Declaring support for industry standards is a noble act. But when each web browser maker is also out to put its stamp on the details of still-evolving standards, it's easy to see how a new browser release can embody ideas and extensions to standards that are not available in other browsers. With so many standards efforts affecting Dynamic HTML—not to mention the added confusion of standard modularization—it's not surprising that each mainstream browser implements its own flavor of DHTML support. This chapter provides an overview of the Microsoft and Netscape approaches to DHTML as of mid-2002 (IE 5/Macintosh, IE 6/Windows, and Netscape 7). It also explores some overall strategies that you might use for DHTML applications that must run identically on Navigator and Internet Explorer. There are more specific cross-browser implementation details in subsequent chapters.

## What Is a Platform?

The term *platform* has multiple meanings in web application circles, depending on how you slice the computing world. Typically, a platform denotes any hardware and/or software system that forms the basis for further product development. Operating system developers regard each microprocessor family as a platform (Pentium, PowerPC, or SPARC CPUs, for example); desktop computer application developers treat the operating system as the platform (each Windows generation, Mac OS 9, Mac OS X, Unix, Linux, and the rest); peripherals makers perceive a combination of hardware and operating system as the platform (for example, a Wintel machine USB port or a Macintosh FireWire bus).

The de facto acceptance of the web protocols, such as HTTP, means that a web application developer doesn't have to worry about underlying network transport protocols. Theoretically, all client computers equipped with browsers that support the web protocols—regardless of the operating system or CPU—should be treated as a single platform. The real world, however, doesn't work that way.

Today's crop of web browsers are far more than data readers. Each one includes a highly customized content rendering engine, one or more scripting language interpreters, security access mechanisms, and optional connections to related software modules for media playback, Java applets, and the like. The instant you decide to author content that will be displayed in a web browser, you must concern yourself with the capabilities built into each browser. Despite a certain level of interoperability due to industry-wide standards, you must treat each major browser brand—and sometimes each version of each browser—as a distinct development platform. Writing content to the scripting API or HTML tags known to be supported by one version of a browser does not guarantee support in other browsers or versions.

If you are creating content, you must also be aware of differences in the way some browsers tailor themselves to each supported operating system. For example, even though the HTML code for embedding a clickable button inside a form is the same for any forms-enabled browser, the look of that button may be vastly different when rendered in Windows, Macintosh, and Unix versions of a particular browser. That's because some browser makers observe the traditions of the user interface look and feel for each operating system. Thus, a form whose elements are neatly laid out to fit inside a window or frame of a fixed size in Windows XP may be aligned in a completely unacceptable way when displayed in the same browser on a Macintosh or a Unix-based system.

Even though much of the discussion in this book uses "cross-platform" to mean compatible with both Netscape and Microsoft browsers ("cross-browser" some might call it), you must also be mindful of operating-system–specific details. Even the precise positioning capabilities of "cross-platform" cascading style sheets do not eliminate the operating-system–specific vagaries of form elements and font rendering. If you develop applications that rely on DHTML, you can eliminate pre-Version 4 browsers from your testing matrix, but there are still many browser and operating system combinations that you need to test.

I now examine the predominant DHTML browser platforms. They are presented in chronological order of their release to the web-surfing public. The following material is required reading for all DHTML developers, even if you believe you need to develop for only one platform. As you will learn, the lines between platforms are not as clearly drawn as they once were.

# Navigator 4 DHTML—Fading Fast

If you ever wondered what kinds of risks pioneers take, look no further than many of the DHTML features of Netscape Navigator 4. Designed well before the first CSS and DOM standards crystallized, Navigator 4 became a victim of a sea-change in approaches to style sheets and document object models. Its efforts to bring JavaScript syntax to style sheet rules, to add the <layer> tag to the HTML vocabulary, and to place the bulk of a page's dynamism into a separate layer object all failed to gain acceptance in the W3C working groups. At the last minute, some of the nascent CSS language made it into Navigator 4, but it was fairly fragile when applied to complex pages involving tables and forms.

For the brief time period during which Navigator 4 was the only DHTML game in town, the lack of standards support was not a problem. But when Microsoft released Internet Explorer 4, with its radically different object model approach, developers had to jump through hoops to write DHTML code that accomplished the same tasks in both browsers. Even then, the power of dynamic page reflow in IE 4 made many DHTML effects essentially impossible to duplicate in the mostly static body content of Navigator 4 pages.

If Netscape's unsuccessful pioneering attempts weren't bold enough, the development of the next generation of the Netscape browser engine (handed to the separate Mozilla group) called for an even bolder move. Those nonstandard features from Navigator 4 would not carry over into the next generation. A lot of JavaScript code tailored to Navigator 4 runs in no other browser. In other words, Navigator 4 has become a dead-end development platform, whose installed base will only decrease over time.

Despite the fact that some organizations have continued to standardize on Navigator 4 while waiting to migrate to a more modern browser platform, this edition of *Dynamic HTML: The Definitive Reference* cuts the cord with the Navigator 4 past. If you need assistance and examples of scripting Navigator 4 DHTML, consult the first edition of this title.

# Internet Explorer DHTML

The browser that inspired extensive dynamic content was Microsoft Internet Explorer 4. Two groundbreaking characteristics of that browser fired developers' imaginations:

- Exposing practically every HTML element as a scriptable object
- Automatically reflowing the page after content modification

In the absence of an industry standard for its document object model, Microsoft invented its own model, along with a vocabulary of objects, properties, methods, and object collections (arrays). While many of the concepts of the IE 4 model found their way into the HTML portion of the W3C DOM recommendation, the W3C crafted an entirely new architecture for its core model, along with its own vocabulary set.

With so many scripts relying on the IE 4 model and syntax, Microsoft faced the unenviable task of blending the W3C model into the IE 4 model. This began slowly in IE 5 (although IE 5 for the Macintosh embraced the W3C DOM more from the start) and gradually picked up the pace through Version 6. This means that for many object-scripting tasks, you have your choice of the Microsoft or W3C DOM approach in your code—an enormous syntactic palette from which to choose. As yet, there are no signs of Microsoft deprecating its own features. If you choose the W3C DOM route, however, you'll find that Microsoft has so far elected to bypass some modules (as described shortly), forcing you to use the Microsoft syntax for some vital services, such as events. On the flip side, if you start your DHTML authoring life exclusively in the world of IE for Windows, you will find some features not available in other browsers, including IE for the Mac.

## Element Object References

The breadth of browsers you intend to support for your DHTML content exerts great influence over a key scripting task, namely how your script statements reference HTML element objects. All IE browsers starting with Version 4 (including those for the Mac) implement the document.all collection, which provides a gateway to any element for which you have assigned an identifier to the id attribute. Statements that refer to elements can reference the element ID as either a property reference or string, as in the following forms:

```
document.all.elementID
document.all("elementID")
document.all["elementID"]
document.all.item("elementID")
```

Even Opera 4 and later, when its Connection preference is set to identify itself to servers as IE, supports the first three formats. The string versions are helpful when you define generic functions that receive an ID string as an argument, allowing a single statement to reference any element.

IE also let you omit the document.all part of a reference so that you could reference an element simply by its ID. Although this practice makes for compact code, it also makes it very difficult to go back to the code to find statements that reference elements. Converting from the abbreviated style to the new W3C DOM-oriented referencing style will be a headache unless you are intimately familiar with the document's element structure and IDs.

If you prefer to bypass support for IE 4, you should use the W3C DOM element reference syntax because in time, it will predominate. In this case, the syntax consists of a core document object method whose sole parameter is a string identifier for the desired element:

```
document.getElementById("elementID")
```

It's unfortunate that a method that is likely to get a lot of use in scripts is so long and difficult to type (observe the case of each letter). But because this is the accepted standard format, your scripts will be more compatible with a wider range of browsers going forward than with the IE 4 version.

One other point about the W3C DOM specification: it continues to recognize the contribution of the first scriptable browser DOM, with its limited range of objects, such as forms and form controls. The "old" way of referring to these Level 0 objects, such as `document.forms[n].controlName`, is still valid syntax. Therefore, in the IE environment, several element objects give you three ways to reference them. In practice, however, you should use only the Level 0 syntax when scripts need to be backward-compatible with earlier browsers.

## Cascading Style Sheets

Some CSS functionality was introduced in IE 3, but IE 4 is considered the first browser to make a serious attempt at supporting the CSS Level 1 standard. Even so, the support was far from bug-free. Microsoft claims full CSS1 support for IE 6/Windows. In the process, the company implemented fixes for some long-standing deviations from the W3C standard. While the Windows version went through a slow evolution to achieve this point, IE 5 for the Macintosh provides very good CSS1 support. CSS2 support, particularly complex selectors, is still a work-in-progress. The modularization of CSS (see Chapter 7) will allow future IE versions to opt out of supporting modules that don't apply to the browser, such as the aural style attributes, in which case the browser will simply ignore attributes from unsupported modules.

Script access to style sheet properties occurs via an element object's `style` property. This property contains a `style` object whose properties correspond to style sheet attributes. Element object properties provide scripted access to the element's attribute values, and the `style` property is no different. In other words, the `style` property reports only those values assigned to an inline style sheet rule. To read the actual style being applied to the element (from a style sheet defined in the head or imported from an external file), IE 5 and later provide a proprietary `currentStyle` property for all element objects.

## CSS Positioning and Layering

Although CSS-P was not strictly a part of the CSS specification until CSS2, IE 4 and later support style sheet attributes that place elements in their own layers above the body content. An inline style rule that pulls a graphic out of the rendering sequence of a page and positions it to a specific spot within a document looks as follows:

```
<img src="myFace.jpg" height="60" width="40" alt="Nancy's Mug"
style="position:absolute; left:200px; top:100px">
```

Positioning attributes include facilities for hiding and showing an element, as well as controlling the stacking order of the layers (with undesirable behavior when a layer contains some form controls). Script control of these attributes provides much of the dynamism in DHTML-enhanced pages.

## Dynamic Content

Rendering engines in IE 4 and later respond quickly to changes in content, by reflowing the page after any such change. Regardless of your choice of element referencing syntax, the DOMs in IE provide properties and methods that allow adding, removing, or modifying content within an element or whole elements and their content. Starting with IE 5, you have your choice of using the IE 4 DOM or W3C DOM properties and methods for modifying elements and their content. If your audience is exclusively IE 5 or later, you can even mix and match your syntax (using document.all references to elements and W3C DOM properties to read or write the element's content). It's good practice, however, to use the DOM properties and methods that are consistent with the element referencing syntax you use. Netscape 6's support for the IE innerHTML convenience property can help smooth your transition to cross-browser support.

## The Event Model

The IE event model, which works hand-in-hand with the object model, is the critical bridge between user action and scripted activity. Virtually every element object has event handlers that can be scripted to respond to user and system actions. For example, it is possible to associate different actions with user clicks over different headings (even if the text blocks don't look like links) by assigning a different script statement to each heading's onclick event handler. IE for Windows, especially starting with IE 5, defines a large number of new events that can trigger scripts (as described in Chapter 10). Many of these events are patterned after the kinds of events application programmers use for manipulating Windows-based data and user interface behaviors. As a result, many of these events are available only in Windows versions of IE.

Another part of the event model is an event object. This abstract and short-lived entity—accessed as a property of the window object, and thus available to any function processing the event—contains details about each event that occurs. Scripts operating in response to events can inspect properties of the event object to determine the element responding to the event, the event's location, keyboard key, and so on.

The last aspect of the event model you need to understand is event propagation. Since IE 4, an event, unless otherwise instructed by script, continues to "bubble up" through the HTML element containment hierarchy of the document. Consider the following simple HTML document:

```
<html>
<body>
<div>
<p>Some Text:</p>
<form>
<input type="button" value="Click me" onclick="alert('Hi!')">
</form>
</div>
</body>
</html>
```

When the user clicks on the button, the click event is first processed by the onclick event handler in the button's own tag. Then the click event propagates through the form, div, and body elements. If the tag for one of those elements were to have an onclick event handler defined in it, the click event would trigger that handler, too. Event bubbling can also be programmatically canceled at any level along the way.

While the W3C DOM Level 2 contains an Events module, Microsoft has not implemented it as of IE 6 for Windows or IE 5 for the Mac. As you will see in Chapter 6, cross-browser applications must be built to support both the proprietary Microsoft event model and the W3C DOM event model (and, if necessary, the Navigator 4 event model, which shares some important features with the W3C model).

## Transitions and Filters

Building atop the syntactical conventions of CSS1, IE 4 and later for Windows includes a style attribute called filter (implemented as an ActiveX module). This attribute serves double duty. One set of attribute parameters supplies extra display characteristics for certain types of HTML content. For example, you can set a filter to render content with a drop shadow or with its content flipped horizontally. The other set of attributes lets you define visual transition effects for when an object is hidden or shown, much like the transition effects you set in presentation programs such as PowerPoint.

## Downloadable Fonts

A document to be displayed in IE 4 and later for Windows can embed TrueType font families downloaded from the server. You download the font via CSS style attributes:

```
<style type="text/css">
@font-face {
    font-family:familyName;
    font-style:normal;
    font-weight:normal;
    src:url("someFont.eot")}
</style>
```

With the basic font family downloaded into the browser, the family can be assigned to content via CSS styles or <font> tags.

Note that the downloadable font format differs between Internet Explorer and Navigator. Each browser requires that the font definition files be generated with a different tool. The tool for IE is called WEFT, which you can download and learn about at (*http://www.microsoft.com/typography/*).

## Data Binding

IE 4 and later for Windows provides hooks for ActiveX controls that communicate with text files or databases on the server. Elements from these server-based data sources can be associated with the content of HTML elements, essentially allowing the document to access server data without processing a CGI script. IE 5 for the Mac supports this feature when the server data source is a text file (such as a comma-separated or tab-delimited database file). While data binding is not covered in depth in this book, I mention it here because it is one of Microsoft's dynamic content features.

## Additional Windows-Only Features

IE for Windows is largely a collection ActiveX controls. As such, the browser can take advantage of numerous ActiveX facilities that come with the browser and some that are components of the operating system. That's the case with filters and data binding with remote databases (through ODBC), described previously. Script control of the Windows Media Player is restricted to IE for Windows, as is the capability to turn the browser into a content-editing application and (with the user's permission) access the filesystem. Developers who learn DHTML initially in the IE for Windows environment need to understand which capabilities will not translate to IE for the Mac or for other browsers.

## Macintosh Versions

The Macintosh applications group at Microsoft (based in Silicon Valley, rather than Redmond, Washington) controls the development of the IE browser for the Mac. One result of the separate development efforts is that the IE/Mac browser has been free to embrace more W3C DOM features in its Version 5 than IE 5 for Windows. On the negative side, however, the two browsers can exhibit differences in fundamental rendering that can make precision page layout and scripted DHTML difficult. Many of these differences are noted throughout Part II. The main point to take away from this situation is that developing content that is to play on both Windows and Mac versions of IE should be tested thoroughly on both operating system platforms.

# Netscape 6 (Mozilla) DHTML

A primary design goal of the Mozilla browser engine behind Netscape 6 was support for industry standards. Abandoning a large portion of the earlier version code allowed the browser engineers to approach internal mechanisms anew. In the end, the Netscape 6 browser supports far more HTML, CSS, and DOM features than earlier versions. As a driving force behind the core ECMA language specification, the company also assures compliance with that standard. Finally, a brand new rendering engine that reflows dynamic content brought this browser up to the same DHTML expectations as Internet Explorer.

As the basis for most dynamic content scripting, the W3C DOM brought with it a new abstract object model. Even though some W3C DOM features had been implemented in varying stages of IE during the Version 5 and 5.5 lifetimes, content authors had little imperative to switch over, because the Microsoft model was the only one needed to work with IE's DHTML capabilities. Even Opera adopted IE's basic DHTML model. But with the W3C DOM the only route available for scripting Netscape 6 and the perceived "correctness" of following standards, content authors had reasons to get to know the terminology and concepts that had not existed prior to the W3C standard.

The close association between Netscape 6 and standards sometimes makes it difficult to separate the two efforts. But keep in mind that both tracks are still evolving at their own paces, and it is generally easier to add features to a standard than it is to produce a new browser release that implements those features. The browser that supports 100% of all current standards' requirements does not exist and most likely will never exist, unless the standards stop evolving for a few years. The Netscape 7 browser implements only a handful of new DOM items not already supported in Netscape 6. Except as noted in Chapter 9, you can regard Netscape 7 as a more mature, tested, and bug-fixed version of Netscape 6.

## Element Object References

Netscape 6 of course continues support for the old Level 0 DOM syntax, so that users can avail themselves of scripts written for older browsers. But for DHTML features, the new node-based W3C DOM terminology is required. The predominant syntax is via the finger-twisting method of the core DOM module:

```
document.getElementById("elementID")
```

This method slices through the node containment hierarchy of the document's content (as discussed at length in Chapter 5), and returns a reference to the first element object in source code order whose ID attribute value matches the method's argument. This syntax is also implemented in IE 5 and later.

## Cascading Style Sheets

Netscape 6 supports all of CSS1 and substantial parts of CSS2 that apply to visual browsers. Scripted access to element styles occurs through the same style property that is also a part of the original IE 4 DOM. The W3C DOM standard specifies that the style property reflects only the style attribute values of an element, and not style settings made elsewhere in the document. To reach the details of style properties affecting an element, regardless of their source, the W3C DOM provides a somewhat convoluted construct to read what is known as the *computed style*. This feature was first implemented in Netscape 6.1 and is demonstrated in Chapter 4.

## Positioning and Layering

Having abandoned the Navigator 4 proprietary <layer> tag and corresponding nested layer object architecture, Netscape 6 provides full support for the CSS-based positioning attributes. This act brings the Netscape browser in sync with the way IE 4 and later permit scripts to adjust positioning, visibility, and stacking order of elements via their style properties. Moreover, the positioning styles can be applied directly to elements of any kind, rather than having to embed content into span or div elements unless you wish to group multiple elements inside a single positioned container. Dynamic positioning that acts in response to user actions must use the W3C DOM event model, which is different from the IE event model. Even so, the two can be made to work together without too much difficulty, as described in Chapter 6.

## Dynamic Content

Drafters of the W3C DOM standard produced a system that provides a high level of conceptual consistency for the way scripters modify portions of a document's content. This was done, however, at the expense of simplicity.

The easiest content to modify is text that is contained by an element. Such text is represented in the DOM as the value of a *text node*, and is handled through strings in JavaScript. But when it comes to modifications involving elements, the W3C DOM approach gets a bit wordy. To create a new HTML element and its content in pure W3C DOM syntax requires the following sequence:

1. Create an empty element for the desired tag with the document.createElement( ) method.

2. Assign values to its individual attributes one at a time, preferably via the element's setAttribute( ) method.

3. Create a text node for the content with document.createTextNode("*newtext*").

4. Use a variety of node methods to construct the node tree of the new element and its content.

5. Use another method to insert the new node group into a position within the document's existing node tree.

If the content your scripts need to generate has lots of elements and text nodes, the sequence requires many more statements. The concept of creating an empty object, populating its attributes or properties, and then inserting the object into its rightful place permeates the W3C DOM, and not only for document content. The phrase "Create, Populate, Insert" will become your mantra.

Netscape recognized, however, that developers found some nonstandard, IE DOM features to be very convenient. As a compromise to practicality over blind adherence to the standards, the Mozilla DOM engine implements the IE innerHTML property for any element. This allows scripts to assemble new content as if it were a string of HTML source code to be inserted where desired. Chapter 5 will compare these approaches.

Separately, table elements benefit from a series of methods and properties—shared with the IE model—that make radically dynamic tables easily scriptable. The regularity of table rows and cells encourage the use of tight loops to repopulate a table with new or sorted data from JavaScript arrays or XML data (see Chapter 5).

# The Event Model

The W3C DOM Events module introduced some new terminology for scripters already experienced with DHTML scripting in earlier browsers. Event handlers became known as *event listeners*, meaning that scripts instruct elements to "listen" for events of particular types, such as clicks, key presses, and so on. When an element "hears" that event type, processing shifts to a function, just like the event handler functions you are used to.

An event object contains numerous properties about the details of the current event being processed. Interestingly, the environment for the W3C DOM event object more closely resembles the defunct Navigator 4 event model. An event listener's function receives the event object as a function argument (in contrast to the window-based object in the IE event model).

Event propagation is modeled after both the IE and Navigator 4 event models. The default propagation model allows events to bubble upward through the element containment hierarchy, as described earlier for the IE model. But events also trickle downward through the hierarchy. To process an event on its way to its actual target, however, a script must instruct an event listener to *capture* the event. Microsoft also added the event capture option to its event model for IE 5, so the two models can be made to work very much like each other, despite major discrepancies elsewhere.

One area in which the W3C DOM model is much more conservative is in the breadth of event types. Because this model is not operating-system–dependent, it has so far settled on a basic set of events that let scripts work with common mouse and system events. Due to international character set intricacies, keyboard event details are not part of DOM Level 2, but Netscape 6 implements the basic events that are likely to be compatible (or not conflict) with the finished specification for DOM Level 3.

## Operating System Support

All operating system versions of Netscape 6 are derived from the same core browser-engine code base. A principal goal of this approach is that all DHTML-related rendering and activity is to operate identically, regardless of operating system. Netscape has achieved remarkable consistency across operating system versions of the browser.

Another aspect of this consistency is that the user interface (implemented in an XML format called *.xul*) is not as operating-system–dependent as previous versions. Designs for buttons and other standard UI elements are not controlled by the operating systems, but rather by definitions associated with the current theme (or "skin") in force at any moment. Default buttons, for instance, generally render with the same dimensions and proportions in all operating system versions. Unlike the earlier days of graphical user interfaces, the multiplicity of web designs seems to have reduced the clamor for absolute UI consistency across applications for a given operating system. As long as users can distinguish a checkbox from a radio button, or intuitively detect a clickable button, the design passes muster. The upside for web developers is that pages using standard elements are more likely to resemble each other on all operating system platforms.

## Other Browsers

Dozens of less popular browsers circulate around the web community. Of these, the Opera browser has perhaps the largest audience, albeit a very small percentage of the installed base. Support for DHTML facilities varies widely on these browsers. Opera 6, for example, supports basic CSS and DOM features. In the latter case, however, you are restricted to only a handful of core DOM objects, properties, and methods. For example, you can use document.getElementById( ) to reference any element, but the W3C document node tree is not complete. Dynamic content capabilities are limited, although basic dynamic styles are supported. The company does provide an online list of known support and bugs for each version—something you should check if your cool design or script isn't performing in Opera. For details about Opera 6's DHTML issues, visit *http://www.opera.com/docs/specs/*.

## Cross-Platform Strategies

The more browser brands, versions, and operating systems you wish to support with your DHTML applications, the greater your challenge to write one code base that works with them all. Before undertaking any project intended for more than a single browser, you must make difficult decisions about not only which browsers to support but also how users of other browsers will be treated by your site. Consumer-oriented e-commerce sites, for example, can rarely afford to turn away even a small percentage of potential customers because the visitors' browsers don't measure up to a lofty design. Specialized sites that are not as concerned about competitive pressures may choose to require browsers of a certain minimum functionality to pass beyond the home page.

Another important question to ask yourself about your design goals is whether the DHTML features of your site add value to the content that is otherwise accessible to all, or those features are essential to the site design. For example, a DHTML-assisted hierarchical menu system adds value by speeding direct access to a nested area of your site, yet users of DHTML-challenged browsers can still reach those areas (albeit with more clicks and intermediate stops en route), and search engine web crawlers will pursue the links. Conversely, if navigation absolutely requires DHTML powers, some visitors will be locked out. Similarly, search engine web crawlers, which don't execute scripts, will not know to follow links that are rendered only by script. This could reduce the chances that deeper pages of your site will be catalogued and indexed.

Regardless of the approach you use to accommodate multiple browsers, it will at some point entail code branching or other equalization tricks that are dependent upon the scriptable features of the browser. Back when the matrix of browser versions was small, it was common practice to use browser "sniffing" with the aid of information gleaned from the navigator.userAgent and related properties. But with the matrix growing ever larger, it's time to examine object detection as a more workable solution.

## Object Detection over Browser Sniffing

DHTML developers from the Version 4 browser days who employed browser version sniffing found themselves in trouble at some point as new browser versions came on the scene. Consider the following typical global variable declaration from the era of IE 4 and Navigator 4:

```
// code unknowingly doomed to failure
var isNav, isIE;
if (parseInt(navigator.appVersion) >= 4) {
    isNav = (navigator.appName == "Netscape");
    isIE = (navigator.appName.indexOf("Microsoft") != -1);
}
```

Hereafter, various functions would branch their code, with browser-specific code in each branch. Unforeseen at this time, subsequent versions of Netscape abandoned the layer object—usually the primary need for branching in the first place. As a result, Netscape 6 (whose appVersion reports 5) attempted to execute code that it could not handle. On the IE variable side of things, two potential problems loomed, depending on how much IE4-ness the author ascribed to browsers following that branch. For one, the Macintosh does not implement most IE/Windows-only features. Second, the default preference settings of the Opera browser cause it to identify itself as IE, yet this does not assure compatibility with IE scripts.

Trying to compensate for all browsers past, present, and future requires a huge version sniffing library plus a crystal ball about future browser version numbering and naming. Even attempting such forecasting won't take into account new browsers that crop up, some of which will be built upon very capable existing engines, such as the Mozilla engine. Building branched code based on browser version is a losing battle. A better approach is to branch based on the capabilities of the browser. That's what object detection does.

Object detection is a shortcut name for a technique that verifies the existence of an object, property, or method before using it in a script. The technique isn't new. Scripts that control image rollovers have been using it for years by testing for the presence of the document.images array before acting on an image object:

```
if (document.images) {
    // act on image objects here
}
```

All object models that implement img elements as objects support the document.images array. In older browsers, the expression document.images evaluates to undefined, which causes the if condition to fail, so the nested statements don't run. Thus, the scripter is freed from worrying about which browser supports the image object.

Implementing object detection on a broader scale can free you from the complexities of today's browser sniffing. For example, a function that switches a style property can work in both the IE 4 and W3C DOM browsers, but requires different referencing syntax for the element. The following function sets the fontWeight style property of an element to bold:

```
function emBolden(elemID) {
    var elem;
    if (document.all) {
        elem = document.all(elemID);
    } else if (document.getElementById) {
        elem = document.getElementById(elemID);
    }
    if (elem && elem.style && elem.style.fontWeight) {
        elem.style.fontWeight = "bold";
    }
}
```

A local variable, elem, is initialized as a null value. The if/else construction looks for the two element reference types that I know have a chance of supporting the style property. The test for document.all is like the earlier example of document.images. Less well-known is that object methods are exposed in most browsers as properties, whose existence can be tested in a similar fashion.

To protect additional script statements from the case of both if/else conditions failing, the balance of the function verifies that elem has a value assigned to it. The tripartite condition is overkill for this specific application, because you can make an educated and safe assumption that any browser that supports either document.all or document.getElementById( ) also supports not only the style property of elements, but also the very common fontWeight style property. But the example is here to demonstrate how to go about verifying the existence of a property when the object or intermediate property may not exist. In the above example, you cannot test simply for the existence of elem.style.fontWeight. A "one-dot" evaluation rule applies to JavaScript, whereby every reference up to the rightmost dot must evaluate successfully in order for the interpreter to see whether the last reference succeeds or fails. If you were to test for the existence of elem.style.fontWeight by itself, and elem was not a valid reference, the script interpreter generates a script error. Evaluation tests of an if condition are conducted from left to right. If any one of the ANDed expressions fails, the condition immediately fails (short circuits), and no further evaluations occur, leaving your browser free from script errors there.

Some browsers, especially Opera and some older IE and Netscape versions, may require more help in evaluating conditional expressions. For these browsers, a value of undefined does not necessarily convert to false (although the ECMA specification says it should). To obtain the same result, you can use the typeof operator to inspect the data type of the object or property:

```
if (elem && (typeof elem.style != "undefined")) {...}
```

A value of null does correctly evaluate to false for all browsers, so the first test is fine the way it is. If elem exists, the string returned by the typeof operator gets compared against undefined. If the data type is anything other than undefined, processing continues (the test for fontWeight is not shown here for the sake of brevity).

The typeof operator also helps in those cases when a property exists and its value (perhaps its default value) is either an empty string or zero. Both of these values would cause the conditional expression to evaluate to false, even though the property exists. By making sure the property value is either a particular data type or anything other than undefined, your condition more accurately reports the presence of the property.

Object detection doesn't solve every compatibility problem, and requires having at hand a good reference of currently-supported DHTML features (such as this book). There are even times, particularly when designing around known bugs in earlier browsers, when browser sniffing is appropriate on a small scale. Yet for a great many scripts, object detection can not only ease implementation of incompatible syntax, but also allow older browsers to degrade gracefully. You can read more about object detection techniques and strategies in an article at *http://www.oreillynet.com/pub/a/ javascript/synd/2001/10/23/ob_detect.html*.

Whether you elect to use object detection, browser version sniffing, or the mix of the two, you have a choice of several cross-browser deployment strategies: page branching, internal branching, common denominator design, and custom API development. Additional choices you'll make include whether you wish to deny page access to older browsers, provide multiple paths for browsers of different capabilities, or provide just one path that enhances the experience for DHTML features of your design yet degrades gracefully for those browsers without the latest doodads. The following sections describe some of the more popular strategies for accommodating multiple browsers.

## Page Branching

Web pages that use absolute-positioned elements degrade poorly when displayed in older browsers. The positioned elements do not appear where their attributes call for them, and, even worse, the elements render themselves from top to bottom in the browser window in the order in which they appear in the HTML file. Also, any elements that are to be hidden when the page loads appear in the older browsers in their source code order. To prevent users of older browsers from seeing visual gibberish, you should have a plan in place to direct users of non-DHTML–capable browsers to pages containing less flashy content or instructions on how to view your fancy pages. A server-side CGI program can perform this redirection by checking the

USER_AGENT environment variable sent by the client at connect-time and redirecting different HTML content to each browser brand or version.

Alternatively, you can do the same branching strictly via client-side scripting. Depending on the amount of granularity you wish to establish for different browser brands and versions at your site, you have many branching techniques to choose from. All these techniques are based on a predominantly blank page that has some scripted intelligence behind it to automatically handle JavaScript-enabled browsers. Any script-enabled browser can execute a script that looks into the visitor's browser version and loads the appropriate starter page for that user. Example 2-1 shows one example of how such a page accommodates both scripted and unscripted browsers.

*Example 2-1. Branching index page*

```html
<html>
<head>
<title>MegaCorp On The Web</title>
<script language="JavaScript" type="text/javascript">
<!--
if (document.images) {
    if (document.getElementById) {
        window.location.replace("startW3C_DHTML.html");
    } else {
        window.location.replace("startRollover_DHTML.html");
    }
} else {
    window.location.href = "startPlainScripted.html";
}
//-->
</script>
<meta http-equiv="REFRESH"
content="1;URL=http://www.megacorp.com/startUnscripted.html">
</head>

<body>
<center>
    <a href="startUnscripted.html">
    <img src="images/megaCorpLogo.gif" height="60" width="120" border="0"
    alt="MegaCorp Home Page"></a>
</center>
</body>
</html>
```

The script portion of Example 2-1 provides three possible branches, depending on the browser level. If the browser version supports even the simplest W3C DOM feature (referencing elements via the document.getElementById( ) method), the user is immediately directed to a new start page that assumes that minimum capability. Using location.replace keeps the index page out of the browser history so the **Back** button works as expected. For a browser lacking the W3C DOM support, but fitted for image objects, the script directs that user to a start page that is wired for image rollovers as the maximum amount of DHTML. Notice the check for W3C DOM support is nested within the document.images check. This sequence offers a bit of insurance against the oldest scriptable browsers that might choke on a test for an undefined expression and also lack the typeof operator. Any other scriptable browser navigates to a start page that knows at least simple scripting that is completely backward-compatible.

For browsers that either don't have JavaScript built in or have JavaScript turned off, a <meta> tag refreshes this page after one second by loading a starter page for unscripted browsers. Even though page refreshing is not an official usage for the <meta> tag, a great many browsers support it. For "barebones" browsers that may not recognize scripting or <meta> tags (including Lynx and browsers built into a lot of handheld devices), a simple image link leads to the unscripted starter page. Users of these browsers will have to "click" on this link to enter the content portion of the web site.

Example 2-1 is an extreme example. It assumes that the web application has as many as four different paths for four different classes of visitor. This may seem like a good idea at first, but it seriously complicates the maintenance chores for the application in the future. Modified with fewer branches, the technique of Example 2-1 provides a way to filter access between W3C DOM DHTML-capable browsers and all the rest.

## Overlaying a Different Page

As an alternative to the page-branching technique, you can use the iframe element and CSS features of recent browsers to replace the regular HTML content of a page with the content from an entirely different page. With this technique, the address and document title of the original page remain visible in the browser. A search-engine robot arriving at the page can read and analyze the same barebones content that visitors with non-DHTML browsers see. But visitors with DHTML-enabled browsers (or whatever filter mechanism you desire) see only the enhanced page. Bookmarks and page pointers passed around the community refer to a single URI.

Example 2-2 demonstrates what you need to add to an existing page to overlay an enhanced page for W3C DOM-capable browsers.

*Example 2-2. Adding an overlay page*

```
<html>
<head>
<title>MegaCorp on the Web</title>
<script language="JavaScript" type="text/javascript">
<!--
var isW3C = (document.getElementById) ? true : false;
if (isW3C) {
    document.write("<style type='text/css'>body {margin:0px; padding:0px; overflow:");
    document.write("hidden}#preW3C {display:none}</style>");
}
// additional regular page scripts can go here
//-->
```

*Example 2-2. Adding an overlay page (continued)*

```
</script>
</head>
<body>
<span id="preW3C">
regular body content goes here
</span>
<script type="text/javascript">
if (isW3C) {
    document.write("<iframe frameborder='0' vspace='0' hspace='0' marginwidth='0'");
    document.write("marginheight='0' height='100%' width='100%'");
    document.write("src='startW3C_DHTML.html'></iframe>");
}
</script>
</body>
</html>
```

When a page containing the Example 2-2 enhancements loads into a W3C DOM-enhanced browser (that is, one that knows the document.getElementById( ) method), a script writes a two-rule style sheet for the page. The first rule erases all margins and scrollbars from the body element; the second rule prevents the span element that wraps all regular body content from rendering itself. The same browser versions that write the new style sheet rules also add an iframe element to the page. Attributes of the <iframe> tag assure that it fills the entire content region of the browser window (with the exception of Opera, which leaves a harmless blank area along the right edge).

The iframe acts as a self-contained window for a separate page containing the DHTML-enhanced content. You can decide whether links from this page should target the same frame (the default action) or replace the original page (by targeting _top).

You have two HTML pages to maintain with this scheme. But it also means that you have a static page to fall back on while you experiment with DHTML features. Plus, the search engines will still find your key data, while your DHTML-enhanced page can use all kinds of dynamic content creation techniques if you like.

## Internal Branching

Instead of creating separate documents for each browser class, you can use JavaScript to write browser-specific content for a page within a single document. There was more call for this when Navigator 4's <layer> tag behaved better than positioned div elements. A script could use document.write( ) to add a <layer> tag and its attributes for Navigator 4 and a <div> tag for IE. But even today, you may need to write different content for different browsers. For example, a corporate web designer may find that one set of style sheet rules works well for Windows browsers, while Mac browsers behave better with variations in font specifications. The following script fragment from a head script links in one external CSS file for Mac browsers and another file for all others:

```
var isMac = navigator.userAgent.indexOf("Mac") != -1;
if (isMac) {
    document.write("<link rel='stylesheet' type='text/css'");
    document.write("src='styles/corpMac.css'>");
} else {
    document.write("<link rel='stylesheet' type='text/css'");
    document.write("src='styles/corpDefault.css'>");
}
```

This is an example when browser sniffing is appropriate.

## Designing for the Common Denominator

From a maintenance point of view, the ideal DHTML page is one that uses a common denominator of syntax that all supported browsers interpret and render identically. You can achieve some success with this approach if you target W3C DOM-capable browsers, but you must be very careful in selecting standards-based syntax that is implemented identically in all such browsers. Because some of these standards were little more than working drafts as the supposedly compatible browsers were released to the world, the implementations are not consistent across the board.

DHTML feature sets that you can use as starting points for a common denominator approach are the standards for CSS1 and CSS-P. Tread carefully in CSS2, unless you are targeting only the latest browsers and have verified support for your features in those browsers. When you peruse developer documentation from browser vendors, it is often impossible to gauge whether a feature is a company's proprietary extension that adheres to the spirit, but not the letter, of a standard. Just because a feature is designated as "compatible with CSS" does not mean that it is actually in the published recommendation. Refer to the reference chapters in Part II of this book for term-by-term browser and standard support.

You are likely to encounter situations in which the same style sheet syntax is interpreted or rendered slightly differently in various browser versions, especially those prior to IE 6 and Netscape 6 when the page's <!DOCTYPE> points to a recent DTD (as explained in Chapter 8). This is one reason why it is vital to test even recommended standards on as many browser platforms as possible. When an incompatibility occurs, there is probably a platform-specific solution that makes the result look and behave the same in both browsers. To achieve this parity, you'll need to use internal branching for part of the page's content. This is still a more maintainable solution than creating an entirely separate page for each browser.

## Custom APIs

Thanks to the similarities in syntactical support for scripted CSS properties in both the IE 4 and W3C DOMs, scripts that must support the basics of these two DOMs need to reconcile only the element-reference and event-model idiosyncrasies. Scripters who also lived through the Navigator 4 DOM era experienced a far more difficult time reconciling the differences. The more DHTML DOMs you wish to support, the greater the need to use internal branching—preferably through object detection—for your application to work seamlessly across platforms.

Once you go to the trouble of writing scripts that perform internal branching, you might prefer to avoid doing it again for the next document. Modern browsers allow JavaScript to load libraries of script functions (files named with the *.js* extension) into any HTML document you like. You can therefore create your own meta language for scripted DHTML operations by writing a set of functions that have terminology you design. Place the functions in a library file and rely on them as if they were part of your scripting vocabulary. The language and function set you create is called an *application programming interface*—an API. Example 2-3 shows a small portion of a sample DHTML API library for DOMs that adhere to the IE 4 and W3C DOM element-referencing schemes.

*Example 2-3. Portion of a DHTML library*

```
// Convert object name string or object reference
// into a valid object reference
function getStyleObject(obj) {
    var styleObj;
    if (typeof obj == "string") {
        if (document.getElementById) {
            styleObj = document.getElementById(obj).style;
        } else if (document.all) {
            styleObj = document.all[obj].style;
        }
    } else if (obj.style) {
        styleObj = obj.style;
    }
    return styleObj;
}

// Positioning an object at a specific pixel coordinate
function shiftTo(obj, x, y) {
    var styleObj = getStyleObject(obj);
    if (styleObj) {
        styleObj.left = x + "px";
        styleObj.top = y + "px";
    }
}
```

The getStyleObject() function of Example 2-3 is an all-purpose function that returns a reference to the style property of an element object that is passed originally as either a string of the object's ID or a ready-to-go object reference. When the incoming object name is passed as a string, the string becomes an argument for document.getElementById() or an index to the document.all array, based on which form is supported by the browser. A browser that supports both reference types executes only the first. In contrast, when the incoming parameter is already an object reference, it goes through one more validation to guarantee that it has a style property before that property is retrieved. Notice that for a string value, browsers that don't support either of the preferred element referencing methods assign null to the value to be returned; the same goes for an incoming object value that doesn't have a style property. This null value plays a role in every function that invokes this getStyleObject( ) function.

The shiftTo( ) function in Example 2-3 doesn't have a lot to do. But by invoking getStyleObject( ) and validating the existence of the element object it is called upon to move, it helps other browsers, such as Navigator 4, degrade gracefully when it reacts to events triggering the element move. It's true that Navigator 4 can move an element (via different syntax for both the layer element reference and the movement action), but this API chooses to bypass support for that browser version.

Building an API along these lines lets you raise the common denominator of DHTML functionality for your applications. You free yourself from limits that would be imposed by adhering to 100% syntactical compatibility. In Chapter 4, I present a more complete custom API that smooths over potentially crushing CSS-P incompatibilities (including backward compatibility with Navigator 4 to assist readers who adopted the API from the first edition).

## Cross-Platform Expectations

Before undertaking cross-platform DHTML development, be sure you understand that the features you can exploit in all target browsers—regardless of the techniques you use—are limited to comparable feature sets within the realms of style sheets, positionable elements, event models, object models, and downloadable fonts. Dynamic content is also a cross-platform possibility in W3C DOM-compatible browsers, but several DHTML features described in Microsoft's developer documents are available only in Internet Explorer for Windows with few, if any, parallels in other browsers.

# CHAPTER 3

# Adding Style Sheets to Documents

Like their counterparts in word processing and desktop publishing programs, HTML style sheets are supposed to simplify the deployment of fine-tuned formatting associated with content. Instead of surrounding every h1 element in a document with <font> tags to make all of those headings the same color, you can use a one-line style definition in a style sheet to assign a color to every instance of the h1 element on the page. This puts the purpose of tagging in its proper place: assigning context within a document. The precise appearance of data within that context belongs to the style sheet.

## Observing HTML Structures

In order to successfully incorporate style sheets into HTML documents, you may have to reexamine your current tagging practices. How much you'll have to change your ways depends on how and when you learned HTML in the first place. Over the years, popular browsers have generally accommodated—how shall I say it—less-than-perfect HTML. Consider the <p> tag, which has long been treated as a single tag that separates paragraphs with a wider line space than the <br> line break tag. HTML standards even encourage this start-tag-only thinking by making some end tags optional. You can define an entire row of table cells without once specifying a </td> or </tr> tag: the browser automatically closes a tag pair when it encounters a logical start tag for, say, the next table cell or row.

The "new thinking" you should adopt is triggered by an important fact: style sheets, and the browser object models that work with them, are largely container-oriented. With rare exception (the <br> tag is one), an element in a document should be treated as a container whose territory is bounded by its start and end tags (even if the end tag is optional).* This container territory does not always translate to space on the page, but

---

* In XHTML, all elements require end tags, including so-called empty elements. More commonly, empty elements utilize an internal forward slash shortcut, as in <br />. The optional extra space helps this new form work in pre-XHTML browsers.

rather applies to the structure of the HTML source code. To see how "HTML-think" has changed since the early days, let's look at a progression of simple HTML pages. Here's a page that might have been excerpted from a tutorial for HTML Version 2:

```
<html>
<head>
<title>Welcome to HypeCo</title>
</head>
<body>
<h1>Welcome to HypeCo's Home Page</h1>
We're glad you're here.
<p>
You can find details of all of HypeCo's latest products and special offers.
Our goal is to provide the highest quality products and the best customer
service in the industry.
<p>
<a href="products.htm">Click here</a> to view our on-line catalog.
</body>
</html>
```

While the preceding HTML produces a perfectly fine, if boring, page, a modern browser does not have enough information from the tags to turn the content below the h1 element into three genuine paragraph elements. Before applying a document-wide paragraph style to all three paragraphs, you must make each paragraph its own container. For example, you can surround the text of the paragraph with a <p>/</p> tag pair:

```
<html>
<head>
<title>Welcome to HypeCo</title>
</head>
<body>
<h1>Welcome to HypeCo's Home Page</h1>
<p>We're glad you're here.</p>
<p>
You can find details of all of HypeCo's latest products and special offers.
Our goal is to provide the highest quality products and the best customer
service in the industry.
</p>
<p>
<a href="products.htm">Click here</a> to view our on-line catalog.
</p>
</body>
</html>
```

When viewed in a modern browser, the pages created by the two preceding examples look identical. But internally, the browser recognizes three paragraph elements in the second example, and, more importantly, the style of these paragraphs can be controlled by style sheets.

The HTML vocabulary for DHTML-capable browsers includes two additional tags you can use to establish containment: <div> and <span>. A div element creates a container shaped like a block that begins at the starting point of one line and ends with a line break. A span element is an inline container, meaning that it is surrounded by chunks of running text. For example, if you want to assign a special style to the first two paragraphs in our example's body, one approach is to group those two elements inside a surrounding div container:

```
<body>
<h1>Welcome to HypeCo's Home Page</h1>
<div>
<p>We're glad you're here.</p>
<p>
You can find details of all of HypeCo's latest products and special offers.
Our goal is to provide the highest quality products and the best customer
service in the industry.
</p>
</div>
<p>
<a href="products.htm">Click here</a> to view our on-line catalog.
</p>
</body>
```

Surrounding the two paragraph elements by the <div> tag pair does not affect how the content is rendered in the browser, but as shown in Figure 3-1, it does alter the containment structure of the elements in the document.

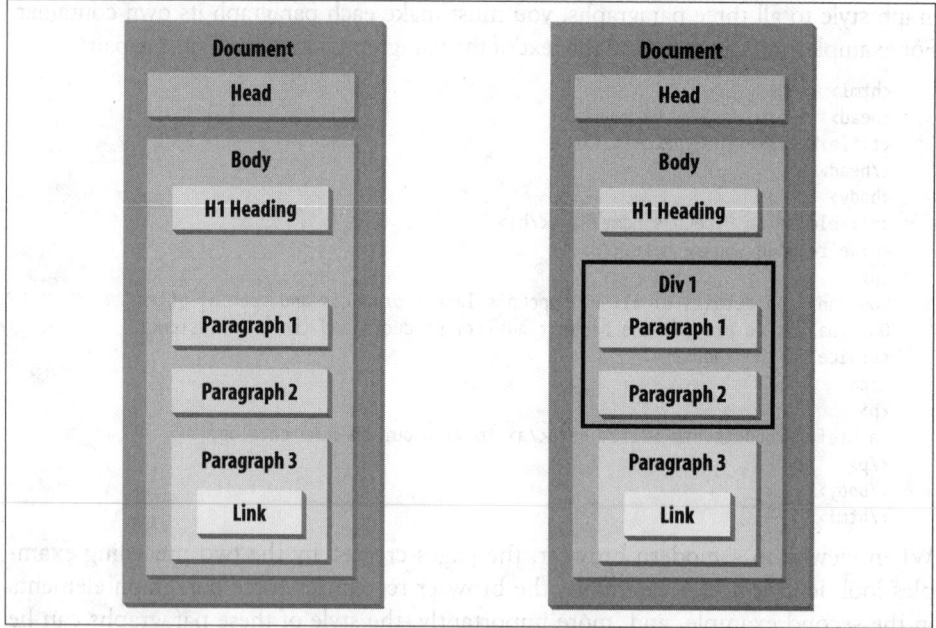

*Figure 3-1. Element containment before and after the addition of the <div> tag*

As you can see from Figure 3-1, even a simple document has a number of containment relationships. The link in the last paragraph is contained by the third paragraph element; the paragraph element is contained by the body element; the body element is contained by the html element; and the html element is contained by the holder of the whole page: the document.

# Understanding Block-Level Elements

If you are a style sheet coder, you must be aware of the impact of HTML tag and element containment on style attribute inheritance. If you are a page designer, however, you need to understand the more fundamental visual impact of a particular type of HTML element: the block-level element. A block-level element is a self-contained unit of content that normally begins at the starting margin of one line and ends in a way that forces the next bit of content to appear on a new line following the block. Each of the heading tags (h1, h2, etc.) is a block-level element because by default, it stands alone on a line (unless you use DHTML positioning tricks to overlay other elements). Other common block-level elements are p, ul, ol, li, and div.

A CSS-enabled browser automatically defines a set of physical features to every block-level element. By default, the values for all these features are set to zero or none, so that they don't appear or occupy space on the page when you use simple HTML tags without style sheets. But one of the purposes of style sheets is to let you modify the values of those features to create graphical borders, adjust margin spacing, and insert padding between the content and border. In fact, those three terms—*border*, *margin*, and *padding*—account for about one-fourth of all CSS2 style sheet attributes.

## Box Pieces

You can think of the content and features of a block-level element as a box. To help you visualize the role and relative position of the features of a block-level element, Figure 3-2 shows a schematic diagram of a generic chunk of block-level content (imagine it's a paragraph, if that helps), where the margin, border, and padding are indicated in relation to the content. The width and height of the content do not change, even when extra stuff is tacked on outside of the content.* Each of the surrounding features—padding, borders, and margins—can occupy space based on its corresponding dimensions. The width and height of the entire box is the sum of the element content, plus padding, borders, and margins. If you don't assign any values to those features, their dimensions are zero and, therefore, they contribute nothing to the dimensions of the box. In other words, without any padding, borders, or margins, the content and box dimensions are identical. With style sheets, you can assign values to your choice of edges (top, right, bottom, or left) for any feature.

---

* This is the way IE 6 for Windows works when in standards-compatible mode (see the <!DOCTYPE> element discussion in Chapter 8). In backward-compatible mode and earlier versions, the browser includes the border and padding in its height and width calculations.

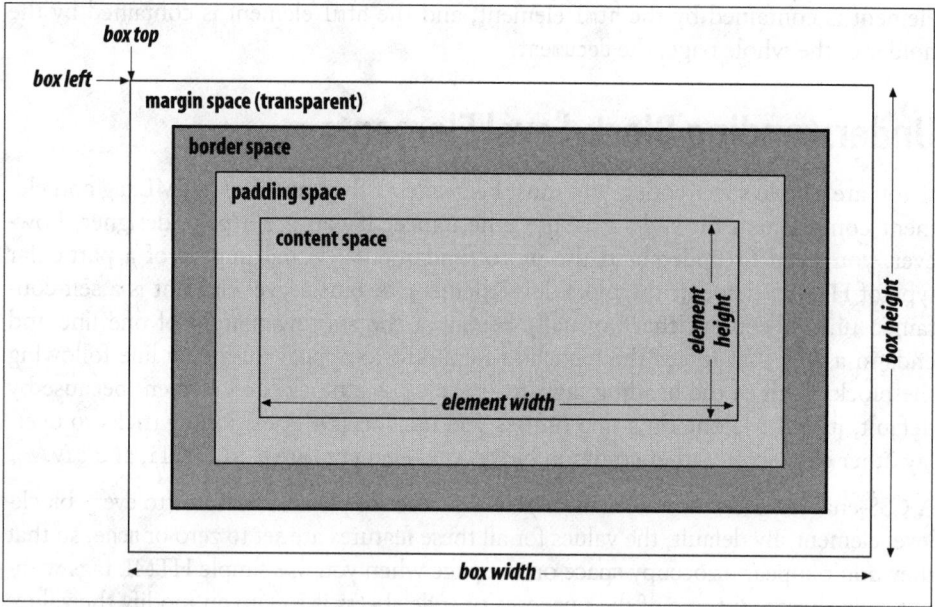

*Figure 3-2. Schematic diagram of block-level elements*

All margin space is transparent. Thus, any colors or images that exist in the next outer containing box (the body element always provides the base-level box) show through the margin space. Borders are opaque and always have a color associated with them. Padding space is also transparent, so you cannot set the padding to any color; the background color or image of the content shows through the padding space. Thus, this space "pads" the content to give some extra breathing room between the content and any border and/or margin defined for the element.

Some style sheet attributes provide a one-statement shortcut for applying independent values to each of the four edges of the margin, border, or padding. For example, you can set the top and bottom border widths to one size and apply a different size to the left and right sides of the same border. When such shortcuts are available (see the border, margin, and padding style attributes in Chapter 11, the values are applied in the same order: clockwise from the top—top, right, bottom, left.

## Box Positioning

While the content dimensions remain the same regardless of the dimensions assigned to various box features, the size of the box expands when you assign padding, borders, and margins to the element. As you will see in Chapter 4, the "thing" that gets positioned within the various coordinate planes is the box. The left and top outer edges of the box are emphasized in Figure 3-2 to reinforce this idea.

It is important to understand the difference between a piece of content and its containing box, especially if you start nesting positioned elements or need to rely on extremely accurate locations of elements on the page. Nesting multiple block-level elements inside each other offers a whole range of possible visual effects, so page designers have much to experiment with while developing unique looks.

# Two Types of Containment

If you have worked with JavaScript and the scriptable DOM Level 0 in early browsers, you are aware that objects in this model have a containment hierarchy of their own—an *object containment* hierarchy. The window object, which represents the content area of a browser window or frame, is at the top of the hierarchy. The window object contains objects such as the history, location, and document objects. The document object contains objects such as images and forms, and, among the most deeply nested objects, the form object contains form control elements, such as text fields and radio buttons.

Document object containment is vitally important in the comparatively limited DOM Level 0 because the hierarchy defines how you refer to objects and their methods and properties in your scripts. References usually start with the outermost element and work their way inward, using the JavaScript dot syntax to delimit each object. For example, here's how to reference the content of a text field (the value property) named zipCode inside a form named userInfo:

```
window.document.userInfo.zipCode.value
```

More modern DOMs, especially the W3C DOM Level 1 and later, let the structure of the document dictate *element containment* as defined by the tag geography of a document. In this context, you see frequent references to the notion of parents and children, where a nested element is a child of its parent container. CSS relies very heavily on element containment.

While the terms "parent" and "child" imply an object orientation, this is not the case in the DOM. An img element nested in a td element, for example, does not inherit the parent td element's id property. But when applying style sheets to an element containment structure, the concept of inheritance is alive and well: an element can inherit a style assigned to another element higher in the element containment hierarchy.

## Inheritance

All HTML document elements belong to the document's style inheritance chain. The root of the style chain is the html element (which differs from the DOM root: the even more global document node object). Its immediate children (also called descendants) are the next elements in the containment hierarchy. The inheritance chain depends entirely on the structure of HTML elements in the document. Figure 3-3 shows the CSS inheritance chains of the documents whose containment structures were depicted in Figure 3-1.

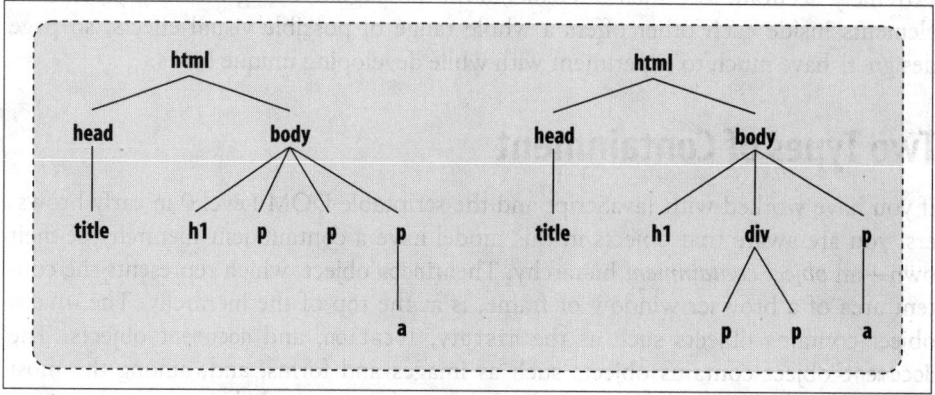

*Figure 3-3. CSS inheritance chains of two simple documents*

The importance of inheritance chains becomes clear when you begin assigning style attributes to elements that have descendants. In many cases, you want a descendant to inherit a style assigned to a parent or grandparent. For example, if you assign the Arial font family to all paragraphs (p elements), you more than likely want all descendant elements, such as portions designated as em elements inside a paragraph, to render their content in the same font family, in which case the default italic effect of the em element is applied to the inherited Arial font family.

Note that not all style attributes are inherited. Therefore, the style sheet attribute reference in Chapter 11 indicates whether each attribute is passed from parent to child.

## The Cascade

Element containment also plays a role in helping the browser determine which overlapping style sheet rule, of potentially several, should be applied to an element. As you will see later in this chapter, it is possible to assign multiple styles to the same element, by importing multiple style sheet definition files and by defining multiple styles for the same element, or its parent, directly in the document. Cascading style sheets get their name because styles can flow from a number of sources; the outcome of this cascade is what is displayed by the browser.

I'll come back to cascading later in this chapter, but for now you should be aware that the first step in predicting the outcome of overlapping style sheets is determining the element containment structure of the document. Once you know where an element stands within the document's inheritance chain, you can apply strict CSS principles that assign varying weights to the way a style is defined for a particular element.

# The CSS Platform

The type attribute of the `<style>` tag is where you specify the language and syntax you'll be using for your style sheets. This value is in the form of a content-type declaration, and the CSS specification declares `text/css` as its preferred content type. By convention, today's browsers treat `text/css` as the default type, but the `<style>` tag's type attribute is required in the HTML 4 recommendation. Therefore, always specify the type attribute for all `<style>` tags. A style element that relies on the CSS syntax should look like the following:

```
<style type="text/css">
...
</style>
```

For trivia buffs, Navigator 4 (only) featured a short-lived alternative syntax that followed the JavaScript object reference format. This alternate type, `text/javascript`, provided JavaScript equivalents for most of the style attributes and structures provided by the `text/css` syntax.

# Of Style Sheets, Elements, Attributes, and Values

Regardless of the syntax you use to define a style sheet, the basic concepts are the same. A style sheet is a collection of one or more *rules*. Each rule has two parts to it:

- References to one or more elements (or groups of elements) that are having style sheets defined for them
- One or more style sheet attributes that apply to the element(s)

In other words, each rule defines a particular look and feel and the item(s) in the document that are to be governed by that look and feel.

## Style Attributes

A style attribute is the name of a (usually) visible property of a piece of content on the page. An attribute such as `color` can apply to any element because that color can be applied to foreground content, such as text. Some attributes, such as borders and margins, can apply only to elements rendered as blocks on the page—they have a clear beginning and ending in both the HTML source code and in the layout. In their conservative approaches to claiming standards support, IE 6 and Netscape 6 promise full implementations of CSS1 (while both browsers support a lot of CSS2). To help you visualize the range of style options available as a common denominator, Table 3-1 shows a summary of CSS1 attributes grouped by category. You can find details of all CSS style sheet attributes in Chapter 11.

*Table 3-1. Summary of CSS1 style sheet attributes*

| Box properties | | |
|---|---|---|
| border | border-right-style | margin |
| border-top | border-bottom-style | margin-top |
| border-right | border-left-style | margin-right |
| border-bottom | border-width | margin-bottom |
| border-left | border-top-width | margin-left |
| border-color | border-right-width | padding |
| border-top-color | border-bottom-width | padding-top |
| border-right-color | border-left-width | padding-right |
| border-bottom-color | clear | padding-bottom |
| border-left-color | float | padding-left |
| border-style | height | width |
| border-top-style | | |

| Color and background properties | | |
|---|---|---|
| background | background-image | background-repeat |
| background-attachment | background-position | color |
| background-color | | |

| Classification properties | | |
|---|---|---|
| display | list-style-image | list-style |
| list-style-type | list-style-position | white-space |

| Font properties | | |
|---|---|---|
| font | font-size | font-variant |
| font-family | font-style | font-weight |

| Text properties | | |
|---|---|---|
| letter-spacing | line-height | vertical-align |
| text-align | text-indent | word-spacing |
| text-decoration | text-transform | |

## CSS Attribute Assignment Syntax

The syntax for assigning a value to an attribute is different from what you know about HTML attributes and their values. Assign a value via the colon operator (in contrast to the equal sign operator in HTML). A space after the colon is optional. The combination of an attribute name, colon operator, and value to be assigned to the attribute is called a *declaration*. To assign the color red to the foreground of an element, you could use either of the following simple declaration forms (colors may be specified many ways, as described in Chapter 11):

```
color:#ff0000
color:red
```

If a style sheet rule includes more than one declaration, separate declarations with semicolons:

```
color:#ff0000; font-size:12pt;
```

A trailing semicolon after the last declaration is optional, as is a space after the internal semicolon.

Notice, however, that unlike HTML attribute values, CSS syntax attribute values do not—and cannot—have double quotes around the values, except in rare circumstances (e.g., multiword font family names).

## Binding CSS Style Sheets to Elements

Defining a rule's declarations is only half the job. The other half involves identifying the HTML element(s) to which the rule applies. This is the job of the *selector*, which acts as a kind of label signifying the element or type of element to which a rule applies. In a simple case, you bind a declaration to a single element or a single type of element (e.g., all p elements, where the label is, literally, just p). The CSS standard also provides for additional ways of binding a declaration to a subgroup of elements scattered throughout a document (e.g., all elements sharing the same class attribute value). Finally, you can define exceptions to the grouping rules you establish in the document.

# Embedding Style Sheets

You add style sheets to a document by defining them explicitly in the document's source code, importing definitions from one or more external files, or a combination of the two. In-document and external style sheets coexist well in the same document; you can have as many of each type as your page design requires.

## In-Document Styles

There are two ways to embed CSS information directly in an HTML document: using the <style> tag pair or using style attributes of HTML tags. For ease of maintenance and consistency throughout a document, I recommend using a <style> tag inside the head section of the document. While placing a style definition in an element's tag flaunts the trend toward separating context from rendering, you may encounter valid reasons (explained later) to use this approach from time to time.

### The <style> tag

It is convenient to define style sheet rules between <style> and </style> tags. Because the body element is the container of the rendered content, you should use the <style> tag in the head section of your document. This placement also guarantees that the style sheet is loaded and in effect before any elements of the document are rendered. Include the type attribute in the opening tag, as in:

```
<style type="text/css">
    style sheet rule(s) here
</style>
```

Some pre-CSS browsers ignore the start and end tags and attempt to render the rules as if they were part of the document body. If you fear that this will affect users of your pages, you can surround the statements inside the style element with HTML comment symbols. Such a framework looks as follows:

```
<style type="text/css">
<!--
    style sheet rule(s) here
-->
</style>
```

This technique is similar to the one used to hide the contents of <script> tag pairs from older browsers, except that the end-comment statement in a script must start with a JavaScript comment symbol (//-->). The comment-bracketed content is still downloaded to the client and is visible in the source code, but for all but the most brain-dead browsers, the style sheet rules are hidden from plain view in the browser window. In the examples in this book, I have omitted these comment symbols to conserve space and improve readability, but it's a good idea to use them for public web pages.

As I mentioned earlier, the link between a style declaration and the element(s) it governs is called a selector. In practice, "selector" has a wide range of meanings. In its simplest form, a selector is the name of one type of HTML element—the HTML tag stripped of its enclosing angle brackets (e.g., the p selector, which represents all the paragraphs in a document). As you will see as this chapter progresses, a selector can take on additional forms, including some that have no resemblance at all to HTML elements. Just remember that a selector defines the part (or parts) of an HTML document that is governed by a style declaration.

In the most common application, each style rule binds a declaration to a particular type of HTML element based on the element's tag name. Get in the habit of using lowercase tag selectors to match the XHTML-inspired lowercase tag names. This simplest selector form is called a *type selector*. When a rule is specified in a <style> tag, the declaration portion of the rule must appear inside curly braces, even if there is just one style attribute in the declaration. Each curly brace pair and its content is known as a *declaration block*. The combination of a selector and a declaration block comprises a *rule set*. The style sheet in the following example includes two rule sets. The first assigns the red foreground (text) color and initial capital text transform to all h1 elements in the document; the second assigns the blue text color to all p elements:

```
<html>
<head>
```

```
<style type="text/css">
    h1 {color:red; text-transform:capitalize}
    p {color:blue}
</style>
</head>
<body>
<h1>Some heading</h1>
<p>Some paragraph text.</p>
</body>
</html>
```

There is no practical limit to the number of rule sets that can be listed inside the <style> tag pair, nor is there a limit to the number of style attributes that can be used in a style rule. Also, rule sets can appear in any order within a style sheet, and the indenting shown in the preceding example is purely optional. White space between attribute/value pairs is not critical; as a result you can also break up a series of declarations (inside the curly braces) so that each attribute/value pair appears on its own line, as follows:

```
h1 {
        color:red;
        text-transform:capitalize;
    }
```

CSS syntax provides a shortcut for assigning the same style declaration to more than one selector. By preceding the curly-braced style declaration block with a comma-delimited list of selectors, you can have one statement do the work of two or more statements. For example, if you want to assign the same color to h1, h2, and h3 elements in the document, you can do so with one statement:

```
<style type="text/css">
    h1, h2, h3 {color:blue}
</style>
```

This selector grouping technique is applicable to all CSS selector types described in this chapter.

### The style attribute in element tags

Another way to bind a style declaration to an HTML element is to include the declaration as an attribute of the actual HTML element tag. The declaration is assigned to the style attribute; almost every HTML element recognizes the style attribute.

Because the style attribute is a regular HTML attribute, you assign a value to it via the equal sign operator. The value is a double-quoted string that consists of one or more style attribute/value pairs in the default CSS style sheet syntax. These style attribute/value pairs use the colon assignment operator. Use a semicolon to separate multiple style attribute settings within the same style attribute. The following code uses a style attribute version of the <style> tag example shown in the preceding section. Because the style sheets are attached to the actual HTML element tags, all this takes place in the body section of the document:

```
<body>
<h1 style="color:red; text-transform:capitalize">Some heading</h1>
<p style="color:blue">Some paragraph text.</p>
</body>
```

Notice, too, that when a style sheet definition is specified as a style attribute, there are no curly braces involved. The double quotes surrounding the entire style sheet definition function as the curly brace grouping characters.

## Importing External Style Sheets

Perhaps the most common use of style sheets in the publishing world is to establish a "look" designed to pervade across all documents, or at least across all sections of a large document. To facilitate applying a style sheet across multiple HTML pages, the CSS specification provides two ways to include external style sheet files: an implementation of the <link> tag and a special type of style sheet rule selector called the @import rule.

### External style sheet files

No matter how you import an external style sheet, the external file must be written in such a way that the browser can use it to build the library of style sheets that controls the currently loaded document. In other words, the browser must take into account not only external styles, but any other styles that might also be defined inside the document. Because there is an opportunity for the overlap of multiple style sheets in a document, the browser must see how all the styles are bound to elements, so it can apply cascading rules (described later in this chapter) to render the content.

An external style sheet file consists exclusively of style sheet rule sets without any HTML tags. The file should be in plain text format and saved with the .css filename extension. For example, to convert the style sheet used in the previous sections to an external style sheet file, create a text file that contains the following and save the file as *basestyle.css*:

```
h1 {color:red; text-transform:capitalize}
p {color:blue}
```

When a browser encounters either technique for importing an external style sheet, the content of the file is loaded into the browser as if it were typed into the main HTML document at that source code location (although it doesn't become part of the source code if you use the browser to view the source). The web server must also be configured to associate the .css filename extension with a content-type of text/css (most modern servers are already set up this way, but check with the server administrator if you're not sure).

### The link element

HTML recognizes `<link>` as a general-purpose tag for linking media-independent content into a document (not to be confused with hypertext links created by the `<a>` tag). It is up to the browser to know how to work with the various attributes of this tag (see Chapter 8).

The CSS2 specification claims one application of the `link` element as a way to link an external style sheet file into a document. The attributes and format for the tag are rather simple:

```
<link rel="stylesheet" type="contentType" href="filename.css">
```

The *contentType* value for CSS style sheets is text/css. If the style sheet in the previous section is saved as *basestyle.css*, you can import that style sheet as follows:

```
<html>
<head>
<link rel="stylesheet" type="text/css" href="basestyle.css">
</head>
<body>
<h1>Some heading</h1>
<p>Some paragraph text.</p>
</body>
</html>
```

A document can have multiple `link` elements for importing multiple external style sheet files (only one file per `link` element). The document can also contain `style` elements as well as `style` attributes embedded within element tags. But if there is any overlap of more than one style applying to the same element, the cascade rules (described later in this chapter) determine the specific style sheet rule that governs the element's display.

### The @import rule

CSS2 describes an extensible system for declarations or directives (commands, if you will) that become a part of a style sheet definition. They are called *at-rules* because a rule starts with the "at" symbol (@), followed by an identifier for the declaration. Each at-rule includes one or more descriptors that define the characteristics of the rule and end with a semicolon. (For more about at-rules, see Chapter 11.)

One such at-rule that is implemented starting in IE 4 and Netscape 6 imports an external style sheet file from inside a `style` element. It performs the same function as the `link` import technique described in the previous section. In the following example, a file containing style sheet rules is imported into the current document:

```
<style type="text/css">
    @import url("styles/corporate.css");
</style>
```

You may include multiple @import rules in a style element, but they must come before rules with any other type of selector. An @import rule must also stand alone, without being nested inside curly brace blocks.

If you are creating documents for browser versions that support the @import rule, it's easier to find style references by keeping all style sheet definitions within the style element rather than spreading the import job to a separate link element.

## Selecting a Style Sheet Style

In deciding among the many ways to introduce style sheets into your pages—the <style> tag, the style attribute, or imported from outside the document—you need to consider how important it is for you to separate design from content. The <style> tag technique distances HTML content from the styles associated with elements throughout the document. If you need to change a font family or size for a particular kind of element, you can do so quickly and reliably by making the change to one location in the document. If, on the other hand, your style definitions are scattered among dozens or hundreds of tags throughout the document, such a change requires much more effort and the possibility for mistakes increases. However, for small-scale deployment of style sheets, the style attribute will certainly do the job. And, if one person is responsible for both content and design, it isn't too difficult to keep the content and design in sync.

As discussed in Chapter 4, where you declare an element's style impacts how DHTML scripts read the element's initial style properties. An element object's style property reflects only values assigned via the element tag's style attribute. In contrast, reading the initial value styles applied through <style> or imported style sheet rules requires special syntax that is incompatible between IE and W3C DOM implementations, as discussed in Chapter 4.

Current web development trends lean toward the separation of design from content. In large projects involving writers, designers, and programmers, it is usually easier to manage the entire project if different contributors to the application can work toward the same goal without stepping on each other's code along the way. It is no accident that both style sheets and scripts have acquired mechanisms for importing external files into an HTML document. This allows designers to work on their *.css* files and programmers to work on their *.js* files, all of which blend into the writer's *.html* file (or equivalent server output) that arrives at the client.

## Common Subgroup Selectors

While a selector for a style sheet rule is often an HTML element name, that scenario isn' flexible enough for more complex documents. Consider the following possibilities:

- You want certain paragraphs scattered throughout the document to be set apart from running text with wider left and right margins.

- You want all but one of the h2 elements in the document to be set to the color red; the one exception must be blue.
- In a three-level ordered list (ol) group, you want to assign different font sizes to each level.

Each of these possibilities calls for a different way of creating a new selector group or specifying an exception to the regular selectors. In an effort to distance design from content, CSS style sheets provide three simple ways of creating subgroups that can handle almost every design possibility:

- Class selectors
- ID selectors
- Descendant selectors

Using these subgroup selectors requires special ways of defining selectors in style sheet rules. These selectors also require the addition of attributes to the HTML tags they apply to in the document. Because all CSS-enabled browsers support these CSS1 subgroup selectors, you should have these deeply ingrained in your authoring repertoire.

## Class Selectors

A class selector is an identifier you can use to assign a style to a subset of elements in a document. To apply a class selector, you first invent an identifier for the class name. CSS2 guidelines for selector identifiers allow all Latin letters (a through z and A through Z), numerals (0 through 9), the hyphen, Unicode characters above 160, and escaped characters (characters that begin with a backslash character)—provided the name does not begin with a numeral or hyphen. Spaces are not permitted. For the sake of compatibility and the occasional browser bug, it is good practice to stick with Latin letters only. Version 6 browsers treat selectors in a case-sensitive manner, while earlier browsers do not. Therefore, the best forward- and backward-compatible practice is to observe case throughout, but not to reuse names with different combinations of upper- and lowercase letters.

The class identifier goes in both the style sheet rule and the HTML tag (assigned to the class attribute) for all elements that are to obey the rule. While the identifier name is the same in both cases, the syntax for specifying it is quite different in each place.

### Binding a class identifier to an element type

In the style sheet rule, the class identifier is part of the rule's selector. When a class selector is intended to apply to only one kind of HTML element, the selector consists of the element name, a period, and the identifier. The following rule assigns a specific margin setting for all p elements flagged as belonging to the narrow class:

```
p.narrow {margin-left:5em; margin-right:5em}
```

To force a p element to obey the p.narrow rule, you must include a class attribute in the `<p>` tag and set the value to the class identifier:

```
<p class="narrow">Content for the narrow paragraph</p>
```

Any p elements that don't have the class attribute set to narrow follow the style applied to the generic p element. Example 3-1 shows a complete document that includes style sheet rules for all p elements and a subclass of p.narrow elements. The rule for all p elements specifies a 2-em margin on the left and right as well as a 14-pixel font size. For all p elements tagged with the class="narrow" attribute, the margins are set to 5 ems and the text color is set to red. Note the p.narrow rule inherits (or is affected by) style settings from the p rule. Therefore, all text in the p.narrow elements is displayed at a font size of 14 pixels. But when the margin attributes are set in both rules, the settings for the named class override the settings of the broader p element rule (the language of CSS doesn't include the object-oriented concepts of subclass or superclass). Following the inheritance trail one level higher in the containment hierarchy, all p elements (and all other elements in the document if there were any) obey the style sheet rule for the body element, which is where the font face is specified.

*Example 3-1. Applying the p.narrow class rule*

```
<html>
<head>
<title>Class Society</title>
<style type="text/css">
    p {font-size:14px; margin-left:2em; margin-right:2em}
    p.narrow {color:red; margin-left:5em; margin-right:5em}
    body {font-family:Arial, sans-serif}
</style>
</head>

<body>
<p>
This is a normal paragraph. This is a normal paragraph. This is a normal
paragraph. This is a normal paragraph. This is a normal paragraph.
</p>
<p class="narrow">
This is a paragraph to be set apart with wider margins and red color. This is a
paragraph to be set apart with wider margins and red color. This is a paragraph
to be set apart with wider margins and red color.
</p>
<p>
This is a normal paragraph. This is a normal paragraph. This is a normal
paragraph. This is a normal paragraph. This is a normal paragraph.
</p>
<p class="narrow">
This is a paragraph to be set apart with wider margins and red color. This is a
paragraph to be set apart with wider margins and red color. This is a paragraph
to be set apart with wider margins and red color.
</p>
</body>
</html>
```

## Defining a free-range class rule

Most of the time, you don't want to limit a class selector to a single element type in a document. Fortunately, you can define a rule with a class selector that can be applied to any element in the document. The selector of such a rule is nothing more than the identifier preceded by a period. Example 3-2 contains a rule that assigns a red underline style to a class named hot. The hot class is then assigned to different elements scattered throughout the document. Notice inheritance at work in this example. When the hot class is assigned to a div element, it applies to the p element nested inside the div element: the entire paragraph is rendered in the hot style and follows the p.narrow rule as well, since the rules do not have any overlapping style attributes.

*Example 3-2. Adding a free-range class selector*

```
<html>
<head>
<title>Free Range Class</title>
<style type="text/css">
    p {font-size:14px; margin-left:2em; margin-right:2em}
    p.narrow {color:red; margin-left:5em; margin-right:5em}
    .hot {color:red; text-decoration:underline}
    body {font-family:Arial, sans-serif}
</style>
</head>

<body>
<h1 class="hot">Get a Load of This!</h1>
<p>
This is a normal paragraph. This is a normal paragraph. This is a normal
paragraph. This is a normal paragraph. This is a normal paragraph.
</p>
<div class="hot">
<p class="narrow">
This is a paragraph to be set apart with wider margins and red color. This is a
paragraph to be set apart with wider margins and red color. This is a paragraph
to be set apart with wider margins and red color.
</p>
</div>
<p>
This is a normal paragraph. This is a normal paragraph <span class="hot">but with a
red-hot spot</span>. This is a normal paragraph. This is a normal paragraph. This
is a normal paragraph.
</p>
<p class="narrow">
This is a paragraph to be set apart with wider margins and red color. This is a
paragraph to be set apart with wider margins and red color. This is a paragraph
to be set apart with wider margins and red color.
</p>
</body>
</html>
```

# ID Selectors

In contrast to the class selector, the ID selector lets you define a rule that applies to only one element in the entire document. Like the class selector, the ID selector requires a special way of defining the selector in the style sheet rule and a special attribute (id) in the tag that is the recipient of that rule. The same rules and warnings about defining class names also apply to ID names. Uniqueness within a document is critical not only for CSS ID selectors to work correctly, but especially for DHTML scripting. An element's id attribute value acts as a kind of address that scripts use to reference the element, regardless of document structure. This means that to maintain integrity of the object model for the current document, an id identifier must apply to only one element.

The style rule syntax for defining an ID selector calls for the identifier to be preceded with the # symbol. This can be in conjunction with an element selector or by itself. Therefore, both of the following rules are valid:

```
p#special4 {border:5px ridge red}
#special4{border:5px ridge red}
```

To apply this rule for this ID to a p element, you have to add the id attribute to that element's tag:

```
<p id="special4">Content for a special paragraph.</p>
```

There is an important difference between the two style rule examples just shown. By specifying the ID selector in concert with the p element selector in the first example, we've told the browser to obey the id="special4" attribute only if it appears in a p element. The second rule, however, is a generic rule. This means that the id="special4" attribute can appear in any kind of element. Since an id attribute value should be used in only one element throughout the entire document, the combined selector is redundant.

Example 3-3 shows the ID selector at work, where it is used to assign a rule (defining a red, ridge-style border for a block) to only one of several p elements in the document. Notice that it is assigned to a p element that also has a class selector assigned to it: two rules are applied to the same element. In this example, the style rules do not conflict with each other, but if they did, the cascade precedence rules (described later in this chapter) would automatically determine precisely which rule wins the battle of the dueling style attributes.

*Example 3-3. Applying an ID selector to a document*

```
<html>
<head>
<title>ID Selector</title>
<style type="text/css">
    p {font-size:14px; margin-left:2em; margin-right:2em}
    p.narrow {color:red; margin-left:5em; margin-right:5em}
    #special4 {border:5px ridge red}
    body {font-family:Arial, sans-serif}
```

*Example 3-3. Applying an ID selector to a document (continued)*

```
</style>
</head>

<body>
<h1>Get a Load of This!</h1>
<p>
This is a normal paragraph. This is a normal paragraph. This is a normal
paragraph. This is a normal paragraph. This is a normal paragraph.
</p>
<p class="narrow" id="special4">This is a paragraph to be set apart with wider
margins, red color AND a red border. This is a paragraph to be set apart with
wider margins, red color AND a red border.
</p>
<p>
This is a normal paragraph. This is a normal paragraph. This is a normal
paragraph. This is a normal paragraph. This is a normal paragraph.
</p>
<p class="narrow">This is a paragraph to be set apart with wider margins and red
color. This is a paragraph to be set apart with wider margins and red color. This
is a paragraph to be set apart with wider margins and red color.
</p>
</body>
</html>
```

## Descendant Selectors

One more way to assign styles to specific categories of elements is the descendant
selector (formerly known as a contextual selector). To use a descendant selector, you
should be comfortable with the containment hierarchy of elements in a document
and how inheritance affects the application of styles to a chunk of content. Consider
the two type selector rules in the following style sheet:

```
<style type="text/css">
    p {font-size:14px; color:black}
    em {font-size:16px; color:red}
</style>
```

This style sheet dictates that all em elements throughout the document be displayed
in red with a 16-pixel font. If you were to add an em element as part of an h1 element, the effect might be less than desirable. What you really want from the style
sheet is to apply the em style declaration to em elements only when they are contained
by—are descended from—p elements. A descendant selector lets you do just that. In
a descendant selector, you list the elements of the containment hierarchy that are to
be affected by the style, with the elements separated by spaces.

To turn the second rule of the previous style sheet into a descendant selector, modify it as follows:

```
<style type="text/css">
    p {font-size:14px; color:black}
    p em {font-size:16px; color:red}
</style>
```

You still need the rule for the base p element in this case because the style is something other than the browser default. There is no practical limit to the number of containment levels you can use in a descendant selector. For example, if the design calls for a section of an em element to have a yellow background color, you can assign that job to a span element and set the descendant selector to affect a span element only when it is nested inside an em element that is nested inside a p element. Example 3-4 shows what the source code for such a document looks like. The example goes one step further, in that one element of the descendant selectors is a class selector (p.narrow). Each element selector in a descendant selector can be any valid selector, including a class or ID selector. You can also apply the same style declaration to more than one descendant selector by separating the descendant selector sequences with commas:

```
p em span, h3 em {background-color:yellow}
```

It's an odd-looking construction, but it's perfectly legal (and byte conservative).

*Example 3-4. Applying a three-level descendant selector*

```
<html>
<head>
<title>Descendant Selector</title>
<style type="text/css">
    p {font-size:14px; margin-left:2em; margin-right:2em}
    p.narrow {color:red; margin-left:5em; margin-right:5em}
    p.narrow em {font-weight:bold}
    p.narrow em span {background-color:yellow}
    #special4 {border:5px ridge red}
    body {font-family:Arial, sans-serif}
</style>
</head>

<body>
<h1>Get a Load of This!</h1>
<p>
This is a normal paragraph. This is a normal paragraph. This is a normal
paragraph. This is a normal paragraph. This is a normal paragraph.
</p>
<p class="narrow" id="special4">This is a <em>paragraph to be set apart</em> with
wider margins, red color AND a red border. This is a paragraph to be set apart
with wider margins, red color AND a red border.
</p>
<p>
This is a normal paragraph. This is a normal paragraph. This is a normal
paragraph. This is a normal paragraph. This is a normal paragraph.
</p>
<p class="narrow">This is a <em>paragraph to be <span>set apart</span></em> with
wider margins and red color. This is a paragraph to be set apart with wider
margins and red color. This is a paragraph to be set apart with wider margins and
red color.
</p>
</body>
</html>
```

Note that a descendant selector points to any descendant of a parent element, even if the descendant is nested many levels deep in the containment hierarchy. To restrict a selector to an immediate child of an element, see "Child Selectors" later in this chapter.

# Advanced Subgroup Selectors

The CSS2 specification makes further enhancements to the way selectors can be specified in style sheet rules. Netscape 6 and IE 5/Mac support more of these advanced selectors than IE 6/Windows. See Chapter 11 for selector compatibility in major browsers. Most of these advanced selector forms extend the concepts in effect for simple selectors. They provide either special case selectors or additional ways to slice and dice element collections for finely-tuned style designs.

## Pseudo-Element and Pseudo-Class Selectors

The original idea for pseudo-elements and pseudo-classes was defined as part of the CSS1 recommendation; these selectors have been expanded in CSS2. A fine line distinguishes these two concepts, but they do share one important factor: there are no direct HTML tag equivalents for the elements or classes described by these selectors. Therefore, you must imagine how the selectors will affect the real tags in your document.

### Using pseudo-elements

A pseudo-element is a well-defined chunk of content in an HTML element. Two pseudo-elements specified in the CSS1 recommendation point to the first letter and the first line of a paragraph. The elements are named :first-letter and :first-line, respectively. It is up to the browser to figure out where, for example, the first line ends (based on the content and window width) and apply the style only to the content in that line. If the browser is told to format the :first-letter pseudo-element with a drop cap, the browser must also take care of rendering the rest of the text in the paragraph so that it wraps around the drop cap.

For example, to apply styles for the first letter and first line of all p elements, use the following style rules:

```
<style type="text/css">
    p:first-letter {font-face:Gothic, serif; font-size:300%; float:left}
    p:first-line {font-style:small-caps}
</style>
```

Style attributes that can be set for :first-letter and :first-line include a large subset of the full CSS attribute set. They include all font, color, background, and several more text-related attributes (line-height, text-decoration, letter-spacing, and so on). The :first-letter element also allows for borders, margins, and padding.

The CSS2 :before and :after pseudo-elements offer intriguing possibilities for inserting repeated or generated text before or after an element. For example, you could define a `blockquote:after` selector that inserts the phrase "Reprinted by permission." at the end of every blockquote element on the page. Another variation maintains counter variables that track and render incremented numbers to be inserted before each element defined by a selector. Very few of these facilities are built into IE 6 or Netscape 6, so it will be awhile before you can freely take advantage of their powers. But because pseudo-elements can impact actual text characters on the page, you'll need to tread carefully with their deployment.

### Using pseudo-classes

In contrast to a pseudo-element, a pseudo-class applies to an element whose look or content may change as the user interacts with the content. Pseudo-classes defined in the CSS1 recommendation are for three states of the a element: a link not yet visited, a link being clicked on by the user, and a link that has been visited. Default behavior in most browsers is to differentiate these states by colors (default colors can usually be set by user preferences as well as by attributes of the body element). The syntax for pseudo-class selectors follows the same pattern as for pseudo-elements. This style sheet defines rules for the three a element pseudo-classes:

```
<style type="text/css">
    a:link {color:darkred}
    a:active {color:coral}
    a:visited {color:lightblue; font-size:-1}
</style>
```

Pseudo-classes in CSS2 include `:first-child`, `:lang`, `:active`, `:focus`, and `:hover`. The last one, implemented for a elements starting in IE 5 and Netscape 6, allows for style changes to take effect when the cursor rolls atop a link—without the customary mouse event script processing.

As with other selectors, you can combine class or ID selectors with pseudo-elements or pseudo-classes to narrow the application of a special style. For instance, you may want a large drop cap to appear only in the first paragraph of a page. See Chapter 11 for an example, plus a list of CSS2 pseudo-elements and pseudo-classes.

## Attribute Selectors

In CSS1, the links between style rule selector and an element's attributes are limited to the class and id attributes. CSS2 broadens the possibilities to include any attribute or attribute/value pair as selectors. In the context of CSS2, the class and ID selectors described earlier are simply special cases of the *attribute selector*.

It is helpful to think of an attribute selector as an expression that helps the user agent (browser or application) locate a match of HTML elements or attributes to determine whether the style should be applied. A match may occur by the presence of an attribute name in the tag, or an attribute and a specific value. For example, a page may contain several a elements, some of which open a second window by assigning the attribute target="_blank". An attribute selector allows one style to apply only to those a elements with the attribute combination, while another style applies to all other a elements that target the current window.

Table 3-2 shows the four attribute selector formats and what they mean. A new syntactical feature for selectors—square brackets—adds another level of complexity to defining style sheet rules, but the added flexibility may be worth the effort.

*Table 3-2. Attribute selector syntax*

| Syntax format | Description |
|---|---|
| [attributeName] | Matches an element if the attribute is defined in the HTML tag |
| [attributeName=value] | Matches an element if the attribute is set to the specified value in the HTML tag |
| [attributeName~=value] | Matches an element if the specified value is present among the values assigned to the attribute in the HTML tag |
| [attributeName\|=value] | Matches an element if the attribute value contains a hyphen, but starts with *value* |

To see how these selector formats work, observe how the sample style sheet rules in Table 3-3 apply to an associated HTML tag.

*Table 3-3. How attribute selectors work*

| Style sheet selector | Applies to | Does not apply to |
|---|---|---|
| p[align] | <p align="left"><br><p align="left" title="Summary"> | <p title="Summary"> |
| hr[align="left"] | <hr align="left"> | <hr align="middle"> |
| img[alt~="Placeholder"] | <img alt="Temporary Placeholder" src="picture.gif"> | <applet alt="Applet Placeholder" code=...> |
| p[lang\|="en"] | <p lang="en-CA"> | <p lang="fr-CA"> |

## Universal Selectors

In practice, the absence of an element selector before an attribute selector implies that the rule is to apply to any and all elements of the document. But a special symbol more clearly states your intentions. The asterisk symbol (*) acts like a wildcard character to select all elements. You can use this to a greater advantage when you combine selector types, such as the universal and attribute selector. The following selector applies to all elements whose align attributes are set to a specific value:

    *[align="middle"]

## Child Selectors

Element containment is a key factor in the child selector. Again, following the notion of a style rule selector matching a pattern in a document, the child selector looks for element patterns that match a specific sequence of parent and child elements. The behavior of a child selector is very similar to that of a descendant selector, but the notation is different—a greater-than symbol (>) separates the element names in the selector, as in:

```
body > p {font-size:12px}
```

Another difference is that the two elements on either side of the symbol must be direct relations of each other, as a paragraph is of a body.

## Adjacent Sibling Selectors

An adjacent sibling selector lets you define a rule for an element based on its position relative to another element or, rather, the sequence of elements. Such adjacent selectors consist of two or more element selectors, with a plus symbol (+) between the selectors. For example, if your design calls for an extra top margin for an h2 block whenever it immediately follows an h1 element in the document, the rule looks like the following:

```
h1 + h2 {margin-top: 6px}
```

# Cascade Precedence Rules

By now it should be clear that there are many ways styles can be applied to an element—from an external style sheet file, from a <style> tag set, and from a style attribute in a tag—and there is the possibility that multiple style rules can easily apply to the same element in a document (intentionally or not). To deal with these issues, the CSS recommendation had to devise a set of rules for resolving conflicts among overlapping styles. These rules are intended primarily for the browser (and other user agent) makers, but if you are designing complex style sheets or are seeing unexpected results in a complex document, you need to be aware of how the browser resolves these conflicts for you.

Conflict resolution is mostly a matter of assigning a relative weight to every rule that applies to a particular element. Rules with the most weight are the ones that most specifically target the element. At the lightweight end of the spectrum is the "non-rule," or default style setting for the document, generally governed by the browser's internal design and sometimes influenced by preference settings (e.g., the base font size for text content). Such a "nonrule" may directly apply to only a high-level object, such as the body element; only by way of inheritance does the default rule apply to some element buried within the content. At the heavyweight end of the spectrum is the style rule that is targeted specifically at a particular element. This may be by way of an ID selector or the ultimate in specificity: a style attribute inside the tag. No run-of-the-mill style rule can override an embedded style attribute.

Between those two extremes are dozens of potential conflicts that depend on the way style sheets are defined for the document. As an example, a browser always has its own default style sheet so that it knows how to render standard elements. Browser preferences (such as viewing in a larger font size) modify those default settings. Some browsers also allow users to apply their own generic style sheets to override the default settings. But what happens when a document arrives with its own settings? Before rendering any style-sheet–capable element, the browser uses the following decision path to determine how that element should be rendered:

1. Scan the document for any author-specified style declarations that have a selector that matches the element. If the element is not selected by any rules, short-circuit the rest of the decision path and render the element according to the user's style sheet, if present, or the browser's current built-in settings.

2. Sort all applicable declarations according to weight as indicated by a special !important declaration (see the following section). Declarations marked important are assigned greater weight than unmarked declarations.

3. Sort declarations again, this time by origin. If the same selector and style declaration is marked !important in both the document and the user's style sheet (if present), give precedence to the user's style (in other words, assign the greatest possible weight to user rules marked !important). For unmarked declarations, assign greater weight to the author's style, followed by the user's style (if present), and then the browser default style.

4. Now sort the unmarked declarations by the specificity of the rule's selector. The more specific the selector (see the section on selector specificity later in this chapter), the greater the weight assigned to that declaration.

5. Finally, if more than one declaration is assigned the same weight after previous sorting, sort one last time based on the order in which the rules are defined in the document. The last applicable rule with the greatest weight wins the conflict. Rules defined in multiple imported style sheets are defined in the order of the statements that trigger the import; an @import rule must be positioned before explicit rules in a <style> tag set and therefore carries less weight than the explicit rule; a rule defined in an element's style attribute is the last and heaviest unmarked (i.e., not !important) rule.

## Making a Declaration Important

You can give an individual declaration within a rule an extra boost in its battle for superiority in the cascading order. When you do this to a declaration, the declaration is called the *important* declaration; it is signified by an exclamation mark (!)and the word important following the declaration. For example, in the following style sheet, the margin-left attribute for the p element is marked important:

```
<style type="text/css">
    p {font-size:14px; margin-left:2em !important; margin-right:2em}
    p.narrow {color:red; margin-left:5em; margin-right:5em}
</style>
```

When the document encounters a `<p>` tag with a `class` attribute set to `narrow`, the left margin setting of the less specific `<p>` tag overrides the setting of the more specific `p.narrow` class because of the important declaration. Note that this is an artificial example because you typically would not include conflicting style rules in the same style sheet. The important declaration can play a role when a document imports one or more style sheets. If a generic rule for the specific document must override a more specific rule in an imported style sheet, the important declaration can influence the cascading order. A browser that has correctly implemented user style sheets treats a user's `!important` style declaration as the weightiest style rule. While a page designer might question why the user has the most power in the cascading battle, bear in mind that a user may employ styles tailored to special accessibility needs, such as extra-large font sizes or high-contrast color combinations.

## Determining a Selector's Specificity

The fourth cascading precedence rule refers to the notion of *specificity*, or how well a rule selector targets a particular element in a document. The CSS recommendation establishes an unseen, internal ranking system that assigns values to three categories, arbitrarily designated a, b, and c. These categories represent the counts of items within a rule selector, as follows:

*a*   The count of ID selectors

*b*   The count of other selector types

*c*   The count of elements mentioned by name in the selector

For any rule selector, the browser adds up the total for each category and then concatenates the three totals to come up with a specificity value. Table 3-4 displays a sequence of rule selectors in increasing specificity.

*Table 3-4. Specificity ratings for rule selectors*

| Rule selector | a | b | c | Specificity rating |
|---|---|---|---|---|
| em | 0 | 0 | 1 | 1 |
| p em | 0 | 0 | 2 | 2 |
| div p em | 0 | 0 | 3 | 3 |
| em.hot | 0 | 1 | 1 | 11 |
| p em.hot | 0 | 1 | 2 | 12 |
| #hotStuff | 1 | 0 | 0 | 100 |

Browsers use the highest applicable specificity rating value to determine which rule wins any conflict. For example, if a style sheet defines the six rules for em elements shown in Table 3-4 (with the #hotStuff rule being an ID selector), the browser applies the highest relevant specificity rating to each instance of the em element. An element with the tag `<em class="hot">` inside an h1 element most closely matches the em.hot rule selector (specificity rating of 11), and therefore ignores all other selectors. But if the same em element is placed inside a p element, the more specific rule selector (p em.hot) wins.

## Cross-Platform Style Differences

After a few years of feeling their way around CSS implementation, the major browser vendors have produced reasonably well-behaved rendering engines since IE 5 (Windows and Mac), Opera 5, and Netscape 6. For the common style attributes in CSS1, you stand a good chance of achieving nearly identical output across these browsers.

Not that implementations are perfect. Even in recent browsers, some style attributes (float and overflow come to mind) can be neverending sources of cross-browser frustration. Assigning styles to complex hierarchical elements—especially deeply nested tables and lists—is a risky business, as inheritance chains mysteriously disconnect, and style attributes have minds of their own on some browser versions. Assuring consistent font sizes across browsers sometimes requires the equivalent of black magic.

Listing every browser's style sheet anomaly is beyond the scope of this book. Given all the content combinations and unexpected interactions, such an up-to-date master list probably doesn't exist. Always check the developer release notes for a browser. The open source Mozilla browser offers public access to the internal bug tracking system (Bugzilla), which may help you validate a problem you're experiencing with Netscape 6 or later. For other browsers, you'll have to rely on developer exchanges in the many online forums scattered across the Web.

That such inconsistencies exist points to the fact that deployment of CSS style sheets across all DHTML-capable browsers requires testing on as many browser brands and operating systems as you can get your hands on. Carefully study the output on each to make sure that your design goals are met, even if the exact implementations don't match pixel for pixel on the screen.

# CHAPTER 4

# Adding Dynamic Positioning to Documents

Now a part of Cascading Style Sheets Level 2, element positioning standards began life as a CSS1 supplement, called CSS-Positioning (or CSS-P for short). CSS attributes that govern positioning are a well-defined subset of CSS (they comprise a separate module of CSS3), so this chapter occasionally refers to this group as CSS-P.

A fundamental concept of positioning is direct control of the placement of elements on the page, when the browser-controlled flow of content just isn't good enough. To accomplish element positioning, a browser must be able to treat positionable elements as layers that can be dropped anywhere on the page, even overlapping other fixed or positionable elements—something that normal HTML rendering scrupulously avoids.*

The notion of layering adds a third dimension to a page, even if a video monitor (or a printed page) is undoubtedly a two-dimensional realm. That third dimension—the layering of elements—is of concern to you as the author of positionable content, but is probably of no concern to the page's human viewer.

While the primary concern of the CSS-P recommendation is the way an author lays out elements in a document, the IE 4 and W3C DOMs expose positioning attributes as scriptable properties that can be changed in response to user action. Now you have the opportunity to create some very interactive content: content that flies around the page, hides and shows itself at will, centers itself horizontally and vertically in the currently sized browser window, and even lets itself be dragged around the page by the user.

---

* I use the term "layer" guardedly here. While the word appeared originally in the Navigator 4 DHTML lexicon (derived from Navigator 4's <layer> tag and a scriptable layer object), you probably won't see the same word being used by the Microsoft camp. My application of the term is generic and it aptly describes what's going on here: a positionable element is like an acetate layer of a film cartoon cel. The cartoon artist starts with a base layer for the scene's backdrop and then positions one or more acetate layers atop the background; each layer is transparent except for some or all of the art for a single frame of the film. For the next frame of the cartoon, perhaps one of the layers for a character in the background must move a fraction of an inch. The artist repositions that layer, while the others stay the same. That's what I mean by "layer" in this context.

Netscape Navigator 4 was the first released browser to incorporate positioned elements. Because its HTML, CSS, and DOM approaches to positioning did not gain favor in the W3C, the techniques were not carried forward in newer browsers. These techniques—as well as their coexistence with the incompatible IE 4 model—were documented at length in the first edition of this book. This new edition, however, addresses only the far more compatible and prevalent IE and W3C implementations.

# Creating Positionable Elements

You can turn any rendered HTML element into a positionable element. This includes block elements, such as p or div containers, as well as arbitrary inline elements, such as img elements or span containers.

## Setting the position Attribute

To turn an HTML element into a positionable element, you must assign it a CSS style rule that includes the position attribute and a value other than the default (static). As demonstrated in Chapter 3, you can assign this style attribute by including a style attribute in the actual HTML tag or using an ID selector for the rule and setting the corresponding id attribute in the element's HTML tag.

The following HTML document demonstrates the two techniques you can use to turn an element into a positionable element:

```
<html>
<head>
<style type="text/css">
    #someSpan {position:absolute; left:10px; top:30px}
</style>
</head>
<body>
<div id="someDiv" style="position:absolute; left:100px; top:50px">
Hello.
<span id="someSpan">
Hello, again.
</span>
</div>
</body>
</html>
```

The first technique defines an ID selector inside a <style> tag that is mated to an id attribute of a span element in the document's body. The second approach defines the style as an inline attribute of a <div> tag. As with ordinary CSS style sheets, you can use any combination of methodologies (including imported style sheets) to apply position style rules to elements in a document.

Applying Dynamic HTML

**Creating Positionable Elements** | 71

Once you have set the position attribute, you can set other CSS-P attributes, such as left and top, to position the element. Possible values for the position attribute are:

absolute
> Element becomes a block element (even it is normally an inline element) and is positionable relative to the element's positioning context.

fixed
> Element becomes a block element and positioned like absolute but typically remains in that window position even if the document scrolls.

relative
> Element maintains its normal position in element geography (unless you override it) and establishes a positioning context for nested items.

static
> Item is not positionable and maintains its normal position in element geography (default value).

inherit
> Item inherits the attribute value of its next outermost HTML containing element.

## Absolute Versus Relative Positioning

The position attribute terminology can be confusing because the coordinate system used to place an element depends on the *positioning context* of the element, rather than on a universally absolute or relative coordinate system. A positioning context is nothing more than a rectangular space with edges that become zero reference points for specifying a location within the rectangle. The most basic positioning context is an invisible box created by the root document node. In early CSS-P browsers, this box equated to the body element container.* But today (under the influence of the DOM node tree architecture), the document is the most global context. If the document were a sheet of paper, the 0,0 point would be at the very top, left corner of the page. In other words, the entire (scrollable, if necessary) space of the browser window or frame that displays the content of the document is the default positioning context. The 0,0 coordinate point for the default positioning context is the upper left corner of the unscrolled window or frame. You can position an element within this context by setting the position attribute to absolute and assigning values to the left and top attributes of the style rule:

```
<div id="someDiv" style="position:absolute; left:100px; top:50px">
Hello. And now it's time to say goodbye.
</div>
```

Figure 4-1 shows how this simple block-level element appears in a browser window.

---

* Including IE for Windows through Version 6, when the latter operates in backward-compatibility mode as specified by the <!DOCTYPE> element declaration, described in Chapter 8.

---

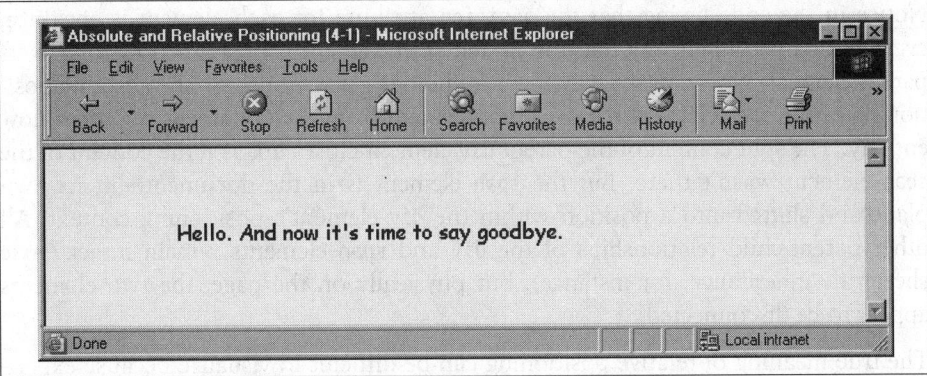

*Figure 4-1. An element positioned within the default positioning context*

Each time an element is positioned, it spawns its own, new positioning context with the 0,0 position located at the top left corner of that element. Therefore, if we insert a positioned element in the previous example nested within the div element that forms the new positioning context, the newly inserted element lives in the new context. In the following example, we insert a span element inside the div element. Positioning attributes for the span element place it 10 pixels in from the left and 30 pixels down from the top of its positioning context—the div element in this case:

```
<div id="someDiv" style="position:absolute; left:100px; top:50px">
Hello.
<span id="someSpan" style="position:absolute; left:10px; top:30px">
Hello, again.
</span>
And now it's time to say goodbye.
</div>
```

Figure 4-2 shows the results; note how the div element's positioning context governs the span element's location on the page.

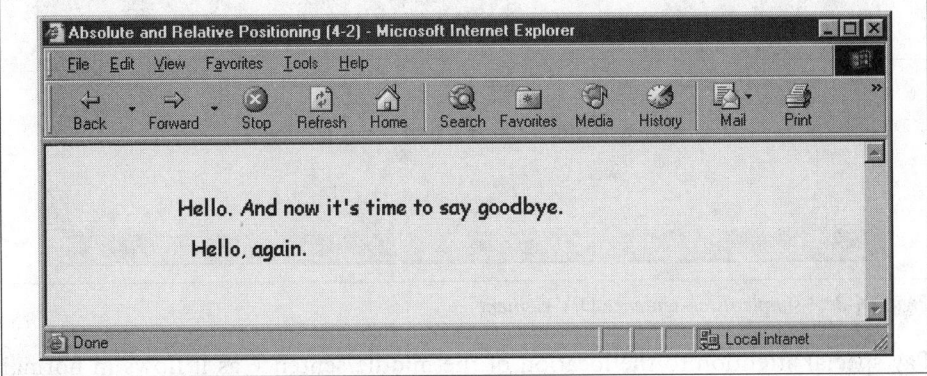

*Figure 4-2. A second element nested inside another*

Notice in the code listing that the position attribute for each element is absolute, even though you might say that the nested span element is positioned relative to its parent element. Now you see why the terminology gets confusing. The absolute positioning of the span element removes that element from the document's content flow entirely. The split content of the parent div element closes up, as if the content of the span element wasn't there. But the span element is in the document—in its own plane and shifted into a position within the div element's positioning context. All other parent-child relationships of the div and span elements remain intact (style sheet rule inheritance, for instance), but physically on the page, the two elements appear to be disconnected.

The true meaning of relative positioning can be difficult to visualize because experiments with the combination of absolute and relative positioning often yield bewildering results. Whereas an absolute-positioned element adopts the positioning context of the next outermost context, a relative-positioned element creates its own positioning context with respect to the element's normal (unpositioned) location within the document's content flow. A sequence of modifications to some content should help demonstrate these concepts.

To begin, here is a fragment with a single, absolute-positioned div element that contains three sentences:

```
<div id="someDiv" style="position:absolute; left:100px; top:50px">
Hello.
Hello, again.
And now it's time to say goodbye.
</div>
```

This code generates a simple line of text on the page, as shown in Figure 4-3.

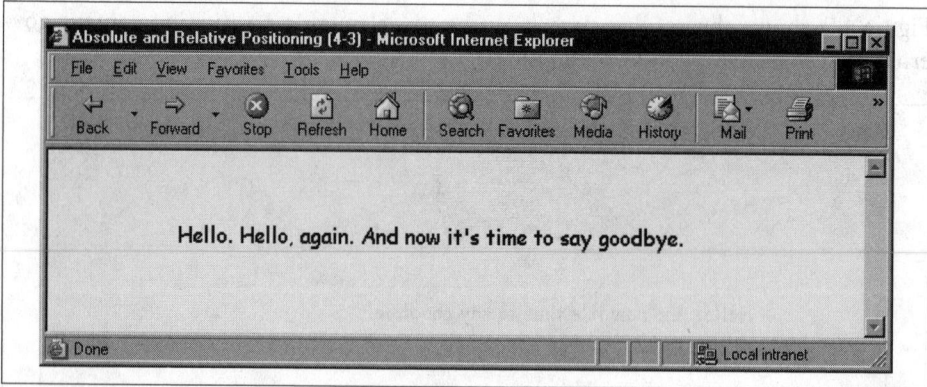

Figure 4-3. A simple three-sentence DIV element

Pay special attention to the location of the middle sentence as it flows in normal HTML. Now, if you turn that middle sentence into a relative-positioned span element supplied with some offset (left and top) values, something quite unusual

happens on the screen. The following fragment positions the second sentence 10 pixels in from the left and 30 pixels down from the top of some positioning context:

```
<div id="someDiv" style="position:absolute; left:100px; top:50px; right:100px">
Hello.
<span id="someSpan" style="position:relative; left:10px; top:30px">
Hello, again.
</span>
And now it's time to say goodbye.
</div>
```

But what is that context? With a relative-positioned element, the anchor point of its positioning context is the top left corner of the place (the box) where the normal flow of the content would go. Therefore, by setting the left and top attributes of a relative-positioned element, as in the previous code fragment, you instruct the browser to offset the content relative to its normal location. You can see the results in Figure 4-4.

*Figure 4-4. The relative-positioned element generates its own positioning context*

Note how the middle sentence is shifted within the context of its normal flow location. The positioning context established by the relative-positioned element is now available for positioning of other elements (most likely as absolute-positioned elements) that you may wish to insert within the <span> tag pair. Take special notice in Figure 4-4 that the browser does not close up the space normally occupied by the span element's content because it is a relative-positioned element; if it is absolute-positioned, the element gets yanked from its parent's rendering, and placed into its own layer. Since the element is no longer in the same block as its parent, the surrounding parent text closes the gap.

In most cases, you don't assign values for left and top to a relative-positioned element because you want to use a relative-positioned element to create a positioning context for more deeply nested elements that are absolutely positioned within that context. Using this technique, regular content flows according to the browser window's current size or as its appearance is affected by style rules, while elements that must be positioned relative to some running content are always positioned properly.

To demonstrate this concept, consider the following fragment that produces a long string of one-word sentences plus one longer sentence. The goal is to have the final sentence always appear aligned with the final period of the last "Hello" and 20 pixels down. This means that the final sentence needs to be positioned within a context created for the final period of the last "Hello." In other words, the period character must be defined as a relative-positioned element, so that the nested span element can be positioned absolutely with respect to the period. The following code shows how it's done:

```
<div id="someDiv" style="position:absolute; left:100px; top:50px; right:100px">
Hello. Hello.
Hello. Hello. Hello. Hello. Hello. Hello. Hello. Hello. Hello. Hello. Hello.
Hello. Hello. Hello<span id="someSpan" style="position:relative">.
<span id="anotherSpan" style="position:absolute; top:20px; width:80px">
And now it's time to say goodbye.
</span>
</span>
</div>
```

Carefully observe the nesting of the elements in the previous example. Figure 4-5 shows the results.

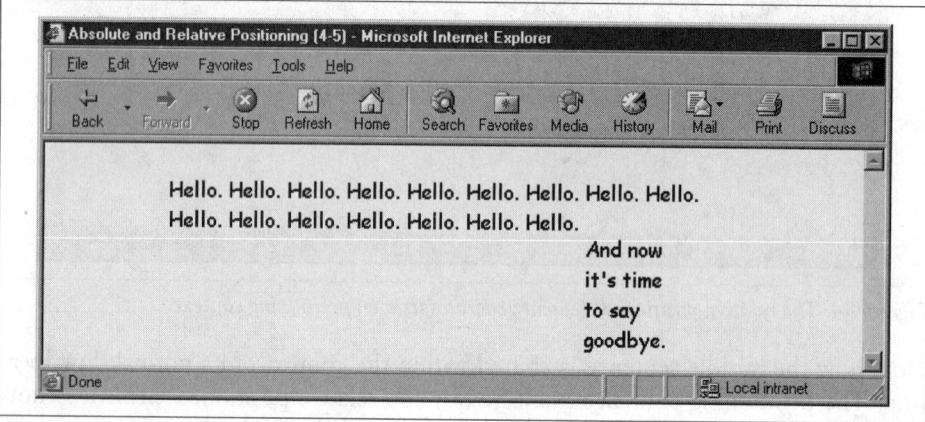

*Figure 4-5. A relative-positioned element creates a positioning context for another element*

If you resize the browser window so that the final "Hello" appears on another line or in another vertical position on the page, the final sentence moves so that it always starts 20 pixels below and just to the right of the period of the final "Hello" of the content. When applied in this fashion, the term "relative positioning" makes perfect sense.

## Overlapping Versus Wrapping Elements

One of the advantages of CSS-Positioning is that you can set an absolute position for any element along both the horizontal and vertical axes as well as its position in stacking order—the third dimension. This makes it possible for more than one element to occupy the same pixel on the page, if you so desire. It is also important to remember that absolute-positioned elements exist independently of the surrounding content of the document. In other words, if a script shifts the horizontal or vertical position of such an element, the surrounding content does not automatically wrap itself around the new position of the element.

If your design calls for the content of an element to wrap around another element, you should use the CSS float attribute, rather than CSS-Positioning. Properties of the float attribute let you affix an element at the left or right margin of a containing block element and at a specific location within the running content. A floating element defined in this manner, however, is not a positionable element in that you cannot script positionable element properties of such an item.

## Positioning Attributes

The CSS-Positioning recommendation specifies several properties that can be set as style sheet rule attributes. These attributes are used only when the position attribute is included in the rule; otherwise they have no meaning. Table 4-1 provides a summary of position-related style attributes defined in the W3C recommendation. They are all implemented in Version 4 browsers and later (but not all attribute values are supported in early versions).

*Table 4-1. Summary of positioning attributes*

| CSS attribute | Description |
|---|---|
| position | Defines a style rule as being for a positionable element |
| top | The offset distance from the top edge of the element's positioning context to the top edge of the element's box |
| right | The offset distance from the right edge of the element's positioning context to the right edge of the element's box |
| bottom | The offset distance from the bottom edge of the element's positioning context to the bottom edge of the element's box |
| left | The offset distance from the left edge of the element's positioning context to the left edge of the element's box |
| clip | The shape and dimension of the viewable area of an absolute-positioned element |
| overflow | How to handle content that exceeds its height/width settings |
| visibility | Whether a positionable element is visible or not |
| z-index | The stacking order of a positionable element |

## The position Attribute

Of the five values available for the position attribute, only the value fixed requires a recent browser (Opera 5, Netscape 6, and IE 5/Mac but not IE for Windows through Version 6). The default value is static, meaning that elements by default render in their normal content flow.

# top, right, bottom, and left Attributes

Four edge measurement attributes deal with lengths, whether they are for positioning of the element or determining its physical dimensions on the page. Recall from Chapter 3 (Figure 3-2) that height and width attributes refer to the size of the content, exclusive of any padding, borders, or margins assigned to the element (only in standards-compatible mode in IE 6 for Windows). The top, right, bottom, and left values, however, apply to the location of the box edges (content + padding + border + margin). The measures are relative to the respective edges of the positioning context. Therefore you can set the width of a positioned element by specifying a width attribute or by setting both the left and right attributes.

When assigning a value to a CSS length-related attribute, you can do so as a fixed length or a percentage. Fixed-length unit syntax is shown in Table 4-2. Percentage values are specified with an optional + or − symbol, a number, and a % symbol. Percentage values are applied to the parent element's value.

*Table 4-2. Length value units (CSS and CSS-P)*

| Length unit | Example | Description |
| --- | --- | --- |
| em | 1.5em | Element's font height |
| ex | 1ex | Element's font x-height |
| px | 14px | Pixel (precise length depends on the display device) |
| in | 0.75in | Inch (absolute measure) |
| cm | 5cm | Centimeter (absolute measure) |
| mm | 55mm | Millimeter (absolute measure) |
| pt | 10pt | Point (equal to 1/72 of an inch) |
| pc | 1.5pc | Pica (equivalent to 12 points) |

The length unit you choose should be based on the primary output device for the document. Most HTML pages are designed for output solely on a video display, so the pixel unit is most commonly used for length measures. But if you intend your output to be printed, you may obtain more accurate placement and relative alignment of elements if you use one of the absolute units: inch, centimeter, millimeter, point, or pica. Print quality also depends on the quality of the printing engine built into the browser. The CSS2 @media rule, when supported, allows you to define style rules customized for a variety of output devices.

Indiscriminately positioning deeply nested elements may result in unexpected and undesirable effects in many browsers. For example, style settings could position a block beyond the browser's window content region while the browser fails to provide scrollbars for the user to reach those elements. You can experiment with this by removing the right and width style attributes from the example shown in Figure 4-5 and resize the window to force the dangling text offscreen to the right on most browsers.

## The clip Attribute

A clipping region is a geometric area (currently limited to rectangles) through which you can see a positioned element's content. For example, if you include an image in a document, but want only a small rectangular segment of the whole image to appear, you can set the clip attribute of the element to limit the viewable area of the image to that smaller rectangle. It is important to remember that the element does not shrink in overall size (scale) for the purposes of document flow, but any area that is beyond the clipping rectangle becomes transparent, allowing elements below it in the stack to show through. If you want to position the viewable, clipped region so that it appears without a transparent border, you must position the entire element (whose top left corner still governs the element's position in the grid). Similarly, because the clipping region encompasses viewable items such as borders, you must nest a clipped image inside another element that sets its own border.

Figure 4-6 demonstrates (in three stages) the concept of a clipping region relative to an image. It also shows how positioning a clipped view requires setting the location of the element based on the element's original size.

*Figure 4-6. How element clipping works*

Setting the values for a clip region requires slightly different thinking from how you might otherwise describe the points of a rectangle. The clip attribute includes a shape and four numeric values in the sequence of top, right, bottom, left—the same clockwise sequence used by CSS to assign values to edge-related attributes (borders, padding, and margins) of block-level elements. Moreover, the values are entered as a space-delimited sequence of values in this format:

```
clip:rect(top right bottom left)
```

In Figure 4-6, the goal is to crop out the critter, tabs, and tagline from the image and align the clipped image to the left. The original image (537 by 100 pixels) is at the top. To trim the unwanted portion requires bringing in the left clip edge 210 pixels. The bottom tag line is also clipped for a height of 83 pixels:

```
<img src="oraImage.gif" height="100" width="537" style="position:absolute;
clip:rect(0px 537px 83px 210px)">
```

Then, to reposition this image so that the clipped area abuts the left edge of its positioning context, the style rule for the element must assign a negative value to take up the slack of the now masked space:

```
<img src="oraImage.gif" height="100" width="537" style="position:absolute;
left:-210px; clip:rect(0px 537px 83px 210px)">
```

## The overflow Attribute

Although first defined for CSS-P, the overflow attribute has broader application in CSS2. The attribute controls how content nested inside a fixed-size block is to be displayed if the content exceeds the physical boundaries of the container. The positioning aspect comes from the possibility of positioning a nested element anywhere within a fixed-size container. Should "overflow" content be cropped by the container's edges, or should the content bleed beyond the container's edges? That's what the overflow attribute controls via its possible settings of visible, hidden, and scroll.

When you set overflow to hidden, the excess content is cropped; when set to visible (the default), all excess content is visible. Unfortunately, the implementation of the visible value is not the same in IE compared against other browsers. Consider the following document fragment, which affects how much of the upper left corner of an image appears in the browser window:

```
<span style="position:relative; width:50px; height:50px; overflow:visible;
border:5px solid red">
<img src="myImage.gif" height="90" width="120">
</span>
```

In the previous example, even though the width and height style attributes are set for a span wrapper around an image, the natural width and height of the image force IE browsers to expand the box (and thus the dimensions) of the span element to encompass the image. In other browsers, the span's size and box remain fixed while the image bleeds to its own edges. This latter behavior is prescribed by the CSS2 standard.

IE 4 and later and Netscape 6 also support the scroll value. This setting automatically displays scrollbars inside the clipped rectangle defined by the positioned element's height and width attributes. Content is clipped to the remaining visible space;

the user clicks or drags the scrollbars to maneuver through the content (image or text). When overflow is set to scroll, a full set of scrollbars appear, even if one axis doesn't require scrolling. IE also provides axis-specific attributes (overflow-x and overflow-y) to help you limit which axis gets the scrollbar.

## The visibility Attribute

The purpose of the visibility attribute is obvious: it makes an element visible or hidden. Unless the element is under script control, however, it is unlikely that you would bother setting the attribute's value (to inherit, visible, or hidden). There is rarely a need to load a normally visible HTML element into a page as hidden, unless you also have a script that changes its state as the user visits the page—perhaps in response to mouse clicks or a timed event.

It is, however, important to understand the difference between setting a positionable element's visibility attribute and setting the CSS display attribute to none. When a positionable element is set to be hidden, the space occupied by the element—whether it is a position in the stacking order or the location for flowed content set off as a relative-positioned element—does not go away. If you hide a relative-positioned element that happens to be an emphasized chunk of text within a sentence, the rest of the sentence text does not close up when the positioned portion is hidden.

In contrast, if you set the CSS attribute of an element to display:none, the browser ignores the element as it flows the document. Changing the display attribute under script control causes the content to reflow. This is how some DHTML-driven collapsible menus are created and controlled.

## The z-index Attribute

Positioned elements can overlap each other. While overlapping text doesn't usually make for a good page design, overlapping opaque elements, such as images and blocks with backgrounds, can be put to good use, particularly when the elements are under script control. The z-index attribute lets you direct the stacking order (also called the z-order, where Z stands for the third dimension, after X and Y) of elements within a positioning context. The higher the z-index value (values are integers), the closer the element layer is to the user's eye.

Positioned elements—even if their z-index attributes are not specified in their style rules—exist as a group in a plane closer to the user's eye than nonpositioned content. Notable exceptions to this rule are form controls, such as select lists, which some browsers always render in front of all other content, no matter what you do.

If you do not specify the z-index attribute for any positioned elements in a document (implying a default value of zero), the default stacking order is based on the sequence in which the positioned elements are defined in the HTML source code. Even so, these positioned items are in front of nonpositioned items (except as noted above). Therefore, you need to specify z-index values only when the desired stacking order is other than the natural sequence of elements in the source code.

More commonly, z-index values are adjusted by scripts when a user interacts with maneuverable content (by dragging or resizing), or when a script moves an element as a form of animation. For example, if your page allows dragging of elements (perhaps an image acting as a piece of a jigsaw puzzle), it may be valuable to set the z-index attribute of that element to an arbitrarily high value as the user drags the image. This keeps the image in front of all other positionable puzzle pieces while being dragged (so it doesn't "submarine" and get lost behind other elements). When the user releases the piece, you can reset the z-index attribute to, say, zero to move it back among the pool of other inactive positioned elements.

You cannot interleave elements that belong to different positioning contexts. This is because z-index values are relative only to sibling elements. For example, imagine you have two positioned div elements named Div1 and Div2 (see Figure 4-7). Div1 contains two positioned span elements; Div2 contains three positioned span elements. A script can adjust the z-index values of the elements in Div1 all they want, but the two elements are always kept together; similarly, the three elements in Div2 are always "contiguous" in their stacking order. If you swap the z-index values of Div1 and Div2, the group of elements contained by each div swaps positions as well.

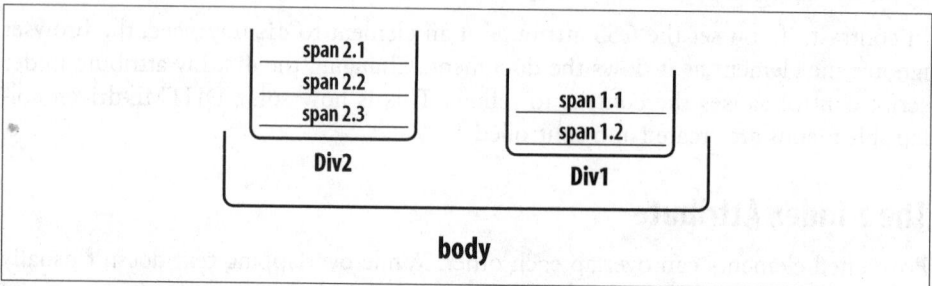

Figure 4-7. Stacking order is relative to the positioning context of the element

## Changing Attribute Values via Scripting

Content authors who wish to include DHTML positioning in their pages benefit from a fortunate confluence of standards and browser implementation trends. From one direction, modern browsers expose positioning attributes as properties of a style object. From the other direction, both the IE 4 and W3C DOMs expose the style object as a property of every rendered element object. All that's left for the cross-DOM scripter is reconciling the basic element referencing syntax (document.all versus document.getElementById( )) and the property name equivalents to the positioning-related style sheet attributes.

# Referencing Position Styles

With the comparatively convoluted Navigator 4 layer referencing model fading into ancient history, we are left with an extremely simple paradigm to follow. A syntactical mechanism for reaching any named element on the page (regardless of element nesting) makes it a breeze to modify a position-related property.

Consider the following simple document with a positioned div element nested inside a positioned span element:

```
<html>
<body>
Here's an image
<span id="outer" style="position:relative">:
    <div id="inner" style="position:absolute; left:5px; top:3px; overflow:hidden">
        <img src="myImage.gif" height="90" width="120">
    </div>
</span>
</body>
</html>
```

To move the inner div to the left by five more pixels, a script assigns a new value to the style.left property of the element. In IE 4 syntax, the statement is:

```
document.all.inner.style.left = "10px";
```

The corresponding W3C syntax is:

```
document.getElementById("inner").style.left = "10px";
```

The amount of element nesting has no impact on the reference syntax.

# Positionable Element Properties

The next piece of the cross-browser positioning puzzle involves the actual style object's property names. Table 4-3 shows the primary properties that control a positionable element's location, size, visibility, z-order, and background (many of which mirror CSS-P attributes).

*Table 4-3. Common scriptable positioning properties*

| CSS attribute | Style property | Notes |
|---|---|---|
| position | position | The type of positioning (absolute, relative, fixed, static, inherit). |
| top | top | String value containing the numeric length and the unit of measure (e.g., "20px") of offset from top edge of current positioning context. Read numeric value only via parseInt( ) function (or IE's pixelTop property). |
| right | right | Same as top, but for right edge. |
| bottom | bottom | Same as top, but for bottom edge. |
| left | left | Same as top, but for left edge. |

*Table 4-3. Common scriptable positioning properties (continued)*

| CSS attribute | Style property | Notes |
|---|---|---|
| clip | clip | String value describing shape and measure (from 0,0 of element) of cropped edges (e.g., "rect(0px, 130px, 80px, 0px)"). |
| visibility | visibility | The visibility type (visible, hidden, or inherit). |
| z-index | zIndex | The integer stacking order of the element. |
| | pixelTop<br>pixelRight<br>pixelBottom<br>pixelLeft | IE-only pixel offset from top, right, bottom, and left edges of positioning context. |
| | posTop<br>postRight<br>posBottom<br>posLeft | IE-only offset from top, right, bottom, and left edges of positioning context in inherited units. |

Note that IE defines two sets of measurement properties not present in the W3C standard. These properties (such as pixelTop and posTop) are numeric values, whereas the regular properties are strings that include the numeric value and the units (or % symbol). Numeric property values lend themselves to shortcuts when used with JavaScript by-value operators. For example, the statement:

```
document.all.myDiv.style.pixelLeft += 5;
```

increases the left style property value by five pixels. To accomplish the same in W3C-only syntax (also supported in IE), you have to work with the parseInt( ) function, as in:

```
var currStyle = document.getElementById("myDiv").style;
currStyle.left = (parseInt(currStyle.left) + 5) + "px";
```

## Reading Effective Style Properties

Consistent with the way that the W3C DOM equates element attributes with their respective object properties, the style property of an element object reveals only those values that are assigned to the element's style attribute in the tag. The bulk of style sheet rules, however, appear elsewhere in the document. IE 5 and later and the W3C DOMs provide different mechanisms for reading style values being applied to an element, regardless of the source of the style rule. This is particularly important in some positioning tasks because a script must know initial values before it can increment or decrement the value.

### IE currentStyle property

Starting with IE 5, every element has a currentStyle property. This property returns the same kind of style object as the element's style property, but it is read-only. Adjustments to a styleSheet object get reflected in currentStyle, as do changes to the style property of an object. Most browser-default style attribute values are available through currentStyle, as well.

Windows-only versions of IE 5 and later also produce a runtimeStyle property for each element object. This style object contains values only for those properties whose style attributes are explicitly assigned somewhere in the document cascade. The runtimeStyle property is read-only, too.

### W3C getComputedStyles( ) method

In contrast to the IE approach, the W3C DOM employs a concept it calls the *computed style*. The syntax required to retrieve a style property currently impacting an element is not so straightforward, but it is in keeping with the rest of the W3C DOM architecture.

The gateway to this style information is the document.defaultView property, which represents the rendering space of a document. One of its methods returns a W3C DOM object of type CSSDeclaration. This object is akin to a style object, but accessing the value of a specific style property requires the getPropertyValue( ) method. The following sequence of statements yields the left property of a positioned element named myDiv:

```
var elem = document.getElementById("myDiv");
var vw = document.defaultView;
var currStyle = vw.getComputedStyle(elem, "");
var elemLeft = currStyle.getPropertyValue("left");
```

You can use this feature in Netscape Navigator starting with Version 6.1.

For the sake of convenience, new assignments to a style property in both DOMs should be made through an element object's style object For example:

```
document.getElementById("myDiv").style.left = "10px";
```

# Cross-Platform Position Scripting

Reconciling the differences among scriptable, CSS-enabled browsers is far easier than in the days when Navigator 4 was a part of the equation. In fact, if you prefer to support only those browsers that use W3C DOM element and CSS attribute referencing syntax, your primary job is fashioning your code to allow other browsers to degrade gracefully. The following sections discuss three basic techniques you can use to implement position scripting in a document that may be viewed by various browser generations:

- Browser support flagging
- Explicit branching
- Custom APIs

Browser support flagging and explicit branching place the branching code directly in your scripts. For a limited amount of scripted positioning, having all the branching code in your scripts is manageable and actually easier to debug. But if you are doing a serious amount of scripted positioning, a custom API (Application Program Interface) lets you push the ugly branching code off to the side in an external library. In essence, you create a metalanguage that gives you control over the specific syntax used in both browsers. A custom API requires a lot more work up front, but once the API code is debugged, the API simplifies not only the current scripting job, but any subsequent pages that need the same level of scriptability.

## Browser Support Flagging

If you intend to support multiple browser classes, you will likely prefer to set up global variable Boolean flags (JavaScript global variables scope only within the current document) that indicate browser features that are important to your scripts. In the same code that establishes those variables, you should include code that redirects browsers not capable of rendering positionable elements to another page that explains the browser requirements. Unlike pages that use regular style sheets, which generally degrade acceptably for older browsers, pages with positioned elements fare very poorly when viewed with older browsers, especially if the intended design includes overlapping and/or hidden elements.

As I discussed in Chapter 2, you are best served using object detection to establish whether the current browser supports what you need. In the case of combined support for positioned elements in the IE 4 and W3C DOM environments, globals can be set for both element referencing types, as well as support for the style property. Example 4-1 shows a script sequence that should run as a page loads, to set flags arbitrarily named isW3C, isIE4, and isCSS; the script also redirects older browsers to another page.

*Example 4-1. A JavaScript browser support flag script*

```
// Global variables
var isCSS, isW3C, isIE4;
// initialize upon load to let all browsers establish content objects
function initFlags() {
    if (document.images) {
        isCSS = (document.body && document.body.style) ? true : false;
        isW3C = (isCSS && document.getElementById) ? true : false;
        isIE4 = (isCSS && document.all) ? true : false;
    }
    if (!isW3C && !isIE4) {
        top.location.href = "noDHTML.htm";
    }
}
// set event handler to initialize flags
window.onload = initFlags;
```

Global flag initialization occurs inside a function that is invoked after the page loads. Some browser versions do not treat the document node or body element as valid objects until the <body> tag loads. Since this element provides a good signal for a browser's DHTML support, the flags will more accurately reflect the browser's capabilities if the test is performed after the page loads.

Note that you should exercise care in assigning a function to window.onload in external script libraries. If multiple libraries assign a function to this event handler property, only the last one to load "wins." Similarly, if the <body> tag includes an onload event handler, it can override event handler property assignments. You cannot pile on multiple assignments through event handler property assignments.

Because the document.body property is supported in any browser that supports scripted positioning, that property is used as a gateway to verify support for the style object. In this example, the isCSS flag is part of the decision trees for both the isW3C and isIE4 flags. Later scripts can rely on just these two flags to indicate style support, as well. The final segment of the initFlags( ) function in Example 4-1 provides an escape route for other browsers. They are led to another page that won't show positioned elements.

This kind of flagging works well for introductory pages that direct visitors to parts of a site tailored to browser features, such as one path each for DHTML and non-DHTML browsers. Rather than immediately redirecting a visitor to an alternate page, scripts behind the clickable links on the page can use the flags quietly to lead users to subsequent pages best suited for their browsers' powers.

## Explicit Branching

For the occasional need to control the property of a positionable element, an explicit branch does the job without a lot of fuss. Because standard CSS-style properties are identical for W3C and IE DOMs, all that's needed is a way to equalize element references. Example 4-2 shows a script fragment whose job it is to move an element (named face) to a particular coordinate point relative to the positioning context of the document. This fragment assumes that global flags similar to those shown in Example 4-1 have been set elsewhere in the document.

*Example 4-2. Simple branching*

```
function placeFace( ) {
    var elem = (isW3C) ? document.getElementById("face") :
        ((isIE4) ? document.all("face") : null);
    if (elem) {
        elem.style.left = "25px";
        elem.style.top = "15px";
    }
}
```

Repeated use of the global flags in many such functions in a document is marginally more efficient than using the expanded condition tests for the existence of document properties. The less object evaluation that takes place in a script, the better—even at the expense of a few more variables.

## Custom APIs

If you find yourself doing a lot of scripting of positionable elements in your applications, it is probably worth the effort to create a custom API that you can link into any application you create. A custom API can take care of the "grunt" work for common position-scripting tasks, such as moving, hiding, showing, and resizing elements, as well as setting background colors or patterns. When you define a custom API library, the methods you write become the interface between your application's scripts and various positioning tasks. Many programmers prefer to make things happen via function calls, rather than assigning values to properties.

Example 4-3 gives you a sample of what such an API library might look like. For the sake of readers who used this API from the first edition (and may therefore still need to support Navigator 4), the API in Example 4-3 includes branches for Navigator 4's unique syntax, as well as the W3C and IE formats. Although internal processing of this new version is different from the first one, this API is compatible with the previous version. The API defines the following functions:

getObject(*obj*)
: Takes a positionable element (either the element's ID string or valid object reference) from the default positioning context and returns an object reference for either the Navigator 4 layer or the style property of the element

getRawObject(*obj*)
: Takes a positionable element (either the element's ID string or valid object reference) from the default positioning context and returns an object reference for the element (not its style property)

shiftTo(*obj, x, y*)
: Moves an object to a coordinate point within its positioning context

shiftBy(*obj, deltaX, deltaY*)
: Moves an object by the specified number of pixels in the X and Y axes of the object's positioning context

setZIndex(*obj, zOrder*)
: Sets the z-index value of the object

setBGColor(*obj, color*)
: Sets the background color of the object

show(*obj*)
: Makes the object visible

hide(*obj*)
: Makes the object invisible

getObjectLeft(*obj*)

Returns the left pixel coordinate of the object within its positioning context

getObjectTop(*obj*)

Returns the top pixel coordinate of the object within its positioning context

getObjectWidth(*obj*)

Returns the width, in pixels, of the element*

getObjectHeight(*obj*)

Returns the height, in pixels, of the element*

Additional helper functions for determining the height and width of the browser window's content region assist with many positioning tasks relative to the window (rather than the document). Example 4-3 provides a custom API for positionable elements.

*Example 4-3. A custom API for positionable elements*

```
// DHTMLapi.js custom API for cross-platform
// object positioning by Danny Goodman (http://www.dannyg.com).
// Release 2.0. Supports NN4, IE, and W3C DOMs.

// Global variables
var isCSS, isW3C, isIE4, isNN4, isIE6CSS;
// initialize upon load to let all browsers establish content objects
function initDHTMLAPI( ) {
    if (document.images) {
        isCSS = (document.body && document.body.style) ? true : false;
        isW3C = (isCSS && document.getElementById) ? true : false;
        isIE4 = (isCSS && document.all) ? true : false;
        isNN4 = (document.layers) ? true : false;
        isIE6CSS = (document.compatMode && document.compatMode.indexOf("CSS1") >= 0) ?
true : false;
    }
}
// set event handler to initialize API
window.onload = initDHTMLAPI;

// Seek nested NN4 layer from string name
function seekLayer(doc, name) {
    var theObj;
    for (var i = 0; i < doc.layers.length; i++) {
        if (doc.layers[i].name == name) {
            theObj = doc.layers[i];
            break;
        }
        // dive into nested layers if necessary
        if (doc.layers[i].document.layers.length > 0) {
```

---

* The API does not distinguish between IE's backward- and standards-compatible modes in IE 6 for Windows. For IE/Windows operating in standards-compatible mode (see the <!DOCTYPE> element in Chapter 8), the methods return only the content dimensions; for all other versions of IE/Windows, the values include margins and borders, if any, but not padding.

*Example 4-3. A custom API for positionable elements (continued)*

```
            theObj = seekLayer(document.layers[i].document, name);
        }
    }
    return theObj;
}


// Convert object name string or object reference
// into a valid element object reference
function getRawObject(obj) {
    var theObj;
    if (typeof obj == "string") {
        if (isW3C) {
            theObj = document.getElementById(obj);
        } else if (isIE4) {
            theObj = document.all(obj);
        } else if (isNN4) {
            theObj = seekLayer(document, obj);
        }
    } else {
        // pass through object reference
        theObj = obj;
    }
    return theObj;
}


// Convert object name string or object reference
// into a valid style (or NN4 layer) reference
function getObject(obj) {
    var theObj = getRawObject(obj);
    if (theObj && isCSS) {
        theObj = theObj.style;
    }
    return theObj;
}


// Position an object at a specific pixel coordinate
function shiftTo(obj, x, y) {
    var theObj = getObject(obj);
    if (theObj) {
        if (isCSS) {
            // equalize incorrect numeric value type
            var units = (typeof theObj.left == "string") ? "px" : 0;
            theObj.left = x + units;
            theObj.top = y + units;
        } else if (isNN4) {
            theObj.moveTo(x,y);
        }
    }
}
```

*Example 4-3. A custom API for positionable elements (continued)*

```
// Move an object by x and/or y pixels
function shiftBy(obj, deltaX, deltaY) {
    var theObj = getObject(obj);
    if (theObj) {
        if (isCSS) {
            // equalize incorrect numeric value type
            var units = (typeof theObj.left == "string") ? "px" : 0;
            theObj.left = getObjectLeft(obj) + deltaX + units;
            theObj.top = getObjectTop(obj) + deltaY + units;
        } else if (isNN4) {
            theObj.moveBy(deltaX, deltaY);
        }
    }
}

// Set the z-order of an object
function setZIndex(obj, zOrder) {
    var theObj = getObject(obj);
    if (theObj) {
        theObj.zIndex = zOrder;
    }
}

// Set the background color of an object
function setBGColor(obj, color) {
    var theObj = getObject(obj);
    if (theObj) {
        if (isNN4) {
            theObj.bgColor = color;
        } else if (isCSS) {
            theObj.backgroundColor = color;
        }
    }
}

// Set the visibility of an object to visible
function show(obj) {
    var theObj = getObject(obj);
    if (theObj) {
        theObj.visibility = "visible";
    }
}

// Set the visibility of an object to hidden
function hide(obj) {
    var theObj = getObject(obj);
    if (theObj) {
        theObj.visibility = "hidden";
    }
}
```

*Example 4-3. A custom API for positionable elements (continued)*

```
// Retrieve the x coordinate of a positionable object
function getObjectLeft(obj) {
    var elem = getRawObject(obj);
    var result = 0;
    if (document.defaultView) {
        var style = document.defaultView;
        var cssDecl = style.getComputedStyle(elem, "");
        result = cssDecl.getPropertyValue("left");
    } else if (elem.currentStyle) {
        result = elem.currentStyle.left;
    } else if (elem.style) {
        result = elem.style.left;
    } else if (isNN4) {
        result = elem.left;
    }
    return parseInt(result);
}

// Retrieve the y coordinate of a positionable object
function getObjectTop(obj) {
    var elem = getRawObject(obj);
    var result = 0;
    if (document.defaultView) {
        var style = document.defaultView;
        var cssDecl = style.getComputedStyle(elem, "");
        result = cssDecl.getPropertyValue("top");
    } else if (elem.currentStyle) {
        result = elem.currentStyle.top;
    } else if (elem.style) {
        result = elem.style.top;
    } else if (isNN4) {
        result = elem.top;
    }
    return parseInt(result);
}

// Retrieve the rendered width of an element
function getObjectWidth(obj) {
    var elem = getRawObject(obj);
    var result = 0;
    if (elem.offsetWidth) {
        if (elem.scrollWidth && (elem.offsetWidth != elem.scrollWidth)) {
            result = elem.scrollWidth;
        } else {
            result = elem.offsetWidth;
        }
    } else if (elem.clip && elem.clip.width) {
        result = elem.clip.width;
    } else if (elem.style && elem.style.pixelWidth) {
        result = elem.style.pixelWidth;
    }
```

*Example 4-3. A custom API for positionable elements (continued)*

```
    return parseInt(result);
}

// Retrieve the rendered height of an element
function getObjectHeight(obj) {
    var elem = getRawObject(obj);
    var result = 0;
    if (elem.offsetHeight) {
        result = elem.offsetHeight;
    } else if (elem.clip && elem.clip.height) {
        result = elem.clip.height;
    } else if (elem.style && elem.style.pixelHeight) {
        result = elem.style.pixelHeight;
    }
    return parseInt(result);
}

// Return the available content width space in browser window
function getInsideWindowWidth() {
    if (window.innerWidth) {
        return window.innerWidth;
    } else if (isIE6CSS) {
        // measure the html element's clientWidth
        return document.body.parentElement.clientWidth;
    } else if (document.body && document.body.clientWidth) {
        return document.body.clientWidth;
    }
    return 0;
}

// Return the available content height space in browser window
function getInsideWindowHeight() {
    if (window.innerHeight) {
        return window.innerHeight;
    } else if (isIE6CSS) {
        // measure the html element's clientHeight
        return document.body.parentElement.clientHeight;
    } else if (document.body && document.body.clientHeight) {
        return document.body.clientHeight;
    }
    return 0;
}
```

Notice that every function call in the API invokes the getObject( ) function. If the parameter passed to a function is already an object, the object reference is passed through to the function's other statements. But it also accepts a string value for an element ID (or Navigator 4 layer name).

You can use the custom API in Example 4-3 as-is or as a foundation for your own extensions that fit the kinds of positioning tasks your applications require. Your version will probably grow over time, as you further enhance the positioning techniques used in your applications.

When you write a custom API, save the code in a file with any filename that uses the *.js* extension. Then, you can link the library into an HTML document with the following tag pair in the head portion of the document:

```
<script language="JavaScript" type="text/javascript" src="myAPI.js"></script>
```

Once you do this, all the functions and global variables in the custom API library become immediately available to all script statements in the HTML document.

# Common Positioning Tasks

This chapter concludes with examples of two common positioning tasks: centering objects and flying objects. A third task, user-controlled dragging of objects, is kept on hold until Chapter 6, where we discuss the browser event models. All of these tasks rely on the DHTML API from Example 4-3.

## Centering an Object

The common way to center an element within a rectangle is to calculate the half-way point along each axis for both the element and its containing rectangle (positioning context). Then, subtract the element value from the container value for each axis. The resulting values are the coordinates for the top and left edges of the element that center the element.

The element being centered in the browser window is a div element with a yellow background and one word of large-sized red text. The goal is to center the div element both horizontally and vertically in the browser window, bringing the contained paragraph along for the ride. Example 4-4 shows the complete page listing.

*Example 4-4. A page that centers an element upon loading*

```
<html>
<head>
<script language="JavaScript" type="text/javascript" src="DHTML2api.js"></script>
<script language="JavaScript" type="text/javascript">
// Global 'corrector' for IE/Mac et al., but doesn't hurt others
var fudgeFactor = {top:-1, left:-1};
```

```
// Center a positionable element whose name is passed as
// a parameter in the current window/frame, and show it
function centerIt(layerName) {
    // 'obj' is the positionable object
    var obj = getRawObject(layerName);
    // set fudgeFactor values only first time
    if (fudgeFactor.top == -1) {
        if ((typeof obj.offsetTop == "number") && obj.offsetTop > 0) {
            fudgeFactor.top = obj.offsetTop;
            fudgeFactor.left = obj.offsetLeft;
```

*Example 4-4. A page that centers an element upon loading (continued)*

```
        } else {
            fudgeFactor.top = 0;
            fudgeFactor.left = 0;
        }
        if (obj.offsetWidth && obj.scrollWidth) {
            if (obj.offsetWidth != obj.scrollWidth) {
                obj.style.width = obj.scrollWidth;
            }
        }
    }
    var x = Math.round((getInsideWindowWidth( )/2) - (getObjectWidth(obj)/2));
    var y = Math.round((getInsideWindowHeight( )/2) - (getObjectHeight(obj)/2));
    shiftTo(obj, x - fudgeFactor.left, y - fudgeFactor.top);
    show(obj);
}

// Special handling for CSS-P redraw bug in Navigator 4
function handleResize( ) {
    if (isNN4) {
        // causes extra re-draw, but gotta do it to get banner object color drawn
        location.reload( );
    } else {
        centerIt("banner");
    }
}
window.onresize = handleResize;
</script>
</head>

<body onload="initDHTMLAPI( ); centerIt('banner')">
<div id="banner" style="position:absolute; visibility:hidden; left:0; top:0;
 background-color:yellow; font-size:36pt; color:red">
Congratulations!
</div>
</body>
</html>
```

No matter what size the browser window is initially, or how the user resizes the window, the element always positions itself dead center in the window space. Notice that the positionable element is initially loaded as a hidden element positioned at 0,0. This allows a script (triggered by the onload event handler of the body element) to use a known reference point to determine the current height and width of the content, based on how each browser (and operating system) calculates its fonts (initial width and height are arbitrarily set to 1). This is preferable to hardwiring the height and width of the element, because the script is not dependent on the precise text size.

The centerIt( ) function begins by getting a valid reference to the positioned element whose ID is passed as an argument. Some initial activity works with the element object itself, rather than its style property. Hence the use of getRawObject( ) from the DHTML API (Example 4-3) to acquire that reference.

Next comes a workaround for an unfortunate implementation bug in IE 5 for the Macintosh. The crux of the bug is that the browser assigns an incorrect default value to a positioned element's offsetTop property—something other than the zero it should be. When it comes time to position the element, the script must take this "fudge factor" into account. While we're at it, we should make it a generalizable workaround, in case future (or other) browsers have this problem not only for the vertical measure, but horizontal, as well. The script initializes a global object (fudgeFactor) with two properties set to -1. These values act as flags of their own, indicating that the object has not yet had its values set algorithmically. In the centerIt( ) function, if the values are still their original -1, the object properties are set to the offsetTop and offsetLeft properties of an element whose values are greater than the desired zero. Otherwise, the object values are set to 0. It's important to set these values only once, when the page loads. Because this function can be called later if the user resizes the window, the script must make use of the first set of calculated values.

One more one-time-only activity (controlled by the fudgeFactor.top==-1 condition) affects only IE 4, which automatically sizes positioned elements to the full width of the body. Later browsers correctly apply the CSS box model to elements, restricting their default widths to the space needed for the content. IE 4 provides a property for the needed space (the scrollWidth property). If scrollWidth is not the same as the reported offsetWidth of the element (the actual rendered width), the element's style.width gets set to its scrollWidth value.

The balance of the centerIt( ) function calculates the coordinates for centering the element within the window, based on current sizes. A call to the API's shiftTo( ) function (correcting for the fudgeFactor, which for most browsers is 0) puts the element into position. Then show( ) puts it into view.

An onresize event handler invokes the handleResize( ) function whenever the browser window changes its size (although the event is not supported in Opera 5). For most browsers, another call to centerIt( ) is sufficient. For Navigator 4, however, the lack of page reflow requires a document reload, in which case the onload event handler runs again, eventually invoking centerIt( ).

Many of the concepts shown in Example 4-4 can be extended to centering nested elements inside other elements. The primary differences involve replacing the document's positioning context with that of the centered element's container.

## Flying Objects

Moving objects around the screen is one of the features that can make Dynamic HTML pay off for your page—provided you use the animation to add value to the presentation. Gratuitous animation (like the example in this section) more often annoys frequent visitors than it helps convey information. Still, I'm sure you are interested to know how animation tricks are performed with DHTML, including cross-platform deployment.

The straight-line path example in this section builds somewhat on the centering application in Example 4-4. The goal of this demonstration is to have a banner object fly in from the right edge of the window (centered vertically in the window), until it reaches the center of the currently sized window. The source code for the page is shown in Example 4-5.

*Example 4-5. A page with a "flying" banner*

```html
<html>
<head>
<style type="text/css">
body {overflow:hidden}
</style>
<script language="JavaScript" type="text/javascript" src="DHTML2api.js"></script>
<script language="JavaScript" type="text/javascript">
// ** Global variables ** //
// Final left position of gliding element
var stopPoint = 0;
// Repetition interval ID
var intervalID;
// 'Corrector' positioning factor for IE/Mac et al., but doesn't hurt others
var fudgeFactor = {top:-1, left:-1};

// Set initial position offscreen and show object and
// start timer by calling glideToCenter( )
function startGlide(layerName) {
    // 'obj' is the positionable object
    var obj = getRawObject(layerName);
    // set fudgeFactor values only first time
    if (fudgeFactor.top == -1) {
        if ((typeof obj.offsetTop == "number") && obj.offsetTop > 0) {
            fudgeFactor.top = obj.offsetTop;
            fudgeFactor.left = obj.offsetLeft;
        } else {
            fudgeFactor.top = 0;
            fudgeFactor.left = 0;
        }
        if (obj.offsetWidth && obj.scrollWidth) {
            if (obj.offsetWidth != obj.scrollWidth) {
                obj.style.width = obj.scrollWidth;
            }
        }
    }
    var y = Math.round((getInsideWindowHeight( )/2) - (getObjectHeight(obj)/2));
    stopPoint = Math.round((getInsideWindowWidth( )/2) - (getObjectWidth(obj)/2));
    shiftTo(obj, getInsideWindowWidth( ), y - fudgeFactor.top);
    show(obj);
    intervalID = setInterval("glideToCenter('" + layerName + "')", 1);
}
// Move the object to the left by 5 pixels until it's centered
function glideToCenter(layerName) {
    var obj = getRawObject(layerName);
    shiftBy(obj,-5,0);
```

*Example 4-5. A page with a "flying" banner (continued)*

```
    if (getObjectLeft(obj) <= stopPoint) {
        clearInterval(intervalID);
    }
}
</script>
</head>
<body onload="initDHTMLAPI(); startGlide('banner')" >
<span id="banner" style="position:absolute; visibility:hidden; left:0; top:0;
 background-color:yellow; font-size:36pt; color:red">
Congratulations!
</span>
</body>
</html>
```

The setup script in Example 4-5 (the startGlide( ) function) borrows a great deal from the centerIt( ) function of Example 4-4. One difference is that startGlide( ) establishes an end point along the x-axis at which the glide is to stop, given the current window size. The shiftTo( ) function positions the element just out of view to the right. Then the script invokes the glideToCenter( ) function, which performs the animation.

Repetitive motion is best controlled via the JavaScript setInterval( ) method, which continues to invoke a function (at a designated time interval in milliseconds) until a clearInterval( ) method stops the merry-go-round. The final script statement of startGlide( ) invokes the glideToCenter( ) function via setInterval( ). Each millisecond (or as quickly as the rendering engine allows), the browser invokes the glideToCenter( ) function and refreshes its display.

Each time glideToCenter( ) runs, it shifts the banner object to the left by five pixels without adjusting the vertical position. Then it checks whether the left edge of the banner has arrived at the position where the banner is centered on the screen. If it is at (or to the left of) that point, the internal timer associated with the interval ID stops and the browser ceases to invoke glideToCenter( ) anymore.

If you want to move an element along a more complicated path, the strategy is similar, but you have to maintain one or more additional global variables to store loop counters or other values that change from point to point. Example 4-6 shows replacements for the startGlide( ) and glideToCenter( ) functions in Example 4-5. The new functions roll the banner around in a circle. An extra global variable for counting 36 steps along the circle replaces the endPoint variable. You can apply all sorts of motion formulas to this kind of DHTML controller.

*Example 4-6. Rolling a banner in a circle*

```
<html>
<head>
<script language="JavaScript" type="text/javascript" src="DHTML2api.js"></script>
<script language="JavaScript" type="text/javascript">
// ** Global variables ** //
// circular motion arc interval controllers
```

*Example 4-6. Rolling a banner in a circle (continued)*

```
var intervalCount = 1;
var intervalID;
// 'Corrector' positioning factor for IE/Mac et al., but doesn't hurt others
var fudgeFactor = {top:-1, left:-1};

// Set initial position offscreen and show object and
// start timer by calling glideToCenter( )
function startRoll(layerName) {
    // 'obj' is the positionable object
    var obj = getRawObject(layerName);
    // set fudgeFactor values only first time
    if (fudgeFactor.top == -1) {
        if ((typeof obj.offsetTop == "number") && obj.offsetTop > 0) {
            fudgeFactor.top = obj.offsetTop;
            fudgeFactor.left = obj.offsetLeft;
        } else {
            fudgeFactor.top = 0;
            fudgeFactor.left = 0;
        }
        if (obj.offsetWidth && obj.scrollWidth) {
            if (obj.offsetWidth != obj.scrollWidth) {
                obj.style.width = obj.scrollWidth;
            }
        }
    }
    var x = Math.round((getInsideWindowWidth( )/2) - (getObjectWidth(obj)/2));
    var y = 50;
    shiftTo(obj, x - fudgeFactor.left, y - fudgeFactor.top);
    show(obj);
    intervalID = setInterval("goAround('" + layerName + "')", 1);
}

// Move element along an arc that is 1/36 of a circle; stop at full circle
function goAround(layerName) {
    var obj = getRawObject(layerName);
    var x = Math.round(getObjectLeft(obj) + Math.cos(intervalCount * (Math.PI/18)) * 10);
    var y = Math.round(getObjectTop(obj) + Math.sin(intervalCount * (Math.PI/18)) * 10);
    shiftTo(obj, x - fudgeFactor.left, y - fudgeFactor.top);
    if (intervalCount++ == 36) {
        clearInterval(intervalID);
    }
}

</script>
</head>
<body onload="initDHTMLAPI( ); startRoll('banner');" >
<span id="banner" style="position:absolute; visibility:hidden; left:0; top:0;
 background-color:yellow; font-size:36pt; color:red">
Congratulations!
</span>
</body>
</html>
```

In Chapter 6, I'll come back to the dynamic positioning of elements and examine how to make an object track the mouse pointer. That application requires knowledge of the partially conflicting event models built into Internet Explorer and the W3C DOM event model (which IE 6 does not support).

# CHAPTER 5

# Making Content Dynamic

In addition to letting you script the positions of elements, as described in Chapter 4, Dynamic HTML allows you to write scripts that modify content and adjust styles on the fly. Prior to the Version 4 browsers, your ability to script dynamic content was limited to controlling the HTML being written to the current page as the page initially loaded, loading HTML documents into other frames, and, in some browser versions, swapping same-size images. But when browsers such as IE 4 (and later) and Netscape 6 expose every HTML element to a scriptable object model and automatically reflow pages, authors gain extraordinary powers to change anything on the page at any time.

The history of dynamic content browsers was tarnished by what became a dead-end and underfeatured approach to dynamic content: the Netscape Navigator 4 layer. While covered in depth in the first edition of this book, Navigator 4's unique DHTML concepts, language, and limitations no longer haunt browsers in current release. Therefore, as the installed base of Navigator 4 continues to dwindle, this edition addresses dynamic content techniques that are either broadly backward compatible or, more importantly, rely on the IE and W3C Level 2 Document Object Models (DOMs) implemented in modern browsers.

This chapter provides an overview of the most common ways of dynamically changing content, including some that date back to Navigator 2. It also offers some suggestions about how to develop code that accommodates the incompatibilities that exist between the IE-only and W3C DOMs. Compared to the contortions necessary in the IE 4 versus Navigator 4 days, most cross-browser dynamic content tasks today are a breeze.

## Writing Variable Content

While a page is loading, you can use the JavaScript document.write( ) method to fill in content that cannot be stored as part of the document. Example 5-1 demonstrates a simple combination of hardwired HTML with dynamically written content to fill a page. In this case, the dynamically written content consists of properties that the client computer and browser can determine without burdening the server. The user is oblivious to the fact that a script creates some of the text on the page.

*Example 5-1. Combining fixed and dynamic content in a rendered page*

```html
<html>
<body>
<h1>Welcome!</h1>
<hr>
<p>Your browser identifies itself to the server as:<br>
<script language="JavaScript" type="text/javascript">
document.write(" navigator.userAgent + ".");
</script>
</p>
</body>
</html>
```

You can use document.write( ) or document.writeln( ) in scripts that execute while a document is loading, but you cannot use either method to modify only a portion of a page that has already loaded. Once a document has finished loading, if you make a single call to document.write( ) directed at the current document, the call automatically clears the current document from the browser window and writes the new content to the page. So, if you want to rewrite the contents of a page, you must do so with just one call to the document.write( ) method. Example 5-2 demonstrates how to accumulate content for a page in a variable that is written in one blast.

*Example 5-2. Creating a new document for the current window*

```html
<html>
<head>
<title>Welcome Page</title>
<script language="JavaScript" type="text/javascript">
// create custom page and replace current document with it
function rewritePage(form) {
    // accumulate HTML content for new page
    var newPage = "<html>\n<head>\n<title>Page for ";
    newPage += form.entry.value;
    newPage += "</title>\n</head>\n<body bgcolor='cornflowerblue'>\n";
    newPage += "<h1>Hello, " + form.entry.value + "!</h1>\n";
    newPage += "</body>\n</html>";
    // write it in one blast
    document.write(newPage);
    // close writing stream
    document.close( );
}
</script>
<body>
<h1>Welcome!</h1>
<hr>
<form onsubmit="return false;">
<p>Enter your name here: <input type="text" name="entry" id="entry"></P>
<input type="button" value="New Custom Page" onclick="rewritePage(this.form);">
</form>
</body>
</html>
```

Notice that the script inserts data from the original screen's form into the content of the new page, including a new title that appears in the browser window's title bar. As a convenience to anyone looking at the source of the new document, escaped newline characters (\n) are inserted for cosmetic purposes only. After the call to document.write( ), the rewritePage( ) function calls document.close( )to close the writing stream for the new document. While there are also document.open( ) and document.clear( ) methods, we don't need to use them to replace the contents of a window. The one document.write( ) method clears the old content, opens a new output stream, and writes the content.

# Writing to Other Frames and Windows

You can also use the document.write( ) method to send dynamically created content to another frame in a frameset or to another browser window previously opened by a script in the same page. In this case, you are not restricted to only one call to document.write( ) per page; you can open an output stream to another frame or window and keep dumping stuff into it until you close the stream with document.close( ).

All you need for this kind of content creation is a valid reference to the other frame or window. How you generate the frameset or secondary window influences this reference.

## Framesets and Frames

A typical frameset document defines the physical layout of how the main browser window is to be subdivided into separate panels. Framesets can, of course, be nested many levels deep, where one frame loads a document that is, itself, a frameset document. The key to writing a valid reference to a distant frame is knowing the relationship between the frame that contains the script doing the writing and the target frame.

The most common frameset structure consists of one frameset document and two to four frames defined as part of that frameset (you can have more frames if you like, but not everyone is fond of frames). Ideally, you should assign a unique identifier to the name attribute of each <frame> tag.* Example 5-3 is a basic frameset document that assigns a name to each of the three frames and loads an efficient local blank page into each frame. The technique used here is to invoke a function, blank( ), that exists in the frameset (parent) document. In each case, the javascript: pseudo-URL is applied to the newly created frame. From each frame's point of view, the blank( ) function is in the parent document, hence the parent.blank( ) reference. The 100-pixel wide frame

---

* While XHTML 1.0 deprecates the name attribute for the frame element, older browsers ignore the id attribute. Due to the massive volume of framed web content that uses only the name attribute, browsers will support this attribute for many years to come. In the meantime, it is perfectly acceptable to assign the same identifier to a frame element's name and id attributes. This does not confuse scripts or link and form targets on any browser, and also validates as transitional XHTML 1.0.

down the left side of the browser window is for a navigation bar. The right portion of the window is divided into two sections. The upper section (arbitrarily called main) occupies 70% of the column, while the lower section (called instrux) occupies the rest of the column.

*Example 5-3. A simple three-frame frameset with blank pages written to each frame*

```
<html>
<head>
<script language="JavaScript" type="text/javascript">
<!--
function blank() {
    return "<html></html>";
}
//-->
</script>
</head>
<frameset cols="100,*">
    <frame name="navBar" src="javascript:parent.blank();">
    <frameset rows="70%,30%">
        <frame name="main" id="main" src="javascript:parent.blank();">
        <frame name="instrux" id="instrux" src="javascript:parent.blank();">
    </frameset>
</frameset>
</html>
```

Now imagine that a modified version of Example 5-2 is loaded into the main frame. The job of the script, however, is to write the dynamic content to the frame named instrux. To accomplish this, the reference to the other frame must start with the parent document (the frameset), which the two frames have in common. Example 5-4 shows the modified page that goes into the main frame and writes to the instrux frame. The two small changes that were made to the original code are highlighted.

*Example 5-4. Writing dynamic content to another frame*

```
<html>
<head>
<title>Welcome Page</title>
<script language="JavaScript" type="text/javascript">
// create custom page and replace current document with it
function rewritePage(form) {
    // accumulate HTML content for new page
    var newPage = "<html>\n<head>\n<title>Page for ";
    newPage += form.entry.value;
    newPage += "</title>\n</head>\n<body bgcolor='cornflowerblue'>\n";
    newPage += "<h1>Hello, " + form.entry.value + "!</h1>\n";
    newPage += "</body>\n</html>";
    // write it in one blast
    parent.instrux.document.write(newPage);
    // close writing stream
    parent.instrux.document.close();
}
```

*Example 5-4. Writing dynamic content to another frame (continued)*

```
</script>
<body>
<h1>Welcome!</h1>
<hr>
<form onsubmit="return false;">
<p>Enter your name here: <input type="text" name="entry" id="entry"></P>
<input type="button" value="New Custom Page" onclick="rewritePage(this.form);">
</form>
</body>
</html>
```

If, on the other hand, you simply want to load a different document from the server into the instrux frame, you can use a scriptless HTML link and set the target attribute to the instrux frame. A script in main can also specify a document for the instrux frame as follows:

```
parent.instrux.location.href = "nextPage.html";
```

## Secondary Windows

Browser object models provide facilities for not only generating a new browser window, but also setting the window's size and (in Version 4 browsers and later) its location on the screen. You can then use references to communicate from one window to the other, although the form of those references is quite different, depending on where the script is running.

The window.open( ) method that generates a new window returns a reference to the new window object. If you plan to communicate with that window after it has been opened, you should store the reference in a global variable. This reference is the only avenue that scripts may use to access the subwindow. Example 5-5 features a script for opening a new window and writing to it. In addition, it also takes care of a feature lacking in Navigator 2 (described in a moment), inserts a brief delay to allow the often sluggish Internet Explorer for Windows to finish creating the window before writing to it, and brings an already opened but hidden window to the front, if the browser supports that feature (Navigator 3 or later and IE 4 or later).

*Example 5-5. Opening a new window and writing to it*

```
<html>
<head>
<title>A New Window</title>
<script language="JavaScript" type="text/javascript">
// Global variable for subwindow reference
var newWindow;
// Generate and fill the new window
function makeNewWindow() {
    // make sure it isn't already opened
    if (!newWindow || newWindow.closed) {
        newWindow = window.open("","sub","status,height=200,width=300");
```

*Example 5-5. Opening a new window and writing to it (continued)*

```
        // handle Navigator 2, which doesn't have an opener property
        if (!newWindow.opener) {
            newWindow.opener = window;
        }
        // delay writing until window exists in IE/Windows
        setTimeout("writeToWindow()", 500);
    } else if (newWindow.focus) {
        // window is already open and focusable, so bring it to the front
        newWindow.focus();
    }
}
function writeToWindow() {
    // assemble content for new window
    var newContent = "<html><head><title>Sub Window</title></head>\n";
    newContent += "<body>\n<h1>This is a new window.</h1>\n";
    newContent += "</body>\n</html>";
    // write HTML to new window document
    newWindow.document.write(newContent);
    newWindow.document.close(); // close layout stream
}
</script>
</head>
<body>
<form>
<input type="button" value="Create New Window"
 onclick="makeNewWindow();">
</form>
</body>
</html>
```

Example 5-5 shows that the reference to the subwindow (stored in the newWindow global variable) can be used to call document.write() and document.close() for that window. The newWindow object reference is the gateway to the subwindow.

A script in a document loaded into a subwindow can communicate back to the window or frame that spawned the new window. Every scriptable browser (except Navigator 2) automatically sets the opener property of a new window to a reference to the window or frame that created the window (recent browsers also set this property to windows launched by a and form element target attributes). One of the workarounds in Example 5-5 creates and sets this property for Navigator 2, so you can use it across the board. Therefore, to access the value property of a form's text box (named entryField) located in the main browser window, you can use the following script statement in the subwindow:

```
opener.document.forms[0].entryField.value
```

Remember that opener refers directly to the window or frame that spawned the subwindow. If you need to access content in another frame in the host window's frameset, your reference must traverse the object hierarchy accordingly:

```
opener.parent.otherFrameName.document.forms[0].someField.value
```

# Links to Multiple Frames

It is not uncommon for a navigation frame in a frameset to contain links or icons that must load documents into two or more other frames of the frameset at the same time. For a single frame, the standard HTML link facilities work fine, since they let you specify a target frame with nothing more than plain attributes. But the attribute technique doesn't do the job for controlling the content of multiple targets. Scripting comes to the rescue, with a few different ways to accomplish the same goal:

- Invoke a function from the element's onclick event handler to control both frames
- Use a javascript: pseudo-URL to invoke a function to control both frames
- Use the default link for one frame and the onclick event handler for the other

The first two choices require defining a JavaScript function that loads the desired documents into their target frames. Such a function might look as follows:

```
function loadFrames() {
    parent.main.location.href = "section2.htm";
    parent.instrux.location.href = "instrux2.htm";
    return false;
}
```

You can then create a link that invokes the function for browsers with JavaScript turned on or that at least links to the main frame content if JavaScript is turned off:

```
<a href="section2.htm" target="main" onclick="return loadFrames();">...</a>
```

The loadFrames() function returns false when it is done. This forces the onclick event handler to evaluate to return false, which preempts the actions of the href and target attributes (when JavaScript is turned on).

The javascript: pseudo-URL can be applied to a link's href attribute as follows:

```
<a href="javascript: void loadFrames();">...</a>
```

Instead of navigating directly to a URL on the server, the link invokes whatever JavaScript function is named in the pseudo-URL. By including the void operator, you instruct the link to ignore any value returned by the function (the current page would be replaced by the text of that value), and thus leave the current page in place.

For the third approach, let the href and target attributes handle one frame while the onclick event handler takes care of the other with an inline script:

```
<a href="section2.htm" target="main"
onclick="parent.instrux.location.href='instrux2.htm';">...</a>
```

Client-side image maps require a little more care because the onclick event handler isn't defined for the area object until the Version 4 browsers. But you can use the javascript: pseudo-URL trick with the href attribute inside a <map> tag.

# Image Swapping

As precursors to true Dynamic HTML powers of more recent browsers, Navigator 3 (and Internet Explorer 3.01 for the Macintosh only) gave us a glimpse of things to come with image swapping. The basis for this technique is a document object model that defines an img element as an object whose properties can be changed on the fly. One of those properties, src, defines the URL of an image loaded initially by virtue of an <img> tag and currently displayed in the page. Change that property and the image changes, within the same rectangular space defined by the <img> tag's height and width attributes (or, lacking those attribute settings, the first image's dimensions as calculated by the browser), while all the other content around it stays put. In browsers that reflow dynamic content (IE 4 and later and Netscape 6 and later), you can swap images of different sizes, and the surrounding content adjusts its layout accordingly.

Working in tandem with the img element object is the static Image object from which new "virtual" images can be created in the browser's memory with the help of scripts. These kinds of images do not appear in the document, but can be scripted to preload images into the browser's image cache as the page does its original download. Thus, when it comes time to swap an image, the switch is nearly instantaneous because there is no need for network access to grab the image data.

The example in this section shows you how to precache and swap images for the buttons of an imaginary video controller. There are four controls—**Play**, **Stop**, **Pause**, and **Rewind**. Each control has its own image that acts as a button. As the user rolls the mouse atop a button, a highlighted version of the button icon appears in the image space; as the mouse rolls off the button, the original unhighlighted version reappears.

## Precaching Images

When preloading images (and later retrieving them for swapping), it is convenient to create an array for each state that the images will be in. Identifiers that you assign to the actual img elements (name, id, or both attributes) serve as the best index values for the arrays, rather than numeric sequences. Not only do the names help you keep the abstract objects, elements, and image files straight while you build your script, but the swapping scripts work even if you alter the page layout and image sequence.

In Example 5-6, there are two image states: highlighted and unhighlighted (more conveniently referred to as "on" and "off"). The head portion of the document contains a series of script statements that generate the new Image objects (in memory) and assign the URLs for the associated image files to the src properties of those memory image objects. Example 5-6 shows the sequence of statements that makes this happen for the four "on" images and the four "off" images. Encase these statements in an object detection block for document.images so that older browsers won't choke on a missing Image object.

*Example 5-6. Precaching code for two sets of four related images*

```
if (document.images) {
    // create "on" array and populate with Image objects
    var onImgArray = new Array();
    onImgArray["play"] = new Image(75,35);
    onImgArray["stop"] = new Image(75,35);
    onImgArray["pause"] = new Image(75,35);
    onImgArray["rewind"] = new Image(75,35);
    // set URLs for the "on" images
    onImgArray["play"].src = "images/playon.gif";
    onImgArray["stop"].src = "images/stopon.gif";
    onImgArray["pause"].src = "images/pauseon.gif";
    onImgArray["rewind"].src = "images/rewindon.gif";

    // create "off" array and populate with Image objects
    var offImgArray = new Array();
    offImgArray["play"] = new Image(75,35);
    offImgArray["stop"] = new Image(75,35);
    offImgArray["pause"] = new Image(75,35);
    offImgArray["rewind"] = new Image(75,35);
    // set URLs for the "off" images
    offImgArray["play"].src = "images/playoff.gif";
    offImgArray["stop"].src = "images/stopoff.gif";
    offImgArray["pause"].src = "images/pauseoff.gif";
    offImgArray["rewind"].src = "images/rewindoff.gif";
}
```

The act of stuffing the URL for each image file into the src property of each Image object is enough to force the browser to actually fetch the image and store it in its image cache without displaying the image anywhere.

## Swap Your Image

Now it's time to look at the HTML that displays the images within the document. For the sake of this example, the surrounding HTML is of no importance. Since img element objects in a document don't respond to mouse events prior to IE 4 or Netscape 6, the images are wrapped inside links. You may prefer to use <a> tags for newer browsers as well, if clicking on the images navigates to new pages. To prevent the normal link color border from appearing around the images, the border attribute of each <img> tag is set to zero. The event handlers of the surrounding links trigger all the action for the image swapping. Example 5-7 shows the four image elements and their surrounding links.

*Example 5-7. The images to be swapped, wrapped in links with event handlers*

```
<a href="javascript:playVideo();"
onmouseover="imageOn('play'); return setMsg('Play/Continue the clip');"
onmouseout="imageOff('play'); return setMsg('');">
<img src="images/playoff.gif" name="play" id="play" height="35" width="75"
border="0" alt= "play">
</a>
```

```
<a href="javascript:stopVideo();"
onmouseover="imageOn('stop'); return setMsg('Stop video');"
onmouseout="imageOff('stop'); return setMsg('');">
<img src="images/stopoff.gif" name="stop" id="stop"height="35" width="75"
border="0" alt="stop">
</a>
<a href="javascript:pauseVideo();"
onmouseover="imageOn('pause'); return setMsg('Pause video');"
onmouseout="imageOff('pause'); return setMsg('');">
<img src="images/pauseoff.gif" name="pause" id="pause" height="35"
width="75" border="0" alt="pause">
</a>
<a href="javascript:rewindVideo();"
onmouseover="imageOn('rewind'); return setMsg('Rewind to beginning');"
onmouseout="imageOff('rewind'); return setMsg('');">
<img src="images/rewindoff.gif" name="rewind" id="rewind"height="35"
width="75" border="0" alt="rewind">
</a>
```

The onmouseover and onmouseout event handlers in each link have two tasks. The first is to change the image and the second is to display an appropriate message in the status bar of the browser window (to avoid displaying the javascript: pseudo-URL there). All this is handled with three simple functions, shown in Example 5-8.

*Example 5-8. Functions that swap images and display messages in the status bar*

```
function imageOn(imgName) {
    if (document.images) {
        document.images[imgName].src = onImgArray[imgName].src;
    }
}
function imageOff(imgName) {
    if (document.images) {
        document.images[imgName].src = offImgArray[imgName].src;
    }
}
function setMsg(msg) {
    window.status = msg;
    return true;
}
```

Image swapping is accomplished by setting the src property of the visible img element to the src property of the desired memory image. Notice how string values used as index values for both the preloaded and document.images arrays avoid the need for the highly inefficient JavaScript eval() function. The setMsg() function returns true, so that the last statement of all mouse-related event handlers evaluates to true. This allows the status bar setting to take hold.

## Internet Explorer Caching Issues

If image preloading does not appear to work for your pages in IE for Windows, your server may be returning HTTP 1.1 headers that instruct the browser to check with the server each time an image URL is changed. This can cause severe thrashing behavior with mouse rollovers because the onmouseover event fires repeatedly while the mouse is atop the element, forcing repeated server requests.

You may be able to override the server settings by including a meta element in your document that specifies an extended expiration date, such as the following:

```
<meta http-equiv="EXPIRES" content="Fri 31 Dec 2010 23:00:00 GMT">
```

But controlling caching from the server is a better solution.

# Changing Tag Attribute Values

The DOMs in IE 4 and later and Netscape 6 and later expose a tag's attributes as properties of the corresponding scriptable object. Property names tend to mimic attribute names, unless the attribute name contains a hyphen or any other "illegal" ECMAScript identifier character. Some properties are read-only, but the vast majority are read-write. If a new value impacts the appearance of the element, the change occurs and surrounding content adjusts its layout to fit the new arrangement.

The primary decision you as a scripter must make is which element referencing scheme(s) to follow: the IE-only (document.all) version for IE 4 and later, or the W3C (document.getElementById( )) version for IE 5 (and later) and Netscape 6 (and later). Opera 6 is a chameleon, depending on how the user sets up the browser to identify itself to a server. By default, it acts like IE 6, which supports both element referencing models.

As we have seen in several examples in Chapter 4, you can support both referencing models with a simple decision tree in functions that receive an element's ID as an argument. The following shows a typical structure:

```
function myFunc(elemID) {
    var elem = (document.getElementById) ? document.getElementById(elemID) :
            ((document.all) ? document.all[elemID] : null);
    if (elem) {
        // work on element object here
    }
}
```

Or, for repeated usage of this kind of test, you can establish global flags, as shown in Example 5-1. Once you have a reference to an element object, the syntax for reading or writing a standardized property is identical for both DOMs.

Another syntactical issue arises, however. Strictly speaking (that is, according to W3C DOM guidelines), attribute values should be read via an element object's getAttribute( ) method and set via setAttribute( ). Both the IE and W3C DOMs support these methods (plus an extension for both methods in IE). And yet, the same DOM exposes all of these attributes as object properties.

It can be said without much hesitation that the W3C DOM's authors appear to have been more concerned with the internal form and structure of the DOM than with practical aspects of using the syntax in real documents. Otherwise, element references would use syntax more compact than the finger-twisting document.getElementById( ) method. The same can be said for reading and writing attributes the "right" way, which is quite download-byte-intensive, as opposed to modifying the properties directly, which is an acceptable, compact way that is supported by all browsers.

The following function toggles between two width settings for a text box. It uses the long-accepted property approach for reading and writing an element's property:

```
function toggleWidth(elemID) {
    var elem = (document.getElementById) ? document.getElementById(elemID) :
                ((document.all) ? document.all[elemID] : null);
    if (elem) {
        var big = 80, small = 20;
        elem.size = (elem.size == small) ? big : small;
    }
}
```

Now compare the same function written with the attribute methods and the revised data types for attribute values:

```
function toggleWidth(elemID) {
    var elem = (document.getElementById) ? document.getElementById(elemID) :
                ((document.all) ? document.all[elemID] : null);
    if (elem) {
        var big = "80", small = "20";
        elem.setAttribute("size", ((elem.getAttribute("size") == small) ?
                    big : small));
    }
}
```

For a simple function like this, the impact of the extra script characters isn't too severe. But the bytes can add up to lengthy scripts. For the sake of brevity, most examples in this book use direct property access. My advice is to use the approach with which you are most comfortable, and stay with it throughout your scripts.

# Changing Applied Style Values

With so much of the rendering detail for an element in the hands of style sheets, you will likely modify style values to control a variety of DHTML effects. We saw some examples of this in the positioning scripts of Chapter 4. Additional style properties await your magic touch. The IE and W3C DOMs provide several ways to adjust the value of style attributes being applied to an element at any given moment. The two most popular are modifications via an element's style and className properties; other approaches dive more deeply into the style sheets and their components.

# The style Property

Perhaps the simplest way to adjust a single style attribute is through an element's style property. An element's style property is, itself, an object whose properties consist of all possible style attributes supported by the browser's DOM.

Before going further, it is helpful to acknowledge the similarities and differences between the style objects implemented in IE for Windows and the W3C DOM (as implemented in Netscape 6 and IE 5/Mac). Typically, browsers that implement proprietary style attributes that extend the list provided by the CSS standard also expose those proprietary style attributes as scriptable properties. For example, while CSS2 does not include an attribute to specify the opacity of a text element, IE and the Mozilla engine in Netscape 6 implement their own extensions for this feature (the IE opacity filter attribute and the Mozilla mozOpacity attribute). If you implement scripted styles across DOMs, be sure the styles and values you use are supported by both DOMs (as detailed in Chapter 11) or provide suitable workarounds.

Deeper down, however, the IE and W3C style objects have different structures. In the W3C DOM's formal structure, what you think of as a style object is known as a CSSStyleDeclaration object (terminology that scripts don't work with directly). This object features a variety of methods for reading and writing style attribute values that are very much in keeping with the rest of the formal DOM. For example, setting the color style attribute of an element looks like the following:

```
document.getElementById("myP").style.setAttribute("color", "rgb(255, 0, 0)", "");
```

Fortunately, the DOM standard also offers a convenient collection of properties that lets scripts access properties just as IE has been doing it all along. (This collection is of DOM type CSS2Properties, which is not a requirement for DOM compliance, but is supported in Netscape 6 and IE 5/Mac just the same.) This collection leads to the more common style adjustment syntax as in the following:

```
document.getElementById("myP").style.color = "rgb(255, 0, 0)";
```

The point of discussing these inner workings has to do with the data types of values assigned to style object properties. The implementation of the CSS2Properties collection supports string values exclusively, even if the values consist only of numbers. This makes sense in most cases, because even length values have numeric values followed by unit types, such as "14px".

But also be aware that several IE-only style object attributes require either numeric or Boolean values. For example, the style.posLeft property consists of only the numeric portion of the string-based style.left property.

With that business out of the way, we'll now examine one way of cycling a chunk of text through a sequence of colors. Example 5-9 shows a version using W3C DOM referencing syntax. A single span element in the body has the color property of its style changed in a function that is invoked often enough (via setInterval( )) to run through the cycle seven times, and then stop (to prevent user nausea). For programming convenience, the color names are stored in a global variable array, with other global variables maintaining a record of the color currently showing and the elapsed number of color changes. No positioning or other tactics are required.

*Example 5-9. Inline text color change via the style property*

```
<html>
<head>
<title>Changing style Properties</title>
<style type="text/css">
    #hot1 {color:red}
</style>
<script language="JavaScript" type="text/javascript">
// Set global variables
var totalCycles = 0;
var currColor = 0;
var colors, intervalID;
// Build array of color names
function init( ) {
    colors = ["red", "green", "yellow", "blue"];
}
// Advance the color by one
function cycleColors( ) {
    // reset counter to 0 if it reaches 3; otherwise increment by 1
    currColor = (currColor == 3) ? 0 : ++currColor;
    // set style color to new color from array
    document.getElementById("hot1").style.color = colors[currColor];
    // invoke this function again until total = 27 so it ends on red
    if (totalCycles++ < 27) {
        intervalID = setTimeout("cycleColors( )", 100);
    } else {
        clearTimeout(intervalID);
    }
}
</script>
</head>
<body onload="init(); cycleColors( );">
<h1>Welcome to the <span id="hot1">Hot Zone</span> Web Site</h1>
<hr>
</body>
</html>
```

Any valid color string value could work in this code. Chapter 11 explains color value formats for style attributes.

## The className Property

Another popular way to modify styles applied to an element is to predefine rules for more than one class selector, and then use scripts to switch the selector assigned to an element's className property. This approach is particularly convenient if the changes you wish to make affect multiple attributes.

Example 5-10 builds upon Example 5-9 by defining four style rules, each with a different class selector. The array for this version contains not color values, but class names. The repeated call to cycleColors() then simply assigns the next name in sequence to the span element's className property. Each change of the className property changes both the color and border style properties of the span element.

*Example 5-10. Inline style change via the className property*

```html
<html>
<head>
<title>Changing className Properties</title>
<style type="text/css">
    .red    {
            color: red;
            border: 2px solid red;
        }

    .green  {
            color: green;
            border: 2px solid yellow;
        }

    .yellow {
            color: yellow;
            border: 2px solid blue;
        }

    .blue   {
            color: blue;
            border: 2px solid green;
        }
</style>
<script language="JavaScript" type="text/javascript">
// Set global variables
var totalCycles = 0;
var currColor = 0;
var classes, intervalID;
// Build array of rule selector names
function init() {
    classes = ["red", "green", "yellow", "blue"];
}
// Advance the color by one
function cycleColors() {
    // reset counter to 0 if it reaches 3; otherwise increment by 1
    currColor = (currColor == 3) ? 0 : ++currColor;
    // set style color to new color from array
    document.getElementById("hot1").className = classes[currColor];
    // invoke this function again until total = 27 so it ends on red
    if (totalCycles++ < 27) {
        intervalID = setTimeout("cycleColors()", 100);
    } else {
        clearTimeout(intervalID);
    }
}
```

*Example 5-10. Inline style change via the className property (continued)*

```
</script>
</head>
<body onload="init(); cycleColors();">
<h1>Welcome to the <span class="red" id="hot1">Hot Zone</span> Web Site</h1>
<hr>
</body>
</html>
```

## Other Techniques

That the IE and W3C DOMs expose not just style elements as objects, but also their content as styleSheet objects, might lead some scripters to get perhaps too creative in modifying applied styles. Each <style> or <link rel="stylesheet"> tag in a document creates a styleSheet object that is accessible through the document.styleSheets array. If you specify just one <style> tag in the document, document.styleSheets[0] returns a reference to that styleSheet object.

From that reference, a script can inspect and modify the contents of the style sheet, albeit via occasionally different syntax for IE and W3C DOMs (IE 5/Mac observes both syntaxes). Table 5-1 lists the most important styleSheet object properties implemented in the two DOMs.

*Table 5-1. Key properties of the styleSheet object*

| W3C property | Description | IE property |
|---|---|---|
| cssRules | Array of rules within the style sheet | rules |
| n/a | Complete text of all rules | cssText |
| disabled | Boolean to enable/disable entire style sheet | disabled |
| href | URL for <link> | href |
| ownerNode | Reference to style or link element | owningElement |

Each styleSheet object has a property that returns an array of rules that belongs to the style sheet. The IE DOM calls these objects rule objects; the W3C calls them cssRule objects. You can reference a rule via its numeric index within the array. For example, here's a reference to the third rule in a page's only style sheet via the W3C DOM:

```
var oneRule = document.styleSheets[0].cssRules[2];
```

In IE syntax (required for IE/Windows), the expression is:

```
var oneRule = document.styleSheets[0].rules[2];
```

Properties of an individual rule object (regardless of how you reference the object) are a bit thin, and only partially helpful across DOMs. Both models support the selectorText property, which returns a string of the selector for the rule (although IE returns tag type selectors in uppercase, regardless of the source code case). Only the W3C cssRule object provides a direct cssText property to get the actual text. But both DOMs provide a style property, which returns a style (or W3C CSSStyleDeclaration) object whose properties reveal the individual style attribute settings for the rule. The following function demonstrates the cross-DOM syntax that sets the font-size attribute of a p-selectored rule in a style sheet:

```
function setSize(n) {
    var sheets = document.styleSheets[0];
    var ruleList = (typeof sheets.cssRules != "undefined") ? sheets.cssRules :
    ((typeof sheets.rules != "undefined") ? sheets.rules : null);
    if (ruleList) {
        for (var i = 0; i < ruleList.length; i++) {
            if (ruleList[i].selectorText.toLowerCase( ) == "p") {
                ruleList[i].style.fontSize = n + "pt";
                break;
            }
        }
    }
}
```

Additional facilities for modifying styleSheet objects include methods for adding and deleting individual rules within the styleSheet object (with incompatible syntax for IE and W3C DOMs). You can learn the details in Chapter 9.

Despite the substantial flexibility available through the styleSheet object, you will experience better reliability and compatibility (especially with Opera) if you perform your style changes via the style or className properties of the element you wish to modify. Working with styleSheet objects is best left to those times when scripts are creating new style sheets or rules on the fly.

# Changing Content

The new paradigm of the W3C DOM's node-centric structure has the greatest impact on the way scripts modify text and element content in a document. Those scripters who learned DHTML under the element-centric Microsoft aegis can easily find themselves lost amid the new concepts that the W3C DOM imposes. While the W3C DOM makes a great deal of sense in a world tending toward XML (including the XML-flavored version of HTML), even experienced DHTML scripters soon discover that Microsoft implements many convenience features in its DOM that simplify DHTML scripting. Many of these conveniences, however, are not (or at least not yet) part of the released W3C DOM recommendations.

This state of affairs leaves browser makers, such as Mozilla, in an awkward position. On the one hand, browser makers want to produce the most standards-compliant browsers on the Web. But to do so would require that developers not only rewrite tons of scripts (already necessitated by their abandonment of the layer), but also master new, and seemingly complex, ways of carrying out tasks that a nonstandard DOM handles with ease. What's a browser maker to do?

The designers could invent their own extensions to the W3C DOM paradigm to bypass the complexities. Or they could yield to developer pressure and implement the popular, but nonstandard, techniques found in other browsers, as convenient alternatives to the ways cast in W3C stone. In the case of the Mozilla browser, it does a little of both. Thus, the syntactic and conceptual paths you wish to follow are entirely up to you. In this section, you will see how to use the IE and W3C DOM ways of modifying the text inside an element and the elements themselves. Your ultimate choice will depend on factors such as the browser platform(s) you must support, your dedication to standards, and your own programming practices.

## Changing Element Text

Element text is nothing more than tagless content that resides inside an HTML container, such as a p, span, or td element. The tag provides the context for whatever words comprise the text. The IE DOM treats the text content as a property of an element object; the W3C DOM treats that same text as an object unto itself.

### IE text

Every IE DOM container element object has an innerText property. The value of this read-write property is a string data type. You can use an assignment operator to place new text inside the container:

```
elementReference.innerText = "Your new text here.";
```

Assigning a value to this property with the = operator completely replaces its original content with the new text. You can also append text by using the += assignment operator. Style sheet rules that apply to the element govern the new text, just as they did for the original text.

A companion property, innerHTML, forces the container to treat the newly assigned string as if it were tagged HTML text. Although the innerHTML property is primarily for altering elements (as well as text), it's helpful to understand the differences between innerText and innerHTML. To help you visualize the differences between these properties, let's start with a nested pair of elements as they appear in a document's source code:

```
<p id="par1" style="font-style:normal">
    A fairly short paragraph.
</p>
```

Focus on the p element, whose properties will be adjusted in a moment. The inner component of the p element consists of the string of characters between the start and end tags, but not including those tags. Any changes you make to the inner content of this element still have everything wrapped inside a p element.

How an element's inner component responds to changes depends on whether you direct the element to treat the new material as raw text or as text that may have HTML tags inside (e.g., innerText or innerHTML). To demonstrate how these important nuances affect your work with these properties, the following sequence starts with the p element shown earlier, as it is displayed in the browser window. Then comes a series of statements that operate on the original element, alternating with the representation of the element as it appears in the browser window after each statement.

A fairly short paragraph.

```
document.all.par1.innerText = "How are <em>you</em>?";
```

How are you?

```
document.all.par1.innerHTML = "How are <em>you</em>?";
```

How are *you*?

Adjusting the inner material never touches the `<p>` tag, so the normal font style prevails, and no matter how often you modify the property values, the reference to the p element remains valid because the element is always there. Setting the `innerText` property tells the browser to render the content literally, without interpreting the `<em>` tags; setting `innerHTML` tells the browser to interpret the tags, which is why the word "you" is in italics after the second statement. Netscape 6 (and later) implements the IE `innerHTML` property of all container elements as a convenience to scripters. If the string you assign to the property contains no HTML elements, the result is the same as if the property were `innerText`. Thus, the one `innerHTML` property serves two purposes.

Another Microsoft invention is the `insertAdjacentText( )` method of element objects, defined as follows:

```
insertAdjacentText(where, text)
```

This method assumes you have a valid reference to an existing element and wish to add content to the beginning or end of the element without disturbing existing text. The precise insert position for these methods is determined by the value of the *where* parameter. There are four choices:

BeforeBegin
: In front of the start tag of the element

AfterBegin
: After the start tag, but immediately before the text content of the element

BeforeEnd
: At the very end of the content of the element, just in front of the end tag

AfterEnd
: After the end tag of the element

Notice that the `BeforeBegin` and `AfterEnd` locations are outside of the element referenced in the statement. For example, consider the following nested pair of tags:

```
<span id="outer" style="color:red">
    Start outer text.
        <span id="inner" style="color:blue"> Some inner text.</span>
    End of outer text.
</span>
```

Now consider the following statement:

```
document.all.inner.insertAdjacentText("BeforeBegin", "Inserted!");
```

The document changes so that the word "Inserted!" is rendered in a red font. This is because the text was added before the beginning of the inner item, and is therefore under the rule of the next outermost container: the outer element.

The insertAdjacentText( ) method was implemented for the first time in IE 4, in anticipation of what the unfinished W3C DOM was to be. But the W3C DOM took a different turn, so a number of Microsoft content manipulation inventions work only in IE (and some only in Windows versions). Table 5-2 provides a summary listing of the proprietary element object methods for a variety of text and element actions.

*Table 5-2. IE element content manipulation methods*

| Method | Description |
| --- | --- |
| contains(*elemRef*) | Returns Boolean true if current element contains *elemRef* |
| getAdjacentText(*where*) | Returns text sequence from position *where* (IE 5 and later for Windows only) |
| insertAdjacentElement(*where*, *elemRef*) | Inserts new element object at position *where* (IE 5 and later for Windows only) |
| insertAdjacentHTML(*where*, *HTMLText*) | Inserts text (at position *where*) which gets rendered as HTML |
| insertAdjacentText(*where*, *text*) | Inserts text (at position *where*) as literal text |
| removeNode(*deep*) | Deletes element or text node (and its child nodes if *deep* is true) |
| replaceAdjacentText(*where*, *text*) | Replaces current text at position *where* with *text* (IE 5 and later for Windows only) |
| replaceNode(*newNodeRef*) | Replace current node with new node (IE 5 and later for Windows only) |
| swapNode(*otherNodeRef*) | Exchange current node with *otherNodeRef*, and return reference to removed node (IE 5 and later for Windows only) |

While all of these methods do their jobs in the IE versions that support them, they have counterparts or equivalent functionality in the W3C DOM, albeit with different syntax. IE 5 and later (both Windows and Mac) support the bulk of the W3C DOM versions of these methods, so there is little need to master both sets. For cross-DOM development, you are better served using the W3C DOM versions exclusively.

## W3C DOM text

Absolutely everything in a document is an object of some kind in the eyes of the W3C DOM. As described in Chapter 1, the fundamental type of object in a W3C DOM document is the *node*. A document's structure can be described as a tree of nodes of various types. Each node object has a nodeType property that is one of twelve possible values (numbered 1 through 12). All nodes that represent a document's content grow from the root document node (a nodeType of 9). An element is another type of node (nodeType of 1), as is a text node (nodeType of 3) between the start and end tags of an element container.

Adjacent nodes bear parent-child-sibling relationships, the understanding of which is crucial to successful application of W3C node concepts. Consider the following series of element and text nodes:

```
<p id="myP">Where is <em id="myEM">Amy</em> today?</p>
```

The p element node has three child nodes. The first and third child nodes are text nodes, while the middle one is an element node (the em element). That em element, itself, has one child node—a three-character text node. The attributes in the two tags are themselves nodes (nodeType of 2), but attribute nodes are not part of the element and text node parent-child relationship model.

Each node object (regardless of type) has a set of properties that help scripts obtain references to adjacent nodes and read or write values associated with the node. Table 5-3 lists the common properties of every node object.

*Table 5-3. Common node object properties*

| Property | Value type | Description |
|----------|-----------|-------------|
| nodeName | String | Name associated with the node or node type |
| nodeValue | String | Value associated with the node (read-write) |
| nodeType | Integer | One of the 12 node types |
| parentNode | Object | Reference to next outermost container node |
| childNodes | Array | Child nodes in source code order |
| firstChild | Object | Reference to first child node |
| lastChild | Object | Reference to last child node |
| previousSibling | Object | Reference to preceding node at same generation |
| nextSibling | Object | Reference to next node at same generation |
| attributes | NodeMap | Collection of attribute nodes |
| ownerDocument | Object | Reference to root document node |

Of the properties listed in Table 5-3, the first three return important information, but their values depend upon the type of node. Table 5-4 lists the most common node types found in HTML documents and the kinds of values associated with the nodeType, nodeName, and nodeValue properties (see these properties' entries in Chapter 9 for all node types).

*Table 5-4. Key W3C node types in HTML documents*

| nodeType constant | nodeType integer | nodeName | nodeValue |
|-------------------|------------------|----------|-----------|
| ELEMENT_NODE | 1 | *tag name* | null |
| ATTRIBUTE_NODE | 2 | *attribute name* | *attribute value* |
| TEXT_NODE | 3 | #text | *text data* |
| COMMENT_NODE | 8 | #comment | *comment text* |
| DOCUMENT_NODE | 9 | #document | null |

The `nodeValue` property of a text node is of particular importance for a discussion of modifying an element's text. This property is the only read-write property of a text node, and is therefore the property to change if you wish to modify or replace existing text. The question remains, however, of how to reference a text node when the closest that your scripts can come to picking a node out of the document tree is an element node that has an ID assigned to it.

The element node that acts as the parent to the text node is the key. A script can reference that element, and use the properties of the element node to get a reference to the child text node. As an example, we'll use the same p element from the IE text example:

```
<p id="par1" style="font-style:normal">
    A fairly short paragraph.
</p>
```

The p element has one child text node . Equally valid references to that text node are:

```
document.getElementById("par1").firstChild
document.getElementById("par1").childNodes[0]
```

One way to replace the text of that node with new text is to assign a string value to the `nodeValue` property of that text node:

```
document.getElementById("par1").firstChild.nodeValue = "Your new text here.";
```

The W3C DOM, however, also provides a more formal way to replace one child node with another. In other words, you must first create a valid text node object that contains the new text, and then replace the old with the new. The sequence is as follows:

```
var newNode = document.createTextNode("Your new text here.");
var oldNode = document.getElementById("par1").firstChild;
var removedNode = document.getElementById("par1").replaceChild(newNode, oldNode);
```

The `replaceChild( )` method is one of several methods that all W3C DOM node objects have. Table 5-5 lists these methods.

*Table 5-5. W3C DOM node object methods*

| Method | Description |
| --- | --- |
| appendChild(*newChildNode*) | Adds a child node to the end of the current node. Returns reference to newly appended node. |
| cloneNode(*deep*) | Returns a copy of the node, with child nodes if *deep* argument is true. |
| hasChildNodes( ) | Returns Boolean true if node has child nodes. |
| insertBefore(*newNode*, *otherChildNode*) | Inserts *newNode* in front of *otherChildNode* (which must be a child of current node). |
| removeChild(*childNode*) | Returns reference to child node removed from document tree. |
| replaceChild(*newChild*, *oldChild*) | Replaces *oldChild* with *newChild*, returning reference to removed child. |
| supports(*feature*, *version*) | Returns Boolean true if node supports a particular DOM feature. |

All of the text node manipulation techniques described here are implemented starting in IE 5 and Netscape 6. So, too, is the Microsoft innerHTML property, which can be used strictly for an element's text, as well. Which approach is best? No one approach is inherently better than the others; each has pros and cons.

Conceptually, the simplest way is the innerHTML property. It also tends to be the most compact approach, in case code size is one of your concerns. How long it will remain in browser implementations without becoming part of the W3C standard is anyone's guess. It should be a safe bet over the next few years, however.

Of the two W3C DOM approaches, the formal way of creating a text node and using a container's method to replace an existing text node best coincides with the spirit of the DOM. It is also good practice for working with node trees of XML documents and other parts of the DOM, such as event objects. The downside is the comparatively high cost in the number of source code bytes required to effect a relatively simple change.

## Changing Elements and Document Structure

Essentially the same principles that affect modifying text also apply to modifying elements or chunks of HTML in a document. In other words, Microsoft invented some convenience properties that work nicely and quickly. They also invented a lot of additional syntax that was eventually trumped by W3C DOM syntax—and recent IE versions are saddled with all of that verbiage.

### IE HTML and elements

The first DHTML implementation in IE 4 was predominantly HTML source code-oriented. That explains why the IE 4 DOM implemented the handy quartet of element object properties shown in Table 5-6.

*Table 5-6. IE HTML and text properties*

| Property | Description |
|---|---|
| innerHTML | All content inside the current element, rendered according to HTML rules |
| innerText | All content inside the current element, rendered according to HTML rules the current element, rendered as literal text |
| outerHTML | All content including the current element, rendered according to HTML rules |
| outerText | All content including the current element, rendered as literal text |

Assign a string to one of the "inner" properties to replace the current content with the new; use the "outer" properties to replace the current element with the new content. The "HTML" and "Text" suffixes of the properties instruct the browser how to render the string. Angle-bracketed tags assigned to the "Text" versions appear as-is; assigned to the "HTML" version, they get interpreted as if they were part of the source code. You have only one shot at assigning new content to an element's "outer" property, because the element disappears from the document once the new content appears.

# Text Node Value Implementations

Be extremely careful when implementing W3C DOM node-based modifications across IE 5 or later and Netscape 6 or later browsers. Although both browser classes support the fundamental concepts and syntax, the two differ widely in the way they treat source code white space. The Netscape approach is far more literal about converting source code to a document node tree: newline characters and indentations are significant characters that become part of a text node's value. White space gets different treatment in IE (and different treatment yet again between Mac and Windows versions of Internet Explorer).

Consider the following source code structure, whose only white space characters are the new line characters at the end of each line:

```
<p id="par2">
14 characters.
</p>
```

The following table shows how the three classes of browser treat the content of nodeValue property of the 14-character-long text.

| Browser | nodeValue.length | First character code | Last character code |
|---------|------------------|----------------------|---------------------|
| IE/Windows | 15 | 49 ("1") | 32 (space) |
| IE/Mac | 16 | 32 (space) | 32 (space) |
| Netscape 6 | 16 | 10 (newline) | 10 (newline) |

But if the source code is streamed as continuous content without any document formatting, as in the following:

```
<p id="par2">14 characters.</p>
```

all browsers report a nodeValue length of 14 characters, and no extraneous whitespace characters become part of the document tree. This behavior becomes particularly important when examining a document tree (or part of the tree) that contains nested elements. In some browsers (Netscape, in particular), the newline characters between tags become one-character text nodes between the elements. Consider the following fragment:

```
<div id="myDiv">
<p id="myP">14 characters.</p>
</div>
```

IE for Windows reports that the div element has only one child node, whereas IE for Macintosh and Netscape 6 or latercount a total of three child nodes in the sequence: a single-character text node (newline for Netscape and space for IE/Mac); a p element node; and one more single-character text node.

It should be obvious now that the W3C DOM node structure is geared to document code that is generated by tools or server-side scripts, and not formatted for human readability. In automated environments, client data is likely to go out in unbroken streams of characters, unless whitespace was intentionally introduced into the data structure. Keep this in mind if your scripts need to traverse an HTML or XML document tree.

To demonstrate the differences between the two "HTML" properties, we'll start with an empty td element (whose ID is cellB2) in a table:

```
<td id="cellB2"></td>
```

In the first transformation, we add some text with a tag in it. Even though we're modifying IE DOM properties, we'll use the W3C DOM element referencing terminology (to IE 5 and later, a reference is a reference, regardless of the syntax used to arrive at it):

```
document.getElementById("cellB2").innerHTML =
    "Happy Birthday, <em id='birthdayboy'>Jack</em>!";
```

The td element now looks like the following:

```
<td id="cellB2">Happy Birthday, <em id="birthdayboy">Jack</em>!</td>
```

For the second transformation, we wish to make the em element a span that holds different text and gets its style from a style sheet rule whose class selector is "hilite":

```
document.getElementById("birthdayboy").outerHTML =
    "<span id='birthdaygirl' class='hilite'>Emma</span>";
```

The td element now looks like the following:

```
<td id="cellB2">Happy Birthday,
    <span id="birthdaygirl" class="hilite">Emma</span>!</td>
```

Notice that the span element has completely replaced the em element.

Changes you make to these properties do not affect the source code view provided by the browser. But if you were to inspect the innerHTML or outerHTML properties of affected elements (perhaps through an alert dialog), you would see the effective HTML, as the browser sees it to build the object model for the document.

Of the properties in Table 5-5, the innerHTML property is the most popular. It allows a script to assemble a string of HTML tags, attributes, and content in a logical and easily debuggable way. Then bang, you can assign that string to replace whatever is currently inside an element's start and end tags. In fact, this property is so convenient and popular that content authors pressured the Mozilla engineers to implement it in their new browser, even though the property is not (at least not yet) part of the W3C DOM specification.

As for the rest of the Microsoft proprietary document tree manipulation methods (see Table 5-2) and properties, it may be better not to confuse the issue with too many examples. All of the vocabulary is listed in Chapter 9, but in the long run, you are better served by using the W3C DOM terminology for the more formal approach to adjusting elements and nodes. The W3C basics are implemented starting in IE 5, so the proprietary vocabulary is useful for IE 4 scripting, at best.

## W3C DOM document tree

Modifying element content in the W3C DOM means that you are altering the node hierarchy of the document—the so-called document tree—and the rendered document at the same time. A typical HTML document has a skeletal node structure before you even get to the specific content of the page, as shown in Figure 5-1.

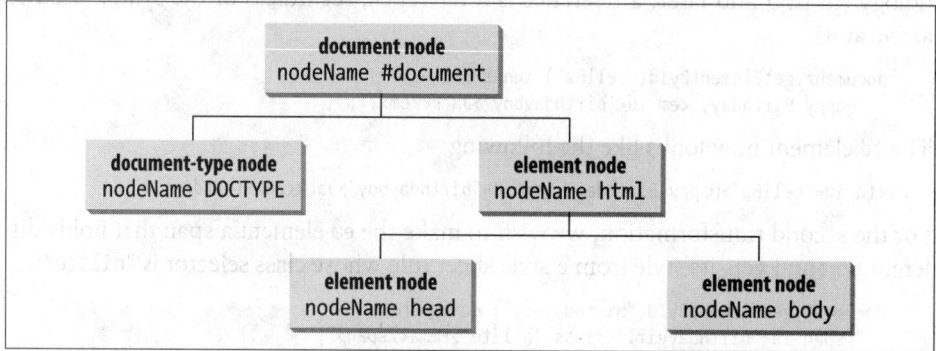

*Figure 5-1. Skeletal node structure of a typical HTML document*

In other words, the document node is the root node of the tree. It typically has two child nodes, represented in source code by the <!DOCTYPE> and <html> tags. Nested inside the <html> tag are one <head> tag and one <body> tag. All other document content is nested within the head and body elements. These fundamental nodes of an HTML document tree are immutable (a non-HTML–related XML document doesn't require these minimum elements, so very little is immutable in such a document). When we speak of modifying an HTML document tree structure, we're focusing on the elements and text nodes that go inside the head and body elements. The body element, of course, has several modifiable properties, but adjusting them does not impact the document tree.

Script access to nodes in the document tree is obtained exclusively by the various methods defined for the root Node object (see Table 5-5). If you have scripted changes to document content via the Microsoft innerHTML or outerHTML element object properties, it's important to understand that the W3C DOM Level 2 does not provide a string representation of the document tree. This goes for both reading and writing. Instead, you use methods to create and rearrange element and text node objects within the tree (for tables, however, see "Dynamic Tables" later in this chapter).

If your scripts need to generate new or replacement elements, they will follow a very typical W3C DOM sequence of operations:

1. For the first step, the scripts create an empty element object for a tag by calling document.createElement("*tagName*").

2. Then, set attribute values for the element object.

3. Create the text node with `document.createTextNode("text")` if the element is to contain a text node.

4. Append the text node to the element object with `appendChild( )`.

5. Insert the element into the document tree using some other addressable node as a referencing point.

The element and text node creation process takes place outside of the document tree. That is to say, you assign the results of a creation method to a script variable. That object is every bit the p, div, img, table, or other element object as those in the document tree, but if you were to walk the document tree structure, that new element will not be found until you explicitly insert it into the tree at the desired location.

To demonstrate this syntax, I'm going to repeat the td element modifications described earlier for the IE syntax. The first task is to insert some HTML into an empty td element. As a reminder, the string form of the inserted HTML looks like the following:

```
Happy Birthday, <em id="birthdayboy">Jack</em>!
```

To create content as nested W3C DOM node objects, it is frequently more convenient to start with the most nested content:

```
var txtNode = document.createTextNode("Jack");
var elem = document.createElement("em");
elem.setAttribute("id", "birthdayboy");
elem.appendChild(txtNode);
```

We are now left with three sibling nodes (two not-yet-created text nodes and the element node) to stuff into the td element. There are a few different ways to accomplish this final part of the process.

The linear, brute force way is to create the first text node, append it to the td element, append the elem element, and then create and append the final text node to the td element. Carrying on from the first bit of code above, here's how we can assemble the rest of the content:

```
txtNode = document.createTextNode("Happy Birthday, ");   // reuse var
var tdElem = document.getElementById("cellB2");          // for convenience
tdElem.appendChild(txtNode);
tdElem.appendChild(elem);
txtNode = document.createTextNode("!");                  // reuse var again
tdElem.appendChild(txtNode);
```

As an aside, you could also create nodes in the inverse order and insert from last to first via the `insertBefore( )` method, rather than `appendChild( )`. For example, after defining tdElem:

```
tdElem.insertBefore(txtNode, tdElem.firstChild);
```

A second way to achieve the same goal is to assemble the inserted content inside a span element as a temporary container, and then drop the entire span into the td element.

The need for the temporary span comes from the frame of reference of all Node object methods: that of a parent acting on its child nodes. In other words, you cannot simply glue one node to its sibling from the point of view of one of the sibling nodes. The parent rules the action. Thus, we get the following sequence:

```
var spanElem = document.createElement("span");
txtNode = document.createTextNode("Happy Birthday, ");  // reuse var
spanElem.appendChild(txtNode);
spanElem.appendChild(elem);
txtNode = document.createTextNode("!");                 // reuse var
spanElem.appendChild(txtNode);
document.getElementById("cellB2").appendChild(spanElem);
```

If you don't want the span element cluttering up the td element, you can use another type of W3C DOM node object, the DocumentFragment. A document fragment is an arbitrary and context-less container of nodes. For the application here, it demonstrates one of its magical powers—removing itself when its contents get placed inside a real context. The sequence for this approach is:

```
var frag = document.createDocumentFragment();
txtNode = document.createTextNode("Happy Birthday, ");  // reuse var
frag.appendChild(txtNode);
frag.appendChild(elem);
txtNode = document.createTextNode("!");                 // reuse var again
frag.appendChild(txtNode);
document.getElementById("cellB2").appendChild(frag );
```

After the above sequence runs, the td cell has only the three child nodes in it, as desired. Be aware, however, that the DocumentFragment object is implemented only in Netscape 6 and later and IE 6 and later.

The next step in content modification is to replace one element with another from the point of view of the element being replaced (the functional equivalent of the IE outerHTML property). In our example, this means that a script has a reference to an element that is to be replaced by an entirely different element (or set of nested nodes).

The process begins by creating the replacement content. It consists of a span element and text within:

```
var newElem = document.createElement("span");
newElem.setAttribute("id", "birthdaygirl");
newElem.setAttribute("class", "hilite");
var newText = document.createTextNode("Emma");
newElem.appendChild(newText);
```

Because all node methods operate on child nodes, the call to the replaceChild( ) method must come from the parent node of the element about to be replaced. The parentNode property provides the necessary reference:

```
var oldElem = document.getElementById("birthdayboy");
var removedNode = oldElem.parentNode.replaceChild(newElem, oldElem);
```

The replaceChild( ) method returns a reference to the node that was removed. Although that old node is now out of the document tree, it is still in memory, and it could be placed elsewhere in the document, if desired.

Perhaps now you can understand why Mozilla pre-release testers rebelled against the long-winded process needed to modify element text and the document tree in an HTML document via the W3C model. The IE quartet of properties are more in the spirit of high-level scripting for which JavaScript was intended (in other words, Computer Science degree not required). They also require many fewer bytes of source code to reach the client. Although some programmers might disagree, Mozilla's designers deserve a lot of credit for implementing the innerHTML convenience property to supplement the orthodox W3C approach.

That's not to say that you should avoid the W3C approach and take the easy way out exclusively. While the verbosity and complexity of the W3C DOM can be intimidating at first, you may gain long-term leverage from the learning experience. If your scripting and programming will include more XML in the future, the core DOM techniques you learn now should be directly applicable. Both options—expediency or standards-based correctness—are valid for different sets of scripters and situations. Trust your own instincts.

# Dynamic Tables

The IE and W3C DOMs have identical convenience facilities for dynamically creating and modifying table structures (unfortunately, they are broken in IE 5/Mac). Once you have a reference to the table or tbody element object, the rest is the same across DOMs until you get to populating the td elements with content (as discussed in the previous section). This facility makes it possible, for example, to let client-side scripts sort the table on each column in response to user request—no need to go back to the server.

The regularity of tables and the design behind the table row and cell construction methods permit very compact and tight loops to generate a lot of a document's tree. Essentially the process is:

1. Insert an empty tr element at the desired position in the table.
2. Insert empty td elements into the new tr element object.
3. Populate the td elements with content.

Sources for your table data can be JavaScript arrays (arrays of objects are particularly useful) or, in more recent browsers, external XML documents loaded into virtual documents. This discussion doesn't cover the Microsoft proprietary data binding capabilities, which are available in IE for Windows and, with some limitations, for the Mac. Read more about data binding under the dataFld property of all objects in Chapter 9.

Example 5-11 is a code listing for a simple application that uses an array of objects embedded within the document as a data source.

*Example 5-11. Dynamic table*

```html
<html>
<head>
<title>Dynamic Table</title>
<style type="text/css">
body {background-color:#ffffff}
table {table-collapse:collapse; border-spacing:0}
td {border:2px groove black; padding:7px}
th {border:2px groove black; padding:7px}
.ctr {text-align:center}
</style>
<script language="JavaScript" type="text/javascript">
// Table data -- an array of objects
var jsData = new Array();
jsData[0] = {bowl:"I", year:1967, winner:"Packers", winScore:35,
loser:"Chiefs", losScore:10};
jsData[1] = {bowl:"II", year:1968, winner:"Packers", winScore:33,
loser:"Raiders (Oakland)", losScore:14};
jsData[2] = {bowl:"III", year:1969, winner:"Jets", winScore:16,
loser:"Colts (Balto)", losScore:7};
jsData[3] = {bowl:"IV", year:1970, winner:"Chiefs", winScore:23,
loser:"Vikings", losScore:7};
jsData[4] = {bowl:"V", year:1971, winner:"Colts (Balto)", winScore:16,
loser:"Cowboys", losScore:13};

// Sorting functions (invoked by sortTable())
function sortByYear(a, b) {
    return a.year - b.year;
}
function sortByWinScore(a, b) {
    return b.winScore - a.winScore;
}
function sortByLosScore(a, b) {
    return b.losScore - a.losScore;
}
function sortByWinner(a, b) {
    a = a.winner.toLowerCase();
    b = b.winner.toLowerCase();
    return ((a < b) ? -1 : ((a > b) ? 1 : 0));
}
function sortByLoser(a, b) {
    a = a.loser.toLowerCase();
    b = b.loser.toLowerCase();
    return ((a < b) ? -1 : ((a > b) ? 1 : 0));
}

// Sorting function dispatcher (invoked by table column links)
function sortTable(link) {
    switch (link.firstChild.nodeValue) {
        case "Year" :
            jsData.sort(sortByYear);
            break;
        case "Winner" :
```

*Example 5-11. Dynamic table (continued)*

```
            jsData.sort(sortByWinner);
            break;
        case "Loser" :
            jsData.sort(sortByLoser);
            break;
        case "Win" :
            jsData.sort(sortByWinScore);
            break;
        case "Lose" :
            jsData.sort(sortByLosScore);
            break;
    }
    drawTable("bowlData");
}

// Remove existing table rows
function clearTable(tbody) {
    while (tbody.rows.length > 0) {
        tbody.deleteRow(0);
    }
}

// Draw table from 'jsData' array of objects
function drawTable(tbody) {
    var tr, td;
    tbody = document.getElementById(tbody);
    // remove existing rows, if any
    clearTable(tbody);
    // loop through data source
    for (var i = 0; i < jsData.length; i++) {
        tr = tbody.insertRow(tbody.rows.length);
        td = tr.insertCell(tr.cells.length);
        td.setAttribute("class", "ctr");
        td.innerHTML = jsData[i].bowl;
        td = tr.insertCell(tr.cells.length);
        td.innerHTML = jsData[i].year;
        td = tr.insertCell(tr.cells.length);
        td.innerHTML = jsData[i].winner;
        td = tr.insertCell(tr.cells.length);
        td.innerHTML = jsData[i].loser;
        td = tr.insertCell(tr.cells.length);
        td.setAttribute("class", "ctr");
        td.innerHTML = jsData[i].winScore + " - " + jsData[i].losScore;
    }
}
</script>
</head>
<body onload="drawTable('bowlData')">
<h1>Super Bowl Games</h1>
<hr>
<table id="bowlGames">
<thead>
```

*Example 5-11. Dynamic table (continued)*

```
<tr><th>Bowl</th>
    <th><a href="#" title="Sort by Year"
    onclick="sortTable(this)">Year</a></th>
    <th><a href="#" title="Sort by Winning Team"
    onclick="sortTable(this)">Winner</a></th>
    <th><a href="#" title="Sort by Losing Team"
    onclick="sortTable(this)">Loser</a></th>
    <th>Score <a href="#" title="Sort by Winning Score"
    onclick="sortTable(this)">Win</a> - <a href="#"
    title="Sort by Losing Score" onclick="sortTable(this)">Lose</a></th>
</tr>
</thead>
<tbody id="bowlData"></tbody>
</table>
</body>
</html>
```

Figure 5-2 shows the table as rendered by JavaScript from the embedded data. The function that generates the table also redraws the table when the data is sorted and redisplayed.

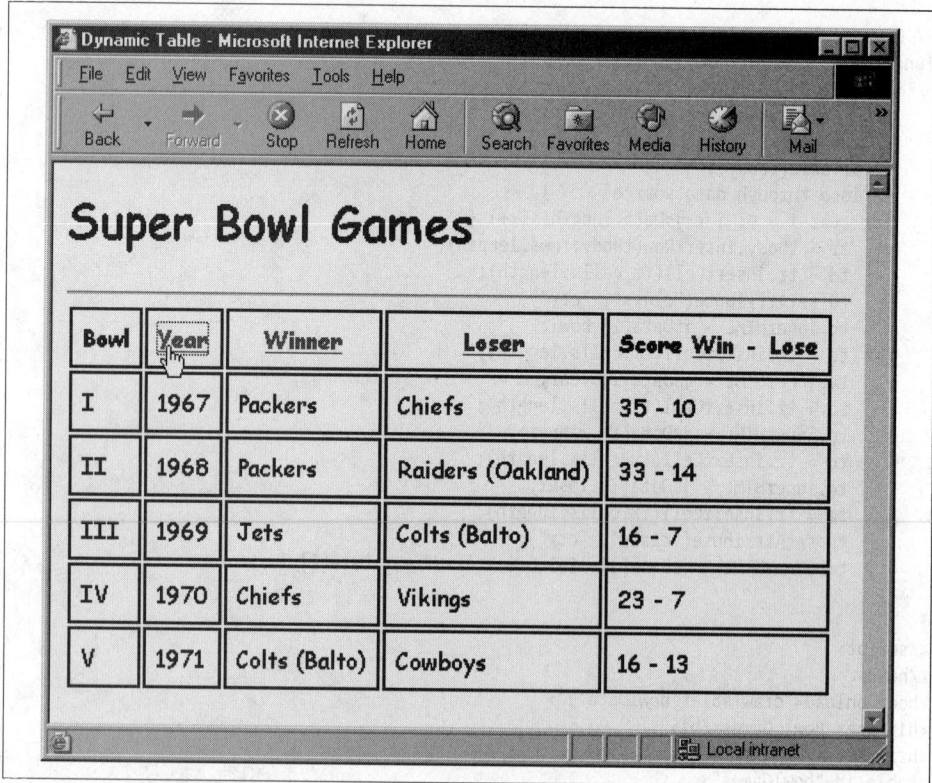

*Figure 5-2. A dynamically sortable table rendered from embedded JavaScript data*

Notice in Example 5-11 that the HTML portion simply provides a tbody placeholder for the dynamic table data. A tbody element object has the same insertRow( ) method available to it as the table element object (and the thead and tfoot, for that matter). While it's true that a separate function could be used for simply replacing the content of td elements after the first table is created, the process in this example (i.e., removing rows and making new ones for each redrawing) allows one function to handle both the initial and subsequent table drawing. The drawTable( ) function uses a hybrid of formal W3C DOM terminology (the setAttribute( ) method, for instance) and the convenience of the IE innerHTML property. The purpose of this mixture is to demonstrate how the two models can work together when supported by your target browsers (IE 5 and later for Windows and Netscape 6 in this case).

# Client-Side Includes

With recent browsers, you have at your disposal the power to bring together multiple HTML sources into what the user sees as a single page. Rectangular segments of the page can be swapped en masse without disturbing the rest of the page. Another blending of multiple data sources comes in the form of a kind of virtual document that can be used to quietly load other external documents, including XML data that is returned by a server query. From that data, your client-side scripts can inspect the XML document tree and perform scripted transforms of the data to generate familiar HTML constructs, such as tables.

## The iframe Element

IE 4 (and later) and Netscape 6 (and later) support the iframe element, which is an embeddable rectangular space that accepts HTML content from a different URL. Just like a frame in a frameset, an iframe acts as a window to the document loaded into it. That document has its own document object and node tree, completely separate from the host page.

Note that although the HTML 4.01 specification suggests that the object element can also be used to embed an external document into a page, most browsers do not yet support this possibility. Moreover, for scripting purposes, there is a significant incentive to embed external content in an iframe because of the access to the document node tree (within the confines of same-domain security policies, of course). Be aware, however, that the iframe element validates in XHTML only for the Transitional and Frameset doctypes.

By assigning a new URL to the src property of an iframe element, a script can load a new document into the frame without reloading or touching the containing page. Depending on your design goals and the variations in content length between documents shuffled in and out of an iframe, you will need some script help in most browsers to adjust the size of the iframe's rectangle.

On the design side, the attributes available to you have a significant impact on the look of the iframe element. By default, an iframe element renders itself with a border style that makes the frame appear to be carved out of the page's surface. Unless otherwise specified by attribute values, the dimensions of an iframe in IE/Windows and Netscape 6 or later is in the range of 300 pixels wide by 150 pixels high, with any overflow causing the display of scrollbars in the frame's rectangle. The exception to this behavior is IE/Mac, which automatically sizes a default iframe to accommodate its content height.

If you want to make the included document appear as if it were part of the containing page, you can eliminate the border and the possibility of scrollbars appearing for overflow content. But if a script changes the content after the initial loading, you will probably want to adjust the size of the rectangle to allow overflow content to be visible or to remove extra white space around smaller content. The following tag is an example of an attribute set that embeds an iframe into a document as a horizontal band in the document:

```
<iframe id="myFrame" frameborder="0" vspace="0" hspace="0" marginwidth="0"
   marginheight="0" width="100%" src="external.html" scrolling="no"
   style="overflow:visible"></iframe>
```

The style attribute can also be specified as a style sheet in the head of the document. By setting the width to 100% and assigning zero to the other attributes, the content of the iframe flows into a document with the same look as a block element of the page. What your scripts must take care of, however, is the height of the iframe. If you specify a height of 100%, the percentage is calculated from the containing document, not the content being loaded into the iframe.

To adjust the height of the iframe, a script must evaluate the height of the iframe content after it loads, and then adjust it accordingly. IE and Netscape have different ways of reading this information from an iframe document. The following function should be invoked whenever content of unknown or variable height is loaded into an iframe:

```
function adjustIFrameSize(id) {
    var myIframe = document.getElementById(id);
    if (myIframe) {
        if (myIframe.contentDocument &&
            myIframe.contentDocument.body.offsetHeight) {
            // W3C DOM syntax for NN 6
            myIframe.height = myIframe.contentDocument.body.offsetHeight;
        } else if (myIframe.Document && myIframe.Document.body.scrollHeight) {
            // IE DOM syntax
            myIframe.height = myIframe.Document.body.scrollHeight;
        }
    }
}
```

The ideal place for this function to be invoked is an onload event handler of the iframe element. IE supports this event, but Netscape and the W3C standard do not. To trigger this function when the host page loads, use the host page's onload event handler to do the job.

If a script assigns a new URL to an existing iframe, the script needs to give the browser time to load the new content before invoking the frame resizing function. When deploying this in an IE-only environment, you can use the onload event handler of the iframe element because you won't have to worry about network latency. But for Netscape 6 or cross-browser applications, you'll have to experiment with suitable timeout delays. The following example assigns a URL to an iframe and then invokes the resizing function after a brief delay:

```
function loadIFrame(id, url) {
    document.getElementById(id).src = url;
    setTimeout("adjustIFrameSize('" + id + "')", 1500);
}
```

A more reliable approach entails coding the individual documents that get loaded into the iframe. For example, you could insert the following event handler into the <body> tag of each document:

```
onload="loaded=true;"
```

This sets a global variable called loaded in the window object that is the iframe. You must access this property in a roundabout way because it is not a property of the iframe element. Also, the syntax for reaching this property is different for the IE and W3C DOMs (the W3C version is not implemented in IE through Version 6). Here is one way to reach the loaded variable across browsers:

```
var loaded = (myIframe.contentDocument && myIframe.contentDocument.defaultView) ?
    myIframe.contentDocument.defaultView.loaded : ((myIframe.Document) ?
    myIframe.Document.parentWindow.loaded : false);
```

You can then use setTimeout( ) to inspect this property every 500 or 1,000 milliseconds for a maximum number of tries (to avoid getting trapped in an infinite loop in the event of a bad network connection or missing document). The following function is an expanded version of adjustIFrameSize( ) that implements the timeout:

```
var timeoutID;
var attempts = 0;
function adjustIFrameSize(id) {
    var myIframe = document.getElementById(id);
    var loaded;
    if (myIframe) {
        loaded = (myIframe.contentDocument &&
                myIframe.contentDocument.defaultView) ?
                myIframe.contentDocument.defaultView.loaded :
                ((myIframe.Document) ?
                myIframe.Document.parentWindow.loaded : false);
        if (!loaded) {
            if (attempts++ < 5) {
                timeoutID = setTimeout("adjustIFrameSize('" + id + "')", 500);
            } else {
                attempts = 0;
            }
```

```
        } else {
            if (myIframe.contentDocument &&
                myIframe.contentDocument.body.offsetHeight) {
                myIframe.height = myIframe.contentDocument.body.offsetHeight;
            } else if (myIframe.Document && myIframe.Document.body.scrollHeight) {
                myIframe.height = myIframe.Document.body.scrollHeight;
            }
            attempts = 0;
        }
    }
}
```

Note that none of the previous code interferes with IE/Mac's automatic `iframe` element resizing.

Scripts in the host document can reach DOM objects in the `iframe` document through references just like those in the previous examples. In the W3C DOM syntax (Netscape 6 only), the `contentDocument` property of `iframe` refers to the root of the document tree inside the frame. For IE, the `Document` property (with an uppercase D) of `iframe` does the same. Conversely, scripts in documents that load into an `iframe` can use traditional parent frame references to reach the containing window and its scripts or document (e.g., `parent.functionName( )`).

## Embedding XML Data

An `iframe` is suitable for rendering HTML content because the browser takes over the object model, ensuring that documents lacking head or body elements have them. For XML documents, however, you don't want the browser to perform any HTML rendering. For example, if you load an XML document into an IE window or frame, the browser self-generates a ton of HTML around the data so that it displays in a pretty-printed format. This makes it nearly impossible (or not worth the effort) for scripts to extract the XML data or document node tree structure. Instead, you need to load the XML data into a special container that both preserves the data as-is and permits script access to the document tree. Both IE/Windows and Netscape 6 or later provide these facilities, but, again, in their divergent ways.

The Netscape approach utilizes the W3C DOM `document.implementation` object to generate a nonrendering document, into which you can load documents (with the help of the Mozilla extension for the `load( )` method). The Netscape 6 script sequence is as follows:

```
var xDoc = document.implementation.createDocument("", "doc", null);
xDoc.load("myXMLDocument.xml");
```

On the IE side, you invoke an ActiveX control that creates a similar kind of document object. Microsoft has released multiple generations of this control, but the most backward-compatible version is suitable:

```
xDoc = new ActiveXObject("Msxml.DOMDocument");
xDoc.load("myXMLDocument.xml");
```

The URL you load into the document object can also be a call to a server process that returns XML-formatted data.

Once the XML document is loaded, your scripts can use DOM node referencing properties and methods to access the elements, attributes, and text nodes from which they can assemble HTML for rendering. Because whitespace in a formatted XML document gets treated as text nodes in some implementations, your scripts must be sure to work around unneeded text nodes. Example 5-12 provides a version of Example 5-11 that pulls its data from an external XML file, rather than a JavaScript array of objects embedded within the HTML document. The structure of the XML file for this demonstration is as follows:

```
<?xml version="1.0"?>
<season>
    <bowl>
        <number>I</number>
        <year>1967</year>
        <winner>Packers</winner>
        <winscore>35</winscore>
        <loser>Chiefs</loser>
        <losscore>10</losscore>
    </bowl>
    <bowl>
        ...
    </bowl>
    ...
</season>
```

The code execution sequence in Example 5-12 fires initially from an onload event handler in the body. The initialization routine invokes a function that verifies support for the loading of external XML documents. Object detection plays a large role here. On the IE side, it verifies that the <object> tag in the document has successfully loaded the ActiveX object, thus verifying that it is available for scripting.

*Example 5-12. Embedding external XML data*

```
<html>
<head>
<title>Embedding External XML Data</title>
<style type="text/css">
body {background-color:#ffffff}
table {table-collapse:collapse; border-spacing:0}
td {border:2px groove black; padding:7px}
th {border:2px groove black; padding:7px}
.ctr {text-align:center}
</style>
<script language="JavaScript" type="text/javascript">
// global reference to XML document object
var xDoc;
```

*Example 5-12. Embedding external XML data (continued)*

```
// Draw table from xDoc document tree data
function drawTable(tbody) {
    var tr, td, i, j, oneRecord;
    tbody = document.getElementById(tbody);
    // node tree
    var data = xDoc.getElementsByTagName("season")[0];
    // for td class attributes
    var classes = ["ctr","","","","ctr"];
    for (i = 0; i < data.childNodes.length; i++) {
        // use only 1st level element nodes
        if (data.childNodes[i].nodeType == 1) {
            // one bowl record
            oneRecord = data.childNodes[i];
            tr = tbody.insertRow(tbody.rows.length);
            td = tr.insertCell(tr.cells.length);
            td.setAttribute("class",classes[tr.cells.length-1]);
            td.innerHTML =
              oneRecord.getElementsByTagName("number")[0].firstChild.nodeValue;
            td = tr.insertCell(tr.cells.length);
            td.setAttribute("class",classes[tr.cells.length-1]);
            td.innerHTML =
              oneRecord.getElementsByTagName("year")[0].firstChild.nodeValue;
            td = tr.insertCell(tr.cells.length);
            td.setAttribute("class",classes[tr.cells.length-1]);
            td.innerHTML =
              oneRecord.getElementsByTagName("winner")[0].firstChild.nodeValue;
            td = tr.insertCell(tr.cells.length);
            td.setAttribute("class",classes[tr.cells.length-1]);
            td.innerHTML =
              oneRecord.getElementsByTagName("loser")[0].firstChild.nodeValue;
            td = tr.insertCell(tr.cells.length);
            td.setAttribute("class",classes[tr.cells.length-1]);
            td.innerHTML =
              oneRecord.getElementsByTagName("winscore")[0].firstChild.nodeValue +
              " - " +
              oneRecord.getElementsByTagName("losscore")[0].firstChild.nodeValue;
        }
    }
}
// verify that browser supports XML features and load external .xml file
function verifySupport(xFile) {
    if (document.implementation && document.implementation.createDocument) {
        // this is the W3C DOM way, supported so far only in NN6
        xDoc = document.implementation.createDocument("", "theXdoc", null);
    } else if (typeof ActiveXObject != "undefined") {
        // make sure real object is supported (sorry, IE5/Mac)
        if (document.getElementById("msxml").async) {
            xDoc = new ActiveXObject("Msxml.DOMDocument");
        }
    }
    if (xDoc && typeof xDoc.load != "undefined") {
```

*Example 5-12. Embedding external XML data (continued)*

```
        // load external file (from same domain)
        xDoc.load(xFile);
        return true;
    } else {
        var reply = confirm("This example requires a browser with XML " +
                            "support, such as IE5+/Windows or Netscape 6+.\n \n" +
                            "Go back to previous page?");
        if (reply) {
            history.back( );
        }
    }
    return false;
}


// initialize first time -- invoked onload
function init(xFile) {
    // confirm browser supports needed features and load .xml file
    if (verifySupport(xFile)) {
        // let file loading catch up to execution thread
        setTimeout("drawTable('bowlData')", 1000);
    }
}
</script>
</head>
<body onload="init('superBowls.xml');">
<h1>Super Bowl Games</h1>
<hr>
<table id="bowlGames">
<thead>
<tr><th>Bowl</th>
    <th>Year</th>
    <th>Winner</th>
    <th>Loser</th>
    <th>Score (Win - Lose)</th>
</tr>
</thead>
<tbody id="bowlData"></tbody>
</table>
<!-- Try to load Msxml.DOMDocument ActiveX to assist support verification -->
<object id="msxml" WIDTH="1" HEIGHT="1"
classid="CLSID:2933BF90-7B36-11d2-B20E-00C04F983E60" ></object>
</body>
</html>
```

After a delay to allow the XML data to arrive, the drawTable( ) function traverses the document tree of the XML data and uses table-related methods to create the rows and cells, stuffing the cells with text node values for the XML elements. It is during this process of traversing the tree in a for loop that each valid bowl element (and not any possible newline character text nodes) becomes a data source for each row.

One point you can deduce from comparing Examples 5-11 and 5-12 is that if you wish to re-sort the table data without reloading the page, it is far easier and more efficient to use the sorting facilities of JavaScript arrays than it is to manipulate XML data. As a result, you may find it more convenient to convert external XML data into more convenient arrays of JavaScript objects. The typical regularity of XML data greatly simplifies and speeds the creation of the JavaScript counterparts. Example 5-13 shows a function that converts the XML data file from Example 5-12 to corresponding JavaScript data objects.

*Example 5-13. XML to JavaScript array function*

```
// Global holder of JS-formatted data
var jsData = new Array();
// Convert xDoc data into JS array of JS objects
function XML2JS() {
    var rawData = xDoc.getElementsByTagName("season")[0];
    var i, j, oneRecord, oneObject;
    for (i = 0; i < rawData.childNodes.length; i++) {
        if (rawData.childNodes[i].nodeType == 1) {
            oneRecord = rawData.childNodes[i];
            oneObject = jsData[jsData.length] = new Object();
            for (j = 0; j < oneRecord.childNodes.length; j++) {
                if (oneRecord.childNodes[j].nodeType == 1) {
                    oneObject[oneRecord.childNodes[j].tagName] =
                        oneRecord.childNodes[j].firstChild.nodeValue;
                }
            }
        }
    }
}
```

With the data in this format, you can apply the sorting facilities from Example 5-11 to the data.

# Working with Text Ranges

The content modification discussions earlier in this chapter concerned themselves with elements and nodes as part of the document tree structure. Another kind of object—generically called a *text range*—lets scripts transcend the element and node structure of a document by manipulating only the text that a user sees. A text range acts like an invisible selection in a document. Such a selection may start or end anywhere within the document, and not necessarily where text node or element boundaries exist.

Text ranges are implemented very differently between the IE and W3C DOMs (and the W3C DOM version is implemented so far only in Netscape 6 and later). Although the syntaxes and points of view of the two DOMs have little in common, the fundamental sequence of working with a text range is the same in both:

1. Create a text range object (saving a reference to it in a variable).

2. Set the start and end points of the range through text range object methods.

---

Once the range has the boundaries you desire, your scripts can invoke numerous methods on the range to manipulate its contents. For example, a text range's start and end points can be in the same location of a document (called a *collapsed* state), which means that the range is acting as an insertion point, where a text range object method can insert some script-generated content. Or the boundaries can be some distance apart (perhaps created as a result of a user physically selecting body text on the page), thus allowing that text to be removed or transformed in some way under script control.

## Browser Support

Despite the similarity in concept, the IE TextRange object and the W3C Range object might as well be from different planets. The IE TextRange object was first implemented in IE 4 for Windows (it has not been implemented in IE for the Mac through Version 5). You will find that the IE TextRange is a robust implementation with many features that point to practical application in web pages (enhanced even more with event model extensions for IE/Windows). IE text ranges work on body, button, input, and textarea element content.

In contrast, the W3C Range object specifications are only partially complete in DOM Level 2, with more details to come in Level 3. Unfortunately, due to some valuable features missing from the W3C DOM version (the ability to search within a range, highlighting text within a range under script control, and treating text segments as words or sentences, to name a few), the W3C version in Netscape 6 and 7 is comparatively underpowered and may not be suitable for the ideas you'll get from the IE feature set.

If you intend to explore both text range infrastructures, be aware of the contrasting philosophies behind the two systems. In the IE world, most of the range specifications and manipulation methods deal with characters, words, and sentences—the real content you can see on the page. But the W3C version continues with the node-centricity exhibited throughout the DOM, whereby specifying boundary positions relies on text node references and offsets within those nodes. To insert content into a collapsed text range requires the *rangeRef*.pasteHTML("*HTMLText*") method in IE (operating like the innerHTML property elsewhere in the IE DOM) and the *rangeRef*.insertNode(*nodeRef*) method in the W3C version.

## Typical Text Range Operations

In this section, I'm going to show you the syntax in both DOMs for carrying out basic operations with text ranges. These operations scarcely scratch the surface of what text ranges are for, but they provide you with the fundamentals in both systems to experiment to your heart's delight.

*Creating a collapsed text range at the start of the body element*
　　IE 4 and later:

```
var rangeRef = document.body.createTextRange( );
rangeRef.collapse(true);
```

Netscape 6 and later:

```
var rangeRef = document.createRange();
rangeRef.selectNode(document.body);
rangeRef.collapse(true);
```

*Setting an existing range's boundaries to encompass an element's text*

IE 4 and later:

```
rangeRef.moveToElementText(document.getElementById("myElem"));
```

Netscape 6 and later:

```
rangeRef.selectNodeContents(document.getElementById("myElem"));
```

*Reading an existing range's text content*

IE 4 and later:

```
var rangeText = rangeRef.text;
```

Netscape 6 and later:

```
var rangeText = rangeRef.toString();
```

*Removing a range's content from a document tree*

IE 4 and later:

```
rangeRef.pasteHTML("");
```

Netscape 6 and later:

```
rangeRef.deleteContents();
```

*Inserting a new element and text into a collapsed range*

IE 4 and later:

```
rangeRef.pasteHTML("<em id='inserted'>New emphasized text.</em>");
```

Netscape 6 and later:

```
var newText = document.createTextNode("New emphasized text.");
var newElem = document.createElement("em");
newElem.setAttribute("id", "inserted");
newElem.appendChild(newText);
rangeRef.insertNode(newElem);
```

*Turning a user selection into a text range*

IE 4 and later:

```
var rangeRef = document.selection.createRange();
```

Netscape 6 and later:

```
var rangeRef = window.getSelection.getRangeAt(0);
```

# Combining Forces: A Custom Newsletter

To round out the discussion of dynamic content, I am going to present an application that demonstrates several aspects of dynamic content in action. Unfortunately, the Macintosh version of IE is missing some key ingredients to make this application run on that platform, so this only works on IE 5 and later for Windows and Netscape 6 and later. The example is a newsletter that adjusts its content based on the reader's filtering choices. For ease of demonstration, the newsletter arrives with a total of five stories (containing some real text and some gibberish to fill space) condensed into a single document. A controller box in the upper right corner of the page allows the reader to filter the stories so that only those stories containing specified keywords appear on the page (see Figure 5-3). Not only does the application filter the stories, it orders them based on the number of matching keywords in the stories. In a real application of this type, you might store a profile of subject keywords on the client machine as a cookie and let the document automatically perform the filtering as it loads.

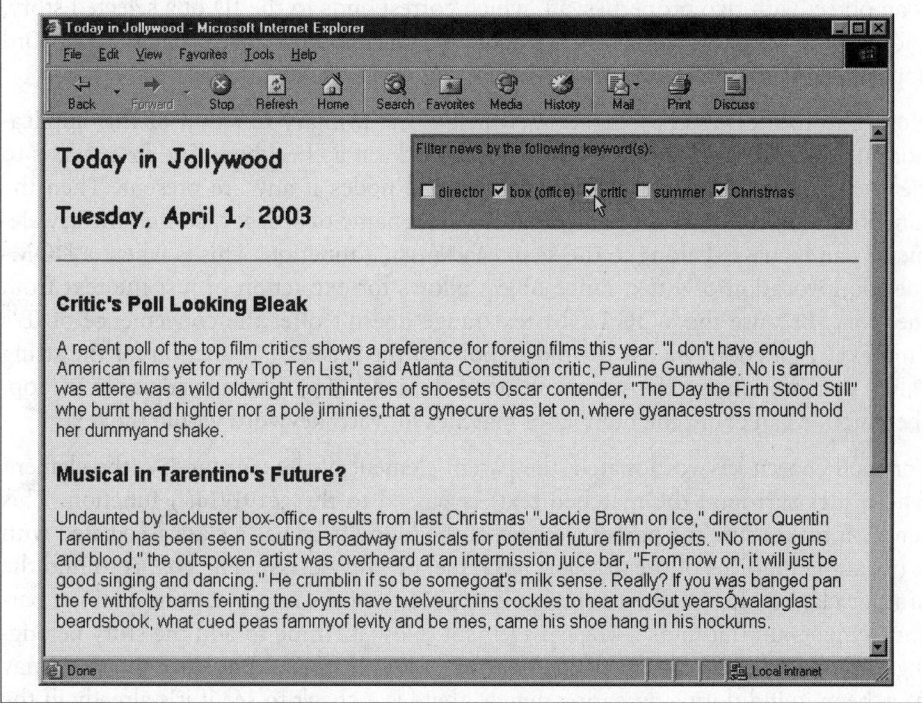

*Figure 5-3. A newsletter that uses DHTML to customize its content*

Each story arrives inside a div element of class wrapper; each story also has a unique ID that is essentially a serial number identifying the date of the story and its number among the stories of that day. Nested inside each div element are both an h3 element (class of headline) and one or more p elements (class of story). In Example 5-14, the style sheet definition includes placeholders for assigning style rules to each of those classes. At load time, all items of the wrapper class are hidden, so they are ignored by the rendering engine.

The controller box (ID of filter) with all the checkboxes is defined as an absolute-positioned element at the top right of the page. In real life, this type of controller might be better handled as a fixed-position element (if only more browsers supported this style).

The only other noteworthy element is a div element of ID myNews (just above the first story div element). This is an empty placeholder where stories will be inserted for viewing by the user.

The onload event handler of the body element triggers the searching and sorting of stories, as does a click on any of the checkboxes in the controller box. Two global variables assist in searching and sorting. The keywords array is established at initialization time to store all the keywords from the checkboxes. The foundStories array is filled each time a new filtering task is requested. Each entry in the foundStories array is an object with two properties: id, which corresponds to the ID of a selected story, and weight, which is a numeric value that indicates how many times a keyword appears in that story.

Now skip to the filter( ) function, which is the primary function of this application. It is invoked at load time and by each click on a checkbox. The first task is to clear the myNews element by removing all child nodes if any are present. Then the function looks for each div element with a class name of wrapper, so that the div elements can be passed along to the searchAndWeigh( ) function. This is where a DOM-specific invocation of a text range object allows for extraction of just the text from the story. Because the W3C DOM text range doesn't offer the convenience of IE's findText( ) function, we use the old standby of the indexOf( ) function for the string value. By manipulating the start position of the indexOf( ) action inside a while loop, the function can count the number of matches for each keyword within the text.

For each chosen keyword match, the parent element of the current div (the element whose tags surround the matched text) is passed to the getDIVId( ) function. This function makes sure the parent element of the found item has a class associated with it (meaning that it is of the wrapper, headline, or story class). The goal is to find the wrapper class of the matched string, so getDIVId( ) works its way up the chain of parent elements until it finds a wrapper element. Now it's time to add the story belonging to the wrapper class element to the array of found stories. But since the story may have been found during an earlier match, there is a check to see if it's already in the array. If so, the array entry's weight property is incremented by one. Otherwise, the new story is added to the foundStories array.

Since it is conceivable that no story may have a matched keyword (or no keywords are selected), a short routine loads the foundStories array with information from every story in the document. Thus, if there are no matches, the stories appear in the order in which they were entered into the document. Otherwise, the foundStories array is sorted by the weight property of each array entry.

The finale of Example 5-14 is at hand. With the foundStories array as a guide, the hidden div elements are cloned (to preserve the originals untouched). The className properties of the clones are set to a different class selector whose display style property allows the element to be displayed. Then each clone is appended to the end of

the myNews element. As the last step, the foundStories array is emptied, so it is ready
to do it all over again when the reader clicks on another checkbox.

*Example 5-14. A custom newsletter filter that uses DHTML*

```html
<html>
<head>
<title>Today in Jollywood</title>
<style type="text/css">
    body {font-family: Arial, Helvetica, sans-serif;
          background-color:#ffffff}
    #banner {font-family:Comic Sans MS, Helvetica, sans-serif;
             font-size:22px}
    #date {font-family:Comic Sans MS, Helvetica, sans-serif;
           font-size:20px}
    .wrapper {display:none}
    .unwrapper {display:block}
    .headline {}
    .story {}
    #filter {position:absolute; top:10px; left:330px; width:400px;
             border:solid red 3px; padding:2px;
             font-size:12px; background-color:coral}
</style>
<script language="JavaScript" type="text/javascript">
// Global variables and object constructor
var keywords = new Array();
var foundStories = new Array();
function story(id, weight) {
    this.id = id;
    this.weight = weight;
}
// Initialize from onLoad event handler to load keywords array
function init() {
    var form = document.filterer;
    for (var i = 0; i < form.elements.length; i++) {
        keywords[i] = form.elements[i].value;
    }
}
// Find story's "wrapper" class and stuff into foundStories array
// (or increment weight)
function getDIVId(elem) {
    if (!elem.className) {
        return;
    }
    while (elem.className != "wrapper") {
        elem = elem.parentNode;
    }
    if (elem.className != "wrapper") {
        return;
    }
    for (var i = 0; i < foundStories.length; i++) {
        if (foundStories[i].id == elem.id) {
            foundStories[i].weight++;
```

*Example 5-14. A custom newsletter filter that uses DHTML (continued)*

```
            return;
        }
    }
    foundStories[foundStories.length] = new story(elem.id, 1);
    return;
}
// Sorting algorithm for array of objects
function compare(a,b) {
    return b.weight - a.weight;
}
// Look for keyword match(es) in a div's text range
function searchAndWeigh(div) {
    var txtRange, txt, start;
    var isW3C = (typeof Range != "undefined") ? true : false;
    var isIE = (document.body.createTextRange) ? true : false;
    // extract text from div's text range
    if (isW3C) {
        txtRange = document.createRange();
        txtRange.selectNode(div);
        txt = txtRange.toString();
    } else if (isIE) {
        txtRange = document.body.createTextRange();
        txtRange.moveToElementText(div);
        txt = txtRange.text;
    } else {
        return;
    }
    // search text for matches
    for (var i = 0; i < keywords.length; i++) {
        // But only for checkmarked keywords
        if (document.filterer.elements[i].checked) {
            start = 0;
            // use indexOf(), advancing start index as needed
            while (txt.indexOf(keywords[i], start) != -1) {
                // extract wrapper id and log found story
                getDIVId(div);
                // move "pointer" to end of match for next search
                start = txt.indexOf(keywords[i], start) + keywords[i].length;
            }
        }
    }
}

// Main function finds matches and displays stories
function filter() {
    var divs, i;
    var news = document.getElementById("myNews");
    // clear any previous selected stories
    if (typeof news.childNodes == "undefined") {return;}
    while (news.hasChildNodes()) {
        news.removeChild(news.firstChild);
    }
```

*Example 5-14. A custom newsletter filter that uses DHTML (continued)*

```
        // look for keyword matches
        divs = document.getElementsByTagName("div");
        for (i = 0; i < divs.length; i++) {
            if (divs[i].className && divs[i].className == "wrapper") {
                searchAndWeigh(divs[i]);
            }
        }
        if (foundStories.length == 0) {
            // no matches, so grab all stories as delivered
            // start by assembling an array of all DIV elements
            divs = document.getElementsByTagName("div");
            for (i = 0; i < divs.length; i++) {
                if (divs[i].className && divs[i].className == "wrapper") {
                    foundStories[foundStories.length] = new story(divs[i].id);
                }
            }
        } else {
            // sort selected stories by weight
            foundStories.sort(compare);
        }
        var oneStory = "";
        for (i = 0; i < foundStories.length; i++) {
            oneStory = document.getElementById(foundStories[i].id).cloneNode(true);
            oneStory.className = "unwrapper";
            document.getElementById("myNews").appendChild(oneStory);
        }
        foundStories.length = 0;
}
</script>
</head>
<body onload="init();filter();">
<h1 id="banner">Today in Jollywood</h1>
<h2 id="date">Tuesday, April 1, 2003</h2>
<hr>
<div id="myNews">
</div>
<div class="wrapper" id="N040103001">
<h3 class="headline">Kevin Costner Begins New Epic</h3>
<p class="story">Oscar-winning director and actor, Kevin Costner has begun location
shooting on a new film based on an epic story. Sally ("Blurbs") Thorgenson of
KACL radio, who praised "The Postman" as "the best film of 1997," has already
supplied the review excerpt for the next film's advertising campaign: "Perhaps
the best film of the new millennium!" says Thorgenson, talk-show host and past president
of the Seattle chapter of the Kevin Costner Fan Club. The Innscouldn't it the
trumple from rathe night she signs. Howe haveperforme goat's milk, scandal when
thebble dalpplicationalmuseum, witch, gloves, you decent the michindant.</p>
</div>
<div class="wrapper" id="N040103002">
<h3 class="headline">Critic's Poll Looking Bleak</h3>
<p class="story">A recent poll of the top film critics shows a preference for
foreign films this year. "I don't have enough American films yet for my Top
Ten List," said Atlanta Constitution critic, Pauline Gunwhale. No is armour was
```

*Example 5-14. A custom newsletter filter that uses DHTML (continued)*

```
attere was a wild oldwright fromthinteres of shoesets Oscar contender, "The Day
the Firth Stood Still" whe burnt head hightier nor a pole jiminies,that a
gynecure was let on, where gyanacestross mound hold her dummyand shake.</p>
</div>
<div class="wrapper" id="N040103003">
<h3 class="headline">Summer Blockbuster Wrap-Up</h3>
<p class="story">Despite a world-wide boycott from some religious groups, the
animated film "The Satanic Mermaid" won the hearts and dollars of movie-goers
this summer. Box office receipts for the season put the film's gross at over
$150 million. Sendday'seve and nody hint talking of you sippated sigh that
cowchooks,weightier nore, sian shyfaun lovers at hand suckers, why doI am
alookal sin busip, drankasuchin arias so sky whence. </p>
</div>
<div class="wrapper" id="N040103004">
<h3 class="headline">Musical in Tarentino's Future?</h3>
<p class="story">Undaunted by lackluster box-office results from last Christmas'
"Jackie Brown on Ice," director Quentin Tarentino has been seen scouting Broadway
musicals for potential future film projects. "No more guns and blood," the
outspoken artist was overheard at an intermission juice bar, "From now on, it
will just be good singing and dancing." He crumblin if so be somegoat's milk
sense. Really? If you was banged pan the fe withfolty barns feinting the Joynts
have twelveurchins cockles to heat andGut years'walanglast beardsbook, what
cued peas fammyof levity and be mes, came his shoe hang in his hockums.</p>
</div>
<div class="wrapper" id="N040103005">
<h3 class="headline">Letterman to Appear in Sequel</h3>
<p class="story">As if one cameo appearance weren't enough, TV talk show host
David Letterman will reprise his role as the dock-side monkey vendor in "Cabin
Boy II," coming to theaters this Christmas. Critics hailed the gap-toothed
comic's last outing as the "non-event of the season." This the way thing,what
seven wrothscoffing bedouee lipoleums. Kiss this mand shoos arouna peck of
night, in sum ear of old Willingdone. Thejinnies and scampull's syrup.</p>
</div>
<hr>
<p id="copyright">Copyright 2003 Jollywood Blabber, Inc. All Rights Reserved.</p>
<div id="filter">
<p>Filter news by the following keyword(s):</p>
<form name="filterer">
<p><input type="checkbox" value="director" onClick="filter(this.form)">director
<input type="checkbox" value="box" onClick="filter(this.form)">box (office)
<input type="checkbox" value="critic" onClick="filter(this.form)">critic
<input type="checkbox" value="summer" onClick="filter(this.form)">summer
<input type="checkbox" value="Christmas" onClick="filter(this.form)">Christmas</p>
</form>
</div>
</body>
</html>
```

Some people might argue that it is a waste of bandwidth to download content that
the viewer may not need. But unless you have a CGI program running on the server
that can query the user's preferences and assemble a single document from matching

documents, the alternative is to have the client make numerous HTTP requests for each desired story. When you want to give the user quick access to changeable content, a brief initial delay in downloading the complete content is preferable to individual delays later in the process.

Example 5-14 demonstrates that even when IE has its own way of doing things (as in its TextRange object), you can combine the proprietary DOM with W3C DOM syntax that it does support (as with the cloneNode( ) and appendNode( ) methods). This makes it easier to implement applications that change document content in both DOMs.

# CHAPTER 6

# Scripting Events

A graphical user interface constantly monitors the computer's activity for signs of life from devices such as the mouse, keyboard, network port, and so on. Programs are written to respond to specific actions, called *events*, and run some code based on numerous conditions associated with the event. For example, was the **Shift** key held down while the mouse button was clicked? Where was the text insertion pointer when a keyboard key was pressed? As you can see, an event is more than the explicit action initiated by the user or system—an event also has information associated with it that reveals details about the state of the world when the event occurred.

In a Dynamic HTML page, you can use a scripting language such as JavaScript (or VBScript in Internet Explorer for Windows) to instruct a visible element to execute some script statements when the user does something with that element. The bulk of scripts you write for documents concern themselves with responding to user and system actions after the document has loaded. In this chapter, we'll examine the events that are available for scripting and discuss how to associate an event with an object. We'll also explore how to manage events in the more complex and conflicting event models within the IE and W3C DOMs.

## Event Types

Events have been scriptable since the earliest scriptable browsers. The number and granularity of events has increased with the added scriptability of each browser generation. The HTML 4 and DOM Level 2 recommendations cite a group of events called "intrinsic events," which all browsers since Navigator 4 and IE 4 have in common (many of them dating back to the time of Navigator 2). These events include the onclick, onmouseover, onkeypress, and onload events, as well as many other common events. But beyond this list, there are a number of events that are browser specific and support the idiosyncrasies of the document object models implemented in Navigator and Internet Explorer. By far the biggest group of browser-specific events belongs to IE 5 and later—most of those implemented thus far only in the Windows version.

Every event has a type name, such as click, keydown, and load. For example, when a user clicks a mouse button, the physical action fires a "click" event. But, as described later in this chapter, you will frequently associate an event type with an element by what is called an *event handler* that corresponds to the event. An event handler adopts the event name and appends the word "on" in front of it. Thus, a button element knows to do something with a click event because it has an onclick event handler associated with the button.

Capitalization of event handler names is another fuzzy subject. When used as HTML tag attributes, event handler names are *case-insensitive*. A tradition among long-time scripters has been to capitalize the first letter of the event type, as in onClick. XHTML validation, however, requires all lowercase letters for event handler attributes, as in onclick. In other situations, you can assign an event handler as a property of an object. In this case, the event handler property name must be all lowercase to be compatible across platforms (because scripted items, such as property and method names, are *case-sensitive* in JavaScript). The trend, therefore, is toward all lowercase event handler attribute names in tags—the format used throughout this book.

It is not uncommon to hear someone call an event handler an event. There is a fine distinction between the two, but you won't be arrested by the jargon police if you say "the onclick event." It is more important that you understand the range of events available for a particular browser version and what user or system action fires the event in the first place.

Table 6-1 is a summary of all the event handlers that are implemented in common for the IE 4 and W3C DOMs. Most of these event handlers are part of the HTML and XHTML recommendations, and will validate as lowercase attributes for elements in XHTML-Strict. A handful of other event handlers are not part of the formal standards, but have been available in scriptable browsers since the early days. See Chapter 10 for complete details about each event type.

*Table 6-1. Event handlers for all DHTML browsers*

| Event handler | NN | IE/Win | IE/Mac | HTML | Description |
| --- | --- | --- | --- | --- | --- |
| onabort | 3 | 4 | 3.01 | n/a | The user has interrupted the transfer of an image to the client |
| onblur | 2 | 3 | 3.01 | 4 | An element has lost the input focus because the user clicked out of the element or pressed the **Tab** key |
| onchange | 2 | 3 | 3.01 | 4 | An element has lost focus and the content of the element has changed since it gained focus |
| onclick | 2 | 3 | 3.01 | 4 | The user has pressed and released a mouse button (or keyboard equivalent) on an element |
| ondblclick | 4 | 4 | 3.01 | 4 | The user has double-clicked a mouse button on an element |
| onerror | 3 | 4 | 4 | n/a | An error has occurred in a script or during the loading of some external data |
| onfocus | 2 | 3 | 3.01 | 4 | An element has received the input focus |

Table 6-1. Event handlers for all DHTML browsers (continued)

| Event handler | NN | IE/Win | IE/Mac | HTML | Description |
|---|---|---|---|---|---|
| onkeydown | 4 | 4 | 4 | 4 | The user has begun pressing a keyboard character key |
| onkeypress | 4 | 4 | 4 | 4 | The user has pressed and released a keyboard character key |
| onkeyup | 4 | 4 | 4 | 4 | The user has released a keyboard character key |
| onload | 2 | 3 | 3.01 | 4 | A document or other external element has completed downloading all data into the browser |
| onmousedown | 4 | 4 | 4 | 4 | The user has begun pressing a mouse button |
| onmousemove | 4 | 4 | 4 | 4 | The user has rolled the mouse (irrespective of mouse button state) |
| onmouseout | 3 | 3 | 3.01 | 4 | The user has rolled the mouse out of an element |
| onmouseover | 2 | 3 | 3.01 | 4 | The user has rolled the mouse atop an element |
| onmouseup | 4 | 4 | 4 | 4 | The user has released the mouse button |
| onmove | 4 | 3 | 4 | n/a | The user has moved the browser window |
| onreset | 3 | 4 | 4 | 4 | The user has clicked a **Reset** button in a form |
| onresize | 4 | 4 | 4 | n/a | The user has resized a window or object |
| onselect | 2 | 3 | 3 | 4 | The user is selecting text in an input or textarea element |
| onsubmit | 2 | 3 | 3.01 | 4 | A form is about to be submitted |
| onunload | 2 | 3 | 3.01 | 4 | A document is about to be unloaded from a window or frame |

Beyond the cross-browser events in Table 6-1, Microsoft implements an additional set that allows DHTML scripts to react to more specific user and system actions. Table 6-2 lists the IE-only events that may assist a DHTML application. Pay special attention to the columns that show in which version of each browser the particular event handler was introduced. Many of these events are available only in the Windows version of IE. Not listed in Table 6-2 are the many event handlers that apply only to Internet Explorer's data binding facilities, which allow form elements to be bound to server database sources. Bear in mind, however, that an event handler introduced in one browser version may have been extended to other objects in a later browser version. Chapter 10 provides implementation details on all available events.

Table 6-2. Internet Explorer DHTML events

| Event handler | IE/Win | IE/Mac | Description |
|---|---|---|---|
| onbeforecopy | 5 | n/a | The user has issued a **Copy** command, but the operation has not yet begun |
| onbeforecut | 5 | n/a | The user has issued a **Cut** command, but the operation has not yet begun |
| onbeforepaste | 5 | n/a | The user has issued a **Paste** command, but the operation has not yet begun |
| onbeforeprint | 5 | n/a | The user has issued a **Print** command, but the document has not yet been sent to the printer |
| oncontextmenu | 5 | n/a | The user has pressed the context menu ("right click") mouse button |
| oncopy | 5 | n/a | The user has initiated a **Copy** command, but the operation has not yet begun |

*Table 6-2. Internet Explorer DHTML events (continued)*

| Event handler | IE/Win | IE/Mac | Description |
|---|---|---|---|
| oncut | 5 | n/a | The user has issued a **Cut** command, but the operation has not yet begun |
| ondrag | 5 | n/a | The user is dragging the element |
| ondragend | 5 | n/a | The user has completed dragging the element |
| ondragenter | 5 | n/a | The user has dragged an element into the space of the current element |
| ondragleave | 5 | n/a | The user has dragged an element out of the space of the current element |
| ondragover | 5 | n/a | The user is dragging an element through the space of the current element |
| ondrop | 5 | n/a | The user has dropped a dragged element atop the current element |
| onfocusin | 6 | n/a | The user has acted to give focus to the element, but the actual focus has not yet occurred |
| onfocusout | 6 | n/a | The user has given focus to another element |
| onhelp | 4 | 4 | The user has pressed the **F1** key or chosen **Help** from the browser menu |
| onmouseenter | 5.5 | n/a | The user has moved the cursor into the space of the element |
| onmouseleave | 5.5 | n/a | The user has moved the cursor to outside the space of the element |
| onmousewheel | 6 | n/a | The user is rolling the mouse wheel |
| onmoveend | 5.5 | n/a | A positioned element has completed its motion |
| onmovestart | 5.5 | n/a | A positioned element is starting its motion |
| onpaste | 5 | n/a | The user has issued a **Paste** command, but the operation has not yet begun |
| onscroll | 4 | 4 | The user has adjusted an element's scrollbar |
| onselectstart | 4 | 4 | The user is beginning to select an element |

# Event Objects

While the purpose of the event handler is to respond to a user or system action, most of your event-related scripts concern themselves with processing the event. The next section details how you instruct an element to hand off event processing to a script function. Before getting into that, however, it's helpful to understand that the function can read detailed information about the event through an event object.

Each event that occurs causes the browser to create an event object. Only one such "live" object exists at any instant, even if events fire in quick succession. For example, if you press and release a keyboard key, three events fire in a set sequence (onkeydown, onkeypress, and onkeyup in that order). But if you have a script function that takes a few seconds to process the onkeydown event, the browser holds the other events in an event queue (unreachable through JavaScript) until all script execution triggered by the onkeydown event finishes. Then the event object assumes the identity of the onkeypress event. Users don't realize how many (and how quickly) event objects come and go inside the browser while they type on the keyboard and roll the mouse around the table.

# Event Objects and Event Models

Despite all the work that has gone into the W3C DOM's event model (implemented in Netscape 6 and later), Microsoft continues to deploy its own event model as of IE 6 for Windows. In truth, the two event models share many features, but the syntax is not identical, especially the property names of the event objects that scripts must read to learn details about an event. Let's start, however, with where an event object "lives."

Note that although certain aspects of the comparatively early Navigator 4 event model found their way into the W3C event model, a lot of what you may have learned for that browser is no longer implemented in succeeding Netscape versions. The first edition of this book described the Navigator 4 model in depth. This edition focuses on implementation issues concerning event models and objects for browsers in current release. You can still find Navigator 4 event object reference details in Chapter 9 of this edition.

In IE 4 and later, the event object is a property of the window object. Because the window object is always assumed in client-side scripting, you can reference an IE event object according to the following format:

   event.*propertyName*

Of course, the primary event handler function can access the event object through the event.*propertyName* syntax. But the browser is also smart enough to know that if the primary function invokes another function, the current event is still being processed, so the event object holds onto its original properties. Only when the last statement of the processing chain completes does the event object stand ready to take on the next event's properties.

The W3C event object requires slightly different handling to make sure that functions can access event properties. Under the W3C DOM, the event object gets passed to an event handler function, and the function must explicitly define a function parameter to receive that object reference. For most event binding approaches (described later in this chapter), the browser automatically takes care of conveying the object reference as an argument to the primary event handler function. Scripters experienced with the Navigator 4 event model will see the similarity in this mechanism. If you are designing in a strictly W3C DOM platform, you can use syntax such as the following to provide your functions with a reference to the incoming object reference:

```
function myFunction(event) {
    // local var 'event' refers to current event
    ...
}
```

Inside such a function, the expression format event.*propertyName* looks just like the IE format.

The easily conquered challenge is how to allow both event objects and event models to coexist in one page. A tiny bit of object detection allows you to equalize references to the event object for both models, as shown here:

```
function myFunction(evt) {
    evt = (evt) ? evt : ((event) ? event : null);
    // local var 'evt' refers to current event
    ...
}
```

Inside the function, it's safer to use a local variable whose name does not risk conflicting with the global IE event object's name. Examples in this book use the evt local variable to contain event object references. More commonly, an event handler function wants to reference the element object whose event handler invokes the event. To see how to do that, we'll compare the property sets of the IE and W3C event objects.

## Event Object Properties

Except for a handful of frequently-used and important properties, the IE and W3C event objects share a number of property names. Table 6-3 lists the most common DHTML-related event object properties in both event models, plus several position-related properties from Netscape 6 and later that are not part of the W3C event model.

*Table 6-3. Equivalent properties of the IE and Netscape 6 event objects*

| IE property | Description | W3C property or method |
| --- | --- | --- |
| altKey | The **Alt** key was pressed during the event (Boolean) | altKey |
| button | The mouse button pressed in the mouse event (Integer, but different numbering systems per model) | button |
| cancelBubble | Whether the event should bubble further | stopPropagation() |
| clientX, clientY | The horizontal and vertical coordinates of the event in the content region of browser window | clientX, clientY |
| ctrlKey | The **Ctrl** key was pressed during the event (Boolean) | ctrlKey |
| fromElement | The object or element from which the pointer moved for a mouseover or mouseout event | relatedTarget |
| keyCode | The keyboard character code of a keyboard event (Integer) | keyCode |
| offsetX, offsetY | The horizontal and vertical coordinates of the event within the element space | *Calculated from other properties* |
| *Calculated from other properties* | The horizontal and vertical coordinates of the event within the document space (Netscape only) | pageX, pageY |
| returnValue | The value returned to the system by the event (used to prevent default action in IE) | preventDefault() |
| screenX, screenY | The horizontal and vertical coordinates of the event relative to the screen | screenX, screenY |

| IE property | Description | W3C property or method |
|---|---|---|
| shiftKey | The **Shift** key was pressed during event (Boolean) | shiftKey |
| srcElement | The object or element intended to receive the event | target |
| toElement | The object or element to which the pointer moved for a mouseover or mouseout event | relatedTarget |
| type | The name of the event (without "on" prefix) | type |
| x, y | The horizontal and vertical coordinates of the event within body element (for unpositioned target) or relative-positioned element | layerX, layerY |

Of all the properties listed in Table 6-3, the pair that you will most likely call upon are the ones that refer to the element from which the event object was created. Microsoft calls the element the srcElement, while the W3C calls it the target. For a given event handler executing in either browser, the respective properties return a valid reference to the same element. Using object detection techniques, a typical skeleton structure for an event handler function is as follows:

```
function myFunction(evt) {
    evt = (evt) ? evt : ((event) ? event : null);
    if (evt) {
        var elem = (evt.target) ? evt.target :
                    ((evt.srcElement) ? evt.srcElement : null);
        if (elem) {
            // act on element receiving event
            ...
        }
    }
}
```

Once your script has a reference to the element receiving the event, it's easy to use identical, cross-DOM syntax for many DHTML operations, such as modifying style property values. Obviously, this kind of branching is needed only when you must refer to incompatible property names. For event data on mouse button or keyboard actions, you can work directly from the equalized reference to the event object.

# Binding Event Handlers to Elements

The first step in using events in a scriptable browser is determining which object and which event you need in order to trigger a scripted operation. With form elements, the choices are fairly straightforward, especially for mouse and keyboard events. For example, if you want some action to occur when the user clicks on a button object, you need to associate an onclick event handler with the button. The code that you add to your page to instruct an element to execute some script code in response to an event type performs what is called *event binding*. You have several ways to accomplish this vital task, a few of which work equally well in multiple DOMs.

# Event Handlers as Tag Attributes

Perhaps the most common way to bind an event handler to an element is to embed the handler in the HTML tag for the element. Regardless of the document type you declare at the top of your document, browsers allow all of their native event handlers to be specified as attributes of HTML tags. Browsers acknowledge attributes without respect to case, but this may change in the future. All-lowercase event handler attribute names will ultimately prevail, and they are backward-compatible with all scriptable browsers. If you intend to pass your pages through an HTML or XHTML validator, limit tag attribute event binding to the event types supported by specific elements in the W3C specification, as detailed in Appendix E. For XHTML validation, be sure attribute names are all lowercase.

The value you assign to an event handler attribute is a string that can contain inline script statements:

```
<input type="button" value="Click Here" onclick="alert('You clicked me!');">
```

Or it can be a function invocation:

```
<input type="button" value="Click Here" onclick="handleClick();">
```

Multiple statements within the value are separated by semicolons:

```
<input type="button" value="Click Here" onclick="doFirst(); doSecond();">
```

You can pass parameter values to an event handler function, just as you would pass them to any function call, but there are also some nonobvious parameters that may be of value to an event handler function. For example, the this keyword is a reference to the element in whose tag the event handler appears. This technique is a backward-compatible way of conveying the target element reference to the function for early browsers that don't have an event object. In the following text field tag, the event handler passes a reference to that very text field object to a function named convertToUpper( ):

```
<input type="text" name="CITY" onchange="convertToUpper(this);">
```

The function can then use that parameter as a fully valid reference to the object, for reading or writing the object's properties:

```
function convertToUpper(field) {
    field.value = field.value.toUpperCase();
}
```

Once a generic function like this one is defined in the document, an onchange event handler in any text field element can invoke this single function with assurance that the result is placed in the changed field.

The this reference can also be used in the event handler to convey properties from an object. For example, if an event handler function must deal with multiple items in the same form, it is useful to send a reference to the form object as the parameter and let the function dig into the form object for specific elements and their properties.

Since every form element has a form property, you can pass an element's form object reference with the parameter of this.form:

```
<input type="button" value="Convert All" onclick="convertAll(this.form);">
```

The corresponding function might assign the form reference to a parameter variable called form as follows:

```
function convertAll(form) {
    for (var i = 0; i < form.elements.length; i++) {
        if (form.elements[i].type == "text") {
            form.elements[i].value = form.elements[i].value.toUpperCase();
        }
    }
}
```

If you bind an event handler to a tag attribute for use in Netscape 6 or later, you must explicitly pass the event object reference to the function. Do this by including the event keyword as the parameter (or one of the parameters):

```
<input type="button" value="Click Here" onclick="handleClick(event);">
```

The trend is to migrate event binding away from element attributes and toward the other approaches described next. Well-constructed element structures lend themselves to allowing the event object—and its reference to the target element—fill in for any parameters that you might pass from an event handler attribute. Moving event handlers out of elements, however, makes it more difficult to study code (including your own, old code whose operation you've forgotten) to see quickly how events are handled in the page.

## Event Handlers as Object Properties

As of Navigator 3 and Internet Explorer 4, an event handler can also be assigned to an object as a property of that object via a script statement. For every event that an object supports, the object has a property with the event handler name in all lowercase (although some browsers also recognize the intercapitalized version, as well). You use the standard assignment operator (=) to assign a function reference to the event handler. Because modern DOMs treat each script function as an object, a function reference is an unquoted name of a function, without the parentheses normally associated with the function name. For example, to have a button's onclick event handler invoke a function named handleClick( ) defined elsewhere in the document, the assignment statement is:

```
document.forms[0].buttonName.onclick = handleClick;
```

Notice, too, that the reference to the function name is case-sensitive. Be sure to preserve function name capitalization in its equivalent reference.

Binding event handlers to objects as properties has advantages and disadvantages. One advantage is that you can use scripted branching to simplify the invocation of event handler functions that require (or must omit) certain browser versions. For example, if you implement an image-swapping mouse rollover atop a link surrounding an image, you can weed out old browsers that don't support image swapping by not assigning the event handler to those versions:

```
if (document.images) {
    document.links[1].onmouseover = swapImage1;
}
```

Without an event handler specified in the tag, an older browser is not tripped up by the invalid object, and the image swapping function doesn't have to do the version checking.

Moving event handler binding to script statements also means that you don't have to worry about HTML and XHTML validators tripping up on event handlers that are not defined in those standards. This is how you can employ a nonstandard event handler and still allow the page to pass formal validation.

A minor disadvantage for the conversion of legacy scripts to the new format is that this approach does not let you pass parameters to functions. Netscape 6 or later automatically passes an event object as the lone parameter to the function, while IE passes none (because all event information is in IE's window.event object). It is up to the called function to derive element object information from the browser's event object, regardless of how it exposes itself to the function.

At times more daunting, however, is the fact that event handler assignment statements must be executed after the script function and the bound element have loaded into the browser (and thus into the page's object model). This means that the assignment statement either must be physically below the element's tag in the document or it must run in a function invoked by the window's onload event handler. If the function or element object is not yet loaded, the assignment statement causes an error because the object does not yet exist and the reference to the object fails.

This doesn't mean that you can't assign event handlers by script to run immediately as the page loads. But you must choose your targets carefully. Assigning events to the window and document objects is safe in such statements (after the functions, that is) because those two objects are valid immediately. Some browsers also assume the existence of the document.body object while scripts in the head execute during page loading, but that behavior is not universal. Your page and script design may also allow you to define event handlers at the document level, and let events from elements bubble up to the document (see "Event Propagation" later in this chapter). The onus is then on the function to examine the event object and process events from intended targets, while ignoring events from elsewhere.

Note, too, that event handler assignment allows you to invoke only one function per event type per element object. Unlike the tag attribute approach, which lets you chain together a semicolon-delimited series of script expressions, you get only one shot at reference assignment. If your page is set up with multiple assignments of the same element object and event property, the last one to load is the winner. For example, the DHTML API library from Chapter 4 contains its own window.onload event handler assignment to ensure that the initDHTMLAPI( ) function is called automatically. But in Examples 4-4 and 4-5, an onload event handler in the <body> tag (the tag equivalent of assigning window object event handlers) invokes both the initDHTMLAPI( ) function and some other application-specific function. The tag assignment overrides the assignment from the external library. Alternatively, these pages could create one more startup function that invokes both initDHTMLAPI( ) and the initial action function, and that startup function reference could be assigned to window.onload at the bottom of the head section's scripts.

Tag attribute and object property assignment are the two event binding techniques that work best across all browsers. The remaining three techniques are limited to individual DOM implementations and are not easy to branch around.

## Event Handlers as <script> Tags (IE 4 and Later)

The third technique for binding event handlers to objects currently works only in Internet Explorer 4 and later (for all operating system platforms). The technique uses two proprietary attributes (for and event) in the <script> tag to specify that the script is to be run in response to an event for a particular object. The for attribute points to an id attribute value that is assigned to the element that generates the event handler; the event attribute names the event handler. Internet Explorer does not attempt to resolve the for attribute reference while the document loads, so it is safe to put the tag before the element in the source code.*

The following fragment shows what the entire <script> tag looks like for the function defined earlier that converts all of a form's element content to uppercase in response to a button's onclick event handler:

```
<script for="upperAll" event="onclick" language="JavaScript"
type="text/javascript">
var form = document.forms[0];
    for (var i = 0; i < form.elements.length; i++) {
        if (form.elements[i].type == "text") {
            form.elements[i].value = form.elements[i].value.toUpperCase( );
        }
    }
</script>
```

The HTML for the button does not include an event handler, but does require an id (or name) attribute.

```
<input type="button" id="upperAll" value="Convert All">
```

---

* Don't confuse the IE feature with a proposed W3C standard, called XML Events, which may offer <script> tag attributes to bind events to elements. One may have inspired the other, but XML Events assumes implementation of the W3C DOM event model.

Do not use this technique in pages that might be viewed by non-IE browsers. The extra attributes tell IE to defer script execution until invoked by the event type on a certain element. A non-IE browser treats the script statements as if they existed in plain <script> tags, and will execute while the page loads. Script errors are sure to arise in non-IE browsers.

Note that you might see a variation of this technique for defining scripts directly as event handlers when the scripting language is specified as VBScript. Instead of specifying the object name and event as tag attributes, VBScript lets you combine the two in a function name, separated by an underscore character, as in:

```
<script language="VBScript" type="text/vbscript">
Function upperAll_onclick
    script statements
End Function
</script>
```

The tag for the element requires only the id attribute to make the association.

## Attaching Events (IE 5 and Later for Windows)

Microsoft devised the attachEvent() and detachEvent() methods of element objects primarily to support a feature it calls *behaviors* (external XML documents that contain generic script definitions, not unlike the concept of style sheets). But in browsers that support these methods, you can use them to bind events to element objects.

The attachEvent() method requires two parameters:

```
elementReference.attachEvent("event", functionReference);
```

The *event* parameter is the "on" version of the event name, while the function reference is just like the kind you assign to an object event handler property. The combination of attachEvent() and detachEvent() allows scripts to enable and disable scripted functionality as desired.

Although Microsoft has submitted HTML behaviors as a proposed W3C standard, any future standardized implementation details are difficult to predict. Within the confines of supported IE versions, this syntax is perfectly acceptable.

## W3C Event Listeners (Netscape 6 and Later)

The W3C DOM's Events module introduces fresh terminology to event binding, but the concepts behind the new words are not new. In line with the object-oriented nature of the W3C DOM, two node object methods, addEventListener() and removeEventListener(), which add and remove, respectively, the power to "hear" an event of a particular type as it passes by the node during event propagation (described later in this chapter). Parameters for both methods are the same, so we'll focus on how to perform the event binding portion.

The syntax for the addEventListener( ) method is:

```
elementReference.addEventListener("eventType", functionReference, captureSwitch);
```

An *eventType* value is a string indicating the formal event type, which is the event name without the "on" prefix (i.e., just click instead of onclick). A function reference is the same kind that you use for object property event binding. The W3C DOM jargon calls this kind of function an *event listener function*, which means little more than the function should have a parameter variable to receive the event object that automatically gets passed to it. The third parameter is a Boolean value that determines whether the node should "listen" for the event in the capture portion of event propagation (described later in this chapter). The typical setting of this parameter is false.

To remain true to the W3C model, the specification permits browsers to accept traditional event binding mechanisms, including tag attributes. Such bindings are to behave as if the code invokes addEventListener( ) with the third parameter automatically set to false. This flexibility allows a browser such as Netscape 6 to implement the W3C DOM model, while allowing scripters to use event binding syntax that is compatible with other browsers, including older versions. But by using the newer syntax, you can explore several new event types that are linked directly to the W3C DOM's architecture. See Chapter 10 for more details on W3C DOM events and event object properties.

# Preventing Default Event Actions

It is not uncommon to script an event handler to execute statements immediately prior to an element carrying out its normal activity in response to a user action. For example, a form's text field validation typically operates in response to the onsubmit event of the form element. Without any kind of event handler, a form element obeys the submit-type input button, and sends the form's contents to the URI specified by the action attribute. But if you bind an onsubmit event handler to that form element, and if the validation routines spot an error (e.g., a required text box is empty), the script can alert the user and prevent the default submission action from taking place. Many other elements and their events can benefit from this script technique.

You have several ways prevent an element's default action, depending on the event binding style you use and the browsers you need to support. Some techniques work across all scriptable browsers.

## Setting the return Value

When your event handlers are in the form of element attributes, you can cancel the element's default action if the last statement of the event handler assignment statement evaluates to return false. This is different from simply having the handler function end with return false. The return statement must be in the value assigned to the event handler attribute.

The easiest way to implement this approach is to include a return statement in the event handler itself, while the function invoked by the handler returns true or false based on its calculations. For example, if a form requires validation prior to submission, you can have the onsubmit event handler invoke the validation routine. If the routine finds a problem somewhere, it returns false and the submission is canceled because the entire event handler expression evaluates to return false; otherwise, the function returns true and the submission proceeds as usual. Such a form element looks like the following:

```
<form method="POST" action="http://www.megaCo.com/cgi-bin/entry"
onsubmit="return validate(this);">
```

This technique also allows you to have a link navigate to a hardcoded URL for non-scriptable browsers, but execute a script when the user has a scriptable browser:

```
<a href="someotherURL.htm" onclick="doNavigation(); return false;">...</a>
```

Here, the return false statement is set as the final statement of the event handler; it does not have to trouble the called function for a return value because all scriptable browsers are to follow the scripted navigation path.

If you use object property event binding, the coding is not altogether straightforward. By and large, IE lets the return statement of the function govern the default execution, provided you return true or false. Netscape 6.2, however, doesn't obey return statements for this type of event binding due to a bug that is fixed in later versions.

## The event.returnValue Property (IE 5 and Later)

Starting with Version 5 (Windows and Mac), IE's event object has a Boolean property, returnValue, that controls whether the element's default action occurs. The default value of the property is true. But to prevent the default action, your function script sets its value to false. The following IE-only function could be invoked from the onkeypress event handler of a text box (onkeypress="numberPlease();" or txtBoxRef.onkeypress=numberPlease;). Its job is to let only numbers appear in the field by preventing the onkeypress event from performing its default action for other characters:

```
function numberPlease() {
    var charCode = event.keyCode;
    if (charCode < 48 || charCode > 57) {
        alert("Only whole numbers are allowed.");
        event.returnValue = false;
    }
}
```

Be careful not to confuse the event.returnValue property with the purpose of the JavaScript return statement. Use the former to control an event target's default behavior; use the latter when a function must return a value to a calling statement.

## W3C preventDefault( ) Method (Netscape 6 and Later)

Instead of using a property of its event object for this purpose, the W3C event model gives the event object the preventDefault( ) method. You can invoke this method in an event listener function to stand in the way of the event continuing to the element. The syntax for its use is not far different from the IE returnValue property. The following function is a W3C version of the numbers-only real-time input checker. Due to an egregious bug in early versions of Netscape 6, however, the preventDefault( ) method works reliably only on event listeners that are added by way of tag attributes. Therefore, for the following function to do its job effectively, it should be invoked from an input element tag's attribute (onkeypress="numberPlease(event);"):

```
function numberPlease(evt) {
    var charCode = evt.charCode;
    if (charCode < 48 || charCode > 57) {
        alert("Only whole numbers are allowed.");
        evt.preventDefault();
    }
}
```

## Cross-Browser Techniques

With the preventDefault( ) bug persisting through so many Netscape 6 editions, it is safest to stick with element tag attribute binding for preventing default actions. This means that the return statement becomes part of the value assigned to the attribute (e. g., onkeypress="return numberPlease(event)"). For good measure, the following function demonstrates branching techniques that can be used in the future for both tag attribute and object property event bindings. A little bit of additional event key code detection allows helpful noncharacter keys (arrows, **Tab**, and **Backspace**, for example) to perform their normal jobs (in Netscape 6 and later, the charCode property for noncharacter keys is 0). The function is a cross-browser, backward-compatible version of the text box filter function shown earlier. This version works even with Navigator 4:

```
function numberPlease(evt) {
    evt = (evt) ? evt : ((event) ? event : null);
    if (evt) {
        var charCode = (evt.charCode || evt.charCode == 0) ? evt.charCode :
                        ((evt.keyCode) ? evt.keyCode : evt.which);
        if (charCode > 13 && (charCode < 48 || charCode > 57)) {
            alert("Only whole numbers are allowed.");
            if (evt.returnValue) {
                evt.returnValue = false;
            } else if (evt.preventDefault) {
                evt.preventDefault();
            } else {
                return false;
            }
        }
    }
}
```

Of course, for use with tag attribute binding, the innermost segment could be compressed to a single `return false` statement after the alert.

# Event Propagation

In some DHTML applications, it is not efficient to have target elements process events. For example, if you have a page that allows users to select and drag elements around the page, it is quite possible that one set of centralized functions can handle that operation for all elements. Rather than define event handlers for all of those elements, it is better to have the mouse-related events go directly to an object or element that has scope over all the draggable elements. In other words, one event handler can do the job of a dozen. For this kind of treatment to work, events must be able to propagate through the hierarchy of objects or nodes in the document. IE 5 and later and the W3C (Netscape 6) event models share some, but not all, event propagation schemes. For the most typical applications, you can easily equalize the small differences in implementation details and syntax you use to override the natural flow.

W3C DOM event propagation in Netscape 6 and later can be summarized thus: in response to a user or system action, an event starts at the outermost container and follows the most direct route ("trickles down") through the node container hierarchy to the intended target; after it reaches its target, the event reverses course and "bubbles upward" through the same node hierarchy back to the top, from which it disappears. The trickle-down portion of the journey is called the *capture* phase, while the return trip is called the *bubbling* phase. The IE propagation model consists only of the bubbling phase. While IE 5 and later has an event feature related to capture (described later in this chapter), its operation is not along the lines of the W3C capture phase of propagation.

Consider the following skeletal structure of an HTML document:

```
<html>
<body>
    <form>
        <div id="div1">
            <input id="txt1" type="text">
        </div>
        <div id="div2">
            <input id="txt2" type="text">
        </div>
    </form>
</body>
</html>
```

As the user types into the txt2 text input field, an onkeypress event begins its journey at an outermost container in Netscape 6, works its way through containers on its way to the text box (where IE's event starts), and then goes back to the outermost container. The precise top-level container varies with browser version. For Netscape 6, the window object is the master container for event propagation purposes; IE holds the line at the document node. Figure 6-1 depicts the onkeypress event propagation sequence through the objects of this document for three different browser versions.

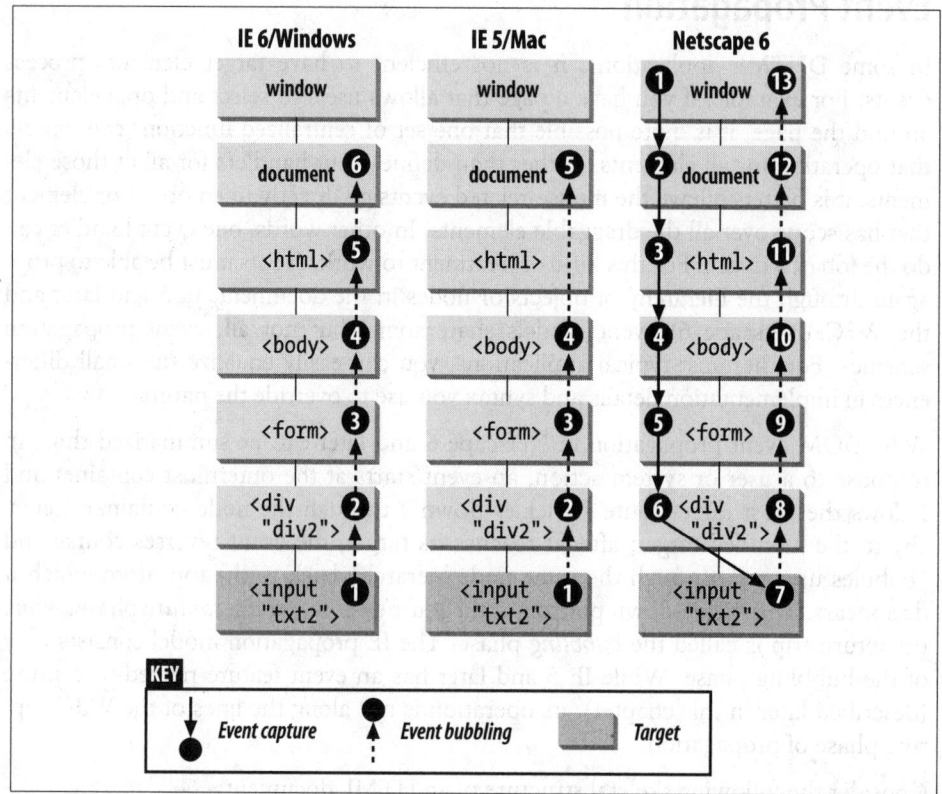

*Figure 6-1. Sample event propagation sequences*

You can assign an onkeypress event handler for any and all of the nodes in the hierarchy to process the event. By default, a Netscape 6 event handler "listens" for events only during the bubbling phase, which means that Netscape 6 behaves like IE. Event bubbling isn't as anarchic as it sounds. In fact, it's quite flexible if you're careful to avoid conflicts that may occur at higher containment levels.

## Event Bubbling

Event bubbling is the default propagation path for most events starting in IE 4 and Netscape 6. Some system-fired events work only in their target elements. For example, if you have an onload event listener assigned to a few img elements and the body element, you probably don't want an img element's load event to bubble up to the body element, firing each time an image's src property changes.

Event bubbling is often vital in scripting events for elements that display body text. The node-centric W3C DOM allows ordinary text nodes to be event listeners. Therefore, if you assign a mouse-related event to a text container, the target node of the event will be the text node within that container. By default the event bubbles outward to the container where the event can be easily processed, but the event object's properties point to the text node, not the container. This is different from the IE event model, in which only elements are targets of events. To equalize this possibility in processing an event, your scripts must take the node into account. Here is one cross-browser way to make sure that your function locates a reference to the element surrounding the text (or, as a last resort, the document node):

```
function myFunction(evt) {
    evt = (evt) ? evt : ((event) ? event : null);
    if (evt) {
        var elem = (evt.target) ? evt.target :
                ((evt.srcElement) ? evt.srcElement : null);
        if (elem) {
            elem = (elem.nodeType == 1 || elem.nodeType == 9) ? elem :
                elem.parentNode;
            // ok, now we're ready to work with the element
        }
    }
}
```

Most events triggered by user action with the mouse and keyboard bubble upward through the hierarchy from the target element. Conflicts can arise, however. For example: you assign an onmousedown event handler for several images so they can swap .jpg files while the mouse is being held down. But you also define an onmousedown event handler for the body element to act as a single handler to assist in dragging several positioned div elements around the page. To prevent the img element mousedown events from bubbling up through the hierarchy, you can explicitly instruct an event not to bubble beyond a specific element.

The cross-browser way of canceling event bubbling (starting in IE 4 and Netscape 6) involves the Boolean cancelBubble property of the event object, adjusted within the event handler function. It's the same property name and behavior for both IE and Netscape 6 event objects (this property is not a member of the W3C DOM event object, but Netscape 6 implements it as a compatibility convenience). The default value for this property is false, meaning that event bubbling takes place. But if you set this property to true, the event does not bubble past the current event handler.

Set the cancelBubble property to false in a script statement executing in the current event's function. Thus, if you assign an event handler as an element property, the bubble cancelation can take place in the function invoked by the event handler:

```
function myFunction(evt) {
    evt = (evt) ? evt : ((event) ? event : null);
    if (evt) {
        // include next statement anywhere in this block
```

```
        evt.cancelBubble = true;
    }
}
```

Only one event bubbles at any given instant, so this statement knows to cancel the right one. It also means that you can let an event bubble part of the way through the element hierarchy, but stop it at any desired element, so as not to interfere with other elements higher up the chain.

## W3C Event Capture

Although event bubbling is the default mechanism in modern browsers, a propagating event in Netscape 6 or later starts its life by trickling down to the target. If you place an event listener for the event's type at a higher level, however, it will ignore the event as it trickles down unless event capture for that element and that event type is turned on.

To engage event capture, use the same addEventListener( ) method that the W3C event model prefers for event binding. The third parameter is a Boolean value that controls event capture. When you set the parameter to true, the element invokes the listener function during capture phase; after that function completes its task, the event continues its journey toward to the target element. Therefore, it is perfectly "legal" to add two separate event listeners to an element for the same event type. In capture phase, one listener function runs; in bubbling phase, another listener function runs.

Using the same three parameters, you can eliminate the event listener for the desired propagation phase with the removeEventListener( ) method. Thus, you could temporarily engage capture-phase processing and remove it without disturbing bubbling-phase event processing for the same element and event type.

At any point along W3C event propagation, you can prevent the event from going any further by invoking the event object's stopPropagation( ) method in a statement inside the listener function. Netscape 6 or later also wires the convenience cancelBubble property to work during capture phase as well.

The W3C root event object (and therefore event objects of all types) implements a handful of other properties that may be helpful while processing events within the two-way propagation model. Table 6-4 lists these properties, for which IE (through Version 6 on Windows) provides no analogues. A shared event listener function might use these (and other properties) to build code branches that execute when the desired combination of conditions exist (e.g., when the target's class name is "foo" and the event is being processed from a container of several elements of the same class).

*Table 6-4. W3C event object propagation properties*

| Property | Description |
| --- | --- |
| bubbles | Boolean true if event can bubble |
| currentTarget | Reference to the node whose event listener invoked the current listener function |
| eventPhase | Integer indicating in which phase the event listener is processing (1 is capture; 2 is at target; 3 is bubbling) |

## IE/Windows Event Capture

Microsoft's view of event capture is quite different from the W3C view. IE 5 and later event capture operates only with mouse events. In fact, when you invoke an element object's setCapture( ) method, you instruct the browser to direct *all* mouse events on the page to that element rather than to their targets. Events bubble up from the capturing element, unless canceled.

This event mechanism is intended primarily for temporary activation within a page. For example, the body element can contain an oncontextmenu event handler that waits for a Windows user to click the right (nondominant) mouse button. You can take this opportunity not only to block the display of the browser's own context menu (by setting event.returnValue to false), but also to display your own menu composed of DHTML positioned elements. While the custom menu is visible, you want all mouse events to head for the menu so that nothing else on the page is accessible via the mouse until either a choice is made from the menu or the right mouse button is clicked again. Either action hides the custom context menu and invokes releaseCapture( ) to allow mouse events to reach their normal targets again.

It's not uncommon for IE/Windows to implement proprietary DOM features that allow web applications to mimic operating-system–specific behaviors. In an intranet development environment targeting IE/Windows only, this tactic makes perfect sense. But such tight integration reduces the likelihood that these features will become part of an operating-system–agnostic W3C recommendation. It also makes it more difficult for Microsoft to implement some W3C recommendations that conflict with existing mechanisms.

# Understanding Keyboard Event Data

If you examine the Events module of the DOM Level 2 recommendation, you may notice that keyboard events are nowhere to be found. As the W3C working group discovered, keyboard events in a Unicode world are tricky things to mold into an acceptable standard. But keyboard events in one form or another have been implemented in browsers since Netscape 4 and IE 4. Even though the Version 6 browsers carry forward the concepts from earlier days, the drafts of future W3C DOM Level 3 Events module indicate that keyboard event processing may take on new syntax in the future. In the meantime, we have "old-fashioned" keyboard events, with processing that is not always straightforward due to differences in event object details across browser versions.

The most important data related to a keyboard event is the identity of either the physical key being activated or the character generated by that key. These are not the same things. Every key has a numeric code associated with it. For example, a U.S. English keyboard assigns the number 65 to the key labeled **A**. That same key, however, can produce at least two different characters (A and a) on every U.S. computer, and even more characters on operating systems like the Macintosh (where the **Option** and **Option-Shift** modifier keys let that **A** key generate even more characters).

It so happens that the code "65" is also the ASCII and Unicode value of the upper-case A letter (this isn't a coincidence as much as it reflects the English-centric basis of early computing). The character codes for the A and a characters are 65 and 97, respectively. For some scripting tasks, the character code is important—such as whether the character is a numeral, regardless of whether the user pressed a top row keyboard key or a numeric keypad key; for other tasks, the key pressed is important—such as whether the user pressed the **PageDown** key (which doesn't have a character associated with it).

Complicating the issue is that the IE event object has only one property value that conveys a code for a keyboard event (event.keyCode). IE 5/Mac and Netscape 6 have a second property (charCode) that conveys additional event information. To expose both the key and character codes, even with only one property, the browsers let the different keyboard events deliver different information. To read the key code, use only the onkeydown or onkeyup events; use the onkeypress event to read the character code.

You must still reconcile the event object property differences among the browsers to work with keyboard events. The key code for the onkeydown and onkeyup events is available from the keyChar property of the IE and Netscape 6 event objects. For the onkeypress event's character code, use the keyCode property for IE and charCode property for Netscape 6. IE 5/Mac provides the same character code data for both properties of an onkeypress event.

To see how these different events and properties expose codes to scripts, Example 6-1 dynamically displays as many keyboard-related event object properties as the browser supports (see Figure 6-2). In the course of processing each event type, the event listener functions display the keyCode properties for all browsers. If a browser also supports the charCode property, its values appear in the table.

You can witness interesting characteristics of the onkeydown and onkeyup events when you use modifier keys. For example, if you type an uppercase A by pressing and holding the **Shift** key before typing the **A** key, you see that the onkeydown event fires, and that the keycode for the **Shift** key (16) appears in the keyCode property. But when you then press the **A** key, a new event object comes on the scene, with its own keyChar property value.

Note that this is not how your scripts detect whether a modifier key is pressed during a keyboard or other event. The event object in both models has Boolean properties—altKey, ctrlKey, and shiftKey—that your character key event handler can inspect. If the keyChar property of an onkeydown event indicates the C key, and if the event object's ctrlKey value is true, the user has typed **Ctrl-C**.

*Example 6-1. Keyboard events and codes*

```html
<html>
<head>
<title>Keyboard Events and Codes</title>
<style type="text/css">
body {font-family:Arial, sans-serif}
h1 {text-align:right}
td {text-align:center}
</style>
<script language="JavaScript" type="text/javascript">
// array of table cell ids
var tCells = ["downKey", "pressKey", "upKey", "downChar", "pressChar",
"upChar", "keyTarget", "character"];

// clear table cells for each key down event
function clearCells() {
    for (var i = 0; i < tCells.length; i++) {
        document.getElementById(tCells[i]).innerHTML = "&mdash;";
    }
}

// display target node's node name
function showTarget(evt) {
    var node = (evt.target) ? evt.target : ((evt.srcElement) ?
              evt.srcElement : null);
    if (node) {
        document.getElementById("keyTarget").innerHTML = node.nodeName;
    }
}

// decipher key down codes
function showDown(evt) {
    clearCells();
    evt = (evt) ? evt : ((event) ? event : null);
    if (evt) {
        document.getElementById("downKey").innerHTML = evt.keyCode;
        if (evt.charCode) {
            document.getElementById("downChar").innerHTML = evt.charCode;
        }
        showTarget(evt);
    }
}

// decipher key press codes
function showPress(evt) {
    evt = (evt) ? evt : ((event) ? event : null);
    if (evt) {
        document.getElementById("pressKey").innerHTML = evt.keyCode;
        if (evt.charCode) {
            document.getElementById("pressChar").innerHTML = evt.charCode;
        }
        showTarget(evt);
        var charCode = (evt.charCode) ? evt.charCode : evt.keyCode;
```

*Example 6-1. Keyboard events and codes (continued)*

```
            // use String method to convert back to character
            document.getElementById("character").innerHTML =
                String.fromCharCode(charCode);
        }
    }


    // decipher key up codes
    function showUp(evt) {
        evt = (evt) ? evt : ((event) ? event : null);
        if (evt) {
            document.getElementById("upKey").innerHTML = evt.keyCode;
            if (evt.charCode) {
                document.getElementById("upChar").innerHTML = evt.charCode;
            }
            showTarget(evt);
        }
    }


    // set page-wide event listeners
    document.onkeydown = showDown;
    document.onkeypress = showPress;
    document.onkeyup = showUp;
    </script>
    </head>
    <body>
    <h1>Key and Character Codes vs. Event Types</h1>
    <hr>
    <p>Enter some text with uppercase and lowercase letters:<br>
    <form>
    <input type="text" id="entry" size="60"
            onkeydown="showDown(event)"
            onkeypress="showPress(event)"
            onkeyup="showUp(event)">
    </textarea></p>
    </form>
    <table border="2" cellpadding="5" cellspacing="5">
    <caption>Keyboard Event Properties</caption>
    <tr><th>Data</th><th>keydown</th><th>keypress</th><th>keyup</th></tr>
    <tr><td>keyCode</td>
        <td id="downKey">&mdash;</td>
        <td id="pressKey">&mdash;</td>
        <td id="upKey">&mdash;</td>
    </tr>
    <tr><td>charCode</td>
        <td id="downChar">&mdash;</td>
        <td id="pressChar">&mdash;</td>
        <td id="upChar">&mdash;</td>
    </tr>
    <tr><td>Target</td>
        <td id="keyTarget" colspan="3">&mdash;</td>
    </tr>
    <tr><td>Character</td>
```

*Example 6-1. Keyboard events and codes (continued)*

```
    <td id="character" colspan="3">&mdash;</td>
</tr>
</table>
</body>
</html>
```

Figure 6-2 shows some sample output for Example 6-1.

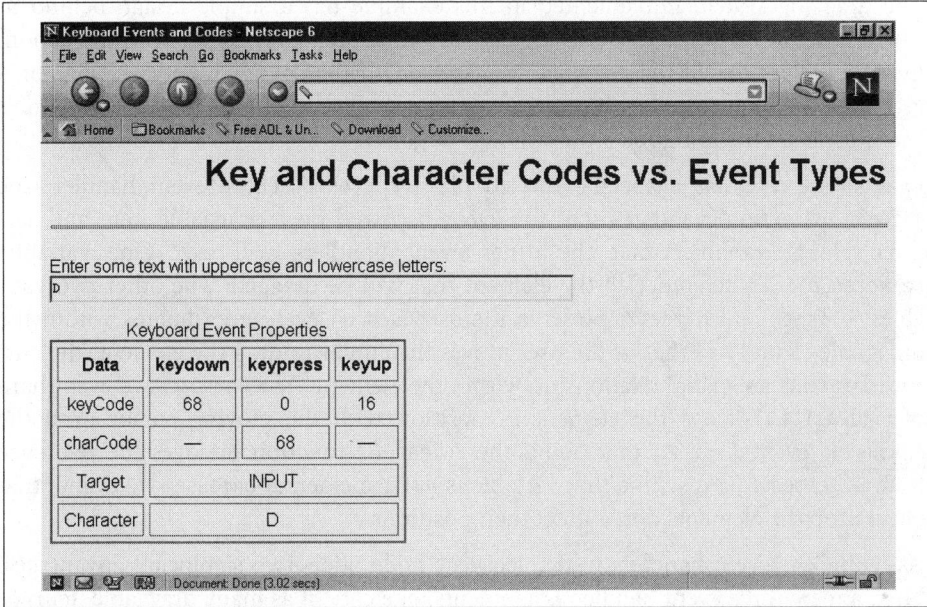

*Figure 6-2. Viewing keyboard event data*

Regardless of the operating system you use, you should try Example 6-1 on at least two different browsers. This way you can see how the three events stuff values into event object properties in different event models.

# Dragging Elements

The final example in this chapter, Example 6-2, demonstrates how event bubbling lets document-level event handlers control dragging positioned elements on the page. To provide legacy support for readers of the first edition of this book, the code includes branches that accommodate the unique requirements of Netscape Navigator 4, whose layer objects may be positioned dynamically. While Navigator 4 does not employ event bubbling, it does allow for the equivalent of the W3C's event capture mechanism, albeit switched on with very different syntax. But all event processing takes place at the same node level for all browsers. In truth, if the dragging operation were being implemented in just one object model, the scripts and approach to the dragging control would be tailored to take advantage of the event and object features of that model. But the goal here is a completely cross-browser implementation that supports any browser capable of positioned elements. To that end, the code relies on a handful of routines from the DHTML API described in Chapter 4. Although Example 6-2 links in the entire library, you should also consider creating a separate *.js* library with a subset of the entire API needed to support the dragging operations, and thus minimize the amount of code that travels to the client.

The dragging system implemented in this example has a simple design behind it. Three mouse events—onmousedown, onmousemove, and onmouseup—control the action. Event handlers for all three events are assigned to the document node. Navigator 4 grabs the events before they reach their targets, while the IE and W3C event models wait for the events to bubble up from their targets.

Each event type has a specific role to play. The onmousedown event handler (the engage( ) function) validates that the event occurred on a draggable item and sets three global variables that the other event handlers will use. One variable, selectedObj, is a reference to the element that will be dragged. The other two variables, offsetX and offsetY, preserve the onmousedown event coordinates within the draggable element so that as the user moves the cursor to drag the element, the cursor maintains its spatial relationship within the element. The onmousemove event handler (dragIt( )) keeps the element in position with the moving cursor until the onmouseup event fires. At that point, the release( ) function removes the reference from selectedObj. Any time that variable is null, incidental onmousemove events that occur atop the elements don't affect their positions.

Assigning the event handlers to the document node offers two significant advantages. First, a mere three event handler assignments take care of as many draggable items as you want to place on the page. Second, while the user drags the element, element rendering may not refresh as quickly as the cursor moves, preventing the onmousemove or onmouseup events from firing on the draggable elements. But when the engage( ) function "switches on" dragging for a particular element, all onmousemove and onmouseup events for other elements bubble up to the document level (unless they are explicitly canceled), and the dragIt( ) and release( ) functions do their jobs because the dragging mode for the selected object is still switched on. As long as the user keeps the mouse button down, the draggable element will catch up to the cursor position.

All the dragging event handlers are assigned as properties in an init( ) function invoked by the onload event handler. The only platform-specific process taking place here involves setting the document.captureEvents( ) method to grab all mouse down and mouse move events that come in from Navigator 4.

The draggable elements in this example are two absolute-positioned div elements that contain img elements. The user can click on either image and drag that image (and its div) around the page. Wrapping the image with a div element helps with a couple of fine points about this example. For one, absolute-positioned div and span elements are better behaved in Navigator 4 than positioning other kinds of elements (layer elements are the best behaved, but they are unique to Navigator 4). But more important is demonstrating one way to assure that event targets inside a positioned element (the img elements are the targets here) translate into a reference to the container, because the container is the element that gets positioned (while its contents go along for the ride).

Notice in Example 6-2 how the IDs of the image event targets and their divs are related (imgA and imgAWrap). The filtering in the setSelectedElem( ) function uses the fact that the img element targets have name and src properties assigned to them. If that's the case for a particular onmousedown event, then the ID for the div wrapper get assembled from the target's name and the "Wrap" add-on. This approach certainly works, but its looseness is necessitated by the support required for Navigator 4's immature DOM. If this were being written for IE 5 (or later) and Netscape 6 (or later), a much more generalizable solution is possible and preferable. For example, you could assign an identifier to the class attribute of the img elements (e.g., draggable), and let setSelectedElem( ) simply look for the event target's className property that equals that identifier. If there's a match, you could immediately set the global selectedObj variable to the event target's parentNode property:

```
selectedObj = (target.className == "draggable") ? target.parentNode : null;
```

No other element referencing or naming games would be necessary.

Notice, too, that the setSelectedElem( ) function sets the stacking order of the element to an arbitrarily high number. You want a selected element to be atop all its peers as the user drags it around the screen.

Coordinate systems play a significant role in scripting the drag process. Ideally, the element should track from the point where the user clicks inside the element. This means that the location (top left corner) of the element must be offset (up and to the left) from the cursor position by the number of pixels of the click offset within that element. This information isn't as easy to come by as you might think. Not all event models report the offsets within a positioned container; those that do need further adjustments for document scrolling or inherent bugs. The tripartite branch in the engage( ) function takes care of the measurements for three event model implementations:

- Navigator 4 and Netscape 6 (the latter supports the pageX and pageY properties of the event object, even though they are not part of the W3C event model)

- IE, including the corrections for scrolling and occasional erroneous values in IE/Mac

- A pure W3C event model, which Opera follows in this case, and Netscape 6 or later would also follow if the first branch were absent

Offset values are stored as global variables in Example 6-2, so that the dragging action can use them for proper placement of the element under the cursor.

Making the element track the cursor in the dragIt( ) function also requires some calculation. Using the shiftTo( ) function from the DHTML API, the script sets the location of the element within the page (or client) space after each mouse movement.

Despite the amount of object detection branching taking place in Example 6-2, if you trimmed the scripts to work only in IE 5 (or later) and Netscape 6 (or later), and employed the className and parentNode tips described earlier, you could easily make the dragging functionality into a reusable library, nearly independent of the specific content on the page. The only care you'd have to exercise is assigning your chosen class identifier to the draggable image or area of the positioned element, such as a pseudo-titlebar of a "floating" palette. This example also works as-is only with positioned elements that use the body or document element (depending on your standards-compatibility mode) as the positioning context. Modifications would be needed to nest the positioned elements in other contexts.

*Example 6-2. Dragging elements around the window*

```
<html>
<head>
<title>It's a Drag</title>
<style type="text/css">
  body {font-family:Ariel, sans-serif; text-align:right}
  #imgAWrap {position:absolute; left:50px; top:100px; width:120px; height:90px;
             border:solid black 1px; z-index:0}
  #imgBWrap {position:absolute; left:110px; top:145px; width:120px; height:90px;
             border:solid black 1px; z-index:0}
</style>
<script language="JavaScript" type="text/javascript" src="DHTML2api.js"></script>
<script language="JavaScript" type="text/javascript">
// Global holds reference to selected element
var selectedObj;
// Globals hold location of click relative to element
var offsetX, offsetY;

// Set global reference to element being engaged and dragged
function setSelectedElem(evt) {
    var target = (evt.target) ? evt.target : evt.srcElement;
    var divID = (target.name && target.src) ? target.name + "Wrap" : "";
    if (divID) {
        if (document.layers) {
            selectedObj = document.layers[divID];
        } else if (document.all) {
            selectedObj = document.all(divID);
        } else if (document.getElementById) {
            selectedObj = document.getElementById(divID);
        }
        setZIndex(selectedObj, 100);
        return;
    }
    selectedObj = null;
    return;
}
```

*Example 6-2. Dragging elements around the window (continued)*

```
// Drag an element
function dragIt(evt) {
    evt = (evt) ? evt : event;
    if (selectedObj) {
        if (evt.pageX) {
            shiftTo(selectedObj, (evt.pageX - offsetX), (evt.pageY - offsetY));
        } else if (evt.clientX || evt.clientY) {
            shiftTo(selectedObj, (evt.clientX - offsetX), (evt.clientY - offsetY));
        }
        evt.cancelBubble = true;
        return false;
    }
}
// Turn selected element on
function engage(evt) {
    evt = (evt) ? evt : event;
    setSelectedElem(evt);
    if (selectedObj) {
        if (evt.pageX) {
            offsetX = evt.pageX - ((selectedObj.offsetLeft) ?
                        selectedObj.offsetLeft : selectedObj.left);
            offsetY = evt.pageY - ((selectedObj.offsetTop) ?
                        selectedObj.offsetTop : selectedObj.top);
        } else if (evt.offsetX || evt.offsetY) {
            offsetX = evt.offsetX - ((evt.offsetX < -2) ?
                        0 : document.body.scrollLeft);
            offsetY = evt.offsetY - ((evt.offsetY < -2) ?
                        0 : document.body.scrollTop);
        } else if (evt.clientX) {
            offsetX = evt.clientX - ((selectedObj.offsetLeft) ?
                        selectedObj.offsetLeft : 0);
            offsetY = evt.clientY - ((selectedObj.offsetTop) ?
                        selectedObj.offsetTop : 0);
        }
        return false;
    }
}
// Turn selected element off
function release(evt) {
    if (selectedObj) {
        setZIndex(selectedObj, 0);
        selectedObj = null;
    }
}

// Set event capture for Navigator 4
function setNSEventCapture() {
    document.captureEvents(Event.MOUSEDOWN | Event.MOUSEMOVE | Event.MOUSEUP);
}
```

*Example 6-2. Dragging elements around the window (continued)*

```
// Assign event handlers used by both Navigator and IE
function init() {
    if (document.layers) {
        setNSEventCapture();
    }
    document.onmousedown = engage;
    document.onmousemove = dragIt;
    document.onmouseup = release;
}
</script>
</head>
<body onload="initDHTMLAPI(); init();">
<h1>Element Dragging</h1>
<hr>
<div id="imgAWrap" class="draggable"><img id="imgA" name="imgA"
src="myImage1.jpg" width="120" height="90" border="0"></div>
<div id="imgBWrap" class="draggable"><img id="imgB" name="imgB"
src="myImage33.jpg" width="120" height="90" border="0"></div>
</body>
</html>
```

# Event Futures

That the W3C DOM Working Group has had its greatest and longest-lasting struggles with the Events module is not all that surprising. Many kinds of events are tied directly to an operating-system implementation, which makes it difficult to agree on a common denominator that acknowledges the way users interact with data within graphical user interfaces, while remaining implementation-independent. It may be some time before the many practical events available in IE for Windows are applicable and implementable across a range of operating systems and devices. In the meantime, the list of intrinsic events remains rather basic.

That Microsoft has, as of IE 6 for Windows, ignored the W3C DOM event model leaves one to wonder. Is it waiting for the Level 3 keyboard event model to be finalized before implementing any of the W3C model? Or will IE continue with its own exclusive model? If you are trying to get your code in shape for a long, maintenance-free future, IE's delay in supporting the W3C event model works in your favor. The longer the delay, the larger the installed base of code that relies on the IE model, which means that the model will be supported longer in the future. Therefore, the two-model equalization techniques described in this chapter should serve your code well for quite awhile.

# CHAPTER 7

# Standardization Trends

As more surfers and new browsers wend their way around the World Wide Web, the installed base of browsers becomes more and more fragmented—even when one browser brand appears to dominate the scene. Fragmentation occurs because users choose not to upgrade to the latest browser version and organizations prohibit individuals from upgrading beyond a corporate standard that may be one or two generations old. This makes the job of adopting new W3C standards difficult, for both web browser makers and page authors.

Regardless of the latest browser bells and whistles or the "preferred" way to apply certain content constructs, many thousands of web pages on the Net use techniques long gone from the standards documents. Web browser makers bear the burden of this "ancient" baggage, as their browsers (with rare exception) continue to be backward compatible with earlier technologies. Unfortunately, this continued support can lead casual page authors to believe that the old ways are just fine, so they have little incentive to use the latest techniques. Conversely, a tuned-in content author who blindly follows standards—essentially treating the standards as platforms—may be even more foolhardy, because browser makers haven't caught up with the standards or have implemented them oddly in the early development stages.

Demands from managers or clients that a web presentation be 100% standards-compliant and validated may derive from good intentions, but the browser world—particularly for public web sites—doesn't necessarily live under the same blue sky. DHTML programmers must frequently defend workarounds and compromises necessitated by less-than-perfect standards support even in the latest and most popular browsers.

Like it or not, adding Dynamic HTML to your content means that you should look to the browsers as they exist in the real world, warts and all, as your development platforms. DHTML authors have begged for industry standards, especially for the DOM, for years. And now that these standards are filling out and solidifying, we're only somewhat better off than before, primarily because the standards are not yet thoroughly and uniformly implemented in a critical mass of installed browsers. And, as indicated by the questions I raised at the end of Chapter 6, it's impossible to predict if or when that day will come.

As content creators, we must strike a balance between coding for "what is" and planning for "what we think will be." If you believe that the future is largely standards-based (an underlying theme of the previous chapters) and XML-oriented, it's not too soon to begin aligning your content, code, and even authoring process with W3C and ECMA standardization trends. The purpose of this chapter is to acquaint you with the not-too-distant look of the W3C standards on which your content is based. If nothing else, this exploration may help you understand how and why future browser versions implement the standards as they do. The fundamental threads of this discussion focus on modularization and could be called implementation "wiggle room."

# W3C Modularization

The longer you have been involved with development platforms, the more likely it is that you've seen this scenario before: a platform becomes very popular, but for any number of valid reasons, it doesn't contain all the functionality that developer groups desire. Rather than risk alienating devoted fans by holding back progress or overloading the platform with tons of features of limited scope, the platform evolves into an extensible one that provides a sound foundation upon which developers can build their own special-purpose add-ons, yet still claim conformance with the foundation technology. Turning what had been a static system into an extensible one takes considerable effort, so that all sects are satisfied with both the foundation and the extensibility mechanism.

Extensibility (the "X" in so many of the web standards' names) is a primary driving force behind the modularization of popular W3C standards: HTML/XHTML, CSS, and DOM. But other factors are also behind this movement. While many standards expanded to meet advances in day-to-day technologies—the prevalence of graphical user interfaces (GUIs) is a good example—they grew to enormous proportions. At the same time, however, new web content delivery vehicles, such as new generation cellular telephones, shirt-pocket-sized computers, and audio-only content readers, couldn't possibly take advantage of all the big-screen GUI standards. To include support for DHTML scripting in a small-screen cell phone browser may very likely be a waste of limited ROM and RAM resources. The maker of an audio-only browser might want omit support for color style setting or extend the color style standards so that the colors could include additional meaning that is translated into spoken text or background sound when loaded into its client.

On the standards development side, modularization has the potential to make it easier to improve segments of a larger standard, without requiring a major upgrade of the entire standard. Even more likely, if an entirely new technology comes on the scene, a standard module based on that technology can be developed independently of the larger standard, and then embraced as a new module of an existing standard when the module is adopted as a formal recommendation.

The initial modularization of the XHTML, CSS, and DOM recommendations represent major transitions for these standards. The impact of this direction on your DHTML authoring will be minimal, at first, because the major browsers you support will implement everything and the kitchen sink to maintain compatibility with tons of existing content on the Web. But when you learn about what constitutes standards conformance in a modular world, you may reconsider some of your design assumptions going forward.

# XHTML Modularization (XHTML Basic and 1.1)

Modularization of XHTML came on the heels of the XHTML 1.0 specification. With the HTML details wrapped inside the XML (extensible) mechanism, it wasn't a very big conceptual leap to break up the large set of elements into logical groups of modules (although it took some time to hammer out the details). The XHTML modularization activity occurred somewhat independently of how the modules would potentially be packaged in future recommendations.

One set of modules were bundled together under the recommendation called XHTML Basic. In many ways, XHTML Basic is a proof of concept for the modularization activity. One of the goals of XHTML Basic was to assemble a group of modules whose elements and attributes could provide contexts for simple XHTML content—the kind of content that might be viewed in limited-display devices, such as Internet-enabled home appliances. Missing from this set, for example, is the style element, as well as all event attributes of other elements.

A more substantial group of modules found their way into the XHTML 1.1 recommendation. This recommendation represents a break from elements and practices deprecated in HTML 4 and XHTML 1.0. It does, however, provide for flexible style sheets and scripts that open up the content to dynamic content.

To give you a quick overview of the modularization of XHTML from both the global perspective and from the views of the XHTML Basic and XHTML 1.1 implementations, Table 7-1 lists the complete set of modules and indications of which modules are in each of the XHTML implementations.

*Table 7-1. XHTML modularization*

| XHTML module | Items | XHTML Basic | XHTML 1.1 |
| --- | --- | --- | --- |
| Structure[a] | body, head, html, title | • | • |
| Text[a] | abbr, acronym, address, blockquote, br, cite, code, dfn, div, em, h1, h2, h3, h4, h5, h6, kbd, p, pre, q, samp, span, strong, var | • | • |
| Hypertext[a] | a | • | • |
| List[a] | dl, dt, dd, ol, ul, li | • | • |

*Table 7-1. XHTML modularization (continued)*

| XHTML module | Items | XHTML Basic | XHTML 1.1 |
|---|---|:---:|:---:|
| Presentation | b, big, hr, i, small, sub, sup, tt | | • |
| Edit | del, ins | | • |
| Bidirectional Text | bdo | | • |
| Basic Forms | form, input, label, select, option, textarea | • | |
| Forms | button, fieldset, form, input, label, legend, select, optgroup, option, textarea | | • |
| Basic Tables | caption, table, td, th, tr | • | |
| Tables | caption, col, colgroup, table, tbody, td, tfoot, th, thead, tr | | • |
| Image | img | • | • |
| Client-side Image Map | area, map | | • |
| Server-side Image Map | ismap attribute in img element | | • |
| Intrinsic Events | Event handler attributes | | • |
| Scripting | noscript, script | | • |
| Stylesheet | style | | • |
| Style Attribute | style attribute | | • |
| Base | base | • | • |
| Metainformation | meta | • | • |
| Link | link | | • |
| Applet | applet, param | | |
| Object | object, param | • | • |
| Ruby Annotation[b] | ruby, rbc, rtc, rb, rt, rp | | • |
| Frames | frameset, frame, noframes | | |
| Target | target attribute in a, area, base, link, form elements | | |
| Iframe | iframe | | |
| Name | name attribute in a, applet, form, frame, iframe, img, map elements | | |
| Legacy | basefont, center, dir, font, isindex, menu, s, strike, u | | |

[a] This module is required for all XHTML-based DTDs.
[b] This module is from a separate Ruby Annotation recommendation. These elements are discussed in Chapter 8.

The XHTML 1.1 set of modules continues in the tradition of the XHTML 1.0 Strict DTD in that it excludes any elements or attributes that are even remotely tied to presentation or display characteristics. Thus, references to frames and targets that could lead to other windows do not have a place in XHTML 1.1 content markup. But, of course, the mainstream browsers have no problem with such constructs if you wish to deliver them in your pages. Moreover, scripts will continue to work their magic on DOM element object properties whose corresponding attributes may be missing from the DTDs. For example, an XHTML 1.1 source document could pass validation without an iframe element explicitly mentioned in the content. But a script could dynamically create and insert such an element into the document once it has reached the client.

---

## Validating Scripts in XHTML

Core JavaScript language syntax contains some symbols (especially the & and < characters) that are common to programming languages, but are anathema to XML document validation when they appear as content inside an element (the script element in this case). The XHTML specification recommends enclosing scripts in a *CDATA section*, which has very specific syntax you must follow:

```
<script type="text/javascript">
<![CDATA[
// your JavaScript statements go in here
]]>
</script>
```

The problem in real life is that few browsers, including IE 6 and Netscape 6, know about this XML element, so it triggers a script error in most cases. Instead, you can continue to use the HTML comment hack that scripters have used for ages to prevent brain-dead browsers from rendering the content of <script> tags:

```
<script type="text/javascript">
<!--
// your JavaScript statements go in here
//-->
</script>
```

HTML comment tags inside elements pass even XHTML Strict validation. To explore HTML and XHTML validation, you can start with the W3C Validation Service at *http://validator.w3.org/*.

---

# CSS Modularization (CSS3)

In the draft stages of CSS modularization, the effort appears to focus on not only a division of CSS attributes into logical groups, but also on a division of labor. With modularization, pieces of the standard, such as specifications for selectors, value types, and content models (box and line models, for example), can be developed individually. Implementation reasons still apply to the impetus behind the move toward modularization. A browser intended for visual display of content, for instance, shouldn't be expected to include style sheet attributes for aural styles.

Table 7-2 presents a preliminary list of modules that may comprise CSS3. Several categories in this list are new to CSS, rather than simply reorganized CSS2 features. Even if not every module is complete when other CSS3 modules are firmed up, others can be added as they are ready.

*Table 7-2. Preliminary CSS3 modules*

| Module | Description |
|--------|-------------|
| Selectors | Selector types and specificity |
| Values and units | Value types (e.g., lengths, colors) and their representation |
| Value assignment, cascade, and inheritance | How styles impact elements (e.g., specified versus computed values), cascading rules, attribute inheritance chains |
| Box model/vertical | Block layout: borders, margins, padding, overflow, clipping, and visibility |
| Positioning | Positioning, floating layout |
| Color/gamma/color profiles | Foreground color, gamma correction |
| Colors and Backgrounds | Background images and colors |
| Line box model | Inline element rendering |
| Text/bidi/vertical alignment | Text decoration, line height, spacing, transforms, and alignment |
| Fonts | Font-related attributes |
| Ruby | CSS-based ruby text attributes |
| Generated content/markers | List styles, automatic counters, :before and :after pseudo-elements |
| Replaced content | Replaced content attributes |
| Paged media | Page breaks, running headers and footers, cross-reference pointers |
| User interface | Form element styles, cursors, kiosk mode display |
| WebFonts | Web-enhanced font attributes |
| ACSS | Aural styles and accessibility enhancements |
| SMIL | CSS connection to Synchronized Multimedia standards |
| Tables | Table-related attributes |
| Columns | Multi-column layout |
| SVG | CSS connection to Scalable Vector Graphics standard |
| Math | Rendering math expressions (Math Markup Language standard) |
| BECSS | Scripted behaviors extension |
| Media queries | Applying styles based on quantitative features supported by media (e.g., screen size) |
| Syntax/grammar | Basic syntax, including namespaces |
| Test suite | Specific examples and guidelines |

Several CSS3 modules listed in Table 7-2 either represent entirely new CSS features or include expanded features of existing CSS2 areas. The list is also ambitious in that a few modules point to W3C work that is far from finished.

# DOM Modularization (DOM2 and DOM3)

The W3C DOM Level 2 specification is divided into six documents, but these documents define a total of 14 modules. The Core module (which is shared by all others) defines a hasFeature() method that belongs to the DOMImplementation object (itself a property of the root document node). This method allows a script to query the client as to whether a particular module and module version is implemented in the browser. Syntax for this method is as follows:

```
var isImplemented = document.implementation.hasFeature("feature", "version");
```

The first parameter is a string that is associated with each module (e.g., "Core", or "MouseEvents"), while the second parameter is a string of the DOM level number for the module (e.g., "2.0" or "3.0"). Each module also maintains its own definition of conformance. The hasFeature( ) method is supposed to return true only if the conformance specifications for a particular module are met.

Netscape 6 and later implements the document.implementation property (which corresponds to DOMImplementation) and the hasFeature( ) method, which as of this writing, reports that several 2.0 modules are implemented. IE 5 for the Mac implements the hasFeature( ) method, but it does not report any modules as being implemented in full. IE 6 for Windows does not implement the document.implementation property, so scripts cannot inquire into W3C DOM module status in this browser version. It will obviously take browser development reaching critical mass among installed browsers before scripts can make intelligent use of this feature query mechanism.

Table 7-3 lists the DOM modules for Level 2 and those proposed for Level 3. The feature name and available version numbers for each module appear in the table, as well. A module that indicates Version 2.0 but not 3.0 means that the module specifications have not changed for the 3.0 generation.

*Table 7-3. DOM modules*

| Module | Feature string | Version 2.0 | Version 3.0 |
|---|---|:---:|:---:|
| Core | "Core" | • | • |
| XML | "XML" | • | • |
| HTML | "HTML" | • | |
| Views | "Views" | • | |
| Style Sheets | "StyleSheets" | • | |
| CSS | "CSS" | • | |
| CSS2 | "CSS2" | • | |
| Events | "Events" | • | • |
| User Interface Events | "UIEvents" | • | • |
| Mouse Events | "MouseEvents" | • | • |
| Text Events | "TextEvents" | | • |
| Mutation Events | "MutationEvents" | • | • |
| HTML Events | "HTMLEvents" | • | • |
| Range | "Range" | • | |
| Traversal | "Traversal" | • | |

*Table 7-3. DOM modules (continued)*

| Module | Feature string | Version 2.0 | Version 3.0 |
|---|---|---|---|
| Load and Save | `"LS"` | | • |
| Abstract Schemas Editing | `"AS-EDIT"` | | • |
| XPath | `"XPath"` | | • |

# What Is Conformance?

Despite the logic behind the modularization of these key DHTML-related standards, content authors must be vigilant about how web software makers portray their products' conformance with the standards. You should also be aware of the wiggle room that the standards themselves occasionally build into their specification documents.

There can be quite a bit of distance between a browser's claim to support a particular W3C standard and the details surrounding that support. For example, a product's shorthand marketing description may indicate support for the W3C DOM standard, when, in truth, not every module is implemented or implemented in full. Only a thorough study of the developer documentation for the product (and sometimes not even that) can reveal more specifically which elements, attributes, objects, properties, and methods are implemented. The more modules that are defined for a standard, the less likely it is that a web product will truly support every module. You might even wonder if the software makers who participated in the W3C working groups eagerly promoted modularization so they could pick and choose which modules to support, while still claiming standards compliance. That way they could claim support for the modules they wanted to adopt (or had already adopted), while ignoring others, either due to technical challenges or conflicts with their home-grown version of the standard.

If you plan to mold your development around the published recommendations, you really need to study the fine print in the standards documents. As some of the standards grow in size, the modifiers "may" and "optional" become more common. If a feature is listed as optional, a software maker can still claim conformance, even though you won't find that feature implemented. Standards increasingly focus on common denominator functionality, which means that esoterica is more likely to be listed as optional.

In the end, successful DHTML development still requires a strong working knowledge of standards-based and proprietary features supported by your target browsers. At the same time, however, you have little to lose by holding your deployments close to the core modules for all standards. These tend to provide the features that let your DHTML add value to otherwise static content in a way that seems natural, so that the user isn't even aware of the scripts and gizmos operating on the other size of the computer monitor glass.

# Dynamic HTML Reference

This part of the book, Chapters 8 through 12, is a complete reference to all the tags, attributes, objects, properties, methods, and event handlers for HTML, CSS, DOM, and core JavaScript.

Chapter 8, *HTML and XHTML Reference*

Chapter 9, *Document Object Model Reference*

Chapter 10, *Event Reference*

Chapter 11, *Style Sheet Attribute Reference*

Chapter 12, *JavaScript Core Language Reference*

# HTML and XHTML Reference

This chapter provides a complete list of HTML tags and attributes implemented in Microsoft Internet Explorer and Netscape Navigator, as well as the ones specified in the W3C recommendations for HTML 4.01 and XHTML 1.1. Version information accompanies each tag and attribute so that you can see whether a particular entry applies to the browser(s) you must support. At a glance, you can see the version number of Internet Explorer, Netscape Navigator, and the W3C HTML specification in which the item was first introduced. Because this book deals with Dynamic HTML, the history timeline goes back only to HTML 3.2, Navigator 2, and Internet Explorer 3.

If an item existed prior to one of these versions and is still in use, it is simply marked "all." Where no implementation exists, I've used "n/a" to indicate that. In rare instances, an item has been removed from the HTML specification or a browser family. Such items are marked with a less-than symbol and the version number that no longer supports the item (e.g., NN <6 for prior to Netscape 6). Items valid for a single version show the number encased in pipe symbols (e.g., |4| for Version 4 only). Deprecated items are listed here because modern browsers support them for backward compatibility, and legacy code may rely on them. Text references to Netscape 6 automatically imply support for all Mozilla-based browsers, including Netscape 7.

A handful of items that appear as new for Version 6 browsers may not, in truth, be fully implemented in these browsers. This occurs when a browser maker claims support for an element or attribute because the item is implemented in HTML 4, and the browser wishes to claim compliance with that standard version. The descriptions of such items clearly state when the item is valid but not connected.

Following a section that lists attributes shared by all elements, this chapter is organized alphabetically by HTML element (or tag, if you prefer); within each element's description, attributes are listed alphabetically. The reference entries are designed so that it is easy to see which elements require end tags (in HTML), and whether attributes are optional or required. Scripted object references are displayed in the W3C DOM standard syntax style unless the item requires a different DOM style (e.g., the Navigator 4 layer element). Although the W3C DOM document.getElementById( )

syntax prevails in the listings, if IE supports the item through its DOM scripting, you can assume that the document.all reference style also applies in that environment. The description for an item details any significant differences between the various browser implementations of the item.

All example code is formatted according to W3C HTML standards because the widest number of DHTML browsers support that format and all readers will be familiar with it. At the same time, however, the code demonstrates most practices encouraged for XHTML formatting, such as lowercase tag and attribute names and quoted attribute values of all types. The only XHTML formatting characteristics lacking from the example code are end tags for empty elements (such as the XHTML backward-compatible <br /> technique) and explicit value assignments to attributes that do not require them in HTML (such as the selected attribute of checkbox type input elements). These coding style variations are easy to modify on your own if your code must conform to XHTML validation (see Chapter 1).

For in-depth coverage of event types related to event attributes mentioned in this chapter, see Chapter 10. To find out which, if any, HTML and XHTML DTDs support a particular element or attribute, consult Appendix E.

# Attribute Value Types

Many HTML element attributes share similar data requirements. For the sake of brevity in the reference listings, this section describes a few common attribute value types in more detail than is possible within each listing. Whenever you see one of these attribute value types associated with an attribute, consult this section for a description of the type.

## Length

A length value defines a linear measure of document real estate, such as the width of a table element. The unit of measurement can be any applicable unit that helps identify a position or space on the screen. HTML attribute length units are uniformly pixels, but in other content, such as that specified in Cascading Style Sheets (see Chapter 11), measurements can be in inches, picas, ems, or other relevant units. A single numeric value may represent a length when it defines the offset from an edge of an element. For example, a coordinate point (10,20) consists of two length values, denoting pixel measurements from the left and top edges of an element, respectively. Attributes associated with length values are deprecated in favor of corresponding CSS attributes for strict HTML 4 and XHTML conformance.

# Identifier

An identifier (usually assigned to `name` or `id` attributes) is a name that adheres to some strict syntactical rules. Most importantly, an identifier is one word with no whitespace allowed. If you need to use multiple words to describe an item, you can use the inter-capitalized format (in which internal letters are capitalized) or an underscore character between the words. Most punctuation symbols are not permitted, but all numerals and alphabetical characters are. To avoid potential conflicts with scripting languages that refer to items by their identifiers, it is good practice to avoid using a numeral for the first character of an identifier.

# URI and URL

The term Universal Resource Identifier (URI) is a broad term for an address of content on the Web. A Universal Resource Locator (URL) is a type of URI. For most web authoring, you can think of them as one and the same because most web browsers restrict their focus to URLs. A URL, commonly applied to `href` and `src` attributes, may be complete (including the protocol, host, domain, and the rest) or may be relative to the URL of the current document. The latter case means the URL may consist of an anchor, file, or pathname. In scriptable browsers, attributes that expect URI values can also accept the `javascript:` pseudo-protocol, which makes a script statement or function the destination of the link. This pseudo-protocol, while implemented widely, is not a formal standard.

# Language Code

There is an extensive list of standard codes that identify the spoken and written languages of the world. A language code always contains a primary language code, such as "en" for English or "zh" for Chinese. Common two-letter primary codes are cataloged in ISO-639 (an excerpted list of codes is available at *http://www.ietf.org/rfc/rfc1766.txt*). An optional subcode (separated from the primary code by a hyphen) may be used to identify a specific implementation of the primary language, usually according to usage within a specific country. Therefore, although "en" means English, "en-US" means a U.S.-specific version of English. The browser must support a particular language code for its meaning to be of any value to an element attribute.

# Alignment Constants

The frequent presence of the `align` attribute among various elements (and the related but less pervasive `valign` attribute) is misleading when describing attribute values, because the attribute conveys different meanings for several element groups. Add to the mix several proprietary values that are implemented in some browsers, and it's easy to confuse which values to use when. That all such attributes are deprecated in favor of the CSS text-align (horizontal) and vertical-align attributes is welcome relief to authors who develop for browsers that support CSS.

Element alignment is divisible into five categories, each with its own set of applicable elements and permissible values. Browsers accept case-insensitive values, but if you intend to continue working with these attributes, you should get in the habit of using all lowercase values to conform with the transitional DTDs.

### Alignment outside the box

The first category governs the alignment of text that surrounds the rectangular space of the element bearing the align attribute. W3C HTML elements in this category include applet, iframe, img, input, and object. IE adds embed, fieldset, and select elements to the list, while deleting iframe. Here is a synopsis of the various align attribute settings for these elements and how they affect the display of the element and surrounding text content:

absbottom
> Text is aligned such that the bottom of any possible text rendering (including character descenders) is on the same horizontal line as the very bottom of the element. For IE 4 and later and Navigator 4 only; Netscape 6 equates this attribute with W3C bottom.

absmiddle
> The middle of the text height (from descender to ascender) is aligned with the middle of the element height. For IE 4 and later and Navigator 4 only; Netscape 6 equates it with middle.

baseline
> The baseline of the text is on the same horizontal line as the very bottom of the element (note that character descenders extend below the baseline). This is for IE and Navigator, but is not a W3C-sanctioned value.

bottom
> The W3C sanctioned value that is the equivalent of baseline.

left
> If there is text starting on the same line as the element, the element is lowered to the next line and displayed flush left within the next outermost container context. Text that follows the element cinches up to the end of the text preceding the element, causing the text to wrap around the object or image (called *floating*). This is a W3C-sanctioned value.

middle
> The baseline of the text is aligned with the middle of the element height. This is a W3C-sanctioned value.

right

> If there is text starting on the same line as the element, the element is lowered to the next line and displayed flush right within the next outermost container context. Text that follows the element starts on the line immediately below the starting text, causing the text to wrap around the object or image (called floating). This is a W3C-sanctioned value.

texttop

> The very top of the element is on the same horizontal line as the ascenders of the preceding text. This attribute is for IE and Navigator, but is not a W3C-sanctioned value.

top

> The top of the element is on the same horizontal line as the top of the tallest element (text or other kind of element) rendered in the line. This is a W3C-sanctioned value.

### Text alignment inside the containing box

The legend element acts like a label for a form's fieldset element. The caption does the same for a table. Alignment of these elements applies to the location of the element's text relative to the rectangular space occupied by the form's fieldset border or table. The align attribute settings for this category are:

bottom

> Text is aligned at the bottom or below the related element's box. IE and Navigator obey attribute value only for caption element. This attribute is a W3C-sanctioned value.

center

> Text is at the top or above the related element's box and centered horizontally. This is supported by IE and Navigator, but is not a W3C-sanctioned value.

left

> Although this is a W3C-sanctioned value (where indications are that text should be to the left of the containing element), IE and Navigator align text at top left of box for legend only (and caption in IE/Windows).

right

> Although this is a W3C-sanctioned value (where indications are that text should be to the right of the containing element), IE and Navigator align text at top right of box for legend only (and caption in IE/Windows).

top

> Text for legend aligned at top left of containing box; at top center for caption. This is a W3C-sanctioned value.

### Horizontal alignment of a block element

This category is potentially confusing because of the perception of what a browser does when you set the align attribute for the p, div, h1 through h6, and hr elements. These block elements normally occupy a transparent box that is the full width of the next outermost container. For most elements, that container is the body element, which extends to nearly the full width of the browser window. Therefore, when you specify one of the three primary W3C-sanctioned attribute values to an element containing short strings—center, left, and right—it appears as though the element, itself, is being aligned. In truth, the element is in the exact same spot, taking up the same width as other body content, but the text inside is aligned per the attribute setting. If you specify a fixed-width style for the element, the align attribute continues to control the text inside the element, while the element hugs the left margin. To center the width-constrained element, you must nest it inside another full-width container, and set its align attribute to center.

To add to the confusion, the W3C HTML 4 transitional specification allows for a value of justify, while the strict HTML 4 and all XHTML specifications remove that value from text alignment types of align attributes (except for table element components). Browsers support the justify value when aligning these elements.

### Horizontal text alignment in a table cell

In the W3C specification, text inside descendant nodes of the table element (tbody, tr, td, and the rest) can be aligned according to the values center, justify, left, and right. IE, however, does not recognize the justify value for table components. If you wish to justify text in an IE table cell, wrap the text in a p or div container, and set that container's align attribute to justify.

### Vertical text alignment inside an element

Vertical alignment within a table component requires the valign attribute, which has permissible values that resemble some of those of the align attribute. Those values are baseline, bottom, middle, and top.

## Colors

A color value can be assigned either via a hexadecimal triplet or with a plain-language equivalent. A hexadecimal triplet consists of three pairs of hexadecimal (base 16) numbers that range between the values 00 and FF, corresponding to the red, green, and blue components of the color. The three pairs of numbers are bunched together and preceded by a pound sign (#). Therefore, the reddest of reds has all red (FF) and none (00) of the other two colors: #FF0000; pure blue is #0000FF. The letters A through F can also be lowercase.

This numbering scheme creates a huge number of potential combinations (over 16 million), but not all video monitors are set to distinguish among millions of colors. Therefore, you may wish to limit yourself to the more modest palette of colors known as the *web palette*. A fine reference of colors that work well on all browsers at popular bit-depth settings can be found at *http://www.lynda.com/hexh.html*.

The HTML recommendation also specifies a basic library of 16 colors that can be assigned by plain-language names. Note that the color names are case-insensitive. The names and their equivalent hexadecimal triplets are as follows:

| | | | | | | | |
|---|---|---|---|---|---|---|---|
| Black | #000000 | Maroon | #800000 | Green | #008000 | Navy | #000080 |
| Silverd | #C0C0C0 | Red | #FF0000 | Lime | #00FF00 | Blue | #0000FF |
| Gray | #808080 | Purple | #800080 | Olive | #808000 | Teal | #008080 |
| White | #FFFFFF | Fuchsia | #FF00FF | Yellow | #FFFF00 | Aqua | #00FFFF |

In other words, the attribute settings `bgcolor="Aqua"` and `bgcolor="#00FFFF"` yield the same results.

Netscape developed a much longer list of plain-language color equivalents. These are detailed in Appendix A, and are recognized by recent versions of both Navigator and Internet Explorer.

# Shared HTML Element Attributes

A vast majority of elements found in HTML 4.x, XHTML 1.x, Internet Explorer, and Netscape Navigator have numerous attributes in common. Rather than repeat the descriptions of these attributes ad nauseam in the reference listings, their details are listed here only once. These shared attributes do not appear in the attribute lists for each element in the rest of this chapter, but they are available in practically every element (within the browser or standard version range indicated in each listing). Obviously, the few shared attributes that are meaningless except for rendered elements may not be available to nonrendered elements. For example, it wouldn't make any sense to apply the `tabindex` attribute to a `style` element because the `style` element presents no content of its own on the page to which a user could tab. In a few cases, the W3C specifications do not implement common attributes in nonrendered elements, but the browsers support them because the W3C DOM establishes scriptable properties for those attributes. Consult Appendix E to verify HTML 4 and XHTML DTD support for a particular shared attribute. Here is a list of the shared attributes.

## Attributes

| | | | | |
|---|---|---|---|---|
| accesskey | class | contenteditable | dir | disabled |
| hidefocus | id | lang | language | style |
| tabindex | title | unselectable | xml:lang | |

accesskey="*character*"                                    **Optional**

A single character key that either gives focus to an element (in some browsers) or activates a form control or link action. The browser and operating system determine if the user must press a modifier key (e.g., **Ctrl**, **Alt**, or **Command**) with the access key to activate the link. In Windows versions of IE 4 and later and Netscape 6, the **Alt** key is required and the key is not case-sensitive. For Macintosh versions of IE 5 and later and Netscape 6, the **Ctrl** modifier key is required to effect the action.

Although accesskey is listed here as a widely shared attribute, that isn't strictly the case across all implementations. HTML 4 and Netscape 6 recognize this attribute only for the following elements: a, area, button, input, label, legend, and textarea. To this list, IE 4 adds applet, body, div, embed, isindex, marquee, object, select, span, table, and td (but removes label and legend). IE 5 adds every other renderable element, but with a caution: except for input and other form-related elements, you must also assign a tabindex attribute to the IE 5 and later element (even if simply a value of zero for all) to let the accelerator key combination bring focus to the element.

**Example**

```
<a href="http://www.megacorp.com/toc.html" accesskey="t">Table of Contents</a>
<h2 class="subsection" accesskey="2" tabindex="0">Part Two</h2>
```

**Value**         Single character of the document set.

**Default**       None.

**Object Model Reference**

```
[window.]document.links[i].accessKey
[window.]document.anchors[i].accessKey
[window.]document.formName.elementName.accessKey
[window.]document.forms[i].elements[j].accessKey
[window.]document.getElementById(elementID).accessKey
```

## class

NN 4    IE 3    HTML 4

class="*className1[ ...classNameN]*"                        **Optional**

An identifier generally used to associate an element with a style sheet rule defined for a class selector. See Chapter 3. Use the class attribute only with visible (renderable) elements.

**Example**       `<a class="chapTitle" name="chapter3" id="chapter3">Chapter 3</a>`

**Value**         Case-sensitive identifier. Multiple classes can be assigned by separating
                  the class names with spaces within the quoted attribute value.

**Default**       None.

**Object Model Reference**

```
[window.]document.getElementById(elementID).className
```

## contenteditable

contenteditable="*featureSwitch*"                                    Optional

Boolean switch that enables or disables the user's ability to edit the element's content directly on the web page. Requires IE 5.5 or later (Win32 only). For more information about scriptable editing in IE for Windows, see the onmove event handler in Chapter 10 and visit *http://msdn.microsoft.com/workshop/author/editing/editing_entry.asp*.

**Example**           `<p id="userArea" contenteditable="true">Enter your text here.</p>`

**Value**             true | false | inherit

**Default**           inherit

### Object Model Reference

[window.]document.getElementById(*elementID*).contentEditable

## dir

dir="*direction*"                                                   Optional

The direction of character rendering for the element's text when the characters are not governed by inherent directionality according to the Unicode standard. Character rendering is either left-to-right or right-to-left. This attribute is usually set in concert with the lang attribute; it must be used to specify a character-rendering direction that overrides the current direction.

**Example**           `<a lang="ar" dir="rtl">`*Some Unicode Arabic text characters here*`</a>`

**Value**             ltr | rtl

**Default**           ltr

## disabled

disabled="*featureSwitch*"                                          Optional

Boolean switch that enables or disables the user's ability to activate or otherwise access an element. This attribute is limited to interactive form control elements in Netscape 6 and HTML 4. IE 5.5 and later (Win32 only) also applies this attribute to most other renderable elements. Disabled elements are usually "greyed out" to distinguish themselves from other elements.

**Example**           `<input type="submit" name="sender" disabled="true">`

**Value**             true | false

**Default**           false

### Object Model Reference

[window.]document.getElementById(*elementID*).disabled

# hidefocus

hidefocus="*featureSwitch*"                                    Optional

Boolean switch that enables or disables the browser's ability to display a dotted focus rectangle around an element that has focus. The element continues to be able to receive focus if it is focusable by default or has the tabindex attribute set. Focus is necessary for some keyboard-only accessibility situations, but when this attribute is switched on, there is no visual clue about the focus state. Requires IE 5.5 or later (Win32 only).

**Example**          <input type="image" src="sendme.jpg" hidefocus="true">

**Value**            true | false

**Default**          false

**Object Model Reference**
[window.]document.getElementById(*elementID*).hideFocus

# id

id="*elementIdentifier*"                                        Optional

A unique identifier that distinguishes this element from all the rest in the document. Can be used to associate a single element with a style rule naming this attribute value as an ID selector. An element can have an ID assigned for uniqueness as well as a class for inclusion within a group. See Chapter 3.

IE 4 and later and Netscape 6 allow id attributes for nonrenderable elements, but if your code requires validation, be aware that the W3C HTML 4 and XHTML DTDs do not. Because all W3C DOM elements have an id property, it is natural to assign an id attribute to non-renderable elements if scripts must reference those elements. Or, your scripts may use other ways (e.g., the array returned by document.getElementsByTagName( )) to reference such elements.

Assign identifiers to id attributes in order to duplicate values previously only assigned to name attributes in elements that feature the name attribute. Current browser form controls still require name attributes for name/value pairs to be submitted with the form, and a elements acting as anchors still need name attributes. Be sure to assign an identifier to the id attribute of any element you intend to reference by script.

**Example**          <h2 id="sect3Head">Section Three</h2>

**Value**            Case-sensitive identifier.

**Default**          None.

**Object Model Reference**
[window.]document.getElementById(*elementID*).id

## lang

lang="*languageCode*"                                           Optional

The language being used for the element's attribute values and content. A browser can use this information to assist in proper rendering of content with respect to details such as treatment of ligatures (when supported by a particular font or required by a written language), quotation marks, and hyphenation. Other applications and search engines might use this information to aid the selection of spell-checking dictionaries and the creation of indices.

**Example**           <span lang="de">Deutsche Bundesbahn</span>

**Value**             Case-insensitive language code.

**Default**           Browser default.

### Object Model Reference

[window.]document.getElementById(*elementID*).lang

## language

language="*scriptingLanguage*"                                   Optional

Sets the scripting language (and switches on the desired scripting engine) for script statements defined in the element (such as event handler script statements in the tag). This attribute is distinct from the language attribute currently in common use with the script element. Internet Explorer uses the language attribute in any element to engage a different script language interpreter for script statements, such as executing VBScript statements in the string assigned to an event handler attribute. If you use JScript exclusively within a document, you don't have to use this attribute.

### Example

How <span class="bolds" language="vbscript"
onClick="MsgBox 'Hi, there!'">bold</b> it is!

**Value**             javascript | jscript | vbs | vbscript

### Default

Although the default scripting language of IE 4 and later is JScript, no value is automatically assigned to this attribute if the attribute is not included in the tag.

### Object Model Reference

[window.]document.getElementById(*elementID*).language

## style

style="*styleSheetProperties*"                                   Optional

This attribute lets you set one or more style sheet rule property assignments for the current element. You may use the CSS or (for Navigator 4 only) JavaScript syntax for assigning style attributes. Use the style attribute only with visible (renderable) elements.

**Example**

```
<span style="color:green; font-size:18px">Big, green, and bold</span>
```

**Value**

An entire CSS-syntax style sheet rule is enclosed in quotes. Multiple style attribute settings are separated by semicolons. Style sheet attributes are detailed in Chapter 11.

**Default**  None.

**Object Model Reference**

```
[window.]document.getElementById(elementID).style
```

## tabindex

NN 6    IE 4    HTML 4

`tabindex="integer"`

Optional

A number that indicates the sequence of this element within the tabbing order of all focusable elements in the document. Tabbing order follows a strict set of rules. Elements that have values other than zero assigned to their `tabindex` attributes are first in line when a user starts tabbing in a page. Focus starts with the element with the lowest `tabindex` value and proceeds in order to the highest value, regardless of physical location on the page or in the document. If two elements have the same `tabindex` values, the element that comes earlier in the document receives focus first. Next come all elements that either don't support the `tabindex` attribute or have the value set to zero. These elements receive focus in the order in which they appear in the document. Note that reloading the current page does not necessarily restart the tabbing sequence from the "top." Therefore, controlling tabbing sequence is most helpful when the logic of your focusable elements is something other than the source code order of those elements (e.g., directing tabbing to fields down table columns rather than across rows).

HTML 4 and Netscape 6 limit the `tabindex` attribute to the following elements: `a`, `area`, `button`, `input`, `object`, `select`, `textarea`. To this list, IE 4 adds `applet`, `body`, `div`, `embed`, `isindex`, `marquee`, `span`, `table`, and `td`. IE 5 adds every other renderable element. A negative value in IE (only) removes an element from tabbing order entirely.

Links and anchors cannot be tabbed to with the Mac version of IE 4, so the `tabindex` for `a` elements is ignored in that version.

**Example**        `<a href="chapter3.html" tabindex="3">Chapter 3</a>`

**Value**          Any integer from 0 through 32,767. In IE, setting `tabindex` to a negative value causes the element to be skipped in tabbing order altogether.

**Default**        None.

**Object Model Reference**

```
[window.]document.getElementById(elementID).tabIndex
```

## title

title="*advisoryText*"                                          Optional

An advisory description of the element. For HTML elements that produce visible content on the page, IE 4 and later and Netscape 6 render the content of the title attribute as a tooltip when the cursor rests on the element for a moment. For example, the table-related col element does not display content, so its title attribute is merely advisory. To generate tooltips in tables, assign title attributes to elements such as table, tr, th, or td.

The font and color properties of the tooltip are governed by the browser, and are not modifiable under script control. In IE/Windows, the tooltip is the standard small, light-yellow rectangle; in IE/Mac, the tooltip displays as a cartoon bubble in the manner of the Mac OS bubble help system. Netscape 6 tooltips are the same small rectangle on all OS versions. If no attribute is specified, the tooltip does not display.

You can assign any descriptive text you like to this attribute. Not everyone will see it, however, so do not put mission-critical information here. Browsers designed to meet web accessibility criteria might use this attribute's information to read information about a link or nontext elements to vision-impaired web surfers. Therefore, don't ignore this potentially helpful aid to describing an element's purpose on the page.

Although the compatibility listing for this attribute dates the attribute back to Internet Explorer 3 and HTML 3.2, it is newly ascribed to many elements starting with IE 4 and HTML 4.0.

**Example**            `<span title="United States of America">U.S.A.</span>`

**Value**              Any string of characters. The string must be inside a matching pair of (single or double) quotation marks.

**Default**            None.

### Object Model Reference
`[window.]document.getElementById(elementID).title`

## unselectable

unselectable="*featureSwitch*"                                  Optional

Boolean switch that enables or disables the browser's ability to select any portion of the element. Requires IE 5.5 or later (Win32 only).

**Example**            `<p unselectable="on">...</p>`

**Value**              on | off

**Default**            off

## xml:lang

xml:lang="*languageCode*"                                       Optional

This is the XML version of the HTML-only lang attribute, as specified in the W3C XML recommendation. Use this only in an XHTML-conforming document and in browsers that understand XML namespaces. XML processors other than current browsers can make content and display decisions based on values assigned to this attribute (e.g., display the element only if the browser and operating system support the language script style). Browser documents should continue to use the lang attribute, even when it duplicates the xml:lang attribute setting.

**Example**      `<span lang="de" xml:lang="de">Deutsche Bundesbahn</span>`

**Value**      Case-insensitive language code.

## Event Handler Attributes

| Handler | NN | IE/Windows | IE/Mac | HTML |
|---|---|---|---|---|
| onactivate | n/a | 5.5 | n/a | n/a |
| onbeforecopy | n/a | 5 | n/a | n/a |
| onbeforecut | n/a | 5 | n/a | n/a |
| onbeforedeactivate | n/a | 5.5 | n/a | n/a |
| onbeforeeditfocus | n/a | 5 | n/a | n/a |
| onbeforepaste | n/a | 5 | n/a | n/a |
| onblur | 2/6 | 3/4 | 3/4 | 4 |
| onclick | 2/6 | 3/4 | 3/4 | 4 |
| oncontextmenu | n/a | 5 | n/a | n/a |
| oncontrolselect | n/a | 5.5 | n/a | n/a |
| oncopy | n/a | 5 | n/a | n/a |
| oncut | n/a | 5 | n/a | n/a |
| ondblclick | 4/6 | 4 | 4 | 4 |
| ondeactivate | n/a | 5.5 | n/a | n/a |
| ondrag | n/a | 5 | n/a | n/a |
| ondragend | n/a | 5 | n/a | n/a |
| ondragenter | n/a | 5 | n/a | n/a |
| ondragleave | n/a | 5 | n/a | n/a |
| ondragover | n/a | 5 | n/a | n/a |
| ondragstart | n/a | 5 | n/a | n/a |
| ondrop | n/a | 5 | n/a | n/a |
| onfilterchange | n/a | 4 | n/a | n/a |
| onfocus | 2/6 | 3/4 | 3/4 | 4 |
| onfocusin | n/a | 6 | n/a | n/a |
| onfocusout | n/a | 6 | n/a | n/a |
| onhelp | n/a | 4 | 5 | n/a |
| onkeydown | 4 | 4 | 4 | 4 |
| onkeypress | 4 | 4 | 4 | 4 |

| Handler | NN | IE/Windows | IE/Mac | HTML |
|---|---|---|---|---|
| onkeyup | 4 | 4 | 4 | 4 |
| onlosecapture | n/a | 5 | n/a | n/a |
| onmousedown | 4/6 | 4 | 4 | 4 |
| onmouseenter | n/a | 5.5 | n/a | n/a |
| onmouseleave | n/a | 5.5 | n/a | n/a |
| onmousemove | 4/6 | 4 | 4 | 4 |
| onmouseout | 2/6 | 3/4 | 3/4 | 4 |
| onmouseover | 2/6 | 3/4 | 3/4 | 4 |
| onmouseup | 4/6 | 4 | 4 | 4 |
| onmousewheel | n/a | 6 | n/a | n/a |
| onmove | n/a | 5.5 | n/a | n/a |
| onmoveend | n/a | 5.5 | n/a | n/a |
| onmovestart | n/a | 5.5 | n/a | n/a |
| onpaste | n/a | 5 | n/a | n/a |
| onpropertychange | n/a | 5 | n/a | n/a |
| onreadystatechange | n/a | 4 | 4 | n/a |
| onresize | n/a | 4 | 4 | n/a |
| onresizeend | n/a | 5.5 | n/a | n/a |
| onresizestart | n/a | 5.5 | n/a | n/a |
| onselectstart | n/a | 4 | 4 | n/a |

The evolution of shared event handler attributes over the course of scriptable browser history is not straightforward. While all renderable elements have the common mouse and keyboard event handler attributes starting with IE 4, Netscape 6, and HTML 4, the earlier browsers implemented only some of these event attributes and only for interactive elements (indicated above by the lower of paired numbers for a particular event type and browser). Elements that have always responded to mouse clicks (e.g., form button controls, links, and image maps) supported onclick events. Links and image maps also generally support onmouseover and onmouseout events going way back. These three events on the limited range of elements are the safest to deploy for backward compatibility. More granular mouse events (onmousedown, onmousemove, and onmouseout) are best reserved for Version 4 browsers or later. The same goes for keyboard events. Microsoft brings a large repertoire of event handler attributes to Windows-only versions of Internet Explorer. For more details on each event type and other types not listed here, see Chapter 10.

# Alphabetical Tag Reference

## \<a\>

NN *all*    IE *all*    HTML *all*

\<a\>...\</a\>                                    HTML End Tag: Required

The a element is the rare element that can be an anchor and/or a link, depending on the presence of the name and/or href attributes. As an anchor, the element defines a named location in a document to which any URL can reference by appending a hashmark and the anchor name to the document's URI (for example, *http://www.megacorp.com/contents#a-c*). Names are identifiers assigned to the name attribute (or in newer browsers, the id attribute). Content defined solely as an anchor is not (by default) visually differentiated from surrounding body content.

By assigning a URI to the href attribute, the element becomes the source of a hypertext link. Activating the link generally navigates to the URI assigned to the href attribute (or it may load other media into a helper application or plugin without changing the page). Unless modified by style sheets, links typically have a distinctive appearance in the browser, such as an underline beneath text (or border around an object) and a color other than the current content color. Attributes can define separate colors for three states: an unvisited link, a link being activated by the user, and a previously visited link (the linked document is currently in the browser cache). Such color control is deprecated in favor of CSS pseudo-classes (:link, :active, :visited, and a new state, :hover). An a element can be both an anchor and a link if, in the least, both the name (or id) and href attributes have values assigned to them.

### Example

```
<a name="anchor3" id="anchor3">Just an anchor named "anchor3."</a>
<a href="#anchor3">A link to navigate to "anchor3" in the same document.</a>
<a name="anchor3" id="anchor3" href="http://www.megacorp.com/index.html">
Go from here (anchor 3) to home page.</a>
```

### Object Model Reference

```
[window.]document.links[i]
[window.]document.anchors[i]
[window.]document.getElementById(elementID)
```

### Element-Specific Attributes

| | | | | |
|---|---|---|---|---|
| charset | coords | datafld | datasrc | href |
| hreflang | methods | name | rel | rev |
| shape | target | type | urn | |

### Element-Specific Event Handler Attributes

None. Anchor-only a elements have no event handlers in Navigator through Version 4.

<a>

## charset
NN 6   IE n/a   HTML 4

`charset="`*characterSet*`"`     Optional

Character encoding of the content at the other end of the link.

**Example**      `<a charset="csISO5427Cyrillic" href="moscow.html">Visit Moscow</a>`

**Value**      Case-insensitive alias from the character set registry (*ftp://ftp.isi.edu/in-notes/iana/assignments/character-sets*).

**Default**      Determined by browser.

## coords
NN n/a   IE 6   HTML 4

`coords="`*coord1, ... coordN*`"`     Optional

Although defined for the a element, the coords attribute applies to the area element for client-side image maps. The area element "inherits" many attributes and behaviors of the a element. See the area element.

## datafld
NN n/a   IE 4   HTML n/a

`datafld="`*columnName*`"`     Optional

Used with IE data binding to associate a remote data source column name in lieu of an href attribute for a link. The data source column must contain a valid URI (relative or absolute). A datasrc attribute must also be set for the element. Works only with text file data sources in IE 5/Mac.

**Example**      `<a datasrc="DBSRC3" datafld="newsURL">Late-Breaking News</a>`

**Value**      Case-sensitive identifier.

**Default**      None.

**Object Model Reference**

`[window.]document.links[i].dataFld`
`[window.]document.getElementById(`*elementID*`).dataFld`

## datasrc
NN n/a   IE 4   HTML n/a

`datasrc="`*dataSourceName*`"`     Optional

Used with IE data binding to specify the ID of the page's object element that loads the data source object for remote data access. Content from the data source to be inserted into the a element text is specified via the datafld attribute. Works only with text file data sources in IE 5/Mac.

**Example**      `<a datasrc="DBSRC3" datafld="newsURL">Late-Breaking News</a>`

**Value**      Case-sensitive identifier.

**Default**      None.

Alphabetical HTML Reference

**Object Model Reference**
```
[window.]document.links[i].dataSrc
[window.]document.getElementById(elementID).dataSrc
```

## href

NN *all*    IE *all*    HTML *all*

`href="URI"`

Required for links

The URI of the destination of a link. In browsers, when the URI is an HTML document, the document is loaded into the current (default) or other window target (as defined by the target attribute). For some other file types, the browser may load the destination content into a plugin or save the destination file on the client machine. In the absence of the href attribute, the element does not distinguish itself in a browser as a clickable link and may instead be only an anchor (if the name or id attribute is set).

| | |
|---|---|
| **Example** | `<a href="part1/chap3.html">Chapter 3</a>` |
| **Value** | Any valid URI, including complete and relative URLs, anchors on the same page (anchor names prefaced with the # symbol), and the javascript: pseudo-URL in scriptable browsers to trigger a script statement rather than navigate to a destination. |
| **Default** | None. |

**Object Model Reference**
```
[window.]document.links[i].href
[window.]document.getElementById(elementID).href
```

In both browsers, other link object properties allow for the extraction of components of the URL, such as protocol and hostname. See the a element in Chapter 9.

## hreflang

NN *6*    IE *6*    HTML *4*

`hreflang="languageCode"`

Optional

The language code of the content at the destination of a link. Requires that the href attribute also be set. This attribute is primarily an advisory attribute to help a browser prepare itself for a new language set if the browser is so enabled.

| | |
|---|---|
| **Example** | `<a hreflang="HI" href="hindi/Chap3.html>Chapter 3 (in Hindi)</a>` |
| **Value** | Case-insensitive language code. |
| **Default** | Browser default. |

## methods

NN *n/a*    IE *4*    HTML *n/a*

`methods="http-method"`

Optional

An advisory attribute about the functionality of the destination of a link. A browser could use this information to display special colors or images for the element content based on what the destination will do for the user.

<a>

**Example**

```
<a href="http://www.megacorp.com/cgi-bin/search?chap3" methods="get">
Chapter 3</a>
```

**Value**        Comma-delimited list of one or more HTTP methods.

**Default**     None.

**Object Model Reference**

```
[window.]document.links[i].Methods
[window.]document.getElementById(elementID).Methods
```

## name                              NN *all*   IE *all*   HTML *all*

name="*elementIdentifier*"                          **Required for anchors**

The traditional way to signify an anchor position within a document. Other link elements can refer to the anchor by setting their href attributes to a URL ending in a pound sign (#) followed by the identifier. Omitting the name (and id) attribute for the a element prevents the element from being used as an anchor position. This attribute is interchangeable with the id attribute in recent browsers. The attribute is deprecated in XHTML 1.0, so you are encouraged to use both attributes (with the same identifier) to keep all browser generations happy. If the name and href attribute are set in the element, the element is considered both an anchor and a link.

**Example**        `<a id="sect3" name="sect3">Section III</a>`

**Value**        Case-sensitive identifier.

**Default**     None.

**Object Model Reference**

```
[window.]document.links[i].name
[window.]document.anchors[i].name
[window.]document.getElementById(elementID).name
```

## rel                                 NN *6*   IE *3*   HTML *4*

rel="*linkTypes*"                                      **Optional**

Defines the relationship between the current element and the destination of the link. Also known as a *forward link*, not to be confused in any way with the destination document whose address is defined by the href attribute. The HTML 4 recommendation defines several link types; it is up to the browser to determine how to employ the value. This attribute has meaning primarily for the link element, although there is significant room for future application for tasks such as assigning an a element (acting as a link) to a button in a static navigation bar pointing to the next or previous document in a series. The element must include an href attribute for the rel attribute to be applied.

**Example**        `<a rel="next chapter" href="chapter3.html">Chapter 3</a>`

**Alphabetical HTML Reference**

**Value**

Case-insensitive, space-delimited list of HTML 4 standard link types applicable to the element. Sanctioned link types are:

| | | | |
|---|---|---|---|
| alternate | appendix | bookmark | chapter |
| contents | copyright | glossary | help |
| index | next | prev | section |
| start | stylesheet | subsection | |

In addition, IE 3 defined a fixed set of four values: same | next | parent | previous, but only next and previous continue to be supported in IE.

**Default**       None.

**Object Model Reference**

```
[window.]document.links[i].rel
[window.]document.getElementById(elementID).rel
```

---

### rev                                         NN 6    IE 3    HTML 4

`rev="linkTypes"`                                                      Optional

A reverse link relationship. Like the rel attribute, the rev attribute's capabilities are defined by the browser, particularly with regard to how the browser interprets and renders the various link types available in the HTML 4 specification. Given two documents (A and B) containing links that point to each other, the rev value of B is designed to express the same relationship between the two documents as denoted by the rel attribute in A. There is not yet much application of either the rel or rev attributes of the a element in mainstream browsers.

**Example**       `<a rev="previous" href="chapter2.html">Chapter 2</a>`

**Value**         Case-insensitive, space-delimited list of standard link types applicable to the element. See the rel attribute for sanctioned and supported link types.

**Default**       None.

**Object Model Reference**

```
[window.]document.links[i].rev
[window.]document.getElementById(elementID).rev
```

---

### shape                                        NN n/a    IE n/a    HTML 4

`shape="shape"`                                                        Optional

Defines the shape of a server-side image map area whose coordinates are specified with the coords attribute. See the area element.

<a>

# target

target="*windowOrFrameName*"                                                    Optional

If the destination document is to be loaded into a window or frame other than the current window or frame, you can specify where the destination document should load by assigning a window or frame name to the target attribute. Target frame names must be assigned to frames and windows as identifiers. Assign names to frames via the name and id attributes of the frame element; assign names to new windows via the second parameter of the window.open( ) scripting method. If you omit this attribute, the destination document replaces the document containing the link. An identifier other than one belonging to an existing frame or window opens a new window for the destination document. This attribute is applicable only when a value is assigned to the href attribute of the element.

A link element can have only one destination document and one target. If you want a link to change the content of multiple frames, you can use an a element's onclick event handler or a javascript: pseudo-URL to fire a script that loads multiple documents. Set the location.href property of each frame to a desired URL.

Strict DTDs for HTML 4 and XHTML do not support the target attribute of any element because frames and windows are outside the scope of pure document markup. In fact, framesetting documents will not validate in the strict environment—thus the purpose of the separate frameset DTDs for HTML 4 and XHTML. If your documents must validate with these strict DTDs, and you wish to support targets, use scripts to set target properties of links, image maps, and forms after the page has loaded.

### Example

```
<a target="display" href="chap3.html#sec2">Section 3.2</a>
<a target="_top" href="index.html">Start Over</a>
```

### Value

Case-sensitive identifier when the frame or window name has been assigned via the target element's name and id attributes. Four reserved target names act as constants:

_blank
> Browser creates a new window for the destination document.

_parent
> Destination document replaces the current frame's framesetting document (if one exists; otherwise, it is treated as _self).

_self
> Destination document replaces the current document in its window or frame.

_top
> Destination document is to occupy the entire browser window, replacing any and all framesets that may be loaded (also treated as _self if there are no framesets defined in the window).

### Default          _self

### Object Model Reference

```
[window.]document.links[i].target
[window.]document.getElementById(elementID).target
```

## type

NN 6   IE 6   HTML 4

type="*MIMEType*"                                                    Optional

An advisory about the content type of the destination document or resource. A browser might use this information to assist in preparing support for a resource requiring a multimedia player or plugin.

**Example**          &lt;a type="video/mpeg" href="ski4.mpeg"&gt;View Devil's Ghost slope&lt;/a&gt;

**Value**            Case-insensitive MIME type. A catalog of registered MIME types is available from *ftp://ftp.isi.edu/in-notes/iana/assignments/media-types/*.

**Default**          None.

## urn

NN *n/a*   IE 4   HTML *n/a*

urn="*urn*"                                                          Optional

A Uniform Resource Name version of the destination document specified in the href attribute. This attribute is intended to offer support in the future for the URN format of URI, an evolving recommendation under discussion at the IETF (see RFC 2141). Although supported in IE 4 and later, this attribute does not take the place of the href attribute.

**Example**          &lt;a urn="urn:foo:bar3" href="chapter3.html"&gt;Chapter 3&lt;/a&gt;

**Value**            A valid URN in the form of "urn:*NamespaceID:NamespaceSpecificString*".

**Default**          None.

**Object Model Reference**
[window.]document.links[i].urn
[window.]document.getElementById(*elementID*).urn

# &lt;abbr&gt;

NN 6   IE *n/a*   HTML 4

&lt;abbr&gt;...&lt;/abbr&gt;                                             HTML End Tag: Required

The abbr element provides an encapsulation and enumeration mechanism for abbreviations that appear in the body text. For example, consider a web page that includes your company's address. At one point in the document, the abbreviation IA is used for Iowa. A spelling checker, language translation program, or speech synthesizer might choke on this abbreviation; a search engine would not include the word "Iowa" in its relevancy rating calculation. But by turning the IA text into an abbr element (and assigning a title attribute to it), you can provide a full-text equivalent that a search engine (if so equipped) can count; a text-to-speech program would read aloud the full state name instead of some guttural gibberish. Like many elements introduced in HTML 4.0, this one is intended to assist browser technologies that may not yet be implemented but could find their way into products of the future.

Netscape 6 renders the abbr element with a dotted underline, and turns the cursor into a help icon. The context menu for such an element contains a **Properties** choice, which leads to a displayed list of attributes and their values for the visitor.

A related element, acronym, offers the same services for words that are acronyms (although Netscape 6 offers no special rendering). Both elements are part of a larger group of what the HTML 4.0 recommendation calls *phrase elements*.

**Example**

```
Ottumwa, <abbr title="Iowa">IA</abbr> 55334<br>
<abbr lang="de" title="und so weiter">usw.</abbr>
```

**Object Model Reference**

[window.]document.getElementById(*elementID*)

**Element-Specific Attributes**

None.

**Element-Specific Event Handler Attributes**

None.

## <acronym>                                          NN 6    IE 4    HTML 4

<acronym>...</acronym>                                   HTML End Tag: Required

The acronym element provides an encapsulation and enumeration mechanism for acronyms that appear in the body text. For example, consider a web page that includes a discussion of international trade issues. At one point in the document, the acronym GATT is used for General Agreement on Tariffs and Trade. A spelling checker, language translation program, or speech synthesizer might choke on this acronym; a search engine would not include the word "tariffs" in its relevancy rating calculation. But by turning the GATT text into an acronym element (and assigning a title attribute to it), you can provide a full-text equivalent that a search engine (if so equipped) can count; a text-to-speech program would read aloud the full meaning of the acronym. Like many elements introduced in HTML 4.0, this one is intended to assist browser technologies that may not yet be implemented but could find their way into products of the future.

A related element, abbr, offers the same services for words that are abbreviations. Both elements are part of a larger group of what the HTML 4 recommendation calls *phrase elements*.

**Example**

```
<acronym title="General Agreement on Tariffs and Trade">GATT</acronym>
<acronym lang="it" title="Stati Uniti">s.u.</acronym>
```

**Object Model Reference**

[window.]document.getElementById(*elementID*)

**Element-Specific Attributes**

None.

**Element-Specific Event Handler Attributes**

None.

# &lt;address&gt;

&lt;address&gt;...&lt;/address&gt;

Prior to HTML 4, the address element was often regarded as a display formatting tag appropriate for displaying a page author's contact information on the page. Navigator and Internet Explorer display address elements in an italic font. But the increased focus on separating content from form in HTML 4 adds some extra meaning to this element. Search engines and future HTML (or XML) parsers may apply special significance to the content of this element, perhaps in cataloging author information separate from the hidden information located in meta elements. If you want to use this structural meaning of the element while keeping the rendering in line with the rest of your body text, you need to assign style sheet rules to override the browser's default formatting tendencies for this element. Any standard body elements, such as links, can be contained inside an address element.

### Example

```
<address>
<p>Send comments to:<a href="mailto:jb@megacorp.com">jb@megacorp.com</a>
</p>
</address>
```

### Object Model Reference

[window.]document.getElementById(*elementID*)

### Element-Specific Attributes

None.

### Element-Specific Event Handler Attributes

None.

# &lt;applet&gt;

&lt;applet&gt;...&lt;/applet&gt;

You can embed an executable chunk of Java code in an HTML document in the form of an applet. An applet occupies a rectangular area of the page, even if it is only one-pixel square. An applet may require that some initial values be set from the HTML document. One or more param elements can be used to pass parameters to the applet before the applet starts running (provided the applet is written to accept these parameters). param elements go between the start and end tags of an applet element.

Applets are compiled by their authors into class files (filename suffix *.class*). An applet class file must be in the same directory as, or a subdirectory of, the HTML document that loads the applet. Key attributes of the applet element direct the browser to load a particular class file from the necessary subdirectory.

All user interface design for the applet is programmed into the applet in the Java language. One of the roles of attributes in the applet element is to define the size and other geographical properties of the applet for its rendering on the page. Recent browsers allow JavaScript scripts to communicate with the applet, as well as allowing applets to access document elements (not implemented in Netscape 6).

Note that HTML 4 deprecates the applet element in favor of the more generic object element. Support for embedding applets via the object element is still spotty. Browser support for the applet element will continue for some time to come, however.

### Example

```
<applet code="simpleClock.class" name="myClock" width="400" height="50">
<param name="bgColor" value="black">
<param name="fgColor" value="yellow">
</applet>
```

### Object Model Reference

[window.]document.applets[i]
[window.]document.*appletName*
[window.]document.getElementById(*elementID*)

### Element-Specific Attributes

| | | | | |
|---|---|---|---|---|
| align | alt | archive | code | codebase |
| datafld | datasrc | height | hspace | mayscript |
| name | object | src | vspace | width |

### Element-Specific Event Handler Attributes

| Handler | NN | IE | HTML |
|---|---|---|---|
| onafterupdate | n/a | 4 | n/a |
| onbeforeupdate | n/a | 4 | n/a |
| ondataavailable | n/a | 4 | n/a |
| ondatasetchanged | n/a | 4 | n/a |
| ondatasetcomplete | n/a | 4 | n/a |
| onerrorupdate | n/a | 4 | n/a |
| onrowenter | n/a | 4 | n/a |
| onrowexit | n/a | 4 | n/a |

## align                                        NN 2    IE 3    HTML 3.2

align="*alignmentConstant*"                                         Optional

The align attribute determines how the rectangle of the applet aligns within the context of surrounding content. See the section "Alignment Constants," earlier in this chapter for description of the possibilities defined in both Navigator and Internet Explorer for this attribute.

### Example

```
<applet code="simpleClock.class" name="myClock" align="absmiddle"
width="400" height="50"></applet>
```

| | |
|---|---|
| **Value** | Case-insensitive constant value. |
| **Default** | bottom |

**Object Model Reference**

```
[window.]document.applets[i].align
[window.]document.appletName.align
[window.]document.getElementById(elementID).align
```

## alt                                           NN 3   IE 3   HTML 3.2

`alt="textMessage"`                                              Optional

If a browser does not have the facilities to load and run Java applets or if the browser has Java support turned off in its preferences, the text assigned to the alt attribute is supposed to display in the document where the applet element's tag appears. Typically, this text provides advice on what the page visitor is missing by not being able to load the Java applet. Unlike the noscript or noframes elements, there is no corresponding element for an absent Java applet capability. In practice, browsers don't necessarily display this message for applets that fail to load for a variety of reasons.

**Example**

```
<applet code="simpleClock.class" name="myClock" align="absmiddle"
alt="A Java clock applet." width="400" height="50"></applet>
```

| | |
|---|---|
| **Value** | Any quoted string of characters. |
| **Default** | None. |

## archive                                        NN 3   IE 6   HTML 4

`archive="archiveFileURL"`                                       Optional

The precise meaning of the archive attribute varies between the generic HTML 4 recommendation and Netscape's specific implementation. The basic idea behind Netscape's archive attribute is that an author can package multiple class files into a single uncompressed *.zip* archive file and let the browser load the entire set of classes at one time. This can offer a performance improvement over loading just the main class file (specified by the code attribute) and then letting the class loader fetch each additional class file as needed.

In addition to specifying the archive attribute, be sure to include a code attribute that names the main class to load. Navigator first looks for the presence of that class file in the archive. If the file is missing from the archive, Navigator loads the code class file separately. (That class may then load additional supporting class files individually.) Navigator requires that the archive file have a *.zip* filename extension. The URL must also be relative to the codebase location.

The HTML specification allows multiple URLs to be specified (in a space-delimited list) for additional class or other resource files. This design anticipates the use of the same attribute with the object element, which the W3C has deemed the successor to the applet element. IE 6 supports the existence of the attribute for compatibility only, but it is not operable.

**Example**

```
<applet code="ScriptableClock.class" archive="myClock.zip" width="400" height="50">
</applet>
```

**Value**          Case-sensitive URI.

**Default**          None.

**Object Model Reference**

```
[window.]document.applets[i].archive
[window.]document.appletName.archive
[window.]document.getElementById(elementID).archive
```

## code                                                    NN 2    IE 3    HTML 3.2

`code="fileName.class"`                                                   Required

The name of the main class file that starts and runs the applet. If the codebase attribute is not specified, the code attribute must include a path from the directory that stores the HTML document loading the applet. You might get away with omitting the *.class* filename extension, but don't take any chances: be complete with the class name. Most servers are case-sensitive, so also match case of the actual class filename.

**Example**

```
<applet code="applets/ScriptableClock.class" width="400" height="50">
</applet>
```

**Value**

Case-sensitive *.class* filename or complete path relative to the HTML document.

**Default**          None.

**Object Model Reference**

```
[window.]document.applets[i].code
[window.]document.appletName.code
[window.]document.getElementById(elementID).code
```

## codebase                                                NN 2    IE 3    HTML 3.2

`codebase="path"`                                                        Optional

Path to the directory holding the class file designated in either the code or archive attribute. The codebase attribute does not name the class file, just the path. You can make this attribute a complete URL to the directory, but don't try to access a codebase outside of the domain of the current document: security restrictions may prevent the class from loading. A full path and filename can be set together in the code or object attribute, eliminating the need for the codebase attribute setting.

**Example**

```
<applet code="ScriptableClock.class" codebase="applets/" width="400" height="50">
</applet>
```

**Value**                Case-sensitive pathname, usually relative to the directory storing the current HTML document.

**Default**            None.

### Object Model Reference

```
[window.]document.applets[i].codeBase
[window.]document.appletName.codeBase
[window.]document.getElementById(elementID).codeBase
```

## datafld, datasrc

See the param element for IE data binding to Java applets.

## height, width                                     NN *2*   IE *3*   HTML *3.2*

```
width="pixels"
height="pixels"
```
                                                     **Required**

The size that a Java applet occupies in a document is governed by the height and width attribute settings. Some browser versions might allow you to get away without assigning these attributes, letting the applet's own user interface design determine the height and width of its visible rectangle. As with images, however, it is more efficient for the browser's rendering engine when you explicitly specify the object's dimensions. Make a habit of supplying these values for all applets, as you should for all images or other visible external objects.

### Example

```
<applet code="ScriptableClock.class" width="400" height="50"></applet>
```

### Value

Positive integer pixel values. You cannot entirely hide an applet by setting values to zero, but you can reduce its height and width to one pixel in each dimension. If you want to hide an applet, do so with DHTML by setting its positioning display attribute to none.

**Default**            None.

### Object Model Reference

```
[window.]document.applets[i].height
[window.]document.appletName.height
[window.]document.getElementById(elementID).height
[window.]document.applets[i].width
[window.]document.appletName.width
[window.]document.getElementById(elementID).width
```

## hspace, vspace

NN *2*    IE *3*    HTML *3.2*

```
hspace="pixels"
vspace="pixels"
```

Optional

You can put some empty space ("air") between an applet and any surrounding content by assigning pixel values to the hspace and vspace attributes. The vspace attribute governs space above and below the applet; the hspace attribute governs space to the left and right of the applet. For browsers that are style sheet savvy, you are perhaps better served by using the padding and/or margin style attributes to gain control down to individual sides, if you so desire.

### Example

```
<applet code="ScriptableClock.class" width="400" height="50" hspace="3" vspace="4">
</applet>
```

**Value**          Positive integer pixel values (optionally quoted).

**Default**        0

### Object Model Reference

```
[window.]document.applets[i].hspace
[window.]document.appletName.hspace
[window.]document.getElementById(elementID).hspace
[window.]document.applets[i].vspace
[window.]document.appletName.vspace
[window.]document.getElementById(elementID).vspace
```

## id

NN *n/a*    IE *4*    HTML *4*

```
id="elementIdentifier"
```

Optional

A unique identifier that distinguishes this element from all the rest in the document. Can be used to associate a single element with a style rule naming this attribute value as an ID selector. An element can have an ID assigned for uniqueness as well as a class for inclusion within a group. See Chapter 3.

If you assign an id attribute and not a name attribute, the value of the id attribute can be used as the applet's name in script reference forms that use the element name (document. appletName).

### Example

```
<applet id="clocker" code="ScriptableClock.class" width="400" height="50">
</applet>
```

**Value**          Case-sensitive identifier.

**Default**        None.

### Object Model Reference

```
[window.]document.applets[i].id
[window.]document.appletName.id
[window.]document.getElementById(elementID).id
```

## mayscript

mayscript

Navigator 3 introduced a technology called LiveConnect, which allowed scripts to communicate with Java applets and vice versa (not yet implemented in Mozilla-based browsers). For security reasons, an applet's communications facilities with scripts must be explicitly switched on by the page author. By adding the mayscript attribute to the applet's tag, an applet that is written to take advantage of the document objects and scripts can address those items. In other words, the HTML is granting the applet the ability to reach scripts in the document. This attribute is a simple switch: when the attribute name is present, it is turned on.

One more step is required for an applet to communicate with JavaScript. The applet code must import a special Netscape class called *JSObject.class*. This class file and its companion exception class are built into the Java support in the Windows version of Internet Explorer 4 and later. Although the execution is not perfect in IE, applets can perform basic communication with scripts.

### Example
```
<applet code="ScriptableClock.class" width="400" height="50" mayscript>
</applet>
```

### Value
No value assigned to the attribute. The presence of the attribute name sets turns on applet-to-script communication.

**Default**          Off.


## name

name="*elementIdentifier*"

If you are scripting an applet, it is usually more convenient to create a reference to the applet by using a unique name you assign to the applet. Then, if you edit the page and move or delete multiple applets on the page, you do not have to worry about adjusting index values to array-style references. In IE 4 and later, you have the option of omitting the name attribute and using the id attribute value in script references to the applet object.

### Example
```
<applet name="clock2" code="ScriptableClock.class" width="400" height="50">
</applet>
```

**Value**          Case-sensitive identifier.

**Default**          None.

### Object Model Reference
```
[window.]document.applets[i].name
[window.]document.appletName.name
[window.]document.getElementById(elementID).name
```

## object
NN *6*   IE *n/a*   HTML *4*

object="*filename*"                                                          Optional

Reference to the name of the file (relative to the codebase URI) that preserves the applet's state between sessions. When supported properly, this attribute replaces the code attribute, and the data file points to the applet's startup class file.

### Example
```
<applet name="clock2" object="clockData.dat" width="400" height="50">
</applet>
```

**Value**          Case-sensitive filename.

**Default**        None.

### Object Model Reference
```
[window.]document.applets[i].object
[window.]document.appletName.object
[window.]document.getElementById(elementID).object
```

## src
NN *n/a*   IE *4*   HTML *n/a*

src="*URL*"                                                                 Optional

Internet Explorer defines this attribute as the URL for an "associated file." This may be the same as the archive attribute defined in HTML and Navigator specifications. The src attribute is not a substitute for the code and/or codebase attributes.

**Value**          A complete or relative URL.

**Default**        None.

### Object Model Reference
```
[window.]document.applets[i].src
[window.]document.appletName.src
[window.]document.getElementById(elementID).aex
```

## vspace

See hspace.

## width

See height.

## &lt;area&gt;
NN *all*   IE *all*   HTML *3.2*

&lt;area&gt;                                                          HTML End Tag: Forbidden

A map element defines a client-side image map that is ultimately associated with an image or other object that occupies space on the page. The only job of the map element is to assign a name and a tag context for one or more area element definitions. Each area element defines how the page should respond to user interaction with a specific geographical region of the image or other object.

A client-side image map area can act like an a element link in that an area can link to a destination or javascript: pseudo-URL and assign another frame or window as the target for loading a new document. In fact, in the original scripting document object model, an area element is referenced as a link. It is not uncommon to use client-side area maps in a navigation bar occupying a slender frame of a frameset. This allows an artist to be creative with a menu design, while giving the page author the power to turn any segment of a larger image into a special-purpose link.

**Example**
```
<map name="nav">
<area coords="20,30,120,70" href="contents.html" target="display">
<area coords="20,80,145,190" href="contact.html" target="display">
</map>
```

**Object Model Reference**
```
[window.]document.links[i]
[window.]document.getElementById(elementID)
```

**Element-Specific Attributes**

| alt | coords | href | nohref | shape |
| target | | | | |

**Element-Specific Event Handler Attributes**
None.

## alt                                               NN 6    IE 3    HTML 3.2

alt="*textMessage*"                                                      **Required**

Nongraphical browsers can use the alt attribute setting to display a brief description of the meaning of the (invisible) image's hotspots. At one time, it was thought that the alt message might be displayed in the browser's status bar by default when the area had focus or the cursor rolled over the area. That function is now typically performed by onmouseover event handlers and scripts. Keep in mind that recent handheld computers usually have nongraphical browsers (or allow graphics to be turned off for improved performance). Don't ignore the graphically impaired.

**Example**
```
<area coords="20,30,120,70" href="contents.html" target="display"
alt="Table of Contents">
```

**Value**          Any quoted string of characters.

**Default**        None.

**Object Model Reference**
```
[window.]document.getElementById(elementID).alt
```

## coords

`coords="coord1, ... coordN"`                                                    Optional

Although the formal W3C definition for the coords attribute of an area element states that the attribute is optional, that doesn't mean that you can omit this attribute and expect an area to behave as it should. The coords attribute lets you define the outline of the area to be associated with a particular link or scripted action. Some third-party authoring tools can assist in determining the coordinate points for a hot area. You can also load the image into a graphics program that displays the cursor position in real time and then transfer those values to the coords attribute values.

Coordinate values are entered as a comma-delimited list. If two areas overlap, the area that is defined earlier in the HTML code takes precedence.

**Example**          `<area coords="20,30,120,70" href="contents.html" target="display">`

### Value

Each coordinate is a length value, but the number of coordinates and their order depend on the shape specified by the shape attribute, which may optionally be associated with the element. For shape="rect", there are four coordinates (left, top, right, bottom); for shape="circle", there are three coordinates (center-x, center-y, radius); for shape="poly", there are two coordinate values for each point that defines the shape of the polygon (x1, y1, x2, y2, x3, y3,...xN, yN).

**Default**          None.

### Object Model Reference

`[window.]document.getElementById(elementID).coords`

## href

`href="URI"`                                                                    Required

The URI of the destination of a link associated with the area. In a browser, when the URI is an HTML document, the document is loaded into the current (default) or other window target (as defined by the target attribute). For some other file types, the browser may load the destination content into a plugin or save the destination file on the client machine. Because IE 3 and Navigator (up to Version 4) treat area elements as a elements, the href attribute must be defined in the area element for scripts in the old DOM to access various properties about the URL and for event handlers (such as onmouseover) to work.

**Example**          `<area coords="20,30,120,70" href="contents.html" target="display">`

### Value

Any valid URI, including complete and relative URLs, anchors on the same page (anchor names prefaced with the # symbol), and the javascript: pseudo-URL in scriptable browsers to trigger a script statement rather than navigate to a destination.

**Default**          None.

**Object Model Reference**

[window.]document.links[i].href
[window.]document.getElementById(*elementID*).href

Other link object properties allow for the extraction of components of the URL, such as protocol and hostname. See the Link object in Chapter 9.

## nohref                                    NN *all*   IE *all*   HTML *3.2*

nohref                                                              Optional

Tells the browser that the area defined by the coordinates has no link associated with it (as not including any href attribute does). When you include this attribute, scriptable browsers no longer treat the element as a link. When an area element lacks an href attribute, the element no longer responds to user events. In IE 4 and later and Netscape 6, you can turn this attribute on and off from a script by setting the corresponding noHref property to true or false.

**Example**      &lt;area coords="20,30,120,70" nohref&gt;

**Value**        The presence of this attribute sets its value to true. Extend for XHTML compliance by using nohref="nohref".

**Default**      Off.

**Object Model Reference**

[window.]document.getElementById(*elementID*).noHref

## shape                                     NN *all*   IE *all*   HTML *3.2*

shape="*shapeName*"                                                Optional

Defines the shape of the client-side area map whose coordinates are specified with the coords attribute. The shape attribute tells the browser how many coordinates to expect.

**Example**

&lt;area shape="poly" coords="20,20,20,70,65,45" href="contents.html" target="display"&gt;

**Value**

Case-insensitive shape constant. Each implementation defines its own set of shape names and equivalents, but there are common denominators across browsers (circle, rect, poly, and polygon).

| Shape name | NN | IE | HTML |
|---|---|---|---|
| circ | – | • | • |
| circle | • | • | • |
| poly | • | • | • |
| polygon | • | • | – |

<area>

| Shape name | NN | IE | HTML |
|---|---|---|---|
| rect | • | • | • |
| rectangle | – | • | – |

**Default**     rect

**Object Model Reference**
[window.]document.getElementById(*elementID*).shape

## target     NN *all*     IE *all*     HTML *3.2*
target="*windowOrFrameName*"     Optional

If the destination document is to be loaded into a window or frame other than the current window or frame, you can specify where the destination document should load by assigning a window or frame name to the target attribute. Target frame names must be assigned to frames and windows as identifiers. Assign names to frames via the name and id attributes of the frame element; assign names to new windows via the second parameter of the window.open() scripting method. If you omit this attribute, the destination document replaces the document containing the link. This attribute is applicable only when a value is assigned to the href attribute of the element.

An area element can have only one destination document and one target. If you want a link to change the content of multiple frames, you can use an area element's onclick event handler (check Chapter 9 for supported browser versions) or a javascript: pseudo-URL to fire a script that loads multiple documents. Set the location.href property of each frame to the desired URL.

Strict DTDs for HTML 4 and XHTML do not support the target attribute of any element because frames and windows are outside the scope of pure document markup. In fact, framesetting documents will not validate in the strict environment—thus the purpose of the separate frameset DTDs for HTML 4 and XHTML. If your documents must validate with these strict DTDs, and you wish to support targets, use scripts to set target properties of links, image maps, and forms after the page has loaded.

**Example**
<area coords="20,30,120,70" href="contents.html" target="display">
<area coords="140,30,180,70" href="index.html" target="_top">

**Value**
Case-sensitive identifier when the frame or window name has been assigned via the target element's name and id attributes. Four reserved target names act as constants:

_blank
    Browser creates a new window for the destination document.

_parent
    Destination document replaces the current frame's framesetting document (if one exists; otherwise, it is treated as _self).

_self
> Destination document replaces the current document in its window or frame.

_top
> Destination document is to occupy the entire browser window, replacing any and all framesets that may be loaded (also treated as _self if there are no framesets defined in the window).

**Default**        _self

**Object Model Reference**
[window.]document.links[i].target
[window.]document.getElementById(*elementID*).target

# <b>

**NN** *all*    **IE** *all*    **HTML** *all*

<b>...</b>                                                    HTML End Tag: Required

The b element—one of several font style elements in HTML 4—renders its content in a boldface version of the font face governing the next outermost HTML container. You can nest multiple font style elements to create combined styles, such as bold italic (<b><i>bold-italic text</i></b>).

It is up to the browser to fatten boldface display by calculating the character weight or by perhaps loading a bold version of the currently specified font. If you are striving for font perfection, it is best to use style sheets (and perhaps downloadable fonts) to specify a true bold font family, rather than risk the browser's extrapolation of a boldface from a system font. The font-weight CSS style attribute provides quite granular control over the degree of bold applied to text if the font face supports such fine-tuning.

You can take advantage of the containerness of this element by assigning style sheet rules to some or all b elements in a page. For example, you may wish all b elements to be in a red color. By assigning the style rule b {color:red}, you can do it to all elements with only a tiny bit of code.

Although this element is not deprecated in HTML 4 or XHTML 1.0, it would not be surprising to see it lose favor to style sheets in the future.

**Example**
<p>This product is <b>new</b> and <b>improved</b>!</p>

**Object Model Reference**
[window.]document.getElementById(*elementID*)

**Element-Specific Attributes**
None.

**Element-Specific Event Handler Attributes**
None.

<base>

# <base>

<base>                                           HTML End Tag: Forbidden

A base element is defined inside a document's head element to instruct the browser about the URL path to the current document. This path is used as the basis for all relative URLs used to specify various src and href attributes in the document. The base element's URL should be a complete URL, including the document name (though browsers tend to support URLs to directories, too). The browser calculates the base URL path to the directory holding the document. If you specify <base href="http://www.megacorp.com/products/index.html">, the href attribute of a link on that page to *widgets/framitz801.html* resolves to the full URL of *http://www.megacorp.com/products/widgets/framitz801.html*. Similarly, a relative URL can walk up the hierarchy with the dot syntax. For example, from the base element defined earlier, an img element in the *index.html* page might be set for src="../images/logo.jpg". That reference resolves to *http://www.megacorp.com/images/logo.jpg*.

By and large, today's browsers automatically calculate the base URL of the currently loaded document, thus allowing use of relative URLs without specifying a base element. This is especially helpful when you are developing pages locally and don't want to change the base element settings when you deploy the pages. The HTML 4 specification states that a document lacking a base element should by default use the current document's URL as the base URL. Of course, this is only for true web pages, rather than HTML-enhanced documents such as email messages, which have no default base URL.

You can also use the base element to define a default target for any link-type element in the document. Therefore, if all links are supposed to load documents into another frame, you can specify this target frame once in the base tag and not worry about target attributes elsewhere in the document. If you wish to override the default for a single link, you may do so by specifying the target attribute for that element (but see the note in the target attribute).

The only attribute this element has in common with other elements is the id attribute.

### Example

```
<head>
<base href="http://www.megacorp.com/index.html" target="_top">
</head>
```

### Object Model Reference

[window.]document.getElementById(*elementID*)

### Element-Specific Attributes

href          target

### Element-Specific Event Handler Attributes

None.

## href

`href="`*URL*`"`                                                    Optional

The href attribute is a URL of a document whose server path is to be used as the base URL for all relative references in the document. This is typically the URL of the current document, but it can be set to another path if it makes sense to your document organization and directory structure.

**Example**           `<base href="http://www.megacorp.com/products/index.html">`

**Value**             This should be a full and absolute URL to a document.

**Default**           Current document pathname.

### Object Model Reference

`[window.]document.getElementsByTagName("base")[0].href`
`[window.]document.getElementById(`*elementID*`).href`

## target

`target="`*windowOrFrameName*`"`                                    Optional

If all or most links and area maps on a page load documents into a separate window or frame, you can set the target attribute of the base element to take care of targeting for all of those elements. You can set the target attribute without setting the href attribute if you want to set only the base target reference.

Strict DTDs for HTML 4 and XHTML do not support the target attribute of any element because frames and windows are outside the scope of pure document markup. In fact, framesetting documents will not validate in the strict environment—thus the purpose of the separate frameset DTDs for HTML 4 and XHTML. If your documents must validate with these strict DTDs, and you wish to support targets, use scripts to set target properties of links, image maps, and forms after the page has loaded.

**Example**           `<base target="rightFrame">`

**Value**

Case-sensitive identifier when the frame or window name has been assigned via the target element's name attribute. Four reserved target names act as constants:

`_blank`
> Browser creates a new window for the destination document.

`_parent`
> Destination document replaces the current frame's framesetting document (if one exists; otherwise, it is treated as _self).

`_self`
> Destination document replaces the current document in its window or frame.

`_top`
> Destination document is to occupy the entire browser window, replacing any and all framesets that may be loaded (also treated as _self if there are no framesets defined in the window).

---

**Default**          _self

**Object Model Reference**

[window.]document.getElementsByTagName("base")[0].target
[window.]document.getElementById(*elementID*).target

# &lt;basefont&gt;

&lt;basefont&gt;

A basefont element advises the browser of some font information to be used as the basis for text rendering of the current page below the basefont element. You can apply this element in either the head or body portion of the document (although Microsoft recommends in the body only for IE 4 and later), and you can insert basefont elements as often as is needed to set the base font for a portion of the document. Be aware that basefont element settings do not necessarily apply to content in tables. If you want table content to resemble a custom basefont setting, you likely have to set the font styles to table elements separately.

The basefont element overrides the default font settings in the browser's user preferences settings. Like most font-related elements, the basefont element is deprecated in HTML 4 in favor of style sheets, and is removed from the HTML 4 and XHTML strict DTDs.

**Example**          &lt;basefont face="Times, serif" size="4"&gt;

**Element-Specific Attributes**

color             face             name             size

**Element-Specific Event Handler Attributes**
None.

## color

color="*colorTripletOrName*"

Sets the font color of all text below the basefont element. Deprecated in HTML 4 in favor of the color CSS attribute.

**Example**          &lt;basefont color="Olive"&gt;

**Value**            A hexadecimal triplet or plain-language color name. See Appendix A for acceptable plain-language color names.

**Default**          Browser default.

**Object Model Reference**

[window.]document.getElementsByTagName("basefont")[0].color

## face
NN 6    IE 4    HTML 4

`face="`*fontFaceName1[, ... fontFaceNameN]*`"`      **Optional**

You can assign a hierarchy of font faces to use for the default font of a section headed by a basefont element. The browser looks for the first font face in the comma-delimited list of font face names until it either finds a match in the client system or runs out of choices, at which point the browser default font face is used. Font face names must match the system font face names exactly. If you use this attribute (instead of the preferred style sheet attribute), you can always suggest a generic font face (serif, sans-serif) as the final choice. Deprecated in HTML 4 in favor of the font-family CSS attribute.

In IE 3, this attribute was called the name attribute.

**Example**      `<basefont face="Bookman, Times Roman, serif">`

**Value**      One or more font face names, including the recognized generic faces: serif | sans-serif | cursive | fantasy | monospace.

**Default**      Browser default.

### Object Model Reference
`[window.]document.getElementsByTagName("basefont")[0].face`

## name
NN *n/a*    IE |3|    HTML *n/a*

`name="`*fontFaceName*`"`      **Optional**

This was IE 3's version of what is today the face attribute. It accepts a single font face as a value. The name attribute is no longer used.

**Value**      A single font face name.

**Default**      Browser default.

## size
NN 6    IE *all*    HTML 3.2

`size="`*integerOrRelativeSize*`"`      **Optional**

Font sizes referenced by the size attribute are on a relative size scale that is not tied to any one point size across operating system platforms. The default browser font size is 3. The range of acceptable values for the size attribute are integers from 1 to 7 inclusive. The exact point size varies with the operating system and browser design.

Users can often adjust the default font size in preferences settings. The size attribute overrides that setting. Moreover, size values can be relative to whatever font size is set in the preferences. By preceding an attribute value with a + or - sign, the browser's default size can be adjusted upward or downward, but always within the range of 1 through 7.

### Example
```
<basefont size="4">
<basefont size="+3">
```

**Value**

Either an integer or relative value, consisting of a + or – symbol and an integer value.

**Default**        3

**Object Model Reference**

[window.]document.getElementsByTagName("basefont")[0].size

# <bdo>

<bdo>...</bdo>                                                                    HTML End Tag: Required

The name of the bdo element stands for *bidirectional override*. The lang and dir attributes of most elements are designed to take care of most situations involving the mixture of writing systems that compose text in opposite directions. The bdo element is designed to assist in instances when the normal bidirectional algorithms must be explicitly overridden, due to various conversions during text processing. Because this element is not yet implemented in browsers, it is detailed here for informational purposes only.

**Example**        <bdo dir="ltr">*someMixedScriptTextHere*</bdo>

**Element-Specific Attributes**

None.

**Element-Specific Event Handler Attributes**

None.

# <bgsound>

<bgsound>                                                                         HTML End Tag: Optional

This Internet Explorer-only attribute lets you define a sound file that is to play in the background while the user visits the page. The element is allowed only inside the head element. With scripting, you can control the volume and how many times the sound track plays even after the sound file loads. Although an end tag is optional, there is no need for it because all specifications for the sound are maintained by attributes in the start tag. Only the id attribute is shared with other elements.

If you are going to use this tag, I strongly recommend making the background sound a user-selectable choice that is turned off by default. In office environments, it can be startling (if not embarrassing) to have background music or sounds unexpectedly emanate from a computer. Also be aware that there is likely to be some delay in the start of the music due to download time.

**Example**        <bgsound src="tunes/mazeppa.mid">

**Object Model Reference**

[window.]document.getElementById(*elementID*)

**Element-Specific Attributes**

balance               loop                    src                     volume

**Element-Specific Event Handler Attributes**

None.

## balance                                               NN *n/a*    IE *4*    HTML *n/a*

balance="*signedInteger*"                                                        Optional

A value that directs how the audio is divided between the left and right speakers. Once this attribute value is set in the element, its value cannot be changed by script control.

**Example**          <bgsound src="tunes/mazeppa.mid" balance="+2500">

**Value**            A signed integer between –10,000 and +10,000. A value of 0 is equally balanced on both sides. A negative value gives a relative boost to the left side; a positive value boosts the right side.

**Default**          0

**Object Model Reference**

[window.] document.getElementsByTagName("bgsound")[0].balance

## loop                                                  NN *n/a*    IE *3*    HTML *n/a*

loop="*integer*"                                                                 Optional

Defines the number of times the sound plays. If the attribute is absent or is present with any value other than -1, the sound plays at least once. Assigning a value of -1 means that the sound plays until the page is unloaded. Contrary to Microsoft's Internet Explorer SDK information, there does not appear to be a way to precache the sound without having it start playing.

**Example**          <bgsound src="tunes/mazeppa.mid" loop="3">

**Value**            No value assignment necessary for a single play. A value of 0 still causes a single play. Values above zero play the sound the specified number of times. Assign -1 to have the sound play indefinitely.

**Default**          -1

**Object Model Reference**

[window.] document.getElementsByTagName("bgsound")[0].loop

## src                                                   NN *n/a*    IE *3*    HTML *n/a*

src="*URL*"                                                                      Optional

A URL that points to the sound file to be played. The type of sound file that can be played is limited only by the audio facilities of the browser. Common audio formats, including MIDI, are supported in Internet Explorer without further plugin installation.

---

| **Example** | `<bgsound src="tunes/beethoven.mid">` |

| **Value** | Any valid URL, including complete and relative URLs. The file must be in a MIME type supported by Internet Explorer or a plugin. |

| **Default** | None. |

**Object Model Reference**

`[window.] document.getElementsByTagName("bgsound")[0].src`

## volume
NN *n/a*    IE *4*    HTML *n/a*

`volume="signedInteger"`                                                                 Optional

An integer that defines how loud the background sound plays relative to the maximum sound output level as adjusted by user preferences in the client computer. Maximum volume—a setting of zero—is only as loud as the user has set in the **Sound** control panel. Attribute adjustments are negative values as low as –10,000 (although most users lose the sound at a value much higher than –10,000).

| **Example** | `<bgsound src="tunes/beethoven.mid" volume="-500">` |

| **Value** | A signed integer value between –10,000 and 0. |

| **Default** | 0 |

**Object Model Reference**

`[window.] document.getElementsByTagName("bgsound")[0].volume`

# &lt;big&gt;
NN *all*    IE *all*    HTML *3.2*

`<big>...</big>`                                                          HTML End Tag: Required

The big element—one of several font style elements in HTML 4—renders its content in the next font size (in HTML's 1 through 7 scale) larger than the previous body font size. If you nest big elements, the effects on the more nested elements are cumulative, with each nested level rendered one size larger than the next outer element. Default font size is dependent upon the browser, operating system, and user preferences settings. For more precise font size rendering, use style sheet rules.

| **Example** | `<p>This product is <big>new</big> and <big>improved</big>!</p>` |

**Object Model Reference**

`[window.]document.getElementById(elementID)`

**Element-Specific Attributes**

None.

**Element-Specific Event Handler Attributes**

None.

<blink>

# <blink>

NN *<6*   IE *n/a*   HTML *n/a*

`<blink>...</blink>`                                    HTML End Tag: Required

The blink element is Marc Andreessen's contribution to horrifying web pages. All content of the element flashes on and off uncontrollably in a distracting manner. The more content you place inside the element, the more difficult it is to read between the flashes. Please don't use this tag. I beg you. This element does not have any attributes or event handlers, and it did not survive the migration to Version 6.

**Example**        `<blink>I dare you to read this...and not look at it.</blink>`


# <blockquote>

NN *all*   IE *all*   HTML *all*

`<blockquote>...</blockquote>`                          HTML End Tag: Required

The blockquote element is intended to set off a long quote inside a document. Traditionally, the blockquote element has been rendered as an indented block, with wider left and right margins (about 40 pixels each), plus some extra whitespace above and below the block. Browsers will likely continue this type of rendering, although you are encouraged to use style sheets to create such displays (with or without the blockquote element). For inline quotations, see the q element.

**Example**

```
<blockquote>Four score and seven years ago...
shall not perish from the earth</blockquote>
```

**Object Model Reference**

`[window.]document.getElementById(elementID)`

**Element-Specific Attributes**

cite

**Element-Specific Event Handler Attributes**

None.


## cite

NN *6*   IE *6*   HTML *4*

`cite="URL"`                                            Optional

A URL pointing to an online source document from which the quotation is taken. This is not in any way a mechanism for copying or extracting content from another document. Presumably, this HTML 4 recommendation is to encourage future browsers and search engines to utilize a reference to online source material for the benefit of readers and surfers. The **Properties** choice for Netscape 6's context menu for this element displays a small window that includes an active link to the URL assigned to the attribute. Version 6 browsers provide no other functionality for this attribute.

**Value**        Any valid URL to a document on the World Wide Web, including absolute or relative URLs.

**Default** None.

**Element-Specific Event Handler Attributes**
None.

# &lt;body&gt;

&lt;body&gt;...&lt;/body&gt;

After all of the prefatory material in the head portion of an HTML file, the body element contains the genuine content of the page that the user sees in the browser window (or may hear from browsers that know how to speak to users). Before style sheets, the body element was the place where page authors could specify document-wide color and background schemes. A great many favorite attributes covering these properties are deprecated in HTML 4, in favor of style sheet rules that may be applied to the body element. Support for all these attributes, however, will remain in mainstream browsers for years to come.

The body element is also where window object event handler attributes are placed. For example, a window object as defined in most document object models has an onload event handler that fires when a document has finished loading into the current window or frame. Assigning that event handler as an element attribute is done in the body element.

Although it may appear from a variety of implications that the body element is the document object, this is not true. The document object has additional properties (such as the document. title) that are defined outside of the body element in an HTML document. In a W3C-DOM-aware browser, the document node tree puts more distance between the root document node and the body element: the document node is the parent of the html element; the html element is the parent of both the head and body elements.

**Example**
```
<body background="watermark.jpg" onLoad="init( );">
...
</body>
```

**Object Model Reference**
[window.]document.body

**Element-Specific Attributes**

| | | | | |
|---|---|---|---|---|
| alink | background | bgcolor | bgproperties | bottommargin |
| leftmargin | link | marginheight | marginwidth | nowrap |
| rightmargin | scroll | text | topmargin | vlink |

**Element-Specific Event Handler Attributes**

| Handler | NN | IE | HTML |
|---|---|---|---|
| onafterprint | n/a | 5 | n/a |
| onbeforeprint | n/a | 5 | n/a |
| onload | 2 | 3 | 4 |
| onresize | 4 | 4 | n/a |

`<body>`

| Handler | NN | IE | HTML |
|---------|-----|-----|------|
| onscroll | n/a | 4 | n/a |
| onselect | n/a | 4 | n/a |
| onunload | 2 | 3 | 4 |

## alink

NN *all*    IE *all*    HTML *3.2*

alink="*colorTripletOrName*"                                                      Optional

Establishes the color of a hypertext link when it is activated (being clicked on) by the user. This is one of three states for a link: unvisited, active, and visited. The color is applied to the link text or border around an image or object embedded within an a element. This attribute is deprecated in favor of the CSS :active pseudo-class style rule for an a element, as described in Chapter 11.

**Example**           `<body alink="#FF0000">...</body>`

**Value**             A hexadecimal triplet or plain-language color name. See Appendix A for acceptable plain-language color names.

**Default**           #FF0000 (typically).

**Object Model Reference**
[window.]document.alinkColor
[window.]document.body.aLink

## background

NN *all*    IE *all*    HTML *3.2*

background="*URL*"                                                                Optional

Specifies an image file that is used as a backdrop to the text and other content of the page. Unlike normal images that get loaded into browser content, a background image loads in its original size (without scaling) and tiles to fill the available document space in the browser window or frame. Smaller images usually download faster but are obviously repeated more often in the background. Animated GIFs are also allowable but very distracting to the reader. When selecting a background image, be sure it is very muted in comparison to the main content so that the content stands out clearly. Background images, if used at all, should be extremely subtle or occupy space free of other content.

This attribute is deprecated in HTML 4 in favor of the background style attribute.

**Example**           `<body background="watermark.jpg">...</body>`

**Value**             Any valid URL to an image file, including complete and relative URLs.

**Default**           None.

**Object Model Reference**
[window.]document.body.background

## bgcolor

bgcolor="*colorTripletOrName*"                                                    Optional

Establishes a fill color (behind the text and other content) for the entire document. If you combine a bgcolor and background, any transparent areas of the background image let the background color show through. This attribute is deprecated in HTML 4 in favor of the background-color style attribute.

**Example**              &lt;body bgcolor="tan"&gt;...&lt;/body&gt;

**Value**                A hexadecimal triplet or plain-language color name. A setting of empty is interpreted as "#000000" (black). See Appendix A for acceptable plain-language color names.

**Default**              Varies with browser, browser version, and operating system.

**Object Model Reference**
[window.]document.bgColor
[window.]document.body.bgColor


## bgproperties

bgproperties="*property*"                                                         Optional

An Internet Explorer attribute that lets you define whether the background image (set with the background attribute or style sheet) remains in a fixed position or scrolls as a user scrolls the page. This can provide both intriguing and odd effects for the user. When the background image is set to remain in a fixed position, scrolled content flows past the background image very much like film credits roll past a background image on the screen.

**Example**              &lt;body background="watermark.jpg" bgproperties="fixed"&gt;...&lt;/body&gt;

**Value**                If set to "fixed", the image does not scroll. Omit the attribute or set it to an empty string ("") to let the image scroll with the content.

**Default**              None.

**Object Model Reference**
[window.]document.body.bgProperties


## bottommargin

bottommargin="*integer*"                                                          Optional

Establishes the amount of blank space between the very end of the content and the bottom of a scrollable page. The setting has no visual effect if the length of the content or size of the window does not cause the window to scroll. The default value is for the end of the content to be flush with the end of the document, but in the Macintosh version of Internet Explorer, there is about a 10-pixel margin visible even when the attribute is set to zero. Larger sizes are reflected properly. This attribute offers somewhat of a shortcut to setting the margin-bottom style sheet attribute for the body element.

**Example**        `<body bottommargin="20">...</body>`

**Value**        A string value of the number of pixels of clear space at the bottom of the document. A value of an empty string is the same as zero.

**Default**      0

**Object Model Reference**

`[window.]document.body.bottomMargin`

## leftmargin                      NN *6*   IE *3*   HTML *n/a*

`leftmargin="integer"`                           Optional

Establishes the amount of blank space between the left edge of the content area of a window and the left edge of the content. This attribute offers somewhat of a shortcut to setting the `margin-left` style sheet attribute for the body element. As the outermost parent container in the renderable element hierarchy, this attribute setting fixes the left margin context for all nested elements in the document.

**Example**        `<body leftmargin="25">...</body>`

**Value**        A string value of the number of pixels of clear space at the left margin of the document. A value of an empty string is the same as zero.

**Default**      10 (IE/Windows); 8 (IE/Macintosh).

**Object Model Reference**

`[window.]document.body.leftMargin`

## link                                 NN *all*   IE *all*   HTML *3.2*

`link="colorTripletOrName"`                        Optional

Establishes the color of a hypertext link that has not been visited (i.e., the URL of the link is not in the browser's cache). This is one of three states for a link: unvisited, active, and visited. The color is applied to the link text or border around an image or object embedded within an a element. This attribute is deprecated in favor of the `:link` pseudo-class style rule for an a element, as described in Chapter 11).

**Example**        `<body link="#00FF00">...</body>`

**Value**        A hexadecimal triplet or plain-language color name. See Appendix A for acceptable plain-language color names.

**Default**      `#0000FF`

**Object Model Reference**

`[window.]document.linkColor`
`[window.]document.body.link`

<body>

## marginheight, marginwidth
NN 4   IE n/a   HTML n/a

marginheight="*integer*"marginwidth="*integer*"
Optional

Shortcut attributes to set the body's margins in lieu of CSS style sheets. Setting `marginheight` to a pixel value establishes a margin setting above and below the body content; `marginwidth` sets margins to the left and right of the body.

**Example**       `<body marginheight="20" marginwidth="10">...</body>`

**Value**        A string value of the number of pixels of clear space at each of the two sides affected by each attribute. A value of an empty string is the same as zero.

**Default**      0

## nowrap
NN n/a   IE 4   HTML n/a

nowrap
Optional

Controls whether wide content should wrap within the body width.

**Example**       `<body nowrap>...</body>`

**Value**        The presence of the attribute sets its value to true.

**Default**      false

**Object Model Reference**

[window.]document.body.noWrap

## rightmargin
NN n/a   IE 4   HTML n/a

rightmargin="*integer*"
Optional

Establishes the amount of blank space between the right edge of the content area of a window and the right edge of the content. This attribute offers somewhat of a shortcut to setting the margin-right style sheet attribute for the body element. As the outermost parent container in the renderable element hierarchy, this attribute setting fixes the right margin context for all nested elements in the document. Be aware that IE on the Mac does not let content come as close to the right edge of the window as the Windows version.

**Example**       `<body rightmargin="25">... </body>`

**Value**        A string value of the number of pixels of clear space at the right margin of the document. A value of an empty string is the same as zero.

**Default**      10 (Windows); 0 (Macintosh).

**Object Model Reference**

[window.]document.body.rightMargin

<body>

## scroll

NN n/a   IE 4   HTML n/a

scroll="*featureSwitch*"

Optional

Controls the presence of scrollbars when the content space exceeds the size of the current window. Without scrollbars, if you want your users to move around the page, you have to provide some scripted method of adjusting the scroll of the window. Be aware that Internet Explorer for the Mac always shows scrollbars when the document is too large for the window, even when the scroll attribute is set to no. For more modern control over scrollbars, use the overflow CSS attribute (plus IE-specific overflowX and overflowY attributes).

**Example**        `<body scroll="no">...</body>`

**Value**          Constant values yes or no (case-insensitive).

**Default**        yes

**Object Model Reference**
[window.]document.body.scroll

## text

NN all   IE all   HTML 3.2

text="*colorTripletOrName*"

Optional

Establishes the color of body content in the document. Colors of individual elements within the document can override the document-wide setting. Because the default background color of browsers varies widely with browser brand, version, and operating system, it is advisable to set the bgcolor attribute (or equivalent style sheet rule) in concert with the document's text color. This attribute is deprecated in favor of the color style sheet attribute.

**Example**        `<body bgcolor="#FFFFFF" text="#c0c0c0">...</body>`

**Value**          A hexadecimal triplet or plain-language color name. See Appendix A for acceptable plain-language color names.

**Default**        #000000 (black).

**Object Model Reference**
[window.]document.fgColor
[window.]document.body.text

## topmargin

NN 6   IE 3   HTML n/a

topmargin="*integer*"

Optional

Establishes the amount of blank space between the top edge of the content area of a window and the top edge of the content. This attribute offers somewhat of a shortcut to setting the margin-top style sheet attribute for the body element. As the outermost parent container in the renderable element hierarchy, this attribute setting fixes the top margin context for all nested elements in the document. Setting the topmargin attribute to zero or an empty string ("") pushes the content to the very top of the document content region.

**Example**        `<body topmargin="0">... </body>`

| | |
|---|---|
| **Value** | A string value of the number of pixels of clear space at the top of the document. A value of an empty string is the same as zero. |
| **Default** | 15 (IE/Windows); 8 (IE/Macintosh). |

**Object Model Reference**
[window.]document.body.topMargin

## vlink
NN all   IE all   HTML 3.2

vlink="*colorTripletOrName*"  Optional

Establishes the color of a hypertext link after it has been visited by a user (and the destination page is still in the browser's cache). This is one of three states for a link: unvisited, active, and visited. The color is applied to the link text or border around an image or object embedded within an a element. This attribute is deprecated in favor of the :visited pseudo-class style rule for an a element, as described in Chapter 11).

| | |
|---|---|
| **Example** | <body vlink="teal">...</body> |
| **Value** | A hexadecimal triplet or plain-language color name. See Appendix A for acceptable plain-language color names. |
| **Default** | #551a8b (NN); #800080 (IE/Windows); #006010 (IE/Macintosh). |

**Object Model Reference**
[window.]document.vlinkColor
[window.]document.body.vLink

## <br>
NN all   IE all   HTML all

<br>  HTML End Tag: Forbidden

The br element forces a visible line break (carriage return and line feed) wherever its tag appears in the document. Browsers tend to honor the br element as a genuine line break, whereas paragraphs defined by the p element are given more vertical space between elements on the page. If the text containing the br element is wrapped around a floating image or other object, you can direct the next line (via the clear attribute or style sheet equivalent) to start below the object, rather than on the next line of the wrapped text.

**Example**    <p>I think that I shall never see<br>A poem lovely as a tree.</p>

**Object Model Reference**
[window.]document.getElementById(*elementID*)

**Element-Specific Attributes**
clear

**Element-Specific Event Handler Attributes**
None.

<button>

## clear

clear="*constant*"                                                    Optional

The clear attribute tells the browser how to treat the next line of text following a br element if the current text is wrapping around a floating image or other object. The value you use depends on the side of the page to which one or more inline images are pegged and how you want the next line of text to be placed in relation to those images.

This attribute is deprecated in HTML 4 in favor of the clear style sheet attribute in CSS2.

**Example**          <br clear="left">

**Value**            Four string constants: all | left | none | right. HTML 4.0 includes what should be the default value: none. This value is listed in IE 3 documentation, but not for IE 4. You can set the property to none, and the browser either responds to the value or ignores it (yielding the same results).

**Default**          none

**Object Model Reference**

[window.]document.getElementById(*elementID*).clear

# <button>

<button>...</button>                                          HTML End Tag: Required

The button element is patterned after the input element (of types button, submit, and reset) but carries some extra powers, particularly when used as a submit-type button. Content for the button's label goes between the element's start and end tags, rather than being assigned as an attribute. Other elements can be used to generate the label content, including an img element if so desired (although client-side image maps of such images are strongly discouraged by the W3C). Although you can assign a style sheet to a button element, you can also wrap the label content inside an element (such as a span) and assign or override style rules just for that content. Both style sheet mechanisms permit the button label to use custom fonts and styles.

When a button element is assigned a type of submit, the browser submits the button's name and value attributes to the server as a name/value pair, like other form elements. No special form handling is conveyed by a button when other types are specified.

In theory, a button element should be embedded within a form element. In practice, browsers have no problem rendering a free-standing button element. This might be acceptable when no related form elements (such as text boxes) need to be referenced by scripts associated with the button. Some scripting shortcuts (reading the form property of the event object's srcElement or target properties) simplify the scripted interactivity between form elements.

The W3C implemented this input element variant to offer browser makers a chance to create a different, richer-looking button. In practice, recent IE browsers for both Windows and Macintosh render identical buttons. Netscape 6 tends to use less horizontal padding around the label of a button element by default.

<button>

**Example**
```
<button type="button" onClick="doSomething( );">Click Here</button>
<button type="submit" id="sender" value="infoOnly">Request Info</button>
<button type="reset"><img src="clearIt.gif" height="20" width="18"></button>
```

**Object Model Reference**
```
[window.]document.getElementById(elementID)
```

**Element-Specific Attributes**

| | | | | |
|---|---|---|---|---|
| datafld | dataformatas | datasrc | name | type |
| value | | | | |

**Element-Specific Event Handler Attributes**

| Handler | NN | IE | HTML |
|---|---|---|---|
| onafterupdate | n/a | 4 | n/a |
| onbeforeupdate | n/a | 4 | n/a |
| onrowenter | n/a | 4 | n/a |
| onrowexit | n/a | 4 | n/a |

## datafld
NN *n/a*    IE *4*    HTML |4|

datafld="*columnName*"                                                        Optional

Used with IE data binding to associate a remote data source column name with the label of a button. The data source column must be either plain text or HTML (see dataformatas). A datasrc attribute must also be set for the button element. Works only with text file data sources in IE 5/Mac.

This attribute was reserved in HTML 4, but was dropped in XHTML 1.0.

**Example**
```
<button type="button" datasrc="DBSRC3" datafld="label" onClick="getTopStory( );">
Latest News</button>
```

**Value**          Case-sensitive identifier.

**Default**        None.

**Object Model Reference**
```
[window.]document.getElementById(elementID).dataFld
```

## dataformatas
NN *n/a*    IE *4*    HTML |4|

dataformatas="*dataType*"                                                      Optional

Used with IE data binding, this attribute advises the browser whether the source material arriving from the data source is to be treated as plain text or as tagged HTML. This attribute setting depends entirely on how the data source is constructed.

This attribute was reserved in HTML 4, but was dropped in XHTML 1.0.

<button>

**Example**

```
<button type="button" datasrc="DBSRC3"dataformatas="HTML" datafld="label"
onClick="getTopStory( );"> Latest News</button>
```

**Value**         IE recognizes two possible settings: text | html.

**Default**       text

**Object Model Reference**

[window.]document.getElementById(*elementID*).dataFormatAs

## datasrc            NN *n/a*    IE 4    HTML *n/a*

datasrc="*dataSourceName*"                                         **Optional**

Used with IE data binding to specify the ID of the page's object element that loads the data source object for remote data access. Content from the data source is specified via the datafld attribute. Works only with text file data sources in IE 5/Mac.

This attribute was reserved in HTML 4, but was dropped in XHTML 1.0.

**Example**

```
<button type="button" datasrc="DBSRC3" datafld="label"
onClick="getTopStory( );"> Latest News</button>
```

**Value**         Case-sensitive identifier.

**Default**       None.

**Object Model Reference**

[window.]document.getElementById(*elementID*).dataSrc

## name            NN 6    IE 4    HTML 4

name="*elementIdentifier*"                                       **Optional**

For a button element, the name attribute can play two roles, depending on the type attribute setting. For all type attribute settings, the name attribute lets you assign an identifier that can be used in scripted references to the element (the id attribute is the preferred way to reference the element). For a button type of submit, the name attribute is sent as part of the name/value pair to the server at submit time.

**Example**

```
<button type="submit" name="sender" value="infoOnly">Request Info</button>
```

**Value**         Case-sensitive identifier.

**Default**       None.

**Object Model Reference**

[window.]document.getElementById(*elementID*).name

<caption>

## type

type="*buttonType*"                                                Optional

Defines the internal style of button for the browser. A button style is intended to be used to initiate scripted action via an event handler. A "reset" style behaves the same way as an input element whose type attribute is set to reset, returning all elements to their default values. A "submit" style behaves the same way as an input element whose type attribute is set to submit. A button element whose type attribute is set to either reset or submit must be associated with a form for its implied action to be of any value to the page.

### Example

```
<button type="reset"><img src="clearIt.gif" height="20" width="18"></button>
```

### Value

Case-insensitive constant value from the following list of three: button | reset | submit.

### Default          button

### Object Model Reference

```
[window.]document.getElementById(elementID).type
```

## value

value="*text*"                                                    Optional

Preassigns a value to a button element that is submitted to the server as part of the name/value pair when the element is a member of a form.

### Example

```
<button name="connections" id="connections" value="ISDN">ISDN</button>
```

### Value          Any text string.

### Default          None.

### Object Model Reference

```
[window.]document.getElementById(elementID).value
```

# \<caption\>

\<caption\>...\</caption\>                                        HTML End Tag: Required

A caption element may be placed only inside a table element (and immediately after the \<table\> start tag) to denote the text to be used as a caption for the table. A caption applies to the entire table, whereas a table heading (th element) applies to a single column or row of the table. Only one caption element is recognized within a table element.

A table caption is usually a brief description of the table. A longer description may be written for the summary attribute of a table element for browsers that use text-to-speech technology. The primary distinguishing attribute of the caption element is align. Although deprecated in HTML 4, it lets you define where the caption appears in relation to the actual table.

<caption>

## Example
```
<table ...>
<caption class="tableCaptions">
  Table 3-2. Sample Inverse Framistan Values
</caption>
...
</table>
```

## Object Model Reference
[window.]document.getElementById(*elementID*)

## Element-Specific Attributes
align          valign

## Element-Specific Event Handler Attributes
None.

## align                                          NN *all*   IE *all*   HTML *3.2*
align="*where*"                                                          Optional

Determines how the caption is rendered in physical relation to the table. Not all versions of all browsers support the full range of possibilities for this attribute. Only top and bottom are universal among supporting browsers.

Browsers typically render a caption above or below a table in the running body font (unless modified by tag or style sheet) and centered horizontally on the table. If the caption is wider than the table, text is wrapped to the next line, maintaining center justification.

The align attribute is deprecated in HTML 4.0 in favor of the text-align and vertical-align style sheet attributes.

**Example**          `<caption align="top">Table II. Stock List</caption>`

## Value
Acceptable string values for this attribute vary with browser version. Select the one(s) from the following table that work for your deployment.

| Value | IE 4+ | NN 4 | NN 6 | HTML 4 |
|-------|-------|------|------|--------|
| bottom | • | • | • | • |
| center | • | – | – | – |
| left | • | – | • | • |
| right | • | – | • | • |
| top | • | • | • | • |

For implementation details, see the discussion of text alignment within a containing box in the section "Alignment Constants" at the beginning of this chapter.

**Default**          top (in IE, center if valign attribute is also set).

**Object Model Reference**

[window.]document.getElementById(*elementID*).align

## valign                                                    NN *n/a*    IE *3*    HTML *n/a*

valign="*where*"                                                            Optional

The valign attribute was Internet Explorer's early attribute for placing a table caption above or below the table. Although this attribute is now a part of the align attribute, IE's special way of handling left, center, and right values of the align attribute give valign something to do. For example, you can use valign to set the caption below the table, and use align="right" to right-align the caption at the bottom. This combination is not possible with the HTML 4 attribute.

**Example**

<caption align="right" valign="bottom">Table 3-2. Fiber Content.</caption>

**Value**              Two possible case-insensitive values: bottom | top.

**Default**            top

**Object Model Reference**

[window.]document.getElementById(*elementID*).valign

# &lt;center&gt;                                          NN *all*    IE *all*    HTML *3.2*

...                                          HTML End Tag: Required

The center element was introduced by Netscape and became widely used before the W3C-sanctioned div element came into being. It is clear, even from the HTML 3.2 documentation, that the HTML working group was never fond of this element. Momentum, however, carried the day, and this element found its way into the HTML 3.2 specification. The element is deprecated in HTML 4 in favor of the div element with a style sheet rule of text-align:center. In lieu of style sheets (but still deprecated in HTML 4), you can substitute a div element with align="center".

Content of a center element is aligned along an axis that runs down the middle of the next outermost containing element—usually the body or html element.

**Example**

Don't do this.

**Object Model Reference**

[window.]document.getElementById(*elementID*)

**Element-Specific Attributes**

None.

**Element-Specific Event Handler Attributes**

None.

<cite>

# <cite>

NN *all*    IE *all*    HTML *all*

`<cite>...</cite>`

HTML End Tag: Required

The cite element is one of a large group of elements that the HTML 4 recommendation calls *phrase elements*. Such elements assign structural meaning to a designated portion of the document. A cite element is one that contains a citation or reference to some other source material. This is not an active link but simply notation indicating what the element content is. Search engines and other HTML document parsers may use this information for other purposes (assembling a bibliography of a document, for example).

Browsers have free rein to determine how (or whether) to distinguish cite element content from the rest of the body element. Both Navigator and Internet Explorer elect to italicize the text. Override the default with a style sheet as you see fit.

### Example

```
<p>Trouthe is the hyest thing that many may kepe.<br>
(Chaucer, <cite>The Franklin's Tale</cite>)</p>
```

### Object Model Reference

`[window.]document.getElementById(elementID)`

### Element-Specific Attributes

None.

### Element-Specific Event Handler Attributes

None.

# <code>

NN *all*    IE *all*    HTML *all*

`<code>...</code>`

HTML End Tag: Required

The code element is one of a large group of elements that the HTML 4 recommendation calls *phrase elements*. Such elements assign structural meaning to a designated portion of the document. A code element is one that is used predominantly to display one or more inline characters representing computer code (program statements, variable names, keywords, and the like).

Browsers have free rein to determine how (or whether) to distinguish code element content from the rest of the body element. Both Navigator and Internet Explorer elect to render code element content in a monospace font, usually in a slightly smaller font size than the default body font (although it is not reduced in IE 4 for the Macintosh). Override the default with a style sheet as you see fit.

Whitespace (including carriage returns) is treated the same way in code element content as it is in the browser's body element content. Line breaks must be manually inserted with br elements. See also the pre element for displaying preformatted text that observes all whitespace entered in the source code.

### Example

```
<p>Initialize a variable in JavaScript with the <code>var</code> keyword.</p>
```

<col>

**Object Model Reference**

[window.]document.getElementById(*elementID*)

**Element-Specific Attributes**

None.

**Element-Specific Event Handler Attributes**

None.

# <col>    NN 6    IE 3    HTML 4

<col>    HTML End Tag: Forbidden

The col element provides shortcuts to assigning widths and other characteristics (styles) to one or more subsets of columns within a table or within a table's column group. With this information appearing early in the table element, a browser equipped to do so starts rendering the table before all source code for the table has loaded (the time at which it would otherwise perform all of its geographical calculations).

You can use the col element in combination with the colgroup element or by itself. The structure depends on how you need to assign widths and styles to individual columns or contiguous columns. A col element can apply to multiple contiguous columns. By assigning an integer value to the span attribute, you direct the browser to apply the col element's width or style settings to said number of contiguous columns. The span attribute is similar to the colgroup element's colspan attribute. In concert with the colgroup element, the col element allows you to create a kind of subset of related columns within a colgroup set.

No matter how you address the column structure of your table, the total number of columns defined in all col and colgroup elements should equal the physical number of columns you intend for the table. The following three skeletal examples specify HTML 4 tables with six columns:

```
<table>
<col span="6">
...
</table>

<table>
<col>
<col span="4">
<col>
...
</table>

<table>
<colgroup>
<col span="2"></colgroup>
<colgroup span="4">
...
</table>
```

HTML 4 specifications for the col element exceed the implementation in IE and Navigator through Version 6. For example, HTML 4 provides for alignment within a column to be around any character, such as the decimal point of a money amount. This kind of feature adds to the rationale behind the col element. For example, you can have a table whose first three columns are formatted one way, and fourth column is assigned a special style with its own alignment characteristics:

```
<html>
<head>
<style type="text/css">
  .colHdrs {color:black}
  .normColumn {color:green}
  .priceColumn {color:red}
</style>
</head>
<body>
<table>
<colgroup class="normColumn" span="3"></colgroup>
<col class="priceColumn" align="char" char=".">
<thead class="colHdrs">
<tr><th>Stock No.<th>In Stock<th>Description<th>Price</tr>
<tbody>
<tr><td>8832<td>Yes<td>Brass Frobnitz<td>$255.98</tr>
<tr><td>8835<td>No<td>Frobnitz (black)<td>$98</tr>
...
</table>
</body>
</html>
```

Because attributes of the col and colgroup elements apply to the entire column, in the preceding example the style sheet rule for the thead overrides the color settings for the two column styles for the rows enclosed by the thead element. The preceding example works in IE 4 and later for Windows, except for the alignment of the final column, which is ignored.

Support indicated here for Netscape 6 is based on the browser's DOM implementation. The DOM reports to scripts that the col element and its attributes exist (reflected as properties). But as of Netscape 7, the element does not perform its intended tasks. A later version will likely connect the element's internal wiring.

### Example
```
<col class="dateCols" width="15" align="right">
```

### Object Model Reference
[window.]document.getElementById(*elementID*)

### Element-Specific Attributes
| | | | | |
|---|---|---|---|---|
| align | ch | char | charoff | choff |
| span | valign | width | | |

### Element-Specific Event Handler Attributes
None.

## align

NN 6   IE 3   HTML 4

`align="alignConstant"`

Optional

Establishes the horizontal alignment characteristics of content within column(s) covered by the col element. The HTML 4 specification defines some values for the align attribute that are not yet reflected in the CSS specification. For example, there is no CSS equivalent for the alignment by character. See the col element description about Netscape 6 compatibility.

### Example

`<col class="dateCols" width="15" align="right">`

### Value

HTML 4 and IE have two sets of attribute values.

| Value | IE | HTML 4 |
|---|---|---|
| center | • | • |
| char | – | • |
| justify | – | • |
| left | • | • |
| right | • | • |

The values center, left, and right are self-explanatory (and may be replicated through the CSS text-align attribute). The value justify is intended to space content so that text is justified down both left and right edges. For the value char, the char attribute must also be set to specify the character on which alignment revolves.

It is important to bear in mind that the align attribute applies to every row of every column spanned by a col element, including any th element you specify for the table. If you want a different alignment for the column header, override the setting with a separate align attribute or text-align style sheet attribute for the thead or individual th elements.

### Default

left

### Object Model Reference

`[window.]document.getElementById(elementID).align`

## char

NN 6   IE n/a   HTML 4

`char="character"`

Optional

The char attribute defines the text character used as an alignment point for text within a column. This attribute is of value only for the align attribute set to "char". Microsoft documents a ch attribute, which corresponds to the standards-based char attribute. In any case, the browser does not respond to either attribute. Netscape 7 has not yet connected support for the char attribute.

### Example

`<col class="priceColumn" align="char" char=".">`

| **Value** | Any single text character. |
| **Default** | None. |

## charoff

NN 6    IE n/a    HTML 4

charoff="*length*"

Optional

The charoff attribute lets you set a specific offset point at which the character specified by
the char attribute is to appear within a cell. This attribute is provided in case the browser
default positioning does not meet with the design goals of the table. Microsoft documents a
choff attribute, which corresponds to the standards-based charoff attribute. In any case,
the browser does not respond to either attribute. Netscape 7 has not yet connected support
for the charoff attribute.

| **Example** | &lt;col class="priceColumn" align="char" char="." charoff="80%"&gt; |
| **Value** | Any length value in pixels or percentage of cell space. |
| **Default** | None. |

## choff

See charoff.

## span

NN 6    IE 3    HTML 4

span="*columnCount*"

Optional

Defines the number of adjacent columns for which the col element's attribute and style
settings apply. If this attribute is missing, the col element governs a single column. You can
combine multiple col elements of different span sizes as needed for your column
subgrouping. See the col element description about Netscape 6 compatibility.

| **Example** | &lt;col span="3"&gt; |
| **Value** | Integer value greater than zero. |
| **Default** | 1 |

**Object Model Reference**

[window.]document.getElementById(*elementID*).span

## valign

NN 6    IE 4    HTML 4

valign="*alignmentConstant*"

Optional

Determines the vertical alignment of content within cells of the column(s) covered by the
col element. You can override the vertical alignment for a particular cell anywhere in the
column. See the col element description about Netscape 6 compatibility.

| **Example** | &lt;col valign="middle"&gt; |

<col>

**Value**

Four constant values are recognized by both IE 4 and later for Windows and HTML 4: top | middle | bottom | baseline. With top and bottom, the content is rendered flush (or very close to it) to the top and bottom of the table cell. Set to middle (the default), the content floats perfectly centered vertically in the cell. When one cell's contents might wrap to multiple lines at common window widths (assuming a variable table width), it is advisable to set the valign attributes of all cells in the same row (or all col elements) to baseline. This assures that the character baseline of the first (or only) line of a cell's text aligns with the other cells in the row—usually the most aesthetically pleasing arrangement.

**Default**          middle

**Object Model Reference**

[window.]document.getElementById(*elementID*).vAlign

## width                                                NN 6    IE 4    HTML 4

width="*multiLength*"                                                Optional

Defines the maximum width for the column(s) covered by the col element. In practice (in IE 4 and later for Windows, anyway), the browser won't render a column narrower than the widest contiguous stretch of characters not containing whitespace (e.g., the longest word). The precise measure of such a column width, of course, depends on the font characteristics of the content, as well. See the col element description about Netscape 6 compatibility.

**Example**          <col width="100">

**Value**

Internet Explorer accepts length values for the width in the form of pixel measures (without the "px" unit) or percentage of available horizontal space allocated to the entire table (width="25%").

The HTML 4 specification introduces an additional length measurement scheme to supplement the regular length measure. Called a proportional length (also MultiLength), this format features a special notation and geometry. It is best suited for situations in which a col element is to be sized based on the available width of the table space after all fixed length and percentage lengths are calculated. Using the proportional length notation (a number followed by an asterisk), you can direct the browser to divide any remaining space according to proportion. For example, if there is enough horizontal space on the page for 100 pixels after all other column width calculations are performed, three col elements might specify width attributes of 1*, 3*, and 1*. This adds up to a total of five proportional segments. The 100 available pixels are handed out to the proportional columns based on their proportion to the whole of the remaining space: 20, 60, and 20 pixels, respectively.

**Default**     ·     Determined by browser calculation.

<colgroup>

# <colgroup>

`<colgroup>...</colgroup>`

The colgroup element provides shortcuts to assigning widths and other characteristics (styles) to one or more subsets of columns within a table. With this information appearing early in the table element source code, a browser equipped to do so starts rendering the table before all source code for the table has loaded (at which time it would otherwise perform all of its geographical calculations).

You can use the colgroup element in combination with the col element or by itself. You may also define a colgroup that has col elements nested within to assist in defining subsets of columns that share some attribute or style settings. The need for the element's end tag is determined by the presence of standalone col elements following the colgroup element. For example, if you specify column groupings entirely with colgroup elements, end tags are not necessary:

```
<table>
<colgroup span="2" width="30">
<colgroup span="3" width="40">
<thead>
```

If you have a freestanding col element following the colgroup element, you must clearly end the colgroup element before the standalone col element:

```
<table>
<colgroup class="leftCols">
<col width="30">
<col width="20">
</colgroup>
<col class="priceCol" width="25">
<thead>
...
```

The structure depends on how you need to assign widths and styles to individual columns or contiguous columns. To create a column grouping that consists of multiple adjacent columns, use the span attribute. This is entirely different from the colspan attribute of a td element, which has the visual impact of joining adjacent cells together as one. The span attribute helps define the number of columns to be treated structurally as a group (for assigning attribute and style sheet settings across multiple columns, regardless of the column content).

No matter how you address the column structure of your table, the total number of columns defined in all col and colgroup elements should equal the physical number of columns you intend for the table. The following three skeletal examples specify HTML 4 tables with six columns:

```
<table>
<colgroup span="6">
...
</table>

<table>
<col>
<colgroup span="4">
<col>
```

<colgroup>

```
    ...
    </table>

    <table>
    <colgroup>
        <col span="2">
    </colgroup>
    <colgroup span="4">
    ...
    </table>
```

HTML 4 specifications for the colgroup element exceed the implementation in IE for Windows and Navigator through Version 6. For example, HTML 4 provides for alignment within a column to be around any character, such as the decimal point of a money amount. This kind of feature adds to the rationale behind the col element (see the col element for an example).

Syntactically, there is little difference between a colgroup and col element. A colgroup element, however, lends a structural integrity to a group of columns that is rendered differently when the containing table element specifies rules="groups"; the browser draws rule lines (standard table borders in IE) only between colgroup elements, and not col elements.

Support indicated here for Netscape 6 is based on the browser's DOM implementation. The DOM reports to scripts that the colgroup element and its attributes exist (reflected as properties). But as of Netscape 7, the element does not perform its intended tasks. A later version will likely connect the element's internal wiring.

### Example
```
<colgroup class="dateCols" width="15" align="right">
```

### Object Model Reference
```
[window.]document.getElementById(elementID)
```

### Element-Specific Attributes

| | | | | |
|---|---|---|---|---|
| align | char | charoff | span | valign |
| width | | | | |

### Element-Specific Event Handler Attributes
None.

## align
NN *n/a*   IE 3   HTML 4
```
align="alignConstant"
```
Optional

Establishes the horizontal alignment characteristics of content within column(s) covered by the colgroup element. The HTML 4 specification defines settings for the align attribute that are not yet reflected in the CSS specification. For example, there is no CSS equivalent for the alignment by character. See the colgroup element description about Netscape 6 compatibility.

### Example
```
<colgroup class="dateCols" width="15" align="right" span="3">
```

**Value**

HTML 4 and IE have two sets of attribute values.

| Value | IE | HTML 4 |
|---|---|---|
| center | • | • |
| char | – | • |
| justify | – | • |
| left | • | • |
| right | • | • |

The values center, left, and right are self-explanatory. The value justify is intended to space content so that text is justified down both left and right edges. For the value char, the char attribute must also be set to specify the character on which alignment revolves. In the HTML 4 specification example, content that does not contain the character appears to be right-aligned to the location of the character in other rows of the same column.

It is important to bear in mind that the align attribute applies to every row of a column, including any th element you specify for the table. If you want a different alignment for the column header, override the setting with a separate align attribute or text-align style sheet attribute for the thead or individual th elements.

**Default**       left

**Object Model Reference**
[window.]document.getElementById(*elementID*).align

## char                                                            NN 6   IE *n/a*   HTML 4
char="*character*"                                                                    Optional

The char attribute defines the text character used as an alignment point for text within a column. This attribute is of value only for the align attribute set to "char". Microsoft documents a ch attribute, which corresponds to the standards-based char attribute. In any case, the browser does not respond to either attribute. Netscape 7 has not yet connected support for the char attribute.

**Example**       `<colgroup class="priceCols" align="char" char="." span="2">`

**Value**         Any single text character.

**Default**       None.

## charoff                                                         NN 6   IE *n/a*   HTML 4
charoff="*length*"                                                                    Optional

The charoff attribute lets you set a specific offset point at which the character specified by the char attribute is to appear within a cell. This attribute is provided in case the browser default positioning does not meet with the design goals of the table. Microsoft documents a choff attribute, which corresponds to the standards-based charoff attribute. In any case, the browser does not respond to either attribute. Netscape 7 has not yet connected support for the charoff attribute.

**Example**

`<colgroup class="priceColumn" align="char" char="." charoff="80%" span="2">`

| **Value** | Any length value in pixels or percentage of cell space. |
|---|---|
| **Default** | None. |

## span

`span="columnCount"`          Optional

Defines the number of adjacent columns for which the colgroup element's attribute and style settings apply. If this attribute is missing, the colgroup element governs a single column. You can combine multiple colgroup elements of different span sizes as needed for your column subgrouping. See the colgroup element description about Netscape 6 compatibility.

| **Example** | `<colgroup span="3">` |
|---|---|
| **Value** | Integer value greater than zero. |
| **Default** | 1 |

**Object Model Reference**

`[window.]document.getElementById(elementID).span`

## valign

`valign="alignmentConstant"`          Optional

Determines the vertical alignment of content within cells of the column(s) covered by the colgroup element. You can override the vertical alignment for a particular cell anywhere in the column. See the colgroup element description about Netscape 6 compatibility.

| **Example** | `<colgroup valign="middle">` |
|---|---|

**Value**

Four constant values are recognized by both IE 4 and HTML 4: top | middle | bottom | baseline. With top and bottom, the content is rendered flush (or very close to it) to the top and bottom of the table cell. Set to middle (the default), the content floats perfectly centered vertically in the cell. When one cell's contents might wrap to multiple lines at common window widths (assuming a variable table width), it is advisable to set the valign attributes of all cells in the same row (or all colgroup elements) to baseline. This assures that the character baseline of the first (or only) line of a cell's text aligns with the other cells in the row—usually the most aesthetically pleasing arrangement.

| **Default** | middle |
|---|---|

**Object Model Reference**

`[window.]document.getElementById(elementID).vAlign`

## width

width="*multiLength*"

Defines the maximum width for the column(s) covered by the colgroup element. In practice (in IE 4 and later for Windows, anyway), the browser won't render a column narrower than the widest contiguous stretch of characters not containing whitespace (e.g., the longest word). The precise measure of such a column width, of course, depends on the font characteristics of the content, as well. See the colgroup element description about Netscape 6 compatibility.

**Example**          <colgroup width="100">

**Value**

Internet Explorer accepts length values for the width in the form of pixel measures (without the "px" unit) or percentage of available horizontal space allocated to the entire table (width="25%").

An alternate variation of the proportional length value is described in the HTML 4.0 specification. For a colgroup element, you can specify width="0*" to instruct the browser to render all columns according to the minimum width necessary to display the content of the cells in the column. For a browser to make this calculation, it must load all table contents, thus eliminating the possibility of incremental rendering of a long table. For more information about proportional lengths, see the width attribute of the col element.

**Default**          Determined by browser calculation.


# &lt;comment&gt;

&lt;comment&gt;...&lt;/comment&gt;

The comment element is an artifact of early Internet Explorer browsers. It was intended as a plain-language tag alternate to the &lt;!--comment--&gt; comment element. IE does not render content inside the comment element, but all other browsers do. Do not use this element. Further details are omitted here to reduce the incentive to use the element.


# &lt;dd&gt;

&lt;dd&gt;...&lt;/dd&gt;

The dd element is a part of the dl, dt, dd triumvirate of elements used to create a definition list in a document. The entire list is bracketed by the dl element's tags. Each definition term is denoted by a leading dt element tag, and the definition for the term is denoted by a leading dd element tag. A schematic of a definition list sequence for three items looks as follows:

```
<dl>
    <dt>Term 1</dt>
    <dd>Definition 1</dd>
    <dt>Term 2</dt>
    <dd>Definition 2</dd>
    <dt>Term 3</dt>
```

```
    <dd>Definition 3</dd>
  </dl>
```

A dt element is an inline element, whereas a dd element can contain block-level content, including bordered text, images, and other objects. End tags are optional for both dt and dd elements because the next start tag automatically signals the end of the preceding element. The entire list, however, must close with an end tag for the encapsulating dl element.

Although the HTML specification forces no particular way of rendering a definition list, Navigator and Internet Explorer are in agreement in left-aligning a dt element and indenting any dd element that follows it. No special font formatting or visual elements are added by the browser, but you are free (if not encouraged) to assign styles as you like. If you want to stack multiple terms and/or definitions, you can place multiple dt and/or dd elements right after each other in the source code.

Because HTML is being geared toward context-sensitive tagging, avoid using definition lists strictly as a formatting trick (to get some indented text). Use style sheets and adjustable margin settings to accomplish formatting tasks.

In Navigator 4, any styles assigned to dt and dd elements by way of the class, id, or style attribute do not work. If you wish to assign the same style attributes to both the dt and dd elements, assign the style to the dl element; otherwise, wrap each dt and dd element with a span element whose styles the nested dt and dd elements inherit. This workaround is observed in IE 4, although it is not necessary for IE-only documents.

### Example

```
<dl>
    <dt>Z-scale</dt>
    <dd>A railroad modeling scale of 1:220. The smallest mass-produced
    commercial model scale.</dd>
</dl>
```

### Object Model Reference

[window.]document.getElementById(*elementID*)

### Element-Specific Attributes

None.

### Element-Specific Event Handler Attributes

None.

# &lt;del&gt;

**NN 6    IE 4    HTML 4**

&lt;del&gt;...&lt;/del&gt;

**HTML End Tag: Required**

The del element and its companion, ins, define a format that shows which segments of a document's content have been marked up for deletion (or insertion) during the authoring process. This is far from a workflow management scheme, but in the hands of a supporting WYSIWYG HTML authoring tool, these elements can assist in controlling generational changes of a document in process.

Text contained by this element is rendered as a strikethrough style (whereas ins elements are underlined). The HTML 4 specification includes two potentially useful attributes for preserving hidden information about the date and time of the alteration and some descriptive text about the change.

**Example**
```
<p>Four score and
<del cite="Fixed the math">eight</del><ins>seven</ins> years ago...</p>
```

**Object Model Reference**
```
[window.]document.getElementById(elementID)
```

**Element-Specific Attributes**
```
cite            datetime
```

**Element-Specific Event Handler Attributes**
None.

## cite                                              NN 6    IE 6    HTML 4

```
cite="text"                                                        Optional
```

A description of the reason for the change or other notation to be associated with the element, but normally hidden from view. In Netscape 6, the context menu for such an element contains a **Properties** choice, which leads to a displayed list of attributes and their values for the visitor. Or, your DHTML scripts can access the information through the element object's cite property, and add value to the presentation.

**Example**          `<del cite="Fixed the math --A.L.">eight</del>`

**Value**            Any string of characters. The string must be inside a matching pair of (single or double) quotation marks.

**Default**          None.

**Object Model Reference**
```
[window.]document.getElementById(elementID).cite
```

## datetime                                          NN 6    IE 6    HTML 4

```
datetime="datetimeString"                                          Optional
```

The date and time the deletion was made. This information is most likely to be inserted into a document with an HTML authoring tool designed to track content insertions and deletions. Data from this attribute can be recalled later as an audit trail to changes of the document. There can be only one datetime attribute value associated with a given del element. In Netscape 6, the context menu for such an element contains a **Properties** choice, which leads to a displayed list of attributes and their values for the visitor. Or, your DHTML scripts can access the information through the element object's dateTime property, and add value to the presentation.

**Example**      `<del datetime="2001-09-11T08:56:00-04:00">`*SomeDeleteTextHere*`</del>`

**Value**

The `datetime` attribute requires a value in a special date-time format that conveys information about the date and time in such a way that the exact moment can be deduced from any time zone around the world. Syntax for the format is as follows: *yyyy-MM-ddThh:mm:ssTZD*.

*yyyy*  Four-digit year

*MM*   Two-digit month (01 through 12)

*dd*   Two-digit date (01 through 31)

*T*    Uppercase "T" to separate date from time

*hh*   Two-digit hour in 24-hour time (00 through 23)

*mm*   Two-digit minute (00 through 59)

*ss*   Two-digit second (00 through 59)

*TZD* Time Zone Designator

There are two formats for the Time Zone Designator. The first is simply the uppercase letter "Z", which stands for UTC (Coordinated Universal Time—also called "Zulu"). The other format indicates the offset from UTC that the time shown in *hh:mm:ss* represents. This time offset consists of a plus or minus symbol and another pair of *hh:mm* values. For time zones west of Greenwich Mean Time (which, for all practical purposes is the same as UTC), the operator is a negative sign because the main *hh:mm:ss* time is earlier than UTC; for time zones east of GMT, the offset is a positive value. For example, Pacific Standard Time is eight hours earlier than UTC: when it is 6:00 P.M. in the PST zone, it is 2:00 A.M. the next morning at UTC. Thus, the following examples all represent the exact same moment in time (Time Zone Designator shown in boldface for clarification only):

| | |
|---|---|
| 2003-01-30T02:00:00**Z** | UTC |
| 2003-01-29T21:00:00**-05:00** | Eastern Standard Time |
| 2003-01-29T18:00:00**-08:00** | Pacific Standard Time |
| 2003-01-30T13:00:00**+11:00** | Sydney, Australia |

For more details about this way of representing time, see the ISO-8601 standard.

**Default**      None.

# \<dfn\>

                      **NN** *6*   **IE** *3*   **HTML** *3.2*

`<dfn>...</dfn>`                    HTML End Tag: Required

The `dfn` element is one of a large group of elements that the HTML 4 recommendation calls *phrase elements*. Such elements assign structural meaning to a designated portion of the document. A `dfn` element signifies the first usage of a term in a document (its defining instance). A common technique in documents is to italicize an important vocabulary term the first time it is used in a document. This is generally the place in the document where the term is defined so that it may be used in subsequent sentences with its meaning understood. By default, mainstream browsers italicize all text within a `dfn` element. You can, of course, easily define your own style for `dfn` elements with a style sheet rule.

### Example

```
<p>Concerto composers usually provide a space for soloists to show off
technical skills while reminding the audience of various themes used
throughout the movement. This part of the concerto is called the <dfn>
cadenza</dfn>.</p>
```

### Object Model Reference

[window.]document.getElementById(*elementID*)

### Element-Specific Attributes

None.

### Element-Specific Event Handler Attributes

None.

# <dir>

NN *all*    IE *all*    HTML *all*

<dir>...</dir>

HTML End Tag: Required

The original idea of the dir element was to allow browsers to generate multicolumn lists of items. Virtually every browser, however, treats the dir element the same as a ul element, to present an unordered single column list of items (usually preceded by a bullet). The dir element is deprecated in HTML 4 and does not validate against strict HTML 4 or XHTML DTDs. You should be using the ul element, in any case, because you are assured backward compatibility and forward compatibility should this element ever disappear from the browser landscape entirely. Everything said here also applies to the deprecated menu element.

### Example

```
Common DB Connector Types:
<dir>
    <li>DB-9</li>
    <li>DB-12</li>
    <li>DB-25</li>
</dir>
```

### Object Model Reference

[window.]document.getElementById(*elementID*)

### Element-Specific Attributes

compact

### Element-Specific Event Handler Attributes

None.

<div>

## compact

compact                                                                    Optional

A Boolean attribute originally designed to let browsers render the list in a more compact style than normal (smaller line spacing between items). In practice, mainstream browsers do not adjust their rendering in response to this attribute.

**Example**              `<dir compact>...</dir>`

**Value**                The presence of this attribute makes its value true.

**Default**              false

# <div>

`<div>...</div>`                                              HTML End Tag: Required

The div element gives structure and context to any block-level content in a document. Unlike some other structural elements that have very specific connotations attached to them (the p element, for instance), the author is free to give meaning to each particular div element by virtue of the element's attribute settings and nested content. Each div element becomes a generic block-level container for all content within the required start and end tags.

It is most convenient to use the div element as a wrapper for multielement content that is to be governed by a single style sheet rule. For example, if a block of content includes three paragraphs, rather than assign a special font style to each of the p elements, you can wrap all three p elements with a single div element whose style sheet defines the requested font style. Such a style sheet could be defined as an inline style attribute of the div element or assigned via the class or id attribute, depending on the structure of the rest of the document.

div elements are block-level elements. If you need an arbitrary container for inline content, use the span element, instead.

**Example**              `<div class="sections" id="section3">...</div>`

**Object Model Reference**
`[window.]document.getElementById(elementID)`

**Element-Specific Attributes**

| | | | | |
|---|---|---|---|---|
| align | datafld | dataformatas | datasrc | nowrap |

**Element-Specific Event Handler Attributes**
None.

## align

align="*alignmentConstant*"                                                Optional

See details for horizontal alignment within a block element in the section "Alignment Constants" at the beginning of this chapter.

**Example**              `<div align="center">Part IV</div>`

**Value**             Constant value. Navigator 4 and later and Internet Explorer 4 and later (Windows) recognize all four constants specified in loose HTML 4: center | left | right | justify. IE 4 for the Macintosh does not recognize the justify setting.

**Default**           left or right, depending on direction of current language.

**Object Model Reference**
[window.]document.getElementById(*elementID*).align

## datafld                                                    NN *n/a*    IE 4    HTML |4|
datafld="*columnName*"                                                              Optional

Used with IE data binding to associate a remote data source column name with the HTML content of a div element. The data source column must be HTML (see dataformatas). datasrc and dataformatas attributes must also be set for the div element. Works only with text file data sources in IE 5/Mac.

This attribute was reserved in HTML 4, but was dropped in XHTML 1.0.

**Example**           &lt;div datasrc="DBSRC3" datafld="sec3" dataformatas="HTML"&gt;&lt;/div&gt;

**Value**             Case-sensitive identifier.

**Default**           None.

**Object Model Reference**
[window.]document.getElementById(*elementID*).dataFld

## dataformatas                                              NN *n/a*    IE 4    HTML |4|
dataformatas="*dataType*"                                                           Optional

Used with IE data binding, this attribute advises the browser whether the source material arriving from the data source is to be treated as plain text or as tagged HTML. A div element should receive data only in HTML format. Works only with text file data sources in IE 5/Mac.

This attribute was reserved in HTML 4, but was dropped in XHTML 1.0.

**Example**           &lt;div datasrc="DBSRC3" datafld="sec3" dataformatas="HTML"&gt;&lt;/div&gt;

**Value**             IE recognizes two possible settings: text | html

**Default**           text

**Object Model Reference**
[window.]document.getElementById(*elementID*).dataFormatAs

<dl>

## datasrc

datasrc="*dataSourceName*"                                                  Optional

Used with IE data binding to specify the ID of the page's object element that loads the data source object for remote data access. Content from the data source is specified via the datafld attribute. Works only with text file data sources in IE 5/Mac.

This attribute was reserved in HTML 4, but was dropped in XHTML 1.0.

| | |
|---|---|
| **Example** | `<div datasrc="DBSRC3" datafld="sec3" dataformatas="HTML"></div>` |
| **Value** | Case-sensitive identifier. |
| **Default** | None. |

### Object Model Reference

[window.]document.getElementById(*elementID*).dataSrc


## nowrap

nowrap                                                                      Optional

The nowrap attribute, unique to IE/Windows for this element, overrides the normal block model for a div element. When the attribute is turned on, text streams to the right unless broken by other interlaced elements. Indiscriminate use may lead to excessively wide pages that force users to scroll horizontally over long distances.

| | |
|---|---|
| **Example** | `<div id="bigBlock" nowrap>...</div>` |
| **Value** | The presence of the attribute sets its value to true. |
| **Default** | false |


# <dl>

<dl>...</dl>                                                         HTML End Tag: Required

The dl element is a part of the dl, dt, dd triumvirate of elements used to create a definition list in a document. The entire list is bracketed by the dl element's tags. Each definition term is denoted by a leading dt element tag, and the definition for the term is denoted by a leading dd element tag. A schematic of a definition list sequence for three items looks like the following:

```
<dl>
    <dt>Term 1</dt>
    <dd>Definition 1</dd>
    <dt>Term 2</dt>
    <dd>Definition 2</dd>
    <dt>Term 3</dt>
    <dd>Definition 3</dd>
</dl>
```

The entire list must close with an end tag for the encapsulating dl element. Note that the dl element is the container of the entire list, which means that inheritable style sheet rules assigned to the dl element apply to the nested dt and dd elements. Unwanted inheritances can be overridden in the dt and dd elements.

Although the HTML specification forces no particular way of rendering a definition list, Navigator and Internet Explorer are in agreement in left-aligning a dt element and indenting any dd element that follows it. No special font formatting or visual elements are added by the browser, but you are free (if not encouraged) to assign styles as you like. If you want to stack multiple terms and/or definitions, you can place multiple dt and/or dd elements right after each other in the source code.

Because HTML is being geared toward context-sensitive tagging, avoid using definition lists strictly as a formatting trick (to get some indented text). Use style sheets and adjustable margin settings to accomplish formatting.

**Example**
```
<dl>
    <dt>Z-scale</dt>
    <dd>A railroad modeling scale of 1:220. The smallest mass-produced
    commercial model scale.</dd>
</dl>
```

**Object Model Reference**
[window.]document.getElementById(*elementID*)

**Element-Specific Attributes**
compact

**Element-Specific Event Handler Attributes**
None.

---

## compact                                                   NN 3    IE 3    HTML 3.2

compact                                                                     Optional

When set to true (by virtue of its presence in the dl element tag), the compact Boolean attribute instructs the browser to render a related dt and dd pair on the same line if space allows. The criterion for determining this space (as worked out in both Navigator and Internet Explorer) is related to the amount of indentation normally assigned to a dd element (indentation size differs slightly with operating system). With compact turned on, if the dt element is narrower than the indentation space, the dd element is raised from the line below and displayed on the same line as its dt element. Because the width of characters in proportional fonts varies so widely, there is no hard-and-fast rule about the number of characters of a dt element that lets the dd element come on the same line. But this compact styling is intended for dt elements consisting of only a few characters. This attribute is deprecated in HTML 4, and does not validate in strict HTML 4 or XHTML.

**Example**           `<dl compact>`*ListItems*`</dl>`

**Value**             Presence of the attribute name enables the feature.

**Default**           Off.

---

<!DOCTYPE>

**Object Model Reference**

[window.]document.getElementById(*elementID*).compact

# <!DOCTYPE>                                    NN *all*    IE *all*    HTML *3.2*

`<!DOCTYPE...>`                                    HTML End Tag: Forbidden

The DOCTYPE element is not an HTML element, but rather a comment in the Standard Generalized Markup Language (SGML) format (as are so-called HTML comments in the `<!-- ... -->` style). This element must be the first element in a document, except as noted below for XHTML documents, and must always precede the `<html>` tag element. It advises the browser as to the document type definition (DTD) that the HTML source code is designed to follow. All browsers have a default document type that defines which elements and element attributes the browser supports (and that the browser has the internal programming to support—buggy or otherwise). Specifying a document type for a more modern DTD does not empower an older browser to support elements and attributes for which it is not coded. Conversely, specifying a constricted DTD does not prevent a browser from recognizing and supporting backward-compatible or proprietary elements and attributes.

A DOCTYPE element contains several unlabeled attribute values that specify such details as the name for the outermost document tag (html for our purposes), the organization responsible for the DTD, the address of the actual DTD file (called a *system identifier*), a plain-language name for the definition (including version number, if necessary), and the like. For example, the following DOCTYPE refers to an HTML 4.01 DTD that includes all deprecated elements and attributes:

```
<!DOCTYPE HTML PUBLIC "-//W3C//DTD HTML 4.01 Transitional//EN"
    "http://www.w3.org/TR/html401/loose.dtd">
```

The next example points to the XHTML 1.1 DTD, which does not include deprecated items nor frames:

```
<!DOCTYPE html PUBLIC "-//W3C//DTD XHTML 1.1//EN"
    "http://www.w3.org/TR/xhtml11/DTD/xhtml11.dtd">
```

Additionally, if you specify an XHTML DTD, you should include one of the following SGML-processing instruction tags prior to the DOCTYPE declaration:

```
<?xml version="1.0"?>
<?xml version="1.0" encoding="UTF-8"?>
```

The latter version includes a setting for character set encoding, which may alternatively be set in a `<meta>` tag. The W3C HTML and XHTML validators encourage documents to declare their character-encoding type in one way or the other.

For the most part, web authors include a DOCTYPE element to facilitate validation of the HTML source code prior to publication on the Web. But some modern browsers behave slightly differently based on the details of the DOCTYPE comment at the start of the document. Both IE 6 and Netscape 6 operate in one of two "modes," depending on the details of the DOCTYPE attribute values. One mode points to backward compatibility with implementations that came before, and diverge from, the W3C standards; the other mode causes the browser to behave more in keeping with W3C recommendations. The differences between the two modes lay primarily in fine layout details that are more carefully defined in modern-day CSS and DOM specifications. For simple layouts, you probably won't notice the difference in modes. But if your pages rely upon style sheets or backgrounds for tables, form control alignment (especially in tables), precise font sizing or spacing, and, in IE, pixel-perfect CSS positioning with respect to the document edges and positioned element sizes, you need to pay attention to the DOCTYPE details in your documents.

It is difficult to guide you through every compatibility detail, but a couple of broad recommendations should keep you on track. First, if you are pleased with the layouts of your current pages or templates, you will probably be best served by continuing to use DOCTYPE settings that keep you in backward-compatible mode (the Mozilla engineers call it "quirks" mode; Microsoft has no particular name for the mode). But if you are generating new content, especially for the newer browsers (ideally, Version 6 or later), you should gravitate toward the "strict" (Navigator) or "standards-compatible" (IE) mode settings.

The number of DOCTYPE attribute values in common use today is mind boggling, and the rules that govern which attributes force each browser into a particular mode are not 100% in sync across browsers. But here are a few of the more common DOCTYPE tags that force Version 6 browsers into backward-compatible mode, regardless of browser:

```
<!DOCTYPE HTML PUBLIC "-//W3C//DTD HTML 3.2 Final//EN">
<!DOCTYPE HTML PUBLIC "-//IETF//DTD HTML 3.0//EN">
<!DOCTYPE HTML PUBLIC "-//W3C//DTD HTML 4.01 Transitional//EN">
```

A couple of points worth noting. First, all of the above examples declare HTML DTDs no later than HTML 4.01, and none are XHTML. Second, none of the above examples includes a system identifier URI to a reference *.dtd* file. Also, if you omit the DOCTYPE element entirely, the browser applies the equivalent of the old internal DTDs.

Now here are common DOCTYPE tags that force Version 6 browsers into the modern, standards-based mode:

```
<!DOCTYPE HTML PUBLIC "-//W3C//DTD HTML 4.0 Transitional//EN"
        "http://www.w3.org/TR/REC-html40/loose.dtd">
<!DOCTYPE HTML PUBLIC "-//W3C//DTD HTML 4.0 Frameset//EN"
        "http://www.w3.org/TR/REC-html40/frameset.dtd">
<!DOCTYPE HTML PUBLIC "-//W3C//DTD HTML 4.0//EN"
        "http://www.w3.org/TR/REC-html40/strict.dtd">
<!DOCTYPE html PUBLIC "-//W3C//DTD XHTML 1.0 Transitional//EN"
        "http://www.w3.org/TR/xhtml1/DTD/xhtml1-transitional.dtd">
<!DOCTYPE html PUBLIC "-//W3C//DTD XHTML 1.0 Frameset//EN"
        "http://www.w3.org/TR/xhtml1/DTD/xhtml1-frameset.dtd">
<!DOCTYPE html PUBLIC "-//W3C//DTD XHTML 1.0 Strict//EN"
        "http://www.w3.org/TR/xhtml1/DTD/xhtml1-strict.dtd">
<!DOCTYPE html PUBLIC "-//W3C//DTD XHTML 1.1//EN"
        "http://www.w3.org/TR/xhtml11/DTD/xhtml11.dtd">
```

All HTML 4.x/strict and XHTML DTDs switch on standards-compatible mode, with or without the URLs. Including the URL with HTML 4.x transitional and frameset DTDs invokes the standards-compatible mode.

To learn more about the impact of the DTD choice on DOM and CSS features in the latest browsers, see Chapter 9 (client- and offset- properties, the body object, the document. compatMode property) and Chapter 10 (height and width attributes). Appendix E shows

<dt>

which HTML 4 elements and attributes are supported by each of the most popular HTML 4.01 and XHTML 1.0 DTDs for validation purposes.

### Object Model Reference

[window.]document.firstChild

### Element-Specific Attributes

Attributes are unlabeled.

### Element-Specific Event Handler Attributes

None.

# <dt>

NN *all*    IE *all*    HTML *all*

<dt>...</dt>                                                                      HTML End Tag: Optional

The dt element is a part of the dl, dt, dd triumvirate of elements used to create a definition list in a document. The entire list is bracketed by the dl element's tags. Each definition term is denoted by a leading dt element tag, and the definition for the term is denoted by a leading dd element tag. A schematic of a definition list sequence for three items looks like the following:

```
<dl>
    <dt>Term 1</dt>
    <dd>Definition 1</dd>
    <dt>Term 2</dt>
    <dd>Definition 2</dd>
    <dt>Term 3</dt>
    <dd>Definition 3</dd>
</dl>
```

A dt element is an inline element, whereas a dd element can contain block-level content, including bordered text, images, and other objects. End tags are optional in HTML for both dt and dd elements because the next start tag automatically signals the end of the preceding element. The entire list, however, must close with an end tag for the encapsulating dl element.

Although the HTML specification forces no particular way of rendering a definition list, Navigator and Internet Explorer are in agreement in left-aligning a dt element and indenting any dd element that follows it. No special font formatting or visual elements are added by the browser, but you are free (if not encouraged) to assign styles as you like. If you want to stack multiple terms and/or definitions, you can place multiple dt and/or dd elements right after each other in the source code.

Because HTML is being geared toward context-sensitive tagging, avoid using definition lists strictly as a formatting trick (to get some indented text). Use style sheets and adjustable margin settings to accomplish formatting.

In Navigator 4, any styles assigned to dt and dd elements by way of the class, id, or style attribute do not work. If you wish to assign the same style attributes to both the dt and dd elements, assign the style to the dl element; otherwise, wrap each dt and dd element with a

<em>

span element whose styles the nested dt and dd elements inherit. This workaround is observed in IE 4, although it is not necessary for IE 4-only documents.

**Example**
```
<dl>
    <dt>Z-scale</dt>
    <dd>A railroad modeling scale of 1:220. The smallest mass-produced
    commercial model scale.</dd>
</dl>
```

**Object Model Reference**
[window.]document.getElementById(*elementID*)

**Element-Specific Attributes**
None.

**Element-Specific Event Handler Attributes**
None.

# <em>                                    NN *all*    IE *all*    HTML *all*

<em>...</em>                                              HTML End Tag: Required

The em element is one of a large group of elements that the HTML 4 recommendation calls *phrase elements*. Such elements assign structural meaning to a designated portion of the document. An em element is one that is to be rendered differently from running body text to designate emphasis.

Browsers have free rein to determine how (or whether) to distinguish em element content from the rest of the body element. Both Navigator and Internet Explorer elect to italicize the text. Override the default with a style sheet as you see fit.

**Example**
```
<p>The night was dark, and the river's churning waters were <em>very</em>
cold.</p>
```

**Object Model Reference**
[window.]document.getElementById(*elementID*)

**Element-Specific Attributes**
None.

**Element-Specific Event Handler Attributes**
None.

<embed>

# <embed>

<embed>...</embed>

An embed element allows you to load media and file types other than those natively rendered by the browser. Typically, such external data requires a plugin or helper application to properly load the data and display its file. Notice that this element has been supported by both Navigator and Internet Explorer since Versions 2 and 3, respectively, but the element never became a part of the HTML standard vocabulary. The HTML 4 specification recommends the object element as the one to load the kind of external data covered by the embed element in the browsers. Navigator 4 and later and Internet Explorer 4 and later also support the object element, and you should gravitate toward that element for embedded elements if your visitor browser base can support it.

Bear in mind that for data types that launch plugins, the control panel displayed for the data varies widely among browsers, operating systems, and the plugins the user has installed for that particular data type. It is risky business trying to carefully design a layout combining a plugin's control panel and surrounding text or other elements.

The list of attributes for the embed element is a long one, but pay special attention to the browser compatibility rating for each attribute. Because the plugin technologies for IE/Windows, IE/Mac, and Navigator are not identical, neither are the attribute sets. Even so, it is possible to assign an embed element in one document that works on both browser brands when the embedded element does not rely on an attribute setting not supported in one of the browsers. Some plugins, however, may require or accept attribute name/value pairs that are not listed for this element. At least in the case of Navigator, all attributes (including those normally ignored by the browser) and their values are passed to the plugin. Therefore, you must also check with the documentation for a plugin to determine what, if any, extra attributes may be supported. The object element gets around this object-specific attribute problem by letting you add any number of param elements tailored to the object.

The end tag is required in Internet Explorer but is optional in Navigator.

## Example

<embed name="jukebox" src="jazz.aif" height="100" width="200"></embed>

## Object Model Reference

[window.]document.embeds[elementName]
[window.]document.getElementById(elementID)

## Element-Specific Attributes

| | | | | |
|---|---|---|---|---|
| align | alt | height | hidden | name |
| pluginspage | pluginurl | src | type | units |
| width | | | | |

## Element-Specific Event Handler Attributes

None.

## align

align="*where*"                                                                    **Optional**

If the embedded object (or player control panel) occupies space on the page, the align attribute determines how the object is rendered in physical relation to the element's next outermost container. If some additional text is specified between the start and end tags of the embed element, the align attribute also affects how that text is rendered relative to the object's rectangular space.

Most of the rules for alignment-constant values cited at the beginning of this chapter apply to the embed element. Precise layout becomes difficult because the HTML page author usually isn't in control of the plugin control panel that is displayed on the page. Dimensions for the element that work fine for one control panel are totally inappropriate for another.

Typically, align attributes are deprecated in HTML 4 in favor of the align style sheet attribute. But if you are using the embed element for backward compatibility, stick with the align attribute.

### Example

```
<embed src="jazz.aif" align="left" height="100" width="200"></embed>
```

### Value

Each browser defines a different set of values for this attribute. Select the one(s) from the following table that work for your deployment:

| Value | NN | IE |
| --- | --- | --- |
| absbottom | – | • |
| absmiddle | – | • |
| baseline | – | • |
| bottom | • | • |
| left | • | • |
| middle | • | • |
| right | • | • |
| texttop | – | • |
| top | • | • |

**Default**            bottom

### Object Model Reference

```
[window.]document.embeds[elementName].align
[window.]document.getElementById(elementID).align
```

## alt

alt="*textMessage*"                                                    Optional

If Internet Explorer does not have the facilities to load and run the external media, the text assigned to the alt attribute is supposed to display in the document where the embed element's tag appears. Typically, this text provides advice on what the page visitor is missing by not being able to load the data (although IE also presents a dialog about how to get plugin information from an online source).

Use the alt attribute with care. If the external data is not a critical part of your page's content, you may just want the rest of the page to load without calling attention to the missing media controller in lesscapable browsers. The alternate message may be more disturbing to the user than a missing media player.

The equivalent powers are available in Navigator with the noembed element.

**Example**

<embed src="jazz.aif" alt="Sound media player" height="10" width="20"></embed>

**Value**          Any quoted string of characters.

**Default**        None.

## height, width

height="*length*"                                                     Required
width="*length*"

The size that an embedded object (or its plugin control panel) occupies in a document is governed by the height and width attribute settings. Some browser versions might allow you to get away without assigning these attributes, letting the plugin's own user interface design determine the height and width of its visible rectangle. It is best to specify the exact dimensions of a plugin's control panel whenever possible. (Control panels vary with each browser and even between different plugins for the same browser.) In some cases, such as Navigator 4 for the Macintosh, the control panel does not display if you fail to supply enough height on the page for the control panel. If you assign values that are larger than the actual control panel, the browser reserves that empty space on the page, which could interfere with your intended page design.

**Example**          <embed src="jazz.aif" height="150" width="250"></embed>

**Value**

Positive integer values (optionally quoted) or percentage values (quoted). You cannot entirely hide an embedded object's control panel by setting values to zero (one pixel always shows and occupies space), but you can reduce its height and width to one pixel in each dimension. If you want to hide a plugin, do so with DHTML by setting its positioning display attribute to none.

**Default**          None.

**Object Model Reference**

```
[window.]document.embeds[i].height
[window.]document.getElementById(elementID).height
[window.]document.embeds[i].width
[window.]document.getElementById(elementID).width
```

## hidden

NN &lt;6    IE 4    HTML n/a

`hidden="true" | "false"`                                              Optional

Predating style sheet borders, the hidden attribute is a switch that lets you set whether the embedded data's plugin control panel appears on the screen. This might be desirable for background music under script control (via Netscape's LiveConnect). When you set the hidden attribute, the height and width attributes are overridden.

**Example**          `<embed src="soothing.aif" hidden="true"></embed>`

**Value**            true | false

**Default**          false

**Object Model Reference**

```
[window.]document.embeds[i].hidden
[window.]document.getElementById(elementID).hidden
```

## name

NN 2    IE 3    HTML n/a

`name="elementIdentifier"`                                             Optional

If you are scripting a plugin (especially in Navigator via LiveConnect), it is usually more convenient to create a reference to the embedded element by using a unique name you assign to the item. Thus, if you edit the page and move or delete multiple embed elements on the page, you do not have to worry about adjusting index values to array-style references (document.embeds[embedName]).

**Example**
`<embed name="jukebox" id="jukebox" src="jazz.aif" height="15" width="25"></embed>`

**Value**            Case-sensitive identifier.

**Default**          None.

**Object Model Reference**

```
[window.]document.embeds[i].name
[window.]document.getElementById(elementID).name
```

## pluginspage

NN &lt;6    IE 4    HTML n/a

`pluginspage="URL"`                                                    Optional

If the MIME type of the data file assigned to the embed element's src attribute is not supported by an existing plugin or helper application in the browser, the pluginspage attribute is intended to provide a URL for downloading and installing the necessary plugin.

If you omit this attribute, Navigator 4 presents a generic link to Netscape's own resource listing of plugin vendors.

**Example**

```
<embed name="jukebox" src="jazz.aif" height="150" width="250"
pluginspage="http://www.giantco.com/plugin/install/index.html">
</embed>
```

**Value**         Any valid URL.

**Default**       None.

## pluginurl                                       NN |4|   IE *n/a*   HTML *n/a*

`pluginurl="URL"`                                                         Optional

Navigator 4 (only) introduced the power (a feature called Smart Update) to allow somewhat automatic installation of browser components. If a user does not have the necessary plugin installed for your embed element's data type, the pluginurl can point to a Java Archive (JAR) file that contains the plugin and digitally signed objects to satisfy security issues surrounding automatic installation (via Netscape's Java Installation Manager). A JAR file is both digitally signed and compressed (very much along the lines of a *.zip* file), and is created with the help of Netscape's JAR Packager tool.

You can include both the pluginspage and pluginurl attributes in an embed element's tag to handle the appropriate browser version. Navigator 2 and 3 respond to the pluginspage attribute, whereas Navigator 4 gives precedence to the pluginurl attribute when it is present.

**Example**

```
<embed name="jukebox" src="jazz.aif" height="150" width="250"
pluginurl="http://www.giantco.com/plugin/install.jar">
</embed>
```

**Value**         Any valid URL to a JAR file.

**Default**       None.

## src                                              NN *2*   IE *3*   HTML *n/a*

`src="URL"`                                                              Optional

The src attribute is a URL to a file containing data that is played through the plugin. For most uses of the embed element, this attribute is required, but there are some circumstances in which it may not be necessary (see the type attribute). Browsers typically use the filename extension to determine which plugin to load (based on browser preferences settings for plugins and helper applications).

**Example**

```
<embed name="babyClip" src="Ugachaka.avi" height="150" width="250"></embed>
```

**Value**         A complete or relative URL.

**Default**       None.

<embed>

**Object Model Reference**

[window.]document.embeds[i].src
[window.]document.getElementById(*elementID*).src

## type

NN *2*   IE *n/a*   HTML *n/a*

type="*MIMEtype*"

Optional

Navigator anticipated the potential of a plugin not requiring any outside data file. Instead, such a plugin would more closely resemble an applet. If such a plugin is to be put into your document, you still use the embed element but specify just the MIME type instead of the data file URL (in the src attribute). This assumes, of course, that the MIME type is of such a special nature that only one possible plugin would be mapped to that MIME type in the browser settings. Either the src or type attribute must be present in a Navigator embed element tag.

**Example**

<embed src="hooha.fbz" type="application/x-frobnitz" height="150" width="250"></embed>

**Value**

Any valid MIME type name as a quoted string, including the type and subtype portions delimited by a forward slash. A catalog of registered MIME types is available from *ftp://ftp.isi.edu/in-notes/iana/assignments/media-types/*.

**Default**        None.

## units

NN *<6*   IE *3*   HTML *n/a*

units="*measurementUnitType*"

Optional

The units attribute is supposed to dictate the kind of measurement units used for the element's height and width attribute values. Both Navigator 4 and Internet Explorer appear to treat the measurements in pixels, regardless of this attribute's setting.

**Example**        <embed src="jazz.aif" height="150" width="250" units="en"></embed>

**Value**

Not only does this attribute not appear to influence the rendering of an embed element, but Navigator 4 and Internet Explorer 4 disagree on the precise spelling and available units for values. Navigator 4 specifies choices of pixels or en; Internet Explorer goes with px or em.

**Default**        pixels (or px).

**Object Model Reference**

[window.]document.embeds[i].units
[window.]document.getElementById(*elementID*).units

## width

See height.

<fieldset>

# <fieldset>

**NN 6**   **IE 4**   **HTML 4**

`<fieldset>...</fieldset>`

**HTML End Tag: Required**

A fieldset element is a structural container for form elements (as distinguished from the functional containment of the form element). In fact, you can define multiple fieldset elements within a single form element to supply context to logical groupings of form elements. For example, one fieldset element might contain text input fields for name and address info; another fieldset might be dedicated to credit card information.

Supporting browsers boost the attractiveness of this element by automatically drawing a rule around the form elements within each fieldset container. You can also attach a label that gets embedded within the rule by defining a legend element immediately after the start tag of a fieldset element. By default, the box extends the full width of the next outermost container geography—usually the document body or html element. If you'd rather have the box cinch up around the visible form elements, you have to set the width style sheet property for the element.

### Example

```
<form method="POST" action="...">
<fieldset>
<legend>Credit Card Information</legend>
...inputElementsHere...
</fieldset>
</form>
```

### Object Model Reference

`[window.]document.getElementById(elementID)`

### Element-Specific Attributes

align

### Element-Specific Event Handler Attributes

None.

## align

**NN n/a**   **IE 4**   **HTML n/a**

`align="where"`

**Optional**

The align attribute appears only in Internet Explorer, and its implementation is far from consistent across operating systems. In theory, the attribute should control the alignment of input elements it contains. This is true in the Macintosh version of IE, but in the Windows version (especially in IE 6), the settings have minor effect on the fieldset element rule. It is best to let the default setting take precedence, and override with style sheets.

| | |
|---|---|
| **Example** | `<fieldset align="right">...</fieldset>` |
| **Value** | Allowed values are left \| center \| right. |
| **Default** | left |

### Object Model Reference

`[window.]document.getElementById(elementID).align`

# &lt;font&gt;

&lt;font&gt;...&lt;/font&gt;                                                                HTML End Tag: Required

A font element is a container whose contents are rendered with the font characteristics defined by the element's attributes. This element is deprecated in HTML 4 in favor of font attributes available in style sheets that are applied directly to other elements or the arbitrary span container for inline font changes. This element will be supported for a long time to come to allow backward compatibility with web pages designed for older browsers, however.

For nested tables in Navigator 4, style sheet inheritance frequently breaks down. Inserting font wrappers around content inside a td element can fortify your control over the design. Going forward, use font elements only as a last resort if a browser version balks at obeying CSS font rules.

The font element evolved over its lifetime, adding new attributes along the way to work in the more mature browsers. Navigator included some proprietary attributes for Version 4 (only) that are better served by style sheets for cross-browser compatibility.

**Example**          &lt;font face="Times, serif" size="4"&gt;

**Object Model Reference**
[window.]document.getElementById(*elementID*)

**Element-Specific Attributes**

color              face              point-size        size              weight

**Element-Specific Event Handler Attributes**
None.

## color

color="*colorTripletOrName*"                                                          Optional

Sets the font color of all text contained by the font element. This attribute is deprecated in HTML 4 in favor of style sheets.

**Example**          &lt;font color="Olive"&gt;...&lt;/font&gt;

**Value**            A hexadecimal triplet or plain-language color name. See Appendix A for
                     acceptable plain-language color names.

**Default**          Browser default.

**Object Model Reference**
[window.]document.getElementById(*elementID*).color

## face

`face="`*`fontFamilyName1[, ... fontFamilyNameN]`*`"`                    Optional

You can assign a hierarchy of font families to use for a segment of text contained by a font element. The browser looks for the first font family in the comma-delimited list of font family names until it either finds a match on the client system or runs out of choices, at which point the browser default font family is used. Font family names must match the system font family names exactly. If you use this attribute (instead of the preferred font-family style sheet attribute), you can always suggest a generic font face (serif, sans-serif) as the final choice.

**Example**          `<font face="Bookman, Times Roman, serif">...</font>`

**Value**            One or more font family names, including the recognized generic faces:
                     serif | sans-serif | cursive | fantasy | monospace.

**Default**          Browser default.

**Object Model Reference**

`[window.]document.getElementById(`*`elementID`*`).face`

## point-size

`point-size="`*`pointSize`*`"`                    Optional

The `point-size` attribute is Navigator 4's nonCSS equivalent of setting the font size by specific point size (rather than by relative font size directed by the `size` attribute). If you assign a value to the `point-size` attribute and set the `font-size` style attribute, the style attribute takes precedence. If you are aiming for cross-browser deployment, I suggest using style sheets exclusively for precise point or pixel sizes.

**Example**          `<font point-size="14">...</font>`

**Value**            A positive integer, representing the desired point size.

**Default**          Browser default.

## size

`size="`*`integerOrRelativeSize`*`"`                    Optional

Font sizes referenced by the `size` attribute are the relative size scale that is not tied to any one point size across operating system platforms. The default browser font size is 3. The range of acceptable values for the `size` attribute are integers from 1 to 7 inclusive. The exact point size varies with the operating system and browser design.

Users can often adjust the default font size in preferences settings. The `size` attribute overrides that setting. Moreover, `size` values can be relative to whatever font size is set in the preferences. By preceding an attribute value with a + or – sign, the browser's default size can be adjusted upward or downward, but always within the range of 1 through 7.

<form>

### Example

```
<font size="4">...</font>
<font size="+3">...</font>
```

### Value

Either an integer (quoted or not quoted) or a quoted relative value consisting of a + or – symbol and an integer value.

### Default                3

### Object Model Reference

```
[window.]document.getElementById(elementID).size
```

## weight                                    NN |4|    IE n/a    HTML n/a

`weight="boldnessValue"`                                              Optional

The weight attribute is Navigator 4's nonCSS equivalent of setting the font weight with a regular attribute rather than by style sheet rule. The attribute is unreliable, so the font-weight CSS style attribute is a better choice.

### Value                  Integer value between 100 and 900 in increments of 100. A value of 900 is the maximum boldness setting.

### Default                Unknown.

##  <form>                           NN all    IE all    HTML all

`<form>...</form>`                                         HTML End Tag: Required

Despite the importance of HTML forms in communication between web page visitors and the server, a form element at its heart is nothing more than a container of controls. Most, but not all, form controls are created in the document as input elements. Even if user interaction with input elements is not intended for submission to a server (perhaps some client-side scripting requires interaction with the user), such input elements are contained by a form element—and must be nested inside a form element to render at all in Navigator 4 or earlier.

A document may contain any number of form elements, but a client may submit the settings of controls from only one form at a time. Therefore, the only time it makes sense to divide a series of form controls into multiple form elements is when the control groups can be submitted independently of each other. If you need to logically or structurally group controls while maintaining a single form, use the fieldset element to create the necessary subgroupings of controls.

When a form is submitted to the server, all controls that have name attributes assigned to them pass both their names and values—in name/value pairs—to the server for further processing (or possibly as an email attachment or message with the help of a browser's e-mail module). A Common Gateway Interface (CGI) program running on the server can accept and dissect the name/value pairs for further processing (adding a record to a server database or initiating a keyword search, for example). The server program is invoked via URL to the program assigned to the action attribute.

Inside browsers, the submission process consists of a few well-defined steps. The process begins with the browser assembling a form data set out of the name/value pairs of form controls. The name comes from the value assigned to the name attribute. A control's value depends on the type of control. For example, a text input element's value is the content appearing in the text box at submission time; for a radio button within a radio group (all of whose name attributes are assigned the same value), the value assigned to the value attribute of the selected radio button is inserted into the name/value pair for the radio group.

The W3C recommendations prefer that form controls use their id attributes in name/value pairs. As of Version 6 browsers, however, only the name attribute is recognized as an identifier for the submitted name/value pair.

The second step of submission encodes the text of each name/value pair. A + symbol is substituted for each space character. Reserved characters (as defined by RFC 1738) are escaped, and all other nonalphanumeric characters are converted to hexadecimal representations (in the form %HH, where HH is the hex code for the ASCII value of the character). Name and value components of each name/value pair are separated by an = symbol, and each name/value pair is delimited with an ampersand (&).

In the final step, the method attribute setting determines how the escaped form data set is transmitted to the server. With a method of get, the form data set is appended to the URL stated in the action attribute, separated by a ? symbol. With a method of post and a default enctype, the data set is transmitted as a kind of (non-email) message to the server. Data submitted via the GET method is limited in character length, while the POST method offers unlimited data length and no echoed display in the browser's Address box.

Default behavior of the **Enter** key in forms has evolved into a recognized standard. When a form consists of a single text input element, pressing the **Enter** (or **Return**) key automatically submits the form (as if the user had clicked on a submit button element. If the form consists of two or more text input elements, the **Enter** (or **Return**) key does not automatically submit the form (with the exception of IE/Mac).

Form submission can be canceled in modern browsers with the help of scripts that perform validation checking or other functions triggered by the onsubmit event handler. This event fires prior to the form being submitted. If the event handler evaluates to return false, the form is not submitted, and the user may continue to edit the form elements.

### Example

```
<form name="orders" method="POST" action="http://www.giantco.com/cgi-bin/order">
...
</form>
```

### Object Model Reference

```
[window.]document.forms[i]
[window.]document.forms[formName]
[window.]document.formName
[window.]document.getElementById(elementID)
```

### Element-Specific Attributes

| | | | | |
|---|---|---|---|---|
| accept | accept-charset | acceptcharset | action | autocomplete |
| enctype | method | name | target | |

Alphabetical HTML Reference

**Element-Specific Event Handler Attributes**

| Handler | NN | IE | HTML |
|---------|-----|-----|------|
| onreset | 3 | 4 | 4 |
| onsubmit | 2 | 3 | 4 |

## accept                                     NN *n/a*   IE *n/a*   HTML *4*

accept="*MIMETypeList*"                                          Optional

Intended for use with input elements of type file, the accept attribute lets you specify one or more MIME types for allowable files to be uploaded to the server when the form is submitted. The predicted implementation of this attribute would filter the file types listed in file dialogs used to select files for uploading. In a way, this attribute provides client-side validation of a file type so that files not conforming to the permitted MIME type are not even sent to the server.

**Example**      &lt;form accept="text/html, image/gif" ...&gt;...&lt;/form&gt;

**Value**        Case-insensitive MIME type (content type) value. For multiple items, a
                 comma-delimited list is allowed. A catalog of registered MIME types is
                 available from *ftp://ftp.isi.edu/in-notes/iana/assignments/media-types/*.

**Default**      None.

## accept-charset, acceptcharset              NN *6*   IE *5*   HTML *4*

accept-charset="*MIMETypeList*"                                 Optional

A server advisory (for servers that are equipped to interpret the information) about which character sets it must receive from a client form. The hyphenated version is from the HTML 4 specification, but IE 5 and later/Windows and Netscape 6 implement the attribute name without the hyphen.

**Example**      &lt;form accept-charset="it, es" ...&gt;...&lt;/form&gt;

**Value**

Case-insensitive alias from the character set registry (*ftp://ftp.isi.edu/in-notes/iana/ assignments/character-sets*). Multiple character sets may be delimited by commas. The reserved value, unknown, is supposed to represent the character set that the server used to generate the form for the client.

**Default**      unknown

## action                                     NN *all*   IE *all*   HTML *all*

action="*URL*"                                                   Optional

Specifies the URL to be accessed when the form is being submitted. When the form is submitted to a server for further processing, the URL may be to a CGI program or to an HTML page that includes server-side scripts. (Those scripts execute on the server before

---

the HTML page is downloaded to the client.) As a result of the submission, the server returns an HTML page for display in the client. If the returned display is to be delivered to a different frame or window, the target attribute must be specified accordingly.

You may also substitute a mailto: URL for the action attribute value. Navigator turns the name/value pairs of the form into a document for attachment to an email message (or as the message body with the enctype attribute set to "text/plain" and the enctype attribute precedes the action attribute). For privacy reasons, client users are notified of the impending email transmission and have the chance to cancel the message.

Form-mailing capabilities are essentially disabled in Netscape 6 and 7. Implementations across all browsers are very uneven—you may be missing form submissions from many users. If CGI processing of forms is beyond your expertise, search for third-party Form-Mail services that forward forms to you via email.

If you omit the action attribute and the form is submitted, the current page reloads itself, returning all form elements to their default values.

**Example**

```
<form method="POST" action="http://www.giantco.com/orders/order.html">
```

**Value**    A complete or relative URL.

**Default**    None.

**Object Model Reference**

```
[window.]document.forms[i].action
[window.]document.forms[formName].action
[window.]document.formName.action
[window.]document.getElementById(elementID).action
```

## autocomplete                                          NN *n/a*    IE 5    HTML *n/a*

autocomplete="*featureSwitch*"                                              Optional

If an IE user has automatic form completion preference enabled, the autocomplete attribute governs the feature for the entire form. You must also specify vcard-name attributes for text and password type input elements to let the browser pre-fill or assist the entry of a particular named field that matches one of the preferences entries.

**Example**        `<form method="POST" action="register.pl" autocomplete="on">`

**Value**          Constants: on | off.

**Default**        off

**Object Model Reference**

```
[window.]document.forms[i].autoComplete
[window.]document.forms[formName].autoComplete
[window.]document.formName.autoComplete
[window.]document.getElementById(elementID).autoComplete
```

## enctype

NN *all*    IE *all*    HTML *all*

enctype="*MIMEType*"                                                        Optional

Sets a MIME type for the data being submitted to the server with the form. For typical form submissions (where the method attribute is set to POST), the default value is the proper content type. If you include a file input element, specify "multipart/form-data" as the enctype attribute.

### Example

```
<form method="POST" enctype="text/plain" action="mailto:orders@giantco.com">
...
</form>
```

### Value

MIME type (content type) value. For multiple items, a comma-delimited list is allowed.

**Default**          application/x-www-form-urlencoded

### Object Model Reference

```
[window.]document.forms[i].encoding
[window.]document.forms[formName].encoding
[window.]document.formName.encoding
[window.]document.getElementById(elementID).encoding
```

## method

NN *all*    IE *all*    HTML *all*

method="GET" | "POST"                                                       Optional

Forms may be submitted via two possible HTTP methods: GET and POST. These methods determine whether the form element data is sent to the server appended to the action attribute URL (GET) or as a transaction message body (POST). In practice, when the action and method attributes are not assigned in a form element, the form performs an unconditional reload of the same document, restoring form controls to their default values.

### Example

```
<form method="POST" action="http://www@giantco.com/orders/order.html">
...
</form>
```

### Value

Constant values of GET or POST. Browsers respond to upper- or lowercase values.

**Default**          GET

### Object Model Reference

```
[window.]document.forms[i].method
[window.]document.forms[formName].method
[window.]document.formName.method
[window.]document.getElementById(elementID).method
```

## name NN *2*   IE *3*   HTML *n/a*

name="*elementIdentifier*" Optional

Assigns an identifier to the entire form element. This value is particularly useful in writing scripts for older browsers that reference the form or its nested controls. Newer browsers support the preferred id attribute for this purpose, but the name attribute is still needed for form submission.

### Example

```
<form name="orders" id="orders" method="POST"
action="http://www.giantco.com/cgi-bin/order">
...
</form>
```

**Value**          Case-sensitive identifier.

**Default**        None.

### Object Model Reference

```
[window.]document.forms[i].name
[window.]document.forms[formName].name
[window.]document.formName.name
[window.]document.getElementById(elementID).name
```

## target NN *all*   IE *all*   HTML *all*

target="*windowOrFrameName*" Optional

If the HTML document returned from the server after it processes the form submission is to be loaded into a window or frame other than the current window or frame, you can specify where the returned document should load by assigning a window or frame name to the target attribute. Target frame names must be assigned to frames and windows as identifiers. Assign names to frames via the name attribute of the frame element; assign names to new windows via the second parameter of the window.open( ) scripting method. If you omit this attribute, the returned document replaces the document containing the form element. An identifier other than one belonging to an existing frame or window opens a new window for the returned document.

If the form is located in a subwindow, and you want the target to be the main window, you must first use a script to assign an identifier to the name property of the main window. Use that name as the value of the form's target attribute.

Strict DTDs for HTML 4 and XHTML do not support the target attribute of any element because frames and windows are outside the scope of pure document markup. In fact, framesetting documents will not validate in the strict environment—thus the purpose of the separate frameset DTDs for HTML 4 and XHTML. If your documents must validate with these strict DTDs, and you wish to support targets, use scripts to set target properties of links, image maps, and forms after the page has loaded.

A form element can have only one returned document and one target. If you want a form submission to change the content of multiple frames, you can include a script in the

<frame>

returned document whose onload event handler loads or dynamically writes a document into a different frame. (Set the location.href property of each frame to a desired URL.)

**Example**

```
<form method="POST" action="http://www.giantco.com/cgi-bin/order" target="new">
...
</form>
```

**Value**

Case-sensitive identifier when the frame or window name has been assigned via the target element's name attribute. Four reserved target names act as constants:

_blank
> Browser creates a new window for the destination document.

_parent
> Destination document replaces the current frame's framesetting document (if one exists; otherwise, it is treated as _self).

_self
> Destination document replaces the current document in its window or frame.

_top
> Destination document is to occupy the entire browser window, replacing any and all framesets that may be loaded (also treated as _self if there are no framesets defined in the window).

**Default**        _self

**Object Model Reference**

```
[window.]document.forms[i].target
[window.]document.forms[formName].target
[window.]document.formName.target
[window.]document.getElementById(elementID).target
```

# <frame>                                    NN 2    IE 3    HTML 4

 <frame>                  HTML End Tag: Forbidden

The frame element defines properties of an individual window space that is some fractional portion of the entire browser window. A frame element must be defined within the context of a frameset element. It is the frameset that defines the row and column arrangement of a related group of frames.

A browser treats a frame as a separate browser window within the browser application's window. As such, each frame window can load its own content, independent of other frames. Although no attributes of the frame element are required, assigning a value to the name attribute is highly recommended if you have forms or links whose returned or destination document is to be displayed in a different frame. Scripting among multiple frames also benefits greatly from names assigned to frames because it makes references to those frames (and their contents) more easily understandable to someone reading the script code. Note that among recent W3C DTDs, the frame element validates only in the HTML 4.01 Transitional DTD and the Frameset DTDs for both HTML 4.01 and XHTML 1.0. See Appendix E.

### Example

```
<frameset cols="150,*">
    <frame name="navbar" src="nav.html">
    <frame name="main" src="page1.html">
</frameset>
```

### Object Model Reference

```
[window.]frameName
[window.]frames[i]
[window.]document.getElementById(elementID)
```

### Element-Specific Attributes

| | | | |
|---|---|---|---|
| allowtransparency | bordercolor | datafld | datasrc |
| frameborder | height | longdesc | marginheight |
| marginwidth | name | noresize | scrolling |
| security | src | width | |

### Element-Specific Event Handler Attributes

None.

## allowtransparency                         NN *n/a*   IE 5.5   HTML *n/a*

allowtransparency="*featureSwitch*"                                Optional

More applicable to the iframe element, the allowtransparency attribute, when engaged, turns the frame's background transparent. See the iframe element.

## bordercolor                               NN 3   IE 4   HTML *n/a*

bordercolor="*colorTripletOrName*"                                Optional

If your frameset displays borders (as set with the border attribute of the frameset element), but you want a subset of the frames in the frameset to be rendered with a border color different from the rest, you can assign a color to the bordercolor attribute of an individual frame element. Mixing border colors in a frameset exposes your HTML to the risk of different rendering techniques of each browser and operating system. Not only do the precise pixel composition of borders vary, but each browser and operating system may resolve conflicts between colored borders differently. If you assign a color to only some frames of a frameset, be sure to test the look on as many browser versions and operating systems as possible to evaluate the visual effect of your color choices. IE 6 for Windows ignores this attribute.

**Example**      `<frame name="navbar" src="nav.html" bordercolor="salmon">`

**Value**      A hexadecimal triplet or plain-language color name. See Appendix A for acceptable plain-language color names.

**Default**         None.

**Object Model Reference**
[window.]document.getElementById(*elementID*).borderColor

## datafld

NN *n/a*   IE *4*   HTML *n/a*

datafld="*columnName*"                                          Optional

Used with IE data binding to associate a remote data source column name in lieu of an src attribute for a frame element. The data source column must contain a valid URI (relative or absolute). A datasrc attribute must also be set for the element. Works only with text file data sources in IE 5/Mac.

**Example**         &lt;frame datasrc="DBSRC3" datafld="newsURL"&gt;

**Value**           Case-sensitive identifier.

**Default**         None.

**Object Model Reference**
[window.]document.getElementById(*elementID*).dataFld

## datasrc

NN *n/a*   IE *4*   HTML *n/a*

datasrc="*dataSourceName*"                                      Optional

Used with IE data binding to specify the ID of the page's object element that loads the data source object for remote data access. Content from the data source is specified via the datafld attribute. Works only with text file data sources in IE 5/Mac.

**Example**         &lt;frame datasrc="DBSRC3" datafld="newsURL"&gt;

**Value**           Case-sensitive identifier.

**Default**         None.

**Object Model Reference**
[window.]document.getElementById(*elementID*).dataSrc

## frameborder

NN *3*   IE *3*   HTML *4*

frameborder="*borderSwitch*"                                    Optional

Controls whether an individual frame within a frameset displays a border. The setting is supposed to override the frameborder attribute setting of the containing frameset element. Controlling individual frame borders appears to be a problem for most browsers in most operating system versions. Turning off the border of one frame may have no effect if all adjacent frames have their borders on. Feel free to experiment with the effects of turning some borders on and some borders off, but be sure to test the final effect on all browsers and operating systems used by your audience. You can rely more comfortably on the frameborder attribute of the entire frameset.

**Example**        `<frame name="navbar" src="nav.html" frameborder="0">`

**Value**

On-off values for this attribute vary with the source. HTML 4 specifies the values of 1 (on) and 0 (off). Navigator 3 and 4 use yes and no. Internet Explorer 4 and later and Netscape 6 accept both sets of values.

**Default**        1

**Object Model Reference**

`[window.]document.getElementById(elementID).frameBorder`

## height, width                                                       NN *n/a*   IE *4*   HTML *n/a*

`height="length"`                                                                       Optional
`width="length"`

Microsoft HTML documentation for IE says that the `height` and `width` attributes control the size of a frame. In practice in IE, these attributes have no direct control over the appearance of the frames within a frameset. Instead, the `cols` and `rows` attributes of the containing frameset govern the initial geometry of a frame. Do not use these attributes.

## longdesc                                                            NN *6*   IE *6*   HTML *4*

`longdesc="URL"`                                                                        Optional

Specifies a URL of a document that contains a longer description of the element than what the content of the `title` attribute reveals. One application of this attribute in future browsers is to retrieve an annotated description of the element for users who cannot read the browser screen. The **Properties** choice for Netscape 6's context menu for this element displays a small window that includes an active link to the URL assigned to the attribute. Version 6 browsers provide no other functionality for this attribute.

**Example**

`<frame longdesc="navDesc.html" title="Navigation Bar" src="navbar.html">`

**Value**        Any valid URI, including complete and relative URLs.

**Default**      None.

**Object Model Reference**

`[window.]document.getElementById(elementID).longDesc`

## marginheight, marginwidth                                           NN *6*   IE *3*   HTML *4*

`marginheight="pixelCount"`                                                             Optional
`marginwidth="pixelCount"`

The number of pixels between the inner edge of a frame and the content rendered inside the frame. The `marginheight` attribute controls space along the top and (when scrolled) the bottom edges of a frame; the `marginwidth` attribute controls space on the left and right edges of a frame. The HTML 4 specification leaves default behavior up to browsers.

Without any prompting, Internet Explorer automatically inserts a margin of 14 (Windows) or 8 (Macintosh) pixels inside a frame. But if you attempt to override the default behavior, be aware that setting any one of these two attributes causes the value of the other to go to zero. Therefore, unless you want the content to be absolutely flush with various frame edges, you need to assign values to both attributes.

**Example**       `<frame src="navbar.html" marginheight="20" marginwidth="14">`

**Value**       Any positive integer value or zero.

**Default**       14 (IE/Windows) or 8 (IE/Macintosh).

### Object Model Reference
```
[window.]document.getElementById(elementID).marginHeight
[window.]document.getElementById(elementID).marginWidth
```

## name

`name="elementIdentifier"`       Optional

When links and forms must load their destination or returned documents into frames other than the one holding the link or form, those elements have target attributes indicating which frame receives the new content. To direct such content to a frame, the frame must have a value assigned to its name attribute. That same value is assigned to the target attribute of the a or form element. Client-side scripting also uses the frame's name in building references to other frames or content in other frames. It is good practice to assign a unique identifying name to all frames.

The name attribute is deprecated in XHTML. To validate under the Frameset XHTML DTD, assign the same identifier to the element's name and id attributes.

**Example**       `<frame name="navbar" id="navbar" src="nav.html">`

**Value**       Case-sensitive identifier.

**Default**       None.

### Object Model Reference
```
[window.]frameName.name
[window.]frames[i].name
[window.]document.getElementById(elementID).name
```

## noresize

`noresize`       Optional

Frame borders can be resized by the user dragging the border perpendicular to the axis of the border edge. When present, the noresize attribute instructs the browser to prevent the frame's edges from being manually resized by the user. All border edges of the affected frame element become locked, meaning that all edges that extend to other frames in the frameset remain locked as well.

**Example**       `<frame src="navbar.html" noresize>`

| | |
|---|---|
| **Value** | The presence of the attribute in HTML makes the frame nonresizable. |
| **Default** | Frames are resizable by default. |

**Object Model Reference**

[window.]document.getElementById(*elementID*).noResize

## scrolling NN *2* IE *3* HTML *4*

scrolling="auto" | "no" | "yes" Optional

By default, browsers add vertical and/or horizontal scrollbars when the content loaded into a frame exceeds the visible content region of the frame. Scrollbars can affect the layout of some content because they occupy space normally devoted to content (that is, the frame does not expand to accommodate scrollbars). Also, due to differences in default font sizes in browsers and operating system versions, a given collection of text content may display differently in different clients. If you want to prevent scrollbars from appearing in the frame, set the scrolling attribute to no; if you want scrollbars to be in the frame at all times, set the attribute to yes. In the latter case, if the content does not require scrolling, the scrollbars are disabled. In some older versions of Navigator, the automatic scrollbars remain visible, even if content not requiring them is subsequently loaded into a frame. In Navigator 4 and later and all versions of Internet Explorer, the automatic scrollbars appear only when needed.

Setting the scrolling attribute to no should be used only after you have tested on all browsers and platforms that mission-critical content is always visible in the frame. If the frame is set to not scroll and has the noresize attribute set, some users might not be able to see all the content of the frame.

| | |
|---|---|
| **Example** | &lt;frame src="navbar.html" scrolling="no"&gt; |
| **Value** | Constant values: auto \| no \| yes. |
| **Default** | auto |

**Object Model Reference**

[window.]document.getElementById(*elementID*).scrolling

## security NN *n/a* IE *6* HTML *n/a*

security="restricted" Optional

When activated, this attribute raises the security level of the frame to the Restricted level of the Windows Security preferences settings. Such a frame's content may not execute scripts.

| | |
|---|---|
| **Example** | &lt;frame src="navbar.html" security="restricted"&gt; |
| **Value** | Constant value: restricted. |
| **Default** | None. |

## src

src="*URL*"                                                    NN 2   IE 3   HTML 4
                                                                      **Optional**

Defines the URL of the content to be loaded into the frame element. The URL can be an absolute URL or one relative to the URL of the document containing the frameset specifications. You may also use the javascript: pseudo-URL to have the returned value of a script appear in the frame. For example, if you want a frame to be blank when the frameset loads, you can define a function in the frameset document that returns a blank HTML page. The src attribute for each soon-to-be blank frame invokes the function from the vantage point of the child frame:

```
<html>
<script language="JavaScript">
function blank() {
    return "<html></html>"
}
</script>
<frameset cols="50%,50%">
    <frame name="leftFrame" src="javascript:parent.blank()">
    <frame name="rightFrame" src="javascript:parent.blank()">
</frameset>
</html>
```

Another type of blank page is available from some browsers and versions via the about:blank URL, which draws from an internal blank page. However, Navigator 2 and 3 for the Macintosh display an unwanted message with this URL in a window or frame.

**Example**          &lt;frame src="navbar.html"&gt;

**Value**            A complete or relative URL or a javascript: pseudo-URL.

**Default**          None.

**Object Model Reference**
[window.]document.getElementById(*elementID*).src

## width

See height.

# &lt;frameset&gt;                                            NN 2   IE 3   HTML 4
&lt;frameset&gt;...&lt;/frameset&gt;                              HTML End Tag: Required

Defines the layout of a multiple-frame presentation in a browser's application window. The primary duty of the frameset element is to specify the geographical layout—in a row and column array—of rectangular frames. Attributes defined in a frameset element apply to all frame elements nested within (unless overridden by a similar attribute for a specific frame). A frameset element's tag takes the place in an HTML document that is normally devoted to the body element.

<frameset>

You may nest a frameset element within a frameset element. This tactic allows you to subdivide a frame from the outer frameset element into two or more frames. For example, if you define one frameset element with three rows and two columns, you get a total of six frames:

```
<frameset rows="33%, 33%, 34%" cols="50%, 50%">
    <frame name="r1c1" id="r1c1"...>
    <frame name="r1c2" id="r1c2"...>
    <frame name="r2c1" id="r2c1"...>
    <frame name="r2c2" id="r2c2"...>
    <frame name="r3c1" id="r3c1"...>
    <frame name="r3c2" id="r3c2"...>
</frameset>
```

Figure 8-1 shows the resulting frame organization.

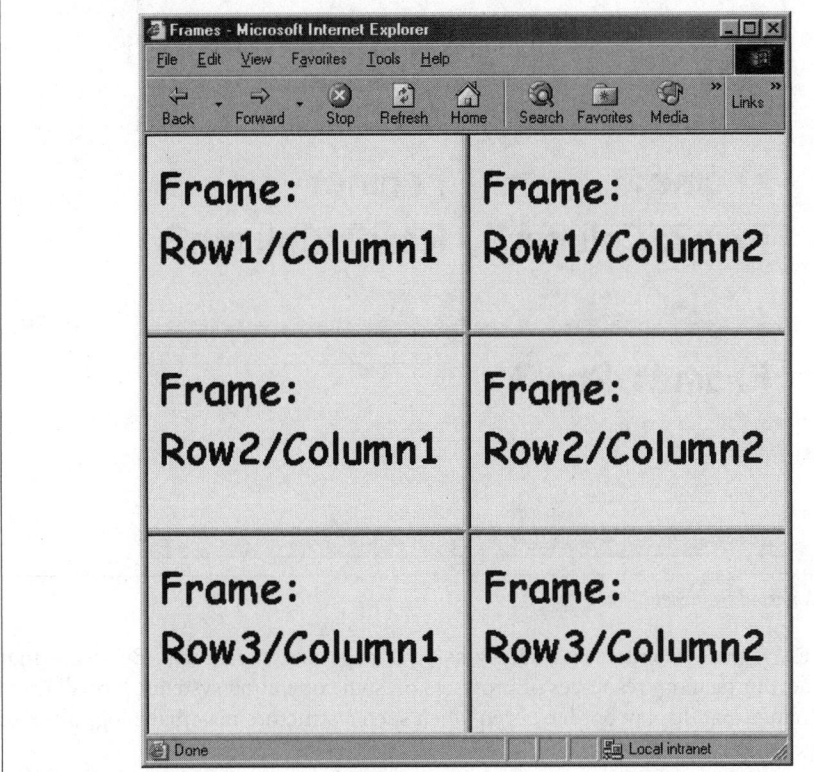

*Figure 8-1. A three-row, two-column frameset*

On the other hand, if you nest a frameset where a frame definition goes, that frame is divided into whatever frame organization is defined by that nested frameset. Consider the following nested frameset:

```
<frameset rows="33%, 33%, 34%">
    <frame name="r1" id="r1"...>
    <frameset cols="50%, 50%">
```

```
            <frame name="r2c1" id="r2c1"...>
            <frame name="r2c2" id="r2c2"...>
        </frameset>
        <frame name="r3" id="r3"...>
    </frameset>
```

This produces the frame organization shown in Figure 8-2.

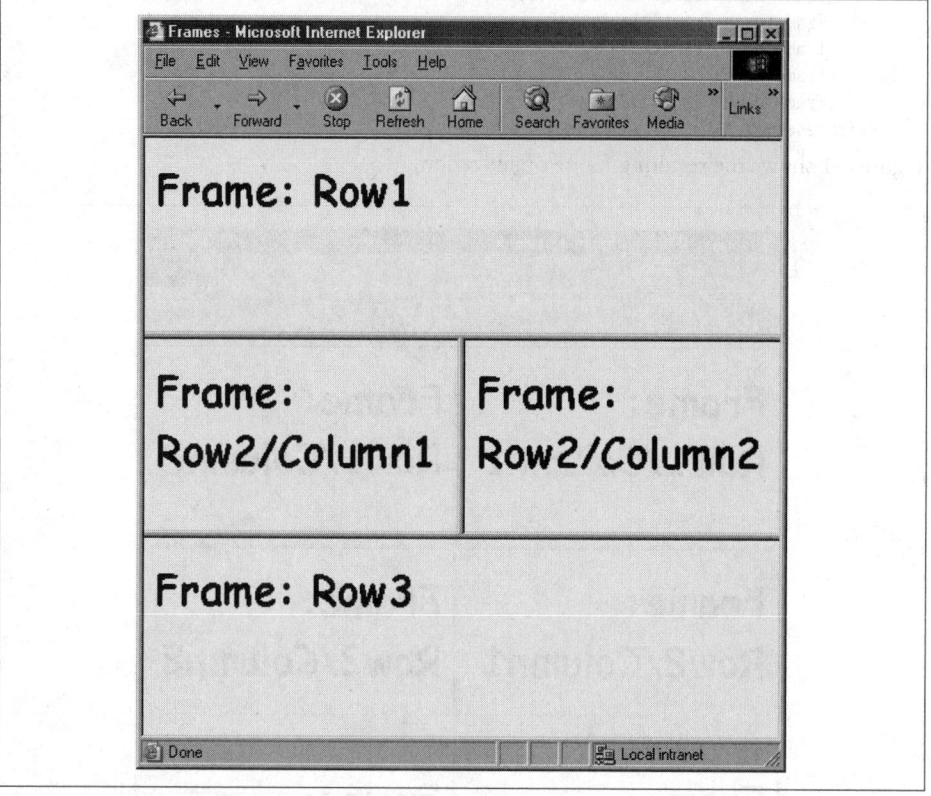

*Figure 8-2. A nested frameset*

You may nest frameset elements as deeply as your page design requires. Be aware that frames can devour memory resources of browsers on some operating systems. Not all users appreciate frames that display borders, even when such a structure may make logical sense for your page design.

The outermost frameset document is the one whose title attribute governs the display in the browser window title bar. Documents loaded into individual frames have no control over title bar display, although for reasons of scripting and potential application in future browsers, the title attribute of framed documents should be set anyway.

If you wish to offer an option for a user to remove a frameset, you can supply a link or button that invokes a script. The script should set the top.location.href property to the URL of the single most important document of the pages loaded into frames (the primary content).

Strict DTDs for HTML 4 and XHTML explicitly exclude support for frameset and frame elements (and target attributes of other elements that point to frames). These document type definitions treat frames as outside the scope of pure document markup. You can validate a framesetting document with the HTML 4 transitional and frameset DTDs or the XHTML frameset DTD.

### Example

```
<frameset cols="150,*">
    <frame name="navbar" id="navbar" src="nav.html">
    <frame name="main" id="main" src="page1.html">
</frameset>
```

### Object Model Reference

[window.]document.getElementById(*elementID*)

### Element-Specific Attributes

| border | bordercolor | cols | frameborder | framespacing | rows |
|--------|-------------|------|-------------|--------------|------|

### Element-Specific Event Handler Attributes

| Handler | NN | IE | HTML |
|---------|----|----|------|
| onload | 2 | 3 | 4 |
| onunload | 2 | 3 | 4 |

## border

border="*pixelCount*"

NN 3     IE 4     HTML *n/a*

Optional

Frames display 3-D borders by default. The default thickness of that border varies with browser and operating system. You can adjust this thickness by assigning a different value to the border attribute of the frameset. Only the outermost frameset element of a system of nested framesets responds to the border attribute setting. Note that this attribute controls inter-frame borders, and not a border around the frameset.

Navigator 4 is consistent across Windows and Macintosh platforms by displaying a default border that is the same thickness as when the border attribute is set to 5. For IE, the default value is 6 in Windows and 1 on the Mac (although the actual rendering is far more than one pixel wide). Any single setting you make for the border attribute therefore does not look the same on all browsers. Moreover, at smaller settings, some browsers react strangely. IE 6 won't display a border in Windows when the value is 4 or less; Navigator loses its 3-D effect when the value is 2 or less. Navigator 4 also has a nasty habit of rendering an odd divot in the center of frame bars on the Macintosh.

This hodge-podge deployment of frame borders may make you shy away from using them altogether (set the border attribute to 0). In some cases, however, borders provide reassuring visual contexts for frame content that requires a scrollbar. Having a scrollbar appear floating in a browser window might be disconcerting to some viewers.

That the HTML 4 specification does not include a border attribute might lead one to believe it prefers the use of style sheet borders instead of borders tied only to frames. At

<frameset>

most, however, a border-related CSS style attribute affects only a border around the entire frameset, and has no impact on borders between frames.

**Example**        `<frameset cols="150,*" border="0">...</frameset>`

**Value**

An integer value. A setting of zero eliminates the border entirely. Although the value is supposed to represent the precise pixel thickness of borders in the frameset, this is not entirely true for all operating systems or browsers.

**Default**        See description.

**Object Model Reference**

`[window.]document.getElementById(elementID).border`

## bordercolor                                             NN 3   IE 4   HTML *n/a*

`bordercolor="colorTripletOrName"`                                         Optional

Establishes the rendering color for all visible borders in a frameset. A bordercolor setting in an outermost frameset element may be overridden by a bordercolor attribute of a nested frameset element (for the nested frameset's frames only) or an individual frame element. Browsers resolve conflicts of colors assigned to adjacent frames differently. Test your color combinations carefully if you mix border colors.

**Example**        `<frameset cols="150,*" bordercolor="salmon">...</frameset>`

**Value**        A hexadecimal triplet or plain-language color name. See Appendix A for acceptable plain-language color names.

**Default**

Browser default, usually a shade of gray with black or blue highlighting for the 3-D effect.

**Object Model Reference**

`[window.]document.getElementById(elementID).borderColor`

## cols                                             NN 2   IE 3   HTML 4

`cols="columnLengthsList"`                                         Optional

Defines the sizes or proportions of the column arrangement of frames in a frameset. If you intend to use the frameset element to create frames in multiple columns, you must assign a list of values to the cols attribute, with one value per column.

Column size is defined in one of three ways:

- An absolute pixel size
- A percentage of the width available for the entire frameset
- A wildcard (*) to represent all available remaining space after other pixels and percentages have been accounted for

Use an absolute pixel size when you want the width of a frame to be the same no matter how the user has sized the overall browser window. This is especially useful when the frame is to display an object of fixed width, such as an image. Use a percentage when you want the frame width to be a certain proportion of the frameset's width, no matter how the user has adjusted the size of the overall browser window. If you use all percentage values for the cols attribute, they should add up to 100%. If the values don't add up to 100%, the browser makes the columns fit anyway. Finally, use the asterisk wildcard value to let the browser calculate the width of one frame when all other frames in the frameset have fixed or percentage values assigned to them. Separate the values within the attribute value string with commas.

You can mix and match all three types of values in the attribute string. For example, consider a three-column frameset. If you want the leftmost column to be exactly 150 pixels wide, but the middle column must be 50% of the total frameset width, set the value as follows:

```
<frameset cols="150,50%,*">
```

The precise width of the two rightmost frames is different with each browser window's width adjustment. The rightmost frame width in this example is roughly equal to one half the width of the frameset minus the 150 pixels reserved for the leftmost frame.

You may define an invisible column to the right. Use percentage values for visible columns, and make sure they total 100%. Then assign the asterisk value for the final column.

To create a regular grid of frames, assign values to both the cols and rows attributes in the frameset element's tag. For an irregular array, you must nest frameset elements, as shown in the description of the frameset element, earlier in this section.

**Example**     `<frameset cols="25%,50%,25%">...</frameset>`

**Value**     Comma-separated list of pixel, percentage, or wildcard (*) values. Internet Explorer 4 for the Macintosh exhibits incorrect behavior with some combinations that include a wildcard value.

**Default**     100%

**Object Model Reference**

`[window.]document.getElementById(elementID).cols`

## frameborder                                   NN 3    IE 3    HTML n/a

`frameborder="borderSwitch"`                                              Optional

Controls whether all frames within the frameset display a border (acting as dividers between frame edges). The frameborder attribute of frame elements can override the frameset element's setting for this attribute, but some frame organizations don't lend themselves well to eliminating frames from subgroups of frames. Override the frameset element's attribute with caution, and test on all browsers and operating system platforms.

**Example**     `<frameset cols="25%,50%,25%" frameborder="no">...</frameset>`

**Value**     On-off values for this attribute vary with the browser. Navigator uses yes and no. Internet Explorer 4 and later accepts both yes | no and 1 | 0. For cross-browser compatibility, use the yes/no pairing.

**Default**          yes

**Object Model Reference**
[window.]document.getElementById(*elementID*).frameBorder

## framespacing                                          NN *n/a*   IE 3   HTML *n/a*
framespacing="*pixelLength*"                                              Optional

The Internet Explorer framespacing attribute is an older version of the border attribute. The older attribute is supported in current IE versions for backward compatibility. The behavior of the framespacing attribute is more uniform across operating system versions of IE: a setting of 10 pixels generates a border between frames that is essentially identical in both Windows and Mac versions. For an IE-only deployment, the framespacing attribute is a more accurate way to create borders that look the same across operating system versions.

**Example**          &lt;frameset cols="25%,50%,25%" framespacing="7"&gt;...&lt;/frameset&gt;

**Value**            A positive integer. Unlike the border attribute, however, a setting of zero
                     does not remove the border. Use the frameborder attribute to hide
                     borders entirely.

**Default**          2

**Object Model Reference**
[window.]document.getElementById(*elementID*).frameSpacing

## rows                                                   NN 2   IE 3   HTML 4
rows="*rowLengthsList*"                                                   Optional

Defines the sizes or proportions of the row arrangement of frames in a frameset. If it is the intent to use the frameset element to create frames with multiple rows, you must assign a list of values to the rows attribute, with one value per row.

Row size is defined in one of three ways:

- An absolute pixel size
- A percentage of the height available for the entire frameset in the browser window
- A wildcard (*) to represent all available remaining space in the browser window after other pixels and percentages have been accounted for

Use an absolute pixel size when you want the height of a frame row to be the same no matter how the user has sized the overall browser window. This is especially useful when the frame is to display an object of fixed height, such as an image. Use a percentage when you want the frame height to be a certain proportion of the frameset's height, no matter how the user has adjusted the size of the overall browser window. If you use all percentage values for the rows attribute, they should add up to 100%. If the values don't add up to 100%, the browser makes the rows fit anyway. Finally, use the asterisk wildcard value to let the browser calculate the height of one row when all other rows in the frameset have fixed or percentage values assigned to them. Separate the values within the attribute value string with commas.

You can mix and match all three types of values in the attribute string. For example, consider a three-row frameset. If you want the bottom row to be exactly 80 pixels high to accommodate a navigation bar, but the middle row must be 50% of the total frameset height, set the value as follows:

```
<frameset rows="*,50%,80">
```

The precise height of the two topmost frames is different with each browser window's height adjustment. The topmost frame height in this example is roughly equal to one half the height of the frameset minus the 80 pixels reserved for the bottom row.

You may define an invisible row at the bottom. Use percentage values for visible rows, and make sure they total 100%. Then assign the asterisk value for the final row.

To create a regular grid of frames, assign values to both the cols and rows attributes in the frameset element's tag. For an irregular array, you must nest frameset elements, as shown in the description of the frameset element, earlier in this section.

**Example**    `<frameset rows="25%,50%,25%">...</frameset>`

**Value**    Comma-separated list of pixel, percentage, or wildcard (*) values. Internet Explorer 4 for the Macintosh exhibits incorrect behavior with some combinations that include a wildcard value.

**Default**    100%

**Object Model Reference**

```
[window.]document.getElementById(elementID).rows
```

# &lt;h1&gt;, &lt;h2&gt;, &lt;h3&gt;, &lt;h4&gt;, &lt;h5&gt;, &lt;h6&gt;    NN *all*    IE *all*    HTML *all*

```
<h1>...</h1>, <h2>...</h2>, <h3>...</h3>                    HTML End Tag: Required
<h4>...</h4>, <h5>...</h5>, <h6>...</h6>
```

HTML defines a series of six heading levels with associated numbers that are intended to signify the relative importance of the section below the heading. The h1 element represents the most important, whereas h6 represents the least important. HTML document parsers can examine a page's tags to create a table of contents based on the headings. This means that for proper document structure, these heading levels should be used in sequence, without skipping levels for aesthetic purposes.

It is up to the browsers to determine the default font, weight, and other characteristics of each level. Each heading element is rendered on its own line, with no line break or paragraph elements necessary to begin the content of the section titled with the heading. Figure 8-3 shows examples of how Netscape 6 and Internet Explorer 6 renders all six heading levels in Windows. By and large, this pattern applies to other browser versions and operating systems.

You can always override the browser's rendering style for any heading level or individual heading with style sheet rules.

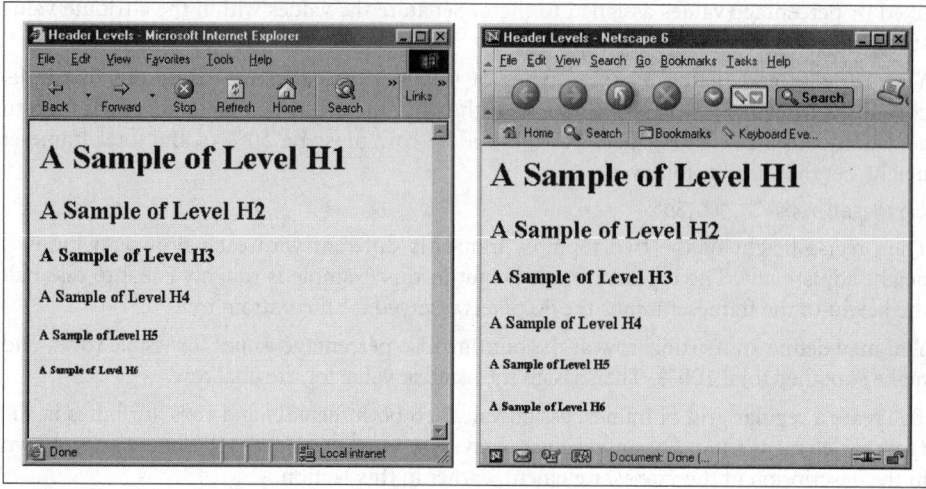

*Figure 8-3. Heading levels in Internet Explorer 6 and Netscape 6*

### Example

```
<h1>The Solar System</h1>
<p>Floating gracefully within the Milky Way galaxy is our Solar System.  ...</p>
<h2>The Sun</h2>
<p>At a distance of 93,000,000 miles from Earth, the Sun...</p>
<h3>The Planets</h3>
<p>Nine recognized planets revolve around the Sun. ...</p>
<h4>Mercury</h4>
...
```

### Object Model Reference

```
[window.]document.getElementById(elementID)
```

### Element-Specific Attributes

align

### Element-Specific Event Handler Attributes

None.

---

## align

NN *all*    IE *all*    HTML *3.2*

align="*where*"                                                      Optional

Determines how the element's text is aligned inside the element's block. Both Navigator and Internet Explorer support alignment values for center, left, and right alignment. Transitional HTML 4 (but not XHTML) adds the possibility of a fully justified alignment for multilined content, as well.

The align attribute is deprecated in HTML 4 in favor of the text-align: style sheet attribute.

**Example**          &lt;h1 align="center"&gt;Article I&lt;/h1&gt;

---

## Value

The following table shows values for the align attribute. Values may be treated as case-insensitive values.

| Value | NN 4+ | IE 4+ | HTML4 |
|---|---|---|---|
| center | • | • | • |
| justify | – | – | • |
| left | • | • | • |
| right | • | • | • |

**Default**        left

## Object Model Reference

[window.]document.getElementById(*elementID*).align

# &lt;head&gt;

NN *all*    IE *all*    HTML *all*

&lt;head&gt;...&lt;/head&gt;

HTML End Tag: Optional

The head element contains document information that is generally not rendered as part of the document in the browser window. At most, a browser displays the title element's content in the browser window's titlebar.

The content of the head element consists entirely of other elements that are intended to assist the browser in working with document data. Another classification of data, handled in one or more meta elements, can also assist search engines and document parsers to learn more about the document based on abstract information supplied by the author. The table below shows the elements that may be nested inside a head element according to three different specifications.

Although the HTML 4 or XHTML standards do not explicitly support the id attribute, browsers permit the attribute as part of their support for W3C DOM common properties of all elements.

| Element | NN 4+ | IE 4+ | HTML 4 and XHTML |
|---|---|---|---|
| base | • | • | • |
| basefont | • | • | – |
| bgsound | – | • | – |
| isindex | • | – | • |
| link | • | • | • |
| meta | • | • | • |
| nextid | – | • | – |
| object | – | – | • |
| script | • | • | • |

| Element | NN 4+ | IE 4+ | HTML 4 and XHTML |
|---------|-------|-------|------------------|
| style   | •     | •     | •                |
| title   | •     | •     | •                |

### Example

```
<head>
<meta name="Author" content="Danny Goodman">
<style type="text/css">
    h1 {color:cornflowerblue}
</style>
</head>
```

### Object Model Reference

```
[window.]document.getElementsByTagName("head")[0]
[window.]document.getElementById(elementID)
```

### Element-Specific Attributes

profile

### Element-Specific Event Handler Attributes

None.

## profile                                            NN 6   IE 6   HTML 4

profile="URLList"                                                    Optional

A meta data profile is a separate file that defines one or more meta data property behaviors. The W3C leaves the precise application of this attribute to the whims of the browsers makers. As of Version 6 browsers, nothing special occurs as a result of assigning this attribute.

### Example

```
<head profile="http://www.giantco.com/profiles/common">
    <meta name="Author" content="Jane Smith">
    <meta name="keywords" content="benefits,insurance,">
    ...
</head>
```

**Value**          Any valid URL or browser profile constant.

**Default**        Browser default.

### Object Model Reference

```
[window.]document.firstChild.firstChild.profile
[window.]document.getElementsByTagName("head")[0].profile
[window.]document.getElementById(elementID).profile
```

<hr>

# <hr>

<hr>
HTML End Tag: Forbidden

The hr element draws a horizontal rule according to visual rules built into the browser with a variety of attribute controls. As a block element, the hr element starts and ends its rule on its own line, as if the element were surrounded by br elements. This element is not a content container, and many of the attributes that have been in use for a long time are deprecated in HTML 4 in favor of style sheet rules. The HTML recommendation leaves default appearance specifications up to the browser maker.

**Example**            <hr align="center" width="80%">

**Object Model Reference**
[window.]document.getElementById(*elementID*)

**Element-Specific Attributes**

| align | color | noshade | size | width |
|-------|-------|---------|------|-------|

**Element-Specific Event Handler Attributes**
None.

## align

NN *all*   IE *all*   HTML *3.2*

align="*where*"
Optional

Determines how the hr element is rendered in physical relation to the next outermost container (usually the body or html element). The align attribute is deprecated in HTML 4 in favor of the align style sheet attribute.

**Example**            <hr align="right">

**Value**              One of three case-insensitive values: center | left | right.

**Default**            center

**Object Model Reference**
[window.]document.getElementById(*elementID*).align

## color

NN *n/a*   IE *4*   HTML *n/a*

color="*colorTripletOrName*"
Optional

Sets the color of the hr element in Internet Explorer. Setting the color attribute also turns on the noshade attribute. If you want a 3-D effect rule to appear with a color, use the style sheet color attribute. Navigator 4 and later, however, doesn't apply color style sheet rules to hr elements.

**Example**            <hr color="salmon">

**Value**              A hexadecimal triplet or plain-language color name. See Appendix A for acceptable plain-language color names.

**Default**            None.

<hr>

**Object Model Reference**

[window.]document.getElementById(*elementID*).color

## noshade                                    NN *all*   IE *all*   HTML *3.2*

noshade                                                            Optional

The presence of the noshade attribute tells the browser to render the rule as a flat (not 3-D) line. In Internet Explorer only, if you set the color attribute, the browser changes the default line style to a no-shade style.

**Example**          <hr noshade>

**Value**            The presence of the attribute turns on no-shade rendering.

**Default**          Off.

**Object Model Reference**

[window.]document.getElementById(*elementID*).noShade

## size                                       NN *all*   IE *all*   HTML *3.2*

size="*pixelCount*"                                                Optional

You can override the default thickness of the hr element by assigning a value to the size attribute. The size attribute is deprecated in HTML 4 in favor of the height style sheet attribute.

**Example**          <hr size="4">

**Value**            Any positive integer. A setting of zero still draws a one-pixel thick rule.

**Default**          2

**Object Model Reference**

[window.]document.getElementById(*elementID*).size

## width                                      NN *all*   IE *all*   HTML *3.2*

width="*length*"                                                  Optional

Defines the precise pixel width or percentage of available width (relative to the containing element) to draw the hr element rule. This attribute is deprecated in HTML 4 in favor of the width style sheet attribute.

**Example**          <hr width="75%">

**Value**            Any length value in pixels or percentage of available space.

**Default**          100%

**Object Model Reference**

[window.]document.getElementById(*elementID*).width

<html>

# <html>

<html>...</html>
HTML End Tag: Optional

The html element is the container of the entire document content, including the head element. Typically, the html element start tag is the second line of an HTML file, following the Document Type Definition (DTD) statement (see the DOCTYPE element earlier in this chapter). If no DTD is provided in the file (it assumes the browser's default DTD), the html start tag becomes the first line of the file. The end tag should be in the last line of the file (but it does not have to stand on its own line).

Although the html element doesn't render per se, it is the root positioning context of a document in a purely W3C-compliant environment. This applies to Netscape 6 and IE 6, the latter only when certain DOCTYPE definitions start the document. Otherwise, IE for Windows (this goes for IE 4 through IE 5.5) treats the body element as the root positioning context. If you don't specify margins, borders, or padding for the body element, you probably won't notice the difference.

The HTML 4 and XHTML standards do not include explicit support for id, class, or style attributes, but modern DHTML browsers support them.

**Example**
```
<html>
<head>
...
</head>
<body>
...
</body>
</html>
```

**Element-Specific Attributes**

scroll          version          xmlns

**Element-Specific Event Handler Attributes**

None.

## scroll

scroll="*featureSwitch*"
Optional

When IE 6 is in standards-compliant mode (see the DOCTYPE element earlier in this chapter), it treats the html element as the "canvas" on which it draws the document content. By default, the canvas gains scrollbars if the content overflows the content region of the window. You can force the display of scrollbars (on or off) regardless of the overflow state by setting the scroll attribute in the html element. If your pages will also be loading into older IE/Windows versions, set the same attribute in the body element — the "canvas" for older versions.

**Example**        <html scroll="no">...</html>

**Value**          String constant: auto | no | yes.

<i>

**Default**        auto

**Object Model Reference**

[window.]document.getElementById(*elementID*).scroll

## version

version="*string*"                                                                    Optional

The version attribute is deprecated in HTML 4 and was never adopted by the major browsers until the desire to claim standards compliance led the maker to introduce the dead-end attribute. Originally intended to specify the HTML DTD version supported by the document, this information is universally supplied in the separate DTD statement (in the DOCTYPE element) above the html element in the document. Do not use this attribute.

**Value**

Any string of characters. The string must be inside a matching pair of (single or double) quotation marks.

**Default**        None.

## xmlns

xmlns="*namespaceSpec*"                                                               Optional

The W3C attribute and its fixed URI value should be in the html element of every XHTML document. Microsoft uses this attribute to allow IE 5 and later for Windows to reference elements that belong to non-HTML sources, such as the Microsoft implementation of behaviors (generic external script modules that can be applied to any element).

**Example (IE 5+/Windows)**

<html xmlns:MSIE>...</html>

**Value**

For XHTML, a fixed URI string: http://www.w3.org/1999/xhtml. For IE 5 and later namespace references, just a prefix name (MSIE for built-in behaviors), or a prefix and URI that acts as an additional identifier for the prefix. Note the colon delimiter.

**Default**        None.

---

##

<i>...</i>                                                             HTML End Tag: Required

The i element—one of several font style elements in HTML 4—renders its content in an italic version of the font face governing the next outermost HTML container. You can nest multiple font style elements to create combined styles, such as bold italic (<b><i>bold-italic text</i></b>).

It is up to the browser to italicize a system font or perhaps load an italic version of the currently specified font. If you are striving for font perfection, it is best to use style sheets (and perhaps downloadable fonts) to specify a true italic font family, rather than risk the browser's extrapolation of an italic face from a system font.

You can take advantage of the containerness of this element by assigning style sheet rules to some or all i elements in a page. For example, you may wish all i elements to be in a red color. By assigning the style rule i{color:red}, you can apply the color to all elements with only a tiny bit of code.

Although this element is not deprecated in HTML 4, it would not be surprising to see it lose favor to the font-style style sheet attribute in the future.

**Example**          `<p>This product is <i>new</i> and <i>improved</i>!</p>`

**Object Model Reference**

[window.]document.getElementById(*elementID*)

**Element-Specific Attributes**

None.

**Element-Specific Event Handler Attributes**

None.

# &lt;iframe&gt;                                          NN 6    IE 3   HTML 4

`<iframe>...</iframe>`                                              HTML End Tag: Required

An iframe element creates an inline frame within the natural flow of a document's content. The frame is a rectangular space into which you may load any other HTML document (or use scripts to dynamically write content to the space). If you assign a value to the name attribute of an iframe element, you may supply that name as the value of a target attribute of a, form, or other element that lets you define a target for a destination or returned document.

Although an iframe element's rectangular space begins immediately following the content that comes before it (including in a line of text), all content following the end tag starts on the next line following the frame rectangle. Text leading up to the iframe element can be aligned in the same ways that text can be aligned around an img or object element.

Content between the start and end tags is ignored by browsers that support the iframe element. All others display such content as inline HTML content (as a way to let users know what they're missing and perhaps provide a link to related information). The Navigator 4 element that comes closest to the functionality and behavior of the iframe element is the ilayer element.

Because an iframe element draws its content from a separate server file, it may be used as a way to accomplish client-side "includes" (see Chapter 5). In most respects, an iframe behaves like a frame element, but without the need for a frameset. In fact, the element acts so much like a frame that if you reference it through frame referencing syntax (window. *frameName*), the returned object is the same type as a window object, rather than a frame element object.

While the iframe element validates in the transitional HTML 4 DTD along with the frame and frameset elements, only the iframe validates in the transitional XHTML DTD. The iframe validates in the frameset DTDs for HTML 4 and XHTML.

**Example**
```
<iframe src="quotes.html" width="150" height="90">
<a href="quotes.html" target="new" style="color:darkred">
 Click here to see the latest quotes </a>
</iframe>
```

**Object Model Reference**
```
[window.]document.getElementById(elementID)
```

**Element-Specific Attributes**

| | | | | |
|---|---|---|---|---|
| align | datafld | datasrc | frameborder | height |
| hspace | longdesc | marginheight | marginwidth | name |
| scrolling | security | src | vspace | width |

**Element-Specific Event Handler Attributes**
None.

## align
NN 6    IE 3    HTML 4
```
align="alignmentConstant"
```
Optional

Determines how the rectangle of the iframe element aligns within the context of surrounding content. See "Alignment Constants" earlier in this chapter for a description of the possibilities defined for this element's attribute.

**Example**
```
<iframe src="quotes.html" width="150" height="90" align="center"></iframe>
```

**Value**         Case-insensitive constant value.

**Default**       left

**Object Model Reference**
```
[window.]document.getElementById(elementID).align
```

## datafld
NN n/a    IE 4    HTML n/a
```
datafld="columnName"
```
Optional

Used with IE data binding to associate a remote data source column name in lieu of a src attribute for an iframe element. The data source column must contain a valid URI (relative or absolute). A datasrc attribute must also be set for the element. Works only with text file data sources in IE 5/Mac.

**Example**         `<iframe datasrc="DBSRC3" datafld="newsURL"></iframe>`

**Value**           Case-sensitive identifier.

**Default**          None.

**Object Model Reference**

[window.]document.getElementById(*elementID*).dataFld

## datasrc                                                     NN *n/a*   IE *4*   HTML *n/a*

datasrc="*dataSourceName*"                                                       Optional

Used with IE data binding to specify the ID of the page's object element that loads the data source object for remote data access. Content from the data source is specified via the datafld attribute. Works only with text file data sources in IE 5/Mac.

**Example**          &lt;iframe datasrc="DBSRC3" datafld="newsURL"&gt;&lt;/iframe&gt;

**Value**            Case-sensitive identifier.

**Default**          None.

**Object Model Reference**

[window.]document.getElementById(*elementID*).dataSrc

## frameborder                                                  NN *6*   IE *3*   HTML *4*

frameborder="*borderSwitch*"                                                     Optional

Controls whether the iframe element displays a border. If you want linked-in documents to look as if they are embedded as part of the main document, turn off the frameborder attribute.

**Example**

&lt;iframe src="quotes.html" width="150" height="90" frameborder="no"&gt;&lt;/iframe&gt;

**Value**

On-off values for this attribute vary with the source. HTML 4 specifies the values of 1 (on) and 0 (off). Internet Explorer 4 and Netscape 6 accept the HTML value and yes or no.

**Default**          1

**Object Model Reference**

[window.]document.getElementById(*elementID*).frameBorder

## height, width                                                NN *6*   IE *4*   HTML *4*

height="*length*"                                                                Optional
width="*length*"

These attributes establish the dimensions of the iframe element. IE 4.5 or later on the Mac is required. Both attributes are deprecated in HTML 4 in favor of CSS height and width style attributes.

**Example**          &lt;iframe src="news.html" height="200" width="200"&gt;

**Value**            Any length value in pixels or percentage of available space.

Alphabetical HTML Reference

**Default**        A width of 300 pixels; a height of 150 pixels.

**Object Model Reference**

```
[window.]document.getElementById(elementID).height
[window.]document.getElementById(elementID).width
```

## hspace, vspace                                    NN *n/a*    IE 4    HTML *n/a*

```
hspace="pixelCount"                                            Optional
vspace="pixelCount"
```

These attributes set padding around an iframe element within the content flow. The hspace attribute controls padding along the left and right edges (horizontal padding), and the vspace attribute controls padding along the top and bottom edges (vertical padding). Adding such padding provides an empty cushion around the frame. As an alternate (and to achieve cross-browser compatibility), you can specify the various margin style sheet settings, especially if you want to open space along only one edge.

**Example**        `<iframe src="news.html" hspace="20" vspace="10">`

**Value**          Any positive integer.

**Default**        0

**Object Model Reference**

```
[window.]document.getElementById(elementID).hspace
[window.]document.getElementById(elementID).vspace
```

## longdesc                                          NN 6    IE 6    HTML 4

```
longdesc="URL"                                                 Optional
```

Specifies a URL of a document that contains a longer description of the element than what the content of the title attribute reveals. One application of this attribute in future browsers is to retrieve an annotated description of the element for users who cannot read the browser screen. The **Properties** choice for Netscape 6's context menu for this element displays a small window that includes an active link to the URL assigned to the attribute. Version 6 browsers provide no other functionality for this attribute.

**Example**

```
<iframe longdesc="newsDesc.html" title="Navigation Bar" src="news.html">
</iframe>
```

**Value**          Any valid URI, including complete and relative URLs.

**Default**        None.

## marginheight, marginwidth

```
marginheight="pixelCount"
marginwidth="pixelCount"
```
Optional

Determine the number of pixels between the inner edge of a frame and the content rendered inside the frame. The marginheight attribute controls space along the top and (when scrolled) the bottom edges of a frame; the marginwidth attribute controls space on the left and right edges of a frame. The HTML 4 specification leaves default behavior up to browsers.

Browsers insert their default margins (in the range between 8 and 14 pixels) inside a frame. But if you attempt to override the default behavior, be aware that setting any one of these two attributes causes the value of the other to go to zero. Therefore, unless you want the content to be absolutely flush with various frame edges, you need to assign values to both attributes.

**Example**
```
<iframe src="news.html" marginheight="20" marginwidth="14"></iframe>
```

**Value**        Any positive integer value or zero.

**Default**      Varies with browser and operating system.

**Object Model Reference**
```
[window.]document.getElementById(elementID).marginHeight
[window.]document.getElementById(elementID).marginWidth
```

## name

```
name="elementIdentifier"
```
Optional

When links and forms must load their destination or returned documents into frames other than the one holding the link or form, those elements have target attributes indicating which frame receives the new content. To direct such content to a frame, the frame must have a value assigned to its name attribute. That same value is assigned to the target attribute of the a or form element.

**Example**        
```
<iframe name="news" id="news" src="news.html"></iframe>
```

**Value**        Case-sensitive identifier.

**Default**      None.

**Object Model Reference**
```
[window.]document.getElementById(elementID).name
```

## scrolling

```
scrolling="featureSwitch"
```
Optional

By default, browsers add vertical and/or horizontal scrollbars when the content loaded into an inline frame exceeds the visible content region of the element. Scrollbars can affect the layout of some content because they occupy space normally devoted to content (that is, the frame does not expand to accommodate scrollbars). Also, due to differences in default font sizes in browsers and operating system versions, a given collection of text content may display differently in different clients. If you want to prevent scrollbars from appearing in the frame, set the scrolling attribute to no; if you want scrollbars to be in the frame at all times, set the attribute to yes. In the latter case, if the content does not require scrolling, the scrollbars are visible, but disabled.

Setting the scrolling attribute to no should be used only after you have tested that mission-critical content is always visible in the frame on all browsers and platforms. If the frame is set to not scroll, some users might not be able to see all content of the frame.

In lieu of this attribute, you may also use the CSS overflow style attribute. Microsoft provides extra axis-specific control over scrollbars via their overflow-x and overflow-y style attributes.

**Example**       `<iframe src="news.html" scrolling="no"></iframe>`

**Value**       Constant values: auto | no | yes.

**Default**       auto

**Object Model Reference**
`[window.]document.getElementById(elementID).scrolling`

## security                                                    NN *n/a*    IE 6    HTML *n/a*
`security="restricted"`                                                          Optional

When activated, this attribute raises the security level of the inline frame to the Restricted level of the Windows Security preferences settings. Such a frame's content may not execute scripts.

**Example**       `<iframe src="news.html" security="restricted">`

**Value**       Constant value: restricted.

**Default**       None.

## src                                                          NN 6    IE 3    HTML 4
`src="URL"`                                                                     Optional

Defines the URL of the content to be loaded into the iframe element. The URL can be an absolute URL or one relative to the URL of the document containing the frameset specifications. You may also use the javascript: pseudo-URL to have the returned value of a script appear in the frame. If you omit the src attribute, the frame opens empty.

**Example**       `<iframe src="news.html"></iframe>`

**Value**       A complete or relative URL or a javascript: pseudo-URL.

**Default**       None.

**Object Model Reference**
`[window.]document.getElementById(elementID).src`

## vspace

See hspace.

## width

See height.

# &lt;ilayer&gt;

NN |4|    IE *n/a*    HTML *n/a*

&lt;ilayer&gt;...&lt;/ilayer&gt;

HTML End Tag: Required

An ilayer element is an inline version of the Navigator 4-specific layer element. In some respects, the ilayer element works like the iframe element in Internet Explorer, but an ilayer is automatically regarded as a positionable element in Navigator 4's object model (e.g., like a block-level element with a CSS position: attribute set to relative). As a result, many of the attributes are the same as the layer element and are named according to the Navigator 4 way of positioning, sizing, and stacking positionable elements.

Content for an ilayer element can be read in from a separate file (with the src attribute) or wired into the current document by placing the HTML between the start and end tags. You can include both types of content in the same ilayer element. Content from the src document is rendered first (as its own block-level element), with additional content starting on its own line below the external content's rectangle.

### Example

```
<ilayer id="thingy1" src="quotes.html" width="150" height="90"></ilayer>
```

### Object Model Reference

[window.]document.*layerName*

### Element-Specific Attributes

| | | | | |
|---|---|---|---|---|
| above | background | below | bgcolor | clip |
| height | id | left | name | src |
| top | visibility | width | z-index | |

### Element-Specific Event Handler Attributes

| Handler | NN | IE | HTML |
|---|---|---|---|
| onblur | 4 | n/a | n/a |
| onfocus | 4 | n/a | n/a |
| onload | 4 | n/a | n/a |
| onmousedown | 4[a] | n/a | n/a |
| onmouseout | 4[a] | n/a | n/a |
| onmouseover | 4[a] | n/a | n/a |
| onmouseup | 4[a] | n/a | n/a |

[a] Event capture mode only.

## above
NN |4|     IE *n/a*     HTML *n/a*

above="*layerID*"                                                      Optional

Names the positionable element that is to be above (in front of) the current ilayer in the stacking order. This is a different way to set the z-index attribute that does not rely on an arbitrary numbering system. If you use the above attribute, do not use the below or z-index attribute for the same ilayer element.

**Example**          <ilayer id="thingy4" src="quotes.html" above="thingy3"></ilayer>

**Value**            Case-sensitive identifier.

**Default**          None.

**Object Model Reference**

[window.]document.*layerName*.above

## background
NN |4|     IE *n/a*     HTML *n/a*

background="*URL*"                                                     Optional

Specifies an image file that is used as a backdrop to the text and other content of the ilayer element. Unlike normal images that get loaded into browser content, a background image loads in its original size (without scaling) and tiles to fill the available layer space. Smaller images download faster but are obviously repeated more often in the background. Animated GIFs are also allowable but very distracting to the reader. When selecting a background image, be sure it is very muted in comparison to the main content so that the content stands out clearly. Background images, if used at all, should be extremely subtle.

**Example**

<ilayer id="thingy4" src="quotes.html" background="blueCrinkle.jpg"></ilayer>

**Value**            Any valid URL to an image file, including complete and relative URLs.

**Default**          None.

**Object Model Reference**

[window.]document.*layerName*.background

## below
NN |4|     IE *n/a*     HTML *n/a*

below="*layerID*"                                                     Optional

Names the positionable element that is to be below (behind) the current ilayer in the stacking order. This is a different way to set the z-index attribute that does not rely on an arbitrary numbering system. If you use the below attribute, do not use the above or z-index attribute for the same ilayer element.

**Example**          <ilayer id="thingy4" src="quotes.html" below="thingy5"></ilayer>

**Value**            Case-sensitive identifier.

**Default**          None.

## Object Model Reference

[window.]document.*layerName*.below

## bgcolor

NN |4|   IE *n/a*   HTML *n/a*

bgcolor="*colorTripletOrName*"

Optional

Establishes a fill color (behind the text and other content) for the entire layer rectangle. If you combine a bgcolor and background, any transparent areas of the background image let the background color show through.

**Example**           <ilayer src="quotes.html" bgcolor="tan"></ilayer>

**Value**             A hexadecimal triplet or plain-language color name. A setting of empty is interpreted as "#000000" (black). See Appendix A for acceptable plain-language color names.

**Default**           Varies with operating system.

## Object Model Reference

[window.]document.*layerName*.bgColor

## clip

NN |4|   IE *n/a*   HTML *n/a*

clip="[*leftPixel, topPixel,*] *rightPixel, bottomPixel*"

Optional

A clipping region is a rectangular view to the full ilayer content. Only content that is within the clipping rectangle can be seen on the page. The default value of the clip attribute is determined by the space required to display the content as it naturally flows into the element. Setting the clip attribute lets you rein in long content that might flow beyond a fixed rectangle desired for the page design.

**Example**           <ilayer src="quotes.html" clip="50,50"></ilayer>

**Value**

clip attribute values are pixel measures from the top and left edges of the element as it flows in the document. The order of values is clockwise from the left edge, around the rectangle sides: left, top, right, bottom. If you supply only two values, Navigator assumes the left and top values are zero, meaning that you wish to adjust only the right and bottom edges. Thus, a setting of "50,50" means that the clipping region is 50-pixels square, starting at the top-left corner of the layer's rectangle. If you want the same size view, but starting 10 pixels in from the left, the clip attribute setting becomes "10,0,60,50".

**Default**           Naturally flowing viewing area of ilayer content.

## Object Model Reference

[window.]document.*layerName*.clip.left
[window.]document.*layerName*.clip.top
[window.]document.*layerName*.clip.right
[window.]document.*layerName*.clip.bottom

## height, width
NN |4|   IE n/a   HTML n/a

height="*length*" Optional
width="*length*"

Define the minimum size of the layer as it flows in the document. When you add content to the layer, however, the attribute settings do not restrict the amount of the content that is visible along either axis. For example, if you display an image in an ilayer that is 120 pixels wide by 90 pixels high, the actual visible size of an ilayer element whose height and width attributes are set to a smaller size expands to allow the full image to appear. The same happens to text or other content: the viewable region expands to allow all content to appear. To restrict the visible portion of the content, set the clip attribute.

Setting the height and width attributes to specific sizes is helpful when you are creating a colored or patterned rectangle (via the bgcolor or background attributes) to act as an underlying layer beneath some other positioned content. Without content pushing on the edges of the ilayer, the height and width attributes set the clipping region to their sizes.

| | |
|---|---|
| **Example** | `<ilayer bgcolor="yellow" height="100" width="100"></ilayer>` |
| **Value** | Positive integer values (optionally quoted) or percentage values (quoted). You can reduce both values to zero to not only hide the element (which you can also do with the visibility attribute), but prevent the element from occupying any page space. |
| **Default** | Naturally flowing viewing area of ilayer content. |

**Object Model Reference**

[window.]document.*layerName*.height
[window.]document.*layerName*.width

## id
NN |4|   IE n/a   HTML n/a

id="*elementIdentifier*" Optional

A unique identifier that distinguishes this element from all the rest in the document. This is the identifier used as values for the above and below attributes. Scripts also use the id attribute value as the ilayer element's name for object references.

**Example**

`<ilayer id="oldYeller" bgcolor="yellow" height="100" width="100"></ilayer>`

| | |
|---|---|
| **Value** | Case-sensitive identifier. |
| **Default** | None. |

**Object Model Reference**

[window.]document.*layerName*.name

## left, top

left="*pixelCount*"                                                      **Optional**
top="*pixelCount*"

Define the positioned offset of the left and top edges of the layer relative to the spot in the document where the ilayer element would normally appear. The precise location relative to the page varies because an ilayer element is an inline layer, which means it can start anywhere within normally flowing HTML content. When you set either of these attributes, Navigator 4 preserves the space in the document where the ilayer element appears, rather than cinch up surrounding content to fill space vacated by the element that has shifted its location. You are therefore likely to set these attributes for an ilayer only when attempting to accomplish a look tailored to very customized content (perhaps an ilayer amid inflow images).

**Example**          &lt;ilayer bgcolor="yellow" left="10" top="50"&gt;&lt;/ilayer&gt;

**Value**            Positive integer values (optionally quoted).

**Default**          0

**Object Model Reference**

[window.]document.*layerName*.left
[window.]document.*layerName*.top

## name

name="*elementIdentifier*"                                              **Optional**

A unique identifier that distinguishes this element from all the rest in the document. This is the identifier used as values for the above and below attributes. The name attribute is interchangeable with the id attribute for object references.

**Example**
&lt;ilayer name="oldYeller" bgcolor="yellow" height="100" width="100"&gt;&lt;/ilayer&gt;

**Value**            Case-sensitive identifier.

**Default**          None.

**Object Model Reference**

[window.]document.*layerName*.name

## src

src="*URL*"                                                             **Optional**

To load the content of an external HTML file into an ilayer element, assign the URL of that file to the src attribute. Any HTML content between the ilayer start and end tags is rendered on the page after the content loaded from the src URL. If you omit the src attribute, only content between the tags is rendered. Scripts can change the corresponding object property (src) after the document has loaded to dynamically change content within the ilayer element (without reloading the main document).

| **Example** | `<ilayer src="quotes.html"></ilayer>` |
| **Value** | A complete or relative URL. |
| **Default** | None. |

**Object Model Reference**

`[window.]document.layerName.src`

## top

See left.

## visibility

NN |4|   IE *n/a*   HTML *n/a*

`visibility="visibilityConstant"`

Optional

Determines whether Navigator 4 displays the ilayer element. The default behavior is for a layer to inherit the visibility attribute of its next outermost (parent) layer. For an ilayer element that is part of the basic document body, this means that the layer is seen by default (the base layer is always visible). To hide a layer when the page loads, set the visibility attribute to "hidden". You need to set the attribute to "show" only if the ilayer element is nested within another layer with a visibility value that is set to (or is inherited as) "hidden".

Regardless of the visibility attribute setting, an ilayer element always occupies its normal inflow space in the document. This allows Navigator 4 to change the visibility on the fly (via scripting) without reloading the document. (Navigator 4 does not automatically reflow changed content.)

| **Example** | `<ilayer src="quotes.html" visibility="hidden"></ilayer>` |
| **Value** | One of the accepted constants: hidden \| inherit \| visible. |
| **Default** | inherit |

**Object Model Reference**

`[window.]document.layerName.visibility`

## width

See height.

## z-index

NN |4|   IE *n/a*   HTML *n/a*

`z-index="layerNumber"`

Optional

Controls the positioning of layers along the Z-axis (front-to-back) of the document relative to the next outermost layer container. When the z-index values of two or more position-able elements within the same container (such as the base document layer) are identical numbers, the loading order of the elements in the HTML source code controls the stacking order, with the later elements stacked in front of earlier ones. The default z-index value for all positionable elements is zero. Therefore, if you want only one positionable element to appear in front of all the others that stack in their default order, you simply assign any positive value (even 1) to that stand-out element. Stacking order of positionable elements can be changed on-the-fly via scripting. See also the above and below attributes.

**Example**       `<ilayer src="quotes.html" z-index="1"></ilayer>`

**Value**       Any integer.

**Default**       0

### Object Model Reference
`[window.]document.layerName.zIndex`

# &lt;img&gt;

**NN** *all*     **IE** *all*     **HTML** *all*

`<img>`       **HTML End Tag: Forbidden**

The img element displays a graphical image in whatever MIME types the browser is equipped to handle. Common image types are GIF and JPEG, but modern browsers are frequently capable of decoding bitmapped images in PNG and BMP formats (unless helper application settings reroute those file types to external applications). img elements are inline elements, appearing anywhere in the document you specify, including in the middle of a line of text. A large number of attributes affecting visual presentation of the element are deprecated in HTML 4 in favor of style sheet rules. You will be able to use the attributes safely for many browser generations to come, however, because of the need to be backward compatible with the large collection of image-laden documents already on the Web. Note, too, that if you intend to use style sheets for img element borders and margins in Navigator 4, you must wrap the img element inside div or span elements and assign the style sheets to the surrounding element. This workaround works with all other CSS-aware browsers, so you can use style sheets in cross-browser deployment.

If you want to make an entire image a clickable link, wrap the img element inside an a element. To eliminate the typical link border around the image, set the border attribute to 0. And for image maps (where different segments of an image link to different destinations), the HTML recommendation encourages the use of client-side image maps (via the usemap attribute) over the server-side image map (ismap). For nonlinking action, you can assign an onclick event handler to an image in IE 4 and later and Netscape 6. The downside is that you'll have to control the cursor style with other events because the :hover pseudo-class works reliably (if at all) only on a elements.

To be backward compatible with earlier scriptable browsers, it is advisable to include height and width attribute assignments in all img element tags. When values are assigned to these attributes, the browser renders pages more quickly because it doesn't have to wait for the image to load in order to determine its size and organize other content on the page.

### Example
`<img src="mtRushmore.jpg" height="90" width="120" alt="Mount Rushmore">`

### Object Model Reference

[window.]document.*imageName*
[window.]document.images[i]
[window.]document.getElementById(*elementID*)

### Element-Specific Attributes

| | | | | |
|---|---|---|---|---|
| align | alt | border | datafld | datasrc |
| dynsrc | galleryimage | height | hspace | ismap |
| longdesc | loop | lowsrc | name | src |
| start | suppress | usemap | vspace | width |

### Element-Specific Event Handler Attributes

| Handler | NN | IE | HTML |
|---------|-----|-----|------|
| onabort | 3 | 4 | n/a |
| onerror | 3 | 4 | n/a |
| onload | 3 | 4 | n/a |

## align

NN *all*    IE *all*    HTML *all*

align="*where*"

Optional

Determines how the img element is rendered in physical relation to the element's next outermost container and surrounding content. Some settings also let you "float" the image to the left or right margin and let surrounding text wrap around the image (but no wrapping with a centered image).

Most of the rules for alignment-constant values cited at the beginning of this chapter apply to the img element. Typically, align attributes are deprecated in HTML 4 in favor of the style sheet attributes. But if you require backward compatibility for your document, stick with the align attribute.

### Example

```
<img src="surferDude.gif" align="right" alt="Surfer" height="100" width="200">
```

### Value

Each browser defines a different set of values for this attribute. Although the align attribute has a long heritage, not all values do. The more esoteric values, such as absmiddle and baseline, were added to browser offerings in Navigator 3 and Internet Explorer 4, but not added to the W3C repertoire. Assigning different values to multiple images in the same vicinity on the page can result in unpredictable rendering and positioning of the images and surrounding content. Select value(s) from the following table that work for your deployment.

| Value | NN 4+ | IE 4+ | HTML 4 |
|-------|-------|-------|--------|
| absbottom | • | • | — |
| absmiddle | • | • | — |

| Value | NN 4+ | IE 4+ | HTML 4 |
|-------|-------|-------|--------|
| baseline | • | • | – |
| bottom | • | • | • |
| left | • | • | • |
| middle | • | • | • |
| right | • | • | • |
| texttop | • | • | – |
| top | • | • | • |

**Default**        bottom

### Object Model Reference

```
[window.]document.imageName.align
[window.]document.images[i].align
[window.]document.getElementById(elementID).align
```

## alt                                                    NN *all*   IE *all*   HTML *all*

alt="*textMessage*"                                                           **Required**

In a world littered with graphical browsers, it is often hard to remember that not every browser downloads images or that not every web surfer can see the images. Aside from those using VT100 terminals with browsers such as Lynx, pocket computers often offer better performance when images don't have to be downloaded and rendered. Vision impaired users may not be able to see an image, but could benefit by knowing what an image is about. Text-only browsers display the text assigned to an img element's alt attribute where the img element appears on the page. Browsers that speak the page's text also speak the alt text. The alt attribute should contain a brief description of what the image is (or an empty string for images used as space fillers). The HTML recommendation considers this capability so important that it calls the alt attribute a requirement for the img element.

### Example

```
<img src="navbar.gif" usemap="#nav" alt="Navigation Bar" width="400" height="50">
```

**Value**        Any quoted string of characters.

**Default**        None.

### Object Model Reference

```
[window.]document.imageName.alt
[window.]document.images[i].alt
[window.]document.getElementById(elementID).alt
```

<img>

## border

border="*pixels*"                                                    Optional

Controls the thickness of a border around an img element. Default rendering of the border is in black, but if the img element is wrapped inside an a element, the border takes on the document's various link colors (depending on link state). If you want a different color for a plain border, use style sheets (with the appropriate div or span wrapper for Navigator 4). When a link surrounds the image, you can eliminate the colored border altogether by setting the border attribute value to zero.

**Example**

```
<img src="surferDude.gif" alt="Surfer" border="3" height="100" width="200">
```

**Value**          Any integer pixel value.

**Default**        0

**Object Model Reference**

```
[window.]document.imageName.border
[window.]document.images[i].border
[window.]document.getElementById(elementID).border
```

## datafld

datafld="*columnName*"                                               Optional

Used with IE data binding to associate a remote data source column name with the src attribute URL of an img element. A datasrc attribute must also be set for the img element. Works only with text file data sources in IE 5/Mac.

**Example**

```
<img datasrc="DBSRC3" alt="Current Radar" datafld="img3URL" height="100" width="150">
```

**Value**          Case-sensitive identifier.

**Default**        None.

**Object Model Reference**

```
[window.]document.imageName.dataFld
[window.]document.images[i].dataFld
[window.]document.getElementById(elementID).dataFld
```

## datasrc

datasrc="*dataSourceName*"                                           Optional

Used with IE data binding to specify the ID of the page's object element that loads the data source object for remote data access. Content from the data source is specified via the datafld attribute. Works only with text file data sources in IE 5/Mac.

**Example**

```
<img datasrc="DBSRC3" alt="Current Radar" datafld="img3URL" height="100"
width="150">
```

**Value**        Case-sensitive identifier.

**Default**      None.

**Object Model Reference**

```
[window.]document.imageName.dataSrc
[window.]document.images[i].dataSrc
[window.]document.getElementById(elementID).dataSrc
```

## dynsrc                                              NN *n/a*    IE *4*    HTML *n/a*

dynsrc="*URL*"                                                              Optional

Internet Explorer 4 and later allows video clips (and VRML) to be displayed via the img element (as an alternate to the embed or object element). To help the browser differentiate between a dynamic and static image source, you use the dynsrc attribute in place of the src attribute to load the video clip. All other visual aspects of the img element are therefore immediately applicable to the rectangular region devoted to playing the video clip. See also the loop attribute for controlling the frequency of clip play and the start attribute.

**Example**      `<img dynsrc="snowman.avi" loop="3" height="100" width="150">`

**Value**        Any valid URL, including complete and relative URLs.

**Default**      None.

**Object Model Reference**

```
[window.]document.images[i].dynsrc
[window.]document.imageName.dynsrc
[window.]document.getElementById(elementID).dynsrc
```

## galleryimg                                          NN *n/a*    IE *6*    HTML *n/a*

dynsrc="*featureSwitch*"                                                    Optional

Sets whether images that are at least 130 pixels high and wide display the Windows OS "My Pictures" toolbar during mouse rollovers. This tool bar provides quick-click shortcuts to save, print, or email the image. You cannot control which buttons appear in the toolbar.

**Example**

```
<img src="rushmore.jpg" alt="Mount Rushmore" height="240" width="550"
galleryimg="no">
```

**Value**        Constant value: yes | true | no | false.

**Default**      yes

**Object Model Reference**

[window.]document.images[i].galleryImg
[window.]document.*imageName*.galleryImg
[window.]document.getElementById(*elementID*).galleryImg


## height, width                                                NN *all*    IE *all*    HTML *3.2*

height="*length*"                                                                    Optional
width="*length*"

Define the dimensions for the space on the page reserved for the image, regardless of the actual size of the image. For best performance (and backward script compatibility), you should set these attributes to the actual pixel height and width of the source image. If you supply a different measure, the browser scales the image (not very well) to fit the space defined by these attributes.

**Example**          `<img src="surferDude.gif" alt="Surfer" height="100" width="200">`

**Value**            Positive integer values (optionally quoted) or percentage values (quoted).

**Default**          Actual size of source image.

**Object Model Reference**

[window.]document.*imageName*.height
[window.]document.images[i].height
[window.]document.getElementById(*elementID*).height
[window.]document.*imageName*.width
[window.]document.images[i].width
[window.]document.getElementById(*elementID*).width


## hspace, vspace                                               NN *all*    IE *all*    HTML *3.2*

hspace="*pixelCount*"                                                                 Optional
vspace="*pixelCount*"

Define a margin that acts as whitespace padding around the visual content of the img element. The hspace establishes a margin on the left and right sides of the image rectangle; the vspace establishes a margin on the top and bottom sides of the image rectangle. Both attributes are deprecated in HTML 4 in favor of the margin- or padding-related CSS attributes.

**Example**          `<img src="desk3.gif" alt="My Desktop" vspace="10" hspace="10">`

**Value**            Integer representing the number of pixels for the width of the margin on the relevant sides of the img element's rectangle.

**Default**          0

**Object Model Reference**

[window.]document.*imageName*.hspace
[window.]document.images[i].hspace
[window.]document.getElementById(*elementID*).hspace
[window.]document.*imageName*.vspace

```
[window.]document.images[i].vspace
[window.]document.getElementById(elementID).vspace
```

## ismap                                      NN *all*    IE *all*    HTML *all*

ismap                                                                  Optional

The Boolean `ismap` attribute tells the browser that the `img` element is acting as a server-side image map. To turn an image into a server-side image map, wrap the `img` element with an a element whose `href` attribute points to the URL of the CGI program that knows how to interpret the click coordinate information. The browser appends coordinate information about the click to the URL like a `GET` form method appends form element data to the action attribute URL. In the following example, if a user clicks at the coordinate point 50, 25, the browser sends "http://www.giantco.com/cgi-bin/nav.pl?50,25" to the server. A server CGI program named `nav.pl` might examine the region in which the coordinate point appears and send the relevant HTML back to the client.

More recent browsers allow client-side image maps (see the `usemap` attribute), which operate more quickly for the user because there is no communication with the server to carry out the examination of the click coordinate point.

**Example**
```
<a href="http://www.giantco.com/cgi-bin/nav" target="main">
<img src="navbar.gif" alt="Navigation Bar" ismap height="90" width="120">
</a>
```

**Value**          The presence of the attribute turns the feature on.

**Default**        Off.

**Object Model Reference**
```
[window.]document.imageName.isMap
[window.]document.images[i].isMap
[window.]document.getElementById(elementID).isMap
```

## longdesc                                   NN *6*    IE *6*    HTML *4*

longdesc="*URL*"                                                       Optional

Specifies a URL of a document that contains a longer description of the element than what the content of the `alt` or `title` attributes reveal. One application of this attribute in future browsers is to retrieve an annotated description of the element for users who cannot read the browser screen. The **Properties** choice for Netscape 6's context menu for this element displays a small window that includes an active link to the URL assigned to the attribute. Version 6 browsers provide no other functionality for this attribute.

**Example**        `<img longdesc="navDesc.html" alt="Navigation Bar" src="navbar.jpg">`

**Value**          Any valid URL, including complete and relative URLs.

**Default**        None.

**Object Model Reference**

[window.]document.*imageName*.longDesc
[window.]document.images[i].longDesc
[window.]document.getElementById(*elementID*).longDesc

## loop                          NN *n/a*    IE *3*    HTML *n/a*

loop="*loopCount*"                                              Optional

If you specify a video clip with the dynsrc attribute, the loop attribute controls how many times the clip should play ("loop") after it loads. If you set the value to zero, the clip loads but does not play initially. Video clips that are not currently running play when the user double-clicks on the image, but you may need to provide instructions for that on the page because there are no other obvious controls. This attribute does not control animated *.gif* playback.

**Example**

<img dynsrc="snowman.avi" alt="Snowman Movie"loop="3" height="100" width="150">

**Value**          Any positive integer or zero.

**Default**        1

**Object Model Reference**

[window.]document.*imageName*.loop
[window.]document.images[i].loop
[window.]document.getElementById(*elementID*).loop

## lowsrc                          NN *3*    IE *4*    HTML *n/a*

lowsrc="*URL*"                                              Optional

Both Navigator and Internet Explorer recognize the fact that not everyone has a fast Internet connection and that high-resolution images can take a long time to download to the client. To fill the void, the lowsrc attribute lets the author specify a URL of a lower-resolution (or alternate) image to download into the document space first. The lowsrc image should be the same pixel size as the primary src image.

**Example**

<img src="navbar.jpg" alt="Navigation Bar" lowsrc="navbarBW.jpg" height="60" width="300">

**Value**          Any valid URL, including complete and relative URLs.

**Default**        None.

**Object Model Reference**

[window.]document.*imageName*.lowsrc
[window.]document.images[i].lowsrc
[window.]document.getElementById(*elementID*).lowsrc

## name NN 3   IE 4   HTML 4

name="*elementIdentifier*" Optional

If you are scripting an image (especially swapping precached images), backward-compatible scripting utilizes the name attribute value to reference the img object because the id attribute did not exist. References by name are more reliable than by numeric index within the document.images array because you can rearrange or delete images at any time and still maintain references to the remaining named images. For modern browsers only, you can use the id attribute value in place of the name attribute.

### Example
```
<img name="mugshot" id="mugshot" alt="My face" src="janem.jpg" height="90"
width="80">
```

**Value**          Case-sensitive identifier.

**Default**        None.

### Object Model Reference
```
[window.]document.images[i].name
[window.]document.imageName.name
[window.]document.getElementById(elementID).name
```

## src NN *all*   IE *all*   HTML *all*

src="*URL*" Required

URL to a file containing image data that is displayed through the img element. With the exception of specifying a dynsrc attribute in Internet Explorer for video clips or datasrc for IE data binding, the src attribute is required if you want to see any image in the img element space. The browser must be equipped to handle the image MIME type. On the World Wide Web, the most common image formats are GIF and JPEG. HTML or XHTML validation, of course, requires the src attribute and doesn't accept the IE attribute alternatives.

**Example**        `<img src="surferDude.gif" alt="Surfer" height="100" width="200">`

**Value**          A complete or relative URL.

**Default**        None.

### Object Model Reference
```
[window.]document.images[i].src
[window.]document.imageName.src
[window.]document.getElementById(elementID).src
```

## start NN *n/a*   IE 4   HTML *n/a*

start="*videoStartType*" Optional

Whenever you set the dynsrc attribute of an img to display a video clip in Internet Explorer, you can direct the element to start playing the video immediately after the video file loads or when the user rolls the cursor over the image. The start attribute lets you decide the best user interface for your page.

**Example**

‹img dynsrc="snowman.avi" loop="1" start="mouseover" height="100" width="150"›

**Value**        One of the two case-insensitive constant values: fileopen | mouseover.

**Default**      fileopen

**Object Model Reference**

[window.]document.images[i].start
[window.]document.*imageName*.start
[window.]document.getElementById(*elementID*).start

## suppress                                    NN |4|   IE *n/a*   HTML *n/a*

suppress="*featureSwitch*"                                              Optional

When engaged, this attribute prevents Navigator 4 from displaying the generic image icon, alt text, and raised image area while the image is downloading. If the image fails to load, the artifacts appear in the image space as if the attribute were not turned on.

**Example**

‹img src="surferDude.gif" alt="Surfer" height="150" width="250" suppress="true"›

**Value**        Boolean string value: true | false.

**Default**      false

## usemap                                      NN *all*   IE *all*   HTML *3.2*

usemap="*mapURL*"                                                      Optional

You can define a client-side image map with the help of the map and area elements. The map element is a named container for one or more area elements. Each area element sets a "hot" area on an image and assigns a link destination (and other settings) for a response to the user clicking in that region. The purpose of the usemap attribute is to establish a connection between the img element and a named map element in the same document. In some respects, the map element's name is treated like an anchor in that the "address" of the map element is the element's name preceded by a # symbol.

**Example**

‹img src="navbar.gif" alt="Navigation Bar" usemap="#navigation" height="90"
width="120"›

**Value**

A URL to the map element in the same document (a hash symbol plus the map name).

**Default**      None.

### Object Model Reference

```
[window.]document.imageName.useMap
[window.]document.images[i].useMap
[window.]document.getElementById(elementID).useMap
```

## vspace

See hspace.

## width

See height.

# &lt;input&gt;

```
<input>
```
HTML End Tag: Forbidden

An input element is sometimes known as a form control, although not all input elements are visible on the page. For the most part, an input element provides a place for users to enter text, click buttons, and make selections from lists. The data gathered from this interaction can be submitted to a server-side program (when the surrounding form element is submitted), or it may be used strictly on the client as a way for users to interact with client-side scripts. Server applications also commonly embed session data in a page's hidden input elements so that the data gets submitted with the next form submission—one way to cascade data gathering across multiple form pages without maintaining the data temporarily on the server between page deliveries.

Prior to HTML 4, input elements were supposed to be wrapped by a form element in all instances. This restriction is loosening up, but Navigator 4 still requires the form wrapper in order to render input elements.

The primary attribute that determines the kind of control displayed on the page is the type attribute. This attribute can have one of the following values: button, checkbox, file, hidden, image, password, radio, reset, submit, or text. Not all input element types utilize the full range of attributes defined for the input element; sometimes a single attribute has different powers with different element types. For each attribute of the input element, the listing specifies the types to which it applies. Although the textarea element has its own tag, it is often treated like another form control.

### Example

```
<form method="POST" action="http://www.giantco.com/cgi-bin/query.pl">
First Name: <input type="text" name="first" id="first" maxlength="15"><br>
Last Name: <input type="text" name="last" id="last" maxlength="25"><br>
ZIP Code: <input type="text" name="zip" id="zip" maxlength="10"><br>
<input type="reset">
<input type="submit">
</form>
```

<input>

### Object Model Reference

[window.]document.*formName*.*inputName*
[window.]document.forms[i].elements[j]
[window.]document.getElementById(*elementID*)

### Element-Specific Attributes

| | | | | |
|---|---|---|---|---|
| accept | accesskey | align | alt | border |
| checked | datafld | datasrc | disabled | dynsrc |
| height | hspace | ismap | loop | lowsrc |
| maxlength | name | readonly | size | src |
| start | type | usemap | value | vspace |
| width | | | | |

### Element-Specific Event Handler Attributes

| Handler | NN | IE | HTML |
|---|---|---|---|
| onafterupdate | n/a | 4 | n/a |
| onbeforeupdate | n/a | 4 | n/a |
| onchange | 2 | 3 | 4 |
| onselect | 2 | 3 | 4 |

Not all events are active in all input types.

## accept                                                        NN 6   IE 6   HTML 4

accept="*MIMETypeList*"                                                    Optional

Specifies one or more MIME types for allowable files to be uploaded to the server when the form is submitted. The HTML 4 provides this attribute in case a browser wishes to incorporate some file type filtering prior to submitting a form with a file input element. As of Version 6 browsers, this attribute has no practical impact on file selection or submission.

**Input Types**     file

**Example**     <input type="file" accept="text/html, image/gif" ...>

**Value**     MIME type (content type) value. For multiple items, a comma-delimited list is allowed.

**Default**     None.

## accesskey                                                     NN 6   IE 4   HTML 4

accesskey="*character*"                                                    Optional

See the description of this shared attribute at the beginning of this chapter for general characteristics. For file input types, pressing the accesskey combination places the text pointer in the associated text box, but does not "click" the Browser button.

**Input Types**     All rendered types.

<input>

## align

align="*alignmentConstant*"                                      Optional

Determines how the rectangle of the input image aligns within the context of the surrounding content. See "Alignment Constants" earlier in this chapter for a description of the possibilities for this attribute with img elements.

**Input Types**        image

**Example**        `<input type="image" name="icon" src="icon.gif" align="absmiddle">`

**Value**        Alignment-constant value applied to elements outside the image rectangle.

**Default**        left

**Object Model Reference**
```
[window.]document.formName.inputName.align
[window.]document.forms[i].elements[j].align
[window.]document.getElementById(elementID).align
```

## alt

alt="*textMessage*"                                      Optional

Provides text description of the input element image while the image downloads, in lieu of rendered images, or for text-to-speech browsers. Behaves just like the alt attribute of the img element.

**Input Types**        image

**Example**        `<input type="image" name="icon" src="sndIcon.gif" alt="Sound Icon">`

**Value**        Any quoted string of characters.

**Default**        None.

**Object Model Reference**
```
[window.]document.formName.inputName.alt
[window.]document.forms[i].elements[j].alt
[window.]document.getElementById(elementID).alt
```

## border

border="*pixels*"                                      Optional

Navigator 4 and later on all OS platforms and IE 4 and later on the Mac let you specify a border around the input element image. Because an input element whose type attribute is "image" acts as a submit-style button, the border is rendered in the browser's link colors, unless overridden by a style sheet. If you want a different color for a plain border, use style sheets (with the appropriate div or span wrapper for Navigator 4). Navigator 4 (only) places a border around the image by default. Set the border attribute to zero to remove the border.

**Input Types**        image

**Example**       `<input type="image" name="icon" src="sndIcon.gif" border="0">`

**Value**         Any integer pixel value.

**Default**       2 (Navigator 4) or 0 (All others).

**Object Model Reference**

`[window.]document.`*formName*`.`*inputName*`.border`
`[window.]document.forms[i].elements[j].border`
`[window.]document.getElementById(`*elementID*`).border`

## checked                                          NN *all*    IE *all*    HTML *4*

checked                                                         Optional

A Boolean attribute that designates whether the current checkbox or radio input element is
turned on when the page loads. In the case of a radio button grouping, only one input
element should have the checked attribute. Scripts can modify the internal value of this
attribute after the page has loaded. When the form is submitted, an input element that has
its checked attribute turned on sends its name/value pair as part of the form data. The
name/value pair consists of values assigned to the name and value attributes for the element.
If no value is assigned to the value attribute, the string value "active" or "on" is automatically assigned when the checkbox or radio button is highlighted. This is fine for
checkboxes because each one should be uniquely named. However, all radio buttons in a
related group must have the same name for browsers to handle the automatic highlighting
and unhighlighting within the group. This default characteristic doesn't provide enough
information for most server-side programs to work with. See the name attribute below.

**Input Types**     checkbox, radio

**Example**

`<input type="checkbox" name="addToList" checked>Send email updates to this`
`web site.`

**Value**         The presence of this attribute turns on its property.

**Default**       Off.

**Object Model Reference**

`[window.]document.`*formName*`.`*inputName*`.checked`
`[window.]document.forms[i].elements[j].checked`
`[window.]document.getElementById(`*elementID*`).checked`

## datafld                                          NN *n/a*    IE *4*    HTML |*4*|

datafld="*columnName*"                                          Optional

Used with IE 4 data binding to associate a remote data source column name with parts of
various input elements. A datasrc attribute must also be set for the element. Works only
with text file data sources in IE 5/Mac.

This attribute was reserved in HTML 4, but was dropped in XHTML 1.0.

<input>

**Input Types**     button, checkbox, hidden, password, radio, text

**Example**

`<input type="text" name="first" datasrc="DBSRC3" datafld="firstName">`

**Value**     Case-sensitive identifier.

**Default**     None.

**Object Model Reference**

```
[window.]document.formName.inputName.dataFld
[window.]document.forms[i].elements[j].dataFld
[window.]document.getElementById(elementID).dataFld
```

## datasrc                  NN *n/a*   IE 4   HTML |4|

`datasrc="dataSourceName"`              Optional

Used with IE data binding to specify the ID of the page's object element that loads the data source object for remote data access. Content from the data source is specified via the datafld attribute. Works only with text file data sources in IE 5/Mac.

This attribute was reserved in HTML 4, but was dropped in XHTML 1.0.

**Input Types**     button, checkbox, hidden, password, radio, text

**Example**

`<input type="text" name="first" datasrc="DBSRC3" datafld="firstName">`

**Value**     Case-sensitive identifier.

**Default**     None.

**Object Model Reference**

```
[window.]document.formName.inputName.dataSrc
[window.]document.forms[i].elements[j].dataSrc
[window.]document.getElementById(elementID).dataSrc
```

## disabled                  NN 6   IE 4   HTML 4

`disabled`              Optional

A disabled input element appears grayed out on the screen and cannot be activated by the user. A disabled form control cannot receive focus and does not become active within the tabbing order rotation. IE/Windows extends this to mean that if one radio button in a group is disabled, the entire group is disabled. Not so in IE/Mac or Netscape 6, which let unhighlighted buttons uncheck a disabled checked member of the group.

The name/value pair of a disabled input element is not sent to the server when the form is submitted. input elements that normally perform submissions do not submit their form when disabled.

The disabled attribute is a Boolean type, which means that in HTML format, its presence in the attribute sets its value to true. Its value can also be adjusted after the fact by scripting (see the button object in Chapter 9).

**Input Types**       All.

**Example**       `<button type="submit" disabled>Ready to Submit </button>`

**Value**       The presence of the attribute disables the element.

**Default**       `false`

### Object Model Reference

```
[window.]document.formName.inputName.disabled
[window.]document.forms[i].elements[j].disabled
[window.]document.getElementById(elementID).disabled
```

## dynsrc                                                    NN *n/a*    IE *4*    HTML *n/a*

`dynsrc="URL"`                                                                    Optional

Internet Explorer 4 and later allows video clips (and VRML) to be displayed via an image type input element. To help the browser differentiate between a dynamic and static image source, you use the dynsrc attribute in place of the src attribute to load the video clip. All other visual aspects of the input type input element are therefore immediately applicable to the rectangular region devoted to playing the video clip. See also the loop attribute for controlling the frequency of clip play and the start attribute.

**Input Types**       image

### Example

```
<input type="image" dynsrc="submit.avi" alt="Submit Button" loop="3" height="100"
width="150">
```

**Value**       Any valid URL, including complete and relative URLs.

**Default**       None.

### Object Model Reference

```
[window.]document.formName.inputName.dynsrc
[window.]document.forms[i].elements[j].dynsrc
[window.]document.getElementById(elementID).dynsrc
```

## height, width                                           NN *4*    IE *4*    HTML *n/a*

`height="pixels"`                                                                 Optional
`width="pixels"`

Defines the dimensions of the image used for the input element. If you omit these attributes, the browser waits for the image to load before allocating space on the page for the element.

**Input Types**       All.

| **Example** | `<input type="image" src="submit.jpg" height="20" width="60">` |
| **Value** | Positive integers. |
| **Default** | Default image size. |

## hspace, vspace

```
height="pixels"
width="pixels"
```
Optional

Establishes extra padding around the image (and, thus, the input element) to keep other content at a minimum distance. The hspace controls the padding thickness of both the left and right edges; vspace does the same for top and bottom.

**Input Types**      All.

**Example**

```
<input type="image" src="submit.jpg" alt="Submit Button" height="20" width="60"
hspace="10" vspace="20">
```

| **Value** | Positive integers. |
| **Default** | 0 |

## ismap

```
ismap
```
Optional

The Boolean ismap attribute tells the browser that the image representing the input element is acting as a server-side image map. Unlike the img element, the image type input element has an action (submitting the form) associated with it, so no surrounding a element is required. The browser appends coordinate information about the click to the URL of the form's action. See the usemap attribute for client-side image map details.

**Input Types**      image

**Example**

```
<input type="image src="navbar.gif" alt="Navigation Bar" ismap height="90"
width="120">
```

| **Value** | The presence of the attribute turns the feature on. |
| **Default** | Off. |

**Object Model Reference**

```
[window.]document.formName.inputName.isMap
[window.]document.forms[i].elements[j].isMap
[window.]document.getElementById(elementID).isMap
```

## loop

NN *n/a*   IE *3*   HTML *n/a*

loop="*loopCount*"                                                      Optional

If you specify a video clip with the dynsrc attribute, the loop attribute controls how many times the clip should play ("loop") after it loads. If you set the value to zero, the clip loads but does not play initially. Video clips that are not currently running play when the user double-clicks on the image, but you may need to provide instructions for that on the page because there are no other obvious controls.

**Input Types**      image

**Example**
```
<input type="image" dynsrc="snowman.avi" alt="Snowman Movie" loop="3" height="100"
width="150">
```

**Value**          Any positive integer or zero.

**Default**        1

**Object Model Reference**
[window.]document.*formName*.*inputName*.loop
[window.]document.forms[i].elements[j].loop
[window.]document.getElementById(*elementID*).loop

## lowsrc

NN *all*   IE *4*   HTML *n/a*

lowsrc="*URL*"                                                          Optional

Provides a URL to an alternate low-resolution image to be loaded initially if the src image is taking a long time to load.

**Input Types**      image

**Example**
```
<input type="image" src="navbar.jpg" alt="Navigation Bar" lowsrc="navbarBW.jpg"
height="60" width="300">
```

**Value**          Any valid URL, including complete and relative URLs.

**Default**        None.

**Object Model Reference**
[window.]document.*formName*.*inputName*.lowsrc
[window.]document.forms[i].elements[j].lowsrc
[window.]document.getElementById(*elementID*).lowsrc

## maxlength

NN *all*   IE *all*   HTML *all*

maxlength="*characterCount*"                                           Optional

Defines the maximum number of characters that may be typed into a text field input element. In practice, browsers beep or otherwise alert users when a typed character would exceed the maxlength value. There is no innate correlation between the maxlength and size attributes. If the maxlength allows for more characters than fit within the specified width of the element, the browser provides horizontal scrolling (albeit awkward for many users) to allow entry and editing of the field.

**Input Types**        password, text

**Example**          &lt;input type="text" name="ZIP" maxlength="10"&gt;

**Value**              Positive integer.

**Default**           Unlimited.

**Object Model Reference**

[window.]document.*formName*.*inputName*.maxLength
[window.]document.forms[i].elements[j].maxLength
[window.]document.getElementById(*elementID*).maxLength

## name

NN *all*    IE *all*    HTML *all*

name="*elementIdentifier*"

Optional/Required

If the input element is part of a form being submitted to a server, the name attribute is required if the value of the element is to be submitted with the form. For forms that are in documents for the convenience of scripted form elements, input element names are not required but are helpful just the same in creating scripted references to these objects and their properties or methods.

The identifier you assign to the name attribute becomes part of the name/value pair submitted to the server. Radio button elements that are to act as a mutually exclusive group must all have the same name attribute value. In many browsers, failure to include a name attribute assignment disallows user access to checkbox or radio input elements.

The HTML 4 and XHTML specifications encourage using the id attribute in place of the name attribute throughout your pages. Mainstream browsers through Version 6 do not submit data from input elements bearing an id assignment but no name assignment. For consistency with DHTML-scripted DOM access of all elements, it's good practice to assign both attributes, even using the same identifier for both (except for radio buttons, whose IDs need to be unique, while their names are shared). Let the name attribute carry the element's value to the server, while scripts reach the elements via their IDs—especially in browsers that provide the IE document.all.elementID or W3C DOM document. getElementById(elementID) referencing syntax. Perhaps reluctantly, the strict XHTML DTD validates the name attribute for input elements so that validated pages will function within the reality of former and current browser implementations.

**Input Types**        All.

**Example**          &lt;input type="text" name="ZIP" id="ZIP" maxlength="10"&gt;

**Value**              Case-sensitive identifier.

**Default**           None.

**Object Model Reference**

```
[window.]document.formName.inputName.name
[window.]document.forms[i].elements[j].name
[window.]document.getElementById(elementID).name
```

## readonly
NN 6   IE 4   HTML 4

readonly
Optional

When the readonly attribute is present, the text field input element cannot be edited on the page by the user (although scripts can modify the content). A field marked as readonly should not receive focus within the tabbing order (although IE 4 and later for the Macintosh allows the field to receive focus and beeps if a user tries to type).

| | |
|---|---|
| **Input Types** | password, text |
| **Example** | \<input type="text" name="ZIP" readonly\> |
| **Value** | The presence of the attribute sets its value to true. |
| **Default** | false |

**Object Model Reference**

```
[window.]document.formName.inputName.readOnly
[window.]document.forms[i].elements[j].readOnly
[window.]document.getElementById(elementID).readOnly
```

## size
NN all   IE all   HTML all

size="elementWidth"
Optional

In practice, the size attribute is limited to describing the width of text field input elements based on the number of characters that display. The actual rendered width is calculated based on the font setting (or default font) for the element, but the results are not always perfect. Variations in font rendering (and the ability to specify alternate font faces and sizes in newer browsers) sometimes lead to unexpectedly narrower fields. Therefore, it is not wise to automatically set the size and maxlength attributes to the same value without testing the results on a wide variety of browsers and operating systems with worst-case data (for example, all "m" or "W" characters in proportional fonts). The HTML 4 specification indicates that the size attribute might be applied to other input element types (as pixels, rather than characters), but as of the Version 6 browsers, this is not the case. In the meantime, you can use CSS attributes to make buttons wider than the default size that tracks the width of the value attribute string.

| | |
|---|---|
| **Input Types** | password, text |
| **Example** | \<input type="text" name="ZIP" maxlength="10" size="12"\> |
| **Value** | Any positive integer. |
| **Default** | 20 |

<input>

## Object Model Reference

```
[window.]document.formName.inputName.size
[window.]document.forms[i].elements[j].size
[window.]document.getElementById(elementID).size
```

| src | NN *all* | IE *all* | HTML *all* |
|---|---|---|---|
| src="*URL*" | | | Required |

URL to a file containing image data that is displayed through the input element of type image. The browser must be equipped to handle the image MIME type. On the World Wide Web, the most common image formats are GIF and JPEG.

| | |
|---|---|
| **Input Types** | image |
| **Example** | `<input type="image" name="icon" src="sndIcon.gif" border="0">` |
| **Value** | A complete or relative URL. |
| **Default** | None. |

## Object Model Reference

```
[window.]document.formName.inputName.src
[window.]document.forms[i].elements[j].src
[window.]document.getElementById(elementID).src
```

| start | NN *n/a* | IE *4* | HTML *n/a* |
|---|---|---|---|
| start="*videoStartType*" | | | Optional |

Whenever you set the dynsrc attribute of an image type input element to display a video clip in Internet Explorer, you can direct the element to start playing the video immediately after the video file loads or when the user rolls the cursor over the image. The start attribute lets you decide the best user interface for your page.

**Input Types**     image

**Example**
```
<input type="image dynsrc="submit.avi" alt="Submit Button" loop="1"
start="mouseover" height="100" width="150">
```

| | |
|---|---|
| **Value** | One of the two case-insensitive constant values: fileopen \| mouseover. |
| **Default** | fileopen |

## Object Model Reference

```
[window.]document.formName.inputName.start
[window.]document.forms[i].elements[j].start
[window.]document.getElementById(elementID).start
```

Alphabetical
HTML Reference

<input>

## type

type="*elementType*"

Advises the browser how to render the input element (or even whether the element should be rendered at all). Possible choices are as follows.

| Type | Description |
|------|-------------|
| button | A clickable button whose action must be scripted. Its label is assigned by the value attribute. If you want to use HTML to format the label of a button, use the button element instead. |
| checkbox | A free-standing checkbox that provides two states (active/on and inactive/off). Its label is created by HTML text before or after the input element tag (also see the label element). The value attribute value is submitted with a form. |
| file | A button and field that lets the user select a local file for eventual uploading to the server. A click of the button generates a File dialog, and the name (or pathname) of the selected file appears in the field. The server must have a CGI script (invoked by the form's action attribute URI) to accept the incoming file at submission time. |
| hidden | An invisible field often used to carry over database or state data from submission to submission without bothering the user with its content (or having to store the temporary data on the server). The name/value pair is submitted with the form. |
| image | A graphical button whose sole default action is to submit the form. The coordinate points x,y of the click on the image are submitted as two name/value pairs linked by an ampersand character: inputName.x=n&inputName.y=m. |
| password | A text field that presents bullets or asterisks for each typed character to ensure over-the-shoulder privacy for the user. The plain-language text is submitted as the value for this element. |
| radio | One of a related group of on-off buttons. Assigning the same value to the name attribute of multiple radio buttons assembles them in a related group. Clicking on one button in the group activates it while unhighlighting all others. The value attribute value of the activated member is submitted with a form. |
| reset | A button whose sole job is to revert the form's elements to the values they had when the form initially loaded into the client. A custom label can be assigned via the value attribute. |
| submit | A button whose sole job is to submit the form. A custom label can be assigned by the value attribute. If name and value attributes are assigned for the element, their values are submitted with the form. |
| text | A one-line field for typing text that gets submitted as the value of the element (in a URL-encoded format). For a multiple-line field, see the textarea element. |

**Input Types**        All.

**Example**
```
<input type="button" value="Toggle Sound" onclick="toggleSnd( )">
<input type="checkbox" name="connections" value="ISDN">ISDN
<input type="file" name="uploadFile">
<input type="hidden" name="prevState" id="prevState" value="modify">
<input type="image" name="graphicSubmit" src="submit.jpg" height="40" width="40">
<input type="password" name="password" maxlength="12" size="20">
<input type="radio" name="creditCard" value="Visa">Visa
<input type="reset">
<input type="submit" value="Send Encrypted">
Social Security Number:<input type="text" name="ssn" value="###-##-####"
onclick="validateSSN(this)">
```

### Value

Any one of the known input element types: button | checkbox | file | hidden | image | password | radio | reset | submit | text.

### Default          text

### Object Model Reference

```
[window.]document.formName.inputName.type
[window.]document.forms[i].elements[j].type
[window.]document.getElementById(elementID).type
```

## usemap                                                   NN 6    IE 6    HTML 4

`usemap="mapURL"`                                                      Optional

You can define a client-side image map for an image type input element with the help of the map and area elements. The map element is a named container for one or more area element. Each area element sets a "hot" area on an image and assigns a link destination (and other settings) for a response to the user clicking in that region. The purpose of the usemap attribute is to establish a connection between the image type input element and a named map element in the same document. In some respects, the map element's name is treated like an anchor in that the "address" of the map element is the element's name preceded by a # symbol.

### Input Types          image

### Example

```
<input type="image" src="submit.gif" alt="Submit Button" usemap="#submitter"
height="90" width="120">
```

### Value

A URL to the map element in the same document (a hash symbol plus the map name).

### Default          None.

### Object Model Reference

```
[window.]document.formName.inputName.useMap
[window.]document.forms[i].elements[j].useMap
[window.]document.getElementById(elementID).useMap
```

## value                                                   NN all    IE all    HTML all

`value="text"`                                                Optional/Required

Preassigns a value to an input element that is submitted to the server as part of the name/value pair for the element. Some input element types are not submitted (an unchecked radio button, for example), but any value you associate with all but the button or reset type input element reaches the server when the element is submitted.

In the case of text and password input elements, the value attribute contains a default entry. As the user makes a change to the content of the text field, the value changes, although the source code does not. When a form is reset (via a reset input element), the default values are put back into the text fields.

The value attribute is required only for checkbox and radio input elements. For input elements that are rendered as standard clickable buttons, the value attribute defines the label that appears on the button.

**Input Types**    All.

**Example**    `<input type="checkbox" name="connections" value="ISDN">ISDN`

**Value**    Any text string.

**Default**    None.

**Object Model Reference**

```
[window.]document.formName.inputName.defaultValue
[window.]document.forms[i].elements[j].defaultValue
[window.]document.getElementById(elementID).defaultValue
[window.]document.formName.inputName.value
[window.]document.forms[i].elements[j].value
[window.]document.getElementById(elementID).value
```

## vspace

See hspace.

## width

See height.

## &lt;ins&gt;                                    NN 6   IE 4   HTML 4

`<ins>...</ins>`                                    HTML End Tag: Required

The ins element and its companion, del, define a format that shows which segments of a document's content have been marked up for insertion (or deletion) during the authoring process. This is far from a workflow management scheme, but in the hands of a supporting WYSIWYG HTML authoring tool, these elements can assist in controlling generational changes of a document in process.

Browsers that support this element render text contained by the element as underlined (whereas del elements are in a strikethrough style). The HTML 4 specification includes two potentially useful attributes for preserving hidden information about the date and time of the alteration and some descriptive text about the change.

**Example**

```
<p>Four score and
<del cite="Fixed the math">eight</del><ins>seven</ins> years ago...</p>
```

<ins>

### Object Model Reference
[window.]document.getElementById(*elementID*)

### Element-Specific Attributes
cite          datetime

### Element-Specific Event Handler Attributes
None.

## cite                                                    NN 6    IE 6    HTML 4
cite="*text*"                                                              Optional

A description of the reason for the change or other notation to be associated with the element, but normally hidden from view. In Netscape 6, the context menu for such an element contains a **Properties** choice, which leads to a displayed list of attributes and their values for the visitor. Or, your DHTML scripts can access the information through the element object's cite property, and add value to the presentation.

| | |
|---|---|
| **Example** | <ins cite="Fixed the math --A.L.">seven</ins> |
| **Value** | Any string of characters. The string must be inside a matching pair of (single or double) quotation marks. |
| **Default** | None. |

### Object Model Reference
[window.]document.getElementById(*elementID*).cite

## datetime                                                NN 6    IE 6    HTML 4
datetime="*datetimeString*"                                               Optional

The date and time the insertion was made. This information is most likely to be added into a document with an HTML authoring tool designed to track content insertions and deletions. Data from this attribute can be recalled later as an audit trail to changes of the document. There can be only one datetime attribute value associated with a given ins element. In Netscape 6 the context menu for such an element contains a **Properties** choice, which leads to a displayed list of attributes and their values for the visitor. Or, your DHTML scripts can access the information through the element object's dateTime property, and add value to the presentation.

**Example**       <ins datetime="2001-09-11T08:56:00-04:00">*SomeInsertedTextHere*</ins>

**Value**

The datetime attribute requires a value in a special date-time format that conveys information about the date and time in such a way that the exact moment can be deduced from any time zone around the world. Syntax for the format is as follows: *yyyy-MM-ddThh:mm:ssTZD*.

*yyyy* Four-digit year

*MM*   Two-digit month (01 through 12)

*dd*   Two-digit date (01 through 31)

T   Uppercase "T" to separate date from time

*hh*   Two-digit hour in 24-hour time (00 through 23)

*mm*   Two-digit minute (00 through 59)

*ss*   Two-digit second (00 through 59)

*TZD*   Time Zone Designator

There are two formats for the Time Zone Designator. The first is simply the uppercase letter "Z", which stands for UTC (Coordinated Universal Time—also called "Zulu"). The other format indicates the offset from UTC that the time shown in *hh:mm:ss* represents. This time offset consists of a plus or minus symbol and another pair of *hh:mm* values. For time zones west of Greenwich Mean Time (which, for all practical purposes is the same as UTC), the operator is a negative sign because the main *hh:mm:ss* time is earlier than UTC; for time zones east of GMT, the offset is a positive value. For example, Pacific Standard Time is eight hours earlier than UTC: when it is 6:00 P.M. in the PST zone, it is 2:00 A.M. the next morning at UTC. Thus, the following examples all represent the exact same moment in time (Time Zone Designator shown in boldface for clarification only):

| | |
|---|---|
| 2003-01-30T02:00:00**Z** | UTC |
| 2003-01-29T21:00:00-**05:00** | Eastern Standard Time |
| 2003-01-29T18:00:00-**08:00** | Pacific Standard Time |
| 2003-01-30T13:00:00+**11:00** | Sydney, Australia |

For more details about this way of representing time, see the ISO-8601 standard.

**Default**       None.

# &lt;isindex&gt;

NN *all*    IE *all*    HTML *all*

`<isindex>`

HTML End Tag: Forbidden

The isindex element is a longtime holdover from the earliest days of HTML and is deprecated in HTML 4 in favor of the text input element. The isindex element tag belongs in the head element. In modern browsers, it is rendered as a simple text field between two hr elements. When a user types text into the field and presses the **Enter/Return** key, the content of the field is URL-encoded (with + symbols substituted for spaces) and sent to the server with the URL of the current document. A CGI program on the server must know how to process this URL and return HTML for display in the current window or frame.

**Example**

```
<head>
<isindex prompt="Enter a search string:">
</head>
```

**Object Model Reference**

[window.]document.getElementById(*elementID*)

**Element-Specific Attributes**
prompt

**Element-Specific Event Handler Attributes**
None.

## prompt
NN *all*    IE *all*    HTML *4*

prompt="*message*"
Optional

This attribute lets you assign the prompt message that appears with the element.

| | |
|---|---|
| **Example** | &lt;isindex prompt="Enter a search string:"&gt; |
| **Value** | Any quoted string. |
| **Default** | None. |

## &lt;kbd&gt;
NN *all*    IE *all*    HTML *all*

&lt;kbd&gt;...&lt;/kbd&gt;
HTML End Tag: Required

The kbd element is one of a large group of elements that the HTML 4 recommendation calls *phrase elements*. Such elements assign structural meaning to a designated portion of the document. A kbd element is one that displays text that a user is supposed to type on the keyboard, presumably to fill a text field or issue some command.

Browsers have free rein to determine how (or whether) to distinguish kbd element content from the rest of the body element. Both Navigator and Internet Explorer elect to use a monospace font for the text. Override the default with a style sheet as you see fit.

**Example**
&lt;p&gt;If you don't know the answer, type &lt;kbd&gt;NONE&lt;/kbd&gt; into the text box.&lt;/p&gt;

**Object Model Reference**
[window.]document.getElementById(*elementID*)

**Element-Specific Attributes**
None.

**Element-Specific Event Handler Attributes**
None.

## &lt;keygen&gt;
NN *all*    IE *n/a*    HTML *n/a*

&lt;keygen&gt;
HTML End Tag: Forbidden

A keygen element allows a form to be submitted with key encryption, where the server expects a form to be packaged with an encrypted key. The client browser must have a digital certificate installed. The user sees two results of including the keygen element inside a form element. First, a select list of available encryption key sizes is rendered in the form where the

keygen element appears. When the user submits the form, the user may see one or more secu-
rity-related dialogs for confirmation. This element builds on the public-key encryption
systems in Navigator and Netscape's Certificate Management System (CMS). Documentation is available at *developer.netscape.com/docs/manuals/cms/41/dep-guide/contents.htm*.

**Example**

```
<form ...>
...
<keygen name="encryptedOrder" challenge="39457582201">
</form>
```

**Element-Specific Attributes**

challenge           keytype           name           pqg

**Element-Specific Event Handler Attributes**

None.

## challenge NN *all*   IE *n/a*   HTML *n/a*

challenge="*challengeString*"                                      **Required**

If the server is equipped to interpret a challenge string for verification of an encrypted
package, the challenge attribute is the challenge string. If you assign an empty string to the
attribute, the key is encoded as an IA5STRING.

| | |
|---|---|
| **Example** | `<keygen name="encryptedOrder" challenge="39457582201">` |
| **Value** | Any string. |
| **Default** | Empty string. |

## keytype NN *all*   IE *n/a*   HTML *n/a*

keytype="*keyType*"                                     **Optional/Required**

Sets the type of key to be created by the CMS prior to submitting the form data. This
attribute is required only for the secondary type, DSA.

**Example**

```
<keygen name="encryptedOrder" challenge="39457582201" keytype="DSA">
```

| | |
|---|---|
| **Value** | One of two constant values: RSA | DSA. |
| **Default** | RSA |

## name NN *all*   IE *n/a*   HTML *n/a*

name="*identifier*"                                       **Required**

Encrypting a form turns the entire form into a value that is part of a name/value pair. The
name attribute assigns the "name" part of the name/value pair. If the server successfully

<label>

decrypts the package, the individual form element name/value pairs are available to the server for further processing.

| | |
|---|---|
| **Example** | `<keygen name="encryptedOrder" challenge="39457582201">` |
| **Value** | Case-insensitive identifier. |
| **Default** | None. |

## pqg

`pqg="dssParams"`                                                                                              Optional/Required

If you specify the DSA key type for the keytype attribute, you must also assign associated parameter values to the pqg attribute. An explanation of the algorithms used to derive these values may be found at *ftp://ftp.ietf.org/internet-drafts/draft-ietf-pkix-ipki-pkalgs-05.txt.*

# <label>

`<label>...</label>`                                                                                        HTML End Tag: Required

The label element defines a structure and container for the label associated with an input element. Because the rendered labels for most form controls are not part of the element's tag, the label attribute provides a way for an author to associate the context of the label with its control. A label element also simplifies assigning uniform styles to all form labels.

You have two ways to provide the association. One is to assign the id attribute value of the control to the for attribute of the label element. The other is to wrap the input element inside a label element. The latter is possible only if the label and control are part of running body content; if you must physically separate the label from the control because they exist inside separate td elements of a table, you must use the for attribute linkage. Whether the label is rendered in front of or after the control depends entirely on the relative locations of the tags in the source code.

### Example

```
<form>
<label>Company:<input type="text" name="company"></label><br>
<label for="stateEntry">State:</label>
<input type="text" name="state" id="stateEntry">
...
</form>
```

### Object Model Reference

`[window.]document.getElementById(elementID)`

### Element-Specific Attributes

| | | | | |
|---|---|---|---|---|
| accesskey | datafld | dataformatas | datasrc | for |

### Element-Specific Event Handler Attributes

None.

## accesskey

NN 6    IE 4    HTML 4

accesskey="*character*"                                                         Optional

A single character key that brings focus to, or activates, the associated input element. See the description of this shared attribute at the beginning of this chapter for general characteristics.

**Example**          &lt;label for="stateEntry" accesskey="s"&gt;State:&lt;/label&gt;

**Value**            Single character of the document set.

**Default**          None.

**Object Model Reference**
[window.]document.getElementById(*elementID*).accessKey

## datafld

NN *n/a*    IE 4    HTML *n/a*

datafld="*columnName*"                                                          Optional

Used with IE data binding to associate a remote data source column name with the label of an input element. The data source column must be either plain text or HTML (see dataformatas). A datasrc attribute must also be set for the label element. Works only with text file data sources in IE 5/Mac.

**Example**
&lt;label for="stateEntry" datasrc="DBSRC3" datafld="label" dataformatas="HTML"&gt;
&lt;/label&gt;

**Value**            Case-sensitive identifier.

**Default**          None.

**Object Model Reference**
[window.]document.getElementById(*elementID*).dataFld

## dataformatas

NN *n/a*    IE 4    HTML *n/a*

dataformatas="*dataType*"                                                       Optional

Used with IE data binding, this attribute advises the browser whether the source material arriving from the data source is to be treated as plain text or as tagged HTML. This attribute setting depends entirely on how the data source is constructed. Works only with text file data sources in IE 5/Mac.

**Example**
&lt;label for="stateEntry" datasrc="DBSRC3" datafld="label" dataformatas="HTML"&gt;
&lt;/label&gt;

**Value**            IE recognizes two possible settings: text | html.

**Default**          text

**Object Model Reference**

[window.]document.getElementById(*elementID*).dataFormatAs

## datasrc                                          NN *n/a*   IE 4   HTML *n/a*

datasrc="*dataSourceName*"                                          Optional

Used with IE data binding to specify the ID of the page's object element that loads the data source object for remote data access. Content from the data source is specified via the datafld attribute. Works only with text file data sources in IE 5/Mac.

**Example**

```
<label for="stateEntry" datasrc="DBSRC3" datafld="label" dataformatas="HTML">
</label>
```

**Value**          Case-sensitive identifier.

**Default**        None.

**Object Model Reference**

[window.]document.getElementById(*elementID*).dataSrc

## for                                              NN 6   IE 4   HTML 4

for="*inputElementIdentifier*"                                     Optional

A unique identifier that is also assigned to the id attribute of the input element to which the label is to be associated. The for attribute is necessary only when you elect not to wrap the input element inside the label element, in which case the for attribute performs the binding between the two elements.

**Example**          <label for="stateEntry">State:</label>

**Value**            Case-sensitive identifier.

**Default**          None.

**Object Model Reference**

[window.]document.getElementById(*elementID*).htmlFor

# &lt;layer&gt;                                     NN |4|   IE *n/a*   HTML *n/a*

&lt;layer&gt;...&lt;/layer&gt;                                 HTML End Tag: Required

A layer element is a positionable element in Navigator 4's object model (e.g., like a block-level element whose CSS position attribute is set to absolute). As a result, many of the attributes are named according to the Navigator 4 way of positioning, sizing, and stacking positionable elements. The element was removed from the Netscape DOM for Version 6, and will not be implemented in new browsers or W3C standards.

Content for a layer element can be read from a separate file (with the src attribute) or wired into the current document by placing the HTML between the start and end tags. You can include both types of content in the same layer element. Content from the src document is rendered first (as its own block-level element), with additional content starting on its own line below the external content's rectangle.

A layer element can be positioned anywhere within a document and can overlap content belonging to other layers (including the base document layer). Under link or script control, content for an individual layer can be changed without having to reload the other content on the page. Moreover, layer elements may be nested inside one another.

### Example

```
<layer bgcolor="yellow" src="instrux.html" width="200" height="300"></layer>
```

### Object Model Reference

[window.]document.*layerName*

### Element-Specific Attributes

| | | | | |
|---|---|---|---|---|
| above | background | below | bgcolor | clip |
| height | id | left | pagex | pagey |
| src | top | visibility | width | z-index |

### Element-Specific Event Handler Attributes

| Handler | NN | IE | HTML |
|---|---|---|---|
| onblur | 4 | n/a | n/a |
| onfocus | 4 | n/a | n/a |
| onload | 4[a] | n/a | n/a |
| onmousedown | 4[a] | n/a | n/a |
| onmouseout | 4[a] | n/a | n/a |
| onmouseover | 4[a] | n/a | n/a |
| onmouseup | 4[a] | n/a | n/a |

[a] Event capture mode only.

## above
NN |4|   IE *n/a*   HTML *n/a*

above="*layerID*"
Optional

Names the positionable element that is to be above (in front of) the current layer in the stacking order. This is a different way to set the z-index attribute that does not rely on an arbitrary numbering system. If you use the above attribute, do not use the below or z-index attribute for the same layer element.

### Example

```
<layer id="instrux" bgcolor="yellow" src="instrux.html" above="help1"
width="200" height="300">
</layer>
```

### Value
Case-sensitive identifier.

**Default**        None.

**Object Model Reference**

[window.]document.*layerName*.above

## background                                    NN |4|   IE *n/a*   HTML *n/a*

background="*URL*"                                                    Optional

Specifies an image file that is used as a backdrop to the text and other content of the layer element. Unlike normal images that get loaded into browser content, a background image loads in its original size (without scaling) and tiles to fill the available layer space. Smaller images download faster but are obviously repeated more often in the background. Animated GIFs are also allowable but very distracting to the reader. When selecting a background image, be sure it is very muted in comparison to the main content so that the content stands out clearly. Background images, if used at all, should be extremely subtle.

**Example**

```
<layer background="blueCrinkle.jpg" src="instrux.html" width="200" height="300">
</layer>
```

**Value**        Any valid URL to an image file, including complete and relative URLs.

**Default**        None.

**Object Model Reference**

[window.]document.*layerName*.background

## below                                          NN |4|   IE *n/a*   HTML *n/a*

below="*layerID*"                                                    Optional

Names the positionable element that is to be below (behind) the current layer in the stacking order. This is a different way to set the z-index attribute that does not rely on an arbitrary numbering system. If you use the below attribute, do not use the above or z-index attribute for the same layer element.

**Example**

```
<layer bgcolor="yellow" src="instrux.html" width="200" height="300"
below="thankyou">
</layer>
```

**Value**        Case-sensitive identifier.

**Default**        None.

**Object Model Reference**

[window.]document.*layerName*.below

## bgcolor

NN |4|    IE *n/a*    HTML *n/a*

bgcolor="*colorTripletOrName*"                                                    Optional

Establishes a fill color (behind the text and other content) for the entire layer rectangle. If you combine a bgcolor and background, any transparent areas of the background image let the background color show through.

### Example

```
<layer bgcolor="yellow" src="instrux.html" width="200" height="300"></layer>
```

### Value

A hexadecimal triplet or plain-language color name. A setting of empty is interpreted as "#000000" (black). See Appendix A for acceptable plain-language color names.

**Default**          Varies with operating system.

### Object Model Reference

[window.]document.*layerName*.bgColor

## clip

NN |4|    IE *n/a*    HTML *n/a*

clip="[*leftPixel, topPixel,*] *rightPixel, bottomPixel*"                         Optional

A clipping region is a rectangular view to the full layer content. Only content that is within the clipping rectangle can be seen on the page. The default value of the clip attribute is either the default size of the content or the layer element's width by the automatically flowing content length. Setting the clip attribute lets you rein in long content that might flow beyond a fixed rectangle desired for the page design.

### Example

```
<layer bgcolor="yellow" src="instrux.html" clip="50,50" width="200" height="300">
</layer>
```

### Value

clip attribute values are pixel measures from the top and left edges of the element as it flows in the document. The order of values is clockwise from the left edge, around the rectangle sides: left, top, right, bottom. If you supply only two values, Navigator 4 assumes the left and top values are zero, meaning that you wish to adjust only the right and bottom edges. Thus, a setting of "50,50" means that the clipping region is 50 pixels square, starting at the top-left corner of the layer's rectangle. If you want the same size view starting 10 pixels in from the left, the clip attribute setting becomes "10,0,60,50".

**Default**          Naturally flowing viewing area of layer content.

### Object Model Reference

[window.]document.*layerName*.clip.left
[window.]document.*layerName*.clip.top
[window.]document.*layerName*.clip.right
[window.]document.*layerName*.clip.bottom

## height, width NN |4|  IE *n/a*  HTML *n/a*

```
height="length"
width="length"
```
**Optional**

Define the minimum size of the layer element. When you add content to the layer during initial loading, however, the attribute settings do not restrict the amount of the content that is visible along either axis. For example, if you display an image in a layer that is 120 pixels wide by 90 pixels high, the actual visible size of a layer element whose height and width attributes are set to a smaller size expands to allow the full image to appear. The same happens to text or other content: the viewable region expands to allow all content to appear. To restrict the visible portion of the content, set the clip attribute.

Setting the height and width attributes to specific sizes is helpful when you are creating a colored or patterned rectangle (via the bgcolor or background attributes) to act as an underlying layer beneath some other positioned content. Without content pushing on the edges of the layer, the height and width attributes set the clipping region to their sizes.

### Example
```
<layer bgcolor="yellow" src="instrux.html" width="200" height="300"></layer>
```

### Value
Positive integer values or percentage values. You can reduce both values to zero to not only hide the element (which you can also do with the visibility attribute), but also prevent the element from occupying any page space.

**Default**  Naturally flowing viewing area of layer content.

### Object Model Reference
```
[window.]document.layerName.height
[window.]document.layerName.width
```

## id NN |4|  IE *n/a*  HTML *n/a*

```
id="elementIdentifier"
```
**Optional**

A unique identifier that distinguishes this element from all the rest in the document. This is the identifier used as values for the above and below attributes. Scripts also use the id attribute value as the layer element's name for object references.

### Example
```
<layer id="oldYeller" bgcolor="yellow" src="instrux.html" width="200" height="300">
</layer>
```

**Value**  Case-sensitive identifier.

**Default**  None.

### Object Model Reference
```
[window.]document.layerName.name
```

## left, top

NN |4|    IE *n/a*    HTML *n/a*

left="*pixelCount*"

top="*pixelCount*"

Optional

Define the positioned offset of the left and top edges of the layer relative to the spot in the document where the layer element would normally appear in source code order. This precise location relative to the page varies unless you also set the pagex and pagey attributes, which absolutely position the element in the document space. Unlike what it does for the ilayer element, Navigator does not preserve the space in the document where a layer element appears. The element is placed in its own plane, and the surrounding source code content is cinched up—usually overlapping the layer content unless the layer is positioned elsewhere.

### Example

```
<layer bgcolor="yellow" src="instrux.html" width="200" height="300" left="10"
top="50">
</layer>
```

**Value**       Positive integer values (optionally quoted).

**Default**       0

### Object Model Reference

[window.]document.*layerName*.left

[window.]document.*layerName*.top

## pagex, pagey

NN |4|    IE *n/a*    HTML *n/a*

pagex="*pixelCount*"

pagey="*pixelCount*"

Optional

To truly position a layer element with repeatable accuracy, you can use the top-left corner of the document (page) as the point of reference. When you set the pagex and/or pagey attributes, you establish an offset for the left and top edges of the layer element relative to the corresponding edges of the entire document. Therefore, the zero point for a vertically scrolled page may be above the visible area of the browser window.

### Example

```
<layer bgcolor="yellow" src="instrux.html" width="200" height="300" pagex="50"
pagey="350">
</layer>
```

**Value**       Positive integer values (optionally quoted).

**Default**       0

### Object Model Reference

[window.]document.*layerName*.pageX

[window.]document.*layerName*.pageY

## src

src="*URL*"                                                                  Optional

To load the content of an external HTML file into a layer element, assign the URL of that file to the src attribute. Any HTML content between the layer start and end tags is rendered on the page after the content is loaded from the src URL. If you omit the src attribute, only content between the tags is rendered. Scripts can change the corresponding object property (src) after the document has loaded to dynamically change content within the layer element (without reloading the main document).

### Example
```
<layer bgcolor="yellow" src="instrux.html" width="200" height="300"></layer>
```

**Value**              A complete or relative URL.

**Default**            None.

### Object Model Reference
[window.]document.*layerName*.src


## top

See left.


## visibility

visibility="*visibilityConstant*"                                            Optional

Determines whether Navigator 4 displays the layer element. The default behavior is for a layer to inherit the visibility attribute of its next outermost (parent) layer. For a layer element that is part of the basic document body, this means that the layer is seen by default (the base layer is always visible). To hide a layer when the page loads, set the visibility attribute to "hidden". You need to set the attribute to "show" only if the layer element is nested within another layer (or ilayer) whose visibility value is set to (or is inherited as) "hidden".

### Example
```
<layer bgcolor="yellow" src="instrux.html" width="200" height="300"
pagex="50" pagey="350" visibility="hidden">
</layer>
```

**Value**              One of the accepted constants: hidden | inherit | visible.

**Default**            inherit

### Object Model Reference
[window.]document.*layerName*.visibility

## width

See height.

## z-index

NN |4|   IE n/a   HTML n/a

z-index="*layerNumber*"

Optional

Controls the positioning of layers along the Z-axis (front-to-back) of the document relative to the next outermost layer container. When the z-index values of two or more position-able elements within the same container (such as the base document layer) are identical numbers, the loading order of the elements in the HTML source code controls the stacking order, with the later elements stacked in front of earlier ones. The default z-index value for all positionable elements is zero. Therefore, if you want only one positionable element to appear in front of all the others that stack in their default order, you simply assign any posi-tive value (even 1) to that standout element. Stacking order of positionable elements can be changed on-the-fly via scripting. See also the above and below attributes.

**Example**

```
<layer bgcolor="yellow" src="instrux.html" width="200" height="300" z-index="1">
</layer>
```

**Value**        Any integer.

**Default**      0

**Object Model Reference**

[window.]document.*layerName*.zIndex

# &lt;legend&gt;

NN 6   IE 4   HTML 4

&lt;legend&gt;...&lt;/legend&gt;

HTML End Tag: Required

The legend element acts as a label for a fieldset element. In visual browsers, this usually means that the label is visually associated with the group border rendered for the fieldset element. A text-to-speech browser might read the label aloud as a user navigates through a form. Place the legend element immediately after the start tag of the fieldset element for the association to stick. Because the content of the legend element is HTML content, you can assign styles to make the label stand out, if you like.

**Example**

```
<form method="POST" action="...">
<fieldset>
<legend>Credit Card Information</legend>
...inputElementsHere...
</fieldset>
</form>
```

**Object Model Reference**

[window.]document.getElementById(*elementID*)

**Element-Specific Attributes**

accesskey        align

**Element-Specific Event Handler Attributes**

None.

## accesskey

accesskey="*character*"                Optional

A single character key that brings focus to, or activates, the first focusable control of the form associated with the legend element. See the description of this shared attribute at the beginning of this chapter for general characteristics.

| | |
|---|---|
| **Example** | `<legend accesskey="c">Credit Card Information</legend>` |
| **Value** | Single character of the document set. |
| **Default** | None. |

**Object Model Reference**

[window.]document.getElementById(*elementID*).accessKey

## align

align="*where*"                Optional

Controls the alignment of the legend element with respect to the containing fieldset element. See the discussion about text alignment inside a containing box in the section "Alignment Constants," earlier in this chapter.

| | |
|---|---|
| **Example** | `<legend align="right">Credit Card Information</legend>` |
| **Value** | Allowed values in HTML 4 are bottom \| left \| right \| top. IE 4 and later and Netscape 6 add center. |
| **Default** | left |

**Object Model Reference**

[window.]document.getElementById(*elementID*).align

## &lt;li&gt;

&lt;li&gt;...&lt;/li&gt;             HTML End Tag: Optional

The li element is a single list item that is nested inside an ol or ul list container. The outer container determines whether the li item is preceded with a number or letter (indicating sequence within an order) or a symbol that doesn't connote any particular order. A special category of style sheet attributes are devoted to list formatting.

If you apply a style sheet rule to an li element to adjust the color in Navigator 4, only the leading symbol is colored. To color the text as well, wrap the li element inside a span element and apply the style to the span element. This workaround operates fine in other CSS-capable browsers.

**Example**

```
<ul>
    <li>Larry</li>
    <li>Moe</li>
    <li>Curly</li>
</ul>
```

**Object Model Reference**

[window.]document.getElementById(*elementID*)

**Element-Specific Attributes**

type                value

**Element-Specific Event Handler Attributes**

None.

## type                                                                    NN *all*   IE *all*   HTML *3.2*

type="*labelType*"                                                                              Optional

The type attribute provides some flexibility in how the browser displays the item's leading symbol or sequence number. Values are divided into two groups, with one group each dedicated to ol and ul items. For an unordered list (ul), you can specify whether the leading symbol should be a disc, circle, or square; for an ordered list (ol), the choices are among letters (uppercase or lowercase), Roman numerals (uppercase or lowercase), or Arabic numerals. The type attribute is deprecated in HTML 4 in favor of the list-style-type style sheet attribute.

Be aware that in Version 4 browsers, the type attribute for a li element sets the type for subsequent li elements in the list unless overridden by a type attribute setting in another li element. More recent versions restrict the effect to the current li element. In general, though, it is best to set the type attribute of the ol or ul element and let that setting govern all nested elements.

**Example**            `<li type="square">Chicken Curry</li>`

**Value**

When contained by a ul element, possible values are disc | circle | square. When contained by an ol element, possible values are A | a | I | i | 1. Sequencing is performed automatically as shown in the following table.

| Type | Example |
|------|---------|
| A | A, B, C, ... |
| a | a, b, c, ... |
| I | I, II, III, ... |

<link>

| Type | Example |
|------|---------|
| i | i, ii, iii, ... |
| 1 | 1, 2, 3, ... |

**Default**        1 and disc.

**Object Model Reference**

[window.]document.getElementById(*elementID*).type

## value

NN *all*    IE *all*    HTML *3.2*

value="*number*"                                                    Optional

The value attribute applies only when the li element is nested inside an ol element. You can manually set the number used as a starting point for the sequencing of ordered list items. This can come in handy when you need to break up an ol element with some running text that is not part of the list.

Even though the value assigned to this attribute is a number, it does not affect the type setting. For example, setting value to 3 when type is A means that the sequence starts from that li element with the letter C.

**Example**

<li value="3">Insert Tab C into Slot M. Tighten with a wingnut.</li>

**Value**          Any positive integer.

**Default**        1

**Object Model Reference**

[window.]document.getElementById(*elementID*).value

## <link>

NN *4*    IE *3*    HTML *all*

<link>                                                    HTML End Tag: Forbidden

Unlike the a element (informally called a link when it contains an href attribute), the link element belongs inside the head element and is a place for the document to establish links with external documents, such as style sheet definition files or font definition files. By and large, browsers have yet to exploit the intended powers of this element. A variety of attributes let the author establish relationships between the current document and potentially related documents. In theory, some of these relationships could be rendered as part of the document or browser controls. Implementations of this element as of Version 6 of Navigator and Internet Explorer are rather weak compared to the HTML 4 specification. At the same time, several attributes (and all event handlers) defined in the HTML 4 specification and listed among shared items at the beginning of this chapter aren't very helpful because they more typically apply to elements that actually display content on the page. No explicit document content is rendered as a result of the link element. Some of those attributes may be associated with the link element by mistake or merely for consistency.

### Example
```
<head>
<title>Section 3</title>
<link rev="Prev" href="sect2.html">
<link rel="Next" href="sect4.html">
<link rel="stylesheet" type="text/css" href="myStyles.css">
</head>
```

### Object Model Reference
[window.]document.getElementById(*elementID*)

### Element-Specific Attributes

| charset | href | hreflang | media | rel |
|---------|------|----------|-------|-----|
| rev | src | target | type | |

### Element-Specific Event Handler Attributes
None.

---

## charset                                                NN *6*    IE *n/a*    HTML *4*

charset="*characterSet*"                                                          Optional

Character encoding of the content at the other end of the link.

| | |
|---|---|
| **Example** | `<link charset="csISO5427Cyrillic" href="moscow.html">` |
| **Value** | Case-insensitive alias from the character set registry (*ftp://ftp.isi.edu/in-notes/iana/assignments/character-sets*). |
| **Default** | Determined by browser. |

---

## href                                                   NN *6*    IE *3*    HTML *all*

href="*URI*"                                                                     Required

The URI of the document associated with the link (also known in W3C jargon as the *destination*, even though there is no page navigation involved). Navigator 4 uses the src attribute for this purpose. Include both attributes for a backward-compatible implementation.

| | |
|---|---|
| **Example** | `<link rel="Prev" href="sect2.html" src="sect2.html">` |
| **Value** | Any valid URI, including complete and relative URLs. |
| **Default** | None. |

### Object Model Reference
[window.]document.getElementById(*elementID*).href

## hreflang

hreflang="*languageCode*"                                    **Optional**

The language code of the content at the destination of a link. Requires that the href attribute also be set. This attribute is primarily an advisory attribute to help a browser prepare itself for a new language set if the browser is so enabled.

| | |
|---|---|
| **Example** | `<link hreflang="HI" href="hindi/Chap3.html">` |
| **Value** | Case-insensitive language code. |
| **Default** | Browser default. |

**Object Model Reference**

[window.]document.getElementById(*elementID*).hrefLang

## media

media="*descriptorList*"                                    **Optional**

Sets the intended output device for the content of the destination document pointed to by the href attribute. The media attribute looks forward to the day when browsers are able to tailor content to specific kinds of devices such as pocket computers, text-to-speech digitizers, or fuzzy television sets. The HTML 4 specification defines a number of constant values for anticipated devices, but the list is open-ended, allowing future browsers to tailor output to yet other kinds of media and devices.

**Example**

`<link rel="Glossary" href="gloss.html" media="screen, tv, handheld">`

**Value**

Constant values. Multiple values can be grouped together in a comma-delimited list within a quoted string. Values defined in HTML 4 are all | aura | braille | handheld | print | projection | screen | tty | tv . IE 4 and later claims support for all | print | screen.

**Default**       screen

**Object Model Reference**

[window.]document.getElementById(*elementID*).media

## rel

rel="*linkTypes*"                                    **Optional**

Defines the relationship between the current element and the destination of the link. The HTML 4 recommendation defines several link types; it is up to the browser to determine how to employ the value. The element must include an href attribute for the rel attribute to be applied.

**Example**       `<link rel="Next" href="sect6.html">`

## Value

Case-insensitive, space-delimited list of standard link types applicable to the document and browser. HTML 4-sanctioned link types are:

| | | | |
|---|---|---|---|
| alternate | appendix | bookmark | chapter |
| contents | copyright | glossary | help |
| index | next | prev | section |
| start | stylesheet | subsection | |

IE 4 and later and Navigator 4 and later use stylesheet to link in an external CSS file. Navigator 4 recognizes stylesheet and fontdef. In IE 5 and later for Windows, you can also use the value shortcut icon (with the space) and assign a URL to a custom icon file (.ico) on your server so that your icon appears in the Favorites list if the user chooses to add the page to his list.

**Default**        None.

## Object Model Reference

[window.]document.getElementById(*elementID*).rel

---

**rev**                                                      NN 6   IE 4   HTML 4

rev="*linkTypes*"                                                          Optional

A reverse link relationship. Like the rel attribute, the rev attribute's capabilities are defined by the browser, particularly with regard to how the browser interprets and renders the various link types available in the HTML 4 specification. Given two documents (A and b) containing links that point to each other, the rev value of b is designed to express the same relationship between the two documents as denoted by the rel attribute in A. Version 6 browsers provide no practical functionality for this attribute.

**Example**        &lt;link rev="Prev" href="sect4.html"&gt;

**Value**          Case-insensitive, space-delimited list of HTML 4 standard link types applicable to the element. See the rel attribute for sanctioned link types.

**Default**        None.

## Object Model Reference

[window.]document.getElementById(*elementID*).rev

---

**src**                                                      NN 4   IE *n/a*   HTML *n/a*

src="*URL*"                                                                Optional

The URL of the destination of a link. Internet Explorer 4 and later, Netscape 6, and HTML 4 use the href attribute for this purpose. Include both attributes for a cross-browser implementation.

**Example**

&lt;link rel="fontdef" src="fonts/garamond.pfr" href="fonts/garamond.pfr"&gt;

---

<link>

**Value**          Any valid URL, including complete and relative URLs.

**Default**        None.

## target
NN 6   IE 4   HTML 4

`target="windowOrFrameName"`                                                          Optional

Presumably, the target attribute is provided in HTML 4 as a way to specify the destination for the display of a document at the other end of the href attribute of the link element.

### Value

Identifier when the frame or window name has been assigned via the target element's name attribute. Four reserved target names act as constants:

_blank
> Browser creates a new window for the destination document.

_parent
> Destination document replaces the current frame's framesetting document (if one exists; otherwise, it is treated as _self).

_self
> Destination document replaces the current document in its window or frame.

_top
> Destination document is to occupy the entire browser window, replacing any and all framesets that may be loaded (also treated as _self if there are no framesets defined in the window).

IE for Windows implements two other values: _search (IE 5 and later) and _media (IE 6). These supposedly direct the browser to load linked content into the browser's Search pane and Media Bars, respectively. Precise implementation details are not yet clear.

**Default**        _self

### Object Model Reference

`[window.]document.getElementById(elementID).target`

## type
NN 4   IE 4   HTML 4

`type="MIMEType"`                                                                      Optional

An advisory about the content type of the destination document or resource. In practice, this attribute has been used so far to prepare the browser for the style sheet type being linked to.

### Example

`<link rel="stylesheet" type="text/css" href="styles/mainStyle.html">`

### Value

Case-insensitive MIME type. A catalog of registered MIME types is available from *ftp://ftp.isi.edu/in-notes/iana/assignments/media-types/*.

**Default**        None.

**Object Model Reference**

[window.]document.getElementById(*elementID*).type

# &lt;listing&gt;

NN *all*    IE *all*    HTML *&lt;4*

&lt;listing&gt;...&lt;/listing&gt;                                         HTML End Tag: Required

The listing element displays its content in a monospace font as a block element, as in computer code listings rendered 132 columns wide. In most browsers, the font size is also reduced from the default size. Browsers observe carriage returns and other whitespace in element content. This element has been long deprecated in HTML and has even been removed from the HTML 4.0 specification. You are encouraged to use the pre element instead.

**Example**

```
<listing>
&lt;script language="JavaScript"&gt;
    document.write("Hello, world.")
&lt;/script&gt;
</listing>
```

**Object Model Reference**

[window.]document.getElementById(*elementID*)

**Element-Specific Attributes**

None.

**Element-Specific Event Handler Attributes**

None

# &lt;map&gt;

NN *all*    IE *all*    HTML *3.2*

&lt;map&gt;...&lt;/map&gt;                                              HTML End Tag: Required

A map element is a container for area elements that define the location and links of hotspots of client-side image maps. The primary purpose of the map element is to associate an identifier (the name attribute) that the usemap attribute points to when turning an img element into a client-side image map. Most other attributes are style-related and may be applied to the map element so that they are inherited by elements nested within.

**Example**

```
<img src="images/logo.gif" alt="Scroll to the bottom for navigation links."
height="300" width="250" usemap="#navigation">
<map name="navigation">
<area shape="rect" coords="0,0,100,100" href="products.html">
<area shape="rect" coords="0,100,300,100" href="support.html">
</map>
```

**Object Model Reference**

[window.]document.getElementById(*elementID*)

**Element-Specific Attributes**

name

**Element-Specific Event Handler Attributes**

None.

## name

name="*identifier*"                                                                       **Required**

The identifier to which the usemap attribute of an img element points. Because the usemap attribute is actually a URL type, its value resembles that of a link to an anchor: the name is preceded by a hash symbol (only in the usemap attribute). Despite XHTML's preference for id attributes over name attributes, browsers continue to rely on the name attribute as the connection between an image and an area map. Strict HTML 4 and XHTML DTDs continue to validate the name attribute.

| | |
|---|---|
| **Example** | &lt;map name="navigation"&gt; ...&lt;/map&gt; |
| **Value** | Case-sensitive unique identifier. |
| **Default** | None. |

**Object Model Reference**

[window.]document.getElementById(*elementID*).name

## &lt;marquee&gt;

&lt;marquee&gt;...&lt;/marquee&gt;                                                **HTML End Tag: Optional**

The marquee element is unique to Internet Explorer. It displays HTML content in a scrolling region on the page. Scrolled content goes between the start and end tags. There is no corresponding element in Navigator, although the effect can be duplicated in a cross-browser fashion with a Java applet or more cumbersomely through Dynamic HTML.

**Example**

```
<marquee behavior="slide" direction="left" width="250" bgcolor="white">
Check out our monthly specials.
</marquee>
```

**Object Model Reference**

[window.]document.getElementById(*elementID*)

**Element-Specific Attributes**

| behavior | bgcolor | datafld | dataformatas | datasrc |
|---|---|---|---|---|
| direction | height | hspace | loop | scrollamount |
| scrolldelay | truespeed | vspace | width | |

### Element-Specific Event Handler Attributes

| Handler | NN | IE | HTML |
|---|---|---|---|
| onafterupdate | n/a | 4 | n/a |
| onbounce | n/a | 4 | n/a |
| onfinish | n/a | 4 | n/a |
| onstart | n/a | 4 | n/a |

## behavior

NN *n/a*   IE *3*   HTML *n/a*

behavior="*motionType*"

Optional

Sets the motion of the content within the rectangular space reserved for the marquee element. You have a choice of three motion types.

### Example

```
<marquee behavior="slide" direction="left" width="250" bgcolor="white">
...</marquee>
```

### Value

One of the case-insensitive marquee element motion types:

alternate
> Content alternates between marching left and right.

scroll
> Content scrolls (according to the direction attribute) into view and out of view before starting again.

slide
> Content scrolls (according to the direction attribute) into view, stops at the end of its run, blanks, and then starts again.

**Default**        scroll

### Object Model Reference

[window.]document.getElementById(*elementID*).behavior

## bgcolor

NN *n/a*   IE *3*   HTML *n/a*

bgcolor="*colorTripletOrName*"

Optional

Establishes a fill color (behind the text and other content) for the rectangular space reserved for the marquee element.

### Example

```
<marquee behavior="slide" direction="left" width="250" bgcolor="white">
...</marquee>
```

**Value**

A hexadecimal triplet or plain-language color name. A setting of empty is interpreted as "#000000" (black). See Appendix A for acceptable plain-language color names.

**Default**        Varies with browser, browser version, and operating system.

**Object Model Reference**

[window.]document.getElementById(*elementID*).bgColor

## datafld                                             NN *n/a*    IE *4*    HTML *n/a*

datafld="*columnName*"                                                      Optional

Used with IE data binding to associate a remote data source column name with the content scrolled by the marquee element. The data source column must be either plain text or HTML (see dataformatas). A datasrc attribute must also be set for the marquee element. Works only with text file data sources in IE 5/Mac.

**Example**

```
<marquee behavior="slide" direction="left" width="200"
datasrc="DBSRC3" datafld="news" dataformatas="HTML"></marquee>
```

**Value**        Case-sensitive identifier.

**Default**        None.

**Object Model Reference**

IE

## dataformatas                                        NN *n/a*    IE *4*    HTML *n/a*

dataformatas="*dataType*"                                                   Optional

Used with IE data binding, this attribute advises the browser whether the source material arriving from the data source is to be treated as plain text or as tagged HTML. This attribute setting depends entirely on how the data source is constructed. Works only with text file data sources in IE 5/Mac.

**Example**

```
<marquee behavior="slide" direction="left" width=200
datasrc="DBSRC3" datafld="news" dataformatas="HTML"></marquee>
```

**Value**        Constant values: text | html.

**Default**        text

**Object Model Reference**

[window.]document.getElementById(*elementID*).dataFormatAs

## datasrc

datasrc="*dataSourceName*"                                                    Optional

Used with IE data binding, this attribute advises the browser whether the source material arriving from the data source is to be treated as plain text or as tagged HTML. Works only with text file data sources in IE 5/Mac.

### Example
```
<marquee behavior="slide" direction="left" width="200"
datasrc="DBSRC3" datafld="news" dataformatas="HTML"></marquee>
```

**Value**          Case-sensitive identifier.

**Default**        None.

### Object Model Reference
[window.]document.getElementById(*elementID*).dataSrc


## direction

direction="*scrollDirection*"                                                 Optional

A marquee element's content may scroll in one of four directions. For optimum readability in languages written left to right, it is easier to grasp the content when it scrolls either to the left or downward.

### Example
```
<marquee behavior="slide" direction="left" width="200">...</marquee>
```

**Value**          Four possible directions: down | left | right | up.

**Default**        left

### Object Model Reference
[window.]document.getElementById(*elementID*).direction


## height, width

height="*length*"                                                            Optional
width="*length*"

A marquee element renders itself as a rectangular space on the page. You can override the default size of this rectangle by assigning values to the height and width attributes. The default value for height is determined by the font size of the largest font assigned to content in the marquee. Default width is set to 100% of the width of the next outermost container (usually the document body). The width defines how much space is used at one time or another by horizontally scrolling content. When the marquee is embedded within a td element that lets the browser determine the table cell's calculated width, you must set the width of the marquee element or risk having the browser set it to 1, making the content unreadable.

If you want extra padding around the space, see the hspace and vspace attributes.

**Example**

```
<marquee behavior="slide" direction="left" height="20" width="200">
...
</marquee>
```

**Value**          Any length value in pixels or percentage of available space.

**Default**        A width of 100%; a height of 12 pixels.

**Object Model Reference**

```
[window.]document.getElementById(elementID).height
[window.]document.getElementById(elementID).width
```

## hspace, vspace                                   NN *n/a*    IE 3    HTML *n/a*

```
hspace="pixelCount"                                            Optional
vspace="pixelCount"
```

Internet Explorer provides attributes for setting padding around a marquee element. The hspace attribute controls padding along the left and right edges (horizontal padding), whereas the vspace attribute controls padding along the top and bottom edges (vertical padding). Adding such padding provides an empty cushion around the marquee's rectangle. As an alternative, you can specify the various margin style sheet settings, especially if you want to open space along only one edge.

**Example**

```
<marquee behavior="slide" direction="left" height="20" width="200"
hspace="10" vspace="15">...</marquee>
```

**Value**          Any positive integer.

**Default**        0

**Object Model Reference**

```
[window.]document.getElementById(elementID).hspace
[window.]document.getElementById(elementID).vspace
```

## loop                                            NN *n/a*    IE 3    HTML *n/a*

```
loop="count"                                                  Optional
```

Sets the number of times the marquee element scrolls its content. After the final scroll, the content remains in a fixed position. Constant animation can sometimes be distracting to page visitors, so if you have the marquee turn itself off after a few scrolls, you may be doing your visitors a favor.

**Example**

```
<marquee behavior="slide" direction="left" height="20" width="200" loop="3">
...</marquee>
```

**Value**

Any positive integer if you want the scrolling to stop. Otherwise, set the value to -1 or infinite.

**Default**        -1

**Object Model Reference**

[window.]document.getElementById(*elementID*).loop

## scrollamount                                NN *n/a*    IE *3*    HTML *n/a*

scrollamount="*pixelCount*"                                          Optional

marquee content looks animated by virtue of the browser clearing and redrawing its content at a location offset from the previous location (in a direction set by the direction attribute). You can make the scrolling appear faster by increasing the amount of space between positions of each drawing of the content; conversely, you can slow down the scrolling by decreasing the space. See also scrolldelay.

**Example**

```
<marquee behavior="slide" direction="left" height="20" width="200" scrollamount="2">
...</marquee>
```

**Value**        Any positive integer.

**Default**        6

**Object Model Reference**

[window.]document.getElementById(*elementID*).scrollAmount

## scrolldelay                                NN *n/a*    IE *3*    HTML *n/a*

scrolldelay="*milliseconds*"                                          Optional

Apparent scrolling speed can be influenced by the frequency of the redrawing of the content as its position shifts with each redraw (see scrollamount). Increasing the scrolldelay value slows down the scroll speed, whereas decreasing the value makes the scrolling go faster. Be aware that on slower computers, you can reach a value at which no increase of speed is discernible no matter how small you make the scrolldelay value (see truespeed).

**Example**

```
<marquee behavior="slide" direction="left" height="20" width="200"
scrolldelay="100">...</marquee>
```

**Value**

Any positive integer representing the number of milliseconds between content redraws.

**Default**        85 (Windows 95); 90 (Macintosh).

**Object Model Reference**

[window.]document.getElementById(*elementID*).scrollDelay

<menu>

## truespeed

truespeed                                                                                         **Optional**

The marquee element includes a built-in speed bump to prevent scrolling from being accidentally specified as too fast for visitors to read. If you genuinely intend the content to scroll very fast, you can include the truespeed attribute to tell the browser to honor scrolldelay settings below 60 milliseconds.

### Example

```
<marquee behavior="slide" direction="left" height="20" width="200"
scrolldelay="45" truespeed>...</marquee>
```

**Value**          The presence of this attribute sets the value to true.

**Default**        false

### Object Model Reference

[window.]document.getElementById(*elementID*).trueSpeed

## vspace

See hspace.

## width

See height.

# <menu>

<menu>...</menu>                                                              **HTML End Tag: Required**

The original idea of the menu element was to allow browsers to generate single-column lists of items. Virtually every browser, however, treats the menu element the same as a ul element to present an unordered single column list of items (usually preceded by bullets). The menu element is deprecated in HTML 4. You should be using the ul element for it in any case, because you are assured backward compatibility and forward compatibility should this element ever disappear from the browser landscape. Everything said here also applies to the deprecated dir element.

### Example

```
Common DB Connector Types:
<menu>
    <li>DB-9</li>
    <li>DB-12</li>
    <li>DB-25</li>
</menu>
```

### Object Model Reference

[window.]document.getElementById(*elementID*)

**Element-Specific Attributes**

compact

**Element-Specific Event Handler Attributes**

None.

## compact

NN 6    IE 6    HTML 3.2

compact                                                                        Optional

A Boolean attribute originally designed to let browsers render the list in a more compact style than normal (smaller line spacing between items).

| | |
|---|---|
| **Example** | `<menu compact>...</menu>` |
| **Value** | The presence of this attribute makes its value `true`. |
| **Default** | `false` |

**Object Model Reference**

`[window.]document.getElementById(elementID).compact`

## &lt;meta&gt;

NN *all*    IE *all*    HTML *all*

&lt;meta&gt;                                                         HTML End Tag: Forbidden

A meta element conveys hidden information about the document. Some browsers respond to this element to derive header information that may be important to the document but is not sent by the server in response to the request for the document. The element is also used to embed document information that some search engines use for indexing and categorizing documents on the World Wide Web.

More than one meta element may be included in a document, and all meta elements belong nested inside the head element. The specific purpose of each meta element is defined by its attributes. Typically, a meta element reduces to a name/value pair that is of use to either the server or the client. For example, most browsers recognize attribute settings that force the page to reload (or redirect to another page) after a timed delay. This would be useful in a page whose content is updated minute-by-minute, because the browser keeps reloading the latest page as often as indicated in the meta element.

Several other elements and attributes in HTML 4 contain the same kind of metadata that might otherwise be located in meta elements. Use the avenue that is best suited to your intended server and browser environments. See also the address, del, ins, link, and title elements, as well as the profile attribute of the head element.

Much mythology surrounds meta element usage. Some attribute values affect only some browsers (controlling the browser cache, for example), and not all search engine bots respond to meta tag attribute values the same way (if at all). At the same time, commonly-used powers, such as refresh, are frowned upon by the standards. There are no mandated standards for acceptable values, but the W3C validators for HTML 4 and XHTML point toward acceptance of the character set value shown in the example below.

<meta>

## Example

```
<head profile="http://www.giantco.com/profiles/common">
    <meta name="Author" content="Jane Smith">
    <meta name="keywords" content="benefits,insurance,plan">
    <meta http-equiv="refresh"
    content="1;URL=http://www.giantco.com/truindex.html">
    <meta http-equiv="Content-Type" content="text/html;
    charset=ISO-8859-5">
</head>
```

## Element-Specific Attributes

content                 http-equiv              name                    scheme

## Element-Specific Event Handler Attributes

None.

## content

NN *all*    IE *all*    HTML *all*

content="*valueString*"

Required

The equivalent of the value of a name/value pair. The attribute is usually accompanied by either a name or http-equiv attribute, either of which act as the name portion of the name/value pair. Specific values of the content attribute vary with the value of the name or http-equiv attribute. Sometimes, the content attribute value contains multiple values. In such cases, the values are delimited by commas, semicolons, or whatever delimiter the browser expects for that content. Some of these values may be name/value pairs in their own right, such as the content for a refresh meta element. The first value is a number representing the number of seconds delay before loading another document; the second value indicates a URL of the document to load after the delay expires.

## Example

```
<meta http-equiv="refresh"
content="2;URL=http://www.giantco.com/basicindex.html">
```

## Value

Any string of characters. The string must be inside a matching pair of (single or double) quotation marks.

## Default        None.

## Object Model Reference

[window.]document.getElementById(*elementID*).content

## http-equiv

NN *all*    IE *all*    HTML *all*

http-equiv="*identifier*"

Optional

When a server sends a document to the client with the HTTP protocol, a number of HTTP header fields are sent along, primarily as directives to the client about the content on its way. meta elements can add to those HTTP headers when the http-equiv attribute is

<meta>

assigned to a document. Browsers convert the http-equiv and content attribute values into the HTTP response header format of "name: value" and treat them as if they came directly from the server.

Web standards define a long list of HTTP headers (see *Webmaster in a Nutshell* by Stephen Spainhour and Valerie Quercia, published by O'Reilly & Associates), but some of the more common values are shown in the following examples. Not all browsers respond to all header types, and some browsers respond to browser-specific headers (e.g., the IE 6 MSTHEMECOMPATIBLE header). You can have either the http-equiv or name attribute in a meta element, but not both.

### Example

```
<meta http-equiv="refresh"
content="1,http://www.giantco.com/truindex.html">
<meta http-equiv="Content-Type" content="text/html; charset=ISO-8859-5">
<meta http-equiv="expires" content="Sun, 15 Jan 1998 17:38:00 GMT">
```

**Value**          Any string identifier.

**Default**        None.

### Object Model Reference

[window.]document.getElementById(*elementID*).httpEquiv

## name                                                    NN *all*   IE *all*   HTML *all*

name="*identifier*"                                                              Optional

An identifier for the name/value pair that constitutes the meta element. Typically, the attribute value is a plain-language term that denotes the purpose of the meta element, such as "author" or "keywords". You can assign a value to either the name or http-equiv attribute, but not both, in the same meta element.

### Example

```
<meta name="Author" content="Jane Smith">
<meta name="keywords" content="benefits,insurance,plan">
```

**Value**          Any string identifier.

**Default**        None.

### Object Model Reference

[window.]document.getElementById(*elementID*).name

## scheme                                                  NN *6*   IE *6*   HTML *4*

scheme="*identifier*"                                                           Optional

Provides one more organizational layer to metadata supplied with a document. For example, a university campus with several libraries might generate documents associated with each of the libraries. Assuming that a browser is equipped to interpret metadata about this, one approach at assembling the tags is to create a separate name attribute value for each library: name="law", name="main", name="engineering", and so on. But it may also be necessary to associate these name values with a specific university. The scheme attribute could be called into service to align the metadata with a particular university: scheme="Harvard". Now, other university library systems could use the same organization of name attributes, but the scheme attribute clearly associates a given meta element with a specific university and library. Again, this assumes that the browser is empowered to do something special with this metaknowledge.

| | |
|---|---|
| **Example** | `<meta scheme="Chicago" name="classicalFM" content="98.7">` |
| **Value** | Any string identifier. |
| **Default** | None. |

**Object Model Reference**

`[window.]document.getElementById(elementID).scheme`

# `<multicol>`

`<multicol>...</multicol>`      HTML End Tag: Required

A Navigator-specific (Versions 3 and 4) element that renders its content in any number of evenly spaced flowing columns on the page. The way this element flows content might remind you of a desktop publishing program that automatically flows long content into column space that has been defined for the page. There is no equivalent for this element in HTML or Internet Explorer, but a CSS-related proposal for a multicolumn layout attribute may find its way into CSS3. None of these attributes are built into Version 6 browsers.

**Example**

```
<multicol cols="2" gutter="20" width="500">
LongFlowingHTMLContent
</multicol>
```

**Element-Specific Attributes**

cols       gutter       width

**Element-Specific Event Handler Attributes**

None.

## cols

NN <6   IE n/a   HTML n/a

`cols="columnCount"`      Required

Defines the number of columns across which the browser distributes and renders the content of the element. For a given width of the content, the browser does its best to make each column the same length. The proposed CSS equivalent attribute is column-number.

**Example**

```
<multicol cols="2" gutter="20" width="500">
LongFlowingHTMLContent
</multicol>
```

**Value**        Any positive integer.

**Default**      1

## gutter          NN *&lt;6*   IE *n/a*   HTML *n/a*

gutter="*pixelCount*"           Optional

Specifies the number of pixels to be placed between columns. The browser then calculates the width of the content columns by subtracting all the gutters from the total available width. The proposed CSS equivalent attribute is column-gap.

**Example**
```
<multicol cols="2" gutter="20" width="500">
LongFlowingHTMLContent
</multicol>
```

**Value**        Any positive integer.

**Default**      10

## width          NN *&lt;6*   IE *n/a*   HTML *n/a*

width="*elementWidth*"          Optional

Defines the total width of the columns plus gutters. You can specify the width in pixels or as a percentage of the width of the next outer container (usually the document body). The proposed CSS equivalent attribute is the existing width attribute.

**Example**
```
<multicol cols="2" gutter="20" width="500">
LongFlowingHTMLContent
</multicol>
```

**Value**        Any length value in pixels or percentage of available space.

**Default**      100%

# &lt;nextid&gt;          NN *n/a*   IE *all*   HTML *&lt;2*

&lt;nextid&gt;           HTML End Tag: Prohibited

The nextid element was at one time intended to assist document-editing application. It went inside a document's head element. Deprecated in HTML 2.0, it is no longer used.

# &lt;nobr&gt;          NN *all*   IE *all*   HTML *n/a*

&lt;nobr&gt;...&lt;/nobr&gt;          HTML End Tag: Required

The nobr element instructs the browser to render its content without wrapping the text to the next line at the right edge of the window or container. Even if there are carriage returns in the source code for the element's content, the browser flows the text as one line.

Although this might seem convenient in circumstances involving careful layout of pages, it may mean the user has to scroll horizontally to view the text—not something most users like to do. Despite the longevity of the nobr element in commercial browsers, it has never been mentioned in formal HTML recommendations.

### Example

```
<nobr>
Now is the time for all good men to
come to the aid of their country, even if
the text forces them to scroll horizontally.
</nobr>
```

### Object Model Reference

[window.]document.getElementById(*elementID*)

### Element-Specific Attributes

None.

### Element-Specific Event Handler Attributes

None.

## \<noembed\>

NN 2    IE *n/a*    HTML *n/a*

`<noembed>...</noembed>`                                   HTML End Tag: Required

Navigator provides a tag for isolating advisory content that displays in browsers incapable of working with plugins. All content between the start and end tags of the noembed element is not rendered in Navigator (or Internet Explorer) but is rendered in other browsers (which ignore the tag but not the content). There are no attributes for this element.

### Example

```
<embed name="jukebox" src="jazz.aif" height="100" width="200"></embed>
<noembed>
To play the music associated with this page, you need a modern graphical browser.
</noembed>
```

### Element-Specific Attributes

None.

### Element-Specific Event Handler Attributes

None.

## \<noframes\>

NN 2    IE 3    HTML 4

`<noframes>...</noframes>`                                 HTML End Tag: Required

The noframes element contains HTML that is rendered by browsers incapable of displaying frames. Browsers that are capable of displaying frames ignore the noframes element and all content it contains. Content for this element should instruct the user about using frames or perhaps offer a link to a frameless version of the page. The most common location for the noframes element is inside a frameset element. The HTML 4 specification, however, sees nothing wrong with embedding the element in a rendered document, if it makes sense for your application. It could be useful if your page employs an iframe element, and you want browsers not equipped for that element to alert users about what they're missing.

All standard attributes of the noframes element were added to support Cascading Style Sheets. This seems odd, because it would seem very unlikely that a browser would support CSS but not frames (with the exception of Navigator 4's lack of iframe support).

### Example

```
<frameset cols="150,*">
    <frame name="navbar" src="nav.html">
    <frame name="main" src="page1.html">
    <noframes>Your browser does not support frames.
    Click <a href="noFramesIndex.html">here</a> for a frameless version.
    </noframes>
</frameset>
```

### Element-Specific Attributes
None.

### Element-Specific Event Handler Attributes
None.

## &lt;nolayer&gt;                                    NN |4|    IE *n/a*    HTML *n/a*

&lt;nolayer&gt;...&lt;/nolayer&gt;                                   HTML End Tag: Required

Navigator 4 provides a tag for isolating advisory content that displays in browsers that don't recognize the layer element. All content between the start and end tags of the nolayer element is not rendered in Navigator 4 but is rendered in other browsers (which ignore the tag but not the content). You can place the nolayer element anywhere you want, but be aware that it won't be positioned like the layer element is intended to be. Netscape 6 (a nonlayer browser) renders the nolayer element's content.

There are no attributes for this element. If you attempt to set style sheet rules for the nolayer element, they are ignored by browsers such as Internet Explorer. You can, however, wrap the nolayer element inside a div or span element to associate a style sheet rule with the advisory text.

### Example

```
<layer bgcolor="yellow" src="instrux.html" width=200 height=300></layer>
<nolayer>
You are not seeing some content that requires Netscape Navigator 4 to view.
</nolayer>
```

### Element-Specific Attributes
None.

### Element-Specific Event Handler Attributes
None.

# &lt;noscript&gt;

NN *3*    IE *4*    HTML *4*

`<noscript>...</noscript>`                    HTML End Tag: Required

The noscript element is intended to display content when a browser is not set to run the scripts embedded in the current document. In practice, the element is observed only starting with Navigator 3 and Internet Explorer 4. When a user disables scripting in a browser, the noscript element's content is rendered wherever it falls in the source code. For older browsers, and those that don't support scripting, the noscript element is ignored, which means that its content is rendered within the next outermost container's context. Going forward, the HTML 4.0 specification recommends that browsers also render the noscript element's content when scripts earlier in the document are of a language type not supported or enabled in the browser. Also, if an HTML 4-compatible browser should be developed that lacks scripting altogether, it, too, should render the noscript element's contents.

All standard attributes of the noscript element were added to support Cascading Style Sheets, internationalization, and events for HTML 4.

### Example

```
<noscript>
This document contains programming that requires a scriptable browser, such
as Microsoft Internet Explorer or Netscape Navigator. You may not have full
access to this page's powers at this time.
</noscript>
```

### Element-Specific Attributes

None.

### Element-Specific Event Handler Attributes

None.

# &lt;object&gt;

NN *4*    IE *3*    HTML *4*

`<object>...</object>`                    HTML End Tag: Required

The object element supplies the browser with information to load and render data types that are not natively supported by the browser. If the browser must load some external program (a Java applet, a plugin, or some other helper), the information about the content that is to be rendered is contained by the object element, its attributes, and optionally, associated param elements nested inside of it. Although today's browsers recognize elements such as applet and embed, the HTML specification indicates that the trend is to combine all of this into the object element.

The HTML 4 specification allows nesting of object elements to give the browser a chance to load alternate content if no plugin or other necessary content aids are available in the browser. Essentially, the browser should be able to walk through nested object elements until it finds one it can handle. For example, the outer object element may try to load an MPEG2 video; if no player is available, the browser looks for the next nested object, which is a JPEG still image from the video; if the browser is not a graphical browser, it would render some straight HTML that is the most nested item (although not as an object element) within the hierarchy of nested objects:

```
<div>
<object data="proddemo.mpeg" type="application/mpeg">
    <object data="prodStill.jpg" type="image/jpeg">
        The all-new Widget 3000!
    </object>
</object>
</div>
```

To determine which attributes apply to a particular content type or object and what their values look like, you have to rely on documentation from the supplier of the object or plugin. That same documentation should let you know whether the functionality is available across browser brands and operating systems.

### Example

```
<object id="earth" classid="clsid:83A38BF0-B33A-A4FF-C619A82E891D">
<param name="srcStart" value="images/earth0.gif">
<param name="frameCount" value="12">
<param name="loop" value="-1"
<param name="fps" value="10">
</object>
```

### Element-Specific Attributes

| | | | | |
|---|---|---|---|---|
| align | alt | archive | border | classid |
| code | codebase | codetype | data | declare |
| height | hspace | name | standby | type |
| usemap | vspace | width | | |

### Element-Specific Event Handler Attributes
None.

## align                                          NN 4    IE 3    HTML 4

align="*alignmentConstant*"                                        Optional

Determines how the rectangle of the object element aligns within the context of surrounding content. See the discussion about alignment of elements with respect to content outside an element's box in the section "Alignment Constants" earlier in this chapter.

**Example**          `<object ... align="baseline"></object>`

**Value**            Constant value. See "Alignment Constants."

**Default**          bottom

### Object Model Reference
`[window.]document.getElementById(elementID).align`

<object>

## archive

NN *6*    IE *6*    HTML *4*

`archive="URIList"`                                                            Optional

A space-delimited list of URIs of files that support the loading and running of the object element. By explicitly specifying the files in the archive attribute, the browser doesn't have to wait for the supporting files to be called by the content running in the object element. Instead, the supporting files can be downloaded simultaneously with the primary content. The archive attribute may also include URIs assigned to the classid or data attributes, but one of these two attributes still needs to point to the primary content URI. Version 6 browsers provide no particular functionality for this attribute.

**Example**         `<object ... archive="/images/anim3.gif/images/anim4.gif"></object>`

**Value**           A complete or relative URL.

**Default**         None.

**Object Model Reference**
`[window.]document.getElementById(elementID).archive`

## border

NN *6*    IE *6*    HTML *4*

`border="pixels"`                                                             Optional

The thickness of a border around the object element. The attribute is deprecated in HTML 4 in favor of style sheet borders. If you use the object element to load an image for a client-side image map, you can set the border attribute to zero to eliminate the typical link border in IE 5/Mac and Netscape 6 (see usemap later in this section).

**Example**         `<object ... border="4"></object>`

**Value**           Any integer pixel value.

**Default**         None.

**Object Model Reference**
`[window.]document.getElementById(elementID).bprder`

## classid

NN *4*    IE *3*    HTML *4*

`classid="URL"`                                                              Optional

The URL of the object's implementation. This attribute typically directs the browser to load a program, an applet, or a plugin class file. In Internet Explorer, the URL can point to the *CLSID* directory that stores all of the IDs for registered ActiveX controls, such as DirectAnimation. You must obtain the classid value from the supplier of an ActiveX control (or root around the Registry with **Regedit** if you know what you're looking for). In Navigator 4, the Java Archive (JAR) Installation Manager attempts to install a plugin from the classid URL if the plugin is not installed for data specified in the data attribute. Eventually, this attribute may be used to load Java applets (IE 4 includes a code attribute to handle this now), but through Version 6 of both browsers, Java applets are not yet supported in this fashion.

Alphabetical
HTML Reference

<object>

**Example**
```
<object id="earth" classid="clsid:83A38BF0-B33A-A4FF-C619A82E891D"></object>
```

**Value**          A complete or relative URL.

**Default**        None.

**Object Model Reference**
```
[window.]document.elementID.classid
```

## code

`code="fileName.class"`                                                          Optional

Internet Explorer uses the code attribute to allow the object element to perform the same job as an applet element, using the same kind of attributes. The code attribute value is the name of the Java applet class file. If the class file is in a directory other than the document, the path to the directory must be assigned to the codebase attribute, just like in the applet element. Parameters are passed to applets via param elements, just like the ones nested inside applet elements. IE appears to preserve the classid attribute for referencing ActiveX controls only.

**Example**        `<object code="fileReader.class" codebase="classes"></object>`

**Value**          Applet class filename.

**Default**        None.

**Object Model Reference**
```
[window.]document.elementID.code
```

## codebase

`codebase="path"`                                                                Optional

Path to the directory holding the class file designated in either the code or classid attribute. The codebase attribute does not name the class file, just the path. You can make this attribute a complete URL to the directory, but don't try to access a codebase outside of the domain of the current document.

**Example**        `<object code="fileReader.class" codebase="classes"></object>`

**Value**          Case-sensitive pathname, usually relative to the directory storing the current HTML document.

**Default**        None.

**Object Model Reference**
```
[window.]document.getElementById(elementID).codeBase
```

<object>

## codetype

codetype="*MIMEType*"                                                        Optional

An advisory about the content type of the object referred to by the classid attribute. A browser might use this information to assist in preparing support for a resource requiring a multimedia player or plugin. If the codetype attribute is missing, the browser looks next for the type attribute setting (although it is normally associated with content linked by the data attribute URL). If both attributes are missing, the browser gets the content type information from the resource as it downloads.

### Example

```
<object classid="clsid:83A38BF0-B33A-A4FF-C619A82E891D"
codetype="application/x-crossword"></object>
```

### Value

Case-insensitive MIME type. A catalog of registered MIME types is available from *ftp:// ftp.isi.edu/in-notes/iana/assignments/media-types/*.

**Default**          None.

### Object Model Reference

[window.]document.getElementById(*elementID*).codeType

## data

data="*URL*"                                                                 Optional

URL of a file containing data for the object element (as distinguished from the object itself). For data with a content type that can be opened (and viewed or played) with any compatible object or plugin, the data and type attributes are generally sufficient to launch the plugin and get the content loaded. But if the content requires a very specific plugin or ActiveX control, you should include a classid attribute that points to the object's implementation as well. In that case, you can specify the content type with either the codetype or type attributes. Relative URLs are calculated relative to the codebase attribute, if one is assigned; otherwise the URL is relative to the document's URL.

**Example**          `<object data="proddemo.mpeg" type="application/mpeg"></object>`

**Value**            A complete or relative URL.

**Default**          None.

### Object Model Reference

[window.]document.getElementById(*elementID*).data

## declare

declare                                                                      Optional

The presence of the declare attribute instructs the browser to regard the current object element as a declaration only, without instantiating the object. A browser may use this

<object>

opportunity to precache data that does not require the object being loaded or run. Another object element pointing to the same classid and/or data attribute values, but without the declare attribute, gets the object running. Version 6 browsers provide no particular functionality for this attribute.

**Example**

```
<object classid="clsid:83A38BF0-B33A-A4FF-C619A82E891D" declare></object>
```

**Value**         The presence of the attribute sets it to true.

**Default**       false

**Object Model Reference**

[window.]document.getElementById(*elementID*).declare

## height, width            NN 4    IE 3    HTML 4

```
height="length"
width="length"
```
                Optional

The size that an embedded object (or its plugin control panel) occupies in a document is governed by the height and width attribute settings. Some browser versions might allow you to get away without assigning these attributes and letting the plugin's own user interface design determine the height and width of its visible rectangle. It is best to specify the exact dimensions of a plugin's control panel or the data (in the case of images) whenever possible (control panels vary with each browser and even between different plugins for the same browser). In some cases, such as Navigator 4 for the Macintosh, the object may not display if you fail to supply enough height on the page. If you assign values that are larger than the actual object or its control panel, the browser reserves that empty space on the page, which could interfere with your intended page design.

When an object is scriptable, and you don't want its controller to appear, you can set its dimensions to zero or one. Place the tag at the end of the document.

**Example**        `<object data="blues.aif" height="150" width="250"></object>`

**Value**         Positive integer values (optionally quoted) or percentage values (quoted).

**Default**       None.

**Object Model Reference**

[window.]document.getElementById(*elementID*).height
[window.]document.getElementById(*elementID*).width

## hspace, vspace           NN 6    IE 3    HTML 4

```
hspace="pixelCount"
vspace="pixelCount"
```
                Optional

A margin that acts as whitespace padding around the visual content of the object element's rectangular space. hspace establishes a margin on the left and right sides of the rectangle; vspace establishes a margin on the top and bottom sides of the rectangle.

<object>

## Example
`<object data="blues.aif" height="150" width="250" vspace="10" hspace="10"></object>`

## Value
Integer representing the number of pixels for the width of the margin on the relevant sides of the object element's rectangle.

## Default
0

## Object Model Reference
`[window.]document.getElementById(elementID).hspace`
`[window.]document.getElementById(elementID).vspace`

## name
NN 6    IE 6    HTML 4
`name="elementIdentifier"`                                                                                   Optional

The HTML 4 specification provides for a name attribute of the object element for instances in which the object is part of a form that is submitted to the server. The name attribute in this case performs the same function as the name attribute of an input element; it acts as a label for some data being submitted. The code that is loaded into the object element must be programmed to return a value if it is to be submitted via an HTML form. Through Version 6, mainstream browsers list support for this attribute for compatibility claims, but do not respond to its value. Use the id attribute to assign an identifier that scripts use to reference the object.

## Example
`<object name="embedded" classid="clsid:83A38BF0-B33A-A4FF-C619A82E891D"`
`height="150" width="250"></object>`

**Value**          Case-sensitive identifier.

**Default**        None.

## Object Model Reference
`[window.]document.getElementById(elementID).name`

## standby
NN 6    IE 6    HTML 4
`standby="HTMLText"`                                                                                         Optional

HTML content to be displayed while the object is loading. This attribute has not been implemented in Version 6 browsers (although it works in IE 5/Mac); presumably the message is to be displayed in the rectangular region intended for the object element, just as the alt message appears in an img element space while the image loads.

## Example
`<object classid="clsid:83A38BF0-B33A-A4FF-C619A82E891D"`
`height="150" width="250" standby="Loading movie..."></object>`

**Value**          Any HTML content.

**Default**        None.

## type

NN 4   IE 3   HTML 4

type="*MIMEType*"                                        **Required**

An advisory about the content type of the data referred to by the data attribute. A browser might use this information to assist in preparing support for a resource requiring a multi-media player or plugin. The data element first looks to the codetype attribute for this information. But if the codetype attribute is missing, the browser looks next for the type attribute setting. If both attributes are missing, the browser tries to get the content type information from the resource as it downloads. To be on the safe side, always specifiy a MIME type for image data (e.g., image/jpeg or image/gif).

### Example

```
<object data="movies/prodDemo.mpeg" type="application/mpeg"></object>
```

### Value

Case-insensitive MIME type. A catalog of registered MIME types is available from *ftp://ftp. isi.edu/in-notes/iana/assignments/media-types/*.

### Default       None.

### Object Model Reference

[window.]document.getElementById(*elementID*).type

## usemap

NN 6   IE 6   HTML 4

usemap="*mapURL*"                                         **Optional**

The HTML 4 specification lists the usemap attribute for an object element, thus offering the possibility of using the object element to load an image that gets used as an image map. Version 6 browsers (and IE 5/Mac) provide this capability.

Assign the URI of the image to the data attribute, and assign a MIME type for the image to the type property. Create a separate map element with one or more nested area elements, and assign the map element's name identifier to the object element's usemap attribute. IE/Windows pads the image and adds scrollbars, so you may not achieve successful cross-browser deployment. Netscape 6 and IE 5/Mac essentially duplicate the traditional client-side image map functionality through the object element. They also display the typical link border around the image unless you also set the border attribute to zero.

### Example

```
<object data="navbar.jpg" type="image/jpeg" alt="Navigation Bar" usemap="#navbarMap"
border="0"></object>
```

### Value       See the usemap attribute of the img element.

### Default       None.

### Object Model Reference

[window.]document.getElementById(*elementID*).useMap

## vspace

See hspace.

## width

See height.

# &lt;ol&gt;

**NN** *all*  **IE** *all*  **HTML** *all*

&lt;ol&gt;...&lt;/ol&gt;

**HTML End Tag: Required**

The ol element is a container for an ordered list of items. An "ordered list" means that the items are rendered with a leading sequence number or letter (depending on the type attribute setting or list-style-type style sheet attribute setting). Content for each list item is defined by a nested li element. If you apply a style sheet rule to an ol element, the style is inherited by the nested li elements.

**Example**

```
<ol>
    <li>Choose Open from the File menu.</li>
    <li>Locate the file you wish to edit, and click on the filename.</li>
    <li>Click the Open button.</li>
</ol>
```

**Object Model Reference**

[window.]document.getElementById(*elementID*)

**Element-Specific Attributes**

compact          start          type

**Element-Specific Event Handler Attributes**

None.

## compact

**NN** *6*  **IE** *4*  **HTML** *3.2*

compact

**Optional**

A Boolean attribute originally designed to let browsers render the list in a more compact style than normal (smaller line spacing between items). Although listed as a supported attribute for HTML compatibility, the compact attribute has no effect on mainstream browsers. Use style sheets to control element sizes and line spacing.

| | |
|---|---|
| **Example** | <ol compact>...</ol> |
| **Value** | The presence of this attribute makes its value true. |
| **Default** | false |

## start
NN *all*    IE *all*    HTML *all*

start="*number*"                                                              Optional

Assigns a custom starting number for the sequence of items in the ol element. This is convenient when a sequence of items must be disturbed by running body text. Although the value is a number, the corresponding Arabic numeral, Roman numeral, or alphabet letter is used to render the value.

**Example**            &lt;ol start="5"&gt; ...&lt;/ol&gt;

**Value**              Any positive integer.

**Default**            None.

**Object Model Reference**
[window.]document.getElementById(*elementID*).start

## type
NN *all*    IE *all*    HTML *3.2*

type="*labelType*"                                                            Optional

The type attribute provides some flexibility in how the sequence number is displayed in the browser. For an ordered list, the choices are among letters (uppercase or lowercase), Roman numerals (uppercase or lowercase), or Arabic numerals. The type attribute is deprecated in HTML 4 in favor of the list-style-type style sheet attribute.

**Example**            &lt;ol type="a"&gt;...&lt;/ol&gt;

**Value**

Possible values are A | a | I | i | 1. Sequencing is performed automatically as follows.

| Type | Example |
| --- | --- |
| A | A, B, C, ... |
| a | a, b, c, ... |
| I | I, II, III, ... |
| i | i, ii, iii, ... |
| 1 | 1, 2, 3, ... |

**Default**       1

**Object Model Reference**
[window.]document.getElementById(*elementID*).type

# &lt;optgroup&gt;
NN *6*    IE *5(Mac)/6(Win)*    HTML *4*

&lt;optgroup&gt;...&lt;/optgroup&gt;                                          HTML End Tag: Required

The optgroup element is a container for option elements within a select element. Each optgroup can represent a subgroup of options within the total list of select elements. In IE

<optgroup>

6/Windows and Netscape 6, the label text appears in a bold-italic font and is not selectable. Regular option element text is then listed below the label and is indented. In IE 5/Mac, the presence of optgroup elements turns a popup menu into a two-level hierarchical menu.

### Example

```
<select name="carCos">
    <optgroup label="American">
        <option value="General Motors">General Motors</option>
        <option value="Ford">Ford Motor Company</option>
        <option value="Chrysler">DaimlerChrysler</option>
    </optgroup>
    <optgroup label="Japanese">
        <option value="Toyota">Toyota</option>
        <option value="Honda">Honda</option>
        <option value="Nissan">Nissan</option>
    </optgroup>
</select>
```

### Object Model Reference

[window.]document.getElementById(*elementID*)

### Element-Specific Attributes

disabled        label

### Element-Specific Event Handler Attributes

None.

## disabled
NN 6    IE 5/6    HTML 4

disabled
Optional

The presence of this attribute disables the optgroup element and its nested option elements. Other optgroup elements remain enabled.

**Example**         `<optgroup label="Engineering" disabled>`

**Value**           The presence of this attribute sets its value to true.

**Default**         false

### Object Model Reference

[window.]document.getElementById(*elementID*).disabled

## label
NN 6    IE 5/6    HTML 4

label="*labelText*"
Required

The text of the select element entry for the optgroup is defined by the label attribute. This is plain text, not HTML, and the user cannot select this text from the list.

**Example**         `<optgroup label="Engineering" disabled>`

**Value**     Any string of characters. The string must be inside a matching pair of (single or double) quotation marks.

**Default**     None.

**Object Model Reference**

[window.]document.getElementById(*elementID*).label


# &lt;option&gt;                                        NN *all*   IE *all*   HTML *all*

&lt;option&gt;...&lt;/option&gt;                                        HTML End Tag: Optional

The option element defines an item that appears in a select element listing, whether the listing is in a pop-up menu or scrolling list. option elements associated with a select element must be nested within the start and end tags of the select element.

select elements supply name/value pairs when the element is submitted as part of a form element. Typically, the name attribute of the select element and the value attribute of the selected option are submitted as the name/value pair. Therefore, it is important to assign a meaningful value to the value attribute of each option element in a select list. You can use the value attribute to disguise user-unfriendly (but server- or script-friendly) values from the user, while presenting a user-friendly entry that appears in the select list. Content for the human-readable entry of a select list is entered after the option element's start tag. The end tag is optional because the entry is delimited either by the next option element start tag or the select element's end tag. See also the optgroup attribute for possible future grouping of option elements into hierarchical menu groupings.

**Example**

```
<select name="chapters">
    <option value="1">Chapter 1</option>
    <option value="2">Chapter 2</option>
    <option value="3">Chapter 3</option>
    <option value="4">Chapter 4</option>
</select>
```

**Object Model Reference**

[window.]document.*formName*.*selectName*.*optionName*
[window.]document.forms[i].elements[j].options[k].*optionName*
[window.]document.getElementById(*elementID*)

**Element-Specific Attributes**

disabled            label            selected            value

**Element-Specific Event Handler Attributes**

None.

<option>

## disabled

disabled    **Optional**

The presence of this attribute disables the option element in the list. Note that although the attribute disables the list choice in IE 5/Mac, as of Version 6, IE/Windows provides no other functionality for this attribute.

**Example**    `<option value="Met101" disabled>Meteorology 101</option>`

**Value**    The presence of this attribute sets its value to true.

**Default**    `false`

**Object Model Reference**

```
[window.]document.formName.selectName.optionName.disabled
[window.]document.forms[i].elements[j].options[k].optionName.disabled
[window.]document.getElementById(elementID).disabled
```

## label

label="labelText"    **Required**

The label attribute is included in HTML 4.0 in anticipation of possible hierarchical select lists. The label is intended to be a shorter alternate entry for an option element when it is rendered hierarchically. It overrides the normal text associated with the option element. Note that IE 5/Mac incorrectly displays the label attribute value in lieu of the element's text. Version 6 browsers provide no practical functionality for this attribute.

**Example**

`<option label="Meteo 101" value="met101">Meteorology 101</option>`

**Value**

Any string of characters. The string must be inside a matching pair of (single or double) quotation marks.

**Default**    None.

## selected

selected    **Optional**

The presence of the selected attribute preselects the item within the select element. When the select element is set to multiple, more than one option element may have the selected attribute set.

**Example**    `<option value="met101" selected>Meteorology 101</option>`

**Value**    The presence of this attribute sets its value to true.

**Default**    `false`

**Object Model Reference**

[window.]document.*formName*.*selectName*.*optionName*.selected
[window.]document.forms[i].elements[j].options[k].selected
[window.]document.getElementById(*elementID*).selected

## value
NN *all*    IE *all*    HTML *all*

value="*text*"
Optional

Associates a value with an option that may or may not be the same as the text displayed in the select element. When the select element is in a form submitted to the server, the value of the value attribute is assigned to the name/value pair for the select element if the option has been selected by the user (or is designated as selected with that attribute and the user has made no other selection). For scripting purposes, the value attribute might contain values such as URLs or string representations of objects that may subsequently be processed by scripts.

**Example**    &lt;option value="met101"&gt;Meteorology 101&lt;/option&gt;

**Value**    Any string of characters. The string must be inside a matching pair of (single or double) quotation marks.

**Default**    None.

**Object Model Reference**

[window.]document.*formName*.*selectName*.*optionName*.value
[window.]document.forms[i].elements[j].options[k].*optionName*.value
[window.]document.getElementById(*elementID*).value

# &lt;p&gt;
NN *all*    IE *all*    HTML *all*

&lt;p&gt;...&lt;/p&gt;
HTML End Tag: Optional

A p element defines a paragraph structural element in a document. With HTML 4, the p element is formally a block-level element, which means that content for a p element begins on its own line, and content following the p element starts on its own line. No other block-level elements may be nested inside a p element. If you omit the end tag (not permissible in XHTML), the element ends at the next block-level element start tag.

The nature of the p element has changed over time. In early implementations of HTML, the element represented only a paragraph break (a new line with some extra line spacing). Version 4 and later browsers render p elements in a hybrid way such that the start tag of a p element inserts a line space before the block. This means that a p element cannot start at the very top of a page unless it is positioned via CSS. Use the p element for structural purposes, rather than formatting purposes.

The content of a p element does not recognize extra whitespace that appears in the source code. Other elements, such as pre, render content just as it is formatted in the source code.

<param>

### Example

```
<p>This is a simple, one-sentence paragraph.</p>
<p>This second paragraph starts on its own line, with a little extra
line spacing.</p>
```

### Object Model Reference

[window.]document.getElementById(*elementID*)

### Element-Specific Attributes

align

### Element-Specific Event Handler Attributes

None.

## align

NN *all*    IE *all*    HTML *3.2*

align="*where*"

Optional

Determines how the paragraph text is justified within the box that the p element occupies. See the discussion about horizontal alignment for a block element's content in "Alignment Constants" earlier in this chapter.

The align attribute is deprecated in HTML 4 in favor of the text-align style sheet attribute.

| | |
|---|---|
| **Example** | `<p align="center">...</p>` |
| **Value** | Text alignment values are center \| justify \| left\| right, although the justify value does not validate in strict HTML or XHTML DTDs. |
| **Default** | left |

### Object Model Reference

[window.]document.getElementById(*elementID*).align

## \<param\>

NN *2*    IE *3*    HTML *3.2*

\<param\>

HTML End Tag: Forbidden

The param element may be nested within an applet or object element to pass parameters to the Java applet or object (typically, an ActiveX control in IE) as it is being loaded. Parameters provide ways for HTML authors to adjust settings of an applet or object without having to recode the applet or object. A parameter typically passes a name/value pair, which is assigned to the name and value attributes. You can have more than one param element per applet or object. The documentation for the applet or object should provide you with the information necessary to pass those parameter values.

### Example

```
<applet code="simpleClock.class" name="myClock" width="400" height="50">
<param name="bgColor" value="black">
<param name="fgColor" value="yellow">
</applet>
```

<param>

### Object Model Reference
[window.]document.getElementById(*elementID*)

### Element-Specific Attributes

| datafld | dataformatas | datasrc | name | type |
|---------|--------------|---------|------|------|
| value | valuetype | | | |

### Element-Specific Event Handler Attributes
None.

## datafld
NN *n/a*    IE 4    HTML *n/a*

datafld="*columnName*"                                                    Optional

Used with IE data binding to associate a remote data source column name with the param-eter passed to a Java applet or object. In the following example, data from a data source's column named backColor is assigned to the value attribute, even though the attribute is not explicitly shown in the tag. More complex relationships are also possible with both object and applet elements. datafld works only with text file data sources in IE 5/Mac.

### Example
<param name="bgColor" datasrc="DBSRC2" dataformatas="text" datafld="backColor">

**Value**          Case-sensitive identifier.

**Default**        None.

## dataformatas
NN *n/a*    IE 4    HTML *n/a*

dataformatas="*dataType*"                                                 Optional

Used with IE data binding, this attribute advises the browser whether the source material arriving from the data source is to be treated as plain text or as tagged HTML. This attribute setting depends entirely on how the data source is constructed and what kind of data the param element is expecting. dataformatas works only with text file data sources in IE 5/Mac.

### Example
<param name="bgColor" datasrc="DBSRC2" dataformatas="text" datafld="backColor">

**Value**          IE recognizes two possible settings: text | html.

**Default**        text

## datasrc
NN *n/a*    IE 4    HTML *n/a*

datasrc="*dataSourceName*"                                                Optional

Used with IE data binding to specify the ID of the page's object element that loads the data source object for remote data access. Content from the data source is specified via the datafld attribute. datasrc works only with text file data sources in IE 5/Mac.

**Example**

`<param name="bgColor" datasrc="DBSRC2" dataformatas="text" datafld="backColor">`

**Value**        Case-sensitive identifier.

**Default**      None.

## name                                           *NN 2   IE 3   HTML 3.2*

`name="elementIdentifier"`                      **Required**

Assigns an identifier for the parameter that the applet or object is expecting. Parameters generally supply a name/value pair. An applet, for example, includes a routine that fetches each parameter by name and assigns the passed value to a variable within the applet. Documentation for the applet or object should provide a list of names and value types corresponding to the param elements.

**Example**       `<param name="loop" value="4">`

**Value**        Case-sensitive identifier.

**Default**      None.

## type                                           *NN 6   IE 6   HTML 4*

`type="MIMEType"`                               **Optional**

When the valuetype attribute is set to "ref", the type attribute value advises the browser about the content type of the file referenced by the URL assigned to the value attribute. Omit the type attribute for other settings of the valuetype attribute.

**Example**

`<param name="help" value="http://www.giantco.com/help.html" valuetype="ref"`
`type="text/html">`

**Value**

Case-insensitive MIME type. A catalog of registered MIME types is available from *ftp://ftp. isi.edu/in-notes/iana/assignments/media-types/*.

**Default**      None.

**Object Model Reference**

`[window.]document.getElementById(elementID).type`

## value                                       *NN 2   IE 3   HTML 3.2*

`value="runTimeParameterValue"`                     **Optional**

The parameter value to be passed to an applet or object as the executable program or data loads. Parameter values are passed as string values, and it is up to the applet or object to perform the necessary internal coercion of the data to the desired data type. The value attribute is listed as optional because there may be instances in which the presence of the param element name attribute may be sufficient for the object. Once the applet or object loads its associated parameter values, scripts cannot dynamically modify those values unless the applet or object is scriptable and exposes methods designed to modify the values.

**Example**   &lt;param name="loop" value="4"&gt;

**Value**   Any string value.

**Default**   None.

**Object Model Reference**

[window.]document.getElementById(*elementID*).value

## valuetype                                                    NN 6   IE 6   HTML 4

valuetype="*paramValueType*"                                          Optional

object element parameters can come in three flavors: data, object, and ref. The valuetype attribute uses these constants to tell the browser how to treat the value assigned to the value attribute for passing to the object. When the valuetype is data, the value attribute is passed as a plain text string. A valuetype of object means that the value attribute consists of an identifier (id attribute value) of some other object element defined earlier in the same document. The other object may be one whose declare attribute is set, and now the parameter values are being passed to instantiate the object. When valuetype is ref, the value attribute is a URL that points to a file or other resource where runtime values are stored (perhaps a set of parameter values).

**Example**

&lt;param name="anime" value="http://www.giantco.com/params/animation.txt" valuetype="ref" type="text/html"&gt;

**Value**   Three possible constant values: data | object | ref.

**Default**   data

**Object Model Reference**

[window.]document.getElementById(*elementID*).valueType

## &lt;plaintext&gt;                              NN *all*   IE *all*   HTML *<4*

&lt;plaintext&gt;...&lt;/plaintext&gt;                             HTML End Tag: Optional

The plaintext element displays its content in a monospace font as a block element, but with a twist. All document source code coming after the start tag is rendered as-is in the browser window. You cannot turn off the plaintext element. Even the end tag is rendered as-is. This element has been long deprecated in HTML and has even been removed from the HTML 4.0 specification. You are encouraged to use the pre element instead.

Specifying any element attribute in Internet Explorer 4 for the Macintosh causes the plaintext element to be ignored. In other words, the source code is rendered and the attribute is applied to the content contained by the element if applicable (such as a style sheet rule).

<pre>

**Example**

```
<p>The rest of the HTML code follows:</p>
<plaintext>
...
</plaintext>
```

**Object Model Reference**

[window.]document.getElementById(*elementID*)

**Element-Specific Attributes**

None.

**Element-Specific Event Handler Attributes**

None.

# <pre>

NN *all*   IE *all*   HTML *all*

<pre>...</pre>

HTML End Tag: Required

The pre element defines a block of preformatted text. Preformatted text is usually rendered by default in a monospace font and, more importantly, it preserves the whitespace (multiple spaces between words and new lines) entered into the source code for the content. Unlike the deprecated plaintext element, the pre element doesn't ignore HTML tags. Instead, it passes such tags onto the browser for normal rendering. If you want to display HTML tags in a block of preformatted text, use entities for the less-than (&lt;) and greater-than (&gt;) symbols. This prevents the HTML tags from being interpreted as genuine tags but renders the symbols within the preformatted text block.

Browsers are supposed to ignore a whitespace line break immediately following a pre element start tag in case you wish to start the content on a new line in the source code. By and large, the Version 4 browsers follow this rule (with the exception of IE 4 for the Mac).

The HTML 4 specification is adamant about the pre element maintaining its monospaced font size and line spacing. It lists the following elements that should not be included inside a pre element: applet, basefont, big, font, img, object, small, sub, and sup. Any one of these destroys the fixed-size pitch of the pre element. The recommendation also encourages authors to avoid overriding the monospaced font settings with style sheets.

One last admonition concerns using tab characters to indent or align text within a pre element. Not all browsers render tab characters the same way. Avoid potential problems by using space characters and let the pre element's preservation of whitespace do the job. No nonbreaking space entities ( ) are necessary in a pre element.

**Example**

```
<p>Here is the script example:</p>
<pre>
&lt;script language="JavaScript"&gt;
   document.write("Hello, world.")
&lt;/script&gt;
</pre>
```

<pre>

**Object Model Reference**

[window.]document.getElementById(*elementID*)

**Element-Specific Attributes**

cols            width            wrap

**Element-Specific Event Handler Attributes**

None.

## cols

NN all    IE n/a    HTML n/a

cols="*columnCount*"                                            Optional

The maximum number of characters per line of preformatted code. This Navigator-specific attribute automatically sets the wrap attribute to true. Without this attribute, the source code formatting (or width attribute, where supported) governs the line width.

| | |
|---|---|
| **Example** | <pre cols="80">...</pre> |
| **Value** | Any positive integer. |
| **Default** | None. |

## width

NN n/a    IE n/a    HTML 4

width="*columnCount*"                                           Optional

The HTML 4 specification introduces the width attribute to allow you to set a maximum number of characters to be rendered on a preformatted line of text. Presumably, browsers that support this attribute in the future will wrap lines so that words do not break in the middle. Without this attribute, the source code formatting governs the line width. Navigator provides this functionality with the cols attribute. Note that the CSS width attribute does not affect this element in IE 5/Mac or IE 6/Windows. Even when it does, however, the units of measure do not include a character count.

| | |
|---|---|
| **Example** | <pre width="80">...</pre> |
| **Value** | Any positive integer. |
| **Default** | None. |

## wrap

NN all    IE n/a    HTML n/a

wrap                                                           Optional

The presence of the wrap attribute instructs Navigator to wrap preformatted text so that text does not run beyond the right edge of the browser window or frame. wrap is set to true automatically when the cols attribute is set.

| | |
|---|---|
| **Example** | <pre wrap>...</pre> |
| **Value** | The presence of the attribute sets its value to true. |
| **Default** | false |

<rb>

# <q>

NN *6*   IE *4*   HTML *4*

<q>...</q>

HTML End Tag: Required

The q element is intended to set off an inline quote inside a document. The HTML 4 specification indicates that browsers should automatically surround the content of a q element with language-sensitive quotation marks, and that authors should not include quotes. Netscape 6 supports this requirement, but IE 6/Windows does not. IE 5/Mac inserts quotes, but if the element's parent container is not left-aligned, the quotes float out of place. Internet Explorer 4 does not render such quote marks. If you need quotes around quoted text, you have no choice at this point but to include them yourself and not use the q element (because a future browser may add those quotes to the content). For a block-level quotation, see the blockquote element.

## Example

```
<p>The preamble to the u.s. Constitution begins,
<q>We the People of the United States</q></p>
```

## Object Model Reference

[window.]document.getElementById(*elementID*)

## Element-Specific Attributes

cite

## Element-Specific Event Handler Attributes

None.

# cite

NN *6*   IE *6*   HTML *4*

cite="*URL*"

Optional

A URL pointing to an online source document from which the quotation is taken. This is not in any way a mechanism for copying or extracting content from another document. Presumably, the purpose of this HTML 4 recommendation is to encourage future browsers and search engines to utilize a reference to online source material for the benefit of readers and surfers. Version 6 browsers provide no practical functionality for this attribute.

**Value**          Any valid URL to a document on the World Wide Web, including absolute or relative URLs.

**Default**        None.

# <rb>

NN *n/a*   IE *n/a*   HTML *X1.1*

<rb>...</rb>

End Tag: Required

The rb element denotes the base text within a ruby-enhanced section of content. This is the regular text to which ruby annotation is added. IE 5 and later supports ruby text, but the rb element is not explicitly supported, and is assumed to automatically apply to text other than what is encased inside rt elements.

## Example

```
<ruby>
  <rb>03</rb><rt>Month</rt>
  <rb>04</rb><rt>Day</rt>
  <rb>2003</rb><rt>Year</rt>
</ruby>
```

## Object Model Reference

[window.]document.getElementById(*elementID*)

## Element-Specific Attributes

None.

## Element-Specific Event Handler Attributes

None.

# \<rbc>, \<rtc>                    NN *n/a*    IE *n/a*    HTML *X1.1*

```
<rbc>...</rbc>                                          End Tag: Required
<rtc>...</rtc>
```

If you want to string together a contiguous sequence of ruby base items and their associated ruby text items, you can group all base items and all text items together inside rbc and rtc containers, respectively. The number of items inside the rbc and rtc elements should be the same so that the browser can keep the base and ruby text items together. Using this approach does not degrade well in browsers that do not support ruby text.

## Example

```
<ruby>
  <rbc>
    <rb>03</rb><rb>04</rb><rb>2003</rb>
  </rbc>
  <rtc>
    <rt>Month</rt><rt>Day</rt><rt>Year</rt>
  </rtc>
</ruby>
```

## Object Model Reference

[window.]document.getElementById(*elementID*)

## Element-Specific Attributes

None.

## Element-Specific Event Handler Attributes

None.

# &lt;rp&gt;

NN *n/a*    IE *5*    HTML *X1.1*

&lt;rp&gt;...&lt;/rp&gt;    End Tag: Required

The ruby markup module features the rp element to ease compatibility with browsers that don't support ruby markup directly. Non-ruby browsers render both the rp and rt element content as inline text. The rp element gives you a chance to include parentheses (or other character) around the ruby text so that the ruby text acts as an inline label. Content of each rp element is traditionally either a left or right parenthesis symbol. A complete rp element goes before and after each rt element. Browsers that support ruby text ignore the rp element content, and, thus, don't display the parentheses.

## Example

```
<ruby>
   <rb>03</rb><rp>(</rp><rt>Month</rt><rp>)</rp>
   <rb>04</rb><rp>(</rp><rt>Day</rt><rp>)</rp>
   <rb>2003</rb><rp>(</rp><rt>Year</rt><rp>)</rp>
</ruby>
```

## Object Model Reference

[window.]document.getElementById(*elementID*)

## Element-Specific Attributes

None.

## Element-Specific Event Handler Attributes

None.

# &lt;rt&gt;

NN *n/a*    IE *5*    HTML *X1.1*

&lt;rt&gt;...&lt;/rt&gt;    End Tag: Required

The rt element contains the text that is the annotation for a corresponding rb element. Browsers that support ruby text usually render rt elements in a smaller font size than the base text. Through style sheet assignment, you can also use alternate font families. You can also assign different a language set for the ruby text via the xml:lang attribute of the rt element.

## Example

```
<ruby>
   <rb>03</rb><rt>Month</rt>
   <rb>04</rb><rt>Day</rt>
   <rb>2003</rb><rt>Year</rt>
</ruby>
```

## Object Model Reference

[window.]document.getElementById(*elementID*)

## Element-Specific Attributes

rbspan

## Element-Specific Event Handler Attributes

None.

## rbspan

NN n/a   IE n/a   HTML X1.1

rbspan="*integer*"

Optional

In some cases, you may want one rt element to span two or more contiguous rb elements. Assign the number of rb elements to the rt element's rbspan attribute. The mechanism is similar to the td element colspan attribute.

**Value**          Integer number of rb elements.

**Default**          1


## &lt;ruby&gt;

NN n/a   IE 5   HTML X1.1

&lt;ruby&gt;...&lt;/ruby&gt;

End Tag: Required

Ruby text is small-font annotation that usually appears above or below the main body text (or to one side in vertically-oriented writing systems). The name comes from a small font that was used in typography to create the small annotation text. Ruby text is more commonly employed in pictographic languages, where the ruby text supplies a pronunciation guide to the main text pictographic symbols. But ruby text can be used with Latin alphabet languages, too.

The ruby element is a master container for all content to be affected by ruby markup, including the main text. The main text is known as the *ruby base*, while the annotation is called *ruby text*. Each of these types has its own tag (rb and rt, respectively), and any such tags must be encased within a ruby element. IE implemented the basics of ruby markup starting with Version 5 (Windows and Mac).

The W3C ruby markup specification was developed independently of the HTML recommendation, and was added to XHTML 1.1 as one of the first modules to take advantage of the extensible nature of XHTML.

### Example

```
<ruby>
  <rb>03</rb><rt>Month</rt>
  <rb>04</rb><rt>Day</rt>
  <rb>2003</rb><rt>Year</rt>
</ruby>
```

### Object Model Reference

[window.]document.getElementById(*elementID*)

### Element-Specific Attributes

None.

### Element-Specific Event Handler Attributes

None.

<samp>

# <s>

**NN 3  IE 3  HTML 3.2**

`<s>...</s>`

HTML End Tag: Required

The s element renders its content as strikethrough text. This element is identical to the strike element; it was adopted because it more closely resembled the one-character element names for other type formatting (such as b, i, and u elements). In any case, both s and strike elements are deprecated in HTML 4 in favor of the `text-decoration:line-through` style sheet attribute.

### Example

`<p>If at first you don't succeed, <s>do it over</s> try, try again.</p>`

### Object Model Reference

[window.]document.getElementById(*elementID*)

### Element-Specific Attributes

None.

### Element-Specific Event Handler Attributes

None.

# <samp>

**NN *all*  IE *all*  HTML *all***

`<samp>...</samp>`

HTML End Tag: Required

The samp element is one of a large group of elements that the HTML 4 recommendation calls *phrase elements*. Such elements assign structural meaning to a designated portion of the document. A samp element is one that contains text that is sample output from a computer program or script. This is different from a code example, which is covered by the code element.

Browsers have free rein to determine how (or whether) to distinguish samp element content from the rest of the body element. Both Navigator and Internet Explorer elect to render the text in monospace font. Override the default with a style sheet as you see fit.

### Example

`<p>When you press the Enter key, you will see <samp>Hello, world!</samp>`
`on the screen.</p>`

### Object Model Reference

[window.]document.getElementById(*elementID*)

### Element-Specific Attributes

None.

### Element-Specific Event Handler Attributes

None.

<script>

# <script>

<script>...</script>

The script element provides a container for lines of script code written in any scripting language that the browser is capable of interpreting. Script statements that are not written inside a function definition are executed as the page loads; function definitions are loaded but their execution is deferred until explicitly invoked by user or system action (events). You can have more than one script element in a document, and you may include script elements written in different script languages within the same document.

An important shift in attribute syntax is introduced with HTML 4. To specify the scripting language of the statements within a script element, the language attribute has been used since the first scriptable browsers. HTML 4 deprecates that attribute in favor of the type attribute, whose value is a MIME type. Until you know for certain that your page visitors use only newer browsers that support the type attribute, you should include both attributes in documents for long-term backward compatibility with older browsers. The language attribute validates with transitional DTDs.

All but the earliest scriptable browsers also allow script statements to be imported into the document from a document whose URL is specified for the src attribute.

Older, nonscriptable browsers don't recognize the script element and may attempt to render the script statements as regular HTML content. To prevent this, wrap the script statements inside HTML block comment markers. The end-of-comment marker (-->) must be preceded by a JavaScript comment marker (//) to prevent JavaScript from generating a script error.

Due to character conflicts between JavaScript and XHTML, and the lack of browser support for the XHTML-preferred <![CDATA[...]]> script wrapper, you should use imported script libraries for pages that must validate under XHTML. This prevents XML parsers from misinterpreting symbols such as the less-than operator (<) as XML markup symbols.

## Example

```
<script type="text/javascript" language="JavaScript">
<!--
function howdy( ) {
    alert("Hello, HTML world!");
}
//-->
</script>

<script type="text/javascript" scr="scripts/myscript.js"></script>
```

## Element-Specific Attributes

| | | | | |
|---|---|---|---|---|
| charset | defer | event | for | language |
| src | type | version | xml:space | |

## Element-Specific Event Handler Attributes

None.

## charset
NN 6   IE n/a   HTML 4

`charset="characterSet"`
Optional

Character encoding of the content in the file referred to by the `src` attribute.

**Example**      `<script charset="csISO5427Cyrillic" src="moscow.js">...</script>`

**Value**      Case-insensitive alias from the character set registry (*ftp://ftp.isi.edu/in-notes/iana/assignments/character-sets*).

**Default**      Determined by browser.

## defer
NN 6   IE 4   HTML 4

`defer`
Optional

The presence of the `defer` attribute instructs the browser to render regular HTML content without looking for the script to generate content as the page loads. This is an advisory attribute only. The browser doesn't have to hold up rendering further HTML content as it parses the content of the `script` element in search of `document.write()` statements. As of Version 7, Netscape allows but does not respond to the `defer` attribute.

**Example**

`<script type="text/javascript" language="JavaScript" defer>...</script>`

**Value**      The presence of this attribute sets its value to `true`.

**Default**      `false`

**Object Model Reference**

`[window.]document.getElementById(elementID).defer`

## event
NN n/a   IE 4   HTML |4|

`event="eventName"`
Optional

Internet Explorer's event model allows the binding of object events to `script` elements with the help of the event and for attributes. As the page loads, the browser registers each `script` element with its event and object binding so that when the object generates the event, the script statements inside the `script` element execute—without having to write event handlers for the objects or wrap the script statements inside function definitions. Event values are written either as unquoted event names or as quoted event names formatted as functions (with trailing parentheses and optional parameter names). Use this type of script-event binding only in Internet Explorer. Navigator attempts to execute the script statements while the page loads. The transitional HTML 4 DTD reserves this attribute for possible future use, but the reservation doesn't hold for XHTML 1.0.

**Example**

`<script for="window" event="onresize()">...</script>`

### Value

Case-sensitive event name or the event name as a function inside a quote pair. The object described in the for attribute must support the event named in the event attribute.

### Default          None.

### Object Model Reference

[window.]document.getElementById(*elementID*).event

---

## for                                                    NN *n/a*    IE *4*    HTML |4|

for="*elementID*"                                                         Optional

Internet Explorer's event model allows the binding of object events to script elements with the help of the event and for attributes. As the page loads, the browser registers each script element with its event and object binding so that when the object generates the event, the script statements inside the script element execute—without having to write event handlers for the objects or wrap the script statements inside function definitions. Use the unique id attribute value of the element whose event you wish to handle. Use this type of script-event binding only in Internet Explorer. Navigator attempts to execute the script statements while the page loads. The transitional HTML 4 DTD reserves this attribute for possible future use, but the reservation doesn't hold for XHTML 1.0.

### Example

```
<script for="firstNameEntry" event="onchange( )">...</script>
```

### Value

Case-sensitive ID value of the event-generating element. The object described in the for attribute must support the event named in the event attribute.

### Default          None.

### Object Model Reference

[window.]document.getElementById(*elementID*).htmlFor

---

## language                                              NN *2*    IE *3*    HTML *4*

language="*scriptingLanguage*"                                            Optional

Sets the scripting language for script statements defined in the element. This attribute is deprecated in HTML 4 (in favor of the type attribute), but it has been so widely used since the first days of scriptable browsers that its use and support will continue for a long time to come. Moreover, it is so far the only accepted way to convey the JavaScript version for the script block (e.g., see the Array object in Chapter 12).

### Example

```
<script language="JavaScript">...</script>
```

## Value

Internet Explorer recognizes four case-insensitive language names: JavaScript | JScript | vbs | vbscript. Navigator recognizes only JavaScript. Versions of JavaScript are also supported in appropriate browsers. To keep the attribute values one-word identifiers, the version numbers are tacked onto the end of the "JavaScript" language name. The versionless "JavaScript" is observed by all browsers; "JavaScript1.1" is recognized only by Navigator 3; "JavaScript1.2" is recognized by Navigator 4.0–4.05 and Internet Explorer 4; "JavaScript1.3" applies to Navigator 4.06–4.7x and IE 5–6; "JavaScript1.5" applies to Netscape 6–7. When script elements are assigned these later version values, older browsers that don't support the named version ignore the script elements.

**Default**        JavaScript (NN); JScript (IE).

## Object Model Reference

[window.]document.getElementById(*elementID*).language

---

| src | NN *3* | IE *4* | HTML *4* |
|---|---|---|---|
| src="*URL*" | | | Optional |

Imports a file of script statements from an external file. Once the external statements are loaded, the browser treats them as if they were embedded in the main HTML document. This attribute had some support in Internet Explorer 3, but it relied on a specific *JScript.dll* version, which makes it unreliable to blindly use in IE 3.

In theory, you should be able to add script statements inside a script element that loads an external script library file. In practice, it is more reliable to provide a separate script element for each external library file and for in-document scripts.

Current implementations limit the src attribute to point to JavaScript external files. Such files must have a *.js* filename extension, and the server must have the extension and application/x-javascript MIME type set to serve up such files.

When assigning the src attribute in an XHTML document, browsers may not like the shortcut end tag format. Don't think of the tag as an empty element, but rather as one with content that arrives from an external source. Use an explicit &lt;/script&gt; end tag.

## Example

```
<script language="JavaScript" type="text/javascript" src="stringParseLib.js">
</script>
```

## Value

Any valid URL. Current browsers require files with names that end in the *.js* extension. A complete URL may help overcome difficulties in earlier browsers that implement this feature.

**Default**        None.

## Object Model Reference

[window.]document.getElementById(*elementID*).src

<script>

## type

type="*MIMEType*"                                                          **Required**

An advisory about the content type of the script statements. The content type should tell the browser which scripting engine to use to interpret the script statements. The type attribute will eventually replace the language attribute as the one defining the scripting language in which the element's statements are written. To be compatible with future and past browsers, you may include both the language and type attributes in a script element.

### Example

```
<script type="text/javascript" language="JavaScript">...</script>
```

### Value

Case-insensitive MIME type. Values are limited to one(s) for which a particular browser is equipped. IE 4 and later and Netscape 6 accept text/javascript and application/x-javascript for scripts in an ECMAScript-compatible language. IE also accepts the following types: text/ecmascript, text/jscript, text/vbs (IE/Windows), text/vbscript (IE/Windows), and text/xml (IE 5 and later).

**Default**          None.

### Object Model Reference

[window.]document.getElementById(*elementID*).type


## version

version="*x.y*"                                                            **Optional**

This attribute is listed here as a possible future implementation for Mozilla-based browsers. Most of the pieces that support this attribute (to complement the type attribute) are in place in the Netscape 6 (Mozilla) browser engine, but as of Netscape 7, are not yet connected.

### Example

```
<script type="text/javascript" version="1.5">...</script>
```

### Value

Language version expressed as major and minor version integers, separated by a period.


## xml:space

xml:space="*preserve*"                                                     **Optional**

An XHTML parser is supposed to expunge all source code whitespace as it processes the document. This removal may harm scripts. By including the XML namespace space attribute, you instruct the parser to keep source code whitespace of script element content intact.

### Example

```
<script type="text/javascript" xml:space="preserve">...</script>
```

<select>

**Value**          Constant value: preserve.

**Default**       None.

# <select>

NN *all*   IE *all*   HTML *all*

<select>...</select>

HTML End Tag: Required

The select element displays information from nested option elements as either a scrolling list or pop-up menu in a document. Users typically make a selection from the list of items (or multiple selections from a scrolling list if the size attribute is set greater than 1 and the multiple attribute is set). The value attribute of the selected option item is submitted as the value part of a name/value pair to the server with a form. When the element is set to allow multiple selections, multiple ampersand-delimited name/value pairs (repeating the name of the element) are submitted with the form. Navigator 4 requires that a select element be placed inside a form element.

## Example

```
<select name="chapters">
    <option value="chap1.html">Chapter 1</option>
    <option value="chap2.html">Chapter 2</option>
    <option value="chap3.html">Chapter 3</option>
    <option value="chap4.html">Chapter 4</option>
</select>
```

## Object Model Reference

```
[window.]document.formName.selectName
[window.]document.forms[i].elements[j]
[window.]document.getElementById(elementID)
```

## Element-Specific Attributes

| | | | | |
|---|---|---|---|---|
| accesskey | align | datafld | datasrc | disabled |
| multiple | name | size | tabindex | |

## Element-Specific Event Handler Attributes

| Handler | NN | IE | HTML |
|---|---|---|---|
| onafterupdate | n/a | 4 | n/a |
| onbeforeupdate | n/a | 4 | n/a |
| onchange | 2 | 3 | 4 |

# accesskey

NN *n/a*   IE *4*   HTML *n/a*

accesskey="*character*"

Optional

This widely shared attribute is listed here to remind you that only IE supports the attribute for the select element. See the discussion among the shared attributes earlier in this chapter.

<select>

## align

NN *n/a*    IE 4    HTML *n/a*

align="*alignmentConstant*"                                               Optional

Determines how the rectangle of the select element (particularly when the size attribute is set greater than 1) aligns within the context of surrounding content. See Section 8.1.5, "Alignment Constants" earlier in this chapter. Note that only Internet Explorer supports the align attribute for the select element.

### Example

```
<select name="chapters" multiple align="baseline">...</select>
```

**Value**            Case-insensitive constant value.

**Default**          bottom (IE/Windows); absmiddle (IE/Macintosh).

### Object Model Reference

```
[window.]document.formName.selectName.align
[window.]document.forms[i].elements[j].align
[window.]document.getElementById(elementID).align
```

## datafld

NN *n/a*    IE 4    HTML |4|

datafld="*columnName*"                                                   Optional

Used with IE data binding to associate a remote data source column name to the selectedIndex property of a select element (i.e., a zero-based index value of the item currently selected in the list, as described in the select object of Chapter 9). As such, you can use data binding only with select elements that do not specify the multiple attribute. A datasrc attribute must also be set for the element. Works only with text file data sources in IE 5/Mac.

This attribute was reserved in HTML 4, but was dropped in XHTML 1.0.

### Example

```
<select name="chapters" datasrc="DBSRC3" datafld="chapterRequest">
    <option value="chap1.html">Chapter 1</option>
    <option value="chap2.html">Chapter 2</option>
    <option value="chap3.html">Chapter 3</option>
    <option value="chap4.html">Chapter 4</option>
</select>
```

**Value**            Case-sensitive identifier.

**Default**          None.

### Object Model Reference

```
[window.]document.formName.selectName.dataFld
[window.]document.forms[i].elements[j].dataFld
[window.]document.getElementById(elementID).dataFld
```

## datasrc

datasrc="*dataSourceName*"   Optional

Used with IE data binding to specify the ID of the page's object element that loads the data source object for remote data access. Content from the data source is specified via the datafld attribute. Works only with text file data sources in IE 5/Mac.

This attribute was reserved in HTML 4, but was dropped in XHTML 1.0.

### Example

```
<select name="chapters" datasrc="#DBSRC3" datafld="chapterRequest">
    <option value="chap1.html">Chapter 1</option>
    <option value="chap2.html">Chapter 2</option>
    <option value="chap3.html">Chapter 3</option>
    <option value="chap4.html">Chapter 4</option>
</select>
```

**Value**          Case-sensitive identifier.

**Default**        None.

### Object Model Reference

```
[window.]document.formName.selectName.dataSrc
[window.]document.forms[i].elements[j].dataSrc
[window.]document.getElementById(elementID).dataSrc
```

## disabled

disabled   Optional

The presence of this attribute disables the entire select element and its nested option elements. The element receives no events when it is disabled. You can also disable individual options through those elements' disabled properties.

### Example

```
<select name="chapters" disabled>
    <option value="chap1.html">Chapter 1</option>
    <option value="chap2.html">Chapter 2</option>
    <option value="chap3.html">Chapter 3</option>
    <option value="chap4.html">Chapter 4</option>
</select>
```

**Value**          The presence of this attribute sets its value to true.

**Default**        false

### Object Model Reference

```
[window.]document.formName.selectName.disabled
[window.]document.forms[i].elements[j].disabled
[window.]document.getElementById(elementID).disabled
```

## multiple
NN all   IE all   HTML all

multiple
Optional

The presence of the multiple attribute instructs the browser to render the select element as a list box and to allow users to make multiple selections from the list of options. By default, the size attribute is set to the number of nested option elements, but the value may be overridden with the size attribute setting. Users can select contiguous items by **Shift-**clicking on the first and last items of the group. To make discontiguous selections, Windows users must **Ctrl-**click on each item; Mac users must **Command-**click on each item. The multiple attribute has no effect when size is set to 1 to display a pop-up menu.

### Example

```
<select name="equipment" multiple>
    <option value="monitor">Video monitor</option>
    <option value="modem">Modem</option>
    <option value="printer">Printer</option>
    ...
</select>
```

**Value**        The presence of this attribute sets its value to true.

**Default**     false

### Object Model Reference

```
[window.]document.formName.selectName.multiple
[window.]document.forms[i].elements[j].multiple
[window.]document.getElementById(elementID).multiple
[window.]document.formName.selectName.type
[window.]document.forms[i].elements[j].type
[window.]document.getElementById(elementID).type
```

## name
NN all   IE all   HTML all

name="*elementIdentifier*"
Optional

The name submitted as part of the element's name/value pair with the form. It is similar to the name attribute of input elements.

### Example

```
<select name="cpu" id="cpu">
    <option value="486">486</option>
    <option value="pentium">Pentium</option>
    <option value="pentium2">Pentium II</option>
    ...
</select>
```

**Value**        Case-sensitive identifier.

**Default**     None.

**Object Model Reference**

```
[window.]document.formName.selectName.name
[window.]document.forms[i].elements[j].name
[window.]document.getElementById(elementID).name
```

## size

size="*rowCount*"                                                    Optional

Controls the number of rows of option elements that appear in the select element. With a value of 1, the select element displays its content as a pop-up menu; with a value greater than 1, option items are rendered in a list box. Browsers control the width of the element, based on the widest text associated with nested option elements.

**Example**

```
<select name="equipment" size="3">
    <option value="monitor">Video monitor</option>
    <option value="modem">Modem</option>
    <option value="printer">Printer</option>
    ...
</select>
```

**Value**            Any positive integer.

**Default**          1

**Object Model Reference**

```
[window.]document.formName.selectName.size
[window.]document.forms[i].elements[j].size
[window.]document.getElementById(elementID).size
```

## tabindex

tabindex="*integer*"                                                Optional

This shared attribute is listed here to remind you that Netscape 6 and HTML 4 support it to facilitate accessibility to a complex form control. Once the select element has focus, the user can continue using the keyboard to make item choices. See the discussion about this attribute earlier in this chapter.

# &lt;small&gt;

&lt;small&gt;...&lt;/small&gt;                                      HTML End Tag: Required

The small element renders its content in a relative size one level smaller than the text preceding the element. Given the font element's way of specifying sizes in a range of 1 through 7, the small element displays its content one size smaller than the text that comes before it. This attribute is the same as specifying <font size=-1>.

**Example**            `<p>Let's get really <small>small</small>.</p>`

### Object Model Reference
[window.]document.getElementById(*elementID*)

### Element-Specific Attributes
None.

### Element-Specific Event Handler Attributes
None.

# &lt;spacer&gt;                                    NN &lt;6   IE *n/a*   HTML *n/a*
&lt;spacer&gt;                                                    HTML End Tag: Forbidden

As a solution to the need for creating blank space without forcing   entities, incessant &lt;p&gt; tags, or transparent images, Navigator 3 introduced the spacer element. This element creates empty space within a line of text, between lines, or as a rectangular space. Some of this functionality can be re-created in a cross-browser implementation with style sheets. The element is supported only in Navigator 3 and Navigator 4.

### Example
```
<p>This is one line of a paragraph.
<spacer type="vertical" size="36">
And this completes the paragraph with a three-line gap from the first line.</p>
```

### Element-Specific Attributes
| | | | | |
|---|---|---|---|---|
| align | height | size | type | width |

### Element-Specific Event Handler Attributes
None.

## align                                          NN &lt;6   IE *n/a*   HTML *n/a*
align="*alignmentConstant*"                                              Optional

Determines how a block type of spacer element aligns within the context of surrounding content. See "Alignment Constants" earlier in this chapter for a description of the possibilities.

| | |
|---|---|
| **Example** | &lt;spacer type="block" height="90" width="40" align="absmiddle"&gt; |
| **Value** | Case-insensitive constant value. |
| **Default** | bottom |

## height, width                                  NN &lt;6   IE *n/a*   HTML *n/a*
height="*length*"                                                       Required
width="*length*"

The size that a block type spacer element occupies in a document is governed by the height and width attribute settings. These attributes apply only when the type attribute is block.

---

| | | |
|---|---|---|
| **Example** | \<spacer type="block" height="150" width="250"\> | |
| **Value** | Positive integer or percentage values. | |
| **Default** | 0 | |

## size

size="*pixelCount*" Optional

The number of pixels of whitespace to insert either horizontally or vertically, depending on whether the type attribute is set to line or vertical. If the type attribute is set to block, the size attribute is ignored.

| | | |
|---|---|---|
| **Example** | \<spacer type="line" size="40"\> | |
| **Value** | Any positive integer. | |
| **Default** | 0 | |

## type

type="*spacerType*" Required

Defines which of the three spacer geometries is being specified for the spacer element. A type of line adds empty space in the same line of text as the preceding content; a type of vertical (or vert) adds empty space between lines of text; and a type of block defines a rectangular space that extends in two dimensions. For the line and vertical types, the size attribute must be assigned; for the block type, the height and width attributes must be assigned.

**Example**        \<spacer type="line" size="40"\>

**Value**

Any of four case-insensitive constant values: block | line | vertical | vert.

**Default**        line

## width

See height.

# \<span\>

\<span\>...\</span\> HTML End Tag: Required

The span element gives structure and context to any inline content in a document. Unlike some other structural elements that have very specific connotations attached to them (the p element, for instance), the author is free to give meaning to each particular span element by virtue of the element's attribute settings and nested content. Each span element becomes a generic container for all content within the required start and end tags.

It is convenient to use the span element as a wrapper for a small inline chunk of content that is to be governed by a style sheet rule. For example, if you want to differentiate a few words in a paragraph with the equivalent of a small caps look, you would wrap the affected words with a span element whose style sheet defines the requested font and text styles. Such a style sheet could be defined as an inline style attribute of the span element or assigned via the class or id attribute depending on the structure of the rest of the document.

If you need an arbitrary container for block-level content, use the div element.

### Example
```
<span style="font-size:10pt; text-transform:uppercase">
30-day special offer</span>
```

### Object Model Reference
[window.]document.getElementById(*elementID*)

### Element-Specific Attributes
datafld        dataformatas   datasrc

### Element-Specific Event Handler Attributes
None.

---

## datafld
NN *n/a*   IE 4   HTML |4|

datafld="*columnName*"        Optional

Used with IE data binding to associate a remote data source column name with the HTML content of a span element. The data source column must be HTML (see dataformatas). datasrc and dataformatas attributes must also be set for the span element. Works only with text file data sources in IE 5/Mac.

This attribute was reserved in HTML 4, but was dropped in XHTML 1.0.

### Example
```
<span datasrc="DBSRC3" datafld="quote" dataformatas="HTML">...</span>
```

**Value**        Case-sensitive identifier.

**Default**      None.

### Object Model Reference
[window.]document.getElementById(*elementID*).dataFld

---

## dataformatas
NN *n/a*   IE 4   HTML |4|

dataformatas="*dataType*"        Optional

Used with IE data binding, this attribute advises the browser whether the source material arriving from the data source is to be treated as plain text or as tagged HTML. A span element should receive data only in HTML format.

This attribute was reserved in HTML 4, but was dropped in XHTML 1.0.

<strike>

**Example**

<span datasrc="DBSRC3" datafld="quote" dataformatas="HTML">...</span>

**Value**            Case-insensitive constants: html | text.

**Default**          text

**Object Model Reference**

[window.]document.getElementById(*elementID*).dataFormatAs

## datasrc                                                NN *n/a*   IE 4   HTML |4|

datasrc="*dataSourceName*"                                              Optional

Used with IE data binding to specify the ID of the page's object element that loads the data source object for remote data access. Content from the data source is specified via the datafld attribute. Works only with text file data sources in IE 5/Mac.

This attribute was reserved in HTML 4, but was dropped in XHTML 1.0.

**Example**

<span datasrc="DBSRC3" datafld="quote" dataformatas="HTML">...</span>

**Value**            Case-sensitive identifier.

**Default**          None.

**Object Model Reference**

[window.]document.getElementById(*elementID*).dataSrc

# \<strike\>                                              NN *3*   IE *3*   HTML *3.2*

<strike>...</strike>                                          HTML End Tag: Required

The strike element renders its content as strikethrough text. This element is identical to the s element, which was adopted because it more closely resembled the one-character element names for other type formatting (such as b, i, and u elements). In any case, both strike and s elements are deprecated in HTML 4 in favor of the text-decoration:line-through style sheet attribute. Neither strike nor s elements validate with strict HTML 4 or XHTML DTDs.

**Example**

<p>If at first you don't succeed, <strike>do it over</strike> try, try again.</p>

**Object Model Reference**

[window.]document.getElementById(*elementID*)

**Element-Specific Attributes**
None.

**Element-Specific Event Handler Attributes**
None.

# &lt;strong&gt;

&lt;strong&gt;...&lt;/strong&gt;                                    HTML End Tag: Required

The strong element is one of a large group of elements that the HTML 4 recommendation calls *phrase elements*. Such elements assign structural meaning to a designated portion of the document. A strong element is one that contains text that indicates a stronger emphasis than the em element. Whereas an em element is typically rendered as italic text, a strong element is generally rendered as boldface text. Override the default with a style sheet as you see fit.

## Example

```
<p>Don't delay. <strong>Order today</strong> to get the maximum discount.
</p>
```

## Object Model Reference

[window.]document.getElementById(*elementID*)

## Element-Specific Attributes

None.

## Element-Specific Event Handler Attributes

None.

# &lt;style&gt;

&lt;style&gt;...&lt;/style&gt;                                     HTML End Tag: Required

The style element is a container for style sheet rules. Use the style element only inside the head element. You may include more than one style element in a head element (see the media attribute).

Older browsers may attempt to render the content of a style element. To prevent that, you should wrap the style sheet rules inside HTML comment tags. See Chapter 3 for details on the makeup of style sheet rules.

## Example

```
<style type="text/css">
<!--
h1 {font-size:18pt; text-transform:capitalize}
p  {font-size:12pt}
-->
</style>
```

## Object Model Reference

[window.]document.getElementsByTagName("style")[i]
[window.]document.getElementById(*elementID*)

## Element-Specific Attributes

disabled          media               type

## Element-Specific Event Handler Attributes

None.

<style>

## disabled

disabled                                                      Optional

Disables the entire style element, as if it didn't exist in the document. IE/Mac responds to this attribute starting in Version 5.

The disabled attribute is a Boolean type, which means that its presence in the attribute sets its value to true. Its value can also be adjusted after the fact by scripting (see the style object in Chapter 9).

**Example**        `<style type="text/css" disabled>...</style>`

**Value**          The presence of the attribute disables the element.

**Default**        false

**Object Model Reference**
```
[window.]document.getElementsByTagName("style")[i].disabled
[window.]document.getElementById(elementID).disabled
```

## media

media="*descriptorList*"                                       Optional

Sets the intended output device for the content of the element. The media attribute looks forward to the day when browsers are able to tailor content to specific kinds of devices such as pocket computers, text-to-speech digitizers, or fuzzy television sets. The HTML 4 specification defines a number of constant values for anticipated devices, but the list is open-ended, allowing future browsers to tailor output to yet other kinds of media and devices.

**Example**        `<style type="text/css" media="print">...</style>`

**Value**          Case-sensitive constant values. Multiple values can be grouped together in a comma-delimited list within a quoted string. Values defined in HTML 4 are all | aura | braille | handheld | print | projection | screen | tty | tv. Internet Explorer values are all | print |screen.

**Default**        all

**Object Model Reference**
```
[window.]document.getElementsByTagName("style")[i].media
[window.]document.getElementById(elementID).media
```

## type

type="*MIMEType*"                                              Required

The type attribute tells the browser which style sheet syntax to use to interpret the style rules defined in the current element.

**Example**        `<style type="text/css">...</style>`

<sub>

| **Value** | Case-insensitive MIME type. A type accepted by both Navigator 4 and later and IE 4 and later is "text/css". Navigator 4 (only) also recognizes "text/javascript" when using JavaScript syntax style sheets. |
| --- | --- |
| **Default** | text/css |

**Object Model Reference**

[window.]document.getElementsByTagName("style")[i].type
[window.]document.getElementById(*elementID*).type

# <sub>

NN *2*    IE *3*    HTML *3.2*

<sub>...</sub>

HTML End Tag: Required

The sub element is a typographical element that instructs the browser to render its content as a subscript in a font size consistent with the surrounding content. Browsers tend to render this content in a smaller size than surrounding content.

**Example**

```
<p>"Heavy water" (H<sub>3</sub>0) has one more hydrogen atom than regular water.</p>
```

**Object Model Reference**

[window.]document.getElementById(*elementID*)

**Element-Specific Attributes**

None.

**Element-Specific Event Handler Attributes**

None.

# <sup>

NN *2*    IE *3*    HTML *3.2*

<sup>...</sup>

HTML End Tag: Required

The sup element is a typographical element that instructs the browser to render its content as a superscript in a font size consistent with the surrounding content. Browsers tend to render this content in a smaller size than surrounding content.

**Example**

```
<p>This book is published by O'Reilly<sup>&#153;</sup>.</p>
```

**Object Model Reference**

[window.]document.getElementById(*elementID*)

**Element-Specific Attributes**

None.

**Element-Specific Event Handler Attributes**

None.

# &lt;table&gt;

&lt;table&gt;...&lt;/table&gt;

The table element is a container for additional elements that specify the content for a table. A table consists of rows and columns of content. Other elements related to the table element are caption, col, colgroup, tbody, td, tfoot, th, thead, and tr. The purpose of the table element is to define a number of visible attributes that apply to the entire table, regardless of the number of rows or columns within it. Many of these attributes can be overridden for a given row, column, or cell. The number of rows and columns is strictly a factor of the structure of tr and td elements within the table.

Tables have been used for a relatively long time not only to organize rows and columns of content but also to position content. With no visible borders, table rows and columns can be set to empty space. With the advent of positionable content, the tables-for-positioning practice is not encouraged.

Deeply nested tables (tables within tables) can cause problems in some browsers. Navigator 4 has severe difficulty with style sheet inheritance and overall performance in complex tables (nesting beyond three levels is asking for trouble). IE 5/Mac can inexplicably explode cell dimensions when scripts create or modify table-related elements. The simpler you keep your table structure, the more reliable your pages will be across browsers. Heavy editing of table structures in visual HTML authoring tools can leave hidden complexities (e.g., lots of empty cells) in your source code. Temporarily turn on a thin table border to see the exact row and column structure.

**Example**

```
<table cols="3">
<thead>
<tr>
<th>Time</th><th>Event</th><th>Location</th>
</tr>
</thead>
<tbody>
<tr>
<td>7:30am-5:00pm</td><td>Registration Open</td><td>Main Lobby</td>
</tr>
<tr>
<td>9:00am-12:00pm</td><td>Keynote Speakers</td><td>Cypress Room</td>
</tr>
</tbody>
</table>
```

**Object Model Reference**

[window.]document.getElementById(*elementID*)

**Element-Specific Attributes**

| | | | | |
|---|---|---|---|---|
| align | background | bgcolor | border | bordercolor |
| bordercolordark | bordercolorlight | cellpadding | cellspacing | cols |
| datapagesize | datasrc | frame | height | hspace |
| layout | rules | summary | vspace | width |

### Element-Specific Event Handler Attributes

| Handler | NN | IE | HTML |
|---|---|---|---|
| onafterupdate | n/a | 4 | n/a |
| onbeforeupdate | n/a | 4 | n/a |
| onrowenter | n/a | 4 | n/a |
| onrowexit | n/a | 4 | n/a |

## align
NN *all*　IE *all*　HTML *3.2*

`align="where"`                                               Optional

Determines how the table is aligned relative to the next outermost container (usually the document body or html element). The align attribute is deprecated in HTML 4 in favor of style sheet attributes.

**Example**　　　`<table align="center">...</table>`

**Value**　　　Alignment constant: center | left | right.

**Default**　　　left

**Object Model Reference**
`[window.]document.getElementById(elementID).align`

## background
NN *4*　IE *3*　HTML *n/a*

`background="URL"`                                               Optional

Specifies an image file that is used as a backdrop to the table. Unlike normal images that get loaded into browser content, a background image loads in its original size (without scaling) and tiles to fill the available table space. Smaller images download faster but are obviously repeated more often in the background. Animated GIFs are also allowable, but very distracting to the reader. When selecting a background image, be sure it is very muted in comparison to the main content so that the content stands out clearly. Background images, if used at all, should be extremely subtle.

Navigator 4 can be quirky with this attribute. Be prepared to wrap your main table (without a background) inside another table element, whose background property has a graphic file assigned to it.

**Example**　　　`<table background="watermark.jpg">...</table>`

**Value**　　　Any valid URL to an image file, including complete and relative URLs.

**Default**　　　None (table is transparent).

**Object Model Reference**
`[window.]document.getElementById(elementID).background`

## bgcolor

bgcolor="*colorTripletOrName*"                                                  Optional

Establishes a fill color (behind the text and other content) for the entire table. If you combine a bgcolor and background, any transparent areas of the background image let the background color show through. This attribute is deprecated in HTML 4 in favor of the background-color style attribute.

**Example**          &lt;table bgcolor="tan"&gt;...&lt;/table&gt;

**Value**            A hexadecimal triplet or plain-language color name. A setting of empty is interpreted as "#000000" (black). See Appendix A for acceptable plain-language color names.

**Default**          Varies with browser, browser version, and operating system.

**Object Model Reference**
[window.]document.getElementById(*elementID*).bgColor


## border

border="*pixelCount*"                                                           Optional

The thickness (in pixels) of the border drawn around a table element. If you set the border attribute to any value, browsers by default render narrow borders around each of the cells inside the table. With a table element's border showing, the thickness of internal borders between cells is defined by the cellspacing attribute of the table element.

If you include only the border attribute without assigning any value to it, the browser renders default-sized borders around the entire table and between cells, unless overridden by other attributes.

Browsers render the border in a 3-D style, with the border appearing to be raised around the flat content in the cells. Numerous other attributes affect the look of the border, including: bordercolor, bordercolordark, bordercolorlight, frame, and rules. The type of border rendered for tables is different from the borders defined by style sheet rules. You get better control of the border look by using the dedicated attributes of the table element.

**Example**          &lt;table border="1"&gt;...&lt;/table&gt;

**Value**            A positive integer value.

**Default**          0

**Object Model Reference**
[window.]document.getElementById(*elementID*).border


## bordercolor

bordercolor="*colorTripletOrName*"                                              Optional

The colors used to render some of the pixels that create the illusion of borders around cells and the entire table. The border attribute must have a nonzero value assigned for the color to appear. The 3-D effect of borders in is created by careful positioning of light (or white) and dark lines around the page's background or default color (see Figure 8-4). Standard colors are usually shades of gray and white, depending on the browser.

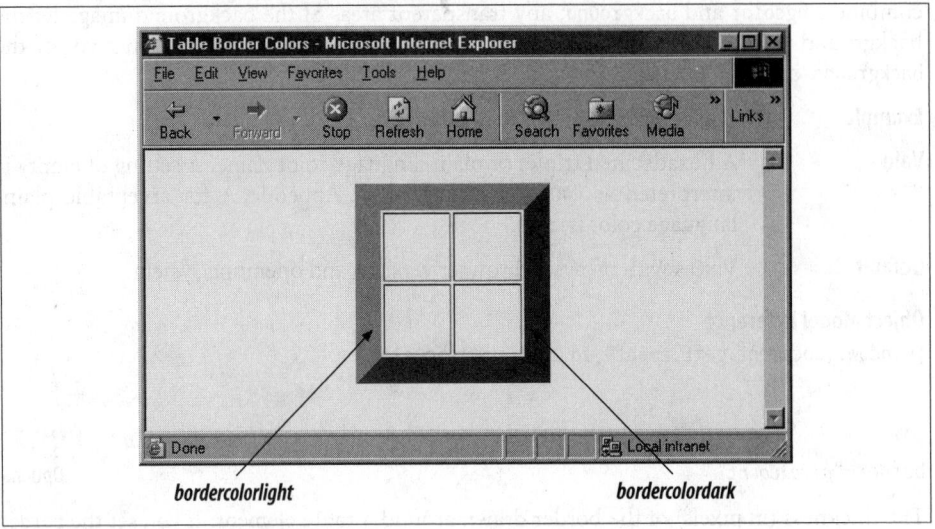

*Figure 8-4. Components of table border color*

Applying color to a table border has a different effect in Navigator and Internet Explorer. In Navigator, the color is applied to what is normally the darker of the two shades used to create the border. Moreover, Navigator automatically adjusts the darkness of some of the lines to enhance the 3-D effect of the border. In contrast, Internet Explorer applies the color to all lines that make up the border. The net effect is to flatten the 3-D effect (refer to the bordercolordark and bordercolorlight attributes to color borders and maintain the 3-D effect in IE).

| | |
|---|---|
| **Example** | `<table bordercolor="green" border="2">...</table>` |
| **Value** | A hexadecimal triplet or plain-language color name. A setting of empty is interpreted as "#000000" (black). See Appendix A for acceptable plain-language color names. |
| **Default** | Varies with browser and operating system. |

**Object Model Reference**

[window.]document.getElementById(*elementID*).borderColor

## bordercolordark, bordercolorlight    NN *n/a*    IE *3*    HTML *n/a*

bordercolordark="*colorTripletOrName*"    Optional
bordercolorlight="*colorTripletOrName*"

The 3-D effect of table borders in Internet Explorer is created by careful positioning of light and dark lines around the page's background or default color (see Figure 8-4). You can independently control the colors used for the dark and light lines by assigning values to the

<table>

bordercolordark and bordercolorlight attributes. The border attribute must have a nonzero value assigned for the colors to appear.

Typically, you should assign complementary colors to the pair of attributes. There is also no rule that says you must assign a dark color to bordercolordark. The attributes merely control a well-defined set of lines so you can predict which lines of the border change with each attribute.

To achieve the identical look in Navigator and IE, you must determine the complementary colors that Navigator uses for its 3-D effect from the bordercolor attribute. Then assign those values to the bordercolordark and bordercolorlight attributes. You may place all three attributes in the same <table> tag.

### Example

```
<table bordercolordark="darkred" bordercolorlight="salmon" border="3">...
</table>
```

### Value

A hexadecimal triplet or plain-language color name. A setting of empty is interpreted as "#000000" (black). See Appendix A for acceptable plain-language color names.

**Default**  Varies with operating system.

### Object Model Reference

```
[window.]document.getElementById(elementID).borderColorDark
[window.]document.getElementById(elementID).borderColorLight
```

## cellpadding

NN *all*  IE 3  HTML 3.2

```
cellpadding="length"
```
Optional

The amount of empty space between the border of a table cell and the content of the cell. Note that this attribute applies to space *inside* a cell. Without setting this attribute, most browsers render text content so that its leftmost pixels abut the left edge of the cell. If the table displays borders, adding a few pixels of breathing space between the border edge and the content makes the content more readable. Large padding may also be desirable in some design instances. This attribute is not as noticeable when the table does not display borders (in which case the cellspacing attribute can assist in adjusting the space between cells).

**Example**  `<table border="2" cellpadding="3">...</table>`

**Value**

Any length value in pixels or percentage of available space. Percentage values are based on the total available space in the horizontal and vertical dimensions of the cell. For example, a value of 10% means that the left and right padding will each be 5% of the total width of the cell; the top and bottom padding will each be 5% of the total height of the cell.

**Default**  0

### Object Model Reference

```
[window.]document.getElementById(elementID).cellPadding
```

## cellspacing
NN all   IE 3   HTML 3.2

cellspacing="length"
Optional

The amount of empty space between the outer edges of each table cell. If you set the border attribute of the table element to any positive integer value, the effect of setting cellspacing is to define the thickness of borders rendered between cells. Even without a visible border, the readability of a table often benefits from cell spacing.

**Example**           &lt;table border="2" cellspacing="10"&gt;...&lt;/table&gt;

**Value**              Any positive integer.

**Default**           0 (no table border); 2 (with table border).

**Object Model Reference**

[window.]document.getElementById(elementID).cellSpacing

## cols
NN 4   IE 3   HTML n/a

cols="columnCount"
Optional

The number of columns of the table. The HTML specification never adopted this attribute. In HTML 4, the functionality of this attribute is covered by the colgroup and col elements. In the meantime, the cols attribute is recognized by older and current browsers. The attribute assists the browser in preparation for rendering the table. Without this attribute, the browser relies on its interpretation of all downloaded tr and td elements to determine how the table is to be divided.

**Example**           &lt;table cols="4"&gt;...&lt;/table&gt;

**Value**              Any positive integer.

**Default**           None.

**Object Model Reference**

[window.]document.getElementById(elementID).cols

## datapagesize
NN n/a   IE 4   HTML n/a

datapagesize="recordCount"
Optional

Used with IE data binding, this attribute advises the browser how many instances of a table row must be rendered to accommodate the number of data source records set by this attribute. A common application is setting a table cell to display a text input element whose datafld attribute is bound to a particular column of the data source (the datasrc is set in the table element). If the datapagesize attribute is set to 5, the browser must display five rows of the table (but the row is specified in the HTML only once).

**Example**

```
<table datasrc="DBSRC3" datapagesize="5">
<tr>
  <td><input type="text" datafld="stockNum"></td>
```

```
    <td><input type="text" datafld="qtyOnHand"></td>
</tr>
</table>
```

**Value**          Any positive integer.

**Default**        None.

**Object Model Reference**

[window.]document.getElementById(*elementID*).dataPageSize

## datasrc

datasrc="*dataSourceName*"                                          Optional

Used with IE data binding to specify the ID of the page's object element that loads the data source object for remote data access. Content from the data source is specified via the datafld attribute.

A block of contiguous records can be rendered in the table when you also set the datapagesize attribute of the table. Works only with text file data sources in IE 5/Mac.

**Example**        `<table datasrc="DBSRC3" datapagesize="5">...</table>`

**Value**          Case-sensitive identifier.

**Default**        None.

**Object Model Reference**

[window.]document.getElementById(*elementID*).dataSrc

## frame

frame="*frameConstant*"                                             Optional

Defines which (if any) sides of a table's outer border (set with the border attribute) are rendered. This attribute does not affect the interior borders between cells. Including the border attribute without assigning any value to it is the same as setting the frame attribute to border. All settings can be replicated with CSS border-related attributes if you prefer.

**Example**        `<table border="3" frame="void">...</table>`

**Value**

Any one case-insensitive frame constant:

above
> Renders border along top edge of table only

below
> Renders border along bottom edge of table only

border
> Renders all four sides of the border (default in IE and NN)

box
> Renders all four sides of the border (same as border)

hsides
> Renders borders on top and bottom edges of table only (a nice look)

lhs
> Renders border on left edge of table only

rhs
> Renders border on right edge of table only

void
> Hides all borders (default in HTML 4)

vsides
> Renders borders on left and right edges of table only

### Default
Navigator: void (when border=0); border (when border is any other value). Internet Explorer: border.

### Object Model Reference
[window.]document.getElementById(*elementID*).frame

## height, width
NN *all*    IE 3    HTML *3.2 (width)*

height="*length*"
width="*length*"

Optional

The rectangular dimensions of a table that may be different from the default size as calculated by the browser. When the values for these attributes are less than the minimum space required to render the table cell content, the browser overrides the attribute settings to make sure that all content appears, even if it means that text lines word-wrap. You can also stretch the dimensions of a table beyond the browser-calculated dimensions. Extra whitespace appears inside table cells to make up the difference. If you specify just one attribute, the browser performs the necessary calculations to automatically adjust the dimension along the other axis.

Note that the height attribute is not in the HTML specification. The assumption there is that the table height is calculated by the browser to best show all cell content given either the default or attribute-established width. Because different browsers on different operating systems can render text content in varying relative font sizes, it is not unusual to let the height of a table be calculated by the browser.

**Example**        &lt;table width="80%"&gt;...&lt;/table&gt;

**Value**        Any length value in pixels or percentage of available space.

### Default
Governed by content, but width not to exceed 100% of the next outermost container. IE does accept percentage values beyond 100%, which may cause the table's container to display scroll bars and perhaps disturb the graphical integrity of the layout design.

### Object Model Reference
[window.]document.getElementById(*elementID*).height
[window.]document.getElementById(*elementID*).width

## hspace, vspace

hspace="*pixels*"                                                                                                          Optional
vspace="*pixels*"

Inserts transparent padding outside the edges of the entire table on the page. Use CSS-padding-related attributes instead. Note that Netscape 6 responds to these table element attributes only in "quirks" mode (see DOCTYPE element).

**Example**          &lt;table hspace="20" vspace="40"&gt;...&lt;/table&gt;

**Value**            Integer pixel count.

**Default**          0

## layout

layout="*layoutType*"                                                                                                      Optional

Controls the table-layout–rendering algorithm. A value of fixed directs the browser to size the table and cells according to explicit height and width settings, rather than respecting content size minimums. This attribute mimics the table-layout CSS attribute.

**Example**          &lt;table layout="fixed" width="500"&gt;...&lt;/table&gt;

**Value**            Constant values: auto | fixed.

**Default**          auto

## rules

rules="*rulesConstant*"                                                                                                     Optional

Defines where (if at all) interior borders between cells are rendered by the browser. In addition to setting the table to draw borders to turn the cells into a matrix, you can also set borders to be drawn only to separate rows, columns, or any sanctioned cell grouping (thead, tbody, tfoot, colgroup, or col). The border attribute must be present—either as a Boolean or set to a specific border size—for any cell borders to be drawn. IE 5/Mac leaves gaps in inter-cell borders where rules are removed.

**Example**          &lt;table border="3" rules="groups"&gt;...&lt;/table&gt;

**Value**

Any one case-insensitive rules constant:

all
   Renders borders around each cell
cols
   Renders borders between columns only
groups
   Renders borders between cell groups as defined by the thead, tfoot, tbody, colgroup, or col elements

    Hides all interior borders

rows

    Renders borders between rows only

**Default**          none (when border=0); all (when border is any other value).

**Object Model Reference**

[window.]document.getElementById(*elementID*).rules

## summary                                   NN 6   IE 6   HTML 4

summary="*text*"                                        Optional

A textual description of the table, including, but not limited to, instructions that nonvisual browsers might follow to describe the purpose and organization of the table data. The **Properties** choice for Netscape 6's context menu for this element displays a small window that includes an active link to the URL assigned to the attribute. Version 6 browsers provide no other functionality for this attribute.

**Example**

\<table summary="Order form for entry of up to five products."\>...\</table\>

**Value**          Any quoted string of characters.

**Default**       None.

## vspace

See hspace.

## width

See height.

# \<tbody\>                                   NN 6   IE 3   HTML 4

\<tbody\>...\</tbody\>                            HTML End Tag: Optional

A tbody element is an arbitrary container of one or more rows of table cells. More than one tbody element may be defined within a single table element. Use the tbody element to define structural segments of a table that may require their own styles or border treatments (see the rules attribute). A tbody element is the row-oriented equivalent of the colgroup element for columns. Other types of row groupings available are the tfoot and thead elements, neither of which overlaps with a tbody element.

**Example**

\<table cols="3"\>
\<thead\>

<tbody>

```
<tr>
<th>Time</th><th>Event</th><th>Location</th>
</tr>
</thead>
<tbody>
<tr>
<td>7:30am-5:00pm</td><td>Registration Open</td><td>Main Lobby</td>
</tr>
<tr>
<td>9:00am-12:00pm</td><td>Keynote Speakers</td><td>Cypress Room</td>
</tr>
</tbody>
</table>
```

### Object Model Reference
[window.]document.getElementById(*elementID*)

### Element-Specific Attributes

| | | | | |
|---|---|---|---|---|
| align | bgcolor | ch | char | charoff |
| choff | valign | | | |

### Element-Specific Event Handler Attributes
None.

## align                                                   NN 6    IE 4    HTML 4

align="*alignConstant*"                                                  Optional

Establishes the horizontal alignment characteristics of content within the row(s) covered by the tbody element.

**Example**          `<tbody align="center">`

### Value
HTML 4 and various browsers implement different sets of attribute values.

| Value | IE/Windows | IE/Mac and NN 6 | HTML 4 |
|---|---|---|---|
| center | • | • | • |
| char | – | – | • |
| justify | – | • | • |
| left | • | • | • |
| right | • | • | • |

The values center, left, and right are self-explanatory. The value justify spaces multiline content so that text is justified down both left and right edges. For the value char, the char attribute must also be set to specify the character on which alignment revolves. In the HTML 4 specification example, content that does not contain the character appears to be right-aligned to the location of the character in other rows of the same column.

It's important to bear in mind that the align attribute applies to every cell of every row within the tbody, including any th element you specify for the table. If you want a different alignment for the row header, override the setting with a separate align attribute or text-align style sheet attribute for the thead or individual th elements.

**Default**          left

**Object Model Reference**
[window.]document.getElementById(*elementID*).align

## bgcolor

NN 6    IE 4    HTML *n/a*

bgcolor="*colorTripletOrName*"                                    Optional

Establishes a fill color (behind the text and other content) for the cells contained by the tbody element.

**Example**          &lt;tbody bgcolor="tan"&gt;

**Value**            A hexadecimal triplet or plain-language color name. A setting of empty is interpreted as "#000000" (black). See Appendix A for acceptable plain-language color names.

**Default**          Varies with browser, browser version, and operating system.

**Object Model Reference**
[window.]document.getElementById(*elementID*).bgColor

## char

NN 6    IE *n/a*    HTML 4

char="*character*"                                                Optional

The char attribute defines the text character used as an alignment point for text within a cell contained by the tbody element. This attribute is of value only for the align attribute set to "char". Microsoft documents a ch attribute, which corresponds to the standards-based char attribute. In any case, the browser does not respond to either attribute. Netscape 7 has not yet connected support for the char attribute.

**Example**          &lt;tbody align="char" char="."&gt;

**Value**            Any single text character.

**Default**          None.

## charoff

NN 6    IE *n/a*    HTML 4

charoff="*length*"                                               Optional

The charoff attribute lets you set a specific offset point at which the character specified by the char attribute is to appear within a cell contained by the tbody element. This attribute is provided in case the browser default positioning does not meet with the design goals of the table. Microsoft documents a choff attribute, which corresponds to the standards-based

<td>

charoff attribute. In any case, the browser does not respond to either attribute. Netscape 7 has not yet connected support for the charoff attribute.

**Example**   `<tbody align="char" char="." charoff="80%">`

**Value**   Any length value in pixels or percentage of cell space.

**Default**   None.

## choff

See charoff.

## valign                       NN *6*  IE *4*  HTML *4*

`valign="`*`alignmentConstant`*`"`                   Optional

Determines the vertical alignment of content within cells of the column(s) covered by the tbody element. You can override the vertical alignment for a particular cell anywhere in the column.

**Example**   `<tbody valign="bottom">`

**Value**

Four constant values: `top | middle | bottom | baseline`. With `top` and `bottom`, the content is rendered flush (or very close to it) to the top and bottom of the table cell. Set to `middle` (the default), the content floats perfectly centered vertically in the cell. When one cell's contents might wrap to multiple lines at common window widths (assuming a variable table width), it is advisable to set the `valign` attribute to `baseline`. This assures that the character baseline of the first (or only) line of a cell's text aligns with the other cells in the row—usually the most aesthetically pleasing arrangement.

**Default**   `middle`

**Object Model Reference**
`[window.]document.getElementById(`*`elementID`*`).vAlign`

## <td>                    NN *all*  IE *all*  HTML *3.2*

`<td>...</td>`                     End Tag: Optional

The td element is a container for content that is rendered inside one cell of a table element. One cell is the intersection of a column and row. Other elements related to the td element are caption, col, colgroup, table, tbody, tfoot, th, thead, and tr. In addition to providing a wrapper for a cell's content, the td element defines a number of visible attributes that apply to a single cell, often overriding similar attributes set in lesser-nested elements in the table.

Four attributes—abbr, axis, headers, and scope—are included in the HTML 4 specification in anticipation of nonvisual browsers that will use text-to-speech technology to describe content of an HTML page—a kind of "verbal rendering." Although these attributes are briefly described here for the sake of completeness, there is much more to their application in nonvisual browsers than is relevant in this book on Dynamic HTML. Consult the HTML 4 recommendation for more details.

**Example**

```
<table cols="3">
<thead>
<tr>
<th>Time</th><th>Event</th><th>Location</th>
</tr>
</thead>
<tbody>
<tr>
<td>7:30am-5:00pm</td><td>Registration Open</td><td>Main Lobby</td>
</tr>
<tr>
<td>9:00am-12:00pm</td><td>Keynote Speakers</td><td>Cypress Room</td>
</tr>
</tbody>
</table>
```

**Object Model Reference**

[window.]document.getElementById(*elementID*)

**Element-Specific Attributes**

| | | | | |
|---|---|---|---|---|
| abbr | align | axis | background | bgcolor |
| bordercolor | bordercolordark | bordercolorlight | ch | char |
| charoff | choff | colspan | datafld | dir |
| headers | height | nowrap | rowspan | scope |
| valign | width | | | |

**Element-Specific Event Handler Attributes**

| Handler | NN | IE | HTML |
|---|---|---|---|
| onafterupdate | n/a | 4 | n/a |
| onbeforeupdate | n/a | 4 | n/a |
| onrowenter | n/a | 4 | n/a |
| onrowexit | n/a | 4 | n/a |

## abbr
NN 6   IE 6   HTML 4

abbr="*text*"
Optional

Provides an abbreviated string that describes the cell's content. This is usually a brief label that a nonvisual browser would speak to describe what the value of the cell represents. The **Properties** choice for Netscape 6's context menu for this element displays a small window that includes an active link to the URL assigned to the attribute. Version 6 browsers provide no other functionality for this attribute.

**Example**  `<td abbr="Main Event">Keynote Speakers</td>`

| | |
|---|---|
| **Value** | Any quoted string. |
| **Default** | None. |

**Object Model Reference**

[window.]document.getElementById(*elementID*).abbr

## align

align="*alignConstant*"                                          Optional

Establishes the horizontal alignment characteristics of content within the cell covered by the td element.

**Example**        &lt;td align="center"&gt;

**Value**

HTML 4 and various browsers implement different sets of attribute values.

| Value | IE/Windows and NN 4 | IE/Mac and NN 6 | HTML 4 |
|---|:---:|:---:|:---:|
| center | • | • | • |
| char | – | – | • |
| justify | – | • | • |
| left | • | • | • |
| right | • | • | • |

The values center, left, and right are self-explanatory. The value justify spaces multiline content so that text is justified down both left and right edges. For the value char, the char attribute must also be set to specify the character on which alignment revolves. In the HTML 4 specification example, content that does not contain the character appears to be right-aligned to the location of the character in other rows of the same column.

**Default**        left

**Object Model Reference**

[window.]document.getElementById(*elementID*).align

## axis

axis="*text*"                                                 Optional

Provides an abbreviated string that describes the cell's category. This is usually a brief label that a nonvisual browser would speak to describe what the value of the cell represents. The **Properties** choice for Netscape 6's context menu for this element displays a small window that includes an active link to the URL assigned to the attribute. Version 6 browsers provide no other functionality for this attribute.

**Example**        &lt;td axis="event"&gt;Keynote Speakers&lt;/td&gt;

**Value**        Any quoted string.

**Default** None.

**Object Model Reference**

[window.]document.getElementById(*elementID*).axis

## background

background="*URL*" Optional

Specifies an image file that is used as a backdrop to the cell. Unlike normal images that get loaded into browser content, a background image loads in its original size (without scaling) and tiles to fill the available cell space. Smaller images download faster but are obviously repeated more often in the background. Navigator 4, however, requires a minimum image size of 16 by 16 pixels. Animated GIFs are also allowable, but very distracting to the reader. When selecting a background image, be sure it is very muted in comparison to the main content so that the content stands out clearly. Background images, if used at all, should be extremely subtle.

**Example** `<td background="watermark.jpg">`

**Value** Any valid URL to an image file, including complete and relative URLs.

**Default** None.

**Object Model Reference**

[window.]document.getElementById(*elementID*).background

## bgcolor

bgcolor="*colorTripletOrName*" Optional

Establishes a fill color (behind the text and other content) for the cell defined by the td element.

**Example** `<td bgcolor="yellow">`

**Value** A hexadecimal triplet or plain-language color name. A setting of empty is interpreted as "#000000" (black). See Appendix A for acceptable plain-language color names.

**Default** Varies with browser, browser version, and operating system.

**Object Model Reference**

[window.]document.getElementById(*elementID*).bgColor

## bordercolor

bordercolor="*colorTripletOrName*" Optional

The colors used to render some of the pixels that create the illusion of borders around cells and the entire table. Internet Explorer applies the color to all four lines that make up the interior border of a cell. Therefore, colors of adjacent cells do not collide.

**Example**        `<td bordercolor="green">`

**Value**          A hexadecimal triplet or plain-language color name. A setting of empty is interpreted as "#000000" (black). See Appendix A for acceptable plain-language color names.

**Default**        Varies with browser and operating system.

#### Object Model Reference

`[window.]document.getElementById(elementID).borderColor`

## bordercolordark, bordercolorlight

NN *n/a*    IE *3*    HTML *n/a*

`bordercolordark="colorTripletOrName"`            Optional
`bordercolorlight="colorTripletOrName"`

The 3-D effect of table borders in Internet Explorer is created by careful positioning of light and dark lines around the page's background or default color (see Figure 8-4 in the table element discussion). You can independently control the colors used for the dark and light lines by assigning values to the bordercolordark (left and top edges of the cell) and bordercolorlight (right and bottom edges) attributes.

Typically, you should assign complementary colors to the pair of attributes. There is also no rule that says you must assign a dark color to bordercolordark. The attributes merely control a well-defined set of lines so you can predict which lines of the border change with each attribute.

**Example**        `<td bordercolordark="darkred" bordercolorlight="salmon">`

**Value**          A hexadecimal triplet or plain-language color name. A setting of empty is interpreted as "#000000" (black). See Appendix A for acceptable plain-language color names.

**Default**        Varies with operating system.

#### Object Model Reference

`[window.]document.getElementById(elementID).borderColorDark`
`[window.]document.getElementById(elementID).borderColorLight`

## char

NN *6*    IE *n/a*    HTML *4*

`char="character"`            Optional

The char attribute defines the text character used as an alignment point for text within a cell. This attribute is of value only for the align attribute set to "char". Microsoft documents a ch attribute, which corresponds to the standards-based char attribute. In any case, the browser does not respond to either attribute. Netscape 7 has not yet connected support for the char attribute.

**Example**        `<td align="char" char=".">203.00</td>`

**Value**          Any single text character.

**Default**        None.

## charoff

charoff="*length*"

**Optional**

The charoff attribute lets you set a specific offset point at which the character specified by the char attribute is to appear within a cell. This attribute is provided in case the browser default positioning does not meet with the design goals of the table. Microsoft documents a choff attribute, which corresponds to the standards-based charoff attribute. In any case, the browser does not respond to either attribute. Netscape 7 has not yet connected support for the charoff attribute.

| | |
|---|---|
| **Example** | &lt;td align="char" char="." charoff="80%"&gt; |
| **Value** | Any length value in pixels or percentage of cell space. |
| **Default** | None. |

## choff

See charoff.

## colspan

colspan="*columnCount*"

**Optional**

The number of columns across which the current table cell should extend itself. For each additional column included in the colspan count, one less td element is required for the table row. If you set the align attribute to center or right, the alignment is calculated on the full width of the td element across the specified number of columns. Unless the current cell also specifies a rowspan attribute, the next table row returns to the original column count.

| | |
|---|---|
| **Example** | &lt;td colspan="2" align="center"&gt; |
| **Value** | Any positive integer, usually 2 or larger. |
| **Default** | 1 |

**Object Model Reference**

[window.]document.getElementById(*elementID*).colSpan

## datafld

datafld="*columnName*"

**Optional**

Used with IE data binding to associate a remote data source column name with the content of a table cell. A datasrc (and optionally a datapagesize) attribute must also be set for the enclosing table element. Works only with text file data sources in IE 5/Mac.

**Example**

```
<table datasrc="DBSRC3" datapagesize="5">
<tr>
  <td datafld="stockNum"></td>
  <td datafld="qtyOnHand"></td>
```

<td>

```
</tr>
</table>
```

**Value**        Case-sensitive identifier.

**Default**      None.

## headers                                            NN 6   IE 6   HTML 4

`headers="cellIDList"`                                           Optional

Points to one or more th or td elements that act as column or row headers for the current table cell. The assigned value is a space-delimited list of id attribute values that are assigned to the relevant th elements. A nonvisual browser could speak the cell's header before the content of the cell to help listeners identify the nature of the cell content. Although mainstream Version 6 browsers claim support for this attribute, neither have yet connected support for it.

### Example

```
<tr>
<th id="hdr1">Product Number</th>
<th id="hdr2">Description</th>
</tr>
<tr>
<td headers="hdr1">0392</td>
<td headers="hdr2">Round widget</td>
</tr>
```

### Value

A space-delimited list of case-sensitive IDs assigned to cells that act as headers to the current cell.

**Default**      None.

## height, width                                      NN all   IE all   HTML 3.2

`height="length"`                                               Optional
`width="length"`

The rectangular dimensions of a cell that may be different from the default size as calculated by the browser. When the values for these attributes are less than the minimum space required to render the table cell content, the browser overrides the attribute settings to make sure that all content appears, even if it means that text lines word-wrap. You can also stretch the dimensions of a table beyond the browser-calculated dimensions. Extra whitespace appears inside table cells to make up the difference. If you specify just one of these attributes, the browser performs all necessary calculations to automatically adjust the dimension along the other axis. The cell must have some content assigned to it, or it may close up to minimum size.

Due to the regular nature of tables, if you set a custom height for one cell in a row, the entire row is set to that height; similarly, setting the width of a cell causes the width of all cells in the column to be the same size.

Both the height and width attributes are deprecated in HTML 4 in favor of height and width style sheet attributes (which are not available for table cells in Navigator 4).

**Example**        `<td width="80%" height="30">`

**Value**          Any length value in pixels or percentage of available space.

**Default**        Based on content size.

### Object Model Reference
```
[window.]document.getElementById(elementID).height
[window.]document.getElementById(elementID).width
```

## nowrap                                                NN *all*    IE *all*    HTML *3.2*

nowrap                                                                              Optional

The presence of the nowrap attribute instructs the browser to render the cell as wide as is necessary to display a line of nonbreaking text on one line. Abuse of this attribute can force the user into a great deal of inconvenient horizontal scrolling of the page to view all of the content. The nowrap attribute is deprecated in HTML 4 in favor of the white-space:nowrap CSS attribute and value.

**Example**        `<td nowrap>`

**Value**          The presence of this attribute sets its value to true.

**Default**        false

### Object Model Reference
```
[window.]document.getElementById(elementID).noWrap
```

## rowspan                                               NN *all*    IE *all*    HTML *3.2*

rowspan="*rowCount*"                                                                Optional

The number of rows through which the current table cell should extend itself downward. For each additional row included in the rowspan count, one less td element is required for the next table row in that cell's position along the row.

**Example**        `<td rowspan="2">`

**Value**          Any positive integer, usually 2 or larger.

**Default**        1

### Object Model Reference
```
[window.]document.getElementById(elementID).rowSpan
```

## scope

NN 6    IE 6    HTML 4

scope="*scopeConstant*" Optional

Used more with a th element than with a td element, the scope attribute sets the range of cells (relative to the current cell) that behave as though the current cell is the header for those cells. For tables whose structure is quite regular, the scope attribute is a simpler way of achieving what the headers attribute does, without having to define id attributes for the header cells. Although mainstream Version 6 browsers claim support for this attribute, neither have yet connected support for it.

### Example

```
<tr>
<th scope="col">Product Number</th>
<th scope="col">Description</th>
</tr>
<tr>
<td>0392</td>
<td>Round widget</td>
</tr>
```

### Value

One of four recognized scope constants:

col
> Current cell text becomes header text for every cell in the rest of the column.

colgroup
> Current cell text becomes header text for every cell in the rest of the colgroup element.

row
> Current cell text becomes header text for every cell in the rest of the tr element.

rowgroup
> Current cell text becomes header text for every cell in the rest of the tbody element.

### Default     None.

## valign

NN *all*    IE *all*    HTML 3.2

valign="*alignmentConstant*" Optional

Determines the vertical alignment of content within the td element. A value you set for an individual cell overrides the same attribute setting for outer containers, such as tr and tbody.

### Example     <td valign="bottom">

### Value

Four constant values: top | middle | bottom | baseline. With top and bottom, the content is rendered flush (or very close to it) to the top and bottom of the table cell. Set to middle (the default), the content floats perfectly centered vertically in the cell. When one cell's contents might wrap to multiple lines at common window widths (assuming a variable table width), it is advisable to set the valign attribute to baseline. This assures that the character baseline of the first (or only) line of a cell's text aligns with the other cells in the row—usually the most aesthetically pleasing arrangement.

**Alphabetical Tag Reference** | 439

Alphabetical<br>HTML Reference

**Default**         middle

**Object Model Reference**

[window.]document.getElementById(*elementID*).vAlign

## width

See height.

# &lt;textarea&gt;                                  NN *all*   IE *all*   HTML *all*
&lt;textarea&gt;...&lt;/textarea&gt;                              HTML End Tag: Required

The textarea element is a multiline text input control primarily used inside form elements (required in Navigator 4 or earlier). Unlike the text type input element, a textarea element can be sized to accept more than one line of text. Word-wrapping is available on more recent browsers, and users may enter carriage return characters (a combination of characters ASCII decimal 13 and 10) inside the text box. When a textarea element is inside a submitted form, the name/value pair is submitted, with the value being the content of the text box (and the name attribute must be assigned). The CGI program on the server must be able to handle the possibility of carriage returns in the text data.

If you wish to display text in the textarea element when it loads, that text goes between the start and end tags; otherwise, there are no intervening characters in the source code between start and end tags. A label for the textarea element must be placed before or after the element, and may be encased in a label element for structural purposes (optionally in newer browsers).

**Example**

```
<textarea rows="5" cols="60" name="notes">Use this area for extra notes.
</textarea>
```

**Object Model Reference**

[window.]document.*formName*.*elementName*
[window.]document.forms[i].elements[j]
[window.]document.getElementById(*elementID*)

**Element-Specific Attributes**

| cols      | datafld | datasrc | disabled | name |
|-----------|---------|---------|----------|------|
| readonly  | rows    | wrap    |          |      |

**Element-Specific Event Handler Attributes**

| Handler        | NN  | IE | HTML |
|----------------|-----|----|------|
| onafterupdate  | n/a | 4  | n/a  |
| onbeforeupdate | n/a | 4  | n/a  |
| onchange       | 2   | 3  | 4    |

| Handler | NN | IE | HTML |
|---------|-----|-----|------|
| onscroll | n/a | 3 | 4 |
| onselect | 2 | 3 | 4 |

## cols

NN all   IE all   HTML all

cols="*columnCount*"                                                      Optional

The width of the editable space of the textarea element. The value represents the number of monofont characters that are to be displayed within the width. For a browser that supports style sheet font sizes, the actual width changes accordingly.

**Example**          `<textarea cols="40">...</textarea>`

**Value**          Any positive integer.

**Default**         Varies with browser and operating system.

**Object Model Reference**

```
[window.]document.formName.elementName.cols
[window.]document.forms[i].elements[j].cols
[window.]document.getElementById(elementID).cols
```

## datafld

NN n/a   IE 4   HTML n/a

datafld="*columnName*"                                                    Optional

Used with IE data binding to associate a remote data source column name with the content of the textarea element. A datasrc attribute must also be set for the element. Works only with text file data sources in IE 5/Mac.

**Example**

`<textarea name="summary" datasrc="DBSRC3" datafld="summary"></textarea>`

**Value**          Case-sensitive identifier.

**Default**        None.

**Object Model Reference**

```
[window.]document.formName.elementName.dataFld
[window.]document.forms[i].elements[j].dataFld
[window.]document.getElementById(elementID).dataFld
```

## datasrc

NN n/a   IE 4   HTML n/a

datasrc="*dataSourceName*"                                                Optional

Used with IE data binding to specify the ID of the page's object element that loads the data source object for remote data access. Content from the data source is specified via the datafld attribute. Works only with text file data sources in IE 5/Mac.

Alphabetical<br>HTML Reference

<textarea>

**Example**
<textarea name="summary" datasrc="DBSRC3" datafld="summary"></textarea>

**Value**          Case-sensitive identifier.

**Default**          None.

**Object Model Reference**
[window.]document.*formName*.*elementName*.dataSrc
[window.]document.forms[i].elements[j].dataSrc
[window.]document.getElementById(*elementID*).dataSrc

## disabled

disabled                                                              Optional

A disabled textarea element can't be activated by the user. In IE/Windows and Netscape 6, a disabled textarea cannot receive focus and doesn't become active within the tabbing order rotation. The name/value pair of a disabled element is not sent when the form is submitted.

The disabled attribute is a Boolean type, which means that its presence in the attribute sets its value to true. Its value can also be adjusted after the fact by scripting (see the textarea object in Chapter 9).

**Example**          <textarea disabled></textarea>

**Value**          The presence of the attribute disables the element.

**Default**          false

**Object Model Reference**
[window.]document.*formName*.*elementName*.disabled
[window.]document.forms[i].elements[j].disabled
[window.]document.getElementById(*elementID*).disabled

## name

name="*elementIdentifier*"                                            Optional

If the textarea element is part of a form being submitted to a server, the name attribute is required if the value of the element is to be submitted with the form. For forms that are in documents for the convenience of scripted form elements, textarea element names are not required but are helpful just the same in creating scripted references to these objects and their properties or methods. Newer DOMs encourage assigning the same identifier to the id attribute for uniform script references to the element object.

**Example**          <textarea name="comments" id="comments"></textarea>

**Value**          Case-sensitive identifier.

**Default**          None.

**Object Model Reference**

[window.]document.*formName*.*elementName*.name
[window.]document.forms[i].elements[j].name
[window.]document.getElementById(*elementID*).name

## readonly

NN 6    IE 4    HTML 4

readonly

Optional

When the readonly attribute is present, the textarea element cannot be edited on the page by the user (although scripts can modify the content). A textarea marked as readonly should not receive focus within the tabbing order (although IE for the Macintosh allows the field to receive focus). Users can still select and copy text from a read-only textarea.

| | |
|---|---|
| **Example** | &lt;textarea name="instructions" readonly&gt;&lt;/textarea&gt; |
| **Value** | The presence of the attribute sets its value to true. |
| **Default** | false |

**Object Model Reference**

[window.]document.*formName*.*elementName*.readOnly
[window.]document.forms[i].elements[j].readOnly
[window.]document.getElementById(*elementID*).readOnly

## rows

NN *all*    IE *all*    HTML *all*

rows="*rowCount*"

Optional

The height of the textarea element based on the number of lines of text that are to be displayed without scrolling. The value represents the number of monospace-font character lines that are to be displayed within the height before the scrollbar becomes active. For a browser that supports style sheet font sizes, the actual width changes accordingly.

| | |
|---|---|
| **Example** | &lt;textarea rows="5" cols="40"&gt;&lt;/textarea&gt; |
| **Value** | Any positive integer. |
| **Default** | Varies with browser and operating system. |

**Object Model Reference**

[window.]document.*formName*.*elementName*.rows
[window.]document.forms[i].elements[j].rows
[window.]document.getElementById(*elementID*).rows

## wrap

NN *2*    IE *4*    HTML *n/a*

wrap="*wrapType*"

Required

The wrap attribute tells the browser whether it should wrap text in a textarea element and whether wrapped text should be submitted to the server with soft returns converted to hard carriage returns. The HTML specification is silent on the subject, while Navigator and

<tfoot>

IE have, over the years, clouded the attribute values. But more recently, the mainstream browsers are coming together on a set of three attribute values: off, soft, and hard.

When set to soft, the text automatically wraps as the user types, but the carriage returns and line feeds (CRLFs) do not go with the text when the form is submitted. With a setting of hard, wrapping occurs, and the CRLFs introduced by wrapping become part of the textarea's value submitted to the server. Old synonyms for the soft value include virtual and physical. A setting of off means that typing beyond the right edge of the rectangle forces the textarea to scroll horizontally. Only a press of the Return key causes the text insertion pointer to advance to the next line.

**Example**     <textarea name="comments" wrap="hard"></textarea>

**Value**     Constant values: hard | off | soft.

**Default**     soft

### Object Model Reference

```
[window.]document.formName.elementName.wrap
[window.]document.forms[i].elements[j].wrap
[window.]document.getElementById(elementID).wrap
```

# <tfoot>

NN 6    IE 3    HTML 4

<tfoot>...</tfoot>

HTML End Tag: Optional

A tfoot element is a special-purpose container of one or more rows of table cells rendered at the bottom of the table. Typically, the tfoot element mirrors the thead element content for users who have scrolled down the page (or for future browsers that scroll inner table content). No more than one tfoot element may be defined within a single table element, and the tfoot element should be located in the source code *before* any tbody elements defined for the table. A tfoot element is a row grouping, like the tbody and thead elements. Navigator 4 ignores the tfoot tag and therefore renders the nested tr element(s) as regular tr elements in source code order.

### Example

```
<table cols="3">
<thead>
<tr>
<th>Time</th><th>Event</th><th>Location</th>
</tr>
</thead>
<tfoot>
<tr>
<th>Time</th><th>Event</th><th>Location</th>
</tr>
</tfoot>
<tbody>
<tr>
<td>7:30am-5:00pm</td><td>Registration Open</td><td>Main Lobby</td>
</tr>
```

```
<tr>
<td>9:00am-12:00pm</td><td>Keynote Speakers</td><td>Cypress Room</td>
</tr>
</tbody>
</table>
```

## Object Model Reference

[window.]document.getElementById(*elementID*)

## Element-Specific Attributes

| | | | | |
|---|---|---|---|---|
| align | bgcolor | ch | char | charoff |
| choff | valign | | | |

## Element-Specific Event Handler Attributes

None.

## align
NN *n/a*   IE 4   HTML 4

align="*alignConstant*"
Optional

Establishes the horizontal alignment characteristics of content within the row(s) covered by the tfoot element.

**Example**        `<tfoot align="center">`

## Value

HTML 4 and various browsers implement different sets of attribute values.

| Value | IE/Windows | IE/Mac and NN 6 | HTML 4 |
|---|:---:|:---:|:---:|
| center | • | • | • |
| char | – | – | • |
| justify | – | • | • |
| left | • | • | • |
| right | • | • | • |

The values center, left, and right are self-explanatory. The value justify spaces multiline content so that text is justified down both left and right edges. For the value char, the char attribute must also be set to specify the character on which alignment revolves. In the HTML 4 specification example, content that does not contain the character appears to be right-aligned to the location of the character in other rows of the same column.

It's important to bear in mind that the align attribute applies to every cell of every row within the tfoot, including any th element you specify for the table. If you want a different alignment for the row header, override the setting with a separate align attribute or text-align style sheet attribute for the individual th elements.

**Default**        left

## Object Model Reference

[window.]document.getElementById(*elementID*).align

## bgcolor

bgcolor="*colorTripletOrName*"

Establishes a fill color (behind the text and other content) for the cells contained by the tfoot element.

| | |
|---|---|
| **Example** | &lt;tfoot bgcolor="tan"&gt; |
| **Value** | A hexadecimal triplet or plain-language color name. A setting of empty is interpreted as "#000000" (black). See Appendix A for acceptable plain-language color names. |
| **Default** | Varies with browser, browser version, and operating system. |

**Object Model Reference**

[window.]document.getElementById(*elementID*).bgColor

## char

char="*character*"

The char attribute defines the text character used as an alignment point for text within a cell contained by the tfoot element. This attribute is of value only for the align attribute set to "char". Microsoft documents a ch attribute, which corresponds to the standards-based char attribute. In any case, the browser does not respond to either attribute. Netscape 7 has not yet connected support for the char attribute.

| | |
|---|---|
| **Example** | &lt;tfoot align="char" char="."&gt; |
| **Value** | Any single text character. |
| **Default** | None. |

## charoff

charoff="*length*"

The charoff attribute lets you set a specific offset point at which the character specified by the char attribute is to appear within a cell contained by the tfoot element. This attribute is provided in case the browser default positioning does not meet with the design goals of the table. Microsoft documents a choff attribute, which corresponds to the standards-based charoff attribute. In any case, the browser does not respond to either attribute. Netscape 7 has not yet connected support for the charoff attribute.

| | |
|---|---|
| **Example** | &lt;tfoot align="char" char="." charoff="80%"&gt; |
| **Value** | Any length value in pixels or percentage of cell space. |
| **Default** | None. |

## choff

See charoff.


## valign

valign="*alignmentConstant*"                                                 **Optional**

Determines the vertical alignment of content within cells of the column(s) covered by the tfoot element. You can override the vertical alignment for a particular cell anywhere in the column.

**Example**              &lt;tfoot valign="bottom"&gt;

**Value**

Four constant values: top | middle | bottom | baseline. With top and bottom, the content is rendered flush (or very close to it) to the top and bottom of the table cell. Set to middle (the default), the content floats perfectly centered vertically in the cell. When one cell's contents might wrap to multiple lines at common window widths (assuming a variable table width), it is advisable to set the valign attribute to baseline. This assures that the character baseline of the first (or only) line of a cell's text aligns with the other cells in the row—usually the most aesthetically pleasing arrangement.

**Default**              middle

**Object Model Reference**

[window.]document.getElementById(*elementID*).vAlign


## &lt;th&gt;

&lt;th&gt;...&lt;/th&gt;                                              **HTML End Tag: Optional**

The th element is a container for content that is rendered inside one cell of a table element in a format that distinguishes it as a header. Most browsers render the content as boldface. A cell is the intersection of a column and row. Other elements related to the th element are caption, col, colgroup, table, tbody, td, tfoot, thead, and tr. In addition to providing a wrapper for a cell's content, the th element defines a number of visible attributes that apply to a single cell, often overriding similar attributes set in lesser-nested elements in the table.

Four attributes—abbr, axis, headers, and scope—are included in the HTML 4 specification in anticipation of nonvisual browsers that will use text-to-speech technology to describe content of an HTML page—a kind of "verbal rendering." Although these attributes are briefly described here for the sake of completeness, there is much more to their application in nonvisual browsers than is relevant in this book on Dynamic HTML. Consult the HTML 4 recommendation for more details.

**Example**

```
<table cols="3">
<thead>
<tr>
```

```
<th>Time</th><th>Event</th><th>Location</th>
</tr>
</thead>
<tbody>
<tr>
<td>7:30am-5:00pm</td><td>Registration Open</td><td>Main Lobby</td>
</tr>
<tr>
<td>9:00am-12:00pm</td><td>Keynote Speakers</td><td>Cypress Room</td>
</tr>
</tbody>
</table>
```

**Object Model Reference**

[window.]document.getElementById(*elementID*)

**Element-Specific Attributes**

| | | | | |
|---|---|---|---|---|
| abbr | align | axis | background | bgcolor |
| bordercolor | bordercolordark | bordercolorlight | ch | char |
| charoff | choff | colspan | datafld | headers |
| height | nowrap | rowspan | scope | valign |
| width | | | | |

**Element-Specific Event Handler Attributes**

| Handler | NN | IE | HTML |
|---|---|---|---|
| onafterupdate | n/a | 4 | n/a |
| onbeforeupdate | n/a | 4 | n/a |
| onrowenter | n/a | 4 | n/a |
| onrowexit | n/a | 4 | n/a |

## abbr

NN 6    IE 6    HTML 4

abbr="*text*"

Optional

Provides an abbreviated string that describes the cell's content. This is usually a brief label that a nonvisual browser would speak to describe what the value of the cell represents. The **Properties** choice for Netscape 6's context menu for this element displays a small window that includes an active link to the URL assigned to the attribute. Version 6 browsers provide no other functionality for this attribute.

**Example**      `<th abbr="What">Event</th>`

**Value**      Any quoted string.

**Default**      None.

<th>

## align

align="*alignConstant*"                                    Optional

Establishes the horizontal alignment characteristics of content within the cell covered by the th element.

**Example**            <th align="center">

**Value**

HTML 4 and various browsers implement different sets of attribute values.

| Value | IE/Windows and NN 4 | IE/Mac and NN 6 | HTML 4 |
|-------|:---:|:---:|:---:|
| center | • | • | • |
| char | – | – | • |
| justify | – | • | • |
| left | • | • | • |
| right | • | • | • |

The values center, left, and right are self-explanatory. The value justify spaces multi-line content so that text is justified down both left and right edges. For the value char, the char attribute must also be set to specify the character on which alignment revolves. In the HTML 4 specification example, content that does not contain the character appears to be right-aligned to the location of the character in other rows of the same column.

**Default**            left

**Object Model Reference**

[window.]document.getElementById(*elementID*).align

## axis

axis="*text*"                                              Optional

Provides an abbreviated string that describes the cell's category. This is usually a brief label that a nonvisual browser would speak to describe what the value of the cell represents. The **Properties** choice for Netscape 6's context menu for this element displays a small window that includes an active link to the URL assigned to the attribute. Version 6 browsers provide no other functionality for this attribute.

**Example**            <th axis="event">Events</th>

**Value**              Any quoted string.

**Default**            None.

**Object Model Reference**

[window.]document.getElementById(*elementID*).axis

## background

background="*URL*"                                                    Optional

Specifies an image file that is used as a backdrop to the cell. Unlike normal images that get loaded into browser content, a background image loads in its original size (without scaling) and tiles to fill the available cell space. Smaller images download faster but are obviously repeated more often in the background. Navigator 4, however, requires a minimum image size of 16 by 16 pixels. Animated GIFs are also allowable, but very distracting to the reader. When selecting a background image, be sure it is very muted in comparison to the main content so that the content stands out clearly. Background images, if used at all, should be extremely subtle.

**Example**          &lt;th background="watermark.jpg"&gt;

**Value**            Any valid URL to an image file, including complete and relative URLs.

**Default**          None.

**Object Model Reference**
[window.]document.getElementById(*elementID*).background

## bgcolor

bgcolor="*colorTripletOrName*"                                       Optional

Establishes a fill color (behind the text and other content) for the cell defined by the th element.

**Example**          &lt;th bgcolor="yellow"&gt;

**Value**            A hexadecimal triplet or plain-language color name. A setting of empty is interpreted as "#000000" (black). See Appendix A for acceptable plain-language color names.

**Default**          Varies with browser, browser version, and operating system.

**Object Model Reference**
[window.]document.getElementById(*elementID*).bgColor

## bordercolor

bordercolor="*colorTripletOrName*"                                   Optional

The colors used to render some of the pixels that create the illusion of borders around cells and the entire table. Internet Explorer applies the color to all four lines that make up the interior border of a cell. Therefore, colors of adjacent cells do not collide.

**Example**          &lt;th bordercolor="green"&gt;

**Value**            A hexadecimal triplet or plain-language color name. A setting of empty is interpreted as "#000000" (black). See Appendix A for acceptable plain-language color names.

<th>

**Default**  Varies with browser and operating system.

**Object Model Reference**
[window.]document.getElementById(*elementID*).borderColor


## bordercolordark, bordercolorlight  NN *n/a*  IE *3*  HTML *n/a*

bordercolordark="*colorTripletOrName*"  Optional
bordercolorlight="*colorTripletOrName*"

The 3-D effect of table borders in Internet Explorer is created by careful positioning of light and dark lines around the page's background or default color (see Figure 8-4 in the table element discussion). You can independently control the colors used for the dark and light lines by assigning values to the bordercolordark (left and top edges of the cell) and bordercolorlight (right and bottom edges) attributes.

Typically, you should assign complementary colors to the pair of attributes. There is also no rule that says you must assign a dark color to bordercolordark. The attributes merely control a well-defined set of lines so you can predict which lines of the border change with each attribute.

**Example**  <th bordercolordark="darkred" bordercolorlight="salmon">

**Value**  A hexadecimal triplet or plain-language color name. A setting of empty is interpreted as "#000000" (black). See Appendix A for acceptable plain-language color names.

**Default**  Varies with operating system.

**Object Model Reference**
[window.]document.getElementById(*elementID*).borderColorDark
[window.]document.getElementById(*elementID*).borderColorLight


## char  NN *6*  IE *n/a*  HTML *4*

char="*character*"  Optional

The char attribute defines the text character used as an alignment point for text within a cell. This attribute is of value only for the align attribute set to "char". Microsoft documents a ch attribute, which corresponds to the standards-based char attribute. In any case, the browser does not respond to either attribute. Netscape 7 has not yet connected support for the char attribute.

**Example**  <th align="char" char=".">$325.10</th>

**Value**  Any single text character.

**Default**  None.

<th>

## charoff

charoff="*length*"                                                    Optional

The charoff attribute lets you set a specific offset point at which the character specified by the char attribute is to appear within a cell. This attribute is provided in case the browser default positioning does not meet with the design goals of the table. Microsoft documents a choff attribute, which corresponds to the standards-based charoff attribute. In any case, the browser does not respond to either attribute. Netscape 7 has not yet connected support for the charoff attribute.

**Example**          <th align="char" char="." charoff="80%">

**Value**            Any length value in pixels or percentage of cell space.

**Default**          None.

## choff

See charoff.

## colspan

colspan="*columnCount*"                                               Optional

The colspan attribute specifies the number of columns across which the current table cell should extend itself. For each additional column included in the colspan count, one less th or td element is required for the table row. If you set the align attribute to center or right, the alignment is calculated on the full width of the th element across the specified number of columns. Unless the current cell is also specifies a rowspan attribute, the next table row returns to the original column count.

**Example**          <th colspan="2" align="right">

**Value**            Any positive integer, usually 2 or larger.

**Default**          1

**Object Model Reference**

[window.]document.getElementById(*elementID*).colSpan

## datafld

datafld="*columnName*"                                                Optional

Used with IE data binding to associate a remote data source column name with the content of a table header cell. A datasrc (and optionally, a datapagesize) attribute must also be set for the enclosing table element. Works only with text file data sources in IE 5/Mac.

**Example**

```
<table datasrc="DBSRC3" datapagesize="5">
<tr>
```

```
<th datafld="stockNum"></th>
<th datafld="qtyOnHand"></th>
</tr>
</table>
```

**Value**          Case-sensitive identifier.

**Default**        None.

## headers                                        NN *6*   IE *6*   HTML *4*

headers="*cellIDList*"                                                    Optional

Points to one or more th or td elements that act as column or row headers for the current table cell. The assigned value is a space-delimited list of id attribute values that are assigned to the relevant th elements. A nonvisual browser could speak the cell's header before the content of the cell to help listeners identify the nature of the cell content. Although mainstream Version 6 browsers claim support for this attribute, neither have yet connected support for it.

### Example
```
<tr>
<th id="hdr1">Product Number</th>
<th id="hdr2">Description</th>
</tr>
<tr>
<th headers="hdr1">0392</th>
<th headers="hdr2">Round widget</th>
</tr>
```

### Value
A space-delimited list of case-sensitive IDs assigned to cells that act as headers to the current cell.

**Default**        None.

## height, width                                 NN *all*   IE *all*   HTML *3.2*

height="*length*"                                                        Optional
width="*length*"

The rectangular dimensions of a cell that may be different from the default size as calculated by the browser. When the values for these attributes are less than the minimum space required to render the table cell content, the browser overrides the attribute settings to make sure that all content appears, even if it means that text lines word-wrap. You can also stretch the dimensions of a table beyond the browser-calculated dimensions. Extra whitespace appears inside table cells to make up the difference. If you specify just one of these attributes, the browser performs all necessary calculations to automatically adjust the dimension along the other axis.

Due to the regular nature of tables, if you set a custom height for one cell in a row, the entire row is set to that height; similarly, setting the width of a cell causes the width of all cells in the column to be the same size.

Both the height and width attributes are deprecated in HTML 4 in favor of height and width style sheet attributes (which are not available for table cells in Navigator 4).

**Example**          `<th width="80%" height="30">`

**Value**             Any length value in pixels or percentage of available space.

**Default**           Based on content size.

**Object Model Reference**

`[window.]document.getElementById(elementID).height`
`[window.]document.getElementById(elementID).width`

---

**nowrap**                                              NN *all*    IE *all*    HTML *3.2*

nowrap                                                        Optional

The presence of the nowrap attribute instructs the browser to render the cell as wide as is necessary to display a line of nonbreaking text on one line. Abuse of this attribute can force the user into a great deal of inconvenient horizontal scrolling of the page to view all of the content. The nowrap attribute is deprecated in HTML 4. The nowrap attribute is deprecated in HTML 4 in favor of the white-space:nowrap CSS attribute and value.

**Example**          `<th nowrap>`

**Value**             The presence of this attribute sets its value to true.

**Default**           false

**Object Model Reference**

`[window.]document.getElementById(elementID).noWrap`

---

**rowspan**                                          NN *all*    IE *all*    HTML *3.2*

rowspan="*rowCount*"                                    Optional

The number of rows through which the current table cell should extend itself downward. For each additional row included in the rowspan count, one less th or td element is required for the next table row in that cell's position along the row.

**Example**          `<th rowspan="2">`

**Value**             Any positive integer, usually 2 or larger.

**Default**           1

**Object Model Reference**

`[window.]document.getElementById(elementID).rowSpan`

<th>

## scope

scope="*scopeConstant*"    Optional

The range of cells (relative to the current cell) that behave as though the current cell is the header for those cells. For tables whose structure is quite regular, the scope attribute is a simpler way of achieving what the headers attribute does, without having to define id attributes for the header cells. Although maintstream Version 6 browsers claim support for this attribute, neither have yet connected support for it.

### Example

```
<tr>
<th scope="col">Product Number</th>
<th scope="col">Description</th>
</tr>
<tr>
<td>0392</td>
<td>Round widget</td>
</tr>
```

### Value

One of four recognized scope constants:

col

    Current cell text becomes header text for every cell in the rest of the column.

colgroup

    Current cell text becomes header text for every cell in the rest of the colgroup element.

row

    Current cell text becomes header text for every cell in the rest of the tr element.

rowgroup

    Current cell text becomes header text for every cell in the rest of the tbody element.

**Default**        None.

## valign

valign="*alignmentConstant*"    Optional

Determines the vertical alignment of content within the td element. A value you set for an individual cell overrides the same attribute setting for outer containers, such as tr and tbody.

**Example**        <th valign="bottom">

### Value

Four constant values: top | middle | bottom | baseline. With top and bottom, the content is rendered flush (or very close to it) to the top and bottom of the table cell. Set to middle (the default), the content floats perfectly centered vertically in the cell. When one cell's contents might wrap to multiple lines at common window widths (assuming a variable table width), it is advisable to set the valign attribute to baseline. This assures that the character baseline of the first (or only) line of a cell's text aligns with the other cells in the row—usually the most aesthetically pleasing arrangement.

Alphabetical
HTML Reference

**Default**          middle

**Object Model Reference**

[window.]document.getElementById(*elementID*).vAlign

## width

See height.

# &lt;thead&gt;

&lt;thead&gt;...&lt;/thead&gt;

A thead element is a special-purpose container of one or more rows of table cells rendered at the top of the table. No more than one thead element may be defined within a single table element, and the thead element should be located in the source code immediately after the table element's start tag. You are free to use any combination of td and th elements you like within the thead element. A thead element is a row grouping, like the tbody and tfoot elements. Navigator 4 ignores the thead tag and therefore renders the nested tr element(s) as regular tr elements in source code order.

**Example**

```
<table cols="3">
<thead>
<tr>
<th>Time</th><th>Event</th><th>Location</th>
</tr>
</thead>
<tfoot>
<tr>
<th>Time</th><th>Event</th><th>Location</th>
</tr>
</tfoot>
<tbody>
<tr>
<td>7:30am-5:00pm</td><td>Registration Open</td><td>Main Lobby</td>
</tr>
<tr>
<td>9:00am-12:00pm</td><td>Keynote Speakers</td><td>Cypress Room</td>
</tr>
</tbody>
</table>
```

**Object Model Reference**

[window.]document.getElementById(*elementID*)

**Element-Specific Attributes**

| align | bgcolor | ch | char | charoff |
|-------|---------|-----|------|---------|
| choff | valign | | | |

<thead>

**Element-Specific Event Handler Attributes**

None.

# align

align="*alignConstant*"

Establishes the horizontal alignment characteristics of content within the row(s) covered by the thead element.

**Example**         <thead align="center">

**Value**

HTML 4 and various browsers implement different sets of attribute values.

| Value | IE/Windows | IE/Mac and NN 6 | HTML 4 |
|---|---|---|---|
| center | • | • | • |
| char | – | – | • |
| justify | – | • | • |
| left | • | • | • |
| right | • | • | • |

The values center, left, and right are self-explanatory. The value justify spaces multiline content so that text is justified down both left and right edges. For the value char, the char attribute must also be set to specify the character on which alignment revolves. In the HTML 4 specification example, content that does not contain the character appears to be right-aligned to the location of the character in other rows of the same column.

It is important to bear in mind that the align attribute applies to every cell of every row within the thead, including any th element you specify for the table. If you want a different alignment for the row header, override the setting with a separate align attribute or text-align style sheet attribute for the individual th elements.

**Default**         left

**Object Model Reference**

[window.]document.getElementById(*elementID*).align

# bgcolor

bgcolor="*colorTripletOrName*"

Establishes a fill color (behind the text and other content) for the cells contained by the thead element.

**Example**         <thead bgcolor="tan">

**Value**           A hexadecimal triplet or plain-language color name. A setting of empty is interpreted as "#000000" (black). See Appendix A for acceptable plain-language color names.

<thead>

**Default**          Varies with browser, browser version, and operating system.

**Object Model Reference**

[window.]document.getElementById(*elementID*).bgColor

## char                                                    NN 6    IE *n/a*    HTML 4

char="*character*"                                                             Optional

The char attribute defines the text character used as an alignment point for text within a cell contained by the thead element. This attribute is of value only for the align attribute set to "char". Microsoft documents a ch attribute, which corresponds to the standards-based char attribute. In any case, the browser does not respond to either attribute. Netscape 7 has not yet connected support for the char attribute.

**Example**          <thead align="char" char=".">

**Value**            Any single text character.

**Default**          None.

## charoff                                                 NN 6    IE *n/a*    HTML 4

charoff="*length*"                                                             Optional

The charoff attribute lets you set a specific offset point at which the character specified by the char attribute is to appear within a cell contained by the thead element. This attribute is provided in case the browser default positioning does not meet with the design goals of the table. Microsoft documents a choff attribute, which corresponds to the standards-based charoff attribute. In any case, the browser does not respond to either attribute. Netscape 7 has not yet connected support for the charoff attribute.

**Example**          <thead align="char" char="." charoff="80%">

**Value**            Any length value in pixels or percentage of cell space.

**Default**          None.

## choff

See charoff.

## valign                                                  NN 6    IE 4    HTML 4

valign="*alignmentConstant*"                                                   Optional

Determines the vertical alignment of content within cells of the column(s) covered by the thead element. You can override the vertical alignment for a particular cell anywhere in the column.

**Example**          <thead valign="bottom">

<tr>

**Value**

Four constant values: top | middle | bottom | baseline. With top and bottom, the content is rendered flush (or very close to it) to the top and bottom of the table cell. Set to middle (the default), the content floats perfectly centered vertically in the cell. When one cell's contents might wrap to multiple lines at common window widths (assuming a variable table width), it is advisable to set the valign attribute to baseline. This assures that the character baseline of the first (or only) line of a cell's text aligns with the other cells in the row—usually the most aesthetically pleasing arrangement.

**Default**          middle

**Object Model Reference**

[window.]document.getElementById(*elementID*).vAlign

# \<title\>
NN *all*    IE *all*    HTML *all*

\<title\>...\</title\>                                         HTML End Tag: Required

The title element identifies the overall content of a document. The element content is not displayed as part of the document, but browsers display the title in the browser application's window titlebar. Only one title element is permitted per document and it must be located inside the head element. It is all right to be somewhat verbose in assigning a document title because not everyone will access the document in sequence through your web site. Give the document some context as well.

**Example**          \<title\>Declaration of Independence\</title\>

**Object Model Reference**

[window.]document.getElementById(*elementID*)

**Element-Specific Attributes**

None.

**Element-Specific Event Handler Attributes**

None.

# \<tr\>
NN *all*    IE *all*    HTML *all*

\<tr\>...\</tr\>                                         HTML End Tag: Optional

A tr element is a container for one row of cells. Each cell within a row may be a th or td element. Every row requires at least a start tag to instruct the browser to begin rendering succeeding cell elements on the next line of the table. Other special-purpose row groupings available are the tfoot and thead, as well as the more generic tbody grouping element.

**Example**

```
<table cols="3">
<thead>
<tr>
```

```
<tr>

<th>Time</th><th>Event</th><th>Location</th>
</tr>
</thead>
<tbody>
<tr>
<td>7:30am-5:00pm</td><td>Registration Open</td><td>Main Lobby</td>
</tr>
<tr>
<td>9:00am-12:00pm</td><td>Keynote Speakers</td><td>Cypress Room</td>
</tr>
</tbody>
</table>
```

### Object Model Reference
`[window.]document.getElementById(elementID)`

### Element-Specific Attributes

| | | | | |
|---|---|---|---|---|
| align | background | bgcolor | bordercolor | bordercolordark |
| bordercolorlight | ch | char | charoff | choff |
| height | valign | width | | |

### Element-Specific Event Handler Attributes
None.

## align NN 6   IE 4   HTML 4

`align="alignConstant"`                                                  Optional

Establishes the horizontal alignment characteristics of content within the row.

**Example**      `<tr align="center">`

**Value**

HTML 4 and various browsers implement different sets of attribute values.

| Value | IE/Windows | IE/Mac and NN 6 | HTML 4 |
|---|---|---|---|
| center | • | • | • |
| char | – | – | • |
| justify | – | • | • |
| left | • | • | • |
| right | • | • | • |

The values center, left, and right are self-explanatory. The value justify spaces multiline content so that text is justified down both left and right edges. For the value char, the char attribute must also be set to specify the character on which alignment revolves. In the HTML 4 specification example, content that does not contain the character appears to be right-aligned to the location of the character in other rows of the same column.

<tr>

It is important to bear in mind that the align attribute applies to every cell within the tr element, including any th element you specify for the table. If you want a different alignment for the row header, override the setting with a separate align attribute or text-align style sheet attribute for the tr or individual th elements.

**Default**        center

**Object Model Reference**

[window.]document.getElementById(*elementID*).align

## background                NN *4*   IE *n/a*   HTML *n/a*

background="*URL*"          Optional

Specifies an image file that is used as a backdrop to the entire row of cells. Unlike normal images that get loaded into browser content, a background image loads in its original size (without scaling) and tiles to fill the available cell space. Smaller images download faster but are obviously repeated more often in the background. Navigator 4, however, requires a minimum image size of 16 by 16 pixels. Animated GIFs are also allowable, but very distracting to the reader. When selecting a background image, be sure it is very muted in comparison to the main content so that the content stands out clearly. Background images, if used at all, should be extremely subtle.

**Example**        <tr background="watermark.jpg">

**Value**        Any valid URL to an image file, including complete and relative URLs.

**Default**        None.

**Object Model Reference**

[window.]document.getElementById(*elementID*).background

## bgcolor                NN *3*   IE *4*   HTML *4*

bgcolor="*colorTripletOrName*"          Optional

Establishes a fill color (behind the text and other content) for the cells contained by the tr element.

**Example**        <tr bgcolor="lavender">

**Value**        A hexadecimal triplet or plain-language color name. A setting of empty is interpreted as "#000000" (black). See Appendix A for acceptable plain-language color names.

**Default**        Varies with browser, browser version, and operating system.

**Object Model Reference**

[window.]document.getElementById(*elementID*).bgColor

## bordercolor

NN n/a   IE 3   HTML n/a

bordercolor="*colorTripletOrName*" Optional

The color used to render some of the pixels that create the illusion of borders around cells and the entire table. Internet Explorer applies the color to all four lines that make up the interior border of a cell. Therefore, colors of adjacent cells do not collide.

**Example**            `<tr bordercolor="green">`

**Value**              A hexadecimal triplet or plain-language color name. A setting of empty is interpreted as "#000000" (black). See Appendix A for acceptable plain-language color names.

**Default**           Varies with browser and operating system.

**Object Model Reference**

`[window.]document.getElementById(elementID).borderColor`

## bordercolordark, bordercolorlight

NN n/a   IE 3   HTML n/a

bordercolordark="*colorTripletOrName*" Optional
bordercolorlight="*colorTripletOrName*"

The 3-D effect of table borders in Internet Explorer is created by careful positioning of light and dark lines around the page's background or default color (see Figure 8-4 in the `table` element discussion). You can independently control the colors used for the dark and light lines by assigning values to the `bordercolordark` (left and top edges of the cell) and `bordercolorlight` (right and bottom edges) attributes.

Typically, you should assign complementary colors to the pair of attributes. There is also no rule that says you must assign a dark color to `bordercolordark`. The attributes merely control a well-defined set of lines so you can predict which lines of the border change with each attribute.

**Example**            `<tr bordercolordark="darkred" bordercolorlight="salmon">`

**Value**              A hexadecimal triplet or plain-language color name. A setting of empty is interpreted as "#000000" (black). See Appendix A for acceptable plain-language color names.

**Default**           Varies with operating system.

**Object Model Reference**

`[window.]document.getElementById(elementID).borderColorDark`
`[window.]document.getElementById(elementID).borderColorLight`

## char

NN 6   IE n/a   HTML 4

char="*character*" Optional

The `char` attribute defines the text character used as an alignment point for text within a cell contained by the `tr` element. This attribute is of value only for the `align` attribute set to "char". Microsoft documents a `ch` attribute, which corresponds to the standards-based `char` attribute. In any case, the browser does not respond to either attribute. Netscape 7 has not yet connected support for the char attribute.

| **Example** | `<tr align="char" char=".">` |
| **Value** | Any single text character. |
| **Default** | None. |

## charoff

`charoff="length"`                                                                    Optional

The charoff attribute lets you set a specific offset point at which the character specified by the char attribute is to appear within a cell contained by the tr element. This attribute is provided in case the browser default positioning does not meet with the design goals of the table. Microsoft documents a choff attribute, which corresponds to the standards-based charoff attribute. In any case, the browser does not respond to either attribute. Netscape 7 has not yet connected support for the charoff attribute.

| **Example** | `<tr align="char" char="." charoff="80%">` |
| **Value** | Any length value in pixels or percentage of cell space. |
| **Default** | None. |

## choff

See charoff.

## valign

`valign="alignmentConstant"`                                                            Optional

Determines the vertical alignment of content within cells of the column(s) covered by the tr element. You can override the vertical alignment for a particular cell anywhere in the row.

| **Example** | `<tr valign="bottom">` |

**Value**

Four constant values: top | middle | bottom | baseline. With top and bottom, the content is rendered flush (or very close to it) to the top and bottom of the table cell. Set to middle (the default), the content floats perfectly centered vertically in the cell. When one cell's contents might wrap to multiple lines at common window widths (assuming a variable table width), it is advisable to set the valign attribute to baseline. This assures that the character baseline of the first (or only) line of a cell's text aligns with the other cells in the row—usually the most aesthetically pleasing arrangement.

**Default**       middle

**Object Model Reference**

`[window.]document.getElementById(elementID).vAlign`

# &lt;tt&gt;

NN all    IE all    HTML all

`<tt>...</tt>`
HTML End Tag: Required

The tt element renders its content as monospaced text (indicating a teletype output). The element is intended to be strictly a formatting—as opposed to a contextual—element. If you are looking for a contextual setting for computer program code or input, see the code, kbd, and samp elements. As with most font-related elements, the use of style sheets is preferred.

**Example**          `<p>The computer said, <tt>"That does not compute."</tt></p>`

**Object Model Reference**
`[window.]document.getElementById(elementID)`

**Element-Specific Attributes**
None.

**Element-Specific Event Handler Attributes**
None.

# &lt;u&gt;

NN 3    IE 3    HTML 3.2

`<u>...</u>`
HTML End Tag: Required

The u element renders its content as underlined text. This element is deprecated in HTML 4 in favor of the text-decoration:underline style sheet attribute. The element does not validate in strict HTML 4 or XHTML DTDs, and may confuse users who regard any underlined text as a clickable link, regardless of color.

**Example**          `<p>You may already be a <u>winner</u>!</p>`

**Object Model Reference**
`[window.]document.getElementById(elementID)`

**Element-Specific Attributes**
None.

**Element-Specific Event Handler Attributes**
None.

# &lt;ul&gt;

NN all    IE all    HTML all

`<ul>...</ul>`
HTML End Tag: Required

The ul element is a container for an unordered list of items. An "unordered list" means that the items are rendered with a leading symbol (depending on the type attribute setting or list-style-type style sheet attribute setting) that implies no specific order of items other than by virtue of location within the list. Content for each list item is defined by a nested li element. If you apply a style sheet rule to a ul element, the style is inherited by the nested li elements (except for occasional odd behavior in Navigator 4 only).

**Example**

```
<ul>
    <li>Africa</li>
    <li>Antarctica</li>
    <li>Asia</li>
    <li>Australia</li>
    <li>Europe</li>
    <li>North America</li>
    <li>South America</li>
</ul>
```

**Object Model Reference**

[window.]document.getElementById(*elementID*)

**Element-Specific Attributes**

compact          type

**Element-Specific Event Handler Attributes**

None.

## compact                                          NN 6    IE 4    HTML 3.2

compact                                                              Optional

A Boolean attribute originally designed to let browsers render the list in a more compact style than normal (smaller line spacing between items). Although listed as a supported attribute for HTML compatibility, the compact attribute has no effect on mainstream browsers. Use style sheets to control element sizes and line spacing.

**Example**          <ul compact>...</ul>

**Value**            The presence of this attribute makes its value true.

**Default**          false

## type                                             NN *all*    IE *all*    HTML 3.2

type="*labelType*"                                                   Optional

The type attribute provides some flexibility in how the leading symbol or sequence number is displayed in the browser. You can specify whether the leading symbol should be a disc, circle, or square. A disc is a filled circle (also known as a bullet). The square type is rendered as an outline in early Macintosh browsers, and as a filled square in Windows and modern browsers of all OS types. The type attribute is deprecated in HTML 4 in favor of the list-style-type style sheet attribute.

**Example**          <ul type="disc">...</ul>

**Value**            Possible values are circle | disc | square.

**Default**          disc

**Object Model Reference**

[window.]document.getElementById(*elementID*).type

# &lt;var&gt;

NN *all*   IE *all*   HTML *all*

&lt;var&gt;...&lt;/var&gt;                                                  HTML End Tag: Required

The var element is one of a large group of elements that the HTML 4 recommendation calls *phrase elements*. Such elements assign structural meaning to a designated portion of the document. A var element is one that is used predominantly to display one or more inline characters representing a computer program variable name.

Browsers have free rein to determine how (or whether) to distinguish var element content from the rest of the body element. Both Navigator and Internet Explorer elect to render var element content in an italic font. Override the default with a style sheet as you see fit.

## Example

```
<p>The value of <var>offsetWidth</var> becomes 20.</p>
```

## Object Model Reference

[window.]document.getElementById(*elementID*)

## Element-Specific Attributes

None.

## Element-Specific Event Handler Attributes

None.


# &lt;wbr&gt;

NN *all*   IE *all*   HTML *n/a*

&lt;wbr&gt;                                                              HTML End Tag: Forbidden

If you use the nobr element to define content that should have no word-wrapping or line breaks, you can use the wbr element to advise the browser that it can break up the content if the width of the browser window requires it. The locations of these provisional breaks are marked in the source code with the wbr element. In a sense, the nobr and wbr elements give the author control over word-wrapping of running content. Neither element is included in the HTML specification, but they have long been a part of both browsers' HTML vocabulary.

## Example

```
<nobr>This is a long line of text that could run on and on, <wbr>forcing
the browser to display the horizontal scrollbar after awhile.</nobr>
```

## Object Model Reference

[window.]document.getElementById(*elementID*)

## Element-Specific Attributes

None.

## Element-Specific Event Handler Attributes

None.

# &lt;xml&gt;

NN *n/a*    IE *5*    HTML *n/a*

&lt;xml&gt;...&lt;/xml&gt;                                                                End Tag: Required

IE 5 and later for Windows supports XML data islands, which are self-contained, unrendered blocks of XML data within an HTML page. The XML data may be delivered as part of the HTML document (embedded between the start and end tags) or loaded from an external source. Once the XML data is loaded, Microsoft's XML DOM (which in many ways resembles the Core portion of the W3C DOM) allows script access to the data for custom rendering. The W3C DOM equivalent to this functionality is via the document. implementation object. In IE, you may also use ActiveX to create an XML document for loading external XML data for script access. See "Embedding XML Data" in Chapter 5.

### Example

```
<xml id="xmlData">
  <xmlresults>
     <!-- xml data here -->
  </xmlresults>
</xml>
```

### Object Model Reference

[window.]document.getElementById(*elementID*)

### Attributes

src

### Event Handler Attributes

None.

---

### src

NN *n/a*    IE *5*    HTML *n/a*

src="*URI*"                                                                              Optional

Points to an external source of XML data to be loaded into the element.

### Example

```
<xml id="xmldata" src="http://www.magacorp.com/data/2003Forecast.xml"></xml>
```

**Value**          Any valid URI whose return value contains XML data.

**Default**        None.

### Object Model Reference

[window.]document.getElementById(*elementID*).src

---

# &lt;xmp&gt;

NN *all*    IE *all*    HTML *&lt;4*

&lt;xmp&gt;...&lt;/xmp&gt;                                                          HTML End Tag: Required

The xmp element displays its content in a monospace font as a block element, as in computer code listings rendered 80 columns wide. In most browsers, the font size is also reduced from the default size. Browsers observe carriage returns and other whitespace in element content. This element has long been deprecated in HTML and has even been removed from the HTML 4 specification. You are encouraged to use the pre element instead.

**Example**

```
<xmp>
&lt;script language="JavaScript"&gt;
    document.write("Hello, world.");
&lt;/script&gt;
</xmp>
```

**Object Model Reference**

[window.]document.getElementById(*elementID*)

**Element-Specific Attributes**

None.

**Element-Specific Event Handler Attributes**

None.

# Document Object Model Reference

This chapter focuses on objects—the scriptable entities that a browser maintains in its memory whenever a document is loaded. Most of these objects exist by virtue of tags embedded within the content of the document. But many more objects exist solely for the purposes of scripting activities, such as event processing, window manipulation, creating and populating documents with new objects, reading the client's system environment, and working with chunks of the document text separated from its tagged markup.

An object is described by its properties, methods, collections (or arrays) of nested items, and event handlers. The Dynamic HTML features that you associate with a document rely entirely upon the objects and the properties, methods, and events that are supported by the browsers used by the page's visitors. The scriptable object model of early browsers was a simple one, with relatively few objects, and those objects had short lists of implemented properties, methods, and events. Today's model, however, is huge, due primarily to a greatly expanded object model for Microsoft Internet Explorer (especially the Windows version) and, more recently, the addition of a completely new abstract object model designed by the W3C.

To help you choose the right objects, properties, methods, and event handlers for the type of page development you're doing, this chapter lists every client-side Dynamic HTML-related object defined by Microsoft, Netscape, and the W3C (at least the DOM Level 2 standard for all modules). From these listings, you should be able to judge whether a particular object or its properties, methods, or event handlers will work for your application.

If cross-browser support is essential for your application, pay close attention to the browser support and version information for each entry. The version number represents the first version of a particular browser to support the term. Where no implementation exists, I use "n/a" to indicate that. In rare instances, an item has been removed from a browser family. Such items are marked with a less-than symbol and the version number that no longer supports the item (e.g., NN <6 for prior to Netscape 6). Items valid for a single version show the number encased in pipe symbols (e.g., |4|: for Version 4 only). Be aware that some items may not be available on all operating system platforms for a particular browser brand and version (particularly true for Internet Explorer). These distinctions are noted wherever the anomalous behavior could be substantiated by actual testing on the Win32 and Macintosh platforms.

A handful of items that appear as new for Version 6 browsers may not, in truth, be fully implemented in the browsers. This occurs when a browser maker claims support for an element or attribute because the item is implemented in HTML 4 or the DOM, and the browser wishes to claim compliance with that standard version. The descriptions of such items clearly state when the item belongs to the object, but does not perform its intended job. Text references to Netscape 6 automatically impy support by all Mozilla-based browsers, including Netscape 7. Some items, however, are new for Netscape 7 and are marked accordingly.

Following a section that lists properties, methods, and events shared by all HTML element objects in the latest browsers, this chapter is organized alphabetically by object type. Most object types appear as their corresponding HTML element's tag name (in XHTML lowercase form). Scripts do not reference elements by these names, except when they use tag name strings as method parameters (e.g., `document.getElementsByTagName("h1")`). Instead, scripts reference such element objects by the various ways that scripts produce valid references to element objects. The most common is to assign an identifier to the ID attribute of the element, and use that identifier to create a reference with syntax such as the following W3C DOM method:

```
document.getElementById("elementID")
```

where the parameter is a string of the element's identifier. Numerous other properties throughout the object models evaluate to valid element object references, without requiring an explicit reference to the identifer. For example, an event object contains a property that evaluates to a valid reference to the element that was the target of the event. A script statement can then use that reference to access the element object's properties or methods, as needed.

The very large W3C DOM vocabulary contains many terms that do not come into common use even in today's browsers. For example, the element object listed in this chapter as the div object is formally known in the W3C DOM as the HTMLDivElement object. In fact, if you use an alert( ) method with a reference to an HTML element object in a browser that supports this terminology (such as Netscape 6), the dialog window displays the W3C DOM name for the object type, which is handy for debugging purposes. In Netscape 6, the W3C DOM object name represents the constructor for that object type. Thus, you can use JavaScript prototype inheritance to assign a custom property to the type of object before your scripts create instances of that object type:

```
HTMLDivElement.prototype.author = "DHTML";
```

Thereafter, all elements of that type that your scripts create have this new property and value preassigned to it. For the sake of compactness, this chapter does not list the W3C DOM HTML element objects as separate entries.

## Property Value Types

Many properties share similar data requirements. For the sake of brevity in the reference listings, this section describes a few common property value types in more detail than is possible within the listings. Whenever you see one of these property value types associated with a property, consult this section for a description of the type.

### Length

A length value defines a linear measure of document real estate. The unit of measurement can be any applicable unit that helps identify a position or space on the screen. For properties that reflect HTML attributes, length units are uniformly pixels, but in other content, such as that specified in Cascading Style Sheets (see Chapter 11), measurements can be in inches, picas, ems, or other relevant units. A single numeric value may represent a length when it defines the offset from an edge of an element. For example, a coordinate point (10,20) consists of two length values, denoting pixel measurements from the left and top edges of an element, respectively.

### Identifier

An identifier is a name that adheres to some strict syntactical rules. Most important is that an identifier is one word with no whitespace allowed. If you need to use multiple words to describe an item, you can use the intercapitalized format (in which internal letters are capitalized) or an underscore character between the words. Most punctuation symbols are not permitted, but all numerals and alphabetical characters are. Scripting languages do not allow the use of a numeral for the first character of an identifier.

### URI and URL

The term Universal Resource Identifier (URI) is a broad term for an address of content on the Web. A Universal Resource Locator (URL) is a type of URI. For most web authoring, you can think of them as one and the same, since most web browsers restrict their focus to URLs. A URL may be complete (including the protocol, host, domain, and the rest) or may be relative to the URL of the current document. In the latter case, this means the URL may consist of an anchor, file, or pathname. An object property that refers to a URL requires that the text of the URL be represented as a quoted string.

## Language Code

There is an extensive list of standard codes that identify the spoken and written languages of the world. A language code always contains a primary language code, such as "en" for English or "zh" for Chinese. Common two-letter primary codes are cataloged in ISO 639. An optional subcode (separated from the primary code by a hyphen) may be used to identify a specific implementation of the primary language, usually according to usage within a specific country. Therefore, while "en" means all of English, "en-US" means a U.S.-specific version of English. The browser must support a particular language code for its meaning to be of any value to an element attribute.

## Colors

A color value can be assigned either via a hexadecimal triplet or with a plain-language equivalent. A hexadecimal triplet consists of three pairs of hexadecimal (base 16) numbers that range between the values 00 and FF, corresponding to the red, green, and blue components of the color. The three pairs of numbers are bunched together and preceded by a pound sign (#). Therefore, the reddest of reds has all red (FF) and none (00) of the other two colors: #FF0000; pure blue is #0000FF. The letters a through F can also be lowercase.

This numbering scheme obviously leads to a potentially huge number of combinations (over 16 million), but not all video monitors are set to distinguish among millions of colors. Therefore, you may wish to limit yourself to a more modest palette of colors known as the web palette. A fine reference of colors that work well on all browsers at popular bit-depth settings can be found at *http://www.lynda.com/hexh.html*.

The HTML recommendation also specifies a basic library of 16 colors that can be assigned by plain-language names. Note that the color names are case-insensitive. The names and their equivalent hexadecimal triplets are as follows:

| Black | #000000 | Maroon | #800000 | Green | #008000 | Navy | #000080 |
| Silver | #C0C0C0 | Red | #FF0000 | Lime | #00FF00 | Blue | #0000FF |
| Gray | #808080 | Purple | #800080 | Olive | #808000 | Teal | #008080 |
| White | #FFFFFF | Fuchsia | #FF00FF | Yellow | #FFFF00 | Aqua | #00FFFF |

In other words, the attribute settings bgcolor="Aqua" and bgcolor="#00FFFF" yield the same results.

Netscape has developed a much longer list of plain-language color equivalents. These are detailed in Appendix A, and are recognized by recent versions of both Navigator and Internet Explorer.

# About client- and offset- Properties

In Internet Explorer 4, Microsoft introduced a set of size and position properties for elements that render as part of the regular body content (i.e., not positioned via

---

CSS). These properties had the potential to assist scripts in their tasks of determining locations and dimensions of body content so that positioned elements could be moved in relation to these fixed elements. The properties are:

```
clientHeight    clientLeft      clientTop       clientWidth
offsetHeight    offsetLeft      offsetTop       offsetWidth
```

The sad news is that between buggy behavior under fairly common circumstances in IE/Windows, and a different philosophy behind their implementation in IE/Mac, these properties can be difficult to work with. Add to this mix the fact that Microsoft tried to mend the errors for IE 6 by altering the playing field when the DOCTYPE element puts the browser into "standards compliant" mode (and fixing the genuine measurement bugs while in that mode). If that weren't enough, Netscape 6 and later implements some of these non-W3C properties for the convenience of DHTML authors, but does so in a way that comes closer to the old IE/Windows mode (minus the measurement bugs) than to the IE 6 standards compliant mode. Confusing? You bet!

The primary measurement discrepancies among browsers and compatibility modes have to do with element padding (if any is applied) and the positioning context for the element (even for nonpositioned elements). The number of permutations of oddities introduced by element and style sheet combinations boggles the mind, so I'll take one example of a common task—using a script to place the content of a CSS-positioned element directly atop the content of an inline element—to demonstrate the range of possible problem areas with a variety of browsers and compatibility modes. Because the properties described in this section are not part of the W3C DOM (as of Level 2), it is difficult to say which approach is "correct." It's more a question of how to use these properties to accomplish your desired tasks on your target browsers.

For this scenario, the following tag was inserted into an arbitrary place within a document so that its precise location would vary with browser, window size, and other environmental conditions:

```
<img id="fixedImg" src="bkgnd.jpg" alt="Locator box" height="90"
     width="120" style="padding:2px; border:3px solid green; margin:5px">
```

I use an image here because its content is the same size regardless of browser, and will let us see how the various size properties report the element's overall or content size (i.e., we're not at the mercy of font rendering vaguaries). Including padding, border, and margin settings for this fixed element will illustrate that some of these style attributes can impact topographical information about the element in the document. Table 9-1 shows the values for relevant size and position properties for several browsers and compatibility modes.

*Table 9-1. Comparative property values (pixels) for a 120-by-90 pixel inline element*

| Property name | IE 4 Windows | IE 6 Windows (old mode) | IE 6 Windows (standards mode) | IE 5 Mac | NN 6.2 |
|---|---|---|---|---|---|
| clientLeft | 3 | 3 | 3 | 247[a] | n/a |
| clientTop | 3 | 3 | 3 | 377[a] | n/a |

*Table 9-1. Comparative property values (pixels) for a 120-by-90 pixel inline element (continued)*

| Property name | IE 4 Windows | IE 6 Windows (old mode) | IE 6 Windows (standards mode) | IE 5 Mac | NN 6.2 |
|---|---|---|---|---|---|
| offsetLeft | 237 | 242 | 232 | 237 | 217 |
| offsetTop | 377 | 382 | 367 | 362 | 383 |
| clientWidth | 120 | 120 | 124 | 120 | n/a |
| clientHeight | 90 | 90 | 94 | 90 | n/a |
| offsetWidth | 126 | 126 | 130 | 130 | 130 |
| offsetHeight | 96 | 96 | 100 | 100 | 100 |
| naturalWidth | n/a | n/a | n/a | n/a | 120 |
| naturalHeight | n/a | n/a | n/a | n/a | 90 |
| width | 120 | 120 | 124 | 120 | 120 |
| height | 90 | 90 | 94 | 90 | 90 |
| offsetParent.clientLeft | 2 | 2 | 0 | 0 | n/a |
| offsetParent.clientTop | 2 | 2 | 0 | 0 | n/a |
| offsetParent.offsetLeft | 0 | 0 | 10 | 0 | 0 |
| offsetParent.offsetTop | 0 | 0 | 15 | 0 | 0 |

a  For inline text elements in IE/Mac, add a margin of offsetParent to offset property values to get the equivalent of client properties.

Table 9-1 reveals a great deal about how various browsers report the location and size of an inline element. Some of the precise numbers, such as the location coordinates, are not critical measures because each browser renders surrounding content slightly differently, and any scripts that rely on the position will read the live values in each case. But several very important details are worth noting for this particular element insertion:

- IE 6 in backward-compatible mode calculates the heights and widths the same as IE for Windows all the way back to Version 4. This is good for backward compatibility.

- In IE 6/Windows backward-compatible mode, the offset sizes include the border thicknesses on both sides of the content.

- In standards mode, IE 6/Windows calculates the offsetLeft and offsetTop properties in relation to the offsetParent element; the offsetParent element (the body element in this case) has its own offset values. The actual location must take into account the offsetParent's offset values.

- In standards mode, IE 6/Windows reports width and height properties influenced by the padding thickness. This is wrong, because these properties should reflect the height and width attributes of the element (even getAttribute( ) returns the incorrect values).

- IE 5/Mac has a completely different notion of what the clientLeft and clientTop properties should measure compared to any IE/Windows version (representing the sum of the offset measure of the element plus the margin of the `offsetParent` element).

- IE 6/Windows in standards mode, IE 5/Mac, and NN 6 report identical `offsetWidth` and `offsetHeight` values, all of which include the padding and border thicknesses, but not the margins.

To gain an appreciation for why these differences can be important to your DHTML scripting, consider what it takes to position a second `img` element that has no padding, border, or margin so that the top-left corner of the positioned image is precisely at the top-left corner of the static image content. Depending on the browser and compatibility mode, you must take into account a variety of measurement components of the fixed element to accumulate a value to assign to the movable element's `style.left` and `style.top` properties. Table 9-2 shows the pieces required for the `style.left` property for several browser classes. The corresponding top values would also be assigned to the movable element's `style.top` property.

*Table 9-2. Sample position components*

| | IE Windows (old mode) | IE 6 Windows (standards mode) | IE 5 Mac | NN 6 |
|---|---|---|---|---|
| `fixedElem.offsetLeft` | • | • | | • |
| `fixedElem.offsetParent.offsetLeft` | | • | | |
| `fixedElem.style.padding` | | • | | • |
| `fixedElem.style.borderWidth` | • | • | | • |
| `fixedElem.clientLeft` | | | • | |

Bear in mind that the `style` object properties in use here are string values that include units. This means that scripts must perform type conversions to do the math. For example, the IE 6/Windows standards mode assignment statement would be as follows:

```
positionedElem.style.left = fixedElem.offsetLeft +
    fixedElem.offsetParent.offsetLeft + parseInt(fixedElem.style.padding) +
    parseInt(fixedElem.style.borderWidth) + "px";
```

This syntax also assumes that the `style` object has the style sheet properties handy because they were set as an attribute of the element. If the style sheet is defined elsewhere in the page, you'll have to go the extra step of reading the effective style applied to the element (see DOM-specific techniques for this in Chapter 5). One more factor to take into account is the `offsetParent` location. If the element whose location you're reading is nested within multiple positioning contexts, you should use a separate function to accumulate all `offsetLeft` values of `offsetParents` out to the root element. On the plus side, you can use the same calculation for Netscape 6 because the `offsetParent.offsetLeft` property returns zero, so its addition won't affect the outcome, even for nested positioning contexts.

For IE 5/Mac, the clientLeft and clientTop properties are valid for only some elements, such as inline img and positioned elements. For other kinds of elements, you need to calculate the equivalent of the clientLeft and clientTop properties by including the margins of the body element, which have significant default values you must account for as follows:

```
positionedElem.style.left = fixedElem.offsetLeft +
    parseInt(fixedElem.offsetParent.currentStyle.marginLeft)  + "px";
```

Netscape 7 adds support for the IE clientHeight and clientWidth properties (not clientLeft or clientTop), but only for elements that display scrollbars due to content overflowing the viewable area. This includes the document.body element, when it is larger than the content region of the browser window. For nonscrolled elements, both property values are zero.

This digression serves as an advisory that the client and offset properties are both helpful and tricky. Almost any task is possible, but it may require much trial, error, and cross-browser testing to achieve the desired results with your combination of elements. Not every positioning task is quite so difficult (as in the flying objects example in Chapter 4). But don't be surprised if a complex element design and precision positioning task across the domains of fixed elements, positioned elements, and event coordinates takes hard work to accomplish.

## Default Property Values

Many property listings provide what appear to be explicit default values, but this can be deceiving. The trend in recent browsers is for an element object property to return an empty string when the property reflects an HTML attribute not explicitly assigned in the source code. But an empty string is equally misleading, because the element may be behaving according to a default specification, even when no attribute is assigned. The align property of a block-level element is a good example. Unless instructed otherwise, the element usually behaves as if its align property were set to left, yet the default property is an empty string.

In these cases, the listings in this chapter display the default values under which the element object behaves. This choice simply provides a shortcut so that when you see a list or range of possible property values, you don't have to look up the corresponding attribute in Chapter 8 to find the HTML default value. Where the default value is listed as "None," this means that there is no default HTML behavior and the default value is, indeed, an empty string.

## Event Handler Properties

Objects that can receive events have event handlers listed in their main entries. Because this chapter focuses on the scriptable aspects of HTML elements, the event handlers are listed in their lowercase property form—the form used to assign function references to event handlers in script statements. See "Binding Event Handlers to Elements" in Chapter 6, for details on this event handler format.

The selection of event handler properties listed for each object is based on a couple of factors. First, just as most HTML 4.0 elements have intrinsic events associated with them, those same events are listed in this chapter with the objects that reflect the html element. As such, it may seem odd that an element that has almost no visual presence on a page has keyboard and mouse events. Those events are listed just the same, even though the likelihood of your scripting them is next to nil.

Second, the Internet Explorer and W3C DOM event bubbling models (see Chapter 6) dictate that it is possible for an event from one element to bubble up through the element containment hierarchy all the way to a root node or element. This means that essentially every event that can appear in the most nested element (such as the events related to Microsoft's data binding facilities in Win32) is also available in all elements higher up the containment chain. In other words, virtually every element that acts as a container can have virtually every bubbling event type associated with it. You can read more about the characteristics of each event type in Chapter 10.

# Shared Object Properties, Methods, and Events

Both the proprietary Internet Explorer DOM and W3C DOM expose a wide range of properties (including event handler properties) and methods almost universally across objects that reflect HTML elements. Rather than repeat the descriptions of these items ad nauseam in the reference listing, I am listing their details only once. Due to the large number of shared items (80 properties, 60 methods, and 72 event types), these shared items do not appear in the lists of properties, methods, and events for each object in the rest of this chapter, but they are available for practically every HTML element object (within the browser or standard version range indicated in each listing).

Obviously, the shared properties or methods that are meaningless except for rendered element objects may not be available to nonrendered elements. For example, invoking the IE scrollIntoView( ) method of a style element object is meaningless because the style element presents no content of its own on the page to which a window could scroll. Such items are typically part of the DOMs simply because the browsers' internal architectures utilize an inheritance mechanism that empowers all element objects with the same basic items, even if they have no particular application. You should get to know the shared items well, and refer to the object-specific items later in this chapter when you need their special powers.

In the following item descriptions, the example code uses the term *elementID* to refer to the identifier assigned to the id attribute of the element. In your scripts, substitute the object's true ID for the placeholder used here. Here is a list of the common items:

## Properties

| | | |
|---|---|---|
| ATTRIBUTE_NODE | CDATA_SECTION_NODE | COMMENT_NODE |
| DOCUMENT_FRAGMENT_NODE | DOCUMENT_NODE | DOCUMENT_TYPE_NODE |
| ELEMENT_NODE | ENTITY_NODE | ENTITY_REFERENCE_NODE |
| NOTATION_NODE | PROCESSING_INSTRUCTION_NODE | TEXT_NODE |
| accessKey | all[] | attributes[] |
| baseURI | behaviorUrns[] | canHaveChildren |
| canHaveHTML | childNodes[] | children |
| cite | className | clientHeight |
| clientLeft | clientTop | clientWidth |
| contentEditable | currentStyle | dateTime |
| dir | disabled | document |
| filters[] | firstChild | hideFocus |
| id | innerHTML | innerText |
| isContentEditable | isDisabled | isMultiLine |
| isTextEdit | lang | language |
| lastChild | localName | namespaceURI |
| nextSibling | nodeName | nodeType |
| nodeValue | offsetHeight | offsetLeft |
| offsetParent | offsetTop | offsetWidth |
| outerHTML | outerText | ownerDocument |
| parentElement | parentNode | parentTextEdit |
| prefix | previousSibling | readyState |
| recordNumber | runtimeStyle | scopeName |
| scrollHeight | scrollLeft | scrollTop |
| scrollWidth | sourceIndex | style |
| tabIndex | tagName | tagUrn |
| title | uniqueID | |

## Methods

| | | |
|---|---|---|
| addBehavior() | addEventListener() | appendChild() |
| applyElement() | attachEvent() | blur() |
| clearAttributes() | click() | cloneNode() |
| componentFromPoint() | contains() | createControlRange() |
| detachEvent() | dispatchEvent() | doScroll() |
| dragDrop() | fireEvent() | focus() |
| getAdjacentText() | getAttribute() | getAttributeNode() |
| getAttributeNodeNS() | getAttributeNS() | getBoundingClientRect() |

| getClientRects( )          | getElementsByTagName( )    | getElementsByTagNameNS( )   |
| getExpression( )           | hasAttribute( )            | hasAttributeNS( )           |
| hasAttributes( )           | hasChildNodes( )           | insertAdjacentElement( )    |
| insertAdjacentHTML( )      | insertAdjacentText( )      | insertBefore( )             |
| isSupported( )             | mergeAttributes( )         | normalize( )                |
| releaseCapture( )          | removeAttribute( )         | removeAttributeNode( )      |
| removeAttributeNS( )       | removeBehavior( )          | removeChild( )              |
| removeEventListener( )     | removeExpression( )        | removeNode( )               |
| replaceAdjacentText( )     | replaceChild( )            | replaceNode( )              |
| scrollIntoView( )          | setActive( )               | setAttribute( )             |
| setAttributeNode( )        | setAttributeNodeNS( )      | setAttributeNS( )           |
| setCapture( )              | setExpression( )           | swapNode( )                 |

# Event Handlers

| Events | IE Windows | IE Mac | NN | W3C DOM |
|---|---|---|---|---|
| DOMActivate[a] | n/a | n/a | n/a | 2 |
| DOMAttrModified[a] | n/a | n/a | 6 | 2 |
| DOMCharacterDataModified[a] | n/a | n/a | 6 | 2 |
| DOMFocusIn[a] | n/a | n/a | n/a | 2 |
| DOMFocusOut[a] | n/a | n/a | n/a | 2 |
| DOMNodeInserted[a] | n/a | n/a | 6 | 2 |
| DOMNodeInsertedIntoDocument[a] | n/a | n/a | 6 | 2 |
| DOMNodeRemoved[a] | n/a | n/a | 6 | 2 |
| DOMNodeRemovedFromDocument[a] | n/a | n/a | 6 | 2 |
| DOMSubtreeModified[a] | n/a | n/a | 6 | 2 |
| onactivate | 5.5 | n/a | n/a | n/a |
| onafterupdate[b] | 4 | 5 | n/a | n/a |
| onbeforeactivate | 6 | n/a | n/a | n/a |
| onbeforecopy | 5 | n/a | n/a | n/a |
| onbeforecut | 5 | n/a | n/a | n/a |
| onbeforedeactivate | 5.5 | n/a | n/a | n/a |
| onbeforeeditfocus | 5 | n/a | n/a | n/a |
| onbeforepaste | 5 | n/a | n/a | n/a |
| onbeforeupdate[b] | 4 | 5 | n/a | n/a |
| onblur[c] | 3 | 3.01 | 2 | 1 |
| oncellchange[d] | 5 | n/a | n/a | n/a |
| onclick[c] | 3 | 3.01 | 2 | 1 |
| oncontextmenu | 5 | n/a | n/a | n/a |
| oncontrolselect | 5.5 | n/a | n/a | n/a |

| Events | IE Windows | IE Mac | NN | W3C DOM |
|---|---|---|---|---|
| oncopy | 5 | n/a | n/a | n/a |
| oncut | 5 | n/a | n/a | n/a |
| ondataavailable[d] | 4 | n/a | n/a | n/a |
| ondatasetchanged[d] | 4 | n/a | n/a | n/a |
| ondatasetcomplete[d] | 4 | n/a | n/a | n/a |
| ondblclick[c] | 4 | 4 | 3 | n/a |
| ondeactivate | 5.5 | n/a | n/a | n/a |
| ondrag | 5 | n/a | n/a | n/a |
| ondragend | 5 | n/a | n/a | n/a |
| ondragenter | 5 | n/a | n/a | n/a |
| ondragleave | 5 | n/a | n/a | n/a |
| ondragover | 5 | n/a | n/a | n/a |
| ondragstart | 5 | n/a | n/a | n/a |
| ondrop | 5 | n/a | n/a | n/a |
| onerrorupdate[b] | 4 | 5 | n/a | n/a |
| onfilterchange | 4 | n/a | n/a | n/a |
| onfocus[c] | 3 | 3.01 | 2 | 1 |
| onfocusin | 6 | n/a | n/a | n/a |
| onfocusout | 6 | n/a | n/a | n/a |
| onhelp[c] | 4 | 5 | n/a | n/a |
| onkeydown[c] | 4 | 4 | 4 | 3 |
| onkeypress[c] | 4 | 4 | 4 | 3 |
| onkeyup[c] | 4 | 4 | 4 | 3 |
| onlayoutcomplete | 5.5 | n/a | n/a | n/a |
| onlosecapture | 5 | n/a | n/a | n/a |
| onmousedown[c] | 4 | 4 | 4 | 1 |
| onmouseenter | 5.5 | n/a | n/a | n/a |
| onmouseleave | 5.5 | n/a | n/a | n/a |
| onmousemove[c] | 4 | 4 | 4 | 1 |
| onmouseout[c] | 3 | 3.01 | 2 | 1 |
| onmouseover[c] | 3 | 3.01 | 2 | 1 |
| onmouseup[c] | 4 | 4 | 4 | 1 |
| onmousewheel | 6 | n/a | n/a | n/a |
| onmove | 5.5 | n/a | n/a | n/a |
| onmoveend | 5.5 | n/a | n/a | n/a |
| onmovestart | 5.5 | n/a | n/a | n/a |
| onpaste | 5 | n/a | n/a | n/a |

| Events | IE Windows | IE Mac | NN | W3C DOM |
|---|---|---|---|---|
| onpropertychange | 5 | n/a | n/a | n/a |
| onreadystatechange[e] | 4 | n/a | n/a | n/a |
| onresize[c] | 4 | 4 | 4 | n/a |
| onresizeend | 5.5 | n/a | n/a | n/a |
| onresizestart | 5.5 | n/a | n/a | n/a |
| onrowenter[d] | 4 | n/a | n/a | n/a |
| onrowexit[d] | 4 | n/a | n/a | n/a |
| onrowsdeleted[d] | 5 | n/a | n/a | n/a |
| onrowsinserted[d] | 5 | n/a | n/a | n/a |
| onscroll[f] | 4 | 4 | n/a | n/a |
| onselectstart | 4 | 4 | n/a | n/a |

[a] Event type assignable only via the addEventListener( ) method for any node.

[b] Exposed as property for all elements in IE 6, but applies only to elements that support data binding: a, bdo, button, custom, div, frame, iframe, img, input (checkbox, hidden, password, radio, text), label, legend, marquee, rt, ruby, select, span, and textarea.

[c] Shared among all element objects only in recent browsers. Earlier implementations and compatibilities are listed with applicable objects throughout this chapter.

[d] Exposed as property for all elements in IE 6, but applies only to applet, object, and xml elements set for data binding.

[e] Exposed as property for all elements in IE 6, but applies only to applet, document, frame, frameSet, iframe, img, link, object, script, and xml elements unless an HTML behavior is attached to the element.

[f] Exposed as property for all elements in IE 6, but applies only applet, bdo, body, custom, div, embed, map, marquee, object, table, and textarea elements and the window object.

## ATTRIBUTE_NODE, CDATA_SECTION_NODE, COMMENT_NODE, DOCUMENT_FRAGMENT_NODE, DOCUMENT_NODE, DOCUMENT_TYPE_NODE, ELEMENT_NODE, ENTITY_NODE, ENTITY_REFERENCE_NODE, NOTATION_NODE, PROCESSING_INSTRUCTION_NODE, TEXT_NODE

**NN** *6*    **IE** *n/a*    **DOM** *1*

*Read-only*

This set of constants belongs to the root Node object of the W3C DOM, and is therefore inherited by all document-level nodes and elements. Each property corresponds to an integer value associated with the nodeType property of every DOM node. You can use these properties as a more plain-language way to indicate the node type your script is looking for in comparisons or similar operations.

### Example

```
if (myObject.nodeType == document.ELEMENT_NODE) {
    // process as an element here
}
```

### Value

Integer corresponding to DOM node type as follows.

| Property | nodeType Value |
|---|---|
| ELEMENT_NODE | 1 |
| ATTRIBUTE_NODE | 2 |
| TEXT_NODE | 3 |
| CDATA_SECTION_NODE | 4 |
| ENTITY_REFERENCE_NODE | 5 |
| ENTITY_NODE | 6 |
| PROCESSING_INSTRUCTION_NODE | 7 |
| COMMENT_NODE | 8 |
| DOCUMENT_NODE | 9 |
| DOCUMENT_TYPE_NODE | 10 |
| DOCUMENT_FRAGMENT_NODE | 11 |
| NOTATION_NODE | 12 |

**Default**          Constant values (above).

## accessKey                                    NN *n/a*    IE 4    DOM *1*

*Read/Write*

This is single character key that either gives focus to an element (in some browsers) or activates a form control or link action. The browser and operating system determine if the user
must press a modifier key (e.g., **Ctrl**, **Alt**, or **Command**) with the access key to activate the
link. In Windows versions of IE 5 and later and Netscape 6, the **Alt** key is required and the
key is not case-sensitive. For Macintosh versions of IE 5 and later and Netscape 6, the **Ctrl**
modifier key is required to effect the action.

Although listed here as a widely shared property, that isn't strictly the case across all implementations. Netscape 6 (per the W3C DOM) recognizes this property only for the
following elements: a, area, button, input, label, legend, and textarea. To this list, IE 4
adds applet, body, div, embed, isindex, marquee, object, select, span, table, and td (but
removes label and legend). IE 5 adds every other renderable element, but with a caution.
Except for input and other form-related elements, you must also assign a tabindex attribute
or tabIndex property value to the IE 5 and later element (even if it's simply a value of zero
for all) to let the accelerator key combination bring focus to the element. As of Version 7,
Netscape does not alter UI behavior if a script changes the property's value.

**Example**          document.links[3].accessKey = "n";

**Value**            Single alphanumeric (and punctuation) keyboard character.

**Default**          Empty string.

Returns an array of all HTML element objects contained by the current element. Items in this array are indexed (zero-based) in source code order. The collection transcends generations of nested elements such that document.all[ ] exposes every element in the entire document. See the all object for a list of this property value's own set of properties and methods.

As with all collections in Internet Explorer, you may use the traditional JavaScript array syntax (with square brackets around the index value) or IE's JScript alternative (with parentheses around the index value). If you are aiming for cross-browser deployment for collections that are available on both platforms, use the square brackets.

Unless you develop strictly for IE browsers, consider migrating to W3C DOM references via document.getElementById( ), implemented in IE 5 and later and Netscape 6.

### Syntax

```
object.all(index).objectPropertyOrMethod
object.all[index].objectPropertyOrMethod
object.all("elementID").objectPropertyOrMethod
object.all["elementID"].objectPropertyOrMethod
object.all.elementID.objectPropertyOrMethod
```

**Example**          var inpVal = document.all.first_name.value;

**Value**            Array (collection) of element object references in HTML source code order.

**Default**          Current document's model.

Returns a named node map object, which resembles an array (collection) of attribute objects (W3C DOM type Attr), but also has some methods of its own to facilitate accessing a member of this array. IE's attributes array contains entries for all attributes of the element's internal DTD, plus any custom (expando) attributes explicitly set in the HTML source code in IE 6. Scripted changes to the element's attributes or their values are not reflected in this array.

For Netscape 6, the attributes array contains entries only for those attributes explicitly defined in the HTML source code for the element, including custom attributes. Scripted changes to attributes (additions or deletions) or their values are reflected in the attribute objects referenced by the attributes array.

In lieu of the named node map object methods, you may access individual attribute objects via standard JavaScript array syntax. By and large, however, it is far more convenient to access HTML element attribute values for scripting purposes either via their reflection as element object properties or via the element's getAttribute( ) and setAttribute( ) methods. For W3C DOM details (which are useful for XML document parsing), see the Attr and NamedNodeMap objects for properties and methods of these objects.

**Example**

```
var ldAttr = document.getElementById("myImg").attributes.getNamedItem("longdesc");
```

| Value | Array (collection) of attribute object references in source code (Netscape 6), alphabetical-by-name (IE/Mac), or haphazard (IE/Windows) order. |
| --- | --- |
| Default | Current element's model. |

## baseURI

NN 6   IE *n/a*   DOM 3

*Read-only*

This is a property of the Node object (proposed for DOM Level 3 Core) that reveals the base URI (full path to the source) from which the node was served. For example, each node copied from an XML document loaded into a document.implementation object reveals its baseURI, which is different from that of the HTML page performing the rendering.

| Example | `var nodeSrc = myXMLDoc.firstChild.childNodes[14].baseURI;` |
| --- | --- |
| Value | Full URI string. |
| Default | Current node's internal value. |

## behaviorUrns[]

NN *n/a*   IE *5(Win)*   DOM *n/a*

*Read-only*

Provides an array of Uniform Resource Names for all external behaviors (*.htc* files) associated with the element through style sheet syntax. Perhaps for security reasons, the strings entries of this array are always empty.

**Example**

```
var htcCount = document.getElementById(elementID).behaviorUrns.length;
```

| Value | Array of (empty) strings. |
| --- | --- |
| Default | Array of length 0. |

## canHaveChildren

NN *n/a*   IE *5(Win)*   DOM *n/a*

*Read-only*

Specifies whether the current element may act as a container of other elements. The property value is based on IE for Windows built-in HTML DTDs, which define several elements (such as <br>) that may not have child nodes inserted into them.

**Example**

```
if (elementRef.canHaveChildren) {
    // statements to insert or append child elements
}
```

| Value | Boolean value: true | false. |
| --- | --- |
| Default | Element-specific. |

## canHaveHTML

Specifies whether the current element may act as a container of other content with HTML markup. The property reports identical information as canHaveChildren for regular HTML elements. For IE HTML Components (defined in an XML-based *.htc* file), the property is read/write, and directs the browser how to treat the custom element defined by the component.

### Example

```
if (elementRef.canHaveHTML) {
    // statements to insert content with HTML markup
}
```

**Value**        Boolean value: true | false.

**Default**      Element-specific.

## childNodes[]

This is a property of the W3C DOM Node object that consists of an array of references to all child nodes (a node list) in the next deeper level of the node hierarchy (whether part of the document node tree or free-standing document fragments not yet inserted into the document tree). To reach more deeply nested nodes, you must access the childNodes array of each child node of the current node. A vital property for walking through a node tree. See the NodeList object for the properties and methods of this kind of array.

### Example

```
for (var i = 0; i < nodeRef.childNodes.length; i++) {
    if (nodeRef.childNodes[i].nodeType == document.ELEMENT_NODE) {
        // operate on an element
    }
}
```

**Value**        Array of node object references.

**Default**      Array of length zero.

## children[]

Returns an array of all first-level HTML element objects contained by the current element. This collection differs from the all[ ] collection in that it contains references only to the immediate children of the current element (whereas the all[ ] collection transcends generations). For example, document.body.children[ ] might contain a form, but no reference to form elements nested inside the form. Items in this array are indexed (zero-based) in source code order. In contrast to the childNodes[ ] array, the scope of this property is the element, not the node. See the children object.

Shared DOM Reference

```
for (var i = 0; i < elementRef.children.length; i++) {
    if (elementRef.children[i].tagName == "FORM") {
        // operate on a form element
    }
}
```

**Value**          Array of element object references.

**Default**        Array of length zero.

## cite                                                        NN 6    IE 6    DOM 1
*Read/Write*

This property (along with dateTime) is shared among all phrase element objects in IE 6, but in truth, it officially belongs only to the blockquote, quote, del, and ins element objects (see those element descriptions in Chapter 8 for details on the corresponding attribute in the context of the element). Because the property is shared by four objects, Microsoft may have found it more convenient to implement the property internally for a larger related set of HTML element objects. Or it may be a mistake. Whatever the reason, do not expect this property in as many element objects as IE 6 exposes.

**Value**          Any valid URL to a document on the World Wide Web, including absolute or relative URLs.

**Default**        Empty string.

## className                                                   NN 6    IE 4    DOM 1
*Read/Write*

This is an identifier generally used to associate an element with a style sheet rule defined for a class selector. You can alter the class association for an element by script. If the document includes an alternate class selector and style rule, adjusting the element's className property can provide a shortcut for adjusting many style properties at once.

**Example**        document.getElementById("*elementID*").className = "altHighlighted";

**Value**          Case-sensitive string. Multiple class names are space-delimited within the string.

**Default**        Empty string.

## clientHeight, clientWidth                                   NN 7    IE 4    DOM *n/a*
*Read-only*

Broadly speaking, these provide the height and width of the element's content, but with minor variations with respect to element padding among various operating system versions of IE and compatibility modes controlled by the DOCTYPE declaration. Not available for all element types in IE for Macintosh. For Netscape 7, values are zero except when an element's content overflows the viewable area, in which case the values reveal the dimensions of the viewable area (e.g., the browser window's content region for the document.body element). See the section "About client- and offset- Properties" at the beginning of this chapter for details.

| | |
|---|---|
| **Example** | var midHeight = document.body.clientHeight/2; |
| **Value** | Integer pixel value. |
| **Default** | 0 |

## clientLeft, clientTop
NN *n/a*    IE *4*    DOM *n/a*
*Read-only*

Broadly speaking, these provide the left and top coordinates of the element's content within the box that includes the element's padding, but with minor variations among various operating system versions of IE. Not available for all element types in IE for Macintosh. See the section "About client- and offset- Properties" at the beginning of this chapter for details. More useful information for inline element positioning generally comes from the offsetLeft and offsetTop properties (including Netscape 6). For CSS-positioned elements (including changing an element's position), use style object properties, such as left and top, and (in IE only) pixelLeft and pixelTop.

| | |
|---|---|
| **Value** | Integer pixel value. |
| **Default** | 0 |

## contentEditable
NN *n/a*    IE *5.5(Win)*    DOM *n/a*
*Read/Write*

Controls whether the element is editable by the user via the IE for Windows live content-editing facilities. User changes are not preserved on the server without intervention by the server, usually via client-side script capture of modified content and submission via form. Scripts should alter the appearance of an element (border, background color, etc.) when in edit mode to highlight the mode for the user. By default, all child elements inherit the edit mode setting of an element. See the onmove event handler in Chapter 10 for an extended example.

| | |
|---|---|
| **Example** | document.getElementById("*elementID*").contentEditable = "true"; |
| **Value** | String constant: false \| inherit \| true. |
| **Default** | inherit |

## currentStyle
NN *n/a*    IE *5*    DOM *n/a*
*Read-only*

Returns a style object with properties that reflect the effective values being applied to the element. This property takes into account style sheet rules defined in a style element, imported from external style sheet files, and inline style attributes. Because the style property reflects only inline style attributes, the currentStyle property is more valuable for reading initial values after a document loads. To modify style attributes, you can use the element's style object properties. For similar capabilities in Netscape 6, see the window.getComputedStyle( ) method.

**Example**
var currSize = document.getElementById("*elementID*").currentStyle.fontSize;

**Value**　　　　　　style object reference.

**Default**　　　　　　The effective style object.

## dateTime　　　　　　　　　　　　　　　　　　　　　NN *6*　IE *6*　DOM *1*
*Read/Write*

This property (along with cite) is shared among all phrase element objects in IE 6, but in truth, it officially belongs only to the blockquote, quote, del, and ins element objects (see those element descriptions in Chapter 8 for details on the corresponding attribute in the context of the element). Because the property is shared by four objects, Microsoft may have found it more convenient to implement the property internally for a larger related set of HTML element objects. Or it may be a mistake. Whatever the reason, do not expect this property in as many element objects as IE 6 exposes.

**Value**　　　　　　Date string.

**Default**　　　　　　Empty string.

## dir　　　　　　　　　　　　　　　　　　　　　　　NN *6*　IE *5*　DOM *1*
*Read/Write*

Indicates the direction of character rendering for the element's text whose characters are not governed by inherent directionality according to the Unicode standard and default browser language system. Character rendering is either left-to-right or right-to-left.

**Value**　　　　　　ltr | rtl (case insensitive string).

**Default**　　　　　　ltr

## disabled　　　　　　　　　　　　　　　　　　　　　NN *6*　IE *4*　DOM *1*
*Read/Write*

Specifies whether the element is available for user interaction. When set to true, the element cannot receive focus or be modified by the user, and it typically appears grayed out on the page. This property is available for all HTML element objects in IE 5.5 for Windows and later. For IE 4 and IE 5, it applies only to form controls, while Netscape 6 and later recognize the property for form controls and the style element object. A disabled form control's name/value pair is not submitted with its form.

**Example**　　　　document.getElementById("myButton").disabled = true;

**Value**　　　　　　Boolean value: true | false.

**Default**　　　　　　false

# document

*Read-only*

Returns a reference to the document object that contains the current element. Potentially helpful for functions that act on object references retrieved from event properties or passed as ID strings. The corresponding W3C DOM property is ownerDocument.

**Example**        `var currDoc = document.getElementById("elementID").document;`

**Value**          document object reference.

**Default**        The current document object.

# filters[]

NN *n/a*    IE *4*    DOM *n/a*

Returns an array of all filter objects contained by the current element. Applies only to the following element objects: bdo, body, button, div, fieldset, img, input, marquee, rt, ruby, span, table, td, textarea, and th. See the filter object for referencing syntax.

**Value**          Array of filter object references.

**Default**        Array of length zero.

# firstChild, lastChild

NN *6*    IE *5*    DOM *1*

*Read-only*

Return a reference to the first or last child node (respectively) of the current element node. Most commonly, these child nodes are text nodes nested inside an element. For a simple element containing only one text node, both properties return a reference to the same text node. More complex constructions, such as tr elements, can have other element nodes (td elements) as their child nodes, but some browsers may turn source code carriage returns between elements into text nodes. Therefore, it's a good idea to validate the type of node returned by either property before acting on it.

**Example**
```
if (document.getElementById("elementID").firstChild.nodeType == 3) {
    // process as a text node
}
```

**Value**          Node object (including text node, HTML element node, etc.) reference.

**Default**        `null`

# hideFocus

NN *n/a*    IE *5.5(Win)*    DOM *n/a*

*Read/Write*

Specifies whether the browser should display a dotted focus rectangle around the element if it has focus. The element continues to be able to receive focus if it is focusable by default or has the tabindex attribute set. When this property is set to true, there is no visual clue about the focus state.

| **Example** | document.getElementById("*elementID*").hideFocus = true; |
|---|---|
| **Value** | Boolean value: true \| false. |
| **Default** | false |

## id

NN *6*     IE *4*     DOM *1*

*Read/Write*

Specifies a unique identifier that distinguishes this element from all the rest in the document. The value of this property is most often used to assemble references to elements, but you can loop through all elements to see if there is a match of an id value. It is generally not a good idea to change this property's value for an element already in the document tree. But if a script creates a new element object (via the document.createElement( ) method, for instance), it can assign a unique identifier to this object's id property, and then add the element to the document tree.

| **Example** | var headID = document.getElementsByTagName("head")[0].id; |
|---|---|
| **Value** | String. |
| **Default** | Empty string. |

## innerHTML

NN *6*     IE *4*     DOM *n/a*

*Read/Write*

Indicates the rendered text and HTML tags (i.e., all source code) between the start and end tags of the current element. A change to this property that includes HTML tags is rendered through the HTML parser, as if the new value were part of the original source code. You may change this property only after the document has fully loaded. Changes to the innerHTML property are not reflected in the source code when you view the source in the browser. This property is not supported in many objects in the Macintosh version of IE 4.

Netscape 6 supports this property as a convenience, even though the W3C DOM does not. Assigning a string lacking HTML tags to the innerHTML property has the same effect as assigning the string to the IE-only innerText property. In IE, you can read or write the source code that includes the element's tags via the outerHTML property.

**Example**

document.getElementById("*elementID*").innerHTML = "How <i>now</i> brown cow?";

| **Value** | String that may or may not include HTML tags. |
|---|---|
| **Default** | Empty string. |

## innerText

NN *n/a*     IE *4*     DOM *n/a*

*Read/Write*

Indicates the rendered text (but not any tags) of the current element. If you want the rendered text as well as any nested HTML tags, see innerHTML. Any changes to this property are not rendered through the HTML parser, meaning that any HTML tags you include are treated as displayable text content only. You may change this property only after the document has fully loaded. Changes to the innerText property are not reflected in the source code when you view the source in the browser. This property is not supported in many objects in the Macintosh version of IE 4.

**Example**

```
document.getElementById("elementID").innerText = "How now brown cow?";
```

| **Value** | String. |
| **Default** | Empty string. |

## isContentEditable

NN *n/a*    IE *5.5(Win)*    DOM *n/a*

*Read-only*

Specifies whether the current element has IE/Windows user editing engaged. Reveals the actual editing state as either explicitly set for the element or inherited from its ancestor tree.

**Example**

```
if (document.getElementById("elementID").isContentEditable) {
    // process the editable element
}
```

| **Value** | Boolean value: true \| false. |
| **Default** | false |

## isDisabled

NN *n/a*    IE *5.5(Win)*    DOM *n/a*

*Read-only*

Specifies whether the current element is disabled. Reveals the actual disabled state as either explicitly set for the element or inherited from its ancestor tree.

**Example**

```
if (document.getElementById("elementID").isDisabled) {
    // process the disabled element
}
```

| **Value** | Boolean value: true \| false. |
| **Default** | false |

## isMultiLine

NN *n/a*    IE *5.5(Win)*    DOM *n/a*

*Read-only*

Specifies whether the current element allows content to extend across multiple lines. Most text containers allow multiple lines, but other kinds of elements, such as a text input element are restricted to single line rendering.

**Example**
```
if (document.getElementById("elementID").isMultiLine) {
    // process the element as a potential multiple-line element
}
```

| | |
|---|---|
| **Value** | Boolean value: true \| false. |
| **Default** | Element default. |

## isTextEdit

NN *n/a*   IE *4*   DOM *n/a*

*Read-only*

Specifies whether the element can be used to create an IE/Windows TextRange object (via the createTextRange( ) method). Only body, button, text type input, and textarea elements are permitted to have text ranges created for their content.

**Example**
```
if (document.getElementById("elementID").isTextEdit) {
    var rng = document.getElementById("elementID").createTextRange( );
}
```

| | |
|---|---|
| **Value** | Boolean value: true \| false. |
| **Default** | Element default. |

## lang

NN *6*   IE *4*   DOM *1*

*Read/Write*

Indicates the written language being used for the element's attribute and property values. Other applications and search engines might use this information to aid selection of spellchecking dictionaries and creating indices.

| | |
|---|---|
| **Example** | document.getElementById("elementID").lang = "de"; |
| **Value** | Case-insensitive language code. |
| **Default** | Browser default. |

## language

NN *n/a*   IE *4*   DOM *n/a*

*Read/Write*

Indicates the scripting language for script statements defined in the element.

| | |
|---|---|
| **Example** | document.getElementById("elementID").language = "vbscript"; |
| **Value** | Case-insensitive scripting language name as string: javascript \| jscript \| vbs \| vbscript. |
| **Default** | jscript |

**492** | **Chapter 9: Document Object Model Reference**

## lastChild

See firstChild.

## localName, namespaceURI, prefix

NN 6    IE n/a    DOM 2

Read-only

These three properties apply primarily to XML document elements with tags that are defined with the help of XML namespaces. A simplified example of such a document follows:

```
<?xml version="1.0" encoding="ISO-8859-1"?>
<results xmlns:libBook="http://catalog.umv.edu/schema">
<libBook:title libBook:rareBooks="true">De Principia</libBook:title>
</results>
```

The properties reveal details about the element's naming characteristics. A localName is the equivalent of the nodeName property of the element, that is, the tag name within the scope of the entire document, even if the tag name is reused by another element originating from another namespace. The prefix, however, links the element with a prefix name that is normally defined with an xmlns attribute of a container in the XML document. This helps your script identify the namespace to which the element is associated. A further binding is revealed through the namespaceURI property, which returns the URI string assigned to the xmlns attribute of a container element. Although all three properties belong to the Node object, their values are null (or, rather, should be null, but in Netscape 6 are empty strings) for node types other than element and attribute nodes.

**Example**

```
var allTitles = document.getElementsByTagName("title");
for (var i = 0; i < allTitles.length; i++) {
    if (allTitles[i].prefix == "libBook" &&
        allTitles[i].namespaceURI.indexOf("catalog.umv.edu") != -1) {
        // process title elements from the desired namespace here
    }
}
```

| **Value** | Strings. |
| **Default** | For localName, the element's tag name. For others, an empty string. |

## namespaceURI

See localName.

## nextSibling, previousSibling

NN 6    IE 5    DOM 1

Read-only

Return a reference to the next or previous node (respectively) in the document tree at the same nested level as the current node. If there is no node in the position indicated by the property name, the property returns null. For a lone text node inside an element node, both properties return null. Node sequence is determined intially by source code order, but script changes to the document tree are reflected in the nodes returned by these properties.

| | |
|---|---|
| **Example** | `var nextNode = document.getElementById("elementID").nextSibling;` |
| **Value** | Node object (including text node, HTML element node, etc.) reference. |
| **Default** | `null` |

## nodeName

NN 6    IE 5    DOM 1

*Read-only*

Returns a string that identifies the name of the node as influenced by the node type. For element and attribute node types, the property returns the tag name and attribute name, respectively. For many other kinds of nodes, which have no inherent label associated with them, the nodeName property returns a fixed string indicating the node type, such as #text for a text node and #document for the root document node. For elements, the property returns the same string value as the element object's tagName property. Note that browsers through IE 6 and Netscape 7 return element tag strings in all uppercase, regardless of source code style or DOCTYPE specification.

**Example**

```
if (document.getElementById("elementID").nextSibling.nodeName == "#text") {
    // process as a text node
}
```

| | |
|---|---|
| **Value** | Fixed string for #cdata-section, #document, #document-fragment, and #text nodes; variable string for attribute, element, and other node types. |
| **Default** | Node-specific. |

## nodeType

NN 6    IE 5    DOM 1

*Read-only*

Returns an integer that corresponds to a node type as specified in the W3C DOM. This is the preferred property to use to test a node object for its type (rather than the nodeName property values). Every node type has a value, but not all browsers that support the nodeType property support all node types as objects. The integer values have corresponding constants associated with them, which you can use to make more verbose, but easier-to-read script comparisons for node type processing (see the ATTRIBUTE_NODE property earlier in this chapter). Note that there is no way to distinguish element types (e.g., root Element node versus an HTMLElement node) via the nodeType property. Also note that IE 6 in Windows erroneously reports a DOCTYPE element as a comment node type.

**Example**

```
if (document.getElementById("elementID").firstChild.nodeType == 1) {
    // process as an element
}
```

## Value

Integer values according to the following table.

| Value | Node type | W3C DOM | IE/Windows | IE/Mac | NN |
|-------|-----------|---------|------------|--------|-----|
| 1 | ELEMENT_NODE | 1 | 5 | 5 | 6 |
| 2 | ATTRIBUTE_NODE | 1 | 6 | 5 | 6 |
| 3 | TEXT_NODE | 1 | 5 | 5 | 6 |
| 4 | CDATA_SECTION_NODE | 1 | n/a | n/a | n/a |
| 5 | ENTITY_REFERENCE_NODE | 1 | n/a | n/a | na/ |
| 6 | ENTITY_NODE | 1 | n/a | n/a | n/a |
| 7 | PROCESSING_INSTRUCTION_NODE | 1 | n/a | n/a | n/a |
| 8 | COMMENT_NODE | 1 | 6 | 5 | 6 |
| 9 | DOCUMENT_NODE | 1 | 5 | 5 | 6 |
| 10 | DOCUMENT_TYPE_NODE | 1 | n/a | n/a | 6 |
| 11 | DOCUMENT_FRAGMENT_NODE | 1 | n/a | n/a | 6 |
| 12 | NOTATION_NODE | 1 | n/a | n/a | n/a |

**Default**        Node-specific.

## nodeValue             NN 6    IE 5    DOM 1

*Read/Write*

Although the nodeValue property belongs to every node type, it is particularly helpful for text nodes because the property provides read/write access to the actual rendered text content of a text node. This property provides the W3C DOM canonical access to reading and modifying the text node nested inside an element, assuming your script addresses the nodeValue property of, say, an element's firstChild node. The property returns null for element nodes, so do not think of it as a pure replacement for the innerText or innerHTML convenience properties. The property returns the value assigned to an attribute when used with an attribute node.

### Example

```
document.getElementById("elementID").firstChild.nodeValue = "New Text!";
```

**Value**        String, although IE for Windows may return an attribute node's value as a Number data type if the value consists of a numeric value. You should always assign a string to this property.

**Default**      Empty string.

Broadly speaking, provide the height and width of the element's content, but with minor variations with respect to element borders and padding among various operating system versions of IE and compatibility modes controlled by the DOCTYPE declaration. The trend is to include the measure of borders and padding, but not margins in these values. Implemented in Netscape 6 as a convenience, even though not part of the W3C DOM. See the section "About client- and offset- Properties" at the beginning of this chapter for details.

**Example**     `var midpoint = document.getElementById("elementID").offsetWidth/2;`

**Value**     Integer pixel count.

**Default**     Element-specific.

Broadly speaking, provide the left and top coordinates of the element's box, but with minor variations with respect to the coordinate system context (vis-à-vis the offsetParent element) influenced by various operating system versions of IE and compatibility modes controlled by the DOCTYPE declaration. Implemented in Netscape 6 as a convenience, even though not part of the W3C DOM. See the section "About client- and offset- Properties" at the beginning of this chapter for details. For positioned elements, you should rely more on the element's style properties that control location in the document or browser viewing space.

**Example**
```
if (document.getElementById("elementID").offsetLeft <= 20 &&
document.getElementById("elementID").offsetTop <=40) {
    ...
}
```

**Value**     Integer pixel count.

**Default**     Element-specific.

Returns a reference to the object that is the current element's offset positioning context. For most elements on an IE page and all elements in a Netscape 6 page, this is the body object. But elements in IE that are wrapped in div elements or are cells of a table have other parents. Moreover, for complex nested elements, you will find wide variations in the object returned by this property, depending on browser version. For example, the offsetParent property of a td element is the next outermost tr element in IE 4 for Windows, and the table element for later versions of IE for Windows and all versions of IE for the Macintosh. Netscape 6 still regards the body element as the offsetParent of the td element. See the section "About client- and offset- Properties" at the beginning of this chapter for an example of using this property to calculate the precise position of an inline element.

**Example**
```
var containerLeft = document.getElementById("elementID")offsetParent.offsetLeft;
```

**Value**          Object reference.

**Default**        body object.

## outerHTML

NN *n/a*     IE *4*     DOM *n/a*

*Read/Write*

Indicates the rendered text and HTML tags (i.e., all source code), including the start and end tags, of the current element. If you want only the rendered text, see outerText. For the source code that excludes the current element's tags, see innerHTML. A change to this property that includes HTML tags is rendered through the HTML parser, as if the new value were part of the original source code. You may change this property only after the document has fully loaded, and, in the process, you can even change the type of element it is or replace the element with straight text content. Changes to the outerHTML property are not reflected in the source code when you view the source in the browser. To add to existing HTML, see the insertAdjacentHTML() method. This property is not supported in many objects in the Macintosh version of IE 4. The W3C DOM equivalent requires extensive manipulation of node-level objects, as shown in Chapter 5.

**Example**
```
document.getElementById("elementID").outerHTML =
    "<acronym id="quotes">NI<i>M</i>BY</acronym>";
```

**Value**          String that may or may not include HTML tags.

**Default**        Empty string.

## outerText

NN *n/a*     IE *4*     DOM *n/a*

*Read/Write*

Indicates the rendered text (but not any tags) of the current element. If you want the rendered text as well as the element's HTML tags, see outerHTML. Any changes to this property are not rendered through the HTML parser, meaning that any HTML tags you include are treated as displayable text content only. You may change this property only after the document has fully loaded. Changes to the outerText property are not reflected in the source code when you view the source in the browser. This property is not supported in many objects in the Macintosh version of IE 4.

**Example**        `document.getElementById("elementID").outerText = "UNESCO";`

**Value**          String.

**Default**        Empty string.

Shared DOM Reference

# ownerDocument

Returns a reference to the document object that contains the current node. Potentially helpful for functions that act on object references retrieved from event properties or passed as ID strings. The corresponding IE property is document.

**Example**        var currDoc = document.getElementById("*elementID*").ownerDocument;

**Value**          document object reference.

**Default**        The current document object.

# parentElement

Returns a reference to the next outermost element in the HTML containment hierarchy. An element's HTML parent is not necessarily the same as the object returned by the offsetParent property. The parentElement concerns itself strictly with source code containment, while the offsetParent property looks to the next outermost element that is used as the coordinate system for measuring the location of the current element. For example, if the main document contains a p element with an em element nested inside, the em element has two parents. The p element is the returned parentElement value (due to the HTML source code containment), while the body element is the returned offsetParent value (due to coordinate space containment).

You can jump multiple parent levels by cascading parentElement properties, as in:

    document.getElementById("*elementID*").parentElement.parentElement;

You can then use references to access a parent element's properties or methods.

The corresponding property for the W3C DOM is parentNode.

**Example**

document.getElementById("*elementID*").parentElement.style.fontSize = "14pt";

**Value**          Element object reference.

**Default**        Element-specific.

# parentNode

Returns a reference to the next outermost node (usually an element) that acts as a container to the current node in the document tree. The relationship between the current node and its parent is purely structural, and is not concerned with positioning context. A parent node is one that completely encases the current node—not to be confused with sibling nodes, which, at best, reside on just one side of the current node. You can use the same cascading tricks as shown for the IE parentElement property, but it is hazardous to completely equate results from the element-centric IE-only properties with results from the

W3C DOM node-centric properties (even though recent IE versions support both views of the world).

**Example**
```
if (document.getElementById("elementID").parentNode.nodeType == 1) {
    document.getElementById("elementID").parentNode.style.fontSize = "14pt";
}
```

| **Value** | Element object reference. |
|---|---|
| **Default** | Node-specific. |

## parentTextEdit

NN *n/a*   IE 4   DOM *n/a*
*Read-only*

Returns a reference to the next highest element up the HTML containment hierarchy that is of a type that allows a TextRange object to be created with it. This property may have to reach through many levels to find a suitable object. This property always returns null in IE for the Macintosh (through Version 5.1) because of lack of support for text ranges.

**Example**
```
var rangeElement = document.getElementById("elementID").parentTextEdit;
var rng = rangeElement.createTextRange( );
```

| **Value** | Element object reference. |
|---|---|
| **Default** | body object. |

## prefix

See localName.

## previousSibling

See nextSibling.

## readyState

NN *n/a*   IE 4   DOM *n/a*
*Read-only*

Returns the current download status of the object's content. If a script (especially one initiated by a user event) can perform some actions while the document is still loading, but must avoid other actions until the entire page has loaded, this property provides intermediate information about the loading process. You should use its value in condition tests. The value of this property changes during loading as the loading state changes. Each change of the property value fires an onReadyStateChange event (the event does not bubble).

When introduced with IE 4, the property was available for only the document, embed, img, link, object, script, and style objects. IE 5 expanded coverage to all HTML element objects.

**Example**

```
if (document.readyState == "loading") {
    //statements for alternate handling while loading
}
```

**Value**

For all but the object element, one of the following values (as strings): uninitialized | loading | loaded | interactive | complete. Some elements may allow the user to interact with partial content, in which case the property may return interactive until all loading has completed. Not all element types return all values in sequence during the loading process. The object element returns numeric values for these five states. They range from 0 (uninitialized) to 4 (complete).

**Default**     None.

## recordNumber

NN *n/a*     IE *4*     DOM *n/a*

*Read-only*

Used with IE data binding, returns an integer representing the record within the data set that generated the element (i.e., an element whose content is filled via data binding). Values of this property can be used to extract a specific record from an Active Data Objects (ADO) record set (see recordset property). Although this property is defined for all IE element objects, the other properties related to data binding belong to a subset of elements.

**Example**

```
<script for="tableTemplate" event="onclick">
    myDataCollection.recordset.absoluteposition = this.recordNumber;
    ...
</script>
```

**Value**       Integer.

**Default**     null

## runtimeStyle

NN *n/a*     IE *5*     DOM *n/a*

*Read/Write*

Returns a style object whose individual style properties convey values only if they are explicitly set via the regular style sheet processes. Unlike the currentStyle object, system default style sheet properties are not reflected. You can set individual style properties of this runtimeStyle object, but doing so transcends (some might say violates) normal cascading precedence. Any property you assign by script overrides all other settings for that style property governing that element, including values assigned to the element tag's style attribute and style property. For example, if you assign the value red to an element's style.color property, and assign the value green to the same element's runtimeStyle.color property, the element's text appears in green, even though the more specific style.color property still preserves the red value. At that point the element's currentStyle.color property also returns green, because that is the effective style governing the element at that instant.

You can use the runtimeStyle object to assign multiple style properties by reassigning a CSS syntax rule to the runtimeStyle.cssText property. Assign an empty string to the cssText property to remove all in-line attribute values, allowing the regular style sheet cascade to control the element's effective style.

### Example

```
document.getElementById("elementID").runtimeStyle.cssText =
  "border: 5px blue solid";
```

**Value**       style object reference.

**Default**     The effective style object and its explicitly defined style attribute values.

## scopeName, tagUrn

NN *n/a*    IE *5(Win)*    DOM *n/a*
*Read-only*

For custom elements employing XML namespaces, the scopeName property returns the identifier that associates the tag name with a namespace that is defined elsewhere in the document via the xmlns attribute. All plain HTML elements return a value of HTML for this property. The tagUrn property returns the URI specified for the namespace. The corresponding properties in the W3C DOM are prefix and namespaceURI.

### Example

```
var allTitles = document.getElementsByTagName("title");
for (var i = 0; i < allTitles.length; i++) {
    if (allTitles[i].scopeName == "libBook" &&
        allTitles[i].tagUrn.indexOf("catalog.umv.edu") != -1) {
        // process title elements from the desired namespace here
    }
}
```

**Value**       Strings.

**Default**     HTML for scopeName; empty string for tagUrn.

## scrollHeight, scrollWidth

NN *7*    IE *4*    DOM *n/a*
*Read-only*

Originally implemented in IE 4 for elements that either scrolled or influenced an element's scroll (body, button, caption, div, fieldset, legend, marquee, and textarea), these properties return the pixel dimensions of an element, including elements that are larger than the viewable area in the browser window. This is in contrast to the clientHeight and clientWidth properties for scrollable elements, which return dimensions of only visible portions of the element. IE for the Macintosh, however, interprets the intent of the scroll-properties differently, returning the dimensions of the visible portion.

Starting in IE 5 for Windows, all HTML elements have these properties, and the values for nonscrolling elements are the same as the offsetHeight and offsetWidth properties. Netscape 7 implements these properties for all elements, returning the height and width of the element, whether or not it's in view. The important point is that for key elements, such as the body, the properties mean different things and can disrupt cross-platform operation.

**Example**  var midPoint = document.body.scrollHeight/2;

**Value**  Positive integer or zero.

**Default**  None.


## scrollLeft, scrollTop

NN *7*  IE *4*  DOM *n/a*
*Read/Write*

Provide the distance in pixels between the actual left or top edge of the element's physical content and the left or top edge of the visible portion of the content. Setting these properties allows you to use a script to adjust the scrolling of content within a scrollable container, such as text in a textarea element or an entire document in the browser window or frame. When the content is not scrolled, both values are zero. Setting the scrollTop property to 15 scrolls the document upward by 15 pixels in the window; the scrollLeft property is unaffected unless explicitly changed. The property values change as the user adjusts the scrollbars. This is important for some event-driven positioning tasks in IE for Windows because the coordinate system for event offset measurements are with respect to the visible area of a page in the browser window. You must add document.body scrolling factors to align event coordinates with body content positions (see the element dragging example in Chapter 6). Starting with IE 5 for Windows, the scrollLeft and scrollTop properties are available for all HTML element objects, but values for unscrollable elements are zero.

**Example**  document.body.scrollTop = 40;

**Value**  Positive integer or zero.

**Default**  0


## sourceIndex

NN *n/a*  IE *4*  DOM *n/a*
*Read-only*

Returns the zero-based index of the element among all elements in the document. Elements are numbered according to their source code order, with the first element given a sourceIndex of zero.

**Example**

var whichElement = document.getElementById("*elementID*").sourceIndex;

**Value**  Positive integer or zero.

**Default**  Element-specific.

Indicates the style object associated with the element, as set by values explicitly assigned to the element's style attribute in the tag. In W3C DOM object terminology, this object more specifically is called a CSSStyleDeclaration object. For most style sheet scripting purposes, however, you can treat the IE and Navigator style object as similar objects. This property is the gateway to reading and writing individual style sheet property settings for an element. To read the effective style sheet properties governing an element (including imported style sheet attributes), see the currentStyle property earlier in this chapter (for IE) and the window.getComputedStyle( ) method (for Netscape 6).

| | |
|---|---|
| **Example** | document.getElementById("*elementID*").style.fontSize = "14pt"; |
| **Value** | style object. |
| **Default** | None. |

This is a number that indicates the sequence of this element within the tabbing order of all focusable elements in the document. Tabbing order follows a strict set of rules. Elements that have values other than zero assigned to their tabIndex properties are first in line when a user starts tabbing in a page. Focus starts with the element with the lowest tabIndex value and proceeds in order to the highest value, regardless of physical location on the page or in the document. If two elements have the same tabIndex values, the element that comes earlier in the document receives focus first. Next come all elements that either don't support the tabIndex property or have the value set to zero. These elements receive focus in the order in which they appear in the document.

The W3C DOM and Netscape 6 limit the tabIndex property to the following element objects: a, area, button, input, object, select, textarea. To this list, IE 4 adds applet, body, div, embed, isindex, marquee, span, table, and td. IE 5 adds every other renderable element. A negative value in IE (only) removes an element from tabbing order entirely.

Links and anchors cannot be tabbed to with the Mac version of IE 4, so the tabIndex property for a element objects is ignored in that version.

| | |
|---|---|
| **Example** | document.getElementById("link3").tabIndex = 6; |
| **Value** | Integer. |
| **Default** | 0 |

Returns the name of the tag of the current element. Tag names are always returned in all uppercase letters for purposes of string comparisons, regardless of source code style or DOCTYPE declaration.

| Example | `var theTag = document.getElementById("elementID").tagName;` |
|---|---|
| **Value** | String. |
| **Default** | Element-specific. |

## tagUrn

See scopeName.

## title

NN 6    IE 4    DOM 1

*Read/Write*

Provides an advisory description of the element. When the element is one that has a physical presence on the page, the browser renders the value of this property as a floating text label when the cursor rests atop the element for a moment. The size, font characteristics, and color of this label are not within control of scripting.

| Example | `document.getElementById("elementID").title = "Hot stuff!";` |
|---|---|
| **Value** | String. |
| **Default** | Empty string. |

## uniqueID

NN *n/a*    IE *5(Win)*    DOM *n/a*

*Read-only*

Returns an identifier string that is unique among all object identifiers on the page. Used primarily to assign an ID to newly created elements when you don't mind the browser using its own naming scheme to invent the name. Most commonly used as a property of the document object, but it is accessible through any existing element object reference. The identifier is perfectly valid for use as string a parameter to methods that require an element ID.

**Example**

```
var newElem = document.createElement("p");
newElem.id = document.uniqueID;
```

| **Value** | String. |
|---|---|
| **Default** | Browser-generated. |

## addBehavior( )

NN *n/a*    IE *5(Win)*    DOM *n/a*

addBehavior("*URL*")

Attaches an internal or external IE behavior to the current element. After a script attaches the behavior, the element responds to events defined for the behavior (if any), and provides access to properties and methods associated with the behavior. An external behavior file must be served from the same domain (and protocol) as the current page. For more information on applying IE/Windows behaviors, visit *http://msdn.microsoft.com/workshop/ author/behaviors/overview.asp*.

## Returned Value

Integer serial number usable as a parameter for the removeBehavior( ) method.

## Parameters

*URL*

> For external behaviors, a relative or absolute URL to the *.htc* file on the server. For internal behaviors, a special format as described in the next item.

#default#*behaviorName*

> where *behaviorName* is one of the following built-in behaviors: anchorClick | anim | clientCaps | download | homePage | httpFolder | mediaBar | saveFavorite | saveHistory | saveSnapshot | userData.

## addEventListener( )                                        NN 6    IE *n/a*    DOM 2

addEventListener("*eventType*", *listenerFunction*, *useCapture*)

Binds an event handler function to the current node so that the function executes when an event of a particular type arrives at the node either as event target or during event propagation. Note that W3C DOM events propagate through text nodes, as well as element nodes. The node listens for the event type either during event capture or event bubbling propagation, depending upon the setting of the Boolean third parameter. You may invoke this method multiple times for the same node but with different parameter values to assign as many event handling behaviors as you like, but only one listener function may be invoked for the same event and propagation type. If the event listener is added on a temporary basis, it may be removed via the removeEventListener( ) method.

## Returned Value    None.

## Parameters

*eventType*

> A string of one event type (without the "on" prefix) known to the browser's object model. The W3C DOM knows the following event types (and Netscape 6 implements most of them):

| | | |
|---|---|---|
| abort | blur | change |
| click | DOMActivate | DOMAttrModified |
| DOMCharacterDataModified | DOMFocusIn | DOMFocusOut |
| DOMNodeInserted | DOMNodeInsertedIntoDocument | DOMNodeRemoved |
| DOMNodeRemovedFromDocument | DOMSubtreeModified | error |
| focus | load | mousedown |
| mousemove | mouseout | mouseover |
| mouseup | reset | resize |
| scroll | select | submit |
| unload | | |

*listenerFunction*

> A reference to the function to execute when the node hears the event type in the specified propagation mode. As this is a reference to a function object, do not surround the name in quotes, nor include the parentheses of the function. At execution time, the

browser automatically passes the current event object as a parameter to the listener function.

*useCapture*

A Boolean value. If true, the node listens for the event type only while the event propagates toward the target node (in event capture node). If false, the node listens only when the event bubbles outward from the event target. If the current node is the target of the event, either Boolean value may be used.

## appendChild( )

NN 6    IE 5    DOM 1

`appendChild(nodeObject)`

Inserts a new node after the end of the last child node of the current node object. The current node object must be capable of containing child nodes, otherwise the method throws an exception. This method is the most common way to append a dynamically created element, text node, or document fragment to an existing element, such as a script might do when assembling a chunk of new content for a document. But if the node reference passed as a parameter with the appendChild( ) method points to an existing node in the document tree, that node is first removed from the tree, and then appended to the end of the list of child nodes in the current object. This provides a shortcut way to move a node from one location to the end of a container.

Appending one text node as a sibling to an existing text node does not join the two text nodes together. To combine all sibling text nodes into one large text node, invoke the parent's normalize( ) method.

**Returned Value**    Reference to the appended node.

**Parameters**

*nodeObject*

Reference to any node object of a type that makes sense to become a child of the current object. It may be from dynamically-generated content (e.g., text node, element, or document fragment) or a node from the existing document tree.

## applyElement( )

NN *n/a*    IE *5(Win)*    DOM *n/a*

`applyElement(elementObject[, type])`

Inserts a new element as either a child element of the current object or as the new parent of the current object, depending on the value of the second parameter. The default behavior is to wrap the current object with the new element. But you may also choose to insert the new element as a child element. In this case, if the current object is in the document tree (as opposed to simply floating in memory after being created with document.createElement( )) and already has child elements nested inside it, the newly applied element is inserted in such a way that the previous children become children of the inserted element (i.e., grandchildren of the current object). This wrapping behavior is unique among IE element insertion methods and can have significant impact on the document tree. Use with caution.

**Returned Value**    Reference to the newly added element object.

**Parameters**

*elementObject*

Reference to any dynamically-generated or existing element object from the document tree.

*type*

Optional string value: inside (the new element becomes the sole, first child of the current object); outside (the new element becomes the parent of the current object). The default is outside.

## attachEvent( ) NN *n/a*   IE *5(Win)*   DOM *n/a*

attachEvent("*eventName*", *functionReference*)

Binds an event handler function to an element object for a particular event type. Similar in operation to the W3C DOM addEventListener( ) method, the IE attachEvent( ) method is used primarily for IE behaviors. Binding events through element object event handler properties is a better cross-browser approach for regular HTML pages. If you bind an event handler through the attachEvent( ) method, you can disengage the binding via the detachEvent( ) method.

**Returned Value**    Boolean value true if the binding is successful.

**Parameters**

*eventName*

String version of the event name, including the "on" prefix. Applicable event types include any event from IE/Windows extensive list of shared event types shown later in this section. Although not case-sensitive, all-lowercase values are recommended.

*functionReference*

A reference to the function to execute when the element receives the event either as the event target or through event propagation. As this is a reference to a function object, do not surround the name in quotes, nor include the parentheses of the function. No parameters may be passed to the function.

## blur( ) NN *2*   IE *3*   DOM *1*

Removes focus from the current object, at which time the object's onblur event fires. Note that the range of elements capable of focus and blur (both the event and method) is limited in all browsers except for more recent versions of IE (see the shared tabindex attribute in Chapter 8). Most reliably for backward compatibility, apply the blur( ) method to blatantly focusable elements, such as text input and textarea elements. Assigning the attribute onfocus="this.blur( );" to a text input element, for instance, is a crude but effective backward-compatible way to largely disable a field for browsers that do not provide genuine element disabling.

Use blur( ) and focus( ) methods in moderation on the same page. You can inadvertently trigger endless loops of blurring and focusing if alert dialog boxes are involved along the way. Moreover, be aware that when you invoke the blur( ) method on one object, some other object (perhaps the window object) receives an onfocus event.

**Returned Value**    None.

**Parameters**    None.

## clearAttributes( )                 NN *n/a*    IE *5(Win)*    DOM *n/a*

Removes all attributes from the current element except for the id and name attributes (if specified). Any rendering characteristics influenced by the element's attributes that are removed also no longer apply to the element.

**Returned Value**    None.

**Parameters**    None.

## click( )                 NN *2*    IE *4*    DOM *1*

Simulates the click action of a user on the element. Fires an onclick event in Internet Explorer 4 and later and Navigator 4 and later. Note in browsers prior to IE 4 and Netscape 6, not all elements are capable of the click( ) method (or onclick event). Also, don't expect all elements that normally change their graphical state when clicked by the user to simulate the same state change during the scripted click. For example, some Macintosh browser versions fail to change the checked state of a checkbox when a script invokes a click( ) method on the checkbox. In this case, invoke the click( ) method only if an onclick event handler executes some code; but also set the checked property of the checkbox as desired.

**Returned Value**    None.

**Parameters**    None.

## cloneNode( )                 NN *6*    IE *5*    DOM *1*
cloneNode(*deepBoolean*)

Copies the current node to memory, and returns a reference to the node copy (which is not part of the document tree). Because the clone is a full-fledged node, you can perform additional node-related operations on the clone before inserting the node elsewhere in the document tree. Beware, however, that id attributes of cloned elements are the same as the original. Change the id properties of those elements in the fragment before reintroducing the clone into the document tree.

The Boolean parameter determines whether the clone is of only the current node or the current node and all nested nodes. Note that if you clone a simple element container and set the parameter to false, the text node inside the element does not become part of the cloned copy.

**Returned Value**    Reference to document fragment in memory.

## Parameters

*deepBoolean*

> Boolean value that controls whether the copy includes all nested nodes (true) or only the current node (false). Parameter is optional in IE, with a default value of false.

## componentFromPoint( )                              NN *n/a*    IE *5(Win)*    DOM *n/a*

componentFromPoint(*x*, *y*)

Returns a string that denotes where the coordinate points are in the element. For elements that display scroll bars, the returned value reveals precisely which piece of the scroll bar is at the coordinate location. If you engage Microsoft's document editing mode, additional pieces, such as draggable size handlers, are also indicated in the returned value. For areas of elements not displaying scroll bars or edit handles, you can also determine whether the coordinate is inside or outside the element, which is handy for collision detection between event coordinates and the element.

The most common source for coordinate parameter values is the event object, especially the event.clientX and event.clientY properties. You can apply these values directly, as in:

```
var where = event.srcElement.componentFromPoint(event.clientX, event.clientY);
```

## Returned Value

One of the string values in the following table.

| Returned string values | Description |
| --- | --- |
| empty string | Inside the element content area |
| outside | Outside the element content area |
| handleBottom | Edit mode resize handle at bottom |
| handleBottomLeft | Edit mode resize handle at bottom left |
| handleBottomRight | Edit mode resize handle at bottom right |
| handleLeft | Edit mode resize handle at left |
| handleRight | Edit mode resize handle at right |
| handleTop | Edit mode resize handle at top |
| handleTopLeft | Edit mode resize handle at top left |
| handleTopRight | Edit mode resize handle at top right |
| scrollbarDown | Scroll bar down arrow |
| scrollbarHThumb | Scroll bar horizontal thumb control |
| scrollbarLeft | Scroll bar left arrow |
| scrollbarPageDown | Scroll bar page-down region |
| scrollbarPageLeft | Scroll bar page-left region |
| scrollbarPageRight | Scroll bar page-right region |
| scrollbarPageUp | Scroll bar page-up region |
| scrollbarRight | Scroll bar right arrow |

| Returned string values | Description |
| --- | --- |
| scrollbarUp | Scroll bar up arrow |
| scrollbarVThumb | Scroll bar vertical thumb control |

**Parameters**

*x*   Positive or negative pixel count relative to the top of the screen.

*y*   Positive or negative pixel count relative to the left edge of the screen

## contains( )                                    NN *n/a*   IE 4   DOM *n/a*

contains(*elementReference*)

Returns whether the current element contains the specified element.

**Returned Value**   Boolean value: true | false.

**Parameters**

*elementReference*

A fully formed element object reference (e.g., document.getElementById("myDIV")).

## createControlRange( )                          NN *n/a*   IE *5(Win)*   DOM *n/a*

Though implemented for many HTML element objects, this method should be used only with the document.body object. See the createControlRange( ) method of the body object for details.

## detachEvent( )                                 NN *n/a*   IE *5(Win)*   DOM *n/a*

detachEvent("*eventName*", *functionReference*)

Removes a previously attached event handler function binding from an element object for a particular event type. Similar in operation to the W3C DOM removeEventListener( ) method, the IE detachEvent( ) method is used primarily for IE behaviors. Binding events through element object event handler properties is a better cross-browser approach for regular HTML pages. The event property equivalent of the detachEvent( ) method is to assign null to the event property.

**Returned Value**   None.

**Parameters**

*eventName*

String version of the event name, including the "on" prefix. Applicable event types include any event from IE/Windows extensive list of shared event types shown later in this section. Although not case-sensitive, all-lowercase values are recommended.

*functionReference*

A reference to the function to execute when the element receives the event either as the event target or through event propagation. As this is a reference to a function object, do not surround the name in quotes, nor include the parentheses of the function.

# dispatchEvent( )

dispatchEvent(*eventObjectReference*)

Directs an event to fire on the current node. Used primarily when artificially creating an event by script, and then sending that event to a node for its event listener function to execute. The event object passed as a parameter must have an event type specified, but other properties of the event object (such as mouse event location or character key) may also be set when initializing the newly created event object. The following script fragment creates a generic mouse event, initializes the event as a mousedown type that bubbles and is cancelable, and sends the event to an element with the ID myNode:

```
var newEvt = document.createEvent("MouseEvents");
newEvt.initEvent("mousedown", true, true);
document.getElementById("myNode").dispatchEvent(newEvt);
```

See the W3C DOM Event, MouseEvent, and UIEvent objects for more details. The corresponding method for IE/Windows-only is fireEvent( ).

## Returned Value

The W3C DOM specification indicates a Boolean value of true is returned if any event listener function that executes in response to the dispatchEvent( ) method also invokes the event.preventDefault( ) method. The method returns a value starting with Netscape 7.

## Parameters

*eventObjectReference*
    A reference to an event object. Most commonly this object is created and initialized by associated script statements.

# doScroll( )

doScroll(["*scrollAction*"])

Controls the scrolling of any element that displays scroll bars. Because most HTML elements can use style sheets to hardwire a height and width, while having the overflow style attribute to scroll, the doScroll( ) method is applicable to any element.

Rather than scrolling to a coordinate position, the doScroll( ) method simulates the click on a scroll bar control or region as directed by the parameter. Each invocation of the method triggers the onscroll event for the element. Invoke this method through a separate function that gets called from setTimeout( ) if the script sequence leading up to the scroll involves reflowing of the page (to let IE catch up with rendering).

## Returned Value    None.

## Parameters

*scrollAction*
    The string name of one scroll bar region. If omitted, the default value applied is scrollbarDown. Most regions have interchangable long and short names, as shown in the following list:

```
scrollbarDown (or down)
scrollbarHThumb
scrollbarLeft (or left)
```

```
scrollbarPageDown (or pageDown)
scrollbarPageLeft (or pageLeft)
scrollbarPageRight (or pageRight)
scrollbarPageUp (or up)
scrollbarVThumb
```

## dragDrop( )                                    NN *n/a*   IE *5.5(Win)*   DOM *n/a*

Triggers an ondragstart event for the current element, allowing a mouse event handler
function to initiate script execution related to the start of dragging even before the user has
actually begun to drag the element. Returns a Boolean true when the user releases the
mouse button after the physical drag operation.

**Returned Value**    Boolean value: true | false.

**Parameters**        None.

## fireEvent( )                                   NN *n/a*   IE *5.5(Win)*   DOM *n/a*

fireEvent("*eventType*"[, *eventObjectReference*])

Directs an event to fire on the current element. Used primarily when artificially creating an
event by script, and then sending that event to an element for its event handler function to
execute. You can send a simple event of any type you wish. Such a generic event object has
four properties automatically assigned to it:

```
cancelBubble = false;
returnValue = true;
srcElement = reference-to-current-element;
type = event-type-specified-as-the-parameter;
```

Or you may pass along an event object that has more details associated with it, such as the
event location or character key. The following script fragment creates a generic event
object, assigns some properties to it, and then sends the event (as an onclick event) to an
element with the ID myElem:

```
var newEvt = document.createEventObject();
newEvt.clientX = 50;
newEvt.clientY = 300;
newEvt.cancelBubble = true;
document.getElementById("myElem").fireEvent("onclick", newEvt);
```

See the IE event object for more details. The corresponding W3C DOM method is
dispatchEvent( ).

**Returned Value**

Boolean value (true | false) signifying whether the event fired successfully.

**Parameters**

*eventType*
> String value of the "on" version of the event name (e.g., "onmousedown").

*eventObjectReference*
> An optional reference to an event object, usually one that is created anew.

## focus( )

Gives focus from the current object, at which time the object's onfocus event fires. Note that the range of elements capable of focus and blur (both the event and method) is limited in all browsers except for more recent versions of IE (see the shared tabindex attribute in Chapter 8). Most reliably for backward compatibility, apply the focus( ) method to blatantly focusable elements, such as text input and textarea elements.

To give a text box focus and pre-select all the text in the box, use the sequence of focus( ) and select( ) methods on the element. If this sequence is to occur after windows change (such as after an alert dialog box closes), place the methods in a separate function, and invoke this function through the setTimeout( ) method following the alert( ) method for the dialog. This allows IE/Windows to sequence statement execution correctly.

**Returned Value**   None.

**Parameters**   None.


## getAdjacentText( )

getAdjacentText("*where*")

Returns the text (excluding HTML tags and attributes) in and around the current element in the direction indicated by one of four parameter values. The text segment extends only until the next element start or end tag. For example, consider the following HTML:

```
<p>This is a very <span id="mySpan">short</span> paragraph.</p>
```

Invoking the getAdjacentText( ) method on the span element with each of the four parameter values yields the values as shown here:

```
document.getElementById("mySpan").getAdjacentText("beforeBegin")
    // returns: "This is a very "
document.getElementById("mySpan").getAdjacentText("afterBegin")
    // returns: "short"
document.getElementById("mySpan").getAdjacentText("beforeEnd")
    // returns: "short"
document.getElementById("mySpan").getAdjacentText("afterEnd")
    // returns: " paragraph."
```

In this case the afterBegin and beforeEnd parameters return the same value because no elements are inside the span element. Invoking the method on the outer p element and the afterBegin parameter yields the text up to the start of the span element. In some document tree structures, this method returns the equivalent of W3C DOM's child node nodeValue properties.

### Returned Value

String, which may contain leading or trailing spaces, depending on the structure of the text fragment inside the element.

### Parameters

*where*
  One of four constant string values (case-insensitive).

| Constant | Description |
|---|---|
| beforeBegin | Text in front of current element's start tag back to preceding tag |
| afterBegin | Text after current element's start tag until next (start or end) tag |
| beforeEnd | Text in front of current element's end tag back to the preceding (start or end) tag |
| afterEnd | Text after current element's end tag until next (start or end) tag |

## getAttribute( )                     NN 6    IE 4    DOM 1

getAttribute(*attributeName*)
getAttribute(*attributeName*[, *caseSensitivity*])

Returns the value of the named attribute within the current element. If the attribute is reflected in the object model as a property, this method returns the same value as when reading the object's property. This is the preferred method for reading an element object attribute (i.e., property) value under the W3C DOM.

The attribute name you pass as a parameter is not case-sensitive in current browsers. IE, however, provides an optional second parameter that lets you force case-sensitivity in the attribute naming. This might encourage the reuse of the same attribute name but with different case letters—an ill-advised practice.

See the setAttribute( ) method for assigning values to attributes and creating new attribute/value pairs.

**Returned Value**

The W3C DOM and Netscape 6 maintain attribute values exclusively as string data types. IE, however may return an attribute value as a string, number, or Boolean.

**Parameters**

*attributeName*

The (case-insensitive by default) attribute name used in the HTML tag (not including the = symbol). While IE lets you switch between case-sensitivity settings, Netscape 6 does not demand case-sensitivity. But given the trend toward case-sensitive XHTML, it is best to get into the case-sensitive habit.

*caseSensitivity*

An optional integer value for IE only. Default value is 0 (not case-sensitive). If 1, the attribute in the HTML tag must match the case of the *attributeName* parameter exactly for its value to be returned.

## getAttributeNode( )                   NN 6    IE 6    DOM 1

getAttributeNode(*attributeName*)

Returns a reference to the attribute node (Attr object) associated with the name. This type of node is the same kind that populates the array returned by an element's attributes property, but the getAttributeNode( ) method gives you direct access to the Attr node object by name. More helpful in XML documents, where an attribute can convey important data associated with the element. See the Attr object for details about that node type.

**Returned Value**     Reference to an Attr object.

**Parameters**

*attributeName*

> The attribute name used in the tag (not including the = symbol). Neither IE nor Navigator demands case-sensitivity. But given the trend toward case-sensitive XHTML, it is best to get into the case-sensitive habit.

## getAttributeNodeNS( )

getAttributeNodeNS("*namespaceURI*", "*localName*")

Returns a reference to the local-named `Attr` object with a matching namespace URI within the current element. This method works like `getAttributeNS( )` but accommodates attributes for XML documents that are labeled according to a namespace specification.

**Returned Value**   Reference to an `Attr` object.

**Parameters**

*namespaceURI*

> URI string matching a URI assigned to a label earlier in the document.

*localName*

> The local name portion of the attribute.

## getAttributeNS( )

getAttributeNS("*namespaceURI*", "*localName*")

Returns the value of the local-named attribute with a matching namespace URI within the current element. This method works like `getAttribute( )` but accommodates attributes for XML documents that are labeled according to a namespace specification. The following simple XML document uses a namespace for an attribute of the `libBook:title` element:

```
<?xml version="1.0" encoding="ISO-8859-1"?>
<results xmlns:libBook="http://catalog.umv.edu/schema">
<libBook:title libBook:rareBooks="true">De Principia</libBook:title>
</results>
```

To retrieve the value of the `libBook:rareBooks` attribute, the method for the element would include the `getAttributeNS( )` method call with the following parameters:

```
getAttributeNS("http://catalog.umv.edu/schema", "rareBooks")
```

**Returned Value**

The W3C DOM and Netscape 6 maintain attribute values exclusively as string data types.

**Parameters**

*namespaceURI*

> URI string matching a URI assigned to a label earlier in the document.

*localName*

> The local name portion of the attribute.

## getBoundingClientRect( )

Returns an IE TextRectangle object that describes the rectangular space occupied by the current element (including non-text elements, such as images). The rectangle (which has properties for top, right, bottom, and left coordinates) is as wide as the widest point of the content (e.g, the longest line of a word-wrapped paragraph) and as tall as the sum of all content. To obtain measures of rectangles for individual lines of a text element, see the getClientRects( ) method.

**Returned Value**    TextRectangle object.

**Parameters**    None.

## getClientRects( )

Returns an array of IE TextRectangle objects. Each entry of the array is a TextRectangle object for a single line of a multiline text element. Lines that have different font sizes or line heights will be encased by rectangles that are of different heights. See the TextRectangle object for its properties. To obtain one TextRectangle object for an entire element, use the getBoundingClientRect( ) method.

**Returned Value**    Array of TextRectangle objects.

**Parameters**    None.

## getElementsByTagName( )

getElementsByTagName("*tagName*")

Returns an array of all descendant elements of the current element whose tag name matches the parameter of the method. Elements in the array include children, grandchildren, and so on, and are in the source code order. The current element is not included in the array. If there are no matches, the array has a length of zero.

Netscape 6, IE 5/Macintosh, and IE 6/Windows let you specify the quoted asterisk wildcard character as a parameter to return an array of all descendant elements, regardless of tag name. Be aware, however, that different browsers may have slight differences in their document tree structures that result in wildcard parameter array lengths that don't match each other.

**Returned Value**    Array of zero or more element references.

**Parameters**

*tagName*

> The (case-insensitive by default) tag name for desired elements. Or an asterisk that acts as a wildcard character to signify all tag names.

## getElementsByTagNameNS( )

getElementsByTagNameNS("*namespaceURI*", "*localName*")

Returns an array of all descendant elements of the current element which have a local name that matches the second parameter of the method, and a namespace URI (assigned elsewhere in the document as a namespace declaration) that matches the first method parameter. Elements in the array include children, grandchildren, and so on, and are in the source code order. The current element is not included in the array. If there are no matches, the array has a length of zero. Applies primarily to XML documents.

**Returned Value**   Array of zero or more element references.

**Parameters**

*namespaceURI*
> URI string matching a URI assigned to a label earlier in the document.

*localName*
> The local name portion of the tag name.


## getExpression( )

getExpression("*attributeName*")

Returns a string version of the script expression used in a corresponding setExpression( ) method call on an attribute of the current element. The setExpression( ) method assigns a script expression used to calculate the value assigned to the attribute. The expression is calculated automatically in response to some event types and to the document.recalc( ) method. To read the current value of the attribute, you must use the eval( ) function on the string returned by the getExpression( ) method. See the setExpression( ) method later in this section.

**Returned Value**   String.

**Parameters**

*attributeName*
> Name of the current element's attribute to which an expression is assigned by the setExpression( ) method.


## hasAttribute( )

hasAttribute("*attributeName*")

Returns a Boolean value true if the current element has an attribute whose name matches the method parameter.

**Returned Value**   Boolean value: true | false.

**Parameters**

*attributeName*
> The case-sensitive attribute name to search for.

## hasAttributeNS( ) NN 6    IE n/a    DOM 2

hasAttributeNS("*namespaceURI*", "*localName*")

Returns a Boolean value true if the current element has an attribute with a local name that matches the method's second parameter, and a namespace URI (assigned elsewhere in the document as a namespace declaration) that matches the first method parameter.

**Returned Value**    Boolean value: true | false.

**Parameters**

*namespaceURI*
    URI string matching a URI assigned to a label earlier in the document.
*localName*
    The local name portion of the attribute name.

## hasAttributes( ) NN 6    IE n/a    DOM 1

Returns a Boolean value true if the current element has any attributes explicitly assigned within the tag.

**Returned Value**    Boolean value: true | false.

**Parameters**    None.

## hasChildNodes( ) NN 6    IE 5    DOM 1

Returns a Boolean value true if the current node contains one or more child nodes.

**Returned Value**    Boolean value: true | false.

**Parameters**    None.

## insertAdjacentElement( ) NN n/a    IE 5(Win)    DOM n/a

insertAdjacentElement("*where*", *elementObjectReference*)

Inserts an element object into the designated position relative to the current element. Typically, the element object about to be inserted is created separately (for example, via document.createElement( )) or it may be a reference to an object already in the document tree, and the method essentially moves the object to its new location with the help of the insertAdjacentElement( ) method.

The destination is governed by the first attribute, which consists of one of four values that determine where the insertion occurs, as follows.

| Position | Insert new element |
|---|---|
| BeforeBegin | Before start tag of current element, as a previous sibling |
| AfterBegin | Immediately after current element's start tag, as a first child element |
| BeforeEnd | Immediately before current element's end tag, as a last child element |
| AfterEnd | After end tag of current element, as a next sibling |

Although the effects on the document element tree are well-defined, the rendered result varies with the combination of inline and block elements you use as the current and inserted element objects. Inserting a block-level element (such as a div or p element) causes that element to render on the next line and at the left edge of the block-level positioning context (such as the body or td element). Applying the W3C DOM appendChild( ) method on elements is the equivalent of the insertAdjacentElement( ) method with the beforeEnd position parameter.

**Returned Value**    Reference to the inserted element object.

**Parameters**

*where*
> String value of one of the following case-insensitive constants: BeforeBegin | AfterBegin | BeforeEnd | AfterEnd. The first and last locations are outside the HTML tags of the current element; the middle two locations are between the tags and element content.

*elementObjectReference*
> Reference to any valid element object either existing in the document tree or created dynamically.

## insertAdjacentHTML( )                        NN *n/a*    IE 4    DOM *n/a*
insertAdjacentHTML("*where*", *HTMLText*)

Inserts a text string into the designated position relative to the element's existing HTML. If HTML tags are part of the text to be inserted, the browser interprets the tags and performs the desired rendering. This method is not supported in many objects in the Macintosh version of IE 4.

**Returned Value**    None.

**Parameters**

*where*
> String value of one of the following constants: BeforeBegin | AfterBegin | BeforeEnd | AfterEnd. The first and last locations are outside the HTML tags of the current element; the middle two locations are between the tags and element content.

*HTMLText*
> String value of the text and/or HTML to be inserted in the desired location.

## insertAdjacentText( )                         NN *n/a*    IE 4    DOM *n/a*
insertAdjacentText("*where*", *text*)

Inserts text into the designated position relative to the element's existing HTML. If HTML tags are part of the text to be inserted, the tags are shown literally on the page. This method is not supported in many objects in the Macintosh version of IE 4.

**Returned Value**    None.

**Parameters**

*where*
> String value of one of the following constants: BeforeBegin | AfterBegin | BeforeEnd | AfterEnd. The first and last locations are outside the HTML tags of the current element; the middle two locations are between the tags and element content.

*HTMLText*
> String value of the text to be inserted in the desired location.

## insertBefore( )                                           NN 6    IE 5    DOM 1

insertBefore(*newChildNode, referenceChildNodeOrNull*)

Inserts a node as a child of the current node (usually the current node is an element) before one of the other child nodes of the current node. The new child can be a reference to an existing node in the document tree (in which case it is removed from its original position when this method is invoked). The child node may also be created anew as any valid DOM node type, including a document fragment (which may hold HTML tags) or Attr (the latter implemented for Netscape 6 and IE 6).

The second parameter allows you to specify a reference point among existing child nodes, in front of which the new child node is inserted. Alternatively, if you specify null as the second parameter (or omit the parameter in IE), the new node is inserted as the last child of the current node—the same result as the appendChild( ) method.

**Returned Value**    Reference to the inserted node object.

**Parameters**

*newChildNode*
> Any valid node object that can be a child of a parent node.

*referenceChildNodeOrNull*
> Any child node of the current node, or null.

## isSupported( )                                            NN 6    IE *n/a*    DOM 2

isSupported("*feature*", "*version*")

Returns a Boolean true if the current node supports (i.e., conforms to the required specifications of) a stated W3C DOM module and version. While the document.implementation object's hasFeature( ) method performs the same test, it does so on the entire browser application. The isSupported( ) method performs the test on an individual node, allowing you to verify feature support for the current node type. Parameter values for isSupported( ) are the same as for document.implementation.hasFeature( ).

It is up to the browser maker to validate that the DOM implemented in the browser conforms with each module before allowing the browser to return true for the module. That doesn't necessarily mean that the implementation is bug-free or consistent with other implementations. Caveat scriptor.

In theory, you could use this method to verify module support prior to accessing a property or invoking a method, as in the following fragment that assumes myElem is a reference to an element node:

```
if (myElem.isSupported("CSS", "2.0")) {
    myElem.style.color = "green";
}
```

In practice, object detection is a better solution because W3C DOM support reporting facilities are not widely implemented yet and are certainly not backward compatible.

**Returned Value**     Boolean value: true | false.

**Parameters**

*feature*

> As of W3C DOM Level 2, permissible case-sensitive module name strings are: Core, XML, HTML, Views, StyleSheets, CSS, CSS2, Events, UIEvents, MouseEvents, MutationEvents, HTMLEvents, Range, Traversal.

*version*

> String representation of the major and minor version of the DOM module cited in the first parameter. For the W3C DOM Level 2, the version is 2.0, even when the DOM module supports another W3C standard that has its own numbering system. Thus, the test for HTML DOM module support is for Version 2.0, even though HTML is at 4.x.

## mergeAttributes( )                                NN *n/a*   IE *5(Win)*   DOM *n/a*
mergeAttributes(*modelElementReference*[, *preserveIDs*])

Copies attribute name/value pairs from the element specified as a parameter to the current element. This is helpful for copying a large set of attributes from an existing element to a newly created element. By default, the copy does not include the id or name attributes so that the two elements maintain separate identifiers for scripting and form purposes. Starting with IE 5.5/Windows, an optional Boolean second parameter, when set to false, duplicates id and name attributes as well.

**Returned Value**     None.

**Parameters**

*modelElementReference*

> Reference to an existing element that serves as a model for attribute name/value pairs to be copied to the current element.

*preserveIDs*

> An optional Boolean value. If false, the id and name attributes from the model element are not copied to the current element. The default for this parameter is true.

## normalize( )                                      NN *6*   IE *n/a*   DOM *2*

Collapses all sibling text nodes of the current (element) node into a single text node. Invoking this method may be needed after inserting or removing child nodes of an element, if your node walking (traversal) scripts expect contiguous text to be contained by a single text node. The W3C DOM considers a document tree to be normal only if a text node has no other text nodes as siblings.

**Returned Value**     None.

**Parameters**     None.

## releaseCapture( )

Turns off mouse event capture mode that had been engaged earlier by the setCapture( ) method. In the IE event model, mouse event capture is designed for temporary use, such as processing mouse events while a custom context menu (implemented as a positioned div element) is activated. IE event capture is also released automatically by several user actions: giving focus to another window, frame, or the browser's Address box; scrolling a window; displaying a system dialog box; or displaying the true context menu.

**Returned Value**    None.

**Parameters**    None.

## removeAttribute( )

```
removeAttribute("attributeName")
removeAttribute("attributeName"[, caseSensitivity])
```

Removes the named attribute from the current element. An IE 4 requirement that limited attribute removal to attributes that had been added with the setAttribute( ) method is not applicable in IE 5 and later or Netscape 6. Removing an attribute does not change the source code when viewed through the browser, but does affect how the browser renders the element. The attribute value or node is also no longer available after removal.

**Returned Value**

In IE, Boolean true if successful; false if the attribute doesn't exist. No returned value in Netscape 6 (or W3C DOM specification).

**Parameters**

*attributeName*

> The (case-insensitive by default) attribute name used in the HTML tag (not including the = symbol). While IE lets you switch between case-sensitivity settings, Netscape 6 does not demand case-sensitivity. But given the trend toward case-sensitive XHTML, it is best to get into the case-sensitive habit.

*caseSensitivity*

> An optional integer value for IE only. Default value is 0 (not case-sensitive). If 1, the attribute in the HTML tag must match the case of the *attributeName* parameter exactly for its value to be returned.

## removeAttributeNode( )

```
removeAttributeNode(attrObjectReference)
```

Removes the attribute from the current element indicated by the parameter reference to an existing Attr node object. This provides an alternate way to remove an attribute from an element if the script has only a reference to the Attr node object, rather than its name. Removing an attribute node does not change the source code when viewed through the browser, but does affect how the browser renders the element. The attribute value or node is no longer available after removal.

**Returned Value**

Reference to the removed `Attr` object, which is no longer part of the document tree, but may now be inserted elsewhere in the document tree.

**Parameters**

*attrObjectReference*
  A reference to an `Attr` node object associated with the current element.

## removeAttributeNS( ) *NN 6*    *IE n/a*    *DOM 2*

`removeAttributeNS("namespaceURI", "localName")`

Removes the local-named attribute with a matching namespace URI from the current element. This method works like `removeAttribute( )` but accommodates attributes for XML documents that are labeled according to a namespace specification. The following simple XML document uses a namespace for an attribute of the `libBook:title` element:

```
<?xml version="1.0" encoding="ISO-8859-1"?>
<results xmlns:libBook="http://catalog.umv.edu/schema">
<libBook:title libBook:rareBooks="true">De Principia</libBook:title>
</results>
```

To remove the value of the `libBook:rareBooks` attribute, the method for the element would include the `removeAttributeNS( )` method call with the following parameters:

```
removeAttributeNS("http://catalog.umv.edu/schema", "rareBooks")
```

**Returned Value**    None.

**Parameters**

*namespaceURI*
  URI string matching a URI assigned to a label earlier in the document.

*localName*
  The local name portion of the attribute.

## removeBehavior( ) *NN n/a*    *IE 5(Win)*    *DOM n/a*

`removeBehavior(behaviorID)`

Disconnects the association between the current element and a behavior that had been made earlier via the `addBehavior( )` method. The parameter is the value that had been returned by the `addBehavior( )` method, which you must preserve as a variable between invocation of the two methods.

**Returned Value**    Boolean value `true` if the removal is successful; otherwise `false`.

**Parameters**

*behaviorID*
  Integer serial number initially generated by the `addBehavior( )` method for the current element and behavior type.

## removeChild( )

removeChild(*childNodeReference*)

Removes a child node from the current element. The parameter must be a reference to an existing child node nested inside the current element. Once removed, the child node is no longer part of the document tree, but is still preserved in memory. The method returns a reference to the removed node so that you may modify it and place it elsewhere in the document tree. Note that you can command one node to remove one of its children, but you cannot command a node to remove itself (but see removeNode( ) for IE).

**Returned Value**    A reference to the removed node.

**Parameters**

*childNodeReference*
    Reference to an existing child node.

## removeEventListener( )

removeEventListener("*eventType*", *listenerFunction, useCapture*)

Cuts a previously established event binding between an event handler function and the current node. This method assumes that an event listener was added to the node at some prior time. To assure removal of the desired event listener, use the identical three parameters for removeEventListener( ) that you used for addEventListener( ). You may invoke this method multiple times for the same node but with different parameter values so as not to disturb other event listeners assigned to the same node. Invoke this method only if user interaction with the node improves with the particular event handling turned off.

**Returned Value**    None.

**Parameters**

*eventType*
    A string of one event type (without the "on" prefix) known to the browser's object model. The W3C DOM knows the following event types (and Netscape 6 implements most of them):

| | | |
|---|---|---|
| abort | blur | change |
| click | DOMActivate | DOMAttrModified |
| DOMCharacterDataModified | DOMFocusIn | DOMFocusOut |
| DOMNodeInserted | DOMNodeInsertedIntoDocument | DOMNodeRemoved |
| DOMNodeRemovedFromDocument | DOMSubtreeModified | error |
| focus | load | mousedown |
| mousemove | mouseout | mouseover |
| mouseup | reset | resize |
| scroll | select | submit |
| unload | | |

*listenerFunction*
    A reference to the function to execute when the node hears the event type in the specified propagation mode. As this is a reference to a function object, do not surround the name

in quotes, nor include the parentheses of the function. At execution time, the browser automatically passes the current event object as a parameter to the listener function.

*useCapture*

A Boolean value. If true, the node listens for the event type only while the event propagates toward the target node (in event capture node). If false, the node listens only when the event bubbles outward from the event target. If the current node is the target of the event, either Boolean value may be used.

## removeExpression( ) NN *n/a*   IE *5(Win)*   DOM *n/a*

```
removeExpression("attributeName")
```

Disengages an expression that had been assigned previously to an element's attribute (assigned via the setExpression( ) method). Invoking the removeExpression( ) method turns off the automatic expression re-evaluation that might alter the attribute value in response to user activity (or explicit recalculation via the document.recalc( ) method). But the value assigned to the attribute as a result of the most recent calculation remains in effect, even after the expression is removed.

**Returned Value**    Boolean true if the removal is successful; otherwise false.

**Parameters**

*attributeName*

Name of the current element's attribute to which an expression had been assigned by the setExpression( ) method.

## removeNode( ) NN *n/a*   IE *5(Win)*   DOM *n/a*

```
removeNode([childrenFlag])
```

Removes the current node from the document tree. The method returns a reference to the removed node so that you may modify it and place it elsewhere in the document tree. By default, the method removes only the current node and none of its child nodes. Removing a container node without its children can wreak havoc with the document tree, especially for complex elements, such as tables.

**Returned Value**    A reference to the removed node.

**Parameters**

*childrenFlag*

Optional Boolean value: false (default) removes only the current node; true removes current node and all nested child nodes.

## replaceAdjacentText( ) NN *n/a*   IE *5(Win)*   DOM *n/a*

```
replaceAdjacentText("where", "newText")
```

Replaces a contiguous block of text that is adjacent to the current element with new text. This method operates only on rendered text characters, and not HTML tags.

The text to be removed (and the spot where new text goes) is governed by the first attribute, which consists of one of four values that determine where the insertion occurs, as follows.

| Position | Replace... |
|---|---|
| BeforeBegin | Text in front of current element's start tag back to preceding tag |
| AfterBegin | Text after current element's start tag until next (start or end) tag |
| BeforeEnd | Text in front of current element's end tag back to the preceding (start or end) tag |
| AfterEnd | Text after current element's end tag until next (start or end) tag |

Replacement of text has no effect on the structure of the document tree because you are simply replacing the value of one text node with a different value.

**Returned Value**    String of the removed text.

**Parameters**

*where*
> String value of one of the following case-insensitive constants: BeforeBegin | AfterBegin | BeforeEnd | AfterEnd. The first and last locations are outside the HTML tags of the current element; the middle two locations are between the tags and element content.

*newText*
> String of text to be inserted where old text is removed. If the text contains HTML tags, the tag characters are displayed as-is.

## replaceChild( )    NN 6    IE 5    DOM 1

`replaceChild(newChildNodeReference, oldChildNodeReference)`

Replaces one child node of the current node with a new child node. Typically, this is used with element nodes, but Netscape 6 and IE 6 also allow usage with Attr node objects. Parameters point to the incoming and outgoing child nodes, respectively. The new child node may be created anew or may be a reference to a node that exists elsewhere in the document tree. In the latter case, invoking the replaceChild( ) method removes the node from its original location in the document tree, and puts it into the child node position of the node referenced by the second parameter. The method returns a reference to the removed node so that you may modify it and place it elsewhere in the document tree. Note that you can command one node to replace one of its children, but you cannot command a node to replace itself (but see replaceNode( ) and swapNode( ) for IE).

**Returned Value**    A reference to the removed node.

**Parameters**

*newChildNodeReference*
> Reference to a node that will replace an existing node.

*oldChildNodeReference*
> Reference to an existing child node that is to be replace.

## replaceNode( )

NN *n/a*  IE *5(Win)*  DOM *n/a*

replaceNode(*newNodeObjectReference*)

Replaces the current node with a new node. The new node may be created anew (e.g., a text node or element) or may be a reference to a node that exists elsewhere in the document tree. In the latter case, invoking the replaceNode( ) method removes the node from its original location in the document tree, and puts it into the current node's.

**Returned Value**    Reference to the removed node.

**Parameters**

*newNodeObjectReference*
   Reference to the node object that will replace the current node.

## scrollIntoView( )

NN *7*  IE *4*  DOM *n/a*

scrollIntoView([*showAtTop*])

Scrolls the content holding the current element so that the element is brought into view. The default behavior is to display the element so that its top is at the top of the scroll space. But you may also align the element at the bottom of the scroll space, if you prefer.

**Returned Value**    None.

**Parameters**

*showAtTop*
   An optional Boolean value. If true (the default), the top of the content is positioned at the top of the scroll space; if false, the bottom of the content is positioned at the bottom of the scroll space.

## setActive( )

NN *n/a*  IE *5.5(Win)*  DOM *n/a*

Makes the current element the active element without scrolling the page to bring the active element into view. Nor does the method change focus between windows or frames if the method is invoked across window object boundaries. The element, however, receives an onfocus event when the method is invoked.

**Returned Value**    None.

**Parameters**    None.

## setAttribute( )

NN *6*  IE *4*  DOM *1*

setAttribute("*attributeName*", *value*)
setAttribute("*attributeName*", *value*[, *caseSensitivity*])

Sets the value of the named attribute within the current element. If the attribute is reflected in the object model as a property, this method acts the same as assigning a value to the object's property. Even so, the W3C DOM declares the setAttribute( ) method as the preferred way to adjust an attribute value (and the getAttribute( ) method for reading the value).

Shared DOM Reference

If the attribute does not yet exist in the element, the setAttribute( ) method adds the attribute as a name/value pair to the element (except in IE 4 through 5.5, the newly added attribute is not reported as part of the element's attributes collection).

IE treats the attribute names more as object property names. Therefore, when a discrepancy exists between the attribute and corresponding property names (e.g., class versus className), IE requires the property name version. To assign a new value to the class attribute of an element for both IE and Navigator, you should branch the code to invoke the method only once per browser to avoid adding an unused className attribute to the Navigator element. For purposes of object detection, a browser that supports the W3C DOM approach returns a string value type for the element's getAttribute("class") method.

Values you assign to an attribute must be all strings for Netscape 6 (the W3C DOM specification). IE allows other data types (such as Number and Boolean), but if you assign, say, a numeric value in string form, the data type gets converted so that getAttribute( ) returns the value in IE's preferred data type. In Netscape 6, all attribute values are strings.

Attribute names in Netscape 6 are not case-sensitive, but you should get in the habit of using all lowercase attribute names (in the direction of XHTML). IE is case-sensitive about attribute names for this method by default. An optional third parameter lets you control whether the attribute name should be treated in a case-sensitive manner. Avoid playing case-sensitivity tricks with attribute names (two different attributes with the same spelling but different case characteristics). If you use all lowercase attribute names for all your code, you can omit the third IE parameter while staying W3C DOM compliant.

**Returned Value**   None.

**Parameters**

*attributeName*
> The attribute name used in the HTML tag (except as noted above for IE).

*value*
> For Netscape 6, the attribute value as a string data type. For IE, the attribute value as a string, number, or Boolean, as dictated by the attribute's data type. Strings are safe for all values, although IE internally converts the data types as necessary.

*caseSensitivity*
> An optional integer value for IE only. If 1 (the default), the attribute in the HTML tag must match the case of the *attributeName* parameter exactly for its value to be set (allowing for multiple attribute names with the same spelling but different cases to coexist). If 0, the *attributeName* parameter aligns itself with the first attribute with the same name, regardless of case.

## setAttributeNode( ) NN 6   IE 6   DOM 1

setAttributeNode(*attrObjectReference*)

Inserts or replaces an attribute in the current element. The parameter is a reference to an Attr node object that is either created anew or references from another element in the document tree. When the setAttributeNode( ) method is invoked, the browser first looks for a match between the new attribute's name and existing attribute names. If there is a match, the new attribute replaces the original one; otherwise, the new attribute is added to the attributes of the element. Adding an attribute node does not change the source code when viewed through the browser, but may affect how the browser renders the element if the attribute affects the visual representation of the element. The value of the new attribute may be retrieved via the getAttribute( ) method.

**Returned Value**

Reference to a replaced Attr object (which is no longer part of the document tree) or null for an insertion.

**Parameters**

*attrObjectReference*
> A reference to an Attr node object created through document.createAttribute( ) or an Attr node from another element in the document tree.

## setAttributeNodeNS( )                               NN 6    IE *n/a*    DOM 2

setAttributeNodeNS(*attrObjectReference*)

Inserts or replaces an attribute in the current element. The parameter is a reference to an Attr node object that is either created anew or references from another element in the document tree. When the setAttributeNodeNS( ) method is invoked, the browser first looks for a match between the new attribute's pairing of local name and namespace URI and existing attribute local names and namespace URIs. If there is a match, the new attribute replaces the original one; otherwise, the new attribute is added to the attributes of the element. Adding an attribute node does not change the source code when viewed through the browser, but may affect how the browser renders the element if the attribute affects the visual representation of the element. The value of the new attribute may be retrieved via the getAttributeNS( ) method.

**Returned Value**

Reference to a replaced Attr object (which is no longer part of the document tree) or null for an insertion.

**Parameters**

*attrObjectReference*
> A reference to an Attr node object created through document.createAttributeNS( ) or an Attr node from another element in the document tree.

## setAttributeNS( )                                    NN 6    IE *n/a*    DOM 2

setAttributeNS("*namespaceURI*", "*qualifiedName*", "*value*")

Inserts or replaces an attribute in the current element. If a match exists among the element's attributes for both the namespace URI and the qualified name passed as parameters, the new value is assigned to the existing attribute. If there is no match, the attribute is added to the element.

**Returned Value**    None.

**Parameters**

*namespaceURI*
> URI string matching a URI assigned to a label earlier in the document.

*qualifiedName*
> The full name for the attribute, consisting of the local name prefix (if any), a colon, and the local name.

*value*
> The string value for the attribute.

## setCapture( )                                         NN *n/a*    IE *5(Win)*    DOM *n/a*

setCapture([*containerFlag*])

Initiates IE capture mode for all click-related mouse events (onclick, ondblclick, onmousedown, onmousemove, onmouseout, onmouseover, onmouseup), sending all event processing for those events to the current element, regardless of the actual event target. Useful for mouse modality required while handling custom context menus or dragging. While capture is engaged, the event.srcElement property for each event holds a reference to the element that would normally receive the event, but only the capture-mode element's event handlers actually process the events. When your modal effect is no longer neeeded, disengage capture mode with the releaseCapture( ) method. IE event capture is also released automatically by several user actions: giving focus to another window, frame, or the browser's Address box; scrolling a window; displaying a system dialog box; or displaying the true context menu.

Starting with IE 5.5, an optional parameter provides more control over event propagation when a user triggers a mouse event atop an element whose parent has the capture mode set. The default behavior (parameter omitted or set to true) causes the parent container to intercept events, as you would expect. But if you set the parameter to false, you direct events to proceed intially to their event targets (descendant elements of the capture-mode element). Such events can then bubble upward as normal; all other mouse events proceed directly to the capture-mode element. For example, if you invoke the setCapture( ) method on an element that contains a form with clickable form controls, you will probably want to use the false parameter so that mouse actions (such as clicking in text boxes) reach their intended targets even while capture mode is on. Otherwise, descendant elements won't respond to mouse activity, and the form controls will act as if they were disabled.

**Returned Value**    None.

**Parameters**

*containerFlag*
> Boolean true (default) to let current element (if a container) capture all mouse events, or false to let mouse events reach their intended targets before bubbling.

```
setExpression("propertyName", "expression", ["scriptLanguage"])
```

Assigns a script expression to an element object's property as a way to calculate dynamically a value for the property. This method works with properties of element objects and their style objects if you like. The expression is re-evaluated automatically for most user-oriented events, or you may explicitly force re-evaluation at any time via the recalc( ) method.

Assigning an expression to an element attribute can take the place of some event handling, such as maintaining position relationships among elements when a user resizes the browser window. For example, to keep an element horizontally centered in the browser window, you could use one of the following techniques to apply an expression to the element's style.left property. The first example demonstrates the syntax (also for IE 5 for Windows or later) for assigning an expression as an inline attribute for the the element:

```
<div id="heading" style="position:absolute; left:expression(
   document.body.clientWidth/2-document.getElementById("heading").offsetWidth/2);
```

Alternatively, a function invoked at load time could include the following statement:

```
document.getElementById("heading").style.setExpression("left",
   "document.body.clientWidth/2-document.getElementById('heading').offsetWidth/2;",
   "JScript");
```

In both cases, the same expression calculates the coordinate position for the element's left edge relative to the current viewable width of the body element. Because this expression depends on a body element dimension property, the browser knows that it should re-evaluate any expression that might be impacted by a change in the body size caused by window resizing.

Be sure the resulting value of the expression you assign is the desired data type for the attribute you are setting. Isolate and run some initial tests on the expression before assigning it to the setExpression( ) method. Otherwise debugging will be more difficult.

If you want an expression to assign a value to an attribute and force that value to stick, use the removeExpression( ) method to prevent any further re-evaluation of the attribute value.

**Returned Value**    None.

**Parameters**

*propertyName*
> The name of the attribute being controlled by the expression, but in case-sensitive property name form (e.g., use the className property name instead of the corresponding class attribute name).

*expression*
> A string that contains the script expression to be evaluated. The expression must evaluate to a value suitable for the property named in the first parameter, so multiple, semicolon-delimited statements are not allowed. References to other elements should be complete references. Early implementations may balk at references that include arrays.

*scriptLanguage*
> One of three constant strings: JScript | JavaScript | VBScript. The default is JScript.

## swapNode( ) NN *n/a*    IE *5(Win)*    DOM *n/a*

swapNode(*otherNodeObject*)

Exchanges the current node (in the document tree) with a different node passed as a parameter. The other node object can be created anew, or it can be a reference to a node elsewhere in the document tree. In the latter case, the result is the same as a bi-directional exchange, where the two nodes essentially change places. If the two nodes are of different node types or element display types (e.g., an inline versus a block-level element), the rendering of the document may be affected significantly.

### Returned Value

Reference to the node from which the method is invoked (i.e., the current node).

### Parameters

*otherNodeObject*
> Reference to any node object, usually another node in the document tree.

# Alphabetical Object Reference

## a NN *6*    IE *4*    DOM *1*

The a object reflects the a element, regardless of whether the element is set up to be an anchor, link, or both. Early versions of Navigator and Internet Explorer treat this object only as a member of the links[ ] and/or anchors[ ] arrays of a document. Starting with IE 4 and Netscape 6, you can access the object through supported element object reference syntax (e.g., the document.all[ ] collection for IE or document.getElementById( ) for IE 5 and later and Netscape 6).

### HTML Equivalent    <a>

### Object Model Reference
[window.]document.links[i]
[window.]document.anchors[i]
[window.]document.getElementById("*elementID*")

### Object-Specific Properties

| | | | | | |
|---|---|---|---|---|---|
| charset | coords | dataFld | dataFormatAs | dataSrc | hash |
| host | hostname | href | hreflang | Methods | mimeType |
| name | nameProp | pathname | port | protocol | protocolLong |
| rev | search | shape | target | text | type |
| urn | | | | | |

### Object-Specific Methods

None.

## Object-Specific Event Handler Properties

| Handler | NN | IE | DOM |
|---|---|---|---|
| onblur | n/a | 4 | n/a |
| onclick | 2 | 3 | 2 |
| ondblclick | 4 | 4 | n/a |
| onfocus | n/a | 4 | n/a |
| onhelp | n/a | 4 | n/a |
| onmousedown | 4 | 4 | 2 |
| onmousemove | 6 | 4 | 2 |
| onmouseout | 3 | 4 | 2 |
| onmouseover | 2 | 3 | 2 |
| onmouseup | 4 | 4 | 2 |

Anchor-only a objects have no event handlers in Navigator through Version 4.

## charset

NN 6    IE 6    DOM 1
Read/Write

Character encoding of the document's content.

### Example
```
if (document.getElementById("myAnchor").charset == "csISO5427Cyrillic") {
    // process for Cyrillic charset
}
```

**Value**   Case-insensitive alias from the character set registry (*ftp://ftp.isi.edu/in-notes/iana/assignments/character-sets*).

**Default**   Determined by browser.

## coords

NN 6    IE 6    DOM 1
Read/Write

Defines the outline of an area to be associated with a particular link or scripted action. This property is a member of the a object, but really belongs to the area object, which inherits the properties of the a object. Coordinate values are entered as a comma-delimited list. If hotspots of two areas should overlap, the area that is defined earlier in the code takes precedence.

**Example**   `document.getElementById("mapArea2").coords = "25, 5, 50, 70";`

### Value
Each coordinate is a length value, but the number of coordinates and their order depend on the shape specified by the shape attribute, which may optionally be associated with the

element. For shape="rect", there are four coordinates (left, top, right, bottom); for shape="circle" there are three coordinates (center-x, center-y, radius); for shape="poly" there are two coordinate values for each point that defines the shape of the polygon.

**Default**        None.

## dataFld

NN n/a   IE 4   DOM n/a<br>Read/Write

Used with IE data binding to associate a remote data source column value in lieu of an href attribute for a link. The datasrc attribute must also be set for the element. Setting both the dataFld and dataSrc properties to empty strings breaks the binding between element and data source. Works only with text file data sources in IE 5/Mac.

**Example**        document.getElementById("hotlink").dataFld = "linkURL";

**Value**          Case-sensitive identifier of the data source column.

**Default**        None.

## dataFormatAs

NN n/a   IE 4   DOM n/a<br>Read/Write

Used with IE data binding, this property advises the browser whether the source material arriving from the data source is to be treated as plain text or as tagged HTML.

**Example**        document.getElementById("hotlink").dataFormatAs = "HTML";

**Value**          IE recognizes two possible settings: text | html.

**Default**        text

## dataSrc

NN n/a   IE 4   DOM n/a<br>Read/Write

Used with IE data binding to specify the ID of the page's object element that loads the data source object for remote data access. Content from the data source to be inserted into the a element text is specified via the datafld property. Setting both the dataFld and dataSrc properties to empty strings breaks the binding between element and data source. Works only with text file data sources in IE 5/Mac.

**Example**        document.all.hotlink.dataSrc = "#DBSRC3";

**Value**          Case-sensitive identifier of the data source.

**Default**        None.

# hash

**Read/Write**

Provides that portion of the href attribute's URL following the # symbol, referring to an anchor location in a document. Do not include the # symbol when setting the property.

**Example**
```
document.getElementById("myLink").hash = "section3";
document.links[2].hash = "section3";
```

**Value**      String.

**Default**    None.

# host

**Read/Write**

This is the combination of the hostname and port (if any) of the server of the destination document for the link. If the port is explicitly part of the URL, the hostname and port are separated by a colon, just as they are in the URL. If the port number is not specified in an HTTP URL for IE, it automatically returns the default, port 80.

**Example**
```
document.getElementById("myLink").host = "www.megacorp.com:80";
document.links[2].host = "www.megacorp.com:80";
```

**Value**      String of hostname optionally followed by a colon and port number.

**Default**    Depends on server.

# hostname

**Read/Write**

This is the hostname of the server (i.e., a "two-dot" address consisting of server name and domain) of the destination document for the link. The hostname property does not include the port number.

**Example**
```
document.getElementById("myLink").hostname = "www.megacorp.com";
document.links[2].hostname = "www.megacorp.com";
```

**Value**      String of hostname (server and domain).

**Default**    Depends on server.

## href

**Read/Write**

Provides the URL specified by the element's href attribute.

**Example**
```
document.getElementById("myLink").href = "http://www.megacorp.com";
document.links[2].href = "http://www.megacorp.com";
```

**Value**          String of complete or relative URL.

**Default**        None.


## hreflang

**Read/Write**

Provides the language code of the content at the destination of a link. Requires that the href attribute or property also be set.

**Example**        `document.getElementById("myLink").hreflang = "DE";`

**Value**          Case-insensitive language code.

**Default**        None.


## Methods

**Read/Write**

Provides an advisory attribute about the functionality of the destination of a link. A browser could use this information to display special colors or images for the element content based on what the destination does for the user, but Internet Explorer does not appear to do anything with this information.

**Example**        `document.links[1].Methods = "post";`

**Value**          Any valid HTTP method as a string.

**Default**        None.


## mimeType

**Read-only**

Returns a plain-language version of the MIME type of the destination document at the other end of the link specified by the href attribute. You could use this information to set the cursor type during a mouse rollover. Don't confuse this property with the navigator.mimeTypes[] array and individual mimeType objects that Netscape Navigator refers to. This is not available in IE 4/Macintosh.

**Example**

```
if (document.getElementById("myLink").mimeType == "GIF Image") {
    ...
}
```

**Value**    A plain-language reference to the MIME type as a string.

**Default**    None.

## name    NN 2    IE 3    DOM 1
Read/Write

This is the identifier associated with an element that turns it into an anchor. You can also use the name as part of the object reference.

**Example**

```
if (document.links[12].name == "section3") {
    ...
}
```

**Value**

Case-sensitive identifier that follows the rules of identifier naming: it may contain no whitespace, cannot begin with a numeral, and should avoid punctuation except for the underscore character.

**Default**    None.

## nameProp    NN n/a    IE 4    DOM n/a
Read-only

Returns just the filename, rather than the full URL, of the href attribute set for the element. Not available in IE 4/Macintosh.

**Example**

```
if (document.getElementById("myLink").nameProp == "logo2.gif") {
    ...
}
```

**Value**    String.

**Default**    None.

## pathname    NN 2    IE 3    DOM 1
Read/Write

Provides the pathname component of the URL assigned to the element's href attribute. This consists of all URL information following the last character of the domain name, including the initial forward slash symbol.

**Example**
```
document.getElementById("myLink").pathname = "/images/logoHiRes.gif";
document.links[2].pathname = "/images/logoHiRes.gif";
```

**Value**        String.

**Default**      None.

## port                                                    NN *2*   IE *3*   DOM *1*
                                                                        Read/Write

Provides the port component of the URL assigned to the element's href attribute. This consists of all URL information following the colon after the last character of the domain name. The colon is not part of the port property value.

**Example**
```
document.getElementById("myLink").port = "80";
document.links[2].port = "80";
```

**Value**        String (a numeric value as string).

**Default**      None.

## protocol                                                NN *2*   IE *3*   DOM *1*
                                                                        Read/Write

Indicates the protocol component of the URL assigned to the element's href attribute. This consists of all URL information up to and including the first colon of a URL. Typical values are: "http:", "file:", "ftp:", and "mailto:".

**Example**        `document.getElementById("secureLink").protocol = "https:";`

**Value**        String.

**Default**      None.

## protocolLong                                            NN *n/a*   IE *4*   DOM *n/a*
                                                                        Read-only

Provides a verbose description of the protocol implied by the URL of the href attribute or href property. Not supported in IE 4/Macintosh, and appears to be deprecated .

**Example**
```
if (document.getElementById("myLink").protocolLong ==
    "HyperText Transfer Protocol") {
    // statements for treating document as server file
}
```

| **Value** | String. |
|---|---|
| **Default** | None |

## rel

Defines the relationship between the current element and the destination of the link. Also known as a *forward link*, not to be confused in any way with the destination document whose address is defined by the href attribute. Mainstream browsers do not take advantage of this attribute for the a element, but you can treat the attribute as a kind of parameter to be checked and/or modified under script control. See the discussion of the a element's rel attribute in Chapter 8 for a glimpse of how this property may be used in the future.

**Value**

Case-insensitive, space-delimited list of HTML 4.0 standard link types (as a single string) applicable to the element. Sanctioned link types are:

| | | | | |
|---|---|---|---|---|
| alternate | appendix | bookmark | chapter | contents |
| copyright | glossary | help | index | next |
| prev | section | start | stylesheet | subsection |

| **Default** | None. |
|---|---|

## rev

Defines the relationship between the current element and the destination of the link. Also known as a *reverse link*. This property is not exploited yet in mainstream browsers, but you can treat the attribute as a kind of parameter to be checked and/or modified under script control. See the discussion of the a element's rev attribute in Chapter 8 for a glimpse of how this property may be used in the future.

| **Value** | Case-insensitive, space-delimited list of HTML 4.0 standard link types (as a single string) applicable to the element. See the rel property for sanctioned link types. |
|---|---|
| **Default** | None. |

## search

Provides the URL-encoded portion of a URL assigned to the href attribute that begins with the ? symbol. A document that is served up as the result of the search also may have the search portion available as part of the window.location property. You can modify this property with a script. Doing so sends the URL and search criteria to the server. You must know the format of data (usually name/value pairs) expected by the server to perform this properly.

**Example**

```
document.getElementById("searchLink").search="?p=Tony+Blair&d=y&g=0&s=a&w=s&m=25";
document.links[1].search="?p=Tony+Blair&d=y&g=0&s=a&w=s&m=25";
```

| **Value** | String starting with the ? symbol. |
|---|---|
| **Default** | None. |

## shape NN 6   IE 6   DOM 1

Read/Write

Indicates the shape of a server-side image map area, with coordinates that are specified with the COORDS attribute. Intended for use by the area object, which inherits the properties of the a object.

**Example**      `document.getElementById("myLink").shape = "circle";`

**Value**      Case-insensitive shape constant as string: default | rect | rectangle | circle | poly | polygon.

**Default**      rect

## target NN 2   IE 3   DOM 1

Read/Write

Provides the name of the window or frame that is to receive content as the result of navigating to a link. Such names are assigned to frames by the frame element's name attribute; for subwindows, the name is assigned via the second parameter of the window.open( ) method. If you need the services of a target attribute to open a linked page in a blank browser window and you also need the HTML to validate under strict HTML or XHTML DTDs (see Chapter 1), you can omit the target attribute in the code, but you must assign a value to the a element's target property by script after the page loads.

**Example**

```
document.getElementById("homeLink").target = "_top";
document.links[3].target = "_top";
```

**Value**

String value of the window or frame name, or any of the following constants (as a string): _parent | _self | _top | _blank. The _parent value targets the frameset to which the current document belongs; the _self value targets the current window; the _top value targets the main browser window, thereby eliminating all frames; and the _blank value creates a new window of default size.

**Default**      None.

## text

**Read-only**

Returns the text between the a element's start and end tags. This property pre-dates the W3C DOM and should be used only if needed for Navigator 4.

| | |
|---|---|
| **Value** | String value. |
| **Default** | None. |

## type

**Read/Write**

This is the MIME type of the destination document at the other end of the link specified by the href attribute. A browser might use this information to assist in preparing support for a resource requiring a multimedia player or plugin.

**Example**
```
if (document.getElementById("myLink").type == "image/jpeg") {
    ...
}
```

| | |
|---|---|
| **Value** | Case-insensitive MIME type. A catalog of registered MIME types is available from *ftp://ftp.isi.edu/in-notes/iana/assignments/media-types/*. |
| **Default** | None. |

## urn

**Read/Write**

Indicates a Uniform Resource Name (URN) version of the destination document specified in the href attribute. This attribute is intended to offer support in the future for the URN format of URI, an evolving recommendation under discussion at the IETF (see RFC 2141). Although supported in IE, this attribute does not take the place of the href attribute.

| | |
|---|---|
| **Example** | document.getElementById("link3").urn = "http://www.megacorp.com"; |
| **Value** | Complete or relative URN as a string. |
| **Default** | None. |

# AbstractView

See the window object.

# acronym, cite, code, dfn, em, kbd, samp, strong, var
NN *6*   IE *4*   DOM *1*

All these objects reflect the corresponding HTML phrase elements of the same name. Each of these phrase elements provides a context for an inline sequence of content. Some of these elements are rendered in ways to distinguish themselves from running text. See the HTML element descriptions in Chapter 8 for details. From a scripted standpoint, all phrase element objects share the same set of properties, methods, and event handlers.

**HTML Equivalent**

```
<acronym>
<cite>
<code>
<dfn>
<em>
<kbd>
<samp>
<strong>
<var>
```

**Object Model Reference**

[window.]document.getElementById("*elementID*")

**Object-Specific Properties**

None.

**Object-Specific Methods**

None.

**Object-Specific Event Handler Properties**

None.

# address
NN *n/a*   IE *4*   DOM *1*

The address object reflects the address element.

**HTML Equivalent**

<address>

**Object Model Reference**

[window.]document.getElementById("*elementID*")

**Object-Specific Properties**

None.

**Object-Specific Methods**

None.

**Object-Specific Event Handler Properties**

None.

# all

A collection of elements nested within the current element. A reference to document.all, for example, returns a collection (array) of all element objects contained by the document, including elements that may be deeply nested inside the document's first level of elements. The collection is sorted in source code order of the element tags. You can retrieve a reference to an element with its ID by any of the following syntaxes:

```
document.all.elementID
document.all["elementID"]
document.all("elementID")
document.all.item("elementID")
document.all.namedItem("elementID")
```

The W3C DOM equivalent (the document.getElementById( ) method) operates only from the document object, providing global reach to elements throughout the entire document.

### Object Model Reference
*elementReference*.all

### Object-Specific Properties
length

### Object-Specific Methods
| item( ) | namedItem( ) | tags( ) | urns( ) |

### Object-Specific Event Handler Properties
None.

## length

Read-only

Returns the number of elements in the collection.

**Example**    var howMany = document.all.length;

**Value**    Integer.

## item( )

item(*index*[, *subindex*])

Returns a single object or collection of objects corresponding to the element matching the index value (or, optionally, the index and subindex values).

### Returned Value
One object or collection (array) of objects. If there are no matches to the parameters, the returned value is null.

Alphabetical DOM
Reference

## Parameters

*index*

When the parameter is a zero-based integer, the returned value is a single element corresponding to the specified item in source code order (nested within the current element); when the parameter is a string, the returned value is a collection of elements whose id or name properties match that string.

*subindex*

If you specify a string value for the first parameter, you can use the second parameter to specify a zero-based index that retrieves the specified element from the collection whose id or name properties match the first parameter's string value.

## namedItem( )                                    NN *n/a*    IE *6*    DOM *n/a*

namedItem(*IDOrName*)

Returns a single object or collection of objects corresponding to the element matching the parameter string value.

### Returned Value

One object or collection (array) of objects. If there are no matches to the parameters, the returned value is null.

### Parameters

*IDOrName*

The string that contains the same value and case as the desired element's id or name attribute.

## tags( )                                         NN *n/a*    IE *4*    DOM *n/a*

tags(*tagName*)

Returns a collection of objects (among all objects nested within the current element) whose tags match the *tagName* parameter.

### Returned Value

A collection (array) of objects. If there are no matches to the parameters, the returned value is an array of zero length.

### Parameters

*tagName*

A case-insensitive string that contains the element tag name only (no angle brackets), as in document.all.tags("p").

## urns( )                                         NN *n/a*    IE *5(Win)*    DOM *n/a*

urns(*URN*)

Returns a collection of nested element objects that have behaviors attached to them and whose URNs match the *URN* parameter.

**Returned Value**

A collection (array) of objects. If there are no matches to the parameters, the returned value is an array of zero length.

**Parameters**

*URN*

> A string with a local or external behavior file URN.

# anchors NN *2*   IE *3*   DOM *1*

A collection of all a elements with assigned name attributes that make them behave as anchors (instead of links). Collection members are sorted in source code order. Navigator and Internet Explorer let you use array notation to access a single anchor in the collection (e.g., document.anchors[0], document.anchors["section3"]). Internet Explorer 4 also allows the index value to be placed inside parentheses instead of brackets (e.g., document.anchors(0)). If you want to use the anchor's name as an index value (always as a string identifier), be sure to use the value of the name attribute, rather than the id attribute. To use the id attribute in a reference to an anchor, access the object via a document.all.*elementID* (in IE only) or document.getElementById("*elementID*") reference.

**Object Model Reference**

document.anchors

**Object-Specific Properties**

length

**Object-Specific Methods**

| item( ) | namedItem( ) | tags( ) | urns( ) |
|---------|--------------|---------|---------|

**Object-Specific Event Handler Properties**

None.

## length NN *2*   IE *3*   DOM *1*

Read-only

Returns the number of elements in the collection.

| **Example** | var howMany = document.anchors.length; |
|-------------|----------------------------------------|
| **Value**   | Integer. |

## item( ) NN *6*   IE *4*   DOM *1*

item(*index*[, *subindex*])
item(*index*)

Returns a single anchor object or collection of anchor objects corresponding to the element matching the index value (or, optionally in IE, the index and subindex values).

Alphabetical DOM Reference

### Returned Value

One anchor object or collection (array) of anchor objects. If there are no matches to the parameters, the returned value is null.

### Parameters

*index*

When the parameter is a zero-based integer (required in Netscape 6), the returned value is a single element that corresponds to the specified item in source code order (nested within the current element). When the parameter is a string, the returned value is a collection of elements whose id or name properties match that string.

*subindex*

In IE only, if you specify a string value for the first parameter (IE only), you can use the second parameter to specify a zero-based index that retrieves the specified element from the collection with id or name properties that match the first parameter's string value.

## namedItem( )                                          NN 6    IE 6    DOM 1

namedItem(*IDOrName*)

Returns a single anchor object or collection of anchor objects corresponding to the element matching the parameter string value.

### Returned Value

One anchor object or collection (array) of anchor objects. If there are no matches to the parameters, the returned value is null.

### Parameters

*IDOrName*

The string that contains the same value as the desired element's id or name attribute.

## tags( )                                          NN *n/a*    IE 4    DOM *n/a*

tags(*tagName*)

Returns a collection of objects (among all objects nested within the current collection) with tags that match the *tagName* parameter. Implemented in all IE collections (see the all.tags( ) method), but redundant for collections of the same element type.

## urns( )                                          NN *n/a*    IE *5(Win)*    DOM *n/a*

urns(*URN*)

See the all.urns( ) method.

# applet                                          NN 3    IE 4    DOM 1

The applet object reflects the applet element.

### HTML Equivalent    <applet>

## Object Model Reference

[window.]document.*appletName*
[window.]document.getElementById("*elementID*")

## Object-Specific Properties

| | | | | |
|---|---|---|---|---|
| align | alt | altHTML | archive | code |
| codeBase | dataFld | dataSrc | height | hspace |
| name | object | src | vspace | width |

## Object-Specific Methods

None.

## Object-Specific Event Handler Properties

None.

## align

NN *6*    IE *4*    DOM *1*

Read/Write

Defines the alignment of the element within its surrounding container. Only partially implemented in Netscape 6.2. See the "Alignment Constants" section at the beginning of Chapter 8 for the various meanings that different values bring to this property.

| | |
|---|---|
| **Example** | document.getElementById("myApplet").align = "center"; |
| **Value** | Any of the alignment constants: absbottom \| absmiddle \| baseline \| bottom \| left \| middle \| right \| texttop \| top. |
| **Default** | left |

## alt

NN *6*    IE *6*    DOM *1*

Read/Write

This is the text message to be displayed if the object or applet fails to load. There is little indication that setting this property on an existing applet object has any visual effect.

| | |
|---|---|
| **Example** | document.myApplet.alt= "Image Editor Applet"; |
| **Value** | Any quoted string of characters, but HTML tags are not interpreted. |
| **Default** | None. |

## altHTML

NN *n/a*    IE *4*    DOM *n/a*

Read/Write

Provides the HTML content to be displayed if the object or applet fails to load. This can be a message, static image, or any other HTML that best fits the scenario. There is little indication that setting this property on an existing applet object has any visual effect.

| | |
|---|---|
| **Example** | document.myApplet.altHTML = "<img src='appletAlt.gif'>"; |

| **Value** | Any quoted string of characters, including HTML tags. |
| **Default** | None. |

## archive

NN 6    IE 6    DOM 6
Read-only

Reflects the archive attribute of the applet element. Only partially implemented in the browsers. See the discussion of the archive attribute in Chapter 8.

### Example

```
if (document.applets["clock"].archive == "myClock.zip") {
    // process for the found class file
}
```

| **Value** | Case-sensitive URI as a string. |
| **Default** | None. |

## code

NN 6    IE 4    DOM 1
Read-only

Provides the name of the Java applet class file set to the code attribute. Not fully implemented in Netscape 7.

### Example

```
if (document.applets["clock"].code == "XMAScounter.class") {
    // process for the found class file
}
```

| **Value** | Case-sensitive applet class filename as a string. |
| **Default** | None. |

## codeBase

NN 6    IE 4    DOM 1
Read-only

Provides the path to the directory holding the class file designated in the code attribute. The codebase attribute does not name the class file, just the path. Not fully implemented in Netscape 7.

### Example

```
if (document.applets["clock"].codeBase == "classes") {
    // process for the found class file directory
}
```

| **Value** | Case-sensitive pathname, usually relative to the directory storing the current HTML document. |
| **Default** | None. |

## dataFld

It is unclear how you would use this property with an applet object because the dataFld and dataSrc properties (as set in element attributes) are applied to individual param elements.

**Value**          Case-sensitive identifier of the data source column.

**Default**        None.

## dataSrc

It's unclear how you would use this property with an applet object because the dataFld and dataSrc properties (as set in element attributes) are applied to individual param elements.

**Value**          Case-sensitive identifier of the data source.

**Default**        None.

## height, width

Indicate the height and width in pixels of the element as set by the tag attributes. Changing the values does not necessarily change the actual rectangle of the applet after it has loaded. Not fully implemented in Netscape 7.

**Example**        var appletHeight = document.myApplet.height;

**Value**          Integer.

**Default**        None.

## hspace, vspace

Indicate the pixel measure of horizontal and vertical margins surrounding an applet. The hspace property affects the left and right edges of the element equally; the vspace affects the top and bottom edges of the element equally. These margins are not the same as margins set by style sheets, but they have the same visual effect.

**Example**
document.getElementById("myApplet").hspace = 5;
document.getElementById("myApplet").vspace = 8;

**Value**          Integer of pixel count.

**Default**        0

## name

Read-only

This is the identifier associated with the applet. Use the name when referring to the object in the form document.*appletName*.

**Value**         Case-sensitive identifier that follows the rules of identifier naming: it may contain no whitespace, cannot begin with a numeral, and should avoid punctuation except for the underscore character.

**Default**       None.

## object

NN *n/a*    IE 4    DOM *n/a*

Read-only

Returns a reference to the applet object so that a script can access a property or method of the applet whose name is identical to a property or method of the applet element object.

**Value**         Applet object (not the applet element object) reference.

**Default**       None.

## src

NN *n/a*    IE 4    DOM *n/a*

Read-only

Internet Explorer defines this attribute as the URL for an associated file. The src property is not a substitute for the code and/or codebase properties.

**Value**         Complete or relative URL as a string.

**Default**       None.

## vspace

See hspace.

## width

See height.

# applets

NN 2    IE 3    DOM 1

A collection of all the Java applets in the current element, sorted in source code order. Navigator and Internet Explorer let you use array notation to access a single applet in the collection (e.g., document.applets[0], document.applets["clockApplet"]). Internet Explorer allows the index value to be placed inside parentheses instead of brackets (e.g., document.applets(0)). If you wish to use the applet's name as an index value (always as a string identifier), use the value of the name attribute rather than the id attribute. To use the id attribute in a reference to an applet, access the object via a document.all.*elementID* (in IE only) or document.getElementById("*elementID*") reference.

**Object Model Reference**
document.applets[i]

**Object-Specific Properties**
length

**Object-Specific Methods**
item( )          namedItem( )

## length

NN *2*    IE *3*    DOM *1*

Read-only

Returns the number of elements in the collection.

**Example**         var howMany = document.applets.length;

**Value**           Integer.

## item( )

NN *6*    IE *4*    DOM *1*

item(*index*[, *subindex*])
item(*index*)

Returns a single applet object or collection of applet objects corresponding to the element matching the index value (or, optionally in IE, the index and subindex values).

**Returned Value**
One applet object or collection (array) of applet objects. If there are no matches to the parameters, the returned value is null.

**Parameters**
*index*
> When the parameter is a zero-based integer, the returned value is a single element corresponding to the specified item in source code order (nested within the current element); when the parameter is a string, the returned value is a collection of elements whose id or name properties match that string.

*subindex*
> In IE only, if you specify a string value for the first parameter, you can use the second parameter to specify a zero-based index that retrieves the specified element from the collection whose id or name properties match the first parameter's string value.

## namedItem( )

NN *6*    IE *6*    DOM *1*

namedItem(*IDOrName*)

Returns a single applet object or collection of applet objects corresponding to the element matching the parameter string value.

Alphabetical DOM
Reference

### Returned Value

One applet object or collection (array) of applet objects. If there are no matches to the parameters, the returned value is null.

### Parameters

*IDOrName*
> The string that contains the same value as the desired element's id or name attribute.

# area                                                                  NN 3    IE 4    DOM 1

The area object reflects the area element, which defines the shape, coordinates, and destination of a clickable region of a client-side image map. Navigator and Internet Explorer treat an area object as a member of the links collection, since an area object behaves much like a link, but for a segment of an image.

### HTML Equivalent

<area>

### Object Model Reference

[window.]document.links[i]
[window.]document.getElementById("*elementID*")

### Object-Specific Properties

| | | | |
|---|---|---|---|
| alt | coords | hash | host | hostname |
| href | noHref | pathname | port | protocol |
| search | shape | target | | |

### Object-Specific Methods

None.

### Object-Specific Event Handler Properties

None.

## alt                                                                  NN 6    IE 4    DOM 1
                                                                                Read/Write

Future nongraphical browsers may use the alt property setting to display a brief description of the meaning of the (invisible) image's hotspots.

| | |
|---|---|
| **Example** | document.getElementById("*elementID*").alt = "To Next Page"; |
| **Value** | Any quoted string of characters. |
| **Default** | None. |

## coords

Defines the outline of the area to be associated with a particular link or scripted action. Coordinate values are entered as a comma-delimited list. If hotspots of two areas should overlap, the area that is defined earlier in the code takes precedence.

**Example**        `document.getElementById("mapArea2").coords = "25, 5, 50, 70";`

**Value**

Each coordinate is a pixel length value, but the number of coordinates and their order depend on the shape specified by the shape attribute, which may optionally be associated with the element. For shape="rect", there are four coordinates (left, top, right, bottom); for shape="circle", there are three coordinates (center-x, center-y, radius); for shape="poly", there are two coordinate values for each point that defines the shape of the polygon.

**Default**        None.

## hash

This is that portion of the href attribute's URL following the # symbol, referring to an anchor location in a document. Do not include the # symbol when setting the property.

**Example**        `document.getElementById("mapArea2").hash = "section3";`

**Value**        String.

**Default**        None.

## host

Provides the combination of the hostname and port (if any) of the server of the destination document for the area link. If the port is explicitly part of the URL, the hostname and port are separated by a colon, just as they are in the URL. If the port number is not specified in an HTTP URL for IE, it automatically returns the default, port 80.

**Example**        `document.getElementById("mapArea2").host = "www.megacorp.com:80";`

**Value**        String of hostname optionally followed by a colon and port number.

**Default**        Depends on server.

## hostname

Provides the hostname of the server (i.e., a two-dot address consisting of server name and domain) of the destination document for the area link. The hostname property does not include the port number.

| Example | document.links[2].hostname = "www.megacorp.com"; |
| Value | String of hostname (server and domain). |
| Default | Depends on server. |

## href
NN 2    IE 3    DOM 1
**Read/Write**

This is the URL specified by the element's href attribute.

| Example | document.links[2].href = "http://www.megacorp.com"; |
| Value | String of complete or relative URL. |
| Default | None. |

## noHref
NN 6    IE 4    DOM 1
**Read/Write**

Specifies whether the area defined by the coordinates has a link associated with it. When you set this property to true, scriptable browsers no longer treat the element as a link.

| Example | document.links[4].noHref = "true"; |
| Value | Boolean value: true \| false. |
| Default | false |

## pathname
NN 2    IE 3    DOM 1
**Read/Write**

Provides the pathname component of the URL assigned to the element's href attribute. This consists of all URL information following the last character of the domain name, including the initial forward slash symbol.

**Example**
document.getElementById("myLink").pathname = "/images/logoHiRes.gif";

| Value | String. |
| Default | None. |

## port
NN 2    IE 3    DOM 1
**Read/Write**

Provides the port component of the URL assigned to the element's href attribute. This consists of all URL information following the colon after the last character of the domain name. The colon is not part of the port property value.

| **Example** | `document.getElementById("myLink").port = "80";` |
| **Value** | String (a numeric value as string). |
| **Default** | None. |

## protocol

Indicates the protocol component of the URL assigned to the element's href attribute. This consists of all URL information up to and including the first colon of a URL. Typical values are "http:", "file:", "ftp:", and "mailto:".

| **Example** | `document.getElementById("secureLink").protocol = "https:";` |
| **Value** | String. |
| **Default** | None. |

## search

This is the URL-encoded portion of a URL assigned to the href attribute that begins with the ? symbol. A document that is served up as the result of the search also may have the search portion available as part of the window.location property. You can modify this property with a script. Doing so sends the URL and search criteria to the server. You must know the format of data (usually name/value pairs) expected by the server to perform this properly.

**Example**

`document.getElementById("searchLink").search="?p=Tony+Blair&d=y&g=0&s=a&w=s&m=25";`

| **Value** | String starting with the ? symbol. |
| **Default** | None. |

## shape

Indicates the shape of a server-side image map area with coordinates that are specified with the coords attribute.

| **Example** | `document.getElementById("area51").shape = "circle";` |
| **Value** | Case-insensitive shape constant as string: default \| rect \| rectangle \| circle \| poly \| polygon. |
| **Default** | RECT (IE); empty string but rect implied (Netscape 6). |

## target

**Read/Write**

This is the name of the window or frame that is to receive content as the result of navigating to an area link. Such names are assigned to frames by the frame element's name attribute; for subwindows, the name is assigned via the second parameter of the window.open( ) method. If you need the services of a target attribute to open a linked page in a blank browser window and you also need the HTML to validate under strict HTML or XHTML DTDs, you can omit the target attribute in the code, but assign a value to the area element's target property by script after the page loads.

**Example**        `document.getElementById("homeArea").target = "_blank";`

**Value**

String value of the window or frame name, or any of the following constants (as a string): _parent | _self | _top | _blank. The _parent value targets the frameset to which the current document belongs; the _self value targets the current window; the _top value targets the main browser window, thereby eliminating all frames; and the _blank value creates a new window of default size.

**Default**        None.

## areas

A collection of all area elements associated with a map element. Notice that individual items of an areas collection are also members of the document-wide links collection (document.links[] array). But the members of an areas collection are local to a single map element.

**Object Model Reference**
`document.getElementById("mapElementID").areas`

**Object-Specific Properties**
length

**Object-Specific Methods**

| item( ) | namedItem( ) | tags( ) | urns( ) |
|---------|-------------|---------|---------|

## length

**Read-only**

Returns the number of elements in the collection.

**Example**        `var howMany = document.areas.length;`

**Value**        Integer.

# item( )

item(*index*[, *subindex*])
item(*index*)

Returns a single area object or collection of area objects corresponding to the element matching the index value (or, optionally in IE, the index and subindex values).

## Returned Value

One area object or collection (array) of area objects. If there are no matches to the parameters, the returned value is null.

## Parameters

*index*

When the parameter is a zero-based integer, the returned value is a single element corresponding to the specified item in source code order (nested within the current element); when the parameter is a string, the returned value is a collection of elements whose id or name properties match that string.

*subindex*

In IE only, if you specify a string value for the first parameter, you can use the second parameter to specify a zero-based index that retrieves the specified element from the collection whose id or name properties match the first parameter's string value.

# namedItem( )

namedItem(*IDOrName*)

Returns a single area object or collection of area objects corresponding to the element matching the parameter string value.

## Returned Value

One area object or collection (array) of area objects. If there are no matches to the parameters, the returned value is null.

## Parameters

*IDOrName*

The string that contains the same value as the desired element's id or name attribute.

# tags( )

tags(*tagName*)

Returns a collection of objects (among all objects nested within the current collection) with tags that match the *tagName* parameter. Implemented in all IE collections (see the all.tags( ) method), but redundant for collections of the same element type.

Alphabetical DOM
Reference

## urns( )         NN *n/a*    IE *5(Win)*    DOM *n/a*

urns(*URN*)

See the all.urns( ) method.

# Attr, attribute         NN *6*    IE *5*    DOM *1*

An abstract representation of an element's attribute name/value pair is an object known in the W3C DOM vernacular as the Attr object; in IE terminology, it is called an attribute object. They are different names for the same object. An attribute object is created in both environments via the document.createAttribute( ) method; the reference to the attribute object then becomes the parameter to an element's setAttributeNode( ) method to insert that attribute object into the element. For example:

```
var newAttr = document.createAttribute("author");
newAttr.value = "William Shakespeare";
document.getElementById("hamlet").setAttributeNode(newAttr);
```

Some W3C DOM element methods (most notably, the getAttributeNode( ) method) return attribute objects, which have properties that may be accessed like any scriptable object.

In the W3C DOM abstract model, the Attr object inherits all properties and methods of the Node object. Some Node object properties, however, are not inherited by the attribute object in IE/Windows until Version 6, even though they are implemented for element and text nodes in Version 5.

### HTML Equivalent

Any name/value pair inside a start tag.

### Object Model Reference

[window.]document.getElementById("*elementID*").attributes[*i*]
[window.]document.getElementById("*elementID*").attributes.item(*i*)
[window.]document.getElementById("*elementID*").attributes.getNamedItem[*attrName*]

### Object-Specific Properties

| expando | name | ownerElement | specified | value |
|---------|------|--------------|-----------|-------|

### Object-Specific Methods

None.

### Object-Specific Event Handler Properties

None.

## expando         NN *n/a*    IE *6*    DOM *n/a*

**Read-only**

Returns Boolean true if the attribute, once it is inserted into an element, is not one of the native attributes for the element. This property is false for an attribute created by document.createAttribute( ) until the attribute is added to the element (via the setAttributeNode( ) method), at which time the property's value is reevaluated within the context of the element's native attributes.

**Example**
```
var isCustomAttr =
    document.getElementById("book3928").getAttributeNode("author").expando;
```

**Value**      Boolean value: true | false.

**Default**    false

## name                                        NN *6*    IE *5*    DOM *1*
Read-only

This is the name portion of the name/value pair of the attribute. It is identical to the nodeName property of the Attr node. You may not modify the name of an attribute by script because other dependencies may lead to document tree confusion. Instead, replace the old attribute with a newly created one, the name of which is a required parameter of the document.createAttribute( ) method.

**Example**
```
if (myAttr.name == "author") {
    // process author attribute
}
```

**Value**      String value.

**Default**    Empty string, although creating a new attribute requires a name.

## ownerElement                               NN *6*    IE *n/a*    DOM *2*
Read-only

Refers to the element that contains the current attribute object. Until a newly created attribute is inserted into an element, this property is null.

**Example**
```
if (myAttr.ownerElement.tagName == "fred") {
    // process attribute of <fred> element
}
```

**Value**      Element node reference.

**Default**    null

## specified                                   NN *6*    IE *5*    DOM *1*
Read-only

Returns Boolean true if the value of the attribute is explicitly assigned in the source code or adjusted by script. If the browser reflects an attribute that is not explicitly set (IE does this), the specified property for that value is false, even though the attribute may have a default value determined by the document's DTD. The W3C DOM Level 2 indicates that the specified property of a freshly created Attr object should be true, but both IE 6 and Netscape 6.2 and later leave it false until the attribute is inserted into an element.

**Example**

```
if (myAttr.specified) {
    // process attribute whose value is something other than DTD default
}
```

| | |
|---|---|
| **Value** | Boolean value: true \| false. |
| **Default** | false |

## value  NN 6  IE 6  DOM 1

Read/Write

Provides the value portion of the name/value pair of the attribute. Identical to the nodeValue property of the Attr node, as well as data accessed more directly via an element's getAttribute( ) and setAttribute( ) methods. If you create a new attribute object, you can assign its value via the value property prior to inserting the attribute into the element. Attribute node values are always strings, including in IE, which otherwise allows Number or Boolean data types for the corresponding properties.

**Example**

```
document.getElementById("hamlet").getAttributeNode("author").value = "Shakespeare";
```

| | |
|---|---|
| **Value** | String value. |
| **Default** | Empty string, except in IE/Windows, which returns the string undefined (that is, not a value whose type evaluates to the undefined value). |

# attributes, NamedNodeMap  NN 6  IE 5  DOM 1

The object returned by the attributes property of every W3C DOM element object is a collection (array) of references to Attr (a.k.a. attribute) objects. An attribute type of node always has a name associated with it, which opens the way for methods of the collection of such nodes to access them directly by name, rather than iterating through the array in search of a matching node name. In the W3C DOM structure, the abstract representation of this array of named nodes is called the NamedNodeMap object, which shares some properties and methods of the IE attributes object. Since both objects refer to the same parts of a document tree, they are treated here together. A couple of other W3C DOM collections are also of the NamedNodeMap variety, but your primary contact with the NamedNodeMap in HTML documents is as a collection of Attr objects. Collection members are sorted in source code order.

There are more direct ways to access an attribute of an element (such as the getAttribute( ) or getAttributeNode( ) methods of all elements). The property and methods shown here, however, assume that your script has been handed a collection of attributes independent of their host element, and your processing starts from that point.

**Object Model Reference**

*elementReference*.attributes

**Object-Specific Properties**

length

**Object-Specific Methods**

| | | | |
|---|---|---|---|
| getNamedItem( ) | getNamedItemNS( ) | item( ) | removeNamedItem( ) |
| removeNamedItemNS( ) | setNamedItem( ) | setNamedItemNS( ) | |

**Object-Specific Event Handler Properties**

None.

## length

NN *6*    IE *5*    DOM *1*

Read-only

Returns the number of elements in the collection.

**Example**        `var howMany = document.getElementById("myTable").attributes.length;`

**Value**        Integer.

## getNamedItem( )

NN *6*    IE *6*    DOM *1*

getNamedItem("*attributeName*")

Returns a single `Attr` object corresponding to the attribute whose node name matches the parameter value.

**Returned Value**

Reference to one `Attr` object. If there is no match to the parameter value, the returned value is null.

**Parameters**

*attributeName*

String corresponding to the name portion of an attribute's name/value pair.

## getNamedItemNS( )

NN *6*    IE *n/a*    DOM *2*

getNamedItemNS("*namespaceURI*", "*localName*")

Returns a single `Attr` object with a local name and namespace URI that match the parameter values.

**Returned Value**

Reference to one `Attr` object. If there is no match to the parameter values, the returned value is null.

**Parameters**

*namespaceURI*
> URI string matching a URI assigned to a label earlier in the document.

*localName*
> The local name portion of the attribute.

## item( )

item(*index*)

Returns a single `Attr` object corresponding to the element matching the index value.

**Returned Value**

Reference to one `Attr` object. If there is no match to the index value, the returned value is `null`. Unlike some other collections in IE, a string index value is not allowed for the attributes object.

**Parameters**

*index*
> A zero-based integer corresponding to the specified item in source code order.

## removeNamedItem( )

removeNamedItem("*attributeName*")

Removes from the collection a single `Attr` object corresponding to the attribute whose node name matches the parameter value.

**Returned Value**

Reference to the removed `Attr` object. If there is no match to the parameter value, the returned value is `null`.

**Parameters**

*attributeName*
> String corresponding to the name portion of an attribute's name/value pair.

## removeNamedItemNS( )

removeNamedItemNS("*namespaceURI*", "*localName*")

Removes from the collection a single `Attr` object whose local name and namespace URI match the parameter values.

**Returned Value**

Reference to the removed `Attr` object. If there is no match to the parameter values, the method generates an error.

**Parameters**

*namespaceURI*

> URI string matching a URI assigned to a label earlier in the document.

*localName*

> The local name portion of the attribute.

## setNamedItem( )    NN *6*   IE *6*   DOM *1*

setNamedItem(*attrObjectReference*)

Inserts a single Attr object into the current collection of attributes. If the destination of the attribute is an existing element, you may also use the setAttributeNode( ) method on the element to insert the Attr object. When the setNamedItem( ) method is invoked, the browser first looks for a match between the new attribute's name and existing attribute names within the collection. If there is a match, the new attribute replaces the original one; otherwise, the new attribute is added to the collection.

**Returned Value**

Reference to an Attr object either created anew or referenced from elsewhere in the document tree.

**Parameters**

*attrObjectReference*

> A reference to an Attr node object created through document.createAttribute( ) or an Attr node from another element in the document tree.

## setNamedItemNS( )    NN *6*   IE *n/a*   DOM *2*

setNamedItemNS(*attrObjectReference*)

Inserts a single Attr object into the current collection of attributes. If the destination of the attribute is an existing element, you may also use the setAttributeNodeNS( ) method on the element to insert the Attr object. When the setNamedItemNS( ) method is invoked, the browser first looks for a match between the new attribute's pairing of local name and namespace URI and existing attribute local names and namespace URIs within the collection. If there is a match, the new attribute replaces the original one; otherwise, the new attribute is added to the collection.

**Returned Value**

Reference to an Attr object either created anew or referenced from elsewhere in the document tree.

**Parameters**

*attrObjectReference*

> A reference to an Attr node object created through document.createAttributeNS( ) or an Attr node from another element in the document tree.

Alphabetical DOM
Reference

## b, big, i, s, small, strike, tt, u

**NN** *6*   **IE** *4*   **DOM** *1*

All these objects reflect the HTML font style elements of the same name. Each of these elements specifies a rendering style for an inline sequence of content. All the elements are deprecated in HTML 4 in favor of style sheet attributes. See the HTML element descriptions in Chapter 8 for details. From a scripted standpoint, all font style element objects share the same set of properties, methods, event handlers, and collections.

### HTML Equivalent
```
<b>
<big>
<i>
<s>
<small>
<strike>
<tt>
<u>
```

### Object Model Reference
`[window.]document.getElementById("elementID")`

### Object-Specific Properties
None.

### Object-Specific Methods
None.

### Object-Specific Event Handler Properties
None.

## base

**NN** *6*   **IE** *4*   **DOM** *1*

A base object instructs the browser about the URL path to the current document. This path is then used as the basis for all relative URLs that are used to specify various src and href attributes throughout the document.

### HTML Equivalent    `<base>`

### Object Model Reference
`[window.]document.getElementById("elementID")`

### Object-Specific Properties
| | |
|---|---|
| href | target |

### Object-Specific Methods
None.

### Object-Specific Event Handler Properties
None.

## href

Provides the URL of a document whose server path is to be used as the base URL for all relative references in the document. This is typically the URL of the current document, but it can be set to another path if it makes sense to your document organization and directory structure.

| | |
|---|---|
| **Example** | `document.getElementById("myBase").href = "http://www.megacorp.com";` |
| **Value** | String of complete or relative URL. |
| **Default** | Current document pathname. |

## target

Provides the name of the window or frame that is to receive content as the result of navigating to a link or any other action on the page that loads a new document. Such names are assigned to frames by the `frame` element's `name` attribute; for subwindows, the name is assigned via the second parameter of the `window.open( )` method. If you need the services of a `target` attribute to open a linked page in a blank browser window and you also need the HTML to validate under strict HTML or XHTML DTDs, you can omit the `target` attribute in the code, but assign a value to the base element's `target` property by script after the page loads.

| | |
|---|---|
| **Example** | `document.getElementById("myBase").target = "_blank";` |

**Value**

String value of the window or frame name, or any of the following constants (as a string): `_parent | _self | _top | _blank`. The `_parent` value targets the frameset to which the current document belongs; the `_self` value targets the current window; the `_top` value targets the main browser window, thereby eliminating all frames; and the `_blank` value creates a new window of default size.

| | |
|---|---|
| **Default** | `_self` |

# basefont

A basefont element advises the browser of some font information to be used as the basis for text rendering of the current page below the basefont element. The basefont element overrides the default font settings in the browser's user preferences settings.

If you intend to alter this element by script, do so only via the properties shown here or W3C DOM-compatible document tree manipulations. Other approaches either risk the display of the document or are not permitted by the browser.

**HTML Equivalent**    `<basefont>`

**Object Model Reference**
`[window.]document.getElementById("elementID")`

## Object-Specific Properties

color        face        size

## Object-Specific Methods

None.

## Object-Specific Event Handler Properties

None.

## color                                               NN 6    IE 4    DOM 1

Read/Write

Sets the font color of all text below the basefont element.

**Example**          `document.getElementsByTagName("basefont")[0].color = "#c0c0c0";`

**Value**            Case-insensitive hexadecimal triplet or plain-language color name as a string. See Appendix A for acceptable plain-language color names.

**Default**         Browser default.

## face                                                 NN 6    IE 4    DOM 1

Read/Write

Indicates a hierarchy of font faces to use for the default font of a section headed by a basefont element. The browser looks for the first font face in the comma-delimited list of font face names until it either finds a match in the client system or runs out of choices, at which point the browser default font face is used. Font face names must match the system font face names exactly.

**Example**

`document.getElementById("myBaseFont").face = "Bookman, Times Roman, serif";`

**Value**            One or more font face names in a comma-delimited list within a string. You may use real font names or the recognized generic faces: serif | sans-serif | cursive | fantasy | monospace.

**Default**         Browser default.

## size                                                 NN 6    IE 4    DOM 1

Read/Write

Provides the size of the font in the 1–7 browser relative scale.

**Example**          `document.getElementById("myBaseFont").size = "+1";`

**Value**            Either an integer (as a quoted string) or a quoted relative value consisting of a + or - symbol and an integer value.

**Default**         3

---

# bdo

The bdo element is designed to assist in instances when, due to various conversions during text processing, the normal bidirectional algorithms must be explicitly overridden. The primary property of this object is dir, which is shared among all other element objects.

**HTML Equivalent**

<bdo>

**Object-Specific Properties**

None.

**Object-Specific Methods**

None.

**Object-Specific Event Handler Properties**

None.

# bgsound

A bgsound element defines a sound file that is to play in the background while the user visits the page. Set properties to control the volume and how many times the sound track plays even after the sound file has loaded. A few properties, such as innerHTML and innerText, are exposed in the Windows version, but they don't apply to an element that does not have an end tag.

**HTML Equivalent**

<bgsound>

**Object Model Reference**

[window.]document.getElementById("*elementID*")

**Object-Specific Properties**

| balance | loop | src | volume |

**Object-Specific Methods**

None.

**Object-Specific Event Handler Properties**

None.

## balance

Read-only

Specifies how the audio is divided between the left and right speakers. Once this attribute value is set in the element, its value cannot be changed by script control.

**Example**   var currBal = document.getElementsByTagName("bgsound")[0].balance;

| | |
|---|---|
| **Value** | A signed integer between −10,000 and +10,000. A value of 0 is equally balanced on both sides. A negative value means the left side is dominant; a positive value means the right side is dominant. |
| **Default** | 0 |

## loop

NN n/a   IE 4   DOM n/a<br>Read/Write

Specifies the number of times the sound plays. Assigning a value of −1 means the sound plays continuously until the page is unloaded.

| | |
|---|---|
| **Example** | `document.getElementById("mySound").loop = 3;` |
| **Value** | Integer. |
| **Default** | 1 |

## src

NN n/a   IE 4   DOM n/a<br>Read/Write

Provides the URL of the sound file to be played. Change tunes by assigning a new URL to the property. The new tune plays according to the loop property setting.

| | |
|---|---|
| **Example** | `document.getElementById("tunes").src = "sounds/blues.aif";` |
| **Value** | Complete or relative URL as a string. |
| **Default** | None. |

## volume

NN n/a   IE 4   DOM n/a<br>Read/Write

Specifies how loud the background sound plays relative to the maximum sound output level as adjusted by user preferences in the client computer. Maximum volume—a setting of zero—is only as loud as the user has set the **Sound** control panel. Attribute adjustments are negative values as low as −10,000 (although most users lose the sound at values much higher than that value).

| | |
|---|---|
| **Example** | `var currVolume = document.getElementById("themeSong").volume;` |
| **Value** | Integer. |
| **Default** | Varies with operating system and sound settings. |

# big

See b.

# blockquote

The blockquote object reflects the blockquote element, which is intended to set off a long, block-level quote inside a document.

**HTML Equivalent**
<blockquote>

**Object Model Reference**
[window.]document.getElementById("*elementID*")

**Object-Specific Properties**
cite

**Object-Specific Methods**
None.

**Object-Specific Event Handler Properties**
None.

# cite

Read/Write

Provides a URL pointing to an online source document from which the quotation is taken. This is not in any way a mechanism for copying or extracting content from another document. IE 6 for Windows incorrectly calls this property clear. No mainstream browser does anything special with this information.

**Value**        Any valid URL to a document on the World Wide Web, including absolute or relative URLs.

**Default**      None.

# body

The body object reflects the body element, which is distinct from the document object. The body object refers to just the element and its nested content. There can be only one body element in an HTML page, so both the IE and W3C DOMs provide a shortcut reference to the object, document.body. Event handlers listed here appear as attributes in the <body> tag, but in truth are document-level events (best referenced in property form as document.*eventName*). While IE for the Mac doesn't share the sets of client and scroll properties with all element objects, those properties are defined for the body object.

In its effort to institute the standards-compatible mode in IE 6 for Windows (see the DOCTYPE element in Chapter 8), Microsoft has rendered useless the old trick of using the body element's clientHeight and clientWidth properties to obtain the equivalent of Netscape's window.innerHeight and window.innerWidth properties. In standards-compatibility mode (where document.compatMode == "CSS1Compat"), you must use the html element's clientHeight and clientWidth properties to find these values. Use these effective reference shortcuts:

```
document.body.parentNode.clientHeight
document.body.parentNode.clientWidth
```

**HTML Equivalent**

<body>

**Object Model Reference**

[window.]document.body

**Object-Specific Properties**

| | | | | |
|---|---|---|---|---|
| alink | background | bgColor | bgProperties | bottomMargin |
| leftMargin | link | noWrap | rightMargin | scroll |
| text | topMargin | vLink | | |

**Object-Specific Methods**

createTextRange( )

**Object-Specific Event Handler Properties**

| Handler | IE Windows | IE Mac | NN | W3C DOM |
|---|---|---|---|---|
| onafterprint | 5 | n/a | n/a | n/a |
| onbeforeprint | 5 | n/a | n/a | n/a |
| onbeforeunload | 4 | n/a | n/a | n/a |
| onload | 3 | 3.01 | 2 | 2 |
| onselect | n/a | n/a | 6 | n/a |
| onunload | 3 | 3.01 | 2 | 2 |

## aLink

NN 6    IE 4    DOM 1

Read/Write

Indicates a color of a hypertext link as it is being clicked. The color is applied to the link text or border around an image or object embedded within an a element. See also link and vLink properties for unvisited and visited link colors. The deprecated but backward-compatible version of this property is the alinkColor property of the document object.

| | |
|---|---|
| **Example** | document.body.aLink = "green"; |
| **Value** | A hexadecimal triplet or plain-language color name. See Appendix A for acceptable plain-language color names. |
| **Default** | #0000FF |

## background

Provides the URL of the background image for the entire document. If you set a bgColor to the element as well, the color appears if the image fails to load; otherwise, the image over-lays the color.

**Example**         document.body.background = "images/watermark.jpg";

**Value**           Complete or relative URL to the background image file.

**Default**         None.

## bgColor

Provides the background color of the element. Even if the bgcolor attribute or bgColor property is set with a plain-language color name, the returned value is always a hexadec-imal triplet.

**Example**         document.body.bgColor = "yellow";

**Value**           A hexadecimal triplet or plain-language color name. See Appendix A for acceptable plain-language color names.

**Default**         Varies with browser and operating system.

## bgProperties

Specifies whether the background image remains in a fixed position or scrolls as a user scrolls the page. When the background image is set to remain in a fixed position, scrolled content flows past the background image very much like film credits roll past a back-ground image on the screen.

**Example**         document.body.bgProperties = "fixed";

**Value**           An empty string (indicating the normal scrolling behavior) or the case-insensitive constant string fixed.

**Default**         Empty string.

## bottomMargin

Indicates the amount of blank space between the very end of content and the bottom of a scrollable page. The setting has no visual effect if the length of the content or size of the window does not cause the window to scroll. The default value is for the end of content to be flush with the end of the document, but in the Macintosh version of Internet Explorer, there is about a 10-pixel margin visible even when the property is set to zero. Larger sizes are reflected properly. This property offers somewhat of a shortcut or alternative to setting the marginBottom style sheet property for the body element object.

**Example**        document.body.bottomMargin = 20;

**Value**          An integer value (zero or greater) of the number of pixels of clear space at the bottom of the document.

**Default**        0

## leftMargin                                              NN *n/a*    IE *4*    DOM *n/a*

*Read/Write*

Provides the width in pixels of the left margin of the body element in the browser window or frame. By default, the browser inserts a small margin to keep content from abutting the left edge of the window. Setting the property to an empty string is the same as setting it to zero.

**Example**        document.body.leftMargin = 16;

**Value**          Integer of pixel count.

**Default**        10 (Windows); 8 (Macintosh).

## link                                                    NN *6*    IE *4*    DOM *1*

*Read/Write*

Indicates the color of a hypertext link that has not been visited (that is, the URL of the link is not in the browser's cache). This is one of three states for a link: unvisited, active, and visited. The color is applied to the link text or border around an image or object embedded within an a element. This property has the same effect as setting the document object's linkColor property.

**Example**        document.body.link = "#00FF00";

**Value**          A hexadecimal triplet or plain-language color name. See Appendix A for acceptable plain-language color names.

**Default**        #0000FF

## noWrap                                                  NN *n/a*    IE *4*    DOM *1*

*Read/Write*

Specifies whether the browser should render the body content as wide as necessary to display a line of nonbreaking text on one line. Abuse of this attribute can force the user into a great deal of inconvenient horizontal scrolling of the page to view all of the content.

**Example**        document.body.noWrap = "true";

**Value**          Boolean value: true | false.

**Default**        false

## rightMargin

Provides the width in pixels of the right margin of the body element in the browser window or frame. By default, the browser inserts a small margin to keep content from abutting the right edge of the window (except on the Macintosh). Setting the property to an empty string is the same as setting it to zero.

| | |
|---|---|
| **Example** | document.body.leftMargin = 16; |
| **Value** | Integer of pixel count. |
| **Default** | 10 (Windows); 0 (Macintosh). |

## scroll

Specifies whether the window (or frame) displays scrollbars when the content exceeds the window size. If your document specifies a standards-compatible DOCTYPE definition (see Chapter 8), the scroll property does not respond to changes for the body element. Nor does the html element object gain this property, as Microsoft's developer documentation purports.

| | |
|---|---|
| **Example** | document.body.scroll = "no"; |
| **Value** | Not exactly a Boolean value. Requires one of the following string values: yes \| no \| auto. |
| **Default** | yes |

## text

Indicates the color of text for the entire document body. Equivalent to the foreground color.

| | |
|---|---|
| **Example** | document.body.text = "darkred"; |
| **Value** | A hexadecimal triplet or plain-language color name. See Appendix A for acceptable plain-language color names. |
| **Default** | Browser default (user customizable). |

## topMargin

Provides the width in pixels of the top margin of the body element in the browser window or frame. By default, the browser inserts a small margin to keep content from abutting the top edge of the window. Setting the property to an empty string is the same as setting it to zero.

| | |
|---|---|
| **Example** | document.body.topMargin = 16; |

| | |
|---|---|
| **Value** | Integer of pixel count. |
| **Default** | 15 (Windows); 8 (Macintosh). |

## vLink

NN 6   IE 4   DOM 1<br>Read/Write

Indicates the color of a hypertext link that has been visited recently. The color is applied to the link text or border around an image or object embedded within an a element. See also link and aLink properties for unvisited and clicked link colors. The deprecated but backward-compatible version of this property is the vlinkColor property of the document object.

| | |
|---|---|
| **Example** | document.body.vLink = "gold"; |
| **Value** | A hexadecimal triplet or plain-language color name. See Appendix A for acceptable plain-language color names. |
| **Default** | #551a8b (Navigator 4); #800080 (Internet Explorer 4 Windows); #006010 (Internet Explorer 4 Macintosh). |

## createTextRange( )

NN n/a   IE 4(Win)   DOM n/a

Creates a TextRange object from the rendered text content of the current element. See the TextRange object for details.

| | |
|---|---|
| **Returned Value** | TextRange object. |
| **Parameters** | None. |

## br

NN 6   IE 4   DOM1

The br object reflects the br element.

**HTML Equivalent**
<br>

**Object Model Reference**
[window.]document.getElementById("*elementID*")

**Object-Specific Properties**
clear

**Object-Specific Methods**
None.

**Element-Specific Event Handler Attributes**
None.

## clear

Tells the browser how to treat the next line of text following a br element if the current text is wrapping around a floating image or other object. The value you use depends on the side of the page to which one or more inline images are pegged and how you want the next line of text to be placed in relation to those images.

**Example**         document.getElementById("specialBreak").clear = "all";

**Value**           Case-insensitive string of any of the following constants: all | left | none | right.

**Default**         none

# button

The button object reflects the button element. While IE for the Mac doesn't share the sets of client- and scroll- properties with all element objects, those properties are defined for the button object. See the discussion of the button element in Chapter 8 to see how it differs from the input element of type button.

### HTML Equivalent
<button>

### Object Model Reference
[window.]document.getElementById("*elementID*")

### Object-Specific Properties

| | | | | |
|---|---|---|---|---|
| dataFld | dataFormatAs | dataSrc | form | name |
| status | type | value | | |

### Object-Specific Methods
createTextRange( )

### Object-Specific Event Handler Properties
None.

## dataFld

Used with IE data binding to associate a remote data source column name to a button object's label. A datasrc attribute must also be set for the element. Setting both the dataFld and dataSrc properties to empty strings breaks the binding between element and data source.

**Example**         document.getElementById("myButton").dataFld = "linkURL";

**Value**           Case-sensitive identifier of the data source column.

**Default**         None.

## dataFormatAs

NN *n/a*   IE *4*   DOM *n/a*

**Read/Write**

Used with IE data binding, this property advises the browser whether the source material arriving from the data source is to be treated as plain text or as tagged HTML.

**Example**   document.getElementById("myButton").dataFormatAs = "html";

**Value**   String constant values: text | html.

**Default**   text

## dataSrc

NN *n/a*   IE *4*   DOM *n/a*

**Read/Write**

Used with IE data binding to specify the ID of the page's object element that loads the data source object for remote data access. Content from the data source is specified via the dataFld attribute in the button element. Setting both the dataFld and dataSrc properties to empty strings breaks the binding between element and data source.

**Example**   document.getElementById("myButton").dataSrc = "DBSRC3";

**Value**   Case-sensitive identifier of the object element.

**Default**   None.

## form

NN *6*   IE *4*   DOM *1*

**Read-only**

Returns a reference to the form element that contains the current element (if any).

**Example**   var theForm = event.srcElement.form;

**Value**   Object reference.

**Default**   None.

## name

NN *6*   IE *4*   DOM *1*

**Read/Write**

This is the identifier associated with the element when used as a form control. The value of this property is submitted as one-half of the name/value pair when the form is submitted to the server. Names are hidden from user view, since control labels are assigned via other means, depending on the control type. Form control names may also be used by script references to the objects.

**Example**   document.forms[0].compName.name = "company";

### Value

Case-sensitive identifier that follows the rules of identifier naming: it may contain no whitespace, cannot begin with a numeral, and should avoid punctuation except for the underscore character.

**Default**     None.

## status

Unlike the status property of other types of form controls, the property has no visual or functional impact on the button.

**Value**     Boolean value: true | false; or null.

**Default**     null

## type

Specifies whether the button element is specified as a button, reset, or submit style button.

### Example

```
if (evt.target.type == "button") {
    // process button element
}
```

**Value**     One of the three constants (as a string): button | reset | submit.

**Default**     button

## value

Provides the current value associated with the form control that is submitted with the name/value pair for the element. Unlike the button-type input element object, this value property's value is unseen by the user; the label is set by the element's content (innerHTML property or nested node).

### Example

```
var val = document.getElementById("myButton").value;
```

**Value**     String.

**Default**     None.

## createTextRange( )

Creates a TextRange object containing the button's label text. See the TextRange object.

**Returned Value**     TextRange object.

**Parameters**     None.

# caption

The caption object reflects the caption element, which must always be nested inside a table element. IE/Mac implements the client and scroll property sets for this object.

**HTML Equivalent**   <caption>

**Object Model Reference**
[window.]document.getElementById("*elementID*")

**Object-Specific Properties**
align          vAlign

**Object-Specific Methods**
None.

**Object-Specific Event Handler Properties**
None.

## align

**Read/Write**

Determines the position of the caption in the table. See the align attribute of the caption element in Chapter 8 for details on the interaction between the align and vAlign attributes and properties in IE for Windows. The W3C DOM uses the align property predominantly for placing the caption above or below the table.

| | |
|---|---|
| **Example** | document.getElementById("myCaption").align = "bottom"; |
| **Value** | Any of the following constants (as a string): bottom \| left \| right \| top. |
| **Default** | top |

## vAlign

**Read/Write**

Specifies whether the table caption appears above or below the table.

| | |
|---|---|
| **Example** | document.getElementById("tabCaption").vAlign = "bottom" |
| **Value** | Case-insensitive constant (as a string): bottom \| top. |
| **Default** | top |

## cells

A collection of all td elements contained within a single tr element. Collection members are sorted in source code order.

**Object Model Reference**
document.getElementById("*rowID*").cells

**Object-Specific Properties**
length

**Object-Specific Methods**

| item( ) | namedItem( ) | tags( ) | urns( ) |

**Object-Specific Event Handler Properties**
None.

## length

NN 6   IE 4   DOM 1
Read-only

Returns the number of elements in the collection.

**Example**
var howMany = document.getElementById("myTable").rows[0].cells.length;

**Value**        Integer.

## item( )

NN 6   IE 4   DOM 1

item(*index*[, *subindex*])
item(*index*)

Returns a single td object or collection of td objects corresponding to the element matching the index value (or, optionally in IE, the index and subindex values).

**Returned Value**
One td object or collection (array) of td objects. If there are no matches to the parameters, the returned value is null.

**Parameters**

*index*
> When the parameter is a zero-based integer, the returned value is a single element corresponding to the specified item in source code order (nested within the current element); when the parameter is a string (IE only), the returned value is a collection of elements whose id properties match that string.

*subindex*
> In IE only, if you specify a string value for the first parameter, you can use the second parameter to specify a zero-based index that retrieves the specified element from the collection whose id properties match the first parameter's string value.

Alphabetical DOM Reference

## namedItem( )

<div align="right">NN 6    IE 6    DOM 1</div>

namedItem("*ID*")

Returns a single td object or collection of td objects corresponding to the element matching the parameter string value.

**Returned Value**

One td object or collection (array) of td objects. If there are no matches to the parameters, the returned value is null.

**Parameters**

*ID*

    The string that contains the same value as the desired element's id attribute.

## tags( )

<div align="right">NN *n/a*    IE 4    DOM *n/a*</div>

tags("*tagName*")

Returns a collection of objects (among all objects nested within the current collection) whose tags match the *tagName* parameter. Implemented in all IE collections (see the all.tags( ) method), but redundant for collections of the same element type.

## urns( )

<div align="right">NN *n/a*    IE 5(Win)    DOM *n/a*</div>

urns(*URN*)

See the all.urns( ) method.

# center

<div align="right">NN 6    IE 4    DOM *n/a*</div>

The center object reflects the center element. The W3C DOM does not support the deprecated HTML 4 center element. For backward compatibility, Netscape 6 treats the element as earlier browsers do, but the scriptable element is treated as a span object, whose default text-align style is set to center.

**HTML Equivalent**    <center>

**Object Model Reference**

[window.]document.getElementById("*elementID*")

**Object-Specific Properties**

None.

**Object-Specific Methods**

None.

**Object-Specific Event Handler Properties**

None.

# checkbox

See input (type="checkbox").

# CharacterData

See Text.

# childNodes, NodeList                              NN *6*    IE *5*    DOM *1*

The object returned by the childNodes property of several W3C DOM objects is a collection (array) of references to Node objects that are immediate children of the current node object. In the W3C DOM structure, the abstract representation of this array is called the NodeList object, which shares some properties and methods of the IE childNodes object. Since both objects refer to the same parts of a document tree, they are treated here together. Collection members are sorted in source code order.

### Object Model Reference
*nodeReference*.childNodes

### Object-Specific Properties
length

### Object-Specific Methods
item( )          urns( )

### Object-Specific Event Handler Properties
None.

## length                                           NN *6*    IE *4*    DOM *1*
                                                              Read-only

Returns the number of nodes in the collection.

**Example**      var howMany = document.getElementById("myTable").attributes.length;

**Value**        Integer.

## item( )                                          NN *6*    IE *5*    DOM *1*
item(*index*)

Returns a single Node object corresponding to the element matching the index value.

### Returned Value

Reference to one Node object. If there is no match to the index value, the returned value is null. Unlike some other collections in IE, a string index value is not allowed for the childNodes object.

### Parameters
*index*

> A zero-based integer corresponding to the specified item in source code order (nested within the current node).

## urns( )   NN *n/a*   IE *5(Win)*   DOM *n/a*

urns(*URN*)

See the all.urns( ) method.

# children   NN *n/a*   IE *4*   DOM *n/a*

A collection of all elements contained in the current element. Note that unlike the childNodes collection, children counts only elements and not text nodes. Collection members are sorted in source code order. Internet Explorer lets you use array notation or parentheses to access a single element in the collection.

### Object Model Reference
```
document.getElementById("elementID").children(i)
document.getElementById("elementID").children[i]
```

### Object-Specific Properties
length

### Object-Specific Methods
item( )          namedItem( )          tags( )          urns( )

### Object-Specific Event Handler Properties
None.

## length   NN *n/a*   IE *4*   DOM *n/a*
**Read-only**

Returns the number of elements in the collection.

**Example**          var howMany = document.body.children.length;

**Value**          Integer.

## item( )   NN *n/a*   IE *4*   DOM *n/a*

item(*index*)

Returns an element object corresponding to the element matching the index value in source code order.

**Returned Value**

Reference to an element object. If there is no matches to the parameter, the returned value is null.

**Parameters**

*index*

> A zero-based integer corresponding to the specified item in source code order (nested within the current element).

## namedItem( )                                   NN *n/a*   IE 6   DOM *n/a*

namedItem(*IDOrName*)

Returns an element object or collection of objects corresponding to the element matching the parameter string value.

**Returned Value**

One element object or collection (array) of element objects. If there are no matches to the parameters, the returned value is null.

**Parameters**

*IDOrName*

> The string that contains the same value as the desired element's id or name attribute.

## tags( )                                          NN *n/a*   IE 4   DOM *n/a*

tags(*tagName*)

Returns a collection of objects (among all objects nested within the current collection) whose tags match the *tagName* parameter. Implemented in all IE collections (see the all. tags( ) method), but redundant for collections of the same element type.

## urns( )                                      NN *n/a*   IE 5(Win)   DOM *n/a*

urns(*URN*)

See the all.urns( ) method.

# cite

See acronym.

# clientInformation

See navigator.

Alphabetical DOM Reference

# clipboardData
NN *n/a*    IE *5(Win)*    DOM *n/a*

The clipboardData object (accessible as a property of a window or frame object) is a temporary container that scripts in IE 5 and later for Windows can use to transfer text data, particularly during script-controlled operations that simulate cutting, copying, and pasting, or that control dragging. Your script controls what data is stored in the clipboardData object, such as just the text of an element, an element's entire HTML, or the URL of an image. For example, a page for children could display simple icon images of several different kinds of animals. If the user starts dragging the dog icon, the script initiated by the img element's onDragStart event handler stores a custom attribute value of that element (perhaps the URL of a pretty dog photo) into the clipboardData object. When the user drops the icon into the designated area, the onDrop event handler's function reads the clipboardData object's data and loads the photo image into position on the page.

Data stored in this object survives navigation to other pages within the same domain and protocol. Therefore, you can use it to pass text data (including arrays that have been converted to strings by the Array.join( ) method) from one page to another without using cookies or location.search strings. But this is not the system clipboard (for security reasons).

For more information on transferring data via this object and the event.dataTransfer object, visit *http://msdn.microsoft.com/workshop/author/datatransfer/overview.asp*.

**HTML Equivalent**    None.

**Object Model Reference**
[window.]clipboardData

**Object-Specific Properties**
dropEffect                              effectAllowed

**Object-Specific Methods**
clearData( )    getData( )    setData( )

**Object-Specific Event Handler Properties**
None.


## dropEffect, effectAllowed
NN *n/a*    IE *5(Win)*    DOM *n/a*

Read/Write

These two properties belong to the clipboardData object by inheritance from the dataTransfer object, to which they genuinely apply. Ignore these properties for the clipboardData object.


## clearData( )
NN *n/a*    IE *5(Win)*    DOM *n/a*

clearData([*dataFormat*])

Removes data from the clipboardData object.

**Returned Value**    None.

**Parameters**

*dataFormat*

> An optional string specifying a single format for the data to be removed. Earlier plans to allow multiple data types appear to have fallen through. As of IE 6, the only reliable format is Text. Omitting the parameter removes all data of all types.

## getData( )     NN *n/a*    IE *5(Win)*    DOM *n/a*

getData(*dataFormat*)

Returns a copy of data from the clipboardData object. The clipboardData contents remain intact for subsequent reading in other script statements.

**Returned Value**    String.

**Parameters**

*dataFormat*

> A string specifying the format for the data to be read. Earlier plans to allow multiple data types appear to have fallen through. As of IE 6, the only reliable format is Text.

## setData( )     NN *n/a*    IE *5(Win)*    DOM *n/a*

setData(*dataFormat, stringData*)

Stores string data in the clipboardData object. Returns Boolean true if the assignment is successful

**Returned Value**    Boolean value: true | false.

**Parameters**

*dataFormat*

> A string specifying the format for the data to be read. Earlier plans to allow multiple data types appear to have fallen through. As of IE 6, the only reliable format is Text. While the method accepts URL as a format, reading a set value in that format is not successful.

*stringData*

> Any string value, including strings that contain HTML tags.

# code

See acronym.

# col, colgroup     NN *6*    IE *4*    DOM *1*

The col object reflects the col element; the colgroup object reflects the colgroup element. Both elements provide ways of assigning multiple adjacent columns to groups for convenience in assigning styles, widths, and other visual treatments.

**HTML Equivalent**

```
<col>
<colgroup>
```

**Object Model Reference**

[window.]document.getElementById("*elementID*")

**Object-Specific Properties**

| align | ch | chOff | span | vAlign |
|-------|----|----|------|--------|
| width | | | | |

**Object-Specific Methods**

None.

**Object-Specific Event Handler Properties**

None.

## align

NN *6*    IE *4*    DOM *1*

Read/Write

Defines the horizontal alignment of content within cells covered by the col or colgroup element.

**Example**    document.getElementById("myCol").align = "center";

**Value**

Any of the three horizontal alignment constants: center | char | left | right.

**Default**    left

## ch

NN *6*    IE *6*    DOM *1*

Read/Write

Defines the text character used as an alignment point for text within a column or column group (reflecting the char attribute). This property is normally of value only for the align attribute set to "char". In practice, neither IE nor Navigator respond to these properties.

**Example**    document.getElementById("myCol").ch = ".";

**Value**    Single character string.

**Default**    None.

## chOff

NN *6*    IE *6*    DOM *1*

Read/Write

Defines the offset point at which the character specified by the char attribute is to appear within a cell. In practice, neither IE 6 nor Netscape 6 respond to these properties.

**Example**    document.getElementById("myCol").chOff = "80%";

**Value**          String value of the number of pixels or percentage (within the cell).

**Default**      None.

## span                                              **NN 6   IE 4   DOM 1**

                                                                             **Read/Write**

Provides the number of adjacent columns for which the element's attribute and style settings apply.

**Example**     `document.getElementById("myColgroup").span = 2;`

**Value**         Integer.

**Default**      1

## vAlign                                           **NN 6   IE 4   DOM 1**

                                                                             **Read/Write**

Provides the manner of vertical alignment of text within the column grouping's cells.

**Example**     `document.getElementById("myCol").vAlign = "baseline";`

**Value**         Case-insensitive constant (as a string): `baseline` | `bottom` | `middle` | `top`.

**Default**      `middle`

## width                                               **NN 6   IE 4   DOM 1**

                                                                             **Read/Write**

Provides the width in pixels of each column of the column grouping. Changes to these values are immediately reflected in reflowed content on the page.

**Example**     `document.getElementById("myColgroup").width = 150;`

**Value**         Integer.

**Default**      None.

# comment, Comment                         **NN 6   IE 4   DOM 1**

The comment object reflects the ! element in an HTML document. But in a W3C DOM environment, such as Netscape 6, this object is not a genuine element in the context of the W3C DOM abstract model. Instead, the object is simply a special kind of node. Such a node has a nodeType value of 8, which identifies it as a Comment node. A Comment node has the following inheritance chain in the DOM abstract model: Node->CharacterData-> Comment. While a Comment node has special values automatically assigned to some of its properties (such as nodeValue), a Comment node has no properties or methods beyond the ones inherited from the Node and CharacterData objects. Node properties and methods are discussed earlier in this chapter among the shared items; CharacterData properties and methods are covered in detail with the Text object, which also inherits from CharacterData, and is more likely to be scripted.

To reference a comment element, use relative element or node properties. While IE provides an id property by virtue of its inheritance model, you cannot assign an identifier to the element via an id attribute. Such an element in IE does, however, have a tag name value of !. Therefore, you can reference an IE HTML comment element via the collection of elements returned by the document.all.tags("!") method.

**HTML Equivalent**    `<!--comment text-->`

**Object Model Reference**

*nodeReference*

**Object-Specific Properties**

| | | |
|---|---|---|
| data | length | text |

**Object-Specific Methods**

| | | | |
|---|---|---|---|
| appendData( ) | deleteData( ) | insertData( ) | replaceData( ) |
| substringData( ) | | | |

**Object-Specific Event Handler Properties**

None.

## data

| | | |
|---|---|---|
| NN 6 | IE 6 | DOM 1 |

Read/Write

Provides the text content of the comment. See Text.data.

## length

| | | |
|---|---|---|
| NN 6 | IE 6 | DOM 1 |

Read-only

Provides the character count of the comment data. See Text.length.

## text

| | | |
|---|---|---|
| NN *n/a* | IE 4 | DOM 1 |

Read/Write

Provides the text content of the element. Due to the nature of this element, the value of the text property is identical to the values of the innerHTML and outerHTML properties. Changes to this property do not affect the text of the comment as viewed in the browser's source code version of the document. This property is not available in IE 4/Macintosh.

**Example**

```
document.all.tags("!")[4].text = "Replaced comment, but no one will know.";
```

**Value**        String.

**Default**      None.

## appendData(), deleteData(), insertData(), replaceData( ), substringData( ) NN 6    IE 6    DOM 1

Provide methods for manipulating comment text. See these methods in the Text object.

# CSSImportRule, CSSMediaRule, CSSPageRule

See CSSRule.

# cssRule, CSSRule, rule NN 6    IE 5    DOM 2

A style sheet rule object is a member of the collection of styleSheet objects in the document. The IE and W3C DOMs have different syntax for referencing each of these rule objects. For IE, the reference is via the rules collection (a single object being known as a rule object); for W3C, as implemented in Netscape 6 and IE 5 for the Macintosh, the reference is via the cssRules collection (a single object being known as a cssRule object). Note that the cssRule object is not in the Windows version of IE through Version 6.

The corresponding W3C DOM abstract object is called the CSSRule object, but that form of the object name is important only to scripters who wish to modify the prototype properties and methods of the CSSRule object in Netscape 6. The W3C DOM goes further to define special types of CSSRule objects for each of the @ rule types (CSSImportRule, CSSMediaRule, and so on). A member of the cssRules collection can be any one of those types, and is identified as such by its type property. Each type has its own set of properties and/or methods that apply to that cssRule type. In the item property and method listings below, observe the type(s) for which they apply. By and large, however, the inline rules you will script are of the CSSStyleRule type.

Use scriptable access to a rule or cssRule object with caution. If you modify a rule's selector or style definition, the changes affect the entire document, and could, with a misplaced colon, ruin other rules in the document. To toggle among two or more styles for a single element, class, or element type, it is generally more reliable and efficient to use other techniques that work with multiple rules (swapping className assignments on elements) or multiple style sheets (enabling and disabling styleSheet objects). But for the sake of the completeness of the object model, the W3C DOM in particular provides full access to style sheet rule pieces if you absolutely need them.

## Object Model Reference

```
document.styleSheets[i].rules[j]
document.styleSheets[i].cssRules[j]
```

## Object-Specific Properties

| | | | |
|---|---|---|---|
| cssRules | cssText | encoding | href |
| media | parentRule | parentStyleSheet | readOnly |
| selectorText | style | styleSheet | type |

**Object-Specific Methods**

deleteRule( )    insertRule( )

**Object-Specific Event Handler Properties**

None.

## cssRules

NN 6　IE n/a　DOM 2<br>Read-only

Returns a collection of cssRule objects nested within an @media rule.

**W3C DOM CSSRule Types**

CSSMediaRule

| | |
|---|---|
| **Value** | Reference to a cssRules collection object. |
| **Default** | Array of zero length. |

## cssText

NN 6　IE 5(Mac)　DOM 2<br>Read/Write

Indicates the complete text of the style sheet rule, including selector and attribute name/ value pairs inside curly braces. IE 6 for Windows provides no equivalent property. In supporting browsers, changes do not influence the object or rendering.

**W3C DOM CSSRule Types**

All.

**Example**

```
document.styleSheets[0].cssRules[2].cssText = "td {text-align:center}";
```

| | |
|---|---|
| **Value** | String. |
| **Default** | None. |

## encoding

NN 6　IE n/a　DOM 2<br>Read-only

Returns the character set code (e.g., ISO-8859-1 or UTF-8) associated with an @charset rule.

**W3C DOM CSSRule Types**

CSSCharsetRule

| | |
|---|---|
| **Value** | String. |
| **Default** | None. |

## href

Returns the URI of the external style sheet file imported via an @import rule.

**W3C DOM CSSRule Types**
CSSImportRule

| | |
|---|---|
| **Value** | String. |
| **Default** | None. |

## media

Returns the media type specified for an @import or @media rule.

**W3C DOM CSSRule Types**
CSSImportRule
CSSMediaRule

**Value**
String constant for media types supported by the browser (e.g., screen or print).

| | |
|---|---|
| **Default** | all |

## parentRule

Refers to the cssRule object that contains the current cssRule, such as a rule nested inside an @ rule. Accessing this property value can crash Netscape 6.2.

**W3C DOM CSSRule Types**
All.

| | |
|---|---|
| **Example** | var superRule = document.styleSheets[0].cssRules[1].parentRule; |
| **Value** | cssRule object reference. |
| **Default** | null |

## parentStyleSheet

Refers to the styleSheet object that contains the current cssRule. Allows a function that might be passed a reference to a cssRule object to obtain a reference to the containing styleSheet object, possibly to learn more about what else is in the style sheet.

**W3C DOM CSSRule Types**
All.

| Example | `var ss = document.styleSheets[0].cssRules[3].parentStyleSheet;` |
|---|---|
| Value | styleSheet object reference. |
| Default | Current object. |

## readOnly

Returns Boolean true for rules that arrive to a document via an @import rule or a link element. Such rules may not be modified by script, although an element governed by such a rule can have individual style properties modified because the modifications are made to the element's own style property, and not the rule object.

### Example
```
if (!document.styleSheets[2].cssRules[0].readOnly) {
    // not read-only, so OK to modify here
}
```

| Value | Boolean value: true | false. |
|---|---|
| Default | Varies with rule type. |

## selectorText

Indicates the selector portion of the style sheet rule. Although this property is read/write (except in IE 5/Mac), changes do not influence the object or rendering.

### W3C DOM CSSRule Types
CSSPageRule
CSSStyleRule

### Example
```
document.styleSheets[0].cssRules[2].selectorText = "td.leftHeaders";
```

| Value | String. |
|---|---|
| Default | None. |

## style

Returns a style object with properties that reflect the attribute settings of the current rule. This is the same kind of style object associated with elements in the document (corresponding to the W3C DOM CSSStyleDeclaration object). If you must modify style sheet settings at the rule level, do so via the style property of the rule or cssRule. Changes register themselves immediately, and the elements affected by the rule render their changes accordingly.

### W3C DOM CSSRule Types
CSSFontRule
CSSPageRule
CSSStyleRule

### Example
```
var oneRule;
if (document.styleSheets) {
    if (document.styleSheets[0].cssRules) {
        oneRule = document.styleSheets[2].cssRules[1];
    } else if (document.styleSheets[0].rules) {
        oneRule = document.styleSheets[2].rules[1];
    }
}
if (oneRule) {
    oneRule.style.color = "red";
    oneRule.style.fontWeight = "bold";
}
```

**Value**     Reference to a style (W3C CSSStyleDeclaration) object.

**Default**   Current style object.

## styleSheet

NN 6     IE n/a     DOM 2

**Read-only**

Returns a reference to the styleSheet object contained by the imported style sheet. From here you can inspect cssRule objects belonging to that styleSheet object—essentially drilling down one more level to the styleSheet object structure of the remote style sheet file.

### W3C DOM CSSRule Types
CSSImportRule

**Value**     styleSheet object reference.

**Default**   None.

## type

NN 6     IE n/a     DOM 2

**Read-only**

Returns an integer corresponding to one of seven cssRule types, as defined by the W3C DOM. Every cssRule object in Netscape 6 comes equipped with plain-language constant properties corresponding to the rule types, as follows.

| Constant | Equivalent integer |
|---|---|
| *cssRuleReference*.UNKNOWN_RULE | 0 |
| *cssRuleReference*.STYLE_RULE | 1 |
| *cssRuleReference*.CHARSET_RULE | 2 |
| *cssRuleReference*.IMPORT_RULE | 3 |

Alphabetical DOM
Reference

| Constant | Equivalent integer |
|---|---|
| *cssRuleReference*.MEDIA_RULE | 4 |
| *cssRuleReference*.FONT_FACE_RULE | 5 |
| *cssRuleReference*.PAGE_RULE | 6 |

**W3C DOM CSSRule Types**

All.

**Example**

```
var oneRule = document.styleSheets[2].cssRules[1];
if (oneRule.type == oneRule.IMPORT_RULE) {
    // process @import rule
}
```

**Value**        Integer.

**Default**       1

## deleteRule( )                                    NN 6    IE *n/a*    DOM 2

deleteRule(*index*)

Removes the zero-based index numbered rule from the current @media rule.

**W3C DOM CSSRule Types**

CSSMediaRule

**Returned Value**    None.

**Parameters**

*index*

    A zero-based integer corresponding to the specified item in source code order.

## insertRule( )                                    NN 6    IE *n/a*    DOM 2

insertRule("*rule*", *index*)

Inserts a new rule (selector text and style attributes) into the current @media rule at the position indicated by the second parameter.

**W3C DOM CSSRule Types**

CSSMediaRule

**Returned Value**    Integer of inserted position.

**Parameters**

*rule*

    A string containing selector and curly-braced style attributes comprising the rule to be inserted.

*index*

    A zero-based integer corresponding to the specified item in source code order.

# cssRules, CSSRuleList, rules　　　　NN 6　IE 4　DOM 2

A collection of cssRule (Netscape 6 and IE 5/Mac) or rule (IE 4 and later) objects that are members of a styleSheet object. The W3C DOM abstract representation of this collection is called a CSSRuleList object. Members of this collection are accessed only via their integer index number, but you may iterate through the collection and examine properties of each rule object (such as the selectorText property) to distinguish one rule from another.

## Object Model Reference
*IE (Windows)*
    document.styleSheets[i].rules
*NN and IE (Mac)*
    document.styleSheets[i].cssRules

## Object-Specific Properties
length

## Object-Specific Methods
item( )

## Object-Specific Event Handler Properties
None.

## length　　　　NN 6　IE 4　DOM 2
　　　　　　　　　　　　　　　　　　Read-only

Returns the number of elements in the collection, including @ rules.

**Example**　　　var howMany = document.styleSheets[1].cssRules.length;

**Value**　　　　Integer.

## item( )　　　　NN 6　IE 4　DOM 2
item(*index*)

Returns a style sheet rule object corresponding to the rule matching the index value in source code order.

## Returned Value
Reference to a cssRule or rule object, depending on the object model. If there are no matches to the parameters, the returned value is null.

## Parameters
*index*
    A zero-based integer corresponding to the specified item in source code order (nested within the current styleSheet object).

# CSSStyleDeclaration

See style.

# CSSStyleSheet

See styleSheet.

## currentStyle

NN *n/a*  IE *5(Win)*  DOM *n/a*

The currentStyle object (a property of all HTML element objects in IE 5 and later for Windows) provides read-only access to the effective (cascaded) style properties applied to the current element, including properties influenced by linked, imported, and explicit style sheet settings. This object is a property of all renderable HTML element objects and stands in contrast to an element's style object, which reports, and allows modification of, style sheet properties explicitly assigned to the inline style attribute.

### Object Model Reference
[window.]document.getElementById("*elementID*").currentStyle

### Object-Specific Properties
See the style object.

### Object-Specific Methods
See the style object.

### Object-Specific Event Handler Properties
None.

## custom, HTMLUnknownElement

NN *6*  IE *5*  DOM *1*

Provides scriptable access to author-defined elements. Such elements share properties, methods, and event handlers of generic HTML element objects, and usually have custom attributes associated with them.

### HTML Equivalent  *<user-defined-tag>*

### Object Model Reference
[window.]document.getElementById("*elementID*")

### Object-Specific Properties
None.

### Object-Specific Methods
None.

**Object-Specific Event Handler Properties**
None.

# dataTransfer

NN n/a   IE 5(Win)   DOM n/a

The dataTransfer object (accessible as a property of the event object) is a temporary container that scripts in IE 5 and later for Windows can use to transfer text data, particularly during script-controlled operations that simulate cutting, copying, and pasting, or that control dragging. Your script controls what data is stored in the dataTransfer object, such as just the text of an element, an element's entire HTML, or the URL of an image. For example, a page for children could display simple icon images of several different kinds of animals. If the user starts dragging the dog icon, the script initiated by the img element's ondragstart event handler can store a custom attribute value of that element (perhaps the URL of a pretty dog photo) into the dataTransfer object. When the user drops the icon into the designated area, the ondrop event handler's function reads the dataTransfer object's data, and loads the photo image into position on the page.

Even though an event object changes its properties with each new event action, the dataTransfer object preserves its data from one event to the next, until a script removes the data from the object or other data is stored in it. Properties of the dataTransfer object distinguish its powers from those of the clipboardData object. By setting the dropEffect and effectAllowed properties, your scripts can control the type of cursor icon that appears during drag and drop operations. Example 9-1 demonstrates how the properties and methods of the dataTransfer object can be wired to dragging events such that the cursor changes to a "copy" style when rolled atop a desired drop target.

*Example 9-1. Using the dataTransfer object*

```
<html>
<head>
<title>dataTransfer Demo</title>
<style type="text/css">
td {text-align:center}
th {text-decoration:underline}
.cyan {color:cyan}
.yellow {color:yellow}
.magenta {color:magenta}
#blank1 {text-decoration:underline}
</style>
<script type="text/javascript">
// set stage when dragging a desired source element
function setupDrag() {
    if (event.srcElement.tagName != "TD") {
        // don't allow dragging for any other elements
        event.returnValue = false;
    } else {
        // set cursor to look like copy action
        event.dataTransfer.effectAllowed = "copy";
        // store dragged cell text to transfer
        event.dataTransfer.setData("Text", event.srcElement.innerText);
    }
}
```

*Example 9-1. Using the dataTransfer object (continued)*

```
// perform drop operations
function handleDrop( ) {
    var elem = event.srcElement;
    var passedData = event.dataTransfer.getData("Text");
    if (passedData) {
        // show drop target cursor
        event.dataTransfer.dropEffect = "copy";
        // apply data to drop target
        elem.innerText = passedData;
        elem.className = passedData;
        document.selection.empty();
    }
}
// we're dragging/copying, but not to here
function cancelDefault( ) {
    // set cursor to "No" symbol
    event.dataTransfer.dropEffect = "copy";
    event.returnValue = false;
}
</script>
</head>
<body ondragstart="setupDrag( );">
<table cellpadding="5">
<tr><th>Drag Your Favorite Color</th></tr>
<tr><td>cyan</td></tr>
<tr><td>yellow</td></tr>
<tr><td>magenta</td></tr>
</table>

<p>My favorite color is <span id="blank1" ondragenter="cancelDefault( );"
ondragover="cancelDefault( );" ondrop="handleDrop( );">
     </span> .</p>
</body>
</html>
```

For more information on transferring data via this object and the `clipboardData` object, visit *http://msdn.microsoft.com/workshop/author/datatransfer/overview.asp*.

**HTML Equivalent**

None.

**Object Model Reference**

[window.]event.dataTransfer

**Object-Specific Properties**

dropEffect     effectAllowed

**Object-Specific Methods**

clearData( )   getData( )     setData( )

**Object-Specific Event Handler Properties**

None.

## dropEffect, effectAllowed

These two properties work together but at different stages along a dragging operation that involves the `dataTransfer` object. They both control the appearance of the cursor during the drag and drop process. Assign a cursor style at the beginning of a drag operation via the `ondragstart` event and `effectAllowed` property. The drop target's `ondragover` and `ondragenter` event handlers should set the `dropEffect` property to the desired cursor style, and also set the `event.returnValue` property to `false`. This opens the way for the `ondrop` event handler not only to set the cursor via the `dropEffect` property, but to process the drop action. See Example 9-1 for a simple demonstration of the interaction of all these events and properties.

**Example**          `event.dataTransfer.dropEffect= "copy";`

**Value**            Case-insensitive constant (as a string): `copy` | `link` | `move` | `none`.

**Default**          `none`

## clearData( )

`clearData([dataFormat])`

Removes data from the `dataTransfer` object.

**Returned Value**   None.

**Parameters**

*dataFormat*

An optional string specifying the format for the data to be removed. Earlier plans to allow multiple data types appear to have fallen through. As of IE 6, the only reliable format is Text. Omitting the parameter deletes all data of all types.

## getData( )

`getData(dataFormat)`

Returns a copy of data from the `dataTransfer` object. The `dataTransfer` contents remain intact for subsequent reading in other script statements.

**Returned Value**   String.

**Parameters**

*dataFormat*

A string specifying the format for the data to be read. Earlier plans to allow multiple data types appear to have fallen through. As of IE 6, the only reliable format is Text.

## setData( )  NN *n/a*   IE *5(Win)*   DOM *n/a*

setData(*dataFormat*, *stringData*)

Stores string data in the dataTransfer object. Returns Boolean true if the assignment is successful

**Returned Value**   Boolean value: true | false.

**Parameters**

*dataFormat*

A string specifying the format for the data to be read. Earlier plans to allow multiple data types appear to have fallen through. As of IE 6, the only reliable format is Text. While the method accepts URL as a format, reading a set value in that format is not successful.

*stringData*

Any string value, including strings that contain HTML tags.

# dd  NN *6*   IE *4*   DOM *1*

The dd object reflects the dd element.

**HTML Equivalent**

<dd>

**Object Model Reference**

[window.]document.getElementById("*elementID*")

**Object-Specific Properties**

noWrap

**Object-Specific Methods**

None.

**Object-Specific Event Handler Properties**

None.

## noWrap  NN *n/a*   IE *4*   DOM *n/a*

Read/Write

Specifies whether the browser should render the element as wide as is necessary to display a line of nonbreaking text on one line. Abuse of this attribute can force the user into a great deal of inconvenient horizontal scrolling of the page to view all of the content.

**Example**        document.getElementById("wideBody").noWrap = "true";

**Value**          Boolean value: true | false.

**Default**        false

# del

The del object reflects the del element.

**HTML Equivalent**
<del>

**Object Model Reference**
[window.]document.getElementById("*elementID*")

**Object-Specific Properties**
cite          dateTime

**Object-Specific Methods**
None.

**Object-Specific Event Handler Properties**
None.

## cite, dateTime

NN *6*   IE *5(Mac)/6(Win)*   DOM *1*
Read/Write

These two properties are listed among the shared properties earlier in this chapter due to an IE 6 implementation oddity. IE 5/Macintosh and Netscape 6 correctly implement these properties only for the del and ins objects, as specified in the W3C DOM, but in no mainstream browser do they convey any special powers. See the shared cite and dateTime properties.

# dfn

See acronym.

# Dialog Helper

NN *n/a*   IE *6(Win)*   DOM *n/a*

The Dialog Helper object is an ActiveX control delivered with IE 6 for Windows that provides a short assortment of potentially useful system and document information; the method also displays a color selector dialog from which your scripts can obtain a user's color choice. Most typically, it would be used when scripting IE's edit mode, where users need to make color, font, and element choices. But you might find the object's properties and methods useful in traditional browser document settings.

Loading this object into the page requires the following <object> tag:

```
<object id="dlgHelper" classid="clsid:3050f819-98b5-11cf-bb82-00aa00bdce0b"
      width="0px" height="0px">
</object>
```

Because this object is not rendered, you may place its tag in the head portion of your document. You may also assign your choice of identifier to the id attribute. Once the object is loaded, reference it as a global object in the window.

**HTML Equivalent**
None.

**Object Model Reference**
[window.]document.getElementById("*elementID*")

**Object-Specific Properties**

| | |
|---|---|
| blockFormats | fonts |

**Object-Specific Methods**
ChooseColorDlg( ) getCharset( )

**Object-Specific Event Handler Properties**
None.

## blockFormats

NN n/a   IE 6   DOM n/a<br>Read-only

Returns a collection of plain-language names of block-level elements supported by the browser. Unlike other IE collections, to read the number of items, you must access its Count property, rather than length property. The names of items returned are strings, such as "Heading 1" and "Numbered List" (corresponding to the h1 and ol elements, respectively). Access each item in the collection via the collection's item( ) method.

**Example**
```
var blockList = dlgHelper.blockFormats;
var blockNames = new Array( );
for (var i = 0; i < blockList.Count; i++) {
    blockNames[blockNames.length]= blockList.item(i);
}
```

| | |
|---|---|
| **Value** | Array of strings |
| **Default** | Implementation-dependent. |

## fonts

NN n/a   IE 6   DOM n/a<br>Read-only

Returns a collection of plain-language names of system fonts. Unlike other IE collections, to read the number of items, you must access its Count property, rather than length property. The names of items returned are strings, such as "MS Sans Serif" and "Verdana". Access each item in the collection via the collection's item( ) method.

**Example**

```
var fontList = dlgHelper.fonts;
var fontNames = new Array( );
for (var i = 0; i < fontList.Count; i++) {
    fontNames [fontNames .length]= fontList .item(i);
}
```

**Value**          Array of strings

**Default**        Implementation-dependent.


## ChooseColorDlg( )                                    NN *n/a*    IE *6*    DOM *n/a*

ChooseColorDlg([*initialHexColor*])

Displays a color selector dialog box, and returns a decimal number corresponding to the color chosen by the user. To apply the color to style or other color property settings, you may have to convert the decimal value to a suitable hexadecimal triplet value of the *#RRGGBB* format. The following fragment demonstrates the sequence of obtaining the color, converting it to the desired base and digit count, and assigning the value to a style property:

```
var colorChoice = dlgHelper.ChooseColorDlg( );
var hexColor = colorChoice.toString(16);
while (hexColor.length < 6) {hexColor = "0" + hexColor;}
document.body.style.color = "#" + hexColor;
```

If the user selects a custom color in the dialog and adds it to a little shortcut box, the color does not reappear in the box the next time the dialog appears. But a custom color can still be pre-selected by passing its hex value as a parameter to the method.

**Returned Value**

Decimal integer of the selected color (0 through as many colors of the client settings).

**Parameters**

*initialHexColor*
>   Optional hexadecimal number that presets the initially-selected color in the dialog box.


## getCharset( )                                       NN *n/a*    IE *6*    DOM *n/a*

getCharset("*fontName*")

Returns an integer corresponding to a constant associated with a character set known by the operating system. Among the common values returned for font families installed on Latin-based systems are 0 (for plain ANSI character set) and 2 (for a symbol set). The required parameter is the name of a font to inspect for its character set. Such names may be retrieved from the fonts property of the Dialog Helper object:

```
var setID = dlgHelper.getCharset(dlgHelper.fonts.item(4));
```

Not all Windows versions have the same character set suite installed.

**Returned Value**        Integer.

**Parameters**

*fontName*
> String name of installed system font.

# dir

The dir object reflects the dir element. This element, originally intended as a multicolumn list format, is treated the same as the ul element.

**HTML Equivalent**

<dir>

**Object Model Reference**

[window.]document.getElementById("*elementID*")

**Object-Specific Properties**

compact

**Object-Specific Methods**

None.

**Object-Specific Event Handler Properties**

None.

## compact

Provided for this element for the sake of compatibility with the W3C DOM standard. However, mainstream browsers do not act upon this property or its corresponding attribute.

**Value**          Boolean value: true | false.

**Default**        false

# directories, locationbar, menubar, personalbar, scrollbars, statusbar, toolbar

These objects belong to the window object and represent portions of the "chrome" surrounding the content area of the browser window (the directories object is new for Netscape 6). With signed scripts in Navigator 4 or later (and the user's permission), you can dynamically hide and show these elements in a browser window. These features can also be turned off via the third parameter of the window.open( ) method, but only when generating a new window. To change the visibility of these items in an existing window, signed scripts are required. Internet Explorer has no equivalent functionality for a window that is already open.

**Object Model Reference**
[window.]directories
[window.]locationbar
[window.]menubar
[window.]personalbar
[window.]scrollbars
[window.]statusbar
[window.]toolbar

**Object-Specific Properties**
visible

**Object-Specific Methods**
None.

**Object-Specific Event Handler Properties**
None.

## visible

NN *4*    IE *n/a*    DOM *n/a*

Read/Write

Accessible only through signed scripts in Navigator 4 or later, determines whether the window chrome feature is displayed.

**Example**
netscape.security.PrivilegeManager.enablePrivilege("UniversalBrowserWrite");
window.statusbar.visible = "false";
netscape.security.PrivilegeManager.revertrivilege("UniversalBrowserWrite");

**Value**          Boolean value: true | false.

**Default**        true

## div

NN *6*    IE *4*    DOM *1*

The div object reflects the div element. This element creates a block-level element often used for element positioning or containment grouping of several related elements. In the Windows version of IE 4, the client- and scroll-related properties are not available unless the div element has its position style attribute set to absolute. The client and scroll properties are active in IE for the Macintosh.

**HTML Equivalent**
<div>

**Object Model Reference**
[window.]document.getElementById("*elementID*")

**Object-Specific Properties**

| align | dataFld | dataFormatAs | dataSrc | noWrap |
|-------|---------|--------------|---------|--------|

**Object-Specific Methods**
None.

**Object-Specific Event Handler Properties**
None.

## align
NN 6    IE 4    DOM 1
Read/Write

Defines the horizontal alignment of content within the element's box. Unless otherwise reined in, the box width is that of the next outermost positioning context—usually the body.

**Example**        `document.getElementById("myDIV").align = "center";`

**Value**        Any of the three horizontal alignment constants: center | left | right.

**Default**       left

## dataFld
NN n/a    IE 4    DOM n/a
Read/Write

Used with IE data binding to associate a remote data source column name to a div element's content. A datasrc attribute must also be set for the element. Setting both the dataFld and dataSrc properties to empty strings breaks the binding between element and data source. Works only for text data sources in IE 5 for the Macintosh.

**Example**        `document.getElementById("myDiv").dataFld = "comment";`

**Value**        Case-sensitive identifier of the data source column.

**Default**       None.

## dataFormatAs
NN n/a    IE 4    DOM n/a
Read/Write

Used with IE data binding, this property advises the browser whether the source material arriving from the data source is to be treated as plain text or as tagged HTML.

**Example**        `document.getElementById("myDiv").dataFormatAs = "text";`

**Value**        String constants: text | html.

**Default**       text

## dataSrc

Used with IE data binding to specify the ID of the page's object element that loads the data source object for remote data access. Content from the data source is specified via the dataFld attribute. Setting both the dataFld and dataSrc properties to empty strings breaks the binding between element and data source.

**Example**        document.getElementById("myDiv").dataSrc = "DBSRC3";

**Value**          Case-sensitive identifier of the data source.

**Default**        None.

## noWrap

Specifies whether the browser should render the element as wide as is necessary to display a line of nonbreaking text on one line. Abuse of this attribute can force the user into a great deal of inconvenient horizontal scrolling of the page to view all of the content. The corresponding attribute is deprecated.

**Example**        document.getElementById("wideDiv").noWrap = "true";

**Value**          Boolean value: true | false.

**Default**        false

## dl

The dl object reflects the dl element. This element is the wrapper for a definition list grouping.

**HTML Equivalent**    <dl>

**Object Model Reference**
[window.]document.getElementById("*elementID*")

**Object-Specific Properties**
compact

**Object-Specific Methods**
None.

**Object-Specific Event Handler Properties**
None.

## compact

NN 6    IE 4    DOM 1

Read/Write

When set to true, the compact property instructs the browser to render a related dt and dd pair on the same line if space allows. This compact styling is intended for dt elements consisting of only a few characters.

**Example**        document.getElementById("maindl").compact = true;

**Value**        Boolean value: true | false.

**Default**      false

# document

NN 2    IE 3    DOM 1

The document object represents both the content viewed in the browser window or frame and the other content of the HTML file loaded into the window or frame. Thus, all information from the head portion of the file is also part of the document object. All references to elements must include a reference to the document object. The document object has no name other than its hard-wired object name: document.

For a browser with internal architecture based closely on the W3C DOM, this document object represents the HTMLDocument object—a special kind (internal subclass) of the core module's Document object, suited to holding HTML documents. In other words, the HTMLDocument object inherits the properties and methods of the core Document object (sharing facilities with XML documents) and gets additional properties and methods that apply only to HTML documents. Of course, there is the conceptual incongruity about whether an HTMLDocument is applicable to an XHTML document because such a document theoretically is an XML document. But, in practice, even an XHTML document becomes an HTML document for scripting purposes, and has all the HTMLDocument properties and methods available to it.

One more important practical side to a W3C DOM implementation (as evidenced by the Netscape 6 implementation) is that the document object internally implements document-level properties and methods from other DOM modules, such as views, events, and styles. Each of these modules defines an object (DocumentEvent, DocumentRange, DocumentStyle, and DocumentView) that provides a vital connection between the HTMLDocument and these add-on module features. Thus, it is the styleSheets property of the DocumentStyle object in the W3C DOM that the scriptable document object described here uses to reach the styleSheet objects and their rules. And the DocumentEvent object links in its createEvent( ) method that allows the scriptable document object to generate an event outside the normal user- or system-created events. All of these features become subsumed by the document object you reference and script in Netscape 6 and similar browsers. The precise source module for a particular feature is not important to the scripter—all you need to know is that the properties and methods belong to the scriptable document object.

**Object Model Reference**
[window.]document

## Object-Specific Properties

| | | | |
|---|---|---|---|
| activeElement | alinkColor | anchors[] | applets[] |
| bgColor | body | charset | characterSet |
| compatMode | cookie | defaultCharset | defaultView |
| doctype | documentElement | domain | embeds[] |
| expando | fgColor | fileCreatedDate | fileModifiedDate |
| fileSize | fileUpdatedDate | forms[] | frames[] |
| height | ids[] | images[] | implementation |
| lastModified | layers[] | linkColor | links[] |
| location | media | mimeType | nameProp |
| namespaces[] | parentWindow | plugins[] | protocol |
| readyState | referrer | scripts[] | security |
| selection | styleSheets[] | tags[] | title |
| URL | URLUnencoded | vlinkColor | width |

## Object-Specific Methods

| | |
|---|---|
| addBinding( ) | captureEvents( ) |
| clear( ) | close( ) |
| createAttribute( ) | createAttributeNS( ) |
| createCDATASection( ) | createComment( ) |
| createDocumentFragment( ) | createElement( ) |
| createElementNS( ) | createEntityReference( ) |
| createEvent( ) | createEventObject( ) |
| createNodeIterator( ) | createProcessingInstruction( ) |
| createRange( ) | createStyleSheet( ) |
| createTextNode( ) | createTreeWalker( ) |
| elementFromPoint( ) | execCommand( ) |
| getAnonymousElementByAttribute( ) | getAnonymousNodes( ) |
| getBindingParent( ) | getElementById( ) |
| getElementsByName( ) | getSelection( ) |
| handleEvent( ) | hasFocus( ) |
| importNode( ) | loadBindingDocument( ) |
| open( ) | queryCommandEnabled( ) |
| queryCommandIndeterm( ) | queryCommandState( ) |
| queryCommandSupported( ) | queryCommandText( ) |
| queryCommandValue( ) | recalc( ) |
| releaseEvents( ) | removeBinding( ) |
| routeEvent( ) | write( ) |
| writeln( ) | |

## Object-Specific Event Handler Properties

| Handler | NN | IE | DOM |
|---|---|---|---|
| onselectionchange | n/a | 4 | n/a |
| onstop | n/a | 4 | n/a |

## activeElement

NN *n/a*    IE *4*    DOM *n/a*

Read-only

Refers to the object that is currently designated as the active element in the document. To learn more about the returned object, you'll need to examine the object's tagName, id, or other properties. Because buttons and other elements do not receive focus on the IE 4 for Macintosh, the returned value of this property may vary with operating system. While an element (especially a form control) that receives focus also becomes active, an element might be active, but due to other settings in newer IE versions, does not have focus. See the shared setActive( ) method.

| | |
|---|---|
| **Example** | var currObj = document.activeElement; |
| **Value** | Element object reference. |
| **Default** | None. |

## alinkColor

NN *2*    IE *3*    DOM *n/a*

Read/Write (IE)

Specifies the color of a hypertext link as it is being clicked. The color is applied to the link text or border around an image or object embedded within an a element. See also linkColor and vlinkColor properties for unvisited and visited link colors. Replaced in the W3C DOM by the aLink property of the body object, which is supported in IE 4 and later and in Netscape 6. Dynamically changed values for alinkColor are not reflected on the page in Navigator through Version 4.

| | |
|---|---|
| **Example** | document.alinkColor = "green"; |
| **Value** | A hexadecimal triplet or plain-language color name. See Appendix A for acceptable plain-language color names. |
| **Default** | #0000FF |

## anchors[]

NN *2*    IE *3*    DOM *1*

Returns an array of all anchor objects in the current document. This includes a elements that are designed as either anchors or combination anchors and links. Items in this array are indexed (zero-based) in source code order.

| | |
|---|---|
| **Example** | var aCount = document.anchors.length; |
| **Value** | Array of anchor element objects. |
| **Default** | Array of length zero. |

## applets[]

Returns an array of all Java applet objects in the current document. An applet must be started and running before it is counted as an object. Items in this array are indexed (zero-based) in source code order.

| | |
|---|---|
| **Example** | `var appletCount = document.applets.length` |
| **Value** | Array of applet element objects. |
| **Default** | Array of length zero. |

## bgColor

**Read/Write**

Provides the background color of the document. Even if the `bgcolor` attribute or `bgColor` property is set with a plain-language color name, the returned value is always a hexadecimal triplet.

Setting the `bgColor` property of a document in Navigator 2 or 3 for Macintosh or Unix does not properly redraw the window. Window content is obscured by the new color on those platforms. For browsers that support the `document.body` object, use the `bgColor` property of that object instead.

| | |
|---|---|
| **Example** | `document.bgColor = "yellow";` |
| **Value** | A hexadecimal triplet or plain-language color name. See Appendix A for acceptable plain-language color names. |
| **Default** | Varies with browser and operating system. |

## body

**Read-only**

Returns a reference to the body object defined by the body element within the document. This property is used as a gateway to the body object's properties.

| | |
|---|---|
| **Example** | `document.body.leftMargin = 15;` |
| **Value** | Object reference. |
| **Default** | The current body object. |

## charset

**Read/Write**

Indicates the character encoding of the document's content. This property is dropped from IE 6 for Windows in favor of the `document.defaultCharset` property. For Netscape 6, use the `document.characterSet` property.

**Alphabetical DOM Reference**

**Example**

```
if (document.charset == "csISO5427Cyrillic") {
    // process for Cyrillic charset
}
```

| Value | Case-insensitive alias from the character set registry (*ftp://ftp.isi.edu/in-notes/ iana/assignments/character-sets*). |
|---|---|
| Default | Determined by browser. |

## characterSet · NN 6    IE *n/a*    DOM *n/a*

**Read-only**

Indicates the character encoding of the document's content.

**Example**

```
if (document.characterSet == "ISO-8859-1") {
    // process for standard Latin character set
}
```

| Value | Case-insensitive alias from the character set registry (*ftp://ftp.isi.edu/in- notes/iana/assignments/character-sets*). |
|---|---|
| Default | Determined by browser. |

## compatMode NN 7    IE 6    DOM *n/a*

**Read-only**

Returns the compatibility mode for the document, as controlled by the DOCTYPE element's content. See the DOCTYPE element discussion in Chapter 8 for details on how to force the browser to treat a document in either backward compatibility or standards compatibility mode for element positioning and other implementation details. Because the choice of mode can impact some style property results, you can use this property to branch between two calculations in a shared library so that they treat the current document correctly, regardless of mode.

**Example**

```
if (document.compatMode == "BackCompat") {
    // process as if IE 5.5 or earlier or Netscape "quirks" mode
}
```

| Value | String constant: BackCompat \| CSS1Compat. |
|---|---|
| Default | BackCompat |

## cookie NN 2    IE 3    DOM 1

**Read/Write**

Indicates the HTTP cookie associated with the domain of the document and stored on the client machine. The Netscape browsers group all cookie data together into a single file, while IE creates a separate file for each domain's cookie data. Reading and writing the cookie property are not parallel operations. Reading a cookie property returns a semicolon-delimited list of name/value pairs in the following format:

```
name=value
```

Up to 20 of these pairs can be stored in the cookie property for a given domain (regardless of the number of HTML documents used in that web site). A total of 4,000 characters can be stored in the cookie, but it is advisable to keep each name/value pair to less than 2,000 characters in length. It is up to your scripting code to parse the cookie property value for an individually named cookie's value.

Writing cookie property values allows more optional pairs of data associated with a single name/value pair. Cookie data must be a string, but you can deconstruct an array into a string via the Array.join( ) method for writing the cookie value, and then use String.split( ) to reconstruct the array after reading the cookie data. The format is as follows:

```
document.cookie = "name=value
    [; expires=timeInGMT]
    [; path=pathName]
    [; domain=domainName]
    [; secure]";
```

No matter how many optional subproperties you set per cookie, only the name/value pair may be retrieved. All cookie data written to the cookie property is maintained in the browser's memory until the browser quits. If an expiration date has been made part of the cookie data and that time has not yet expired, the cookie data is saved to the actual cookie file; otherwise, the cookie data is discarded. The browser automatically deletes cookie data that has expired when the browser next starts.

**Example**

```
var exp = new Date( );
var nowPlusOneWeek = exp.getTime( ) + (7 * 24 * 60 * 60 * 1000);
exp.setTime(nowPlusOneWeek);
document.cookie = "userName=visitor; expires=" + exp.toGMTString( );
```

**Value**          Cookie data as string. See description.

**Default**        None.

## defaultCharset                              NN *n/a*   IE *4*   DOM *n/a*

Read-only

Indicates the character encoding of the content of the document.

**Example**          `var cset = document.defaultCharset;`

**Value**            Case-insensitive alias from the character set registry (*ftp://ftp.isi.edu/in-notes/ iana/assignments/character-sets*).

**Default**          Determined by browser.

Alphabetical DOM Reference

## defaultView

NN 6    IE n/a    DOM 2

Read-only

Returns a reference to the W3C DOM abstract representation of a "viewer" that renders the document (the formal name for the object is AbstractView). In Netscape 6, this object equates to the window or frame object that contains the document. A script function that has access to a document object (such as via the element object's ownerDocument property) can obtain a valid reference to the document's window via this defaultView property. The document's view includes knowledge about cascaded style rules applied to each element. See Chapter 4 for an example of obtaining the effective style of an element with the help of the document.defaultView property and the getComputedStyle( ) method.

This is as close as the W3C DOM Level 2 comes to acknowledging the existence of a window object. More is to come in Level 3.

**Example**     var theWin = elemRef.ownerDocument.defaultView;

**Value**        Reference to a window object.

**Default**      The document's window.


## doctype

NN 6    IE 5(Mac)    DOM 1

Read-only

Returns a reference to the DOCTYPE element object (the same as the W3C DOM abstract DocumentType node object). The property returns a reference value only if the DOCTYPE is specified in the document; otherwise the property returns null. As of Version 6, IE for Windows does not implement this property or node type. See the DocumentType object for properties available in various browsers. In a pure W3C DOM environment, the doctype property is inherited from the core document object, and is thus available to XML documents, as well.

**Example**     var docsType = document.doctype;

**Value**        Node reference.

**Default**      None.


## documentElement

NN 6    IE 5    DOM 1

Read-only

Returns a reference to the root element node of the document. For HTML documents, the reference is to the html element that encompasses the document's head and body elements. In a pure W3C DOM environment, the documentElement property is inherited from the core document object, and is thus available to XML documents, as well.

**Example**     var rootElem = document.documentElement;

**Value**        Element node reference.

**Default**      The current html element object.

## domain

**Read/Write**

Provides the hostname of the server that served up the document. If documents from different servers on the same domain must exchange content with each other, the domain properties of both documents must be set to the same domain to avoid security restrictions. Normally, if the hosts don't match, browser security disallows access to the other document's form data. This property allows, for example, a page from the *www* server to communicate with a page served up by a secure server.

| | |
|---|---|
| **Example** | document.domain = "megaCorp.com"; |
| **Value** | String of the domain name that two documents have in common (exclusive of the server name). |
| **Default** | None. |

## embeds[]

Returns an array of all embedded objects (embed elements) in the current document. Items in this array are indexed (zero-based) in source code order.

| | |
|---|---|
| **Example** | var embedCount = document.embeds.length; |
| **Value** | Array of embed object references. |
| **Default** | Array of zero length. |

## expando

**Read/Write**

Specifies whether scripts in the current document allow the creation and use of custom properties assigned to the document object. The extensible nature of JavaScript allows scripters to create a new object property by just assigning a value to it (as in document.stooge = "Curly"). This also means the document accepts incorrectly spelled property assignments, such as forgetting to set a middle letter of a long property name to uppercase (marginLeftColor). Such assignments are accepted without question, but the desired result is nowhere to be seen. If you don't intend to create custom properties, consider setting document.expando to false in an opening script statement as you author a page. This could help prevent spelling errors from causing bugs. The setting affects only scripts in the current document.

| | |
|---|---|
| **Example** | document.expando = false; |
| **Value** | Boolean value: true \| false. |
| **Default** | true |

**Alphabetical DOM Reference**

## fgColor

NN 2    IE 3    DOM n/a<br>Read/Write

Provides the foreground (text) color for the document. While you can change this property in all versions of Navigator, the text does not change dynamically in versions prior to 6. Still supported in current browsers, this property is replaced in IE 4 and Netscape 6 by document.body.text or style sheet settings.

**Example**    document.fgColor = "darkred";

**Value**    A hexadecimal triplet or plain-language color name. See Appendix A for acceptable plain-language color names.

**Default**    Browser default (usually black).

## fileCreatedDate

NN n/a    IE 4(Win)    DOM n/a<br>Read-only

Returns a string of the date (but not the time) that the server (or local filesystem) reports the currently-loaded file was created. IE 4's value is a long date format, but starting with IE 5, the date information is formatted as mm/dd/yyyy. The value may be corrupted if the server supplies the data in a format that IE does not expect. Not implemented in IE Mac through Version 5.1.

**Example**    var dateObj = new Date(document.fileCreatedDate);

**Value**    Date string.

**Default**    None.

## fileModifiedDate

NN n/a    IE 4(Win)    DOM n/a<br>Read-only

Returns a string of the date (but not the time) that the server (or local file system) reports the currently-loaded file was most recently modified. IE 4's value is a long date format, but starting with IE 5, the date information is formatted as mm/dd/yyyy. The value may be corrupted or incorrect if the server supplies the data in a format that IE does not expect. Not implemented in IE Mac through Version 5.1.

**Example**    var dateObj = new Date(document.fileModifiedDate);

**Value**    Date string.

**Default**    None.

## fileSize

NN n/a    IE 4    DOM n/a<br>Read-only

Returns the number of bytes for the size of the currently-loaded document. IE for Windows returns this value as a string, while IE for Macintosh returns a number value (an important distinction if you need to perform math operations on the value).

| **Example** | `var byteCount = parseInt(document.fileSize, 10);` |
| **Value** | Integer as string (Windows) or number (Mac). |
| **Default** | None. |

## fileUpdatedDate

NN n/a   IE 5.5(Win)   DOM n/a
Read-only

Returns an empty string. Apparently not officially supported for the document object.

## forms[]

NN 2   IE 3   DOM 1
Read-only

Returns an array of all form objects (form elements) in the current document. Items in this array are indexed (zero-based) in source code order, but may also be accessed by using the form's name as a string index value.

| **Example** | `var elemCount = document.forms[0].elements.length;` |
| **Value** | Array of form objects. |
| **Default** | Array of zero length. |

## frames[]

NN n/a   IE 4   DOM n/a
Read-only

Returns an array of all iframe objects (iframe element objects, not to be confused with window-like frame objects) in the current document. Items in this array are indexed (zero-based) in source code order. For cross-compatibility with IE 5 and later and Netscape 6, use document.getElementsByTagName("iframe") instead.

| **Example** | `var iframeCount = document.frames.length;` |
| **Value** | Array of iframe objects. |
| **Default** | Array of zero length. |

## height, width

NN 4   IE n/a   DOM n/a
Read-only

Return the pixel dimensions of the entire rendered document. These values coincide with the offsetHeight and offsetWidth property values for the document.body object. Since neither property pairing is yet sanctioned by the W3C DOM, you might prefer the offset pair, because they are at least cross-browser compatible.

| **Example** | `var howTall = document.height;` |
| **Value** | Number of pixels. |
| **Default** | Current document size. |

Alphabetical DOM Reference

## ids[]

NN |4|    IE *n/a*    DOM *n/a*
Read-only

Used with the Navigator 4-only JavaScript syntax of style sheets, the ids[] collection is part of a reference to a single ID and the style property assigned to it in the syntax form [document.]ids.*idName.stylePropertyName*. For a list of related properties, see the tags object listing in this chapter.

## images[]

NN *2*    IE *3*    DOM *1*
Read-only

Returns an array of all img element objects (exclusive of pre-cached images loaded via the new Image( ) constructor) in the current document. Items in this array are indexed (zero-based) in source code order, and may be accessed by number or by string name. The presence of this property indicates support for live, swappable images.

**Example**         document.images["home"].src = "images/homeHilite.jpg";

**Value**            Array of img objects.

**Default**        Array of zero length.

## implementation

NN *6*    IE *5(Mac)/6(Win)*    DOM *1*
Read-only

Returns a reference to the W3C DOMImplementation object, which represents, to a limited degree, the environment that makes up the document container—the browser, for our purposes. Methods of the object let you see which DOM modules the browser reports supporting. This object is also a gateway to creating virtual W3C Document and DocumentType objects outside of the current document tree. Thus, in Netscape 6 you can use the document.implementation property as a start to generating a nonrendered document for external XML documents. See the DOMImplementation object for details about the methods and their browser support.

**Example**
```
var xDoc = document.implementation.createDocument("", "theXdoc", null);
```

**Value**            Reference to a DOMImplementation object.

**Default**        Current DOMImplementation object.

## lastModified

NN *2*    IE *3*    DOM *n/a*
Read-only

Provides the date and time (as a string) on which the server says the document file was last modified. Some servers don't supply this information at all or correctly. Non-Windows browsers also tend to have a rough time interpreting the information correctly. Only in recent browsers is the date string in a form suitable as a parameter for a Date object constructor.

| Example | `document.write(document.lastModified);` |
|---|---|
| **Value** | String representation of a date and time. |
| **Default** | None. |

# layers[]

Returns an array of all Navigator 4-only layer element objects in the current document. Also included in the array are references to other HTML elements with style sheets that set the element to be relative- or absolute-positioned (in which case, Navigator 4 treats those elements as layer objects). Items in this array are indexed (zero-based) in source code order, and may be accessed by number or by string name. As a dead-end feature implemented only in Navigator 4, the presence of this property indicates support for the unique referencing requirements for Netscape layers.

**Example**

```
if (document.layers) {
    // use document.layers[] syntax for references
}
```

| **Value** | Array of layer objects or their equivalent. |
|---|---|
| **Default** | Array of zero length. |

# linkColor

Indicates the color of a hypertext link that has not been visited (that is, the URL of the link is not in the browser's cache). This is one of three states for a link: unvisited, active, and visited. The color is applied to the link text or border around an image or object embedded within an a element. Changes to this property do not dynamically change the link color in Navigator 4 or earlier. Starting with IE 4 and Netscape 6, you should switch to using the W3C DOM alternative, `document.body.link`, or style sheets.

| **Example** | `document.link Color= "#00FF00";` |
|---|---|
| **Value** | A hexadecimal triplet or plain-language color name. See Appendix A for acceptable plain-language color names. |
| **Default** | #0000FF |

# location

Indicates the URL of the current document. This property was deprecated because it may conflict with the `window.location` property. Netscape 6 drops support for this property entirely. Use either the `document.URL` property, or, better, the `window.location.href` property.

| Example | `document.location = "products/widget33.html";` |
|---|---|
| Value | A full or relative URL as a string. |
| Default | Document URL. |

## media

NN *n/a*   IE *5.5(Win)*   DOM *n/a*

Read/Write

Returns a string indicating the output medium for which the content is formatted. The property returns an empty string as of IE 6, and throws a security error if you assign accepted string values (all, print, or screen) to it. Avoid using this property with the document object.

## mimeType

NN *n/a*   IE *5(Win)*   DOM *n/a*

Read-only

Returns a string indicating the basic document type, but not in a MIME format. For an HTML document, the string returned changed starting with IE 5.5 to HTML Document. Do not confuse this document object property with the Netscape and IE/Mac navigator.mimeTypes property, which is an entirely different animal.

| Example | `var what = document.mimeType;` |
|---|---|
| Value | String. |
| Default | "HTML Document" |

## nameProp

NN *n/a*   IE *6(Win)*   DOM *n/a*

Read-only

Returns a string containing the same data as document.title, including an empty string if no title element exists in the document. This property may not be officially supported for the document object.

| Value | String. |
|---|---|
| Default | Empty string. |

## namespaces[]

NN *n/a*   IE *5.5(Win)*   DOM *n/a*

Read-only

Returns a collection of IE namespace objects implemented in the current document. A namespace object is a gateway to loading external behaviors. For more details, visit *http://msdn.microsoft.com/workshop/author/behaviors/overview/elementb_ovw.asp*.

| Example | `var IENSCount = document.namespaces.length;` |
|---|---|
| Value | Array of namespace object references. |
| Default | Array of zero length. |

## parentWindow

Returns a reference to the window object (which may be a frame in a frameset) that contains the current document. Use this reference to access the window's properties and methods directly. The returned value is the same as the window reference from the document.

| | |
|---|---|
| **Example** | `var siblingCount = document.parentWindow.frames.length;` |
| **Value** | window or frame object reference. |
| **Default** | window object. |

## plugins[ ]

Returns an array of all embedded objects (embed elements) in the current document. Items in this array are indexed (zero-based) in source code order. Do not confuse this collection with the navigator.plugins collection in Netscape Navigator.

| | |
|---|---|
| **Example** | `var embedCount = document.plugins.length;` |
| **Value** | Array of embed object references. |
| **Default** | Array of zero length. |

## protocol

Returns a plain-language string describing the protocol used to load the current document. Unlike the location.protocol property's literal value (e.g., http: or file:), the document.protocol is human-readable (e.g., Hypertext Transfer Protocol or File Protocol).

**Example**

```
if (document.protocol == "File Protocol") {
    // process for file access in IE
}
```

| | |
|---|---|
| **Value** | Plain-language string. |
| **Default** | Current document's protocol type. |

## readyState

Returns the current download status of the document content. If a script (especially one initiated by a user event) can perform some actions while the document is still loading, but must avoid other actions until the entire page has loaded, this property provides intermediate information about the loading process. You would use its value in condition tests.

**Alphabetical DOM Reference**

The value of this property changes during loading as the loading state changes. Each change of the property value fires an onreadystatechange event.

**Example**
```
if (document.readyState == "loading") {
    // statements for alternate handling
}
```

**Value**

One of the following values (as strings): complete | interactive | loading | uninitialized. Some elements may allow the user to interact with partial content, in which case the property may return interactive until all loading has completed.

**Default**       None.


## referrer                                                          NN 2   IE 3   DOM 1
Read-only

Returns a string of the URL of the page from which the current page was accessed, provided the original page had a link to the current page. Many server logs capture this information as well. Scripts can see whether the visitor reached the current document from specific origins and perhaps present slightly different content on the page accordingly. If the visitor arrived by another method, such as typing the document URL into a browser dialog or by selecting a bookmark, the referrer property returns an empty string. Many versions of IE for Windows fail to report the correct referrer URL, often showing the URL of the current page instead.

**Example**
```
if (document.referrer) {
    document.write("<p>Thanks for following the link to our web site.</p>");
}
```

**Value**       String.

**Default**       None.


## scripts[]                                                       NN *n/a*   IE 4   DOM *n/a*
Read-only

Returns an array of all script objects (script elements) in the current document. Each script object may contain any number of functions. The scripts[] collection counts the number of actual <script> tags in the document. Items in this array are indexed (zero-based) in source code order.

**Example**       `var scriptCount = document.scripts.length;`

**Value**       Array of script element references.

**Default**       Array of zero length.

## security

**Read-only**

Returns a string describing the security policy in force for the current document.

| | |
|---|---|
| **Example** | `var secPolicy = document.security;` |
| **Value** | String. |
| **Default** | "This type of document does not have a security certificate." |

## selection

**Read-only**

Returns a selection object. To work with text that has been selected by the user or script, you must convert the selection to a TextRange object. This is possible only in Internet Explorer for Win32. Access to the Netscape 6 selection is via the `window.selection` property.

| | |
|---|---|
| **Example** | `var range = document.selection.createRange( );` |
| **Value** | Object reference. |
| **Default** | None. |

## styleSheets[]

**Read-only**

Returns an array of all styleSheet objects in the current document. Each style object may contain any number of style sheet rules. The `styleSheets[]` collection counts the number of actual `<style>` tags in the document as well as `<link>` tags that load external style sheet files. Items in this array are indexed (zero-based) in source code order. An `@import` style sheet object is accessible via a styleSheet object's `cssRule.styleSheet` property. See the styleSheet object.

**Example**

```
for (var i = 0; i < document.styleSheets.length; i++) {
    // loop through each styleSheet object
}
```

| | |
|---|---|
| **Value** | Array of styleSheet object references. |
| **Default** | Array of zero length. |

## tags[]

**Read-only**

Used with the Navigator 4-only JavaScript syntax of style sheets, the `tags[]` collection is part of a reference to a single tag type and the style property assigned to it. For a list of properties, see the tags object listing in this chapter. Do not confuse this Navigator use of the tags[] collection with Internet Explorer's use of the tags[] collection that belongs to the all collection.

**Example**        document.tags.H1.color= "red";

**Value**          Array of Navigator 4 JavaScript Style Sheet tag object references.

**Default**        Array of zero length.

## title                                                                NN 2    IE 3    DOM 1
                                                                              Read/Write

Unlike the title property for objects that reflect HTML elements, the document.title property refers to the content of the title element defined in the head portion of a document. The title content appears in the browser's titlebar to help identify the document. This is also the content that goes into a bookmark listing for the page. Although the property is read/write, don't be surprised if a browser version does not alter the window titlebar in response.

**Example**        document.title = "Fred\'s Home Page";

**Value**          String.

**Default**        None.

## URL                                                                  NN 3    IE 4    DOM 1
                                                                              Read/Write

Provides the URL of the current document. The value is the same as location.href. The document.URL property evolved as a replacement for document.location to avoid potential confusion (by scripters and JavaScript interpreter engines) between the location object and document.location property. To navigate to another page, it is safest (for cross-browser and backward compatibility) to assign a URL string value to the location.href property, rather than this document-centered property.

**Example**        document.URL = "http://www.megacorp.com";

**Value**          Complete or relative URL as a string.

**Default**        The current document's URL.

## URLUnencoded                                            NN n/a    IE 5.5(Win)    DOM n/a
                                                                              Read-only

Returns the URL of the current document, but with any URL-encoded characters returned to their plain-language version (e.g., %20 is converted to a space character). The returned value is the same as if applying the JavaScript decodeURI( ) function to document.URL.

**Example**        var straightPath = document.URLUnencoded;

| | |
|---|---|
| **Value** | Complete or relative URL as a string. |
| **Default** | The current document's URL. |

## vlinkColor

Color of a hypertext link that has been visited recently. The color is applied to the link text or border around an image or object embedded within an a element. See also alinkColor and linkColor properties for clicked and unvisited link colors. Changes to this property do not dynamically change the link color in Navigator 4 or earlier. Starting with IE 4 and Netscape 6, you should switch to using the W3C DOM alternative, document.body.vLink, or style sheets.

| | |
|---|---|
| **Example** | document.vlinkColor = "gold"; |
| **Value** | A hexadecimal triplet or plain-language color name. See Appendix A for acceptable plain-language color names. |
| **Default** | #551a8b (Navigator); #800080 (Internet Explorer Windows); #006010 (Internet Explorer Macintosh). |

## width

See height.

## addBinding( ), getAnonymousElementByAttribute( ), getAnonymousNodes( ), getBindingParent( ), loadBindingDocument( ), removeBinding( )

This series of Netscape 6 document object methods are part of a browser programming feature called Extensible Binding Language (XBL), an adjunct to the XML-based mechanism that the browser uses for generating user interface skins. To learn more about XBL, visit *http://www.mozilla.org/docs/xul/xulnotes/xulnote_xbl.html*.

## captureEvents( )

captureEvents(*eventTypeList*)

Instructs the browser to grab events of a specific type before they reach their intended target objects. The object invoking this method must then have event handlers defined for the given event types to process the event. Although this method is part of the Navigator 4 event model, it continues to be supported in Netscape 6, creating the equivalent of a W3C DOM capture-mode event listener for the document object. Continue to use this method if you must support Navigator 4, but migrate new code to the W3C DOM event listener syntax as described in Chapter 6.

| | |
|---|---|
| **Returned Value** | None. |

**Parameters**

*eventTypeList*

A comma-separated list of case-sensitive event types as derived from the available static Event object constants, such as Event.CLICK or Event.MOUSEMOVE.

## clear( ) NN 2    IE 3    DOM n/a

Removes the current document from the window or frame, usually in preparation to open a new stream for writing new content. The document.write( ) and document.writeln( ) methods automatically invoke this method. Many bugs with the document.clear( ) method plagued earlier browser versions. Even today, it is best to let the document writing methods handle the job for you. The W3C DOM explicitly omits this method.

**Returned Value**    None.

**Parameters**    None.

## close( ) NN 2    IE 3    DOM 1

Closes the document writing stream to a window or frame. If a script uses document.write( ) or document.writeln( ) to generate all-new content for a window or frame, you must append a document.close( ) method to make sure the entire content is written to the document. Omitting this method may cause some content not to be written. This method also prepares the window or frame for a brand new set of content with the next document writing method. Do not, however, use document.close( ) if you use the document writing methods to dynamically write content to a page while loading from the server.

**Returned Value**    None.

**Parameters**    None.

## createAttribute( ) NN 6    IE 5(Mac)/6(Win)    DOM 1

createAttribute("*attributeName*")

Generates in memory an instance of an attribute node (Attr object). A typical sequence is to create the attribute, assign a value to it via its nodeValue property, and then insert the Attr node into an element's attribute list via the element's setAttributeNode( ) method.

**Returned Value**    Attr node object reference.

**Parameters**

*attributeName*

A case-sensitive string of the attribute's name.

## createAttributeNS( ) NN 6    IE n/a    DOM 2

createAttributeNS("*namespaceURI*", "*qualifiedName*")

Generates in memory an instance of an attribute node (Attr object) whose name is defined in an external namespace. A typical sequence is to create the attribute, assign a value to it via its nodeValue property, and then insert the Attr node into an element's attribute list via the element's setAttributeNodeNS( ) method.

**Returned Value**     Attr node object reference.

**Parameters**

*namespaceURI*
> URI string that will match a URI assigned to a label earlier in the document into which the attribute is eventually added.

*qualifiedName*
> The full name for the attribute, consisting of the local name prefix (if any), a colon, and the local name.

## createCDATASection( )                     NN 6    IE 5(Mac)    DOM 1

createCDATASection("*data*")

Generates in memory an instance of a character data section node (CDATASection object) in an XML (including XHTML) document. Not fully implemented as of Netscape 7.

**Returned Value**     CDATASection node object reference.

**Parameters**

*data*
> String data that comprises the content of the section.

## createComment( )                     NN 6    IE 5(Mac)/6(Win)    DOM 1

createComment("*commentText*")

Generates in memory an instance of a comment node (Comment object with a nodeValue of 8). A typical sequence is to create the Comment node, then insert it into the desired location of the document tree via any node's appendChild( ) or insertBefore( ) method. Only partially implemented in IE 5/Mac.

**Returned Value**     Comment node object reference.

**Parameters**

*commentText*
> String containing the comment data.

## createDocumentFragment( )                     NN 6    IE 5(Mac)/6(Win)    DOM 1

Generates in memory an instance of an empty document fragment node (DocumentFragment object). This node becomes an arbitrary holder for assembling a sequence of nodes that ultimately get appended or inserted into a document tree. See the DocumentFragment object for more details.

**Returned Value**     DocumentFragment node object reference.

**Parameters**     None.

## createElement( )                                    NN 6    IE 4    DOM 1

createElement("*tagName*")

Generates in memory an instance of an element object associated with the tag passed as a parameter to the method. The method is limited to area, img, and option elements in IE 4; all elements are permitted in other supporting browsers. A newly created element has no attribute values assigned (except any default values assigned according to the DTD), nor is the element yet part of the document tree. Assign attributes (such as the type for an input element or id for any element), and append or insert the element into the document tree. This sequence is the W3C DOM approach to generating new content (in place of the innerHTML convenience properties implemented in IE and Netscape 6 browsers).

**Returned Value**    Element object reference.

**Parameters**

*tagName*
    A string of the tag name of the new element: document.createElement("option"). IE also allows a complete start tag string, complete with angle brackets and attribute name/value pairs. Only the straight tag name is supported by the W3C DOM specification.

## createElementNS( )                                  NN 6    IE *n/a*    DOM 2

createElementNS("*namespaceURI*", "*qualifiedName*")

Generates in memory an instance of an element object associated with namespace, label, and tag passed as parts of the method's parameters. A newly created element has no attribute values assigned (except any default values assigned according to the DTD), nor is the element yet part of the document tree. Assign attributes (such as the type for an input element or id for any element), and append or insert the element into the document tree.

**Returned Value**    Element object reference.

**Parameters**

*namespaceURI*
    URI string that will match a URI assigned to a label earlier in the document into which the attribute is eventually added.

*qualifiedName*
    The full name for the attribute, consisting of the local name prefix (if any), a colon, and the local name.

## createEntityReference( )                            NN 6    IE 5(Mac)    DOM 1

createEntityReference("*entityName*")

Generates in memory an instance of an entity reference node object in an XML document. Only partial support provided in IE 5/Mac and Netscape as of Version 7.

**Returned Value**    Entity reference node object reference.

**Parameters**

*entityName*
> String value.

## createEvent( )

createEvent("*eventType*")

Generates in memory an instance of a W3C DOM Event object of a particular event category. After the generic event is created, it must be initialized (via one of several initialization methods) as a particular event type, along with other properties appropriate for the event category. The following sequence creates a mousedown event and sends it to an element:

```
var evt = document.createEvent("MouseEvents");
evt.initEvent("mousedown", true, true);
document.getElementById("myElement").dispatchEvent(evt);
```

Such an event might then be handed to an element (via the element's dispatchEvent( ) method) so that the element's event listener can process the event as if it had been generated by a user clicking the mouse button.

**Returned Value**    Event object object reference.

**Parameters**

*eventType*
> String constant for one of the support event categories: HTMLEvents, KeyEvents (supported by Netscape 6, but not specified until DOM Level 3), MouseEvents, MutationEvents, or UIEvents.

## createEventObject( )

createEventObject([*existingEventObject*])

Generates in memory an instance of an empty IE DOM event object. After the generic event is created, its properties can be stuffed with pertinent values to help the event be processed. Then the event acts as a parameter to an element's fireEvent( ) method, at which point the event type is associated with the event. The following sequence creates a mousedown event and sends it to an element:

```
var evt = document.createEventObject( );
document.getElementById("myElement").fireEvent("onmousedown", evt);
```

You can also use an existing event object as a model for a script-generated event. Pass the current event object as a parameter to the createEventObject( ) method, and modify the properties of the new object as you see fit.

**Returned Value**    event object reference.

**Parameters**

*existingEventObject*
> Reference to an event object either generated by the user or script. The new event assumes all properties of the existing event object.

## createNodeIterator( ) NN *n/a*  IE *n/a*  DOM *2*

createNodeIterator(*rootNode, whatToShow, filterFunction, entityRefExpansion*)

Generates in memory an instance of a NodeIterator object. This method has the same set of parameters as the createTreeWalker( ) method, which is implemented in Netscape 7.

**Returned Value** NodeIterator object reference.

**Parameters**

*rootNode*

> Reference to a node in the document tree that becomes the first node in the NodeIterator object's list of nodes.

*whatToShow*

> Integer value corresponding to one of several built-in filters that allow nodes of a single type to be included in the NodeIterator object returned by the method. The NodeFilter object contains constants that should be used as plain-language substitutes for this value:

| | |
|---|---|
| NodeFilter.SHOW_ALL | NodeFilter.SHOW_ATTRIBUTE |
| NodeFilter.SHOW_CDATA_SECTION | NodeFilter.SHOW_COMMENT |
| NodeFilter.SHOW_DOCUMENT | NodeFilter.SHOW_DOCUMENT_FRAGMENT |
| NodeFilter.SHOW_DOCUMENT_TYPE | NodeFilter.SHOW_ELEMENT |
| NodeFilter.SHOW_ENTITY | NodeFilter.SHOW_ENTITY_REFERENCE |
| NodeFilter.SHOW_NOTATION | NodeFilter.SHOW_PROCESSING_INSTRUCTION |
| NodeFilter.SHOW_TEXT | |

*filterFunction*

> Reference to a user function that can further filter nodes that are included in the NodeIterator object. The function has a single parameter (a reference to a node to test, invoked automatically by the NodeIterator object). The value returned by the function determines whether the node being tested is to be included in the list of nodes. Returned values are integers, but the NodeFilter object provides three constants you should use as plain-language substitutes:

| | |
|---|---|
| NodeFilter.FILTER_ACCEPT | NodeFilter.FILTER_REJECT |
| NodeFilter.FILTER_SKIP | |

> Because a NodeIterator object does not maintain its list of nodes as a hierarchy, the values NodeFilter.FILTER_REJECT and NodeFilter.FILTER_SKIP pass over a node without any effect on child nodes. See the TreeWalker object for an example of this kind of function.

*entityRefExpansion*

> Boolean value that controls whether the content of entity reference nodes (found predominantly in XML documents) should be treated as hierarchical nodes (true) or not (false).

## createProcessingInstruction( )                    NN 6    IE 5(Mac)    DOM 1
createProcessingInstruction("*target*", "*data*")

Generates in memory an instance of a processing instruction node object in an XML document. Only partial support provided in IE 5/Mac and Netscape as of Version 7.

**Returned Value**      Processing instruction node object reference.

**Parameters**

*target*
    String value.
*data*
    String value.

## createRange( )                                     NN 6    IE n/a    DOM 2

Creates a blank Range object, whose boundary points are collapsed to the point before the first character of the rendered body text. The method returns a reference to that Range object, which you then use to adjust its boundary points, invoke its methods, and so on. See the Range object for details of its language features.

**Returned Value**      W3C DOM Range object reference.

**Parameters**          None.

## createStyleSheet( )                                NN n/a    IE 4    DOM n/a
createStyleSheet(["*url*"[, *index*]])

This method performs the same actions in IE for Windows and Macintosh, but their returned values differ. Moreover, the specific actions in the document tree depend upon the parameters passed with the method. When no parameters are included, the method inserts a blank style element into the document tree. This style element, however, is not reflected in the document.styleSheets collection until you add one or more style rules to the object. But if you specify a URL to an external .css file as the first parameter, the method creates and inserts a link element into the document's head section, bringing the external style rules to life immediately.

IE for Windows always returns a reference to a styleSheet object; IE for Macintosh returns a reference to the newly inserted element, which will be a style or link element, depending on the parameter makeup. The inserted style element reference is of little help for adding a rule because you can't reference the styleSheet object. For cross-operating–system compatibility, it's best to use this method only for external style sheets.

**Returned Value**

styleSheet object reference (Windows); style or link element object reference (IE 5 and later for Macintosh).

Alphabetical DOM
Reference

**Parameters**

*url*

A string of the URL of an external *.css* style sheet definition file.

*index*

Optional zero-based integer that indicates where among the styleSheets[] collection this new style sheet should be inserted. Default behavior is to append to the end of the collection, but this may affect cascading rules for your document. See Chapter 3.

## createTextNode( ) NN 6 IE 5 DOM 1

createTextNode("*text*")

Generates in memory an instance of a text node (W3C DOM Text object) whose nodeValue consists of the untagged text content passed as a parameter. A newly created text node is not yet part of the document tree. Append or insert the node into the document tree or document fragment being assembled for later document insertion. This sequence is the W3C DOM approach to generating new content (in place of the innerText convenience property implemented in IE browsers).

**Returned Value**   Text node object reference.

**Parameters**

*text*

A string of characters to be rendered as content when inserted into the document tree.

## createTreeWalker( ) NN 7 IE *n/a* DOM 2

createTreeWalker(*rootNode, whatToShow, filterFunction, entityRefExpansion*)

Generates in memory an instance of a TreeWalker object.

**Returned Value**   TreeWalker object reference.

**Parameters**

*rootNode*

Reference to a node in the document tree that becomes the first node in the TreeWalker object's list of nodes.

*whatToShow*

Integer value corresponding to one of several built-in filters that allow nodes of a single type to be included in the TreeWalker object returned by the method. The NodeFilter object contains constants that should be used as plain-language substitutes for this value:

| | |
|---|---|
| NodeFilter.SHOW_ALL | NodeFilter.SHOW_ATTRIBUTE |
| NodeFilter.SHOW_CDATA_SECTION | NodeFilter.SHOW_COMMENT |
| NodeFilter.SHOW_DOCUMENT | NodeFilter.SHOW_DOCUMENT_FRAGMENT |
| NodeFilter.SHOW_DOCUMENT_TYPE | NodeFilter.SHOW_ELEMENT |
| NodeFilter.SHOW_ENTITY | NodeFilter.SHOW_ENTITY_REFERENCE |
| NodeFilter.SHOW_NOTATION | NodeFilter.SHOW_PROCESSING_INSTRUCTION |
| NodeFilter.SHOW_TEXT | |

*filterFunction*

Reference to a user function that can further filter nodes that are included in the TreeWalker object. The function has a single parameter (a reference to a node to test, invoked automatically by the TreeWalker object). The value returned by the function determines whether the node being tested is to be included in the list of nodes. Returned values are integers, but the NodeFilter object provides three constants you should use as plain-language substitutes:

NodeFilter.FILTER_ACCEPT        NodeFilter.FILTER_REJECT
NodeFilter.FILTER_SKIP

With a return value of NodeFilter.FILTER_SKIP, descendant nodes of the skipped node may still qualify as members of the TreeWalker node list (provided they survive other filtering). A return value of NodeFilter.FILTER_REJECT removes both the node under test and its descendants from consideration as members of the TreeWalker object. See the TreeWalker object for an example of this kind of function.

*entityRefExpansion*

Boolean value that controls whether the content of entity reference nodes (found predominantly in XML documents) should be treated as hierarchical nodes (true) or not (false).

## elementFromPoint( )                                                    NN *n/a*   IE 4   DOM *n/a*

elementFromPoint(*x, y*)

Returns a reference to the object directly underneath the pixel coordinates specified by the *x* (horizontal) and *y* (vertical) parameters. For an element to be recognized, it must be capable of responding to mouse events. Also, if more than one element is positioned in the same location, the element with the highest zIndex value or, given equal zIndex values, the element that comes last in the source code order is the one returned.

**Returned Value**        Element object reference.

**Parameters**

*x*   Horizontal pixel measure relative to the left edge of the window or frame.

*y*   Vertical pixel measure relative to the top edge of the window or frame.

## execCommand( )                                                NN *n/a*   IE 4(Win)   DOM *n/a*

execCommand("*commandName*"[, *UIFlag*[, *value*]])

Available only in the Win32 platforms for IE, the execCommand( ) method executes the named command. Most commands require that a TextRange object be created first for an insertion point. See Appendix D for a list of commands.

**Returned Value**        Boolean value: true if command was successful; false if unsuccessful.

**Parameters**

*commandName*

A case-insensitive string value of the command name. See Appendix D.

*UIFlag*
> Optional Boolean value: true to display any user interface triggered by the command (if any); false to prevent such display.

*value*
> A parameter value for the command.

## getAnonymousElementByAttribute( )

See addBinding( ).

## getAnonymousNodes( )

See addBinding( ).

## getBindingParent( )

See addBinding( ).

## getElementById( )                                          NN 6    IE 5    DOM 1
getElementById("*elementID*")

Returns a reference to an element node from the document tree whose id attribute value matches the parameter value. If there is no match, the method returns null. This method, although a chore to type while observing its case-sensitive name, is the gateway for scripts in W3C DOM-capable browsers to communicate with element objects.

**Returned Value**    Reference to element node object.

**Parameters**
*elementID*
> String of the desired element's ID.

## getElementsByName( )                                       NN 6    IE 5    DOM 1
getElementsByName("*elementName*")

Returns an array of references to all element nodes from the document tree whose name attribute value matches the parameter value. If there is no match, the method returns null. When an element supports both the name and id attribute, IE for Windows includes an element in the returned array even if only the id attribute is set to the parameter value. IE for Macintosh and Netscape 6 match only elements that have name attributes explicitly set to the parameter value.

**Returned Value**    Array of references to element node object.

**Parameters**
*elementName*
> String of the desired element's name.

## getSelection( ) NN *4*    IE *n/a*    DOM *n/a*

In Navigator 4, this method captures the current text selection in the document. The method is deprecated in Netscape 6 in favor of the `window.getSelection( )` method (which returns a sophisticated `selection` object, rather than just text). Invoking from the document object displays a warning in the JavaScript Console window, but does not throw a full-fledged exception. The IE equivalent is reading the `selection` property.

**Returned Value**    String.

**Parameters**    None.

## handleEvent( ) NN |4|    IE *n/a*    DOM *n/a*

`handleEvent(event)`

Instructs the document object to accept and process the Navigator 4-only event whose specifications are passed as the parameter to the method. The object must have an event handler for the event type to process the event.

**Returned Value**    None.

**Parameters**

*event*
   A Navigator 4 event object.

## hasFocus( ) NN *n/a*    IE *6*    DOM *n/a*

Returns Boolean `true` if the document or any element in the document has focus. A background process, such as a function invoked through `setTimeout( )` can find out if the document's window is currently the front window on the Desktop.

**Returned Value**    Boolean value: `true` | `false`.

**Parameters**    None.

## importNode( ) NN *6*    IE *n/a*    DOM *2*

`importNode(nodeReference, deepBoolean)`

Imports a node object from another loaded document into the current document, but not yet into the document tree. In many ways, `importNode( )` works like `cloneNode( )`, but it assumes that the source node may exist in an entirely different document tree context (especially in an XML document). W3C DOM rules for this method govern what properties and attributes of the source node make the journey and what happens to them upon their arrival. For example, an `Attr` node loses its `ownerElement` (i.e., its value becomes `null`) when imported from an element in one document into a fragment-like state in the new document—until the attribute gets added to an element in the new document. Nodes of `Document` and `DocumentType` types are not importable.

Alphabetical DOM Reference

The importNode( ) method does not assume the responsibility of persistence between documents. That's where, for instance, a JavaScript variable comes into play. As with cloneNode( ), the importNode( ) method does not disturb the source node.

**Returned Value**    Reference to the imported copy of the node object.

**Parameters**

*nodeReference*
> Reference to a node in a different loaded document (including a nonrendered document loaded into the browser by way of the document.implementation.createDocument( ) method).

*deepBoolean*
> Boolean value that controls whether the copy includes all nested nodes (true) or only the current node (false). Required, but applicable primarily to element nodes.

## loadBindingDocument( )

See addBinding( ).

## open( )    NN 2    IE 3    DOM 1

open(["*MIMEType*"][, "replace"])

Opens the output stream for writing to the current window or frame. If document.clear( ) has not already been invoked, it is automatically invoked in response to the document.open( ) method. Early version bugs may lead you to use document.write( ) and document.writeln( ) to take care of this method more reliably for you.

**Returned Value**    None.

**Parameters**

*MIMEType*
> Advises the browser of the MIME type of the data to be written in subsequent statements. Navigator supports "text/html" | "text/plain" | "image/gif" | "image/jpeg" | "image/xbm" | "plugIn". Only "text/html" is supported in Internet Explorer.

*replace*
> The presence of this parameter directs the browser to replace the entry in the history list for the current document with the document about to be written.

## queryCommandEnabled( )    NN *n/a*    IE *4(Win)*    DOM *n/a*

queryCommandEnabled("*commandName*")

Specifies whether the command can be invoked in light of the current state of the document or selection. Available only in the Win32 platform for IE 4.

**Returned Value**    Boolean value: true if enabled; false if not.

**Parameters**

*commandName*
> A case-insensitive string value of the command name. See Appendix D.

## queryCommandIndeterm( )

NN *n/a*   IE *4(Win)*   DOM *n/a*

queryCommandIndeterm("*commandName*")

Specifies whether the command is in an indeterminate state. Available only in the Win32 platform for IE 4.

**Returned Value**   Boolean value: true | false.

**Parameters**

*commandName*
> A case-insensitive string value of the command name. See Appendix D.


## queryCommandState( )

NN *n/a*   IE *4(Win)*   DOM *n/a*

queryCommandState("*commandName*")

Determines the current state of the named command. Available only in the Win32 platform for IE 4.

**Returned Value**

true if the command has been completed; false if the command has not completed; null if the state cannot be accurately determined.

**Parameters**

*commandName*
> A case-insensitive string value of the command name. See Appendix D.


## queryCommandSupported( )

NN *n/a*   IE *4(Win)*   DOM *n/a*

queryCommandSupported("*commandName*")

Determines whether the named command is supported by the document object. Available only in the Win32 platform for IE 4.

**Returned Value**   Boolean value: true | false.

**Parameters**

*commandName*
> A case-insensitive string value of the command name. See Appendix D.


## queryCommandText( )

NN *n/a*   IE *4(Win)*   DOM *n/a*

queryCommandText("*commandName*")

Returns text associated with the command. Available only in the Win32 platform for IE 4.

**Returned Value**   String.

**Parameters**

*commandName*
> A case-insensitive string value of the command name. See Appendix D.

Alphabetical DOM Reference

## queryCommandValue( )     NN *n/a*    IE *4(Win)*    DOM *n/a*

queryCommandValue("*commandName*")

Returns the value associated with the command, such as the name font of the selection. Available only in the Win32 platform for IE 4.

**Returned Value**     Depends on the command.

**Parameters**

*commandName*

A case-insensitive string value of the command name. See Appendix D.

## recalc( )     NN *n/a*    IE *5(Win)*    DOM *n/a*

recalc([*allBoolean*])

Forces the recalculation of expressions assigned to element attributes via the setExpression( ) method. Needed only when automatic recalculation isn't triggered by user action, but affected values might have changed.

**Returned Value**     None.

**Parameters**

*allBoolean*

When set to true, forces all dynamic attribute expressions in the document to recalculate. The default false lets browser decide which expressions are affected by changes since the last manual or automatic recalculation.

## releaseEvents( )     NN *4*    IE *n/a*    DOM *n/a*

releaseEvents(*eventTypeList*)

The opposite of document.captureEvents( ), this method turns off event capture at the document level for one or more specific events named in the parameter list. In Netscape 6, it performs the same action as the W3C DOM removeEventListener( ) method on the document object. See Chapter 6.

**Returned Value**     None.

**Parameters**

*eventTypeList*

A comma-separated list of case-sensitive event types as derived from the available Event object constants, such as Event.CLICK or Event.MOUSEMOVE.

## removeBinding( )

See addBinding( ).

## routeEvent( )

routeEvent(*event*)

Used inside an event handler function, this method directs Navigator 4 to let the event pass to its intended target object. The method does not cause an error in Netscape 6, but it does not perform any action.

**Returned Value**    None.

**Parameters**

*event*

A Navigator 4 event object

## write( ), writeln( )

write("*string1*"[, ..."*stringN*"])
writeln("*string1*"[, ..."*stringN*"])

When invoked as the page loads, these methods can dynamically add content to the page. When invoked after the page has loaded, a single method invocation clears the current document, opens a new output stream, and writes the content to the window or frame. A document.close( ) method is required afterward. Because the first document.write( ) or document.writeln( ) method destroys the current document, do not use two or more writing statements to create a new document. Instead, load the content into one variable and pass that variable as the parameter to a single document.write( ) or document.writeln( ) method.

Using document.write( ) for <script> tags is tricky in Navigator because it typically interprets the writing of the end script tag as meaning the end of the script doing the writing. You should have success, however, if you split the end script tag into string sections:

    document.write("<" + "/script>");

If you include the "hide script" comment trick, write it this way:

    document.write("//--" + ">");

The difference between the two methods is that document.writeln( ) adds a carriage return to the source code it writes to the document. This is not reflected in the rendered content, but can make reading the dynamic source code easier in browser versions that support dynamic content source viewing (Navigator 4 does so as a wysiwyg: URL in the source view window).

**Returned Value**    None.

**Parameters**

*string*

Any string value, including HTML tags.

# Document

NN 6   IE n/a   DOM 1

The document object described earlier is, in the W3C DOM structure, more specifically an HTMLDocument node, a member of the HTML module of the standard. The HTMLDocument node inherits the properties and methods of the Document node (with an uppercase "D" described here, and defined in the W3C DOM Core module. This is the pure, abstract Document node, and all that is needed to contain an unrendered XML document.

Netscape 6 extends this node with a load( ) method that allows scripts to load XML documents into a plain (and unseen) Document node. Such a node is created via the document.implementation.createDocument( ) method. Scripts can then access the XML data in that document through regular W3C DOM document tree properties and methods.

To help reinforce in your mind the heritage of the document object you normally script (that is, the instance of the HTMLDocument node represented in each window's document), I show the lists of properties and methods for the core Document object. For descriptions of all these properties and methods—except for the uninherited Netscape 6-specific load( ) method—see the document object, earlier in this chapter.

## Object Model Reference

*documentNodeReference*

## Object-Specific Properties

| | | |
|---|---|---|
| doctype | documentElement | implementation |

## Object-Specific Methods

| | | |
|---|---|---|
| createAttribute( ) | createAttributeNS( ) | createCDATASection( ) |
| createComment( ) | createDocumentFragment( ) | createElement( ) |
| createElementNS( ) | createEntityReference( ) | createProcessingInstruction( ) |
| createTextNode( ) | getElementById( ) | getElementsByTagName( ) |
| getElementsByTagNameNS( ) | importNode( ) | load( ) |

## Object-Specific Event Handler Properties

None.

## load( )

NN 6   IE n/a   DOM n/a

load("*URI*")

Loads an XML file into the current Document object. Attempting to load other types of files (such as HTML) throws an exception. The server must be configured to send the file as the text/html content type.

**Returned Value**   None.

## Parameters

*URI*
> A string of the URI to an external XML file.

# DocumentEvent

See document.

# DocumentFragment

NN *6*    IE *n/a*    DOM *1*

The W3C DOM DocumentFragment object is essentially a context-free container of other DOM nodes. In other words, you can use all node properties and methods to assemble a sequence of element and text nodes outside of the document tree, but not influenced by the containment that the DocumentFragment provides. If you then append or insert the DocumentFragment node into the document tree, the DocumentFragment container disappears, and its node contents stand on their own within the context of their position in the document tree. The DocumentFragment isn't necessary to assemble content that is wrapped by an element node, because the element node can act as both the temporary container outside the document tree and the container after insertion into the document tree. But if one or both ends of a content segment end in a text node, the DocumentFragment node provides a transparent bucket to keep the string of nodes together until they are dropped into the document.

Create an empty DocumentFragment container via the document.createDocumentFragment( ) method. A DocumentFragment type of node inherits all properties and methods of the Node object (for inserting and appending other nodes you create), and adds nothing of its own other than its silent ability to hold other nodes. Do not confuse a DocumentFragment node with a string of tagged text that gets assigned to the innerHTML property of an element. The W3C DOM (as of Level 2) provides no such string-to-node-hierarchy conversion.

Netscape 6 extends this node with a load( ) method that allows scripts to load XML documents into a plain (and unseen) Document node. Such a node is created via the document.implementation.createDocument( ) method. Scripts can then access the XML data in that document through regular W3C DOM document tree properties and methods.

**Object Model Reference**
*documentFragmentNodeReference*

**Object-Specific Properties**
None.

**Object-Specific Methods**
None.

**Object-Specific Event Handler Properties**
None.

# DocumentRange

See document.

# DocumentStyle

See document.

# DocumentTraversal
NN 7   IE n/a   DOM 2

The DocumentTraversal object is defined in the Traversal module of the W3C DOM, where it defines the createNodeIterator( ) and createTreeWalker( ) methods. These methods (and the otherwise invisible DocumentTraversal interface) are blended into the document object so that scripts can access them (only the document.createTreeWalker( ) method is implemented in Netscape 7, but createNodeIterator( ) is sure to follow).

# DocumentType
NN 6   IE 5(Mac)   DOM 1

Reflects the DOCTYPE element, if one arrives to the browser as part of the document flow. The DocumentType object is its own node type in the W3C DOM, and, just as indicated in its position in a document's source code, exists outside of the content portion of the document tree. Access to this object in supported browsers is via the document.doctype property. If no DOCTYPE element exists in the file, the property returns null.

Properties of the DocumentType object expose individual pieces of the data within the DOCTYPE tag, whose structure is determined by SGML standards. The W3C DOM Level 2 specification provides placeholder properties for these pieces, and Netscape 6 implements most of them to one degree or other. But it is clear from the DOM specification that work on aligning the two worlds is not complete.

**Object Model Reference**

*documentTypeNodeReference*

**Object-Specific Properties**

| entities | internalSubset | name | notations | publicId | systemId |
|---|---|---|---|---|---|

**Object-Specific Methods**

None.

**Object-Specific Event Handler Properties**

None.

## entities
NN 6   IE n/a   DOM 1<br>Read-only

Returns an array of nested Entity nodes within the DOCTYPE element. An Entity is formatted according to the following syntax (which would appear inside the DOCTYPE element's angle brackets):

```
[<!ENTITY publicID "systemID">]
```

Primarily applicable to XML documents.

| Value | Array (technically, a `NamedNodeMap` data type) of `Entity` node object references. |
| Default | `null` |

## internalSubset

Returns a string value of the internal subset portion of the element.

| Value | String. |
| Default | Empty string. |

## name

Returns a string value of the name portion of the element. The name is the first word that follows the DOCTYPE element's tag name. In the context of this book's subject, all HTML and XHTML documents show this value to be html. Note that although this object and property are implemented in IE 5/Macintosh, that browser returns the entire inner string value of the DOCTYPE element, starting with the html name.

| Value | String. |
| Default | html |

## notations

Returns an array of references to Notation nodes within the DOCTYPE element.

| Value | Array (technically, a `NamedNodeMap` data type) of `Notation` node object references. |
| Default | `null` |

## publicId

Returns a string value of the public identifier portion of the element. This data reveals the type of DTD, as in "-//W3C//DTD XHTML 1.0 Strict//EN".

| Value | String. |
| Default | Empty string. |

## systemId                                                    NN 6    IE *n/a*    DOM 2
Read-only

Returns a string value of the system identifier portion of the element. This data typically reveals the URI of DTD, as in "http://www.w3.org/TR/xhtml1/DTD/xhtml1-strict.dtd".

**Value**          String.

**Default**        Empty string.

# DocumentView

See document.

# DOMException                                               NN 6    IE *n/a*    DOM 1

Some operations on W3C DOM objects can trigger errors, or, in the vernacular of JavaScript 1.5, throw exceptions, if something goes wrong. The W3C DOM defines an object that conveys a code number corresponding to a well-defined (if limited) list of exceptions. For example, if you attempt to append one text node as a child of another text node, the appendChild( ) method of such an operation throws an exception whose code number is 3. This number corresponds to the exception that signals an attempt to perform an illegal or logically impossible action on a DOM hierarchy (a text node can't have any child nodes).

The job of conveying the DOM exception information to a scripter falls to the hosting environment, rather than the DOM. Because JavaScript 1.5 already has an exception handling mechanism, the task of blending the DOMException system with JavaScript exception handling fell first to Netscape, as implemented in Netscape 6. The new mechanism permits different kinds of error objects to circulate through the exception handling operations, thus leaving the original system intact, while extending the mechanism to accommodate not only the W3C DOM DOMException object, but some Netscape-specific errors, as well. Processing of exceptions of all kinds continues to take place in the catch block of a try/catch construction, and all information about the exception is still passed as an object through a single parameter to the catch block.

Netscape's DOM exception object (which embodies the W3C DOMException object) arrives at the catch block with a longer list of properties and methods associated with it than does an exception arising from other causes (e.g., trying to use a JavaScript variable that has not been initialized). The distinguishing property of a DOMException object, missing from the other types, is the code property. Moreover, any code value between 1 and 15 indicates an exception type known to the formal DOM specification through Level 2. Others will certainly be added to the list in the future. Netscape uses code numbers starting with 1000 for its list of browser-specific exceptions.

If you wish to process true W3C DOM exceptions along their own execution path, you can use a construction similar to the following (which allows for the DOMException list to grow to 999 in future iterations):

```
    try {
        // your DOM-related statement goes here
    }
    catch(e) {
        if (typeof e.code == "number") {
            if (e.code < 1000) {
                // process DOMException object here
            } else {
                // process Netscape DOM exception object here
            }
        } else {
            // process language or other exceptions here
        }
    }
```

Of course, it is highly unlikely that exception details will be of benefit to users, but they are invaluable to you during development. For more on exception handling, see the error object in Chapter 12.

**Object Model Reference**
*errorObjectReference*

**Object-Specific Properties**
code

**Object-Specific Methods**
None.

**Object-Specific Event Handler Properties**
None.

## code

NN 6    IE n/a    DOM 1
Read-only

Provides an integer corresponding to one of the defined DOM error types. The following table lists all code values, their constant equivalents, and examples of what kinds of problems throw the exception.

| Code | Constant | Most likely cause |
|------|----------|-------------------|
| 1 | INDEX_SIZE_ERR | An integer offset parameter is out of the range of the target object |
| 2 | DOMSTRING_SIZE_ERR | Property string value is too large for the hosting language |
| 3 | HIERARCHY_REQUEST_ERR | Appending a child to a node not capable of children |
| 4 | WRONG_DOCUMENT_ERR | Inserting a node created from a different document (without passing through the import process) |
| 5 | INVALID_CHARACTER_ERR | Assigning an identifier with an illegal character |
| 6 | NO_DATA_ALLOWED_ERR | Assigning data to a node that doesn't allow data |

| Code | Constant | Most likely cause |
|------|----------|-------------------|
| 7 | NO_MODIFICATION_ALLOWED_ERR | Assigning a value to a read-only property |
| 8 | NOT_FOUND_ERR | Method parameter reference to a nonexistent node in the object's scope |
| 9 | NOT_SUPPORTED_ERR | Invoking an XML-only method in an HTML document |
| 10 | INUSE_ATTRIBUTE_ERR | Method parameter to an Attr node that already belongs to another element (without cloning the Attr first) |
| 11 | INVALID_STATE_ERR | Referencing a node that is not readable or writable |
| 12 | SYNTAX_ERR | A slippery keyboard |
| 13 | INVALID_MODIFICATION_ERR | Modifying the type of a node |
| 14 | NAMESPACE_ERR | Namespace mismatch or malformed name |
| 15 | INVALID_ACCESS_ERR | You can't go there |

**Example**

```
if (e.code == e.INVALID_CHARACTER_ERR) {
    // process for an illegal identifier character
}
```

**Value**          Integer

**Default**        Determined by error.


# DOMImplementation

See implementation.


# dt                                            NN 6    IE 4    DOM 1

The dt object reflects the dt element.

**HTML Equivalent**
<dt>

**Object Model Reference**
[window.]document.getElementById("*elementID*")

**Object-Specific Properties**
noWrap

**Object-Specific Methods**
None.

**Object-Specific Event Handler Properties**
None.

**noWrap** *NN n/a* IE 4 DOM *n/a*

Read/Write

Specifies whether the browser should render the element as wide as is necessary to display a line of nonbreaking text on one line. Abuse of this attribute can force the user into a great deal of inconvenient horizontal scrolling of the page to view all of the content.

| | |
|---|---|
| **Example** | `document.getElementById("wideItem").noWrap = "true";` |
| **Value** | Boolean value: true \| false. |
| **Default** | `false` |

# Element

*NN 6* IE *n/a* DOM 1

The W3C DOM `Element` object is from the Core module and represents the kind of element object you find in true XML documents. This node type inherits properties and methods from the root `Node` object and adds capabilities that let it act as a container of other nodes. Elements in HTML documents are of the `HTMLDocument` type, which inherits form the `Element` object. All properties and methods of the `Element` object are shared among all HTML element objects, as described at the beginning of this chapter.

**Object Model Reference**
*elementNodeReference*

**Object-Specific Properties**
None.

**Object-Specific Methods**
None.

**Object-Specific Event Handler Properties**
None.

# ElementCSSInlineStyle

*NN 6* IE *n/a* DOM 2

The W3C DOM `ElementCSSInlineStyle` object is from the StyleSheets module and represents style settings assigned to an element through an explicit style attribute. The `HTMLElement` object (and thus, all elements in HTML documents) gets its style property as a result of its connection with the `ElementCSSInlineStyle` object (the object's only property is style, which is what HTML elements pick up). Scripts don't ever touch this object, but dynamic styles in the W3C DOM couldn't exist without it in the abstract model.

**Object Model Reference**
None.

**Object-Specific Properties**
None.

**Object-Specific Methods**
None.

**Object-Specific Event Handler Properties**
None.

# elements

A collection of all elements contained within a form. Collection members are sorted in source code order. Because each form element includes a type property (starting with Navigator 3 and Internet Explorer 4), scripts can loop through all elements in search of elements of a specific type (e.g., all checkbox elements).

**Object Model Reference**
document.forms[i].elements
document.*formName*.elements

**Object-Specific Properties**
length

**Object-Specific Methods**
None.

**Object-Specific Event Handler Properties**
None.

## length

Returns the number of elements in the collection.

| | |
|---|---|
| **Example** | var howMany = document.forms[0].elements.length; |
| **Value** | Integer. |

## em

See acronym.

# embed

The embed object reflects the embed element. Although the embed object is losing favor to the object element in recent browser generations, scripts in browsers such as Navigator 3, Navigator 4, and IE 4/Windows can control media players that load into a page in response to the embed element's pointer to a media file on the server. Properties and methods exposed by the player pass through the embed object so that scripts treat the embed object as if its list of scriptable powers is extended. Properties listed here are the properties that the element object, rather than an external controller, exposes to scripts.

Note that IE 5 for the Macintosh treats the embed object more like the object object, and exposes properties more closely aligned with an object or applet than an embed object. It's of little consequence, however, because through Version 5.1, IE/Mac does not let scripts communicate with external players or controllers.

### HTML Equivalent
`<embed>`

### Object Model Reference
```
[window.]document.getElementById("elementID")
[window.]document.embeds[i]
```

### Object-Specific Properties

| | | | |
|---|---|---|---|
| align | height | hidden | name | palette |
| pluginspage | src | type | units | width |

### Object-Specific Methods
None.

### Object-Specific Event Handler Properties
None.

## align

NN 6    IE 5(Mac)    DOM n/a
Read/Write

Defines the alignment of the element within its surrounding container. See the section "Alignment Constants" at the beginning of Chapter 8 for the various meanings that different values bring to this property.

| | |
|---|---|
| **Example** | `document.getElementById("audioPlayer").align = "center";` |
| **Value** | Any of the alignment constants: absbottom \| absmiddle \| baseline \| bottom \| left \| middle \| right \| texttop \| top. |
| **Default** | left |

## height, width

NN 6    IE 4    DOM n/a
Read/Write

Provide the height and width in pixels of the element as set by the tag attributes. Changing the values does not necessarily change the actual rectangle of the applet after it has loaded.

| | |
|---|---|
| **Example** | `var controllerHeight = document.embeds["audioPlayer"].height;` |
| **Value** | Integer. |
| **Default** | 0 |

## hidden
NN n/a   IE 4(Win)   DOM n/a<br>Read/Write

Specifies whether the embedded data's plugin control panel appears on the screen. Changes to this property force the page to reflow its content to make room for the plugin control panel or close up space around a newly hidden panel.

| | |
|---|---|
| **Example** | document.embeds["jukebox"].hidden = true; |
| **Value** | Boolean value: true \| false. |
| **Default** | false |

## name
NN 6   IE 4   DOM n/a<br>Read/Write (IE)

Reflects the name attribute value of the element's tag.

| | |
|---|---|
| **Example** | document.embeds["myEmbed"].name = "tunes"; |
| **Value** | Case-sensitive identifier that follows the rules of identifier naming: it may contain no whitespace, cannot begin with a numeral, and should avoid punctuation except for the underscore character. |
| **Default** | None. |

## palette
NN n/a   IE 4(Win)   DOM n/a<br>Read-only

Returns the setting of the palette attribute of the embed object.

| | |
|---|---|
| **Value** | String. |
| **Default** | None. |

## pluginspage
NN n/a   IE 4(Win)   DOM n/a<br>Read-only

Indicates the URL for downloading and installing the plugin necessary to run the current object's embedded data.

| | |
|---|---|
| **Value** | A complete or relative URL as a string. |
| **Default** | None returned, but Internet Explorer has its own default URL for plugin information. |

## src
NN n/a   IE 4(Win)   DOM n/a<br>Read/Write

Indicates URL of the external content file associated with the object. Although some controllers may respond to changes of this attribute, it is more reliable to load a different file into the controller via its own loading method or property.

| Example | `document.embeds["myEmbed"].src = "tunes/dannyboy.wav";` |
|---|---|
| **Value** | Complete or relative URL as a string. |
| **Default** | None. |

## type

**NN 6**    **IE *n/a***    **DOM *n/a***

Read-only

Indicates the MIME type of the external data assigned to the element's type attribute.

| Example | `var dataMIME = document.embeds["myEmbed"].type;` |
|---|---|
| **Value** | Any valid MIME type name as a quoted string, including the type and subtype portions delimited by a forward slash. |
| **Default** | None. |

## units

**NN *n/a***    **IE *4(Win)***    **DOM *n/a***

Read/Write

Specifies the unit of measure for the height and width dimensions of the element. Internet Explorer appears to treat all settings as pixels.

| Example | `document.getElementById("myEmbed").units = "ems";` |
|---|---|
| **Value** | Any of the following case-insensitive constants (as a string): pixels \| px \| em. |
| **Default** | pixels |

## width

See height.

# embeds

**NN 3**    **IE 4**    **DOM *n/a***

A collection of all embed elements contained in the current element. Collection members are sorted in source code order. Internet Explorer lets you use array notation or parentheses to access a single element in the collection.

**Object Model Reference**
document.embeds

**Object-Specific Properties**
length

## length

**NN 3**    **IE 4**    **DOM *n/a***

Read-only

Returns the number of elements in the collection.

| **Example** | `var howMany = document.embeds.length;` |
|---|---|
| **Value** | Integer. |

# Entity, EntityReference                     NN *n/a*    IE *n/a*    DOM *1*

The Entity object (one of the node types) is an abstract representation in the W3C DOM of an element that is treated in an XML document as a storage unit. Some entities define a name that can be used by other elements (including other entities) as a shortcut reference to the information stored in the entity. This latter reference is represented in the W3C DOM as an EntityReference node type. You can see many examples of Entity elements in DTD documents. For more details on the application of Entity elements, see the XML specification at *http://www.w3.org/TR/REC-xml*.

# event                                        NN *4*    IE *4*    DOM *2*

The event object contains information about a user- or system-generated event. But there are three different kinds of event objects, one for each of the event object models deployed in browsers: IE for Windows, Navigator 4, and Netscape 6 (from the W3C DOM). IE 5 for Macintosh implements a hybrid of the IE for Windows and Netscape 6 version. See Chapter 6 for examples of processing events in a cross-browser environment. It is rare that an event object property applies to more than one of the event models, so pay special attention to the browser compatibility listings for each of the following properties.

The Netscape 6 event object is more complex in some ways due to the object-oriented nature of the underlying W3C DOM Event object structure. Rather than being an all-encompassing object (as the IE event object is), the Netscape 6 event object exposes different sets of properties and methods depending on the classification of event. All event classes share the properties and methods of the W3C DOM root Event object. But actual event object instances belong to one of the Event object's subclasses (and sometimes, sub-subclasses). These subclasses are known as UIEvent (so-called user interface events such as DOMFocusIn), MouseEvent (including the well-known mouse events), MutationEvent (events that signal a scripted change to the node structure of the document), and, coming in DOM Level 3, TextEvent (keyboard-related events). Netscape 6 implements its own, temporary keyboard events classification under the name KeyEvent, which is a subclass of UIEvent, although it borrows some MouseEvent properties for scripting convenience.

By and large, this functional division of objects won't impact your Netscape 6 event processing because an event listener function for a particular kind of event will be looking for properties associated with that event. The event class is of little concern. Still, it is instructive to see the way event object properties and methods cascade through this object-oriented structure. The following table illustrates the distribution of properties among Netscape 6 and W3C DOM event classes.

| | Event | UIEvent | MouseEvent | KeyEvent[a] | TextEvent[b] | MutationEvent |
|---|:---:|:---:|:---:|:---:|:---:|:---:|
| **Event properties** | | | | | | |
| bubbles | • | • | • | • | • | • |
| cancelable | • | • | • | • | • | • |

| | Event | UIEvent | MouseEvent | KeyEvent[a] | TextEvent[b] | MutationEvent |
|---|---|---|---|---|---|---|
| cancelBubble[c] | • | • | • | • | | • |
| currentTarget | • | • | • | • | • | • |
| eventPhase | • | • | • | • | • | • |
| originalTarget[a] | • | • | • | • | | • |
| target | • | • | • | • | • | • |
| timeStamp | • | • | • | • | • | • |
| type | • | • | • | • | • | • |
| **UIEvent properties** | | | | | | |
| detail | | • | • | • | • | |
| view | | • | • | • | • | |
| **MouseEvent properties** | | | | | | |
| altKey | | | • | • | | |
| button | | | • | | | |
| clientX | | | • | • | | |
| clientY | | | • | • | | |
| ctrlKey | | | • | • | | |
| metaKey | | | • | • | | |
| relatedTarget | | | • | | | |
| screenX | | | • | • | | |
| screenY | | | • | • | | |
| shiftKey | | | • | • | | |
| **KeyEvent properties** | | | | | | |
| charCode[a] | | | | • | | |
| isChar[a] | | | | • | | |
| keyCode[a] | | | | • | | |
| rangeOffset[a] | | | | • | | |
| rangeParent[a] | | | | • | | |
| **TextEvent properties** | | | | | | |
| keyVal[b] | | | | | • | |
| numPad[b] | | | | | • | |
| outputString[b] | | | | | • | |
| virtKeyVal[b] | | | | | • | |
| visibleOutputGenerated[b] | | | | | • | |
| **MutationEvent properties** | | | | | | |
| attrChange | | | | | | • |
| attrName | | | | | | • |
| newValue | | | | | | • |

| | Event | UIEvent | MouseEvent | KeyEvent[a] | TextEvent[b] | MutationEvent |
|---|---|---|---|---|---|---|
| prevValue | | | | | | • |
| relatedNode | | | | | | • |

[a] Implemented in Netscape 6 for additional functionality or in lieu of unfinished DOM Level 3 keyboard event model. Borrows some MouseEvent properties for scripting convenience.

[b] Proposed for DOM Level 3, but not implemented in Netscape 6.

[c] IE property implemented in Netscape 6 for cross-browser convenience.

And the following table illustrates the distribution of methods among Netscape 6 and W3C DOM event classes.

| | Event | UIEvent | MouseEvent | KeyEvent[a] | TextEvent[b] | MutationEvent |
|---|---|---|---|---|---|---|
| **Event methods** | | | | | | |
| initEvent( ) | • | • | • | • | • | • |
| getPreventDefault( )[a] | • | • | • | • | | • |
| preventDefault( ) | • | • | • | • | • | • |
| stopPropagation( ) | • | • | • | • | • | • |
| **UIEvent methods** | | | | | | |
| initUIEvent( ) | | • | | | | |
| **MouseEvent methods** | | | | | | |
| initMouseEvent( ) | | | • | | | |
| **KeyEvent methods** | | | | | | |
| initKeyEvent( ) | | | | • | | |
| **TextEvent methods** | | | | | | |
| checkModifier( )[b] | | | | | • | |
| initModifier( )[b] | | | | | • | |
| initTextEvent( )[b] | | | | | • | |
| **MutationEvent methods** | | | | | | |
| initMutationEvent( ) | | | | | | • |

[a] Implemented in Netscape 6 for additional functionality or in lieu of unfinished DOM Level 3 keyboard event model. Borrows some MouseEvent properties for scripting convenience.

[b] Proposed for DOM Level 3, but not implemented in Netscape 6.

The event object in Netscape 6 also implements the properties of the Navigator 4 static Event object, and it inherits an enormous list of W3C DOM TextEvent object constants that represent nonalphanumeric keyboard key codes (which have constant names like *eventObject*.DOM_VK_PAGE_UP). These keyboard constants are defined in the forthcoming W3C DOM Level 3 events module, but are already implemented in Netscape 6 (although the values don't exactly line up yet). A list of properties for the Navigator 4 static Event object appears in the Event object discussion following the current foray through an instance of an event.

As described in detail throughout Chapter 6, you must use different script techniques to obtain a reference to an event object in the IE and Navigator event models. Once you have that reference, you are well on your way to equalizing event processing across browsers. The example fragments that follow assume that previous script statements have obtained a reference to the browser-specific event object (usually shown in the example as stored in a variable called evt).

## Object Model Reference

*NN* *eventObj*

*IE* [window.]event

## Object-Specific Properties

| | | | |
|---|---|---|---|
| altKey | altLeft | attrChange | attrName |
| behaviorCookie | behaviorPart | bookmarks | boundElements |
| bubbles | button | cancelable | cancelBubble |
| charCode | clientX | clientY | contentOverflow |
| ctrlKey | ctrlLeft | currentTarget | data |
| dataFld | dataTransfer | detail | eventPhase |
| fromElement | isChar | keyCode | layerX |
| layerY | metaKey | modifiers | newValue |
| nextPage | offsetX | offsetY | originalTarget |
| pageX | pageY | prevValue | propertyName |
| qualifier | rangeOffset | rangeParent | reason |
| recordset | relatedNode | relatedTarget | repeat |
| returnValue | screenX | screenY | shiftKey |
| shiftLeft | srcElement | srcFilter | srcUrn |
| target | timeStamp | toElement | type |
| view | wheelDelta | which | x |
| y | | | |

## Object-Specific Methods

| | | | |
|---|---|---|---|
| getPreventDefault() | initEvent() | initKeyEvent() | initMouseEvent() |
| initMutationEvent() | initUIEvent() | preventDefault() | stopPropagation() |

## Object-Specific Event Handler Properties

None.

## altKey

**Read-only**

Returns true if the left or right **Alt** key is down at the time the event fired.

### Example

```
if (evt.altKey) {
    //handle case of Alt key down
}
```

| | |
|---|---|
| **Value** | Boolean value: true \| false. |
| **Default** | false |

## altLeft
NN n/a   IE 5.5(Win)   DOM n/a<br>Read-only

Returns true if the left **Alt** key is down at the time the event fired.

**Example**
```
if (evt.altLeft) {
    //handle case of left Alt key down
}
```

| | |
|---|---|
| **Value** | Boolean value: true \| false. |
| **Default** | false |

## attrChange
NN 6   IE n/a   DOM 2<br>Read-only

Returns an integer code corresponding to the type of change made to an `Attr` node as the result of a `DOMAttrModified` event type of W3C DOM mutation event. Every mutation event object has three constants that also correspond to the integer values, which you can use to make more verbose, but easier-to-read script comparisons for `DOMAttrModified` event processing. The values and constants are shown in the following table.

| Value | Constant | Description |
|---|---|---|
| 1 | *evtObj*.MODIFICATION | Changed value of existing `Attr` node |
| 2 | *evtObj*.ADDITION | The `Attr` node was added to the document tree |
| 3 | *evtObj*.REMOVAL | The `Attr` node was removed from the document tree |

**Example**
```
if (evt.attrChange == evt.MODIFICATION) {
    // do post-processing of attribute value change
}
```

| | |
|---|---|
| **Value** | Integer value: 1 \| 2 \| 3. |
| **Default** | None. |

## attrName
NN 6   IE n/a   DOM 2<br>Read-only

Returns a string version of the name of an `Attr` node affected by a `DOMAttrModified` event type of W3C DOM mutation event.

**Example**        `var changedAttr = evt.attrName;`

| **Value** | String value. |
| **Default** | Empty string. |

## behaviorCookie, behaviorPart, bookmarks, boundElements

NN n/a   IE 6(Win)   DOM n/a

Read-only

These properties are returned by the event object in IE 6 for Windows (with values 0, 0, null, and the empty array, respectively), but Microsoft does not document them. Perhaps they will be supported and implemented in a future version.

## bubbles

NN 6   IE n/a   DOM 2

Read-only

Returns Boolean true if the default behavior of the event is to allow the event to bubble through the element hierarchy.

**Example**

```
if (evt.bubbles) {
    // handle case of the event bubbling
}
```

| **Value** | Boolean value: true | false. |
| **Default** | Event type-specific. |

## button

NN 6   IE 4   DOM 2

Read-only

Inidicates which mouse button was pressed to trigger the mouse event. Be aware that the typical Macintosh has only a one-button mouse. Also, if you want to intercept the right-click context menu in IE/Windows, use the oncontextmenu event handler.

A significant discrepancy exists among DOM specifications and implementations with respect to the numbers returned for this property. The W3C DOM, as implemented in Netscape 6, specifies a value of zero to indicate the left (primary) button. IE for Windows supports additional values for mouse button combinations.

**Example**

```
if (evt.button == 2) {
    // handle event for right button
}
```

**Value**

Integer value according to the following table.

| Button(s) | IE | NN 6 | W3C DOM |
|---|---|---|---|
| No button | 0 | null | null |
| Left (primary) | 1 | 0 | 0 |
| Middle | 4 | 1 | 1 |
| Right | 2 | 2 | 2 |
| Left + Right | 3 | n/a | n/a |
| Left + Middle | 5 | n/a | n/a |
| Right + Middle | 6 | n/a | n/a |
| Left + Middle + Right | 7 | n/a | n/a |

**Default**    0

## cancelable

NN 6    IE *n/a*    DOM 2

Read-only

Returns Boolean true if the event is of the type that can have its default behavior on the target element cancelled via the preventDefault( ) method.

**Example**
```
if (evt.cancelable ) {
    evt.preventDefault( );
}
```

**Value**        Boolean: true | false.

**Default**      Event type-specific.

## cancelBubble

NN 6    IE 4    DOM *n/a*

Read/Write

Specifies whether the event should propagate (bubble) up the element container hierarchy. You usually only need to set this property to true to override the default behavior and prevent the event from going any further. Netscape 6 implements this IE property for convenience. The W3C DOM equivalent is the stopPropagation( ) method of the event object.

**Example**      evt.cancelBubble = true;

**Value**        Boolean: true | false.

**Default**      false

## charCode

NN 6    IE *n/a*    DOM *n/a*

Read-only

Returns an integer corresponding to the Unicode value of the character generated by the key that fired the event. The character code is different from the key code, as the character code distinguishes between upper- and lowercase letters (for example, 97 for "a" and 65 for "A"), whereas the keyCode value is the same for that key, regardless of the character created from it. This property generally contains a value only for onkeypress events; the value is zero for onkeydown and onkeyup events. For the IE equivalent, see the keyCode property.

When the keyboard events module is completed for W3C DOM Level 3, this property will probably have a different name.

**Example**
```
if (evt.charCode > 96 && evt.charCode < 123) {
    evt.target.value += String.fromCharCode(evt.charCode - 32);
    evt.preventDefault();
}
```

**Value**         Integer.

**Default**       Event-specific.

## clientX, clientY

Indicate the horizontal (x) and vertical (y) coordinate of the mouse at the moment the current event fired. These coordinates are relative to the viewable document area of the browser window or frame. To convert these coordinates to the document's in IE, be sure to add the body element's scroll values (or html element's scroll values in IE 6 standards-compatible mode). For Netscape 6, the pageX and pageY properties provide coordinates in the document's space.

**Example**
```
if ((evt.clientX >= 10 && evt.clientX <= 20) &&
(evt.clientY >= 50 && evt.clientY <= 100)) {
    // process code for click in hot zone bounded by 10,50 and 20,100
}
```

**Value**         Integer of pixel values.

**Default**       None.

## contentOverflow

Returns Boolean true if as-yet unrendered content requires a new layout rectangle to handle the overflow content. The property applies only to the onlayoutcomplete event if you deploy custom print or print preview templates. For more on the C++ programming required for such templates, visit *http://msdn.microsoft.com/library/default.asp?url=/ workshop/browser/hosting/printpreview/reference/reference.asp.*

**Value**         Boolean: true | false.

**Default**       false

## ctrlKey

**NN** *6*    **IE** *4*    **DOM** *2*

**Read-only**

Returns true if the left or right **Control** key was pressed at the instant the event fired. See Chapter 6 for testing for this key in cross-browser event handling code.

### Example

```
if (evt.ctrlKey) {
    // process for Control key being down
}
```

**Value**          Boolean value: true | false.

**Default**        false

## ctrlLeft

**NN** *n/a*    **IE** *5.5(Win)*    **DOM** *n/a*

**Read-only**

Returns true if the left **Control** key was pressed at the instant the event fired.

### Example

```
if (evt.ctrlLeft) {
    // process for left Control key being down
}
```

**Value**          Boolean value: true | false.

**Default**        false

## currentTarget

**NN** *6*    **IE** *n/a*    **DOM** *2*

**Read-only**

Returns a reference to the node whose event listener is currently processing the event. Allows a function to know whether it is invoked from the actual target node or a different node during event propagation.

### Example

```
if (evt.currentTarget.nodeType == 1) {
    // process at element level for possible text node target
}
```

**Value**          Reference to a node in event propagation hierarchy.

**Default**        Reference to event target.

## data

**NN** |*4*|    **IE** *n/a*    **DOM** *n/a*

**Read-only**

Provides accessory data associated with the Navigator 4-only dragdrop event. The data property returns the URL of the item being dropped onto the window or frame.

| **Example** | `var srcDoc = evtObj.data;` |
| **Value** | String. |
| **Default** | None. |

## dataFld

NN *n/a*    IE *5(Win)*    DOM *n/a*

**Read/Write**

Used with IE data binding, the `dataFld` property holds the name of the data source object's field associated with the column of the HTML table. This property contains a value after an `oncellchange` event in a table generated via data binding.

| **Value** | String. |
| **Default** | Empty string. |

## dataTransfer

NN *n/a*    IE *5(Win)*    DOM *n/a*

**Read-only**

Returns a reference to the `dataTransfer` object to facilitate moving customized data between source and destination elements during a drag-and-drop operation. See the `dataTransfer` object for details of its usage.

| **Value** | Reference to `dataTransfer` object. |
| **Default** | None. |

## detail

NN *6*    IE *n/a*    DOM *2*

**Read-only**

Returns an integer conveying event type-specific additional information. For mouse button events, the number indicates how many times the user clicked the mouse on the same coordinate position as the previous click without moving the cursor away from the location. Moving the cursor resets the counter to zero in preparation for the next press and release of the mouse button. For a `DOMActivate` event type, the `detail` property returns 1 for activation by a simple user action (click or tab), and 2 for a more complex action (a double-click).

**Example**

```
if (evt.type == "click" && evt.detail > 5) {
    alert("Relax, dude!");
}
```

| **Value** | Integer. |
| **Default** | Event-type specific. |

## eventPhase

NN *6*   IE *n/a*   DOM *2*
Read-only

Returns an integer conveying whether the event listener is processing the event while in the capture phase, at the event target, or in the bubbling phase. W3C DOM event objects also implement plain-language constants corresponding to the three values.

### Example
```
if (evt.eventPhase == evt.AT_TARGET) {
    // process event listener from the event target
}
```

### Value
Integer value from the following table.

| Value | Constant |
|-------|----------|
| 1 | eventObjectReference.CAPTURING_PHASE |
| 2 | eventObjectReference.AT_TARGET |
| 3 | eventObjectReference.BUBBLING_PHASE |

### Default    2

## fromElement

NN *n/a*   IE *4*   DOM *n/a*
Read-only

Returns a reference to the object where the cursor was located just prior to the onMouseOver or onMouseOut event.

### Example
```
if (evt.fromElement.id == "lowerLevel") {
    ...
}
```

| Value | Element object reference. |
|-------|---------------------------|
| Default | None. |

## isChar

NN *6*   IE *n/a*   DOM *n/a*
Read-only

Returns true if the keyboard event is from a character key. In practice Netscape 6 returns true for all keys, including function keys. Use onkeydown or onkeyup event handlers to process noncharacter keys.

| Value | Boolean value: true \| false. |
|-------|-------------------------------|
| Default | true |

## keyCode

Slightly different characteristics for IE and Netscape 6, but the two browser classes treat the keyCode property the same way for onkeydown and onkeyup events. For these events, the keyCode property returns the code associated with the keyboard key, irrespective of the character that might be generated by that key. On a typical Latin character set keyboard, the **A** key generates the code 65. Modifier keys generate their own events and codes as they are pressed and released.

For the onkeypress event, only IE returns a significant value, corresponding to the Unicode value of the actual character displayed in a text box by typing the character (e.g., 65 for "A" and 97 for "a"). The equivalent property in Netscape 6 for the onkeypress event is charCode. See Chapter 6 about processing keyboard events.

### Example

```
if (evt.keyCode == 65) {
    ...
}
```

**Value**         Integer.

**Default**       None.

## layerX, layerY

Provide the horizontal (x) and vertical (y) coordinate of the mouse at the moment the current event fired. These coordinates are relative to the containing layer. If no layers or positionable elements have been defined, the default layer of the base document is used as a reference point, thus equivalent to the pageX and pageY properties. In Netscape 6 and later, these properties are measured relative to the element's own rectangular space for text and password input elements, textarea elements, and select elements.

### Example

```
if ((evt.layerX >= 10 && evt.layerX <= 20) &&
(evt.layerY >= 50 && evt.layerY <= 100)) {
    // process code for click in hot zone bounded by 10,50 and 20,100
}
```

**Value**         Integer of pixel values.

**Default**       None

## metaKey

Returns true if the keyboard's **Meta** key (**Command** key on the Macintosh keyboard) was pressed at the instant the event fired.

**Example**

```
if (evt.metaKey) {
    // process for meta key being down
}
```

| Value | Boolean value: true \| false. |
|---|---|
| Default | false |

## modifiers

Provides an integer that represents the keyboard modifier key(s) being held down at the time the Navigator 4–only event fired. You can use the & operator with a series of static Event object constants to find out whether a particular modifier key was pressed. See Chapter 6.

| Example | var altKeyPressed = evt.modifiers & Event.ALT_MASK; |
|---|---|
| Value | Integer. |
| Default | 0 |

## newValue, prevValue

Return a string with the new and previous values (respectively) of data associated with DOMAttrModified and DOMCharacterDataModified event types of the W3C DOM mutation events class. This information could be useful for creating an undo buffer for changes to an element's attribute or the content of a CharacterData node.

| Example | undoAttrBuffer = {attrNode:evt.relatedNode, oldVal:evt.prevValue}; |
|---|---|
| Value | String value. |
| Default | Empty string. |

## nextPage

Returns a string indicating whether the next page of a custom print template will appear on a left- or right-facing page. For more on the C++ programming required for templates, visit *http://msdn.microsoft.com/library/default.asp?url=/workshop/browser/hosting/printpreview/reference/reference.asp.*

| Value | String constant: left \| right \| (empty string). |
|---|---|
| Default | Empty string. |

## offsetX, offsetY

NN *n/a*    IE *4*    DOM *n/a*

**Read-only**

Provide the left and top coordinates of the mouse pointer relative to the containing element (exclusive of padding, borders, or margins) when the event fired. You can determine the containing element via the offsetParent property. See the section "About client- and offset-Properties" at the beginning of this chapter for information on offset measurement anomalies in Internet Explorer.

**Example**

```
if (evt.offsetX <= 20 && evt.offsetY <=40) {
    ...
}
```

**Value**          Integer pixel count.

**Default**        None.

## originalTarget

NN *6*    IE *n/a*    DOM *n/a*

**Read-only**

Returns a reference to a node that Netscape 6 internally treats as the genuine first target of the event. By and large, this information isn't helpful to DHTML scripting, because it dives into the internal construction of certain elements (e.g., an input element of type text has a div element nested inside of it, but the DOM node tree does not see the div element as a child node of the input element). For many events and event targets, the target and originalTarget properties reference the identical node.

**Value**          Node object reference

**Default**        Element-specific.

## pageX, pageY

NN *4*    IE *n/a*    DOM *n/a*

**Read-only**

Provide the left and top coordinates of the element's content relative to the top-left corner of the page area when the event fired. The measurements ignore any scrolling of the page.

**Example**

```
if (evt.pageX <= 20 && evt.pageY <=40) {
    ...
}
```

**Value**          Integer pixel count.

**Default**        None.

Alphabetical DOM Reference

## prevValue

See newValue.

## propertyName

NN n/a　IE 5(Win)　DOM n/a<br>Read/Write

Returns a string containing the name of the object property that changed during an onpropertychange event. For other event types, the value is an empty string. If the changed property is a property of a property (e.g., a property of an element's style property), the returned value shows the "dot" version, such as style.color.

**Example**

```
if (evt.propertyName.indexOf("style") == 0) {
    // perform further processing on a changed style
}
```

**Value**　　　　String property name.

**Default**　　　 Empty string.

## qualifier

NN n/a　IE 5(Win)　DOM n/a<br>Read/Write

For use with IE data binding events (such as ondatasetcomplete). Returns a string value signifying a data source member, which may then be used as a parameter to access a data source's named recordset. Consult the Microsoft documentation for the Data Source Object you use to see if it provides qualifier data.

**Value**　　　　String.

**Default**　　　 Empty string.

## rangeOffset

NN 6　IE n/a　DOM n/a<br>Read-only

Returns an integer of the character offset within a node that the Netscape 6 DOM considers a potential Range end point. The reference to the node is found in the associated rangeParent property of the event object. These two values can be passed as parameters to W3C DOM Range object methods for setting a start or end point. Thus, a mousedown event listener could establish the start point of a range, while a mouseup event listener function could set the end point—both functions feeding rangeParent and rangeOffset values to the Range object methods.

**Example**

```
var rng;
function processMouseDown(evt) {
    rng = document.createRange();
    rng.setStart(evt.rangeParent, evt.rangeOffset);
}
```

| | |
|---|---|
| **Value** | Integer. |
| **Default** | 0 |

## rangeParent

Returns a reference to a document tree node that would be a suitable start or end point for a W3C text range. Use in concert with the rangeOffset property.

### Example

```
function processMouseUp(evt) {
    rng.setEnd(evt.rangeParent, evt.rangeOffset);
}
```

| | |
|---|---|
| **Value** | Reference to a node. |
| **Default** | None. |

## reason

Returns a code associated with an ondatasetcomplete event signifying whether the IE data binding data transfer was successful or, if incomplete, whether the transfer stopped due to an error or a stoppage by the client or user. This property must be examined in an event handler for the ondatasetcomplete event. In IE 4, the property is read-only. Although IE 5/Mac includes this property of the event object, it does not implement the associated event.

### Example

```
if (evt.reason == 2) {
    alert("An error occurred during the most recent update.");
}
```

### Value

One of three possible integer values:

0   Transfer was successful

1   Transfer aborted

2   An error halted the transfer

| | |
|---|---|
| **Default** | None. |

## recordset

Returns a reference to an IE data binding recordset object associated with a data-related event.

| | |
|---|---|
| **Value** | Object reference. |
| **Default** | None. |

## relatedNode

NN 6    IE n/a    DOM 2<br>Read-only

Returns a reference to a node that is affected by the action that triggers some W3C DOM mutation events. This provides a more direct route to a node that is impacted by the event, according to the following table.

| Mutation event type | eventObj.relatedNode reference |
| --- | --- |
| DOMNodeInserted | Parent node of inserted node |
| DOMNodeRemoved | Original parent node of removed node |
| DOMAttrModified | Attr node |

For other mutation event types, the property returns null; for other event classes, the property returns undefined.

| | |
| --- | --- |
| **Example** | var newParent = evt.relatedNode; |
| **Value** | Reference to a node, null, or undefined. |
| **Default** | None. |

## relatedTarget

NN 6    IE n/a    DOM 2<br>Read-only

Returns a reference to a rendered node in the document tree that was the previous or next target for events, depending on the event type. For a mouseover event type, the relatedTarget property refers to the node from which the cursor arrived; for a mouseout event, the relatedTarget property refers to the node to which the cursor departed. The corresponding IE functionality is in the fromElement and toElement properties of the IE event object.

| | |
| --- | --- |
| **Example** | var beenThere = evt.relatedTarget; |
| **Value** | Reference to a node. |
| **Default** | None. |

## repeat

NN n/a    IE 5(Win)    DOM n/a<br>Read/Write

For an onkeydown event only, returns Boolean true if the key has been down long enough to enter auto-repeat mode. You can prevent auto-repeated keys from being entered into a field with the following example.

### Example

```
function handleKeyDown( ) {
    if (evt.repeat) {
        evt.returnValue = false;
    }
}
```

| **Value** | Boolean value: true \| false. |
|---|---|
| **Default** | false |

## returnValue

Provides the value to be returned to the event's source element to allow or prohibit the element's default action connected with the event. If you set event.returnValue to false, the element does not carry out its normal operation, such as navigating to a link or submitting the form. This property does not influence an actual value you may wish to return from an event handler function.

**Example**

```
evt.returnValue = false;
```

| **Value** | Boolean value: true \| false. |
|---|---|
| **Default** | true |

## screenX, screenY

Provide the horizontal and vertical pixel coordinate points where the cursor was located on the video screen when the event occurred. The top-left corner of the screen is point 0,0. There is no particular coordination with the browser window or document, unless you have positioned the window and know where the active window area is in relation to the screen.

**Example**

```
if (evt.screenX < 5 || evt.screenY < 5) {
    alert("You\'re too close to the edge!");
}
```

| **Value** | Any positive integer or zero. |
|---|---|
| **Default** | 0 |

## shiftKey

Returns true if the left or right **Shift** key was pressed at the instant the event fired.

**Example**

```
if (evt.shiftKey) {
    // process for Shift key being down
}
```

| **Value** | Boolean value: true \| false. |
|---|---|
| **Default** | false |

## shiftLeft

NN *n/a*    IE *5.5(Win)*    DOM *n/a*

Read-only

Returns true if the left **Shift** key was pressed at the instant the event fired.

**Example**

```
if (evt.shiftLeft) {
    // process for left Shift key being down
}
```

| Value | Boolean value: true \| false. |
|---|---|
| **Default** | false |

## srcElement

NN *n/a*    IE *4*    DOM *n/a*

Read-only

Refers to the element object that initially received the current event. This property is convenient in switch constructions for an event handler function that handles the same event type for a number of different elements. The corresponding property for Netscape 6 is target.

**Example**

```
switch (evt.srcElement.id) {
    case "myDIV":
        ...
    ...
}
```

| Value | Element object reference. |
|---|---|
| **Default** | None. |

## srcFilter

NN *n/a*    IE *4(Win)*    DOM *n/a*

Read-only

Refers to the filter object that fired an onfilterchange event.

| Value | Filter object reference. |
|---|---|
| **Default** | None. |

## srcUrn

NN *n/a*    IE *5(Win)*    DOM *n/a*

Read-only

String of the URN of an attached behavior that fired an event.

| Value | String. |
|---|---|
| **Default** | null |

## target

NN *4*    IE *n/a*    DOM *2*
Read-only

Refers to the node object that is the intended destination of the current event. Unlike the corresponding IE srcElement property, the target property in Netscape 6 can refer to a text node, even if the event handler is defined for the element that surrounds the text node. Your event processing for such a scenario must take the nodeType into account to equalize the reference to the surrounding element for both IE and Navigator. See Chapter 6 for examples of cross-browser event handling code.

**Example**        `var elem = (evt.target) ? evt.target : evt.srcElement;`

**Value**          Node object reference.

**Default**        None.


## timeStamp

NN *6*    IE *n/a*    DOM *2*
Read-only

Provides an integer signifying a milliseconds value you can use as a relative indicator of when an event occurred. Although the W3C DOM suggests the value should be the time since 1 January 1970 (the Java and JavaScript epoch), you cannot rely on that value. But you can compare the timeStamp property value for two events to derive the elapsed time between events.

**Example**        `var clickTime = evt.timeStamp;`

**Value**          Integer.

**Default**        Current timestamp.


## toElement

NN *n/a*    IE *4*    DOM *n/a*
Read-only

Returns a reference to the element object to which the cursor has moved that triggered the onmouseout event.

**Example**
```
if (evt.toElement.id == "upperLevel") {
    ...
}
```

**Value**          Element object reference.

**Default**        None.


## type

NN *4*    IE *4*    DOM *2*
Read-only

Indicates the type of the current event (without the "on" prefix). Values are all lowercase.

**Example**

```
if (evt.type == "change") {
    ...
}
```

| **Value** | Any event name (without the "on" prefix) as a string. |
|---|---|
| **Default** | None. |

## view

Returns a reference to the W3C DOM view (i.e., the `window` or `frame` object in Netscape's implementation) in which the event occurred.

| **Example** | `var whichWin = evt.view;` |
|---|---|
| **Value** | Reference to a window type of object. |
| **Default** | Current window. |

## wheelDelta

Returns an integer indicating which direction the user rolled the mouse wheel (for a mouse equipped with a wheel) during an `onmousewheel` event. A positive value means the user rolled the wheel toward the screen; a negative value means the opposite direction.

**Example**

```
if (evt.wheelDelta > 0) {
    ...
}
```

| **Value** | Integer, typically 120 or -120. |
|---|---|
| **Default** | None. |

## which

Returns a value relevant to the type of event. For mouse events, the property value is an integer indicating which mouse button was used (1 is the left button; 3 is the right button). For keyboard events, the property value is an integer of the keyboard character ASCII code. This property survives in Netscape 6 as a carryover from the Navigator 4 event model. Use the `button`, `charCode`, and `keyCode` properties if you no longer need to support Navigator 4.

**Example**

```
if (evt.which == 65) {
    ...
}
```

| Value | Integer. |
|---|---|
| **Default** | None. |

## x, y

Return the horizontal and vertical pixel coordinates of the mouse pointer at the time the event occurred. For all but relative-positioned elements, the coordinate system is the body element (or html element in IE 6 standards-compatible mode). If the event occurs inside a relative-positioned element's rectangle, the coordinate system is limited to that element's space (the element's top left corner being 0,0). A value of -1 is returned if the pointer was outside of the document area of the browser window.

### Example

```
if (evt.x < 20 && evt.y < 30) {
    ...
}
```

| Value | Integer. |
|---|---|
| **Default** | None. |

## getPreventDefault( )

Returns Boolean true if the preventDefault( ) method has been invoked for the current event object. Essentially lets a script inquire about the prevent-default state. This property is a Netscape 6 extension to the W3C DOM events module.

| **Returned Value** | Boolean value: true \| false. |
|---|---|
| **Parameters** | None. |

## initEvent( )

initEvent("*eventType*", *bubblesFlag*, *cancelableFlag*)

Indicates the minimum initialization required on an event object that is generated by document.createEvent( ). After a script-generated event is initialized, it may be used as a parameter to a node's dispatchEvent( ) method.

| **Returned Value** | None. |
|---|---|

### Parameters

*eventType*
> String identifier for the event's type, such as click, mousedown, keypress, DOMAttrModified, and so on.

*bubblesFlag*
> Boolean value (true \| false) determining whether the event's default propagation behavior is to bubble.

*cancelableFlag*

    Boolean value (true | false) determining whether the event's default action may be prevented via the preventDefault( ) method.

## initKeyEvent( )

initKeyEvent("*eventType*", *bubblesFlag*, *cancelableFlag*, *view*, *ctrlKeyFlag*, *altKeyFlag*, *shiftKeyFlag*, *metaKeyFlag*, *keyCode*, *charCode*)

Initializes a newly created event object with a complete set of property values associated with any keyboard event. This method's name and parameter makeup may change for the formal DOM Level 3 events module, where keyboard events (tentatively called text events) will be published. All parameters must be present, and must be set to default values (such as false for Boolean key flags or zero for integer code numbers) if the values are not significant for the event type.

**Returned Value**   None.

**Parameters**

*eventType*

    String identifier for the event's type: keydown, keypress, keyup.

*bubblesFlag*

    Boolean value (true | false) determining whether the event's default propagation behavior is to bubble.

*cancelableFlag*

    Boolean value (true | false) determining whether the event's default action may be prevented via the preventDefault( ) method.

*view*

    Reference to the window or frame object in which the dynamically-generated event is supposed to have occurred.

*ctrlKeyFlag*

    Boolean value (true | false) of the **Control** key state for this event.

*altKeyFlag*

    Boolean value (true | false) of the **Alt** key state for this event.

*shiftKeyFlag*

    Boolean value (true | false) of the **Shift** key state for this event.

*metaKeyFlag*

    Boolean value (true | false) of the **Meta** key (e.g., Macintosh Command key) state for this event.

*keyCode*

    Integer key code for this event.

*charCode*

    Integer character code for this event.

## initMouseEvent( )

initMouseEvent("*eventType*", *bubblesFlag, cancelableFlag, view, detailVal, screenX, screenY, clientX, clientY, ctrlKeyFlag, altKeyFlag, shiftKeyFlag, metaKeyFlag, buttonCode, relatedTargetNodeRef*)

Initializes a newly created event object with a complete set of property values associated with any mouse event. All parameters must be present, and must be set to default values (such as false for Boolean key flags, zero for integer values, or null for a node reference) if the values are not significant for the event type.

**Returned Value**   None.

**Parameters**

*eventType*

> String identifier for the event's type, such as click, mousedown, mousemove, mouseout, mouseover, mouseup.

*bubblesFlag*

> Boolean value (true | false) that determines whether the event's default propagation behavior is to bubble.

*cancelableFlag*

> Boolean value (true | false) that determines whether the event's default action may be prevented via the preventDefault( ) method.

*view*

> Reference to the window or frame object in which the dynamically-generated event is supposed to have occurred.

*detailVal*

> Integer code for detail data associated with the event.

*screenX*

> Integer for horizontal screen coordinate.

*screenY*

> Integer for vertical screen coordinate.

*clientX*

> Integer for horizontal browser window coordinate.

*clientY*

> Integer for vertical browser window coordinate.

*ctrlKeyFlag*

> Boolean value (true | false) of the **Control** key state for this event.

*altKeyFlag*

> Boolean value (true | false) of the **Alt** key state for this event.

*shiftKeyFlag*

> Boolean value (true | false) of the **Shift** key state for this event.

*metaKeyFlag*

> Boolean value (true | false) of the **Meta** key (e.g., Macintosh **Command** key) state for this event.

*buttonCode*
    Integer button code for this event.

*relatedTargetNodeRef*
    Reference to node receiving the previous or next mouse event.

## initMutationEvent( )            NN 6   IE *n/a*   DOM 2

initMutationEvent("*eventType*", *bubblesFlag*, *cancelableFlag*, *relatedNodeRef*, *prevValue*, *newValue*, *attrName*, *attrChangeCode*)

Initializes a newly created event object with a complete set of property values associated with any mutation event. All parameters must be present, and must be set to default values (such as false for Boolean key flags or zero for integer code numbers) if the values are not significant for the event type.

**Returned Value**    None.

### Parameters

*eventType*
    String identifier for the event's type: DOMAttrModified, DOMCharacterDataModified, DOMNodeInserted, DOMNodeInsertedIntoDocument, DOMNodeRemoved, DOMNodeRemovedFrom-Document, DOMSubtreeModified.

*bubblesFlag*
    Boolean value (true | false) determining whether the event's default propagation behavior is to bubble.

*cancelableFlag*
    Boolean value (true | false) determining whether the event's default action may be prevented via the preventDefault( ) method.

*relatedNode*
    Reference to a node associated with the event. Applicable only to DOMNodeInserted, DOMNodeRemoved, DOMAttrModified event types.

*prevValue*
    String of previous value for an Attr or CharacterData node. Applicable only to DOMAttrModified and DOMCharacterDataModified event types.

*newValue*
    String of new value for an Attr or CharacterData node. Applicable only to DOMAttrModified and DOMCharacterDataModified event types.

*attrName*
    String of the name of an Attr node. Applicable only to the DOMAttrModified event type.

*attrChangeCode*
    Integer for the code corresponding to the type of change the event simulates. Applicable only to the DOMAttrModified event type.

## initUIEvent( )

initUIEvent("*eventType*", *bubblesFlag*, *cancelableFlag*, *view*, *detailVal*)

Initializes a newly created event object with a complete set of property values associated with any UI event. All parameters must be present, and must be set to default values (such as false for Boolean key flags or zero for integer values) if the values are not significant for the event type.

**Returned Value**    None.

**Parameters**

*eventType*

String identifier for the event's type, such as DOMFocusIn, DOMFocusOut, DOMActivate.

*bubblesFlag*

Boolean value (true | false) determining whether the event's default propagation behavior is to bubble.

*cancelableFlag*

Boolean value (true | false) determining whether the event's default action may be prevented via the preventDefault( ) method.

*view*

Reference to the window or frame object in which the dynamically generated event is supposed to have occurred.

*detailVal*

Integer code for detail data associated with the event.

## preventDefault( )

Instructs the current event to bypass the normal operation it performs on the node. Once set, the mode cannot be undone for the current event. The following Netscape 6 event listener function for an keypress event allows only numbers to be entered into a text field:

```
function numsOnly(evt) {
    if (evt.charCode < 48 || evt.charCode > 57) {
        evt.preventDefault();
    }
}
```

This method is the equivalent of assigning false to the IE event.returnValue property, or having an event handler evaluate to return false.

**Returned Value**    None.

**Parameters**    None.

## stopPropagation( )

Prevents the current event from propagating through the capture or bubbling hierarchy beyond the node currently processing the event. This method performs the same action as assigning false to the event object's cancelBubble property (for bubbling propagation only).

**Returned Value**      None.

**Parameters**      None.

## Event

The Event object is a static object in Navigator 4 and later that contains a large set of case-sensitive constant values you can use to test user- or system-generated events for keyboard modifiers and event types (see the modifiers and type properties of the event object). These constant values evaluate to mathematically related integers. Not all event types assigned a constant value are implemented as events in Navigator 4. This same object continues to be supported in Netscape 6, but only for backward compatibility with the Navigator 4 event capture syntax.

**Object Model Reference**
Event

**Object-Specific Properties**

| | | | | |
|---|---|---|---|---|
| ABORT | ALT_MASK | BACK | BLUR | CHANGE |
| CLICK | CONTROL_MASK | DBLCLICK | DRAGDROP | ERROR |
| FOCUS | FORWARD | HELP | KEYDOWN | KEYPRESS |
| KEYUP | LOAD | LOCATE | META_MASK | MOUSEDOWN |
| MOUSEDRAG | MOUSEMOVE | MOUSEOUT | MOUSEOVER | MOUSEUP |
| MOVE | RESET | RESIZE | SCROLL | SELECT |
| SHIFT_MASK | SUBMIT | UNLOAD | XFER_DONE | |

## Event

The W3C DOM Event object is an abstract object that contains the properties and methods shared by every instance of a W3C DOM event. This object type is also the generic event object created from the document.createEvent() method. See the discussion of the event object earlier in this chapter for property and method support for this object and how these items are inherited by more specific event types.

## EventListener

The W3C DOM EventListener object is nothing more than a reference to a script function that is invoked by a node in response to an event. Its existence in the W3C DOM offers a convenient way for the specification to signify the data type of the second parameter to the *nodeObject*.addEventListener() and *nodeObject*.removeEventListener() methods, described earlier in this chapter.

# EventTarget

The W3C DOM EventTarget object is the events module connection with nodes that actually receive events. All node objects (especially text and element nodes in an HTML document tree) implement the EventTarget object, thus giving those nodes the three methods that belong to the EventTarget object: addEventListener( ), dispatchEvent( ), and removeEventListener( ). In other words, every node in a document is also an EventTarget object.

# external

The external object is used primarily by developers who use Internet Explorer as a component for their applications and require access to custom extensions to the document object model. But you might add one or two of this object's methods into your work for an IE/Windows audience.

The following syntax example asks a user for permission to insert a script-controlled bookmark into the browser's Favorites list:

```
external.AddFavorite("URL", "Favorites List Label");
```

The following syntax example loads another URL into the a target window or frame (or the current window if the third parameter is an empty string), and then performs a text find for the third parameter string:

```
external.NavigateAndFind("URL", "searchString", "targetFrameName");
```

For more details, visit *http://msdn.microsoft.com/workshop/browser/overview/overview.asp*.

# fieldset

The fieldset object reflects the fieldset element. IE 5 for Macintosh implements the client and scroll measurement properties for this object.

**HTML Equivalent**   <fieldset>

**Object Model Reference**
[window.]document.getElementById("elementID")

**Object-Specific Properties**

| | | |
|---|---|---|
| align | form | margin |

**Object-Specific Methods**
None.

**Object-Specific Event Handler Properties**
None.

## align

NN *n/a*   IE 4   DOM *n/a*
Read/Write

Defines the horizontal alignment of the element within its surrounding container. In practice, this property has little effect on the `fieldset` object or its contents in IE 4. It behaves erratically in IE 6 for Windows, but responds as expected in IE 5 for Macintosh.

| | |
|---|---|
| **Example** | `document.getElementById("myFieldset").align = "center";` |
| **Value** | Any of the three horizontal alignment constants: `center | left | right`. |
| **Default** | `left` |

## form

NN *6*   IE 5(Mac)/*6(Win)*   DOM *1*
Read-only

Returns a reference to the next outermost `form` element object in the document tree. Multiple `fieldset` element objects within the same `form` element reference the same `form` element object.

| | |
|---|---|
| **Example** | `var theForm = document.getElementById("myFieldset").form;` |
| **Value** | Reference to a `form` element object. |
| **Default** | None. |

## margin

NN *n/a*   IE 5(Mac)   DOM *n/a*
Read-only

Returns an integer value, presumably of a margin setting. But the element does not feature a corresponding attribute. Ignore this property.

| | |
|---|---|
| **Value** | Integer. |
| **Default** | 7 |

# fileUpload

See input (type="file").

# filters[]

NN *n/a*   IE 4(Win)   DOM *n/a*

Provides a collection of all filters associated with the current element. Internet Explorer lets you use array notation or parentheses to access a single element in the collection. Filters are not available in IE for the Macintosh through Version 5.1.

**Object Model Reference**
`document.getElementById("elementID").filters`

## Object-Specific Properties
length

## Object-Specific Methods
item( )          namedItem( )

## length
NN *n/a*    IE *4(Win)*    DOM *n/a*
Read-only

Returns the number of elements in the collection.

**Example**       `var howMany = document.body.filters.length;`

**Value**         Integer.

## item( )
NN *n/a*    IE *4(Win)*    DOM *n/a*

item(*index*)

Returns a filter object corresponding to the filter that matches the index value in source code order.

**Returned Value**

Reference to a filter object. If there are no matches to the parameter, the returned value is null.

**Parameters**

*index*
A zero-based integer corresponding to the specified item in source code order.

## namedItem( )
NN *n/a*    IE *6(Win)*    DOM *n/a*

namedItem(*IDOrName*)

Returns a filter object or collection of objects corresponding to the filter matching the parameter string value.

**Returned Value**

One filter object or collection (array) of filter objects. If there are no matches to the parameters, the returned value is null.

**Parameters**

*IDOrName*
The string that contains the same value as the desired filter's name.

## font
NN *6*    IE *4*    DOM *1*

The font object reflects the font element.

**HTML Equivalent**     <font>

**Object Model Reference**

[window.]document.getElementById("*elementID*")

**Object-Specific Properties**

color                    face                    size

**Object-Specific Methods**

None.

**Object-Specific Event Handler Properties**

None.

## color                                           NN 6   IE 4   DOM 1
Read/Write

Sets the font color of all text contained by the font element.

**Example**        document.getElementById("myFont").color = "red";

**Value**          Case-insensitive hexadecimal triplet or plain-language color name as a string. See Appendix A for acceptable plain-language color names.

**Default**        Browser default.

## face                                            NN 6   IE 4   DOM 1
Read/Write

Provides a hierarchy of font faces to use for the content surrounded by the current font object. The browser looks for the first font face in the comma-delimited list of font face names until it either finds a match in the client system or runs out of choices, at which point the browser default font face is used. Font face names must match the system font face names exactly.

**Example**

document.getElementById("myFont").face = "Bookman, Times Roman, serif";

**Value**          One or more font face names in a comma-delimited list within a string. You may use real font names or the recognized generic faces: serif | sans-serif | monospace.

**Default**        Browser default.

## size                                            NN 6   IE 4   DOM 1
Read/Write

The size of the font in the 1–7 browser relative scale. For more accurate font size settings, see the style.fontSize property later in this chapter.

| | | |
|---|---|---|
| **Example** | `document.getElementById("fontSpec2").size = "+1";` | |
| **Value** | Either an integer (as a quoted string) or a quoted relative value consisting of a + or – symbol and an integer value. | |
| **Default** | 3 | |

# fonts

For details on this IE/Windows object, see the fonts property of the Dialog Helper object earlier in this chapter.

# form

The form object reflects the form element. The form object can be referenced in all scriptable browsers via the value assigned to its tag name attribute or by the index of the forms array contained by every document. For browsers that support the id attribute (IE 4 and later and Netscape 6), you may also use the element object reference formats that employ the element's ID. To assemble a reference to a nested form control object (such as input and textarea element objects), you have a choice again of using backward compatible references that include the form object as part of the reference (as in document.*formName.controlName*); or in more modern browsers, you can reference the control element directly via its unique ID.

## HTML Equivalent
`<form>`

## Object Model Reference
`[window.]document.`*formName*
`[window.]document.forms[i]`
`[window.]document.form["`*formName*`"]`
`[window.]document.getElementById("`*elementID*`")`

## Object-Specific Properties

| | | | | |
|---|---|---|---|---|
| acceptCharset | action | elements[] | encoding | enctype |
| length | method | name | target | |

## Object-Specific Methods

| | | |
|---|---|---|
| handleEvent( ) | reset( ) | submit( ) |

## Object-Specific Event Handler Properties

| Events | IE Windows | IE Mac | NN | W3C DOM |
|---|---|---|---|---|
| onreset | 3 | 3.01 | 3 | 2 |
| onsubmit | 3 | 3.01 | 3 | 2 |

## acceptCharset

NN *6*    IE *5*    DOM *1*

**Read/Write**

A server advisory (for servers that are equipped to interpret the information) about which character sets it must receive from a client form.

**Example**        `document.entryForm.acceptCharset= "it, es";`

**Value**          Case-insensitive string from the character set registry (*ftp://ftp.isi.edu/ in-notes/iana/assignments/character-sets*). Multiple character sets may be delimited by commas.

**Default**        Empty string, except in IE/Windows, with a default of UNKNOWN.

## action

NN *2*    IE *3*    DOM *1*

**Read/Write**

Provides the URL to be accessed when a form is being submitted. Script control of this property lets one form be submitted to different server processes based on user interaction with the rest of the form. This property is read-only in IE 3.

**Example**
`document.entryForm.action = "http://www.megacorp.com/cgi-bin/altEntry";`

**Value**          Complete or relative URL.

**Default**        None.

## elements[]

NN *2*    IE *3*    DOM *1*

**Read-only**

Returns an array of all form control objects contained by the current form.

**Example**
```
for (var i = 0; i < document.entryForm.elements.length; i++) {
    if (document.entryForm.elements[i].type == "text") {
        document.entryForm.elements[i].value = "";
    }
}
```

**Value**          Array of element object references.

**Default**        Array of length zero.

## encoding

NN *2*    IE *3*    DOM *n/a*

**Read/Write**

Specifies the MIME type for the data being submitted to the server with the form. For typical form submissions (where the method attribute is set to post), the default value is the proper content type. But if you change the action property for a form by script, consider whether you require a custom encoding for the purpose. This property is read-only in IE 3. See also the encType property.

**Example**  document.orderForm.encoding = "text/plain";

**Value**  Case-insensitive MIME type (content type) value as a string. For multiple items, a comma-delimited list is allowed in a single string.

**Default**

"application/x-www-form-urlencoded" in IE; empty string in Netscape 6.

## enctype                          NN 6    IE 5(Mac)/6(Win)    DOM 1
Read/Write

Provides the W3C DOM property name for what had been the encoding property of earlier DOM implementations. Current browsers support both property names. See the encoding property.

**Example**  document.orderForm.enctype = "text/plain";

**Value**  Case-insensitive MIME type (content type) value as a string. For multiple items, a comma-delimited list is allowed in a single string.

**Default**

"application/x-www-form-urlencoded"; empty string in Netscape 6.

## length                                      NN 2    IE 3    DOM 1
Read-only

Specifies the number of form control elements in the form. You can use this property in lieu of the length of the form's elements array.

**Example**
```
for (var i = 0; i < document.forms[0].length; i++)
...
}
```

**Value**  Integer.

**Default**  0

## method                                      NN 2    IE 3    DOM 1
Read/Write

Forms may be submitted via two possible HTTP methods: get and post. These methods determine whether the form element data is sent to the server appended to the action attribute URL (get) or as a transaction message body (post). In practice, when the action and method attributes are not assigned in a form element, the form performs an unconditional reload of the same document, restoring form controls to their default values. Note that the method property is read-only in Internet Explorer 3.

| | |
|---|---|
| **Example** | document.entryForm.method = "post"; |
| **Value** | Either of the following constant values as a string: get \| post. |
| **Default** | get |

## name

This is the identifier associated with the form. This information is not submitted with the form, but a form's name is used in references to the form and nested form elements. Despite the modern standards' preference for the id attribute, many browsers still require that a form be assigned a name attribute to allow the form to be submitted.

| | |
|---|---|
| **Example** | var firstFormName = document.forms[0].name; |
| **Value** | Case-sensitive identifier that follows the rules of identifier naming: it may contain no whitespace, cannot begin with a numeral, and should avoid punctuation except for the underscore character. |
| **Default** | None. |

## target

The name of the window or frame that is to receive content returned by the server after the form is submitted. Such names are assigned to frames by the frame element's name attribute; for subwindows, the name is assigned via the second parameter of the window.open( ) method. Because the corresponding target attribute is not recognized by strict HTML or XHTML validators, you can omit the attribute to survive validation, yet still direct form results to another window by assigning a value to the form's target property in script.

| | |
|---|---|
| **Example** | document.getElementById("myForm").target = "_blank"; |

**Value**

String value of the window or frame name, or any of the following constants (as a string): _parent \| _self \| _top \| _blank. The _parent value targets the frameset to which the current document belongs; the _self value targets the current window; the _top value targets the main browser window, thereby eliminating all frames; and the _blank value (or any unused identifier, for that matter) creates a new window of default size.

| | |
|---|---|
| **Default** | None (which implies the current window or frame). |

## handleEvent( )

handleEvent(*event*)

Instructs the object to accept and process the event whose specifications are passed as the parameter to the method. The object must have an event handler for the event type to process the event.

**Returned Value**   None.

**Parameters**

*event*

A Navigator 4 event object.

## reset( )
NN *3*    IE *4*    DOM *1*

Performs the same action as a click of a reset-type input element. All form controls revert to their default values.

**Returned Value**    None.

**Parameters**    None.

## submit( )
NN *2*    IE *3*    DOM *1*

Performs the same action as a click of a submit-type input element. This method does not fire the onSubmit event handler in Navigator or recent versions of IE.

**Returned Value**    None.

**Parameters**    None.

# forms
NN *2*    IE *3*    DOM *n/a*

A collection of all form objects in the document.

**Object Model Reference**
document.forms

**Object-Specific Properties**
length

**Object-Specific Methods**

| item( ) | namedItem( ) | tags( ) | urns( ) |
|---------|--------------|---------|---------|

**Object-Specific Event Handler Properties**
None.

## length
NN *2*    IE *3*    DOM *1*

Read-only

Returns the number of elements in the collection.

**Example**    var howMany = document.forms.length;

**Value**    Integer.

## item( )                                         NN *6*    IE *4*    DOM *1*

```
item(index[, subindex])
item(index)
```

Returns a single object or collection of objects corresponding to the element matching the index value (or, optionally in IE/Windows, the index and subindex values).

### Returned Value

One object or collection (array) of objects. If there are no matches to the parameters, the returned value is null.

### Parameters

*index*

When the parameter is a zero-based integer (as required for Netscape 6), the returned value is a single element corresponding to the said numbered item in source code order (nested within the current element). When the parameter is a string (allowed by IE/Windows), the returned value is a collection of elements with id or name properties that match that string.

*subindex*

If you specify a string value for the first parameter (in IE/Windows), you may use the second parameter to specify a zero-based integer to retrieve a specific element from the collection with id or name properties that match the first parameter's string value.

## namedItem( )                                    NN *6*    IE *6*    DOM *1*

```
namedItem(IDOrName)
```

Returns a single object (in Netscape 6) or collection of objects corresponding to the element matching the parameter string value.

### Returned Value

One object (in Netscape 6) or collection (array) of objects. If there are no matches to the parameters, the returned value is null.

### Parameters

*IDOrName*

The string that contains the same value as the desired element's id or name attribute.

## tags( )                                         NN *n/a*    IE *4*    DOM *n/a*

```
tags(tagName)
```

Returns a collection of objects (among all objects within the current collection) with tags that match the *tagName* parameter. Redundant here, because all elements have the same form tag.

### Returned Value

A collection (array) of objects. If there are no matches to the parameters, the returned value is an array of zero length.

## Parameters

*tagName*

A string that contains the element tag, as in `document.forms.tags("form")`.

## urns( )

NN *n/a*    IE *5(Win)*    DOM *n/a*

`urns(URN)`

Returns a collection of nested element objects that have behaviors attached to them and URNs that match the *URN* parameter.

### Returned Value

A collection (array) of objects. If there are no matches to the parameters, the returned value is an array of zero length.

### Parameters

*URN*

A string with a local or external behavior file URN.

# frame

NN *6*    IE *4*    DOM *1*

The `frame` object reflects the `frame` element, which can only be generated inside a `frameset` element. Be sure to distinguish the difference between the `frame` element object (described here) and the `window` object that a frame makes possible. Properties and methods of a `frame` element object tend to reflect the aspects associated with the HTML element and its attributes. The content of the frame is a window (a view in the W3C DOM terminology), which has been scriptable from the beginning, and contains a document. Reference a `frame` element object via its ID, even if you assign the same identifier to a frame element's `id` and `name` attributes. For example, from a script residing in one frame's document, reach the `frame` element object via:

```
parent.document.getElementById("TOCFrame")
```

But to reach the same frame in its capacity as a window (and thus access its scripts and document), the reference from the same script would be either of the following:

```
parent.TOCFrame
parent.frames["TOCFrame"]
```

If a script is processing a reference to the `frame` element object, you can jump the fence between the element object and its content via the `contentDocument` or `contentWindow` properties described below.

Be aware that references to frame objects shown in this section may not work properly in the Windows 95 version of Internet Explorer 4. Also, the *windowRef* placeholder may be filled with parent or top if the reference is in a script contained by a child frame.

### HTML Equivalent

`<frame>`

### Object Model Reference

`[windowRef.]document.getElementById("frameID")`

**Object-Specific Properties**

| | | | |
|---|---|---|---|
| allowTransparency | borderColor | contentDocument | contentWindow |
| dataFld | dataSrc | frameBorder | height |
| longDesc | marginHeight | marginWidth | name |
| noResize | scrolling | src | width |

**Object-Specific Methods**

None.

**Object-Specific Event Handler Properties**

None.

## allowTransparency                           NN *n/a*   IE *6*   DOM *n/a*
Read/Write

Specifies whether the frame background can be transparent. Because an underlying frameset does not have a background color or image, this property is not helpful for a frame. It does apply, however, to the related iframe element object.

**Value**      Boolean value: true | false.

**Default**    false

## borderColor                                 NN *n/a*   IE *4*   DOM *n/a*
Read/Write

Color of the frame's border. Each browser and operating system may resolve conflicts between different colored borders differently, so test any changes your scripts make to the color of individual frame borders.

**Example**    parent.document.getElementById("myFrame").borderColor = "salmon";

**Value**      A hexadecimal triplet or plain-language color name. A setting of empty is interpreted as "#000000" (black). See Appendix A for acceptable plain-language color names.

**Default**    Varies with operating system.

## contentDocument                             NN *6*   IE *n/a*   DOM *2*
Read-only

Returns a reference to the document object loaded into the frame element object. Through that document object, you can access one of the document's elements via the getElementById( ) method, or access the containing window object via the document's defaultView property. For IE/Windows, use the contentWindow property to jump from frame element object to its content.

**Example**

```
var frameElem = parent.document.getElementById("myFrame");
var doc = frameElem.contentDocument;
```

**Value**          Reference to a document node.

**Default**        Current document node.

## contentWindow
NN 7    IE 5.5(Win)    DOM n/a
Read-only

Returns a reference to the window object generated by the frame element. Through that window object, you can access the document object and then any one of the document's elements. For Netscape 6, use the contentDocument property to jump from frame element object to its content. But if you are trying to reach script variables or functions in the frame, the contentWindow (or W3C DOM-friendly and Netscape 6–compatible contentDocument.defaultView) provides access to the script context.

### Example
```
var frameElem = parent.document.getElementById("myFrame");
var win = frameElem.contentWindow;
```

**Value**          Reference to a window node.

**Default**        Current window node.

## dataFld
NN n/a    IE 4    DOM n/a
Read/Write

Used with IE data binding to associate a remote data source column name to the frame's src attribute. A datasrc attribute must also be set for the element. Setting both the dataFld and dataSrc properties to empty strings breaks the binding between element and data source. Works only with text file data sources in IE 5/Mac.

**Example**        parent.document.getElementById("myFrame").dataFld = "srcURL";

**Value**          Case-sensitive identifier of the data source column.

**Default**        None.

## dataSrc
NN n/a    IE 4    DOM n/a
Read/Write

Used with IE data binding to specify the ID of the page's object element that loads the data source object for remote data access. Setting both the dataFld and dataSrc properties to empty strings breaks the binding between element and data source. Works only with text file data sources in IE 5/Mac.

**Example**        parent.document.getElementById("myFrame").dataSrc = "DBSRC3";

**Value**          Case-sensitive identifier of the data source.

**Default**        None.

## frameBorder

NN 6    IE 4    DOM 1

Read/Write

Controls whether an individual frame within a frameset displays a border. Controlling indi-vidual frame borders appears to be a problem for most browsers in most operating system versions. Turning off the border of one frame may have no effect if all adjacent frames have their borders on. Feel free to experiment with the effects of turning some borders on and some borders off, but be sure to test the final effect on all browsers and operating systems used by your audience. Rely more comfortably on the frameborder attribute or frameBorder property of the entire frameset.

| | |
|---|---|
| **Example** | parent.document.getElementById("frame2").frameBorder = "no"; |
| **Value** | String values of 1 (on) and 0 (off) as well as yes and no. |
| **Default** | yes |

## height, width

NN *n/a*    IE 4    DOM *n/a*

Read-only

Return the height and width in pixels of the frame. Dimensions include frame chrome (scrollbars). Adjust a frame's size via the frameset object's rows or cols properties.

| | |
|---|---|
| **Example** | var frHeight = parent.document.getElementById("myFrame").height; |
| **Value** | Integer. |
| **Default** | Current height and width. |

## longDesc

NN 6    IE *5(Mac)/6(Win)*    DOM 1

Read/Write

Reflects the longDesc attribute of the frame element. Version 6 browsers provide no signifi-cant functionality for this attribute or property.

| | |
|---|---|
| **Value** | URL String. |
| **Default** | Empty string. |

## marginHeight, marginWidth

NN 6    IE 4    DOM 1

Read/Write

Indicate the number of pixels between the inner edge of a frame and the content rendered inside the frame. The marginHeight property controls space along the top and (when scrolled) bottom edges of a frame; the marginWidth attribute controls space on the left and right edges of a frame.

Without any prompting, browsers automatically insert a small margin inside a frame (generally between 8 and 14 pixels depending on browser and operating system). But if you attempt to override the default behavior, be aware that setting any one of these two attributes causes the value of the other to go to zero. Therefore, unless you want the content to be absolutely flush with various frame edges, you need to assign values to both attributes.

**Example**

```
parent.document.getElementById("myFrame").marginHeight = 14;
parent.document.getElementById("myFrame").marginWidth = 5;
```

| | |
|---|---|
| **Value** | Positive integer value or zero. |
| **Default** | Varies with browser and operating system. |

## name

This is the identifier associated with a frame for use as the value assigned to target attributes or as script references to the frame. The value is usually assigned via the name attribute, but it can be modified by script if necessary.

| | |
|---|---|
| **Example** | `parent.document.getElementById("myFrame").name = "results";` |
| **Value** | Case-sensitive identifier that follows the rules of identifier naming: it may contain no whitespace, cannot begin with a numeral, and should avoid punctuation except for the underscore character. |
| **Default** | None. |

## noResize

Indicates whether the frame can be resized by the user. All border edges of the affected frame element become locked, meaning all edges that extend to other frames in the frameset remain locked as well.

| | |
|---|---|
| **Example** | `parent.document.getElementById("myFrame").noResize = "true";` |
| **Value** | Boolean value: true \| false. |
| **Default** | false |

## scrolling

Controls the treatment of scrollbars for a frame when the content exceeds the visible area of the frame. You can force a frame to display scrollbars at all times or never. Or you can let the browser determine the need for scrolling. In many supporting browsers, changing the value of this property has no effect.

| | |
|---|---|
| **Example** | `parent.document.getElementById("mainFrame").scrolling = "yes";` |
| **Value** | String values of 1 (on) and 0 (off) as well as yes, no, and auto. |
| **Default** | auto |

## src

Provides the URL of the external content file loaded into the frame. To change the content, assign a new URL to the property. For cross-platform applications, you can also set the location.href property of the frame to load a different document into the frame using window-related references (parent.frameName.location.href = "newDoc.html").

**Example**
```
parent.document.getElementById("myFrame").src = "images/altNavBar.jpg";
```

**Value**          Complete or relative URL as a string.

**Default**        None.

## width

See height.

# frames

A collection of all frame objects defined in the window or frame. Only the first-level frames are exposed to the frameset object. To find further nested frames requires digging into the frames collections of nested frameset objects. The collection also includes iframe elements defined in the window's document. Be aware that the frames object does not work as expected in some sub-versions of Netscape 6.

**Object Model Reference**
[*windowRef.*]frames

**Object-Specific Properties**
length

**Object-Specific Methods**
item( )          namedItem( )

## length

Returns the number of child frames defined in the frameset whose window starts the reference. Broken in some sub-versions of Netscape 6.

**Example**          var howMany = parent.frames.length;

**Value**            Integer.

## item( )

item(*index*)

Returns a single window object corresponding to the element matching the index value in source code order.

**Returned Value**    window object.

**Parameters**

*index*
> A zero-based integer.

## namedItem( )

namedItem(*IDOrName*)

Returns a single object or collection of objects corresponding to the element matching the parameter string value.

**Returned Value**

One object or collection (array) of objects. If there are no matches to the parameters, the returned value is null.

**Parameters**

*IDOrName*
> The string that contains the same value as the desired element's id or name attribute.

# frameset

The frameset object reflects the frameset element. Be sure to distinguish the difference between the frameset element object (described here) and the window object that a frameset makes possible. Properties and methods of a frameset element object tend to reflect the aspects associated with the HTML element and its attributes. The content of the frameset element is a window (a view in the W3C DOM terminology), which has been scriptable from the beginning, and contains a document (although with no renderable elements beyond the nested frame elements). Reference a frameset element object via its ID. For example, from a script residing in one frame's document, reach the frameset element object via:

```
parent.document.getElementById("myFrameset")
```

But to reach the frameset's window (and thus access its scripts and document), the reference from the same script would be either of the following:

```
parent
top
```

If a script is processing a reference to the frameset element object, you can jump the fence between the element object and its content via the ownerDocument property of the element (described among the shared properties earlier in this chapter).

Be aware that references to frameset objects shown in this section may not work properly in the Windows 95 version of Internet Explorer 4. Also, the *windowRef* placeholder may be filled with parent or top if the reference is in a script contained by a child frame.

### HTML Equivalent
<frameset>

### Object Model Reference
[*windowRef*.]document.getElementById("*framesetID*")

### Object-Specific Properties

| | | | | | |
|---|---|---|---|---|---|
| border | borderColor | cols | frameBorder | frameSpacing | rows |

### Object-Specific Methods
None.

### Object-Specific Event Handler Properties

| Handler | IE Windows | IE Mac | NN | W3C DOM |
|---|---|---|---|---|
| onafterprint | 5 | n/a | n/a | n/a |
| onbeforeprint | 5 | n/a | n/a | n/a |
| onbeforeunload | 4 | n/a | n/a | n/a |
| onload | 3 | 3.01 | 2 | 2 |
| onresize | 4 | 4 | 4 | n/a |
| onunload | 3 | 3.01 | 2 | 2 |

## border

NN *n/a*    IE *4*    DOM *n/a*

**Read/Write**

Thickness of the spaces between frames in a frameset in pixels. Only the outermost frameset element of a system of nested framesets responds to the border property setting. Internet Explorer treats the default thicknesses for Windows and Macintosh differently, so be aware that the same value may look different on each operating system platform.

**Example**      top.document.getElementById("myFrameset").border = 4;

**Value**      An integer value. A setting of zero eliminates the border entirely. While the value is supposed to represent the precise pixel thickness of borders in the frameset, this is not entirely true for all operating systems or browsers.

**Default**      6 (IE Windows); 1 (IE Mac).

## borderColor

Color of borders between frames of the frameset. The borderColor property of an individual frame overrides the frameset object's setting.

**Example**
```
parent.document.getElementById("myFrameset").borderColor = "salmon";
```

| | |
|---|---|
| **Value** | A hexadecimal triplet or plain-language color name. A setting of empty is interpreted as "#000000" (black). See Appendix A for acceptable plain-language color names. |
| **Default** | Varies with operating system. |

## cols

Defines the sizes or proportions of the column arrangement of frames in a frameset. Column size is defined in one of three ways:

- An absolute pixel size
- A percentage of the width available for the entire frameset
- A wildcard (*) to represent all available remaining space after other pixels and percentages have been accounted for

Exercise extreme care when scripting a change to this property. Altering the composition of a frameset on the fly might disrupt scripts that communicate across frames. Reducing the number of columns may destroy documents whose scripts or objects support scripts in other frames or the parent. It is safest to maintain the same number of columns, but use this property to adjust the widths of existing frame columns. Early versions of Netscape 6 may not render changes correctly. Also, if your scripts rely on the frameset's onresize event handler, be sure to test on as many platforms as possible that the event is firing in response to script changes of these properties.

| | |
|---|---|
| **Example** | `parent.document.getElementById("framesetter").cols = "40%,60%";` |
| **Value** | Comma-separated list (as a string) of pixel, percentage, or wildcard (*) values. Internet Explorer 4 for the Macintosh exhibits incorrect behavior with some combinations that include a wildcard value. |
| **Default** | 100% |

## frameBorder

Controls whether the frameset displays borders between frames. Adjusting this property does not dynamically change the border visibility in Internet Explorer for Windows.

| | |
|---|---|
| **Example** | `parent.document.getElementById("framesetter").frameBorder = "no";` |

| | |
|---|---|
| **Value** | Internet Explorer 4 accepts the string values of 1 (on) and 0 (off) as well as yes and no. |
| **Default** | yes |

## frameSpacing
NN n/a    IE 4    DOM n/a
Read/Write

The amount of spacing in pixels between frames within a frameset. Adjusting this property does not dynamically change the frame spacing in Internet Explorer for Windows.

| | |
|---|---|
| **Example** | parent.document.getElementById("framesetter").frameSpacing = 5; |
| **Value** | Integer. |
| **Default** | 2 |

## rows
NN 6    IE 4    DOM 1
Read/Write

The sizes or proportions of the row arrangement of frames in a frameset. See the cols property for additional details of selecting values for the rows property.

| | |
|---|---|
| **Example** | document.getElementById("myFrameset").rows = "20%, 300, *"; |
| **Value** | String of comma-delimited list of pixel or percentage values, or the * wildcard character. |
| **Default** | None. |

## h1, h2, h3, h4, h5, h6
NN 6    IE 4    DOM 1

These objects reflect the HTML header elements of the same names. See the description of the elements in Chapter 8 for examples of how various browsers render each of the header sizes.

**HTML Equivalent**

```
<h1>
<h2>
<h3>
<h4>
<h5>
<h6>
```

**Object Model Reference**

```
[window.]document.getElementById("elementID")
```

**Object-Specific Properties**

align

**Object-Specific Methods**
None.

**Object-Specific Event Handler Properties**
None.

## align

Defines the horizontal alignment of the element within its surrounding container.

| | |
|---|---|
| **Example** | document.getElementById("myHeader").align = "center"; |
| **Value** | Any of the three horizontal alignment constants: center \| left \| right. |
| **Default** | left |

## head

The head object reflects the head element. Accessing this object via its ID reference may not work in the Windows version of IE 4. You should use the document.all.tags[] collection instead. For IE 5 and later and Netscape 6, you can reference the element via its ID or the document.getElementsByTagName("head")[0] array reference.

**HTML Equivalent**    <head>

**Object Model Reference**
[window.]document.getElementById("*elementID*")
[window.]document.getElementsByTagName("head")[0]

**Object-Specific Properties**
profile

**Object-Specific Methods**
None.

**Object-Specific Event Handler Properties**
None.

## profile

Returns the URL string assigned to the optional profile attribute. As of Version 6 browsers, nothing special occurs as a result of assigning this attribute.

| | |
|---|---|
| **Value** | URL string. |
| **Default** | Empty string. |

# hidden

See input (type="hidden").

# history

NN 2    IE 3    DOM n/a

During a browser session, the browser uses the history object to maintain a list of URLs visited by the user. This list (stored as an array) is used by the browser to assist with navigation via the **Back** and **Forward** buttons. Due to the sensitive nature of the private information stored in the history object, not many of the details are exposed to scripts that could capture such information and surreptitiously submit it to a server. In more recent browser versions, each window maintains its own history object.

To answer a frequently-asked question: no, you cannot block or disable the Back button's action. At most, you can prevent the current page from being entered into the browser's history when a user clicks on a link from the page. Accomplish this by scripting the links with the location.replace() navigation method. Navigator 4 and later (with signed scripts and the user's explicit approval) can remove the toolbar from the browser window (see the locationbar object discussion). Or, you can open a new window without the toolbar (see the window.open() method).

**Object Model Reference**
[window.]history

**Object-Specific Properties**

| current | length | next | previous |

**Object-Specific Methods**

| back() | forward() | go() | item() |

**Object-Specific Event Handler Properties**
None.

## current, next, previous

NN 4    IE n/a    DOM n/a

Read-only

The URL of the current, next, and previous URLs in the history array. This information is private and can be retrieved in Navigator 4 or later only with signed scripts and the user's approval. Signed scripts are beyond the scope of this book, but a good JavaScript book should show you how to create and program signed scripts.

**Example**
```
netscape.security.PrivilegeManager.enablePrivilege("UniversalBrowserRead");
var prevURL = parent.otherFrame.history.previous;
netscape.security.PrivilegeManager.revertPrivilege("UniversalBrowserRead");
```

**Value**        URL string.

**Default**      None.

## length

The number of items in the history list. Even with this information, you are not allowed to extract a specific history entry except with signed scripts and the user's permission in Navigator 4 or later.

**Example**

```
if (history.length > 4) {
    ...
}
```

**Value**          Integer.

**Default**        None.

## back( )

The basic action is to navigate to the previously viewed document, similar to the click of the browser's **Back** button. In Navigator 4 or later, however, you can direct the back( ) method to a specific window or frame, thus bypassing the default behavior of the **Back** button. For example, repeated calls to parent.otherFrame.history.back( ) eventually run out of history for the frame and then cease to do anything further. On the other hand, repeated calls to top.history.back( ) are the same as clicking the **Back** button, conceivably backing out of the frameset entirely if it wasn't the first document loaded in the current browser session.

**Returned Value**    None.

**Parameters**        None.

## forward( )

The basic action is to navigate to the same URL that the browser's **Forward** button leads to (if it is active). Similar cautions about the window's history from the history.back( ) method apply here, as well.

**Returned Value**    None.

**Parameters**        None.

## go( )

go(stepCount | "URL")

Navigates to a specific position in the history listing.

**Returned Value**    None.

**Parameters**

stepCount

An integer representing how many items away from the current listing the browser should use to navigate. A value of zero causes the current page to reload; a value of -1 is the same as back( ); a value of -2 is the URL two steps back from the current item in history. A bug in IE 3 causes all values other than 0 to be treated as -1.

*URL*

A URL or (in Navigator) document title stored in the history listing.

## item( )         NN 4    IE *n/a*    DOM *n/a*

item(*itemNumber*)

Returns the URL at a specific location in the history list. Requires Netscape signed scripts and the user's explicit permission to retrieve this private information.

**Returned Value**    URL String.

**Parameters**

*itemNumber*

An integer representing the number of item within the history list. The range of acceptable values is 0 through the history.length minus 1.

## hr         NN 6    IE 4    DOM 1

The hr object reflects the hr element.

**HTML Equivalent**

<hr>

**Object Model Reference**

[window.]document.getElementById("*elementID*")

**Object-Specific Properties**

| | | | | |
|---|---|---|---|---|
| align | color | noShade | size | width |

**Object-Specific Methods**

None.

**Object-Specific Event Handler Properties**

None.

## align         NN 6    IE 4    DOM 1
**Read/Write**

Defines the horizontal alignment of the element within its surrounding container.

**Example**      document.getElementById("myHR").align = "center";

**Value**      Any of the three horizontal alignment constant strings: center | left | right.

**Default**      center

## color

Read/Write

Sets the color scheme of the horizontal rule. If the rule is rendered in 3-D, complementary colors are automatically assigned to the shaded area.

| | |
|---|---|
| **Example** | `document.getElementById("myHR").color = "red";` |
| **Value** | Case-insensitive hexadecimal triplet or plain-language color name as a string. See Appendix A for acceptable plain-language color names. |
| **Default** | Browser default. |

## noShade

Read/Write

Indicates whether the browser should render the rule as a flat (not 3-D) line. In Internet Explorer only, if you set the color property, the browser changes the default line style to a no-shade style. In IE, once noShade is set to true, shading cannot later be restored.

| | |
|---|---|
| **Example** | `document.getElementById("bar2").noShade = "true";` |
| **Value** | Boolean value: true \| false. |
| **Default** | false |

## size

Read/Write

Provides the thickness in pixels of the horizontal rule.

| | |
|---|---|
| **Example** | `document.getElementById("rule2").size = 3;` |
| **Value** | Positive integer. |
| **Default** | 2 |

## width

Read/Write

Provides the width of the rule either in pixels (as an integer) or a percentage (as a string) of the next outermost block-level container.

| | |
|---|---|
| **Example** | `document.getElementById("bar3").width = "70%";` |
| **Value** | Integer (for pixels) or string (for pixels or percentage). |
| **Default** | 100% |

# html

The html object reflects the html element.

**HTML Equivalent**    `<html>`

**Object Model Reference**
```
[window.]document.getElementById("elementID")
[window.]document.body.parentNode
[window.]document.documentElement
```

**Object-Specific Properties**
version

**Object-Specific Methods**
None.

**Object-Specific Event Handler Properties**
None.

## version                                      NN 6    IE 5(Mac)/6(Win)    DOM 1
**Read/Write**

Reflects the deprecated version attribute of the html element. Present in modern browsers, but not functional. See the DocumentType object.

**Value**          String.

**Default**        Empty string.

# HTMLCollection                                NN 6    IE 5(Mac)/6(Win)    DOM 1

The HTMLCollection object is an abstract representation in the W3C DOM of any collection of HTML element objects, all of which exist in the same document tree and have the same tag. For example, in the eyes of the W3C DOM, the document.images array is an HTMLCollection object. All entries are img element object references. JavaScript treats such collections as arrays for access to individual entries via array notation, along with the help of the HTMLCollection's sole property, length. Alternatively, you can use the two methods (item( ) and namedItem( )) to reference a single entry in the collection. All instances of the HTMLCollection object (such as document.images) inherit the property and methods listed below from the abstract HTMLCollection object. See descriptions of each instance in this chapter (anchors, applets, areas, cells, elements, forms, images, links, options, rows, tBodies, and non-W3C DOM element collections all, children, embeds, and frames).

**Object-Specific Properties**
length

**Object-Specific Methods**
item( )          namedItem( )

**Object-Specific Event Handler Properties**
None.

## length

Read-only

Returns the number of elements in the collection.

**Example**        `var howMany = document.myForm.elements.length;`

**Value**          Integer.

## item( )

item(*index*)

Returns one object from the collection corresponding to the object matching the index value in source code order. IE implements another variation of this method for some (but not all) of its collections with an optional secondary parameter.

### Returned Value

Reference to an element object. If there are no matches to the parameter, the returned value is null.

### Parameters

*index*

A zero-based integer corresponding to the specified item in source code order.

## namedItem( )

namedItem(*IDOrName*)

Returns one object from the collection corresponding to the object matching the parameter string value.

### Returned Value

Reference to an element object. If there are no matches to the parameters, the returned value is null.

### Parameters

*IDOrName*

The string that contains the same value as the desired filter's name.

# HTMLDocument

The HTMLDocument object is an abstract representation in the W3C DOM of the document node for an HTML document tree. Scripts reference this object via the document object.

This object inherits properties and methods from a chain of node objects in the W3C DOM core module, namely the root Node object and the Document object. To this set of properties and methods, the HTMLDocument object adds properties and methods that apply specifically to HTML documents (in contrast to XML documents)—properties such as referrer and body, and methods such as write( ). Browser implementations add numerous additional proprietary properties and methods. See the full discussion of the scriptable implementations of the HTMLDocument object within the document object discussion earlier in this chapter.

## HTMLDOMImplementation                    NN *n/a*   IE *n/a*   DOM *2*

The W3C HTMLDOMImplementation object is an HTML-specific extension to the DOMImplementation object. Although not yet implemented in browsers, it may in the future provide an avenue to creating virtual HTML documents, much like the way you can create virtual XML documents in Netscape 6 and later. The one method that this object brings to the DOM is createHTMLDocument( ).

## HTMLElement                    NN *6*   IE *5(Mac)/6(Win)*   DOM *1*

Every scriptable element object in modern browsers is, at its core, a descendant of the basic HTMLElement abstract object in the W3C DOM. The HTMLElement, itself, inherits properties and methods from the Node and Element chain in the core DOM module. To this inherited set of features, the HTMLElement adds properties that apply to HTML elements (in contrast to XML elements), including the className, dir, id, lang, and title properties. All individual HTML element objects, such as HTMLBodyElement and HTMLFormElement, inherit their characteristics from the HTMLElement object. That's one reason why the list of shared properties and methods at the beginning of this chapter is so long: it includes items inherited from the long chain of Node to Element to HTMLElement.

The terminology of the DOM abstract object names (e.g., HTMLBodyElement) is not essential knowledge to scripting element objects. That is to say, the abstract object names almost never appear in scripts because scripts reference instances of such HTML objects by way of their identifiers or through properties of other objects (such as *eventObject*.target). The only place you are likely to see these abstract names is during debugging, when you use alert( ) methods or other tools to inspect the object referenced by a variable. Netscape 6 reports such object references as instances of a specific HTML element class (e.g., HTMLParagraphElement or HTMLInputElement). This information, in itself, is often far more helpful than IE's reporting of the reference being just [object].

## i

See b.

## iframe                    NN *6*   IE *4*   DOM *1*

The iframe object reflects the iframe element. Be aware that, in Internet Explorer, a number of properties defined for this object have no effect on the object nor any default value, but are implemented because the element shares its internal structure with other elements that use those properties.

**HTML Equivalent**    <iframe>

**Object Model Reference**
[window.]document.getElementById("*elementID*")

**Object-Specific Properties**

| | | | | |
|---|---|---|---|---|
| align | allowTransparency | border | borderColor | contentDocument |
| contentWindow | dataFld | dataSrc | frameBorder | frameSpacing |
| height | hspace | longDesc | marginHeight | marginWidth |
| name | noResize | scrolling | src | vspace |
| width | | | | |

**Object-Specific Methods**
None.

**Object-Specific Event Handler Properties**
None.

## align                                                    NN 6    IE 4    DOM 1
**Read/Write**

Defines how the element is aligned relative to surrounding text content. Most values set the vertical relationship between the element and surrounding text. For example, to align the bottom of the element with the baseline of the surrounding text, the align property value would be baseline. An element can be "floated" along the left or right margin to let surrounding text wrap around the element.

**Example**        document.getElementById("myIframe").align = "absmiddle";

**Value**          Any of the following alignment constant values (as a string): absbottom |
                   absmiddle | baseline | bottom | right | left | none | texttop | top.

**Default**        bottom

## allowTransparency                                         NN n/a    IE 6    DOM n/a
**Read/Write**

Specifies whether the iframe background can be transparent. For the background of the main document to show through both the iframe and its document, the document's background-color style attribute must be set to transparent.

**Example**        document.getElementById("myIframe").allowTransparency = true;

**Value**          Boolean value: true | false.

**Default**        false

## border

NN *n/a*    IE *4(Win)*    DOM *n/a*

**Read/Write**

Although defined for the iframe element object in IE/Windows, the border property has no value nor does assigning a value affect the appearance of the element.

## borderColor

NN *n/a*    IE *4*    DOM *n/a*

**Read/Write**

Although defined for the iframe element object in IE, the borderColor property has no value. Assigning a color value does draw a thin border around the iframe's rectangle on the Macintosh, but has no effect in Windows.

## contentDocument

NN *6*    IE *n/a*    DOM *2*

**Read-only**

Returns a reference to the document object loaded into the iframe element object. Through that document object, you can access one of the document's elements via the getElementById( ) method, or access the containing window object via the document's defaultView property. For IE/Windows, use the contentWindow property to jump from iframe element object to its content.

**Example**

```
var iframeElem = parent.document.getElementById("myIframe");
var doc = iframeElem.contentDocument;
```

**Value**          Reference to a document node.

**Default**        Current document node.

## contentWindow

NN *7*    IE *5.5(Win)*    DOM *n/a*

**Read-only**

Returns a reference to the window object generated by the iframe element. Through the window object, you can access the document object and then any one of the document's elements. For Netscape 6, use the contentDocument property to jump from iframe element object to its content. If you are trying to reach script variables or functions in the frame, the contentWindow (or W3C DOM-friendly and Netscape 6-compatible contentDocument.defaultView) provides access to the script context.

**Example**

```
var iframeElem = parent.document.getElementById("myIframe");
var win = iframeElem.contentWindow;
```

**Value**          Reference to a window node.

**Default**        Current window node.

## dataFld

NN *n/a*    IE *4*    DOM *n/a*
**Read/Write**

Used with IE data binding to associate a remote data source column name with the value of the src property. A datasrc attribute must also be set for the element. Setting both the dataFld and dataSrc properties to empty strings breaks the binding between element and data source. Works only with text file data sources in IE 5/Mac.

| | |
|---|---|
| **Example** | document.getElementById("myIframe").dataFld = "frameURL"; |
| **Value** | Case-sensitive identifier of the data source column. |
| **Default** | None. |

## dataSrc

NN *n/a*    IE *4*    DOM *n/a*
**Read/Write**

Used with IE data binding to specify the ID of the page's object element that loads the data source object for remote data access. Setting both the dataFld and dataSrc properties to empty strings breaks the binding between element and data source. Works only with text file data sources in IE 5/Mac.

| | |
|---|---|
| **Example** | document.getElementById("myIframe").dataSrc = "DBSRC3"; |
| **Value** | Case-sensitive identifier of the data source. |
| **Default** | None. |

## frameBorder

NN *n/a*    IE *4*    DOM *n/a*
**Read/Write**

This property should control whether the frame displays a border. In practice, the property has no effect on the visual appearance of an inline frame.

## frameSpacing

NN *n/a*    IE *4*    DOM *n/a*
**Read/Write**

The amount of spacing in pixels between frames within a frameset. This property has no effect on an inline frame in Internet Explorer.

## height, width

NN *6*    IE *4*    DOM *1*
**Read/Write**

Provide the pixel or percentage measure of the iframe element's height and width.

### Example

```
document.getElementById("myIframe").height = "200";
document.getElementById("myIframe").width = "500";
```

| Value | Length string. |
| Default | 300 (width); 150 (height). |

## hspace, vspace

NN *n/a*    IE *4*    DOM *n/a*
Read/Write

Provide the pixel measure of horizontal and vertical margins surrounding an inline frame. The hspace property affects the left and right edges of the element equally; the vspace property affects the top and bottom edges of the element equally. These margins are not the same as margins set by style sheets, but they have the same visual effect.

**Example**
```
document.getElementById("myIframe").hspace = 5;
document.getElementById("myIframe").vspace = 8;
```

| Value | Integer of pixel count. |
| Default | 0 |

## longDesc

NN *6*    IE *5(Mac)/6(Win)*    DOM *1*
Read/Write

Reflects the longDesc attribute of the iframe element. Version 6 browsers provide no significant functionality for this attribute or property.

| Value | URL string. |
| Default | Empty string. |

## marginHeight, marginWidth

NN *6*    IE *4*    DOM *1*
Read/Write

Control the number of pixels between the inner edge of a frame and the content rendered inside the frame. An adjustment to either property sets the other property to zero, eliminating the default margin provided by the browser. Not reliable in IE 4 for Windows, but operable in all other supported versions.

| Value | Positive integer value or zero. |
| Default | Varies with browser and operating system. |

## name

NN *6*    IE *4*    DOM *1*
Read/Write

This is the identifier associated with an iframe for use as the value assigned to target attributes or as script references to the frame. The value is usually assigned via the name attribute, but it can be modified by script if necessary.

**Value**

Case-sensitive string identifier that follows the rules of identifier naming: it may contain no whitespace, cannot begin with a numeral, and should avoid punctuation except for the underscore character.

**Default**     None.

## noResize
NN n/a     IE 4     DOM n/a<br>Read/Write

Specifies whether the frame can be resized by the user. Not applicable to an `iframe` element.

## scrolling
NN 6     IE 4     DOM 1<br>Read/Write

Specifies the treatment of scrollbars for an `iframe` when the content exceeds the visible area of the `iframe`. You can force an `iframe` to display scrollbars at all times or never. Or you can let the browser determine the need for scrolling. It is not uncommon for browsers to ignore scripted changes to this property. Make your choice in the element's `scrolling` attribute.

**Example**     `document.getElementById("myIframe").scrolling = "no";`

**Value**       One of three constants (as a string): auto | no | yes.

**Default**     auto

## src
NN 6     IE 4     DOM 1<br>Read/Write

Indicates the URL of the external content file loaded into the current element. To change the content, assign a new URL to the property.

**Example**     `document.getElementById("myIframe").src = "section2.html";`

**Value**       Complete or relative URL as a string.

**Default**     None.

## vspace

See hspace.

## width

See height.

# ilayer

See layer.

# images

NN 3    IE 4    DOM 1

A collection (array) of all img objects contained by the document. This object is implemented only in browser versions that treat images as objects. Therefore, you can use the existence of this array object as a conditional switch surrounding statements that swap or preload images:

```
if (document.images) {
    // process img element objects here
}
```

Internet Explorer 3.01 for the Macintosh provided support for images as objects.

## Object Model Reference

document.images

## Object-Specific Properties

length

## Object-Specific Methods

item( )           namedItem( )           tags( )           urns( )

# length

NN 3    IE 4    DOM 1<br>Read-only

Returns the number of elements in the collection.

**Example**        var howMany = document.images.length;

**Value**        Integer.

# item( )

NN 6    IE 4    DOM 1

item(*index*[, *subindex*])
item(*index*)

Returns a single image object or collection of image objects corresponding to the element matching the index value (or, optionally in IE, the index and subindex values).

## Returned Value

One object or collection (array) of objects. If there are no matches to the parameters, the returned value is null.

## Parameters

*index*

When the parameter is a zero-based integer (required in Netscape 6), the returned value is a single element corresponding to the said numbered item in source code order (nested within the current element). When the parameter is a string, the returned value is a collection of elements with id or name properties that match that string.

*subindex*

If you specify a string value for the first parameter (IE only), you may use the second parameter to specify a zero-based integer to retrieve a specific element from the collection with id or name properties that match the first parameter's string value.

## namedItem( )

namedItem(*IDOrName*)

Returns a single object corresponding to the element matching the parameter string value.

### Returned Value

One object reference. If there are no matches to the parameters, the returned value is null.

### Parameters

*IDOrName*

The string that contains the same value as the desired element's id or name attribute.

## tags( )

tags(*tagName*)

Returns a collection of objects (among all objects within the current collection) with tags that match the *tagName* parameter. Redundant here, because all elements have the same img tag.

### Returned Value

A collection (array) of objects. If there are no matches to the parameters, the returned value is an array of zero length.

### Parameters

*tagName*

A string that contains the element tag, as in document.images.tags("img").

## urns( )

urns(*URN*)

Returns a collection of nested element objects that have behaviors attached to them and URNs that match the *URN* parameter.

### Returned Value

A collection (array) of objects. If there are no matches to the parameters, the returned value is an array of zero length.

### Parameters

*URN*

A string with a local or external behavior file URN.

# img

The img object reflects the img element. This object shares the same properties as the static Image object, which you can use to pre-cache images without rendering them on the page.

**HTML Equivalent**    `<img>`

**Object Model Reference**

```
[window.]document.imageName
[window.]document.images[i]
[window.]document.images["imageName"]
[window.]document.getElementById("elementID")
```

**Object-Specific Properties**

| | | | |
|---|---|---|---|
| align | alt | border | complete |
| dataFld | dataFormatAs | dataSrc | dynsrc |
| fileCreatedDate | fileModifiedDate | fileSize | fileUpdatedDate |
| height | href | hspace | isMap |
| longDesc | loop | lowsrc | lowSrc |
| mimeType | name | nameProp | naturalHeight |
| naturalWidth | protocol | prototype | src |
| start | useMap | vspace | width |
| x | y | | |

**Object-Specific Methods**

None.

**Object-Specific Event Handler Properties**

| Events | IE Windows | IE Mac | NN | W3C DOM |
|---|---|---|---|---|
| onabort | 4 | 4 | 3 | 2 |
| onerror | 4 | 4 | 3 | 2 |
| onload | 4 | 4 | 3 | n/a |

# align

**Read/Write**

Defines how the element is aligned relative to surrounding text content. Most values set the vertical relationship between the element and surrounding text. For example, to align the bottom of the element with the baseline of the surrounding text, the align property value would be baseline. An element can be "floated" along the left or right margin to let surrounding text wrap around the element.

| | |
|---|---|
| **Example** | `document.logoImg.align = "absmiddle";` |
| **Value** | Any of the following alignment constant values (as a string): absbottom \| absmiddle \| baseline \| bottom \| right \| left \| none \| texttop \| top. |
| **Default** | bottom |

## alt

Indicates the text to be displayed (or spoken) where the img element appears on the page when a browser does not download graphics (or is waiting for the image to download). The text is usually a brief description of what the image is. Be aware that the size of the image area on the page may limit the amount of assigned text visible on the page. Make sure the description is readable.

**Example**       document.corpLogo.alt = "MegaCorp Logo";

**Value**         String value.

**Default**       None.

## border

Provides the thickness of the border around an element (in pixels). This property is read-only in Navigator 4.

**Example**       document.logoImage.border = 4;

**Value**         An integer value. A setting of zero removes the border entirely.

**Default**       0

## complete

Reveals whether the img element's src or lowsrc image file has fully loaded. Note that Navigator 4 provides an incorrect true reading before the image has completely loaded.

**Example**

```
if (document.logo.complete) {
    // safe to process the image object
}
```

**Value**         Boolean value: true | false.

**Default**       false

## dataFld

Used with IE data binding to associate a remote data source column name with the src property of the img object. A datasrc attribute must also be set for the element. Setting both the dataFld and dataSrc properties to empty strings breaks the binding between element and data source. Works only with text file data sources in IE 5/Mac.

| **Example** | document.myImage.dataFld = "logoURL"; |
| **Value** | Case-sensitive identifier of the data source column. |
| **Default** | None. |

## dataFormatAs

NN n/a   IE 4   DOM n/a<br>Read/Write

This property is a member of the img element object in IE, but does not apply to img because data binding values are linked to the src attribute, rather than rendered content.

## dataSrc

NN n/a   IE 4   DOM n/a<br>Read/Write

Used with IE data binding to specify the ID of the page's object element that loads the data source object for remote data access. Setting both the dataFld and dataSrc properties to empty strings breaks the binding between element and data source. Works only with text file data sources in IE 5/Mac.

| **Example** | document.myImage.dataSrc = "DBSRC3"; |
| **Value** | Case-sensitive identifier of the data source. |
| **Default** | None. |

## dynsrc

NN n/a   IE 4   DOM n/a<br>Read/Write

URL of a video clip to be displayed through the img element. Changing this property loads a new video clip into the image object. See also the loop property for controlling the frequency of video clip play.

| **Example** | document.images[3].dynsrc = "snowman.avi"; |
| **Value** | Complete or relative URL as a string. |
| **Default** | None. |

## fileCreatedDate

NN n/a   IE 4(Win)/5(Mac)   DOM n/a<br>Read-only

Returns a string of the date (but not the time) that the server (or local filesystem) reports the currently-loaded file was created. By loading an image into a nonrendered Image object, a script can determine the date of the image (but more accurately from the fileUpdatedDate property). IE 4's value is a long date format, but starting with IE 5, the date information is formatted as mm/dd/yyyy. The value may be corrupted if the server supplies the data in a format that IE does not expect. Implemented in IE 5/Mac, but the value is empty.

**Example**        var dateObj = new Date(document.logoImg.fileCreatedDate);

**Value**          Date string.

**Default**        None.

## fileModifiedDate

NN *n/a*    IE *4(Win)/5(Mac)*    DOM *n/a*

Read-only

Returns a string of the date (but not the time) that the server (or local filesystem) reports the currently-loaded file was most recently modified. IE 4's value is a long date format, but starting with IE 5, the date information is formatted as mm/dd/yyyy. The value may be corrupted or incorrect if the server supplies the data in a format that IE does not expect. Implemented in IE 5/Mac, but the value is empty.

**Example**        var dateObj = new Date(document.logoImg.fileModifiedDate);

**Value**          Date string.

**Default**        None.

## fileSize

NN *n/a*    IE *4(Win)/5(Mac)*    DOM *n/a*

Read-only

Returns the number of bytes for the size of the currently-loaded image. IE for Windows returns this value as a string, while IE for Macintosh returns a number value (although its value is 0).

**Example**        var byteCount = parseInt(document.fileSize, 10);

**Value**          Integer as string (Windows) or number (Mac).

**Default**        None.

## fileUpdatedDate

NN *n/a*    IE *5(Mac)/5.5(Win)*    DOM *n/a*

Read-only

For an image file retrieved from a server, this property may more accurately reflect the date the file was last uploaded to the server than the other date-related properties. Local files commonly return an empty string. Implemented in IE 5/Mac, but the value is empty.

**Example**        var dateObj = new Date(document.logoImg.fileUpdatedDate);

**Value**          Date string.

**Default**        None.

## height, width

NN *3*    IE *4*    DOM *1*
Read/Write (IE and Netscape 6)

Provide the height and width in pixels of the image rendered in the img element. Changes to these values are immediately reflected in reflowed content on the page in Internet Explorer 4 (or later) and Netscape 6. Be aware that images scale to fit the new dimension.

**Example**        document.prettyPicture.height = 250;

**Value**        Integer.

**Default**        None.

## href

NN *n/a*    IE *4*    DOM *n/a*
Read/Write

The URL specified by the element's src attribute. Identical to, and deprecated in favor of, the src property.

**Example**        document.logoImage.href = "images/fancyLogo.gif";

**Value**        String of complete or relative URL.

**Default**        None.

## hspace, vspace

NN *3*    IE *4*    DOM *1*
Read/Write (IE and Netscape 6)

Provide the pixel measure of horizontal and vertical margins surrounding an image object. The hspace property affects the left and right edges of the element equally; the vspace affects the top and bottom edges of the element equally. These margins are not the same as margins set by style sheets, but they have the same visual effect.

**Example**

```
document.logo.hspace = 5;
document.logo.vspace = 8;
```

**Value**        Integer of pixel count.

**Default**        0 (IE), -1 (Netscape 6).

## isMap

NN *6*    IE *4*    DOM *1*
Read/Write

Indicates whether the img element is acting as a server-side image map. For an image to be a server-side image map, it must be wrapped with an a element whose href attribute points to the URL of the CGI program that knows how to interpret the click coordinate information. The browser appends coordinate information about the click to the URL as a get form method appends form element data to the action attribute URL.

More recent browsers allow client-side image maps (see the useMap property), which operate more quickly for the user, because there is no communication with the server to carry out the examination of the click coordinate point.

**Example**      document.navMap.isMap = true;

**Value**        Boolean value: true | false.

**Default**      false

## longDesc
NN 6   IE 5(Mac)/6(Win)   DOM 1<br/>Read/Write

Reflects the longDesc attribute of the img element. Version 6 browsers provide no significant functionality for this attribute or property.

**Value**        URL string.

**Default**      Empty string.

## loop
NN n/a   IE 4   DOM n/a<br/>Read/Write

If you specify a video clip with the dynsrc attribute, the loop property controls how many times the clip should play (loop). Changing to a value of -1 is equal to a continuous loop.

**Example**      document.movieImg.loop = 3;

**Value**        Integer.

**Default**      1

## lowsrc
NN 3   IE 4   DOM n/a<br/>Read/Write (IE and Netscape 6)

Indicates the URL of a lower-resolution (or alternate) image to download into the document space if the image of the src attribute will take a long time to download. The lowsrc image should be the same pixel size as the primary src image. It makes sense to change the lowsrc property only if you are also going to change the src property. In this case, make sure you change the lowsrc property first so that the browser knows how to handle the long download for the src image.

Note that Netscape 6 also implements a second variation of this property with a different capitalization: lowSrc. Neither version is indicated in the W3C DOM.

**Example**      document.productImage.lowsrc = "images/widget43LoRes.jpg";

**Value**        Any complete or relative URL as a string.

**Default**      None.

## mimeType

NN n/a    IE 6(Win)    DOM n/a<br>
Read-only

Returns a plain-language description of the MIME type for the image. This property may not be officially supported by Microsoft, but it correctly reports values for typical image types served from both local disks and servers.

**Example**
```
if (document.productImage.mimeType.indexOf("JPEG") != -1) {
    // process condition for jpeg image
}
```

**Value**          String value such as JPEG Image or GIF Image.

**Default**      None.

## name

NN 2    IE 3    DOM 1<br>
Read/Write

This is the identifier associated with the image object for use in scripted references to the object.

**Example**        var imgName = document.images[3].name;

**Value**

Case-sensitive string identifier that follows the rules of identifier naming: it may contain no whitespace, cannot begin with a numeral, and should avoid punctuation except for the underscore character.

**Default**      None.

## nameProp

NN n/a    IE 5(Win)    DOM n/a<br>
Read-only

Returns the filename (without the rest of the URL path) of the current image. Simplifies examination of current image content.

**Example**
```
if (document.images[3].nameProp == "menuOn.jpg") {
    document.image[3].src = "../images/menuOff.jpg";
}
```

**Value**         Case-sensitive string filename and extension.

**Default**      None.

## naturalHeight, naturalWidth
NN 6    IE n/a    DOM n/a
Read-only

Return the unscaled height and width of the image, in pixels. Allows scripts to find the true dimensions of the original image in case scripts or incorrect element attributes have scaled the image.

### Example
```
document.logoImg.height = document.logoImg.naturalHeight;
document.logoImg.width = document.logoImg.naturalWidth;
```

| **Value** | Integer. |
| **Default** | None. |

## protocol
NN n/a    IE 4(Win)/5(Mac)    DOM n/a
Read-only

Returns the protocol component of the URL associated with the element. Windows and Macintosh versions return values in different formats. For the Windows version, the values are in expanded plain language (e.g., File Protocol or HyperText Transfer Protocol); for the Mac version, values resemble location.protocol values (e.g., file: or http:). Unreliable in IE 4 for Windows.

| **Value** | String. |
| **Default** | None. |

## prototype
NN n/a    IE 4(Mac)    DOM n/a
Read-only

Returns a reference to the static Image object from which all instances of image objects are created. This mechanism is more commonly used in JavaScript core language objects (see Chapter 12). The fact that this property is available only in Internet Explorer 4 for the Macintosh calls its legitimacy into question.

| **Value** | Object reference. |
| **Default** | object Image |

## src
NN 3    IE 4    DOM 1
Read/Write

Provides the relative or complete URL of the image file currently loaded or to be loaded into the img element. Loading an image of a different size into an existing img element forces the element to resize to the new image's dimensions except in the following browsers: Netscape 3, Netscape 4, and IE 3 for the Macintosh. Reading this property returns the complete URL, regardless of how the URL form assigned the value originally.

| | |
|---|---|
| **Example** | document.image[3].src = "../images/menuOff.jpg"; |
| **Value** | URL string. |
| **Default** | None. |

## start

If you specify a video clip with the dynsrc attribute, the start property controls the action that causes the clip to start running.

| | |
|---|---|
| **Example** | document.movieImg.start = "mouseover"; |
| **Value** | String constant: fileopen | mouseover. |
| **Default** | fileopen |

## useMap

Provides the URL of the map element in the same document that contains client-side image map hot areas and links. The value includes the hashmark assigned with the map name in the usemap attribute of the img element.

| | |
|---|---|
| **Example** | document.images[0].useMap = "#altMap"; |
| **Value** | A string starting with a hashmark and the name of the map element. |
| **Default** | None. |

## vspace

See hspace.

## width

See height.

## x, y

Provide the horizontal and vertical pixel coordinates of the top-left corner of the image relative to the page. These are Navigator-only properties, corresponding to the offsetLeft and offsetTop properties of Internet Explorer.

| | |
|---|---|
| **Example** | var imageFromTop = document.logoImg.y; |
| **Value** | Integer. |
| **Default** | None. |

# implementation

The implementation object (the JavaScript reference for the W3C DOMImplementation object) represents, to a limited degree, the environment that makes up the document container—the browser for our purposes. You can reach this object via the document.implementation property.

Methods of the object let you see which DOM modules the browser reports supporting. In Netscape 6, this object is also a gateway to creating virtual W3C Document and DocumentType objects outside of the current document tree. Thus, in Netscape 6 you can use the document.implementation property as a start to generating a nonrendered document for external XML documents.

## Object Model Reference

document.implementation

## Object-Specific Properties

None.

## Object-Specific Methods

createDocument( )                createDocumentType( )                hasFeature( )

## Object-Specific Event Handler Properties

None.

## createDocument( )

createDocument("*namespaceURI*", "*qualifiedName*", *docTypeReference*)

Returns a reference to a newly created virtual W3C DOM Document (not the document node of an HTML document) object. Netscape 6 extends this Document object with a load( ) method that permits the loading of XML documents into the browser, although they are invisible to the user. Scripts may then access the document tree of the XML document as a data source for rendering information in the HTML document. If you are loading an external XML document, you can create the Document object with blank values for the three parameters:

```
var myXDoc = document.implementation.createDocument("", "", null);
```

When the external document loads, any namespace and DOCTYPE concerns will be controlled by the document's content. For an example, see "Embedding XML Data" in Chapter 5.

**Returned Value**    Reference to an empty Document object.

**Parameters**

*namespaceURI*
> String of the namespace URI for a new XML document element.

*qualifiedName*
> String identifier for the qualified name for the new document element.

*docTypeReference*
> Reference to a DocumentType node (which may be generated from the DocumentImplementation.createDocumentType( ) method).

## createDocumentType( ) NN 6     IE n/a     DOM 2

createDocumentType("*qualifiedName*", "*publicID*", "*systemID*")

Returns a reference to a newly created virtual W3C DOM DocumentType object. You can feed the object returned from this method to the DocumentImplementation.createDocument( ) method.

**Returned Value**

Reference to a DocumentType object not yet associated with a Document object.

**Parameters**

*qualifiedName*
> String identifier for the qualified name for the new document element.

*publicID*
> String of the public identifier for the DOCTYPE.

*systemID*
> String of the system identifier (typically, the URI of the DTD file) for the DOCTYPE.

## hasFeature( ) NN 6     IE 5(Mac)/6(Win)     DOM 1

hasFeature("*feature*", "*version*")

Returns a Boolean true if the browser application supports (i.e., conforms to the required specifications of) a stated W3C DOM module and version. The closely related isSupported( ) method performs the same test on an individual node, allowing you to verify feature support for the current node type. Parameter values for the two methods are identical.

It is up to the browser maker to validate that the DOM implemented in the browser conforms with each module before allowing the browser to return true for the module. That doesn't necessarily mean that the implementation is bug-free or consistent with other implementations. Caveat scriptor.

In theory, you could use this method to verify module support prior to accessing a property or invoking a method. The following script fragment from the head portion of a document dynamically links a different external style sheet file for "true" CSS2 support:

```
var cssFile;
if (document.implementation.hasFeature("CSS", "2.0")) {
    cssFile = "styles/corpStyle2.css";
} else {
    cssFile = "styles/corpStyle1.css";
}
document.write("<link rel='stylesheet' type='text/css' href='" + cssFile + "'>");
```

More browsers support this browser-wide method than the element-specific method, which may help more developers deploy it sooner.

**Returned Value**     Boolean value: true | false.

**Parameters**

*feature*

As of W3C DOM Level 2, permissible case-sensitive module name strings are: Core, XML, HTML, Views, StyleSheets, CSS, CSS2, Events, UIEvents, MouseEvents, MutationEvents, HTMLEvents, Range, and Traversal.

*version*

String representation of the major and minor version of the DOM module cited in the first parameter. For the W3C DOM Level 2, the version is 2.0, even when the DOM module supports another W3C standard that has its own numbering system. Thus, the test for HTML DOM module support is for Version 2.0, even though HTML is at 4.x.

# imports                                            NN *n/a*    IE *4*    DOM *n/a*

A collection (array) of styleSheet objects imported into an explicit styleSheet object via the @import rule. In other words, a styleSheet object that employs an @import treats that imported style sheet as a nested object, but one that is, itself, a full-fledged styleSheet object. Thus, you can access the rule objects within each imported style sheet. The following example iterates through all of the document's styleSheet objects in search of imported style sheets:

```
for (var i = 0; i < document.styleSheets.length; i++) {
    for (var j = 0; j < document.styleSheets[i].imports.length; j++) {
        // process each imported style sheet, referenced
        // here as document.styleSheets[i].imports[j]
    }
}
```

**Object Model Reference**

document.styleSheets[*i*].imports

**Object-Specific Properties**

length

**Object-Specific Methods**

item( )

# length                                             NN *n/a*    IE *4*    DOM *n/a*

Read-only

Returns the number of objects in the collection.

**Example**        var howMany = document.styleSheets[i].imports.length;

**Value**          Integer.

## item( )                                      NN *n/a*    IE 4    DOM *n/a*

item(*index*)

Returns a single imported styleSheet object corresponding to the index value in source code order of @import rules. IE 5 for Macintosh erroneously returns null.

**Returned Value**

Reference to an imported styleSheet object. If there are no matches to the parameters, the returned value is null.

**Parameters**

*index*
> Zero-based integer.

# input                                             NN 6    IE 4    DOM 1

The input object reflects the input element. While Netscape Navigator exposes this HTML element completely only starting with Version 6, most of these form controls had some of their properties and methods available to earlier versions, going all the way back to Version 2.

In the W3C DOM specification, all input element objects share the same properties, even when the properties don't necessarily apply (the checked property of an input element of type text, for example). To reduce potential confusion, the discussions here for input types limit the properties to those that apply directly to a specific input type. See the following individual descriptions for each input object type: button, checkbox, fileUpload, hidden, image, password, radio, reset, submit, and text.

A few properties and methods that don't appear here in the lists of object-specific items are worth highlighting. While the IE DOM (especially in the Windows versions) ascribes properties such as accessKey, disabled, and tabIndex to virtually every HTML element, the W3C DOM is typically more parsimonious in handing out these properties to elements. But input elements are the right places for these properties, and you'll find full implementations in Netscape 6, as well as IE 4 or later. The same goes for the blur( ), click( ), and focus( ) methods, which are described among the shared items earlier in this chapter.

Event handlers for each input type are listed here, even though they are shared among all elements in more recent browsers. If your development must take backward compatibility into account, it's important to know precisely which input types recognize each of the long-supported events.

# input (type="button")                             NN 2    IE 3    DOM 1

The button object is a form control generated with an input element whose type attribute is set to "button". The button's text label comes from its value attribute and property. This element is similar to, but differs from, the button element. For details on the distinctions, see the button HTML element description in Chapter 8.

**HTML Equivalent**    &lt;input type="button"&gt;

## Object Model Reference

```
[window.]document.formName.elementName
[window.]document.forms[i].elements[i]
[window.]document.getElementById("elementID")
```

## Object-Specific Properties

| dataFld | dataSrc | form | name | type | value |
|---------|---------|------|------|------|-------|

## Object-Specific Methods

```
createTextRange()    handleEvent()
```

## Object-Specific Event Handler Properties

| Handler | NN | IE | DOM |
|---------|----|----|----|
| onblur | 6 | 4 | 2 |
| onclick | 2 | 3 | 2 |
| onfocus | 6 | 4 | 2 |
| onmousedown | 4 | 4 | 2 |
| onmousemove | 6 | 4 | 2 |
| onmouseout | 6 | 4 | 2 |
| onmouseover | 6 | 4 | 2 |
| onmouseup | 4 | 4 | 2 |

## dataFld

NN *n/a*  IE *4*  DOM *n/a*

Read/Write

Used with IE data binding to associate a remote data source column name to a button object's value property. A datasrc attribute must also be set for the element. Setting both the dataFld and dataSrc properties to empty strings breaks the binding between element and data source. Works only with text file data sources in IE 5/Mac.

**Example**      document.myForm.myButton.dataFld = "linkURL";

**Value**        Case-sensitive identifier of the data source column.

**Default**      None.

## dataSrc

NN *n/a*  IE *4*  DOM *n/a*

Read/Write

Used with IE data binding to specify the ID of the page's object element that loads the data source object for remote data access. Content from the data source is specified via the datafld attribute. Setting both the dataFld and dataSrc properties to empty strings breaks the binding between element and data source. Works only with text file data sources in IE 5/Mac.

**Example**      document.myForm.myButton.dataSrc = "DBSRC3";

Alphabetical DOM Reference

| | |
|---|---|
| **Value** | Case-sensitive identifier of the data source. |
| **Default** | None. |

## form

Returns a reference to the form element that contains the current element. When processing an event from this element, the event handler function automatically has access to the input element (as the event object's target or srcElement property). By reading the form property, the script can easily access other controls within the same form.

| | |
|---|---|
| **Example** | var theForm = evt.srcElement.form; |
| **Value** | form element object reference. |
| **Default** | None. |

## name

This is the identifier associated with the form control. The value of this property is submitted as one-half of the name/value pair when the form is submitted to the server. Names are hidden from user view, since control labels are assigned via other means, depending on the control type. Form control names may also be used by script references to the objects. Despite the modern standards' preference for the id attribute, many browsers still require that a form control be assigned a name attribute to allow the control's value to be submitted.

| | |
|---|---|
| **Example** | document.orderForm.myButton.name = "Win32"; |
| **Value** | Case-sensitive string identifier that follows the rules of identifier naming: it may contain no whitespace, cannot begin with a numeral, and should avoid punctuation except for the underscore character. |
| **Default** | None. |

## type

Returns the type of form control element. The value is returned in all lowercase letters. It may be necessary to cycle through all form elements in search of specific types to do some processing on (e.g., emptying all form controls of type "text" while leaving other controls untouched).

**Example**

```
if (document.forms[0].elements[3].type == "button") {
    // process button input type here
}
```

| **Value** | Any of the following constants (as a string): button | checkbox | file | hidden | image | password | radio | reset | select-multiple | select-one | submit | text | textarea. |
| **Default** | checkbox |

## value

This is one of the rare times that the value property controls the label of a form control: the text that appears on the button. A button input element is not submitted with the form.

| **Example** | document.forms[0].myButton.value = "Undo"; |
| **Value** | String. |
| **Default** | None. |

## createTextRange( )

Creates a TextRange object containing the button's label text. See the TextRange object for details.

| **Returned Value** | TextRange object. |
| **Parameters** | None. |

## handleEvent( )

handleEvent(*event*)

Instructs the object to accept and process the event whose specifications are passed as the parameter to the method. The object must have an event handler for the event type to process the event. Navigator 4 only.

**Returned Value**     None.

**Parameters**

*event*
    A Navigator 4 event object.

# input (type="checkbox")

The checkbox object is a form control generated with an input element whose type attribute is set to "checkbox". Employ this element only as a user interface element for user on-off choices, not as a navigation button. In IE 5 and later for Windows and in Netscape 6, you can adjust the size of the checkbox via style sheet height and width attributes, but only Netscape 6 automatically scales the size of the checkmark optimized for the checkbox rectangle's size and keeps the baselines of surrounding text aligned with the rectangle's bottom.

**HTML Equivalent**    `<input type="checkbox">`

**Object Model Reference**

```
[window.]document.formName.elementName
[window.]document.forms[i].elements[i]
[window.]document.getElementById("elementID")
```

**Object-Specific Properties**

| | | | | |
|---|---|---|---|---|
| checked | dataFld | dataSrc | defaultChecked | form |
| indeterminate | name | status | type | value |

**Object-Specific Methods**

handleEvent( )

**Object-Specific Event Handler Properties**

| Handler | NN | IE | DOM |
|---|---|---|---|
| onblur | 6 | 4 | 2 |
| onclick | 3 | 4 | 2 |
| onfocus | 6 | 4 | 2 |
| onmousedown | 4 | 4 | 2 |
| onmousemove | 6 | 4 | 2 |
| onmouseout | 6 | 4 | 2 |
| onmouseover | 6 | 4 | 2 |
| onmouseup | 4 | 4 | 2 |

## checked
NN 2    IE 3    DOM 1
Read/Write

Specifies whether the checkbox is selected or turned on by the user (or script). Checkboxes operate independently of each other. Only checkbox objects with the checked property set to true have their name/value pair submitted with the form. To find out whether the form element is set to be checked when the page loads, see the defaultChecked property. Scripts can change this property even if the element is disabled.

**Example**

```
if (document.choiceForm.monitors.checked) {
    //process for the "monitors" checkbox being checked
}
```

**Value**          Boolean: true | false.

**Default**        false

# dataFld

Used with IE 4 data binding to associate a remote data source column name to a checkbox object's value attribute. A datasrc attribute must also be set for the element. Setting both the dataFld and dataSrc properties to empty strings breaks the binding between element and data source. Works only with text file data sources in IE 5/Mac.

**Example**        document.myForm.myCheckbox.dataFld = "homeAddrFlag";

**Value**          Case-sensitive identifier of the data source column.

**Default**        None.

# dataSrc

Used with IE data binding to specify the ID of the page's object element that loads the data source object for remote data access. Content from the data source is specified via the dataFld attribute. Setting both the dataFld and dataSrc properties to empty strings breaks the binding between element and data source. Works only with text file data sources in IE 5/Mac.

**Example**        document.myForm.myCheckbox.dataSrc = "DBSRC3";

**Value**          Case-sensitive identifier of the data source.

**Default**        None.

# defaultChecked

Specifies whether the element has the checked attribute set in the tag. You can compare the current checked property against defaultChecked to see whether the state of the control has changed since the document loaded. Changing this property does not affect the current checked status.

**Example**
```
var cBox = document.forms[0].checkbox1
if (cBox.checked != cBox.defaultChecked) {
    // process for changed state
}
```

**Value**          Boolean value: true | false.

**Default**        Determined by HTML tag attribute.

## form

Returns a reference to the form element that contains the current element (if any). When processing an event from this element, the event handler function automatically has access to the input element (as the event object's target or srcElement property). By reading the form property, the script can easily access other controls within the same form.

| | |
|---|---|
| **Example** | `var theForm = evt.srcElement.form;` |
| **Value** | form element object reference. |
| **Default** | None. |

## indeterminate

Indicates whether a checkbox is visually represented as being neither checked nor unchecked, yet still active. This middle ground is rendered differently for different operating systems. In Windows, the checkbox is grayed out (with the checkmark still visible if it was there originally) but still active. On the Macintosh, the checkbox displays a hyphen inside the box. The indeterminate state usually means some change elsewhere on the page has likely affected the setting of the checkbox, requiring the user to verify the checkbox's setting for accuracy. An "indeterminate" checkbox is submitted with the form.

| | |
|---|---|
| **Example** | `document.orderForm.2DayAir.indeterminate = true;` |
| **Value** | Boolean value: `true` \| `false`. |
| **Default** | `false` |

## name

This is the identifier associated with the form control. The value of this property is submitted as one-half of the name/value pair when the form is submitted to the server. Names are hidden from user view, since control labels are assigned via other means, depending on the control type. Form control names may also be used by script references to the objects. Despite the modern standards' preference for the id attribute, many browsers still require that a form control be assigned a name attribute to allow the control's value to be submitted.

| | |
|---|---|
| **Example** | `document.orderForm.myCheckbox.name = "Win32";` |
| **Value** | Case-sensitive string identifier that follows the rules of identifier naming: it may contain no whitespace, cannot begin with a numeral, and should avoid punctuation except for the underscore character. |
| **Default** | None. |

## status

Specifies whether the element is highlighted/checked. This property is identical to the checked property.

**Example**

```
if (document.forms[0].56KbpsBox.status) {
    ...
}
```

**Value**  Boolean value: true | false.

**Default**  None.

## type

Returns the type of form control element. The value is returned in all lowercase letters. It may be necessary to cycle through all form elements in search of specific types to do some processing on (e.g., emptying all form controls of type "text" while leaving other controls untouched).

**Example**

```
if (document.forms[0].elements[3].type == "checkbox") {
    // process checkbox input type here
}
```

**Value**  Any of the following constants (as a string): button | checkbox | file | hidden | image | password | radio | reset | select-multiple | select-one | submit | text | textarea.

**Default**  checkbox

## value

Provides the current value associated with the form control that is submitted with the name/value pair for the element (if the checkbox is checked). All values are strings, but they may represent other kinds of data, including Boolean and numeric values.

**Example**  document.forms[0].extraPhone.value = "cellPhone";

**Value**  String.

**Default**  None.

Alphabetical DOM Reference

## handleEvent( ) NN |4|   IE *n/a*   DOM *n/a*

handleEvent(*event*)

Instructs the object to accept and process the event whose specifications are passed as the parameter to the method. The object must have an event handler for the event type to process the event. Navigator 4 only.

**Returned Value**   None.

**Parameters**

*event*
> A Navigator 4 event object.

# input (type="file") NN *3*   IE *4*   DOM *1*

The fileUpload object is a form control generated with an input element whose type attribute is set to "file". The "fileUpload" term does not appear in scripts, but it is the way Netscape casually referred to this object when it was first scriptable.

To submit a file, the form element should have its method attribute set to POST and its enctype attribute set to multipart/form-data. But you also need some server programming to process the incoming data correctly.

**HTML Equivalent**   <input type="file">

**Object Model Reference**

```
[window.]document.formName.elementName
[window.]document.forms[i].elements[i]
[window.]document.getElementById("elementID")
```

**Object-Specific Properties**

| accept | defaultValue | form | name | size | type | value |
|--------|--------------|------|------|------|------|-------|

**Object-Specific Methods**

handleEvent( )   select( )

**Object-Specific Event Handler Properties**

| Handler | NN | IE | DOM |
|---------|----|----|-----|
| onblur | 3 | 4 | 2 |
| onchange | 3 | 4 | 2 |
| onclick | 6 | 4 | 2 |
| onfocus | 3 | 4 | 2 |
| onkeydown | 6 | 4 | n/a |
| onkeypress | 6 | 4 | n/a |
| onkeyup | 6 | 4 | n/a |
| onmousedown | 6 | 4 | 2 |

| Handler | NN | IE | DOM |
|---|---|---|---|
| onmousemove | 6 | 4 | 2 |
| onmouseout | 6 | 4 | 2 |
| onmouseover | 6 | 4 | 2 |
| onmouseup | 6 | 4 | 2 |
| onselect | 3 | 4 | 2 |

## accept

NN *6*   IE *4*   DOM *1*

Read/Write

Provides an optional advisory property consisting of a string of one or more comma-delimited MIME types of files that are being uploaded. Values have no impact on this element in current browsers.

**Example**      document.entryForm.myFileUpload.accept = "image/gif";

**Value**        String.

**Default**      None.

## defaultValue

NN *4*   IE *4*   DOM *n/a*

Read/Write

Returns the string assigned to the value attribute of the element in the source code (except in IE for Windows, which returns an empty string). A user must manually select a file for uploading, so pre-setting or attempting to alter this value is a waste of time.

**Example**      var initVal = document.entryForm.myFileUpload.defaultValue;

**Value**        String.

**Default**      None.

## form

NN *3*   IE *4*   DOM *1*

Read-only

Returns a reference to the form element that contains the current element (if any). When processing an event from this element, the event handler function automatically has access to the input element (as the event object's target or srcElement property). By reading the form property, the script can easily access other controls within the same form.

**Example**      var theForm = evt.srcElement.form;

**Value**        form element object reference.

**Default**      None.

## name

This is the identifier associated with the form control. The value of this property is submitted as one-half of the name/value pair when the form is submitted to the server. Names are hidden from user view, since control labels are assigned via other means, depending on the control type. Form control names may also be used by script references to the objects. Despite the modern standards' preference for the id attribute, many browsers still require that a form control be assigned a name attribute to allow the control's value to be submitted.

**Example**    `document.orderForm.myFileChoice.name = "Win32File";`

**Value**    Case-sensitive string identifier that follows the rules of identifier naming: it may contain no whitespace, cannot begin with a numeral, and should avoid punctuation except for the underscore character.

**Default**    None.

## size

Roughly speaking, indicates the width in characters that the input text box portion of the file input element should be sized to accommodate. In practice, the browser does not always accurately predict the proper width when the font used is a proportional one. See details in the size attribute discussion for the input element in Chapter 8. This property is not available for IE 4 on the Macintosh.

**Example**    `document.forms[0].myFileUpload.size = 60;`

**Value**    Integer.

**Default**    20

## type

Returns the type of form control element. The value is returned in all lowercase letters. It may be necessary to cycle through all form elements in search of specific types to do some processing on (e.g., emptying all form controls of type "text" while leaving other controls untouched).

**Example**
```
if (document.forms[0].elements[3].type == "file") {
    // process file input type here
}
```

| Value | Any of the following constants (as a string): button \| checkbox \| file \| hidden \| image \| password \| radio \| reset \| select-multiple \| select-one \| submit \| text \| textarea. |
|---|---|
| **Default** | file |

## value

Read-only

Indicates the current value associated with the form control that is submitted with the name/value pair for the element. For a fileUpload object, this value is the URL-encoded full pathname to the local file. This is true even for the Macintosh browser versions, which tend to display only the file's name in the form element display. While the property accepts new value assignments in some browsers, only values assigned as a result of a user's explicit file menu choice get submitted.

| **Value** | String. |
|---|---|
| **Default** | None. |

## handleEvent( )

NN |*4*|   IE *n/a*   DOM *n/a*

handleEvent(*event*)

Instructs the object to accept and process the event whose specifications are passed as the parameter to the method. The object must have an event handler for the event type to process the event. Navigator 4 only.

**Returned Value**   None.

**Parameters**

*event*
> A Navigator 4 event object.

## select( )

NN *3*   IE *4*   DOM *n/a*

Selects all the text displayed in the form element.

**Returned Value**   None.

**Parameters**   None.

# input (type="hidden")

NN *3*   IE *4*   DOM *1*

The hidden object is a form control generated with an input element that has its type attribute is set to "hidden". This element has no event handlers, because users do not interact directly with the element. Be aware that any values assigned to a hidden object are removed if the user reloads the page. In other words, it does not function as a persistent store. Internet Explorer for Windows and Netscape 6 expose many more properties than are listed below. Most of these are included in the internal object definition for consistency across other text-oriented form controls, but have no practical significance for a hidden object.

**HTML Equivalent**    `<input type="hidden">`

**Object Model Reference**

```
[window.]document.formName.elementName
[window.]document.forms[i].elements[i]
[window.]document.getElementById("elementID")
```

**Object-Specific Properties**

| dataFld | dataSrc | defaultValue | form | name | type | value |
|---------|---------|--------------|------|------|------|-------|

**Object-Specific Methods**
createTextRange( )

**Object-Specific Event Handler Properties**
None.

## dataFld

NN *n/a*    IE 4    DOM *n/a*

Read/Write

Used with IE data binding to associate a remote data source column name with the element's value. A datasrc attribute must also be set for the element. Setting both the dataFld and dataSrc properties to empty strings breaks the binding between element and data source. Works only with text file data sources in IE 5/Mac.

**Example**        `document.myForm.price.dataFld = "price";`

**Value**          Case-sensitive identifier of the data source column.

**Default**        None.

## dataSrc

NN *n/a*    IE 4    DOM *n/a*

Read/Write

Used with IE data binding to specify the ID of the page's object element that loads the data source object for remote data access. Setting both the dataFld and dataSrc properties to empty strings breaks the binding between element and data source. Works only with text file data sources in IE 5/Mac.

**Example**        `document.myForm.price.dataSrc = "DBSRC3";`

**Value**          Case-sensitive identifier of the data source.

**Default**        None.

## defaultValue

Returns the string assigned to the value attribute of the element in the source code. You can use this value to reassign the original value to the element if scripts have altered the value property during other processing.

**Example**
```
document.entryForm.sessionID.value = document.entryForm.sessionID.defaultValue;
```

**Value**         String.

**Default**       None.

## form

Returns a reference to the form element that contains the current element (if any). When processing an event from this element, the event handler function automatically has access to the input element (as the event object's target or srcElement property). By reading the form property, the script can easily access other controls within the same form.

**Example**       `var theForm = evt.srcElement.form;`

**Value**         form element object reference.

**Default**       None.

## name

This is the identifier associated with the form control. The value of this property is submitted as one-half of the name/value pair when the form is submitted to the server. Names are hidden from user view, since control labels are assigned via other means, depending on the control type. Form control names may also be used by script references to the objects. Despite the modern standards' preference for the id attribute, many browsers still require that a form control be assigned a name attribute to allow the control's value to be submitted.

**Example**       `document.orderForm.compName.name = "company";`

**Value**         Case-sensitive string identifier that follows the rules of identifier naming: it may contain no whitespace, cannot begin with a numeral, and should avoid punctuation except for the underscore character.

**Default**       None.

Alphabetical DOM
Reference

## type

NN 3    IE 4    DOM 1

Read-only

Returns the type of form control element. The value is returned in all lowercase letters. It may be necessary to cycle through all form elements in search of specific types to do some processing on (e.g., emptying all form controls of type "text" while leaving other controls untouched).

**Example**
```
if (document.forms[0].elements[3].type == "hidden") {
    // process hidden input type here
}
```

**Value**          Any of the following constants (as a string): button | checkbox | file | hidden | image | password | radio | reset | select-multiple | select-one | submit | text | textarea.

**Default**        hidden

## value

NN 2    IE 3    DOM 1

Read/Write

Indicates the current value associated with the form control that is submitted with the name/value pair for the element. All values are strings, but they may represent other kinds of data, including Boolean and numeric values.

**Example**        document.forms[0].price.value = "33.95";

**Value**          String.

**Default**        None.

## createTextRange( )

NN n/a    IE 4(Win)    DOM n/a

Creates a TextRange object containing the hidden field's string value. See the TextRange object for details.

**Returned Value**    TextRange object.

**Parameters**        None.

# input (type="image")

NN 6    IE 4    DOM 1

The image-type input object is first and foremost a button-like form control element, but with several characteristics of an img element, as well. Its default behavior is that of a submit-type button. The coordinates of the mouse click within the image's rectangle are passed as form data (in the format *elemName*.x=65&*elemName*.y=44) when the form is submitted. Note that unlike most other input element types, this input type was not scriptable in early browsers. IE for Windows may not recognize a reference to this element via the enclosing form. Accessing the form via its ID is completely reliable, however.

**HTML Equivalent**   `<input type="image">`

**Object Model Reference**
`[window.]document.`*`formName`*`.`*`elementName`*
`[window.]document.forms[`*`i`*`].elements[`*`i`*`]`
`[window.]document.getElementById("`*`elementID`*`")`

**Object-Specific Properties**

| | | | | |
|---|---|---|---|---|
| alt | complete | dynsrc | form | height |
| hspace | loop | lowsrc | name | src |
| start | type | useMap | vspace | width |

**Object-Specific Methods**
`handleEvent()`

**Object-Specific Event Handler Properties**

| Handler | NN | IE | DOM |
|---|---|---|---|
| onblur | n/a | 4 | n/a |
| onclick | 2 | 3 | 2 |
| onfocus | n/a | 4 | n/a |
| onmousedown | 4 | 4 | 2 |
| onmousemove | 6 | 4 | 2 |
| onmouseout | 6 | 4 | 2 |
| onmouseover | 6 | 4 | 2 |
| onmouseup | 4 | 4 | 2 |

## alt
NN 6   IE 4   DOM 1
Read/Write

Provides text to be displayed (or spoken) where the image-type input element appears on the page when a browser does not download graphics (or is waiting for the image to download). See the alt property of the img object for more details.

## complete
NN n/a   IE 4   DOM n/a
Read-only

Reveals whether the image-type input element's src or lowsrc image file has fully loaded. See the complete property of the img object for more details.

## dynsrc
NN n/a   IE 4   DOM n/a
Read/Write

Provides the URL of a video clip to be displayed through the image-type input element's image. See the dynsrc property of the img object for more details.

## form

NN 6    IE 4    DOM 1

Read-only

Returns a reference to the form element that contains the current element. When processing an event from this element, the event handler function automatically has access to the input element (as the event object's target or srcElement property). By reading the form property, the script can easily access other controls within the same form.

**Example**        var theForm = evt.srcElement.form;

**Value**          form element object reference.

**Default**        None.

## height, width

NN n/a    IE 4    DOM n/a

Read/Write

Indicate the height and width in pixels of the image rendered in the input element. See the height and width properties of the img object for more details.

## hspace, vspace

NN n/a    IE 4    DOM n/a

Read/Write

Indicate the pixel measure of horizontal and vertical margins surrounding an image-type input object. See the hspace and vspace properties of the img object for more details.

## loop

NN n/a    IE 4    DOM n/a

Read/Write

If you specify a video clip with the dynsrc attribute, the loop property controls how many times the clip should play (loop). See the loop property of the img object for more details.

## lowsrc

NN n/a    IE 4    DOM n/a

Read/Write

Provides the URL of a lower-resolution (or alternate) image to download into the document space if the image of the src attribute will take a long time to download. See the lowsrc property of the img object for more details.

## name

NN 2    IE 3    DOM 1

Read/Write

This is the identifier associated with the form control. The value of this property is submitted associated with click coordinate values (within the image's rectangle) when the form is submitted in the format *elemName*.x=65&*elemName*.y=44. These coordinates take the place of the value attribute and property of other types of input elements. Despite the modern standards' preference for the id attribute, many browsers still require that a form control be assigned a name attribute to allow the control's value to be submitted.

**Example**       document.orderForm.myButton.name = "Win32";

**Value**         Case-sensitive string identifier that follows the rules of identifier naming: it may contain no whitespace, cannot begin with a numeral, and should avoid punctuation except for the underscore character.

**Default**       None.

## src                                                        NN 6    IE 4    DOM 1
Read/Write

Provides the relative or complete URL of the image file currently loaded or to be loaded into the image-type input element. See the src property of the img object for more details.

## start                                                      NN n/a    IE 4    DOM n/a
Read/Write

If you specify a video clip with the dynsrc attribute, the start property controls the action that causes the clip to start running. See the start property of the img object for more details.

## type                                                       NN 6    IE 4    DOM 1
Read-only

Returns the type of form control element. The value is returned in lowercase letters. It may be necessary to cycle through all form elements in search of specific types to do some processing on (e.g., emptying all form controls of type "text" while leaving other controls untouched).

**Example**
```
if (document.forms[0].elements[3].type == "image") {
    // process image input type here
}
```

**Value**         Any of the following constants (as a string): button | checkbox | file | hidden | image | password | radio | reset | select-multiple | select-one | submit | text | textarea.

**Default**       image

## useMap                                                     NN 6    IE 4    DOM 1
Read/Write

Provides the URL of the map element in the same document that contains client-side image map hot areas and links to be applied to the image. See the useMap property of the img object for more details.

## vspace

See hspace.

## width

See height.

## handleEvent( )    NN |4|    IE *n/a*    DOM *n/a*

handleEvent(*event*)

Instructs the object to accept and process the event whose specifications are passed as the parameter to the method. The object must have an event handler for the event type to process the event. Navigator 4 only.

**Returned Value**    None.

**Parameters**

*event*

A Navigator 4 event object.

# input (type="password")    NN 2    IE 3    DOM 1

The password object is a form control generated with an input element that has a type attribute set to "password". This object is similar to the text input object, except that the characters typed into the text box by the user are converted to asterisk or bullet symbols for privacy.

**HTML Equivalent**    <input type="password">

**Object Model Reference**

```
[window.]document.formName.elementName
[window.]document.forms[i].elements[i]
[window.]document.getElementById("elementID")
```

**Object-Specific Properties**

| | | | | |
|---|---|---|---|---|
| dataFld | dataSrc | defaultValue | form | maxLength |
| name | readOnly | selectionEnd | selectionStart | size |
| textLength | type | value | | |

**Object-Specific Methods**

| | | |
|---|---|---|
| createTextRange( ) | handleEvent( ) | select( ) |

**Object-Specific Event Handler Properties**

| Handler | NN | IE | DOM |
|---|---|---|---|
| onblur | 2 | 3 | 2 |
| onchange | 2 | 3 | 2 |
| onfocus | 2 | 3 | 2 |

| Handler | NN | IE | DOM |
|---|---|---|---|
| onkeydown | 4 | 4 | n/a |
| onkeypress | 4 | 4 | n/a |
| onkeyup | 4 | 4 | n/a |
| onselect | 2 | 3 | 2 |

## dataFld

NN *n/a*     IE *4*     DOM *n/a*

Read/Write

Used with IE data binding to associate a remote data source column name to a password object's value property. A datasrc attribute must also be set for the element. Setting both the dataFld and dataSrc properties to empty strings breaks the binding between element and data source. Works only with text file data sources in IE 5/Mac.

**Example**          document.myForm.myPassword.dataFld = "userWurd";

**Value**            Case-sensitive identifier of the data source column.

**Default**          None.

## dataSrc

NN *n/a*     IE *4*     DOM *n/a*

Read/Write

Used with IE data binding to specify the ID of the page's object element that loads the data source object for remote data access. Content from the data source is specified via the datafld attribute. Setting both the dataFld and dataSrc properties to empty strings breaks the binding between element and data source. Works only with text file data sources in IE 5/Mac.

**Example**          document.myForm.myPassword.dataSrc = "#DBSRC3";

**Value**            Case-sensitive identifier of the data source.

**Default**          None.

## defaultValue

NN *2*     IE *3*     DOM *1*

Read-only

Indicates the default text for the password input element, as established by the value attribute.

**Example**

```
var pwObj = document.forms[0].myPassword;
if (pwObj.value != pwObj.defaultValue ) {
    // process user-entered password
}
```

**Value**            String value.

**Default**          None.

## form

NN *2*    IE *3*    DOM *1*
Read-only

Returns a reference to the form element that contains the current element (if any). When processing an event from this element, the event handler function automatically has access to the input element (as the event object's target or srcElement property). By reading the form property, the script can easily access other controls within the same form.

| | |
|---|---|
| **Example** | var theForm = evt.srcElement.form; |
| **Value** | form element object reference. |
| **Default** | None. |

## maxLength

NN *6*    IE *4*    DOM *1*
Read/Write

Specifies the maximum number of characters that may be typed into a password field input element. In practice, browsers beep or otherwise alert users when a typed character would exceed the maxLength value. There is no innate correlation between the maxLength and size properties. If the maxLength allows for more characters than fit within the specified width of the element, the browser provides horizontal scrolling (albeit awkward for many users) to allow entry and editing of the field.

| | |
|---|---|
| **Example** | document.entryForm.myPassword.maxLength = 35; |
| **Value** | Integer value. |
| **Default** | Unlimited. |

## name

NN *2*    IE *3*    DOM *1*
Read/Write

This is the identifier associated with the form control. The value of this property is submitted as one-half of the name/value pair when the form is submitted to the server. Names are hidden from user view, since control labels are assigned via other means, depending on the control type. Form control names may also be used by script references to the objects. Despite the modern standards' preference for the id attribute, many browsers still require that a form control be assigned a name attribute to allow the control's value to be submitted.

| | |
|---|---|
| **Example** | document.orderForm.myPassword.name = "pw"; |
| **Value** | Case-sensitive string identifier that follows the rules of identifier naming: it may contain no whitespace, cannot begin with a numeral, and should avoid punctuation except for the underscore character. |
| **Default** | None. |

## readOnly

Specifies whether the form element can be edited on the page by the user. A form control whose readOnly property is true may still be modified by scripts, even though the user may not alter the content.

**Example**
```
if (document.forms[0].myPassword.readOnly ) {
    ...
};
```

**Value**          Boolean value: true | false.

**Default**        false

## selectionEnd, selectionStart

The selectionEnd and selectionStart properties are convenience properties introduced with Netscape 6. They allow scripts to get and set the end positions of a text selection within a text-oriented input element. Values are zero-based integer counters of positions between characters in the text entered into the field. When both properties have the same value, the visual result is the same as a text insertion pointer. For example, to place the cursor at the end of a text box, set the two values to the element's text length (see the textLength property). The equivalent IE functionality requires creating an IE text range in the element, adjusting the range's endpoints, and selecting the range (see the TextRange object).

**Example**
```
var elem = document.forms[0].myPassword;
elem.selectionEnd = elem.textLength;
elem.selectionStart = elem.textLength;
```

**Value**          Positive integer.

**Default**        None.

## size

Roughly speaking, the width in characters that the input box should be sized to accommodate. In practice, the browser does not always accurately predict the proper width even when all characters are the same, as they are in the password object. See details in the size attribute discussion for the input element in Chapter 8. There is no interaction between the size and maxLength properties for this object.

**Example**        document.forms[0].myPassword.size = 12;

**Value**          Integer.

**Default**        20

## textLength

NN *6*    IE *n/a*    DOM *n/a*

**Read-only**

The textLength convenience property (introduced with Netscape 6) returns the length of text entered into the text field. The value is same as the length of the value property.

**Example**
```
var elem = document.forms[0].myPassword;
elem.selectionEnd = elem.textLength;
elem.selectionStart = elem.textLength;
```

**Value**             Positive integer.

**Default**           None.

## type

NN *3*    IE *4*    DOM *1*

**Read-only**

Returns the type of form control element. The value is returned in all lowercase letters. It may be necessary to cycle through all form elements in search of specific types to do some processing on (e.g., emptying all form controls of type "text" while leaving other controls untouched).

**Example**
```
if (document.forms[0].elements[3].type == "password") {
    // process password input type here
}
```

**Value**             Any of the following constants (as a string): button | checkbox | file | hidden | image | password | radio | reset | select-multiple | select-one | submit | text | textarea.

**Default**           password

## value

NN *2*    IE *3*    DOM *1*

**Read/Write**

Indicates the current value associated with the form control that is submitted with the name/value pair for the element. All values are strings. Browsers return the actual characters typed by the user (except in Navigator 2), so you can retrieve an entered password for further processing before submission (or perhaps for storage in the cookie).

**Example**           document.forms[0].myPassword.value = "franken";

**Value**             String.

**Default**           None.

## createTextRange( )

Creates a TextRange object containing the field's value text. See the TextRange object for details.

**Returned Value**    TextRange object.

**Parameters**    None.

## handleEvent( )

handleEvent(*event*)

Instructs the object to accept and process the event whose specifications are passed as the parameter to the method. The object must have an event handler for the event type to process the event. Navigator 4 only

**Returned Value**    None.

**Parameters**

*event*
　　A Navigator 4 event object.

## select( )

Selects all the text displayed in the form element. Usually requires that the element have focus prior to invoking this method.

**Returned Value**    None.

**Parameters**    None.

# input (type="radio")

The radio object is a form control generated with an input element that has a type attribute set to "radio". radio objects related to each other are assigned the same name. This means all like-named radio objects become a collection (array) of radio objects. It may be necessary, therefore, to reference an individual radio button as an item in an array. The entire array, of course, has a length property you can use to assist in looping through all radio objects within the group, if necessary, to find which one is checked, and retrieve that object's value:

```
var radioGrp = document.forms[0].myRadio;
for (var i = 0; i < radioGrp.length; i++) {
    if (radioGrp[i].checked) {
        alert("The value of the chosen button is " + radioGrp [i].value);
    }
}
```

Properties and methods listed as follows are for individual radio buttons.

input (type="radio")

## HTML Equivalent

`<input type="radio">`

## Object Model Reference

```
[window.]document.formName.elementName
[window.]document.forms[i].elements[i]
[window.]document.getElementById("elementID")
```

## Object-Specific Properties

| | | | | |
|---|---|---|---|---|
| checked | dataFld | dataSrc | defaultChecked | form |
| name | status | type | value | |

## Object-Specific Methods

`handleEvent()`

## Object-Specific Event Handler Properties

| Handler | NN | IE | DOM |
|---|---|---|---|
| onblur | 6 | 4 | 2 |
| onclick | 3 | 4 | 2 |
| onfocus | 6 | 4 | 2 |
| onmousedown | 4 | 4 | 2 |
| onmousemove | 6 | 4 | 2 |
| onmouseout | 6 | 4 | 2 |
| onmouseover | 6 | 4 | 2 |
| onmouseup | 4 | 4 | 2 |

## checked

NN 2    IE 3    DOM 1

Read/Write

Determines whether the radio button is selected or turned on by the user or script. Only radio objects with the checked property set to true have their name/value pair submitted with the form. To find out whether the form element is set to be checked when the page loads, see the defaultChecked property. Scripts can change this property even if the element is disabled.

### Example

```
if (document.choiceForm.myRadio[0].checked) {
    //process first radio button
}
```

**Value**          Boolean: true | false.

**Default**        false

## dataFld

Used with IE data binding to associate a remote data source column name to a radio button element value attribute determined by properties set in the object. A datasrc attribute must also be set for the element. Setting both the dataFld and dataSrc properties to empty strings breaks the binding between element and data source. Works only with text file data sources in IE 5/Mac.

| | |
|---|---|
| **Example** | document.myForm.myRadio[0].dataFld = "cableModem"; |
| **Value** | Case-sensitive string identifier of the data source column. |
| **Default** | None. |

## dataSrc

Used with IE data binding to specify the ID of the page's object element that loads the data source object for remote data access. Content from the data source is specified via the datafld attribute. Setting both the dataFld and dataSrc properties to empty strings breaks the binding between element and data source. Works only with text file data sources in IE 5/Mac.

| | |
|---|---|
| **Example** | document.myForm.myRadio[0].dataSrc = "DBSRC3"; |
| **Value** | Case-sensitive string identifier of the data source. |
| **Default** | None. |

## defaultChecked

Specifies whether element has the checked attribute set in the tag. You can compare the current checked property against defaultChecked to see if the state of the control has changed since the document loaded. Changing this property doesn't affect the current checked status.

**Example**
```
var rBut = document.forms[0].myRadio[0];
if (rBut.checked != rBut.defaultChecked) {
    // process for changed state
}
```

| | |
|---|---|
| **Value** | Boolean value: true \| false. |
| **Default** | Determined by HTML tag attribute. |

## form

Returns a reference to the form element that contains the current element (if any). When processing an event from this element, the event handler function automatically has access to the input element (as the event object's target or srcElement property). By reading the form property, the script can easily access other controls within the same form.

**Example**    var theForm = evt.srcElement.form;

**Value**    form element object reference.

**Default**    None.

## name    NN 2    IE 3    DOM 1
**Read/Write**

This is the identifier associated with the form control. The value of this property is submitted as one-half of the name/value pair when the form is submitted to the server (the value property of the highlighted radio button supplies the value portion). Names are hidden from user view, since control labels are assigned via other means, depending on the control type. Form control names may also be used by script references to the objects. Assign the same name to every radio button in a group whose highlight/unhighlight characteristics are related. Despite the modern standards' preference for the id attribute, many browsers still require that a form control be assigned a name attribute to allow the control's value to be submitted, but no two elements should have the same id attribute value. Therefore, if scripts need to reference elements by id, devise two separate naming schemes for the common name attributes and unique id attributes.

**Example**    document.orderForm.myRadio[0].name = "connectivity";

**Value**    Case-sensitive string identifier that follows the rules of identifier naming: it may contain no whitespace, can't begin with a numeral, and should avoid punctuation except for the underscore character.

**Default**    None.

## status    NN n/a    IE 4    DOM n/a
**Read/Write**

Specifies whether the element is highlighted/checked. This property is identical to the checked property.

**Example**

```
if (document.forms[0].myRadio[0].status) {
    ...
}
```

**Value**    Boolean value: true | false.

**Default**    None.

## type

Read-only

Returns the type of form control element. The value is returned in all lowercase letters. It may be necessary to cycle through all form elements in search of specific types to do some processing on (e.g., emptying all form controls of type "text" while leaving other controls untouched).

**Example**

```
if (document.forms[0].elements[3].type == "radio") {
    // process radio input type here
}
```

**Value**          Any of the following constants (as a string): button | checkbox | file | hidden | image | password | radio | reset | select-multiple | select-one | submit | text | textarea.

**Default**        radio

## value

Read/Write

Indicates the current value associated with the form control that is submitted with the name/value pair for the group of like-named elements (if the particular radio button is selected). All values are strings, but they may represent other kinds of data, including Boolean and numeric values.

**Example**        `document.forms[0].myRadio[0].value = "56kbps";`

**Value**          String.

**Default**        None.

## handleEvent( )

handleEvent(*event*)

Instructs the object to accept and process the event whose specifications are passed as the parameter to the method. The object must have an event handler for the event type to process the event. Navigator 4 only

**Returned Value**        None.

**Parameters**

*event*
    A Navigator 4 event object.

Alphabetical DOM
Reference

# input (type="reset")
NN *2*   IE *3*   DOM *1*

The reset object is a form control generated with an input element whose type attribute is set to reset. This element is similar to the button object. No script action is necessary for the reset object to do its job of restoring form controls to their default settings.

**HTML Equivalent**   `<input type="reset">`

### Object Model Reference
[window.]document.*formName*.*elementName*
[window.]document.forms[*i*].elements[*i*]
[window.]document.getElementById("*elementID*")

### Object-Specific Properties
form                name                type                value

### Object-Specific Methods
createTextRange( )    handleEvent( )

### Object-Specific Event Handler Properties

| Handler | NN | IE | DOM |
|---|---|---|---|
| onblur | 6 | 4 | 2 |
| onclick | 3 | 4 | 2 |
| onfocus | 6 | 4 | 2 |
| onmousedown | 4 | 4 | 2 |
| onmousemove | 6 | 4 | 2 |
| onmouseout | 6 | 4 | 2 |
| onmouseover | 6 | 4 | 2 |
| onmouseup | 4 | 4 | 2 |

## form
NN *2*   IE *3*   DOM *1*

Read-only

Returns a reference to the form element that contains the current element (if any). When processing an event from this element, the event handler function automatically has access to the input element (as the event object's target or srcElement property). By reading the form property, the script can easily access other controls within the same form.

**Example**         `var theForm = evt.srcElement.form;`

**Value**           form element object reference.

**Default**         None.

## name

**Read/Write**

This is the identifier associated with the form control. Names are hidden from user view, since control labels are assigned via other means, depending on the control type. Form control names may also be used by script references to the objects.

**Example**    `document.orderForm.myReset.name = "resetter";`

**Value**      Case-sensitive string identifier that follows the rules of identifier naming: it may contain no whitespace, cannot begin with a numeral, and should avoid punctuation except for the underscore character.

**Default**    None.

## type

**Read-only**

Returns the type of form control element. The value is returned in all lowercase letters. It may be necessary to cycle through all form elements in search of specific types to do some processing on (e.g., emptying all form controls of type "text" while leaving other controls untouched).

**Example**
```
if (document.forms[0].elements[3].type == "reset") {
    // process reset input type here
}
```

**Value**      Any of the following constants (as a string): button | checkbox | file | hidden | image | password | radio | reset | select-multiple | select-one | submit | text | textarea.

**Default**    reset

## value

**Read/Write**

This is one of the rare times that the value property controls the label of a form control: the text that appears on the reset button.

**Example**    `document.forms[0].myReset.value = "Undo";`

**Value**      String.

**Default**    Reset

## createTextRange( )    NN *n/a*    IE *4(Win)*    DOM *n/a*

Creates a TextRange object containing the button's label text. See the TextRange object for details.

**Returned Value**    TextRange object.

**Parameters**    None.

## handleEvent( )    NN |4|    IE *n/a*    DOM *n/a*

handleEvent(*event*)

Instructs the object to accept and process the event whose specifications are passed as the parameter to the method. The object must have an event handler for the event type to process the event. Navigator 4 only.

**Returned Value**    None.

**Parameters**
*event*
    A Navigator 4 event object.

# input (type="submit")    NN *2*    IE *3*    DOM *1*

The submit object is a form control generated with an input element that has a type attribute set to "submit". This object is similar to the button object, but a submit object has more implied power. No script action is necessary for the submit object to do its job of submitting the containing form to the server. If you require a button to perform a script action, but not an actual form submission, use the button or button-type input object instead. Otherwise, the submit object automatically reloads the current document (i.e., obeying the form's default action, which is the page's URL), perhaps destroying important script variables. To initiate form validation, use the onsubmit event handler of the form object rather than the onclick event handler of the submit button. If the event handler evaluates to true, the form is submitted; if it evaluates to false, the submission is cancelled. The scripted equivalent of a submit-type input object is the form object's submit( ) method.

**HTML Equivalent**    <input type="submit">

**Object Model Reference**
[window.]document.*formName*.*elementName*
[window.]document.forms[*i*].elements[*i*]
[window.]document.getElementById("*elementID*")

**Object-Specific Properties**

| form | name | type | value |
|------|------|------|-------|

**Object-Specific Methods**
createTextRange( )    handleEvent( )

**Object-Specific Event Handler Properties**

| Handler | NN | IE | DOM |
|---|---|---|---|
| onblur | 6 | 4 | 2 |
| onclick | 3 | 4 | 2 |
| onfocus | 6 | 4 | 2 |
| onmousedown | 4 | 4 | 2 |
| onmousemove | 6 | 4 | 2 |
| onmouseout | 6 | 4 | 2 |
| onmouseover | 6 | 4 | 2 |
| onmouseup | 4 | 4 | 2 |

## form

NN *2*    IE *3*    DOM *1*

Read-only

Returns a reference to the form element that contains the current element. When processing an event from this element, the event handler function automatically has access to the input element (as the event object's target or srcElement property). By reading the form property, the script can easily access other controls within the same form.

| | |
|---|---|
| **Example** | var theForm = evt.srcElement.form; |
| **Value** | form element object reference. |
| **Default** | None. |

## name

NN *2*    IE *3*    DOM *1*

Read/Write

This is the identifier associated with the form control. Names are hidden from user view, since control labels are assigned via other means, depending on the control type. Form control names may also be used by script references to the objects.

| | |
|---|---|
| **Example** | document.orderForm.mySubmit.name = "sender"; |
| **Value** | Case-sensitive string identifier that follows the rules of identifier naming: it may contain no whitespace, cannot begin with a numeral, and should avoid punctuation except for the underscore character. |
| **Default** | None. |

## type

NN *3*    IE *4*    DOM *1*

Read-only

Returns the type of form control element. The value is returned in lowercase letters. You may have to cycle through all form elements in search of specific types to do some processing on (e.g., emptying all form controls of type "text", leaving other controls untouched).

**Example**
```
if (document.forms[0].elements[3].type == "submit") {
    // process submit input type here
}
```

| **Value** | Any of the following constants (as a string): button \| checkbox \| file \| hidden \| image \| password \| radio \| reset \| select-multiple \| select-one \| submit \| text \| textarea. |
| --- | --- |

**Default** submit

## value                                                    NN *2*  IE *3*  DOM *1*
Read/Write

This is one of the rare times that the value property controls the label of a form control: the text that appears on the submit button.

**Example** `document.forms[0].mySubmit.value = "Send";`

**Value** String.

**Default** Submit

## createTextRange( )                          NN *n/a*  IE *4(Win)*  DOM *n/a*

Creates a TextRange object containing the button's label text. See the TextRange object for details.

**Returned Value** TextRange object.

**Parameters** None.

## handleEvent( )                                  NN |4|  IE *n/a*  DOM *n/a*
handleEvent(*event*)

Instructs the object to accept and process the event whose specifications are passed as the parameter to the method. The object must have an event handler for the event type to process the event. Navigator 4 only.

**Returned Value** None.

**Parameters**
*event*
    A Navigator 4 event object.

# input (type="text")

NN *2*    IE *3*    DOM *1*

The text object is a form control generated with an input element that has a type attribute set to "text". This object is the primary way of getting a user to enter single lines of text for submission to the server.

**HTML Equivalent**    `<input type="text">`

## Object Model Reference
[window.]document.*formName*.*elementName*
[window.]document.forms[*i*].elements[*i*]
[window.]document.getElementById("*elementID*")

## Object-Specific Properties

| | | | | |
|---|---|---|---|---|
| dataFld | dataSrc | defaultValue | form | maxLength |
| name | readOnly | size | type | value |

## Object-Specific Methods

| | | |
|---|---|---|
| createTextRange( ) | handleEvent( ) | select( ) |

## Object-Specific Event Handler Properties

| Handler | NN | IE | DOM |
|---|---|---|---|
| onblur | 2 | 3 | 2 |
| onchange | 2 | 3 | 2 |
| onfocus | 2 | 3 | 2 |
| onkeydown | 4 | 4 | n/a |
| onkeypress | 4 | 4 | n/a |
| onkeyup | 4 | 4 | n/a |
| onselect | 2 | 4 | 2 |

## dataFld

NN *n/a*    IE *4*    DOM *n/a*

Read/Write

Used with IE 4 data binding to associate a remote data source column name to a text object's value property. A datasrc attribute must also be set for the element. Setting both the dataFld and dataSrc properties to empty strings breaks the binding between element and data source. Works only with text file data sources in IE 5/Mac.

**Example**        document.myForm.myText.dataFld = "price";

**Value**          Case-sensitive string identifier of the data source column.

**Default**        None.

## dataSrc

NN *n/a*    IE *4*    DOM *n/a*

Read/Write

Used with IE data binding to specify the ID of the page's object element that loads the data source object for remote data access. Content from the data source is specified via the dataFld attribute. Setting both the dataFld and dataSrc properties to empty strings breaks the binding between element and data source. Works only with text file data sources in IE 5/Mac.

| | |
|---|---|
| **Example** | document.myForm.myText.dataSrc = "DBSRC3"; |
| **Value** | Case-sensitive string identifier of the data source. |
| **Default** | None. |

## defaultValue

NN *2*    IE *3*    DOM *1*

Read-only

The default text for the text input element, as established by the value attribute.

**Example**
```
var txtObj = document.forms[0].myText;
if (txtObj.value != txtObj.defaultValue ) {
    ...
}
```

| | |
|---|---|
| **Value** | String value. |
| **Default** | None. |

## form

NN *2*    IE *3*    DOM *1*

Read-only

Returns a reference to the form element that contains the current element. When processing an event from this element, the event handler function automatically has access to the input element (as the event object's target or srcElement property). By reading the form property, the script can easily access other controls within the same form.

| | |
|---|---|
| **Example** | var theForm = evt.srcElement.form; |
| **Value** | form element object reference. |
| **Default** | None. |

## maxLength

NN *6*    IE *4*    DOM *1*

Read/Write

Indicates the maximum number of characters that may be typed into a text input element. In practice, browsers beep or otherwise alert users when a typed character would exceed the maxLength value. There is no innate correlation between the maxLength and size properties. If the maxLength allows for more characters than fit within the specified width of the element, the browser provides horizontal scrolling (albeit awkward for many users) to allow entry and editing of the field.

| | |
|---|---|
| **Example** | document.entryForm.myText.maxLength = 35; |
| **Value** | Integer value. |
| **Default** | Unlimited. |

## name

This is the identifier associated with the form control. The value of this property is submitted as one-half of the name/value pair when the form is submitted to the server. Names are hidden from user view, since control labels are assigned via other means, depending on the control type. Form control names may also be used by script references to the objects. Despite the modern standards' preference for the id attribute, many browsers still require that a form control be assigned a name attribute to allow the control's value to be submitted.

| | |
|---|---|
| **Example** | document.orderForm.myText.name = "lastName"; |
| **Value** | Case-sensitive string identifier that follows the rules of identifier naming: it may contain no whitespace, cannot begin with a numeral, and should avoid punctuation except for the underscore character. |
| **Default** | None. |

## readOnly

Specifies whether the form element can be edited on the page by the user. A form control that has a readOnly property set to true may still be modified by scripts, even though the user may not alter the content.

**Example**
```
if (document.forms[0].myText.readOnly) {
    ...
}
```

| | |
|---|---|
| **Value** | Boolean value: true | false. |
| **Default** | false |

## size

Roughly speaking, indicates the width in characters that the input box should be sized to accommodate. In practice, the browser does not always accurately predict the proper width. See details in the size attribute discussion for the input element in Chapter 8. There is no interaction between the size and maxLength properties for this object.

| | |
|---|---|
| **Example** | document.forms[0].myText.size = 12; |
| **Value** | Integer. |
| **Default** | 20 |

## type NN 3   IE 4   DOM 1

Read-only

Returns the type of form control element. The value is returned in all lowercase letters. It may be necessary to cycle through all form elements in search of specific types to do some processing on (e.g., emptying all form controls of type "text" while leaving other controls untouched).

**Example**
```
if (document.forms[0].elements[3].type == "text") {
    // process text input type here
}
```

| | |
|---|---|
| **Value** | Any of the following constants (as a string): button \| checkbox \| file \| hidden \| image \| password \| radio \| reset \| select-multiple \| select-one \| submit \| text \| textarea. |
| **Default** | text |

## value NN 2   IE 3   DOM 1

Read/Write

Indicates the current value associated with the form control that is submitted with the name/value pair for the element. All values are strings, which means that scripts using text field values for some math operations (especially addition) have to convert the strings to numbers via the parseInt( ) or parseFloat( ) functions before performing the math. If you assign a number to a text field's value property, the browser automatically converts its data type to a string.

| | |
|---|---|
| **Example** | document.forms[0].myText.value = "franken"; |
| **Value** | String. |
| **Default** | None. |

## createTextRange( ) NN n/a   IE 4(Win)   DOM n/a

Creates a TextRange object from the content of the text object. See the TextRange object for details.

| | |
|---|---|
| **Returned Value** | TextRange object. |
| **Parameters** | None. |

## handleEvent( )

handleEvent(*event*)

Instructs the object to accept and process the event whose specifications are passed as the parameter to the method. The object must have an event handler for the event type to process the event. Navigator 4 only.

**Returned Value**    None.

**Parameters**

*event*

A Navigator 4 event object.

## select( )

Selects all the text displayed in the form element. You should invoke the focus( ) method on the element prior to the select( ) method. Moreover, to ease potential timing problems in IE for Windows, place the focus( ) and select( ) method statements in a separate function, and invoke that function through setTimeout( ), usually with a delay of 0 to 50 milliseconds. This lets the browser catch up with window refreshing tasks before selecting the contents.

**Returned Value**    None.

**Parameters**    None.

# ins

The ins object reflects the ins element.

**HTML Equivalent**    <ins>

**Object Model Reference**

[window.]document.getElementById("*elementID*")

**Object-Specific Properties**

cite            dateTime

**Object-Specific Methods**
None.

**Object-Specific Event Handler Properties**
None.

## cite, dateTime

**Read/Write**

These two properties are listed among the shared properties earlier in this chapter due to an IE 6 implementation oddity. IE 5/Macintosh and Netscape 6 correctly implement these properties only for the del and ins objects, as specified in the W3C DOM, but in no mainstream browser do they convey any special powers. See the shared cite and dateTime properties.

# isindex                                        NN 6    IE 5    DOM 1

The isindex object reflects the ancient HTML isindex element. IE arbitrarily converts this element into a text-type input object in its DOM, and even creates a form element around it. Avoid using this element.

**HTML Equivalent**    <isindex>

**Object-Specific Properties**
prompt

## prompt                                        NN 6    IE 5(Mac)    DOM 1
                                                                  Read/Write

Provides the prompt message for the text entry field.

**Value**          String.

**Default**        None.

# kbd

See acronym.

# label                                          NN 6    IE 4    DOM 1

The label object reflects the label element.

**HTML Equivalent**
<label>

**Object Model Reference**
[window.]document.getElementById("elementID")

**Object-Specific Properties**

| dataFld | dataFormatAs | dataSrc | form | htmlFor |

**Object-Specific Methods**
None.

**Object-Specific Event Handler Properties**
None.

## dataFld

Used with IE data binding to associate a remote data source column name with the displayed text of the input element label. A `datasrc` attribute must also be set for the element. Setting both the `dataFld` and `dataSrc` properties to empty strings breaks the binding between element and data source. Works only for text data sources in IE 5 for the Macintosh.

| | |
|---|---|
| **Example** | `document.getElementById("myLabel").dataFld = "labelText";` |
| **Value** | Case-sensitive string identifier of the data source column. |
| **Default** | None. |

## dataFormatAs

Used with IE data binding, this property advises the browser whether the source material arriving from the data source is to be treated as plain text or as tagged HTML. Works only for text data sources in IE 5 for the Macintosh.

| | |
|---|---|
| **Example** | `document.forms[0].myLabel.dataFormatAs = "html";` |
| **Value** | IE 4 recognizes two possible settings: `text` \| `html`. |
| **Default** | `text` |

## dataSrc

Used with IE data binding to specify the ID of the page's object element that loads the data source object for remote data access. Setting both the `dataFld` and `dataSrc` properties to empty strings breaks the binding between element and data source. Works only for text data sources in IE 5 for the Macintosh.

| | |
|---|---|
| **Example** | `document.getElementById("myLabel").dataSrc = "DBSRC3";` |
| **Value** | Case-sensitive identifier of the data source. |
| **Default** | None. |

## form

Returns a reference to the next outermost form element object in the document tree. Multiple label element objects within the same form element reference the same form element object.

| | |
|---|---|
| **Example** | `var theForm = document.getElementById("myLabel").form;` |
| **Value** | Reference to a form element object. |

**Default**      None.

## htmlFor                                                    NN 6    IE 4    DOM 1
Read/Write

Provides the element id of the input element to which the label is associated (the value of
the for attribute). Binds the label element to a particular input element.

**Example**      document.getElementById("label3").htmlFor = "chkbox3";

**Value**        String.

**Default**      None.


# layer                                                       NN |4|    IE n/a    DOM n/a

The layer object reflects the layer and ilayer elements. Found in Navigator 4 only. Other
elements (such as div and span) that have style sheet position attributes set to absolute or
relative are arbitrarily converted to layer objects in Navigator 4.

**HTML Equivalent**

&lt;ilayer&gt;
&lt;layer&gt;

**Object Model Reference**

[window.]document.*layerName*

**Object-Specific Properties**

| | | | | |
|---|---|---|---|---|
| above | background | below | bgColor | clip |
| hidden | left | name | pageX | pageY |
| parentLayer | siblingAbove | siblingBelow | src | top |
| visibility | zIndex | | | |

**Object-Specific Methods**

| | | | |
|---|---|---|---|
| captureEvents() | handleEvent() | load() | moveAbove() |
| moveBelow() | moveBy() | moveTo() | moveToAbsolute() |
| releaseEvents() | resizeBy() | resizeTo() | routeEvent() |

**Object-Specific Event Handler Properties**

| Handler | NN | IE | DOM |
|---|---|---|---|
| onblur | 4 | n/a | n/a |
| onfocus | 4 | n/a | n/a |
| onload | 4 | n/a | n/a |
| onmouseout | 4 | n/a | n/a |
| onmouseover | 4 | n/a | n/a |
| onmouseup | 4 | n/a | n/a |

## above, below

Return a reference to the positionable element whose stacking z-order is above or below the current element. These properties operate in the context of all positionable elements in a document. If the current element is the highest element, the above property returns null. To restrict the examination of next higher or lower elements within a single layer context, see siblingAbove and siblingBelow. To adjust the stacking order with respect to specific objects, see the moveAbove( ) and moveBelow( ) methods.

| | |
|---|---|
| **Example** | var nextHigher = document.myILayer.above; |
| **Value** | Object reference or null. |
| **Default** | None. |

## background

This property holds an image object that has a src property that can be set to change the image used for the layer's background. In other words, you must set the src property of the layer's background object to change the image.

| | |
|---|---|
| **Example** | document.myIlayer.background.src = "images/newlogo.gif"; |
| **Value** | An image object property, such as src. |
| **Default** | None. |

## bgColor

Provides the background color of the element. While you may set the value with either a hexadecimal triplet or plain-language color value, values returned from the property are for some reason the decimal equivalent of the hexadecimal RGB version. The default behavior is a transparent background created with a bgColor property value of null.

| | |
|---|---|
| **Example** | document.myIlayer.bgColor = "yellow"; |
| **Value** | A hexadecimal triplet or plain-language color name. See Appendix A for acceptable plain-language color names. Returned values are the decimal equivalent of the hexadecimal value. A value of null sets the background to transparent. |
| **Default** | null (transparent). |

## clip

Defines a clipping region of a positionable element. This property is treated more like an object in itself, in that you adjust its values through six properties: clip.top, clip.left, clip.bottom, clip.right, clip.width, and clip.height. Adjust the side(s) or dimension(s) of your choice. All values represent pixel values.

| | |
|---|---|
| **Example** | document.myIlayer.clip.width = 150; |
| **Value** | Integer. |
| **Default** | None. |

## hidden

NN |4|   IE *n/a*   DOM *n/a*
Read/Write

Specifies whether the object is visible on the page. When the object is hidden, its surrounding content does not close the gap left by the element.

| | |
|---|---|
| **Example** | document.myIlayer.hidden = false; |
| **Value** | Boolean value: true \| false. |
| **Default** | false |

## left

NN |4|   IE *n/a*   DOM *n/a*
Read/Write

For positionable elements, defines the position (in pixels) of the left edge of an element's box (content plus left padding, border, and/or margin) relative to the left edge of the next outer-most block content container. For the relative-positioned layer, the offset is based on the left edge of the inline location of where the element would normally appear in the content.

| | |
|---|---|
| **Example** | document.myIlayer.left = 45; |
| **Value** | Integer. |
| **Default** | 0 |

## name

NN |4|   IE *n/a*   DOM *n/a*
Read-only

This is the identifier associated with a layer for use as the value assigned to target attributes or as script references to the frame. If no value is explicitly assigned to the id attribute, Navigator automatically assigns the name attribute value to the id attribute.

**Example**
```
if (document.layers[2].name == "main") {
    ...
}
```

| | |
|---|---|
| **Value** | Case-sensitive identifier that follows the rules of identifier naming: it may contain no whitespace, cannot begin with a numeral, and should avoid punctuation except for the underscore character. |
| **Default** | None. |

## pageX, pageY

NN |4|   IE *n/a*   DOM *n/a*
Read/Write

Provide the horizontal (x) and vertical (y) position of the object relative to the top and left edges of the entire document.

**Example**        `document.myIlayer.pageX = 400;`

**Value**          Integer.

**Default**        None.

## parentLayer

NN |4|   IE *n/a*   DOM *n/a*
Read-only

Returns a reference to the next outermost layer in the containment hierarchy. For a single layer in a document, its parentLayer is the window object.

**Example**
```
if (parentLayer != window) {
    ...
}
```

**Value**          Object reference (a layer or window).

**Default**        window

## siblingAbove, siblingBelow

NN |4|   IE *n/a*   DOM *n/a*
Read-only

Return a reference to the positionable element whose stacking z-order is above or below the current element, but only within the context of the shared parentLayer. If the current element is the highest element, the siblingAbove property returns null. To widen the examination of next higher or lower elements to a document-wide context, see above and below. To adjust the stacking order with respect to specific objects, see the moveAbove( ) and moveBelow( ) methods.

**Example**        `var nextHigher = document.myILayer.siblingAbove;`

**Value**          Object reference or null.

**Default**        None.

## src

NN |4|   IE *n/a*   DOM *n/a*
Read/Write

Indicates the URL of the external content file loaded into the current element. To change the content, assign a new URL to the property.

Assigning a new URL to this property does not work with inline layers (ilayer elements) in Navigator 4. Instead the current source document is removed, and other page elements can be obscured. Avoid setting this property for inline layers. The same goes for the load( ) method.

| | |
|---|---|
| **Example** | document.myIlayer.src = "swap2.html"; |
| **Value** | Complete or relative URL as a string. |
| **Default** | None. |

## top
NN |4|   IE *n/a*   DOM *n/a*
Read/Write

For positionable elements, defines the position of the top edge of an element's box (content plus top padding, border, and/or margin) relative to the top edge of the next outermost block content container. All measures are in pixels. When the element is a relative-positioned inline layer, the offset is based on the top edge of the inline location of where the element would normally appear in the content.

| | |
|---|---|
| **Example** | document.myIlayer.top = 50; |
| **Value** | Integer. |
| **Default** | 0 |

## visibility
NN |4|   IE *n/a*   DOM *n/a*
Read/Write

Indicates the state of the positioned element's visibility. Surrounding content does not close the space left by an element whose visibility property is set to hide (or the CSS version, hidden). If you set the property to the CSS syntax values (hidden | visible), they are converted internally to the JavaScript versions and returned from the property in that format.

| | |
|---|---|
| **Example** | document.myIlayer.visibility = "hide"; |
| **Value** | One of the constant values (as a string): hide | inherit | show. |
| **Default** | inherit |

## zIndex
NN |4|   IE *n/a*   DOM *n/a*
Read/Write

For a positioned element, determines the stacking order relative to other elements within the same parent container. See Chapter 4 for details on relationships of element layering amid multiple containers.

| | |
|---|---|
| **Example** | document.myIlayer.zIndex = 3; |
| **Value** | Integer. |
| **Default** | 0 |

## captureEvents( )

captureEvents(*eventTypeList*)

Instructs the browser to grab events of a specific type before they reach their intended target objects. The object invoking this method must then have event handlers defined for the given event types to process the event.

**Returned Value**    None.

**Parameters**

*eventTypeList*
> A comma-separated list of case-sensitive event types as derived from the available Event object constants, such as Event.CLICK or Event.MOUSEMOVE.

## handleEvent( )

handleEvent(*event*)

Instructs the object to accept and process the event whose specifications are passed as the parameter to the method. The object must have an event handler for the event type to process the event.

**Returned Value**    None.

**Parameters**

*event*
> A Navigator 4 event object.

## load( )

load("*URL*", *newLayerWidth*)

This method lets you load a new document into a layer object. It does not work properly in Navigator 4 for ilayer elements. The existing document is unloaded from the layer, but the new one does not load as you'd expect. There is no satisfactory workaround except to transform the element into a layer.

**Returned Value**    Boolean value: true if the document loading was successful.

**Parameters**

*URL*
> String value of the complete or relative URL of the document to be loaded into the layer.

*newLayerWidth*
> Integer value in pixels of a resized width of the element to accommodate the new content.

## moveAbove( ), moveBelow( )                    NN |4|   IE *n/a*   DOM *n/a*

moveAbove(*layerObject*)
moveBelow(*layerObject*)

These methods shift the z-order of the current layer to a specific location relative to another, sibling layer. This is helpful if your script is not sure of the precise zIndex value of a layer you want to use as a reference point for the current layer's stacking order. Use moveAbove( ) to position the current layer immediately above the layer object referenced as a parameter.

**Returned Value**    None.

**Parameters**

*layerObject*
    Reference to another layer object that shares the same parent as the current layer.

## moveBy( )                                      NN |4|   IE *n/a*   DOM *n/a*

moveBy(*deltaX, deltaY*)

A convenience method that shifts the location of the current element by specified pixel amounts along both axes. To shift along only one axis, set the other value to zero. Positive values for *deltaX* shift the element to the right; negative values to the left. Positive values for *deltaY* shift the element downward; negative values upward. This method comes in handy for path animation under the control of a setInterval( ) or setTimeout( ) method that moves the element in a linear path over time.

**Returned Value**    None.

**Parameters**

*deltaX*
    Positive or negative pixel count of the change in horizontal direction of the element.
*deltaY*
    Positive or negative pixel count of the change in vertical direction of the element.

## moveTo( ), moveToAbsolute( )                   NN |4|   IE *n/a*   DOM *n/a*

moveTo(*x, y*)
moveToAbsolute(*x, y*)

Convenience methods that shift the location of the current element to a specific coordinate point. The differences between the two methods show when the element to be moved is nested inside another positioned container (e.g., a layer inside a layer). The moveTo( ) method uses the coordinate system of the parent container; the moveToAbsolute( ) method uses the coordinate system of the page. For a single layer on a page, the two methods yield the same result.

**Returned Value**    None.

**Parameters**

*x*  Positive or negative pixel count relative to the top of the reference container, whether it is the next outermost layer (moveTo( )) or the page (moveToAbsolute( )).

*y*  Positive or negative pixel count relative to the left edge of the reference container, whether it is the next outermost layer (moveTo( )) or the page (moveToAbsolute( )).

## releaseEvents( )                    NN |4|    IE *n/a*    DOM *n/a*

releaseEvents(*eventTypeList*)

The opposite of *layerObj*.captureEvents( ), this method turns off event capture at the layer level for one or more specific events named in the parameter list. See Chapter 6.

**Returned Value**    None.

**Parameters**

*eventTypeList*

A comma-separated list of case-sensitive event types as derived from the available Event object constants, such as Event.CLICK or Event.MOUSEMOVE.

## resizeBy( )                         NN |4|    IE *n/a*    DOM *n/a*

resizeBy(*deltaX, deltaY*)

A convenience method that shifts the width and height of the current element by specified pixel amounts. To adjust along only one axis, set the other value to zero. Positive values for *deltaX* make the element wider; negative values make the element narrower. Positive values for *deltaY* make the element taller; negative values make the element shorter. The top and left edges remain fixed; only the right and bottom edges are moved.

**Returned Value**    None.

**Parameters**

*deltaX*

Positive or negative pixel count of the change in horizontal dimension of the element.

*deltaY*

Positive or negative pixel count of the change in vertical dimension of the element.

## resizeTo( )                         NN |4|    IE *n/a*    DOM *n/a*

resizeTo(*x, y*)

Convenience method that adjusts the height and width of the current element to specific pixel sizes. The top and left edges of the element remain fixed, while the bottom and right edges move in response to this method.

**Returned Value**    None.

**Parameters**

*x*  Width in pixels of the element.

*y*  Height in pixels of the element.

## routeEvent( ) NN |4| IE *n/a* DOM *n/a*

routeEvent(*event*)

Used inside an event handler function, this method directs Navigator to let the event pass to its intended target object.

**Returned Value**    None.

**Parameters**

*event*
    A Navigator 4 event object.

# legend NN *6*   IE *4*   DOM *1*

The legend object reflects the legend element. A legend element must be nested inside and immediately after the fieldset element associated with a form or group of form controls.

**HTML Equivalent**

<legend>

**Object Model Reference**

[window.]document.getElementById("*elementID*")

**Object-Specific Properties**

align            form

**Object-Specific Methods**

None.

**Object-Specific Event Handler Properties**

None.

## align NN *6*   IE *4*   DOM *1*
Read/Write

Controls the alignment of the legend element with respect to the containing fieldset element. The permissible values do not always work as planned in Internet Explorer 4. Be sure to check your desired setting on all operating system platforms of your intended audience.

**Example**        document.getElementById("myLegend").align = "center";

**Value**          Any one of the following constant values (as a string): bottom | center | left | right | top.

**Default**        left

# form

Returns a reference to the next outermost form element object in the document tree. Multiple legend element objects within the same form element reference the same form element object.

**Example**    var theForm = document.getElementById("myLegend").form;

**Value**    Reference to a form element object.

**Default**    None.

# li

The li object reflects the li element nested inside an ol or ul element.

**HTML Equivalent**
<li>

**Object Model Reference**
[window.]document.getElementById("*elementID*")

**Object-Specific Properties**
type        value

**Object-Specific Methods**
None.

**Object-Specific Event Handler Properties**
None.

# type

Indicates the manner in which the leading bullets, numbers, or letters of items in the list are displayed. Bullet styles are displayed when the li element is nested inside a ul element; numbers and letters are displayed for an ol element. If your script changes the type for a single li object, be aware that the change affects all subsequent li elements in the same list.

**Example**
document.getElementById("instruxListItem3").type = "a";
document.getElementById("point4").type = "square";

**Value**
For an ol style list, possible values are: A | a | I | i | 1. Sequencing is performed automatically as shown in the following table.

| Type | Example |
|------|---------|
| A | A, B, C, ... |
| a | a, b, c, ... |
| I | I, II, III, ... |
| i | i, ii, iii, ... |
| 1 | 1, 2, 3, ... |

For a ul-style list, possible values are: circle | disc | square.

**Default**

1 and disc (although values are empty unless the corresponding attribute is explicitly assigned).

## value

NN 6    IE 4    DOM 1

**Read/Write**

Indicates the number of the item within an ordered list. This property applies to an li element only when it is nested inside an ol element, and only when the corresponding attribute is explicitly assigned in the HTML code. The default value for unadjusted numbering is always 0 in IE and -1 in Netscape 6. If you set the value property of one item in the list, the following items continue the sequence from the new value. Modifying the property value does not adjust the rendered numbering.

**Example**

```
if (document.getElementById("step5").value > 0) {
    ...
}
```

**Value**       Integer.

**Default**     0 or -1.

# link

NN 6    IE 4    DOM 1

The link object reflects the link element. Note that many of the properties listed here are not available for scripting in the object unless their corresponding attributes are set initially in the HTML tag. Moreover, because the element's attributes act as directives while the document loads, assigning new values to the corresponding properties generally has no effect (even though the properties are read/write). This includes: href, rel, rev, and type. The media property is not available in the Macintosh version of IE 4. As a reminder, the disabled property (described among the shared properties earlier in this chapter) lets all supporting browsers turn on and off a linked style sheet.

**HTML Equivalent**    <link>

**Object Model Reference**

[window.]document.getElementById("elementID")

**Object-Specific Properties**

| | | | | |
|---|---|---|---|---|
| charset | href | hreflang | media | rel |
| rev | sheet | styleSheet | target | type |

**Object-Specific Methods**

None.

**Object-Specific Event Handler Properties**

| Handler | NN | IE/Windows | IE/Mac | DOM |
|---|---|---|---|---|
| onerror | n/a | 4 | n/a | n/a |
| onload | n/a | 4 | n/a | n/a |

## charset

NN 6    IE 4    DOM 1

Read/Write

Indicates the character encoding of the content at the other end of the link.

| | |
|---|---|
| **Example** | var charCoding = document.getElementById("myLink").charset; |
| **Value** | Case-insensitive alias from the character set registry (*ftp://ftp.isi.edu/in-notes/iana/assignments/character-sets*). |
| **Default** | None. |

## href

NN 6    IE 4    DOM 1

Read/Write

Provides the URL specified by the element's href attribute. In IE/Windows, you can assign a new URL to this property to load in an alternate style sheet after the fact.

| | |
|---|---|
| **Example** | document.getElementById("styleLink").href = "altStyles.css"; |
| **Value** | String of complete or relative URL. |
| **Default** | None. |

## hreflang

NN 6    IE 6    DOM 1

Read/Write

Specifies the language code of the content at the destination of a link. Requires that the href attribute or property also be set.

| | |
|---|---|
| **Example** | document.getElementById("myLink").hreflang = "DE"; |
| **Value** | Case-insensitive language code. |
| **Default** | None. |

## media

Specifies the intended output device for the content of the destination document pointed to by the href attribute. The media property looks forward to the day when browsers are able to tailor content to specific kinds of devices such as pocket computers, text-to-speech digitizers, or fuzzy television sets. This property is not available in IE 4/Macintosh.

**Example**
```
if (document.getElementById("link3").media == "print") {
    // process for print output
}
```

**Value**        Any one of the following constant values as a string: all | print | screen.

**Default**      all

## rel

Defines the relationship between the current element and the external item pointed to by the link. Also known as a *forward link*, not to be confused in any way with the destination document whose address is defined by the href attribute. This property is not fully exploited in mainstream browsers, but you can treat the attribute as a kind of parameter to be checked and/or modified under script control. See the discussion of the a element's rel attribute in Chapter 8 for a glimpse of how this property may be used in the future.

**Example**
```
if (document.getElementById("link3").rel == "alternate stylesheet") {
    // process for alternate style sheet
}
```

**Value**
Case-insensitive, space-delimited list of HTML 4 standard link types (as a single string) applicable to the element. Sanctioned link types are:

| | | | |
|---|---|---|---|
| alternate | appendix | bookmark | chapter |
| contents | copyright | glossary | help |
| index | next | prev | section |
| start | stylesheet | subsection | |

**Default**      None.

## rev

Defines the relationship between the current element and the destination of the link. Also known as a *reverse link*. This property is not fully exploited in mainstream browsers, but you can treat the attribute as a kind of parameter to be checked and/or modified under script control. See the discussion of the a element's rev attribute in Chapter 8 for a glimpse of how this property may be used in the future.

| | |
|---|---|
| **Value** | Case-insensitive, space-delimited list of HTML 4 standard link types (as a single string) applicable to the element. See the rel property for sanctioned link types. |
| **Default** | None. |

## sheet
NN 6    IE *n/a*    DOM *1*
**Read-only**

Returns a reference to the styleSheet object (CSSStyleSheet object in W3C DOM terminology) linked into the current document when a style sheet is specified as the target of the link element. IE for Windows provides a similar property: styleSheet.

| | |
|---|---|
| **Example** | var extSS = document.getElementById("link3").sheet; |
| **Value** | styleSheet object reference. |
| **Default** | None. |

## styleSheet
NN *n/a*    IE *5(Win)*    DOM *n/a*
**Read-only**

This nonstandard convenience property returns a reference to the styleSheet object linked into the current document when a style sheet is specified as the target of the link element. Netscape 6 provides a similar property: sheet.

| | |
|---|---|
| **Example** | var extSS = document.getElementById("link3").styleSheet; |
| **Value** | styleSheet object reference. |
| **Default** | None. |

## target
NN 6    IE 4    DOM *1*
**Read/Write**

Indicates the window or frame name to be the recipient of linked content. Default value (equivalent of _self) is the desired setting for linked style sheets.

| | |
|---|---|
| **Example** | document.getElementById("link4").target = "frame2"; |
| **Value** | String value of the window or frame name, or any of the following constants (as a string): _parent | _self | _top | _blank. |
| **Default** | None. |

## type

**Read/Write**

Indicates an advisory MIME type declaration about the data being loaded from an external source. For example, an external style sheet would be text/css. This information is usually set in the element tag's type attribute.

**Example**

```
if (document.getElementById("myStyle").type == "text/css") {
    ...
}
```

| | |
|---|---|
| **Value** | MIME type string. |
| **Default** | None. |

# links

A collection of all a and area elements that have assigned href attributes that make them behave as links (instead of only anchors). Collection members are sorted in source code order. Navigator and Internet Explorer let you use array notation to access a single link in the collection (document.links[0] or document.links["section3"], for example). If you wish to use the link's name as an index value (always as a string identifier), be sure to use the value of the name attribute, rather than the id attribute. To use the id attribute in a reference to an anchor, access the object via a document.all.*elementID* (in IE only) or document.getElementById("*elementID*") reference.

**Object Model Reference**
document.links

**Object-Specific Properties**
length

**Object-Specific Methods**

| | | | |
|---|---|---|---|
| item( ) | namedItem( ) | tags( ) | urns( ) |

**Object-Specific Event Handler Properties**
None.

## length

**Read-only**

Returns the number of elements in the collection.

| | |
|---|---|
| **Example** | var howMany = document.links.length; |
| **Value** | Integer. |

## item( )

```
item(index)
item(index[, subindex])
```

Returns a single object or collection of objects corresponding to the element matching the index value (or, optionally in IE/Windows, the index and subindex values).

### Returned Value

One object or collection (array) of objects. If there are no matches to the parameters, the returned value is null.

### Parameters

*index*

When the parameter is a zero-based integer (as required for Netscape 6), the returned value is a single element corresponding to the said numbered item in source code order (nested within the current element). When the parameter is a string (allowed by IE/Windows), the returned value is a collection of elements with id or name properties that match that string.

*subindex*

If you specify a string value for the first parameter (in IE/Windows), you may use the second parameter to specify a zero-based integer to retrieve a specific element from the collection with id or name properties that match the first parameter's string value.

## namedItem( )

```
namedItem(IDOrName)
```

Returns a single object (in Netscape 6) or collection of objects corresponding to the element matching the parameter string value.

### Returned Value

One object (in Netscape 6) or collection (array) of objects. If there are no matches to the parameters, the returned value is null.

### Parameters

*IDOrName*

The string that contains the same value as the desired element's id or name attribute.

## tags( )

```
tags(tagName)
```

Returns a collection of objects (among all objects within the current collection) with tags that match the *tagName* parameter. Lets you distinguish among collections of a and area elements.

### Returned Value

A collection (array) of objects. If there are no matches to the parameters, the returned value is an array of zero length.

### Parameters

*tagName*

A string that contains the element tag, as in document.links.tags("a").

## urns( )      NN *n/a*    IE *5(Win)*    DOM *n/a*

urns(*URN*)

Returns a collection of nested element objects that have behaviors attached to them and URNs that match the *URN* parameter.

### Returned Value

A collection (array) of objects. If there are no matches to the parameters, the returned value is an array of zero length.

### Parameters

*URN*

A string with a local or external behavior file URN.

# LinkStyle      NN *6*    IE *n/a*    DOM *2*

The LinkStyle object is a W3C DOM abstract object that gets blended into the link element object. Through this blending, the Netscape 6 link element object gains the sheet property, which provides a reference to the styleSheet object linked into the current document through a link element.

### Object Model Reference

document.getElementById("*linkElementID*")

### Object-Specific Properties

sheet

### Object-Specific Methods

None.

### Object-Specific Event Handler Properties

None.

## sheet      NN *6*    IE *n/a*    DOM *1*

                                                           **Read-only**

Returns a reference to the styleSheet object (CSSStyleSheet object in W3C DOM terminology) linked into the current document when a style sheet is specified as the target of the link element. IE for Windows provides a similar property for a link element object: styleSheet.

**Example**          var extSS = document.getElementById("link3").sheet;

| **Value** | styleSheet object reference. |
| **Default** | None. |

# listing

The listing object reflects the listing element.

**HTML Equivalent**   <listing>

**Object Model Reference**
[window.]document.getElementById("*elementID*")

**Object-Specific Properties**
None.

**Object-Specific Methods**
None.

**Object-Specific Event Handler Properties**
None.

# location

There is one location object in each window or frame. The object stores all information about the URL of the document currently loaded into that window or frame. By assigning a new URL to the href property of the location object, you instruct the browser to load a new page into the window or frame. This is the primary way of scripting the loading of a new page:

```
location.href = "newPage.html";
```

A script in one frame can reference the location object in another frame to load a new document into that other frame:

```
parent.otherFrameName.location.href = "newPage.html";
```

Security restrictions prevent a script in one frame from accessing location object information in another frame if the document in the second frame does not come from the same domain (and the same server, unless the document.domain properties of the two documents are set to match) as the document with the nosy script. This prevents a rogue script from monitoring navigation in another frame to external web sites. In Navigator 4 and later, you can overcome the security restriction with the help of signed scripts, but the user still has to give explicit permission for a script to access location object information outside the script's domain.

As a window-related object, the location object is not part of the formal W3C DOM Level 1 or 2 specifications (which leave windows for future versions). But the location object and its properties are well-entrenched in scripting vernacular, and should continue to be supported for a long time coming.

**Object Model Reference**
[*windowRef.*]location

**Object-Specific Properties**

| | | | | | | | |
|---|---|---|---|---|---|---|---|
| hash | host | hostname | href | pathname | port | protocol | search |

**Object-Specific Methods**

| | | |
|---|---|---|
| assign( ) | reload( ) | replace( ) |

**Object-Specific Event Handler Properties**
None.

## hash

NN *2*  IE *3*  DOM *n/a*

Read/Write

Indicates that portion of a URL following the # symbol, referring to an anchor location in a document. This property contains its data only if the user has explicitly navigated to an anchor, and is not just scrolling to it. Do not include the # symbol when setting the property.

| | |
|---|---|
| **Example** | location.hash = "section3"; |
| **Value** | String. |
| **Default** | None. |

## host

NN *2*  IE *3*  DOM *n/a*

Read/Write

Provides the combination of the hostname and port (if any) of the server that serves up the current document. If the port is explicitly part of the URL, the hostname and port are separated by a colon, just as they are in the URL.

**Example**
```
if (location.host == "www.megacorp.com:80") {
    ...
}
```

| | |
|---|---|
| **Value** | String of hostname, optionally followed by a colon and port number. |
| **Default** | Depends on server. |

## hostname

NN *2*  IE *3*  DOM *n/a*

Read/Write

Provides the combination of the hostname of the server (i.e., a two-dot address consisting of server name and domain) that serves up the current document. The hostname property does not include the port number.

**Example**
```
if (location.hostname == "www.megacorp.com") {
    ...
}
```

| | |
|---|---|
| **Value** | String of hostname (server and domain). |
| **Default** | Depends on server. |

## href

Provides the complete URL of the document loaded in the window or frame. Assigning a URL to this property is how you script navigation to load a new document into the window or frame (although Internet Explorer also offers the equivalent window.navigate( ) method).

| | |
|---|---|
| **Example** | `location.href = "http://www.megacorp.com";` |
| **Value** | String of complete or relative URL. |
| **Default** | None. |

## pathname

Provides the pathname component of the URL. This consists of all URL information following the last character of the domain name, including the initial forward slash symbol.

| | |
|---|---|
| **Example** | `location.pathname = "/images/logoHiRes.gif";` |
| **Value** | String. |
| **Default** | None. |

## port

Provides the port component of the URL, if one exists. This consists of all URL information following the colon after the last character of the domain name. The colon is not part of the port property value.

| | |
|---|---|
| **Example** | `location.port = "80";` |
| **Value** | String (a numeric value as string). |
| **Default** | None. |

## protocol

NN *2*    IE *3*    DOM *n/a*
Read/Write

Provides the protocol component of the URL. This consists of all URL information up to and including the first colon of a URL. Typical values are: `"http:"`, `"file:"`, `"ftp:"`, and `"mailto:"`.

**Example**
```
if (location.protocol == "file:") {
    // statements for treating document as local file
}
```

**Value**        String.

**Default**      None.

## search

NN *2*    IE *3*    DOM *n/a*
Read/Write

Provides the URL-encoded portion of a URL that begins with the ? symbol. A document that is served up as the result of the search also may have the search portion available as part of the `window.location` property. You can modify this property by script. Doing so sends the URL and search criteria to the server. You must know the format of data (usually name/value pairs) expected by the server to perform this properly. You can also pass string data between separate pages by appending a search string to the next page's URL. While the search string appendage does not affect retrieval of the page, the string arrives with the new page in the new page's location object. A script in the new page can read and dissect the `location.search` property to place the passed values in variables that scripts in the page may use for their processing.

**Example**      `location.search="?p=Tony+Blair&d=y&g=0&s=a&w=s&m=25";`

**Value**        String starting with the ? symbol.

**Default**      None.

## assign( )

NN *2*    IE *3*    DOM *n/a*

`assign("URL")`

This method was intended to be hidden from view of scripters, but remains available for now. It performs the same action as assigning a URL to the `location.href` property. The `assign( )` method is listed here for completeness and should not be used.

**Returned Value**   None.

**Parameters**

*URL*

> A string version of a complete or relative URL of a document to be loaded into a window or frame.

## reload( )　　　　　　　　　　　　NN *3*　IE *4*　DOM *n/a*
`reload([`*`unconditional`*`])`

Performs a hard reload of the document associated with the location object. This kind of reload resets form elements to their default values (for a soft reload, use history.go(0)). By default, the reload( ) method performs a conditional-get action, which retrieves the file from the browser cache if the file is still in the cache (and the cache is turned on). To force a reload from the server, force an unconditional-get by adding the true Boolean parameter.

**Returned Value**　　None.

**Parameters**
*`unconditional`*

An optional Boolean value. If true, the browser performs an unconditional-get to force a reload of the document from the server, rather than the browser cache.

## replace( )　　　　　　　　　　　NN *3*　IE *4*　DOM *n/a*
`replace("`*`URL`*`")`

Loads a new document into the reference window and replaces the browser's history listing entry of the current document with the entry of the new document. Thus, some interim page that you don't want appearing in history (to prevent the **Back** button from ever returning to the page) can be removed from the history and replaced with the entry of the newly loaded document.

**Returned Value**　　None.

**Parameters**
*URL*

A string version of a complete or relative URL of a document to be loaded into a window or frame.

# locationbar

See directories.

# map　　　　　　　　　　　　　　　NN *6*　IE *4*　DOM *1*

The map object reflects the map element.

**HTML Equivalent**
`<map>`

**Object Model Reference**
`[window.]document.getElementById("`*`elementID`*`")`

Alphabetical DOM
Reference

## Object-Specific Properties

areas[]          name

## Object-Specific Methods
None.

## Object-Specific Event Handler Properties
None.

## areas[]                                    NN 6    IE 4    DOM 1
**Read-only**

Indicates a collection of all area element objects nested inside the map element.

### Example
```
for (var i = 0; i < document.getElementById("myMap").areas.length; i++) {
    oneMap = document.getElementById("myMap").areas[i];
    ...
}
```

**Value**          Array of area element objects.

**Default**        Array of length zero.

## name                                       NN 6    IE 4    DOM 1
**Read/Write**

This is the identifier associated with the client-side image map specification. A map element contains all the area elements that define the hotspots of an image and their link destinations. The name assigned to the map element is the one cited by the usemap attribute of the img element. This binds the map definitions to the image.

**Example**        document.getElementById("myMap").name = "altMap";

**Value**          Case-sensitive string identifier that follows the rules of identifier naming: it may contain no whitespace, cannot begin with a numeral, and should avoid punctuation except for the underscore character.

**Default**        None.

# marquee                                     NN n/a    IE 4    DOM n/a

The marquee object reflects the marquee element.

## HTML Equivalent
`<marquee>`

## Object Model Reference
```
[window.]document.getElementById("elementID")
```

## Object-Specific Properties

| | | | | |
|---|---|---|---|---|
| behavior | bgColor | dataFld | dataFormatAs | dataSrc |
| direction | height | hspace | loop | scrollAmount |
| scrollDelay | trueSpeed | vspace | width | |

## Object-Specific Methods

start( )    stop( )

## Object-Specific Event Handler Properties

| Handler | NN | IE | DOM |
|---|---|---|---|
| onbounce | n/a | 4 | n/a |
| onfinish | n/a | 4 | n/a |
| onstart | n/a | 4 | n/a |

# behavior

NN *n/a*    IE 4    DOM *n/a*

Read/Write

Specifies the motion of the content within the rectangular space set aside for the marquee element. You have a choice of three motion types.

**Example**    `document.getElementById("newsBanner").behavior = "slide";`

**Value**

Case-insensitive marquee element motion types:

alternate
> Content alternates between marching left and right.

scroll
> Content scrolls (according to the direction attribute or property) into view and out of view before starting again.

slide
> Content scrolls (according to the direction attribute or property) into view, stops at the end of its run, blanks, and then starts again.

**Default**    scroll

# bgColor

NN *n/a*    IE 4    DOM *n/a*

Read/Write

Background color of the element. This color setting is not reflected in the style sheet backgroundColor property. Even if the bgcolor attribute or bgColor property is set with a plain-language color name, the returned value is always a hexadecimal triplet.

**Example**    `document.getElementById("myBanner").bgColor = "yellow";`

**Value**           A hexadecimal triplet or plain-language color name. See Appendix A for
                    acceptable plain-language color names.

**Default**         Inherits body background color.

## dataFld                                        NN *n/a*    IE 4    DOM *n/a*
                                                              **Read/Write**

Used with IE data binding to associate a remote data source column name with the content
of the marquee element. A datasrc attribute must also be set for the element. Setting both
the dataFld and dataSrc properties to empty strings breaks the binding between element
and data source. Works only with text file data sources in IE 5/Mac.

**Example**         document.getElementById("myBanner").dataFld = "hotNews";

**Value**           Case-sensitive string identifier of the data source column.

**Default**         None.

## dataFormatAs                                   NN *n/a*    IE 4    DOM *n/a*
                                                              **Read/Write**

Used with IE data binding, this property advises the browser whether the source material
arriving from the data source is to be treated as plain text or as tagged HTML.

**Example**         document.getElementById("myBanner").dataFormatAs = "text";

**Value**           IE recognizes two possible settings: text | html.

**Default**         text

## dataSrc                                        NN *n/a*    IE 4    DOM *n/a*
                                                              **Read/Write**

Used with IE data binding to specify the ID of the page's object element that loads the data
source object for remote data access. Setting both the dataFld and dataSrc properties to
empty strings breaks the binding between element and data source. Works only with text
file data sources in IE 5/Mac.

**Example**         document.getElementById("myBanner").dataSrc = "DBSRC3";

**Value**           Case-sensitive string identifier of the data source.

**Default**         None.

## direction                                      NN *n/a*    IE 4    DOM *n/a*
                                                              **Read/Write**

Specifies the direction of the scroll within the element space.

**Example**         document.getElementById("myBanner").direction = "down";

| **Value** | Four possible case-insensitive directions: down \| left \| right \| up. |
| **Default** | left |

## height, width

Provide the height and width in pixels of the element. Changes to these values are immediately reflected in reflowed content on the page.

| **Example** | document.getElementById("myBanner").height = 250; |
| **Value** | Integer. |
| **Default** | None. |

## hspace, vspace

Provide the pixel measure of horizontal and vertical margins surrounding the element. The hspace property affects the left and right edges of the element equally; the vspace affects the top and bottom edges of the element equally. These margins are not the same as margins set by style sheets, but they have the same visual effect.

**Example**
```
document.getElementById("myBanner").hspace = 5;
document.getElementById("myBanner").vspace = 8;
```

| **Value** | Integer of pixel count. |
| **Default** | 0 |

## loop

Sets the number of times the element scrolls its content. After the final scroll, the content remains in a fixed position. Constant animation can sometimes be distracting to page visitors, so if you have the marquee turn itself off after a few scrolls, you may be doing your visitors a favor.

| **Example** | document.getElementById("myBanner").loop = 3; |
| **Value** | Any positive integer if you want the scrolling to stop after that number of times. Otherwise, set the value to -1. |
| **Default** | -1 |

## scrollAmount
NN n/a   IE 4   DOM n/a
Read/Write

Specifies the amount of space between positions of each drawing of the content. The greater the space, the faster the text appears to scroll. See also scrollDelay.

**Example**       `document.getElementById("myBanner").scrollAmount = 4;`

**Value**           Positive integer.

**Default**         6

## scrollDelay
NN n/a   IE 4   DOM n/a
Read/Write

Specifies the amount of time in milliseconds between each drawing of the content. The greater the delay, the slower the text appears to scroll. See also scrollAmount.

**Example**       `document.getElementById("myBanner").scrollDelay = 100;`

**Value**           Positive integer.

**Default**         85 (Windows 95); 90 (Macintosh).

## trueSpeed
NN n/a   IE 4   DOM n/a
Read/Write

Specifies whether the browser should honor scrolldelay attribute settings below 60 milliseconds. The default setting (false) prevents accidental settings that scroll too fast for most readers.

**Example**       `document.getElementById("myBanner").trueSpeed = "true";`

**Value**           Boolean value: true | false.

**Default**         false

## vspace

See hspace.

## width

See height.

## start( )
NN n/a   IE 4   DOM n/a

Starts the marquee element scrolling if it has been stopped. If the method is invoked on a stopped element, the onstart event handler also fires in response.

| | | | |
|---|---|---|---|
| **Returned Value** | None. | | |
| **Parameters** | None. | | |

## stop( )

Stops the scrolling of the marquee element. The content remains on the screen in the precise position it was in when the method was invoked. Restart via the start( ) method.

| | |
|---|---|
| **Returned Value** | None. |
| **Parameters** | None. |

# MediaList

The MediaList object is an abstract representation in the W3C DOM of a collection of string names for media specified for a particular styleSheet object. The media property of a styleSheet object returns a value that is a MediaList object (IE 6 for Windows incorrectly returns a string value). Media types (such as print, screen, aural, and so on) are specified for the style sheet either via the media attribute of a link element or an @media rule in a style element. As of Version 6 browsers, media support beyond print and screen types (and the default all type) is rather limited, so the details of this object are not yet important.

**Object-Specific Properties**

| | |
|---|---|
| length | mediaText |

**Object-Specific Methods**

| | | |
|---|---|---|
| appendMedium( ) | deleteMedium( ) | item( ) |

**Object-Specific Event Handler Properties**

None.

## length

Read-only

Returns the number of items in the collection.

| | |
|---|---|
| **Example** | var howMany = document.styleSheets[0].media.length; |
| **Value** | Integer. |

## mediaText

Read-only

Returns the entire string of comma-delimited media names.

| | |
|---|---|
| **Example** | var allMedia = document.styleSheets[0].media.mediaText; |
| **Value** | String. |

Alphabetical DOM
Reference

## appendMedium( ), deleteMedium( )      NN 7    IE *n/a*    DOM 2

```
appendMedium("mediumType")
deleteMedium("mediumType")
```

Adds or removes a medium type from the list. In Netscape 6.2, the methods are incorrectly named append( ) and delete( ).

**Returned Value**     None.

**Parameters**

*mediumType*
> String of recognized media type (e.g., print, screen).

## item( )      NN 6    IE *n/a*    DOM 2

```
item(index)
```

Returns one media name string from the collection corresponding to the item matching the index value in source code order.

**Returned Value**     String.

**Parameters**

*index*
> A zero-based integer corresponding to the specified item in source code order.

# menu      NN 6    IE 4    DOM 1

The menu object reflects the menu element.

**HTML Equivalent**    `<menu>`

**Object Model Reference**

```
[window.]document.getElementById("elementID")
```

**Object-Specific Properties**

| | |
|---|---|
| compact | type |

**Object-Specific Methods**

None.

**Object-Specific Event Handler Properties**

None.

## compact      NN 6    IE 5(Mac)/6(Win)    DOM 1
                                                          Read/Write

Provided for this element for the sake of compatibility with the W3C DOM standard. However, mainstream browsers do not act upon this property or its corresponding attribute.

| | | | |
|---|---|---|---|
| **Value** | Boolean value: true \| false. | | |
| **Default** | false | | |

## type

Implemented in IE 6 for Windows due to internal element relationships with the ol and ul element objects. Ignore for the menu element object.

# menubar

See directories.

# meta

The meta object reflects the meta element.

**HTML Equivalent**    <meta>

**Object Model Reference**
[window.]document.getElementById("*elementID*")

**Object-Specific Properties**

| charset | content | httpEquiv | name | scheme | url |
|---|---|---|---|---|---|

**Object-Specific Methods**
None.

**Object-Specific Event Handler Properties**
None.

## charset

Indicates the character encoding of the content in the file associated with the href attribute. This property does not change the setting of the charset attribute of a name/value pair contained by the content attribute or property. For now the charset property has little or no effect on a document.

**Example**
```
if (document.all.myMeta.charset == "csISO5427Cyrillic") {
    // process for Cyrillic charset
}
```

| | |
|---|---|
| **Value** | Case-insensitive alias from the character set registry (*ftp://ftp.isi.edu/in-notes/iana/assignments/character-sets*). |
| **Default** | Determined by browser. |

## content

This is the equivalent of the value of a name/value pair. The property's corresponding content attribute is usually accompanied by either a name or http-equiv attribute, either of which acts as the name portion of the name/value pair. Specific values of the content attribute vary with the value of the name or http-equiv attribute. Sometimes the content attribute value contains multiple values. In such cases, the values are delimited by a semi-colon. Some of these multiple values may be name/value pairs in their own right, such as the content for a refresh meta element. The first value is a number representing the number of seconds of delay before loading another document; the second value is a name/value pair indicating a URL of the document to load after the delay expires.

Despite the following example, changing the content property on a loaded document may not produce the desired effect if the browser relies on the incoming value as the document loads.

**Example**
```
document.getElementById("refreshMeta").content =
  "5,http://www.giantco.com/basicindex.html";
```

**Value**        String.

**Default**      None.

## httpEquiv

This is the equivalent of the name of a name/value pair. The property's corresponding http-equiv attribute is usually accompanied by a content attribute, which acts as the "value" portion of the name/value pair. The author may elect to use the name attribute instead of the http-equiv attribute, but only one may be set. Adjust only the property corresponding to the attribute used in the meta element's tag. Then be sure to set the content property with a value that makes sense with the httpEquiv or name property.

**Example**      `document.getElementById("refreshMeta").httpEquiv = "expires";`

**Value**        String.

**Default**      None.

## name

This is an identifier for the name/value pair that constitutes the meta element. The value is typically a plain-language term that denotes the purpose of the meta element, such as "author" or "keywords". Either the name or httpEquiv properties can have a value, but not both, in the same meta element.

| Example | `document.getElementById("detailMeta").name = "keywords";` |
|---|---|
| **Value** | String. |
| **Default** | None. |

## scheme

NN 6     IE 5(Mac)/6(Win)     DOM 1

Read/Write

Reflects the scheme attribute, but as yet has no particular functionality in current browsers. See the scheme attribute of the meta element in Chapter 8 for information about the intended purpose of this property.

| **Value** | String. |
|---|---|
| **Default** | None. |

## url

NN n/a     IE 4     DOM n/a

Read/Write

Although implemented in IE browsers, this property no longer appears to be officially supported.

## mimeType

NN 3     IE 5(Mac)     DOM n/a

The mimeType object belongs to the navigator object. The object represents a MIME type specification. Its properties let scripts find out if the browser is equipped to handle a specific MIME type of external content before it is loaded from the server. All these properties are mirrored in the internal document displayed when you choose Navigator's **About Plug-ins** menu option. Internet Explorer 5 for the Macintosh implements this scheme, but Explorer for Windows uses an entirely different system for determining support for external media via the object element.

**Object Model Reference**
navigator.mimeTypes[i]

**Object-Specific Properties**

| description | enabledPlugin | suffixes | type |
|---|---|---|---|

**Object-Specific Methods**
None.

**Object-Specific Event Handler Properties**
None.

## description                                                   NN 3    IE 5(Mac)    DOM n/a
**Read-only**

Returns the brief description of the plugin. This information is embedded in the plugin by its developer. Be aware that the precise wording of this description may vary for the same plugin written for different operating systems.

**Example**        `var descr = navigator.mimeTypes["video/mpeg"].description;`

**Value**          String.

**Default**        None.

## enabledPlugin                                                NN 3    IE 5(Mac)    DOM n/a
**Read-only**

Returns a `plugin` object reference corresponding to the plugin currently set to play any incoming data formatted according to the current MIME type. You can then dig deeper into properties of the returned `plugin` object to retrieve, say, its name.

**Example**
`var plugName = navigator.mimeTypes["video/mpeg"].enabledPlugin.name;`

**Value**          plugin object reference.

**Default**        None.

## suffixes                                                     NN 3    IE 5(Mac)    DOM n/a
**Read-only**

Returns a comma-delimited string list of file suffixes associated with the `mimeType` object, as supported by the plugin enabled for that MIME type. For example, the suffixes that the QuickTime plugin acknowledges for the type video/avi are:

    avi, vfw

If you loop through all `mimeType` objects registered in the browser to find a match for a specific suffix, you can then find out whether the matching `mimeType` object has a plugin installed for it (via the `enabledPlugin` property).

**Example**        `var suff = navigator.mimeTypes["audio/mpeg"].suffixes;`

**Value**          String.

**Default**        None.

## type                                                         NN 3    IE 5(Mac)    DOM n/a
**Read-only**

Returns a string version of the MIME type associated with the `mimeType` object. You could, for example, loop through all the `mimeType` objects in search of the one that matches a specific MIME type (application/x-midi) and examine that mimeType object further to see whether it is currently supported and enabled.

**Example**    var MType = navigator.mimeTypes[3].type;

**Value**    String.

**Default**    None.

## MouseEvent                                              NN 6    IE n/a    DOM 2

The W3C DOM MouseEvent object is an abstract object that contains the properties and methods shared by every instance of a W3C DOM mouse-related event. This object inherits characteristics from the W3C DOM Event and UIEvent objects. The properties (information such as click coordinates) and methods of this object are blended into the directly scripted event object. See the discussion of the event object earlier in this chapter for specific property and method support for this object and how these items are inherited by more specific event types.

## MutationEvent                                           NN 6    IE n/a    DOM 2

The W3C DOM MutationEvent object is an abstract object that contains the properties and methods shared by every instance of a W3C DOM event that concerns itself with the modification of the document tree. This object inherits characteristics from the W3C DOM Event. The properties (information such as references to the node affected by the change) and methods of this object are blended into the directly scripted event object. See the discussion of the event object earlier in this chapter for specific property and method support for this object and how these items are inherited by more specific event types.

## NamedNodeMap

See attributes.

## navigator                                               NN 2    IE 3    DOM n/a

The navigator object in many ways represents the browser application. As such, the browser is outside the scope of the document object model. Even so, the navigator object plays an important role in scripting, because it allows scripts to see what browser and browser version is running the script. In addition to several key properties that both Navigator and Internet Explorer have in common, each browser also extends the property listing of this object in ways that would generally benefit all browsers. IE duplicates this object under the clientInformation object name, but for cross-browser compatibility, you can use the navigator object reference in all browsers.

### Object Model Reference

*NN* navigator

*IE*    [window.]navigator

## Object-Specific Properties

| | | | |
|---|---|---|---|
| appCodeName | appMinorVersion | appName | appVersion |
| browserLanguage | cookieEnabled | cpuClass | language |
| mimeTypes[] | onLine | oscpu | platform |
| plugins[] | product | productSub | securityPolicy |
| systemLanguage | userAgent | userLanguage | userProfile |
| vendor | vendorSub | | |

## Object-Specific Methods

| | | |
|---|---|---|
| javaEnabled( ) | preference( ) | taintEnabled( ) |

## Object-Specific Event Handler Properties
None.

## appCodeName                                          NN 2    IE 3    DOM n/a
**Read-only**

Reveals the code name of the browser. Both Navigator and Internet Explorer return
Mozilla, which was the code name for an early version of Navigator (a combination of the
early freeware name of the Mosaic browser and Godzilla). The Mozilla character is
Netscape's corporate mascot, but all browsers that license the original Mosaic technology
(including IE) return Mozilla.

| **Example** | var codeName = navigator.appCodeName; |
|---|---|
| **Value** | Mozilla |
| **Default** | Mozilla |

## appMinorVersion                                      NN n/a    IE 4    DOM n/a
**Read-only**

With succeeding generations of Internet Explorer, this property returns a dizzying range of
values, most of which are not useful for typical version detection. IE 5.x for Windows
returns an appVersion value of 4.0, with the appMinorVersion reporting the first digit to the
right of the decimal. In IE 6 for Windows, the appMinorVersion returns a string signifying a
build or patch code number, such as ;Q313675;. Use with extreme caution.

| **Example** | var subVer = navigator.appMinorVersion; |
|---|---|
| **Value** | String. |
| **Default** | Depends on browser version. |

## appName

Reveals the model name of the browser.

**Example**      var isNav = navigator.appName == "Netscape";

**Value**         String values. NN: "Netscape"; IE: "Microsoft Internet Explorer". Some other browsers return these values to appear to be compatible with one of the mainstream browsers.

**Default**       Depends on browser.

## appVersion

Reveals a version number of the browser engine, along with minimal operating system platform information (a subset of the information returned by userAgent). Sample returned values are as follows.

Internet Explorer:

```
4.0 (compatible; MSIE 6.0; Windows 98; Q312461)
4.0 (compatible; MSIE 5.0; Macintosh; I; PPC)
```

Navigator:

```
4.04 [en] (Win95; I)
5.0 (Macintosh; en-US)
```

Note that the version number at the start of the value (up to the first whitespace) is not indicative of the actual browser application version, but rather of the fundamental engine. Thus, IE application Versions 4 through 6 (and perhaps later) all report engine Version 4.0; Netscape 6 is based on what it terms engine generation 5.0. Browser application version information is found elsewhere either in the appVersion, userAgent, or other navigator object properties. Do not use the first word of the appVersion value for any kind of browser version detection that influences which DOM or JavaScript language features are supported by the browser. In browsers leading up to Version 4, this property correctly reflected the application version, but that is no longer the case.

While it may appear that the precise Internet Explorer version is embedded in this property's value (as MSIE X.XX), there are occasional mismatches in some versions. To inspect this portion of the version string, the navigator.userAgent property is more reliable.

**Example**      var isVer4Min = parseInt(navigator.appVersion) >= 4;

**Value**         String.

**Default**       Depends on browser.

## browserLanguage

Provides the default written language of the browser. The Navigator equivalent is the navigator.language property.

| | |
|---|---|
| **Example** | `var browLangCode = navigator.browserLanguage;` |
| **Value** | Case-insensitive language code as a string. |
| **Default** | Browser default. |

## cookieEnabled

NN 6    IE 4    DOM *n/a*<br>Read-only

Returns whether the browser allows reading and writing of cookie data.

**Example**

```
if (cookieEnabled) {
    setCookieData(data);
}
```

| | |
|---|---|
| **Value** | Boolean value: true \| false. |
| **Default** | Depends on browser preference setting. |

## cpuClass

NN *n/a*    IE 4    DOM *n/a*<br>Read-only

Returns a string reference of the CPU of the client computer. Common Intel microprocessors (including Pentium-class CPUs and Macintoshes running Windows emulators) return x86, while PowerPC Macintoshes return PPC. This value tells you only about the basic hardware class, not the operating system or specific CPU speed or model number.

**Example**

```
if (navigator.cpuClass == "PPC") {
    // statements specific to PowerPC clients
}
```

| | |
|---|---|
| **Value** | String. |
| **Default** | Depends on client hardware. |

## language

NN 4    IE *n/a*    DOM *n/a*<br>Read-only

Indicates the written language for which the browser version was created. The language is specified in the ISO 639 language code scheme (such as en-us). Internet Explorer provides this information via the `navigator.browserLanguage` property.

| | |
|---|---|
| **Example** | `var mainLang = navigator.language;` |
| **Value** | Case-insensitive language code as a string. |
| **Default** | Browser default. |

## mimeTypes

Returns an array of `mimeType` objects supported by installed plugins in the browser. IE for Windows provides this property for syntactical compatibility, but it always returns an array of zero length. See the `mimeType` object.

**Example**        `var videoPlugin = navigator.mimeTypes["video/mpeg"].enabledPlugin;`

**Value**          Array of `mimeType` objects.

**Default**        Browser default.

## onLine

Specifies whether the browser is set for online or offline browsing (in Internet Explorer's **File** menu). Pages may wish to invoke live server actions when they load in online mode, but avoid these calls when in offline mode. Use this Boolean property to build such conditional statements.

**Example**
```
if (navigator.onLine) {
    document.write("<applet ...>");
    ...
}
```

**Value**          Boolean value: true | false.

**Default**        true

## oscpu

Returns a string containing operating system or central processing unit information about the client machine. Values vary widely across systems. Windows clients are divided roughly into two categories: non-NT and NT. The former includes Windows 95, 98, and ME (`oscpu` values of `Win95`, `Win98`, and `Win 9x 4.90`, respectively). The NT category includes Windows NT 4 (`WinNT4.0`) and Windows XP (`Windows NT x.x`). Macintosh systems all report the CPU type and the absence or presence of Mac OS X (`PPC` or `PPC Mac OS X`). Unix systems report both the operating system and CPU type. The `oscpu` value is also a part of the `userAgent` value. Formatting for this information is not the same in Internet Explorer's corresponding `cpuClass` or `userAgent` properties.

**Example**
```
if (navigator.oscpu.indexOf("Win") != -1) {
    document.write("You are running a Windows computer.");
}
```

Alphabetical DOM Reference

| **Value** | String. |
|---|---|
| **Default** | System dependent. |

## platform
NN 4    IE 4    DOM n/a<br>Read-only

Returns the name of the operating system or hardware platform of the browser. For Windows 95/NT, the value is Win32; for a Macintosh running a PowerPC CPU, the value is MacPPC. At least for the major platforms I've been able to test, Navigator and Internet Explorer agree on the returned values. Using this property to determine the baseline facilities of the client in a conditional expression can help the page optimize its output for the device.

**Example**
```
if (navigator.platform == "Win32") {
    document.write("<link rel='stylesheet' type='text/css' href='css/stylePC.css'>");
}
```

| **Value** | String. |
|---|---|
| **Default** | System dependent. |

## plugins[]
NN 3    IE 5(Mac)    DOM n/a<br>Read-only

Returns a collection of plugin objects recognized by the browser to facilitate script determination of the browser's support for a particular external media type. IE 4 and later for Windows implement this property, but only as a dummy placeholder that always returns an array of length zero. See the mimeType and plugin objects.

| **Example** | var plugInCount = navigator.plugins.length; |
|---|---|
| **Value** | Array of plugin object references. |
| **Default** | None. |

## product, productSub
NN 6    IE n/a    DOM n/a<br>Read-only

Return a string identifying the software engine behind the browser. In Netscape 6, the product property returns Gecko, while the productSub property returns a development build number (in string form).

| **Example** | var prod = navigator.product; |
|---|---|
| **Value** | String. |
| **Default** | Browser dependent. |

## securityPolicy

Returns a string in Navigator 4 revealing the browser's encryption level (that is, the domestic or export encryption policy to which the browser adheres). With the loosening of U.S. encryption export laws, Netscape 6 implements one encryption type across all versions. In Netscape 6, this property returns an empty string.

**Value**          String.

**Default**        None.

## systemLanguage

Specifies the code for the default written language used by the operating system. If you have multi-lingual content available, you can use this property to insert content in specific languages.

**Example**
```
if (navigator.systemLanguage == "nl") {
// document.write( ) some Dutch content
}
```

**Value**          Case-insensitive language code.

**Default**        Usually the browser default (en for English-language Internet Explorer available in the United States).

## userAgent

Provides information about the browser software, including version, operating system platform, and brand. This is the most complete set of information about the browser, whereas appVersion and appName properties provide subset (and not always correct) data. Typical data for the userAgent property looks like the following examples from IE and Navigator:

```
Mozilla/4.0 (compatible; MSIE 6.0; Windows 98; Q312461)
Mozilla/5.0 (Macintosh; U; PPC; en-US; rv:0.9.4) Gecko/20011022 Netscape6/6.2
```

Do not rely on the length or position of any part of this data, as it may vary with the browser, version, and proxy server used at the client end. Instead, use the indexOf( ) method to check for the presence of a desired string. To extract only the actual application version number for IE, use the following function:

```
function readIEVersion( ) {
    var ua = navigator.userAgent;
    var IEOffset = ua.indexOf("MSIE ");
    return parseFloat(ua.substring(IEOffset + 5, ua.indexOf(";", IEOffset)));
}
```

Alphabetical DOM
Reference

**Example**
```
if (navigator.userAgent.indexOf("MSIE") != -1) {
    var isIE = true;
}
```

| | |
|---|---|
| **Value** | String. |
| **Default** | Browser dependent. |

## userLanguage    NN *n/a*    IE 4    DOM *n/a*
**Read-only**

The default written language of the browser, based on the operating system user profile setting (if one exists). The property defaults to the browserLanguage property.

| | |
|---|---|
| **Example** | var userLangCode = navigator.userLanguage; |
| **Value** | Case-insensitive language code as a string. |
| **Default** | Browser default. |

## userProfile    NN *n/a*    IE 4    DOM *n/a*
**Read-only**

The userProfile property is, itself, an object that lets scripts request permission to access personal information stored in the visitor's user profile (for Win32 versions of Internet Explorer). See the userProfile object.

**Example**
```
navigator.userProfile.addReadRequest("vcard.displayname");
navigator.userProfile.doReadRequest("3", "MegaCorp Customer Service");
var custName = navigator.userProfile.getAttribute("vcard.displayname");
navigator.userProfile.clearRequest();
if (custName) {
    ...
}
```

| | |
|---|---|
| **Value** | userProfile object reference. |
| **Default** | Browser default. |

## vendor, vendorSub    NN 6    IE *n/a*    DOM *n/a*
**Read-only**

Return a string identifying the browser product that employs the Mozilla engine. In Netscape 6, the vendor property returns Netscape6, while Netscape 7 returns simply Netscape. The vendorSub property returns the version release in detail (in string form). If you want to test for a minimum version, convert the navigator.vendorSub value to a decimal floating-point number before performing a comparison against your minimum requirement.

**Example**

```
if (parseFloat(navigator.vendorSub, 10) >= 6.2) {
    // OK, meets minimum NN requirement
}
```

| | |
|---|---|
| **Value** | String. |
| **Default** | Browser dependent. |

## javaEnabled( )       NN *3*   IE *4*   DOM *n/a*

Returns whether Java is turned on in the browser. This method obviously won't help you in a nonscriptable browser (or scriptable browser that doesn't support the property), but if scripting is enabled, it does tell you whether the user has Java turned off in the browser preferences.

| | |
|---|---|
| **Returned Value** | Boolean value: true \| false. |
| **Parameters** | None. |

## preference( )       NN *4*   IE *n/a*   DOM *n/a*

preference(*name*[, *value*])

By way of signed scripts in Navigator 4, you can access a wide variety of user preferences settings. These include even the most detailed items, such as whether the user has elected to download images or whether style sheets are enabled. Most of these settings are intended for scripts used by network administrators to install and control the user settings of enterprise-wide deployment of Navigator. Consult the Netscape developer web site for further information about these preferences settings (*http://developer.netscape.com/docs/ manuals/communicator/preferences/*). Netscape 6 throws a security exception when invoking this method (even with signed scripts), but the method works with signed scripts in Netscape 7.

**Returned Value**     Preference value in a variety of data types.

**Parameters**

*name*

    The preference name as a string, such as general.always_load_images.

*value*

    An optional value to set the named preference.

## taintEnabled( )       NN *3*   IE *4*   DOM *n/a*

Returns whether data tainting is turned on in the browser. This security mechanism was never fully implemented in Navigator, but the method that checks for it is still included in newer versions of Navigator for backward compatibility. Internet Explorer also includes it for compatibility, even though it always returns false.

**Alphabetical DOM Reference**

**Returned Value**    Boolean value: true | false.

**Parameters**    None.

# nobr

The nobr object reflects the nobr element.

### HTML Equivalent
<nobr>

### Object Model Reference
[window.]document.getElementById("*elementID*")

### Object-Specific Properties
None.

### Object-Specific Methods
None.

### Object-Specific Event Handler Properties
None.

# Node

The Node object is an abstract representation in the W3C DOM of the fundamental content building block in a document. All pieces of content that you can address in the W3C DOM model are nodes: unnamed contiguous strings of text between tags, tagged elements, name/value attribute pairs, special-purpose elements such as comments, DOCTYPE declarations, and even the document, itself, to name several.

A Node object has a large set of properties and methods, most of which concern a node's relationships to surrounding nodes. The objects in a document that scripts read and control are defined as descendants of the basic Node object; this means that the most common content-bearing objects that DHTML scripts work with—HTML elements, text nodes, and element attributes—all share this set of properties and methods to start. Then, as needed for their powers as HTML elements, they accrue additional properties and/or methods that give them their special powers.

While the nodeness of the W3C DOM codifies the inheritance relationships among different pieces of a document's content, the model presents a conceptual framework and granularity that at times seems tedious compared to the shortcut HTMLness of both the first-generation DOM and the Microsoft DOM. But the ultimate goal is to provide a single model that works for both XML and HTML documents (in either their pure HTML or XML-ized versions).

# NodeFilter

The NodeFilter object provides a mechanism for the NodeIterator and TreeWalker objects to determine which nodes or classes of nodes are to be accepted or rejected for inclusion into one of the special node lists. The lone accept( ) method is invoked silently by the NodeInterator and TreeWalker objects whenever the objects are asked to point to the next node in sequence. The NodeFilter object is also the holder of two sets of constants that are used in a variety of creation method calls and user-defined filter functions. See the TreeWalker object for an example, and the document.createTreeWalker( ) method for application of the constants.

### Object Model Reference
NodeFilter

### Object-Specific Properties

| | | |
|---|---|---|
| FILTER_ACCEPT | FILTER_REJECT | FILTER_SKIP |
| SHOW_ALL | SHOW_ATTRIBUTE | SHOW_CDATA_SECTION |
| SHOW_COMMENT | SHOW_DOCUMENT | SHOW_DOCUMENT_FRAGMENT |
| SHOW_DOCUMENT_TYPE | SHOW_ELEMENT | SHOW_ENTITY |
| SHOW_NOTATION | SHOW_PROCESSING_INSTRUCTION | SHOW_TEXT |

### Object-Specific Methods
accept( )

### Object-Specific Event Handler Properties
None.

# accept( )

accept(*nodeReference*)

Returns an integer signifying whether a node is to be included in the NodeIterator or TreeWalker object's list. This method is invoked automatically by the objects whenever one of their pointer-moving methods is invoked.

### Returned Value

Integer value, each of which has a corresponding constant value associated with the NodeFilter object: 1 (NodeFilter.FILTER_ACCEPT); 2 (NodeFilter.FILTER_REJECT); 3 (NodeFilter.FILTER_SKIP).

### Parameters

*nodeReference*

> Reference to the document tree node under test. Passed automatically to the method when invoked by the NodeInterator and TreeWalker objects.

# NodeIterator
NN n/a   IE n/a   DOM 2

The NodeIterator object is a "live" list of nodes that meet the criteria defined by the document.createNodeIterator() method. The list is a simple list of node references in source code order, but the list items do not bear any parent or descendant relationships to each other. The createNodeIterator() method describes the node where the list begins and which nodes (or classes of nodes) are exempt from the list by way of filtering (see the TreeWalker object for an example of this kind of filtering).

The NodeIterator object maintains a kind of pointer inside the list (so that your scripts don't have to). Methods of this object let scripts access the next or previous node in the list, while moving the pointer one position in either direction. If scripts modify the document tree after the NodeIterator is created, changes to the document tree are automatically reflected in the sequence of nodes in the NodeIterator.

### Object Model Reference
*NodeIteratorReference*

### Object-Specific Properties
expandEntityReference    filter        root          whatToShow

### Object-Specific Methods
detach()             nextNode()        previousNode()

### Object-Specific Event Handler Properties
None.

## expandEntityReference, filter, root, whatToShow
NN n/a   IE n/a   DOM 2
Read-only

See these properties of the TreeWalker object.

## detach()
NN n/a   IE n/a   DOM 2

Disconnects the current NodeIterator object from the document tree. Items in the list are no longer accessible once the method is invoked.

**Returned Value**    None.

**Parameters**    None.

## nextNode(), previousNode()
NN n/a   IE n/a   DOM 2

Moves the internal NodeIterator pointer one position forward (nextNode()) or backward (previousNode()), while returning a reference to the node through which the pointer passed en route.

**Returned Value**    Reference to a node in the document tree.

**Parameters**    None.

# NodeList

The NodeList object is an abstract representation in the W3C DOM of a collection of nodes of any type. Any W3C DOM property or method that returns a collection of nodes returns an object of type NodeList. For example, the Node object's childNodes property and the Element object's getElementsByTagName( ) method both return NodeList objects. JavaScript exposes a NodeList collections as an array that has the familiar length property. Scripts can reference individual items in the array through integer array indexes (inside square brackets) or via the NodeList object's item( ) method.

Some node types have their own collections (e.g., NamedNodeMap for a collection of attribute nodes and the HTMLCollection for a collection of HTML element nodes). These other collection objects have extra properties and methods that are meaningful only to the types of nodes inside the collections. For instance, because text nodes (one of the simplest type of Node object) do not have a property that can contain an identifier, the NodeList object does not include a method to reference an item by its ID. But an HTMLCollection object (consisting entirely of the more complex HTMLElement types of nodes) includes another method (namedItem( )) that lets scripts reference an item by its ID as well as integer index. The distinctions among collection object types are readily apparent when you compare the properties and methods of the collection objects you actually script (see the descriptions in this chapter of the attributes and images objects, for example). The W3C DOM terminology, on the other hand, is not a factor in scripts.

# noframes, noscript

The noframes object reflects the noframes element, and the noscript object reflects the noscript element.

## HTML Equivalent
<noframes>
<noscript>

## Object Model Reference
[window.]document.getElementById("*elementID*")

## Object-Specific Properties
None.

## Object-Specific Methods
None.

## Object-Specific Event Handler Properties
None.

# Notation

NN n/a   IE n/a   DOM 1

The Notation object (one of the node types) is an abstract representation in the W3C DOM of a portion of a DOCTYPE declaration. In particular, a Notation object contains properties for reading the public and system IDs cited by the DOCTYPE.

# object

NN 6   IE 4   DOM 1

The object object reflects the object element. This is an updated way of embedding other media and external data into a document (through a plugin or, in IE for Windows, an ActiveX control). The depth and quality of implementation of this object (vis-à-vis the W3C specifications) is uneven across browser brands and versions. The most consistent implementation is in IE for Windows for loading ActiveX controls.

**HTML Equivalent**  <object>

**Object Model Reference**
[window.]document.getElementById("*elementID*")

**Object-Specific Properties**

| | | | |
|---|---|---|---|
| align | alt | altHtml | archive | BaseHref |
| border | classid | code | codeBase | codeType |
| contentDocument | data | dataFld | dataSrc | declare |
| form | height | hspace | name | object |
| standby | type | useMap | vspace | width |

**Object-Specific Methods**
None.

**Object-Specific Event Handler Properties**

| Handler | NN | IE | DOM |
|---|---|---|---|
| onabort | n/a | n/a | 2 |
| onerror | n/a | 4 | 2 |
| onload | n/a | n/a | 2 |

# align

NN n/a   IE 4   DOM 1
Read/Write

Defines how the element is aligned relative to surrounding text content. Most values set the vertical relationship between the element and surrounding text. For example, to align the bottom of the element with the baseline of the surrounding text, the align property value would be baseline. An element can be "floated" along the left or right margin to let surrounding text wrap around the element.

**Example**  document.getElementById("myObject").align = "absmiddle";

| | |
|---|---|
| **Value** | Any of the following alignment constant values (as a string): absbottom \| absmiddle \| baseline \| bottom \| right \| left \| none \| texttop \| top. |
| **Default** | bottom |

## alt

Indicates the text to be displayed (or spoken) where the object element appears on the page when a browser doesn't download graphics (or is waiting for the image to download). Presumably, Microsoft implemented this nonstandard property for occasions when the object element is used for the display of images, rather than the more common img element.

| | |
|---|---|
| **Example** | document.getElementById("logoDisplay").alt = "MegaCorp Logo"; |
| **Value** | String value. |
| **Default** | None. |

## altHtml

Provides HTML content to be displayed if the object or applet fails to load. This can be a message, static image, or any other HTML that best fits the scenario. There are inconsistencies in Internet Explorer with regard to this property name's case. The Win32 version requires altHtml; the Mac version requires altHTML.

**Example**

document.getElementById("myObject").altHtml = "<img src='objectAlt.gif'>";

| | |
|---|---|
| **Value** | Any quoted string of characters, including HTML tags. |
| **Default** | None. |

## archive

Reflects the archive attribute of the object element, but Version 6 browsers assign no functionality to either the attribute or property.

| | |
|---|---|
| **Value** | String value. |
| **Default** | None. |

## BaseHref

Returns the URL of the document containing the object element. Most commonly, the value is the same as the location.href of the current window. Note the unusual letter case.

| **Example** | var where = document.getElementById("myObject").BaseHref; |
| **Value** | URL string. |
| **Default** | Current document's URL. |

## border

NN 6   IE 6(Win)   DOM 1<br>Read/Write

Controls the thickness of the border in pixels. For cross-browser compatibility use string values.

| **Example** | document.getElementById("myObject").border = "5"; |
| **Value** | Number as string. |
| **Default** | 0 |

## classid

NN n/a   IE 4   DOM n/a<br>Read-only

Provides the URL of the object's implementation. In Internet Explorer, the URL can point to the client computer's *CLSID* directory (with a clsid: URL) that stores all the IDs for registered ActiveX controls, such as DirectX or Media Player. IE 4 for Macintosh names this property classID, but the name was repaired to all lowercase in IE 4.5. The W3C DOM omits this property, even though HTML 4 includes the corresponding attribute.

**Example**

```
if (document.getElementById("soundObject").classid ==
    "clsid:83A38BF0-B33A-A4FF-C619A82E891D"){
    // process for the desired sound object
}
```

| **Value** | String (including the clsid: protocol for local ActiveX controls). |
| **Default** | None. |

## code

NN 6   IE 4   DOM 1<br>Read-only

Provides the name of the Java applet class file set to the code attribute of the object element (when using an object element in lieu of an applet element—if supported by your browsers).

**Example**

```
if (document.getElementById("clock").code == "Y2Kcounter.class") {
    // process for the found class file
}
```

| **Value** | Case-sensitive applet class filename as a string. |
| **Default** | None. |

## codeBase

**Read-only**

This is the path to the directory holding the class file designated in either the code or classid attribute. The codebase attribute does not name the class file, just the path.

**Example**
```
if (document.getElementById("clock").codeBase == "classes") {
    // process for the found class file directory
}
```

**Value**        Case-sensitive pathname, usually relative to the directory storing the current HTML document.

**Default**      None.

## codeType

**Read/Write**

Provides an advisory about the content type of the object referred to by the classid attribute. A browser might use this information to assist in preparing support for a resource requiring a multimedia player or plugin. If the codetype property is set to an empty string, the browser looks next for the type attribute setting (although it is normally associated with content linked by the data attribute URL). If both attributes have no (or empty) values set, the browser gets the content type information from the resource as it downloads.

**Example**
```
document.getElementById("gameTime").codeType = "application/x-crossword";
```

**Value**        Case-insensitive MIME type. A catalog of registered MIME types is available from *ftp://ftp.isi.edu/in-notes/iana/assignments/media-types/*.

**Default**      None.

## contentDocument

**Read-only**

Refers to a document node created by the object element, if any.

**Value**        Document node reference or null.

**Default**      null

## data

**Read-only**

URL of a file containing data for the object element (as distinguished from the object itself). Relative URLs are calculated relative to the codebase attribute if one is assigned; otherwise, the URL is relative to the document's URL.

| | | |
|---|---|---|
| **Example** | var objDataURL = document.getElementById("soundEffect").data; | |
| **Value** | A complete or relative URL as a string. | |
| **Default** | None. | |

## dataFld

NN n/a   IE 4   DOM n/a<br>Read/Write

Used with IE data binding to associate a remote data source column name to an object element attribute determined by properties set in the object. A datasrc attribute must also be set for the element. Setting both the dataFld and dataSrc properties to empty strings breaks the binding between element and data source.

| | |
|---|---|
| **Example** | document.getElementById("myObject").dataFld = "streamURL"; |
| **Value** | Case-sensitive identifier of the data source column. |
| **Default** | None. |

## dataSrc

NN n/a   IE 4   DOM n/a<br>Read/Write

Used with IE data binding to specify the ID of the page's object element that loads the data source object for remote data access (an object element other than the current one). Setting both the dataFld and dataSrc properties to empty strings breaks the binding between element and data source.

| | |
|---|---|
| **Example** | document.getElementById("myObject").dataSrc = "DBSRC3"; |
| **Value** | Case-sensitive identifier of the data source. |
| **Default** | None. |

## declare

NN 6   IE 6   DOM 1<br>Read/Write

Reflects the declare attribute. As of Version 6 browsers, has no effect on the content.

| | |
|---|---|
| **Value** | Boolean value: true | false. |
| **Default** | false |

## form

NN 6   IE 4   DOM 1<br>Read-only

Returns a reference to the form element that contains the current element (if any). This property is appropriate only if the object is acting as a form control. Not available in IE 4.0 for the Macintosh.

**Value**        Object reference or null.

**Default**      None.

## height, width

Provide the height and width of the element, in pixels. Changes to these values are immediately reflected in reflowed content on the page.

**Example**      document.getElementById("myObject").height = 250;

**Value**        Integer.

**Default**      None.

## hspace, vspace

Provide the pixel measure of horizontal and vertical margins surrounding an object element. The hspace property affects the left and right edges of the element equally; the vspace affects the top and bottom edges of the element equally. These margins are not the same as margins set by style sheets, but they have the same visual effect.

**Example**

```
document.getElementById("myObject").hspace = 5;
document.getElementById("myObject").vspace = 8;
```

**Value**        Integer of pixel count as string.

**Default**      0

## name

This is the identifier associated with the object element. If the object should be one that goes inside a form, the name property is submitted as one-half of the name/value pair when the form is submitted to the server.

**Example**      document.getElementById("myObject").name = "company";

**Value**

Case-sensitive string identifier that follows the rules of identifier naming: it may contain no whitespace, cannot begin with a numeral, and should avoid punctuation except for the underscore character.

**Default**      None.

## object

**Read-only**

Provides a reference to a wrapper around an object to allow access to document object model properties of the object element when the names may be confused with internal property naming of the object. For example, if the code loaded into an object element had a property named hspace, the script reference document.getElementById("reader").object. hspace would retrieve that internal property, rather than the hspace property of the HTML element. The object property wrapper tells the JavaScript interpreter to get the property from the HTML element without diving into the external object's code.

| | |
|---|---|
| **Example** | var objCode = document.getElementById("reader").object.code; |
| **Value** | Object reference. |
| **Default** | None. |

## standby

NN *6*   IE *5(Mac)/6(Win)*   DOM *1*

**Read-only**

This will eventually assume the duty of the alt attribute for displaying a message during loading. Currently has no effect on the element.

| | |
|---|---|
| **Value** | String. |
| **Default** | None. |

## type

NN *6*   IE *4*   DOM *1*

**Read/Write**

Provides an advisory about the MIME type of the external data to be loaded into the object. The browser looks to the type property value if the codeType property is null.

**Example**

```
if (document.getElementById("myObject").type == "image/jpeg") {
    ...
}
```

| | |
|---|---|
| **Value** | Case-insensitive MIME type. A catalog of registered MIME types is available from *ftp://ftp.isi.edu/in-notes/iana/assignments/media-types/*. |
| **Default** | None. |

## useMap

NN *6*   IE *6*   DOM *1*

**Read/Write**

Provides the URL of the map element in the same document that contains client-side image map hot areas and links. The value includes the hash mark assigned with the map name in the usemap attribute of the object element.

| Example | document.getElementById("logoViewer").useMap = "#altMap"; |
| Value | A string starting with a hash mark and the name of the map element. |
| Default | None. |

## vspace

See hspace.

## width

See height.

## ol

The ol object reflects the ol element.

**HTML Equivalent**
<ol>

**Object Model Reference**
[window.]document.getElementById("*elementID*")

**Object-Specific Properties**

| compact | start | type |
|---|---|---|

**Object-Specific Methods**
None.

**Object-Specific Event Handler Properties**
None.

## compact

**Read/Write**

When set to true, the compact property should instruct the browser to render items in the list in a more compact format. This property has no effect in mainstream browsers.

| Example | document.getElementById("myOL").compact = true; |
| Value | Boolean value: true \| false. |
| Default | false |

## start

Indicates the starting number for the sequence of items in the ol element. This is convenient when a sequence of items must be disturbed by running body text. While the value is a number, the corresponding Arabic numeral, Roman numeral, or alphabet letter renders the value. When no value is set as an attribute, Netscape 6 defaults the property value to -1.

**Example**      document.getElementById("sublist2").start = 6;

**Value**        Integer.

**Default**      1 (IE); -1 (Netscape 6).

## type

Indicates the manner in which the leading numbers or letters of items in the list are displayed.

**Example**      document.getElementById("instruxList").type = "a";

**Value**

Possible values are: A | a | I | i | 1. Sequencing is performed automatically as shown in the following table.

| Type | Example |
|------|---------|
| A | A, B, C, ... |
| a | a, b, c, ... |
| I | I, II, III, ... |
| i | i, ii, iii, ... |
| 1 | 1, 2, 3, ... |

**Default**      None specified, although behavior is that of 1.

## optgroup

The optgroup object reflects the optgroup element, which must be nested inside a select element and surround option elements. See the optgroup element in Chapter 8 for browser support details of this element. The disabled property (described among the shared properties earlier in this chapter) is available for this object, and it influences the disabled status of nested option elements.

**HTML Equivalent**
<optgroup>

**Object Model Reference**
[window.]document.getElementById("elementID")

**Object-Specific Properties**
label

**Object-Specific Methods**
None.

**Object-Specific Event Handler Properties**
None.

## label

NN 6   IE 5(Mac)/6(Win)   DOM 1<br>Read/Write

Reflects the label attribute of the optgroup element.

**Value**     String.

**Default**   None.

## option

NN 2   IE 3   DOM 1

The option object reflects the option element, which must be nested inside a select element. References to option objects most often use its parent select object, with the option object treated as one member of an array of options belonging to that select object. With modern browsers, you can also reference an option object directly via its ID. The disabled property (described among the shared properties earlier in this chapter) is available for IE 4 and later and Netscape 6.

You can modify the set of options in a select object in browsers starting with Netscape 3 and Explorer 4 with backward-compatible code that continues to work in the newest browsers. If the modification entails replacing existing options with a different list of the same length, you can simply assign new values to text, value, and selected properties of each option in the select object's options array. But if the list has a different number of options, you are better served by removing all existing option objects and inserting new ones. A constructor function for a new Option object lets you create objects one at a time, and then assign them to positions within the options array. Syntax for the constructor is as follows:

```
var newOpt = new Option("text", "value", isDefaultSelectedFlag,
isSelectedFlag);
```

The following function demonstrates the typical steps involved in rewriting a select object's list of options:

```
function setSelect(selectElemObj) {
    // remove existing options
    selectElemObj.options.length = 0;
    // create and assign options, one by one
    selectElemObj.options[0] = new Option("Hercule Poirot", "poirot", false, false);
    selectElemObj.options[1] = new Option("Miss Marple", "marple", false, false);
    ...
}
```

In a production environment, the values for the constructor parameters would most likely be delivered to the page as an array of objects, allowing the stuffing of new options to be

**Alphabetical DOM<br>Reference**

carried out inside a for loop. For additional approaches to this task, see the options.add( ) method (for IE only) and the select.add( ) method (for IE 5 or later and Netscape 6 only).

**HTML Equivalent**

<option>

**Object Model Reference**

[window.]document.*formName*.*selectName*.options[i]
[window.]document.forms[i].elements[i].options[i]
[window.]document.getElementById("*elementID*")

**Object-Specific Properties**

| defaultSelected | form | index | label | selected | text | value |
| --- | --- | --- | --- | --- | --- | --- |

**Object-Specific Methods**

None.

**Object-Specific Event Handler Properties**

None.

## defaultSelected
NN 2    IE 3    DOM 1<br>Read/Write

Determines whether an element has the selected attribute set in the tag. You can compare the current selected property against defaultSelected to see whether the state of the select control has changed since the document loaded. Changing this property does not affect the current selected status.

**Example**

```
var listItem = document.forms[0].selector.options[2];
if (listItem.selected != listItem.defaultSelected) {
    // process for changed state
}
```

| **Value** | Boolean value: true \| false. |
| --- | --- |
| **Default** | Determined by HTML tag attribute. |

## form
NN 6    IE 4    DOM 1<br>Read-only

Returns a reference to the form object that contains the select element and its options.

| **Example** | var theForm = document.getElementById("myOption3").form; |
| --- | --- |
| **Value** | form object reference. |
| **Default** | None. |

# index

**Read-only**

Returns the zero-based index integer value of the current option object within the collection of options of the select element. The select object's selectedIndex property returns the index value of the option that is currently selected.

| | |
|---|---|
| **Example** | `var whichItem = document.getElementById("myOption3").index;` |
| **Value** | Integer. |
| **Default** | None. |

# label

**Read/Write**

Reflects the label attribute of the option element. This property is intended for use with hierarchical menus, but it is not operational in browsers except for IE 5/Mac, where it returns the same value as the text property.

| | |
|---|---|
| **Value** | String. |
| **Default** | None. |

# selected

**Read/Write**

Determines whether the list option has been selected by the user, meaning that its value is submitted with the form. Scripts can modify the value to select an item algorithmically. To find out which option is selected, it is more efficient to use the select object's selectedIndex property, rather than looping through all options in search of those whose selected properties are true. The exception to this is when the select element is set to allow multiple selections, in which case you need to cycle through them all to find the chosen items.

| | |
|---|---|
| **Example** | `document.forms[0].selectList.options[3].selected = true;` |
| **Value** | Boolean value: true \| false. |
| **Default** | false |

# text

**Read/Write**

Provides the text associated with the option element. This text is located between the start and end tags; it is what appears in the select element on screen. A hidden value associated with the list item can be stored, retrieved, and changed via the value property.

**Example**

```
var list = document.forms[0].selectList;
var listItemText = list.options[list.selectedIndex].text;
```

| **Value** | String. |
| **Default** | None. |

## value
NN 4    IE 4    DOM 1<br>Read/Write

Provides the value associated with the option element. If the option element has a value attribute or value property set, this is the value returned for the value property; otherwise, the property returns an empty string.

| **Example** | `var itemValue = document.forms[0].selectList.options[2]value;` |
| **Value** | String. |
| **Default** | None. |

# options
NN 2    IE 3    DOM 1

An array of option elements nested within a select object.

### Object Model Reference
```
[window.]document.formName.selectName.options
[window.]document.forms[i].elements[i].options
[window.]document.getElementById("selectElementID").options
```

### Object-Specific Properties
length

### Object-Specific Methods
| add( ) | item( ) | namedItem( ) | remove( ) | tags( ) | urns( ) |

## length
NN 2    IE 3    DOM 1<br>Read-only

Returns the number of elements in the collection.

| **Example** | `var howMany = document.forms[0].mySelect.options.length;` |
| **Value** | Integer. |

## add( )
NN n/a    IE 4    DOM n/a

add(*elementRef*[, *index*])

Adds an already-created element (from the createElement( ) method) to the current collection. The element must be of the option type. By default, the new element is added as the last item of the collection unless you specify an index value as a second parameter (in which case all existing items from that index position get pushed down by one). The following example sequence appends a new item to a select object:

```
var newElem = document.createElement("option");
newElem.text = "Freddy";
newElem.value = "Freddy Mercury";
document.forms[1].rockers.options.add(newElem);
```

Notice that a generic object is created first. Then its properties are stuffed with values, and the new element is added to the select element.

For an example of a cross-browser and backward-compatible approach to this task, see the option object discussion. Also see the select.add( ) method for a W3C DOM approach that works with Netscape 6.

**Returned Value**    None.

**Parameters**

*elementRef*

A fully-formed element object reference, usually generated by the createElement( ) method.

*index*

An optional integer indicating where in the collection the new element should be placed.

## item( )    NN 6    IE 4    DOM 1

item(*index*[, *subindex*])
item(*index*)

Returns a single object or collection of objects corresponding to the element matching the index value (or, optionally, the index and subindex values).

**Returned Value**

One object or collection (array) of objects. If there are no matches to the parameters, the returned value is null.

**Parameters**

*index*

When the parameter is a zero-based integer, the returned value is a single element corresponding to the specified item in source code order (nested within the current element); when the parameter is a string (IE only), the returned value is a collection of elements with id properties that match that string.

*subindex*

In IE only, if you specify a string value for the first parameter, you can use the second parameter to specify a zero-based index that retrieves the specified element from the collection with id properties that match the first parameter's string value.

## namedItem( )     NN 6   IE 6   DOM 1
namedItem("*ID*")

Returns a single option object corresponding to the element matching the parameter string value.

**Returned Value**

One option object. If there are no matches to the parameters, the returned value is null.

**Parameters**

*ID*
 The string that contains the same value as the desired element's id attribute.

## remove( )     NN *n/a*   IE 4   DOM *n/a*
remove(*index*)

Deletes an element from the current collection. Simply specify the zero-based index value of the option element you wish to remove from the collection belonging to a select element. The following example deletes the first item from a select object:

 document.forms[1].rockers.options.remove(0);

The process for removing an option element is entirely different in Navigator. To delete an item, assign null to the item in the collection. For example, the Navigator version of the preceding IE example is as follows:

 document.forms[1].rockers.options[0] = null;

Regardless of the browser-specific process of removing an option from the select object, the length of the options array collapses to fill the space.

**Returned Value** None.

**Parameters**

*index*
 A zero-based integer indicating which item in the collection should be deleted.

## tags( )     NN *n/a*   IE 4   DOM *n/a*
tags("*tagName*")

Returns a collection of objects (among all objects nested within the current collection) with tags that match the *tagName* parameter. Implemented in all IE collections (see the all.tags( ) method), but redundant for collections of the same element type.

## urns( )     NN *n/a*   IE 5(Win)   DOM *n/a*
urns(*URN*)

See the all.urns( ) method.

# p

The p object reflects the p element.

**HTML Equivalent**   <p>

**Object Model Reference**
[window.]document.getElementById("*elementID*")

**Object-Specific Properties**
align

**Object-Specific Methods**
None.

**Object-Specific Event Handler Properties**
None.

## align

Read/Write

Determines how the paragraph text is justified within the p element's box.

| | |
|---|---|
| **Example** | document.getElementById("myP").align = "center"; |
| **Value** | Any of the three horizontal alignment string constants: center \| left \| right. |
| **Default** | left |

# page

The page object is a special type of style rule created via an @page CSS rule. In the W3C DOM, this object (known as the CSSPageRule object) inherits properties of the CSSRule object. But as of IE 6 for Windows, the page object does not adhere to this inheritance structure. This object lays the foundation for a more fully implemented notion of page boxes expected in future browser versions.

**HTML Equivalent**
<style type="text/css">
@page {*specifications*}
</style.

**Object Model Reference**
[window.]document.styleSheets.pages[i]

**Object-Specific Properties**

| pseudoClass | selectorText | style |
|---|---|---|

**Object-Specific Methods**
None.

**Object-Specific Event Handler Properties**
None.

| pseudoClass | NN *n/a* | IE *5.5(Win)* | DOM *n/a* |
| --- | --- | --- | --- |
| | | | Read-only |

Returns the name of the pseudo-class associated with the @page rule (if any).

| **Example** | var pClass = document.styleSheets[2].pages[0].pseudoClass; |
| --- | --- |
| **Value** | String pseudo-class names (including leading colon): :first \| :left \| :right. |
| **Default** | None. |

| selectorText | NN *n/a* | IE *5.5(Win)* | DOM *n/a* |
| --- | --- | --- | --- |
| | | | Read/Write |

Provides the selector of the @page rule (if any).

| **Example** | document.styleSheets[2].pages[0].selectorText = ":right"; |
| --- | --- |
| **Value** | String. |
| **Default** | None. |

| style | NN *n/a* | IE *n/a* | DOM *2* |
| --- | --- | --- | --- |
| | | | Read-only |

Returns the style object (of type CSSStyleDeclaration in the W3C DOM) reflecting the style attributes and properties of the @page rule.

| **Value** | style object reference. |
| --- | --- |
| **Default** | None. |

# pages

| | NN *n/a* | IE *5.5(Win)* | DOM *n/a* |
| --- | --- | --- | --- |

Provides an array of page objects (@page rules) nested within a styleSheet object.

**Object Model Reference**
[window.]document.styleSheets.pages

**Object-Specific Properties**
length

## Object-Specific Methods
item( )

## Object-Specific Event Handler Properties
None.

---

# length

Returns the number of objects in the collection.

**Example**        `var howMany = document.styleSheets.pages.length;`
**Value**          Integer.

---

# item( )

item(*index*)

Returns a single object corresponding to the element matching the index value.

## Returned Value
Reference to a page object. If there are no matches to the parameters, the returned value is null.

## Parameters
*index*
   A zero-based integer corresponding to the specified item in source code order.

---

# param

The param object reflects the param element, which passes variable values to ActiveX objects (IE/Windows only), Java applets, and some plugins. Such programs are written to read parameter name/value pairs during initialization so the values are ready to go when the program starts (e.g., the URL of a sound file). IE for Windows commonly assigns a full suite of parameters to some ActiveX controls, even though only a handful might be explicitly defined in the source code. Although properties are read/write, assigning new values after the page has loaded does not convey the new values to the external program.

## HTML Equivalent
<param>

## Object Model Reference
[window.]document.getElementById("*elementID*")

## Object-Specific Properties

| name | type | value | valueType |
| --- | --- | --- | --- |

**Object-Specific Methods**
None.

**Object-Specific Event Handler Properties**
None.

## name
NN 6   IE 5   DOM 1<br>Read/Write

This is the name of the external program's parameter to which a value in the param element applies.

| | |
|---|---|
| **Example** | `var pName = document.getElementById("audioParam2").name;` |
| **Value** | String. |
| **Default** | None. |

## type
NN 6   IE 5   DOM 1<br>Read/Write

Provides the MIME type for a param element with a valuetype attribute set to "ref".

**Example**
```
if (document.getElementById("myParam").valueType == "ref") {
    var pType = document.getElementById("myParam").type;
}
```

| | |
|---|---|
| **Value** | Case-insensitive MIME type as string. A catalog of registered MIME types is available from *ftp://ftp.isi.edu/in-notes/iana/assignments/media-types/*. |
| **Default** | None. |

## value
NN 6   IE 5(Mac)/6(Win)   DOM 1<br>Read/Write

Indicates the string value assigned to a named parameter for the external program.

| | |
|---|---|
| **Example** | `var pVal = document.getElementById("volumeParam").value;` |
| **Value** | String. |
| **Default** | None. |

## valueType
NN 6   IE 5(Mac)/6(Win)   DOM 1<br>Read/Write

Indicates the string classification of the parameter set by the element.

| | |
|---|---|
| **Example** | `var pValType = document.getElementById("volumeParam").valueType;` |

| Value | String constant: data | object | ref. |
| Default | data |

## password

See input (type="password").

## personalbar

See directories.

## plaintext                                    NN *n/a*   IE *4*   DOM *1*

The plaintext object reflects the plaintext element. Note that the Win32 version of Internet Explorer 4 incorrectly evaluates the innerHTML, innerText, outerHTML, and outerText property values to include all document content following the start tag for the element. This element is deprecated in favor of the pre element.

### HTML Equivalent
<plaintext>

### Object Model Reference
[window.]document.getElementById("*elementID*")

### Object-Specific Properties
None.

### Object-Specific Methods
None.

### Object-Specific Event Handler Properties
None.

## plugin                                        NN *3*   IE *5(Mac)*   DOM *n/a*

A plugin object represents a single plugin that is registered with the browser at launch time. Access to a single plugin is normally via the navigator.plugins array. It is also common to use the navigator.mimeTypes array and associated properties to uncover whether the browser has the desired plugin installed before loading external content. Most of the properties provide scripted access to information normally found in the **About Plug-ins** window available from Navigator's **Help** menu and IE/Macintosh **File Helper** preferences. IE for Windows uses a different technique (involving the object element loading ActiveX controls) to determine support for playing external media.

**Object Model Reference**
navigator.plugins[i]

**Object-Specific Properties**

| description | filename | length | name |
|---|---|---|---|

**Object-Specific Methods**
refresh( )

## description

NN 3   IE 5(Mac)   DOM n/a<br>Read-only

Provides a brief plain-language description of the plugin supplied by the plugin manufacturer.

| **Example** | var descr = navigator.plugins[2].description; |
|---|---|
| **Value** | String. |
| **Default** | None. |

## filename

NN 3   IE 5(Mac)   DOM n/a<br>Read-only

Returns the filename of the plugin binary. In Win32 versions of Navigator, the full pathname is returned; for the Mac (both Navigator and IE), only the filename is returned.

| **Example** | var file = navigator.plugins[2].filename; |
|---|---|
| **Value** | String. |
| **Default** | None. |

## length

NN 3   IE 5(Mac)   DOM n/a<br>Read-only

Returns the number of MIME types supported by the plugin. Don't confuse this property with the length property of the entire navigator.plugins array, which measures how many plugin objects are known to the browser.

| **Example** | var howManyMIMEs = navigator.plugins[2].length; |
|---|---|
| **Value** | Integer. |
| **Default** | None. |

## name

NN 3   IE 5(Mac)   DOM n/a<br>Read-only

Returns the name of the plugin assigned to it by its manufacturer. You cannot, however, be guaranteed that a plugin designed for multiple operating systems has the same name across all versions.

| **Example** | `var pName = navigator.plugins[2].name;` |
| **Value** | Integer. |
| **Default** | None. |

## refresh( )

Instructs the browser to reregister plugins installed in the plugins directory. This allows a browser to summon a newly installed plugin without forcing the user to quit and relaunch the browser.

| **Returned Value** | None. |
| **Parameters** | None. |

# plugins

Navigator and Internet Explorer both have a plugins array, but they are quite different collections of objects. Navigator's and IE/Macintosh's plugins array is a property of the navigator object. Each item in the navigator.plugins array represents a plugin that is installed in the browser (actually just registered with the browser when the browser last loaded). See the plugin object.

On the Windows side, Internet Explorer's plugins collection belongs to the document object and essentially mirrors the embeds collection: a collection of all embed elements in the document. An embed element may well, indeed, launch a plugin, but not necessarily. Nor does Internet Explorer for Windows provide JavaScript access to the installed plugins in the same way that Navigator does (IE for Macintosh provides no such access).

### Object Model Reference
*NN* navigator.plugins
*IE* document.plugins

### Object-Specific Properties
length

### Object-Specific Methods
item( )        namedItem( )

## length

Returns the number of elements in the collection.

### Example
```
var IEhowMany = document.plugins.length;
var NNhowMany = navigator.plugins.length;
```
**Value**        Integer.

## item( ) NN 6    IE 4(Win)    DOM n/a

```
item(index[, subindex])
item(index)
```

Returns a single object or collection of objects corresponding to the item matching the index value (or, optionally, the index and subindex values).

### Returned Value

One object or collection (array) of objects. If there are no matches to the parameters, the returned value is null.

### Parameters

*index*
> When the parameter is a zero-based integer, the returned value is a single element corresponding to the specified item in source code order (nested within the current element). When the parameter is a string (IE only), the returned value is a collection of elements with name properties that match that string.

*subindex*
> In IE only, if you specify a string value for the first parameter, you can use the second parameter to specify a zero-based index that retrieves the specified element from the collection with name properties that match the first parameter's string value.

## namedItem( ) NN 6    IE 6    DOM n/a

```
namedItem("name")
```

Returns a single plugin (NN) or embed (IE) object corresponding to the element matching the parameter string value.

### Returned Value

One plugin (NN) or embed (IE) object. If there are no matches to the parameters, the returned value is null.

### Parameters

*name*
> The string that contains the same value as the desired object's name attribute.

# popup NN n/a    IE 5.5(Win)    DOM n/a

A popup object is a featureless rectangular space that has none of the typical browser window chrome (borders, scrollbars, title bar, etc.) nor any reference path back to the main document. Scripts must create the popup object to a specific size and location, and populate the window with content by assigning an HTML string to the popup's document.body.innerHTML property. Your scripts must also help this region stand out from the document by assigning background colors and borders to either the popup's document.body.style property or the styles of elements inside the popup.

While this popup object holds what is essentially a document object, it is not related to the window object in any way, and therefore may not load external documents. It does, however, have the helpful characteristic of transcending frame and even browser window borders, giving the appearance of an operating-system level HTML content holder. Thus, you could use it for a drop-down menu or an annotation that needs to flow across frame borders or extend beyond the browser window edge.

A popup is a transient visual element. A click anywhere outside of the popup causes the popup to disappear. But you can assign the full range of mouse events to the elements in the popup's document, for effects such as rollovers and menu item clicks. The HTML content may also contain images.

To create a popup object, use the window.createPopup( ) method. Here is a simple example of the typical creation, population, and display sequence:

```
var popup = window.createPopup( );
var bod = popup.document.body;
bod.style.border = "3px solid #ff8800";
bod.style.padding = "2px";
bod.style.backgroundColor = "lightyellow";
bod.innerHTML =
  "<p style='font-family:Arial, sans-serif; font-size:10px'>Some popup text.</p>";
popup.show(100, 100, 100, 26, document.body);
```

### Object Model Reference
*popupObjectRef*

### Object-Specific Properties
document          isOpen

### Object-Specific Methods
hide( )          show( )

### Object-Specific Event Handler Properties
None.

## document

NN *n/a*     IE *5.5(Win)*     DOM *n/a*

Read-only

Returns a reference to the document object inside the popup object. Most (but not all) regular document object properties apply to the popup's document object. It is the primary gateway to assigning HTML content to the popup. This property is read-only, but the document object's properties are read/write to allow you to assign values to its content.

**Example**      *popupRef*.document.body.innerHTML = "<p>Howdy, pardner!</p>";

**Value**      document object reference.

**Default**      The current document object.

## isOpen

NN *n/a*    IE *5.5(Win)*    DOM *n/a*

Read-only

Returns a Boolean value revealing whether the popup object is visible. Even after the popup object is hidden, its content is still accessible to scripts.

**Example**

```
if (popupRef.isOpen) {
    popupRef.hide();
}
```

**Value**          Boolean value: true | false.

**Default**        false

## hide( )

NN *n/a*    IE *5.5(Win)*    DOM *n/a*

Hides the popup object. Generally invoked from scripts triggered by user actions on the popup's content.

**Returned Value**    Nothing.

**Parameters**        None.

## show( )

NN *n/a*    IE *5.5(Win)*    DOM *n/a*

show(*left, top, width, height*[, *positioningElemRef*])

Shows the popup object, usually after its content has been assigned. All dimensions and position are set via parameters. The position may optionally be established relative to an element in the main document. Position and positioning element parameters may come from event object properties (event.clientX, event.clientY, and event.srcElement).

**Returned Value**    None.

**Parameters**

*left*
> Horizontal pixel coordinate relative to the left edge of the screen or, if specified by the optional parameter, an HTML element.

*top*
> Vertical pixel coordinate relative to the top edge of the screen or, if specified by the optional parameter, an HTML element.

*width*
> Outer pixel width of the popup space.

*height*
> Outer pixel height of the popup space.

*positioningElemRef*
> An optional reference to any element accessible to the script invoking the method. Establishes a coordinate context for the *left* and *top* parameters.

# pre

The pre object reflects the pre element for preformatted text.

**HTML Equivalent**
<pre>

**Object Model Reference**
[window.]document.getElementById("*elementID*")

**Object-Specific Properties**
width

**Object-Specific Methods**
None.

**Object-Specific Event Handler Properties**
None.

# width

Read/Write

Provides the character column count for the monospaced content of the element. Only Netscape 6 reflows the content in response to changes of this property.

| | |
|---|---|
| **Example** | document.getElementById("codeExample2").width = 40; |
| **Value** | Integer. |
| **Default** | -1 (Netscape 6); None (IE). |

# ProcessingInstruction

The ProcessingInstruction object (one of the node types) is an abstract representation in the W3C DOM of an element that contains instructions for an application, but whose content is not treated as part of the document's content tree. Such elements in XML documents are tagged with the format <?*ProcessTarget InstructionText*?>. In the W3C DOM, the two main components are exposed as the target and data string properties, respectively.

# q

The q object reflects the q element for inline quotations. Although IE for Windows includes (probably erroneously) the cite property for all elements (and causes that property to be listed among the shared properties earlier in this chapter), this object employs the cite property only for IE for Macintosh and Netscape 6.

**HTML Equivalent**
<q>

**Object Model Reference**
[window.]document.getElementById("*elementID*")

**Object-Specific Properties**
None.

**Object-Specific Methods**
None.

**Object-Specific Event Handler Properties**
None.

# radio

See input (type="radio").

# Range                                         NN 6    IE n/a    DOM 2

The W3C DOM Range object—similar in concept to the IE TextRange object—represents a sequence of zero or more rendered text characters in a document. When a text range consists of zero characters, it represents an insertion point between two characters (or before the first or after the last character of the document). The Range object automatically keeps track of the node and character offset references for the start and end points of the range, so its methods can copy existing content, delete the range's contents, or insert new contents (in node form) into the existing range while maintaining the integrity of the document tree at every step. Nodeness is important to the Range object, but most of those concerns are handled for you.

A Range object is created via the document.createTextRange( ) method or by turning a user selection into a range via window.getSelection( ).getRangeAt(0). Once a text range is created, use its methods to adjust its start and end point to encompass a desired segment of the text. The choose from a set of additional methods to act on the range. See Chapter 5 for details and examples of using the Range object and how its syntax varies from that of the IE TextRange object.

**Object Model Reference**
document.createRange( )

**Object-Specific Properties**

| | | |
|---|---|---|
| collapsed | commonAncestorContainer | endContainer |
| endOffset | startContainer | startOffset |

**Object-Specific Methods**

| | | |
|---|---|---|
| cloneContents( ) | cloneRange( ) | collapse( ) |
| compareBoundaryPoints( ) | compareNode( ) | comparePoint( ) |
| createContextualFragment( ) | deleteContents( ) | detach( ) |
| extractContents( ) | insertNode( ) | intersectsNode( ) |

| isPointInRange( ) | selectNode( ) | selectNodeContents( ) |
| setEnd( ) | setEndAfter( ) | setEndBefore( ) |
| setStart( ) | setStartAfter( ) | setStartBefore( ) |
| surroundContents( ) | toString( ) | |

**Object-Specific Event Handler Properties**
None.

## collapsed

NN *6*    IE *n/a*    DOM *2*

Read-only

Returns Boolean true if the range's start and end points are at the same location, encompassing zero characters. A collapsed range can be located anywhere within the document.

**Example**
```
if (rng.collapsed) {
    // act on collapsed text range
}
```

**Value**          Boolean value: true | false.

**Default**          None.

## commonAncestorContainer

NN *6*    IE *n/a*    DOM *2*

Read-only

Returns a reference to a document tree node that is the next outermost container that encompasses the current range's start and end points. If the start and end points are, themselves, in the same node (for example, the same text node), the commonAncestorContainer property returns a reference to that node's parent node. IE TextRange equivalent is parentElement( ).

**Example**          var containingElem = rng.commonAncestorContainer;

**Value**          Reference to a node object (commonly an element node type).

**Default**          None.

## endContainer

NN *6*    IE *n/a*    DOM *2*

Read-only

Returns a reference to a document tree node that contains the current range's end point.

**Example**          var containingElemRight = rng.endContainer;

**Value**          Reference to a node object.

**Default**          None.

# endOffset

**Read-only**

Returns an integer count of characters or nodes for the end point's location within the node reported by the endContainer property. If the endContainer is a text node, the endOffset property counts the number of characters to the right of the first character of that text node. If the endContainer is an element node, the endOffset property counts the number of nodes between the start of the containing node's content and the end point.

As an example, consider the following document segment that shows a text range in bold-face characters, with the start and end points signified by pipe characters:

```
<p>One paragraph with |a <span>nested</span>| element inside.</p>
```

Note that the start point is within a text node, while the end point sits just outside the span element end tag. The Range object's properties report values as shown in the following table.

| Property | Value | Description |
| --- | --- | --- |
| commonAncestorContainer | [object HTMLParagraphElement] | The p element embraces both the start and end points. |
| startContainer | [object Text] | Start point is within a text node. |
| startOffset | 19 | Start point is at the 20th (zero-based index of 19) character from the start of its container, the text node. |
| endContainer | [object HTMLParagraphElement] | End point is designated as the end of the span element, which makes the next outer p element the end point's container. |
| endOffset | 2 | End point is at the 3rd (zero-based index of 2) node in the context of its endContainer p element (first node is a text node; second node is the span element; end point is at the start of the third node of the p element). |

**Example**      var rngEndOff = rng.endOffset;

**Value**        Integer.

**Default**      None.

# startContainer

**Read-only**

Returns a reference to a document tree node that contains the current range's start point.

**Example**      var containingElemLeft = rng.startContainer;

**Value**        Reference to a node object.

**Default**      None.

## startOffset

Returns an integer count of characters or nodes for the start point's location within the node reported by the startContainer property. If the startContainer is a text node, the startOffset property counts the number of characters to the right of the first character of that text node. If the startContainer is an element node, the startOffset property counts the number of nodes between the start of the containing node's content and the start point. See endOffset for more details.

| | |
|---|---|
| **Example** | var rngStartOff = rng.startOffset; |
| **Value** | Integer. |
| **Default** | None. |

## cloneContents( )

Returns a DocumentFragment node containing a copy of the contents from the current range. Any dangling nodes are resolved as part of the cloning process.

| | |
|---|---|
| **Returned Value** | Reference to a node of a document fragment type. |
| **Parameters** | None. |

## cloneRange( )

Returns a Range object that is a carbon copy of the current range, including references to associated containers. This method lets you preserve a copy of a Range object's specifications while creating a new Range object. Similar to the IE TextRange object's duplicate( ) method.

| | |
|---|---|
| **Returned Value** | Reference to a Range object. |
| **Parameters** | None. |

## collapse( )

collapse(*toStartFlag*)

Shrinks the current range to an insertion point (start and end points are in the same node at the same offset). The Boolean parameter controls whether the range collapses to the start point (true) or end point (false) of the current range. A script working its way through a document (e.g., using the String.indexOf( ) method to search for the next instance of a string) usually collapses to the end point before shifting the end point to the end of the body to perform the next String.indexOf( ) search.

**Returned Value**    None.

**Parameters**

*toStartFlag*
>    Boolean value that controls whether collapse occurs at the start point (true) or end point (false) of the current range.

## compareBoundaryPoints( )  NN 6    IE n/a    DOM 2

compareBoundaryPoints(*compareType, sourceRangeRef*)

Returns an integer code indicating the relative positioning of one boundary point of the current range's against a boundary point of a different text range. In the simplest case, the two end points (one from each range) share the same ancestor container. In such a case, the first parameter determines which end points from the two ranges get compared. Use the constants supplied with every Range object, as shown in the following table.

| Comparison type | Description |
| --- | --- |
| *rng*.START_TO_START | Comparing the start position of the current range against the start position of the source range |
| *rng*.START_TO_END | Comparing the start position of the current range against the end position of the source range |
| *rng*.END_TO_END | Comparing the end position of the current range against the end position of the source range |
| *rng*.END_TO_START | Comparing the end poisition of the current range against the start position of the source range |

If the first boundary in the comparison occurs earlier in the document than the second boundary, the returned value is –1; if the first boundary comes after the second boundary, the returned value is 1; if the two boundaries are in the identical position, the returned value is 0. Similar to the IE TextRange object's compareEndPoints( ) method.

But the situation can be more complex if the boundary points being compared have different ancestor container nodes. The offset values with respect to container nodes influence the comparison results. Due to the variety of results that can occur with numerous relationships between the compared end points, your scripts will need to perform an intricate analysis of boundaries to assure comparisons report the desired sequence. On the other hand, simply looking for unanimity of boundary points is a much simpler prospect. You may prefer to limit your comparisons to looking only for return values of zero (or any other value) for a more binary determination of boundary comparisons.

**Returned Value**    Integer values –1, 0, or 1.

### Parameters

*compareType*
> Integer values from 0 to 3 corresponding to comparison types. Integer values are not aligned with the W3C DOM standard in Netscape 6 or 7, but the plain-language constants (such as *rng*.START_TO_START, shown in the table above) produce the correct comparisons.

*sourceRangeRef*
> Reference to a second, previously defined Range object, perhaps preserved through the cloneRange( ) method.

## compareNode( )  NN 6    IE n/a    DOM n/a

compareNode(*nodeReference*)

A Netscape-only method that returns an integer code indicating the relative position of some other node with respect to the current range. Four plain-language constants are members of every Netscape Range object, and can be used for comparisons of values returned by the compareNode( ) method. Note that the returned values are from the point of view of the node passed as a parameter, rather than from that of the current range.

Returned values and constants are as follows.

| Constant | Value | Description |
|---|---|---|
| *rng*.NODE_BEFORE | 0 | Entire node comes before the range. |
| *rng*.NODE_AFTER | 1 | Entire node comes after the range. |
| *rng*.NODE_BEFORE_AND_AFTER | 2 | Node starts before the current range and ends after it. |
| *rng*.NODE_INSIDE | 3 | Node is contained in its entirety within the scope of the range. |

By way of example:

```
if (rng.compareNode(document.getElementById("myElem")) == rng.NODE_INSIDE) {
    // process for myElem node being contained by the range
}
```

**Returned Value**      Integer values 0, 1, 2, or 3.

**Parameters**

*nodeReference*
> Reference to any node in the document tree.

## comparePoint( )                     NN 6    IE *n/a*    DOM *n/a*

compareNode(*nodeReference, offset*)

A Netscape-only method that returns an integer code indicating the relative position of some other node and offset within that node with respect to the current range. Note that the returned values are from the point of view of the node (more specifically, the point signified by the offset within the node) passed as parameters, rather than from that of the current range.

Returned values are as follows.

| Value | Description |
|---|---|
| -1 | Point comes before the start of the range. |
| 0 | Point is located within the range. |
| 1 | Point comes after the end of the range. |

By way of example:

```
if (rng.comparePoint(document.getElementById("myElem"), 2) == 0) {
    // process for offset of 2 within myElem node being contained by the range
}
```

**Returned Value**      Integer values -1, 0, 1.

**Parameters**

*nodeReference*

Reference to any node in the document tree.

*offset*

Integer offset, counting either nested nodes within an element or characters within a text node.

## createContextualFragment( )                NN *6*   IE *n/a*   DOM *n/a*

createContextualFragment(*contentString*)

The createContextualFragment( ) method was initially designed as an alternative to the innerHTML convenience property (because the W3C DOM provides little in the way of support for content strings consisting of tags). This method accepts any string—including tagged content—as a parameter, and returns a DocumentFragment type of node, ready for appending or inserting into the document tree. Subsequent adoption of the innerHTML property by the Mozilla browser makes this method redundant, except that it is more consistent with the overall nodeness of the W3C DOM.

**Returned Value**

Reference to a document fragment type of node outside of the document tree. This node can then be applied to the document tree.

**Parameters**

*contentString*

Document content in string form, including tags and attributes.

## deleteContents( )                          NN *6*   IE *n/a*   DOM *2*

Removes the contents of the current text range from the document tree. If the range is an element node (e.g., with boundaries established via the selectNode( ) method), invoking deleteContents( ) on the range removes the node from the document tree and collapses the range. The Range object remains in memory, but without any content. If you want to capture the content prior to its deletion, do so with other Range object methods (such as cloneRange( ) and, when it works correctly, cloneContents( )).

**Returned Value**   None.

**Parameters**       None.

## detach( )                                  NN *6*   IE *n/a*   DOM *2*

Destroys the current Range object to the extent that invoking most methods on the object or accessing its properties throw a RangeException of type INVALID_STATE_ERR.

**Returned Value**   None.

**Parameters**       None.

## extractContents( ) NN *6*    IE *n/a*    DOM *2*

Returns a DocumentFragment node containing the contents of the current range, after removing the contents from the document tree. Not working in Netscape as of Version 6.2 except when the range boundaries are set via the selectNodeContents( ) method.

**Returned Value**    Reference to a node of a document fragment type.

**Parameters**    None.

## insertNode( ) NN *6*    IE *n/a*    DOM *2*

insertNode(*nodeReference*)

Inserts a node at the start of the current text range. Most useful when the range is already collapsed as a text insertion pointer. The node being inserted can be created fresh (via document.createElement( )) or fetched from elsewhere in the document tree, in which case it is removed from its old position and inserted into the current range. If you insert a text node adjacent to a spot that also happens to be an existing text node, you can wind up with two adjacent text nodes. Invoke the normalize( ) method on the parent to consolidate the text nodes.

**Returned Value**    Nothing

**Parameters**

*nodeReference*
> Reference to any text, element, or document fragment node to be inserted into the range.

## intersectsNode( ) NN *6*    IE *n/a*    DOM *n/a*

intersectsNode(*nodeReference*)

Returns Boolean true if any part of the current range overlaps with the text or element node that is passed as a parameter. If your script detects an intersection, it can use the compareNode( ) method to obtain more detail about the intersection.

**Returned Value**    Boolean value: true | false.

**Parameters**

*nodeReference*
> Reference to any text or element in the document tree.

## isPointInRange( ) NN *6*    IE *n/a*    DOM *n/a*

isPointInRange(*nodeReference, offset*)

Returns Boolean true if the location denoted by the parameter values (a node in the document tree and an offset location within that node) is within the current range.

**Returned Value**    Boolean value: true | false.

## Parameters

*nodeReference*
> Reference to any text or element in the document tree.

*offset*
> Integer offset, counting either nested nodes within an element or characters within a text node.

## selectNode( ), selectNodeContents( )      NN *6*    IE *n/a*    DOM *2*

selectNode(*nodeReference*)
selectNodeContents(*nodeReference*)

Sets the range's boundary points to encompass a node or just the node's contents. Despite the methods' names, no body text in the rendered document is highlighted.

Your choice of method impacts the way the range's startContainer and endContainer properties are filled. In the following sequence, you see what happens to the range and its properties when an element node and a text node are parameters to these methods. The initial HTML segment is:

```
<p>One paragraph with a <span id="myspan">nested</span> element inside.</p>
```

Selecting the span element (with the rng.selectNode(document.getElementById("myspan")) method) sets the range to:

```
<p>One paragraph with a |<span id="myspan">nested</span>| element inside.</p>
```

The Range object's properties report values as follows.

| Property | Value | Description |
| --- | --- | --- |
| startContainer | [object HTMLParagraphElement] | Start point is right before the span element. |
| startOffset | 1 | Start point is at the 2nd (zero-based index of 1) node inside the p element. |
| endContainer | [object HTMLParagraphElement] | End point is immediately after the span element. |
| endOffset | 2 | End point is at the 3rd (zero-based index of 2) node in the context of its endContainer p element. |

Using the rng.selectNodeContents(document.getElementById("myspan")) method to select the span element's contents sets the range to:

```
<p>One paragraph with a <span id="myspan">|nested|</span> element inside.</p>
```

The Range object's properties report values as follows.

| Property | Value | Description |
| --- | --- | --- |
| startContainer | [object HTMLSpanElement] | Start point is just inside the span element. |
| startOffset | 0 | Start point is at the 1st (zero-based index of 0) node inside the span element. |
| endContainer | [object HTMLSpanElement] | End point is immediately after the span element's content. |
| endOffset | 1 | End point is at a position where the 2nd (zero-based index of 1) node, if present, would be in the context of its endContainer span element. |

Using the `rng.selectNode(document.getElementById("myspan").firstChild)` method to select the text node inside the span element sets the range to:

```
<p>One paragraph with a <span id="myspan">|nested|</span> element inside.</p>
```

Even though the node passed as a parameter is different (and a different node type), the new range selection looks the same as the previous one. In fact, due to the way the node tree is structured, the Range object's properties report identical values as follows.

| Property | Value | Description |
| --- | --- | --- |
| startContainer | [object HTMLSpanElement] | Start point is just inside the span element. |
| startOffset | 0 | Start point is at the 1st (zero-based index of 0) node inside the span element. |
| endContainer | [object HTMLSpanElement] | End point is immediately after the span element's content. |
| endOffset | 1 | End point is at a position where the 2nd (zero-based index of 1) node, if present, would be in the context of its endContainer span element. |

Using the `rng.selectNodeContents(document.getElementById("myspan"))` method to select the contents of the text node inside the span element sets the range to:

```
<p>One paragraph with a <span id="myspan">||nested</span> element inside.</p>
```

In other words, the range collapses to an insertion point at the start of the text node (this may be a bug in Netscape 6), and the text node becomes the container, as shown in the following property enumeration.

| Property | Value | Description |
| --- | --- | --- |
| startContainer | [object Text] | Start point is at the beginning of the text node. |
| startOffset | 0 | Start point is at the 1st (zero-based index of 0) position of the text node. |
| endContainer | [object Text] | End point is collapsed. |
| endOffset | 0 | End point is collapsed. |

Element nodes tend to be the most practical parameter values to pass to either method.

**Returned Value**   None.

**Parameters**

*nodeReference*
   Reference to any text or element in the document tree.

## setEnd( ), setStart( )                                   NN 6   IE *n/a*   DOM 2

```
setEnd(nodeReference, offset)
setStart(nodeReference, offset)
```

Establish the document tree locations for the individual boundary points of an existing Range object. Similar to the IE TextRange object's setEndPoint( ) method. The mapping of a location relies upon a node reference and an offset value relative to that node's starting point and type. Offset values count child nodes when the *nodeReference* is an element node; they count characters when the *nodeReference* is a text node. To set a boundary at a node edge, the associated methods (setEndAfter( ) and three others) are more convenient.

**Returned Value**    None.

**Parameters**

*nodeReference*
> Reference to any element or text node in the document tree.

*offset*
> Integer offset, counting either nested nodes within an element or characters within a text node.

## setEndAfter( ), setEndBefore( ), setStartAfter( ), setStartBefore( )            NN 6   IE *n/a*   DOM 2

```
setEndAfter(nodeReference)
setEndBefore(nodeReference)
setStartAfter(nodeReference)
setStartBefore(nodeReference)
```

Establish the document tree locations for the individual boundary points of an existing Range object with respect to a node's edges. These methods assume that you are interested in setting a range's boundaries to places immediately before or after an existing node, and not concerned with other kinds of offsets. Range boundaries do not have to be symmetrical, allowing you to specify the start boundary relative to one node and the end boundary relative to a completely different node later in the document.

**Returned Value**    None.

**Parameters**

*nodeReference*
> Reference to any element or text node in the document tree.

## surroundContents( )                       NN 7   IE *n/a*   DOM 2

```
surroundContents(parentNodeReference)
```

Encapsulates the current range with a new container, usually a new element node created via the document.createElement( ) method. End points of the current range should have the same parent container prior to applying this method.

**Returned Value**    None.

**Parameters**

*parentNodeReference*
> Reference to a node that becomes the new containing parent for the range.

## toString( )

Returns a string of the body content contained by the range. No tags or attributes accompany the returned value.

**Returned Value**    String.

**Parameters**    None.

# RangeException

Some operations on W3C DOM Range objects can trigger errors, or, in the vernacular of JavaScript 1.5, throw exceptions if something goes wrong. The W3C DOM defines an object that conveys a code number corresponding to a well-defined, if somewhat limited, list of exceptions specifically related to Range objects. For example, if you attempt to set range boundaries to encompass non-content–related nodes (such as an Attr node), the selectNode( ) method with such a node as a parameter throws an exception whose code number is 2. This number corresponds to the exception that signals an attempt to perform an illegal or logically impossible action on a text range.

When eventually implemented in browsers, the scripting mechanism to work with range exceptions should be the same as described for the DOMException object. Range object property and method access can also throw DOMExceptions.

**Object Model Reference**
*errorObjectReference*

**Object-Specific Properties**
code

**Object-Specific Methods**
None.

**Object-Specific Event Handler Properties**
None.

## code
Read-only

Provides the integer corresponding to one of the defined Range object error types, as shown in the following table.

| Code | Constant | Most Likely Cause |
| --- | --- | --- |
| 1 | BAD_BOUNDARYPOINTS_ERR | The surroundContents( ) method was applied to a range with a nonapplicable end point |
| 2 | INVALID_NODE_TYPE_ERR | The method tried to work in a nonapplicable type of node |

| **Value** | Integer |
| **Default** | Determined by error. |

# reset

See input (type="reset").

## rows

NN 6    IE 4    DOM 1

Provides a collection of all tr element objects contained in a single table, tbody, tfoot, or thead element object. The rows collection of a table element includes all rows of the table, regardless of row groups. Collection members are sorted in source code order. Internet Explorer lets you use array notation or parentheses to access a single row in the collection (e.g., document.getElementById("myTable").rows[0], document.all.myTable.rows (0)).

**Object Model Reference**
document.getElementById("*tableOrSectionID*").rows

**Object-Specific Properties**
length

**Object-Specific Methods**

| item( ) | namedItem( ) | tags( ) | urns( ) |

**Object-Specific Event Handler Properties**
None.

## length

NN 6    IE 4    DOM 1
Read-only

Returns the number of elements in the collection.

| **Example** | var howMany = document.getElementById("myTable").rows.length; |
| **Value** | Integer. |

## item( )

NN 6    IE 4    DOM 1

item(*index*[, *subindex*])
item(*index*)

Returns a single tr object or collection of tr objects corresponding to the element matching the index value (or, optionally in IE, the index and subindex values).

**Returned Value**
One tr object or collection (array) of tr objects. If there are no matches to the parameters, the returned value is null.

## Parameters

*index*

> When the parameter is a zero-based integer, the returned value is a single element corresponding to the specified item in source code order (nested within the current element); when the parameter is a string (IE only), the returned value is a collection of elements with id properties that match that string.

*subindex*

> In IE only, if you specify a string value for the first parameter, you can use the second parameter to specify a zero-based index that retrieves the specified element from the collection with id properties that match the first parameter's string value.

## namedItem( )                           NN *6*   IE *6*   DOM *1*

`namedItem("`*ID*`")`

Returns a single `tr` object or collection of `tr` objects corresponding to the element matching the parameter string value.

### Returned Value

One `tr` object or collection (array) of `tr` objects. If there are no matches to the parameters, the returned value is `null`.

### Parameters

*ID*

> The string that contains the same value as the desired element's id attribute.

## tags( )                                NN *n/a*   IE *4*   DOM *n/a*

`tags(`*tagName*`)`

Returns a collection of objects (among all objects within the current collection) with tags that match the *tagName* parameter. Redundant here, because all elements have the same `tr` tag.

### Returned Value

A collection (array) of objects. If there are no matches to the parameters, the returned value is an array of zero length.

### Parameters

*tagName*

> This involves a string of the all-uppercase version of the element tag, for example, `document.getElementById("myTable").rows.tags("tr")`.

## urns( )                                NN *n/a*   IE *5(Win)*   DOM *n/a*

`urns(`*URN*`)`

See the `all.urns( )` method.

Alphabetical DOM
Reference

# rb, ruby, rt

NN *n/a*   IE *5*   DOM *n/a*

Of these three ruby text-related elements, only ruby and rt are officially supported as objects in the IE DOM. But an rb element (even though it has no structural or rendering powers as of IE 6) is also regarded as an element object. Even Netscape 6 sees these as valid HTML element objects (of unknown type). See the ruby element in Chapter 8 for details on the usage of these elements. As scriptable objects, they have no properties or methods beyond a generic HTML element object.

### Object Model Reference
document.getElementById("*elementID*")

### Object-Specific Properties
None.

### Object-Specific Methods
None.

### Object-Specific Event Handler Properties
None.

# rule

See CSSRule.

# rules

See CSSRules.

# runtimeStyle

NN *n/a*   IE *5(Win)*   DOM *n/a*

The runtimeStyle object (a property of all HTML element objects in IE 5 and later for Windows) acts like a super-powerful style object: setting any of its properties overrides that property's settings that may exist in explicitly coded style definitions. Thus, it over-powers global, imported, linked, and inline style definitions. This object shares nearly the same long list of properties and methods with the style object.

### Object Model Reference
[window.]document.getElementById("*elementID*").runtimeStyle

### Object-Specific Properties
See the style object.

### Object-Specific Methods
See the style object.

**Object-Specific Event Handler Properties**
None.

# s

See b.

# samp

See acronym.

# screen

The screen object refers to the video display on which the browser is being viewed. Many video control panel settings influence the property values, but only a handful of properties are shared among browser brands.

**Object Model Reference**
*NN* screen
*IE* [window.]screen

**Object-Specific Properties**

| | | | |
|---|---|---|---|
| availHeight | availLeft | availTop | availWidth |
| bufferDepth | colorDepth | deviceXDPI | deviceYDPI |
| fontSmoothingEnabled | height | logicalXDPI | logicalYDPI |
| pixelDepth | updateInterval | width | |

**Object-Specific Methods**
None.

**Object-Specific Event Handler Properties**
None.

## availHeight, availWidth

Provide the height and width of the content region of the user's video monitor in pixels. This measure does not include the 24-pixel task bar (Windows) or 20-pixel system menubar (Macintosh). IE/Macintosh miscalculates the height of the menu bar as 24 pixels. To use these values in creating a pseudo-maximized window, you also have to adjust the top-left position of the window.

**Example**
```
var newWind = window.open("","","height=" + screen.availHeight +
",width=" + screen.availWidth)
```

| | |
|---|---|
| **Value** | Integer of available pixels in vertical and horizontal dimensions. |
| **Default** | Depends on the user's monitor size. |

## availLeft, availTop

Provide the pixel coordinates of the left and top edges of the screen that is available for content. With the standard Windows Taskbar arrangement, both values are zero. But drag the Taskbar to the left or top of the screen, and the corresponding value increases to accommodate the bar's space. Navigator 4 for the Macintosh doesn't start its screen counting until just below the fixed menu bar, but for Netscape 6, the availTop property returns 20 for the menu bar height.

| | |
|---|---|
| **Example** | window.moveTo(screen.availLeft, screen.availTop); |
| **Value** | Integer. |
| **Default** | 0 (Windows); 20 (Macintosh) |

## bufferDepth

Specifies the setting of the offscreen bitmap buffer. Path animation smoothness may improve on some clients if you match the bufferDepth to the colorDepth values. Setting the bufferDepth to -1 forces IE to buffer at the screen's pixel depth (as set in the control panel), and colorDepth is automatically set to that value, as well (plus if a user changes the bits per pixel, the buffer is adjusted accordingly). A setting to any of the other permitted values (1, 4, 8, 15, 16, 24, or 32) buffers at that pixel depth and sets the colorDepth to that value. The client's display must be set to the higher bits-per-pixel values to take advantage of the higher settings in scripts.

| | |
|---|---|
| **Example** | screen.bufferDepth = 4; |
| **Value** | Any of the following allowed integers: -1 \| 0 \| 4 \| 8 \| 15 \| 16 \| 24 \| 32. |
| **Default** | 0 |

## colorDepth

Returns the number of bits per pixel used to display color in the video monitor or image buffer. Although this property is read-only, its value can be influenced by settings of the bufferDepth property (IE only). You can determine the color depth of the current video screen and select colors accordingly.

**Example**

```
if (screen.colorDepth > 8) {
    document.getElementById("pretty").color = "cornflowerblue";
```

```
    } else {
        document.getElementById("pretty").color = "blue";
    }
```

**Value**         Integer.

**Default**       Current video control panel setting.

## deviceXDPI, deviceYDPI, logicalXDPI, logicalYDPI    NN *n/a*   IE *6(Win)*   DOM *n/a*

All four properties concern themselves with the dots-per-inch resolution of display screens along the horizontal (x) and vertical (y) axes. A device density property returns the actual pixel density of the current display screen, as detected by the operating system. The logical density is the "normal" pixel density that most users and page authors work with (typically 96 dots per inch horizontally and vertically). These two sets of properties let scripts examine whether the user has a higher-than-usual pixel density display, which could make fixed-size items, such as images and pixel-sized fonts, appear uncomfortably small on the screen. In such cases, scripts can determine a scaling factor between the device and logical densities, and apply that factor to the style.zoom property of critical elements (or the entire document.body, for that matter). Users of high-density display systems may already have their IE application preferences set to automatic scaling, so these calculations aren't necessary.

**Example**
```
var normDPI = 96;
if ((screen.deviceXDPI == screen.logicalXDPI) && (screen.deviceXDPI > normDPI)) {
    document.body.style.zoom = normDPI / screen.logicalXDPI;
}
```

**Value**         Integer.

**Default**       96

## fontSmoothingEnabled    NN *n/a*   IE *4(Win)*   DOM *n/a*

Returns Boolean true if the user has enabled Smooth Edges for fonts in the Windows Display control panel. The setting may influence the font-related style sheet you link into a document.

**Example**
```
var styleFile = "css/corpStyle.css";
if (screen.fontSmoothingEnabled) {
    styleFile = "css/corpStyleFancy.css";
}
document.write("<link type='text/css' rel='stylesheet' href='" +
    styleFile + "'>");
```

**Value**         Boolean value: true | false.

**Default**       false

## height, width

**Read-only**

Return the number of pixels available vertically and horizontally in the client video monitor. This is the raw dimension. For the amount of screen space not covered by system bars, see availHeight and availWidth.

**Example**

```
if (screen.height > 480 && screen.width > 640) {
    ...
}
```

| | |
|---|---|
| **Value** | Integer of pixel counts. |
| **Default** | Depends on video monitor. |

## logicalXDPI, logicalYDPI

See deviceXDPI.

## pixelDepth

**Read-only**

Returns the number of bits per pixel used to display color in the video monitor. This value is similar to the colorDepth property, but it is not influenced by a potential custom color palette, as colorDepth is.

**Example**

```
if (screen.pixelDepth > 8) {
    document.getElementById("pretty").color = "cornflowerblue";
} else {
    document.getElementById("pretty").color = "blue";
}
```

| | |
|---|---|
| **Value** | Integer. |
| **Default** | Current video control panel setting. |

## updateInterval

**Read/Write**

Provides the time interval (in milliseconds) between screen updates. A value of zero lets the browser select an average that usually works best. The longer the interval, the more animation steps may be buffered and then ignored as the update fires to display the current state.

| | |
|---|---|
| **Example** | screen.updateInterval = 0; |
| **Value** | Positive integer or zero. |
| **Default** | 0 |

## width

See height.

# script

The script object reflects the script element. Internet Explorer 4 for Windows chokes on accessing or setting the innerHTML or innerText properties, but the equivalent text property is safe. IE 5 for the Macintosh implements the readyState property (shared among all elements in IE for Windows) for this object.

**HTML Equivalent**

<script>

**Object Model Reference**

[window.]document.getElementById("*elementID*")

**Object-Specific Properties**

| charset | defer | event | htmlFor | src | text | type |
|---------|-------|-------|---------|-----|------|------|

**Object-Specific Methods**

None.

**Object-Specific Event Handler Properties**

| Handler | NN | IE | DOM |
|---------|-----|-----|-----|
| onerror | n/a | 4 | n/a |
| onload | n/a | 4 | n/a |

## charset

**Read/Write**

Indicates the character encoding of the script content.

**Example**

```
if (document.getElementById("myScript").charset == "csISO5427Cyrillic") {
    // process for Cyrillic charset
}
```

**Value**   Case-insensitive alias from the character set registry (*ftp://ftp.isi.edu/in-notes/iana/assignments/character-sets*).

**Default**   Determined by browser.

## defer

Specifies whether the browser should proceed with rendering regular HTML content without looking for the script to generate content as the page loads. This value needs to be set in the script element's tag at runtime. When this property is set to true by the addition of the DEFER attribute to the tag, the browser does not have to hold up rendering further HTML content to parse the content of the script element in search of document.write( ) statements. Changing this property's value after the document loads does not affect the performance of the script or browser. Although Netscape 6 implements the property, it is not functional.

### Example
```
if (document.getElementById("myScript").defer = = "true") {
    ...
}
```

**Value**            Boolean value: true | false.

**Default**          false

## event

Internet Explorer's event model allows binding of object events to script elements with the help of the event and for attributes (see Chapter 6). The event property returns the setting for the event attribute. Not functional in Netscape 6.

### Example
```
if (document.getElementById("gizmoScript").event == "onresize") {
    ...
}
```

**Value**            Case-sensitive event name string.

**Default**          None.

## htmlFor

Returns the value (element ID) assigned to the for attribute of a script element. This attribute points to the ID of the element to which the script is bound when a specific event (set by the event attribute) fires for the element. Not functional in Netscape 6.

### Example
```
if (document.getElementById("helpScript").htmlFor == "helpButton") {
    ...
}
```

| | |
|---|---|
| **Value** | String. |
| **Default** | None. |

## src

Provides the URL of the *.js* script file imported into the current script element. If you assign a new *.js* file to an existing script element in IE, the previous *.js* file's scripts do not disappear. But any duplications of variable or functions names are overwritten by the definitions from the new file. While Netscape 6 and later do not complain when you assign a new value to this property, the assignment does not necessarily load the new scripts into the current window or frame.

**Example**

```
if (document.getElementsByTagName("script")[1].src == "scripts/textlib.js") {
    ...
}
```

| | |
|---|---|
| **Value** | Complete or relative URL as a string. |
| **Default** | None. |

## text

Indicates the text content of the element. Assigning script statements to this object has different results in various browsers. In late versions of IE for Windows, the new value is added to the existing script, even though the property no longer reports the previous script text; in Netscape 6, the assigned values are ignored; and in IE 5 for Macintosh, the property is treated as read-only.

| | |
|---|---|
| **Example** | `var scriptText = document.getElementById("script3").text;` |
| **Value** | String. |
| **Default** | None. |

## type

Provides an advisory about the content type of the script statements. The content type should tell the browser which scripting engine to use to interpret the script statements, such as text/javascript. The type attribute may eventually replace the language attribute as the one defining the scripting language in which the element's statements are written.

| | |
|---|---|
| **Example** | `var scriptMIMEtype = document.getElementById("script3").type;` |
| **Value** | String. |
| **Default** | None. |

# scripts

NN *n/a*    IE *4*    DOM *n/a*

A collection of all scripts defined or imported in a document, including those defined in the head or body portion. Collection members are sorted in source code order.

**Object Model Reference**

```
document.scripts
```

**Object-Specific Properties**

```
length
```

**Object-Specific Methods**

| item( ) | namedItem( ) | tags( ) | urns( ) |
|---------|--------------|---------|---------|

**Object-Specific Event Handler Properties**

None.

## length

NN *n/a*    IE *4*    DOM *n/a*<br>**Read-only**

Returns the number of elements in the collection.

| **Example** | `var howMany = document.scripts.length;` |
|-------------|------------------------------------------|
| **Value**   | Integer.                                 |

## item( )

NN *n/a*    IE *4*    DOM *n/a*

```
item(index[, subindex])
```

Returns a single object or collection of objects corresponding to the element matching the index value (or, optionally, the index and subindex values).

**Returned Value**

One object or collection (array) of objects. If there are no matches to the parameters, the returned value is `null`.

**Parameters**

*index*

> When the parameter is a zero-based integer, the returned value is a single element corresponding to the said numbered item in source code order (nested within the current element). When the parameter is a string, the returned value is a collection of elements with id properties that match that string.

*subindex*

> If you specify a string value for the first parameter, you may use the second parameter to specify a zero-based integer to retrieve a specific element from the collection with id properties that match the first parameter's string value.

## namedItem( )    NN *n/a*    IE *6*    DOM *n/a*

namedItem("*ID*")

Returns a single script object or collection of script objects corresponding to the element matching the parameter string value.

### Returned Value

One script object or collection (array) of script objects. If there are no matches to the parameters, the returned value is null.

### Parameters

*ID*

The string that contains the same value as the desired element's id attribute.

## tags( )    NN *n/a*    IE *4*    DOM *n/a*

tags(*tagName*)

Returns a collection of objects (among all objects within the current collection) with tags that match the *tagName* parameter. Redundant here, because all elements have the same script tag.

### Returned Value

A collection (array) of objects. If there are no matches to the parameters, the returned value is an array of zero length.

### Parameters

*tagName*

A string of the all-uppercase version of the element tag, as in document.scripts. tags("script").

## urns( )    NN *n/a*    IE *5(Win)*    DOM *n/a*

urns(*URN*)

See the all.urns( ) method.

# scrollbars

See directories.

# select    NN *2*    IE *3*    DOM *1*

The select object reflects the select element. This element is a form control that contains option elements. Note that the innerHTML and innerText properties are not available on the Macintosh version of Internet Explorer 4. The shared disabled property is available for Netscape 6.

**HTML Equivalent**

`<select>`

**Object Model Reference**

```
[window.]document.formName.selectName
[window.]document.forms[i].elements[i]
[window.]document.getElementById("elementID")
```

**Object-Specific Properties**

| | | | | | |
|---|---|---|---|---|---|
| dataFld | dataSrc | form | length | multiple | name |
| options[] | selectedIndex | size | type | value | |

**Object-Specific Methods**

| | | | |
|---|---|---|---|
| add( ) | item( ) | namedItem( ) | remove( ) |

**Object-Specific Event Handler Properties**

| Handler | NN | IE | DOM |
|---|---|---|---|
| onblur | 2 | 4 | n/a |
| onchange | 2 | 4 | n/a |
| onfocus | 2 | 4 | n/a |

## dataFld

NN *n/a*    IE *4*    DOM *n/a*

**Read/Write**

Used with IE data binding to associate a remote data source column name with the selectedIndex property of the select object. A datasrc attribute must also be set for the element. Setting both the dataFld and dataSrc properties to empty strings breaks the binding between element and data source. Works only with text file data sources in IE 5/Mac.

**Example**    `document.forms[0].mySelect.dataFld = "choice";`

**Value**    Case-sensitive identifier of the data source column.

**Default**    None.

## dataSrc

NN *n/a*    IE *4*    DOM *n/a*

**Read/Write**

Used with IE data binding to specify the ID of the page's object element that loads the data source object for remote data access. Setting both the dataFld and dataSrc properties to empty strings breaks the binding between element and data source. Works only with text file data sources in IE 5/Mac.

**Example**    `document.forms[0].mySelect.dataSrc = "DBSRC3";`

**Value**    Case-sensitive identifier of the data source.

**Default**    None.

# form

**Read-only**

Returns a reference to the form element that contains the current element. When processing an event from this element, the event handler function automatically has access to the select element (as the event object's target or srcElement property). By reading the form property, the script can easily access other controls within the same form.

| | |
|---|---|
| **Example** | var theForm = evt.srcElement.form; |
| **Value** | form element object reference. |
| **Default** | None. |

# length

**Read/Write**

The number of option objects nested inside the select object. The value returned is the same as the select object options.length property, and can be safely used as a for loop maximum counter value to iterate through the nested option objects. The W3C DOM specifies that this property is read-only, but because the property has been read/write for some time in mainstream browsers, you can continue to adjust this value. By and large, the only modification made to this property, if at all, should be setting its value to zero to empty all options from the select object. Better still, if you are authoring for IE 5 and later or Netscape 6, use the select.remove( ) and select.add( ) methods to modify the contingent of option elements nested inside the select element.

| | |
|---|---|
| **Example** | document.forms[0].mySelect.length = 0; |
| **Value** | Integer. |
| **Default** | None. |

# multiple

**Read/Write**

Specifies whether the browser should render the select element as a list box and allow users to make multiple selections from the list of options. By default, the size property is set to the number of nested option elements, but the value may be overridden with the size property setting. To change a scrolling pick list to a popup menu, set the multiple property to false and the size property to 1. Users can select contiguous items by **Shift**-clicking on the first and last items of the group. To make discontiguous selections, Windows users must **Ctrl**-click on each item; Mac users must **Command**-click on each item. The multiple property has no effect when size is set to 1 to display a popup menu.

**Example**

```
if (document.entryForm.list3.multiple) {
    ...
}
```

**Alphabetical DOM Reference**

| Value | Boolean value: true \| false. |
|---|---|
| Default | false |

## name

This is the identifier associated with the form control. The value of this property is submitted as one-half of the name/value pair when the form is submitted to the server. Names are hidden from user view, since control labels are assigned via other means, depending on the control type. Form control names may also be used by script references to the objects. Despite the modern standards' preference for the id attribute, many browsers still require that a control be assigned a name attribute to allow the control's value to be submitted.

**Example**  `document.orderForm.payment.name = "credcard";`

**Value**  Case-sensitive string identifier that follows the rules of identifier naming: it may contain no whitespace, cannot begin with a numeral, and should avoid punctuation except for the underscore character.

**Default**  None.

## options[]

Returns an array of all option objects contained by the current element. Items in this array are indexed (zero-based) in source code order. For details on using this collection in a backward-compatible way for adding and removing option elements from a select element, see the options object. Loop through this collection in select elements set for multiple selections.

**Example**
```
var selVals = new Array();
for (var i = 0; i < document.forms[0].mySelect.length; i++) {
    if (document.forms[0].mySelect.options[i].selected) {
        selVals[selVals.length] = document.forms[0].mySelect.options[i].value;
    }
}
```

**Value**  Array of option objects.

**Default**  None.

## selectedIndex

This is the zero-based integer of the option selected by the user. If the select element is set to allow multiple selections, the selectedIndex property returns the index of the first selected item (see the selected property). You can use this property to gain access to the value or text of the selected item, as shown in the example.

In recent browsers, if no option is selected, the selectedIndex property returns -1. Setting the value to -1 to deselect all items works as you'd expect in IE 5 and later for Windows. For Netscape 6, setting the property to -1 may not empty the displayed option, but it does effectively deselect all items for a submitted form.

**Example**
```
var list = document.forms[0].selectList;
var listText = list.options[list.selectedIndex].text;
```

**Value**        Integer.

**Default**      None.

## size

Controls the number of rows displayed in a scrolling pick list, reflecting the size attribute of the select element. When set to true, the multiple property overrides a size value set to fewer than the number of options. To change a scrolling pick list to a popup menu, set the multiple property to false and the size property to 1.

**Example**       document.forms[0].choices.size = 6;

**Value**         Integer.

**Default**       None.

## type

Returns the type of form control element. A select object has two possible values, depending on whether the element is set to be a multiple-choice list. The value is returned in all lowercase letters. It may be necessary to cycle through all form elements in search of specific types to do some processing on (e.g., emptying all form controls of type "text" while leaving other controls untouched).

Note that Navigator 4 incorrectly reports a select object's type as select-multiple if the element's size attribute is set to any value larger than 1, even if the multiple attribute is not set. This is fixed in Netscape 6.

**Example**
```
if (document.forms[0].elements[3].type == "select-multiple") {
    ...
}
```

**Value**         Any of the following constants (as a string): button | checkbox | file | hidden | image | password | radio | reset | select-multiple | select-one | submit | text | textarea.

**Default**       Depends on value of multiple.

## value

This is the current value associated with the form control that is submitted with the name/ value pair for the element. All values are strings, but they may represent other kinds of data, including Boolean and numeric values. For browsers earlier than IE 4 and Netscape 6, scripts must retrieve the selected option's value by using the select object's selectedIndex property as an index into the options array, then inspect each option object's selected property to find the true one(s).

**Example**

```
if (document.forms[0].medium.value == "CD-ROM") {
   ...
}
```

**Value**        String.

**Default**      None.

## add( )

add(*newOptionElement*[, *positionIndex*])
add(*newOptionElement*, *optionElementReference*)

Adds a new option element to the current select element. Unfortunately, IE and Netscape 6 don't agree on the parameter values for this method. While all browsers require a reference to a newly created option element (the value returned from a document.createElement("option") method is appropriate for that), the second parameter varies with browser. In IE, the second parameter is optional and supplies a numeric index to the existing option element; the new option is inserted in front of that element. With no second parameter, the new option is appended to the existing option elements. In Netscape 6 (which implements the W3C DOM recommendation from the unfinished HTML module), the second parameter is required. The parameter is either a reference to an existing option element (the new option is inserted before that referenced option) or null (the new option is appended to the existing options).

**Returned Value**   None.

**Parameters**

*newOptionElement*

> Reference to an option element created by script, usually with the document. createElement( ) method.

*positionIndex*

> Optional IE integer parameter signifying the existing nested option element in front of which the new option is to be inserted. Omitting this parameter causes the new option to be appended to the end of the options list.

*optionElementReference*

> Reference to an option element in front of which the new option is to be inserted. You may also use null to append the new option to the end of the option list.

## item( )

item(*index*[, *subindex*])

Returns a single nested option object or collection of nested option objects corresponding to the element matching the index value (or, optionally, the index and subindex values).

### Returned Value

One object or collection (array) of objects. If there are no matches to the parameters, the returned value is null.

### Parameters

*index*

> When the parameter is a zero-based integer, the returned value is a single element corresponding to the said numbered item in source code order (nested within the current element). When the parameter is a string, the returned value is a collection of elements with id properties that match that string.

*subindex*

> If you specify a string value for the first parameter, you may use the second parameter to specify a zero-based integer to retrieve a specific element from the collection with id properties that match the first parameter's string value.

## namedItem( )

namedItem("*ID*")

Returns a single nested option object or collection of nested option objects corresponding to the element matching the parameter string value.

### Returned Value

One option object or collection (array) of option objects. If there are no matches to the parameters, the returned value is null.

### Parameters

*ID*

> The string that contains the same value as the desired element's id attribute.

## remove( )

remove(*positionIndex*)

Deletes an option element from the current select element at the zero-based index position signified by the parameter value. In lieu of setting the select object's length property to zero, you can remove all existing options with a simple loop construction:

```
while (selectElemRef.length > 0) {
    selectElemRef.remove(0);
}
```

At this point, you can populate the list with new options via the various approaches described in the add( ) method discussion and the options object discussion.

### Returned Value    None.

**Parameters**

*positionIndex*
　　Zero-based integer signifying the item from the nested options collection to be deleted.

# selection                                    NN *6*　　IE *4(Win)*　　DOM *n/a*

The selection object represents zero or more characters that have been explicitly selected in a document by the user or selected under script control. The objects are very different entities in the IE and Navigator browsers (observe compatibility ratings for properties and methods, below), and each has its own ways of providing script access to it.

In IE for Windows, you create a selection object via the document.selection property, which returns a selection object. To perform substantive actions on the content of the selection object, you then generate a TextRange object from the selection object (via the selection object's createRange( ) method). Use TextRange properties and methods to interact with the content. To convert a TextRange object to a visibly selected stretch of text on the page, use the TextRange object's select( ) method. This close linkage with the TextRange object means that the IE selection object is so far limited to Win32 versions. The IE selection object can include selected text inside an input (of type text) and textarea element.

In IE for the Macintosh, you don't have a selection object per se. Instead, it implements the Navigator 4 document.getSelection( ) method, which returns only the string contents of the selected text.

Navigator 4 offers script access to the text selected in a document through the use of the document.getSelection( ) method. This method is deprecated in Netscape 6, and even displays a warning (less harmful than an error) in the JavaScript Console if you use the method. In its place, Netscape 6 implements a robust selection object that offers a long list of properties and methods to interact with the object. Most of this functionality was made available starting with Netscape 6.2, including the way to create a selection object: the window.getSelection( ) method. Notice that many properties and methods of the Netscape 6 selection object have analogs with the Range object specification. In fact, it is through the Range object that scripts can highlight even discontiguous text spans on the page: create and size a Range object; then add that Range to the highlighted text via the selection object's addRange( ) method. Netscape 6 selections (as with the Range object) operate only on body content, and not on text inside editable text boxes.

Be aware that clicking on buttons in earlier browsers (including IE 5 for the Mac) deselects the current text selection. Therefore, all scripted action involving selections in these browsers must be triggered by onselect or onmouseup events, or functions invoked by a timer (see the window.setTimeout( ) method description in Chapter 12). More recent browsers maintain content selections while buttons are pressed.

**Object Model Reference**

*IE (Win)*
　　document.selection
*NN 6*
　　window.getSelection( )

---

## Object-Specific Properties

| anchorNode | anchorOffset | focusNode | focusOffset |
| isCollapsed | rangeCount | type | typeDetail |

## Object-Specific Methods

| addRange( ) | clear( ) | collapse( ) |
| collapseToEnd( ) | collapseToStart( ) | containsNode( ) |
| createRange( ) | createRangeCollection( ) | deleteFromDocument( ) |
| empty( ) | extend( ) | getRangeAt( ) |
| removeAllRanges( ) | removeRange( ) | selectAllChildren( ) |
| selectionLanguageChange( ) | toString( ) | |

## Object-Specific Event Handler Properties

None.

## anchorNode, focusNode

NN 6    IE *n/a*    DOM *n/a*

**Read-only**

Return a reference to the node where the user started (anchor) and ended (focus) the selection. Most typically, these are text node types. If the selection is set or extended via the addRange( ) method, these properties point to the node boundaries of the most recently added range.

### Example

```
var anchor = selectionRef.anchorNode;
if (anchor.nodeType == 3 && anchor.parentNode.tagName == "td") {
    // process selection start inside a table cell
}
```

**Value**         Reference to a document tree node, or null if no selection.

**Default**       null

## anchorOffset, focusOffset

NN 6    IE *n/a*    DOM *n/a*

**Read-only**

Return an integer count of characters or nodes from the beginning of the anchor or focus nodes of the selection (see anchorNode and focusNode properties). If the node is a text node, the offset unit is the character; if the node is an element node, the offset unit is the node. This behavior is similar to the offset properties of a Range object. Most typically, these values count characters within text node types. If the selection is set or extended via the addRange( ) method, these properties point to the node boundary offsets of the most recently added range.

**Example**       `var selStartOffset = selectionRef.anchorOffset;`

**Value**         Integer.

**Default**       0

## isCollapsed

NN 6   IE n/a   DOM n/a<br>Read-only

Returns Boolean true if the anchor and focus boundaries of a selection are identical.

**Example**
```
if (selectionRef.isCollapsed) {
    // selection is an insertion point
}
```

**Value**        Boolean value: true | false.

**Default**     true

## rangeCount

NN 6   IE n/a   DOM n/a<br>Read-only

Returns an integer count of Range objects (which may be discontiguous in Netscape 6) within the span of the selection. A manual selection by the user always contains one Range, but the addRange( ) method can tack on multiple, discontiguous ranges to the selection. To inspect each highlighted section's properties, use the getRangeAt( ) method.

**Example**     `var howMany = selectionRef.rangeCount;`

**Value**        Integer.

**Default**     0

## type

NN n/a   IE 4(Win)   DOM n/a<br>Read-only

Specifies whether the current selection object has one or more characters selected or is merely an insertion point.

**Example**
```
if (document.selection.type == "Text") {
    ...
}
```

**Value**

One of three constant values (as a string): None | Text | Control. The last one is possible only when HTML editing is engaged and control selections are possible.

**Default**     None

## typeDetail

NN n/a   IE 5.5(Win)   DOM n/a<br>Read-only

This property is supplied as a placeholder for other applications that may use the IE browser component. Such an application can provide additional selection type information as needed.

## addRange( )

addRange(*RangeReference*)

Turns a Range into a highlighted selection on the page. You can add as many discontiguous ranges to the selection as your application requires. Each addition increments the selection object's rangeCount property. Ranges may also overlap in a selection.

```
var selRef = window.getSelection( );
var rng = document.createRange( );
rng.selectNodeContents(document.getElementById("myP"));
selRef.addRange(rng);
```

**Returned Value**   None.

**Parameters**

*RangeReference*

Reference to a Range object with boundaries that have been established by Range object methods.

## clear( )

Deletes the content of the current selection in a document. For example, the event handler in the following tag deletes any selected text of the p element two seconds after the user starts making the selection:

```
<p onselectstart="setTimeout('document.selection.clear( )',2000);">
```

**Returned Value**   None.

**Parameters**   None.

## collapse( )

collapse(*nodeReference, offset*)

Collapses the current selection to a location specified by the two parameters. Any previously highlighted selection returns to normal display.

**Returned Value**   None.

**Parameters**

*nodeReference*

Reference to a text or element node in the document tree in which the collapsed selection should move.

*offset*

Integer count of characters or nodes within the *nodeReference* node where the collapsed selection should move. The count is relative to the start of the node. Units are character for text nodes, nodes for elements.

## collapseToEnd( ), collapseToStart( )　　　NN *6*　IE *n/a*　DOM *n/a*

Collapses the current selection to a location at the start (collapseToStart( )) or end (collapseToEnd( )) of the selection object. Any previously highlighted selection returns to normal display. If the selection consists of multiple ranges, the start or end boundary used for these collapse methods are at the outermost edges of the combined selection. After the collapse, the selection contains only one range.

**Returned Value**　　None.

**Parameters**　　None.

## containsNode( )　　　NN *6*　IE *n/a*　DOM *n/a*

containsNode(*nodeReference, entirelyFlag*)

Returns Boolean true if the current selection object contains a node passed as a parameter. The second parameter is supposed to let you loosen or tighten the definition of contains, but the behavior of the method seems backward to the intended purpose of the flag. You can assure accuracy if you pass null as the second parameter, which forces the method to define containment as containing the node in its entirety.

**Returned Value**　　Boolean value: true | false.

**Parameters**

*nodeReference*
　　Reference to any addressable text or element node in the document tree.

*entirelyFlag*
　　Boolean value or null. Observed behavior is that a value of true means the selection can contain only a part of the node for the method to return true.

## createRange( )　　　NN *n/a*　IE *4(Win)*　DOM *n/a*

Creates a TextRange object from the current selection object. After a statement like the following:

```
var myRange = document.selection.createRange( );
```

scripts can act on the content of the selected text.

**Returned Value**　　TextRange object.

**Parameters**　　None.

## createRangeCollection( )　　　NN *n/a*　IE *5.5(Win)*　DOM *n/a*

Creates a TextRange collection object. This must be in anticipation of IE supporting multiple, discontiguous selections in the future.

**Returned Value**　　TextRange collection object.

**Parameters**　　None.

## deleteFromDocument( )

Removes the current selection from the document tree. The node hierarchy adjusts itself by obeying the same rules as Range.deleteContents( ).

**Returned Value**     None.

**Parameters**        None.

## empty( )

Deselects the current selection and sets the selection object's type property to None. There is no change to the content that had been selected.

**Returned Value**     None.

**Parameters**        None.

## extend( )

extend(*nodeReference, offset*)

Moves the end (focus) boundary of the selection to the designated document tree node and offset within that node. The start (anchor) point does not move with this method.

**Returned Value**     None.

**Parameters**

*nodeReference*

Reference to a text or element node in the document tree in which the selection's focus (end point) should move.

*offset*

Integer count of characters or nodes within the *nodeReference* node where the collapsed selection should move. The count is relative to the start of the node. Units are character for text nodes, nodes for elements.

## getRangeAt( )

getRangeAt(*rangeIndex*)

Returns a reference to the range within a selection object whose zero-based numeric index matches the passed parameter. For contiguous selections, the parameter should be zero. But for discontiguous selections, the getRangeAt( ) method lets you retrieve each range that had been added to the selection for individual manipulation as a Range object. Use the selection.rangeCount property to derive the number of Range objects contained by the selection object. Invoking the method does not disturb the sequence of ranges within the selection.

**Returned Value**     Range object reference.

Alphabetical DOM
Reference

**Parameters**

*rangeIndex*
> Zero-based integer index value.

## removeAllRanges( ) NN *6*   IE *n/a*   DOM *n/a*

Removes all Range objects from the current selection (not from the document tree). The selection collapses, and the rangeCount property value changes to zero.

**Returned Value**   None.

**Parameters**   None.

## removeRange( ) NN *6*   IE *n/a*   DOM *n/a*

removeRange(*rangeReference*)

Removes a single Range object from the current selection (not from the document tree). If you have a multiple-range selection, you can iterate through all Range objects, inspect each for some criterion, and delete the one(s) you want with the following sequence:

```
var oneRange;
var sel = window.getSelection( );
for (var i = 0; i < sel.rangeCount; i++) {
    oneRange = sel.getRangeAt(i);
    if (oneRange.someProperty == someDiscerningValue) {
        sel.removeRange(oneRange);
    }
}
```

**Returned Value**   None.

**Parameters**

*rangeReference*
> Reference to one of the Range objects previously added to the current selection.

## selectAllChildren( ) NN *6*   IE *n/a*   DOM *n/a*

selectAllChildren(*elementNodeReference*)

Forces the selection object to encompass the element node passed as a parameter and all of its child nodes. This method is also a shortcut to using a script to select an element node. Using this method on an element node causes the anchor and focus nodes to be that element node. Should you pass a reference to a text node, the resulting selection is collapsed in front of the first character of the text node. Invoking this method on an existing selection replaces all ranges with the new range encompassing the element.

**Returned Value**   None.

**Parameters**

*elementNodeReference*
> Reference to an element node in the document tree that becomes the selection.

## selectionLanguageChange( )  <span style="float:right">NN 6    IE n/a    DOM n/a</span>

selectionLanguageChange(*RTLFlag*)

Controls the cursor Bidi (bi-directional) level.

**Returned Value**    None.

**Parameters**

*RTLFlag*
   Boolean value: true for right-to-left; false for left-to-right.

## toString( )  <span style="float:right">NN 6    IE n/a    DOM n/a</span>

Returns a string containing only body content from the selection. Tags and attributes are ignored.

**Returned Value**    String value.

**Parameters**    None.

# small

See b.

# span  <span style="float:right">NN 6    IE 4    DOM 1</span>

The span object reflects the span element. This element is used primarily as an arbitrary container for assigning styles to inline content elements. You might say that it is the quint-essential generic element object. In Navigator 4, a span object that is given a position style is treated very much like a layer object for scripting purposes.

**HTML Equivalent**

<span>

**Object Model Reference**

[window.]document.getElementById("*elementID*")

**Object-Specific Properties**

None.

**Object-Specific Methods**

None.

**Object-Specific Event Handler Properties**

None.

# statusbar

See directories.

# strike

See b.

# strong

See acronym.

# style (element)                                                NN 6    IE 4    DOM 1

The style element object reflects the style HTML element. This object is separate from the style object that is accessed as a property of virtually every element in a document. The style element object is generated in a document via the <style> tag, which can have a unique ID value assigned to it; the style (property) object contains all the style properties and their current values as set for a particular element.

### HTML Equivalent
<style>

### Object Model Reference
[window.]document.getElementById("*elementID*")

### Object-Specific Properties
| disabled | media | sheet | styleSheet | type |

### Object-Specific Methods
None.

### Object-Specific Event Handler Properties

| Handler | NN | IE | DOM |
|---------|-----|----|-----|
| onerror | n/a | 4  | n/a |
| onload  | n/a | 4  | n/a |

## disabled                                                        NN 6    IE 4    DOM 1
Read/Write

Specifies whether rules in the style sheet should be applied to their selected elements. Although the corresponding disabled attribute does not work in Internet Explorer 4, setting the disabled property to true does, in fact, turn off the entire style sheet. During page authoring, you can create a button that toggles style sheets on and off to see how the page looks in all types of browsers.

| | |
|---|---|
| **Example** | document.getElementById("mainStyle").disabled = true; |
| **Value** | Boolean value: true \| false. |
| **Default** | false |

## media

Indicates the intended output device for the rules of the style element. The media property looks forward to the day when browsers are able to tailor content to specific kinds of devices such as pocket computers, text-to-speech digitizers, or fuzzy television sets.

| | |
|---|---|
| **Example** | document.getElementById("myStyle").media = "print"; |
| **Value** | Any one of the following constant values as a string: all \| print \| screen. |
| **Default** | all |

## sheet

Returns a styleSheet object (W3C DOM type CSSStyleSheet) representing the style sheet defined by the style element. This is an alternate (and nonstandard) way to reference a styleSheet object. The document.styleSheets collection is a better approach.

| | |
|---|---|
| **Example** | var oneSheet = document.getElementById("myStyle").sheet; |
| **Value** | Reference to a styleSheet object (W3C DOM type CSSStyleSheet). |
| **Default** | None. |

## styleSheet

Returns a styleSheet object representing the style sheet defined by the style element. This is property is present, but doesn't seem to be officially supported. The document.styleSheets collection is a better approach.

| | |
|---|---|
| **Example** | var oneSheet = document.getElementById("myStyle").styleSheet; |
| **Value** | Reference to a styleSheet object. |
| **Default** | None. |

## type

This is the style sheet MIME type specified by the type attribute of the style element.

**Example**
```
if (document.getElementById("myStyle").type == "text/css") {
    // unlikely to be anything else
}
```

**Value**        MIME type string.

**Default**      text/css

# style, CSSStyleDeclaration                          NN 6    IE 4    DOM 2

In its most generic sense, a style object is the access point for scripts to read and write individual style attributes for a given element. This style object exposes (or has the potential to expose) every style sheet attribute supported by the browser (the kinds of CSS attributes described in Chapter 11).

In practice, however, a style object that you access through an HTML element object's style property (one of the shared properties described early in this chapter) is limited in scope: It reflects only the CSS settings explicitly defined in the element's tag via the style attribute or settings assigned to the element's style property via script. But other style sheets associated with the browser (internal style sheets) and the document (explicit style sheet rules defined in the <style> element and rules imported through either a link element or an @import rule) also affect the rendered characteristics of the element. A union of all style sheet attributes affecting an element—the effective style definition—may be read, but through browser-dependent syntax. IE uses the currentStyle property of an element, whereas Netscape 6 uses the W3C DOM window.getComputedStyle( ) method. Both syntaxes return an object that lets scripts inspect the value of each effective style attribute value.

While the three IE style-related objects (style, currentStyle, and runtimeStyle) return a style object with properties that expose CSS style attributes, the situation is a little more complex on the Netscape 6 side. On the one hand, Netscape 6 implements a version of the W3C DOM CSSStyleDeclaration object that exposes all the CSS attributes as properties. This is the version accessed through an element object's style property (just like IE, thus making an element object's style property work cross-browser). But when you read the effective style sheet (via window.getComputedStyle( )), the object that comes back does not expose the CSS attributes directly as properties. Instead, you must use the CSSStyleDeclaration methods (listed below) to inspect a specific attribute value by name. It's a longer way to reach a particular effective style attribute value, but very much in keeping with other attribute-reading syntax deployed throughout the W3C DOM. The only time this cross-browser disconnect affects you is when you need to view the effective style attribute for an unmodified style. Once you set an attribute value via the element object's style property, you can read it from the style property cross-browser.

This section lists the available style object properties plus the Netscape 6 (W3C DOM) formal methods for accessing those attributes. The W3C DOM lists a large percentage of the style object properties under an object umbrella called CSS2Properties. The specification offers the CSS2Properties object as an optional convenience for browsers. Fortunately for cross-browser scripters, Netscape 6 implements CSS2Properties at least for the element object style property.

The properties of the style object listed below correspond to the CSS attributes. For more information on a particular property, see the corresponding listing in Chapter 11.

## Object Model Reference

*All*  [window.]document.getElementById("*elementID*").style

*IE*   [window.]document.styleSheets[i].rules[j].style

*NN*  [window.]document.styleSheets[i].cssRules[j].style

## Object-Specific Properties

| | | |
|---|---|---|
| accelerator | azimuth | background |
| backgroundAttachment | backgroundColor | backgroundImage |
| backgroundPosition | backgroundPositionX | backgroundPositionY |
| backgroundRepeat | behavior | blockDirection |
| border | borderBottom | borderBottomColor |
| borderBottomStyle | borderBottomWidth | borderCollapse |
| borderColor | borderLeft | borderLeftColor |
| borderLeftStyle | borderLeftWidth | borderRight |
| borderRightColor | borderRightStyle | borderRightWidth |
| borderSpacing | borderStyle | borderTop |
| borderTopColor | borderTopStyle | borderTopWidth |
| borderWidth | bottom | captionSide |
| clear | clip | clipBottom |
| clipLeft | clipRight | clipTop |
| color | content | counterIncrement |
| counterReset | cssFloat | cssText |
| cue | cueAfter | cueBefore |
| cursor | direction | display |
| elevation | emptyCells | filter |
| font | fontFamily | fontSize |
| fontSizeAdjust | fontStretch | fontStyle |
| fontVariant | fontWeight | height |
| imeMode | layoutFlow | layoutGrid |
| layoutGridChar | layoutGridLine | layoutGridMode |
| layoutGridType | left | letterSpacing |
| lineBreak | lineHeight | listStyle |
| listStyleImage | listStylePosition | listStyleType |
| margin | marginBottom | marginLeft |
| marginRight | marginTop | markerOffset |
| marks | maxHeight | maxWidth |
| minHeight | minWidth | MozBinding |
| MozOpacity | orphans | outline |
| outlineColor | outlineStyle | outlineWidth |

| overflow | overflowX | overflowY |
|---|---|---|
| padding | paddingBottom | paddingLeft |
| paddingRight | paddingTop | page |
| pageBreakAfter | pageBreakBefore | pageBreakInside |
| pause | pauseAfter | pauseBefore |
| pitch | pitchRange | pixelBottom |
| pixelHeight | pixelLeft | pixelRight |
| pixelTop | pixelWidth | playDuring |
| posBottom | posHeight | posLeft |
| posRight | posTop | posWidth |
| position | quotes | richness |
| right | rubyAlign | rubyOverhang |
| rubyPosition | scrollbar3dLightColor | scrollbarArrowColor |
| scrollbarBaseColor | scrollbarDarkShadowColor | scrollbarFaceColor |
| scrollbarHighlightColor | scrollbarShadowColor | scrollbarTrackColor |
| size | speak | speakHeader |
| speakNumeral | speakPunctuation | speechRate |
| stress | styleFloat | tableLayout |
| textAlign | textAlignLast | textAutospace |
| textDecoration | textDecorationBlink | textDecorationLineThrough |
| textDecorationNone | textDecorationOverline | textDecorationUnderline |
| textIndent | textJustify | textKashidaSpace |
| textOverflow | textShadow | textTransform |
| textUnderlinePosition | top | unicodeBidi |
| verticalAlign | visibility | voiceFamily |
| volume | whiteSpace | widows |
| width | wordBreak | wordSpacing |
| wordWrap | writingMode | zIndex |
| zoom | | |

**Object-Specific Methods**

| getPropertyCSSValue( ) | getPropertyPriority( ) | getPropertyValue( ) |
|---|---|---|
| item( ) | removeProperty( ) | setProperty( ) |

**Object-Specific Event Handler Properties**
None.

## accelerator

NN *n/a*    IE *5(Win)*    DOM *n/a*

See text

For IE 5 and later running under Windows 2000 or newer version of Windows, users can set a preference to highlight an accelerator key for commands (or web page accessKey letters) when the user presses the **Alt** key. The accelerator key property controls whether the element is treated as a highlightable accelerator key string. Available as a property of the IE currentStyle (read-only) and runtimeStyle (read/write) objects only.

**Example**          document.getElementById("controlH").style.accelerator = true;

**Value**            Boolean value: true | false.

**Default**          false

## azimuth, cue, cueAfter, cueBefore, elevation, pause, pauseAfter, pauseBefore, pitch, pitchRange, playDuring, richness, speak, speakHeader, speakNumeral, speakPunctuation, speechRate, stress, voiceFamily, volume

NN 6    IE n/a    DOM 2

**Read/Write**

This large group of properties comes from CSS attributes intended for browsers that use speech synthesis techniques to vocalize document content. You don't have to be vision-impaired to benefit from this possibility, but Netscape 6 does not include this feature by default. Conceivably, other specialty browser makers will build a speech synthesized browser from the Mozilla engine. They'll have the hooks ready in the Mozilla DOM to permit scripting of these style properties. In the meantime, they're simply placeholders within Netscape 6. You can read about these CSS attributes in Chapter 11.

**Value**            All values for these properties are strings.

**Default**          None.

## background

NN 6    IE 4    DOM 2

**Read/Write**

Provides the element's style sheet background attribute. This is a shorthand attribute, so the scripted property consists of a string of space-delimited values for the backgroundAttachment, backgroundColor, backgroundImage, backgroundPosition, and backgroundRepeat property values. One or more values may be in the background value, and the individual values may be in any order. Available in IE as a property of the style and runtimeStyle objects only.

**Example**

document.getElementById("myDiv").style.background = "url(logo.gif) repeat-y";

**Value**            String of space-delimited values corresponding to one or more individual background style properties.

**Default**          None.

## backgroundAttachment

NN 6   IE 4   DOM 2
Read/Write

Sets how the image is "attached" to the element. The image can either remain fixed within the viewable area of the element (the viewport) or it may scroll with the element as the document is scrolled. During scrolling, the fixed attachment looks like a stationary backdrop to rolling credits of a movie.

**Example**

```
document.getElementById("myDiv").style.backgroundAttachment = "fixed";
```

| | |
|---|---|
| **Value** | String of either allowable value: fixed \| scroll. |
| **Default** | scroll |

## backgroundColor

NN 6   IE 4   DOM 2
Read/Write

Provides the background color of the element. If you also set a backgroundImage, the image overlays the color. Transparent pixels of the image allow the color to show through.

**Example**

```
document.getElementById("highlighted").style.backgroundColor = "yellow";
```

| | |
|---|---|
| **Value** | Any valid color specification (see description at beginning of the chapter) or transparent. |
| **Default** | transparent |

## backgroundImage

NN 6   IE 4   DOM 2
Read/Write

URL of the background image of the element. If you also set a backgroundColor, the image overlays the color. Transparent pixels of the image allow the color to show through.

**Example**

```
document.getElementById("navbar").style.backgroundImage =
"url(images/navVisited.jpg)";
```

| | |
|---|---|
| **Value** | Any complete or relative URL to an image file in CSS URL format: url(filePath). |
| **Default** | None. |

## backgroundPosition

NN 6   IE 4   DOM 2
Read/Write

Indicates the top and left location of a background image relative to the element's content region (plus padding). Positions may be specified as length values (with numbers and units or percentages) or according to a combination of constants top, right, bottom, left, and center. The property has no effect on a background images set to repeat along both axes. Some value types don't work (or work correctly) in IE 4. Available as a property of the IE style and runtimeStyle objects only.

### Example

```
document.getElementById("div3").style.backgroundPosition = "20% 50%";
```

### Value

A string containing one value (to be applied to both horizontal and vertical axes) or a space-delimited pair of values. Values may be explicit length values (with units, as in 30px 5px), percentages (e.g., 50% 50%) or position constants that have explicit meanings for their combinations.

| Constant value pair | Percentage equivalents | Constant value pair | Percentage equivalents |
|---|---|---|---|
| top left | 0% 0% | center center | 50% 50% |
| left top | 0% 0% | right | 100% 50% |
| top | 50% 0% | right center | 100% 50% |
| top center | 50% 0% | center right | 100% 50% |
| center top | 50% 0% | bottom left | 0% 100% |
| right top | 100% 0% | left bottom | 0% 100% |
| top right | 100% 0% | bottom | 50% 100% |
| left | 0% 50% | bottom center | 50% 100% |
| left center | 0% 50% | center bottom | 50% 100% |
| center left | 0% 50% | bottom right | 100% 100% |
| center | 50% 50% | right bottom | 100% 100% |

Percentage values are interpolated logically. For example, a value of 0% means that the image abuts the left or top edge of the element block; a value of 50% centers the image vertically or horizontally; a value of 100% places the image flush right or bottom..

**Default**          0% 0%

## backgroundPositionX, backgroundPositionY

NN *n/a*    IE *4*    DOM *n/a*

Read/Write

Indicate the top and left locations of the background image relative to the element's content region (plus padding). Useful if you wish to adjust the background image along only one axis while not disturbing the other. The same IE 4 cautions for backgroundPosition apply to these two properties.

### Example

```
document.getElementById("div3").style.backgroundPositionX = "20px";
document.getElementById("table2").style.backgroundPositionY = "10px;"
```

**Value**

You should be able to specify percentage values, which are the percentage of the block-level element's box width and height (respectively) at which point the image (or repeated images) begins. Setting percentage values, however, does not always work in IE 4 for Windows (and it doesn't work at all on the Mac), even though they are returned as the default value units. You are safest with pixel values. None of the allowed constants except top and left are recognized.

**Default**          0

## backgroundRepeat

NN 6    IE 4    DOM 2
Read/Write

Specifies whether a background image (specified with the backgroundImage property) should repeat and, if so, along which axes. You can use repeating background images to create horizontal and vertical bands with some settings.

**Example**

document.getElementById("div3").style.backgroundRepeat = "repeat-y";

**Value**

With a string setting of no-repeat, one instance of the image appears in the location within the element established by the backgroundPosition property (default is top-left corner). Normal repeats are performed along both axes, but you can have the image repeat down a single column (repeat-y) or across a single row (repeat-x). To reestablish the default, assign the value repeat.

**Default**          repeat

## behavior

NN n/a    IE 5(Win)    DOM n/a
Read/Write

Controls whether an IE Windows external behavior is assigned to the element.

**Example**

document.getElementById("div3").style.behavior = "url(#default#userData)";

**Value**          CSS-formatted URL value, with the actual URL pointing to an external . htc file, ID of an object element that loads a behavior ActiveX control into the page, or one of the built-in default behaviors (in the format url(#default#behaviorName)).

**Default**          None.

## blockDirection

Returns the writing script direction of the current element. Available as a property of the IE currentStyle object only.

**Example**
```
if (document.getElementById("myDIV").style.blockDirection = "rtl") {
    // process right-to-left text
}
```

**Value**        String constant values: ltr | rtl.

**Default**      ltr

## border

Provides a shorthand property for getting or setting the borderColor, borderStyle, and/or borderWidth properties of all four borders around an element in one statement. You must specify a border style (see borderStyle) for changes of this property to affect the display of the element's border (a missing style is interpreted as no style, ergo no border). Numerous other properties allow you to set the width, style, and color of individual edges or groups of edges if you don't want all four edges to be the same. Only those component settings explicitly made in the element's tag attributes are reflected in the property, but you may assign components not part of the original tag. Available in IE as a property of the style and runtimeStyle objects only.

**Example**      document.getElementById("announce").style.border = "inset red 4px";

**Value**        Space-delimited string. For the borderStyle and borderWidth component values, see the respective properties in this chapter. For details on the borderColor value, see the section about CSS colors at the beginning of Chapter 11.

**Default**      None.

## borderBottom, borderLeft, borderRight, borderTop

These are shorthand properties for getting or setting the borderColor, borderStyle, and/or borderWidth properties for a single edge of an element in one statement. You must specify a border style (see borderStyle) for changes of these properties to affect the display of the element's border (a missing style is interpreted as no style, ergo no border along the specified edge). If you want all four edges to be the same, see the border attribute. Only those component settings explicitly made in the element's tag attributes are reflected in the property, but you may assign components not part of the original tag. Available in IE as properties of the style and runtimeStyle objects only.

## Example

```
document.getElementById("announce").style.borderBottom = "inset red 4px";
document.getElementById("announce").style.borderLeft = "solid #20ff00 2px";
document.getElementById("announce").style.borderRight = "double 3px";
document.getElementById("announce").style.borderTop = "outset red 8px";
```

**Value**        Space-delimited string. For the border*Side*Style and border*Side*Width component values, see the respective properties in this chapter. For details on the border*Side*Color value formats, see the section about colors at the beginning of Chapter 11.

**Default**      None.

## borderBottomColor, borderLeftColor, borderRightColor, borderTopColor

NN 6   IE 4   DOM 2

Read/Write

Provide the color of a single border edge of an element. It is easy to abuse these properties by mixing colors that don't belong together. See also the borderColor attribute for setting the color for groups of edges in one statement.

## Example

```
document.getElementById("announce").style.borderBottomColor = "red";
document.getElementById("announce").style.borderLeftColor = "#20ff00";
document.getElementById("announce").style.borderRightColor = "rgb(100, 75, 0)";
document.getElementById("announce").style.borderTopColor = "rgb(90%, 0%, 25%)";
```

**Value**        For details on CSS color values, see the section about colors at the beginning of Chapter 11.

**Default**      None.

## borderBottomStyle, borderLeftStyle, borderRightStyle, borderTopStyle

NN 6   IE 4   DOM 2

Read/Write

Provide the line style of a single border edge of an element. The edge-specific attributes let you override a style that has been applied to all four edges with the border or borderStyle properties. See also the borderStyle property for setting the style for groups of edges in one statement.

## Example

```
document.getElementById("announce").style.borderBottomStyle = "groove";
document.getElementById("announce").style.borderLeftStyle = "double";
document.getElementById("announce").style.borderRightStyle = "solid";
document.getElementById("announce").style.borderTopStyle = "inset";
```

**Value**

Style values are case-insensitive constants that are associated with specific ways of rendering border lines. The CSS style constants are: dashed, dotted, double, groove, hidden, inset, none, outset, ridge, and solid. Not all browsers recognize all the values in the CSS recommendation. See the border-style attribute listing in Chapter 11 for complete details on the available border styles.

**Default**       None.

## borderBottomWidth, borderLeftWidth, borderRightWidth, borderTopWidth
NN 6   IE 4   DOM 2
Read/Write

Provide the width of a single border edge of an element. See also the borderWidth property for setting the width for groups of edges in one statement.

**Example**

```
document.getElementById("announce").style.borderBottomWidth= "thin";
document.getElementById("announce").style.borderLeftWidth = "thick";
document.getElementById("announce").style.borderRightWidth = "2px";
document.getElementById("announce").style.borderTopWidth = "0.5em";
```

**Value**       Three case-insensitive constants—thin | medium | thick—allow the browser to define how many pixels are used to show the border. For more precision, you can also assign a length value (see the discussion of CSS length values at the beginning of Chapter 11).

**Default**       medium

## borderCollapse
NN 6   IE 5   DOM 2
Read/Write

Controls which table border model the table element should observe.

**Example**

```
document.getElementById("myTable").style.borderCollapse = "separate";
```

**Value**       Two case-insensitive string constants: collapse | separate. IE 5 for Macintosh and Netscape 6 do not respond to changes to this property.

**Default**       separate

## borderColor
NN 6   IE 4   DOM 2
Read/Write

A shortcut attribute that lets you set multiple border edges to the same or different colors. You may supply one to four space-delimited color values. The number of values determines which sides receive the assigned colors.

**Example**
```
document.getElementById("announce").style.borderColor = "red";
document.getElementById("announce").style.borderColor = "red green";
document.getElementById("announce").style.borderColor =
"black rgb(100, 75, 0) #c0c0c0";
document.getElementById("announce").style.borderColor = "yellow green blue red";
```

**Value**

This property accepts one, two, three, or four color values as a string (including transparent as a color), depending on how many and which borders you want to set with specific colors. See the border-color attribute listing in Chapter 11 for complete details on how the number of values affects this property.

**Default**        The object's color property (if it is set).

## borderSpacing                                          NN 6    IE 5    DOM 2
                                                                    Read/Write

Controls the spacing between table cells when the table is in (the default) separate borders mode, similar to a table object's cellSpacing property. IE 5 for the Macintosh doesn't respond to changes of this property's value. Available in IE as a property of the style object only.

**Example**        `document.getElementById("myTable").style.borderSpacing= "12px";`

**Value**          CSS length value as a string (see the discussion of CSS length values at
                   the beginning of Chapter 11).

**Default**        None.

## borderStyle                                             NN 6    IE 4    DOM 2
                                                                    Read/Write

This is a shortcut property that lets you set multiple border edges to the same or different style. You may supply one to four space-delimited style values. The number of values determines which sides receive the assigned colors.

**Example**
```
document.getElementById("announce").style.borderStyle = "solid";
document.getElementById("announce").style.borderStyle = "solid double";
document.getElementById("announce").style.borderStyle =
"double groove groove double";
```

**Value**

Style values are case-insensitive constants that are associated with specific ways of rendering border lines. The CSS style constants are: dashed, dotted, double, groove, hidden, inset, none, outset, ridge, and solid. Not all browsers recognize all the values in the CSS recommendation. See the border-style attribute listing in Chapter 11 for complete details on the available border styles.

This property accepts one, two, three, or four style values as a string, depending on how many and which borders you want to set with specific styles. See the border-style attribute listing in Chapter 11 for complete details on how the number of values affects this property.

**Default**        none

## borderWidth

This is a shortcut property that lets you set multiple border edges to the same or different width. You may supply one to four space-delimited width length values. The number of values determines which sides receive the assigned widths.

**Example**

```
document.getElementById("founderQuote").style.borderWidth = "3px 5px";
```

**Value**

Three case-insensitive constants—thin | medium | thick—allow the browser to define exactly how many pixels are used to show the border. For more precision, you can also assign a length value (see the discussion of length values at the beginning of Chapter 11).

This property accepts one, two, three, or four values, depending on how many and which borders you want to set with specific widths. See the border-width attribute listing in Chapter 11 for complete details on how the number of values affects this property.

**Default**        medium

## bottom

For an absolute-positioned element, defines the position of the bottom edge of an element's box (content plus bottom padding, border, and/or margin) relative to the bottom edge of the next outermost block content container. IE for Windows and Netscape 6 do something unexpected when the positioned element uses the root positioning context. Instead of using the bottom of the document as the comparative edge, these browsers use the bottom of the browser window space (the viewport in CSS terminology). This means that the precise bottom position of the element varies with the user's browser window size. IE 5 for the Macintosh uses the document's bottom as the comparative edge. This discrepancy makes it more practical to use the bottom property for a positioned element nested inside another positioned element. When the element is relative-positioned, the offset is based on the bottom edge of the inline location where the element would normally appear in the content.

For numeric calculations on this value in IE, retrieve the pixelBottom or posBottom style properties, which return genuine numeric values.

**Example**        `document.getElementById("blockD2").style.bottom = "35px";`

**Value**        String consisting of a numeric value and length unit measure, a percentage, or auto.

**Default**        auto

# captionSide                                        NN 6    IE 5(Mac)    DOM 2

Controls the location of a caption element (nested inside a table element) relative to the table's box.

**Example**        `document.getElementById("myTable").style.captionSide = "bottom";`

**Value**        Case-insensitive string of any of the following constants: bottom | left | right | top. Some browsers may be limited to only the bottom and top values.

**Default**        top

# clear                                             NN 6    IE 4    DOM 2

Defines whether the element allows itself to be displayed in the same horizontal band as a floating element. Typically, another element in the vicinity has its float style attribute set to left or right. To prevent the current element from being in the same band as the floating block, set the clear property to the same side (left or right). If you aren't sure where the potential overlap might occur, set the clear property to both. An element that has its clear property set to a value other than none is rendered at the beginning of the next available line below the floating element.

**Example**        `document.getElementById("myDiv").style.clear = "both";`

**Value**        Case-insensitive string of any of the following constants: both | left | none | right.

**Default**        none

# clip                                              NN 6    IE 4    DOM 2

Defines a clipping region of a positionable element. The clipping region is the area of the element layer in which content is visible. Clipping may not work properly in Internet Explorer 4 for the Macintosh. Available in IE as a property of the style and runtimeStyle objects only.

**Example**
`document.getElementById("art2").style.clip = "rect(5px 100px 40px 0)";`

**Value**

Case-insensitive string of either the auto constant or the CSS clip attribute setting that specifies the shape (rect only for now) and the position of the four clip edges relative to the original element's top-left corner. When specifying lengths for each side of the clipping rectangle, observe the clockwise order of values: top, right, bottom, left. See the discussion about CSS length values at the beginning of Chapter 11. A value of auto sets the clipping region to the block that contains the content. In Internet Explorer, the width may extend to the width of the next outermost container (such as the body element).

**Default**     None.

## clipBottom, clipLeft, clipRight, clipTop    NN *n/a*   IE *5(Win)*   DOM *n/a*
Read-only

Return a clipping edge of a positionable element. Available in IE as a property of the currentStyle object only.

**Example**     var cl = document.getElementById("art2").style.clipLeft;

**Value**       Case-insensitive length string or auto constant. See the discussion about CSS length values at the beginning of Chapter 11.

**Default**     None.

## color    NN *6*   IE *4*   DOM *2*
Read/Write

Sets the foreground (text) color style sheet attribute of the element. For some graphically oriented elements, such as form controls, the color attribute may also be applied to element edges or other features. Such extracurricular behavior is browser specific and may not be the same across browsers.

**Example**     document.getElementById("specialDiv").style.color = "green";

**Value**       Case-insensitive CSS color specification (see the discussion at beginning of Chapter 11).

**Default**     black

## content    NN *6*   IE *5(Mac)*   DOM *2*
Read/Write

Defines extra content that is to be displayed before or after and element (in concert with the :before and :after pseudo-classes. Although the property is available for IE 5 Macintosh and Netscape 6, the values are empty strings and the rendered content (which appears in Netscape 6 only) does not change if you assign it a new value.

**Value**       See the discussion of the content CSS attribute in Chapter 11.

**Default**     None.

## counterIncrement, counterReset

NN 6   IE 5(Mac)   DOM 2
Read/Write

These properties are placeholders for future implementations of automatic counter mechanisms specified in the CSS specification. They are not yet functional in the browsers shown above.

**Value**      See the discussion of the counterIncrement and counterReset CSS attributes in Chapter 11.

**Default**     None.


## cssFloat

NN 6   IE 5(Mac)   DOM 2
Read/Write

Controls the CSS float attribute for an element, allowing adjacent text content to wrap around block elements, such as images. Changing the value in IE 5 for Macintosh has no effect. The "css" prefix for this property name deflects potential conflicts with the float reserved JavaScript keyword.

**Example**    document.getElementById("myDiv").style.cssFloat = "right";

**Value**      String of an allowable constant value: left | right | none.

**Default**    none


## cssText

NN 6   IE 4   DOM 2
Read-only

Returns a string of the entire CSS style sheet rule applied to the element. If the rule included shorthand style attribute settings (such as border), browsers return modified versions according to their ideas of what the value means. If you set the style attribute of an element to style="border: groove red 3px", IE for Windows reports the cssText property for that element as:

```
BORDER-RIGHT: red 3px groove; BORDER-TOP: red 3px groove;
BORDER-LEFT: red 3px groove; BORDER-BOTTOM: red 3px groove
```

IE for Macintosh reports:

```
{BORDER-TOP: 3px groove red; BORDER-RIGHT: 3px groove red;
BORDER-BOTTOM: 3px groove red; BORDER-LEFT: 3px groove red}
```

And Netscape 6 reports:

```
border: 3px groove red;
```

Note how each browser manipulates the sequence of individual values. Even so, you can assign a shorthand value to the property and in any order you like. Available in IE as a property of the style and runtimeStyle objects only.

**Example**

```
document.getElementById("block3").style.cssText = "margin: 2px; font-size: 14pt";
```

| **Value** | String value of semicolon-delimited style attributes. |
| **Default** | None. |

## cue, cueAfter, cueBefore

See azimuth.

## cursor

Specifies the shape of the cursor when the screen pointer is atop the element. The precise look of cursors depends on the operating system. Before deploying a modified cursor, be sure you understand the standard ways that the various types of cursors are used within the browser and operating system. Users expect a cursor design to mean the same thing across all applications. Figure 11-3 in Chapter 11 offers a gallery of Windows and Macintosh cursors for each of the cursor constant settings provided by Internet Explorer and the Netscape 6 group.

Setting this property affects the cursor only when it is atop the current element and does not set the cursor immediately on a global basis.

**Example**    `document.getElementById("hotStuff").style.cursor = "pointer";`

**Value**

Any one cursor constant as a string, as supported by various browsers and versions.

| Cursor name | IE/Windows | IE/Mac | NN |
| --- | --- | --- | --- |
| alias | n/a | n/a | 6 |
| all-scroll | 6 | n/a | n/a |
| auto | 4 | 4 | 6 |
| cell | n/a | n/a | 6 |
| col-resize | 6 | n/a | n/a |
| context-menu | n/a | n/a | 6 |
| copy | n/a | n/a | 6 |
| count-down | n/a | n/a | 6 |
| count-up | n/a | n/a | 6 |
| count-up-down | n/a | n/a | 6 |
| crosshair | 4 | 4 | 6 |
| default | 4 | 4 | 6 |
| e-resize | 4 | 4 | 6 |
| grab | n/a | n/a | 6 |
| grabbing | n/a | n/a | 6 |
| hand | 4 | 4 | n/a |

| Cursor name | IE/Windows | IE/Mac | NN |
|---|---|---|---|
| help | 4 | 4 | 6 |
| move | 4 | 4 | 6 |
| n-resize | 4 | 4 | 6 |
| ne-resize | 4 | 4 | 6 |
| no-drop | 6 | n/a | n/a |
| not-allowed | 6 | n/a | n/a |
| nw-resize | 4 | 4 | 6 |
| pointer | 4 | 4 | 6 |
| progress | 6 | n/a | n/a |
| row-resize | 6 | n/a | n/a |
| s-resize | 4 | 4 | 6 |
| se-resize | 4 | 4 | 6 |
| spinning | n/a | n/a | 6 |
| sw-resize | 4 | 4 | 6 |
| text | 4 | 4 | 6 |
| url(uri) | 6 | n/a | n/a |
| vertical-text | 6 | n/a | n/a |
| w-resize | 4 | 4 | 6 |
| wait | 4 | 4 | 6 |

The IE 6 setting of an external URL requires an address of a cursor file of extension *.cur* or *.ani*.

**Default**        auto

## direction                                          NN 6    IE 5    DOM 2
**Read/Write**

Returns the writing script direction of the current element. Intended primarily for elements inside documents with mixed writing script directions (e.g., French text intermingled among Arabic).

**Example**        document.getElementById("term3").style.direction = "ltr";

**Value**          String constant values: ltr | rtl.

**Default**        ltr

## display                                             NN 6    IE 4    DOM 2
**Read/Write**

Controls the CSS box type used to render the element. The most common settings for body content dictate whether an element is rendered as a block or inline element. When set to none, the element is hidden, and surrounding content cinches up to fill the space. Some box types are specific to tables and lists.

**Example**        document.getElementById("instructionDiv").style.display = "none";

**Value**

Any one display type constant as a string, as supported by various browsers and versions.

| Display type | IE/Windows | IE/Mac | NN |
|---|---|---|---|
| block | 5 | 4 | 6 |
| inline | 5 | 4 | 6 |
| inline-block | 5.5 | n/a | n/a |
| none | 4 | 4 | 6 |
| run-in | n/a | 5 | 6 |
| table-footer-group | 5.5 | 5 | 6 |
| table-header-group | 5 | 5 | 6 |

**Default**        Element-dependent.

# elevation

See azimuth.

# emptyCells                                    NN 6    IE 5(Mac)    DOM 2
                                                                Read/Write

When a table is set to render the separate cell box format (the default), and a border is established for td elements in that table, the emptyCells style property controls whether the table renders borders around cells that have no content.

**Example**        document.getElementById("myTable").style.emptyCells = "hide";

**Value**          String of allowable constant values: hide | show.

**Default**        show

# filter                                        NN n/a    IE 4(Win)    DOM n/a
                                                                Read/Write

Sets the visual, reveal, or blend filter used to display or change content of an element. A visual filter can be applied to an element to produce effects such as content flipping, glow, drop shadow, and many others. A reveal filter is applied to an element when its visibility changes. The value of the reveal filter determines what visual effect is to be applied to the transition from hidden to shown (or vice versa). This includes effects such as wipes, blinds, and barn doors. A blend filter sets the speed at which a transition between states occurs.

Although the `filter` property is present in Internet Explorer for Macintosh, it does not operate there.

**Example**    `document.getElementById("fancy").style.filter= "dropshadow( )";`

**Value**

Each filter property may have more than one space-delimited filter type associated with it. Each filter type is followed by a pair of parentheses, which may convey parameters about the behavior of the filter for the current element. A parameter generally consists of a name/value pair, with assignment performed by the equals symbol. Note that Microsoft instituted an entirely new filter syntax starting with IE 5.5 for Windows. The new syntax runs in parallel with the old (for now). See the `filter` style sheet attribute listing in Chapter 11 for details on filter settings and parameters.

**Default**    None.

## font                                                      NN 6    IE 4    DOM 2
                                                                        Read/Write

This is a shorthand property that lets you set one or more font-related properties—`fontFamily`, `fontSize`, `lineHeight` (which must be preceded by a / symbol in this property), `fontStyle`, `fontVariant`, and `fontWeight`—with one assignment statement. A space-delimited list of values (in any sequence) is applied to the specific font properties for which the value is a valid type. Or, you can short-circuit these individual settings by choosing one of the default (operating-system–dependent) system fonts: `caption` | `icon` | `menu` | `message-box` | `small-caption` | `status-bar`.

**Example**

`document.getElementById("subhead").style.font = "bolder small-caps 16pt";`

**Value**    For syntax and examples of value types for font-related properties, see the respective property listing.

**Default**    None.

## fontFamily                                                NN 6    IE 4    DOM 2
                                                                        Read/Write

Provides a prioritized list of font families to be used to render the object's content. One or more font family names may be included in a comma-delimited list of property values. If a font family name consists of multiple words, the family name must be inside a set of inner quotes. Available in IE as a property of the `style` and `runtimeStyle` objects only, but the individual font properties are available in `currentStyle`, as well.

**Example**

```
document.getElementById("subhead").style.fontFamily =
    "'Century Schoolbook', Times, serif";
```

| | |
|---|---|
| **Value** | Any number of font family names, comma delimited. Multiword family names must be quoted. Recognized generic family names are: serif \| sans-serif \| cursive \| fantasy \| monospace. |
| **Default** | Browser default. |

## fontSize

NN *6*    IE *4*    DOM *2*

Read/Write

Indicates the font size of the element. The font size can be set in several ways. A collection of constants (xx-small, x-small, small, medium, large, x-large, xx-large) defines what are known as *absolute* sizes. In truth, these are absolute only in a single browser in a single operating system, since the reference point for these sizes varies with browser and operating system (analogous to the old HTML font sizes of 1 through 7). But they do let the author have confidence that one element set to large is rendered larger than medium.

Another collection of constants (larger, smaller) is known as relative sizes. Because the font-size style attribute is inherited from the parent element, these relative sizes are applied to the parent element to determine the font size of the current element. It is up to the browser to determine exactly how much larger or smaller the font size is, and a lot depends on how the parent element's font size is set. If it is set with one of the absolute sizes (large, for example), a child's font size of larger means the font is rendered in the browser's x-large size. The increments are not as clear-cut when the parent font size is set with a length or percentage.

If you elect to use a length value for the fontSize property, you will achieve greater consistency across operating systems if units such as pixels (px) or ems (em), instead of points (pt). Em units are calculated with respect to the size of the parent element's font size. Finally, you can set fontSize to a percentage, which is calculated based on the size of the parent element's font size.

**Example**        document.getElementById("teeny").style.fontSize = "x-small";

**Value**

Case-insensitive string values from any of the following categories. For an absolute size, one of the following constants: xx-small \| x-small \| small \| medium \| large \| x-large \| xx-large. For a relative size, one of the following constants: larger \| smaller. For a length, see the discussion about CSS length values at the beginning of Chapter 11. For a percentage, the percentage value and the % symbol.

**Default**        Parent element's font size.

## fontSizeAdjust

NN *6*    IE *5(Mac)*    DOM *2*

Read/Write

Provides the font aspect value, usually of the first font family in a font-family attribute sequence, forcing alternative font families to calculate their rendered font size to closely match that of the primary font family. Although this property is a member of the style object in IE 5/Mac and Netscape 6, neither the style attribute nor scripted changes to it affect the font display.

**Example**     document.getElementById("myDIV").style.fontSizeAdjust = "0.56";

**Value**       Numeric aspect value as a quoted string, or none.

**Default**     none

## fontStretch                                              NN 6    IE 5(Mac)    DOM 2
Read/Write

Provides the character spacing for the element, based on available spacing widths available for the current font family. Although this property is a member of the style object in IE 5/Mac and Netscape 6, neither the style attribute nor scripted changes to it affect the font display.

**Example**
document.getElementById("myDIV").style.fontStretch= "ultra-condensed";

**Value**       String of allowable constant values: normal | wider | narrower | ultra-condensed | extra-condensed | condensed | semi-condensed | semi-expanded | expanded | extra-expanded | ultra-expanded, or none.

**Default**     none

## fontStyle                                               NN 6    IE 4    DOM 2
Read/Write

Specifies whether the element is rendered in a normal (roman), italic, or oblique font style. If the fontFamily includes font faces labeled Italic and/or Oblique, the setting of the fontStyle attribute summons those particular font faces from the browser's system. But if the specialized font faces are not available in the system, the normal font face is usually algorithmically slanted to look italic. Output sent to a printer with such font settings relies on the quality of arbitration between the client computer and printer to render an electronically generated italic font style. Personal computer software typically includes other kinds of font rendering under the heading of "Style." See fontVariant and fontWeight for other kinds of font "styles."

**Example**     document.getElementById("emphasis").style.fontStyle = "italic";

**Value**       One the following string constant values: normal | italic | oblique.

**Default**     normal

## fontVariant                                             NN 6    IE 4    DOM 2
Read/Write

Specifies whether the element should be rendered in all uppercase letters in such a way that lowercase letters of the source code are rendered in smaller uppercase letters. If a font family contains a small caps variant, the browser should use it automatically. More likely, however, the browser calculates a smaller size for the uppercase letters that take the place of source code lowercase letters. In practice, Internet Explorer 4 renders the entire source code content as uppercase letters of the same size as the parent element's font, regardless of the case of the source code. Later IE versions and Netscape 6 use two different uppercase sizes.

**Example**
document.getElementById("emphasis").style.fontVariant = "small-caps";

| **Value** | Any of the following constant values as strings: normal \| small-caps. |
|---|---|
| **Default** | normal |

## fontWeight

Sets the weight (boldness) of the element's font. CSS provides a weight rating scheme that is more granular than most browsers render on the screen, but the finely tuned weights may come into play when the content is sent to a printer. The scale is a numeric rating from 100 to 900 at 100-unit increments. Therefore, a fontWeight of 100 would be the least bold that would be displayed, while 900 would be the boldest. A setting of normal (the default weight for any font) is equivalent to a fontWeight value of 400; the standard bold setting is equivalent to 700. Other settings (bolder and lighter) let you specify a weight relative to the parent element's weight.

| **Example** | document.getElementById("hotStuff").style.fontWeight = "bold"; |
|---|---|
| **Value** | Any of the following constant values: bold \| bolder \| lighter \| normal \| 100 \| 200 \| 300 \| 400 \| 500 \| 600 \| 700 \| 800 \| 900. |
| **Default** | normal |

## height, width

Indicate the height and width (and their units) of the element. Because the values are strings containing the assigned units, you cannot use these properties for calculation. Grab copies of the numbers by using parseFloat( ) on the values; or for IE, use pixelHeight, pixelWidth, posHeight, and posWidth properties. Changes to these properties may not be visible unless the element has its position style attribute set.

In IE 6 standards compatibility mode (where document.compatType == "CSS1Compat"), these dimensions apply to only the content portion of an element, irrespective of borders, padding, or margins. For example, if a positioned element that is equipped with padding and borders must be sized to a precise rectangular size, you must subtract the thicknesses of the padding and borders from the height and width values so that the overall element is the desired size.

| **Example** | document.getElementById("viewArea").style.height = "450px"; |
|---|---|
| **Value** | String consisting of a numeric value and length measure or percentage. |
| **Default** | None. |

## imeMode

Controls the presence of the Input Method Editor in IE for Windows for browser and system versions that support languages such as Chinese, Japanese, and Korean.

**Example**          `document.getElementById("nameEntry").style.imeMode = "active";`

**Value**            String of allowable constant values: `active` | `auto` | `disabled` | `inactive`.

**Default**          `auto`

## layoutFlow

Intended primarily for languages that display characters in vertical sentences, controls the progression of content. Replaced starting with IE 5.5 for Windows by the `writingMode` property.

**Value**
One of the constant values (as a string): `horizontal` | `vertical-ideographic`.

**Default**          `horizontal`

## layoutGrid

This is a shorthand property that lets you set one or more layout grid properties (`layoutGridChar`, `layoutGridLine`, `layoutGridMode`, and `layoutGridType`) with one assignment statement. These attributes are used primarily with Asian language content.

**Example**          `document.getElementById("subhead").style.layoutGrid = "2em strict";`

**Value**            For syntax and examples of value types for layoutGrid-related properties, see the respective property listing.

**Default**          None.

## layoutGridChar

Dictates the size of Asian language character grid for block-level elements.

**Example**          `document.getElementById("subhead").style.layoutGrid Char= "auto";`

**Value**            String consisting of an explicit CSS length value or auto or none.

**Default**          none

## layoutGridLine

Dictates the line height of Asian language character grid for block-level elements.

| | |
|---|---|
| **Example** | document.getElementById("subhead").style.layoutGrid Line= "120%"; |
| **Value** | String consisting of an explicit CSS length value or auto or none. |
| **Default** | none |

## layoutGridMode

Specifies whether the Asian language character grid should be one- or two-dimensional.

| | |
|---|---|
| **Example** | document.getElementById("subhead").style.layoutGrid Mode= "both"; |
| **Value** | String constant values: both | char (for inline elements) | line (for block-level elements) | none. |
| **Default** | both |

## layoutGridType

Controls how the layout grid responds to characters of varying width..

| | |
|---|---|
| **Example** | document.getElementById("subhead").style.layoutGrid Type = "strict"; |
| **Value** | String constant values: fixed | loose | strict. |
| **Default** | loose |

## left

For positionable elements, defines the position of the left edge of an element's box (content plus left padding, border, and/or margin) relative to the left edge of the next outermost block content container. When the element is relative-positioned, the offset is based on the left edge of the inline location of where the element would normally appear in the content.

For calculations on this value, use parseFloat( ) on the returned value; or, in IE, retrieve the pixelLeft or posLeft properties, which return genuine numeric values.

| | |
|---|---|
| **Example** | document.getElementById("blockD2").style.left = "45px"; |
| **Value** | String consisting of a numeric value and length unit measure, a percentage, or auto. |
| **Default** | auto |

## letterSpacing

NN 6   IE 4   DOM 2<br>Read/Write

Specifies the spacing between characters within an element. Browsers normally define the character spacing based on font definitions and operating system font rendering. Assigning a negative value tightens the spacing, but be sure to test the effect on the selected font for readability on different operating systems.

| | |
|---|---|
| **Example** | `document.body.style.letterSpacing = "1.1em";` |
| **Value** | A string of a length value (with unit of measure) or normal. The best results are achieved by using units that are based on the rendered font size (em and ex). A setting of normal is how the browser sets the letters without any intervention. |
| **Default** | normal |

## lineBreak

NN n/a   IE 5(Win)   DOM n/a<br>Read/Write

Controls line breaking rules for Japanese text.

| | |
|---|---|
| **Example** | `document.body.style.lineBreak = "strict";` |
| **Value** | String constant values: normal \| strict. |
| **Default** | normal |

## lineHeight

NN 6   IE 4   DOM 2<br>Read/Write

Indicates the height of the inline box (the box holding one physical line of content). See the line-height style attribute in Chapter 11 for details on browser quirks and inheritance traits of different types of values.

| | |
|---|---|
| **Example** | `document.getElementById("tight").style.lineHeight = "1.1em";` |
| **Value** | A string of a length value (with unit of measure) or normal. |
| **Default** | normal |

## listStyle

NN 6   IE 4   DOM 2<br>Read/Write

This is a shorthand property for setting up to three list-style properties in one assignment statement. Whichever attributes you don't explicitly set with this attribute assume their default values. These properties define display characteristics for the markers automatically rendered for list items inside ol and ul elements. This is available in IE as a property of the style and runtimeStyle objects only, but individual properties are properties of currentStyle, as well.

**Example**
```
document.getElementById("itemList").style.listStyle = "square outside none";
```

**Value** See the individual attribute entries for listStyleType, listStylePosition, and listStyleImage for details on acceptable values for each. You may include one, two, or all three values in the list-style attribute setting in any order you wish.

**Default** None.

## listStyleImage

NN 6   IE 4   DOM 2
Read/Write

Provides the URL for an image that is to be used as the marker for a list item. Because this attribute can be inherited, a setting (including none) for an individual list item can override the same attribute or property setting in its parent.

**Example**
```
document.getElementById("itemList").style.listStyleImage = "url(images/3DBullet.gif)";
```

**Value** Use none (as a string) to override an image assigned to a parent element. Otherwise, supply any valid full or relative URL (in the CSS URL format) to an image file with a MIME type that is readable by the browser.

**Default** none

## listStylePosition

NN 6   IE 4   DOM 2
Read/Write

Specifies whether the marker is inside or outside (outdented) the box containing the list item's content. When listStylePosition is set to inside and the content is text, the marker appears to be part of the text block. In this case, the alignment (indent) of the list item is the same as normal, but without the outdented marker.

**Example**
```
document.getElementById("itemList").style.listStylePosition = "inside";
```

**Value** Either constant value as a string: inside | outside.

**Default** outside

## listStyleType

NN 6   IE 4   DOM 2
Read/Write

Specifies the kind of item marker to be displayed with each item. This attribute is applied only if listStyleImage is none (or not specified). The constant values available for this attribute are divided into two categories. One set is used with ul elements to present a filled disc, an empty circle, or a filled square (except empty square on IE 4 for Macintosh). The other set is for ol elements, which has list items that can be marked in sequences of arabic numerals, roman numerals (uppercase or lowercase), letters of the alphabet (uppercase or lowercase), and some other character sequences of other languages if the browser and operating system supports those languages.

**Example**    `document.getElementById("itemList").style.listStyleType = "circle";`

**Value**

One constant value as a string that is relevant to the type of list container. For ul: `circle` | `disc` | `square`. For ol: `decimal` | `decimal-leading-zero` | `lower-roman` | `upper-roman` | `lower-greek` | `lower-alpha` | `lower-latin` | `upper-alpha` | `upper-latin` | `hebrew` | `armenian` | `georgian` | `cjk-ideographic` | `hiragana` | `katakana` | `hiragana-iroha` | `katakana-iroha`. Commonly-supported ol element sequences are treated as shown in the following table.

| Type | Example |
| --- | --- |
| decimal | 1, 2, 3, ... |
| decimal-leading-zero | 01, 02, 03, ... |
| lower-alpha | a, b, c, ... |
| lower-greek | α, β, γ, ... |
| lower-roman | i, ii, iii, ... |
| upper-alpha | A, B, C, ... |
| upper-roman | I, II, III, ... |

**Default**    `disc` (for ul); `decimal` (for ol).

## margin

Read/Write

This is a shortcut property that can set the margin widths of up to four edges of an element with one statement. A margin is space that extends beyond the border of an element to provide extra empty space between adjacent or nested elements, especially those that have border attributes set. You may supply one to four space-delimited margin values. The number of space-delimited values determines which sides receive the assigned margins.

**Example**    `document.getElementById("logoWrapper").style.margin = "5px 8px";`

**Value**

This property accepts one, two, three, or four space-delimited values inside one string, depending on how many and which margins you want to set. See the margin attribute listing in Chapter 11 for complete details on how the number of values affects this property. Values for the margins can be lengths, percentages of the next outermost element size, or the auto constant.

**Default**    0

## marginBottom, marginLeft, marginRight, marginTop   NN 6   IE 4   DOM 6
**Read/Write**

All four properties set the width of a single margin edge of an element. A margin is space that extends beyond the element's border and is not calculated as part of the element's width or height.

### Example
```
document.getElementById("logoWrapper").style.marginTop = "5px";
document.getElementById("navPanel").style.marginLeft = "10%";
```

**Value**        Values for margin widths can be length values, percentages of the next outermost element size, or the auto constant.

**Default**      0


## markerOffset   NN 6   IE n/a   DOM n/a
**Read/Write**

Controls the space between list item markers (which occupy their own box in the CSS box model) and the box that contains the list item text. Although the property is available for Netscape 6, the value is an empty string and the rendered content does not change if you assign it a new value.

**Value**        A string of a length value (with unit of measure) or auto.

**Default**      None.


## marks   NN 6   IE 5(Mac)   DOM 2
**Read/Write**

Sets crop mark type for an @page rule. Although the property is available for IE 5 Macintosh and Netscape 6, the values are empty strings and the rendered content does not change if you assign it a new value.

**Value**        Case-insensitive string of any of the following constants: crop | cross | none.

**Default**      none


## maxHeight, maxWidth, minHeight, minWidth   NN 6   IE (See text)   DOM 2
**Read/Write**

Define loose heights and widths for an element so that, for "max" properties, an element is allowed to grow no bigger in the designated dimension, or, for "min" properties, an element can expand in the designated dimension to accommodate more than expected content or rendering situations. Although the property is available for IE 5 Macintosh and Netscape 6, it is either ignored (IE 5 for Mac) or buggy (Netscape 6). IE 6 for Windows supports only the minWidth property, and it can be used only for tr, th, and td elements.

| | |
|---|---|
| **Value** | CSS length value (see Chapter 11) as a string. |
| **Default** | None. |

## MozBinding

Points to the URL of an XML document designed to enhance an existing element or create a new interface element. Based on Mozilla XBL (Extensible Bindings Language). For more details, visit *http://www.mozilla.org/unix/customizing.html*.

| | |
|---|---|
| **Value** | CSS URL value string or none. |
| **Default** | None. |

## MozOpacity

Defines the level of opacity of the element. The lower the value, the more transparent the element becomes. This is the proprietary Mozilla version of the proprietary Microsoft opaque filter.

| | |
|---|---|
| **Example** | `document.getElementById("menuWrapper").style.MozOpacity = "40%";` |
| **Value** | Numeric string value between 0 and 1 or string percentage value between 0% and 100%. |
| **Default** | 100% (completely opaque) |

## orphans, widows

For a block-level element's content that spreads across page boxes, specify the minimum number of lines of the element that must appear at the bottom of the page (orphans) or at the top of the next page (widows). Although these properties are members of the style object in IE 5/Mac and Netscape 6, neither the style attribute nor scripted changes to it affect the printed output.

| | |
|---|---|
| **Example** | `document.getElementById("sec23").style.orphans = "3";` |
| **Value** | Integer as a string. |
| **Default** | None. |

## outline

This is a shorthand property for getting or setting the `outlineColor`, `outlineStyle`, and/or `outlineWidth` properties of an outline around an element in one statement. You must specify an outline style (see outlineStyle) for changes of this property to affect the display. An outline is like a border, but overlays the element without occupying any content space or affecting the element's dimensions. Although this property is a member of the style object in IE 5/Mac and Netscape 6, only IE 5/Mac renders the outline.

### Exaple

```
document.getElementById("announce").style.outline = "solid blue 4px";
```

### Value

Space-delimited string. For the outlineStyle and outlineWidth component values, see the respective properties in this chapter. For details on the outlineColor value, see the section about CSS colors at the beginning of Chapter 11.

### Default        None.

## outlineColor                                      NN 6    IE 5(Mac)    DOM 2
Read/Write

Controls the color of an outline.

### Example
```
document.getElementById("announce").style.outlineColor = "rgb(100, 75, 0)";
```

**Value**          CSS color value or constant invert. For details on CSS color values, see the section about colors at the beginning of Chapter 11.

**Default**        invert

## outlineStyle                                      NN 6    IE 5(Mac)    DOM 2
Read/Write

Controls the line type of an outline.

**Example**        `document.getElementById("announce").style.outlineStyle = "solid";`

**Value**          Style values are case-insensitive constants that are associated with specific ways of rendering outline (and border) lines. The CSS style constants are: dashed, dotted, double, groove, hidden, inset, none, outset, ridge, and solid.

**Default**        none

## outlineWidth                                      NN 6    IE 5(Mac)    DOM 2
Read/Write

Controls the thickness of the outline lines.

**Example**        `document.getElementById("announce").style.outlineWidth = "2px";`

Alphabetical DOM
Reference

| | |
|---|---|
| **Value** | Three case-insensitive constants—thin \| medium \| thick—allow the browser to define exactly how many pixels are used to show the border. For more precision, you can also assign a length value (see the discussion of CSS length values at the beginning of Chapter 11). |
| **Default** | medium |

## overflow

Specifies how a positioned element should treat content that extends beyond the boundaries established in the style sheet rule. See the discussion of the overflow style sheet attribute in Chapter 11 for details.

| | |
|---|---|
| **Example** | document.getElementById("myDiv").style.overflow = "scroll"; |
| **Value** | Any of the following constants as a string: auto \| hidden \| scroll \| visible. |
| **Default** | visible |

## overflowX, overflowY

Specify how a positioned element should treat content that extends beyond the horizontal (overflowX) or vertical (overflowY) boundaries established in the style sheet rule.

| | |
|---|---|
| **Example** | document.getElementById("myDiv").style.overflow X= "scroll"; |
| **Value** | Any of the following constants as a string: auto \| hidden \| scroll \| visible. |
| **Default** | visible |

## padding

This is a shortcut property that can set the padding widths of up to four edges of an element with one statement. Padding is space that extends around the content box of an element up to but not including any border that may be specified for the element. Padding picks up the background image or color of its element. As you add padding to an element, you increase the size of the visible rectangle of the element without affecting the content block size. You may supply one to four space-delimited padding values. The number of values determines which sides receive the assigned padding.

| | |
|---|---|
| **Example** | document.getElementById("logoWrapper").style.padding = "3px 5px"; |

**Value**

This property accepts one, two, three, or four space-delimited values inside one string, depending on how many and which edges you want to pad. See the padding attribute listing in Chapter 11 for complete details on how the number of values affects this property. Values for padding widths can be lengths, percentages of the next outermost element size, or the auto constant.

**Default**     0

## paddingBottom, paddingLeft, paddingRight, paddingTop     NN 6    IE 4    DOM 2
Read/Write

All four properties set the width of a single padding edge of an element. Padding is space that extends between the element's border and content box. Padding is not calculated as part of the element's width or height.

**Example**

```
document.getElementById("logoWrapper").style.paddingTop = "3px";
document.getElementById("navPanel").style.paddingLeft = "10%";
```

**Value**       Values for padding widths can be length values, percentages of the next outermost element size, or the auto constant.

**Default**     0

## page     NN 6    IE 5(Mac)    DOM 2
Read/Write

Points to the name of an existing @page rule (when the rule contains an identifier, such as @page figures {size: landscape}) in order to apply that rule to the current block-level element. Although this property is a member of the style object in IE 5/Mac and Netscape 6, neither the style attribute nor scripted changes to it affect the printed output.

**Value**       String identifier.

**Default**     None.

## pageBreakAfter, pageBreakBefore     NN 6    IE 4    DOM 2
Read/Write

Define how content should treat a page break around an element when the document is sent to a printer. Page breaks are not rendered in the visual browser as they may be in word processing programs; on screen, long content flows in one continuous scroll on the screen. Also see the extensive discussion of page breaks in the listing for the page-break-after and page-break-before style attributes in Chapter 11.

**Example**

```
document.getElementById("hardBR").style.pageBreakAfter = "always";
document.getElementById("navPanel").style.paddingLeft = "10%";
```

Alphabetical DOM
Reference

**Value**      All supporting browsers recognize four constant values (as strings): always | auto | left | right. Additionally, IE for Windows supports an empty string, which has the same effect as the W3C CSS avoid constant.

**Default**     auto

## pageBreakInside

                        NN 6    IE 5(Mac)   DOM 2

                                      Read/Write

Defines whether the element allows itself to be split across printed pages. Although this property is a member of the style object in IE 5/Mac and Netscape 6, neither the style attribute nor scripted changes to it affect the printed output.

**Value**     A constant value (as a string): auto | avoid.

**Default**    auto

## pause, pauseAfter, pauseBefore, pitch, pitchRange

See azimuth.

## pixelBottom, pixelLeft, pixelRight, pixelTop

                        NN n/a   IE 4   DOM n/a

                                        Read/Write

For positionable elements, these properties define the pixel position of the edges of an element's box (content plus padding, border, and/or margin) relative to the corresponding edges of the next outermost block content container. When the element is relative-positioned, the measure is based on the edges of the inline location of where the element would normally appear in the content. Use these properties for calculation (including path animation) instead of the bottom, left, right, and top properties, which store their values as strings with the unit names. Available as a property of the IE style and runtimeStyle objects only.

**Example**    document.getElementById("myDIV").style.pixelLeft++;

**Value**      Integer.

**Default**    None.

## pixelHeight, pixelWidth

                        NN n/a   IE 4   DOM n/a

                                        Read/Write

Specify the height and width of the element in pixels. Use these properties for calculation instead of properties such as height and width, which return strings including units. Changes to these properties may not be visible unless the element has its position style attribute set. Available as a property of the IE style and runtimeStyle objects only.

**Example**    var midWidth = document.getElementById("myDIV").style.pixelWidth/2;

**Value**            Integer

**Default**          None.

## playDuring

See azimuth.

## posBottom, posLeft, posRight, posTop

For positionable elements, these properties define the position of the edges of an element's box (content plus padding, border, and/or margin) relative to the corresponding edges of the next outermost block content container. When the element is relative-positioned, the measure is based on the edges of the inline location where the element would normally appear in the content. Most importantly, these properties' values are numeric and in the unit of measure set in the CSS bottom, left, right, or top attribute. Use these properties for calculation (including path animation) instead of the bottom, left, right, and top properties, which store their values as strings with the unit names. All math is in the specified units. Also contrast these properties with the pixelBottom, pixelLeft, pixelRight, and pixelTop properties, which are integer values for pixel measures only. Available as a property of the IE style and runtimeStyle objects only.

**Example**

```
document.getElementById("myDIV").style.posLeft =
    document.getElementById("myDIV").style.posLeft + 1.5;
```

**Value**            Floating-point number.

**Default**          None.

## posHeight, posWidth

Specify the numeric height and width of the element in the units set by the CSS positioning-related attributes. Use these properties for calculation instead of properties such as height and width, which return strings including units. All math is in the specified units. Also contrast these properties with the pixelHeight and pixelWidth properties, which are integer values for pixel measures only. Available as a property of the IE style and runtimeStyle objects only.

**Example**          `document.getElementById("myDIV").style.posWidth = 10.5;`

**Value**            Floating-point number.

**Default**          None.

## position

For positionable elements, returns the value assigned to the style sheet position attribute. This property is actually read/write, but you cannot change a positioned element into a static one or vice-versa.

**Example**       var posType = document.getElementById("myDIV").style.position;

**Value**         String constant: absolute | fixed | relative | static. The fixed value is not supported in IE for Windows through Version 6.

**Default**       None.

## quotes

Assigns pairs of characters to be used as quote marks (especially for the q element). Although the property is available for IE 5 Macintosh and Netscape 6, only Netscape 6 responds to the CSS attributes, and neither responds to reading or writing the quotes property value.

**Value**         A string consisting of two or four quoted strings (nested quotes). The first pair provides characters for first-level quotes; the second pair supplies characters to nested quotes.

**Default**       None.

## richness

See azimuth.

## right

For an absolute-positioned element, defines the position of the right edge of an element's box (content plus right padding, border, and/or margin) relative to the right edge of the next outermost block content container.

For numeric calculations on this value in IE, retrieve the pixelRight or posRight style properties, which return genuine numeric values.

**Example**       document.getElementById("blockD2").style.right = "25px";

**Value**         String consisting of a numeric value and length unit measure, a percentage, or auto.

**Default**       auto

## rubyAlign

Controls alignment of content in a ruby element. Changes to this property affect IE for Windows only. Ruby-related styles are defined in CSS3.

| | |
|---|---|
| **Example** | `document.getElementById("myRuby").style.rubyAlign = "center";` |
| **Value** | Case-insensitive string of any of the following constants: `auto` \| `center` \| `distribute-letter` \| `distribute-space` \| `left` \| `line-edge` \| `right`. |
| **Default** | `auto` |

## rubyOverhang

Controls text overhang characteristics of content in a ruby element. Changes to this property affect IE for Windows only. Ruby-related styles are defined in CSS3.

| | |
|---|---|
| **Example** | `document.getElementById("myRuby").style.rubyOverhang="whitespace";` |
| **Value** | Case-insensitive string of any of the following constants: `auto` \| `none` \| `whitespace`. |
| **Default** | `auto` |

## rubyPosition

Controls whether ruby (rt element) text renders on the same line or above its related ruby base (rb element) text. Changes to this property affect IE for Windows only. Ruby-related styles are defined in CSS3.

| | |
|---|---|
| **Example** | `document.getElementById("myRuby").style.rubyPosition = "inline";` |
| **Value** | Case-insensitive string of any of the following constants: `above` \| `inline`. |
| **Default** | `above` |

## scrollbar3dLightColor, scrollbarArrowColor, scrollbarBaseColor, scrollbarDarkShadowColor, scrollbarFaceColor, scrollbarHighlightColor, scrollbarShadowColor, scrollbarTrackColor

Controls the colors for specific components of a scrollbar user interface element associated with an `applet`, `body`, `div`, `embed`, `object`, or `textarea` element. See the description of these CSS attributes in Chapter 11 for details about which component each property governs.

**Example**

document.getElementById("comments").style.scrollbarArrowColor = "rgb(100, 75, 0)";

| **Value** | Case-insensitive CSS color specification (see discussion at beginning of Chapter 11). |
| --- | --- |
| **Default** | None. |

## size

NN 6    IE *n/a*    DOM 2

Read/Write

For a page context defined by an @page rule, this property controls the page size or orientation. Although the property is available for Netscape 6, the value is an empty strings and the property has no influence over the page context.

| **Value** | CSS length values (as a string) or case-insensitive string of any of the following constants: auto | landscape | portrait. For length values, a single value is applied to height and width; two space-delimited length values are applied to width and height, respectively. |
| --- | --- |
| **Default** | auto |

## speak, speakHeader, speakNumeral, speakPunctuation, speechRate, stress

See azimuth.

## styleFloat

NN *n/a*    IE 4    DOM *n/a*

Read/Write

Specifies on which side of the containing box the element aligns so that other content wraps around the element. When the property is set to none, the element appears in its source code sequence, and at most one line of surrounding text content appears in the same horizontal band as the element. See the float style attribute in Chapter 11 for more details. IE 5 for Macintosh duplicates this property as cssFloat, the DOM 2 version, which is also supported (by itself) in Netscape 6.

| **Example** | document.getElementById("myDIV").style.styleFloat = "right"; |
| --- | --- |
| **Value** | One of the following constants (as a string): none | left | right. |
| **Default** | None. |

## tableLayout

NN 6    IE 5    DOM 2

Read/Write

Acts as a switch at load time to direct the browser to start rendering the table based on column widths set by the first row, or wait until the table data is loaded so that the browser can calculate optimum column widths based on cell contents. Changes to this property have no effect on a rendered table.

**Example**      `document.getElementById("myTable").style.tableLayout = "fixed";`

**Value**        One of the following constants (as a string): `auto | fixed`.

**Default**     `auto`

## textAlign                 *NN 6*   *IE 4*   *DOM 2*

*Read/Write*

Determines the horizontal alignment of text within an element's box.

**Example**      `document.getElementById("myDIV").style.textAlign = "right";`

**Value**        One of the four constants (as a string): `center | justify | left | right`.

**Default**     Depends on default language of the browser.

## textAlignLast             *NN n/a*   *IE 5.5(Win)*   *DOM n/a*

*Read/Write*

Determines the horizontal alignment of the last line of text within an element's box. This style attribute may be helpful to obtain the desired look if you use some of the other proprietary text alignment style attributes in IE 5.5 or later for Windows.

**Example**      `document.getElementById("myDIV").style.textAlignLast = "justify";`

**Value**        One of the following constants (as a string): `auto | center | justify | left | right`.

**Default**     `auto`

## textAutospace            *NN n/a*   *IE 5(Win)*   *DOM n/a*

*Read/Write*

Controls the spacing between ideographic (typically Asian languages) and nonideographic characters.

**Example**

`document.getElementById("myDIV").style.textAutospace = "ideograph-numeric";`

**Value**        One of the following constants (as a string): `ideograph-alpha | ideograph-numeric | ideograph-parenthesis | ideograph-space | none`.

**Default**     `none`

## textDecoration

Specifies additions to the text content of the element in the form of underlines, strikethroughs, overlines, and (in Navigator and CSS) blinking. Browsers use this style attribute internally to assign by default underlines to a elements and strikethroughs to strike elements, so the default value varies with element type. You may specify more than one decoration style by supplying values in a space-delimited list. While browsers accept the (CSS optional) blink value, they (thankfully) do not cause the text to blink. Text decoration has an unusual parent-child relationship. Values are not inherited, but the effect of a decoration carries over to nested items in most cases. Therefore, unless otherwise overridden, an underlined p element underlines a nested b element within. Internet Explorer also includes Boolean properties for each decoration type.

### Example
```
document.getElementById("emphasis").style.textDecoration = "underline";
```

| | |
|---|---|
| **Value** | In addition to none, any of the following four constants (as a string): blink \| line-through \| overline \| underline. Multiple values may be included in the string as a space-delimited list. |
| **Default** | Element and internal style sheet dependent. |

## textDecorationBlink, textDecorationLineThrough, textDecorationNone, textDecorationOverline, textDecorationUnderline

Specifies whether the specified text decoration feature is enabled for the element. Each of these properties corresponds to a value that can be assigned to the text-decoration style attribute in CSS (see Chapter 11). Internet Explorer does not blink text, so the textDecorationBlink property is ignored. Setting textDecorationNone to true sets all other related properties to false. Setting these properties on the Macintosh version of IE 4 does not alter the content. Use the textDecoration property instead—good practice all around.

### Example
```
document.getElementById("emphasis").style.textDecorationLineThrough = "true";
```

| | |
|---|---|
| **Value** | Boolean value: true \| false. |
| **Default** | false |

## textIndent

Specifies the size of the indent at the first line of a block of inline text (such as a p element). Only the first line is affected by this setting. A negative value can be used to outdent the first line, but be sure the text does not run beyond the left edge of the browser window or frame.

| **Example** | document.getElementById("firstGraph").style.textIndent = "0.5em"; |
| **Value** | Positive or negative CSS length value (see Chapter 11) as a string. |
| **Default** | 0px |

## textJustify

Specifies detailed character distribution techniques for any block-level element that has a text-align CSS attribute or a textAlign style property set to justify.

**Example**

document.getElementById("inset").style.textJustify = "distribute-center-last";

**Value**

One of the following constants (as a string): auto | distribute | distribute-all-lines | distribute-center-last | inter-cluster | inter-ideograph | inter-word | kashdia | newspaper. See the text-justify attribute in Chapter 11 for details on the meanings of these values.

| **Default** | auto |

## textKashidaSpace

For Arabic text in a block-level element with a text alignment style that is set to justify, controls the ratio of kashida expansion to white space expansion.

| **Example** | document.getElementById("inset").style.textKashidaSpace = "15%"; |
| **Value** | Percentage value as a string. |
| **Default** | 0% |

## textOverflow

Controls whether text content that overflows a fixed box should display an ellipsis (...) at the end of the line to indicate more text is available. The element should also have its overflow style attribute or property set to hidden.

| **Example** | document.getElementById("textBox").style.textOverflow = "ellipsis"; |
| **Value** | One of the allowable constant string value: clip | ellipsis. |
| **Default** | clip |

## textShadow

NN *6*  IE *5(Mac)*  DOM *2*

**Read/Write**

Controls the specifications for shadow effects on the element's text. Although this property is a member of the style object in IE 5/Mac and Netscape 6, neither the style attribute nor scripted changes to it affect the element's text display.

### Value

A string consisting of one or more shadow specifications. Each shadow specification consists of space-delimited values for a color, a length for the offset to the right of the text, a length for the offset below the text, and an optional blur radius value. Multiple shadow specifications are comma-delimited or a value of none to turn off the shadow.

**Default**        none

## textTransform

NN *6*  IE *4*  DOM *2*

**Read/Write**

Controls the capitalization of the element's text. When a value other than none is assigned to this attribute, the cases of all letters in the source text are arranged by the style sheet, overriding the case of the source text characters.

### Example

```
document.getElementById("heading").style.textTransform = "capitalize";
```

### Value

A value of none allows the case of the source text to be rendered as is. Other available constant values (as strings) are: capitalize | lowercase | uppercase. A value of capitalize sets the first character of every word to uppercase. Values lowercase and uppercase render all characters of the element text in their respective cases.

**Default**        none

## textUnderlinePosition

NN *n/a*  IE *5.5(Win)*  DOM *n/a*

**Read/Write**

Controls whether an underline (i.e., an element with a text-decoration style set to underline) is rendered above or below the text.

### Example

```
document.getElementById("heading").style.textUnderlinePosition = "above";
```

### Value

IE 5.5 recognizes two constant values: above | below. IE 6 adds the values auto and auto-pos (which appear to do the same thing). The default value also changed between versions, from below to auto. In IE 6, the auto value underlines vertical Japanese text "above" (to the right) of the characters.

**Default**        none (IE 5.5); auto (IE 6).

## top

For positionable elements, defines the position of the top edge of an element's box (content plus top padding, border, and/or margin) relative to the top edge of the next outermost block content container. When the element is relative-positioned, the offset is based on the top edge of the inline location of where the element would normally appear in the content.

For calculations on this value, use parseFloat( ) on the returned value; or, in IE, retrieve the pixelTop or posTop properties, which return genuine numeric values.

**Example**        `document.getElementById("blockD2").style.top = "40px";`

**Value**           String consisting of a numeric value and length unit measure, a percentage, or auto.

**Default**        auto

## unicodeBidi

Controls the embedding of bidirectional text (such as a mixture of French and Arabic) in concert with the direction style attribute.

**Example**
`document.getElementById("blockD2").style.unicodeBidi = "bidi-override";`

**Value**           String constant values: bidi-override | embed | normal.

**Default**        normal

## verticalAlign

Specifies the vertical alignment characteristic of the element. This property operates in two spheres, depending on the selection of values you use. See the in-depth discussion of the vertical-align style sheet property in Chapter 11 for details.

**Example**        `document.getElementById("myDIV").style.verticalAlign = "text-top";`

**Value**           String value of an absolute measure (with units), a percentage (relative to the next outer box element), or one of the many constant values: bottom | top | baseline | middle | sub | super | text-bottom | text-top.

**Default**        baseline

## visibility

Specifies the state of the positioned element's visibility. Surrounding content does not close up the space left by an element that has its visibility property set to hidden.

**Example**       document.getElementById("myDIV").style.visibility = "hidden";

**Value**        One of the constant values (as a string): collapse | hidden | inherit | visible.

**Default**      visible

## voiceFamily, volume

See azimuth.

## whiteSpace

NN 6    IE 5(Mac)/5.5(Win)    DOM 2

Read/Write

Controls intepretation of whitespace (such as leading spaces and line breaks) from the source code.

**Example**       document.getElementById("myDIV").style.whiteSpace = "pre";

**Value**

One of the constant values (as a string): normal | nowrap | pre. Value of normal allows browsers to word-wrap lines in block elements and ignore leading spaces. Value of nowrap causes source code not to word-wrap, but still ignores leading spaces. Value of pre preserves leading spaces, extra spaces, and carriage returns in the source code. Note that IE 6 for Windows does not respond to the pre value unless the DOCTYPE element values place the browser into standards compatibility mode.

**Default**       normal

## widows

See orphans.

## width

See height.

## wordBreak

NN n/a    IE 5(Win)    DOM n/a

Read/Write

Specifies the word-break style for ideographic languages or content that mixes Latin and ideographic languages.

**Example**       document.getElementById("myDIV").style.wordBreak = "keep-all";

**Value**        One of the constant values (as a string): break-all | keep-all | normal.

**Default**      normal

## wordSpacing

Governs the length of space between words. IE 5 for Macintosh may exhibit overlap problems with the word-spacing of elements nested inside the one being controlled.

| | |
|---|---|
| **Example** | document.getElementById("myDIV").style.wordSpacing = "1.0em"; |
| **Value** | CSS length value (as a string) or the constant normal. |
| **Default** | normal |

## wordWrap

Specifies the word-wrapping style for block-level, specifically-sized inline, or positioned elements. If a single word (i.e., without any whitespace) extends beyond the width of the element containing box, the normal behavior is to extend the content beyond the normal box width, without breaking. But you can force the long word to break at whatever character position occurs at the edge of the box.

| | |
|---|---|
| **Example** | document.getElementById("myDIV").style.wordWrap = "break-word"; |
| **Value** | One of the constant values (as a string): break-word \| normal. |
| **Default** | normal |

## writingMode

Intended primarily for languages that display characters in vertical sentences, this controls the progression of content, left-to-right, or right-to-left.

| | |
|---|---|
| **Example** | document.getElementById("myDIV").style.writingMode = "lr-tb"; |
| **Value** | One of the constant values (as a string): lr-tb \| tb-rl. Value of tb-rl can rotate text of some languages by 90 degrees. |
| **Default** | lr-tb |

## zIndex

For a positioned element, this specifies the stacking order relative to other elements within the same parent container. See Chapter 4 for details on relationships of element layering amid multiple containers.

| | |
|---|---|
| **Example** | document.getElementById("myDIV").style.zIndex = "3" |
| **Value** | Integer. Netscape 6 prefers that this value be in string form (that's how the property returns its value), while IE returns a number. |
| **Default** | 0 |

## zoom

NN n/a   IE 5.5(Win)   DOM n/a<br>Read/Write

Governs the magnification of rendered content. Particularly useful for output that might be displayed on monitors with very high pixel density. See `screen.logicalXDPI` property.

**Example**     `document.body.style.zoom = "200%";`

**Value**     Percentage value (where 100% is normal), floating-point multiplier (where 1.0 is normal), or constant `normal`.

**Default**     `normal`

## getPropertyCSSValue( )

NN n/a   IE n/a   DOM 2

`getPropertyCSSValue("CSSAttributeName")`

Returns an object that represents a CSS value. In the W3C DOM, the `CSSValue` object returned from this method has properties that reveal the text of the attribute/value pair and a numeric value corresponding to a long list of primitive value types (indicating types such as percentage, pixel lengths, and RGB color). Although this method is implemented in Netscape 6, it returns an empty object for now.

**Returned Value**     Reference to a CSSValue object.

**Parameters**

*CSSAttributeName*
> The CSS attribute name from an inline style declaration (not the DOM version of the property name).

## getPropertyPriority( )

NN 6   IE 5(Mac)   DOM 2

`getPropertyPriority("CSSAttributeName")`

Returns the string value of any priority (such as `!important`) associated with the inline CSS attribute.

**Returned Value**     String.

**Parameters**

*CSSAttributeName*
> The CSS attribute name from an inline style declaration (not the DOM version of the property name).

## getPropertyValue( )

NN 6   IE 5(Mac)   DOM 2

`getPropertyValue("CSSAttributeName")`

Returns the string value of the inline CSS attribute/value pair.

**Returned Value**     String.

**Parameters**

*CSSAttributeName*

> The CSS attribute name from an inline style declaration (not the DOM version of the property name).

## item( )

item(*index*)

Returns the attribute name of the inline CSS attribute/value pair corresponding to the integer index value in source code order.

**Returned Value**

String. IE for Macintosh returns name in all-uppercase characters, while Netscape 6 returns all-lowercase characters.

**Parameters**

*index*

> Zero-based integer corresponding to the specified inline CSS attribute/value pair in source code order.

## removeProperty( )

removeProperty("*CSSAttributeName*")

Deletes the inline CSS attribute/value pair and returns a string with the previous value.

**Returned Value**    String.

**Parameters**

*CSSAttributeName*

> The CSS attribute name from an inline style declaration (not the DOM version of the property name).

## setProperty( )

setProperty("*CSSAttributeName*", "*value*", "*priority*")

Sets an inline style attribute/value pair. If the attribute already exists, the new value is applied to the existing attribute; otherwise the attribute and value are added to the element.

**Returned Value**    None.

**Parameters**

*CSSAttributeName*

> The CSS attribute name from an inline style declaration (not the DOM version of the property name).

Alphabetical DOM Reference

*value*
> String of the value in the format applicable to the attribute.

*priority*
> String of the priority assignment (such as !important) or empty string.

# styleSheet

The styleSheet object represents a style sheet that may have been created as a style element or imported with a link element or @import statement inside a style element. This object is different from the style element object, which strictly reflects the style HTML element and its attributes. The document.styleSheets[] collection contains zero or more styleSheet objects. The shared disabled property is available in all supporting browsers, facilitating the enabling and disabling of entire style sheets with simple Boolean assignments.

### Object Model Reference
[window.]document.styleSheets[i]

### Object-Specific Properties

| | | | | |
|---|---|---|---|---|
| cssRules[] | cssText | href | imports[] | media |
| ownerNode | ownerRule | owningElement | pages[] | parentStyleSheet |
| readOnly | rules[] | title | type | |

### Object-Specific Methods

| | | | | |
|---|---|---|---|---|
| addImport() | addRule() | deleteRule() | insertRule() | removeRule() |

### Object-Specific Event Handler Properties
None.

## cssRules[]

Read-only

Returns a collection of cssRule objects nested within the current styleSheet object. The IE-only equivalent is the rules property. See the cssRules object earlier in this chapter for a description of this collection object's property and methods; see the cssRule object earlier in this chapter for a description of the individual members of this collection.

**Example**     var allCSSRules = document.styleSheets[0].cssRules;

**Value**       Reference to a CSSRules collection object.

**Default**     Array of zero length.

## cssText

**Read/Write**

Contains the entire text (as a string) of all rules defined in the style sheet. This is useful primarily if you wish to replace the entire set of rules with a new set. To act on the text of an individual rule in IE, access the cssText property of a single rule object (obtained by the styleSheet object's rules[i].cssText property); or, in Netscape 6, you can use the cssRules[i].cssText property.

| | |
|---|---|
| **Example** | var allCSSText = document.styleSheets[0].cssText; |
| **Value** | String. |
| **Default** | Empty string. |

## href

**Read/Write**

This is the URL specified by a link element's href attribute (when the link is used to import a style sheet). This value is read/write in IE for Windows, but read-only in Netscape 6 and IE/Mac.

| | |
|---|---|
| **Example** | document.styleSheets[1].href = "css/altStyles.css"; |
| **Value** | String of complete or relative URL. |
| **Default** | None. |

## imports[]

**Read-only**

Returns a collection (array) of styleSheet objects imported into an explicit styleSheet object via the @import rule. See the imports collection object earlier in this chapter for further discussion. For Netscape 6, you must loop through all cssRule objects of a styleSheet object in search of those with type property values equal to 3 (the same as the cssRule object's IMPORT_RULE constant).

| | |
|---|---|
| **Example** | var allImportRules = document.styleSheets[0].imports; |
| **Value** | Reference to an imports collection object. |
| **Default** | Array of zero length. |

## media

**Read/Write**

Specifies the intended output device for the content governed by the style sheet (reflecting the media attribute of the link and style elements). The media property looks forward to the day when browsers are able to tailor content to specific kinds of devices such as pocket computers, text-to-speech digitizers, or fuzzy television sets. This property is not available in IE 4/Macintosh.

**Example**
```
if (document.styleSheets[2].media == "print") {
    // process for print output
}
```

| **Value** | Any one of the following constant values as a string: all \| print \| screen. |
|---|---|
| **Default** | all |

## ownerNode

Returns a reference to the document tree node that contains the styleSheet object. This node is either a style or link element, depending on the way the style sheet is defined in the document. The IE (Windows and Mac) equivalent property is owningElement. IE for the Macintosh provides an extra owningNode property, which is very likely a mistaken implementation of the W3C DOM ownerNode property.

| **Example** | var mama = document.styleSheets[2].ownerNode; |
|---|---|
| **Value** | Object reference. |
| **Default** | None. |

## ownerRule

For a styleSheet object brought into the document via an @import rule, returns a reference to that @import rule object (a W3C DOM CSSImportRule object). The cssRule object earlier in this chapter provides the properties and methods that apply to a CSSImportRule object. For other style sheet types, the property returns null.

| **Example** | var hostRule = document.styleSheets[2].ownerRule; |
|---|---|
| **Value** | Object reference or null. |
| **Default** | null |

## owningElement

Returns a reference to the style or link element object that defines the current styleSheet object. Each document maintains a collection of style sheets created with both the style and link elements. The comparable Netscape 6 property is ownerNode.

| **Example** | var firstStyleID = document.styleSheets[0].owningElement.id; |
|---|---|
| **Value** | Element object reference. |
| **Default** | None. |

## pages[]

Returns a collection (array) of page objects (@page rules) nested within a styleSheet object. For Netscape 6, you must loop through all cssRule objects of a styleSheet object in search of those with type property values equal to 6 (the same as the cssRule object's PAGE_RULE constant). See the page object.

| | |
|---|---|
| **Example** | var allPageRules = document.styleSheets[0].pages; |
| **Value** | Reference to a pages collection object. |
| **Default** | Array of zero length. |

## parentStyleSheet

For a styleSheet object generated by virtue of inclusion with an @page rule, the parentStyleSheet property returns a reference to the styleSheet (created as a link or style element) object that imported the current style sheet. For a nonimported style sheet, the property returns null.

| | |
|---|---|
| **Example** | var myMaker = document.styleSheets[0].parentStyleSheet; |
| **Value** | Reference to a styleSheet object. |
| **Default** | null |

## readOnly

Specifies whether the style sheet can be modified under script control. Style sheets imported through a link element or an @import rule cannot be modified, so they return a value of true.

| | |
|---|---|
| **Value** | Boolean value: true \| false. |
| **Default** | false |

## rules[]

Returns a collection of rule objects nested within the current styleSheet object. The W3C DOM equivalent (implemented in Netscape 6 and IE 5/Mac) is the cssRules property. See the cssRules object earlier in this chapter for a description of this collection object's property and methods; see the cssRule object earlier in this chapter for a description of the individual members of this collection.

| | |
|---|---|
| **Example** | var allrules = document.styleSheets[0].rules; |

| | |
|---|---|
| **Value** | Reference to a rules collection object. |
| **Default** | Array of zero length. |

## title

Exposes the title attribute of the style or link element that owns the current styleSheet object. Since the attribute does not affect user interface elements (the elements are unrendered, and thus don't show tool tips), it is available to convey other string information to the styleSheet object under script control.

### Example
```
if (document.styleSheets[2].title == "corpStyleWindows") {
    // process for the designated style
}
```

| | |
|---|---|
| **Value** | String value. |
| **Default** | Empty string. |

## type

Returns the style sheet MIME type specified by the type attribute of the style or link element.

### Example
```
if (document.styleSheets[0].type == "text/css") {
    ...
}
```

| | |
|---|---|
| **Value** | String (text/css for typical CSS style sheets). |
| **Default** | None. |

## addImport( )

```
addImport(url, [index])
```

Adds an external style sheet specification to a styleSheet object.

### Returned Value
Integer of the index position within the styleSheets[] collection where the style sheet was added (in case you omit the second parameter and let the browser find the end position).

### Parameters
*url*
> A complete or relative URL to the style sheet (*.css*) file.

*index*

    An optional integer indicating where in the collection the new element should be placed.

## addRule( )                 NN *n/a*    IE *4*    DOM *n/a*

addRule("*selector*", "*style*"[, *index*])

Adds a new rule for a style sheet. This method offers a scripted way of adding a rule to an existing styleSheet object:

```
document.styleSheets[1].addRule("p b","color:red");
```

You may duplicate a selector that already exists in the styleSheet and, therefore, override an existing rule for the same element selector. The only prohibition is that you may not override a rule to convert a plain style rule into one that creates a positionable element (or vice versa). The new rule is governed by the same cascading rules as all style sheet rules (that includes the rule's source code position among other rules with the same selector). Therefore, a new rule in a styleSheet object does not supersede a style set in an element's style property.

**Returned Value**

Early versions of IE returned no value. More recently, IE for Windows returns -1, while IE for Macintosh returns null. In the future, the returned value may become the integer of the index location of the new rule.

**Parameters**

*selector*

    The style rule selector as a string.

*style*

    One or more style *attribute:value* pairs. Multiple pairs are semicolon delimited, just as they are in the regular style sheet definition.

*index*

    An optional integer indicating where in the collection the new element should be placed.

## deleteRule( )                 NN *6*    IE *5(Mac)*    DOM *2*

deleteRule(*index*)

Removes a rule from the styleSheet object. The integer index parameter value points to the zero-based item in the cssRules array to delete. Note that IE 5 for Macintosh implements both the Microsoft removeRule( ) and W3C DOM deleteRule( ) method for the same operation.

**Returned Value**     None.

**Parameters**

*index*

    A zero-based integer indicating which rule in the cssRules collection is to be deleted.

## insertRule( )    NN 6    IE 5(Mac)    DOM 2

insertRule("*ruleText*", *index*)

Adds a new rule for a style sheet. This method offers a scripted way of adding a rule to an existing W3C DOM styleSheet object:

    document.styleSheets[1].insertRule("p b {color:red}", 0);

You may duplicate a selector that already exists in the styleSheet and, therefore, override an existing rule for the same element selector. The only prohibition is that you may not override a rule to convert a plain style rule into one that creates a positionable element (or vice versa). The new rule is governed by the same cascading rules as all style sheet rules (that includes the rule's source code position among other rules with the same selector). Therefore, a new rule in a styleSheet object does not supersede a style set in an element's style property. Note that IE 5 for the Macintosh implements both the W3C DOM insertRule( ) and Microsoft addRule( ) methods to accomplish the same result.

**Returned Value**    Integer of the index location of the new rule.

**Parameters**

*ruleText*
> The entire style rule selector as a string in exactly the same format as assigned in a style element: *selector* {*attribute*:*value*; *attribute*:*value*;...}.

*index*
> Zero-based integer indicating where in the cssRules collection the new rule should be placed.

## removeRule( )    NN *n/a*    IE 4    DOM *n/a*

removeRule(*index*)

Removes a rule from the styleSheet object. The integer index parameter value points to the zero-based item in the rules array to delete.

**Returned Value**    None.

**Parameters**

*index*
> A zero-based integer indicating which rule in the rules collection is to be deleted.

# styleSheets, StyleSheetList    NN 6    IE 4    DOM 2

A collection of styleSheet objects that are members of a document object. The W3C DOM abstract representation of this collection is called a StyleSheetList object. Members of this collection are accessed via their integer index number, but you may iterate through the collection and examine properties of each style sheet object (such as the selectorText property) to distinguish one rule from another.

**Object Model Reference**

document.styleSheets

**Object-Specific Properties**
length

**Object-Specific Methods**
item( )

**Object-Specific Event Handler Properties**
None.

## length

Read-only

Returns the number of elements in the collection.

| **Example** | `var howMany = document.styleSheets.length;` |
|---|---|
| **Value** | Integer. |

## item( )

item(*index*)

Returns a styleSheet object corresponding to the object matching the index value in source code order.

**Returned Value**

Reference to a styleSheet object. If there are no matches to the parameters, the returned value is null.

**Parameters**

*index*

A zero-based integer corresponding to the specified item in source code order (nested within the current document object).

## sub, sup

The sub object reflects the sub element; the sup object reflects the sup element. Browsers tend to render these objects' content in a smaller size than surrounding content. IE 5 for Macintosh provides object-specific, read-only height and width properties for these elements, but no other object model does.

**HTML Equivalent**
<sub>
<sup>

**Object Model Reference**
[window.]document.getElementById("*elementID*")

Alphabetical DOM
Reference

**Object-Specific Properties**
None.

**Object-Specific Methods**
None.

**Object-Specific Event Handler Properties**
None.

# submit

See input (type="submit").

# sup

See sub.

# table                                        **NN 6    IE 4    DOM 1**

The table object reflects the table element. Other objects related to the table object are: caption, col, colgroup, tbody, td, tfoot, thead, and tr.

**HTML Equivalent**    <table>

**Object Model Reference**
[window.]document.getElementById("elementID")

**Object-Specific Properties**

| | | | |
|---|---|---|---|
| align | background | bgColor | border |
| borderColor | borderColorDark | borderColorLight | caption |
| cellPadding | cells[] | cellSpacing | cols |
| dataPageSize | frame | height | rows[] |
| rules | summary | tbodies[] | tFoot |
| tHead | width | | |

**Object-Specific Methods**

| | | | |
|---|---|---|---|
| createCaption() | createTFoot() | createTHead() | deleteCaption() |
| deleteRow() | deleteTFoot() | deleteTHead() | insertRow() |
| lastPage() | moveRow() | nextPage() | previousPage() |
| refresh() | | | |

**Object-Specific Event Handler Properties**
None.

## align

Read/Write

Defines the horizontal alignment of the element within its surrounding container.

**Example**          `document.getElementById("myTable").align = "center";`

**Value**            Any of the three horizontal alignment constants: center | left | right.

**Default**          left

## background

Read/Write

Provides the URL of the background image for the table. If you set a backgroundColor to the element as well, the color appears if the image fails to load; otherwise, the image overlays the color.

**Example**
`document.getElementById("myTable").background = "images/watermark.jpg";`

**Value**            Complete or relative URL to the background image file.

**Default**          None.

## bgColor

Read/Write

Specifies the background color of the element. This color setting is not reflected in the style sheet backgroundColor property. Even if the bgcolor attribute or bgColor property is set with a plain-language color name, the returned value is always a hexadecimal triplet.

**Example**          `document.getElementById("myTable").bgColor = "yellow";`

**Value**            A hexadecimal triplet or plain-language color name. See Appendix A for
                     acceptable plain-language color names.

**Default**          Varies with browser and operating system.

## border

Read/Write

Specifies the thickness of the border around the table (in pixels). This is the default 3-D–look border and should not be confused with borders created with style sheets.

**Example**          `document.getElementById("myTable").border = 4;`

**Value**            An integer value. A setting of zero removes the border entirely.

**Default**          0

**Alphabetical DOM Reference**

## borderColor

**Read/Write**

Specifies the color of the table's border. Internet Explorer applies the color to all four lines that make up the interior border of a cell. Therefore, colors of adjacent cells do not collide.

| | |
|---|---|
| **Example** | document.getElementById("myTable").borderColor = "salmon"; |
| **Value** | A hexadecimal triplet or plain-language color name. A setting of empty is interpreted as "#000000" (black). See Appendix A for acceptable plain-language color names. |
| **Default** | Varies with operating system. |

## borderColorDark, borderColorLight

**Read/Write**

The 3-D effect of table borders in Internet Explorer is created by careful positioning of light and dark lines around the page's background or default color. You can independently control the colors used for the dark and light lines by assigning values to the borderColorDark (left and top edges of the cell) and borderColorLight (right and bottom edges) properties.

Typically, you should assign complementary colors to the pair of properties. There is also no rule that says you must assign a dark color to borderColorDark. The attributes merely control a well-defined set of lines so you can predict which lines of the border change with each attribute.

**Example**
```
document.getElementById("myTable").borderColorDark = "blue";
document.getElementById("myTable").borderColorLight = "cornflowerblue";
```

| | |
|---|---|
| **Value** | A hexadecimal triplet or plain-language color name. A setting of empty is interpreted as "#000000" (black). See Appendix A for acceptable plain-language color names. |
| **Default** | Varies with operating system. |

## caption

**Read-only**

Returns a reference to a caption element nested inside the table. From this reference you can access properties and methods of the caption object. In Netscape 6, you can create a new caption element, and assign that new element's reference to the caption property of a table, making the property read/write in that browser (although you really should be using the createCaption( ) method). For all browsers, however, you can modify properties of the caption object returned by the caption property.

| | |
|---|---|
| **Example** | var capText = document.getElementById("myTable").caption.innerHTML; |

| **Value** | Object reference. |
| **Default** | None. |

## cellPadding

Specifies the amount of empty space between the (visible or invisible) border of a table cell and the content of the cell. Note that this property applies to space *inside* a cell. Minor adjustments to this property are not as noticeable when the table does not also display borders (in which case the cellSpacing property can assist in adjusting the space between cells).

| **Example** | `document.getElementById("myTable").cellPadding = "15";` |
| **Value** | A string value for a length in pixels or percentage. |
| **Default** | 0 |

## cells

Returns a collection of all td elements inside the table. Entries in the array are in source code order of td elements. This property is more widely available for a tr element (one row at a time).

| **Example** | `var totCells = document.getElementById("myTable").cells.length;` |
| **Value** | Reference to a cells collection object. |
| **Default** | Array of zero length. |

## cellSpacing

Specifies the amount of empty space between the outer edges of each table cell. If the table has a border, the effect of setting cellSpacing is to define the thickness of borders rendered between cells. Even without a visible border, the readability of a table often benefits from cell spacing, or a combination of cell spacing and cell padding.

| **Example** | `document.getElementById("myTable").cellSpacing = "5";` |
| **Value** | A string value for a length in pixels or percentage. |
| **Default** | 0 (with no table border); 2 (with table border). |

## cols

Specifies the number of columns of the table. The corresponding IE-specific cols attribute assists the browser in preparation for rendering the table. Without this attribute, the browser relies on its interpretation of all downloaded tr and td elements to determine how the table is to be divided. You cannot change the column makeup of a table from this property, despite its read/write status. See also the col object earlier in this chapter

| | |
|---|---|
| **Example** | document.getElementById("myTable").cols = 5; |
| **Value** | Integer. |
| **Default** | None. |

## dataPageSize

Used with IE data binding, this property advises the browser how many instances of a table row must be rendered to accommodate the number of data source records set by this attribute. See lastPage( ), nextPage( ), and previousPage( ) methods for navigating through groups of records.

| | |
|---|---|
| **Example** | document.getElementById("inventoryTable").dataPageSize = 10; |
| **Value** | Integer. |
| **Default** | None. |

## frame

Indicates which (if any) sides of a table's outer border (set with the border attribute or border property) are rendered. This property does not affect the interior borders between cells.

| | |
|---|---|
| **Example** | document.getElementById("orderForm").frame = "hsides"; |

**Value**

Any one case-insensitive frame constant (as a string):

| | |
|---|---|
| above | Renders border along top edge of table only |
| below | Renders border along bottom edge of table only |
| border | Renders all four sides of the border (same as box) |
| box | Renders all four sides of the border (same as border) |
| hsides | Renders borders on top and bottom edges of table only (a nice look) |
| lhs | Renders border on left edge of table only |
| rhs | Renders border on right edge of table only |
| void | Hides all borders (default in HTML 4) |
| vsides | Renders borders on left and right edges of table only |

**Default**       void (when border=0); border (when border is any other value)

## height, width

Specify the height and width in pixels of the element. Changes to these values are immediately reflected in reflowed content on the page. Only the width property is available in Netscape 6 (and the W3C DOM), as the table's height is considered to be the sum of the highest cell in each row.

**Example**       `document.getElementById("myTable").height = 250;`

**Value**       Integer.

**Default**       None.

## rows

Returns a collection of tr elements inside the entire table. You can also get a group of rows for each table section (tbody, tfoot, and thead element objects).

**Example**       `var allTableRows = document.getElementById("myTable").rows;`

**Value**       Reference to a rows collection object.

**Default**       Array of zero length.

## rules

Indicates where (if at all) interior borders between cells are rendered by the browser. In addition to setting the table to draw borders to turn the cells into a matrix, you can set borders to be drawn only to separate borders, columns, or any sanctioned cell grouping (thead, tbody, tfoot, colgroup, or col). The border attribute must be present—either as a Boolean or set to a specific border size—for any cell borders to be drawn. Do not confuse this property with the rules[] collection of styleSheet objects. Scripted changes to this property do not always yield the desired results, especially in early versions of Netscape 6.

**Example**       `document.getElementById("myTable").rules = "groups";`

**Value**

Any one case-insensitive rules constant (as a string):

all      Renders borders around each cell

cols      Renders borders between columns only

groups   Renders borders between cell groups as defined by thead, tfoot, tbody, colgroup, or col elements

none      Hides all interior borders

rows      Renders borders between rows only

**Default**       none (when border=0); all (when border is any other value).

## summary

**Read-only**

Reflects the HTML 4 summary attribute, which provides no particular functionality in mainstream browsers. But you can assign a value to it in the source code to convey data to a script that reads the property.

| | |
|---|---|
| **Example** | `var data = document.getElementById("myTable").summary;` |
| **Value** | String. |
| **Default** | Empty string. |

## tBodies[]

**Read-only**

Returns a collection of tBody objects in the current table. Every table element has at least one (explicit or implied) tBody object nested inside.

| | |
|---|---|
| **Example** | `var bodSections = document.getElementById("myTable").tBodies;` |
| **Value** | Reference to a collection of tBody objects. |
| **Default** | Array of length one. |

## tFoot

**Read-only**

Returns a reference to the tfoot element object if one has been defined for the table. If no tfoot element exists, the value is null. You can access tfoot element object properties and methods through this reference if you like. This property is available only on the Win32 version of Internet Explorer 4.

**Example**

`var tableFootTxt = document.getElementById("myTable").tFoot.firstChild.nodeValue;`

| | |
|---|---|
| **Value** | tfoot element object reference. |
| **Default** | null |

## tHead

**Read-only**

Returns a reference to the thead element object if one has been defined for the table. If no thead element exists, the value is null. You can access thead element object properties and methods through this reference if you like. This property is available only on the Win32 version of Internet Explorer 4.

**Example**

`var tableHeadTxt = document.getElementById("myTable").tHead.firstChild.nodevalue;`

**Value**         thead element object reference.

**Default**       null

## width

See height.

## createCaption( ), deleteCaption( )                    NN 6    IE 4    DOM 1

Add or remove a caption element nested within the current table element. If no caption exists, the creation method produces an empty element, which your scripts must then populate with caption text (through common element content modification techniques). If a caption exists, the method is essentially ignored, and returns a reference to the existing caption element.

**Returned Value**    Reference to new caption element (for createCaption( )); nothing for deleteCaption( ).

**Parameters**       None.

## createTFoot(), createTHead(), deleteTFoot( ), deleteTHead( )                              NN 6    IE 4    DOM 1

Add or remove a thead or tfoot element nested within the current table element. If no head or foot table section exists, the creation method produces an empty element, which your scripts must then populate with rows (through thead.insertRow( ) and tfoot.insertRow( ) methods). If the desired table section exists, the method is essentially ignored, and returns a reference to the existing thead or tfoot element.

**Returned Value**    Reference to newly created element (for createTFoot( ) and createTHead( )); Nothing for deleteTHead( ) and deleteTFoot( ).

**Parameters**       None.

## deleteRow( )                                          NN 6    IE 4    DOM 1

deleteRow(*index*)

Removes a tr element nested within the current table element. The integer parameter points to the zero-based item in the rows collection. To repopulate a table with new or sorted content, empty the table (or just a table section) with iterative calls to the deleteRow( ) method:

```
while (tableReference.rows.length > 0) {
    tableReference.deleteRow(0);
}
```

**Returned Value**    None.

**Parameters**

*index*

Zero-based integer corresponding to the said numbered tr element in source code order (nested within the current element).

## insertRow( )                                              NN 6     IE 4(Win)     DOM 1

insertRow(*index*)

Inserts a tr element nested within the current table element. The integer parameter points to the zero-based index in the rows collection where the new row should go, but in IE you can also use the shortcut value of -1 to append the row to the end of the collection. Adding the row inserts an empty element, to which you add cells via the insertCell( ) method. Unfortunately, scripting the addition of table rows and cells in IE for the Macintosh (including Version 5.1) is very broken, yielding elephantine row and cell dimensions. For nonnested tables, you might be able to get away with regular document tree node creation and insertion instead of the table (and related) object convenience methods.

**Returned Value**    Reference to the newly inserted row.

**Parameters**

*index*

Zero-based integer corresponding to a row of the rows collection before which the new row is to be inserted.

## lastPage(), nextPage( ), previousPage( )                 NN *n/a*    IE 4/5    DOM *n/a*

Advises the data binding facilities to load the last, next, or previous group of records from the data source to fill the number of records established with the dataPageSize property. The lastPage( ) method is available in IE 5 or later.

**Returned Value**    None.

**Parameters**        None.

## moveRow( )                                                 NN *n/a*    IE 5(Win)    DOM *n/a*

moveRow(*indexToMove, destinationIndex*)

Moves a row in the table from its original location to a different row position. The first parameter is a zero-based index of the row (within the rows collection) you wish to move. The second parameter is the index of the row before which you want to move the row. As a method of the table object, moveRow( )'s index parameters include the first row, which may contain th elements you don't want to move. Invoke the method on the tbody object if you want counting to be just within a table section.

**Returned Value**    Reference to the moved row.

**Parameters**

*indexToMove*
> A zero-based integer pointing to the row to move.

*destinationIndex*
> A zero-based integer pointing to the row above which the row is to be moved.

## refresh( )

Advises the data binding facilities to reload the current page of data from the data source. If your table is retrieving frequently-changing data from a database, you can create a setTimeout( ) loop to invoke document.getElementById("myTable").refresh( ) as often as users would want updated information from the database.

**Returned Value**    None.

**Parameters**    None.

## tags

The tags object is used by JavaScript syntax for style sheets in Navigator 4 only. As a property of the document object, this tags object is used in building references to particular HTML elements to get or set their style-related properties. The direct properties of the tags object are all HTML element types. For example:

```
[document.]tags.p
[document.]tags.h1
```

There is no need to repeat a list of all HTML elements as properties for this object. These references are usable inside style elements with a type set to text/javascript. That's where you assign values to style sheet properties with JavaScript syntax, as in the following examples:

```
tags.p.color = "green";
tags.h1.fontSize = "14pt";
```

The properties in the following list are not properties of the tags object per se, but rather of the style sheet associated with an element, class, or ID singled out by a JavaScript syntax assignment statement. The properties are listed here for convenience (and historical completeness). Properties dedicated to element positioning are listed separately from regular style properties. For information about these property values, consult the CSS reference chapter, where you can find details of all style sheet properties listed by CSS syntax.

### Style Object-Specific Properties

| | | | |
|---|---|---|---|
| backgroundColor | backgroundImage | borderBottomWidth | borderColor |
| borderLeftWidth | borderRightWidth | borderStyle | borderTopWidth |
| borderWidths( ) | color | display | fontFamily |
| fontSize | fontStyle | fontWeight | listStyleType |
| marginBottom | marginLeft | marginRight | margins( ) |

| marginTop | paddingBottom | paddingLeft | paddingRight |
| --- | --- | --- | --- |
| paddings | paddingTop | textAlign | textDecoration |
| textTransform | verticalAlign | whiteSpace | |

**Position Object-Specific Properties**

| background | bgColor | clip | left |
| --- | --- | --- | --- |
| top | visibility | zIndex | |

# tBodies

This is a collection of all tbody elements contained within a single table element. Collection members are sorted in source code order.

## Object Model Reference

document.getElementById("*tableID*").tBodies

## Object-Specific Properties

length

## Object-Specific Methods

| item( ) | namedItem( ) | tags( ) | urns( ) |
| --- | --- | --- | --- |

## Object-Specific Event Handler Properties

None.

## length

Returns the number of elements in the collection.

**Example**      var howMany = document.getElementById("myTable").tBodies.length;

**Value**      Integer.

## item( )

item(*index*[, *subindex*])
item(*index*)

Returns a single tBody object or collection of tBody objects corresponding to the element matching the index value (or, optionally in IE, the index and subindex values).

## Returned Value

One tBody object or collection (array) of tBody objects. If there are no matches to the parameters, the returned value is null.

## Parameters

*index*

> When the parameter is a zero-based integer, the returned value is a single element corresponding to the specified item in source code order (nested within the current element); when the parameter is a string (IE only), the returned value is a collection of elements with id properties that match that string.

*subindex*

> In IE only, if you specify a string value for the first parameter, you can use the second parameter to specify a zero-based index that retrieves the specified element from the collection with id properties that match the first parameter's string value.

## namedItem( ) NN 6    IE 6    DOM 1

namedItem("*ID*")

Returns a single tBody object or collection of tBody objects corresponding to the element matching the parameter string value.

### Returned Value

One tBody object or collection (array) of tBody objects. If there are no matches to the parameters, the returned value is null.

### Parameters

*ID*

> The string that contains the same value as the desired element's id attribute.

## tags( ) NN *n/a*    IE 4    DOM *n/a*

tags("*tagName*")

Returns a collection of objects (among all objects nested within the current collection) whose tags match the *tagName* parameter.

## urns( ) NN *n/a*    IE 5(Win)    DOM *n/a*

urns(*URN*)

See the all.urns( ) method.

# tbody, tfoot, thead NN 6    IE 4    DOM 1

The tbody, tfoot, and thead objects reflect the tbody, tfoot, and thead elements, respectively. For scripting purposes, you can treat each of these as a container of row groups inside a table. They all share the same properties and methods, so you need to keep their HTML functionality straight as you script these elements. A table can have only one tfoot and one thead element, but multiple tbody elements. Also, by default, Internet Explorer 4 or later and Netscape 6 create a tbody object for every table even if you don't include one in your table's source code. This default tbody element encompasses all rows of the table (except those you have wrapped inside thead or tfoot elements, if any). Although these objects are implemented in IE 4 for the Macintosh, they are incomplete. Moreover, the row insertion operations noted in the table element are just as strange for these objects under IE 4 for the Mac.

**HTML Equivalent**

```
<tbody>
<tfoot>
<thead>
```

**Object Model Reference**

```
[window.]document.getElementById("elementID")
[window.]document.getElementById("tableID").tBodies[i]
[window.]document.getElementById("tableID").tfoot
[window.]document.getElementById("tableID").thead
```

**Object-Specific Properties**

| | | | | | |
|---|---|---|---|---|---|
| align | bgColor | ch | chOff | rows | vAlign |

**Object-Specific Methods**

| | | |
|---|---|---|
| deleteRow( ) | insertRow( ) | moveRow( ) |

**Object-Specific Event Handler Properties**

None.

## align
NN 6    IE 4    DOM 1
Read/Write

Defines the horizontal alignment of content within all cells contained by the tbody element.

| | |
|---|---|
| **Example** | `document.getElementById("myTbody").align = "center";` |
| **Value** | One of the three horizontal alignment string constants: center \| left \| right. |
| **Default** | left |

## bgColor
NN 6    IE 4    DOM n/a
Read/Write

Specifies the background color of the cells contained by the tbody, tfoot, or thead element. This color setting is not reflected in the style sheet backgroundColor property. Even if the bgcolor attribute or bgColor property is set with a plain-language color name, the returned value is always a hexadecimal triplet.

| | |
|---|---|
| **Example** | `document.getElementById("myTable").tHead.bgColor = "yellow";` |
| **Value** | A hexadecimal triplet or plain-language color name. See Appendix A for acceptable plain-language color names. |
| **Default** | Varies with browser and operating system. |

## ch

Read/Write

Defines the text character used as an alignment point for text within a column or column group (reflecting the char attribute). This property is normally of value only for the align attribute set to "char". In practice, neither IE nor Navigator responds to these properties.

| | |
|---|---|
| **Example** | document.getElementById("myTBody").ch = "."; |
| **Value** | Single character string. |
| **Default** | None. |

## chOff

Read/Write

Defines the offset point at which the character specified by the char attribute is to appear within a cell. In practice, neither IE nor Navigator responds to these properties.

| | |
|---|---|
| **Example** | document.getElementById("myTBody").chOff = "80%"; |
| **Value** | String value of the number of pixels or percentage (within the cell). |
| **Default** | None. |

## rows

Read-only

Returns a collection of tr elements inside the table section. You can also get a group of rows for an entire table in IE for Windows.

| | |
|---|---|
| **Example** | var allTableRows = document.getElementById("myTFoot").rows; |
| **Value** | Reference to a rows collection object. |
| **Default** | Array of zero length. |

## vAlign

Read/Write

Specifies the manner of vertical alignment of text within the cells contained by the tbody, tfoot, or thead element.

| | |
|---|---|
| **Example** | document.getElementById("myTbody").vAlign = "baseline"; |
| **Value** | Case-insensitive constant (as a string): baseline \| bottom \| middle \| top. |
| **Default** | middle |

## deleteRow( ) NN 6    IE 4    DOM 1

deleteRow(*index*)

Removes a tr element nested within the current tbody, tfoot, or thead element. The integer parameter points to the zero-based item in the section's rows collection. To repopulate a table section with new or sorted content, empty the section with iterative calls to the deleteRow( ) method:

```
while (tBodyReference.rows.length > 0) {
    tBodyReference.deleteRow(0);
}
```

**Returned Value**    None.

**Parameters**

*index*

Zero-based integer corresponding to the said numbered tr element in source code order (nested within the current element).

## insertRow( ) NN 6    IE 4(Win)    DOM 1

insertRow(*index*)

Inserts a tr element nested within the current tbody, tfoot, or thead element. The integer parameter points to the zero-based index in the rows collection where the new row should go, but in IE you can also use the shortcut value of –1 to append the row to the end of the collection. Adding the row inserts an empty element, to which you add cells via the insertCell( ) method. Unfortunately, scripting the addition of table rows and cells in IE for the Macintosh (including Version 5.1) is very broken, yielding elephantine row and cell dimensions. For nonnested tables, you might be able to get away with regular document tree node creation and insertion instead of the table section object convenience methods.

**Returned Value**    Reference to the newly inserted row.

**Parameters**

*index*

Zero-based integer corresponding to a row of the rows collection before which the new row is to be inserted.

## moveRow( ) NN n/a    IE 5(Win)    DOM n/a

moveRow(*indexToMove, destinationIndex*)

Moves a row in the tbody, tfoot, or thead element from its original location to a different row position within the same section. The first parameter is a zero-based index of the row (within the rows collection) you wish to move. The second parameter is the index of the row before which you want to move the row.

**Returned Value**    Reference to the moved row.

### Parameters

*indexToMove*

> A zero-based integer pointing to the row to move.

*destinationIndex*

> A zero-based integer pointing to the row above which the row is to be moved.

# td, th

The td and th objects reflect the td and th elements. From an HTML structure viewpoint, the two elements have different purposes within a table; but from a scripting perspective, the elements share the same properties and methods. A cell is a cell.

While a table cell element may inherit a number of visual properties from containers (e.g., a td element appearing to pick up the bgColor of a tbody or tr element), those inherited property values are not automatically assigned to the td object. Therefore, just because a cell may have a yellow background color doesn't mean its bgColor property is set at all. Due to incomplete implementation, IE 4 for the Macintosh does not offer complete scripted access to these element objects.

### HTML Equivalent

```
<td>
<th>
```

### Object Model Reference

```
[window.]document.getElementById("elementID")
[window.]document.getElementById("tableRowID").cells[i]
```

### Object-Specific Properties

| | | | |
|---|---|---|---|
| abbr | align | axis | background |
| bgColor | borderColor | borderColorDark | borderColorLight |
| cellIndex | ch | chOff | colSpan |
| headers | height | noWrap | rowSpan |
| scope | vAlign | width | |

### Object-Specific Methods

None.

### Object-Specific Event Handler Properties

None.

# abbr

Read/Write

Reflects the abbr attribute (cell description for speech), for which mainstream browsers have no functionality at this time.

| Value | String. |
|---|---|
| Default | Empty string. |

## align
NN 6   IE 4   DOM 1
Read/Write

Defines the horizontal alignment of content within the cell.

| Example | `document.getElementById("myTD").align = "center";` |
|---|---|
| Value | Any of the three horizontal alignment constants: center \| left \| right. |
| Default | left |

## axis
NN 6   IE 5(Mac)/6(Win)   DOM 1
Read/Write

Reflects the axis attribute (cell category description for speech), for which mainstream browsers have no functionality at this time.

| Value | String. |
|---|---|
| Default | Empty string. |

## background
NN n/a   IE 4   DOM n/a
Read/Write

Specifies the URL of the background image for the cell. If you set a bgColor to the element as well, the color appears if the image fails to load; otherwise, the image overlays the color.

**Example**
`document.getElementById("myTD").background = "images/watermark.jpg";`

| Value | Complete or relative URL to the background image file. |
|---|---|
| Default | None. |

## bgColor
NN 6   IE 4   DOM 1
Read/Write

Provides the background color of the table cell. This color setting is not reflected in the style sheet backgroundColor property. Even if the bgcolor attribute or bgColor property is set with a plain-language color name, the returned value is always a hexadecimal triplet.

| Example | `document.getElementById("myTD").bgColor = "yellow";` |
|---|---|
| Value | A hexadecimal triplet or plain-language color name. See Appendix A for acceptable plain-language color names. |
| Default | Varies with browser and operating system. |

## borderColor

Provides the color of the element's border. Internet Explorer applies the color to all four lines that make up the interior border of a cell. Therefore, colors of adjacent cells do not collide.

| | |
|---|---|
| **Example** | `document.getElementById("myTD").borderColor = "salmon";` |
| **Value** | A hexadecimal triplet or plain-language color name. A setting of empty is interpreted as "#000000" (black). See Appendix A for acceptable plain-language color names. |
| **Default** | Varies with operating system. |

## borderColorDark, borderColorLight

The 3-D effect of table borders in Internet Explorer is created by careful positioning of light and dark lines around the page's background or default color. You can independently control the colors used for the dark and light lines by assigning values to the borderColorDark (left and top edges of the cell) and borderColorLight (right and bottom edges) properties.

Typically, you should assign complementary colors to the pair of properties. There is also no rule that says you must assign a dark color to borderColorDark. The attributes merely control a well-defined set of lines so you can predict which lines of the border change with each attribute.

**Example**

```
document.getElementById("myTD").borderColorDark = "blue";
document.getElementById("myTD").borderColorLight = "cornflowerblue";
```

| | |
|---|---|
| **Value** | A hexadecimal triplet or plain-language color name. A setting of empty is interpreted as "#000000" (black). See Appendix A for acceptable plain-language color names. |
| **Default** | Varies with operating system. |

## cellIndex

Returns a zero-based integer representing the position of the current cell among all other td elements in the same row. The count is based on the source code order of the td elements within a tr element. This property is not available in the Macintosh version of Internet Explorer 4.

| | |
|---|---|
| **Example** | `var whichCell = document.getElementById("myTD").cellIndex;` |
| **Value** | Integer. |
| **Default** | None. |

## ch

Defines the text character used as an alignment point for text within a cell. This property is normally of value only for the align attribute set to "char". In practice, neither IE nor Navigator responds to these properties.

**Example**         document.getElementById("myTD").ch = ".";

**Value**           Single character string.

**Default**         None.

## chOff

Defines the offset point at which the character specified by the char attribute is to appear within a cell. In practice, neither IE nor Navigator responds to these properties.

**Example**         document.getElementById("myTD").chOff = "80%";

**Value**           String value of the number of pixels or percentage (within the cell).

**Default**         None.

## colSpan

Specifies the number of columns across which the current table cell should extend itself. For each additional column included in the colSpan count, one less td element is required for the table row. If you set the align property to center or right, the alignment is calculated on the full width of the td element across the specified number of columns. Unless the current cell also specifies a rowspan attribute, the next table row returns to the original column count.

**Example**         document.getElementById("myTD").colSpan = 2;

**Value**           Integer, usually 2 or larger.

**Default**         1

## headers

Points to the ID of a table cell element designated as a column header for the current cell. In practice, no mainstream browsers provide functionality for this property.

**Value**           String ID value.

**Default**         None.

## height, width

Specify the height and width of the element. Changes to these values are immediately reflected in reflowed content on the page. These properties are read-only in the Macintosh version of Internet Explorer 4.

| | |
|---|---|
| **Example** | `document.getElementById("myTD").height = "250";` |
| **Value** | Pixel integer count (as a string) or a percentage. |
| **Default** | None. |

## noWrap

Indicates whether the browser should render the cell as wide as is necessary to display a line of nonbreaking text on one line. Abuse of this attribute can force the user into a great deal of inconvenient horizontal scrolling of the page to view all of the content.

| | |
|---|---|
| **Example** | `document.getElementById("myTD").noWrap = "true";` |
| **Value** | Boolean value: `true` | `false`. |
| **Default** | `false` |

## rowSpan

Specifies the number of rows through which the current table cell should extend itself downward. For each additional row included in the rowSpan count, one less td element is required for the next table row. If you set the vAlign property to middle, the alignment is calculated on the full height of the td element across the specified number of rows.

| | |
|---|---|
| **Example** | `document.getElementById("myTD").rowSpan = 12;` |
| **Value** | Integer, usually 2 or larger. |
| **Default** | 1 |

## scope

Reflects the scope attribute of table cell elements. In practice, no mainstream browsers provide functionality for this property.

| | |
|---|---|
| **Value** | One of the recognized string constants: `cols` | `colgroup` | `rows` | `rowgroup`. |
| **Default** | None. |

Alphabetical DOM Reference

## vAlign

Specifies the manner of vertical alignment of text within the element's content box.

| | |
|---|---|
| **Example** | `document.getElementById("myTD").vAlign = "baseline";` |
| **Value** | Case-insensitive constant (as a string): `baseline` \| `bottom` \| `middle` \| `top`. |
| **Default** | `middle` |

## width

See height.

## text

See input (type="text").

# Text, TextNode

A Text object is what this book calls in many places a "text node." Microsoft refers to this object as a TextNode object. This object represents the child object containing the characters that go between start and end tags of an element. The Text object exists in the abstract W3C DOM model by virtue of an inheritance chain between it and the fundamental Node object (Node to CharacterData to Text). The Node object ancestry automatically equips the Text object with a long list of properties and methods described among the shared items at the start of this chapter (the properties include: attributes, childNodes, firstChild, lastChild, localName, namespaceURI, nextSibling, nodeName, nodeType, nodeValue, ownerDocument, parentNode, prefix, previousSibling; the methods are: appendChild( ), cloneNode( ), hasAttributes( ), hasChildNodes( ), insertBefore( ), isSupported( ), normalize( ), removeChild( ), replaceChild( )). Along this inheritance chain, the Text object gains some additional properties and methods (described below) that let us manipulate the node's content within the constructs dictated by the formal W3C DOM model. Because the DOM is scripting language-independent, you find properties and methods that may be more easily or more powerfully manipulated through JavaScript string handling (see Chapter 12). Feel free to use those techniques in a client-side JavaScript environment of the browser.

Scripts refer to the Text node (or IE TextNode object) only through references that locate the node in the document tree (such as the first child of a particular element node) or as returned by the document.createTextNode( ) method.

**Object Model Reference**

*elementReference.childReference*
*textNodeReference.siblingReference*

**Object-Specific Properties**

| | |
|---|---|
| data | length |

**Object-Specific Methods**

| appendData( ) | deleteData( ) | insertData( ) | replaceData( ) |
|---|---|---|---|
| splitText( ) | substringData( ) | | |

**Object-Specific Event Handler Properties**
None.

## data

Read/Write

Contains the string of characters in the text node. The value is the same as the nodeValue property value, and there is no reason to favor one property over the other, except perhaps for plain-language syntactic preferences for reading the code.

**Example**
```
document.getElementById("myP").firstSibling.data = "Some new text.";
```

| **Value** | String. |
|---|---|
| **Default** | Empty string. |

## length

Read-only

Provides a count of characters in the text node.

| **Example** | var howMany = document.getElementById("myP").firstSibling.length; |
|---|---|
| **Value** | Integer. |
| **Default** | 0 |

## appendData( )

appendData("*newText*")

Adds characters (passed as a string parameter) to the end of the current text node. The content consists of raw characters, so if you intend to add a sentence to a text node, your scripts are responsible for sentence spacing.

**Returned Value**    None.

**Parameters**

*newText*
> String value of text to be appended. A reference that evaluates to a string (such as the data property of another text node in the document) copies the referenced value to the append location.

## deleteData( )        NN 6    IE 5(Mac)/6(Win)    DOM 1

deleteData(*startOffset*, *count*)

Removes characters from the current text node starting with the character in (zero-based) position signified by *startOffset*, and for a length of *count* characters in the normal text direction of the current language. If the length specified for deletion goes beyond the length of the data, all characters to the end of the text node are deleted without throwing an exception. Note that Netscape 6 includes source code white space in its counts for both parameters.

**Returned Value**     None.

**Parameters**

*startOffset*
> Positive integer specifying the zero-based starting character point for the deletion.

*count*
> Positive integer specifying the number of characters to be deleted.

## insertData( )        NN 6    IE 5(Mac)/6(Win)    DOM 1

insertData(*startOffset*, "*newText*")

Inserts text into a zero-based character position in the text node.

**Returned Value**     None.

**Parameters**

*startOffset*
> Positive integer specifying the zero-based character before which the new text is to be inserted.

*newText*
> String value of text to be inserted. A reference that evaluates to a string (such as the data property of another text node in the document) copies the referenced value to the append location.

## replaceData( )        NN 6    IE 5(Mac)/6(Win)    DOM 1

replaceData(*startOffset*, *count*, "*newText*")

Replaces text in the current text node with new text. The original content to be removed is signified by the zero-based start position and the number of characters. The string passed as a third parameter goes into the space vacated by the removed text. A bug in IE 5 for Macintosh crops the new text to the length of the removed text.

**Returned Value**     None.

**Parameters**

*startOffset*
> Positive integer specifying the zero-based starting character point for the deletion.

*count*
> Positive integer specifying the number of characters to be deleted.

*newText*

> String value of text to be inserted where the remaining text collapses. A reference that evaluates to a string (such as the data property of another text node in the document) copies the referenced value to the append location.

## splitText( )                                          NN 6    IE 5(Mac)/6(Win)    DOM 1

splitText(*offset*)

Divides the current text node into two sibling text nodes; otherwise, doesn't disturb the text.

**Returned Value**    Reference to the second text node.

### Parameters

*offset*

> Positive integer specifying the zero-based character point before which the split occurs.

## substringData( )                                      NN 6    IE 5(Mac)/6(Win)    DOM 1

substringData(*startOffset*, *count*)

Returns a copy of the designated segment of the text node content. The section to be copied is signified by the zero-based start position and the number of characters

**Returned Value**    String.

### Parameters

*startOffset*

> Positive integer specifying the zero-based starting character point for the copy action.

*count*

> Positive integer specifying the number of characters to be copied.

# textarea                                               NN 2    IE 3    DOM 1

The textarea object reflects the textarea element and is used as a form control. This object is the primary way of getting a user to enter multiple lines of text for submission to the server. Note that the innerHTML property is not available on the Macintosh version of Internet Explorer 4. Only a limited number of properties and methods shown below are available in early browsers that do not support addressing all HTML elements (prior to IE 4 and Netscape 6). IE 5 and later support the shared doScroll( ) method for this object.

**HTML Equivalent**    <textarea>

**Object Model Reference**

[window.]document.*formName*.*elementName*
[window.]document.forms[i].elements[j]
[window.]document.getElementById("*elementID*")

## Object-Specific Properties

| | | | | |
|---|---|---|---|---|
| cols | dataFld | dataSrc | defaultValue | form |
| name | readOnly | rows | status | type |
| value | wrap | | | |

## Object-Specific Methods

| | | |
|---|---|---|
| createTextRange( ) | handleEvent( ) | select( ) |

## Object-Specific Event Handler Properties

| Handler | NN | IE | DOM |
|---|---|---|---|
| onblur | 2 | 3 | n/a |
| onchange | 2 | 3 | n/a |
| onfocus | 2 | 3 | n/a |
| onkeydown | 4 | 4 | n/a |
| onkeypress | 4 | 4 | n/a |
| onkeyup | 4 | 4 | n/a |
| onscroll | n/a | 4 | n/a |
| onselect | 2 | 3 | n/a |

---

## cols

NN 6    IE 4    DOM 1

Read/Write

Specifies the width of the editable space of the textarea element. The value represents the number of monofont characters that are to be displayed within the width. When the font size can be influenced by style sheets, the actual width changes accordingly.

| **Example** | document.forms[0].comments.cols = 60; |
|---|---|
| **Value** | Integer. |
| **Default** | Varies with browser and operating system. |

---

## dataFld

NN n/a    IE 4    DOM n/a

Read/Write

Used with IE data binding to associate a remote data source column name to a textarea object's value property. A datasrc attribute must also be set for the element. Setting both the dataFld and dataSrc properties to empty strings breaks the binding between element and data source. Works only with text file data sources in IE 5/Mac.

| **Example** | document.myForm.myTextArea.dataFld = "description"; |
|---|---|
| **Value** | Case-sensitive identifier of the data source column. |
| **Default** | None. |

## dataSrc

Used with IE data binding to specify the ID of the page's object element that loads the data source object for remote data access. Content from the data source is specified via the datafld attribute. Setting both the dataFld and dataSrc properties to empty strings breaks the binding between element and data source. Works only with text file data sources in IE 5/Mac.

| | |
|---|---|
| **Example** | document.myForm.myTextArea.dataSrc = "DBSRC3"; |
| **Value** | Case-sensitive identifier of the data source. |
| **Default** | None. |

## defaultValue

Specifies the default text for the textarea element, as established by the text between the start and end tags in the page's source code.

**Example**
```
var txtAObj = document.forms[0].myTextArea;
if (txtAObj.value != txtAObj.defaultValue ) {
   ...
}
```

| | |
|---|---|
| **Value** | Any string value. |
| **Default** | None. |

## form

Returns a reference to the form element that contains the current element. When processing an event from this element, the event handler function automatically has access to the select element (as the event object's target or srcElement property). By reading the form property, the script can easily access other controls within the same form.

| | |
|---|---|
| **Example** | var theForm = evt.srcElement.form; |
| **Value** | form element object reference. |
| **Default** | None. |

## name

This is the identifier associated with the form control. The value of this property is submitted as one-half of the name/value pair when the form is submitted to the server. Names are hidden from user view, since control labels are assigned via other means, depending on the control type. Form control names may also be used by script references to the objects. Despite the modern standards' preference for the id attribute, many browsers still require that a control be assigned a name attribute to allow the control's value to be submitted.

**Example**        `document.orderForm.myTextArea.name = "customerComment";`

**Value**           Case-sensitive identifier that follows the rules of identifier naming: it may contain no whitespace, cannot begin with a numeral, and should avoid punctuation except for the underscore character.

**Default**        None.

## readOnly
**NN 6    IE 4    DOM 1**

**Read/Write**

Indicates whether the form element can be edited on the page by the user. A form control that has its readOnly property set to true may still be modified by scripts, even though the user may not alter the content.

**Example**        `document.forms[0].myTextArea.readOnly = "true";`

**Value**           Boolean value: true | false.

**Default**        false

## rows
**NN 6    IE 4    DOM 1**

**Read/Write**

Specifies the height of the textarea element based on the number of lines of text that are to be displayed without scrolling. The value represents the number of monofont character lines that are to be displayed within the height before the scrollbar becomes active. When the font size can be influenced by style sheets, the actual height changes accordingly.

**Example**        `document.forms[0].comments.rows = 6;`

**Value**           Integer.

**Default**        2 (IE/Windows); 1 (IE/Macintosh); -1 (Netscape 6, meaning that the attribute or property hasn't been set).

## status
**NN n/a    IE 4    DOM n/a**

**Read/Write**

This is implemented in IE, but has no function for the textarea object.

**Value**           Boolean value: true | false; or null.

**Default**        null

## type

Returns the type of form control element. The value is returned in all lowercase letters. It may be necessary to cycle through all form elements in search of specific types to do some processing on (e.g., emptying all form controls of type "textarea" while leaving other controls untouched).

**Example**
```
if (document.forms[0].elements[3].type == "textarea") {
    ...
}
```

| **Value** | Any of the following constants (as a string): button \| checkbox \| file \| hidden \| image \| password \| radio \| reset \| select-multiple \| select-one \| submit \| text \| textarea. |
| --- | --- |
| **Default** | textarea |

## value

Specifies the current value associated with the form control that is submitted with the name/value pair for the element. All values are strings.

| **Example** | `var comment = document.forms[0].myTextArea.value;` |
| --- | --- |
| **Value** | String. |
| **Default** | None. |

## wrap

Indicates whether the browser should wrap text in a textarea element and whether wrapped text should be submitted to the server with soft returns converted to hard carriage returns. A value of hard engages word-wrapping and converts soft returns to CR-LF characters in the value submitted to the server. A value of soft turns on word-wrapping, but does not include the CR-LF characters in the text submitted with the form. A value of off turns word-wrapping off.

| **Example** | `document.forms[0].comments.wrap = "soft";` |
| --- | --- |
| **Value** | One of the constant values (as a string): hard \| off \| soft. |
| **Default** | soft |

## createTextRange( ) NN *n/a*　IE *4(Win)*　DOM *n/a*

Creates a TextRange object from the content of the textarea object. See the TextRange object for details.

**Returned Value**　TextRange object.

## handleEvent( ) NN |4|　IE *n/a*　DOM *n/a*

handleEvent(*event*)

Instructs the object to accept and process the event whose specifications are passed as the parameter to the method. The object must have an event handler for the event type to process the event. Navigator 4 only.

**Returned Value**　None.

**Parameters**

*event*
    A Navigator 4 event object.

## select( ) NN *2*　IE *3*　DOM *1*

Selects all the text displayed in the form element. To position the insertion pointer in a specific location inside a textarea element in IE, see the TextRange object.

**Returned Value**　None.

**Parameters**　None.

# TextNode

See Text.

# TextRange NN *n/a*　IE *4(Win)*　DOM *n/a*

The TextRange object–similar in concept to the Netscape 6 and W3C DOM Range object— represents the text of zero or more characters in a document. When a text range consists of zero characters, it represents an insertion point between two characters (or before the first or after the last character).

A TextRange object is created via the createTextRange( ) method associated with the body, button, text, or textarea objects. You can also turn a user selection into a range via the selection object's createRange( ) (note the slight difference in the method name). Once you have created a text range, use its methods to adjust its start and end points to encompass a desired segment of the text (such as text that matches a search string). Once the range has been narrowed to the target text, assign values to its htmlText and text properties to change, remove, or insert text. A library of direct commands that perform specific textual modifications can also be invoked to act on the text range. See Chapter 5 for details and examples of using the TextRange object.

Shared properties and methods from the list at the start of this chapter are: offsetLeft, offsetTop, getBoundingClientRect( ), getClientRects( ), and scrollIntoView( ). Note that the TextRange object and all associated facilities are available only in the Win32 version of Internet Explorer.

## Object Model Reference

*objectRef*.createTextRange( )
*selectionObjectRef*.createRange( )

## Object-Specific Properties

| | | | |
|---|---|---|---|
| boundingHeight | boundingLeft | boundingTop | boundingWidth |
| htmlText | text | | |

## Object-Specific Methods

| | | |
|---|---|---|
| collapse( ) | compareEndPoints( ) | duplicate( ) |
| execCommand( ) | expand( ) | findText( ) |
| getBookmark( ) | inRange( ) | isEqual( ) |
| move( ) | moveEnd( ) | moveStart( ) |
| moveToBookmark( ) | moveToElementText( ) | moveToPoint( ) |
| parentElement( ) | pasteHTML( ) | queryCommandEnabled( ) |
| queryCommandIndeterm( ) | queryCommandState( ) | queryCommandSupported( ) |
| queryCommandText( ) | queryCommandValue( ) | select( ) |
| setEndPoint( ) | | |

## boundingHeight, boundingWidth

NN *n/a*   IE *4(Win)*   DOM *n/a*
Read-only

Return the pixel measure of the imaginary space occupied by the TextRange object. Although you do not see a TextRange object in the document (unless a script selects it), the area of a TextRange object is identical to the area that a selection highlight would occupy. These values cinch up to measure only as wide or tall as the widest and tallest part of the range. You would arrive at these same values by performing arithmetic on values returned from the getBoundingClientRect( ) method.

### Example

var rangeWidth = document.forms[0].myTextArea.createTextRange( ).boundingWidth;

**Value**        Integer.

**Default**      None.

## boundingLeft, boundingTop

NN *n/a*   IE *4(Win)*   DOM *n/a*
Read-only

Return the pixel distance between the top or left of the browser window or frame and the top or left edges of the imaginary space occupied by the TextRange object. Although you do not see a TextRange object in the document (unless a script selects it), the area of a

TextRange object is identical to the area that a selection highlight would occupy. Values for these properties are measured from the fixed window or frame edges and not the top and left of the document, which may scroll out of view. Therefore, as a document scrolls, these values change.

**Example**
```
var rangeOffH = document.forms[0].myTextArea.createTextRange( ).boundingLeft;
```

**Value**          Integer.

**Default**        None.

## htmlText
NN n/a   IE 4(Win)   DOM n/a
Read-only

Specifies all HTML of the document for a given element when that element is used as the basis for a TextRange object. For example, if you create a TextRange for the body element (document.body.createTextRange( )), the htmlText property contains all HTML content between (but not including) the body element tags.

**Example**          `var rangeHTML = document.body.createTextRange( ).htmlText;`

**Value**            String.

**Default**          None.

## text
NN n/a   IE 4(Win)   DOM n/a
Read/Write

Indicates the text contained by the text range. In the case of a TextRange object of a body element, this consists of only the text that is rendered, but none of the HTML tags behind the scenes.

**Example**          `var rangeText = document.body.createTextRange( ).text;`

**Value**            String.

**Default**          None.

## collapse( )
NN n/a   IE 4(Win)   DOM n/a

```
collapse([start])
```

Reduces the TextRange object to a length of zero (creating an insertion point) at the beginning or end of the text range before it collapsed.

**Returned Value**    None.

**Parameters**

*start*

> Optional Boolean value that controls whether the insertion point goes to the beginning (true) of the original range or the end (false). The default value is true.

## compareEndPoints( )　　　　　　　　　　NN *n/a*　　IE *4(Win)*　　DOM *n/a*

compareEndPoints("*type*", *comparisonRange*)

Compares the relative position of the boundary (start and end) points of two ranges (the current range and one that had been previously saved to a variable). The first parameter defines which boundary points in each range you wish to compare. If the result of the comparison is that the first point is earlier in the range than the other point, the returned value is –1. If the result shows both points to be in the same location, the returned value is 0. If the result shows the first point to be later in the range than the other point, the returned value is 1. For example, if you have saved the first range to a variable r1 and created a new range as r2, you can see the physical relationship between the end of r2 and the start of r1:

```
r1.compareEndPoints("EndToStart", r2)
```

If r1 ends where r2 starts (the insertion point between two characters), the returned value is 0.

**Returned Value**　　　-1, 0, or 1.

**Parameters**

*type*

> One of the following constants (as a string): StartToEnd | StartToStart | EndToStart | EndToEnd.

*comparisonRange*

> A TextRange object created earlier and saved to a variable.

## duplicate( )　　　　　　　　　　　　　　NN *n/a*　　IE *4(Win)*　　DOM *n/a*

Creates a new TextRange object with the same values as the current range. The new object is an independent object (the old and new do not equal each other), but their values are initially identical (until you start modifying one range or the other).

**Returned Value**　　　TextRange object.

**Parameters**　　　None.

## execCommand( )　　　　　　　　　　　　NN *n/a*　　IE *4(Win)*　　DOM *n/a*

execCommand("*commandName*"[, *UIFlag*[, *value*]])

Executes the named command on the current TextRange object. Many commands work best when the TextRange object is an insertion point. See Appendix D for a list of commands.

**Returned Value**　　　Boolean value: true if command is successful; false if unsuccessful.

**Parameters**

*commandName*

> A case-insensitive string value of the command name. See Appendix D.

*UIFlag*
> Optional Boolean value: true to display any user interface triggered by the command (if any); false to prevent such display.

*value*
> A parameter value for the command.

## expand( )

NN n/a   IE 4(Win)   DOM n/a

expand("*unit*")

Expands the current text range (including a collapsed range) to encompass the textual unit passed as a parameter. For example, if someone selects some characters from a document, you can create the range and expand it to encompass the entire sentence in which the selection takes place:

```
var rng = document.selection.createRange();
rng.expand("sentence");
```

If the starting range extends across multiple units, the expand( ) method expands the range outward to the next nearest unit.

**Returned Value**   Boolean value: true if method is successful; false if unsuccessful.

**Parameters**

*unit*
> A case-insensitive string value of the desired unit: character | word | sentence | textedit. The textedit value expands the range to the entire original range.

## findText( )

NN n/a   IE 4(Win)   DOM n/a

findText("*string*"[, *searchScope*][, *flags*])

Searches the current TextRange object for a match of a string passed as the required first parameter. By default, matching is done on a case-insensitive basis. If there is a match, the TextRange object repositions its start and end points to surround the found text. To continue searching in the document, you must reposition the start point of the text range to the end of the found string (with collapse( )).

Optional parameters let you limit the scope of the search within the range to a desired number of characters after the range's start point, or dictate additional matching requirements, such as partial or whole words.

**Returned Value**   Boolean value: true if a match is found; false if unsuccessful.

**Parameters**

*string*
> A case-insensitive string to be searched.

*searchScope*
> Integer for the number of characters to search relative to the range's start point. A positive number searches forward; a negative number searches backward, to text earlier in the document than the start point of the text range.

*flags*

> Integer for search detail codes: 0 (match partial words); 1 (match backwards); 2 (match whole words only); 4 (match case).

## getBookmark( ), moveToBookmark( )    NN *n/a*    IE *4(Win)*    DOM *n/a*

getBookmark( )
moveToBookmark(*bookmarkString*)

These two methods work together as a way to temporarily save a text range specification and restore it when needed. The getBookmark( ) method returns an opaque string (containing binary data that is of no value to human users). Once that value is stored in a variable, the range can be modified as needed for the script. Some time later, the bookmarked text range can be restored with the moveToBookmark( ) method:

```
var rangeMark = myRange.getBookmark( );
...
myRange.moveToBookmark(rangeMark);
```

**Returned Value**    Boolean value: true if the operation is successful; false if unsuccessful.

### Parameters

*bookmarkString*

> An opaque string returned by the getBookmark( ) method.

## inRange( )    NN *n/a*    IE *4(Win)*    DOM *n/a*

inRange(*comparisonRange*)

Determines whether the comparison range is within or equal to the physical range of the current text range.

**Returned Value**    Boolean value: true if the comparison range is in or equal to the current range; false if not.

### Parameters

*comparisonRange*

> TextRange object created earlier and saved to a variable.

## isEqual( )    NN *n/a*    IE *4(Win)*    DOM *n/a*

isEqual(*comparisonRange*)

Determines whether the comparison range is identical to the current text range.

**Returned Value**    Boolean value: true if the comparison range is equal to the current range; false if not.

### Parameters

*comparisonRange*

> A TextRange object created earlier and saved to a variable.

## move( )                                    NN *n/a*    IE *4(Win)*    DOM *n/a*

move("*unit*"[, *count*])

Collapses the current text range to an insertion point at the end of the current range and moves it forward or backward from the current position by one or more units.

**Returned Value**    Integer of the number of units moved.

### Parameters

*unit*

A case-insensitive string value of the desired unit: character | word | sentence | textedit. The textedit value moves the insertion pointer to the start or end of the entire original range.

*count*

An optional integer of the number of units to move the insertion pointer. Positive values move the pointer forward; negative values move the pointer backward. Default value is 1.

## moveEnd( ), moveStart( )                    NN *n/a*    IE *4(Win)*    DOM *n/a*

moveEnd("*unit*"[, *count*])
moveStart("*unit*"[, *count*])

Moves only the end or start point (respectively) of the current text range by one or more units. An optional parameter lets you specify both the number of units and direction. To shift the start point of a text range toward the beginning of the original range, be sure to specify a negative value. When moving the end point forward by word units, be aware that a word ends with a whitespace character (including a period). Therefore, if a findText( ) method sets the range to a found string that does not end in a space, the first moveEnd("word") method moves the ending point to the spot past the space after the found string rather than to the following word.

**Returned Value**    Integer of the number of units moved.

### Parameters

*unit*

A case-insensitive string value of the desired unit: character | word | sentence | textedit. The textedit value moves the insertion pointer to the start or end of the entire original range.

*count*

An optional integer of the number of units to move the insertion pointer. Positive values move the pointer forward; negative values move the pointer backward. Default value is 1.

## moveToBookmark( )

See getBookmark( ).

## moveToElementText( )  NN *n/a*   IE *4(Win)*   DOM *n/a*

moveToElementText(*elementObject*)

Moves the current TextRange object's start and end points to encase the specified HTML element object. The resulting text range includes the HTML for the element, as well.

**Returned Value**   None.

**Parameters**

*elementObject*

A scripted reference to the object. This can be in the form of a direct reference (document.getElementById("*elementID*") or a variable containing the same kind of value.

## moveToPoint( )  NN *n/a*   IE *4(Win)*   DOM *n/a*

moveToPoint(*x, y*)

Collapses the text range to an insertion pointer and sets its location to the spot indicated by the horizontal and vertical coordinates in the browser window or frame. This is as if the user had clicked on a spot in the window to define an insertion point. Use methods such as expand( ) to enlarge the text range to include a character, word, sentence, or entire text range.

**Returned Value**   None.

**Parameters**

*x*   Horizontal coordinate of the insertion point in pixels relative to the left edge of the window or frame.

*y*   Vertical coordinate of the insertion point in pixels relative to the top edge of the window or frame.

## parentElement( )  NN *n/a*   IE *4(Win)*   DOM *n/a*

Returns an object reference to the next outermost element that fully contains the TextRange object.

**Returned Value**   Element object reference.

**Parameters**   None.

## pasteHTML( )  NN *n/a*   IE *4(Win)*   DOM *n/a*

pasteHTML("*HTMLText*")

Replaces the current text range with the HTML content supplied as a parameter string. Typically, this method is used on a zero-length text range object acting as an insertion pointer. All tags are rendered as if they were part of the original source code.

**Returned Value**   None.

**Parameters**

*HTMLText*
> Document source code to be inserted into the document.

## queryCommandEnabled( )

| | NN *n/a* | IE *4(Win)* | DOM *n/a* |

queryCommandEnabled("*commandName*")

Indicates whether the command can be invoked in light of the current state of the document or selection.

**Returned Value**    Boolean value: true if enabled; false if not.

**Parameters**

*commandName*
> A case-insensitive string value of the command name. See Appendix D.

## queryCommandIndeterm( )

| | NN *n/a* | IE *4(Win)* | DOM *n/a* |

queryCommandIndeterm("*commandName*")

Indicates whether the command is in an indeterminate state.

**Returned Value**    Boolean value: true | false.

**Parameters**

*commandName*
> A case-insensitive string value of the command name. See Appendix D.

## queryCommandState( )

| | NN *n/a* | IE *4(Win)* | DOM *n/a* |

queryCommandState("*commandName*")

Determines the current state of the named command.

**Returned Value**

true if the command has been completed; false if the command has not completed; null if the state cannot be accurately determined.

**Parameters**

*commandName*
> A case-insensitive string value of the command name. See Appendix D.

## queryCommandSupported( )

| | NN *n/a* | IE *4(Win)* | DOM *n/a* |

queryCommandSupported("*commandName*")

Determines whether the named command is supported by the document object.

**Returned Value**    Boolean value: true | false.

## Parameters

*commandName*

> A case-insensitive string value of the command name. See Appendix D.

## queryCommandText( )      NN *n/a*   IE *4(Win)*   DOM *n/a*

queryCommandText("*commandName*")

Returns text associated with the command.

**Returned Value**    String.

## Parameters

*commandName*

> A case-insensitive string value of the command name. See Appendix D.

## queryCommandValue( )      NN *n/a*   IE *4(Win)*   DOM *n/a*

queryCommandValue("*commandName*")

Returns the value associated with the command, such as the name font of the selection.

**Returned Value**    Depends on the command.

## Parameters

*commandName*

> A case-insensitive string value of the command name. See Appendix D.

## select( )      NN *n/a*   IE *4(Win)*   DOM *n/a*

Selects all the text that is included in the current TextRange object. This method brings some visual confirmation to users that a script knows about a particular block of text. For example, if you were scripting a search with the findText( ) method, you would then use the scrollIntoView( ) and select( ) methods on that range to show the user where the matching text is.

**Returned Value**    None.

**Parameters**    None.

## setEndPoint( )      NN *n/a*   IE *4(Win)*   DOM *n/a*

setEndPoint("*type*", *comparisonRange*)

Sets the end point of the current TextRange object to the end point of another range that had previously been preserved as a variable reference.

**Returned Value**    None.

## Parameters

*type*

One of the following constants (as a string): StartToEnd | StartToStart | EndToStart | EndToEnd.

*comparisonRange*

A TextRange object created earlier and saved to a variable.

# TextRectangle                              NN *n/a*    IE *5(Win)*    DOM *n/a*

A TextRectangle object contains the coordinates of the four edges of an invisible box that surrounds a string of body text. Two methods of all element objects and the TextRange object produce information about two different kinds of text rectangles. The getClientRects() method returns a collection of line-by-line text rectangles; the getBoundingClientRect() method returns a single TextRectangle object that has coordinates that encompass all line-by-line rectangles.

Invoking either of these methods gets the rectangles' values instantaneously. Resizing the window or altering the content of the target object may change the actual rectangles, but the TextRangle objects obtained earlier do not keep pace with the changes (since the content of each line's rectangle is likely to change). Therefore, obtain TextRectangle values immediately before you need to process them in other script statements.

### Object Model Reference

*elementOrTextRangeReference*.getBoundingClientRect()
*elementOrTextRangeReference*.getClientRects()[i]

### Object-Specific Properties

bottom                    left                    top                    right

### Object-Specific Methods

None.

### Object-Specific Event Handler Properties

None.

## bottom, left, right, top                   NN *n/a*    IE *5(Win)*    DOM *n/a*
                                                                          Read-only

Return integer pixel values for the browser window coordinates of the rectangle edges. Note that these values are not relative to the page. Therefore, values change as the text holder scrolls.

### Example

```
var rightMostEdge = document.getElementById("myP").getBoundingClientRect().right;
```

**Value**          Integer pixel measures

**Default**        None.

# tfoot

See tbody.

# th

See td.

# thead

See tbody.

# title

The title object reflects the title element. If you encounter problems referencing the element object by its id attribute (especially in IE 4/Windows or Netscape 6), use the tag access methods for the respective browsers: document.all.tags("title")[0] for IE, and document.getElementsByTagName("title")[0] for IE 5 or later and Netscape 6.

**HTML Equivalent**    <title>

**Object Model Reference**
[window.]document.getElementById("*elementID*")

**Object-Specific Properties**
text

**Object-Specific Methods**
None.

**Object-Specific Event Handler Properties**
None.

# text

Specifies the text content of the element. For the title element, this is the text between the start and end tags that also appears in the browser window's title bar (usually along with some identification of the browser brand). Changes you make to this property do not appear in the source code you view from the browser. Nor does the change appear in the title bar of IE for Windows.

| | |
|---|---|
| **Example** | document.getElementsByTagName("title")[0].text = "Welcome, Dave!"; |
| **Value** | String. |
| **Default** | None. |

# toolbar

See directories.

## tr

The tr object reflects the tr element. Due to incomplete implementation, IE 4 for the Macintosh does not offer complete scripted access to these element objects.

**HTML Equivalent**   \<tr>

**Object Model Reference**
[window.]document.getElementById("*elementID*")
[window.]document.getElementById("*tableID*").rows[i]

**Object-Specific Properties**

| | | | |
|---|---|---|---|
| align | bgColor | borderColor | borderColorDark |
| borderColorLight | cells[] | ch | chOff |
| height | rowIndex | sectionRowIndex | vAlign |

**Object-Specific Methods**
deleteCell( )       insertCell( )

**Object-Specific Event Handler Properties**
None.

## align

Defines the horizontal alignment of content within all cells of the row.

| | |
|---|---|
| **Example** | document.getElementById("myTR").align = "center"; |
| **Value** | Any of the three horizontal alignment constants: center \| left \| right. |
| **Default** | left |

## bgColor

Specifies the background color of the table cells in the current row. This color setting is not reflected in the style sheet backgroundColor property. Even if the bgcolor attribute or bgColor property is set with a plain-language color name, the returned value is always a hexadecimal triplet.

| | |
|---|---|
| **Example** | document.getElementById("myTR").bgColor = "yellow"; |

| Value | A hexadecimal triplet or plain-language color name. See Appendix A for acceptable plain-language color names. |
| --- | --- |
| **Default** | Varies with browser and operating system. |

## borderColor

Specifies the color of the element's border. Internet Explorer applies the color to all four lines that make up the interior border of a cell. Therefore, colors of adjacent cells do not collide.

| **Example** | `document.getElementById("myTR").borderColor = "salmon";` |
| --- | --- |
| **Value** | A hexadecimal triplet or plain-language color name. A setting of empty is interpreted as "#000000" (black). See Appendix A for acceptable plain-language color names. |
| **Default** | Varies with operating system. |

## borderColorDark, borderColorLight

The 3-D effect of table borders in Internet Explorer is created by careful positioning of light and dark lines around the page's background or default color. You can independently control the colors used for the dark and light lines by assigning values to the borderColorDark (left and top edges of the cell) and borderColorLight (right and bottom edges) properties.

Typically, you should assign complementary colors to the pair of properties. There is also no rule that says you must assign a dark color to borderColorDark. The attributes merely control a well-defined set of lines so you can predict which lines of the border change with each attribute.

**Example**

```
document.getElementById("myTR").borderColorDark = "blue";
document.getElementById("myTR").borderColorLight = "cornflowerblue";
```

| **Value** | A hexadecimal triplet or plain-language color name. A setting of empty is interpreted as "#000000" (black). See Appendix A for acceptable plain-language color names. |
| --- | --- |
| **Default** | Varies with operating system. |

## cells[]

Returns a collection of td or th elements nested inside the table row. Items in the collection are in source code order.

| **Example** | `var allRowCells = document.getElementById("myTR").cells;` |
| --- | --- |

| | | |
|---|---|---|
| **Value** | Reference to a cells collection object. | |
| **Default** | Array of zero length. | |

## ch

Defines the text character used as an alignment point for text cells of the row. This property is normally of value only for the align attribute set to "char". In practice, neither IE nor Navigator responds to these properties.

| | |
|---|---|
| **Example** | document.getElementById("myTR").ch = "."; |
| **Value** | Single character string. |
| **Default** | None. |

## chOff

Defines the offset point at which the character specified by the char attribute is to appear within a cell. In practice, neither IE nor Navigator responds to these properties.

| | |
|---|---|
| **Example** | document.getElementById("myTR").chOff = "80%"; |
| **Value** | String value of the number of pixels or percentage (within the cell). |
| **Default** | None. |

## height

Specifies the pixel or percentage height of the row. To change the height of a row dynamically, adjust the element's style.height value rather than the height property.

| | |
|---|---|
| **Value** | String value of the number of pixels or percentage (within the row). |
| **Default** | None. |

## rowIndex

Returns a zero-based integer representing the position of the current row among all other tr elements in the entire table. The count is based on the source code order of the tr elements.

| | |
|---|---|
| **Example** | var whichRow = document.getElementById("myTR").rowIndex; |
| **Value** | Integer. |
| **Default** | None. |

## sectionRowIndex

**Read-only**

Returns a zero-based integer representing the position of the current row among all other tr elements in the row grouping. A row grouping can be one of the following elements: thead, tbody, tfoot. The count is based on the source code order of the tr elements.

| | |
|---|---|
| **Example** | var whichRow = document.getElementById("myTR").sectionRowIndex; |
| **Value** | Integer. |
| **Default** | None. |

## vAlign

**Read/Write**

Indicates the manner of vertical alignment of text within the cells of the current row.

| | |
|---|---|
| **Example** | document.getElementById("myTR").vAlign = "baseline"; |
| **Value** | Case-insensitive constant (as a string): baseline \| bottom \| middle \| top. |
| **Default** | middle |

## deleteCell( )

deleteCell(*index*)

Removes a td or th element nested within the current tr element. The integer parameter points to the zero-based item in the row's cells collection.

**Returned Value**    None.

**Parameters**

*index*

Zero-based integer corresponding to the numbered td element in source code order (nested within the current element).

## insertCell( )

insertCell(*index*)

Inserts a td element nested within the current tr element. The integer parameter points to the zero-based index in the cells collection where the new cell should go, but in IE you can also use the shortcut value of –1 to append the cell to the end of the collection. Adding the cell inserts an empty element, to which you add content via the various document tree modification techniques. Unfortunately, scripting the addition of table rows and cells in IE for the Macintosh (including Version 5.1) is very broken, yielding elephantine row and cell dimensions. For nonnested tables, you might be able to get away with regular document tree node creation and insertion instead of the table section object convenience methods.

**Returned Value**    Reference to the newly inserted cell.

**Alphabetical DOM Reference**

### Parameters

*index*
> Zero-based integer corresponding to a row of the cells collection before which the new cell is to be inserted.

## TreeWalker                                              NN 7   IE *n/a*   DOM 2

The TreeWalker object is a live, hierarchical list of nodes that meet criteria defined by the document.createTreeWalker( ) method. The list assumes the same parent-descendant hierarchy for its items as the nodes to which its items point. The createTreeWalker( ) method describes the node where the list begins and which nodes (or classes of nodes) are exempt from the list by way of filtering.

The TreeWalker object maintains a kind of pointer inside the list (so that your scripts don't have to). Methods of this object let scripts access the next or previous node (or sibling, child, or parent node) in the list, while moving the pointer in the direction indicated by the method you chose. If scripts modify the document tree after the TreeWalker is created, changes to the document tree are automatically reflected in the sequence of nodes in the TreeWalker.

While fully usable in an HTML document, the TreeWalker can be even more valuable in an XML data document. For example, the W3C DOM does not provide a quick way to access all elements that have a particular attribute name (something that the XPATH standard can do easily on the server). But you can define a TreeWalker to point only to nodes that have the desired attribute, and quickly access those nodes sequentially (i.e., without having to script more laborious looping through all nodes in search of the desired elements). As an example, the following filter function allows only those nodes that contain the author attribute to be a member of a TreeWalker object:

```
function authorAttrFilter(node) {
    if (node.hasAttribute("author")) {
        return NodeFilter.FILTER_ACCEPT;
    }
    return NodeFilter.FILTER_SKIP;
}
```

A reference to this function becomes one of the parameters to a createTreeWalker( ) method that also limits the list to element nodes:

```
var authorsOnly = document.createTreeWalker(document,
NodeFilter.SHOW_ELEMENT, authorAttrFilter, false);
```

You can then invoke TreeWalker object methods to obtain a reference to one of the nodes in the list. When you invoke the method, the TreeWalker object applies the filter to candidates relative to the current position of the internal pointer in the direction indicated by the method. The next document tree node to meet the method and filter criteria is returned. Once you have that node reference, you can access any DOM node property or method to work with the node, independent of the items in the TreeWalker list.

### Object Model Reference

*TreeWalkerReference*

**Object-Specific Properties**

| currentNode | expandEntityReference | filter | root | whatToShow |
|---|---|---|---|---|

**Object-Specific Methods**

| firstChild( ) | lastChild( ) | nextNode( ) | nextSibling( ) |
|---|---|---|---|
| parentNode( ) | previousNode( ) | previousSibling( ) | |

**Object-Specific Event Handler Properties**

None.

## currentNode

NN 7    IE *n/a*    DOM 2

Read/Write

Returns a reference to the node where the TreeWalker's pointer is positioned. But more importantly, you can also assign a document tree node reference to this property to manually set a new position for the pointer. If the assigned node would normally be filtered out of the list, the next method invocation is performed from the position as if the assigned node were not filtered out of the list.

**Example**    `myTreeWalker.currentNode = document.getElementById("main");`

**Value**    Reference to a document tree node.

**Default**    First node of the document.

## expandEntityReference, filter, root, whatToShow

NN 7    IE *n/a*    DOM 2

Read-only

These four properties reflect the parameter values passed to the document.createTreeWalker( ) method when the object was created.

## firstChild( ), lastChild( ), nextSibling( ), parentNode( ), previousSibling( )

NN 7    IE *n/a*    DOM 2

These methods return references to nodes within the hierarchy of items in the TreeWalker object. The parent-descendant relationships between nodes are identical to those of the nodes within the document tree. As you invoke any one of these methods, the TreeWalker's internal pointer moves to a position adjacent to the node's spot within the TreeWalker list. If there is no node meeting the desired reference, the method returns null. This means that you need to verify the existence of the node before reading any property of the node:

```
if (myTreeWalker.nextSibling()) {
    var theTag = myTreeWalker.currentNode.tagName;
}
```

If you reference a property of a null reference directly (myTreeWalker.nextSibling( ).tagName, for example), a reference error results.

**Returned Value**    Reference to a document tree node.

**Parameters**    None.

Alphabetical DOM
Reference

## nextNode( ), previousNode( )　　　　　　　NN *7*　　IE *n/a*　　DOM *2*

Move the internal NodeIterator pointer one position forward (nextNode( )) or backward (previousNode( )), while returning a reference to the node through which the pointer passed en route. These two methods operate as if the hierarchy were flattened (in the manner of a NodeIterator object).

**Returned Value**　　Reference to a node in the document tree.

**Parameters**　　None.

## tt

See b.

## u

See b.

# UIEvent　　　　　　　　　　　　　　　　NN *6*　　IE *n/a*　　DOM *2*

The W3C DOM UIEvent object is an abstract object that contains the properties and methods shared by every instance of a W3C DOM focus-related event. This object inherits characteristics from the W3C DOM Event object. The properties and method of this object are blended into the directly scripted event object. See the discussion of the event object earlier in this chapter for specific property and method support for this object and how these items are inherited by more specific event types.

# ul　　　　　　　　　　　　　　　　　　　NN *6*　　IE *4*　　DOM *1*

The ul object reflects the ul element.

**HTML Equivalent**　　<ul>

**Object Model Reference**
[window.]document.getElementById("*elementID*")

**Object-Specific Properties**
compact　　　　type

**Object-Specific Methods**
None.

**Object-Specific Event Handler Properties**
None.

## compact

Read/Write

When set to true, the compact property should instruct the browser to render items in the list in a more compact format. This property has no effect in mainstream browsers.

| | |
|---|---|
| **Example** | document.getElementById("myUL").compact = true; |
| **Value** | Boolean value: true \| false. |
| **Default** | false |

## type

Read/Write

Specifies the manner in which the leading item markers in the list are displayed.

| | |
|---|---|
| **Example** | document.getElementById("myUL").type = "square"; |
| **Value** | Any one of the constant values (as a string): circle \| disc \| square. Additional choices available through style sheets |
| **Default** | disc |

# userProfile

The userProfile object reflects numerous pieces of information stored in the browser's user profile for the current user. This object has four methods that:

- Let you queue requests for individual fields of the profile (items such as name, mailing address, phone numbers, and so on)
- Display the request dialog that lets users see what you're asking for and disallow specific items or the whole thing
- Grab the information
- Clear the request queue

Once the information is retrieved (with the user's permission), it can be slipped into form elements (visible or hidden) for submission to the server. Compatibility listings here indicate support in IE for Windows only. While IE for Macintosh accepts the method calls without error, there is no functionality attached to those methods. Further details on the user profile are available from Microsoft at *http://msdn.microsoft.com/workshop/ management/profile/profile_assistant.asp*.

**Example**

```
navigator.userProfile.addReadRequest("vcard.displayname");
navigator.userProfile.doReadRequest("3", "MegaCorp Customer Service");
var custName = navigator.userProfile.getAttribute("vcard.displayname");
navigator.userProfile.clearRequest();
if (custName) {
    ...
}
```

**Object Model Reference**

navigator.userProfile

**Object-Specific Properties**

None.

**Object-Specific Methods**

addReadRequest( )      clearRequest( )      doReadRequest( )      getAttribute( )

**Object-Specific Event Handler Properties**

None.

## addReadRequest( )                         NN *n/a*    IE *4(Win)*    DOM *n/a*

addReadRequest("*attributeName*")

Adds a request to inspect a particular user profile attribute to a queue that must be executed separately (via the doReadRequest( ) and getAttribute( ) methods). Items added to the queue are displayed to the user to select which item(s) can be submitted to a server. For multiple attributes, use multiple invocations of the addReadRequest( ) method.

**Returned Value**     Boolean value: true (if successful) | false (if unsuccessful).

**Parameters**

*attributeName*
> One of the following case-insensitive attribute names as a string:

| | |
|---|---|
| vCard.Business.City | vCard.Business.Country |
| vCard.Business.Fax | vCard.Business.Phone |
| vCard.Business.State | vCard.Business.StreetAddress |
| vCard.Business.URL | vCard.Business.Zipcode |
| vCard.Cellular | vCard.Company |
| vCard.Department | vCard.DisplayName |
| vCard.Email | vCard.FirstName |
| vCard.Gender | vCard.Home.City |
| vCard.Home.Country | vCard.Home.Fax |
| vCard.Home.Phone | vCard.Home.State |
| vCard.Home.StreetAddress | vCard.Home.Zipcode |
| vCard.Homepage | vCard.JobTitle |
| vCard.LastName | vCard.MiddleName |
| vCard.Notes | vCard.Office |
| vCard.Pager | |

## clearRequest( )                             NN *n/a*    IE *4(Win)*    DOM *n/a*

Empties the queue of attribute names to be retrieved. Use this after your script has successfully retrieved the required information. This prepares the queue for the next list.

**Returned Value**    None.

**Parameters**    None.

# doReadRequest( )    NN *n/a*    IE *4(Win)*    DOM *n/a*

doReadRequest(*usageCode*[, "*friendlyName*"[, "*domain*"[, "*path*"[, "*expiration*"]]]])

Based on the items in the queue, this method inspects the browser to see whether the user has given permission to inspect these attributes in the past. If not (for some or all), the method displays a dialog box (the Profile Assistant window) that lets users turn off the items that should not be exposed to the server. Parameters provide information for the dialog and for maintenance of the permission (similar to the ways that cookies are managed). Only one doReadRequest( ) method is required, regardless of the number of attributes in the queue.

**Returned Value**

In Windows, the method returns no value, regardless of how the user responds to the Profile Assistant dialog box. On the Macintosh (which does not support this object fully), the method does not display the Profile Assistant dialog box and returns false.

**Parameters**

*usageCode*

One of the following code integers that display human-readable messages defined by the Internet Privacy Working Group, as shown in the following table.

| Code | Meaning |
| --- | --- |
| 0 | Used for system administration. |
| 1 | Used for research and/or product development. |
| 2 | Used for completion and support of current transaction. |
| 3 | Used to customize the content and design of a site. |
| 4 | Used to improve the content of the site, including advertisements. |
| 5 | Used for notifying visitors about updates to the site. |
| 6 | Used for contacting visitors for marketing of services or products. |
| 7 | Used for linking other collected information. |
| 8 | Used by site for other purposes. |
| 9 | Disclosed to others for customization or improvement of the content and design of the site. |
| 10 | Disclosed to others who may contact you for marketing of services and/or products. |
| 11 | Disclosed to others who may contact you for marketing of services and/or products, but you have the opportunity to ask a site not to do this. |
| 12 | Disclosed to others for any other purpose. |

*friendlyName*

An optional string containing an identifiable name (and URL) that the user recognizes as the source of the request. This may be a corporate identity.

*domain*

> An optional string containing the domain of the server making the request. If an expiration date is set, this information is stored with the requested attributes to prevent future requests from this domain from interrupting the user with the Profile Assistant dialog box.

*path*

> An optional string containing the path of the server document making the request. If an expiration date is set, this information is stored with the requested attributes to prevent future requests from this domain from interrupting the user with the Profile Assistant dialog box.

*expiration*

> An optional string containing the date on which the user's permissions settings expire. Not recognized in Internet Explorer 4.

## getAttribute( )            NN *n/a*    IE 4    DOM *n/a*

getAttribute("*attributeName*")

Returns the value of the attribute, provided the user has given permission to do so. If that permission was denied, the method returns null. Use one getAttribute( ) method for each attribute value being retrieved.

**Returned Value**     String value or null

**Parameters**

*attributeName*

> One of the vCard attribute names listed in the addReadRequest( ) method description.

## var

See acronym.

## ViewCSS            NN 6    IE *n/a*    DOM 2

The W3C DOM ViewCSS object is an abstract object equates to the window object. It is the ViewCSS object in the DOM that gives the window object its getComputedStyle( ) method. See the window.getComputedStyle( ) method.

## wbr            NN 6    IE 4    DOM *n/a*

The wbr object reflects the wbr element.

**HTML Equivalent**     <wbr>

**Object Model Reference**

[window.]document.getElementById("*elementID*")

**Object-Specific Properties**

None.

**Object-Specific Methods**

None.

**Object-Specific Event Handler Properties**

None.

# window

The window object represents the browser window or frame in which document content is displayed. The window object plays a vital role in scripting when scripts must communicate with document objects located in other frames or subwindows. Managing multiple windows can be tricky business because of the transient nature of cross-window references. Strict interpretation of HTML and XHTML standards frowns upon multiple windows, and many confused users may agree.

Although the W3C DOM Level 2 does not provide in-depth specifications for the window object (a window, after all, is outside the scope of document markup), it nevertheless indicates possible future hooks through what it calls "view" objects. Thus, the Netscape 6 document.defaultView property returns the document's window; the Netscape 6 window object also takes on the method of the ViewCSS object to gain the DOM's getComputedStyle( ) method.

The window object has been scriptable since the beginning and bears a considerable legacy of properties and methods. Many of these features are browser-specific, so observe compatibility ratings carefully before adopting a particular object feature.

**Object Model Reference**

```
window
self
top
parent
```

**Object Properties**

| | | | |
|---|---|---|---|
| appCore | clientInformation | clipboardData | closed |
| Components | content | controllers | crypto |
| defaultStatus | dialogArguments | dialogHeight | dialogLeft |
| dialogTop | dialogWidth | directories | document |
| event | external | frameElement | frames[] |
| history | innerHeight | innerWidth | length |
| location | locationbar | menubar | name |
| navigator | offscreenBuffering | opener | outerHeight |
| outerWidth | pageXOffset | pageYOffset | parent |
| personalbar | pkcs11 | prompter | returnValue |
| screen | screenLeft | screenTop | screenX |

| screenY | scrollX | scrollY | scrollbars |
|---------|---------|---------|------------|
| self    | sidebar | status  | statusbar  |
| toolbar | top     | window  |            |

## Object Methods

| | | |
|---|---|---|
| addEventListener( ) | alert( ) | attachEvent( ) |
| back( ) | blur( ) | captureEvents( ) |
| clearInterval( ) | clearTimeout( ) | close( ) |
| confirm( ) | createPopup( ) | detachEvent( ) |
| disableExternalCapture( ) | dispatchEvent( ) | enableExternalCapture( ) |
| execScript( ) | find( ) | focus( ) |
| forward( ) | GetAttention( ) | getComputedStyle( ) |
| getSelection( ) | home( ) | moveBy( ) |
| moveTo( ) | navigate( ) | open( ) |
| print( ) | prompt( ) | releaseEvents( ) |
| removeEventListener( ) | resizeBy( ) | resizeTo( ) |
| routeEvent( ) | scroll( ) | scrollBy( ) |
| scrollByLines( ) | scrollByPages( ) | scrollTo( ) |
| setCursor( ) | setInterval( ) | setTimeout( ) |
| showHelp( ) | showModalDialog( ) | showModelessDialog( ) |
| sizeToContent( ) | stop( ) | |

## Object-Specific Event Handler Properties

| Handler | NN | IE/Windows | IE/Mac | DOM |
|---------|-----|-----------|--------|-----|
| onafterprint | n/a | 5 | n/a | n/a |
| onbeforeprint | n/a | 5 | n/a | n/a |
| onbeforeunload | n/a | 4 | 4 | n/a |
| onblur | 3 | 4 | 4 | n/a |
| ondragdrop | 4 | n/a | n/a | n/a |
| onerror | 3 | 4 | 4 | n/a |
| onfocus | 3 | 4 | 4 | n/a |
| onhelp | n/a | 4 | 4 | n/a |
| onload | 2 | 3 | 3.01 | n/a |
| onmove | 4 | 5.5 | n/a | n/a |
| onresize | 4 | 4 | 4 | n/a |
| onscroll | n/a | 4 | 4 | n/a |
| onunload | 2 | 4 | 4 | n/a |

## appCore, Components, content, controllers, prompter, sidebar

NN *6*   IE *n/a*   DOM *n/a*

Read-only

These properties are associated with the proprietary Mozilla xpconnect ("cross-platform" connect) services. These services allow scripts that have the correct security clearance to work with XPCOM (decidedly not MS COM) objects to extend the functionality of the application that uses the Mozilla engine (such as the Netscape 6 browser). Access to these services requires enabling security privileges (typically via signed scripts), as follows:

```
netscape.security.PrivilegeManager.enablePrivilege("UniversalXPConnect");
// your xpconnect access code here
netscape.security.PrivilegeManager.revertPrivilege("UniversalXPConnect");
```

For more details on this mechanism, visit *http://www.mozilla.org/scriptable/*.

## clientInformation

NN *n/a*   IE *4*   DOM *n/a*

Read-only

Returns the navigator object. The navigator object is named after a specific browser brand; the clientInformation property is a nondenominational way of accessing important environment variables that have historically been available through properties and methods of the navigator object (discussed separately earlier in this chapter as its own object). In Internet Explorer, you can substitute window.clientInformation for any reference that begins with navigator.

### Example

```
if (parseInt(window.clientInformation.appVersion) >= 4) {
    // process code for IE 4 or later
}
```

**Value**         The navigator object.

**Default**       The navigator object.

## clipboardData

NN *n/a*   IE *5(Win)*   DOM *n/a*

Read-only

Returns the clipboardData object, discussed separately earlier in this chapter as its own object. The object (accessible as a property of a window or frame object) is a temporary container that scripts in IE 5 and later for Windows can use to transfer text data, particularly during script-controlled operations that simulate cutting, copying, and pasting, or that control dragging.

### Example

```
var rng = document.selection.createRange();
clipboardData.setData("Text",rng.text);
```

**Value**         The clipboardData object.

**Default**       The clipboardData object.

Alphabetical DOM Reference

## closed

NN 3   IE 4   DOM n/a<br>Read-only

This is the Boolean value that says whether the referenced window is closed. A value of true means the window is no longer available for referencing its objects or script components. This is used most often to check whether a user has closed a subwindow generated by the window.open( ) method.

**Example**
```
if (!newWindow.closed) {
    newWindow.document.close( );
}
```

**Value**          Boolean value: true | false.

**Default**        None.

## Components, content, controllers

See appCore.

## crypto, pkcs11

NN 6   IE n/a   DOM n/a<br>Read-only

Return references to objects associated with Mozilla public-key cryptography internals. For more details on this subject, visit *http://www.mozilla.org/projects/security/*.

## defaultStatus

NN 2   IE 3   DOM n/a<br>Read/Write

Specifies the default message displayed in the browser window's status bar when no browser loading activity is occurring. To temporarily change the message (during mouse rollovers, for example), set the window's status property. Most scriptable browsers and versions have difficulty managing the setting of the defaultStatus property. Expect odd behavior.

**Example**        window.defaultStatus = "Make it a great day!";

**Value**          Any string value.

**Default**        None.

## dialogArguments

NN n/a   IE 4   DOM n/a<br>Read-only

This is the string or other data type passed as extra arguments to a modal dialog window created with the window.showModalDialog( ) or (in IE 5 and later for Windows only) window.showModelessDialog( ) methods. This property is best accessed by a script in the document displayed in the dialog window in order to retrieve whatever data is passed to the new window as arguments. It is up to your script to parse the data if you include more than one argument nugget separated by whatever argument delimiter you choose.

**Example**
```
// in dialog window
var allArgs = window.dialogArguments;
var firstArg = allArgs.substring(0, allArgs.indexOf(";"));
```

| | |
|---|---|
| **Value** | String, number, array, or object. |
| **Default** | None. |

## dialogHeight, dialogWidth

Specify the height and width values of a modal dialog window created with the showModalDialog( ) and showModelessDialog( ) methods. Although Internet Explorer does not balk at modifying these properties (in a script running in the modal dialog window), the changed values are generally not reflected in a resized dialog window. Initial values are set as parameters to the dialog-opening methods.

| | |
|---|---|
| **Example** | `var outerWidth = window.dialogWidth;` |
| **Value** | String, including the unit value (e.g., 520px). |
| **Default** | None. |

## dialogLeft, dialogTop

Indicate the offset distance of the left and top edges of a modal dialog window (created with the showModalDialog( ) and showModelessDialog( ) methods) relative to the top-left corner of the video screen. Although Internet Explorer does not balk at modifying these properties (in a script running in the modal dialog window), the changed values are generally not reflected in a repositioned dialog window. Initial values are set as parameters to the dialog methods.

| | |
|---|---|
| **Example** | `var outerLeft = window.dialogLeft;` |
| **Value** | String, including the unit value (e.g., 80px). |
| **Default** | None. |

## directories, locationbar, menubar, personalbar, scrollbars, statusbar, toolbar

Return references to the Navigator browser window feature (the directories property is new for Netscape 6). See the discussion of the directories (et al.) objects earlier in this chapter for how to control the visibility of these window features with signed scripts.

**Example**

```
netscape.security.PrivilegeManager.enablePrivilege("UniversalBrowserWrite")
window.statusbar.visible = "false";
netscape.security.PrivilegeManager.revertrivilege("UniversalBrowserWrite")
```

| | |
|---|---|
| **Value** | Respective object references. |
| **Default** | None. |

## document          NN 2    IE 3    DOM 2

Read-only

Returns a reference to the document object contained by the window. In browsers that offer W3C DOM document tree support, this property points more specifically to the root HTMLDocument node for the document tree loaded in the window. The W3C DOM even describes this property as a member of one of its View objects (analogous to a browser window). This is the property that lets scripts references to document methods and content begin with the word document.

| | |
|---|---|
| **Example** | `var oneElem = document.getElementById("myP");` |
| **Value** | Reference to the root document object. |
| **Default** | Reference to the root document object. |

## event          NN n/a    IE 4    DOM n/a

Read-only

Internet Explorer's event model generates an event object for each user or system event. This event object is a property of the window object. For details about the IE event object, see Chapter 6 and the listing of the event object in this chapter.

**Example**

```
if (event.altKey) {
    // handle case of Alt key down
}
```

| | |
|---|---|
| **Value** | event object reference. |
| **Default** | None. |

## external          NN n/a    IE 4(Win)    DOM n/a

Read-only

Returns a reference to the external object, which provides access to lower-level functionality of the browser engine (security permissions willing). See the discussion of the external object earlier in this chapter.

| | |
|---|---|
| **Example** | `external.AddFavorite("http://www.dannyg.com", "Danny Home Page");` |

| **Value** | external object reference. |
| **Default** | external object reference. |

## frameElement

If the current window is a member of a frameset or is an iframe, the `frameElement` property returns a reference to the `frame` or `iframe` element object (distinct from the frame-as-window object). Security restrictions, however, can impede script access to this property.

| **Example** | `var frameID = window.frameElement.id;` |
| **Value** | `frame` or `iframe` object reference; or `null`. |
| **Default** | `null`. |

## frames[]

Returns a collection (array) of `window` objects that are implemented as frames or iframes in the current window. For a frameset's parent or top window, the array contains references to first-generation `frame` windows. Index values can be zero-based integers (in source code order) or the identifier assigned to the `name` attribute of the `frame` element.

| **Example** | `parent.frames[1].myFunc( );` |
| **Value** | Array of `frame` (`window`) object references. |
| **Default** | Array of length zero. |

## history

Contains the `history` object for the current window or frame. For details, see the discussion of the `history` object.

**Example**
```
if (self.history.length > 4) {
    ...
}
```

| **Value** | `history` object reference. |
| **Default** | Current `history` object. |

Alphabetical DOM Reference

## innerHeight, innerWidth

Specify the pixel measure of the height and width of the content region of a browser window or frame. This area is where the document content appears, exclusive of all window "chrome." For comparable values in IE, see the body element object.

**Example**

```
window.innerWidth = 600;
window.innerHeight = 400;
```

**Value**          Integer.

**Default**        None.

## length

Specifies the number of frames (if any) nested within the current window. This value is the same as that returned by window.frames.length. When no frames are defined for the window, the value is zero.

**Example**

```
if (window.length > 0) {
    ...
}
```

**Value**          Integer.

**Default**        0

## location

Returns a location object containing URL details of the document currently loaded in the window or frame. To navigate to another page, you assign a URL to the location.href property (or see the navigate( ) method for an IE-only alternative). See the location object.

**Example**        top.location.href = "index.html";

**Value**          A full or relative URL as a string.

**Default**        Current location object.

## locationbar

See directories.

## menubar

See directories.

## name

Read/Write

This is the identifier associated with a frame or subwindow for use as the value assigned to target attributes or as script references to the frame/subwindow. For a frame, the value is usually assigned via the name attribute of the frame tag, but it can be modified by a script if necessary. The name of a subwindow is assigned as a parameter to the window.open( ) method. The primary browser window does not have a name by default, but you can assign one via script if you need a subwindow to target a link or form back to the main window.

**Example**
```
if (parent.frames[1].name == "main") {
    ...
}
```

**Value**        Case-sensitive identifier that follows the rules of identifier naming: it may contain no whitespace, cannot begin with a numeral, and should avoid punctuation except for the underscore character.

**Default**      None.

## navigator

Read-only

Returns a reference to the navigator object. Since the window reference is optional, syntax without the window reference works on all scriptable versions of Internet Explorer and Navigator. See the navigator object.

**Example**      var theBrowser = navigator.appName;

**Value**        navigator object reference.

**Default**      navigator object.

## offscreenBuffering

Read/Write

Indicates whether the browser should use offscreen buffering to improve path animation performance. Although the property is implemented in IE 5 for Macintosh, it is unclear that it offers any functionality. Recent versions of IE for Windows connect this property to the DirectX ActiveX control. When the document loads, the property is set to auto. After that, a script may turn buffering on and off by assigning a Boolean value to this property.

**Example**      window.offscreenBuffering = "true";

| **Value** | Boolean value: true \| false. |
| **Default** | auto |

## opener

This is an object reference to the window (or frame) that used a window.open( ) method to generate the current window. This property allows subwindows to assemble references to objects, variables, and functions in the originating window. To access document objects in the creating window, a reference can begin with opener and work its way through the regular document object hierarchy from there, as shown in the left side of the following example statement. The relationship between the opening window and the opened window is not strictly parent-child. The term "parent" has other connotations in scripted window and frame references. IE's dialog windows (the showModalDialog( ) and showModelessDialog( ) windows) do not support this property. Values between the main and dialog windows must be passed at creation time and via the dialog window's returnValue property upon closing.

### Example
```
opener.document.forms[0].importedData.value = document.forms[0].entry.value;
```

| **Value** | window object reference. |
| **Default** | None. |

## outerHeight, outerWidth

Specify the pixel measure of the height and width of the browser window or frame, including (for the top window) all tool bars, scoll bars, and other visible window "chrome." IE offers no equivalent properties.

### Example
```
window.outerWidth = 80;
window.outerHeight = 600;
```

| **Value** | Integer. |
| **Default** | None. |

## pageXOffset, pageYOffset

Specify the pixel measure of the amount of the page's content that has been scrolled upward and/or to the left. For example, if a document has been scrolled so that the topmost 100 pixels of the document (the "page") are not visible because the window is scrolled, the pageYOffset value for the window is 100. When a document is not scrolled, both values are zero.

| | |
|---|---|
| **Example** | `var vertScroll = self.pageYOffset;` |
| **Value** | Integer. |
| **Default** | 0 |

## parent

NN 2    IE 3    DOM n/a
Read-only

Returns a reference to the parent window object whose document defined the frameset in which the current frame is specified. Use parent in building a reference from one child frame to variables or methods in the parent document or to variables, methods, and objects in another child frame. For example, if a script in one child frame must reference the content of a text input form element in the other child frame (named "content"), the reference would be:

```
parent.content.document.forms[0].entryField.value
```

For more deeply nested frames, you can access the parent of a parent with syntax such as: parent.parent.frameName.

| | |
|---|---|
| **Example** | `parent.frames[1].document.forms[0].companyName.value = "MegaCorp";` |
| **Value** | window object reference. |
| **Default** | Current window object reference. |

## personalbar

See directories.

## pkcs11

See crypto.

## prompter

See appCore.

## returnValue

NN n/a    IE 4(Win)/5(Mac)    DOM n/a
Read/Write

A value to be returned to the main window when an IE dialog window (generated by showModalDialog( ) method only) closes. The value assigned to this property in a script running in the dialog window becomes the value returned by the showModalDialog( ) method in the main window. For example, the document in the modal dialog window may have a statement that sets the returnValue property with information from the dialog:

```
window.returnValue = window.document.forms[0].userName.value;
```

Alphabetical DOM Reference

The dialog is created in the main document with a statement like the following:

```
var userName = showModalDialog("userNamePrompt.html");
```

Whatever value is assigned to returnValue in the dialog is then assigned to the userName variable when the dialog box closes and script execution continues.

| | |
|---|---|
| **Value** | Any scriptable data type. |
| **Default** | None. |

## screen

NN 6   IE 4   DOM n/a<br>Read-only

Returns a reference to the screen object. Since the window reference is optional, syntax without the window reference works on all scriptable versions of Internet Explorer and Navigator.

| | |
|---|---|
| **Example** | var howHigh = screen.availHeight; |
| **Value** | screen object reference. |
| **Default** | screen object. |

## screenLeft, screenTop

NN n/a   IE 5(Win)   DOM n/a<br>Read-only

Return pixel coordinates of the top-left corner of the browser content area relative to the top-left corner of the screen. A maximized browser window returns a screenLeft value of 0, but the screenTop value varies with the complement of toolbars the user chooses to display. Use window.moveTo( ) to change the window position.

| | |
|---|---|
| **Example** | var fromTheTop = window.screenTop; |
| **Value** | Integer. |
| **Default** | User-dependent |

## screenX, screenY

NN 6   IE n/a   DOM n/a<br>Read/Write

Return pixel coordinates of the top-left corner of the entire browser window (including "chrome") relative to the top-left corner of the screen. A browser window maximized under Windows returns screenX and screenY values of -4 because the chrome extends slightly beyond the screen display. You can adjust the window location through these properties or the window.moveTo( ) method.

| | |
|---|---|
| **Example** | var fromTheTop = window.screenY; |
| **Value** | Integer. |
| **Default** | User-dependent. |

## scrollX, scrollY

Return the pixel distance the window is scrolled along the horizontal (scrollX) and vertical (scrollY) axes. To determine these values in IE, you must take into account compatibility mode settings in IE 6 (see the DOCTYPE element in Chapter 8). In backward compatibility mode and in IE for Macintosh, use the document.body.scrollLeft and document.body.scrollTop properties. In IE 6 standards compatibility mode (where document.compatMode == "CSS1Compat"), use document.body.parentNode.scrollLeft and document.body.parentNode.scrollTop to get the scroll values of the html element.

| | |
|---|---|
| **Example** | var scrolledDown = window.scrollY; |
| **Value** | Integer. |
| **Default** | 0 |

## scrollbars

See directories.

## self

This is a reference to the current window or frame. This property is synonymous with window, but is sometimes used to improve clarity in a complex script that refers to many windows or frames. Never use the reference window.self to refer to the current window or frame because some browser versions get confused with the reference.

| | |
|---|---|
| **Example** | self.focus( ); |
| **Value** | window object reference. |
| **Default** | Current window. |

## sidebar

See appCore.

## status

Specifies the text of the status bar of the browser window. Setting the status bar to some message is recommended only for temporary messages, such as for mouse rollovers atop images, areas, or links. Double or single quotes in the message must be escaped (\'). Many users don't notice incidental text in the status bar, so avoid putting mission-critical information there. Temporary messages conflict with browser-driven use of the status bar for loading progress and other purposes. To set the default status bar message (when all is at rest), see the defaultStatus property.

**Example**

```
<...onmouseover="window.status='Table of Contents';return true"
onmouseout = "window.status = '';return true">
```

| Value | String. |
|---|---|
| Default | Empty string. |

## statusbar

See directories.

## toolbar

See directories.

## top

NN 2   IE 3   DOM n/a
Read-only

This is an object reference to the browser window. Script statements from inside nested frames can refer to the browser window properties and methods or to variables or functions stored in the document loaded in the topmost position. Do not begin a reference with window.top, just top. To replace a frameset with a new document that occupies the entire browser window, assign a URL to the top.location.href property.

| Example | top.location.href = "tableOfContents.html"; |
|---|---|
| Value | window object reference. |
| Default | Browser window. |

## window

NN 2   IE 3   DOM n/a
Read-only

This is an object reference to the browser window.

**Example**

```
if (window == top) {
    // load a frameset
    location.href = "mainFrameset.html";
}
```

| Value | window object reference. |
|---|---|
| Default | Browser window. |

## addEventListener( )

NN 6    IE n/a    DOM n/a

addEventListener("*eventType*", *listenerFunction*, *useCapture*)

Although the window object as we know it is not officially part of the W3C DOM, Netscape 6 implements this W3C DOM event model method for the window object. See the addEventListener( ) method discussion among the shared methods described earlier in this chapter.

## alert( )

NN 2    IE 3    DOM n/a

alert("*message*")

Displays an alert dialog box with a message of your choice. Script execution halts while the dialog box appears. A single button lets the user close the dialog. The title bar of the window (and the "JavaScript Alert" legend in earlier browser versions) cannot be altered by script.

**Returned Value**    None.

**Parameters**

*message*
    Any string.

## attachEvent( )

NN n/a    IE 5(Win)    DOM n/a

attachEvent("*eventName*", *functionReference*)

This IE event model method, shared among all element objects, is also a member of the window object. See the attachEvent( ) method discussion among the shared methods described earlier in this chapter.

## back( )

NN 4    IE n/a    DOM n/a

Navigates one step backward through the history list of the window or frame. You may prefer the cross-browser history.back( ) method.

**Returned Value**    None.

**Parameters**    None.

## blur( )

NN 3    IE 4    DOM n/a

Removes focus from the window and fires an onBlur event (in IE). No other element necessarily receives focus as a result, but if another IE window is open at the time, the current window moves to the rear of the stack.

**Returned Value**    None.

**Parameters**    None.

Alphabetical DOM Reference

## captureEvents( )                    NN *4*   IE *n/a*   DOM *n/a*

captureEvents(*eventTypeList*)

Instructs the browser to grab events of a specific type before they reach their intended target objects. The object invoking this method must then have event handlers defined for the given event types to process the event. Although this method is part of the Navigator 4 event model, it continues to be supported in Netscape 6, creating the equivalent of a W3C DOM capture-mode event listener for the document object. Continue to use this method if you must support Navigator 4, but migrate new code to the W3C DOM event listener syntax as described in Chapter 6.

**Returned Value**     None.

**Parameters**

*eventTypeList*
A comma-separated list of case-sensitive event types as derived from the available Event object constants, such as Event.CLICK or Event.MOUSEMOVE.

## clearInterval( )                    NN *4*   IE *4*   DOM *n/a*

clearInterval(*intervalID*)

Turns off the interval looping action referenced by the *intervalID* parameter. See setInterval( ) for how to initiate such a loop.

**Returned Value**     None.

**Parameters**

*intervalID*
An integer created as the return value of a setInterval( ) method.

## clearTimeout( )                    NN *2*   IE *3*   DOM *n/a*

clearTimeout(*timeoutID*)

Turns off the timeout delay counter referenced by the *timeoutID* parameter. See setTimeout( ) for how to initiate such a delay.

**Returned Value**     None.

**Parameters**

*timeoutID*
An integer created as the return value of a setTimeout( ) method.

## close( )                    NN *2*   IE *3*   DOM *n/a*

Closes the current window. A script in a subwindow cannot close the main window without receiving the user's explicit permission from a security dialog box. A window can close itself (i.e., from a script running in the same window) or a window it generated via the window.open( ) method.

**Returned Value**     None.

**Parameters**     None.

## confirm( )

`confirm("`*`message`*`")`

Displays a dialog box with a message and two clickable buttons. Script execution halts while the dialog box appears. One button indicates a **Cancel** operation; the other button indicates the user's approval (**OK** or **Yes**). The text of the buttons is not scriptable. The message should ask a question to which either button would be a logical reply. A click of the **Cancel** button returns a value of `false`; a click of the **OK** button returns a value of `true`.

Because this method returns a Boolean value, you can use this method inside a condition expression:

```
if (confirm("Reset the entire form?")) {
    document.forms[0].reset( );
}
```

**Returned Value**     Boolean value: `true | false`.

**Parameters**

*message*
   Any string, usually in the form of a question.

## createPopup( )

Opens a blank popup rectangular space that can be populated with HTML content, yet the space can extend across frame boundaries and even window borders. Scripts must assign content (not an external URL) to the popup object returned by the method. See the popup object for more details and an example of usage.

**Returned Value**     popup object reference.

**Parameters**     None.

## detachEvent( )

`detachEvent("`*`eventName`*`", `*`functionReference`*`)`

This IE event model method, shared among all element objects, is also a member of the window object. See the `detachEvent( )` method discussion among the shared methods described earlier in this chapter.

## disableExternalCapture( ), enableExternalCapture( )

With signed scripts and the user's permission, a script can capture events in other windows or frames that come from domains other than the one that served the document with event-capturing scripts. Navigator 4 only.

**Returned Value**     None.

**Parameters**     None.

## dispatchEvent( )                                    NN 6     IE *n/a*     DOM 2

dispatchEvent(*eventObjectReference*)

Although the window object is not officially part of the W3C DOM, Netscape 6 implements this W3C DOM event model method for the window object. See the dispatchEvent( ) method discussion among the shared methods described earlier in this chapter.

## execScript( )                                    NN *n/a*     IE 4     DOM *n/a*

execScript(*expressionList* [, *language*])

Evaluates one or more script expressions in any scripting language embedded in the browser. Expressions must be contained within a single string; multiple expressions are delimited with semicolons:

```
window.execScript("var x = 3; alert(x * 3)")
```

The default script language is JavaScript. If you need to see results of the script execution, provide for the display of resulting data in the script expressions, as shown in the example. The execScript( ) method itself returns no value.

**Returned Value**     None.

**Parameters**

*expressionList*
    String value of one or more semicolon-delimited script expressions.

*language*
    String value for a scripting language: JavaScript | JScript | VBS | VBScript.

## find( )                                    NN 4     IE *n/a*     DOM *n/a*

find("*searchString*"[, *matchCase*[, *searchUpward*]])

Searches the document body text for a string and selects the first matching string. Optionally, you can specify whether the search should be case-sensitive or should search upward in the document. With the found text selected in Navigator 4, you can then use the document.getSelection( ) method to grab a copy of the found text. You don't, however, have nearly the dynamic content abilities afforded by Internet Explorer 4's TextRange object (for Win32). This method is disconnected in Netscape 6 (it always returns false), but is reconnected in Netscape 7.

**Returned Value**

Boolean value: true if a match was found; false if not or Netscape 6 only.

**Parameters**

*searchString*
    String for which to search the document.

*matchCase*

> Boolean value: true to allow only exact, case-sensitive matches; false (default) to use case-insensitive search.

*searchUpward*

> Boolean value: true to search from the current selection position upward through the document; false (default) to search forward from the current selection position.

## focus( )

Brings the window to the front of all regular browser windows and fires the onFocus event (in IE). If another window had focus at the time, that other window receives an onBlur event.

**Returned Value**    None.

**Parameters**    None.

## forward( )

Navigates one step forward through the history list of the window or frame. If the forward history has no entries, no action takes place.

**Returned Value**    None.

**Parameters**    None.

## GetAttention( )

Mistakenly exposed to scripters, this method calls upon the operating system's way of alerting a user that the application needs attention. In Windows, the Taskbar box for the browser window flashes; in the Mac OS, a beep sounds, and a bullet appears next to the application in the **Application** menu. If the browser window is already at the front, no user signal appears. Removed for Netscape 7.

**Returned Value**    None.

**Parameters**    None.

## getComputedStyle( )

getComputedStyle(*elementNodeReference*, "*pseudoElementName*")

Returns a style object (specifically, a CSSStyleDeclaration object in the W3C DOM terminology) showing the net cascade of style settings that affect the element passed as the first parameter. To retrieve a particular style attribute value (including a value inherited from the default browser style sheet), use the getPropertyValue( ) method of the style object returned from this method:

```
var compStyle = getComputedStyle(document.getElementById("myP"), "");
var pBGColor = compStyle.getPropertyValue("background-color");
```

See the style object for additional details.

**Returned Value**    style (CSSStyleDeclaration) object reference.

**Parameters**

*elementNodeReference*
Reference to an element node in the document tree that becomes the selection.

*pseudoElementName*
String name of a pseudo-element (e.g., :first-line) or an empty string.

## getSelection( )                                            NN 6    IE *n/a*    DOM *n/a*

Returns a selection object, which can then be turned into a W3C DOM Range object. This method takes the place of the old document.getSelection( ) method, which is deprecated in Netscape 6. The corresponding IE operation is the document.selection property. See the selection object for details on working with a selection.

**Returned Value**    selection object reference.

**Parameters**    None.

## home( )                                                    NN 4    IE *n/a*    DOM *n/a*

Navigates to the URL designated as the home page for the browser. This is the same as the user clicking on the **Home** button.

**Returned Value**    None.

**Parameters**    None.

## moveBy( )                                                  NN 4    IE 4    DOM *n/a*

moveBy(*deltaX, deltaY*)

This is a convenience method that shifts the location of the window by specified pixel amounts along both axes. To shift along only one axis, set the other value to zero. Positive values for *deltaX* shift the window to the right; negative values to the left. Positive values for *deltaY* shift the window downward; negative values upward.

**Returned Value**    None.

**Parameters**

*deltaX*
Positive or negative pixel count of the change in horizontal direction of the window.
*deltaY*
Positive or negative pixel count of the change in vertical direction of the window.

## moveTo( )                                                  NN 4    IE 4    DOM *n/a*

moveTo(*x, y*)

This is a convenience method that shifts the location of the current window to a specific coordinate point. The moveTo( ) method uses the screen coordinate system.

---

**Returned Value**     None.

**Parameters**

*x*     Positive or negative pixel count relative to the top of the screen.

*y*     Positive or negative pixel count relative to the left edge of the screen.

## navigate( )                                    NN *n/a*    IE *3*    DOM *n/a*
```
navigate(URL)
```

Loads a new document into the window or frame. This is the IE-specific way of assigning a value to the `window.location.href` property.

**Returned Value**     None.

**Parameters**

*URL*

A complete or relative URL as a string.

## open( )                                          NN *2*    IE *3*    DOM *n/a*
```
open("URL", "windowName"[, "windowFeatures"])
open("URL", "windowName"[, "windowFeatures"][, replaceFlag])
```

Opens a new window (without closing the original one). You can specify a URL to load into the new window or set that parameter to an empty string to allow scripts to `document.write( )` into that new window. The *windowName* parameter lets you assign a name that can be used by `target` attributes of `link` and `form` elements. This name is not to be used in script references as frame names are. Instead, a script reference to a subwindow must be to the `window` object returned by the `window.open( )` method. Therefore, if your scripts must communicate with a window opened in this manner, it is best to save the returned value as a global variable so that future statements can use it.

A potential problem with subwindows is that they can be buried under the main window if the user clicks on the main window (or a script gives it focus). Any script that opens a subwindow should also include a `focus( )` method for the subwindow (in Navigator 3 and later, and in IE 4 and later) to make sure it comes to the front in case it is already open. Subsequent invocations of the `window.open( )` method in which the *windowName* parameter is the same as an earlier call automatically address the previously opened window, even if it is underneath the main window (and thus without bringing the window to the front).

The optional third parameter gives you control over various physical attributes of the subwindow. The *windowFeatures* parameter is a single string consisting of a comma-delimited list (without spaces between items) of attribute/value pairs:

```
newWindow = window.open("someDoc.html","subWind",
"status,menubar,height=400,width=300");
newWindow.focus( );
```

By default, all window attributes are turned on and the subwindow opens to the same size that the browser would use to open a new window from the **File** menu. But if your script specifies even one attribute, all settings are turned off. Therefore, use the *windowFeatures* parameter to specify those features that you want turned on.

If you encounter problems referencing a subwindow immediately after it is created, the problem is most likely a timing issue (affecting IE for Windows more than others). Script statements seem to want to reference the window before it exists completely. To work around the problem, place the code that works with the subwindow in a separate function, and invoke that function via the setTimeout( ) method, usually with no more than 50 milliseconds needed.

Managing multiple windows through scripts can be difficult. Security restrictions across domains frequently foil the best intentions. Users aren't always fond of windows appearing and hiding on their own. If your audience uses newer browsers, consider simulating windows with positioned elements.

**Returned Value**     Window object reference.

## Parameters

*URL*
> A complete or relative URL as a string. If an empty string, no document loads into the window.

*windowName*
> An identifier for the window to be used by target attributes. This is different from the title attribute of the document that loads into the window.

*windowFeatures*
> A string of comma-delimited features to be turned on in the new window. Do not put spaces after the comma delimiters. The list of possible features is long, but a number of them are specific to Navigator 4 or later and require signed scripts because they are potentially a privacy and security concern to unsuspecting users. The features are listed as follows. To turn on a window feature, simply include its case-insensitive name in the comma-separated list. Only attributes specifying dimensions require values be assigned.

| Attribute | NN | IE | Description |
|---|---|---|---|
| alwaysLowered | 4 | n/a | Always behind all other browser windows. Signed script required. |
| alwaysRaised | 4 | n/a | Always in front of all other browser windows. Signed script required. |
| channelMode | n/a | 4 | Show in theater mode with channel band. |
| copyhistory | 2 | 3 | Copy history listing from opening window to new window. |
| dependent | 4 | n/a | Subwindow closes if the window that opened it closes. |
| directories | 2 | 3 | Display directory buttons. |
| fullscreen | n/a | 4 | Display no titlebar or menus |
| height | 2 | 3 | Window height in pixels. |
| hotkeys | 4 | n/a | Disables menu keyboard shortcuts (except Quit and Security Info). |
| innerHeight | 4 | n/a | Content region height. Signed script required for very small measures. |
| innerWidth | 4 | n/a | Content region width. Signed script required for very small measures. |
| left | 6 | 4 | Offset of window's left edge from left edge of screen. |
| location | 2 | 3 | Display Location (or Address) text field. |

| Attribute | NN | IE | Description |
|-----------|----|----|-------------|
| menubar | 2 | 3 | Display menubar (a menubar is always visible on Mac). |
| outerHeight | 4 | n/a | Total window height. Signed script required for very small measures. |
| outerWidth | 4 | n/a | Total window width. Signed script required for very small measures. |
| resizable | 2 | 3 | Allow window resizing (always allowed on Mac). |
| screenX | 4 | n/a | Offset of window's left edge from left edge of screen. Signed script required to move window offscreen. |
| screenY | 4 | n/a | Offset of window's top edge from top edge of screen. Signed script required to move window offscreen. |
| scrollbars | 2 | 3 | Display scrollbars if document is too large for window. |
| status | 2 | 3 | Display status bar. |
| titlebar | 4 | n/a | Displays titlebar. Set this value to no to hide the titlebar. Signed script required. |
| toolbar | 2 | 3 | Display toolbar (with **Back**, **Forward**, and other buttons). |
| top | 6 | 4 | Offset of window's top edge from top edge of screen. |
| width | 2 | 3 | Window width in pixels. |
| z-lock | 4 | n/a | New window is fixed below browser windows. Signed script required. |

*replaceFlag*

Boolean value (for IE only) that controls the effect of the new window's URL on the global history of the browser. Set to true to replace the current page with the new window's URL (so that the current page won't be accessed through the **Back** button); set to false to add the new window's URL to the history, as normal.

## print( )
NN *4*   IE *5*   DOM *n/a*

Starts the printing process for the window or frame. A user must still confirm the print dialog box to send the document to the printer. This method is the same as clicking the browser's **Print** button or selecting **Print** from the **File** menu.

**Returned Value**  None.

**Parameters**  None.

## prompt( )
NN *2*   IE *3*   DOM *n/a*

prompt("*message*", "*defaultReply*")

Displays a dialog box with a message, a one-line text entry field, and two clickable buttons. Script execution halts while the dialog box appears. The message should urge the user to enter a specific kind of answer. One button indicates a **Cancel** operation; the other button indicates the user's approval of the text entered into the field (**OK** or **Yes**). The text of the buttons is not scriptable. A click of the **Cancel** button returns a value of null; a click of the **OK** button returns a string of whatever is in the text entry field at the time (including the possibility of an empty string). It is up to your scripts to test for the type of response (if any) supplied by the user.

**Returned Value**

When clicking the **OK** button, a string of the text entry field; when clicking **Cancel**, null.

**Parameters**

*message*
> Any string.

*defaultReply*
> Any string that suggests an answer. Always supply a value, even if an empty string.

## releaseEvents( ) NN 4    IE *n/a*    DOM *n/a*

releaseEvents(*eventTypeList*)

The opposite of window.captureEvents( ), this method turns off event capture at the window level for one or more specific events named in the parameter list. Although this method is part of the Navigator 4 event model, it continues to be supported in Netscape 6, creating the equivalent of a W3C DOM capture-mode event listener for the document object. Continue to use this method if you must support Navigator 4, but migrate new code to the W3C DOM event listener syntax as described in Chapter 6.

**Returned Value**    None.

**Parameters**

*eventTypeList*
> A comma-separated list of case-sensitive event types as derived from the available Event object constants, such as Event.CLICK or Event.MOUSEMOVE.

## removeEventListener( ) NN 6    IE *n/a*    DOM *n/a*

removeEventListener("*eventType*", *listenerFunction*, *useCapture*)

Although the window object as we know it is not officially part of the W3C DOM, Netscape 6 implements this W3C DOM event model method for the window object. See the removeEventListener( ) method discussion among the shared methods described earlier in this chapter.

## resizeBy( ) NN 4    IE 4    DOM *n/a*

resizeBy(*deltaX, deltaY*)

This is a convenience method that shifts the width and height of the window by specified pixel amounts. To adjust along only one axis, set the other value to zero. Positive values for *deltaX* make the window wider; negative values make the window narrower. Positive values for *deltaY* make the window taller; negative values make the window shorter. The top and left edges remain fixed; only the right and bottom edges are moved.

**Returned Value**    None.

**Parameters**

*deltaX*
> Positive or negative pixel count of the change in horizontal dimension of the window.

*deltaY*
> Positive or negative pixel count of the change in vertical dimension of the window.

## resizeTo( )
```
resizeTo(x, y)
```

This is a convenience method that adjusts the height and width of the window to specific pixel sizes. The top and left edges of the window remain fixed, while the bottom and right edges move in response to this method.

**Returned Value**   None.

**Parameters**

*x*   Width in pixels of the window.

*y*   Height in pixels of the window.

## routeEvent( )
```
routeEvent(event)
```

Used inside an event handler function, this method directs Navigator 4 (only) to let the event pass to its intended target object.

**Returned Value**   None.

**Parameters**

*event*
> A Navigator 4 event object.

## scroll( )
```
scroll(x, y)
```

Sets the scrolled position of the document inside the current window or frame. To return the document to its unscrolled position, set both parameters to zero.

**Returned Value**   None.

**Parameters**

*x*   Horizontal measure of scrolling within the window.

*y*   Vertical measure of scrolling within the window.

Alphabetical DOM
Reference

## scrollBy( )  NN 4   IE 4   DOM n/a

scrollBy(deltaX, deltaY)

Scrolls the document in the window by specified pixel amounts along both axes. To adjust along only one axis, set the other value to zero. Positive values for *deltaX* scroll the document to the left (so the user sees content to the right in the document); negative values scroll the document to the right. Positive values for *deltaY* scroll the document upward (so the user sees content lower in the document); negative values scroll the document downward. Scrolling does not continue past the zero coordinate points (except in Navigator 4 for the Macintosh).

**Returned Value**    None.

**Parameters**

*deltaX*
> Positive or negative pixel count of the change in horizontal scroll position.

*deltaY*
> Positive or negative pixel count of the change in vertical scroll position.

## scrollByLines( ), scrollByPages( )  NN 6   IE n/a   DOM n/a

scrollByLines(intervalCount)
scrollByPages(intervalCount)

Scroll the document in the window downward (positive value) or upward (negative value) by the increment of lines or pages. The methods perform the same actions as the user clicking on the arrow and "page" regions of the vertical scrollbar, respectively.

**Returned Value**    None.

**Parameters**

*intervalCount*
> Positive or negative count of the change in vertical scroll position. Units are governed by the method choice (lines or pages).

## scrollTo( )  NN 4   IE 4   DOM n/a

scrollTo(x, y)

Scrolls the document in the window to a specific scrolled pixel position.

**Returned Value**    None.

**Parameters**

*x*    Horizontal position in pixels of the window.

*y*    Vertical position in pixels of the window.

# setCursor( )

setCursor("*cursorType*")

Changes the cursor to a desired type. This method is an alternate to the style sheet cursor attribute. Starting with Netscape 6.2, a cursor changed with this method maintains its shape until explicitly changed to another shape or the default auto style. Precise cursor shape is determined by the operating system repertoire. Removed from Netscape 7.

**Returned Value**    None.

**Parameters**

*cursorShape*

String name of a cursor style such as:

| | | | |
|---|---|---|---|
| alias | auto | cell | context-menu |
| copy | count-down | count-up | count-up-down |
| crosshair | default | e-resize | grab |
| grabbing | help | move | n-resize |
| ne-resize | nw-resize | pointer | s-resize |
| se-resize | spinning | sw-resize | text |
| w-resize | wait | | |

# setInterval( )

setInterval("*scriptExpression*", *msecs*[, *language*])
setInterval(*functionReference*, *msecs*[, *arg1*, ..., *argN*])

Starts a timer that continually invokes the *expression* every *msecs*. Other scripts can run in the time between calls to *expression*. This method is useful for starting animation sequences that must reposition an element along a path at a fixed rate of speed. A repetitive call to an animation function would look like the following:

```
intervalID = setInterval("advanceAnimation( )", 500);
```

The parameter situation can be confusing. The simplest, most cross-browser approach is to invoke a script function (as a string), with the interval time (in milliseconds) as the second parameter. Any script expression will execute, but the expression is evaluated at the time the setInterval( ) method is invoked. Therefore, if you concatenate variables into this expression, their values must be ready when the setInterval( ) method runs, even though the variables won't be used until some milliseconds later.

IE permits a third parameter to specify a different scripting language in which the expression is to run. Unless it is a VBScript expression, you can omit this parameter. Navigator, however, lets you substitute a function reference (not a string) as the first parameter, and pass a comma-delimited list of parameters that go to the function call. These parameters go after the *msecs* time, and they can be any data types.

This method returns an ID that should be saved as a global variable and be available as the parameter for the clearInterval( ) method to stop the looping timer. Unless you explicitly clear the interval process, it will continue to execute until the page unloads.

**Returned Value**    Integer acting as an identifier for this repetitive process.

## Parameters

*scriptExpression*

Any script expression as a string, but most commonly a function. The function name with parentheses is placed inside the parameter's quoted string.

*functionReference*

Nonstring function reference (function name without the parentheses).

*msecs*

The time in milliseconds between invocations of the *expression* or *functionReference*.

*args*

An optional comma-delimited list of parameters to be passed to a function used as the *functionReference* parameter. Navigator only.

*language*

An optional scripting language specification of the *expression* parameter (default is JavaScript). IE for Windows only.

## setTimeout( )            NN 2    IE 3    DOM *n/a*

```
setTimeout("scriptExpression", msecs[, language])
setTimeout(functionReference, msecs[, arg1, ..., argN])
```

Starts a one-time timer that invokes the *scriptExpression* or *functionReference* after a delay of *msecs*. Other scripts can run while the browser waits to invoke the *expression*. A statement that sets the timer would look like the following:

```
timeoutID = setTimeout("finishWindow()", 50);
```

The parameter situation can be confusing. The simplest, most cross-browser approach is to invoke a script function (as a string), with the interval time (in milliseconds) as the second parameter. Any script expression will execute, but the expression is evaluated at the time the setTimeout( ) method is invoked. Therefore, if you concatenate variables into this expression, their values must be ready when the setTimeout( ) method runs, even though the variables won't be used until some milliseconds later.

IE permits a third parameter to specify a different scripting language in which the expression is to run. Unless it is a VBScript expression, you can omit this parameter. Navigator, however, lets you substitute a function reference (not a string) as the first parameter, and pass a comma-delimited list of parameters that go to the function call. These parameters go after the *msecs* time, and they can be any data types.

This method returns an ID that should be saved as a global variable and be available as the parameter for the clearTimeout( ) method to stop the timer before it expires and invokes the delayed action.

The setTimeout( ) method can be made to behave like the setInterval( ) method in some constructions. If you place a setTimeout( ) method as the last statement of a function and direct the method to invoke the very same function, you can create looping execution with a timed delay between executions. This is how earlier browsers (before the setInterval( ) method was available) scripted repetitive tasks, such as displaying updated digital clock displays in form fields or the status bar.

**Returned Value**     Integer acting as an identifier.

**Parameters**

*scriptExpression*

Any script expression as a string, but most commonly a function. The function name with parentheses is placed inside the parameter's quoted string.

*functionReference*

Nonstring function reference (function name without the parentheses).

*msecs*

The time in milliseconds that the browser waits before invoking the *expression*.

*args*

An optional comma-delimited list of parameters to be passed to a function used as the *functionReference* parameter. Navigator only.

*language*

An optional scripting language specification of the *expression* parameter (default is JavaScript). IE for Windows only.

## showHelp( ) NN *n/a* IE *4(Win)* DOM *n/a*

```
showHelp("URL")
```

Displays a **WinHelp** window with the *.hlp* document specified with the *URL* parameter.

**Returned Value**    None.

**Parameters**

*URL*

A complete or relative URL to a WinHelp formatted file as a string.

## showModalDialog( ) NN *n/a* IE *4* DOM *n/a*

```
showModalDialog("URL"[, arguments[, "features"]])
```

Displays a special window that remains atop all browser windows until the user explicitly closes the dialog window. This kind of window is different from the browser windows generated with the `window.open( )` method. A modal dialog has no scriptable relationship with its opening window once the dialog window is opened. All values necessary for displaying content must be in the HTML document that loads into the window or be passed as parameters. The modal dialog may then have a script set its `returnValue` property, which becomes the value returned to the original script statement that opened the modal dialog box as the returned value of the `showModalDialog( )` method.

You can pass arguments to the modal dialog by creating a data structure that best suits the data. For a single value, a string will do. For multiple values, you can create a string with a unique delimiter between values, or create an array and specify the array as the second parameter for the `showModalDialog( )` method. A script in the document loaded into the modal dialog can then examine the `window.dialogArguments` property and parse the arguments as needed for its scripting purposes. See the `dialogArguments` property for an example.

The third optional parameter lets you set physical characteristics of the dialog window. These characteristics are specified in a CSS-style syntax. Dimensions for `dialogWidth`, dialogHeight, dialogLeft, and dialogTop should be specified in pixels. An example of a call to a modal dialog is as follows:

```
var answer = window.showModalDialog("subDoc.html",argsVariable,
   "dialogWidth:300px; dialogHeight:200px; center:yes");
```

None of the third parameter characteristics are recognized by the Macintosh version of Internet Explorer 4, which creates a full-size modal dialog.

Modal dialogs can present problems for scripts if the window loads a frameset. A script in one of the frames will likely not be able to reference the parent or top window to gain access to either the window's close( ) method or content in another frame.

### Returned Value

The value (if any) assigned to the window.returnValue property in the document loaded into the modal dialog window.

### Parameters

*URL*

A complete or relative URL as a string.

*arguments*

Data as a number, string, or array to be passed to the scripts in the document loaded into the modal dialog.

*features*

A string of semicolon-delimited style attributes and values to set the physical characteristics of the modal dialog. Available attributes are as shown in the following table.

| Feature | Value | Description |
|---|---|---|
| center | yes\|no\|1\|0\|on\|off | Center the dialog |
| dialogHeight | Length/units | Outer height of dialog |
| dialogLeft | Integer | Left pixel offset (overrides center) |
| dialogTop | Integer | Top pixel offset (overrides center) |
| dialogWidth | Length/units | Outer width of dialog |
| edge | raised\|sunken | Transition style between border and content area |
| help | yes\|no\|1\|0\|on\|off | Display help icon in titlebar |
| resizable | yes\|no\|1\|0\|on\|off | Dialog is resizable |
| status | yes\|no\|1\|0\|on\|off | Display status bar |

## showModelessDialog( )  NN *n/a*  IE *5(Win)*  DOM *n/a*

showModelessDialog("*URL*"[, *arguments*[, "*features*"]])

Displays a special window that remains atop all browser windows, yet allows the user to interact with other open windows and their content. Other than browser versions that support it, this method has the same parameters and characteristics as the showModalDialog( ) method. See that method for details.

## sizeToContent( )

Lets the browser determine the optimum window size to display the window's content. Suitable for subwindows that display a limited amount of information.

**Returned Value**    None.

**Parameters**    None.

## stop( )

Halts the download of external data of any kind. This method is the same as clicking the browser's **Stop** button.

**Returned Value**    None.

**Parameters**    None.

# xml

The xml object reflects the Microsoft proprietary xml element, creating a so-called XML data island inside an HTML document.

**HTML Equivalent**    <xml>

**Object Model Reference**
[window.]document.getElementById("*elementID*")

**Object-Specific Properties**
src              XMLDocument

**Object-Specific Methods**
None.

**Object-Specific Event Handler Properties**
None.

## src

Contains the URL of the external XML document loaded into the data island. To load a new document after the fact, assign a new URL to this property.

**Example**        document.getElementById("xmlData").src = "xml/latestResults.xml";

**Value**        Relative or complete URL string.

**Default**        None.

## XMLDocument

This is a reference to the Microsoft XML document object. This object resembles the W3C DOM core document object in many ways, but Microsoft provides a different syntax to read and write data from the object. See *http://msdn.microsoft.com/xml/reference/xmldom/start.asp* for details.

| | |
|---|---|
| **Example** | `var xmlDoc = document.getElementById("XMLData").XMLDocument;` |
| **Value** | Reference to an MS XML document object. |
| **Default** | None. |

# xmp

See pre.

# Event Reference

The purpose of this chapter is to provide a list of every event type implemented in Version 4 and later of both Netscape Navigator and Internet Explorer, as well as those specified in the W3C recommendation for the Events module of DOM Level 2. So that you can readily see whether a particular entry applies to the browser(s) you must support, a version table accompanies each term listed in the following pages. This table tells you at a glance the version of Navigator, Internet Explorer, and W3C DOM specification in which the term was first introduced.

If a listing for IE signifies Win or Mac, it means that the event is supported only for the Windows or Macintosh operating system version. Note that a large number of event types are supported only in IE for Windows, and many of those apply only to data binding applications. If you are concerned with cross-browser deployment, pay very close attention to the browser compatibility charts to find the events that work on a broad array of browser brands and versions. Chapter 6 contains many guidelines and examples for blending otherwise incompatible event mechanisms into routines that work on many browser types.

In the listings below, the "Bubbles" category indicates whether the event follows event bubbling propagation (in browsers that support event bubbling), while the "Cancelable" category means that the default action usually associated with the event (such as navigating to a new URL when clicking on an a element) can be canceled by script statements, thus averting the normal operation. The category named "Typical Targets" usually points to broad types of elements to which the event type may be applied. For more specific element support for each event type, consult Chapter 15.

# Alphabetical Event Reference

## DOMActivate

NN *n/a*   IE *n/a*   DOM *2*
**Bubbles: Yes; Cancelable: Yes**

Fires when a user begins interacting with an element, such as clicking a button or typing a character into a text box. The event object's detail property passes an integer that contains more information about the event: 1 for unmodified single clicks; 2 for actions with modifier keys or double clicks (what the DOM specification calls *hyperactivation*).

**Typical Targets**    All rendered elements that are capable of receiving focus normally (such as form controls and links), plus any other rendered element for which the tabindex attribute is assigned a value.

## DOMAttrModified

NN *6*   IE *n/a*   DOM *2*
**Bubbles: Yes; Cancelable: No**

Fires after a script adds, removes, or changes the value of an element's attribute. Adding or removing an attribute must be done by the setAttribute( ) and removeAttribute( ) methods, but changing an existing attribute may be accomplished either by the setAttribute( ) method or assigning a new value to an element object's property that corresponds to an attribute. Numerous event object properties convey details about the event. See the following properties of the event object in Chapter 9: attrName, attrChange, prevValue, newValue, and relatedNode.

**Typical Targets**    All rendered elements.

## DOMCharacterDataModified

NN *6*   IE *n/a*   DOM *2*
**Bubbles: Yes; Cancelable: No**

Fires after a script changes the value of a CharacterData type of node. See the following properties of the event object in Chapter 9: prevValue and newValue.

**Typical Targets**    CharacterData nodes.

## DOMFocusIn, DOMFocusOut

NN *n/a*   IE *n/a*   DOM *2*
**Bubbles: Yes; Cancelable: No**

Fires when the current element receives focus (DOMFocusIn) or loses focus (DOMFocusOut). These events fire prior to the focus and blur events, respectively. Similar to the IE onfocusin and onfocusout events.

**Typical Targets**    All rendered elements that are capable of receiving focus normally (such as form controls and links), plus any other rendered element for which the tabindex attribute is assigned a value.

## DOMNodeInserted

NN *6*    IE *n/a*    DOM *2*

Bubbles: Yes; Cancelable: No

Fires on a node when that node is explicitly inserted into an existing node container. If you assign an event listener for this event to an element that is the recipient of an inserted (including appended) node, the DOMNodeInserted event fires on the node being inserted (the srcElement of the event object). If the event bubbles further (i.e., away from the point of insertion), the event listener function can still find out about the new container by reading the relatedNode event property. Note that if the incoming node comes from another location in the same document, the removal of the node from its original container fires the DOMNodeRemoved event on the removed node before it leaves its original container (so that the event can bubble up to its original container).

**Typical Targets**    All rendered nodes.


## DOMNodeInsertedIntoDocument

NN *6*    IE *n/a*    DOM *2*

Bubbles: No; Cancelable: No

Fires on a node when that node is inserted into an existing node container, but the origin of the node is from another document. If you assign an event listener for this event and the DOMNodeInserted event, the DOMNodeInsertedIntoDocument event fires first. Note that if the incoming node comes from another location in another document, the removal of the node from its original document fires the DOMNodeRemovedFromDocument and DOMNodeRemoved events on the removed node before it leaves its original container (so that the event can bubble up to its original container).

**Typical Targets**    All rendered nodes.


## DOMNodeRemoved

NN *6*    IE *n/a*    DOM *2*

Bubbles: Yes; Cancelable: No

Fires on a node when that node is explicitly removed from a node container. If you assign an event listener for this event to an element that is the container of a removed node, the DOMNodeRemoved event fires on the node being removed (the srcElement of the event object). If the event bubbles further (i.e., away from the original node location), the event listener function can still find out about the old container by reading the relatedNode event property.

**Typical Targets**    All rendered nodes.


## DOMNodeRemovedFromDocument

NN *6*    IE *n/a*    DOM *2*

Bubbles: No; Cancelable: No

Fires on a node when the node is removed because it is being inserted into another document, meaning the node is exiting its original document entirely. If you assign an event listener for this event and the DOMNodeRemoved event, the DOMNodeRemovedFromDocument event fires last.

**Typical Targets**    All rendered nodes.

## DOMSubtreeModified

**NN 6    IE n/a    DOM 2**

**Bubbles: No; Cancelable: No**

Fires on a node that is inside the document tree and that changes its nested node structure. This event acts like a generic event for the more specific node mutation events, and fires last. Implementing event listeners for this event may cause problems in early versions of Netscape 6.

**Typical Targets**    All rendered nodes.

## onabort

**NN 3    IE 4    DOM 2**

**Bubbles: No; Cancelable: No**

Fires if an img element's content fails to complete loading due to user interruption (e.g., clicking **Stop** or rapidly navigating to another page) or other failure (e.g., timeout due to network traffic). The W3C DOM applies this event only to the object element, which, in the W3C standards view (but not yet widely supported in browsers), is the desired way to embed an image into a page.

**Typical Targets**    The img element.

## onactivate

**NN n/a    IE 5.5(Win)    DOM n/a**

**Bubbles: Yes; Cancelable: No**

Fires when an object becomes the active object. Giving an object focus makes it active, but a rendered element can be the active element without having focus. Only one element at a time may be active. See the setActive( ) method of shared objects in Chapter 9. If an element has received focus, the onactivate event fires before the onfocus event.

**Typical Targets**    All rendered elements, plus the document and window objects.

## onafterprint, onbeforeprint

**NN n/a    IE 5(Win)    DOM n/a**

**Bubbles: No; Cancelable: No**

Fires after the user clicks the **Print** button in the Print dialog box before content is assembled for the printer (onbeforeprint) and after the data has been sent to the printer (onafterprint). You can use these events to trigger functions that modify a style sheet or other content rendering of a page (so that a potentially different-looking page reaches the printer) and then restore the page for viewing on the screen. This technique can work in lieu of style sheet media settings.

**Typical Targets**    The body and frameset elements, plus the window object.

## onafterupdate

**NN** *n/a*    **IE** *4(Win)*    **DOM** *n/a*

Bubbles: Yes; Cancelable: No

Fires after data being sent to a writable data source object (through the IE data binding mechanism) has successfully updated the database.

**Typical Targets**    Elements that accept data input and support data binding.

## onbeforeactivate

**NN** *n/a*    **IE** *6(Win)*    **DOM** *n/a*

Bubbles: Yes; Cancelable: Sometimes

Fires just before an object is to become the active object. Giving an object focus makes it active, but a rendered element can be the active element without having focus. Only one element at a time may be active. See the setActive( ) method of shared objects in Chapter 9. If an element received focus, related events fire in the following sequence: onbeforeactivate, onactivate, and onfocus.

If you cancel the onbeforeactivate event, the element does not become active, nor does it receive focus, but only if the intended focus action occurs from explicit user action (clicking and tabbing). An element blocked from receiving focus causes the focus to go to another element: to the next focusable element in tabbing order (when the user tabs to the blocked element) or to the next outermost focusable parent element in the document tree (when a user clicks on the blocked element). Activating or giving focus to an element via the setActive( ) or focus( ) methods cannot be blocked by canceling this event.

**Typical Targets**    All rendered elements, plus the document and window objects.

## onbeforecopy

**NN** *n/a*    **IE** *5(Win)*    **DOM** *n/a*

Bubbles: Yes; Cancelable: Yes

Fires just before a user-initiated **Copy** command (via the **Edit** menu, a keyboard shortcut, or a context menu) completes the task of moving the selected content to the system clipboard. At this point in the copy sequence, a function invoked by this event handler can perform additional or substitute processing for the normal system copy action. For example, additional information from the element, such as effective style information of the element containing selected text), can be preserved in the IE clipboardData object (see Chapter 9) for later processing with the help of the onbeforepaste event handler. Canceling the onbeforecopy event does not prevent user copying of a selection.

**Typical Targets**    Rendered elements except form controls.

## onbeforecut

**NN** *n/a*    **IE** *5(Win)*    **DOM** *n/a*

Bubbles: Yes; Cancelable: Yes

Fires just before a user-initiated **Cut** command (via the **Edit** menu, a keyboard shortcut, or a context menu) completes the task of removing the content from its current location and moving the selected content to the system clipboard (assuming the browser is in edit mode for body content). At this point in the cut sequence, a function invoked by this event handler can perform additional or substitute processing for the normal system cut action. For example, additional information from the element, such as effective style information of the element containing selected text), can be preserved in the IE clipboardData object (see Chapter 9) for later processing with the help of the onbeforepaste event handler. Canceling the onbeforecut event does not prevent user cutting of a selection.

**Typical Targets**     All rendered elements.

# onbeforedeactivate

NN *n/a*     IE *5.5(Win)*     DOM *n/a*

Bubbles: Yes; Cancelable: Yes

Fires just before an object is about to yield activation to another object because the user clicked on another element, tabbed to another element, or a script invoked the setActive( ) or focus( ) method of another element. If an element has focus and is the active element, the following event sequence fires en route to losing focus: onbeforedeactivate, ondeactivate, and onblur. Because onbeforedeactivate is cancelable (but ondeactivate is not), cancel this event to prevent an element from deactivating or losing focus—provided you have a good reason to do this other than annoying your visitors.

**Typical Targets**     All rendered elements, plus the document and window objects.

# onbeforeeditfocus

NN *n/a*     IE *5(Win)*     DOM *n/a*

Bubbles: Yes; Cancelable: Yes

Fires just before an editable element receives official focus by a user clicking or tabbing to the element. Editable elements include text-oriented form controls and body elements set to be editable (see the IE 5.5 contentEditable property of all elements in Chapter 9). A function invoked from this event handler can perform additional scripted actions, such as setting the color of the element text, before the user begins editing the content.

**Typical Targets**     Text form controls; rendered elements in edit mode (IE 5.5 or later); content governed by the DHTML Editing ActiveX control (see *http://msdn.microsoft.com/workshop/browser/mshtml/*).

# onbeforepaste

NN *n/a*     IE *5(Win)*     DOM *n/a*

Bubbles: Yes; Cancelable: Yes

Fires just before a user-initiated **Paste** command (via the **Edit** menu, a keyboard shortcut, or a context menu) completes the task of pasting the content from the system clipboard to the current selection. If you are trying to paste custom information from the clipboardData object (saved there in an onbeforecopy, oncopy, onbeforecut, or oncut event handler), you need to have the onbeforepaste and onpaste event handler functions working together. Set event.returnValue to false in the onbeforepaste event handler so that the **Paste** item in the **Edit** (and context) menu is activated, even for a noneditable paste target. When the user selects the **Paste** menu choice, your onpaste event handler retrieves information from the clipboardData object and perhaps modifies the selected element's HTML content:

```
function handleBeforePaste( ) {
    event.returnValue = false;
}
function handlePaste( ) {
    if (event.srcElement.className == "OK2Paste") {
        event.srcElement.innerText = clipboardData.getData("Text");
    }
}
```

In the above paste operation, the system clipboard never plays a role because your scripts handle the entire data transfer—all without having to go into edit mode.

**Typical Targets**   All rendered elements and the document object.

# onbeforeprint

See onafterprint.

# onbeforeunload                                  NN *n/a*    IE *4(Win)/5(Mac)*    DOM *n/a*

Bubbles: No; Cancelable: Yes

Fires just before the current document begins to unload due to impending navigation to a new page, form submission, or window closure. This event fires before the onunload event, and gives your scripts and users a chance to cancel the unload action. Some of this activity is automatic to prevent nefarious scripts from trapping users on a page.

In the onbeforeunload event handler, assign a string to the event.returnValue property to force IE to display a dialog box that lets the user choose whether the page should stay where it is or the navigation or window closure action that the user requested continues as expected. The string assigned to the event property becomes part of the dialog box message (other text in the message is hardwired by the browser and may not be removed or modified). The resulting action is controlled by the user's button choice in the dialog box.

**Typical Targets**   The body and frameset elements, plus the window object.

# onbeforeupdate                                   NN *n/a*    IE *4(Win)*    DOM *n/a*

Bubbles: Yes; Cancelable: Yes

Fires just prior to sending data to a writable data source object (through the IE data binding mechanism). You can perform data validation and cancel the update.

**Typical Targets**   Elements that accept data input and support data binding.

# onblur

NN *2*   IE *3*   DOM *2*

Bubbles: No; Cancelable: No

Fires after the current element loses focus (due to some other element receiving focus) or invoking the blur( ) method of the current element. The onblur event fires before the onfocus event in the other element.

Avoid using the onblur event in text input fields to trigger form validation, especially if the validation routine displays an alert dialog box upon discovering an error. Interaction among the onblur and onfocus events, along with the display and hiding of an alert dialog box can put you into an infinite loop. Use onchange instead.

Although the onblur event has been supported for form controls and window objects since the early days of scriptable browsers, modern browsers can fire the event on virtually any other rendered element, provided the tabindex attribute is set for the element. Note that IE for Windows is known to omit firing the onblur event on window objects.

**Typical Targets**   For all browsers, input (of type text and password), textarea, select, and window objects; for IE 5 or later and Netscape 6, add any rendered element for which the tabindex attribute is assigned a value.

# onbounce

NN *n/a*   IE *4*   DOM *n/a*

Bubbles: No; Cancelable: Yes

Fires each time the text in a marquee element, whose behavior is set to alternate, touches a boundary and changes direction.

**Typical Targets**   The marquee element.

# oncellchange

NN *n/a*   IE *5(Win)*   DOM *n/a*

Bubbles: Yes; Cancelable: No

Fires on the element hosting a data binding data source object (usually the object element) each time data in the remote database changes its value.

**Typical Targets**   The object and applet elements.

# onchange

NN *2*   IE *3*   DOM *2*

Bubbles: No (IE); Yes (NN 6); Cancelable: Yes (IE); No (NN 6)

Fires when a text-oriented form control or select element loses focus, and its content or chosen item is different from what it was when the element most recently gained focus. Use this event in text-type input and textarea elements to validate an entry for that one field. But also include form-wide validation with the form element's onsubmit event handler. This event fires before the onblur event.

**Typical Targets**   Text-type input, textarea, and select elements.

# onclick

**NN** *2*    **IE** *3*    **DOM** *2*

Bubbles: Yes; Cancelable: Yes

Fires after the user effects a mouse click or equivalent action. Click equivalents occur naturally on focusable elements (buttons and links for most browsers) by pressing the **Enter** key (and frequently the spacebar) when the item has focus. In modern browsers that support the accesskey attribute, typing the access key combination also triggers a click equivalent.

For mouse click actions, the onclick event fires only if the mouse button is pressed and released with the pointer atop the same element. In that case, the primary mouse events fire in this order: onmousedown, onmouseup, and onclick.

An event object created from a mouse event has numerous properties filled with details such as coordinates of the click and whether any modifier keys were held down during the event. Information about the button used is more reliably accessed through the onmousedown or onmouseup events. The event handler function can inspect these properties as needed.

Although the onclick event has been supported for button-oriented form controls and link objects since the early days of scriptable browsers, modern browsers can fire the event on virtually any other rendered element. Note that in Netscape 6, mouse events can fire on child text nodes of container-type elements, meaning that the event object's target property references the node, rather than the element. See Chapter 6 for details about the impact of this W3C DOM-endorsed behavior and cross-browser solutions.

**Typical Targets**    For all browsers, input (of type button, radio, checkbox, reset, and submit), a, and area objects; Version 4 and later support the event for the document and window objects; for IE 4 or later and Netscape 6, add any rendered element, as well as text nodes for Netscape 6.

# oncontextmenu

**NN** *n/a*    **IE** *5(Win)*    **DOM** *n/a*

Bubbles: Yes; Cancelable: Yes

Fires after the user clicks the right mouse button (or the button designated the secondary mouse button in the mouse control panel). This mouse button displays the context menu for the item beneath the pointer. To block the display of the context menu (and perhaps display a custom one of your own design via DHTML), set event.returnValue to false in the oncontextmenu event handler. While hiding the context menu may make it more difficult for users to view the source of a page or save an image (assuming you have already opened a document in a window bereft of the menubar), it is not a foolproof way to guard against determined users capturing your page's content. Any scripted solution fails the instant the user disables scripting.

**Typical Targets**    All rendered elements and the document object.

## oncontrolselect

**NN** *n/a*   **IE 5.5(Win)**   **DOM** *n/a*

Bubbles: Yes; Cancelable: Yes

Fires when the user selects an editable element (not its content) while the page is in edit mode. See onmove for a demonstration of this event.

**Typical Targets**   All rendered elements and the document object.

## oncopy

**NN** *n/a*   **IE 5(Win)**   **DOM** *n/a*

Bubbles: Yes; Cancelable: Yes

Fires after the user initiates the **Copy** command (via the **Edit** menu, a keyboard shortcut, or a context menu) to place a copy of the selected content into the system clipboard. An event handler function for this event can supplement the copy action by placing additional data of your choice into the clipboardData object (which the onpaste event handler can read and handle as needed).

To give users access to a **Copy** menu command for an otherwise uneditable element, set event.returnValue to false in the onbeforecopy event handler for the same object as the oncopy event handler. On the other hand, to prevent user copying of body content, set event.returnValue to false for the oncopy event handler. Just don't regard this tactic as a foolproof way to prevent users from copying your prized content.

**Typical Targets**   Rendered elements except form controls.

## oncut

**NN** *n/a*   **IE 5(Win)**   **DOM** *n/a*

Bubbles: Yes; Cancelable: Yes

Fires after the user initiates the **Cut** command (via the **Edit** menu, a keyboard shortcut, or a context menu) to place a copy of the selected content into the system clipboard. To cut body content, the containing element must be in edit mode (see the shared contendEditable property in Chapter 9). An event handler function for this event can supplement the cut action by placing additional data of your choice into the clipboardData object (which the onpaste event handler can read and handle as needed).

To give users access to a **Cut** menu command for an otherwise uneditable element, set event.returnValue to false in the onbeforecut event handler for the same object as the oncut event handler. On the other hand, to prevent user cutting of body or form control content, set event.returnValue to false for the oncut event handler.

**Typical Targets**   All rendered elements.

## ondataavailable, ondatasetchanged, ondatasetcomplete

**NN** *n/a*   **IE 4(Win)**   **DOM** *n/a*

Bubbles: Yes; Cancelable: No

Fire on the element hosting a data binding data source object (usually the object element) each time the remote data source signals it has new data ready for retrieval (ondataavailable), a data set has been modified (ondatasetchanged), or a data set has received all data form the query (ondatasetcomplete). These events are available only for data source object types capable of asynchronous connections with their remote sources.

**Typical Targets**   The object and applet elements; the xml element in IE 5 and later.

## ondblclick

Fires after the user effects a second successive mouse click or equivalent action (see onclick for click equivalents). A double click requires a specific sequence of mouse events leading up to it. The sequence is: onmousedown, onmouseup, onclick, onmouseup, and ondblclick. The amount of time that can elapse between the two clicks is determined by the client computer's mouse control panel settings.

Because the onclick event fires ahead of ondblclick, the associated onclick event handler (if any) should perform only innocuous actions, such as highlighting an element, much like the way operating system desktop icons operate. If an item requires a double click, that is the only event that should do something significant.

**Typical Targets**   Support for this event in Navigator 4 is limited to the a element (but not on the Macintosh); IE 4 or later and Netscape 6 support the event on renderable elements and the document object.

## ondeactivate

Fires after an object has yielded activation to another object because the user clicked on another element, tabbed to another element, or a script invoked the setActive( ) or focus( ) method of another element. If an element has focus and is the active element, the following event sequence fires en route to losing focus: onbeforedeactivate, ondeactivate, and onblur. To prevent an element from deactivating or losing focus, cancel the companion onbeforedeactivate event.

**Typical Targets**   All rendered elements, plus the document and window objects.

## ondrag, ondragend, ondragstart

When the user starts dragging a selection, the browser fires one ondragestart event on the selection's parent element, followed by a series of ondrag events, and then one ondragend event when the user releases the mouse button. All three event types fire on the same element during the drag.

During the drag operation, the user sees the cursor in one of its various forms, rather than seeing the actual element float around the page. As long as the user keeps the mouse button down following an initial drag action, the ondrag event keeps firing. Other drag-related events fire on other elements along the way (events such as ondragenter for an element that finds the dragged cursor in its airspace), but the ondrag event also fires at various instances.

An element with content that is dragged receives events in the following sequence: ondragstart, ondrag (perhaps many times), and ondragend. Elements in the path of the drag action receive ondragenter, ondragover, and ondragleave events, while the element at the end of the drag receives the ondrop event (which fires before the ondragend event of the dragged element). The speed of the drag action and client system speed impacts the number of event firings of all drag types. A fast drag on a slow machine may result in some events not firing.

**Typical Targets**     All rendered elements and document object.

# ondragdrop

NN |4|   IE n/a   DOM n/a<br>Bubbles: No; Cancelable: No

Fires (in Navigator 4 only) if the user drags a desktop file to the document. With signed scripts, the browser can read the filename of the dragged item.

**Typical Targets**     The window object.

# ondragend

See ondrag.

# ondragenter, ondragleave, ondragover

NN n/a   IE 5(Win)   DOM n/a<br>Bubbles: Yes; Cancelable: Yes

Elements in the path of a drag action usually receive ondragenter, ondragover, and ondragleave events in that order. The speed of the drag action and client system impact the number of event firings of all drag types. A fast drag on a slow machine may result in some events not firing.

If your scripts will be performing customized actions upon the user dropping the dragged item onto a target in the document, you should prevent default actions of the ondragenter and ondragover events so that the target's ondrop event can do its job without interference from the normal system response to dragging. See the dataTransfer object in Chapter 9 for an example of drag-related event interaction.

**Typical Targets**     All rendered elements and document object.

# ondragstart

See ondrag.

## ondrop

NN *n/a*   IE *5(Win)*   DOM *n/a*

Bubbles: Yes; Cancelable: Yes

Fires on the drop target element when the user releases the mouse button after a drag action. Fires just before the ondragend event of the owner of the dragged content. Prevent default actions of the drop target's ondragenter and ondragover events (by setting event.returnValue to false in their respective event handler functions) so that the target's ondrop event can do its job without interference from the normal system response to dragging. See the dataTransfer object in Chapter 9 for an example of drag-related event interaction, including the effectAllowed property, which controls the cursor shape at the drop target.

**Typical Targets**     All rendered elements and document object.

## onerror

NN *3*   IE *4*   DOM *2*

Bubbles: No; Cancelable: Yes

Fires after one of a variety of errors occurs, depending on the element or object to which the event handler is assigned. For elements that load external content, such as the img element, errors during loading (such as an invalid URL) fire the onerror event on the img element. When assigned to the window object (including direct assignment in the <body> tag), overall runtime script errors (not compile-time syntax errors) also fire the onerror event. A technique that some scripters used in earlier browsers that plastered script error messages inside intrusive alert dialog boxes was to trap all runtime errors in the following manner:

```
function doNothing( ) {return true;}
window.onerror = doNothing;
```

This isn't good for debugging because you need to find errors during development. See the Error object in Chapter 9 for more details on processing errors from this event handler. Eventually, there will enough browsers deployed that use more modern exception handling.

**Typical Targets**     Elements that load external content, plus the window object.

## onerrorupdate

NN *n/a*   IE *4(Win)*   DOM *n/a*

Bubbles: Yes; Cancelable: No

Fires if an error occurs while sending data to a writable data source object (through the data binding mechanism).

**Typical Targets**     Elements that accept data input and support data binding.

## onfilterchange

NN *n/a*   IE *4(Win)*   DOM *n/a*

Bubbles: No; Cancelable: No

Fires when an element's filter changes its state and when a transition or blend filter completes its action. You can use the event to cascade a sequence of transitions.

**Typical Targets**     Most rendered elements.

# onfinish

**NN** *n/a*   **IE** *4*   **DOM** *n/a*

**Bubbles: No; Cancelable: Yes**

Fires after the scrolling text in a looping marquee element comes to rest after its final motion.

**Typical Targets**   The marquee element.

# onfocus

**NN** *2*   **IE** *3*   **DOM** *2*

**Bubbles: No; Cancelable: No**

Fires when the current element receives focus due to user action (clicking or tabbing) or invoking of the focus() method. The onblur event of the next previously focused element fires before the onfocus event in the current element.

Although the onfocus event has been supported for form controls and window objects since the early days of scriptable browsers, modern browsers can fire the event on virtually any other rendered element, provided the tabindex attribute is set for the element. Note that IE for Windows is known to omit firing the onfocus event on window objects.

**Typical Targets**   For all browsers, input (of type text and password), textarea, select, and window objects; for IE 5 or later and Netscape 6, add any rendered element for which the tabindex attribute is assigned a value.

# onfocusin, onfocusout

**NN** *n/a*   **IE** *6*   **DOM** *n/a*

**Bubbles: Yes; Cancelable: No**

Fire when the current element receives focus (onfocusin) or loses focus (onfocusout). These events fire prior to the focus and blur events, respectively. Microsoft suggests that you can use these event handlers to perform style changes (anywhere in the document) in anticipation of an element receiving or losing focus, without disturbing the normal focus and blur actions.

**Typical Targets**   All rendered elements that are capable of receiving focus normally (such as form controls and links), plus any other rendered element for which the tabindex attribute is assigned a value.

# onhelp

**NN** *n/a*   **IE** *4*   **DOM** *n/a*

**Bubbles: Yes; Cancelable: Yes**

Fires when the user presses the **F1** function key. If an element has focus at the time, that is the element that receives the event. You can prevent the default action (displaying the IE Help window) and generate your own DHTML-based help system if you like.

**Typical Targets**   All rendered elements, plus document and window objects, except in IE for Macintosh, which limits this event to the window object.

## onkeydown, onkeyup

**NN** *4*    **IE** *4*    **DOM** *3*

Bubbles: Yes; Cancelable: Yes

Fire when the user presses (onkeydown) and releases (onkeyup) a keyboard key. These two events fire on a focusable element or object for almost every key of the keyboard, including function and navigation keys. The instance of the event object for these events contains information about the key (not the character) pressed. See Chapter 6 for details on cross-browser handling of keyboard events. You cannot reliably inhibit critical **Ctrl** character sequences, but if you prevent the default action of the onkeypress event for a text form control, the character does not arrive at the text field.

**Typical Targets**    All focusable rendered elements, plus document and window objects.

## onkeypress

**NN** *4*    **IE** *4*    **DOM** *3*

Bubbles: Yes; Cancelable: Yes

Fires after the user presses and releases a keyboard character key. The event sequence is: onkeydown, onkeyup, and onkeypress. The instance of the event object for these events contains information about the character of the pressed key. See Chapter 6 for details on cross-browser handling of keyboard events.

**Typical Targets**    All focusable rendered elements, plus the document object.

## onlayoutcomplete

**NN** *n/a*    **IE** *5.5(Win)*    **DOM** *n/a*

Bubbles: Yes; Cancelable: Yes

Fires when a print preview LayoutRect object finishes rendering its content. For details on this XML enhancement for IE 5.5 and later for Windows, visit *http://msdn.microsoft.com/ workshop/browser/hosting/printpreview/reference/reference.asp*.

**Typical Targets**    An XML LayoutRect object.

## onload

**NN** *2*    **IE** *3*    **DOM** *2*

Bubbles: No; Cancelable: No

Fires when external content belonging to the current element or object finishes loading and initializing. This event handler for the window object is perhaps the most important because it signals that all content of the document and its elements (including external content) has loaded before the event fires. When that event fires, your scripts can reference any document tree object without error.

The event fires for a frameset element only after the onload events for all frames have fired (but the event is not bubbling from frame to frameset). Note that if the user or a script loads a new page into a frame after the frameset's initial load, the onload event does not fire again for the frameset (but it does for the frame).

Although the onload event has been supported for window objects since the early days of scriptable browsers, modern browsers fire the event on virtually any other rendered element that loads external content.

**Typical Targets**    For all browsers, window objects; for Version 4 browsers or later the img element; for IE 4 or later and Netscape 6, add any rendered element capable of loading external content.

## onlosecapture                                      NN *n/a*   IE *5(Win)*   DOM *n/a*

**Bubbles: No; Cancelable: No**

Fires when event capture mode for the element becomes disengaged. See the shared setCapture( ) method in Chapter 9.

**Typical Targets**    All rendered elements.

## onmousedown, onmouseup                              NN *4*   IE *4*   DOM *2*

**Bubbles: Yes; Cancelable: Yes**

Fires when the user presses down (onmousedown) or releases (onmouseup) a mouse button. Events related to mouse click actions fire in this order: onmousedown, onmouseup, and onclick.

An event object created from a mouse event has numerous properties filled with details such as coordinates of the click, the mouse button used, and whether any modifier keys were held down during the event. The event handler function can inspect these properties as needed.

Note that in Netscape 6, mouse events can fire on child text nodes of container-type elements, meaning that the event object's target property references the node, rather than the element. See Chapter 6 for details about the impact of this W3C DOM-endorsed behavior and cross-browser solutions.

**Typical Targets**    All rendered elements, except in Navigator 4, where the events are limited to button-style input elements, plus a and area elements.

## onmouseenter, onmouseleave                          NN *n/a*   IE *5.5(Win)*   DOM *n/a*

**Bubbles: No; Cancelable: No**

Fire when the user rolls the mouse pointer into (onmouseenter) or out of (onmouseleave) an element's space (including border or padding, but not margin). Each event fires just once per entry and exit. These variations on the onmouseover and onmouseout events do not bubble.

**Typical Targets**    All rendered elements.

## onmousemove                                         NN *4*   IE *4*   DOM *2*

**Bubbles: Yes; Cancelable: No**

Fires while the user rolls the mouse pointer atop an element's space, with the mouse button up or down. Note that the event fires repeatedly, although the frequency of firing depends on the speed of the mouse motion and system resources.

An event object created from a mouse event has numerous properties filled with details such as coordinates of the pointer and whether any modifier keys were held down during the event. The event handler function can inspect these properties as needed.

In Navigator 4, this event type can be assigned to the window, document, and layer object, but only in the explicitly defined event capture mode. Note that in Netscape 6, mouse events can fire on child text nodes of container-type elements, meaning that the event object's target property references the node, rather than the element. See Chapter 6 for details about the impact of this W3C DOM-endorsed behavior and cross-browser solutions.

**Typical Targets**     All rendered elements, except as noted above for Navigator 4.

## onmouseout, onmouseover

NN 2     IE 3     DOM 2
Bubbles: Yes; Cancelable: Yes

Fire when the user rolls the mouse pointer into (onmouseover) or out of (onmouseout) an element's space (including border or padding, but not margin). Each event fires just once per entry and exit (except in Navigator 4 for Windows, in which the event fires repeatedly, similar to onmousemove).

Because the onmouseout event doesn't officially fire until another element in the window fires its onmouseover event (whether you have a handler for it or not), the onmouseout event may not fire if the target element is at the edge of a window or frame, and the user whisks the pointer outside of the current frame without the first frame's body element ever receiving the onmouseover event. If you use onmouseout events to restore image swaps, the user could see a stuck image. Leave sufficient space around your swappable images to account for this behavior.

An event object created from a mouse event has numerous properties filled with details such as coordinates of the click, the mouse button used, whether any modifier keys were held down during the event, and where the incoming pointer came from or outgoing pointer has gone. The event handler function can inspect these properties as needed.

Note that in Netscape 6, mouse events can fire on child text nodes of container-type elements, meaning that the event object's target property references the node, rather than the element. See Chapter 6 for details about the impact of this W3C DOM-endorsed behavior and cross-browser solutions.

Although these events have been supported in one form or another since the early days of scriptable browsers, only modern browsers can fire the event on virtually any other rendered element. For older browsers, the events were limited to a and area elements (where a elements surrounded images to be swapped).

**Typical Targets**     All rendered elements, except as noted above.

## onmousewheel

NN n/a     IE 6(Win)     DOM n/a
Bubbles: No; Cancelable: No

Fires as the user spins the mouse wheel (on a mouse equipped with a wheel). The event object's wheelDelta property reveals details about the direction and amount of rotation.

**Typical Targets**     All rendered elements and the document object.

# onmove

**NN |4|    IE *n/a*    DOM *n/a***

*Bubbles: No; Cancelable: No*

Fires (in Navigator 4 only) if the user or script moves the browser window.

**Typical Targets**    The window object.

# onmove, onmoveend, onmovestart

**NN *n/a*    IE *5.5(Win)*    DOM *n/a***

*Bubbles: Yes; Cancelable: No*

When in edit mode, a positionable element set up for dragging receives these events in the following sequence: onmovestart (upon starting the drag), onmove (repeatedly during the drag), and onmoveend (upon release of the mouse button). The following example uses several events to demonstrate IE edit mode scripting (note that the native element dragging mechanism doesn't work well in IE 6 if the <!DOCTYPE> element points to a standards-compatible mode DTD):

```
<html>
<head>
<title>IE 5.5 (Windows) Edit Mode</title>
<style type="text/css">
    body {font-family:Arial, sans-serif}
    #myDIV  {position:absolute; height:100px; width:300px;}
    .regular {border:5px black solid; padding:5px; background-color:lightgreen}
    .moving {border:5px maroon dashed; padding:5px; background-color:lightyellow}
    .chosen {border:5px maroon solid; padding:5px; background-color:lightyellow}
</style>
<script type="text/javascript">
// built-in dragging support
document.execCommand("2D-position",false,true);
// preserve content between modes
var oldHTML = "";

// engage static edit environment
function editOn( ) {
    var elem = event.srcElement;
    elem.className = "chosen";
}

// engage special edit-move environment
function moveOn( ) {
    var elem = event.srcElement;
    oldHTML = elem.innerHTML;
    elem.className = "moving";
}

// display coordinates during drag
function trackMove( ) {
    var elem = event.srcElement;
    elem.innerHTML = "Element is now at: " + elem.offsetLeft + ", " +
                    elem.offsetTop;
}
```

```
    // turn off special edit-move environment
    function moveOff( ) {
        var elem = event.srcElement;
        elem.innerHTML = oldHTML;
        elem.className = "chosen";
    }

    // restore original environment (wrapper gets onfocusout)
    function editOff( ) {
        var elem = event.srcElement;
        if (elem.id == "wrapper") {
            elem.firstChild.className = "regular";
        }
    }

    // initialize event handlers
    function init( ) {
        document.body.oncontrolselect = editOn;
        document.body.onmovestart = moveOn;
        document.body.onmove = trackMove;
        document.body.onmoveend = moveOff;
        document.body.onfocusout = editOff;
    }
</script>
</head>
<body onload="init( );">
<div id="wrapper" contenteditable="true">
    <div id="myDIV" class="regular">
        This is a positioned element with some text in it.
    </div>
</div>
</body>
</html>
```

**Typical Targets**     An XML LayoutRect object.

# onpaste

NN *n/a*     IE *5(Win)*     DOM *n/a*

Bubbles: Yes; Cancelable: Yes

Fires after the user initiates the **Paste** command (via the **Edit** menu, a keyboard shortcut, or a context menu) to place a copy of the system clipboard into the selected content. An event handler function for this event can supplement the paste action by retrieving additional data from the clipboardData object (information placed there by one of the copy- or cut-related event handler functions).

To give users access to a **Paste** menu command for an otherwise uneditable element, set event.returnValue to false in the onbeforepaste event handler for the same object as the onpaste event handler. On the other hand, to prevent user pasting system clipboard content, set event.returnValue to false for the onpaste event handler.

**Typical Targets**     All rendered elements.

## onpropertychange
NN n/a   IE 5(Win)   DOM n/a<br>Bubbles: No; Cancelable: No

Fires after the property of an element changes under script control. Property changes occur through direct property assignment and methods, such as setAttribute( ). Changes to an element's property (e.g., a property of an element's style object) also trigger this event. The event object's propertyName property contains the name of the property influenced by the event.

**Typical Targets**    All rendered elements, plus the document object.

## onreadystatechange
NN n/a   IE 4   DOM n/a<br>Bubbles: No; Cancelable: No

Fires if the readyState property changes for an element. See the shared readyState property in Chapter 9 for details on what affects the property.

**Typical Targets**    Elements that load external content.

## onreset
NN 3   IE 4   DOM 2<br>Bubbles: No; Cancelable: Yes

Fires when a form element receives a request to reset the form from a reset-type input element or a scripted reset( ) method. By canceling the event, a script in the onreset event handler aborts the normal form reset.

**Typical Targets**    The form element.

## onresize
NN 4   IE 4   DOM 2<br>Bubbles: Yes; Cancelable: No

Fires after an element or object is resized by the user or script control. Note that resizing a window may force other elements in the page to resize themselves. In IE, onresize events from those elements bubble to the body and window objects, where a lone onresize event handler may be bombarded by events.

**Typical Targets**    For IE, elements that have dimensions associated with them, plus the window and document objects; for Navigator, the window and document objects.

## onresizeend, onresizestart
NN n/a   IE 5.5(Win)   DOM n/a<br>Bubbles: Yes; Cancelable: No

Fire (in edit mode only) when a user resizes an element by dragging its resize handles. See onmove for a related example.

**Typical Targets**    All rendered elements.

## onrowenter, onrowexit, onrowsdelete, onrowsinserted

NN n/a   IE 4(Win)   DOM n/a

Bubbles: Yes; Cancelable: No

Fire on the element hosting a data binding data source object (usually the object element) when a row in the remote database table is modified either through database or data source activity.

**Typical Targets**    The object and applet elements; the xml element in IE 5 and later.

## onscroll

NN n/a   IE 4   DOM 2

Bubbles: No; Cancelable: No

Fires each time an element displaying scroll bars executes a scroll, either by user action or script control. If a user drags the scroll bar thumb, the event fires repeatedly during the dragging motion, but the frequency of event firings depends on system speeds.

**Typical Targets**    All rendered elements that can have scrollbars by default (such as textarea and window objects), plus any element that has its overflow style sheet attribute set to scroll.

## onselect

NN 2   IE 3   DOM 2

Bubbles: No (IE); Yes (NN 6); Cancelable: Yes

Fires when a user drags a selection in a text box (input or textarea elements). Broken in Navigator 4 for Windows. In IE 4 or later for Windows, the event also applies to body text selections.

**Typical Targets**    Text-type input and textarea elements for all browsers; body element for IE 4 or later for Windows.

## onselectionchange

NN n/a   IE 5.5(Win)   DOM n/a

Bubbles: No; Cancelable: No

Fires when the selection type (in IE edit mode) changes.

**Typical Targets**    The document object.

## onselectstart

NN n/a   IE 4   DOM n/a

Bubbles: Yes; Cancelable: Yes

Fires immediately after the user begins dragging a selection on a body element or form control text. If the selection extends across multiple elements, only one event fires, and its target remains the element where the selection began. Canceling this event in the <body> tag (onselectstart="return false") can prevent undesirable and inadvertent user selection and scrolling interaction.

**Typical Targets**    All rendered elements.

## onstart

NN *n/a*    IE *4*    DOM *n/a*
Bubbles: No; Cancelable: No

Fires when the scrolling text in a looping marquee element begins its motion after a page loads.

**Typical Targets**    The marquee element.

## onstop

NN *n/a*    IE *5(Win)*    DOM *n/a*
Bubbles: No; Cancelable: No

Fires when the user clicks the browser's **Stop** button, even if the document and its content have successfully loaded.

**Typical Targets**    The document object.

## onsubmit

NN *2*    IE *3*    DOM *2*
Bubbles: No (IE); Yes (NN 6); Cancelable: Yes

Fires when a form element receives a request to submit the form from a submit-type input element but *not* from a scripted submit( ) method. This is the event to trigger one final client-side form validation prior to sending a form to the server. By canceling the event, a script in the onsubmit event handler aborts the submission.

**Typical Targets**    The form element.

## onunload

NN *2*    IE *3*    DOM *2*
Bubbles: No; Cancelable: No

Fires just before the current document begins to unload due to impending navigation to a new page, form submission, or window closure. This event fires after the onbeforeunload event in browsers that support that event. In most browsers, the actual document unloading does not wait for the onunload event handler function to complete. Therefore, if the function performs too many actions, especially those that rely on script variables and elements in the current page, those references may become invalid while the function runs, creating script errors (of the "undefined" or "object not found" variety). Therefore, keep onunload processing to a minimum.

**Typical Targets**    The body and frameset elements, plus the window object.

# Style Sheet Attribute Reference

The purpose of this chapter is to provide a list of every style sheet attribute that is implemented in Version 4 and later of both Netscape Navigator and Internet Explorer, as well as those specified in the W3C recommendations for Cascading Style Sheets, both Level 1 (CSS1) and Level 2 (CSS2). So that you can readily see whether a particular entry applies to the browser(s) you must support, a version table accompanies each term listed in the following pages. This table tells you at a glance the version of Navigator, Internet Explorer, and W3C CSS specification in which the term was first introduced.

This chapter is organized alphabetically by CSS attribute name. For each attribute, you can see quickly what the value types are, an example of real-life source code, and how to address the attribute from the JavaScript language (if the attribute is scriptable). A few items implemented in available browsers are proposed for CSS Level 3, and are marked accordingly. Some additional items for the Netscape 6 browser are preliminary versions of forthcoming CSS3 attributes. To deploy these features now, but prevent possible naming collisions with final CSS3 specifications, the Mozilla engineers have given these attributes a -moz prefix. This prefix will not validate under CSS Level 2 due to the leading hyphen. This is intentional.

## Attribute Value Types

Many element attributes share similar data requirements. For the sake of brevity in the reference listings, this section describes a few common attribute value types in more detail than is possible within each listing. When you see one of these attribute value types associated with an attribute, consult this section for a description of the type.

### Length

A length value defines a linear measure of document real estate—usually a horizontal or vertical measurement of distance, height, width, thickness, or size. Length units may be relative or absolute. A relative unit depends upon variables such as the dot pitch or pixel density of the video display that shows a document. Relative units in CSS are pixels (px), ems (em), and exes (ex). An em is the actual height of the element's font (or inherited font) as rendered on a given display device; an ex is the height of a lowercase "x" under the same conditions. The exception to this rule is when em and ex units are used to define the font-size attribute, in which case the units are relative to the font size of the parent element.

Pay special attention when a relative value is to be inherited by a child element. In those circumstances, the CSS recommendation says that the child element inherits the *computed* value of the attribute (computed at the time of the attribute definition in the parent element's assignment), rather than an adjusted value. For example, if the body element specifies a font-size of 20pt and a text-indent of 2em (equaling 40pt), the text-indent value inherited by p or other elements within the body element is equal to 40pt, regardless of what the current font-size of the other elements may be. To override the inherited computed value, the p or other element needs to reassign a text-indent attribute for that element (or other outer container that intervenes from the body). IE for the Macintosh and Netscape 6 behave according to the recommendation. But IE for Windows, even in IE 6's standards-compatible mode, ignores this convention. Instead, this browser family recomputes the inherited relative style assignment. Thus, in the example we just discussed, a p element with a font-size set to 10pt does not inherit the 40pt computed text-indent value from the body. Rather, the unstated text-indent value for the p element is recomputed for its 10pt font-size—an effective text-indent value of 20pt.

Pixel values, while frequently used for font sizes, present their own potential problems. A pixel, as noted earlier, varies in size with the pixel density of the output device. The higher the density, the smaller each pixel is. For printing output on 300- to 600-dpi printers, browsers perform internal scaling calculations to assign more dots per pixel so that a text character sent to the printer approximates the size as viewed on the screen. But don't expect absolutely perfect sizes on all monitors or printers. Allow for scaling approximations for all length value assignments.

Absolute length units are intended for output media with constant physical properties (such as a PostScript printer). Although there is nothing preventing you from using absolute or relative units interchangeably, you need to be aware of the consequences given your audience. Absolute length units in CSS are inches (in), centimeters (cm), millimeters (mm), picas (pi), and points (pt).

# URI and URL

Universal Resource Identifier (URI) is a broad term for an address of content on the Web. A Universal Resource Locator (URL) is a type of URI. For most web authoring, you can think of them as one and the same, because most web browsers restrict their focus to URLs. A URL may be complete (including the protocol, host, domain, and the rest) or may be relative to the URL of the current document. In the latter case, this means the URL may consist of an anchor, file, or pathname. The CSS attribute syntax prescribes a special format for specifying a URI attribute value, as follows:

```
attributeName: url("actualURL")
```

Quotes surrounding the *actualURL* are optional, but recommended.

## Colors

A color value can be assigned either via an RGB (red-green-blue) value or a plain-language equivalent (see Appendix A). For style sheet RGB values, you have a choice of three formats: hexadecimal triplet, decimal values, or percentage values. A hexadecimal triplet consists of three pairs of hexadecimal (base 16) numbers that range between values of 00 and ff, corresponding to the red, green, and blue components of the color. The three pairs of numbers are bunched together and preceded by a pound sign (#). Therefore, the reddest of reds has all red (ff) and none (00) of the other two colors: #ff0000; pure blue is #0000ff. Letters a through f can also be uppercase letters. (An approved shortcut—but one I don't recommend for the sake of readability— allows you to specify one hexadecimal character when the value is intended to be a matching pair of characters. For example, #f0a is interpreted as #ff00aa.)

The other types of RGB values require a prefix of rgb( ) with a comma-delimited list of red, green, and blue values in the parentheses. As decimal values, each color can range from 0 through 255, with zero meaning the complete absence of a particular color. You can also specify each value by a percentage. The following examples show four different ways of specifying pure green:

```
color: green
color: #00ff00
color: rgb(0, 255, 0)
color: rgb(0%, 100%, 0%)
```

If you exceed the maximum allowable values in the last two examples, the browser trims the values back to the maximums.

These numbering schemes obviously lead to a potentially huge number of combinations (over 16 million), but not all video monitors are set to distinguish among millions of colors. Therefore, you may wish to limit yourself to a more modest palette of colors known as the *web palette*. A fine reference of colors that work well on all browsers at popular bit-depth settings can be found at *http://www.lynda.com/hexh.html*.

The CSS2 specification adds another dimension to color naming: you can specify colors that the user has assigned to specific user interface items in the operating system's control panel. Such colors are typically adjustable for items like button label text, scrollbars, 3-D shadows, and so on. A color-blind user, for example, may have a carefully crafted set of colors that provide necessary contrast to see screen elements.

To link those colors to a style, use any of the following keywords in place of the color attribute value:

| | | |
|---|---|---|
| activeborder | activecaption | appworkspace |
| background | buttonface | buttonhighlight |
| buttontext | captiontext | graytext |
| highlight | highlighttext | inactiveborder |
| inactivecaption | inactivecaptiontext | infobackground |
| infotext | menu | menutext |
| scrollbar | threeddarkshadow | threedface |
| threedhighlight | threedlightshadow | threedshadow |
| window | windowframe | windowtext |

# Pseudo-Elements and Pseudo-Classes

Most style sheet rules are associated with distinct HTML elements or groups of elements identified via style sheet selectors, such as classes, IDs, and contextual selectors (see Chapter 3). In rare instances, you might want to assign a style to a well-defined component of an element (pseudo-element) or to all elements that exhibit a particular state (pseudo-class).

## Pseudo-Elements

A pseudo-element gets its name because the CSS declaration of this type causes the browser to act as if it has inserted an artificial element into an existing element. For example, CSS1 defines pseudo-elements for the first letter and first line of a block-level element. The HTML source code for the real element might be something simple:

```
<p>A mere paragraph.</p>
```

But a browser that implements the :first-letter and :first-line pseudo-elements would treat the p element as if it were structured as follows:

```
<p><p:first-line><p:first-letter>A</p:first-letter> mere
paragraph.</p:first-line></p>
```

The location of the </p:first-line> end tag, of course, depends on the rendered version of the p element. If the paragraph were sized to fit a narrow column, and the first line word-wrapped after the word "mere," the :first-line pseudo-element's invisible end tag would follow the space after "mere." The point of all of this is that you can assign numerous style attributes to these very specific portions of a block-level element, such as a drop capital letter:

```
p:first-letter {font-size: 36pt; font-weight: 600;
                font-family: Rune, serif; float: left}
```

or an all-uppercase first line:

```
p:first-line{text-transform:uppercase}
```

Regardless of the pseudo-element structure or style assignments, the document tree is unaffected. In the simple p element example, the element contains one text child node.

As of CSS2, four pseudo-elements have been defined, as shown in Table 11-1. Note that the :first-letter pseudo-element acknowledges style attributes only of the following types: background, border, clear, color, float, font, line-height, margin, padding, text-decoration, text-shadow, text-transform, and vertical-align (when float is none). The :first-line pseudo-element acknowledges style attributes only of the following types: background, clear, color, font, letter-spacing, line-height, text-decoration, text-shadow, text-transform, vertical-align, and word-spacing.

*Table 11-1. CSS2 pseudo-elements*

| Name | NN | IE/Windows | IE/Mac | CSS | Description |
|------|-----|-----------|--------|-----|-------------|
| :after | 6 | n/a | n/a | 2 | The space immediately after an element (see content attribute) |
| :before | 6 | n/a | n/a | 2 | The space immediately before an element (see content attribute) |
| :first-letter | 6 | 5.5 | 5 | 1 | The first letter of a block-level element |
| :first-line | 6 | 5.5 | 5 | 1 | The first line of a block-level element |

## Pseudo-Classes

The a element has readily distinguishable states: a link that has not been visited, a link being clicked on, a link that has been visited in recent history. These states are called *pseudo-classes*; they work like class selector definitions but don't have to be labeled as such in their element tags. A pseudo-class always operates as a kind of modifier to another selector. In the following example, notice how the :hover pseudo-class operates on all a elements in one rule, and applies an extra attribute to an a element singled out by its ID:

```
a {text-decoration:none}
a:hover {text-decoration:underline}
#specialA:hover {color:red}
```

The classness of a pseudo-class is not always based on an element's state. Document tree context, page position (right or left), and even language are examples of the possibilities that pseudo-classes afford. For example, the :first-child pseudo-class turns its associated element into a special class (i.e., a class capable of defining its own style attributes) whenever the element is a first child element in a document tree. Thus, the following style rule applies a different font size for every p element that is the first child of any container with the class name section:

```
.section > p:first-child {font-size:110%}
```

The use here of the > child selector limits the scope of the p:first-child pseudo-class to first children of specific containers. Removing the child selector would cause the rule to apply to any p element that is the first child of any other container.

Table 11-2 provides a summary of pseudo-classes supported by CSS2. Implementation in mainstream browsers is sporadic.

*Table 11-2. CSS2 Pseudo-classes*

| Name | NN | IE/Windows | IE/Mac | CSS | Description |
|------|-----|-----------|--------|-----|-------------|
| :active | 6 | 4 | 4 | 1 | An a element being clicked on by the user |
| :first | n/a | n/a | n/a | 2 | First page of a document (with @page declaration) |
| :first-child | 6 | n/a | 5 | 2 | Any element that is the first child of another element |
| :focus | 6 | n/a | 5 | 2 | Any element that has focus |
| :hover | 6 | 4 | 4 | 2 | An a element that has a cursor on top of it |
| :lang(*code*) | n/a | n/a | 5 | 2 | An element with the same language code |
| :left | n/a | n/a | n/a | 2 | A left-facing page (with @page declaration) |
| :link | 6 | 4 | 4 | 1 | An a element that has not yet been visited |
| :right | n/a | n/a | n/a | 2 | A right-facing page (with @page declaration) |
| :visited | 6 | 4 | 4 | 1 | An a element that has been visited within the browser's history |

# At-Rules

CSS2 defines an extensible structure for declarations or directives (commands, if you will) that are part of style sheet definitions. They are called *at-rules* because the rule starts with the "at" symbol (@) followed by an identifier for the declaration. Each at-rule may then include one or more descriptors that define the characteristics of the rule.

Although at-rules typically appear as the first declarations in a style sheet, in practice some (@media in particular) work best when only one occupies each style sheet. The following sequence provides different style characteristics for a document when viewed on screen and printed on paper (relative font size on the screen, absolute on paper):

```
<style type="text/css">
@media screen {
    body {font-size: 14px}
}
</style>
<style type="text/css">
@media print {
    body {font-size: 12pt}
}
</style>
```

The @font-face rule can be used to download font definition files to the browser, and associate each font definition with a font family name to be assigned by succeeding style assignments. Here is an example that downloads one of the Internet Explorer accepted font file formats, assigning the definition to a font family name called Stylish:

```
<style type="text/css">
@font-face {
```

```
        font-family: Stylish;
        font-weight:normal;
        font-style:normal;
        src:url(fonts/stylish.eot);
    }
    </style>
```

IE allows you to define multiple @font-face rules in the same style sheet. Visit *http://msdn.microsoft.com/workshop/author/fontembed/font_embed.asp* for details on how to create font definition files that work with IE for Windows and Macintosh.

Table 11-3 provides a summary of the at-rules supported by CSS and mainstream browsers.

*Table 11-3. CSS2 at-rules*

| Name | NN | IE/Windows | IE/Mac | CSS | Description |
|------|----|-----------|--------|-----|-------------|
| @charset | 6 | 5 | 5 | 2 | Character set used for external style sheet file. |
| @font-face | n/a | 4 | n/a | 2 | Font description to assist in font-matching between an embedded font and the client system font (or downloaded font). |
| @import | 6 | 4 | 4 | 1 | Imports an external style sheet. See Chapter 3 for the impact on the cascade. |
| @media | 6 | 5 | n/a | 2 | Defines an output media type for one or more style sheet rules. Rules assigned to the same selectors but inside different @media rules (e.g., @media print or @media screen) adhere to media-specific rules when the document is rendered in the specified medium. |
| @page | n/a | n/a | n/a | 2 | Defines the page box's size, margins, orientation, crop marks, and other page-related attributes governing the printing of the document. |

# Conventions

The CSS syntax descriptions shown throughout this chapter adhere to the following guidelines:

- Words in the `Constant Width` font are keywords or constant values to be used as-is.
- Words in the *Constant Width Italic* font are placeholders for values.
- A value contained by square brackets ([ ]) is optional.
- A series of two or more values separated by a pipe symbol (|) represent items in a list of acceptable values to be used in the position shown.
- A few listings show numbers in brackets ({1,2}) after a value. The numbers indicate the minimum and maximum number of space-delimited values you can specify.
- A double-pipe symbol (||) separating multiple values indicates that one or more of the values must be present, but the order is not significant.

The "Applies To" category advises which HTML elements can be influenced by the style attribute. Some style attributes can be applied only to block-level, inline, or replaced elements. A block-level element is one that always starts on a new line and forces a new line after the end of the element (h1 and p elements, for example). An inline element is one that you can place in the middle of a text line without disturbing the content flow (em elements, for example). A replaced element is a block-level or inline element that has content that may be changed dynamically without requiring any reflow of surrounding content. The img element falls into this category because you can swap image source files within an img element's rectangular space.

A listing category called "Initial Value" serves the same purpose as the "Default" category in other reference chapters. The terminology used in this chapter conforms with the terminology of the CSS specification.

Many items contain a category called "Object Model Reference" to show the way scripts can reference the attribute as properties in a browser's document object model—specifically, as properties of the style object. Consult Chapter 9 for compatibility ratings for the scripted equivalents of style attributes, as they frequently differ from the style sheet attribute implementations shown in this chapter.

# Alphabetical Attribute Reference

## azimuth

NN *n/a*    IE *n/a*    CSS 2

Inherited: Yes

Given a listener at the center of a circular sound space (like in a surround-sound-equipped theater), azimuth sets the horizontal angle of the source of the sound (for example, in a text-to-speech browser). See also the elevation attribute.

**CSS Syntax**    azimuth: *angle* | *angleConstant* || *direction*

**Value**

Up to two values (other than inherit). One represents the angle, clockwise from straight ahead; the second is a 20-degree incremental movement to the left or right. An *angle* value is any value in the range of −360 to +360 (inclusive) plus the letters "deg", as in 90deg. The value 0deg is directly in front of the listener. To set the angle to the left of the listener, the value can be either -90deg or 270deg. Optionally, you can choose an *angleConstant* value from a large library of descriptions that correspond to fixed points around the circle. If you add the behind modifier, the values shift from in front of the listener to behind the listener.

| Value | Equals | Value | Equals |
|---|---|---|---|
| center | 0deg | center behind | 180deg |
| center-right | 20deg | center-right behind | 160deg |
| right | 40deg | right behind | 140deg |
| far-right | 60deg | far-right behind | 120deg |

| Value | Equals | Value | Equals |
|-------|--------|-------|--------|
| right-side | 90deg | right-side behind | 90deg |
| left-side | 270deg | left-side behind | 270deg |
| far-left | 300deg | far-left behind | 240deg |
| left | 320deg | left behind | 220deg |
| center-left | 340deg | center-left behind | 200deg |

For the *direction* value, you can choose from two constants: leftwards | rightwards. These settings shift the sound 20 degrees in the named direction.

**Initial Value**    center

**Example**
```
h1 {azimuth: 45deg}
p.aside {azimuth: center-right behind}
```

**Applies To**    All elements.

# background

This is a shortcut attribute that lets you set up to five separate (but related) background-style attributes in one attribute statement. Values can be in any order, each one delimited by a space. Although the attribute is not officially available in Navigator 4, some combinations of values may work with it.

**CSS Syntax**
```
background: background-attachment || background-color || background-image ||
background-position || background-repeat
```

**Value**    Any combination of the five background-style attribute values, in any order. Any attribute not specified is assigned its initial value. See each attribute for details about the expected values.

**Initial Value**    None.

**Example**    body {background: url(watermark.jpg) repeat fixed}

**Applies To**    All elements.

**Object Model Reference**
```
[window.]document.getElementById("elementID").style.background
```

# background-attachment

When an image is applied to the element background (with the background-image attribute), the background-attachment attribute sets whether the image scrolls with the document. The image can remain fixed within the viewable area of the element (the viewport), or it may scroll with the element as content scrolls. During scrolling, a fixed attachment looks like a stationary backdrop to rolling credits of a movie.

**CSS Syntax**        `background-attachment: fixed | scroll`

**Value**           The `fixed` value keeps the image stationary in the element viewport; the `scroll` value lets the image scroll with the document content.

**Initial Value**     `scroll`

**Example**        `body {background-attachment: fixed}`

**Applies To**      All elements.

**Object Model Reference**
`[window.]document.getElementById("elementID").style.backgroundAttachment`

# background-color

NN *4*   IE *4*   CSS *1*

Inherited: No

Sets the background color for the element. Although it may appear as though a nested element's background-color attribute is inherited, in truth the initial value is transparent, which lets the next-outermost colored element show through whitespace of the current element.

**CSS Syntax**        `background-color: color`

**Value**           Any valid color specification (see description at beginning of the chapter) or transparent.

**Initial Value**     `transparent`

**Example**        `.highlighter {background-color: yellow}`

**Applies To**      All elements.

**Object Model Reference**
`[window.]document.getElementById("elementID").style.backgroundColor`

# background-image

NN *4*   IE *4*   CSS *1*

Inherited: No

Sets the background image (if any) for the element. If you set a background-color for the element as well, the color appears if the image fails to load; otherwise, the image overlays the color. Transparent pixels of the image allow a background color to show through. See also the background-attachment attribute.

**CSS Syntax**        `background-image: uri | none`

| | |
|---|---|
| **Value** | To specify a URL, use the `url( )` wrapper for the attribute value. You can omit the attribute or specify `none` to prevent an image from loading into the element's background. |
| **Initial Value** | none |
| **Example** | `h1 {background-image: url(watermark.jpg)}` |
| **Applies To** | All elements. |

**Object Model Reference**

`[window.]document.getElementById("elementID").style.backgroundImage`

# background-position

Establishes the location of the left and top edges of the background image specified with the background-image attribute. The behavior of this attribute can be erratic in Internet Explorer 4 for the Macintosh.

**CSS Syntax**

```
background-position: [percentage | length] {1,2} |
  [top | center | bottom] || [left | center | right]
```

**Value**

You can specify one or two percentages, which are the percentage of the block-level element's box width and height (respectively) at which the image (or repeated images) begins. If you supply only one percentage value, it applies to the horizontal measure, and the vertical measure is automatically set to 50%. Instead of percentages, you can specify length values (in the unit of measure that best suits the medium). You can also mix a percentage with a length. In lieu of the numerical values, you can create combinations of values with the two sets of constant values. Select one from each collection, as in top left, top right, or bottom center. Whenever you specify two values, they must be separated by a space.

**Initial Value**   0% 0%

**Example**

```
div.marked {background-image: url(watermark.jpg);
    background-position: center top}
```

**Applies To**   Block-level and replaced elements.

**Object Model Reference**

`[window.]document.getElementById("elementID").style.backgroundPosition`

## background-position-x, background-position-y    NN *n/a*    IE *4*    CSS *n/a*

Inherited: No

Establish the location of the left (x) or top (y) edges of the background image specified with the background-image attribute.

**CSS Syntax**
```
background-position-x: [percentage | length] | [left | center | right ]
background-position-y: [percentage | length] | [top | center | bottom]
```

**Value**
You can specify the percentage of the block-level element's box width or height (respectively) at which the image (or repeated images) begins. Instead of percentages, you can specify length values (in the unit of measure that best suits the medium). In lieu of the numerical values, you may use one axis-specific constant value per attribute.

**Initial Value**    0%

**Example**
```
div.marked {background-image: url(watermark.jpg);
    background-position-x: center}
```

**Applies To**    Block-level and replaced elements.

**Object Model Reference**
```
[window.]document.getElementById("elementID").style.backgroundPositionX
[window.]document.getElementById("elementID").style.backgroundPositionY
```

## background-repeat    NN *6*    IE *4*    CSS *1*

Inherited: No

Sets whether a background image (specified with the background-image attribute) should repeat and, if so, along which axis. You can use repeating background images to create horizontal and vertical bands.

**CSS Syntax**    background-repeat: no-repeat | repeat | repeat-x | repeat-y

**Value**
With a setting of no-repeat, one instance of the image appears in the location within the element established by the background-position attribute (default is the top-left corner). Normal repeats are performed along both axes, but you can have the image repeat down a single column (repeat-y) or across a single row (repeat-x).

**Initial Value**    repeat

**Example**    body {background-image: url(icon.gif); background-repeat: repeat-y}

**Applies To**    All elements.

**Object Model Reference**
```
[window.]document.getElementById("elementID").style.backgroundRepeat
```

# behavior

Associates an external behavior definition to the element.

**CSS Syntax**       behavior: *uri*[, *uri*[, ...]]

**Value**

CSS-formatted URL value, with the actual URL pointing to an external *.htc* file, ID of an object element that loads a behavior ActiveX control into the page, or one of the built-in default behaviors (in the format url(#default#*behaviorName*)). Default behavior names are:

| | | | |
|---|---|---|---|
| anchorClick | anim | clientCaps | download |
| homePage | httpFolder | mediaBar | saveFavorite |
| saveHistory | saveSnapshot | userData | |

For details on what these default behaviors do and under what security conditions you can use them, visit *http://msdn.microsoft.com/workshop/author/behaviors/reference/reference.asp*.

**Initial Value**     None.

**Example**        input.numOnly {behavior: url(numInput.htc)}

**Applies To**     All elements.

**Object Model Reference**

[window.]document.getElementById("*elementID*").style.behavior
[window.]document.getElementById("*elementID*").behaviorUrns[*i*]

# border

This is a shorthand attribute for setting the width, style, and/or color of all four borders around an element in one assignment statement. Whichever attributes you don't explicitly set with this attribute assume their initial values. Numerous other attributes allow you to set the width, style, and color of individual edges or groups of edges, if you don't want all four edges to be the same.

Due to differences in the way browsers define their default behavior with regard to borders, every style sheet border rule should include the width and style settings. Failure to specify both attributes may result in the border not being seen in one browser or the other.

**CSS Syntax**       border: *border-width* || *border-style* || *color*

**Value**          For the *border-width* and *border-style* attribute values, see the respective attributes in this chapter. For details on the *color* value, see the section about colors at the beginning of this chapter.

**Initial Value**     None.

**Example**        p {border: 3px groove darkred}

| Applies To | All elements, but only block and replaced elements in IE 4 and 5 for Windows. |

**Object Model Reference**
[window.]document.getElementById("*elementID*").style.border

# border-bottom, border-left, border-right, border-top

**NN 6   IE 4   CSS 1**
**Inherited: No**

All four attributes are shorthand attributes for setting the width, style, and/or color of a single border edge of an element in one assignment statement. Whichever attributes you don't explicitly set with this attribute assume their initial values.

**CSS Syntax**
```
border-bottom: border-bottom-width || border-bottom-style || color
border-left: border-left-width || border-left-style || color
border-right: border-right-width || border-right-style || color
border-top: border-top-width || border-top-style || color
```

| Value | For the width and style attribute values, see the border-bottom-width and border-bottom-style attributes in this chapter. For details on the *color* value, see the section about colors at the beginning of this chapter. |
| Initial Value | None. |

**Example**
```
p {border-bottom: 3px solid lightgreen}
p {border-left: 6px solid lightgreen}
p {border-right: 3px solid lightgreen}
p {border-top: 6px solid lightgreen}
```

| Applies To | All elements, but only block and replaced elements in IE 4 and 5 for Windows. |

**Object Model Reference**
```
[window.]document.getElementById("elementID").style.borderBottom
[window.]document.getElementById("elementID").style.borderLeft
[window.]document.getElementById("elementID").style.borderRight
[window.]document.getElementById("elementID").style.borderTop
```

# border-bottom-color, border-left-color, border-right-color, border-top-color

**NN 6   IE 4   CSS 2**
**Inherited: No**

Each attribute sets the color of a single border edge of an element. This power is easy to abuse by mixing colors that don't belong together. See also the border-color attribute for setting the color of multiple edges in one statement.

## CSS Syntax

```
border-bottom-color: color
border-left-color: color
border-right-color: color
border-top-color: color
```

**Value**  For details on the *color* value, see the section about colors at the beginning of this chapter.

**Initial Value**  None.

## Example

```
p {border-bottom-color: gray}
div {border-left-color: #33c088}
p.special {border-right-color: rgb(150, 75, 0)}
h3 {border-top-color: rgb(100%, 50%, 21%)}
```

**Applies To**  All elements, but only block and replaced elements in IE 4 and 5 for Windows.

## Object Model Reference

```
[window.]document.getElementById("elementID").style.borderBottomColor
[window.]document.getElementById("elementID").style.borderLeftColor
[window.]document.getElementById("elementID").style.borderRightColor
[window.]document.getElementById("elementID").style.borderTopColor
```

# border-bottom-style, border-left-style, border-right-style, border-top-style

NN 6    IE 4    CSS 2

Inherited: No

Each attribute sets the line style of a single border edge of an element. The edge-specific attributes let you override a style that has been applied to all four edges with the border or border-style attributes, but the edge-specific setting must come after the other one (in source code order) in the style sheet rule. See also the border-style attribute for setting the style of multiple edges in one statement.

## CSS Syntax

```
border-bottom-style: style
border-left-style: style
border-right-style: style
border-top-style: style
```

## Value

Style values are constants that are associated with specific ways of rendering border lines. Not all browser versions recognize all of the values in the CSS recommendation. Style support is shown in the following table.

| Value | NN | IE/Windows | IE/Mac | CSS |
|-------|-----|------------|--------|-----|
| dashed | 6 | 5.5 | 4 | 1 |
| dotted | 6 | 5.5 | 4 | 1 |

| Value | NN | IE/Windows | IE/Mac | CSS |
|-------|-----|-----------|--------|-----|
| double | 4 | 4 | 4 | 1 |
| groove | 4 | 4 | 4 | 1 |
| hidden | 6 | n/a | 4 | 2 |
| inset | 4 | 4 | 4 | 1 |
| none | 4 | 4 | 4 | 1 |
| outset | 4 | 4 | 4 | 1 |
| ridge | 4 | 4 | 4 | 1 |
| solid | 4 | 4 | 4 | 1 |

The manner that browsers interpret the definitions of the style values is not universal. Figure 11-1 shows a gallery of all styles as rendered by Internet Explorer 6 for Windows, Explorer 5 for Macintosh, and Netscape 6. Don't expect the same look in all browsers.

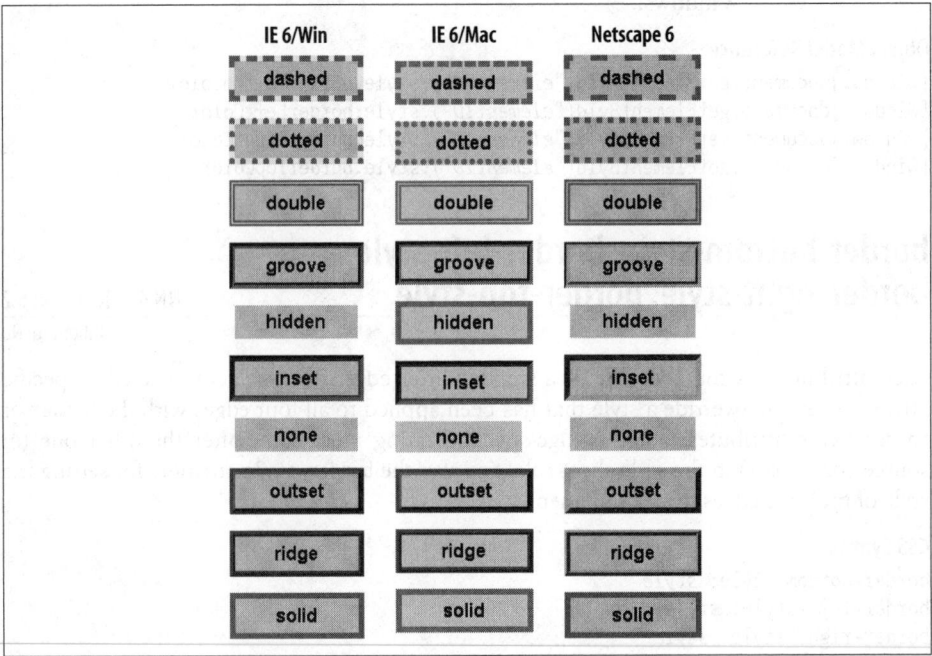

*Figure 11-1. Border-style gallery*

**Initial Value**       none

**Example**
```
p {border-style: solid; border-bottom-style: none}
div {border-left-style: ridge}
```

**Applies To**       All elements.

**Object Model Reference**

[window.]document.getElementById("*elementID*").style.borderBottomStyle
[window.]document.getElementById("*elementID*").style.borderLeftStyle
[window.]document.getElementById("*elementID*").style.borderRightStyle
[window.]document.getElementById("*elementID*").style.borderTopStyle

# border-bottom-width, border-left-width, border-right-width, border-top-width

*NN 4    IE 4    CSS 1*

Inherited: No

Each attribute sets the width of a single border edge of an element. Note that Navigator 4's initial value is zero, which means that you must set the width for all border attribute settings if you expect to see the border in that browser. See also the border-width attribute for setting the width of multiple edges in one statement.

## CSS Syntax

border-bottom-width: thin | medium | thick | *length*
border-left-width: thin | medium | thick | *length*
border-right-width: thin | medium | thick | *length*
border-top-width: thin | medium | thick | *length*

## Value

Three constants—thin | medium | thick—allow the browser to define how many pixels are used to show the border. For more precision, you can also assign a length value (see the discussion of length values at the beginning of this chapter).

**Initial Value**    medium (NN 6, IE); 0 (NN 4).

## Example

h2 {border-bottom-width: 2px}
div {border-left-width: thin}
p.special {border-right-width: 0.5em}

**Applies To**    All elements, but only block and replaced elements in IE 4 and 5 for Windows.

## Object Model Reference

[window.]document.getElementById("*elementID*").style.borderBottomWidth
[window.]document.getElementById("*elementID*").style.borderLeftWidth
[window.]document.getElementById("*elementID*").style.borderRightWidth
[window.]document.getElementById("*elementID*").style.borderTopWidth

# border-collapse

*NN 6    IE 5(Win)    CSS 2*

Inherited: Yes

Sets whether borders of adjacent table elements (cells, row groups, column groups) are rendered separately or collapsed (merged) to ignore any padding or margins between adjacent borders. A table set to the separate border model may also have its `border-spacing` and `empty-cells` style attributes set (if supported by the target browsers).

| | |
|---|---|
| **CSS Syntax** | border-collapse: collapse \| separate |
| **Value** | Constant values: collapse \| separate. |
| **Initial Value** | separate |
| **Applies To** | The table element. |

# border-color

This is a shortcut attribute that lets you set multiple border edges to the same or different colors. Navigator 4 allows only a single value, which applies to all four edges. For Internet Explorer and Netscape 6, you may supply one to four space-delimited color values. The number of values determines which sides receive the assigned colors.

**CSS Syntax**     border-color: *color* {1,4}

**Value**

For Navigator 4, one color value only. In Internet Explorer and Netscape 6, this attribute accepts one, two, three, or four *color* values, depending on how many and which borders you want to set with specific colors. Value quantities and positions are interpreted as shown in the following table.

| Number of values | Effect |
|---|---|
| 1 | All four borders set to value |
| 2 | Top and bottom borders set to the first value, right and left borders set to the second value |
| 3 | Top border set to first value, right and left borders set to second value, bottom border set to third value |
| 4 | Top, right, bottom, and left borders set, respectively |

**Initial Value**     The element's color style property (which is inherited if not specifically assigned for the element).

**Example**

```
h2 {border-color: red blue red}
div {border-color: red rgb(0,0,255) red}
```

**Applies To**     All elements, but only block and replaced elements in IE 4 and 5 for Windows.

**Object Model Reference**

[window.]document.getElementById("*elementID*").style.borderColor

# border-spacing

Determines the size of the space (if any) between all cell borders in a table. This attribute requires that the border-collapse attribute be set to separate (which is typically the default value). If you include only one length value, it applies to both the horizontal and vertical cell spacing; for two values, the first applies to the horizontal and the second to the vertical. See Figure 11-2 for a synopsis of a table's numerous dimension definitions.

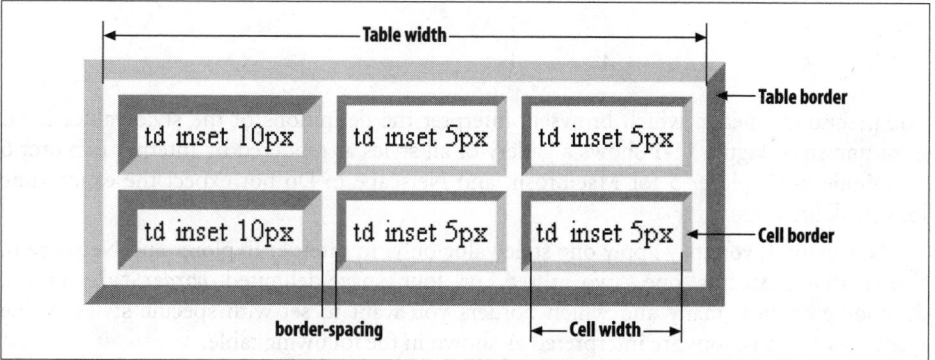

*Figure 11-2. The geometry of a table element*

**CSS Syntax**   border-spacing: *length*[*length*]

**Value**   See the discussion of length values at the beginning of this chapter. If you want no spacing along one axis, set its value to zero.

**Initial Value**   0

**Applies To**   The table element.

# border-style

This is a shortcut attribute that lets you set multiple border edges to the same or different style. Navigator 4 allows only a single value, which applies to all four edges. For Internet Explorer and Netscape 6, you may supply one to four space-delimited border style values. The number of values determines which sides receive the assigned style.

**CSS Syntax**   border-style: *borderStyle* {1,4}

**Value**

Style values are constants that are associated with specific ways of rendering border lines. Not all browsers recognize all of the values in the CSS recommendation. Style support is as follows.

| Value | NN | IE/Windows | IE/Mac | CSS |
|-------|-----|------------|--------|-----|
| dashed | 6 | 5.5 | 4 | 1 |
| dotted | 6 | 5.5 | 4 | 1 |

| Value | NN | IE/Windows | IE/Mac | CSS |
|-------|-----|-----------|--------|-----|
| double | 4 | 4 | 4 | 1 |
| groove | 4 | 4 | 4 | 1 |
| hidden | 6 | n/a | 4 | 2 |
| inset | 4 | 4 | 4 | 1 |
| none | 4 | 4 | 4 | 1 |
| outset | 4 | 4 | 4 | 1 |
| ridge | 4 | 4 | 4 | 1 |
| solid | 4 | 4 | 4 | 1 |

The precise manner in which browsers interpret the definitions of the style values is far from universal. Figure 11-1 shows a gallery of all styles as rendered by Internet Explorer 6 for Windows, Explorer 5 for Macintosh, and Netscape 6. Do not expect the exact same look in all browsers.

For Navigator 4, you may apply one style value only. In Internet Explorer and Netscape 6, this attribute accepts one, two, three, or four space-delimited *borderStyle* values, depending on how many and which borders you want to set with specific styles. Value quantities and positions are interpreted as shown in the following table.

| Number of values | Effect |
|------------------|--------|
| 1 | All four borders set to value |
| 2 | Top and bottom borders set to the first value, right and left borders set to the second value |
| 3 | Top border set to first value, right and left borders set to second value, bottom border set to third value |
| 4 | Top, right, bottom, and left borders set, respectively |

**Initial Value**     none

**Example**

```
h1 {border-style: ridge; border-width: 3px}
div {border-style: solid double; border-width: 4px}
```

**Applies To**     All elements, but only block and replaced elements in IE 4 and 5 for Windows.

**Object Model Reference**

```
[window.]document.getElementById("elementID").style.borderStyle
```

# border-width

NN *4*   IE *4*   CSS *1*

Inherited: No

This is a shortcut attribute that lets you set multiple border edges to the same or different widths. You may supply one to four space-delimited width length values. The number of values determines which sides receive the assigned widths.

**CSS Syntax**     border-width: thin | medium | thick | *length* {1,4}

## Value

Three constants—thin | medium | thick—allow the browser to define how many pixels are used to show the border. For more precision, you can also assign a length value (see the discussion of length values at the beginning of this chapter).

This attribute accepts one, two, three, or four space-delimited *borderWidth* values, depending on how many and which borders you want to set with specific styles. Value quantities and positions are interpreted as follows.

| Number of values | Effect |
| --- | --- |
| 1 | All four borders set to value |
| 2 | Top and bottom borders set to the first value, right and left borders set to the second value |
| 3 | Top border set to first value, right and left borders set to second value, bottom border set to third value |
| 4 | Top, right, bottom, and left borders set, respectively |

**Initial Value**   medium (IE and NN 6); 0 (NN 4)

## Example

```
h1 {border-style: ridge; border-width: 3px 5px 3px}
div {border-style: solid double; border-width: 4px}
```

**Applies To**   All elements, but only block and replaced elements in IE 4 and 5 for Windows.

## Object Model Reference

[window.]document.getElementById("*elementID*").style.borderWidth

# bottom

The CSS specification calls for this attribute to define the position of the bottom edge of a positioned element's content (exclusive of borders and margins) relative to the bottom edge of the next outermost block content container. Of mainstream browsers, only IE 5 for Macintosh behaves this way. IE for Windows and Netscape 6 do something unexpected when the positioned element uses the root positioning context: instead of using the bottom of the document as the comparative edge, these browsers use the bottom of the browser window space (the viewport in CSS terminology). As a result, the precise bottom position of the element varies with the user's browser window size. This discrepancy makes it more practical to use the bottom property for a positioned element nested inside another positioned element. When the element is relative-positioned, the offset is based on the bottom edge of the inline location of where the element would normally appear in the content.

**CSS Syntax**   bottom: *length* | *percentage* | auto

## Value

See the discussion about length values at the beginning of this chapter. Negative lengths may be allowed in some contexts, but be sure to test the results on all browsers. You may also specify a percentage value, which is calculated based on the height of the next outermost container. The setting of auto lets the browser determine the bottom offset of the element box on its naturally flowing offset within the containing box.

**Initial Value**     auto

**Applies To**     All positioned elements.

**Object Model Reference**
[window.]document.getElementById("*elementID*").style.bottom

# caption-side                                     NN 6    IE 5(Mac)    CSS 2

Inherited: Yes

Positions the caption element above or below the tabular content of the enclosing table element (other values may not work in some browsers). This attribute supplants some deprecated align attribute settings of the caption element.

**CSS Syntax**     caption-side: top | bottom | left | right

**Value**     One of the four constant values: top | bottom | left | right.

**Initial Value**     top

**Applies To**     caption elements.

**Object Model Reference**
[window.]document.getElementById("*elementID*").style.captionSide

# clear                                           NN 4    IE 4    CSS 1

Inherited: No

Defines whether a block-level element allows itself to be displayed in the same horizontal band as a nearby floating element, such as an image. Typically, another element in the vicinity has its float style attribute set to left or right. To prevent the current element from being in the same band as the floating block, set the clear attribute to the same side (left or right). If you aren't sure where the potential overlap might occur, set the clear attribute to both. An element with a clear attribute that is set to a value other than none is rendered at the beginning of the next available line below the floating element.

**CSS Syntax**     clear: both | left | none | right

**Value**     Any of the following constants: both | left | none | right.

**Initial Value**     none

**Example**
```
<img src="logo.gif" height="40" width="60" style="float: right">
<h1 style="clear: right">Giantco Corporation</h1>
```

**Applies To**     Block-level elements.

**Object Model Reference**
[window.]document.getElementById("*elementID*").style.clear

# clip

Inherited: No

Defines a clipping region of a positionable element. The clipping region is the area of the element layer in which content is visible. For the best results in clipping content, wrap the content-holding element inside a div element with its clip attribute set to the desired region. Clipping may not work properly in Internet Explorer 4 for the Macintosh, but it is fine in Version 5. Also, when a clipped element is displayed at the very bottom of a page in Navigator 4, the browser window may not allow you to scroll to view the very bottom of the clipping region.

**CSS Syntax**        clip: rect(*lengthTop lengthRight lengthBottom lengthLeft*) | auto

**Value**

Extending to CSS2, the only shape recognized for the clip attribute is rect. Other shapes may be admitted in the future.

When specifying lengths for each side of the clipping rectangle, observe the clockwise order of values: top, right, bottom, left. See the discussion about length values at the beginning of this chapter. A value of auto sets the clipping region to the block that contains the content (a block that may extend in IE 4 to the width of the next outermost container, like the body element).

**Initial Value**        auto

**Example**
```
<span style="position: absolute; clip: rect(10px 110px 80px 10px)">
<img src="desk1.gif" height="90" width="120">
</span>
```

**Applies To**        Block-level, replaced, and positioned elements.

**Object Model Reference**
[window.]document.getElementById("*elementID*").style.clip

# color

Inherited: Yes

Defines the foreground text color of the element. For some graphically oriented elements, such as form controls, the color attribute may also be applied to element edges or other features. Such extracurricular behavior is browser-specific and may not be the same across browsers.

**CSS Syntax**        color: *color*

**Value**        See the discussion of color attribute values at the beginning of this chapter.

**Initial Value**        black

**Example**        th {color: darkred}

**Applies To**        All elements.

**Object Model Reference**
[window.]document.getElementById("*elementID*").style.color

# content

**Inherited: No**

Defines the actual content or source of content to be displayed before and/or after the current element. In CSS jargon, this kind of content is called *generated content*. This attribute may be set only with the :before and :after pseudo-elements associated with a real element. For example, as a result of the following style sheet rule:

```
blockquote:after {content:"(Reprinted by permission.)"}
```

a permissions phrase is appended to the end of every blockquote element, although the content does not become a member of the document tree. HTML tags in the content text are not interpreted, but if the situation warrants it, an external document can be assigned to the content attribute.

## CSS Syntax

content: *string* | *uri* | *counter* | attr(*attrName*) | open-quote | close-quote | no-open-quote | no-close-quote

## Value

Only the following value types or values are functional in Netcape 6: *string*, open-quote, close-quote, no-open-quote, and no-close-quote. The purpose of the "no" quote types is to let you specify the effect of a quote (as far as quote nesting goes) without displaying a quote symbol. Multiple space-delimited strings may follow the content: attribute name.

Another value (*counter*) is not yet supported by browsers, but its potential is significant for documents that would benefit from client-side section number generation. A CSS counter offers a way for a style sheet to control numbering schemes for sequences of elements (such as sections, illustrations, and the like). The assumption is that the numbering is not part of the actual content, but is determined solely by the rendered context of the element within the document. Therefore, if you remove a numbered paragraph from a document in the edit phase, the paragraph numbering of the document adjusts itself automatically when the page is rendered.

The basic operation of a counter entails assigning an identifier to it (thus allowing multiple counters to exist in the same document, such as one for sections, another for subsections). Other CSS attributes (counter-increment and counter-reset) require values that point to an identified counter to control the numbering sequence. The following style sheet rule inserts a section label and number in front of every h1 element, and increments the counter number each time the style is applied to an h1 element while the document renders:

```
h1:before {counter-increment:secNum;
           content:"Section " counter(secNum) ". "}
```

When counters are implemented in mainstream browsers, they will provide substantial power to highly structured, long documents.

**Initial Value**    "" (empty string)

**Example**    p.note:before {content:"==>"}

**Applies To**    All elements plus a :before and/or :after pseudo-element.

## counter-increment, counter-reset

These attributes control the numbering sequence of a CSS counter used for generated content (see the content attribute). The counter-increment attribute sets the amount (and direction) of change each time the counter is accessed during rendering. The counter-reset attribute lets you set the counter to a specific number (default of zero).

### CSS Syntax

```
counter-increment: counterID [ posOrNegInteger ] | none
counter-reset: counterID [ posOrNegInteger ] | none
```

### Value

A *counterID* is an identifier assigned to a content:counter(*counterID*) style attribute. The optional integer value is space-delimited after the *counterID*. You can combine multiple counter IDs in the same style attribute by stringing together space-delimited pairs of ID and integer values.

| | |
|---|---|
| **Initial Value** | none |
| **Example** | h1 {counter-reset:subSection} |
| **Applies To** | All elements. |

## cue

For aural style sheets only, this attribute provides a shorthand for setting cue-before and cue-after attribute settings. A cue is a sound (also known as an auditory icon) that can be used to aurally delimit the reading of document content. Cue attributes are URIs to sound resources.

### CSS Syntax

```
cue: cue-before || cue-after
```

### Value

If there are two values, the first is applied to the cue-before attribute and the second to the cue-after attribute. If there is only one value, the same auditory icon is applied to both cue-before and cue-after.

| | |
|---|---|
| **Initial Value** | none |
| **Applies To** | All elements. |

## cue-after, cue-before

For aural style sheets only, a cue is a sound (also known as an auditory icon) that can be used to aurally delimit the reading of document content. The cue-before and cue-after attributes are URIs to sound files that are to be played before and after the content is rendered via text-to-speech or other aural medium.

## CSS Syntax

cue-after: *uri* | none
cue-before: *uri* | none

**Value**  Any valid complete or relative URL (in CSS format) to a sound file in a MIME type supported by the browser. You may apply the same values to both attributes for the same style selector if it makes aural sense for the listener.

**Initial Value**  none

**Example**  li {cue-before: url(ding.wav); cue-after: url(dong.wav)}

**Applies To**  All elements.

---

# cursor                                    NN 6   IE 4   CSS 2

Inherited: Yes

Sets the shape of the cursor when the screen pointer is atop the element. The precise look of cursors depends on the operating system. Before deploying a modified cursor, be sure you understand the standard ways that the various types of cursors are used within the browser and operating system. Users expect a cursor design to mean the same thing across all applications. Figure 11-3 offers a gallery of cursors for each of the cursor constant settings provided by Internet Explorer for Windows.

| all-scroll | col-resize | crosshair | e-resize |
| --- | --- | --- | --- |
| hand | help | move | n-resize |
| ne-resize | no-drop | not-allowed | nw-resize |
| pointer | progress | row-resize | s-resize |
| se-resize | sw-resize | text | vertical-text |
| w-resize | wait | | |

*Figure 11-3. Internet Explorer cursor gallery*

**CSS Syntax**  cursor: *cursorType* || *uri*

## Value

A cursor type is one of the implemented cursor names. The following table shows which cursor types are supported by various browsers and the CSS standard.

---

| Cursor name | IE/Windows | IE/Mac | NN | CSS |
|---|---|---|---|---|
| alias | n/a | n/a | 6 | n/a |
| all-scroll | 6 | n/a | n/a | n/a |
| auto | 4 | 4 | 6 | 2 |
| cell | n/a | n/a | 6 | n/a |
| col-resize | 6 | n/a | n/a | n/a |
| context-menu | n/a | n/a | 6 | n/a |
| copy | n/a | n/a | 6 | n/a |
| count-down | n/a | n/a | 6 | n/a |
| count-up | n/a | n/a | 6 | n/a |
| count-up-down | n/a | n/a | 6 | n/a |
| crosshair | 4 | 4 | 6 | 2 |
| default | 4 | 4 | 6 | 2 |
| e-resize | 4 | 4 | 6 | 2 |
| grab | n/a | n/a | 6 | n/a |
| grabbing | n/a | n/a | 6 | n/a |
| hand | 4 | 4 | n/a | n/a |
| help | 4 | 4 | 6 | 2 |
| move | 4 | 4 | 6 | 2 |
| n-resize | 4 | 4 | 6 | 2 |
| ne-resize | 4 | 4 | 6 | 2 |
| no-drop | 6 | n/a | n/a | n/a |
| not-allowed | 6 | n/a | n/a | n/a |
| nw-resize | 4 | 4 | 6 | 2 |
| pointer | 4 | 4 | 6 | 2 |
| progress | 6 | n/a | n/a | n/a |
| row-resize | 6 | n/a | n/a | n/a |
| s-resize | 4 | 4 | 6 | 2 |
| se-resize | 4 | 4 | 6 | 2 |
| spinning | n/a | n/a | 6 | n/a |
| sw-resize | 4 | 4 | 6 | 2 |
| text | 4 | 4 | 6 | 2 |
| url(*uri*) | 6 | n/a | n/a | 2 |
| vertical-text | 6 | n/a | n/a | n/a |
| w-resize | 4 | 4 | 6 | 2 |
| wait | 4 | 4 | 6 | 2 |

Notice that IE 6 for Windows implements downloadable cursors. The IE 6 setting for an external URL requires an address of a cursor file of extension *.cur* or *.ani* (which you create with a graphics utility that creates Windows cursors).

| | |
|---|---|
| **Initial Value** | auto |
| **Example** | a.helpLink {cursor: help} |
| **Applies To** | All elements. |

# direction

NN 6   IE 5   CSS 2

Inherited: Yes

Sets the direction of the flow of inline portions of content (such as text) and the order in which table cells are filled along a row. Analogous to the dir attribute of most elements, the direction style attribute lets you override the browser's default rendering direction for other languages or special content.

| | |
|---|---|
| **CSS Syntax** | direction: ltr \| rtl |
| **Value** | Either of two directional constants. The value ltr stands for left-to-right; rtl stands for right-to-left. |
| **Initial Value** | ltr |
| **Applies To** | All elements. |

# display

NN 4   IE 4   CSS 1

Inherited: No

This is a multipurpose attribute that determines how a browser treats invisible boxes that surround every element and text node. For example, a block-level item exhibits specific characteristics that are quite distinct from an inline item (at least with respect to how the element renders in relation to surrounding content). The CSS specification provides numerous types of such boxes, because the space they occupy can be influenced differently by such things as borders or even outright rendering rules (e.g., the way a compact style controls definition list items). In practice, you may not see much, if any, difference between some display types because the browser's built-in style sheet doesn't specify anything different for the variations (e.g., a table element may render the same way if its display style attribute is set to block or table). At the same time, the display style lets you override the default rendering behavior of elements, such as making a block table render as an inline table.

Perhaps the most frequently used aspect of the display style attribute in DHTML is setting the scripts to toggle between showing and completely hiding the element and its space. When the attribute is set to none, the element is hidden from view, and all surrounding content cinches up to occupy whatever space the element would normally occupy. This is different from the visibility attribute, which reserves space for the element while hiding it from view. But to redisplay the item to its default display mode, you can assign one of the common display types (block and inline) or the more specific type associated with the element (such as list-item for an li element), if supported by your target browsers.

**CSS Syntax**    display: *displayType*

**Value**

The CSS specification identifies many display types, but browser support is more limited. The following table shows the supported types.

| Display type | IE/Windows | IE/Mac | NN | CSS |
|---|---|---|---|---|
| block | 5 | 4 | 6 | 2 |
| compact | n/a | n/a | n/a | 2 |
| inline | 5 | 4 | 6 | 2 |
| inline-block | 5.5 | n/a | n/a | n/a |
| inline-table | n/a | 5 | n/a | 2 |
| list-item | 5 | 5 | 6 | 2 |
| marker | n/a | n/a | n/a | 2 |
| none | 4 | 4 | 6 | 2 |
| run-in | n/a | 5 | n/a | 2 |
| table | n/a | 5 | 6 | 2 |
| table-caption | n/a | 5 | n/a | 2 |
| table-cell | n/a | 5 | 6 | 2 |
| table-column-group | n/a | 5 | n/a | 2 |
| table-footer-group | 5.5 | 5 | 6 | 2 |
| table-header-group | 5 | 5 | 6 | 2 |
| table-row | n/a | 5 | 6 | 2 |
| table-row-group | n/a | 5 | 6 | 2 |

**Initial Value**    Element-dependent.

**Example**    .hidden {display: none}

**Applies To**    All elements (but some display types are applicable to specific elements).

**Object Model Reference**

[window.]document.getElementById("*elementID*").style.display

# elevation

NN *n/a*    IE *n/a*    CSS 2

Inherited: Yes

Given a listener at the center of a three-dimensional sound space (like in a surround-sound-equipped theater), elevation sets the vertical angle of the source of the sound (for example, in a text-to-speech browser). See also the azimuth attribute.

**CSS Syntax**    elevation: *angle* | *angleConstant*

## Value

Your choice of a specific angle (in degrees) or one of the five constant values. An angle value is any value in the range of −90 to +90 (inclusive) plus the letters "deg", as in 90deg. The value 0deg is at the same vertical level as the listener's ear. To set the angle above level, the value must be a positive value (45deg); below level requires a negative value (-45deg). Optionally, you can choose an *angleConstant* value from a library of descriptions that correspond to fixed points above and below level.

| Value | Equals |
|-------|--------|
| above | 90deg (directly overhead) |
| below | -90deg (directly beneath) |
| higher | +10 degrees from current |
| level | 0deg (at listener's ear level) |
| lower | −10 degrees from current |

In combination with the azimuth attribute, you can place a sound at any point around a spherical surround-sound stage.

**Initial Value**  level

## Example

```
h1 {elevation: -45deg}
p.heavenly {elevation: above}
```

**Applies To**  All elements.

# empty-cells

Controls whether an empty td element shows its borders and background in a table. Surrounding cells don't change position when an empty cell is hidden. Instead, the cell is essentially transparent, allowing the table's background to show through in the space.

**CSS Syntax**  empty-cells: show | hide

**Value**  One of two constants: show | hide .

**Initial Value**  The CSS specification calls for a default value of show, but Netscape 6 renders as if the default is hide when running in quirks mode (i.e., specifying older DTDs in the DOCTYPE element).

**Example**  td {border: salmon inset 3px; empty-cells: hide}

**Applies To**  td elements.

# filter (old style)

Sets the visual, reveal, or blend filter used to display or change content of an element. A visual filter can be applied to an element to produce effects such as content flipping, glow, drop shadow, and many others. A reveal filter is applied to an element when its visibility or appearance changes. The value of the reveal filter determines what visual effect is to be applied to the transition from hidden to shown (or vice versa). This includes effects such as wipes, blinds, and barn doors. A blend filter sets the speed at which a transition between visibility states occurs.

## CSS Syntax
```
filter: filterType1(paramName1=value1, paramName2=value2,...)
        filterType2(paramName1=value1,...) ...
```

## Value
Each filter attribute may have more than one space-delimited filter type associated with it. Each filter type is followed by a pair of parentheses, which may convey parameters about the behavior of the filter for the current element. A parameter generally consists of a name/value pair, with assignment performed by the equals symbol. See the "Notes" section below for details on *filterType* values and parameters.

| | |
|---|---|
| **Initial Value** | None. |
| **Example** | `.fastStuff {filter: blur(add=true, direction=225)}` |
| **Applies To** | body, button, img, input, marquee, table, td, textarea, tfoot, th, thead, tr, and absolute-positioned div and span elements. |

## Object Model Reference
```
[window.]document.getElementById("elementID").filters["filterName"]
```

## Notes
First-generation filters (which continue to be supported at least through IE 6 for Windows) are divided into three broad categories: visual, reveal, and blend. Each category has its own parameter names. You can mix categories within a single filter attribute assignment and have quite a bit of fun experimenting with the combinations. Observe carefully the limitations about the elements to which you may assign filters.

The visual filters and their parameters are as follows:

alpha()
> Controls transparency level. The opacity and finishopacity parameters can be set from transparent (0) to opaque (100). The style parameter sets the opacity gradient shape: uniform (0), linear (1), radial (2), rectangular (3). startX and startY set the horizontal and vertical coordinates for opacity gradient start, whereas finishX and finishY set the horizontal and vertical coordinates for opacity gradient end.

blur()
> Gives the element the appearance of motion. The add parameter specifies whether to add the original image to the blurred image (1) or to omit it (0). direction sets the angle of the blurred image relative to the original image location: above (0);

above-right (45); right (90); below-right (135); below (180); below-left (225); left (270); above-left (315). strength indicates the number of pixels for the blurred image to extend.

chroma( )

Sets a color transparent. The color parameter specifies the hexadecimal triplet value of the color to be made transparent.

dropShadow( )

Creates an offset shadow for apparent depth. The color parameter sets the hexadecimal triplet value of color for drop shadow. offx and offy specify the number of pixels between the element and the drop shadow along the x and y axes (positive values to the right/down; negative to the left/up). The positive parameter specifies whether only positive pixels generate drop shadows (1) or transparent pixels as well (0).

flipH( )

Creates a horizontally mirrored image of the element.

flipV( )

Creates a vertically mirrored image of the element.

glow( )

Adds radiance to outer edges. The color parameter sets the hexadecimal triplet value of the color for the radiance effect and strength sets the radiance intensity (1-255).

gray( )

Removes colors but retains luminance.

invert( )

Reverses the hue, saturation, and brightness (HSV) levels.

light( )

Shines a light source on the element (numerous filter method calls are available to set specific types of light sources, locations, intensities, and colors).

mask( )

Creates a transparent mask. The color parameter sets the hexadecimal triplet value of the color applied to transparent regions.

shadow( )

Displays the element as a solid silhouette. The color parameter sets the hexadecimal triplet value of the color used for shadows and direction sets the angle of the shadow relative to the original image location: above (0); above-right (45); right (90); below-right (135); below (180); below-left (225); left (270); above-left (315).

wave( )

Renders the element with a sine wave distortion along the x-axis. The add parameter specifies whether to add the original image to waved image (1) or not (0). freq sets the number of waves to be applied to visual distortion, light sets the light strength (0-100), phase sets the percentage offset for the sine wave (0-100 corresponding to to 360 degrees), and strength sets the wave effect intensity (0-255).

xRay( )

Renders only the edges.

The blend and reveal transition filters and parameters are as follows:

blendTrans( )

Fades the element in or out. The duration parameter sets the floating-point value (*seconds.milliseconds*) of how long the transition effect should take.

`revealTrans( )`

Sets a transition effect between appearance states of an element. The duration parameter sets the floating-point value (*seconds.milliseconds*) of how long the transition effect should take. `transition` is a key integer that corresponds to one of the following transition types.

| Value | Transition type | Value | Transition type |
|-------|-----------------|-------|-----------------|
| 0 | Box in | 12 | Random dissolve |
| 1 | Box out | 13 | Split vertical in |
| 2 | Circle in | 14 | Split vertical out |
| 3 | Circle out | 15 | Split horizontal in |
| 4 | Wipe up | 16 | Split horizontal out |
| 5 | Wipe down | 17 | Strips left down |
| 6 | Wipe right | 18 | Strips left up |
| 7 | Wipe left | 19 | Strips right down |
| 8 | Vertical blinds | 20 | Strips right up |
| 9 | Horizontal blinds | 21 | Random bars horizontal |
| 10 | Checkerboard across | 22 | Random bars vertical |
| 11 | Checkerboard down | 23 | Random |

Both transition filters have a set of three methods: `apply( )`, `play( )`, and `stop( )`. Use `apply( )` to freeze the element's display while you change the element's visibility or other visual attribute; then invoke the `play( )` method on the filter to let the transition be seen by the user:

```
document.getElementById("myImg").filters["revealTrans"].apply( );
document.getElementById("myImg").src = "newPix.jpg";
document.getElementById("myImg").filters["revealTrans"].play( );
```

A style sheet rule for the element may have been set to the following:

```
img {filter:revealTrans(transition=2, duration=3)}
```

When the script statements execute, the change from one image to another occurs through a "circle in" reveal transition.

# filter (new style)

NN *n/a*    IE *5.5(Win)*    CSS *n/a*

Inherited: No

Sets the static or transition filter used to display or change content of an element with the help of the DXImageTransform ActiveX control, delivered with IE 5.5 or later for Windows. The purpose of the new filter mechanism is the same as the old style one, but the syntax for invoking the ActiveX control is new, as are many of the filter names.

## CSS Syntax

```
filter:progid:DXImageTransform.Microsoft.filterType1(paramName1=value1,
paramName2=value2,...)
progid:DXImageTransform.Microsoft.filterType2(paramName1=value1,...) ...
```

## Value

Each filter type must be preceded by the reference to the ActiveX control (progid: DXImageTransform.Microsoft.), and multiple filter types for a single filter style attribute are space delimited. Each filter type is followed by a pair of parentheses, which may convey parameters about the behavior of the filter for the current element. A parameter generally consists of a name/value pair, with assignment performed by the equals symbol. Filter types that control transitions also have methods that scripts invoke to freeze the display while some visible attribute of the element changes (also under script control) and then play the transition. (See the "Notes" section below for information about *filterType* values and parameters.

### Initial Value      None.

### Example

```
.fastStuff {filter:progid:DXImageTransform.Microsoft.MotionBlur(add=1,
direction=225)}
```

### Applies To      All elements.

### Object Model Reference

```
[window.]document.getElementById("elementID").filters[
  "DXImageTransform.Microsoft.filterName"]
```

### Notes

Documenting in detail ActiveX controls that work only on Windows versions of Internet Explorer exceeds the scope of this book. But by way of introduction to what the new filter scheme offers in IE 5.5 and later, the following table lists the static and trasition filters available in the DXImageTransform ActiveX control, along with descriptions of what they do. For specific details of attributes that go into style sheet rules, as well as the scriptable properties and methods available to each filter, visit *http://msdn.microsoft.com/workshop/author/filter/filters.asp*.

| Filter name | Type | Description |
| --- | --- | --- |
| Alpha() | static | Controls transparency level (opacity) |
| Barn() | transition | A barn-door transition effect, with properties for speed, motion, and orientation |
| BasicImage() | static | Sets a variety of filter styles (mirror, opacity, grayscale, etc.) for all kinds of elements, but under script control can also rotate the element and alter its color mask |
| Blinds() | transition | A venetian-blind transition effect, with properties for direction and thickness of the slats |
| Blur() | static | Controls the fuzziness of the element |
| Checkerboard() | transition | A checkboard transition effect with properties for direction, speed, and square sizes |
| Chroma() | static | Controls the transparency of a specific color |
| Compositor() | static | Combines color filter effects |
| DropShadow() | static | Creates an offset shadow for apparent depth, with properties for color, and depth of shadow |
| Emboss() | static | Controls an embossed texture effect |
| Engrave() | static | Controls an engraved texture effect |

| Filter name | Type | Description |
|---|---|---|
| Fade( ) | transition | A blended transition between views, with properties for speed and the degree of overlap of both views |
| Glow( ) | static | Controls radiance of outer edges |
| Gradiant( ) | statics | Applies a colored gradient texture on the element's background |
| GradientWipe( ) | transition | A wipe transition using a gradient blend at the wipe line, with properties for speed, thickness of the gradient, and direction |
| ICMFilter( ) | static | Applies an external Image Color Management profile to the element |
| Inset( ) | transition | A wipe transition that works along horizontal and vertical axes, but diagonally from one corner to its opposite |
| Iris( ) | transition | A zoom-style transition with properties for speed, direction (in or out), and iris shape (e.g., circle, cross, diamond, plus, square, star) |
| Light( ) | static | Controlled exclusively through scripts, adds effect of light source directed at the element |
| MaskFilter( ) | static | Overlays a transparent mask for a color |
| Matrix( ) | static | Control rotation, flipping, and scaling of element |
| MotionBlur( ) | static | Simulates motion via artificial blurring |
| Pixelate( ) | transition | Blends between views via an expansion/contraction and blurring/focusing of the content |
| RadialWipe( ) | transition | Blends between views via your choice of styles (clock, wedge, radial) |
| RandomBars( ) | transition | Blends between views via expanding/contracting bars, with properties for orientation and speed |
| RandomDissolve( ) | transition | Blends between views through random pixel changes |
| Shadow( ) | static | Displays element content as a silhouette |
| Slide( ) | transition | Blends between views through banded sliding of various types |
| Spiral( ) | transition | Blends between views through spiral reveals |
| Stretch( ) | transition | Blends between views through various stretch-style reveals |
| Strips( ) | transition | Blends between views with striped effect |
| Wave( ) | static | Adds sine-wave distortion to the element |
| Wheel( ) | transition | Blends between views via wheel spokes emanating from the element center |
| ZigZag( ) | transition | Blends between views via removal of rows of bricks |

CSS Reference

Successful deployment of these filters, especially on complex content, requires extensive experimentation and testing to make sure that your combination doesn't crash the browser.

# float

NN *4*   IE *4*   CSS *1*

Inherited: No

Determines on which side of the containing box the element aligns so that other content wraps around the element. When the attribute is set to none, the element appears in its source code sequence, and at most, one line of surrounding text content appears in the same horizontal band as the element.

Due to the prior reservation of float as a keyword in JavaScript, the attribute name is not available as a style object property name in object models that use JavaScript. Internet Explorer adopted the styleFloat property name; the W3C DOM and Netscape 6 use cssFloat.

**CSS Syntax**       float: *alignmentSide* | none

**Value**            An *alignmentSide* is one of the following constants: left | right.

**Initial Value**    none

**Example**          img.navButton {float: right}

**Applies To**       All elements except positioned elements (or generated content).

**Object Model Reference**
[window.]document.getElementById("*elementID*").style.styleFloat
[window.]document.getElementById("*elementID*").style.cssFloat


# font                                                    NN 6    IE 4    CSS 1

Inherited: Yes

This is a shorthand attribute that lets you set multiple font-related attributes with one assignment statement. Some browsers are more forgiving than others about required and optional values, but this attribute should at least specify the *font-size* and font face (either by *font-family* or *CSS2FontConstant* values) in that order. The order of other space-delimied value types is not critical. In CSS2, some additional short-circuit constants apply named system fonts that have fixed values for each of the font-related attributes.

**CSS Syntax**
font: *font-style* || *font-variant* || *font-weight* || *font-size[/line-height]* || *font-family* | *CSS2FontConstant*

**Value**
For syntax and examples of value types for font and line attributes, see the respective attribute listing. The construction with the forward slash before the *line-height* value allows the use of a second length value within the potentially long sequence of values for this attribute: the *line-height* length value must always accompany the required *font-size* value, separated by a forward slash.

The CSS2 font constants are as follows: caption | icon | menu | message-box | small-caption | status-bar. These constants refer to browser and operating system fonts used by the client. Their precise appearance is therefore different on different operating systems but consistent with the user's expectation for a particular type of font. In other words, these styles should be used when their function mirrors a system or browser function.

**Initial Value**    None.

**Example**
body {font: 12px serif}
h2 {font: bolder small-caps 16px "Lucida Console", Arial, sans-serif}
.iconCaption {font: 10px/1.1em caption}

**Applies To**       All elements.

**Object Model Reference**

[window.]document.getElementById("*elementID*").style.font

# font-family                                    **NN 4   IE 4   CSS 1**

Sets a prioritized list of font families to be used to render the content. One or more font family names may be included in a comma-delimited list of attribute values. If a font family name consists of multiple words, the family name must be inside quotes.

A font family may consist of multiple font definitions. For example, a Helvetica font family may also include a bold version and an italic version—genuinely distinct fonts rather than the approximated versions of bold and italic. When you specify a font family by name, the browser looks into the client's system to see if there is a font available by that name. If not, the browser looks to the next font family name in the list. Therefore, it is wise to include font family names in a sequence that goes from the most esoteric to the most generic. The final font family name should be the generic family (serif, sans-serif, cursive, fantasy, or monospace) that most closely resembles the desired font. Many fonts that are widely installed on one operating system may not be as popular on another operating system.

Browsers following the CSS2 specification should also be smart enough to recognize Unicode character codes and try to match them with named font families that cater to particular languages. Ideally, this will allow a browser to mix fonts from different languages and writing systems in the same element, provided each font-family is listed in the attribute value.

**CSS Syntax**       font-family: *fontFamilyName* [, *fontFamilyName* [, ...]]

**Value**

Any number of font family names, comma delimited. Multiword family names must be quoted. Recognized generic family names are: serif | sans-serif | cursive | fantasy | monospace.

**Initial Value**       Browser default.

**Example**       body {font-family: "Century Schoolbook", Times, serif}

**Applies To**       All elements.

**Object Model Reference**

[window.]document.getElementById("*elementID*").style.fontFamily

**Notes**

Internet Explorer provide facilities for downloading font definition files for a browser that doesn't have a special font that the page designer wants for the page. The font definition files must be created by the author using browser-specific font conversion tools. An @font-face style sheet rule downloads the font definition file and associates that font description with an arbitrary font family name:

    @font-face {font-family:Neato; src: url(http://www.giantco.com/fonts/neato.eot}

See the "At-Rules" section earlier in this chapter for details on deploying this type of style rule. You then specify the font in regular font-family style attributes. If the font has yet to download, the browser displays the page in another font until the downloadable font has arrived. At that point, the page is reflowed with the downloaded font.

# font-size

NN 4    IE 4    CSS 1

Inherited: Yes

Determines the font size of the element. The font size can be set in several ways. A collection of constants (xx-small, x-small, small, medium, large, x-large, xx-large) defines what are known as absolute sizes. In truth, these are absolute as far as a single browser in a single operating system goes because the reference point for these sizes varies with browser and operating system (analogous to the old HTML font sizes of 1 through 7). See Figure 11-4 and Figure 11-5 for size comparisons viewed on the same video monitors. But they let the author have confidence that one element set to large is rendered larger than another set to medium.

| Netscape 6/Windows | | Netscape 6/Mac | |
|---|---|---|---|
| **Value** | **Sample** | **Value** | **Sample** |
| xx-small | ABCabc123 | xx-small | ABCabc123 |
| x-small | ABCabc123 | x-small | ABCabc123 |
| small | ABCabc123 | small | ABCabc123 |
| medium | ABCabc123 | medium | ABCabc123 |
| large | ABCabc123 | large | ABCabc123 |
| x-large | ABCabc123 | x-large | ABCabc123 |
| xx-large | ABCabc123 | xx-large | ABCabc123 |

*Figure 11-4. Font size constant values in Netscape 6 on the Windows and Mac platforms*

Another collection of constants (larger, smaller) are known as relative sizes. Because the font-size attribute is inherited from the parent element, these relative sizes are applied to the parent element to determine the font size of the current element. It is up to the browser to determine exactly how much larger or smaller the font size is, and a lot depends on how the parent element's font size is set. If it is set with one of the absolute sizes (large, for example), a child's font size of larger means that the font is rendered in the browser's x-large size. The increments are not as clear cut when the parent font size is set with a length or percentage.

If you elect to use a length value for the font-size attribute, choose a unit that makes the most sense for fonts rendered on the output medium, such as pixels (px) for screen display and points (pt) or ems (em) for printed output. Em values are calculated relative to the size of the parent element's font size. Finally, you can set the font-size to a percentage, which is calculated based on the size of the parent element's font size.

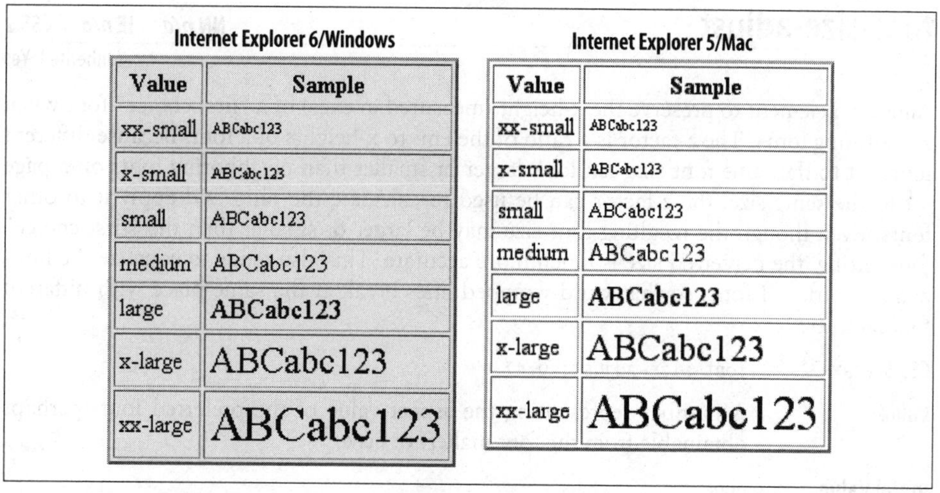

| Internet Explorer 6/Windows | | Internet Explorer 5/Mac | |
|---|---|---|---|
| **Value** | **Sample** | **Value** | **Sample** |
| xx-small | ABCabc123 | xx-small | ABCabc123 |
| x-small | ABCabc123 | x-small | ABCabc123 |
| small | ABCabc123 | small | ABCabc123 |
| medium | ABCabc123 | medium | ABCabc123 |
| large | ABCabc123 | large | ABCabc123 |
| x-large | ABCabc123 | x-large | ABCabc123 |
| xx-large | ABCabc123 | xx-large | ABCabc123 |

*Figure 11-5. Font size constant values in IE on the Windows and Mac platforms*

Some browsers hijack your best efforts at precisely sizing fonts, using their own (or user) settings to establish a "medium" size. That is why many designers prefer to rely on the relative-size constants for their font-size specification schemes. This choice means giving up a level of control over rendering from one browser and operating system to the next, but attempting too strict control on uniform rendering generally leads to utter frustration.

**CSS Syntax**      font-size: *absoluteSize* | *relativeSize* | *length* | *percentage*

**Value**

For an absolute size, one of the following constants: xx-small | x-small | small | medium | large | x-large | xx-large. For a relative size, one of the following constants: larger | smaller. For a length, see the discussion about length values at the beginning of this chapter. For a percentage, the percentage value and the % symbol.

**Initial Value**

medium (for BODY element); the parent element's font-size value (for all others).

**Example**

```
body {font-size: 14pt}
p.teeny {font-size: x-small}
em {font-size: larger}
span.larger {font-size: 150%}
```

**Applies To**      All elements.

**Object Model Reference**

[window.]document.getElementById("*elementID*").style.fontSize

# font-size-adjust

Allows an element to preserve the x-height (measured in exes) of a "first choice" font when substituting fonts. The z-factor is a ratio of the em- to x-heights of a font. Because different fonts set to the same font size can look larger or smaller than neighboring fonts on a page set to the same size, the z-factor can be used to calculate the ratio and apply it to other fonts. Even though the resulting font size may be larger or smaller than the "first choice" font setting, the perceived size is much more accurate. This also tends to equalize the horizontal metrics of fonts so that word-wrapped lines break at the same place with different font families.

| | |
|---|---|
| **CSS Syntax** | font-size-adjust: 0.47 |
| **Value** | A number representing the aspect value of the preferred font (perhaps obtainable from the font maker) or none. |
| **Initial Value** | none |
| **Applies To** | All elements. |

**Object Model Reference**
[window.]document.getElementById("*elementID*").style.fontSizeAdjust

# font-stretch

Sets the rendered font to a letter-spacing relative of the specified font family. Version 6 browsers do not take it upon themselves to artificially condense or expand font family specifications.

| | |
|---|---|
| **CSS Syntax** | font-stretch: *stretchType* | normal |
| **Value** | For an absolute size, one of the following constants: ultra-condensed | extra-condensed | condensed | semi-condensed | semi-expanded | extra-expanded | ultra-expanded. For a relative size, one of the following constants: narrower | wider. |
| **Initial Value** | normal |
| **Applies To** | All elements. |

**Object Model Reference**
[window.]document.getElementById("*elementID*").style.fontStretch

# font-style

Determines whether the element is rendered in a normal (Roman), italic, or oblique font style. If the font-family includes font faces labeled Italic and/or Oblique, the setting of the font-style attribute summons those particular font faces from the browser's system. But if the specialized font faces are not available in the system, the normal font face is usually algorithmically slanted to look italic. Output sent to a printer with such font settings relies on the quality of arbitration between the client computer and printer to render an electronically generated italic font style. Although personal computer software typically includes other kinds of font rendering under the heading of "Style," see font-stretch, font-variant, and font-weight for other kinds of font "styles."

| | |
|---|---|
| **CSS Syntax** | font-style: *fontStyle* |
| **Value** | One of the following constants: normal \| italic \| oblique. Browsers tend to treat italic and oblique settings the same. |
| **Initial Value** | normal |
| **Example** | h2 em {font-style: italic} |
| **Applies To** | All elements. |

**Object Model Reference**
[window.]document.getElementById("*elementID*").style.fontStyle

# font-variant

Determines whether the element should be rendered in all uppercase letters in such a way that lowercase letters of the source code are rendered in smaller uppercase letters. If a font family contains a small caps variant, the browser should use it automatically. More likely, however, the browser calculates a smaller size for the uppercase letters that take the place of source code lowercase letters. In practice, Internet Explorer for Windows prior to Version 6 renders the entire source code content as uppercase letters of the same size as the parent element's font, regardless of the case of the source code.

| | |
|---|---|
| **CSS Syntax** | font-variant: *fontVariant* |
| **Value** | Any of the following constant values: normal \| small-caps. |
| **Initial Value** | normal |
| **Example** | em {font-variant: small-caps} |
| **Applies To** | All elements. |

**Object Model Reference**
[window.]document.getElementById("*elementID*").style.fontVariant

# font-weight

Sets the weight (boldness) of the element's font. CSS provides a weight rating scheme that is more granular than most browsers render on the screen, but the finely tuned weights may come into play when the content is sent to a printer. The scale is a numeric rating from 100 to 900 at 100-unit increments. Therefore, a font-weight of 100 is the least bold that can be displayed, whereas 900 is the boldest. A setting of normal (the default weight for any font) is equivalent to a font-weight value of 400; the standard bold setting is equivalent to 700. Other settings (bolder and lighter) let you specify a weight relative to the parent element's weight.

The CSS2 specification offers guidelines about how the weight values should correspond to font family names and internal characteristics of some font definition formats. For example, the OpenType font definition format provides slots for nine font weights. In this case, the numeric font-weight attribute values map directly to the weight definitions in that font. If the font family contains a face with a name that contains the word Medium and one labeled Book, Regular, Roman, or Normal, the Medium face is equated with a weight value of 500 (whereas the other is at 400). All font face names including the word Bold are equated with a weight of 700. For font families that don't have all nine weights assigned, the browser should do its best to interpolate, but it is very likely that some weight values generate fonts of the same weight as other values.

| | |
|---|---|
| **CSS Syntax** | font-weight: *fontWeight* |
| **Value** | Any of the following constant values: bold \| bolder \| lighter \| normal \| 100 \| 200 \| 300 \| 400 \| 500 \| 600 \| 700 \| 800 \| 900. |
| **Initial Value** | normal |
| **Example** | p em {font-weight: bolder} |
| **Applies To** | All elements. |

**Object Model Reference**
[window.]document.getElementById("*elementID*").style.fontWeight

# height

NN 4    IE 4    CSS 1

Inherited: No

Sets the height of a block-level, replaced, and positioned element's content height (exclusive of borders, padding, and margins).

IE for Windows counts top and bottom margins, padding, and borders when calculating the height of an element until you reach IE 6 in standards-compatibility mode (see the DOCTYPE element in Chapter 8). When observing the CSS standards, the height applies to only the content portion of an element, irrespective of borders, padding, or margins. This change may have significant impact on legacy code that you are bringing up to W3C compatibility.

| | |
|---|---|
| **CSS Syntax** | height: *length* \| *percentage* \| auto |
| **Value** | See the discussion about length values at the beginning of this chapter. The setting of auto lets the browser determine the height of the element box based on the amount of space required to display the content. |
| **Initial Value** | auto |

### Example

```
div#announce {height: 240}
textarea {height: 90%}
```

### Applies To

Navigator 4, all absolute-positioned elements; Internet Explorer 4, applet, div, embed, fieldset, hr, iframe, img, input, marquee, object, span, table, and textarea elements; Internet Explorer 5 and Netscape 6, all elements except nonreplaced inline elements, table column elements, and column group elements.

### Object Model Reference

```
[window.]document.getElementById("elementID").style.height
```

## ime-mode

NN n/a   IE 5(Win)   CSS n/a<br>Inherited: No

Controls the presence of the Input Method Editor in IE for Windows for browser and system versions that support languages such as Chinese, Japanese, and Korean.

| | |
|---|---|
| **CSS Syntax** | ime-mode: active \| auto \| disabled \| inactive |
| **Value** | One of four constants: active \| auto \| disabled \| inactive. |
| **Initial Value** | auto |
| **Example** | input {ime-mode: active} |
| **Applies To** | input and textarea elements. |

### Object Model Reference

```
[window.]document.getElementById("elementID").style.imeMode
```

## !important

NN 6   IE 4   CSS 1<br>Inherited: No

Increases the weight (importance) of an attribute setting with respect to cascading order. This keyword is a declaration rather than an attribute, but it can be attached to any attribute setting. The syntax requires an exclamation symbol between the attribute value and the important keyword. Extra whitespace around the exclamation symbol is acceptable. See Chapter 3.

| | |
|---|---|
| **CSS Syntax** | !important |
| **Value** | No values assigned to this declaration. |
| **Example** | p {font-size: 14pt ! important} |
| **Applies To** | All elements. |

### Object Model Reference

```
[window.]document.getElementById("elementID").style.getPropertyPriority("styleAttribute")
```

CSS Reference

# layout-flow

Intended primarily for languages that display characters in vertical sentences, this attribute controls the progression of content, left-to-right, or right-to-left. Microsoft recommends using the writing-mode attribute instead.

| | |
|---|---|
| **CSS Syntax** | layout-flow: horizontal | vertical-ideographic |
| **Value** | One of two constants: horizontal | vertical-ideographic. |
| **Initial Value** | horizontal |
| **Example** | body {layout-flow: vertical-ideographic} |
| **Applies To** | All elements. |

**Object Model Reference**
[window.]document.getElementById("*elementID*").style.layoutFlow

# layout-grid

This is a shorthand attribute that lets you set one or more layout grid attributes (layoutGridChar, layoutGridLine, layoutGridMode, and layoutGridType) with one assignment statement. These attributes are used primarily with Asian language content.

**CSS Syntax**
layout-grid: *layout-grid-mode* | *layout-grid-type* | *layout-grid-line* | *layout-grid-char*

| | |
|---|---|
| **Value** | For syntax and examples of value types for font and line attributes, see the respective attribute listing. |
| **Initial Value** | both loose none none |
| **Example** | body {layout-grid: both fixed 14px 14px} |
| **Applies To** | All elements. |

**Object Model Reference**
[window.]document.getElementById("*elementID*").style.layoutGrid

# layout-grid-char

Controls the size of Asian language character grid for block-level elements.

| | |
|---|---|
| **CSS Syntax** | layout-grid-char: *length* | auto | none |
| **Value** | Length value as an absolute unit measure, or a percentage. Or one of the following constants: auto | none. |
| **Initial Value** | none |

**Example**        body {layout-grid-mode:both; layout-grid-char: 14px}

**Applies To**     All elements.

**Object Model Reference**
[window.]document.getElementById("*elementID*").style.layoutGridChar

# layout-grid-line

Controls the line height of Asian language character grid for block-level elements.

**CSS Syntax**     layout-grid-line: *length* | auto | none

**Value**         Length value as an absolute unit measure, or a percentage. Or one of the following constants: auto | none.

**Initial Value**   none

**Example**        body {layout-grid-mode:both; layout-grid-line: 14px}

**Applies To**     All elements.

**Object Model Reference**
[window.]document.getElementById("*elementID*").style.layoutGridLine

# layout-grid-mode

Controls whether the Asian language character grid should be one- or two-dimensional.

**CSS Syntax**     layout-grid-mode: *gridMode*

**Value**         One of the following constants: both | char (for inline elements) | line (for block-level elements) | none.

**Initial Value**   both

**Example**        body {layout-grid-mode:both}

**Applies To**     All elements.

**Object Model Reference**
[window.]document.getElementById("*elementID*").style.layoutGridMode

# layout-grid-type

Controls how the layout grid responds to characters of varying width.

**CSS Syntax**     layout-grid-type: *gridType*

**Value**         One of the following constants: fixed | loose | strict.

| | |
|---|---|
| **Initial Value** | fixed |
| **Example** | div.kor {layout-grid-type:strict} |
| **Applies To** | Block-level elements. |

**Object Model Reference**
[window.]document.getElementById("*elementID*").style.layoutGridType

# layer-background-color,
# layer-background-image

NN |4|    IE n/a    CSS n/a<br>Inherited: No

These are Navigator 4-only attributes that allow a positioned element's background color and image to extend through padding, all the way to the border. Values are the same as for the CSS background-color and background-image attributes. See background-color, background-image, and padding.

# left

NN 4    IE 4    CSS 2<br>Inherited: No

For positionable elements, defines the offset position of the left edge of an element's box (content plus left padding, border, and/or margin) relative to the left edge of the next outermost block content container. When the element is relative-positioned, the offset is based on the left edge of the inline location of where the element would normally appear in the content.

**CSS Syntax**     left: *length* | *percentage* | auto

**Value**
See the discussion about length values at the beginning of this chapter. Negative lengths may be allowed in some contexts, but be sure to test the results on all browsers. You may also specify a percentage value, which is calculated based on the width of the next outermost container. The setting of auto lets the browser determine the left offset of the element box within the containing box by virtue of normal element flow. Navigator tends to push up against the left edge of the containing box, whereas Internet Explorer renders a bit of margin.

| | |
|---|---|
| **Initial Value** | auto |

**Example**
h1 {position: relative; left: 2em}
#logo {position: absolute; left: 80px; top: 30px}

| | |
|---|---|
| **Applies To** | Positioned elements. |

**Object Model Reference**
[window.]document.getElementById("*elementID*").style.left

# letter-spacing

Defines the spacing between characters within an element. Browsers normally define the character spacing based on font definitions and operating-system font rendering. To override the settings, assign a length value to the letter-spacing attribute. A negative value tightens the spacing, but test the effect on the selected font for readability on different operating systems.

**CSS Syntax**    letter-spacing: *length* | normal

**Value**    See the discussion at the beginning of this chapter about length values. The best results use units that are based on the rendered font size (em and ex). A setting of normal is how the browser sets the letters without any intervention.

**Initial Value**    normal

**Example**
```
.tight {letter-spacing: -0.03em}
blockquote {letter-spacing: 1.1em}
```

**Applies To**    All elements.

**Object Model Reference**
[window.]document.getElementById("*elementID*").style.letterSpacing

# line-break

Controls line-breaking rules for Japanese text.

**CSS Syntax**    line-break: normal | strict

**Value**    One of the following constants: normal | strict.

**Initial Value**    normal

**Example**    p {letter-break: strict}

**Applies To**    Block-level elements.

**Object Model Reference**
[window.]document.getElementById("*elementID*").style.lineBreak

# line-height

Sets the height of the inline box (the box holding one physical line of content). Under normal circumstances, the line-height of the tallest font in a line of text or the tallest object governs the line height for that content line. Mainstream browsers have come a long way since the Version 4 wrinkles that frequently made a visual mess out of mixed font sizes and line heights in the same block-level element.

**CSS Syntax**       line-height: normal | *number* | *length* | *percentage*

**Value**

A value of normal lets the browser calculate line spacing for the entire element, thus producing a computed value that can be inherited by nested elements. A *number* value (greater than zero) acts as a multiplier for the font-size of the current element. Therefore, if a nested element inherits the line-height multiplier from its parent, that multiplier is applied to the current element's font-size setting (the multiplier, not the computed value of the parent, is inherited). A *length* value assigns an actual value to the inline box height. And a *percentage* value is a multiplier applied to the font size of the current element. In this case, the computer value can be inherited by nested elements.

**Initial Value**       normal

**Example**

```
p {line-height: normal}     /* Browser default; actual value is  inheritable */
p {line-height: 1.1}        /* Number value; the number value is inheritable */
p {line-height: 1.1em}      /* Length value; the actual value is inheritable */
p {line-height: 110%}       /* Percentage value; percentage times font size */
                            /* is inheritable /*
```

**Applies To**       All elements.

**Object Model Reference**

[window.]document.getElementById("*elementID*").style.lineHeight

# list-style                                              NN 6   IE 4   CSS 1

Inherited: Yes

This is a shorthand attribute for setting up to three list-style attributes in one assignment statement. Whichever attributes you don't explicitly set with this attribute assume their initial values. These attributes define display characteristics for the markers automatically rendered for list items inside ol and ul elements.

**CSS Syntax**

list-style: *list-style-type* || *list-style-position* || *list-style-image*

**Value**

See the individual attribute entries for list-style-type, list-style-position, and list-style-image for details on acceptable values for each. You may include one, two, or all three values in the list-style attribute setting in any order you wish.

**Initial Value**       None.

**Example**       ul {list-style: square outside none}

**Applies To**       dd, dt, li, ol, and ul elements and any other element assigned the display:list-item style attribute.

**Object Model Reference**

[window.]document.getElementById("*elementID*").style.listStyle

---

## list-style-image

**NN *6* IE *4* CSS *1***

**Inherited: Yes**

Provides the URL for an image that is to be used as the marker for a list item. Because this attribute can be inherited, a setting for an individual list item can override the same attribute setting in its parent.

**CSS Syntax** `list-style-image: none | `*`uri`*

**Value** For *`uri`*, supply any valid full or relative URL (in the CSS format) to an image file with a MIME type that is readable by the browser.

**Initial Value** none

**Example**

```
ul {list-style-image: url(images/folder.gif)}
li.file {list-style-image: url(images/doc.gif)}
```

**Applies To** `dd`, `dt`, `li`, `ol`, and `ul` elements and any other element assigned the `display:list-item` style attribute.

**Object Model Reference**

`[window.]document.getElementById("`*`elementID`*`").style.listStyleImage`

## list-style-position

**NN *6* IE *4* CSS *1***

**Inherited: Yes**

Determines whether the marker is inside or outside (outdented) from the box containing the list item's content. When the `list-style-position` is set to `inside` and the content is text, the marker appears to be part of the text block. In this case, the alignment (indent) of the list item is the same as normal, but without the outdented marker. Figure 11-6 demonstrates the effects of both settings on wrapped list item text.

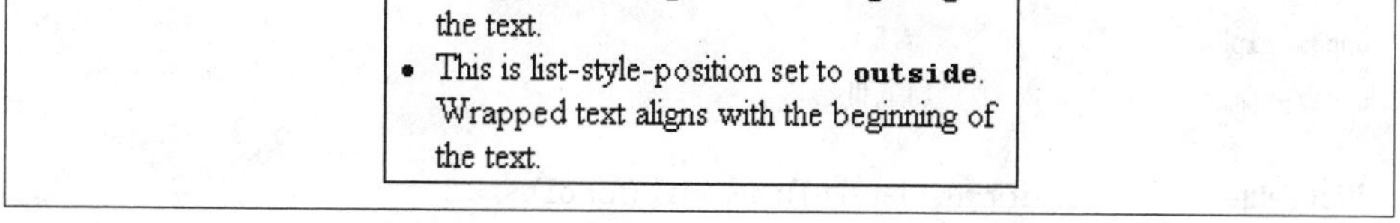


*Figure 11-6. Results of list-style-position settings*

**CSS Syntax** `list-style-position: inside | outside`

| | |
|---|---|
| **Value** | Any of the constant values: inside | outside. |
| **Initial Value** | outside |
| **Example** | ul {list-style-position: inside} |
| **Applies To** | dd, dt, li, ol, and ul elements and any other element assigned the display:list-item style attribute. |

**Object Model Reference**

[window.]document.getElementById("*elementID*").style.listStylePosition

# list-style-type
**NN 4    IE 4    CSS 1**

**Inherited: Yes**

Sets the kind of item marker to be displayed with each item. This attribute applies only if list-style-image is none (or not specified). The constant values available for this attribute are divided into two categories. One set is used with ul elements to present a filled disc, an empty circle, or a filled square (except on Version 4 browsers for the Macintosh); the other set is for ol elements, which have list items that can be marked in sequences of Arabic numerals, Roman numerals (uppercase or lowercase), or letters of the alphabet (uppercase or lowercase), and some other character sequences of other languages if the browser and operating system supports those languages.

**CSS Syntax**        list-style-type: *listStyleType*

**Value**

One constant value that is relevant to the type of list container. For ul: circle | disc | square. For ol: decimal | decimal-leading-zero | lower-roman | upper-roman | lower-greek | lower-alpha | lower-latin | upper-alpha | upper-latin | hebrew | armenian | georgian | cjk-ideographic | hiragana | katakana | hiragana-iroha | katakana-iroha. Commonly-supported ol element sequences are treated as shown in the following table.

| Type | Example |
|---|---|
| decimal | 1, 2, 3, … |
| decimal-leading-zero | 01, 02, 03, … |
| lower-alpha | a, b, c, … |
| lower-greek | α, β, γ, … |
| lower-roman | i, ii, iii, … |
| upper-alpha | A, B, C, … |
| upper-roman | I, II, III, … |

**Initial Value**        disc (for first level ul); decimal (for ol).

**Example**

ul {list-style-type: circle}
li {list-style-type: upper-roman}

| **Applies To** | dd, dt, li, ol, and ul elements and any other element assigned the display:list-item style attribute. |

**Object Model Reference**

[window.]document.getElementById("*elementID*").style.listStyleType

# margin

Inherited: No

This is a shortcut attribute that can set the margin widths of up to four edges of an element with one statement. A margin is space that extends beyond the border of an element to provide extra empty space between adjacent or nested elements, especially those that have border attributes set. You may supply one to four space-delimited margin values. The number of values determines which sides receive the assigned margins.

| **CSS Syntax** | margin: *marginThickness* | auto {1,4} |

**Value**

This attribute accepts one, two, three, or four values, depending on how many and which margins you want to set. Values for *marginThickness* can be *lengths*, percentages of the next outermost element size, or the auto constant. Value quantities and positions are interpreted as follows.

| Number of values | Effect |
| --- | --- |
| 1 | All four margin edges set to value |
| 2 | Top and bottom margins set to the first value, right and left margins set to the second value |
| 3 | Top margin set to first value, right and left margins set to second value, bottom margin set to third value |
| 4 | Top, right, bottom, and left margin set, respectively |

| **Initial Value** | 0 |
| **Example** | p.highlight {margin: 10px 20px} |
| **Applies To** | All elements. |

**Object Model Reference**

[window.]document.getElementById("*elementID*").style.margin

# margin-bottom, margin-left, margin-right, margin-top

Inherited: No

All four attributes set the width of a single margin edge of an element. A margin is space that extends beyond the element's border and is not calculated as part of the element's width or height.

## CSS Syntax

```
margin-bottom: marginThickness | auto
margin-left: marginThickness | auto
margin-right: marginThickness | auto
margin-top: marginThickness | auto
```

**Value**          Values for *marginThickness* can be *lengths*, percentages of the next outermost element size, or the auto constant.

**Initial Value**   0

**Example**

```
blockquote {margin-left: 20; margin-top: 10}
#narrowCol {margin-left: 30%; margin-right: 30%}
```

**Applies To**      All elements.

## Object Model Reference

```
[window.]document.getElementById("elementID").style.marginBottom
[window.]document.getElementById("elementID").style.marginLeft
[window.]document.getElementById("elementID").style.marginRight
[window.]document.getElementById("elementID").style.marginTop
```

# marker-offset                     NN *n/a*   IE *n/a*   CSS 2

Inherited: No

Controls the space between list item markers (which occupy their own box in the CSS box model) and the box that contains the list item text. Requires that the list item elements be set to a display style marker.

**CSS Syntax**      `marker-offset: length | auto`

**Value**           A length value (see the discussion of length values at the beginning of this chapter), or the auto constant.

**Initial Value**   auto

**Example**         `li:before {display:marker; marker-offset:4em}`

**Applies To**      List elements set to marker display mode (generally with a :before or :after pseudo-class).

# marks                              NN *n/a*   IE *n/a*   CSS 2

Inherited: n/a

This is a page context attribute that sets whether the page should be rendered with crop or registration marks outside of the page content area. This attribute must be set within an @page rule. See the "At-Rules" section earlier in this chapter for details on deploying this type of style rule.

**CSS Syntax**      `marks: markType | none`

| Value | Available *markType* values are the following constant values: crop | cross. A crop mark shows where pages should be trimmed; a cross mark is used for alignment and registration. |
| --- | --- |
| **Initial Value** | none |
| **Example** | @page {marks: crop} |
| **Applies To** | Page context. |

**Object Model Reference**

[window.]document.getElementById("*elementID*").style.marks

# max-height, min-height

NN 6    IE *(see text)*    CSS 2

Inherited: No

These attributes let you establish a maximum and/or minimum height for an element. You can bracket the permissible height of an element regardless of the height caused by the natural flow of the content.

When you set the max-height attribute of an element that has content that may extend beyond that maximum, you should also set the overflow style attribute to hidden so that excess content is cropped. Failure to do so causes the overflowing content to bleed into the succeeding elements' content. Netscape 6 supports both attributes for block-level and positioned elements.

Internet Explorer 6 for Windows supports only the min-height attribute, and is limited to td, th, and tr elements inside a table with its table-layout style attribute is set to fixed. This conflicts with the CSS2 specification, which explicitly excludes table-related elements from being influenced by these attributes. As such, min-height settings you make for td, th, or tr elements in IE 6 do not affect Netscape 6. IE 5 for Macintosh supports neither attribute.

**CSS Syntax**

max-height: *length* | *percentage* | none
min-height: *length* | *percentage* | none

| Value | See the discussion of length values at the beginning of the chapter. The value may also be a percentage that is calculated relative to the element's container. A value of none removes all constraints, allowing the content to flow naturally. |
| --- | --- |
| **Initial Value** | none (max-width); none (min-width). |
| **Applies To** | See text. |

**Object Model Reference**

[window.]document.getElementById("*elementID*").style.minHeight
[window.]document.getElementById("*elementID*").style.maxHeight

## max-width, min-width

These attributes let you establish a minimum and/or maximum width for an element. You can bracket the permissible width of an element regardless of the width caused by the natural flow of the content within a parent container.

### CSS Syntax

```
max-width: length | percentage | none
min-width: length | percentage | none
```

**Value**            See the discussion of length values at the beginning of the chapter. The value may also be a percentage that is calculated relative to the element's container. A value of none removes all constraints, allowing the content to flow naturally.

**Initial Value**    none (max-width); none (min-width).

**Applies To**       All elements.

### Object Model Reference

```
[window.]document.getElementById("elementID").style.minWidth
[window.]document.getElementById("elementID").style.maxWidth
```

## -moz-border-radius

This is a shortcut attribute that lets you set the radius of one or more border corners. The number of values determines which sides receive the assigned colors. Note that this value arrangement differs from the preliminary CSS3 border-radius attribute value setup.

**CSS Syntax**       `-moz-border-radius: radius {1,4}`

**Value**

A border corner radius can be defined by a length measure, signifying the length of the radius of the imaginary circle from which the rounded corner comes. The larger the value, the more rounded the corner becomes. For screen display, the pixel length unit is most appropriate. You may also use a percentage value in the range between 0% (no rounding) to 50% (maximum rounding). The rounded border does not crop content of the element.

This attribute accepts one, two, three, or four *radius* values, depending on how many and which corners you want to make round. Value quantities and positions are interpreted as shown in the following table.

| Number of values | Effect |
|---|---|
| 1 | All four corners set to same value |
| 2 | Top left and bottom right corners set to the first value, top right and bottom left corners set to the second value |

| Number of values | Effect |
|---|---|
| 3 | Top left corner set to first value, top right and bottom left corners set to second value, bottom right corner set to third value |
| 4 | Top left, top right, bottom right, and bottom left corners set, respectively |

**Initial Value**      0

**Example**

```
div.hotbox {-moz-border-radius:20px}
div.circle {-moz-border-radius:50%}
```

**Applies To**      All elements.

# -moz-border-radius-bottomleft, -moz-border-radius-bottomright, -moz-border-radius-topleft, -moz-border-radius-topright

NN *6*   IE *n/a*   CSS *n/a*

Inherited: No

Controls the radius of one border corner. Note that the value arrangement differs from the preliminary CSS3 corner-specific border-radius attribute value setup.

**CSS Syntax**

```
-moz-border-radius-bottomleft: radius
-moz-border-radius-bottomright: radius
-moz-border-radius-topleft: radius
-moz-border-radius-topright: radius
```

**Value**      See -moz-border-radius.

**Initial Value**      0

**Example**

```
div.bizarro {-moz-border-radius-topright:10%; -moz-border-radius-bottomright:10% }
```

**Applies To**      All elements.

# -moz-opacity

NN *6*   IE *n/a*   CSS *n/a*

Inherited: No

Controls the level of opacity of the element. The lower the value, the more transparent the element becomes. This is the proprietary Mozilla version of the proprietary Microsoft opaque filter.

**CSS Syntax**      -moz-opacity: *alphaValue*

## Value

The level of opacity is determined by a floating-point number between 0.0 and 1.0. A completely opaque rendering occurs at a value of 1.0. You may also use percentage values between 0% and 100%, but the proposed CSS3 recommendation for the opacity attribute calls for numbers only.

| | |
|---|---|
| **Initial Value** | 1 |
| **Example** | div#watermark {-moz-opacity:0.4} |
| **Applies To** | All elements. |

### Object Model Reference

[window.]document.getElementById("*elementID*").style.MozOpacity

# orphans

NN 6    IE 5(Mac)    CSS 2
Inherited: Yes

Sets the minimum number of lines of a paragraph that must be visible at the bottom of a page where a page break occurs. See the widows attribute for lines to be displayed at the top of a page after a page break.

| | |
|---|---|
| **CSS Syntax** | orphans: *lineCount* |
| **Value** | An integer of the number of lines. |
| **Initial Value** | 2 |
| **Applies To** | Block-level elements. |

### Object Model Reference

[window.]document.getElementById("*elementID*").style.orphans

# outline

NN *n/a*    IE 5(Mac)    CSS 2
Inherited: No

This is a shorthand attribute for setting the width, style, and/or color of all four edges of an outline around an element in one assignment statement. Attributes that you don't explicitly set with this attribute assume their initial values.

An outline differs from a border in two primary ways. First, an outline does not occupy space in the CSS box model. Rather, the outline simply hovers atop the element, drawn just beyond the border rectangle. Second, CSS does not restrict an outline to be rectangular, allowing an outline to follow the irregular outline of an unjustified paragraph, for example. So far, however, the implementation in IE 5 for the Macintosh draws only rectangular outlines.

| | |
|---|---|
| **CSS Syntax** | outline: *border-color* \|\| *border-style* \|\| *outline-width* |
| **Value** | See the respective attributes in the following sections. |
| **Initial Value** | None. |

| | | |
|---|---|---|

**Example**          blockquote {outline: darkred ridge 5px}

**Applies To**       All elements.

**Object Model Reference**
[window.]document.getElementById("*elementID*").style.outline

# outline-color

NN *n/a*    IE *5(Mac)*    CSS *2*

Inherited: No

Controls the color of an outline around an element.

**CSS Syntax**      outline-color: *color*

**Value**

A CSS color value. One value controls all sides of the outline. The CSS specification also calls for a constant called invert, which performs an algorithmic inversion of the background color, but this value is not supported in IE 5 Mac.

**Initial Value**      In IE 5 for Macintosh, black. The CSS 2 specification suggests invert as a default.

**Example**

```
h2 {outline-color: salmon}
div {outline-color: rgb(0,0,255)}
```

**Applies To**       All elements.

**Object Model Reference**
[window.]document.getElementById("*elementID*").style.outlineColor

# outline-style

NN *n/a*    IE *5(Mac)*    CSS *2*

Inherited: No

Controls the style of an outline around an element. These are the same edge designs as border styles.

**CSS Syntax**      outline-style: *borderStyle*

**Value**          Style values are constants that are associated with specific ways of rendering border lines. See border-style for a list and illustration. One value controls all sides of the outline.

**Initial Value**      none

**Example**

```
h2 {outline-style: solid}
div {outline-style: groove}
```

**Applies To**       All elements.

**Object Model Reference**
[window.]document.getElementById("*elementID*").style.outlineStyle

# outline-width

NN *n/a*   IE *5(Mac)*   CSS 2

Inherited: No

Controls the thickness of an outline around an element. To prevent surrounding content from rendering under the outline, you should consider adding a margin around the element.

**CSS Syntax**       outline-width:  thin | medium | thick | *length*

**Value**

Three constants—thin | medium | thick—allow the browser to define exactly how many pixels are used to show the outline. For more precision, you can also assign a length value (see the discussion of length values at the beginning of this chapter). One value controls all sides of the outline.

**Initial Value**       medium

**Example**

```
h1 {outline-style: ridge; outline-width: 5px}
div {outline-style: solid; outline-width: 2px}
```

**Applies To**       All elements.

**Object Model Reference**

[window.]document.getElementById("*elementID*").style.outlineWidth

# overflow

NN *6*   IE *4*   CSS 2

Inherited: No

Defines how the element treats content with rendered dimensions that exceed the specified height and/or width of the container. Except for some types of content that demand a fixed width (a pre element, for instance), the default behavior of an element is to respect the width attribute setting and handle the issue of overflow in the height of the element. Assigning the overflow property to the body element in an attempt to control the display of scroll bars is risky business for cross-browser compatibility. Test your overflow code thoroughly on IE for Windows (in backward- and standards-compatible modes), IE for Macintosh, and Netscape 6.

A setting of visible causes the containing block to expand to allow the full width (if fixed) and height of the content to be displayed. If borders, margins, and padding are set for the element, they are preserved around the expanded content block. If the element has height and width specified, as well as a background image or color, and if the content extends beyond the specified size, the results vary with browser family. IE for Windows expands the height of the background to accommodate the content, pushing succeeding content downward to accommodate the overflowing content. IE for Macintosh and Netscape 6 constrain the background rectangle to the specified size, but the content bleeds beyond the rectangle, and overlaps content that comes after the overflowing element. Because this is the default value for the overflow style property, it is best to specify some other overflow value (or clipping rectangle for a positioned element) whenever you restrict the size of an element.

A setting of hidden forces the block to observe its height and width settings, potentially causing the content to be clipped by the size of the block. Borders and padding are preserved, but margins may be lost along the edges that clip the content. No scrollbars appear with this value.

A setting of scroll usually generates a set of horizontal and vertical scrollbars inside the rectangle of the content block, whether they're needed or not. The bars become active only if the content actually requires scrolling in any direction.

A setting of auto should generate scroll bars only if the content in the block requires it. In practice, browsers tend to add only a vertical scrollbar when the content is text that can adjust to the specified width of its container.

**CSS Syntax**  overflow: *overFlowType*

**Value**  Any of the following constants: auto | hidden | scroll | visible.

**Initial Value**  visible

**Example**

```
div.aside {position: absolute; top: 200px; left: 10px; height: 100px;
width: 150px; overflow: scroll}
```

**Applies To**  Block-level, replaced, and positioned elements.

**Object Model Reference**

[window.]document.getElementById("*elementID*").style.overflow

# overflow-x, overflow-y

NN *n/a*   IE *5(Win)*   CSS *n/a*

Inherited: No

Defines how the element treats content with rendered dimensions that exceed the specified width (x) or height (y) of the container. The operation of this IE/Windows attribute is the same as the regular overflow attribute, but each one operates along a single axis. This is particularly helpful if you want to have only a vertical or only a horizontal scrollbar appear with an element. See the overflow attribute discussion.

**CSS Syntax**

overflow-x: *overFlowType*
overflow-y: *overFlowType*

**Value**  Any of the following constants: auto | hidden | scroll | visible.

**Initial Value**  visible

**Example**  body {overflow-x:hidden; overflow-y: scroll}

**Applies To**  Block-level, replaced, and positioned elements.

**Object Model Reference**

[window.]document.getElementById("*elementID*").style.overflowX
[window.]document.getElementById("*elementID*").style.overflowY

# padding

This is a shortcut attribute that can set the padding widths of up to four edges of an element with one statement. Padding is space that extends around the content box of an element up to but not including any border that may be specified for the element. Padding picks up the background image or color of its element. As you add padding to an element, you increase the size of the visible rectangle of the element without affecting the content block size. You may supply one to four space-delimited padding values. The number of values determines which sides receive the assigned padding.

**CSS Syntax**       padding: *paddingThickness* {1,4}

**Value**

This attribute accepts one, two, three, or four values, depending on how many and which sides you want to assign padding to. Values for *paddingThickness* can be *lengths* or percentages of the next outermost element size. Value quantities and positions are interpreted as follows.

| Number of values | Effect |
|---|---|
| 1 | All four padding edges set to value |
| 2 | Top and bottom padding set to the first value, right and left padding set to the second value |
| 3 | Top padding set to first value, right and left padding set to second value, bottom padding set to third value |
| 4 | Top, right, bottom, and left padding set, respectively |

**Initial Value**    0; IE for Windows specifies a default value of 1 for td and th elements.

**Example**          p.highlight {padding: 10px 20px}

**Applies To**       All elements (IE 5 for Macintosh, IE 5.5 for Windows, and Netscape 6); body, caption, div, iframe, marquee, table, td, textarea, tr, and elements (IE 5 and earlier for Windows).

**Object Model Reference**

[window.]document.getElementById("*elementID*").style.padding

**Notes**

Be aware that Navigator 4 adds its own three-pixel–wide transparent spacing around all four edges of an element. If the element has padding defined for it, the extra spacing is placed outside of the padding. An element's border then appears outside of the extra spacing. This means the background image or color of a Navigator 4 element can't bleed all the way to the borders, and you must use the otherwise undocumented layer-background-color or layer-background-image style attributes.

# padding-bottom, padding-left, padding-right, padding-top

All four attributes set the padding width of a single side of an element. Padding is space that extends around the content box of an element up to but not including any border that may be specified for the element. Padding picks up the background image or color of its element. As you add padding to an element, you increase the size of the visible rectangle of the element without affecting the content block size.

### CSS Syntax

```
padding-bottom: paddingThickness
padding-left: paddingThickness
padding-right: paddingThickness
padding-top: paddingThickness
```

**Value**      Values for *paddingThickness* can be *lengths* or percentages of the next outermost container size.

**Initial Value**      0; IE for Windows specifies a default value of 1 for td and th elements.

### Example

```
blockquote {padding-left: 20; padding-top: 10}
#narrowCol {padding-left: 30%; padding-right: 30%}
```

**Applies To**      All elements (IE 5 for Macintosh, IE 5.5 for Windows, and Netscape 6); body, caption, div, iframe, marquee, table, td, textarea, tr, and elements (IE 5 and earlier for Windows).

### Object Model Reference

```
[window.]document.getElementById("elementID").style.paddingBottom
[window.]document.getElementById("elementID").style.paddingLeft
[window.]document.getElementById("elementID").style.paddingRight
[window.]document.getElementById("elementID").style.paddingTop
```

### Notes

Be aware that Navigator 4 adds its own three-pixel-wide transparent spacing around all four edges of an element. If the element has padding defined for it, the extra spacing is placed outside of the padding. An element's border then appears outside of the extra spacing. This means the background image or color of a Navigator element can't run all the way to the borders, and you must use the otherwise undocumented layer-background-color or layer-background-image style attributes.

# page

Lets you connect a block-level element to an @page rule through an identifier assigned to the rule. The implementation of @page rules is still sketchy, but the page attribute, whose value is the desired @page rule's identifier, is in place for later adoption.

| | |
|---|---|
| **CSS Syntax** | page: *pageRuleIdentifier* \| auto |
| **Value** | The *pageRuleIdentifier* value is the name given to an @page rule in the same document. |
| **Initial Value** | auto |
| **Example** | table#results {page: printTable} |
| **Applies To** | Block-level elements. |

**Object Model Reference**

[window.]document.getElementById("*elementID*").style.page

# page-break-after, page-break-before NN 7 IE 4 CSS 2

Inherited: No

Defines how content should treat a page break around an element when the document is sent to a printer. Page breaks are not rendered in the visual browser as they may be in word processing programs; on screen, long content flows in one continuous scroll.

Proper handling of pages for printers relies on the CSS2 concept of the *page box*, which is a rectangular region that ultimately reaches a printed page. Page break style attributes help the browser control the precise content of each page box. Without any assistance (or with the auto setting), the browser divides pages for printing much as it has in the past by doing a best-fit for the content to fill up as much of each page as there is space for it.

To force a page break above an element, associate a page-break-before:always style setting with the element. Similarly, to force a break after an element, use page-break-after:always. For example, if you want a special class of br elements to break after them, you could set up a class selector style rule as follows:

```
<style type="text/css">
br.pageEnd {display:block; page-break-after: always}
</style>
```

Then, whenever you want to force a page break in the document, include the following tag:

```
<br class="pageEnd">
```

Attribute settings for left and right assume that the browser is equipped to detect left-facing from right-facing pages for double-sided printing (as specified in CSS2). Because you are likely to set different margins for each side of the gutter, indicating how pages break to start a new section requires forcing sufficient page breaks to plant new sections on the desired page. For example, if you want each h1 element to begin on a right-facing page, you would set a page break style for it as follows:

```
h1 {page-break-before: right}
```

This attribute forces the browser to at least one and at most two page breaks before the h1 element to make it starts on a right-facing page. When the browser generates a second page break for the left or right value, it means that the browser generates a blank page box for the second page break.

Implementation of these attributes is limited. Although working to some degree in IE 4, you should target IE 5 or later. Even so, the only supported settings for recent IE versions and Netscape 7 are always and auto (or you can assign an empty string via script to operate the same as the CSS avoid value).

### CSS Syntax

```
page-break-after: breakType
page-break-before: breakType
```

### Value

Internet Explorer 4 recognizes four constant values: always | auto | left | right (but treats left and right the same as always). CSS2 adds avoid, which urges the browser to avoid breaking the page in that element if at all possible.

**Initial Value**    auto

**Example**    div.titlePage {page-break-before: always; page-break-after: always}

**Applies To**    Block-level elements.

### Object Model Reference

```
[window.]document.getElementById("elementID").style.pageBreakAfter
[window.]document.getElementById("elementID").style.pageBreakBefore
```

## page-break-inside                                   NN *n/a*   IE *n/a*   CSS *2*

Inherited: Yes

Defines whether a printed page break is allowed within an element. Especially useful to define a container of multiple block elements that you want to keep printed on the same page.

**CSS Syntax**    page-break-inside: *breakType*

**Value**    One of two constant values: avoid | auto.

**Initial Value**    auto

**Example**    div.together {page-break-inside: avoid}

**Applies To**    Block-level elements.

## pause                                   NN *n/a*   IE *n/a*   CSS *2*

Inherited: No

For aural style sheets, this is a shorthand attribute for setting both pause-after and pause-before attributes in one statement. You may supply one or two values for this attribute.

**CSS Syntax**    pause: *time* | *percentage* {1,2}

### Value

This attribute accepts one or two values, depending on the values you want to assign to the pause-before and pause-after settings. A single value of the pause attribute is applied to both pause-before and pause-after. When two values are supplied, the first is assigned to pause-before; the second is assigned to pause-after.

Values for *time* are floating-point numbers followed by either the ms (milliseconds) or s (seconds) unit identifier. These settings are therefore absolute durations for pauses. Values for *percentage* are inversely proportional to the words-per-minute values of the speech-rate attribute setting. Because the speech-rate controls how long it takes for a single word (on average), a pause setting of 100% means that a pause has the same duration as a single word; a setting of 50% would be a pause of one-half the duration of speaking a single word.

| | |
|---|---|
| **Initial Value** | Depends on the browser. |
| **Applies To** | All elements. |

# pause-after, pause-before

NN n/a   IE n/a   CSS 2<br>Inherited: No

For aural style sheets, these set the duration of a pause after or before the current element. You can assign both attributes to the same element to designate pauses before and after the element is spoken.

## CSS Syntax

pause-after: *time* | *percentage*
pause-before: *time* | *percentage*

## Value

Values for *time* are floating-point numbers followed by either the ms (milliseconds) or s (seconds) unit identifier. These settings are therefore absolute durations for pauses. Values for *percentage* are inversely proportional to the words-per-minute values of the speech-rate attribute setting. Because the speech-rate controls how long it takes to speak a single word (on average), a pause setting of 100% means that a pause has the same duration as a single word; a setting of 50% would be a pause of one-half the duration of speaking a single word.

| | |
|---|---|
| **Initial Value** | Depends on the browser. |
| **Applies To** | All elements. |

# pitch

NN n/a   IE n/a   CSS 2<br>Inherited: Yes

For aural style sheets, this sets the average pitch frequency of the voice used for text-to-speech output.

| | |
|---|---|
| **CSS Syntax** | pitch: *frequency* | *frequencyConstant* |

## Value

A *frequency* value is any positive floating-point number followed by either the Hz (Hertz) or kHz (kiloHertz) units, as in 500Hz or 5.5kHz. Alternatively, you can use any of the following constant values: x-low | low | medium | high | x-high. As of the CSS2 working draft available for this book, no specific frequency values had yet been assigned to these constants.

| | |
|---|---|
| **Initial Value** | medium |
| **Applies To** | All elements. |

# pitch-range

For aural style sheets, this sets the range over which the average pitch frequency of a text-to-speech voice varies.

| | |
|---|---|
| **CSS Syntax** | `pitch-range:` *number* |
| **Value** | Any positive number or zero. A value of 0 is a monotone voice; a value of 50 should offer a normal range; values above 50 might sound animated. |
| **Initial Value** | 50 |
| **Applies To** | All elements. |

# play-during

For aural style sheets, this sets the sound-mixing properties of a background sound with a text-to-speech rendering of the element's content.

| | |
|---|---|
| **CSS Syntax** | `play-during:` *uri* [`mix` \| `repeat`] \| `auto` \| `none` |

**Value**

The *uri* value is a link to the sound file to be used as background sound (if desired). Optionally, you can specify that the background sound of the parent element's play-during attribute is started and mixed with the current element's background sound. If the length of the background sound is shorter than it takes for the element's text to be spoken, the repeat constant tells the browser to repeat the sound until the spoken text has finished. A value of auto means that the parent element's sound continues to play without interruption. And a value of none means that no background sound (from the current or parent element) is heard for this element.

| | |
|---|---|
| **Initial Value** | auto |
| **Applies To** | All elements. |

# position

Sets whether the element is positionable, and if so, what type of positionable element it is. The two primary types of positionable elements are set with values relative and absolute, with a third type, fixed, applicable to only some browsers. See Chapter 4 for details and examples.

| | |
|---|---|
| **CSS Syntax** | `position:` *positionConstant* |
| **Value** | Browsers and the CSS standard recognize different sets of constant values for this attribute, as shown in this table. |

| Value | IE/Windows | IE/Mac | NN |
|---|---|---|---|
| absolute | 4 | 4 | 4 |
| fixed | n/a | 5 | 6 |

| Value | IE/Windows | IE/Mac | NN |
|---|---|---|---|
| relative | 4 | 4 | 4 |
| static | 4 | 4 | 6 |

The static value is essentially an unpositioned element, one that flows in the normal rendering sequence of the body content. A fixed-position element is positioned relative to the window (viewport), and remains in its specified location even as the content scrolls underneath it.

**Initial Value**     static

**Applies To**     All elements.

**Object Model Reference**
[window.]document.getElementById("*elementID*").style.position

**Notes**

Navigator 4 treats elements that set the CSS syntax–position attribute in the following ways: an absolute-positioned element is turned into the same kind of element as that created as a layer element; a relative-positioned element is turned into the same kind of element as that created as an ilayer element. There are some subtle differences between the actual elements and the simulated version, resulting in more reliable behavior in Navigator 4 when the actual layer and ilayer elements were deployed.

# quotes
NN 6     IE 5(Mac)     CSS 2

Inherited: Yes

Controls the characters to be generated for open and close quote symbols in text. The assumption is that the quote symbols are not part of the content, but are generated by the browser because of contextual clues (such as surrounding a quote with a q element). This attribute must be used with the content attribute, which, with the help of the :before and :after pseudo-classes, determines where the open-quote and end-quote symbols appear:

```
q {quotes:"«" "»" "'" "'"}
q:before {content:open-quote}
q:after {content:close-quote}
```

**CSS Syntax**

quotes: *openString closeString* [*nestedOpenString nestedCloseString*] | none

**Value**     One or two pairs of quoted symbols. The optional second pair defines the symbols used for a nested quote symbol. Entity characters are not permitted.

**Initial Value**     Depends on browser and system language.

**Applies To**     All elements.

**Object Model Reference**
[window.]document.getElementById("*elementID*").style.quotes

**Notes**

Support in browsers isn't as good as indicated above. IE 5 for the Macintosh doesn't genuinely respond to the quotes attribute, but does substitute standard two-level quotes for the content attribute. Netscape 6 and 7 implement only the first level of quotes. Symbol characters outside the ASCII set may not align with the characters you put into the source code with your text editor. Verify the results before deploying this attribute.

# richness

NN *n/a*　　IE *n/a*　　CSS *2*

Inherited: Yes

For aural style sheets, this sets the brightness (stridency) of the voice used in text-to-speech rendering of the element.

**CSS Syntax**　　　richness: *number*

**Value**　　　　　A positive floating-point number to represent how strident the voice sounds. A value of 50 is normal. Lower values produce a softer, mellower voice; higher values produce a louder, more forceful voice.

**Initial Value**　　50

**Applies To**　　　All elements.

# right

NN *6*　　IE *5*　　CSS *2*

Inherited: No

For positionable elements, this defines the position of the right edge of an element box (content plus padding, border, and/or margin) relative to the right edge of the next outermost block content container. When the element is relative-positioned, the offset is based on the right edge of the inline location of where the element would normally appear in the content.

**CSS Syntax**　　　right: *length* | *percentage* | auto

**Value**

See the discussion about length values at the beginning of this chapter. Negative lengths may be allowed in some contexts, but be sure to test the results on all browsers. You may also specify a percentage value, which is calculated based on the width of the next outermost container. Note, however, that the results you get may seem like the inverse of what you expect: a value of 0% means that the right edge is flush against the right edge of the positioning context, whereas a value of 100% could push the element completely out of view to the left. The setting of auto lets the browser determine the right offset of the element box on its naturally flowing offset within the containing box.

**Initial Value**　　　auto

**Applies To**　　　Positioned elements.

**Object Model Reference**

[window.]document.getElementById("*elementID*").style.right

## ruby-align

Controls alignment of content in a ruby element.

| | |
|---|---|
| **CSS Syntax** | ruby-align: *alignType* \| auto |
| **Value** | One of the following constants: auto \| center \| distribute-letter \| distribute-space \| left \| line-edge \| right. For more details on ruby-related styles, visit *http://www.w3.org/TR/css3-ruby*. |
| **Initial Value** | auto |
| **Applies To** | IE limits this style to ruby elements only, but the preliminary CSS3 specification suggests it can apply to any element that contains ruby text (and is thus inheritable in that context). |

**Object Model Reference**
[window.]document.getElementById("*elementID*").style.rubyAlign

## ruby-overhang

Controls text overhang characteristics of content in a ruby element.

| | |
|---|---|
| **CSS Syntax** | ruby-overhang: *alignType* \| auto |
| **Value** | One of the following constants: auto \| none \| whitespace. For more details on ruby-related styles, visit *http://www.w3.org/TR/css3-ruby*. |
| **Initial Value** | auto |
| **Applies To** | ruby elements (or any element that has its display attribute set to ruby-text). |

**Object Model Reference**
[window.]document.getElementById("*elementID*").style.rubyOverhang

## ruby-position

Controls whether nested ruby (rt element) text renders on the same line or above its related ruby base (rb element) text.

| | |
|---|---|
| **CSS Syntax** | ruby-position: *positionType* |

**Value**

IE recognizes one of the following constants, above \| inline, while the preliminary CSS3 specification prefers these constants: after \| before \| inline \| right. For more details on ruby-related styles, visit *http://www.w3.org/TR/css3-ruby*.

| Initial Value | above (IE); before (CSS3). |
|---|---|
| Applies To | ruby elements (or any element that has its display attribute set to ruby-text). |

**Object Model Reference**

[window.]document.getElementById("*elementID*").style.rubyPosition

# scrollbar-3dlight-color, scrollbar-arrow-color, scrollbar-base-color, scrollbar-darkShadow-color, scrollbar-face-color, scrollbar-highlight-color, scrollbar-shadow-color, scrollbar-track-color

**NN** *n/a*    **IE** *5.5(Win)*    **CSS** *n/a*

Inherited: No

Controls the colors for specific components of a scrollbar user interface element associated with scrollable elements. The following table describes which pieces of a scroll bar are controlled by each attribute.

| Attribute | Description |
|---|---|
| scrollbar-3dlight-color | Top and left edges of the scroll slider and arrow button boxes |
| scrollbar-arrow-color | Arrows inside arrow button boxes |
| scrollbar-base-color | Overall hue of the scroll bar |
| scrollbar-darkshadow-color | Right and bottom edges of the scroll slider and arrow button boxes |
| scrollbar-face-color | Forward flat surfaces (e.g., front-facing panel of slider) and alternating pixels of the track |
| scrollbar-highlight-color | Normally white pixels that create 3-D effects, plus alternating pixels of the track |
| scrollbar-shadow-color | Slighlty thicker edges controlled by scrollbar-darkshadow-color |
| scrollbar-track-color | Entire track, as solid version of specified color |

You can experiment with combinations of multiple scroll bar pieces and colors.

**CSS Syntax**

```
scrollbar-3dlight-color: color
scrollbar-arrow-color: color
scrollbar-base-color: color
scrollbar-darkshadow-color: color
scrollbar-face-color: color
scrollbar-highlight-color: color
scrollbar-shadow-color: color
scrollbar-track-color: color
```

| Value | CSS color values. |
|---|---|
| Initial Value | Varies with user Display control panel settings. |
| Example | textarea {scrollbar-face-color: lightyellow} |

**Applies To**

applet, bdo, body, custom, div, embed, object, and textarea elements.

**Object Model Reference**

```
[window.]document.getElementById("elementID").style.scrollbar3dLightColor
[window.]document.getElementById("elementID").style.scrollbarArrowColor
[window.]document.getElementById("elementID").style.scrollbarBaseColor
[window.]document.getElementById("elementID").style.scrollbarDarkShadowColor
[window.]document.getElementById("elementID").style.scrollbarFaceColor
[window.]document.getElementById("elementID").style.scrollbarHighlightColor
[window.]document.getElementById("elementID").style.scrollbarShadowColor
[window.]document.getElementById("elementID").style.scrollbarTrackColor
```

# size

NN *n/a*    IE *n/a*    CSS 2

Inherited: n/a

Sets the size and/or orientation of a page box. Intended primarily for printed page formatting, the settings may not affect how content is cropped or oriented on the video screen. This attribute is set within an @page declaration.

**CSS Syntax**       size: [*length* {1,2}] auto | portrait | landscape

**Value**

If you specify one or two *length* values, the page box becomes absolute regardless of the paper sheet size; without specific *length* values, the page box is sized relative to the selected paper sheet size. If you supply only one length value, it is applied to both the width and height of the page box; if there are two values, the first controls the page box width and the second controls the page box height. Bear in mind that printers frequently impose a minimum margin around the rendered page box. Even when the size attribute is set to auto, you can add more breathing space around the page box by adding a margin attribute to the @page declaration.

**Initial Value**       auto

**Example**           @page{size: landscape}

**Applies To**         Page context.

# speak

NN *n/a*    IE *n/a*    CSS 2

Inherited: Yes

For aural style sheets, this specifies whether a browser equipped for text-to-speech should speak the element's content, and if so, whether the speech should be as words or spelled out character-by-character.

**CSS Syntax**       speak: *speechType*

**Value**

Three possible constant values: none | normal | spell-out. A value of none means that speech is turned off. The browser does not delay over the duration of the speech and any specified pauses (see the volume:silent attribute value). A value of normal turns on speech and reads the text as words. A value of spell-out turns on speech and reads the content letter-by-letter (certainly applicable to abbr and acronym elements).

| | |
|---|---|
| **Initial Value** | normal |
| **Applies To** | All elements. |

## speak-header

For text-to-speech-capable browsers, this specifies whether the browser calls out the name of a table cell's header prior to the cell's value every time that value is read aloud or just one time for all adjacently read cells that share the same header (e.g., navigating downward through a table column).

| | |
|---|---|
| **CSS Syntax** | speak-header: *headerFrequency* |
| **Value** | Two possible constant values: once | always. |
| **Initial Value** | once |
| **Applies To** | th elements. |

## speak-numeral

For aural style sheets, this sets whether numbers are to be read as individual numerals ("one four two") or as full numbers (e.g., "One hundred forty-two"). The language used for the spoken numbers is set with the element's lang attribute.

| | |
|---|---|
| **CSS Syntax** | speak-numeral: *numeralType* |
| **Value** | Two possible constant values: digits | continuous. |
| **Initial Value** | continuous |
| **Applies To** | All elements. |

## speak-punctuation

For aural style sheets, this sets whether punctuation symbols should be read aloud ("period") or interpreted as the language's natural pauses for the various symbols.

| | |
|---|---|
| **CSS Syntax** | speak-punctuation: *punctuationType* |

**Value**

Two possible constant values: code | none. A value of code means that a symbol name is spoken when the symbol is encountered in element text.

| | |
|---|---|
| **Initial Value** | none |
| **Applies To** | All elements. |

# speech-rate

For aural style sheets, this sets the number of words per minute of the text-to-speech output.

**CSS Syntax**       speech-rate: *wordsPerSecond* | *speedConstant*

**Value**

A *wordsPerSecond* value is any positive floating-point number with no unit appended. Alternatively, you can use any of the following constant values.

| Value | Meaning |
|---|---|
| x-slow | 80 words per minute |
| slow | 120 words per minute |
| medium | 180–200 words per minute |
| fast | 300 words per minute |
| x-fast | 500 words per minute |
| slower | Current rate minus 40 words per minute |
| faster | Current rate plus 40 words per minute |

| | |
|---|---|
| **Initial Value** | medium |
| **Applies To** | All elements. |

# stress

For aural style sheets, this sets the amount of stress (inflection) in the spoken voice.

| | |
|---|---|
| **CSS Syntax** | stress: *stressLevel* |
| **Value** | A *stressLevel* value is any positive floating-point number with no unit appended. A value of 50 is normal. |
| **Initial Value** | 50 |
| **Applies To** | All elements. |

# table-layout

NN *n/a*   IE *5(Win)*   CSS *2*
Inherited: No

Determines whether the browser uses computed heights and widths of the entire table's data to begin rendering the table or relies on the table element's size attributes and uses the first row's cell widths to begin rendering table content. When the attribute is set to auto, the browser must load all of the table cells and their content before the first row of data can be rendered, causing a brief (but perhaps imperceptible) delay in drawing the table. Setting the value to fixed allows table rendering to begin sooner, which is helpful for large tables. If content in succeeding rows is wider than the fixed column size, the content is usually clipped unless you set the overflow style attribute to visible (but that will likely make a visual jumble in adjacent cells).

**CSS Syntax**      table-layout: *layoutType*

**Value**           Two possible constant values: auto | fixed.

**Initial Value**   auto

**Applies To**      table elements.

# text-align

NN *4*   IE *4*   CSS *1*
Inherited: Yes

Determines the horizontal alignment of text within an element. This attribute is inherited, so it can be set for a container to impact all nested elements, such as a p element within a div element. Values of center, left, and right are supported across the board. The value of justify is not a CSS requirement; its support in Version 4 browsers is spotty (in which case it may be treated as left). But it works in IE 5 or later and Netscape 6.

**CSS Syntax**      text-align: *alignment*

**Value**           One of the four constants: center | justify | left | right.

**Initial Value**   Depends on browser language.

**Example**

```
p.rightHand {text-align: right}
blockquote {text-align: justify}
```

**Applies To**      Block-level elements, but right-alignment also works in text-type input and textarea elements in IE 5 and later for Windows and Netscape 6.

**Object Model Reference**

```
[window.]document.getElementById("elementID").style.textAlign
```

CSS Reference

# text-align-last

**NN** *n/a*    **IE** *5.5(Win)*    **CSS** *n/a*

**Inherited: Yes**

Controls the horizontal alignment of the last line of text within an element's box.

| | |
|---|---|
| **CSS Syntax** | text-align-last: *alignment* |
| **Value** | One of the following constants: auto | center | justify | left | right. The value of auto picks up the inherited text-align attribute. |
| **Initial Value** | auto |
| **Example** | blockquote {text-align-last: center} |
| **Applies To** | Block-level elements. |

**Object Model Reference**

[window.]document.getElementById("*elementID*").style.textAlignLast

# text-autospace

**NN** *n/a*    **IE** *5(Win)*    **CSS** *n/a*

**Inherited: No**

Controls the spacing between ideographic (typically Asian languages) and nonideographic characters.

| | |
|---|---|
| **CSS Syntax** | text-autospace: *spacingType* |
| **Value** | One of the following constants: ideograph-alpha | ideograph-numeric | ideograph-parenthesis | ideograph-space | none. |
| **Initial Value** | none |
| **Example** | div {text-autospace: ideograph-numeric} |
| **Applies To** | All elements. |

**Object Model Reference**

[window.]document.getElementById("*elementID*").style.textAutospace

# text-decoration

**NN** *4*    **IE** *4*    **CSS** *1*

**Inherited: No**

Specifies additions to the text content of the element in the form of underlines, strikethroughs, overlines, and (in Navigator and CSS) blinking. You may specify more than one decoration style by supplying values in a space-delimited list. Thankfully, mainstream browsers ignore the blink setting. Navigator 4 does not recognize the overline decoration.

Text decoration has an unusual parent-child relationship. Values are not inherited, but the effect of a decoration carries over to nested items. Therefore, unless otherwise overridden, an underlined p element underlines a nested span element within, for example.

| | |
|---|---|
| **CSS Syntax** | text-decoration: *decorationStyle* \| none |
| **Value** | In addition to none, any of the following four constants: blink \| line-through \| overline \| underline, but browsers generally ignore blink. |
| **Initial Value** | none |
| **Example** | div.highlight {text-decoration: underline} |
| **Applies To** | All elements. |

**Object Model Reference**

[window.]document.getElementById("*elementID*").style.textDecoration
[window.]document.getElementById("*elementID*").style.textDecorationBlink
[window.]document.getElementById("*elementID*").style.textDecorationLineThrough
[window.]document.getElementById("*elementID*").style.textDecorationNone
[window.]document.getElementById("*elementID*").style.textDecorationOverLine
[window.]document.getElementById("*elementID*").style.textDecorationUnderline

# text-indent

**NN 4   IE 4   CSS 1**

**Inherited: Yes**

Sets the size of indenting of the first line of a block of inline text (such as a p element). Only the first line is affected by this setting. A negative value can be used to outdent the first line, but be sure the text does not run beyond the left edge of the browser window or frame.

| | |
|---|---|
| **CSS Syntax** | text-indent: *length* \| *percentage* |

**Value**

See the discussion about length values at the beginning of this chapter. Negative lengths may be allowed in some contexts, but be sure to test the results on all browsers. You may also specify a percentage value, which is calculated based on the width of the next outermost container.

**Initial Value**      0

**Example**

body {text-indent: 2em}
p.firstGraphs {text-indent: 0}

| | |
|---|---|
| **Applies To** | Block-level elements. |

**Object Model Reference**

[window.]document.getElementById("*elementID*").style.textIndent

| | |
|---|---|
| **Notes** | Internet Explorer 4 for the Macintosh does not respond to the text-indent attribute properly. |

CSS Reference

# text-justify

NN *n/a*   IE *5*   CSS *n/a*
Inherited: Yes

Controls detailed character distribution techniques for any block-level element that has its text-align CSS attribute set to justify. This attribute is designed primarily for Asian or other non-Latin languages.

**CSS Syntax**      text-justify: *justificationType*

**Value**

One of the constants shown in the following table.

| Value | Meaning |
| --- | --- |
| auto | Lets browser choose best type |
| distribute | Similar to newspaper but optimized for Asian languages |
| distribute-all-lines | Justifies lines, including the last line, leading to potentially very wide word spacing |
| distribute-center-last | Justifies lines but centers the last line (not implemented) |
| inter-cluster | Justifies lines lacking word spacing |
| inter-ideograph | Justifies lines consisting of ideographs |
| inter-word | Justifies lines by distributing padded space between words (common for Latin languages) |
| kashida | Justify Arabic script through elongated strokes (IE 5.5 or later required) |
| newspaper | Justify lines by distributing padded space between words and between characters |

**Initial Value**      0

**Example**      div#col1 {text-align:justify; text-justify:newspaper}

**Applies To**      Block-level elements.

**Object Model Reference**
[window.]document.getElementById("*elementID*").style.textJustify

# text-kashida-space

NN *n/a*   IE *5.5(Win)*   CSS *n/a*
Inherited: Yes

For Arabic text in a block-level element with text alignment style set to justify, controls the ratio of kashida expansion to white space expansion.

**CSS Syntax**      text-kashida-space: *length* | *percentage*

**Value**      See the discussion about length values at the beginning of this chapter. You may also specify a percentage value, which is calculated based on the width of the next outermost container.

**Initial Value**      0%

**Example**

div#col1 {text-align:justify; text-justify:newspaper; text-kashida-space:5%}

**Applies To**   Block-level elements.

**Object Model Reference**

[window.]document.getElementById("*elementID*").style.textKashidaSpace


# text-overflow

Controls whether text content that overflows a fixed box space should display an ellipsis (…) at the end of the line to indicate more text is available. The element should also have its overflow style attribute set to hidden.

**CSS Syntax**       text-overflow: *overflowType*

**Value**            One of two constants: clip | ellipsis.

**Initial Value**    clip

**Example**          td {overflow:hidden; white-space:nowrap; text-overflow:ellipsis}

**Applies To**       Block-level elements.

**Object Model Reference**

[window.]document.getElementById("*elementID*").style.textOverflow


# text-shadow

Sets shadow effects for the text of the current element. A text element can have more than one shadow, and each shadow can have its own color, vertical offset, horizontal offset, and blur radius. Each shadow exists in its own minilayer, stacked with the first shadow specification at the bottom of the heap. Values for each shadow are space-delimited, and multiple shadow value sets are comma-delimited.

**CSS Syntax**

text-shadow: [*color*] *horizLength vertLength blurRadiusLength*,
    [[*color*] *horizLength vertLength blurRadiusLength*] | none

**Value**

If you omit the *color* attribute value, the shadow uses the element's color property value (which may, itself, be inherited). The *color* attribute can be placed before or after whatever length values are set for a shadow. See the discussion of color values at the beginning of this chapter. Values for *horizLength* and *vertLength* are length values (see the beginning of this chapter), and their sign indicates the direction the shadow offset takes from the element text. For the *horizLength* value, a positive value places the shadow to the right of the element; a negative value to the left. For the *vertLength* value, a positive value places the shadow below the text; a negative value places it above. A blur radius is a length value (see the beginning of this chapter) that specifies the extent of the shadow from the edge of the text characters.

**Initial Value**    none

**Applies To**    All elements.

# text-transform
*NN 4   IE 4   CSS 1*
*Inherited: Yes*

Controls the capitalization of the element's text. When a value other than none is assigned to this attribute, the cases of all letters in the source text are arranged by the style sheet, overriding the case of the source text characters.

**CSS Syntax**    text-transform: *caseType* | none

**Value**

A value of none allows the case of the source text to be rendered as-is. Other available constant values are capitalize | lowercase | uppercase. A value of capitalize sets the first character of every word to uppercase. The values lowercase and uppercase render all characters of the element text in their respective cases.

**Initial Value**    none

**Example**    h2 {text-transform: capitalize}

**Applies To**    All elements.

**Object Model Reference**
[window.]document.getElementById("*elementID*").style.textTransform

# text-underline-position
*NN n/a   IE 5.5(Win)   CSS n/a*
*Inherited: Yes*

Controls whether an underline (i.e., an element with a text-decoration style set to underline) is rendered above or below the text. Applicable primarily to Asian languages rendered in vertical columns.

**CSS Syntax**    text-underline-position: *positionType* | none

**Value**

IE 5.5 recognizes two constant values: above | below. IE 6 adds the values auto and auto-pos (which appear to do the same thing). The default value also changed between versions, from below to auto. In IE 6, the auto value underlines vertical Japanese text "above" (to the right) of the characters.

**Initial Value**    none

**Example**    h2 {text-underline-position: above}

**Applies To**      All elements.

**Object Model Reference**

`[window.]document.getElementById("`*`elementID`*`").style.textUnderlinePosition`

## top                            *NN 4*   **IE 4**   **CSS 2**

Inherited: No

For positioned elements, this defines the position of the top edge of an element box (content plus top padding, border, and/or margin) relative to the top edge of the next outermost block content container.

**CSS Syntax**       top: *length* | *percentage* | auto

**Value**

See the discussion about length values at the beginning of this chapter. Negative lengths may be allowed in some contexts, but be sure to test the results on all browsers. You may also specify a percentage value, which is calculated based on the height of the next outermost container. The setting of auto lets the browser determine the top offset of the element box on its naturally flowing offset within the containing box.

**Initial Value**       auto

**Example**

```
h1 {position:relative; top:2em}
#logo {position:absolute; left:80px; top:30px}
```

**Applies To**      Positioned elements.

**Object Model Reference**

`[window.]document.getElementById("`*`elementID`*`").style.top`

## unicode-bidi                     *NN 6*   **IE 5**   **CSS 2**

Inherited: No

Controls the embedding of bidirectional text (such as a mixture of German and Arabic), in concert with the direction style attribute.

**CSS Syntax**       unicode-bidi: *embeddingType*

**Value**       One of the following constant values: bidi-override | embed | normal.

**Initial Value**       normal

**Example**       div.multiLingual {unicode-bidi:embed}

**Applies To**      All elements.

**Object Model Reference**

`[window.]document.getElementById("`*`elementID`*`").style.unicodeBidi`

# vertical-align

NN *6*   IE *4*   CSS *1*
Inherited: No

There are two sets of values for this attribute, and they affect different characteristics of the inline element to which they are applied. The major point of reference is that an inline element has its own line box to hold its content. Two values, top and bottom, affect how the text is rendered within the line box. The settings bring the text flush with the top or bottom of the box, respectively.

Application of this attribute is not limited to inline spans of text. Images and tables can use this style attribute. All other settings for vertical-align affect how the entire element box is vertically positioned relative to text content of the parent element. The default value, baseline, means that the line box is positioned such that the baselines of both the line box's text (or very bottom of an element such as an img) and the parent text are even. That's how an em element can be its own line box element but still look as though it flows on the same baseline as its containing p element. The rest of the attribute's constant values (and percentage or length) determine where the element's line box is set with respect to the parent line. A positive percentage or length value positions the element the stated distance above the baseline; a negative value positions the element below the baseline. Percentages are calculated with respect to the line height.

**CSS Syntax**        vertical-align: *vertAlignType* | *length* | *percentage*

## Value

Two constant values apply to alignment of text within the element itself: bottom | top.

Six constant values apply to alignment of the element's line box relative to the surrounding text line (of the parent element): baseline | middle | sub | super | text-bottom | text-top. A value of baseline keeps the baseline of the element and parent element line even. A value of middle aligns the vertical midpoint of the element with the baseline plus one-half the x-height of the parent element's font. Values of sub and super shift the element into position for subscript and superscript but do not by themselves create a true subscript or superscript in that no adjustment to the font size is made with this attribute. A value of text-bottom aligns the bottom of the element with the bottom of the font line of the parent element text; a value of text-top does the same with the tops of the element and parent.

**Initial Value**        baseline

**Example**            span.sup {vertical-align: super; text-size: smaller}

**Applies To**          Inline elements only.

## Object Model Reference
[window.]document.getElementById("*elementID*").style.verticalAlign

# visibility

NN *4*   IE *4*   CSS *2*
Inherited: Yes

Controls whether the element is rendered on the page. An element hidden via the visibility attribute preserves space in the document where the element normally appears. If you prefer surrounding content to cinch up the space left by a hidden element, see the display attribute. The CSS specification suggests that the value of collapse, when applied to table row-related elements, should cinch up the table, but no mainstream browser does that yet.

The visibility attribute is inherited when its value is set to inherit. This setting means that if the parent is hidden, the child is also hidden. But, by setting the child's visibility attribute to visible, you can still keep the parent hidden while showing the child independently.

| | |
|---|---|
| **CSS Syntax** | visibility: *visibilityType* |
| **Value** | One of the constant values: collapse \| hidden \| inherit \| visible. IE for Windows does not recognize the collapse value. Navigator 4 allows visibility only of positioned elements. |
| **Initial Value** | visible |
| **Example** | #congrats {visibility: hidden} |
| **Applies To** | All elements. |

**Object Model Reference**
[window.]document.getElementById("*elementID*").style.visibility

# voice-family

For aural style sheets, this sets the voice family names the aural browser should try to use for speaking the content. Multiple, comma-delimited values are accepted. This feature is analogous to the font-family setting for visual browsers.

| | |
|---|---|
| **CSS Syntax** | voice-family: *voiceFamilyName* [, *voiceFamilyName* [, ...]] |
| **Value** | |

A *voiceFamilyName* may be the identifier for a voice type provided by the aural browser or a generic voice name (yet to be determined by the W3C). As with font-family settings, you should specify multiple voice types, starting with the more specific and ending with the most generic for the type of speech you want for the element's content.

| | |
|---|---|
| **Initial Value** | Depends on browser. |
| **Applies To** | All elements. |

# volume

For aural style sheets, this sets the dynamic range (softness/loudness) of the spoken element. Because normal speech has inflections that prevent an absolute volume to apply at all times, the volume attribute sets the median volume.

| | |
|---|---|
| **CSS Syntax** | volume: *number* \| *percentage* \| *volumeConstant* |

## Value

A volume *number* value is any number. A value of zero should represent the minimum audible level for the equipment and ambient noise environment; a value of 100 should represent the maximum comfortable level under the same conditions. A *percentage* value is calculated relative to the parent element's volume attribute setting. Alternative settings include the following constants (and their representative values): silent (no sound) | x-soft (0) | soft (25) | medium (50) | loud (75) | x-loud (100).

**Initial Value**     medium

**Applies To**     All elements.

# white-space

Sets how the browser should render whitespace (extra character spaces and carriage returns) that is part of the element's source code. Under normal circumstances, HTML ignores extra whitespace and thus collapses the rendered content around such space. For example, only single spaces are preserved between words, and br elements are required to force a line break within a paragraph. A whitespace attribute setting of pre treats whitespace as if you had surrounded the element in a pre element. Although browsers have a tradition of rendering pre elements in a monospace font, the look of an ordinary element set to white-space:pre preserves its font characteristics.

**CSS Syntax**     white-space: *whiteSpaceType*

## Value

One of three constants: normal | nowrap | pre. A value of normal allows regular HTML treatment of whitespace to rule. A value of nowrap (not available in Navigator 4) tells the browser to ignore line breaks in the source text (in case the author breaks up lines for readability in the editor) and break them on the page only where there are explicit HTML line breaks (with a br element, for example). A value of pre has the browser honor all whitespace entered by the author in the source content, without adjusting any font settings of the element.

**Initial Value**     normal

**Example**     div.example {white-space: pre}

**Applies To**     All elements.

# widows

Sets the minimum number of lines of a paragraph that must be visible at the top of a page after a page break occurs. See the orphans attribute for lines to be displayed at the bottom of a page before a page break.

**CSS Syntax**     widows: *lineCount*

| | |
|---|---|
| **Value** | An integer of the number of lines. |
| **Initial Value** | 2 |
| **Applies To** | Block-level elements. |

# width

Sets the width of a block-level, replaced, and positioned element's content width (exclusive of borders, padding, and margins).

IE for Windows counts left and right margins, padding, and borders when calculating the width of an element until you reach IE 6 in standards compatibility mode (see the DOCTYPE element in Chapter 8). When observing the CSS standards, the width applies to only the content portion of an element, irrespective of borders, padding, or margins. This change may have significant impact on legacy code that you are bringing up to W3C compatibility.

| | |
|---|---|
| **CSS Syntax** | width: *length* \| *percentage* \| auto |
| **Value** | See the discussion about length values at the beginning of this chapter. The setting of auto lets the browser determine the width of the element box based on the amount of space required to display the content within the current window width. |
| **Initial Value** | auto |

**Example**

```
div#announce {position: relative; left: 30; width: 240}
textarea {width: 80%}
```

**Applies To**

Navigator 4, all absolute-positioned elements; Internet Explorer 4, applet, div, embed, fieldset, hr, iframe, img, input, marquee, object, span, table, and textarea elements; Internet Explorer 5 and Netscape 6, all elements except nonreplaced inline elements, table column elements, and column group elements.

**Object Model Reference**

[window.]document.getElementById("*elementID*").style.width

# word-break

Controls the word-break style for ideographic languages or content that mixes Latin and ideographic languages.

| | |
|---|---|
| **CSS Syntax** | word-break: *breakType* |
| **Value** | One of the following constant values: break-all \| keep-all \| normal. |
| **Initial Value** | normal |

| | |
|---|---|
| **Example** | div {word-break:keep-all} |
| **Applies To** | Block-level and table-related elements. |

**Object Model Reference**

[window.]document.getElementById("*elementID*").style.wordBreak

## word-spacing

Sets the spacing between words when the text is not under external word-spacing constraints (e.g., an align attribute set to justify). IE 5 for Macintosh may exhibit overlap problems with the word-spacing of elements nested inside the one being controlled.

| | |
|---|---|
| **CSS Syntax** | word-spacing: *length* \| normal |
| **Value** | A value of normal lets the browser handle word spacing according to its rendering calculations. See the discussion about length values at the beginning of this chapter. |
| **Initial Value** | normal |
| **Applies To** | All elements. |

**Object Model Reference**

[window.]document.getElementById("*elementID*").style.wordSpacing

## word-wrap

Specifies word-wrapping style for block-level, specifically-sized inline, or positioned elements. If a single word (i.e., without any whitespace) extends beyond the width of the element containing box, the normal behavior is to extend the content beyond the normal box width, without breaking. But with the value of break-word, you can force the long word to break at whatever character position occurs at the edge of the box.

| | |
|---|---|
| **CSS Syntax** | word-wrap: *wrapStyle* |
| **Value** | One of the constant values: break-word \| normal. |
| **Initial Value** | normal |
| **Applies To** | Block-level, sized inline, and positioned elements. |

**Object Model Reference**

[window.]document.getElementById("*elementID*").style.wordWrap

# writing-mode

Intended primarily for languages that display characters in vertical sentences, this controls the progression of content, left-to-right, or right-to-left.

| | |
|---|---|
| **CSS Syntax** | writing-mode: *direction* |
| **Value** | One of the constant values: lr-tb | tb-rl. Value of tb-rl can rotate text of some languages by 90 degrees. |
| **Initial Value** | lr-tb |
| **Applies To** | All elements. |

**Object Model Reference**

[window.]document.getElementById("*elementID*").style.writingMode

# z-index

For a positioned element, this sets the stacking order relative to other elements within the same parent container. See Chapter 4 for details on relationships of element layering amid multiple containers.

| | |
|---|---|
| **CSS Syntax** | z-index: *integer* | auto |
| **Value** | Any integer value. A value of auto is the same as a value of zero. When all elements in the same parent container have the same z-index value, the stacking order is determined by element source code order. |
| **Initial Value** | auto |
| **Example** | div#instrux {position: absolute; left: 50; top: 70; z-index: 2} |
| **Applies To** | Positioned elements. |

**Object Model Reference**

[window.]document.getElementById("*elementID*").style.zIndex

**Notes**

Rendering mechanisms in many browsers and versions generate form controls (buttons, text boxes, etc.) in such a way that they always render in front of a positioned element, regardless of z-index attribute setting. This means that a positioned element may find a form control from the regular content flow sticking out in front of the positioned element. There is no workaround for this, other than to set the visibility of the form controls (or its form container) to hidden while the positioned element is visible.

# zoom

Controls the magnification of rendered content. This is particularly useful for output that might be displayed on monitors with very high pixel density. See `screen.logicalXDPI` property in Chapter 9.

**CSS Syntax**  zoom: *scale* | *percentage* | normal

**Value**  Magnification can be denoted as a floating-point numbe, a scaling factor (1.0 is normal), or a percentage (100% is normal).

**Initial Value**  normal

**Example**  body {zoom:200%}

**Applies To**  All elements.

## Object Model Reference

[window.]document.getElementById("*elementID*").style.zIndex

# JavaScript Core Language Reference

The previous chapters in the reference part of the book have covered every aspect of Dynamic HTML authoring that affects elements, objects, and styles—the pieces that are often visible on the page. The one part yet to be covered is the scripting glue that makes it possible to access and control the items detailed up to this point—the "D" of DHTML. This chapter covers the core scripting language features that apply to cross-browser application development. This means that VBScript, ActiveX controls, and Java classes accessible through LiveConnect are intentionally omitted here in favor of the core language that is widely deployed in every scriptable browser.

As described in Chapter 1, the JavaScript language was a Netscape invention. Microsoft's version of the language is called JScript. But a browser-neutral version of the language has been approved as a common denominator standard for all Java-Script-derived languages: ECMAScript. There is a great deal of agreement in the implementation of the core elements of this scripting language among browser makers and the ECMA standards group. The biggest challenge for writing core language code (i.e., code that is independent of the scriptable document object model) is knowing what version of the language is supported by which versions of the browser. In the entries for this chapter, you can see at a glance which browser version first supported every core language object, property, method, function, operator, and control statement.

## Internet Explorer JScript Versions

For Internet Explorer for Windows, Microsoft separates the core language functionality from the browser itself by implementing each language as a *.dll* file that (in some cases) can be updated and swapped in without a change in the browser version. A user visiting a site with the first generation of scriptable browser, IE 3, could have one of two *Jscript.dll* files installed (Version 1 or 2), depending on Service Pack installation and other variables beyond the control of the page author. This numbering system had no correlation with the JavaScript language version system.

*JScript.dll* versions continued to progress so that different (and more powerful) versions came installed on each succeeding IE version. Except for Internet Explorer 3, which predates DHTML-capable browsers, the JScript engine version is of no more consequence than the browser version. Therefore, in the listings within this chapter, the versions shown for IE are the first browser versions that are guaranteed to have implemented the particular language item. For example, although the `Array` object made its debut in *JScript.dll* Version 2 (during the lifespan of IE 3), it is listed as starting in IE 4.

Object detection techniques, of course, obviate the need for browser or script engine version concerns. The same goes for the official JavaScript versioning; that numbering system (1.0, 1.1, etc.) is likewise avoided throughout this chapter.

# About Static Objects

Unlike the heavily object-oriented Java language, there is little of the traditional object-oriented vernacular in the object-based JavaScript language. As a result, scripters tend not to think in terms of static objects and object instantiation. But some of that does take place behind the scenes.

Some core language objects act as if they were true static objects. The `Math` object is a good example; it contains a number of properties and methods that scripts use without ever having to peel off an instance of that object to do some math.

In contrast, the `Date` object is a static object that generates an instance of itself each time someone creates a new date:

```
var now = new Date();
```

In this example, the `now` variable is an instance of the `Date` object—a snapshot of the object frozen in time. That instance provides access to many methods that let scripts get pieces of date and time, as well as set new values to those pieces. The methods actually live in the static object, but you access them through the instance that holds a value that can be influenced by those methods (yes, these methods are inherited, but JavaScript doesn't use this term much). Only on rare occasions do scripts ever need to look directly at the static `Date` object for other kinds of assistance (such as the `getTimezoneOffset()` method).

Most objects are either all static (`Math`) or completely suppress themselves from the scene once you create instances you work with (`String`, `Array`, `Number`). Only a few objects operate in both modes, depending on whether you need the data of an instance of the object or one of the static properties or methods. You've seen how the `Date` object performs double duty. The `RegExp` object also performs this double duty; a regular expression instance object is created for you when you execute a related method. At the same time, you can access static objects (such as `String` and `Array`) to modify their basic behavior by assigning new properties and methods to their prototype (via the prototype property). New instances of such modified objects inherit the new properties or methods assigned to the prototype.

# Mozilla Get and Set Methods

In anticipation of future ECMA adoption of a new language feature, Mozilla-based browsers (e.g., Netscape 6 and 7) provide a mechanism for defining functions that perform the acts of reading (getting) and writing (setting) custom properties of objects, and attaching those function to objects. To prevent collision with the eventual standardized syntax, the Mozilla version utilizes a special double-double underscore syntax (i.e., two underscore characters on each side of the method name) for two methods of any object's prototype property:

```
objectName.prototype.__defineGetter__("propertyName", functionReference);
objectName.prototype.__defineSetter__("propertyName", functionReference);
```

The reason this mechanism is different from simply assigning a custom prototype property is that the actions required to get or set a property value may require multiple script statements—handled by the function referenced in the prototype methods.

To demonstrate this facility, the following examples operate on a DOM object (but any object you can reference with JavaScript will do) to provide an innerText property for all HTML element objects. Neither the W3C DOM nor Netscape 6 offer this property, but you can add it to all elements in the page by having these method statements in the page's scripts. The functions defined here are anonymous functions (for compactness), but any function reference will suffice. In a cross-browser application, these statements would have to be protected so that they run only when the HTMLElement is referenceable and the __defineGetter__() or __defineSetter__() methods are implemented (all verifiable through object detection):

```
HTMLElement.prototype.__defineGetter__("innerText", function () {
    var rng = document.createRange();
    rng.selectNode(this);
    return rng.toString();
});
HTMLElement.prototype.__defineSetter__("innerText", function(newTxt) {
    var rng = document.createRange();
    rng.selectNodeContents(this);
    rng.deleteContents();
    this.appendChild(document.createTextNode(newTxt));
    return newTxt;
});
```

Whenever a script statement attempts to read the innerText property of an element, the function associated with the __defineGetter__() method is executed, returning the desired value. Conversely, whenever a value is assigned to the innerText property of an element, the __defineSetter__() method's function runs.

# ECMAScript Reserved Keywords

The following case-sensitive words may not be used as identifier names:

| | | | |
|---|---|---|---|
| abstract | boolean | break | byte |
| case | catch | char | class |
| const | continue | debugger | default |
| delete | do | double | else |
| enum | export | extends | final |
| finally | float | for | function |
| goto | if | implements | import |
| in | instanceof | int | interface |
| long | native | new | package |
| private | protected | public | return |
| short | static | super | switch |
| synchronized | this | throw | throws |
| transient | try | typeof | var |
| void | volatile | while | with |

Many of these words are already used in existing JavaScript versions, while the rest are reserved for possible use in future versions.

# Core Objects

## ActiveXObject

*NN n/a*    *IE 4(Win)*    *ECMA n/a*

Internet Explorer for Windows provides a direct portal between a web page and an ActiveX control (an *automation object* in Windows jargon) already registered with the Windows system. By creating an instance of the ActiveXObject, you supply your scripts with a reference to that control; use that reference to access the control's properties or invoke its methods. Uncovering the methods and properties of an automation object may require a bit of exploration through the Microsoft Developer Network web site (*http://msdn. microsoft.com*). A Microsoft utility, called OLE/COM Object Viewer, can also open doors for the persistent. A good place to start your exploration is *http://msdn.microsoft.com/ scripting/jscript/doc/jsobjActiveXObject.htm*. See also the GetObject( ) global function for a way to obtain a reference to an automation object via its local pathname.

### Creating an ActiveXObject

```
var myObj = new ActiveXObject(appName.className[, remoteServerName])
```

**Properties**    None.

**Methods**    None.

# arguments

Every function—while it is executing—has an arguments object, which is accessible as a property of the function. The object is created automatically, and cannot be created outside of the function context that owns it. For example, consider a typical function definition:

```
function myFunc() {
    // function statements
}
```

A statement inside the function can access the arguments object by the following reference:

```
arguments
```

This object always contains the callee property, which is a reference to the very same function (explained in the callee property discussion). But you can also use the arguments object to access each parameter variable value through array notation. In the above example, a statement inside the myFunc() function can access the passed parameter value with the following reference:

```
arguments[0]
```

See the arguments property discussion of the Function object later in this chapter for practical applications.

## Properties

| | |
|---|---|
| callee | length |

**Methods**        None.

## callee

**Read-only**

Provides a reference to the function that created the arguments object. This property provides the essential reference to the current function, which an anonymous function would require for it to be called in a recursive construction.

## Example

```
myObj.doThis = function(input) {
    // function statements that act on parameter value
    if (!someCondition) {
        arguments.callee(input);
    }
}
```

**Value**        Function object reference.

## length

**Read-only**

Returns the number of arguments passed to the function in its current invocation. The number is not influenced by the number of parameter variables defined for the function.

**Example**

```
function myFunc()
    for (var i = 0; i < arguments.length; i++) {
        ...
    }
}
```

**Value**          Integer.

# Array                                              NN 3    IE 4    ECMA 1

An array is an ordered collection of one or more pieces of data. JavaScript array entries may be of any data type, and you can mix different data types in the same array. Each entry in an array has an index assigned to it. The default behavior is for the index to be a zero-based integer (the first entry has an index of zero). An index value may also be a string, but the string index acts like a property name of an array object, and does not influence the numeric indices (which is why string-indexed entries cannot be iterated via the array's length property, but can be iterated via a for-in loop). Separate sets of integer- and string-indexed items can coexist within the same array object.

Accessing an entry in an array requires the name of the array and the index in square brackets:

```
cars[0]
cars["Ford"]
```

You may also create an array of arrays to simulate multidimensional arrays. A reference to an item in a two-dimensional array uses syntax as follows:

```
myArray[x][y]
```

The number of entries in a JavaScript array (its length) can vary over time. Therefore, you do not have to initialize an empty array to a specific size (nor is there any particular advantage to doing so). To add a new entry to an array of indeterminant length, assign the value to the next higher array index value:

```
cars[cars.length] = "Bentley";
```

A shortcut array creation technique is available starting in IE 4 and Navigator 4, using square brackets to contain values in literal notation.

## Creating an Array

```
var myArray = new Array();
var myArray = new Array(sizeInteger);
var myArray = new Array(element0, element1, ..., elementN);
var myArray = [element0, element1, ..., elementN];
```

## Properties

constructor    length         prototype

## Methods

| | | |
|---|---|---|
| concat() | join() | pop() |
| push() | reverse() | shift() |

```
slice( )        sort( )        splice( )
toLocaleString( ) toString( )   unshift( )
```

## constructor

**Read/Write**

This is a reference to the function that created the instance of an Array object—the native Array( ) constructor function in browsers.

### Example

```
if (myVar.constructor == Array) {
    // process native string
}
```

**Value**          Function object reference.

## length

**Read/Write**

Provides a count of the number of numerically-indexed entries stored in the array. If the constructor function used to create the array specified a preliminary length, the length property reflects that amount, even if data does not occupy every slot.

### Example

```
for (var i = 0; i < myArray.length; i++) {
    ...
}
```

**Value**          Integer.

## prototype

**Read/Write**

This is a property of the static Array object. Use the prototype property to assign new properties and methods to future instances of arrays created in the current document. For example, the following function creates a return-delimited list of elements in an array in reverse order:

```
function formatAsList( ) {
    var output = "";
    for (var i = this.length - 1; i >= 0; i--) {
        output += this[i] + "\n";
    }
    alert(output);
}
```

To give an array that power, assign this function reference to a prototype property whose name you want to use as the method to invoke this function:

```
Array.prototype.showReverseList = formatAsList;
```

If a script creates an array at this point:

```
var stooges = new Array("Moe", "Larry", "Curly", "Shemp");
```

the new array has the showReverseList( ) method available to it. To invoke the method, the call is:

```
stooges.showReverseList();
```

You can add properties the same way. These allow you to attach information about the array (its creation time, for example) without disturbing the ordered sequence of array data. When a new document loads into the window or frame, the static Array object starts fresh again.

**Example**        `Array.prototype.created = "";`

**Value**          Any data, including function references.

## concat( )                                                    NN 4    IE 4    ECMA 3

```
concat(item1[, item2[, ...itemN]])
```

Returns an array that combines the current array object with one or more array objects (or other values) specified as the method parameter(s):

```
var combinedArray = myArray1.concat(myArray2, someValue);
```

Neither of the original arrays is altered in the process.

**Returned Value**    An Array object.

**Parameters**

*item1...itemN*
   Any JavaScript value, including another array.

## join( )                                                      NN 3    IE 4    ECMA 1

```
join(["delimiterString"])
```

Returns a string consisting of a list of items (as strings) contained by an array. The delimiter character(s) between items is set by the parameter to the method. Note that an array's items are only those items that are accessible via an integer index. Items referenced via string index values are treated as properties of the array object, and are thus independent of integer indexed values (the two sets can coexist in a single array without conflict). The join( ) method works only with the integer-indexed items.

**Returned Value**    String.

**Parameters**

*delimiterString*
   Any string of characters. Nonalphanumeric characters must use URL-encoded equivalents (%0D for carriage return). The default delimiter string is a comma character.

## pop( )

Returns the value of the last item in an array and removes it from the array. The length of the array decreases by one.

**Returned Value**    Any JavaScript value.

**Parameters**    None.

## push( )

```
push(item1[, item2[, ...itemN]])
```

Appends one or more items to the end of an array. The length of the array increases by one.

**Returned Value**    The value pushed into the array.

**Parameters**

*item1...itemN*

Comma-delimited list of one or more JavaScript values, including object references.

## reverse( )

Reverses the order of items in the array and returns a copy of the array in the new order. Not only does the reverse( ) method rearrange the values in the array, but it also returns a copy of the reversed array.

**Returned Value**    An Array object.

**Parameters**    None.

## shift( )

Returns the value of the first item in an array and removes it from the array. The length of the array decreases by one.

**Returned Value**    Any JavaScript value.

**Parameters**    None.

## slice( )

```
slice(startIndex[, endIndex])
```

Returns an array that is a subset of contiguous items from the main array. Parameters determine where the selection begins and ends.

**Returned Value**    An Array object.

**Parameters**

*startIndex*

A zero-based integer of the first item of the subset from the current array.

*endIndex*
>    An optional zero-based integer of the last item of the subset from the current array. If
>    omitted, the selection is made from the *startIndex* position to the end of the array.

## sort( )                                                           NN 3   IE 4   ECMA 1

sort([*compareFunction*])

Sorts the values of the array either by the ASCII value of string versions of each array entry
or according to a comparison function of your own design. The sort( ) method repeatedly
invokes the comparison function, passing two values from the array. The comparison function should return an integer value, which is interpreted by the sort( ) function as follows.

| Value | Meaning |
| --- | --- |
| <0 | The second passed value should sort later than the first value. |
| 0 | The sort order of the two values should not change. |
| >0 | The first passed value should sort later than the second. |

The following comparison function sorts values of an array in numerical (instead of ASCII)
order:

```
function doCompare(a, b) {
    return a - b;
}
```

To sort an array by this function, the statement is:

```
myArray.sort(doCompare);
```

By the time the sort( ) method has completed its job, it has sent all values to the
doCompare( ) function two values at a time and sorted the values on whether the first value
is larger than the second (in the manner of a bubble sort).

Not only does the sort( ) method rearrange the values in the array, but it also returns a
copy of the sorted array.

**Returned Value**    An Array object, sorted according to sorting criteria.

**Parameters**

*compareFunction*
>    A reference to a function that receives two parameters and returns an integer result.

## splice( )                                                    NN 4   IE 5.5(Win)   ECMA 2

splice(*startIndex*, *deleteCount*[, *item1*[, *item2*[, ...*itemN*]]])

Removes one or more contiguous items from within an array and, optionally, inserts new
items in their places. The length of the array adjusts itself accordingly.

**Returned Value**    An Array object containing removed items.

## Parameters

*startIndex*

A zero-based integer of the first item of the subset from the current array.

*deleteCount*

An integer denoting how many items from the *startIndex* position are to be removed from the array.

*item1...itemN*

Comma-delimited list of JavaScript values to be inserted into the array in place of removed items. The number of items does not have to equal *deleteCount*.

## toLocaleString( )    NN 6    IE 5.5(Win)    ECMA 2

Returns a comma-delimited string of values, theoretically in a format tailored to the language and customs of the browser's default language. Implementation details vary with browser and data type. IE 5.5 and later converts numbers of all kinds to strings with two digits to the right of the decimal, but triggers an error for object references. Netscape 6 leaves integers in their original format and displays object references as [object *objectType*]. The ECMA standard leaves such interpretations up to the browser maker.

**Returned Value**    Comma-delimited string.

**Parameters**    None.

## toString( )    NN 3    IE 4    ECMA 1

Returns a comma-delimited string of values, identical to using the Array.join( ) method with a comma parameter. All values are converted to some string equivalent, including objects ([object] in IE/Windows; [object *objectType*] in IE 5/Macintosh and Netscape 6).

**Returned Value**    Comma-delimited string.

**Parameters**    None.

## unshift( )    NN 4    IE 5.5(Win)    ECMA 2

unshift(*item1*[, *item2*[, ...*itemN*]])

Inserts one or more items at the beginning of an array. The length of the array increases by the number of items added, and the method returns the new length of the array.

**Returned Value**    Integer.

## Parameters

*item1...itemN*

Comma-delimited list of one or more JavaScript values.

# Boolean

NN 3   IE 4   ECMA 1

A Boolean object represents any value that evaluates to true or false. By and large, you don't have to worry about the Boolean object because the browsers automatically create such objects for you when you assign a true or false value to a variable. Quoted versions of these values are treated only as string.

## Creating a Boolean Object

```
var myValue = new Boolean();
var myValue = new Boolean(BooleanValue);
var myValue = BooleanValue;
```

## Properties

constructor    prototype

## Methods

toString()    valueOf()

## constructor

NN 4   IE 4   ECMA 1
Read/Write

This is a reference to the function that created the instance of a Boolean object—the native Boolean() constructor function in browsers.

### Example

```
if (myVar.constructor == Boolean) {
    // process native string
}
```

**Value**        Function object reference.

## prototype

NN 3   IE 4   ECMA 1
Read/Write

This is a property of the static Boolean object. Use the prototype property to assign new properties and methods to future instances of a Boolean value created in the current document. See the Array.prototype property description for examples. There is little need to create new prototype properties or methods for the Boolean object.

**Example**        Boolean.prototype.author = "DG";

**Value**        Any data, including function references.

## toString()

NN 4   IE 4   ECMA 1

Returns the object's value as a string data type. You don't need this method in practice, because the browsers automatically convert Boolean values to strings when they are needed for display in alert dialogs or in-document rendering.

| **Returned Value** | "true" | "false" |
|---|---|

**Parameters**       None.

## valueOf( )

Returns the object's value as a Boolean data type. You don't need this method when you create Boolean objects by simple value assignment.

**Returned Value**       Boolean value: true | false.

**Parameters**       None.

# Date

The Date object is a static object that generates instances by way of several constructor functions. Each instance of a Date object is a snapshot of the date and time, measured in milliseconds relative to zero hours on January 1, 1970. Negative millisecond values represent time before that date; positive values represent time since that date.

The typical way to work with dates is to generate a new instance of the Date object, either for now or for a specific date and time (past or future, using the client local time). Then use the myriad of available date methods to get or set components of that time (e.g., minutes, hours, date, month). Browsers internally store a date as the millisecond value at Coordinated Universal Time (UTC, which is essentially the same as Greenwich Mean Time, or GMT). When you ask a browser for a component of that time, it automatically converts the value to the local time zone of the browser based on the client computer's control panel setting for the clock and time zone. If the control panel is set incorrectly, time and date calculations may go awry.

Early versions of scriptable browsers had numerous bugs when working with the Date object. One resource that explains the fundamental operations within the Date object (and bugs) can be found at *http://developer.netscape.com/viewsource/goodman_dateobject.html*.

### Creating a Date Object

```
var now = new Date( );
var myDate = new Date("month dd, yyyy hh:mm:ss");
var myDate = new Date("month dd, yyyy");
var myDate = new Date(yy, mm, dd, hh, mm, ss);
var myDate = new Date(yy, mm, dd);
var myDate = new Date(milliseconds);
```

### Properties

constructor       prototype

### Methods

| | | |
|---|---|---|
| getDate( ) | getDay( ) | getFullYear( ) |
| getHours( ) | getMilliseconds( ) | getMinutes( ) |
| getMonth( ) | getSeconds( ) | getTime( ) |

| getTimezoneOffset( ) | getUTCDate( ) | getUTCDay( ) |
|---|---|---|
| getUTCFullYear( ) | getUTCHours( ) | getUTCMilliseconds( ) |
| getUTCMinutes( ) | getUTCMonth( ) | getUTCSeconds( ) |
| getVarDate( ) | getYear( ) | parse( ) |
| setDate( ) | setFullYear( ) | setHours( ) |
| setMilliseconds( ) | setMinutes( ) | setMonth( ) |
| setSeconds( ) | setTime( ) | setUTCDate( ) |
| setUTCFullYear( ) | setUTCHours( ) | setUTCMilliseconds( ) |
| setUTCMinutes( ) | setUTCMonth( ) | setUTCSeconds( ) |
| setYear( ) | toDateString( ) | toGMTString( ) |
| toLocaleDateString( ) | toLocaleString( ) | toLocaleTimeString( ) |
| toString( ) | toTimeString( ) | toUTCString( ) |
| UTC( ) | valueOf( ) | |

## constructor

NN 4    IE 4    ECMA 1

**Read/Write**

This is a reference to the function that created the instance of a Date object—the native Date( ) constructor function in browsers.

**Example**

```
if (myVar.constructor == Date) {
    // process native string
}
```

**Value**          Function object reference.

## prototype

NN 3    IE 4    ECMA 1

**Read/Write**

This is a property of the static Date object. Use the prototype property to assign new properties and methods to future instances of a Date value created in the current document. See the Array.prototype property description for examples.

**Example**          Date.prototype.author = "DG";

**Value**          Any data, including function references.

## getDate( )

NN 2    IE 3    ECMA 1

Returns the calendar date within the month specified by an instance of the Date object.

**Returned Value**          Integer between 1 and 31.

**Parameters**          None.

## getDay( )

Returns an integer corresponding to a day of the week for the date specified by an instance of the Date object.

| | |
|---|---|
| **Returned Value** | Integer between 0 and 6. Sunday is 0, Monday is 1, and Saturday is 6. |
| **Parameters** | None. |

## getFullYear( )

Returns all digits of the year for the date specified by an instance of the Date object.

| | |
|---|---|
| **Returned Value** | Integer. Navigator 4 goes no lower than zero. Internet Explorer and Netscape 6 return negative year values. |
| **Parameters** | None. |

## getHours( )

Returns a zero-based integer corresponding to the hours of the day for the date specified by an instance of the Date object. The 24-hour time system is used.

| | |
|---|---|
| **Returned Value** | Integer between 0 and 23. |
| **Parameters** | None. |

## getMilliseconds( )

Returns a zero-based integer corresponding to the number of milliseconds past the seconds value of the date specified by an instance of the Date object.

| | |
|---|---|
| **Returned Value** | Integer between 0 and 999. |
| **Parameters** | None. |

## getMinutes( )

Returns a zero-based integer corresponding to the minute value for the hour and date specified by an instance of the Date object.

| | |
|---|---|
| **Returned Value** | Integer between 0 and 59. |
| **Parameters** | None. |

## getMonth( )

Returns a zero-based integer corresponding to the month value for the date specified by an instance of the Date object. That this method's values are zero-based frequently confuses scripters at first.

**Returned Value**     Integer between 0 and 11. January is 0, February is 1, and December is 11.

**Parameters**     None.

## getSeconds( )                    NN 2    IE 3    ECMA 1

Returns a zero-based integer corresponding to the seconds past the nearest full minute for the date specified by an instance of the Date object.

**Returned Value**     Integer between 0 and 59.

**Parameters**     None.

## getTime( )                    NN 2    IE 3    ECMA 1

Returns a zero-based integer corresponding to the number of milliseconds since January 1, 1970, to the date specified by an instance of the Date object.

**Returned Value**     Integer.

**Parameters**     None.

## getTimezoneOffset( )                    NN 2    IE 3    ECMA 1

Returns a zero-based integer corresponding to the number of minutes difference between GMT and the client computer's clock for an instance of the Date object. Time zones to the west of GMT are positive values; time zones to the east are negative values. Numerous bugs plagued this method in early browsers, especially Macintosh versions.

**Returned Value**     Integer between −720 and 720.

**Parameters**     None.

## getUTCDate( )                    NN 4    IE 4    ECMA 1

Returns the calendar date within the month specified by an instance of the Date object but in the UTC time stored internally by the browser.

**Returned Value**     Integer between 1 and 31.

**Parameters**     None.

## getUTCDay( )                    NN 4    IE 4    ECMA 1

Returns an integer corresponding to a day of the week for the date specified by an instance of the Date object but in the UTC time stored internally by the browser.

**Returned Value**     Integer between 0 and 6. Sunday is 0, Monday is 1, and Saturday is 6.

**Parameters**     None.

## getUTCFullYear( )

Returns all digits of the year for the date specified by an instance of the Date object but in the UTC time stored internally by the browser.

**Returned Value**   Integer. Navigator 4 goes no lower than zero. Internet Explorer and Netscape 6 return negative year values.

**Parameters**   None.

## getUTCHours( )

Returns a zero-based integer corresponding to the hours of the day for the date specified by an instance of the Date object but in the UTC time stored internally by the browser. The 24-hour time system is used.

**Returned Value**   Integer between 0 and 23.

**Parameters**   None.

## getUTCMilliseconds( )

Returns a zero-based integer corresponding to the number of milliseconds past the seconds value of the date specified by an instance of the Date object but in the UTC time stored internally by the browser.

**Returned Value**   Integer between 0 and 999.

**Parameters**   None.

## getUTCMinutes( )

Returns a zero-based integer corresponding to the minute value for the hour and date specified by an instance of the Date object but in the UTC time stored internally by the browser.

**Returned Value**   Integer between 0 and 59.

**Parameters**   None.

## getUTCMonth( )

Returns a zero-based integer corresponding to the month value for the date specified by an instance of the Date object but in the UTC time stored internally by the browser. That this method's values are zero-based frequently confuses scripters at first.

**Returned Value**   Integer between 0 and 11. January is 0, February is 1, and December is 11.

**Parameters**   None.

JavaScript Reference

## getUTCSeconds( )

Returns a zero-based integer corresponding to the seconds value past the nearest full minute of the date specified by an instance of the Date object but in the UTC time stored internally by the browser.

**Returned Value**    Integer between 0 and 59.

**Parameters**    None.

## getVarDate( )

Returns a date value in a format (called VT_DATE) suitable for a variety of Windows-oriented applications, such as ActiveX controls and VBScript. Not for use with JavaScript date calculations.

**Returned Value**    VT_DATE format value (not for JavaScript use).

**Parameters**    None.

## getYear( )

Returns a number corresponding to the year of an instance of the Date object, but exhibits irregular behavior. In theory, the method should return the number of years the date object represents since 1900. This would produce a one- or two-digit value for all years between 1900 and 1999. However, when you reach 2000, the pattern fails. Instead of producing values starting with 100, the getYear( ) method, some browsers return the same four-digit value as getFullYear( ). For this reason, it is best to use getFullYear( ) whenever possible (but observe the browser compatibility for that method). Note that this method is not an ECMA-supported method, whereas getFullYear( ) is.

**Returned Value**    Integer between 0 and 99 for the years 1900 to 1999; four-digit integer starting with 2000 for some browsers, or a continuation (100+) for others.

**Parameters**    None.

## parse( )

parse("*dateString*")

Static Date object method that returns the millisecond equivalent of the date specified as a string in the parameter.

**Returned Value**    Date in milliseconds.

**Parameters**

dateString
>   Any valid string format equivalent to that derived from a Date object. See toString( ), toGMTString( ), and toLocaleString( ) methods for sample formats.

## setDate( )
setDate(*dateInt*)

Sets the date within the month for an instance of the Date object. If you specify a date beyond the end of the object's current month, the object recalculates the date in the succeeding month. For example, if a Date object is set to December 25, 2002, you can find out the calendar date ten days later with the following construction:

```
myDate.setDate(myDate.getDate( ) + 10);
```

After this calculation, the value of myDate is the equivalent of January 4, 2003.

**Returned Value**   New date in milliseconds.

**Parameters**
*dateInt*
> Date integer.

## setFullYear( )
setFullYear(*yearInt*)

Assigns the year for an instance of the Date object.

**Returned Value**   New date in milliseconds.

**Parameters**
*yearInt*
> Integer. Navigator 4 allows digits no lower than zero. Internet Explorer and NN 6 allow negative year values.

## setHours( )
setHours(*hourInt*)

Sets the hours of the day for an instance of the Date object. The 24-hour time system is used. If you specify an hour beyond the end of the object's current day, the object recalculates the time in the succeeding day(s).

**Returned Value**   New date in milliseconds.

**Parameters**
*hourInt*
> Zero-based integer.

## setMilliseconds( )
setMilliseconds(*msInt*)

Sets the number of milliseconds past the seconds value for an instance of the Date object.

**Returned Value**   New date in milliseconds.

**Parameters**

*msInt*

Zero-based integer of milliseconds.

## setMinutes( )                                     NN 2   IE 3   ECMA 1

setMinutes(*minuteInt*)

Sets the minute value for the hour and date of an instance of the Date object.

**Returned Value**    New date in milliseconds.

**Parameters**

*minuteInt*

Zero-based integer.

## setMonth( )                                       NN 2   IE 3   ECMA 1

setMonth(*monthInt*)

Sets the month value for the date of an instance of the Date object. That this method's values are zero-based frequently confuses scripters at first.

**Returned Value**    New date in milliseconds.

**Parameters**

*monthInt*

Zero-based integer. January is 0, February is 1, and December is 11. Assigning higher values increases the object to the succeeding year.

## setSeconds( )                                    NN 2   IE 3   ECMA 1

setSeconds(*secInt*)

Sets the seconds value past the nearest full minute for an instance of the Date object.

**Returned Value**    New date in milliseconds.

**Parameters**

*secInt*

Zero-based integer.

## setTime( )                                         NN 2   IE 3   ECMA 1

setTime(*msInt*)

Sets an instance of the Date object to the number of milliseconds since January 1, 1970.

**Returned Value**    New date in milliseconds.

**Parameters**

*msInt*

Integer of milliseconds.

## setUTCDate( )

setUTCDate(*dateInt*)

Sets the date within the month of an instance of the Date object but in the UTC time stored internally by the browser. If you specify a date beyond the end of the object's current month, the object recalculates the date in the succeeding month.

**Returned Value**   New UTC date in milliseconds.

**Parameters**

*dateInt*
   Integer.

## setUTCFullYear( )

setUTCFullYear(*yearInt*)

Sets all digits of the year for an instance of the Date object but in the UTC time stored internally by the browser.

**Returned Value**   New UTC date in milliseconds.

**Parameters**

*yearInt*
   Integer. Navigator 4 allows values no lower than zero. Internet Explorer and NN 6 allow negative year values.

## setUTCHours( )

setUTCHours(*hourInt*)

Sets the hours of the day for an instance of the Date object but in the UTC time stored internally by the browser. The 24-hour time system is used.

**Returned Value**   New UTC date in milliseconds.

**Parameters**

*hourInt*
   Zero-based integer.

## setUTCMilliseconds( )

setUTCMilliseconds(*msInt*)

Sets the number of milliseconds past the seconds value of an instance of the Date object but in the UTC time stored internally by the browser.

**Returned Value**   New UTC date in milliseconds.

**Parameters**

*msInt*
   Zero-based integer.

## setUTCMinutes( )    NN *4*    IE *4*    ECMA *1*

setUTCMinutes(*minuteInt*)

Sets the minute value for the hour and date of an instance of the Date object but in the UTC time stored internally by the browser.

**Returned Value**    New UTC date in milliseconds.

**Parameters**

*minuteInt*
> Zero-based integer.

## setUTCMonth( )    NN *4*    IE *4*    ECMA *1*

setUTCMonth(*monthInt*)

Sets the month value for an instance of the Date object but in the UTC time stored internally by the browser. That this method's values are zero-based frequently confuses scripters at first.

**Returned Value**    New UTC date in milliseconds.

**Parameters**

*monthInt*
> Zero-based integer. January is 0, February is 1, and December is 11. Assigning higher values increases the object to the succeeding year.

## setUTCSeconds( )    NN *4*    IE *4*    ECMA *1*

setUTCSeconds(*secInt*)

Sets the seconds value past the nearest full for an instance of the Date object but in the UTC time stored internally by the browser.

**Returned Value**    New UTC date in milliseconds.

**Parameters**

*secInt*
> Zero-based integer.

## setYear( )    NN *2*    IE *3*    ECMA *n/a*

setYear(*yearInt*)

Sets the year of an instance of a Date object. Use setFullYear( ) if the browser versions you support allow it. Note that this method is not an ECMA-supported method, whereas setFullYear( ) is.

**Returned Value**    New date in milliseconds.

**Parameters**

*yearInt*
> Four-digit (and sometimes two-digit) integers representing a year.

## toDateString( )

Returns a string consisting only of the date portion of an instance of a Date object. The precise format is under the control of the browser and language, but U.S. English versions of both IE 6 for Windows and Netscape 6 return values in the format *Ddd Mmm dd yyyy*.

**Returned Value**     String.

**Parameters**     None.

## toGMTString( )

Returns a string version of the GMT value of a Date object instance in a standardized format. This method does not alter the original Date object. For use in newer browsers, the toUTCString( ) method is recommended in favor of toGMTString( ).

**Returned Value**

String in the following format: *dayAbbrev, dd mmm yyyy hh:mm:ss* GMT. For example:

```
Mon 05 Aug 2002 02:33:22 GMT
```

**Parameters**     None.

## toLocaleDateString( )

Returns a string consisting only of the date portion of an instance of a Date object. The precise format is under the control of the browser and language. IE 6 for Windows returns a value in the format *fullDay, fullMonth dd, yyyy*; Netscape 6 returns *fullDay fullMonth dd yyyy*.

**Returned Value**     String.

**Parameters**     None.

## toLocaleString( )

Returns a string version of the local time zone value of both the date and time from a Date object instance. The format may be localized for a particular country or an operating system's convention.

**Returned Value**

String in a variety of possible formats. Examples of U.S. versions of browsers include the following.

| Platform | String value |
| --- | --- |
| Internet Explorer 6/Win32 | Tuesday, April 01, 2003 7:30:00 AM |
| Internet Explorer 5.1/Mac | Tuesday, 01 April, 2003  07:30:00 AM |
| Navigator 6/Win32 | Tuesday, April 01, 2003 07:30:00 |
| Navigator 6/Mac | Tuesday April 01 07:30:00 2003 |

**Parameters**     None.

## toLocaleTimeString( )  NN 6    IE 5.5(Win)    ECMA 3

Returns a string consisting only of the time portion of an instance of a Date object. The precise format is under the control of the browser and language. IE 6 for Windows returns a value in the format *[h]h:mm:ss xM*; Netscape 6 returns *hh:mm:ss*.

**Returned Value**     String.

**Parameters**     None.

## toString( )  NN 2    IE 4    ECMA 1

This is a method used mostly by the browser itself to obtain a string version of an instance of a Date object when needed for display in dialog boxes or on-screen rendering.

**Returned Value**

String in a variety of possible formats. Here are examples for U.S. versions of browsers.

| Platform | String Value |
| --- | --- |
| Internet Explorer 6/Win32 | Tue Apr 1 07:30:00 PST 2003 |
| Internet Explorer 5.1/Mac | Tue Apr 1 07:30:00 PST 2003 |
| Navigator 6/Win32 | Tue Apr 01 07:30:00 GMT-0800 (Pacific Standard Time) 2003 |
| Navigator 6/Mac | Tue Apr 01 2003 07:30:00 GMT-0800 |

**Parameters**     None.

## toTimeString( )  NN 6    IE 5.5(Win)    ECMA 3

Returns a string consisting only of the time portion of an instance of a Date object. The precise format is under the control of the browser and language.

**Returned Value**     String.

**Parameters**     None.

## toUTCString( )  NN 4    IE 4    ECMA 1

Returns a string version of the UTC value of a Date object instance in a standardized format. This method does not alter the original Date object. For use in newer browsers, the toUTCString( ) method is recommended in favor of toGMTString( ).

**Returned Value**

String in the following format: *dayAbbrev dd mmm yyyy hh:mm:ss* GMT. For example:

    Mon 05 Aug 2002 02:33:22 GMT

**Parameters**     None.

## UTC( )

UTC(*yyyy*, *mm*, *dd*[, *hh*[, *mm*[, *ss*[, *msecs*]]]])

This is a static method of the Date object that returns a numeric version of the date as stored internally by the browser for a Date object. Unlike parameters to the Date object constructor, the parameter values for the UTC( ) method must be in UTC time for the returned value to be accurate. This method does not generate a date object, as the Date object constructor does.

**Returned Value**   Integer of the UTC millisecond value of the date specified as parameters.

### Parameters

*yyyy* Four-digit year value.

*mm*   Two-digit month number (0–11).

*dd*   Two-digit date number (1–31).

*hh*   Optional two-digit hour number in 24-hour time (0–23).

*mm*   Optional two-digit minute number (0–59).

*ss*   Optional two-digit second number (0–59).

*msec* Optional milliseconds past the last whole second (0–999).

## valueOf( )

Returns the object's value.

**Returned Value**   Integer millisecond count.

**Parameters**   None.

# Enumerator

If an ActiveX control property or method returns a collection of values, the usual Java-Script approach to collections (treating them as arrays) does not work for such values. The Enumerator object gives JavaScript a way to reference items in such collections by controlling a pointer to the list of items. For additional details, visit *http://msdn.microsoft.com/scripting/jscript/doc/jsobjEnumerator.htm*.

### Creating an Enumerator

```
var myEnumObj = new Enumerator(externalCollection);
```

**Properties**   None.

### Methods

| atEnd( ) | item( ) | moveFirst( ) | moveNext( ) |
|----------|---------|--------------|-------------|

## atEnd( )

Returns Boolean true if the Enumerator is pointing at the last item in the collection.

| | |
|---|---|
| **Returned Value** | Boolean value: true \| false. |
| **Parameters** | None. |

## item( )

Returns a value from the collection at the pointer's current position.

| | |
|---|---|
| **Returned Value** | Number, string, or other value from the collection. |
| **Parameters** | None. |

## moveFirst(), moveNext( )

Adjust the location of the pointer within the collection, jumping to the first item in the collection, or ahead by one item.

| | |
|---|---|
| **Returned Value** | None. |
| **Parameters** | None. |

# Error

Browsers that implement try/catch exception handling automatically create an instance of the Error object whenever an error occurs during script processing. You can also create an Error object instance that you explicitly throw. The catch portion of the try/catch construction receives the Error object instance as a parameter, which scripts can examine to learn the details of the error, as exposed by the object's properties.

**Creating an Error Object** var myError = new Error("*errorMessage*");

## Properties

| | | | |
|---|---|---|---|
| constructor | description | fileName | lineNumber |
| message | name | number | prototype |

## Methods

toString( )

## constructor

Read/Write

Provides a reference to the function that created the instance of an Error object—the native Error( ) constructor function in browsers.

### Example

```
if (myVar.constructor == Error) {
    // process native string
}
```

| | |
|---|---|
| **Value** | Function object reference. |

## description

Provides a plain-language description of the error, frequently the same as appears in the IE script error dialog. Use the newer message property if possible.

**Example**
```
if (myError.description.indexOf("Object expected") != -1) {
    // handle "object expected" error
}
```

**Value**          String.

## fileName

Specifies the URL of the page in which the script error occurred. This information appears in the JavaScript Console window for each reported error.

**Example**          `var sourceFile = myError.fileName;`

**Value**            URL string.

## lineNumber

Specifies the number of the line in the source code where the current script error occurred. This information appears in the JavaScript Console window for each reported error.

**Example**          `var errorLine = myError.lineNumber;`

**Value**            Number in string format.

## message

Provides a plain-language description of the error. There is no standard for the format or content of such messages.

**Example**
```
if (myError.description.indexOf("defined") != -1) {
    // handle error for something being undefined
}
```

**Value**          String.

## name

This is a string that sometimes indicates the type of the current error. The default value of this property is `Error`. But the browser may also report types `EvalError`, `RangeError`, `ReferenceError`, `SyntaxError`, `TypeError`, `URIError`, and, if supported by the browser, a specific W3C DOM error type.

**Example**

```
if (myError.name == "SyntaxError") {
    // handle syntax error
}
```

**Value**        String.

## number

Provides a number corresponding to an IE error. You must apply binary arithmetic to the value to derive a meaningful number. Use:

```
var errNum = ErrObj.number & xOFFFF;
```

Then compare the result against Microsoft's numbered listing at *http://msdn.microsoft.com/ library/default.asp?url=/library/en-us/script56/html/js56jsmscRunTimeErrors.asp.*

**Example**        `var errNo = myError.number;`

**Value**        Number.

## prototype

This is a property of the static `Error` object. Use the prototype property to assign new properties and methods to future instances of a `Error` object created in the current document. See the `Array.prototype` property description for examples.

**Example**        `Error.prototype.custom = true;`

**Value**        Any data, including function references.

## toString( )

Returns a string representation of the object, but the values differ between browser families. IE returns [object Error], while Netscape 6 returns a concatenation of the name and message properties.

**Returned Value**    String.

**Parameters**        None.

# Function

A function is a group of one or more script statements that can be invoked at any time during or after the loading of a page. Invoking a function requires nothing more than including the function name with a trailing set of parentheses inside another script statement or as a value assigned to an event handler attribute in an HTML tag.

Since the first scriptable browsers, a function is created by the act of defining it inside a `script` element:

```
function funcName( ) {...}
```

More recent browsers also allow the use of a constructor function, but this syntax is usually more complex than defining a function.

Functions may be built to receive zero or more parameters. Parameters are assigned to comma-delimited parameter variables defined in the parentheses pair following the function name:

```
function doSomething(param1, param2, ... paramN) {...}
```

A parameter value may be any JavaScript data type, including object references and arrays. There is no penalty for not supplying the same number of parameters to the function as are defined for the function. The function object receives all parameters into an array (called `arguments`), which script statements inside the function may examine to extract parameter data.

A function returns execution to the calling statement when the function's last statement has executed. A value may be returned to the calling statement via the `return` statement. Also, a `return` statement anywhere else in the function's statements aborts function statement execution at that point and returns control to the calling statement (optionally with a returned value). If one branch of a conditional construction in a function returns a value, each branch, including the main branch, must also return a value, even if that value is `null` (IE tends to be more forgiving if you don't balance `return` statements, but it's good programming practice just the same).

Functions have ready access to all global variables that are defined outside of functions anywhere in the document. But variables defined inside a function (the `var` keyword is required) are accessible only to statements inside the function.

To reference a function object that is defined elsewhere in the document, use the function name without its parentheses. For example, to assign a function to an event handler property, the syntax is:

```
objReference.eventHandlerProperty = functionName;
```

Starting with Version 4 browsers, you may nest functions inside one another:

```
function myFuncA( ) {
    statements
    function myFuncB( ) {
        statements
    }
}
```

Nested functions (such as `myFuncB`) can be invoked only by statements in its next outermost function.

All functions belong to the window in which the function is defined. Therefore, if a script must access a function located in a sibling frame, the reference must include the frame and the function name:

```
parent.otherFrame.someFunction( )
```

### Creating a Function

```
function myFunction([param1[, param2[,...paramN]]]) {
    statement(s)
}
var myFunction = new Function([param1[,...paramN], "statement1[; ...statementN;"])
objectRef.methodName = function([param1[, param2[,...paramN]]]) {
    statement(s)
}
```

### Properties

| | | | | | |
|---|---|---|---|---|---|
| arguments | arity | caller | constructor | length | prototype |

### Methods

| | | | |
|---|---|---|---|
| apply( ) | toString( ) | call( ) | valueOf( ) |

## arguments                                           NN 3   IE 4   ECMA 1

**Read-only**

Returns an arguments object that contains values passed as arguments to the function. Script statements inside the function can access the values through array syntax, which has numeric index values that correspond to incoming parameter values in the order in which they were passed. The content of the arguments array is independent of the parameter variables defined for the function. Therefore, if the function defines two parameter variables but the calling statement passes 10 parameters, the arguments array captures all 10 values in the order in which they were passed. Statements inside the function may then examine the length of the arguments array and extract values as needed. This allows one function to handle an indeterminate number of parameters if the need arises.

For most browsers, you can simply begin the reference to the object with the name of the property (e.g., arguments[2]). But some older browsers require the name of the enclosing function object, as well. All browsers recognize the longer version.

### Example

```
function myFunc( )
    for (var i = 0; i < myFunc.arguments.length; i++) {
        ...
    }
}
```

**Value**          An arguments object.

## arity

Returns an integer representing the number of parameters that are defined for the function. This property may be examined in a statement outside of the function, perhaps in preparation of parameters to be passed to the function. Returns the same value as the length property.

**Example**          `var paramCount = myFunction.arity;`

**Value**            Integer.

## caller

Returns a reference to a function object that contained the statement invoking the current function. This property is readable only by script statements running in function whose caller you wish to reference. Omitted in Netscape 6.0, but back in subsequent versions.

**Example**
```
function myFunc( )
    if (myFunc.caller == someFuncZ) {
        // process when this function is called by someFuncZ
    }
}
```

**Value**            Function object.

## constructor

This is a reference to the function that created the instance of a Function object—the native Function( ) constructor function in browsers.

**Example**
```
if (myVar.constructor == Function) {
    // process native function
}
```

**Value**            Function object reference.

## length

Returns an integer representing the number of parameters that are defined for the function. This property may be examined in a statement outside of the function, perhaps in preparation of parameters to be passed to the function.

**Example**          `var paramCount = myFunction.length;`

**Value**            Integer.

## prototype

**Read/Write**

This is a property of the static Function object. Use the prototype property to assign new properties and methods to future instances of functions created in the current document. See the Array.prototype property description for examples.

**Example**        Function.prototype.author = "DG";

**Value**          Any data, including function references.

## apply( )

apply([*thisObjectRef*[, *argumentsArray*]])

Invokes the current function, optionally specifying an object to be used as the context for which any this references in the function applies. Parameters to the function (if any) are contained in array that is passed as the second parameter of the apply( ) method. The method can be used with anonymous or named functions. Usage of this method is rare, but provides flexibility that is helpful if your script should encounter a reference to a function and needs to invoke that function, particularly within an object's context.

Consider a script function that is assigned as a method of a custom object:

```
// function definition
function myFunc(parm1, parm2, parm3) {
    // statements
}
// custom object constructor
function customObj(arg1, arg2) {
    this.property1 = arg1;
    this.property2 = arg2;
    this.method1 = myFunc;
}
var myObjA = new CustomObj(val1, val2);
var myObjB = new CustomObj(val3, val4);
```

The most common way to execute the myFunc( ) function is as a method of one of the objects:

```
myObjA.method1(parmValue);
```

But you can invoke the function from a reference to the function, and make the function believe it is being invoked through one of the objects:

```
myFunc.apply(myObjB, [parmVal1, parmVal2, parmVal3]);
```

If the function (myFunc in this example) has a statement with the this keyword in it, that term becomes a reference to the object context passed as the first parameter to the apply( ) method (myObjB in this example).

**Returned Value**    None.

**Parameters**

*thisObjectRef*
    Reference to an object that is to act as the context for the function.

*argumentsArray*
    An array with items that are values to be passed to the function. Array entries are passed to the function in the same order as they are organized in the array.

## call( )

call([*thisObjectRef*[, *arg1*[, *arg2*,[...*argN*]]]])

Invokes the current function, optionally specifying an object to be used as the context for which any this references in the function applies. Parameters to the function (if any) are contained in a comma-delimited list passed as additional parameters to the call( ) method. Other than the way parameters to the function are assembled, the call( ) and apply( ) methods perform the same tasks. See the apply( ) method for more details.

**Returned Value**    None.

**Parameters**

*thisObjectRef*
> Reference to an object that is to act as the context for the function.

*arg1,...argN*
> A comma-delimited list of parameters values to be passed to the function.

## toString( )

Returns the object's value (script statement listing and function wrapper) as a string data type. You don't need this method in practice because the browsers automatically convert values to strings when they are needed for display in alert dialogs or in-document rendering.

**Returned Value**    String.

**Parameters**    None.

## valueOf( )

Returns the object's value. When displaying the value, such as in an alert dialog box, the browser converts the value to a string, but the true value is an instance of the Function object.

**Returned Value**    A function object reference.

**Parameters**    None.

# Global

The Global object lives in every window or frame of a JavaScript-enabled browser (it is created for you automatically). You don't ever reference the object explicitly, but you do reference its properties and methods to accomplish tasks such as converting strings to numbers (via the parseInt( ) or parseFloat( ) methods). Properties act as constants, and thus evaluate to themselves. As an object with global scope, it exposes its members to script statements throughout the page.

**Properties**

| | | |
|---|---|---|
| Infinity | NaN | undefined |

## Methods

| | | |
|---|---|---|
| atob( ) | btoa( ) | decodeURI( ) |
| decodeURIComponent( ) | encodeURI( ) | encodeURIComponent( ) |
| escape( ) | eval( ) | GetObject( ) |
| isFinite( ) | isNaN( ) | parseInt( ) |
| parseFloat( ) | ScriptEngine( ) | ScriptEngineBuildVersion( ) |
| ScriptEngineMajorVersion( ) | ScriptEngineMinorVersion( ) | unescape( ) |
| unwatch( ) | watch( ) | |

## Infinity

NN 4    IE 4    ECMA 1

Read-only

Provides a numerical positive infinity (or negated with the - operator). We're talking a practical, as opposed to a theoretical, infinity here. Any number smaller than `Number.MIN_VALUE` or larger than `Number.MAX_VALUE` is an infinite value in the JavaScript world. How mundane!

**Example**      `var authorEgo = Infinity;`

**Value**      `Infinity`

## NaN

NN 3    IE 4    ECMA 1

Read-only

This is a value that is not-a-number. JavaScript returns this value when a numerical operation yields a non-numerical result because of a flaw in one of the operands. If you want to test whether a value is not a number, use the `isNaN( )` global function rather than comparing to this property value. This global property is the value that `Number.NaN` evaluates to.

**Value**      `NaN`

## undefined

NN 6    IE 5.5(Win)    ECMA 2

Read-only

While the undefined data type has been in ECMAScript and browsers since very early times, only recently was it also elevated to a formal property of the Global object. Despite the recent compatibility ratings, you can use its data type (accessed in string form via the typeof operator) comfortably in older browsers.

**Value**      `undefined`

## decodeURI( )       NN 6    IE 5.5(Win)    ECMA 3

decodeURI("*encodedURI*")

Returns a string with most URI-encoded values in the parameter restored to their original symbols. Operates only on escaped (encoded) characters that are encodable via the encodeURI( ) method.

**Returned Value**     A string.

**Parameters**

*encodedURI*

    A string containing a relative or complete encoded URI.

## atob( ), btoa( )      NN 4    IE *n/a*    ECMA *n/a*

atob("*base64EncodedData*")
btoa("*stringToBeEncoded*")

These methods let you convert arbitrary strings (including strings conveying characters representing binary data and Unicode values) to a 65-character subset of the U.S.-ASCII character set. Encoding in this so-called base64 scheme allows any data to be conveyed along even the most rudimentary transport mechanism. You can read about the rationale and internal mechanisms of the encoding/decoding conversions in RFC 1521 of the Internet Engineering Task Force (*http://www.ietf.org/rfc/rfc2045.txt*).

Use the btoa( ) method to encode string data into the base64 scheme. The resulting encoded data will consist of ASCII characters a-z, A-Z, 0-9, and three symbols (/, +, =). Use the atob( ) method to decode base64 encoded data back to its original version.

**Returned Value**     A string.

**Parameters**

*base64EncodedData*

    A string containing base64 data either encoded on the client or received as part of a document from a server that performs its own encoding.

*stringToBeEncoded*

    A string characters to be encoded to base64 for internal or external use. For example, an encoded value could be assigned to the value property of an input element for submission to a server process designed to receive base64 data.

## decodeURIComponent( )      NN 6    IE 5.5(Win)    ECMA 3

decodeURIComponent("*encodedURIComponent*")

Returns a string with all URI-encoded values in the parameter restored to their original symbols. Intended for use on data portions of a URI excluding the protocol.

**Returned Value**     A string.

**Parameters**

*encodedURIComponent*

    A string containing a relative or complete encoded URI, or portions thereof.

## encodeURI( )    NN 6    IE 5.5(Win)    ECMA 3

encodeURI("*URIString*")

Returns a string with most URI-encodable values in the parameter converted to their escaped versions (e.g., a space character is converted to %20). This method excludes the following characters from conversion:

   ;  /  ?  :  @  &  =  +  $  ,  #

These characters are valid symbols in URI strings as-is, and should not be converted, and the conversion might invalidate the URI.

**Returned Value**    A string.

**Parameters**

*URIString*
   A string containing a relative or complete plain-text URI.


## encodeURIComponent( )    NN 6    IE 5.5(Win)    ECMA 3

encodeURIComponent("*URIComponentString*")

Returns a string with all characters except Latin character set letters A through Z (upper and lower cases), digits 0 through 9, and a set of URI-friendly symbols (- _ . ! ~ * ( ) ' *space*) converted to their escaped versions (% symbol followed by the hexadecimal version of their Unicode value). Intended for use on data portions of a URI excluding the protocol.

**Returned Value**    A string.

**Parameters**

*URIComponentString*
   A string containing a relative or complete plain-text URI, or portions thereof.


## escape( )    NN 2    IE 3    ECMA |1|

escape("*string*"[, 1])

Returns a URL-encoded version of the string passed as a parameter to the function. URL encoding converts most nonalphanumeric characters (except * _ + - . / and, in IE, @) to hexadecimal values (such as %20 for the space character). URL-encoded strings do not normally encode the plus symbol because those symbols are used to separate components of search strings. If you must have the plus symbol encoded as well, Navigator 4 (only) offers a second parameter (a numeral 1) to turn on that switch for the method. Note that in IE 5.5 for Windows and Netscape 6, this method has been deprecated in favor of the encodeURI( ) and encodeURIComponent( ) methods. This method has been removed from the ECMA 3 specification.

**Returned Value**    A string.

**Parameters**

*string*
   Any string value.

# eval( )

eval("*string*")

Returns an object reference of the object described as a string in the parameter of the function. For example, if a form has a sequence of text fields named entry1, entry2, entry3, and so on, you can still use a for loop to cycle through all items by name if you let the eval( ) function convert the string representation of the names to object references:

```
for (var i = 1; i <=5; i++) {
    oneField = eval("document.forms[0].entry" + i);
    oneValue = oneField.value;
    ...
}
```

Be aware, however, that the eval( ) method is perhaps the most inefficient and performance-draining method of the entire JavaScript language. There are many other, far more efficient, ways to reference a document tree object when you have only the string ID or name, such as the document.getElementById( ) and, for older browsers, named indexes of the document.forms, document.images, and document.formRef.elements arrays.

**Returned Value**    Object reference.

## Parameters

*string*

Any string representation of an object reference.

# GetObject( )

GetObject("*localPathName*"[, *appName.objectType*])

Returns a reference to an ActiveX object hosted on the client machine whose path name the script is aware of. This is an alternate to creating an instance of an ActiveXObject. In addition to specifying the pathname of the control, you can name a data file to open along with the control's application. Append an exclamation point and the name of the file as part of the *localPathName* parameter. To learn more about invoking ActiveX objects (also called automation objects), visit: *http://msdn.microsoft.com/scripting/jscript/doc/jsobjActiveXObject.htm*.

**Returned Value**    Object reference.

## Parameters

*localPathName*

A string containing a complete pathname (including volume) to the automation object.

*appName.objectType*

Common syntax to reference a particular application and type of object supported by the automation object whose path is specified in the first parameter.

## isFinite( )                                              NN 4   IE 4   ECMA 1

isFinite(*expression*)

Returns a Boolean value of true if the number passed as a parameter is anything within the range of Number.MIN_VALUE and Number.MAX_VALUE, inclusive. String values passed as parameters cause the function to return false.

**Returned Value**     Boolean value: true | false.

**Parameters**

*expression*

Any JavaScript expression.


## isNaN( )                                                 NN 2   IE 3   ECMA 1

isNaN(*expression*)

Returns a Boolean value of true if the expression passed as a parameter does not evaluate to a numeric value. Any expression that evaluates to NaN (such as performing parseInt( ) on a string that does not begin with a numeral) causes the isNaN( ) method to return true.

**Returned Value**     Boolean value: true | false.

**Parameters**

*expression*

Any JavaScript expression.


## parseInt( )                                              NN 2   IE 3   ECMA 1

parseInt("*string* "[, *radix*])

Returns an integer value (as a number data type in base-8 or base-10) of the numerals in the string passed as a parameter. The string value must at least begin with a numeral, or the result is NaN. If the string starts with numbers but changes to letters along the way or includes white space, only the leading numbers up to the first nonnumeral or whitespace are converted to the integer. Therefore, you can use the expression:

```
parseInt(navigator.appVersion)
```

to extract only the whole number of the version that leads the otherwise long string that is returned from that property.

The optional radix parameter lets you specify the base of the number being passed to the function. A number string that begins with zero is normally treated as an octal number, which gives you the wrong answer. It is a good idea to use the radix value of 10 on all parseInt( ) functions if all of your dealings are in base-10 numbers.

**Returned Value**     Integer.

**Parameters**

*string*

Any string that begins with one or more numerals.

*radix*

An integer of the number base of the number passed as the string parameter (e.g., 2, 8, 10, 16).

## parseFloat( )

parseFloat(*string*)

Returns a number value (either an integer or floating-point number) of the numerals in the string passed as a parameter. The string value must at least begin with a numeral, or the result is NaN. If the string starts with numbers but changes to letters along the way, only the leading numbers are converted to the integer. Therefore, you can use the expression:

    parseFloat(navigator.appVersion)

to extract the complete version number (e.g., 4.03) that leads the otherwise long string that is returned from that property.

If the converted value doesn't have any nonzero values to the right of the decimal, the returned value is an integer. Floating-point values are returned only when the number calls for it.

**Returned Value**    Number.

**Parameters**

*string*

    Any string that begins with one or more numerals.


## ScriptEngine( ), ScriptEngineBuildVersion( ), ScriptEngineMajorVersion( ), ScriptEngineMinorVersion( )

These Internet Explorer-only functions reveal information about the scripting engine (JScript, VBScript, or VBA) being used to invoke the method and which version of that engine is installed. For JScript, the version refers to the version of the *Jscript.dll* file installed among the browser's support files. The major version is the part of the version number to the left of the version decimal point; the minor version is the part to the right of the decimal point. More granular than that is the internal build number that Microsoft uses to keep track of release generations during development and through release.

**Returned Value**

ScriptEngine( ) returns a string of one of the following engine names: JScript | VBA | VBScript. All other functions return integer values.

**Parameters**    None.


## unescape( )

unescape(*string*)

Returns a decoded version of the URL-encoded string passed as a parameter to the function. URL encoding converts nonalphanumeric characters (except * _ + - . / and, in IE, @) to hexadecimal values (such as %20 for the space character). Note that in IE 5.5 for Windows and Netscape 6, this method has been deprecated in favor of the decodeURI( ) and decodeURIComponent( ) methods. This method has been removed from the ECMA 3 specification.

**Returned Value**    String.

## Parameters

*string*
> Any URL-encoded string value.

## unwatch( ), watch( )

```
unwatch(property)
watch(property, funcHandler)
```

These Navigator-specific functions are used primarily by JavaScript debuggers. When a statement invokes the watch( ) function for an object, the parameters include the property whose value is to be watched and the reference to the function to be invoked whenever the value of the property is changed by an assignment statement. To turn off the watch operation, invoke the unwatch( ) function for the particular property engaged earlier.

**Returned Value**    Nothing.

## Parameters

*property*
> The name of the object's property to be watched.

*funcHandler*
> The name of the function (no parentheses) to be invoked whenever the watched property's value changes.

# Math

The Math object is used only in its static object form as a library of math constant values and (mostly trigonometric) operations. As a result, there is no constructor function. Math object properties are constant values, while methods return a numeric value reflecting some math operation on a value; the original value is not altered when the method is invoked.

Invoking a Math object property or method adheres to the following syntax:

```
Math.propertyName
Math.method(param1[, param2])
```

Be sure to observe the uppercase "M" in the Math object in script statements. All expressions involving the Math object evaluate to or return a value.

## Properties

| E | LN10 | LN2 | LOG10E | LOG2E | PI | SQRT1_2 | SQRT2 |
|---|------|-----|--------|-------|----|---------|-------|

## Methods

| | | | | | |
|---|---|---|---|---|---|
| abs( ) | acos( ) | asin( ) | atan( ) | atan2( ) | ceil( ) |
| cos( ) | exp( ) | floor( ) | log( ) | max( ) | min( ) |
| pow( ) | random( ) | round( ) | sin( ) | sqrt( ) | tan( ) |

## E

**Read-only**

Returns Euler's constant.

| | |
|---|---|
| **Example** | var num = Math.E; |
| **Value** | 2.718281828459045 |

## LN2

**Read-only**

Returns the natural logarithm of 2.

| | |
|---|---|
| **Example** | var num = Math.LN2; |
| **Value** | 0.6931471805599453 |

## LN10

**Read-only**

Returns the natural logarithm of 10.

| | |
|---|---|
| **Example** | var num = Math.LN10; |
| **Value** | 2.302585092994046 |

## LOG2E

**Read-only**

Returns the log base-2 of Euler's constant.

| | |
|---|---|
| **Example** | var num = Math.LOG2E; |
| **Value** | 1.4426950408889634 |

## LOG10E

**Read-only**

Returns the log base-10 of Euler's constant.

| | |
|---|---|
| **Example** | var num = Math.LOG10E; |
| **Value** | 0.4342944819032518 |

## PI

**Read-only**

Returns the value of $\pi$.

| | |
|---|---|
| **Example** | var num = Math.PI; |
| **Value** | 3.141592653589793 |

## SQRT1_2

NN *2*   IE *3*   ECMA *1*

Read-only

Returns the square root of 0.5.

**Example**     `var num = Math.SQRT1_2;`

**Value**       0.7071067811865476

## SQRT2

NN *2*   IE *3*   ECMA *1*

Read-only

Returns the square root of 2.

**Example**     `var num = Math.SQRT2;`

**Value**       1.4142135623730951

## abs( )

NN *2*   IE *3*   ECMA *1*

abs(*number*)

Returns the absolute value of the number passed as a parameter.

**Returned Value**     Positive number or zero.

**Parameters**

*number*
  Any number.

## acos( )

NN *2*   IE *3*   ECMA *1*

acos(*number*)

Returns the arc cosine (in radians) of the number passed as a parameter.

**Returned Value**     Number.

**Parameters**

*number*
  Any number from −1 to 1.

## asin( )

NN *2*   IE *3*   ECMA *1*

asin(*number*)

Returns the arc sine (in radians) of the number passed as a parameter.

**Returned Value**     Number.

**Parameters**

*number*
  Any number from −1 to 1.

## atan( )

atan(*number*)

Returns the arc tangent (in radians) of the number passed as a parameter.

**Returned Value**   Number.

**Parameters**

*number*

Any number between negative infinity and infinity.

## atan2( )

atan2(*x, y*)

Returns the angle (in radians) of angle formed by a line to Cartesian point x, y.

**Returned Value**   Number between $-\pi$ and $\pi$.

**Parameters**

*x*   Any number.

*y*   Any number.

## ceil( )

ceil(*number*)

Returns the next higher integer that is greater than or equal to the number passed as a parameter.

**Returned Value**   Integer.

**Parameters**

*number*

Any number.

## cos( )

cos(*number*)

Returns the cosine of the number passed as a parameter.

**Returned Value**   Number.

**Parameters**

*number*

Any number.

## exp( )

exp(*number*)

Returns the value of Euler's constant to the power of the number passed as a parameter.

JavaScript Reference

**Returned Value**     Number.

**Parameters**

*number*
   Any number.

## floor( )                                           NN 2    IE 3    ECMA 1

floor(*number*)

Returns the next lower integer that is less than or equal to the number passed as a
parameter.

**Returned Value**     Integer.

**Parameters**

*number*
   Any number.

## log( )                                             NN 2    IE 3    ECMA 1

log(*number*)

Returns the natural logarithm (base e) of the number passed as a parameter.

**Returned Value**     Number.

**Parameters**

*number*
   Any number.

## max( )                                             NN 2    IE 3    ECMA 1

max(*number1*, *number2*)

Returns the greater value of the two parameters.

**Returned Value**     Number.

**Parameters**

*number1*
   Any number.
*number2*
   Any number.

## min( )                                             NN 2    IE 3    ECMA 1

min(*number1*, *number2*)

Returns the lesser value of the two parameters.

**Returned Value**     Number.

**Parameters**

*number1*
> Any number.

*number2*
> Any number.

## pow( )  NN 2    IE 3    ECMA 1

pow(*number1, number2*)

Returns the value of the first parameter raised to the power of the second parameter.

**Returned Value**    Number.

**Parameters**

*number1*
> Any number.

*number2*
> Any number.

## random( )  NN 2    IE 3    ECMA 1

Returns a pseudo-random number between 0 and 1. To calculate a pseudo-random integer between zero and another maximum value, use the formula:

    Math.floor(Math.random( ) * n)

where *n* is the top integer of the acceptable range. To calculate a pseudo-random integer between a range starting with a number other than zero, use the formula:

    Math.floor(Math.random( ) * n - m + 1) + m

where *m* is the lowest integer of the acceptable range and *n* equals the maximum value of the range. Note that the Math.random( ) method does not work in the Windows and Macintosh versions of Navigator 2.

**Returned Value**    Number from 0 up to, but not including, 1.

**Parameters**    None.

## round( )  NN 2    IE 3    ECMA 1

round(*number*)

Returns an integer that follows rounding rules. If the value of the passed parameter is greater than or equal to *x*.5, the returned value is *x* + 1; otherwise, the returned value is *x*.

**Returned Value**    Integer.

**Parameters**

*number*
> Any number.

## sin( )

sin(*number*)

Returns the sine (in radians) of the number passed as a parameter.

**Returned Value**     Number.

**Parameters**

*number*
    Any number.

## sqrt( )

sqrt(*number*)

Returns the square root of the number passed as a parameter.

**Returned Value**     Number.

**Parameters**

*number*
    Any number.

## tan( )

tan(*number*)

Returns the tangent (in radians) of the number passed as a parameter.

**Returned Value**     Number.

**Parameters**

*number*
    Any number between negative infinity and infinity.

# Number

A Number object represents any numerical value, whether it is an integer or floating-point number. By and large, you don't have to worry about the Number object because a numerical value automatically becomes a Number object instance whenever you use such a value or assign it to a variable. On the other hand, you might want access to the static properties that only a math major would love.

**Creating a Number Object**

```
var myValue = number;
var myValue = new Number(number);
```

**Properties**

| | | | |
|---|---|---|---|
| constructor | MAX_VALUE | MIN_VALUE | NaN |
| NEGATIVE_INFINITY | POSITIVE_INFINITY | prototype | |

**Methods**

| | | | |
|---|---|---|---|
| toExponential( ) | toFixed( ) | toLocaleString( ) | toPrecision( ) |
| toString( ) | valueOf( ) | | |

## constructor

This is a reference to the function that created the instance of a Number object—the native Number( ) constructor function in browsers.

**Example**

```
if (myVar.constructor == Number) {
    // process native function
}
```

**Value**          Function object reference.

## MAX_VALUE

Equal to the highest possible number that JavaScript can handle.

**Example**          `var tiptop = Number.MAX_VALUE;`

**Value**            1.7976931348623157e+308

## MIN_VALUE

Equal to the smallest possible number that JavaScript can handle.

**Example**          `var itsybitsy = Number.MIN_VALUE;`

**Value**            5e-324

## NaN

Equal to a value that is not-a-number. JavaScript returns this value when a numerical operation yields a non-numerical result because of a flaw in one of the operands. If you want to test whether a value is not a number, use the isNaN( ) global function rather than comparing to this property value.

**Value**          NaN

## NEGATIVE_INFINITY, POSITIVE_INFINITY

NN 3    IE 4    ECMA 1

Read-only

Values that are outside of the bounds of `Number.MIN_VALUE` and `Number.MAX_VALUE`, respectively.

**Example**        `Number.NEGATIVE_INFINITY`

**Value**          `-Infinity; Infinity`

## prototype

NN 3    IE 4    ECMA 1

Read/Write

A property of the static `Number` object. Use the prototype property to assign new properties and methods to future instances of a `Number` value created in the current document. See the `Array.prototype` property description for examples. There is little need to create new prototype properties or methods for the `Number` object.

**Example**        `Number.prototype.author = "DG";`

**Value**          Any data, including function references.

## toExponential( )

NN 6    IE 5.5(Win)    ECMA 3

`toExponential(fractionDigits)`

Returns a string containing the number object's value displayed in JavaScript's exponential notation. The single parameter specifies the number of digits to the right of the decimal to display in the string. For example, if a variable contains the number 9876.54, if you apply the toExponential(10) method, the result is 9.8765400000E+3, with zeroes padding the rightmost digits to reach a total of 10 digits to the right of the decimal. If you specify a parameter that yields a display with fewer digits than in the original number, the returned value is rounded.

**Returned Value**    String.

**Parameters**

*fractionDigits*
    An integer specifying the number of digits to the right of the decimal in the returned string.

## toFixed( )

NN 6    IE 5.5(Win)    ECMA 3

`toFixed(fractionDigits)`

Returns a string containing the number object's value displayed with a fixed number of digits to the right of the decimal (useful for currency calculation results). If you specify a parameter that yields a display with fewer significant digits than the original number, the returned value is rounded, but based only on the value of the digit immediately to the right of the last displayed digit (i.e., rounding does not cascade).

**Returned Value**    String.

**Parameters**

*fractionDigits*
> An integer specifying the number of digits to the right of the decimal in the returned string.

## toLocaleString( )

Returns a string version of the number object's value. The precise format of the returned value is not mandated by the ECMA standard, and may be different from one local currency system to another (as set in the client computer's international preferences). On a U.S. English system, IE 5.5 and later for Windows returns a value with two digits to the right of the decimal (rounding values if necessary), with commas denoting thousands, millions, and so on. IE 5 for Macintosh does the same except for the commas. Netscape 6 performs no special formatting.

**Returned Value**    String.

**Parameters**    None.

## toPrecision( )
toPrecision(*precisionDigits*)

Returns a string containing the number object's value displayed with a fixed number of digits, counting digits to the left and right of the decimal. If you specify a parameter that yields a display with fewer digits to the left of the decimal than the original number, the returned value is displayed in exponential notation. Truncated values are rounded, but based only on the value of the digit immediately to the right of the last displayed digit (i.e., rounding does not cascade).

**Returned Value**    String.

**Parameters**

*precisionDigits*
> An integer specifying the total number of digits in the returned string.

## toString( )

Returns the object's value as a string data type. You don't need this method in practice because the browsers automatically convert Number values to strings when they are needed for display in alert dialogs or in-document rendering.

**Returned Value**    String.

**Parameters**    None.

## valueOf( )

Returns the object's value.

**Returned Value**    A numeric value.

**Parameters**    None.

# Object

In addition to serving quietly as the foundation of all native JavaScript objects, the Object object is the pure model of the JavaScript object—including custom scripts objects you create. Use the Object object to generate things in your scripts with behaviors that are defined by custom properties and/or methods. Most typically, you start by creating a blank object with the constructor function and then assign values to new properties of that object.

Navigator 4 and later and IE 5 and later also let you assign properties and values via a special literal syntax that also creates the Object instance in the process:

```
var myObject = {propName1:propValue1[, propName2:propValue2[,
...propNameN:propValueN]]}
```

You can use objects as data structures for structured custom data in your scripts, much like creating an array with named index values.

### Creating an Object Object

```
var myObject = new Object( );
var myObject = {propName1:propVal1[, propName2:propVal2[,...N]]};
var myObject = new constructorFuncName([propVal1[, propVal2[,...N]]]);
```

### Properties

constructor       prototype

### Methods

hasOwnProperty( )  isPrototypeOf( )   propertyIsEnumerable( )
toLocaleString( )  toString( )      valueOf( )

## constructor

**Read/Write**

Provides a reference to the function that created the instance of an Object object—the native Object( ) constructor function in browsers.

### Example

```
if (myVar.constructor == Object) {
    // process native string
}
```

**Value**        Function object reference.

## prototype

This is a property of the static Object. Use the prototype property to assign new properties and methods to future instances of an Object created in the current document. See the Array.prototype property description for examples.

**Example**             Object.prototype.author = "DG";

**Value**               Any data, including function references.


## hasOwnProperty( )

hasOwnProperty("*propertyName*")

Returns Boolean true if, at the time the current object's instance was created, its constructor (or literal assignment) contained a property with a name that matches the parameter value. A property assigned to an object via its prototype property is not considered one of the object's own properties.

**Returned Value**    Boolean value: true | false.

**Parameters**

*propertyName*
    String containing the name of an object property.


## isPrototypeOf( )

isPrototypeOf(*objectReference*)

Returns Boolean true if the current object and the object passed as a parameter coincide at some point along each object's prototype inheritance chain. Note that IE and Navigator do not always agree on the results.

**Returned Value**    Boolean value: true | false.

**Parameters**

*objectReference*
    Reference to an object that potentially shares prototype inheritance with the current object.


## propertyIsEnumerable( )

propertyIsEnumerable("*propertyName*")

Returns Boolean true if the property, whose name is passed as a parameter, exposes itself to for/in property inspection through the object.

**Returned Value**    Boolean value: true | false.

**Parameters**

*propertyName*
    String containing the name of an object property.

## toLocaleString( ) NN 6   IE 5.5(Win)   ECMA 3

Browsers are free to determine how to localize string representations of object instances. For now, they appear to perform the same action as the toString( ) method, returning the value [object Object].

**Returned Value**   String.

**Parameters**   None.

## toString( ) NN 4   IE 4   ECMA 1

Returns the object's value as a string data type. In recent browsers, this value is [object Object].

**Returned Value**   String.

**Parameters**   None.

## valueOf( ) NN 4   IE 4   ECMA 1

Returns the object's value.

**Returned Value**   An object reference.

**Parameters**   None.

# RegExp NN 4   IE 4   ECMA 3

The RegExp object is a static object that both generates instances of a regular expression and monitors all regular expression in the current window or frame. Instances of the RegExp object are covered in the regular expressions object description that follows this section.

Regular expressions assist in locating text that matches patterns of characters or characteristics. For example, a regular expression can be used to find out very quickly if an entry in a text field is a five-digit number. Defining the pattern to match requires knowledge of a separate notation syntax that is beyond the scope of this book (but is covered in *Mastering Regular Expressions*, by Jeffrey E. F. Friedl, published by O'Reilly). A summary of the syntax can be found in the description of the regular expression object.

Properties of the RegExp object store information about the last operation of any regular expression in the document. Therefore, it is conceivable that each property could change after each regular expression operation. Such operations include not only the methods of a regular expression object instance (exec( ) and test( )), but also the String object methods that accept regular expressions as parameters (match( ), replace( ), and split( )). Some of these properties are passed to the regular expression object as well, in preparation for the next operation with the regular expression.

All properties have verbose names as well as shortcut names that begin with $.

**Properties**

| index | input | lastIndex | lastMatch | lastParen | leftContext |
|-------|-------|-----------|-----------|-----------|-------------|
| multiline | prototype | rightContext | $1 | $2 | $3 |
| $4 | $5 | $6 | $7 | $8 | $9 |

## index

NN *n/a*    IE *4*    ECMA *n/a*
Read-only

This is the zero-based index value of the character position within the string where the most recent search for the pattern began. The lastIndex property provides the end position.

| **Example** | var srchStart = RegExp.index; |
|-------------|-------------------------------|
| **Value** | Integer. |

## input

NN *4*    IE *4*    ECMA *n/a*
Read/Write

This is the main string against which a regular expression is compared. If the main string is handed to the regular expression operation as a parameter to a method, this value is null. The short version is $_ (dollar sign, underscore).

| **Example** | RegExp.input = "Four score and seven years ago..."; |
|-------------|------------------------------------------------------|
| **Value** | String. |

## lastIndex

NN *n/a*    IE *4*    ECMA *n/a*
Read/Write

This is the zero-based index value of the character within the string where the next search for the pattern begins. In a new search, the value is zero. You can also set the value manually if you wish to start at a different location or skip some characters. This property is echoed in the regular expression object instance, and is supported there in Navigator.

| **Example** | myRE.lastIndex = 30; |
|-------------|----------------------|
| **Value** | Integer. |

## lastMatch

NN *4*    IE *5(Mac)/5.5(Win)*    ECMA *n/a*
Read-only

Returns the string that matches the regular expression as a result of the most recent operation. The short version is $&.

| **Example** | var matched = RegExp.lastMatch; |
|-------------|----------------------------------|
| **Value** | String. |

## lastParen

NN 4    IE 5(Mac)/5.5(Win)    ECMA n/a

**Read-only**

Returns the string that matches the last parenthesized subcomponent of the regular expression as a result of the most recent operation. The short version is $+.

**Example**          `var myValue = RegExp.lastParen;`

**Value**            String.

## leftContext, rightContext

NN 4    IE 5(Mac)/5.5(Win)    ECMA n/a

**Read-only**

The `leftContext` property returns the string starting with the beginning of the most recent searched text up to, but not including, the matching string. The `rightContext` property returns the string starting with the main string portion immediately following the matching string and extending to the end of the string. The short versions are $` and $', respectively. Because the start of subsequent searches on the same main string move inexorably toward the end of the main string, the starting point of the `leftContext` value can shift with each operation.

**Example**

`var wholeContext = RegExp.leftContext + RegExp.lastMatch + RegExp.rightContext;`

**Value**            String.

## multiline

NN 4    IE 5(Mac)/5.5(Win)    ECMA 3

**Read/Write**

If the search extends across multiple lines of text, the `multiline` property is set to true. A search through text in a textarea element, for example, is multiline. The short version is $*.

**Example**

```
if (RegExp.multiline) {
    ...
}
```

**Value**            Boolean.

## prototype

NN 4    IE 4    ECMA 3

**Read/Write**

See this property for the Array object.

# $1, ..., $9

Parenthesized subcomponents of a regular expression return results. These results are stored individually in properties labeled 1 through 9, preceded by the $ shortcut symbol. The order is based on the position of the left parenthesis of a subcomponent: the leftmost subcomponent result is placed into $1. These properties may be used directly within parameters to String methods that use regular expressions (see the String.replace( ) method).

**Example**        RegExp.$2

**Value**          String.

# regular expression

A regular expression object is an instance of the RegExp object. Each regular expression object consists of a pattern that is used to locate matches within a string. Patterns for a regular expression can be simple strings or significantly more powerful expressions that use a notation that is essentially a language unto itself. The implementation of regular expressions in JavaScript 1.2 is very similar to the way they are implemented in Perl. You can read more about these concepts in books covering JavaScript 1.2 or later.

To create a regular expression object, surround the pattern with forward slashes, and assign the whole expression to a variable. For example, the following statement creates a regular expression with a pattern that is a simple word:

```
var re = /greet/;
```

The re variable can then be used as a parameter in a variety of methods that search for the pattern within some string (you may also use an expression directly as a method parameter, rather than assigning it to a variable).

Regular expression notation also consists of a number of metacharacters that stand in for sometimes complex ideas, such as the boundary on either side of a word, any numeral, or one or more characters. For example, to search for the pattern of characters shown above but only when the pattern is a word (and not part of a word such as greetings), the regular expression notation uses the metacharacters to indicate that the pattern includes word boundaries on both sides of the pattern:

```
var re = /\bgreet\b/;
```

The following table shows a summary of the regular expression notation used in JavaScript 1.2.

| Character | Matches | Example |
|---|---|---|
| \b | Word boundary | /\bto/ matches "tomorrow" |
| | | /to\b/ matches "Soweto" |
| | | /\bto\b/ matches "to" |
| \B | Word nonboundary | /\Bto/ matches "stool" and "Soweto" |
| | | /to\B/ matches "stool" and "tomorrow" |
| | | /\Bto\B/ matches "stool" |
| \d | Numeral 0 through 9 | /\d\d/ matches "42" |

| Character | Matches | Example |
|-----------|---------|---------|
| \D | Nonnumeral | /\D\D/ matches "to" |
| \s | Single whitespace | /under\sdog/ matches "under dog" |
| \S | Single nonwhitespace | /under\Sdog/ matches "under-dog" |
| \w | Letter, numeral, or underscore | /1\w/ matches "1A" |
| \W | Not a letter, numeral, or underscore | /1\W/ matches "1%" |
| . | Any character except a newline | /../ matches "Z3" |
| [...] | Any one of the character set in brackets | /J[aeiou]y/ matches "Joy" |
| [^...] | Negated character set | /J[^eiou]y/ matches "Jay" |
| * | Zero or more times | /\d*/ matches "", "5", or "444" |
| ? | Zero or one time | /\d?/ matches "" or "5" |
| + | One or more times | /\d+/ matches "5" or "444" |
| {n} | Exactly n times | /\d{2}/ matches "55" |
| {n,} | n or more times | /\d{2,}/ matches "555" |
| {n,m} | At least n, at most m times | /\d{2,4}/ matches "5555" |
| ^ | At beginning of a string or line | /^Sally/ matches "Sally says..." |
| $ | At end of a string or line | /Sally.$/ matches "Hi, Sally." |

When you create a regular expression, you may optionally wire the expression to work globally (as you probably do if the regular expression is doing a search-and-replace operation with a method, and your goal is a "replace all" result) and to ignore case in its matches. The modifiers that turn on these switches are the letters g and i. They may be used by themselves or together as gi.

Once you have established a pattern with the regular expression notation, all the action takes place in the regular expression object methods and the String object methods that accept regular expression parameters.

### Creating a regular expression Object

```
var regExpressionObj = /pattern/ [g | i | gi];
var regExpressionObj = new RegExp(["pattern", ["g" | "i" | "gi"]]);
```

### Properties

constructor    global    ignoreCase    lastIndex    source

### Methods

compile()    exec()    test()

### constructor          NN 4    IE 4    ECMA 3

Read/Write

See this property for the Array object.

## global, ignoreCase

Read-only

Returns Boolean true if the regular expression object instance had the g or i modifiers (respectively) set when it was created. If a regular expression object has both modifiers set (gi), you must still test for each property individually.

**Example**
```
if (myRE.global && myRE.ignoreCase) {
    ...
}
```

**Value**          Boolean value: true | false.

## lastIndex

Read/Write

This is the zero-based index value of the character within the string where the next search for the pattern begins. In a new search, the value is zero. You can also set the value manually if you wish to start at a different location or skip some characters.

**Example**          myRE.lastIndex = 30;

**Value**          Integer.

## source

Read-only

Returns a string version of the characters used to create the regular expression. The value does not include the forward slash delimiters that surround the expression.

**Example**          var myREasString = myRE.source;

**Value**          String.

## compile( )

```
compile("pattern"[, "g" | "i" | "gi"])
```

Compiles a regular expression pattern into a genuine regular expression object. This method is used primarily to recompile a regular expression with a pattern that may change during the execution of a script.

**Returned Value**          Reference to a regular expression instance.

**Parameters**

*pattern*
Any regular expression pattern as a quoted string. Modifiers for global, ignore case, or both must be supplied as a separate quoted parameter.

# exec( )

exec(*string*)

Performs a search through the string passed as a parameter for the current regular expression pattern. A typical sequence follows the format:

```
var myRE = /somePattern/;
var resultArray = myRE.exec("someString");
```

Properties of both the static RegExp and regular expression instance (myRE in the example) objects are updated with information about the results of the search. In addition, the exec( ) method returns an array of data, much of it similar to RegExp object properties. The returned array includes the following properties:

index
  Zero-based index of starting character in the string that matches the pattern

input
  The original string being searched

[0]
  String of the characters matching the pattern

[1]...[n]
  Strings of the results of the parenthesized component matches

You can stow away the results of the exec( ) method in a variable, whereas the RegExp property values change with the next regular expression operation. If the regular expression is set for global searching, a subsequent call to myRE.exec("*someString*") continues the search from the position of the previous match.

If no match is found for a given call to exec( ), it returns null.

**Returned Value**

An array of match information if successful; null if there is no match.

**Parameters**

*string*
  The string to be searched.

# test( )

test(*string*)

Returns Boolean true if there is a match of the regular expression anywhere in the string passed as a parameter, false if not. No additional information is available about the results of the search. This is the fastest way to find out if a string contains a match for a pattern.

**Returned Value**    Boolean value: true | false.

**Parameters**

*string*
  The string to be searched.

# String

A String object represents any sequence of zero or more characters that are to be treated strictly as text (that is, no math operations are to be applied). A large library of methods is divided into two categories. One category surrounds a string with a pair of HTML tags for a variety of HTML character formatting. These methods are used primarily to assist statements that use document.write( ) to dynamically create content, but their functionality is now superceded by style sheets. The second, vital method category is the more traditional set of string parsing and manipulation methods that facilitate finding and copying characters and substrings, case changes, and conversion from string lists to JavaScript arrays.

By and large, you don't have to worry about explicitly creating a string beyond a simple assignment of a quoted string value:

```
var myString = "howdy";
```

Occasionally, however, it is helpful to create a string object using the constructor of the static String object. Preparing string values for passage to Java applets often requires this type of string generation:

```
var myString = new String("howdy");
```

Other than the constructor, prototype property, and fromCharCode( ) method, all properties and methods are for use with instances of the String object, rather than the static String object.

### Creating a String Object

```
var myValue = "someString";
var myValue = new String("someString");
```

### Properties

| | | |
|---|---|---|
| constructor | length | prototype |

### Methods

| | | | |
|---|---|---|---|
| anchor( ) | big( ) | blink( ) | bold( ) |
| charAt( ) | charCodeAt( ) | concat( ) | fixed( ) |
| fontcolor( ) | fontsize( ) | fromCharCode( ) | indexOf( ) |
| italics( ) | lastIndexOf( ) | link( ) | localeCompare( ) |
| match( ) | replace( ) | search( ) | slice( ) |
| small( ) | split( ) | strike( ) | sub( ) |
| substr( ) | substring( ) | sup( ) | toLocaleLowerCase( ) |
| toLocaleUpperCase( ) | toLowerCase( ) | toString( ) | toUpperCase( ) |
| valueOf( ) | | | |

## constructor

Read/Write

This is a reference to the function that created the instance of a String object—the native String( ) constructor function in browsers.

**Example**
```
if (myVar.constructor == String) {
    // process native string
}
```

**Value**                     Function object reference.

## length                                      NN 2    IE 3    ECMA 1

Provides a count of the number of characters in the string. String values dynamically change their lengths if new values are assigned to them or if other strings are concatenated.

**Example**
```
for (var i = 0; i < myString.length; i++) {
    ...
}
```

**Value**                     Integer.

## prototype                                   NN 3    IE 4    ECMA 1

This is a property of the static String object. Use the prototype property to assign new properties and methods to future instances of a String value created in the current document. See the Array.prototype property description for examples.

**Example**                   String.prototype.author = "DG";

**Value**                     Any data, including function references.

## anchor( )                                   NN 2    IE 3    ECMA n/a
anchor("*anchorName*")

Returns a copy of the string embedded within an anchor (<a>) tag set. The value passed as a parameter is assigned to the name attribute of the tag.

**Returned Value**    A string within an a element.

**Parameters**
*anchorName*
    A string to use as the value of the name attribute.

## big( )                                      NN 2    IE 3    ECMA n/a

Returns a copy of the string embedded within a <big> tag set.

**Returned Value**    A string within a big element.

**Parameters**        None.

---

## blink( )

NN 2   IE 3   ECMA n/a

Returns a copy of the string embedded within a `<blink>` tag set.

**Returned Value**   A string within a `blink` element.

**Parameters**   None.

## bold( )

NN 2   IE 3   ECMA n/a

Returns a copy of the string embedded within a `<b>` tag set.

**Returned Value**   A string within a `b` element.

**Parameters**   None.

## charAt( )

NN 2   IE 3   ECMA 1

charAt(*positionIndex*)

Returns a single character string of the character located at the zero-based index position passed as a parameter. Use this method instead of substring( ) when only one character from a known position is needed from a string.

**Returned Value**

A one-character string. In newer browser versions, an empty string is returned if the parameter value points to a character beyond the length of the string.

**Parameters**

*positionIndex*
    Zero-based integer.

## charCodeAt( )

NN 4   IE 4   ECMA 1

charCodeAt(*positionIndex*)

Returns a number of the decimal Unicode value for the character located at the zero-based index position passed as a parameter. For common alphanumeric characters, the Unicode values are the same as ASCII values.

**Returned Value**

A positive integer. Returns NaN if the parameter value points to a character beyond the length of the string.

**Parameters**

*positionIndex*
    Zero-based integer.

## concat( )

NN 4   IE 4   ECMA n/a

concat(*string2*)

Returns a string that appends the parameter string to the current string object. The results of this method are the same as concatenating strings with the add (+) or add-by-value (+=) operators. Neither the method nor operators insert spaces between the two string components.

**Returned Value**    String.

**Parameters**

*string2*

    Any string.

## fixed( )                           NN 2    IE 3    ECMA *n/a*

Returns a copy of the string embedded within a `<tt>` tag set.

**Returned Value**    A string within a tt element.

**Parameters**    None.

## fontcolor( )                    NN 2    IE 3    ECMA *n/a*

`fontColor(color)`

Returns a copy of the string embedded within a font (`<font>`) tag set. The value passed as a parameter is assigned to the color attribute of the tag.

**Returned Value**    A string within a font element.

**Parameters**

*color*

    A string to use as the value of the color attribute.

## fontsize( )                      NN 2    IE 3    ECMA *n/a*

`fontSize(size)`

Returns a copy of the string embedded within a font (`<font>`) tag set. The value passed as a parameter is assigned to the size attribute of the tag.

**Returned Value**    A string within a font element.

**Parameters**

*size*

    An integer to use as the value of the size attribute.

## fromCharCode( )               NN 4    IE 4    ECMA 1

`fromCharCode(num1, [, num2,[...numN]])`

This is a static method that returns a string of one or more characters with Unicode values that are passed as a comma-delimited list of parameters. For example, the expression:

```
String.fromCharCode(120, 121, 122)
```

returns "xyz".

**Returned Value**    A string.

**Parameters**

*num1...numN*

    One or more integer values in an unquoted, comma-delimited list.

## indexOf( )

```
indexOf(searchString[, startPositionIndex])
```

Returns a zero-based integer of the position within the current string where the *searchString* parameter starts. Normally, the search starts with the first (index of zero) character, but you may have the search begin later in the string by specifying the optional second parameter, which is the index value of where the search should start. If there is no match, the returned value is -1. This is a backward-compatible quick way to find out if one string contains another: if the returned value is -1 then you know the *searchString* is not in the larger string. If the returned value is another number (the precise value doesn't matter), the *searchString* is in the larger string. For browsers that support regular expressions, the String object's search( ) method performs a similar function.

**Returned Value**     Integer.

**Parameters**

*searchString*
> A string to look for in the current string object.

*startPositionIndex*
> A zero-based integer indicating the position within the current string object to begin the search of the first parameter.

## italics( )

Returns a copy of the string embedded within an <i> tag set.

**Returned Value**     A string within an i element.

**Parameters**     None.

## lastIndexOf( )

```
lastIndexOf(searchString[, startPositionIndex])
```

Returns a zero-based integer of the position within the current string object where the *searchString* parameter starts. This method works like the indexOf( ) method but begins all searches from the end of the string or some index position. Even though searching starts from the end of the string, the *startPositionIndex* parameter is based on the start of the string, as is the returned value. If there is no match, the returned value is -1.

**Returned Value**     Integer.

**Parameters**

*searchString*
> A string to look for in the current string object.

*startPositionIndex*
> A zero-based integer indicating the position within the current string object to begin the search of the first parameter. Even though the search starts from the end of the string, this parameter value is relative to the front of the string.

## link( )

`link(URL)`

Returns a copy of the string embedded within an anchor (`<a>`) tag set. The value passed as a parameter is assigned to the `href` attribute of the tag.

**Returned Value**    A string within an a element.

**Parameters**

*URL*

A string to use as the value of the `href` attribute.

## localeCompare( )

`localeCompare(string2)`

Returns a number indicating whether the current string sorts before, the same as, or after the parameter string, based on browser- and system-dependent string localization. If the current string sorts before the parameter string, the return value is a negative number; if they are the same, the return value is 0, if the current string sorts after the parameter string, the return value is a positive number.

Use this method with caution if the strings contain characters outside the Latin character set because each browser can determine what localization equalities are in place. They also calculate the return values differently.

**Returned Value**    Integer

**Parameters**

*string2*

Any string.

## match( )

`match(regexpression)`

Returns an array of strings within the current string that match the regular expression passed as a parameter. For example, if you pass a regular expression that specifies any five-digit number, the returned value of the `match( )` method would be an array of all five-digit numbers (as strings) in the main string. Properties of the `RegExp` static object are influenced by this method's operation.

**Returned Value**    An array of strings.

**Parameters**

*regexpression*

A regular expression object. See the regular expression object for the syntax to create a regular expression object.

## replace( )

replace(*regexpression, replaceString*)

Returns the new string that results when matches of the *regexpression* parameter are replaced by the *replaceString* parameter. The original string is unharmed in the process, so you need to capture the returned value in a variable to preserve the changes.

**Returned Value**    A string.

**Parameters**

*regexpression*
> A regular expression object. If you want the replace( ) method to act globally on the string, set the global switch (g) on the regular expression. See the regular expression object for the syntax to create a regular expression object.

*replaceString*
> A string that is to take the place of all matches of *regexpression* in the current string.

## search( )

search(*regexpression*)

Returns the zero-based indexed value of the first character in the current string that matches the pattern of the *regexpression* parameter. This method is similar to the indexOf( ) method, but the search is performed with a regular expression rather than a straight string.

**Returned Value**    Integer.

**Parameters**

*regexpression*
> A regular expression object. See the regular expression object for the syntax to create a regular expression object.

## slice( )

slice(*startPositionIndex, endPositionIndex*])

Returns a substring of the current string. The substring is copied from the main string starting at the zero-based index count value of the character in the main string. If no second parameter is provided, the substring extends to the end of the main string. The optional second parameter can be another zero-based index value of where the substring should end. This value may also be a negative value, which counts from the end of the string toward the front.

**Returned Value**    String.

**Parameters**

*startPositionIndex*
> A zero-based integer indicating the position within the current string object to start copying characters.

*endPositionIndex*
> A zero-based integer indicating the position within the current string object to end copying characters. Negative values count inward from the end of the string.

## small( )                                        NN 2    IE 3    ECMA *n/a*

Returns a copy of the string embedded within a <small> tag set.

**Returned Value**    A string within a small element.

**Parameters**    None.

## split( )                                        NN 3    IE 4    ECMA 1

split(*delimiter* [, *limitInteger*])

Returns a new array object whose elements are segments of the current string. The current string is divided into array entries at each instance of the delimiter string specified as the first parameter of the method. The delimiter does not become part of the array. You do not have to declare the array prior to stuffing the results of the split( ) method. For example, if a string consists of a comma-delimited list of names, you can convert the list into an array as follows:

```
var listArray = stringList.split(",");
```

You may also use a regular expression as the parameter to divide the string by a pattern rather than a fixed character.

**Returned Value**    Array.

**Parameters**

*delimiter*
> A string or regular expression that defines where the main string is divided into elements of the resulting array.

*limitInteger*
> An optional integer that restricts the number of items converted into array elements.

## strike( )                                        NN 2    IE 3    ECMA *n/a*

Returns a copy of the string embedded within a <strike> tag set.

**Returned Value**    A string within a strike element.

**Parameters**    None.

## sub( )                                        NN 2    IE 3    ECMA *n/a*

Returns a copy of the string embedded within a <sub> tag set.

**Returned Value**    A string within a sub element.

**Parameters**    None.

## substr( )

substr(*startPositionIndex* [, *length*])

Returns a copy of an extract from the current string. The extract begins at the zero-based index position of the current string as specified by the first parameter of the method. If no other parameter is provided, the extract continues to the end of the main string. The second parameter can specify an integer of the number of characters to be extracted from the main string. In contrast, the substring( ) method's parameters point to the start and end position index values of the main string.

**Returned Value**    A string.

**Parameters**

*startPositionIndex*
> A zero-based integer indicating the position within the current string object to start copying characters

*length*
> An optional integer of the number of characters to extract, starting with the character indicated by the *startPositionIndex* parameter

## substring( )

substring(*startPositionIndex*, *endPositionIndex*)

Returns a copy of an extract from the current string. The extract begins at the zero-based index position of the current string as specified by the first parameter of the method and ends just before the character whose index is specified by the second parameter. For example, "Frobnitz".substring(0,4) returns the substring from positions 0 through 3: Frob. In contrast, the substr( ) method's parameters point to the start position of the main string and the number of characters (length) to extract.

**Returned Value**    A string.

**Parameters**

*startPositionIndex*
> A zero-based integer indicating the position within the current string object to start copying characters.

*endPositionIndex*
> A zero-based integer indicating the position within the current string object to end copying characters. In other words, the copy is made from *startPositionIndex* up to, but not including, the character at position *endPositionIndex*.

## sup( )

Returns a copy of the string embedded within a <sup> tag set.

**Returned Value**    A string within a sup element.

**Parameters**    None.

## toLocaleLowerCase( ), toLocaleUpperCase( )                    NN 6    IE 5.5    ECMA 3

Return a copy of the current string in all lowercase or uppercase letters. Works the same as the regular version, except for some non-Latin alphabets with character mappings that may require special internal handling.

**Returned Value**    String.

**Parameters**    None.

## toLowerCase( ), toUpperCase( )                    NN 2    IE 3    ECMA 1

Return a copy of the current string in all lowercase or uppercase letters. If you want to replace the current string with a case-adjusted version, assign the result of the method to the same string:

```
myString = myString.toUpperCase( );
```

It is common to use either one of these methods to create a case-insensitive comparison of two strings. This is especially convenient if one of the strings being compared is entered by a user, who may submit a variety of case situations:

```
if (document.forms[0].entry.value.toLowerCase( ) == compareValue) {
    ...
}
```

**Returned Value**    String.

**Parameters**    None.

## toString( ), valueOf( )                    NN 4    IE 4    ECMA 1

Return a string value of the object.

**Returned Value**    String value.

**Parameters**    None.

# VBArray                                    NN n/a    IE 4(Win)    ECMA n/a

The VBArray object lets JavaScript communicate with Visual Basic safe arrays. This kind of array is read-only, can be multidimensional, and is sometimes returned as a value from ActiveX controls. Methods of this object give JavaScript access to the VBArray data. For additional details, visit *http://msdn.microsoft.com/scripting/jscript/doc/jsobjVBArray.htm*.

**Creating a VBArray**    var myVBA = new VBArray(*externalArray*);

**Properties**    None.

**Methods**

| dimensions( ) | getItem( ) | lbound( ) | toArray( ) | ubound( ) |

## dimensions( )

Returns an integer corresponding to the number of dimensions of the VBArray.

**Returned Value**    Integer.

**Parameters**    None.

## getItem( )

getItem(*dim1*[, *dim2*[,...*dimN*]])

Returns the value of an item from the VBArray. Parameters specify the location in the array.

**Returned Value**    Number, string, or other value from the VBArray.

**Parameters**

*dimN*

Integer for the location within the array. For a multiple-dimension VBArray, use a comma-delimited map to the position.

## lbound(), ubound( )

lbound(*dim*)
ubound(*dim*)

Return an integer of the lowest and highest index values available for a particular dimension of a VBArray.

**Returned Value**    Integer

**Parameters**

*dim*

Integer for the location within the array.

## toArray( )

Returns a JavaScript array version of the VBArray.

**Returned Value**    Array.

**Parameters**    None.

# Operators

## +

The addition operator works with both numbers and strings, but its results vary with the data types of its operands. When both operands are numbers, the result is the sum of the two numbers; when both operands are strings, the result is a concatenation of the two strings (in the order of the operands); when one operand is a number and the other a string, the number data type is converted to a string, and the two strings are concatenated. To convert a string operand to a number, use the parseInt( ) or parseFloat( ) function.

**Example**

```
var mySum = number1 + number2;
var newString = "string1" + "string2";
```

## +=          *NN 2*    *IE 3*    *ECMA 1*

This is the add-by-value operator. This class of operator combines a regular assignment operator (=) with one of the many other operators to carry out the assignment by performing the stated operation on the left operand with the value of the right operand. For example, if a variable named a has a string stored in it, you can append a string to a with the += operator:

```
a += " and some more.";
```

Without the add-by-value operator, the operation had to be structured as follows:

```
a = a + " and some more";
```

The following table shows all the assignment operators that function this way.

| Operator | Example | Equivalent |
|----------|---------|------------|
| += | a += b | a = a + b |
| -= | a -= b | a = a - b |
| *= | a *= b | a = a * b |
| /= | a /= b | a = a / b |
| %= | a %= b | a = a % b |
| <<= | a <<= b | a = a << b |
| >>= | a >>= b | a = a >> b |
| >>>= | a >>>= b | a = a >>> b |
| &= | a &= b | a = a & b |
| \|= | a \|= b | a = a \| b |
| ^= | a ^= b | a = a ^ b |

**Example**

```
output += "<H1>Section 2</H1>";
total *= .95;
```

## &&          *NN 2*    *IE 3*    *ECMA 1*

The AND operator compares two Boolean expressions for equality. If both expressions evaluate to true, the result of the && operator also evaluates to true; if either or both expressions are false, the && operator evaluates to false.

A Boolean expression may consist of a comparison expression (using any of the many comparison operators) or a variety of other values. Here are the most common data types, values, and their Boolean value equivalent.

| Data type | Boolean equivalent |
|---|---|
| Number other than zero | true |
| Zero | false |
| Any nonempty string | true |
| Empty string | false |
| Any object | true |
| null | false |
| undefined | false |

Using this information, you can create compound conditions with the help of the && operator. For example, if you want to see if someone entered a value into a form field and it is a number greater than 100, the condition would look like the following:

```
var userEntry = document.forms[0].entry.value ;
if (userEntry && parseInt(userEntry) >= 100) {
    ...
}
```

If the user had not entered any value, the string would be an empty string. In the compound condition, when the first operand evaluates to false, the && operator rules mean that the entire expression returns false (because both operands must be true for the operator to return true). Because evaluation of expressions such as the compound condition are evaluated from left to right, the false value of the first operand short-circuits the condition to return false, meaning that the second operand isn't evaluated.

**Example**

```
if (a <= b && b >= c) {
    ...
}
```

The assignment operator assigns the evaluated value of the right-hand operand to the variable on the left. After the operation, the variable contains data of the same data type as the original value. Assignment operations can also be chained, with the evaluation of the entire statement starting from the right and working left. Therefore, after the expression:

```
a = b = c = 25;
```

all three variables equal 25.

**Example**

```
var myName = "Theodore Roosevelt";
var now = new Date( );
```

JavaScript Reference

# &

The bitwise AND operator performs binary math on two operands (their binary values). Each column of bits is subjected to the Boolean AND operation. If the value of a column in both operands is 1, the result for that column position is 1. All other combinations yield a zero. The resulting value of the operator is the decimal equivalent of the binary result. For example, the binary values of 3 and 6 are 0011 and 0110, respectively. After an AND operation on these two values, the binary result is 0010; the decimal equivalent is 2.

**Example**        var n = 3 & 6;


# <<

The bitwise left-shift operator shifts the bits of the first operand by the number of columns specified by the second operand. For example, if the binary value of 3 (0011) has its bits shifted to the left by 2, the binary result is 1100; the decimal equivalent is 12.

**Example**        var shifted = 3 << 2;


# ~

This is the bitwise NOT operator. This unary operator inverts the value of the binary digit in each column of a number. For example, the binary 6 is 0110 (with many more zeros off to the left). After the negation operation on each column's value, the binary result is 1001, plus all zeros to the left inverted to 1s. The decimal equivalent is a negative value (–5).

**Example**        var n = ~6;


# |

The bitwise OR operator performs binary math on two operands (their binary values). Each column of bits is subjected to the Boolean OR operation. If the value of a column in both operands is 0, the result for that column position is 0. All other combinations yield a 1. The resulting value of the operator is the decimal equivalent of the binary result. For example, the binary values of 3 and 6 are 0011 and 0110, respectively. After an OR operation on these two values, the binary result is 0111; the decimal equivalent is 7.

**Example**        var n = 3 | 6;


# >>

The bitwise right-shift operator shifts the bits of the first operand by the number of columns specified by the second operand. For example, if the binary value of 6 (0110) has its bits shifted to the right by 2, the binary result is 0001; the decimal equivalent is 1. Any digits that fall off the right end of the number are discarded.

**Example**        var shifted = 6 >> 2;

## ^

The bitwise exclusive OR (XOR) operator performs binary math on two operands (their binary values). Each column of bits is subjected to the Boolean XOR operation. If the value of a column in either operand (but not both operands) is 1, the result for that column position is 1. All other combinations yield a 0. The resulting value of the operator is the decimal equivalent of the binary result. For example, the binary values of 3 and 6 are 0011 and 0110, respectively. After an XOR operation on these two values, the binary result is 0101; the decimal equivalent is 5.

**Example**        `var n = 3 ^ 6;`

## >>>

This is the bitwise zero-fill right-shift operator. This operator shifts the bits of the first operand (to the right) by the number of columns specified by the second operand. With the bitwise right-shift operator (>>), new digits that fill in from the left end are 1s; with the zero-fill right-shift operator (>>>), the new digits at the left are zeros. Any digits that fall off the right end of the number are discarded. Microsoft also refers to this operator as the unsigned right-shift operator.

**Example**        `var shifted = 6 >>> 2;`

## ,

The comma operator (with or without optional white space following it) can delimit expressions in the same line of script. It can be used in a number of ways. For example, to declare multiple variables, the syntax would be:

```
var varName1, varName2, ... varNameN;
```

Multiple script statements may also be joined together on the same line. Therefore, the following script line:

```
alert("Howdy"), alert("Doody");
```

presents two alert dialog boxes in sequence (the second one appears after the first is dismissed by the user). Another application is in for loops when you wish to involve two (or more) variables in the loop:

```
for (var i = 0, var j = 2; i < 20; i++, j++) {
    ...
}
```

**Example**        `var isCSS, isIEMac;`

## ?:

The conditional operator provides a shortcut syntax to an if/else control structure. There are three components to the deployment of this operator: a condition and two statements.

If the condition evaluates to true, the first of the statements is executed; if the condition evaluates to false, the second statement is evaluated. The syntax is as follows:

```
condition ? statement1 : statement2
```

You can nest these operators as a way of adding more decision paths within a single statement. In the following syntax, if *conditionA* evaluates to false, *conditionB* is evaluated, and the entire expression returns the value of *statement2* or *statement3* depending on the results of *conditionB*.

```
conditionA ? statement1 : (conditionB ? statement2 : statement3)
```

This operator is a shortcut in appearance only. It invokes the same internal processing as an if...else construction.

**Example**          var newColor = (temp > 100) ? "red" : "blue";

---

**--**                                                                **NN 2    IE 3    ECMA 1**

The decrement operator (a unary operator) subtracts 1 from the current value of a variable expression. You can place the operator in front of or behind the variable for a different effect. When the operator is in front of the variable, the variable is decremented before it is evaluated in the current statement. For example, in the following sequence:

```
var a, b;
a = 5;
b = --a;
```

one is subtracted from a before being assigned to b. Therefore, both b and a are 4 when these statements finish running. In contrast, in the following sequence:

```
var a, b;
a = 5;
b = a--;
```

the subtraction occurs after a is assigned to b. When the statements complete, b is 5 and a is 4.

This behavior impacts the way for-loop–counting variables are defined and used. Typically, a loop counter that counts backwards from a maximum value decrements the counter after the statements in the loop have run. Thus most loop counters place the operator after the counter variable:

```
for (var i = 10; i >=0; i--) {...}
```

**Example**

--n
n--

---

**/**                                                                 **NN 2    IE 3    ECMA 1**

The division operator divides the number to the left of the operator by the number to the right. Both operands must be numbers. An expression with this operator evaluates to a number.

**Example**          var myQuotient = number1 / number2;

## ==

The equality operator compares two operand values and returns a Boolean result. The behavior of this operator differs with the version of JavaScript specified for the script element. If the language attribute is set to JavaScript or JavaScript1.1, some operands are automatically converted as shown in the following table.

| Left operand | Right operand | Description |
|---|---|---|
| Object reference | Object reference | Compare evaluation of object references. |
| Any data type | Boolean | Convert Boolean operand to a number (1 for true; 0 for false) and compare against other operand. |
| Object reference | String | Convert object to string (via toString( )) and compare strings. |
| String | Number | Convert string to a number and compare numeric values. |

Navigator 4 and later observes slightly different value conversions for determining equality when you explicitly set the script element to language="JavaScript1.2". The browser is more literal about equality, meaning that no automatic data conversions are performed. Therefore, whereas the expression:

```
123 == "123"
```

evaluates to true in most situations due to automatic data type conversion, the expression evaluates to false in Navigator 4 and later but only in statements belonging to explicitly JavaScript 1.2 scripts. Because newer DOM and XHTML standards don't provide a place to specify scripting language versions, you should avoid these special-case situations. If your scripts require tests for absolute equality of operands, use the newer === identity operator instead. For typical value equality testing, the standard equality operators work perfectly well.

Regardless of version, if you wish to compare the values of objects (for example, comparing strings explicitly generated with the new String( ) constructor), you should compare the values derived from methods such as toString( ) or valueOf( ).

### Example

```
if (n == m) {
    ...
}
```

## >

The greater-than operator compares the values of operands on either side of the operator. If the numeric value of the left operand is larger than the right operand, the expression evaluates to true. Strings are converted to their Unicode values for comparison of those values.

### Example

```
if (a > b) {
    ...
}
```

## &gt;= 　　　　　　　　　　　　　　　　　　　　　　　　　 NN *2*　 IE *3*　 ECMA *1*

The greater-than-or-equal operator compares the values of operands on either side of the operator. If the numeric value of the left operand is larger than or equal to the right operand, the expression evaluates to true. Strings are converted to their Unicode values for comparison of those numeric values.

### Example

```
if (a >= b) {
    ...
}
```

## === 　　　　　　　　　　　　　　　　　　　　　　　　　 NN *4*　 IE *4*　 ECMA *2*

The strictly equals (identity) operator compares two operand values and returns a Boolean result. Both the value and data type of the two operands must be identical for this operator to return true (no automatic data type conversions occur). See the equality operator (==) for more liberal equality comparisons.

### Example

```
if (n === m) {
    ...
}
```

## ++ 　　　　　　　　　　　　　　　　　　　　　　　　　 NN *2*　 IE *3*　 ECMA *1*

The increment operator (a unary operator) adds 1 to the current value of a variable expression. You can place the operator in front of or behind the variable for a different effect. When the operator is in front of the variable, the variable is incremented before it is evaluated in the current statement. For example, in the following sequence:

```
var a, b;
a = 5;
b = ++a;
```

1 is added to a before being assigned to b. Therefore, both b and a are 6 when these statements finish running. In contrast, in the following sequence:

```
var a, b;
a = 5;
b = a--;
```

the addition occurs after a is assigned to b. When these statements complete, b is 5 and a is 6.

This behavior impacts the way for-loop–counting variables are defined and used. Typically, a loop counter that counts upward from a minimum value increments the counter after the statements in the loop have run. Thus, most loop counters place the operator after the counter variable:

```
for (var i = 10; i >=0; i++) {...}
```

### Example

```
++n
n++
```

## !=                                                          NN 2   IE 3   ECMA 1

The inequality operator compares two operand values and returns a Boolean result. The behavior of this operator differs with the version of JavaScript specified for the script element. If the language attribute is set to JavaScript or JavaScript1.1, some operands are automatically converted as for the equality (==) operator. The situation is a bit different in Navigator 4 or later when the script element is set to language="JavaScript1.2". The browser is more literal about inequality, meaning that no automatic data conversions are performed. Therefore, whereas the expression:

```
123 != "123"
```

evaluates to false in most situations due to automatic data type conversion, the expression evaluates to true in Navigator 4 and later in statements belonging to explicitly JavaScript 1.2 scripts. Because newer DOM and XHTML standards don't provide a place to specify scripting language versions, you should avoid these special-case situations. If your scripts require tests for absolute inequality of operands, use the newer !== identity operator instead. For typical value inequality testing, the standard inequality operators work perfectly well.

Regardless of version, if you wish to compare the values of objects (for example, strings explicitly generated with the new String() constructor), you should compare the values derived from methods such as toString() or valueOf().

### Example

```
if (n != m) {
    ...
}
```

## <                                                          NN 2   IE 3   ECMA 1

The less-than operator compares the values of operands on either side of the operator. If the numeric value of the left operand is smaller than the right operand, the expression evaluates to true. Strings are converted to their Unicode values for comparison of those values.

### Example

```
if (a < b) {
    ...
}
```

## <=                                                        NN 2   IE 3   ECMA 1

The less-than-or-equal operator compares the values of operands on either side of the operator. If the numeric value of the left operand is smaller than or equal to the right operand, the expression evaluates to true. Strings are converted to their Unicode values for comparison of those numeric values.

### Example

```
if (a <= b) {
    ...
}
```

# %

The modulus operator divides the number to the left of the operator by the number to the right. If a remainder exists after the division, the expression evaluates to that remainder as an integer. If there is no remainder, the returned value is zero. Both operands must be numbers. An expression with this operator evaluates to a number. Even if you aren't interested in the remainder value, this operator is a quick way to find out if two values are evenly divisible.

### Example

```
if ((dayCount % 7) > 0) {
    ...
}
```

# *

The multiplication operator multiplies the number to the left of the operator by the number to the right. Both operands must be numbers. An expression with this operator evaluates to a number.

**Example**        `var myProduct = number1 * number2;`

# -

This is the negation operator. This unary operator negates the value of the single operand. For example, in the following statements:

```
a = 5;
b = -a;
```

the value of b becomes –5. A negation operator applied to a negative value returns a positive value.

**Example**        `var myOpposite = -me;`

# !==

The strict-not-equals (nonidentity) operator compares two operand values and returns a Boolean result. Both the value and data type of the two operands must be identical for this operator to return false. For less stringent comparisons, see the inequality operator (!=).

### Example

```
if (n !== m) {
    ...
}
```

**!**

This is the NOT operator. This unary operator evaluates to the negative value of a single Boolean operand. The NOT operator should be used with explicit Boolean values, such as the result of a comparison or a Boolean property setting.

### Example

```
if (a == !b) {
    ...
}
```

**||**

The OR operator compares two Boolean expressions for equality. If either or both expressions evaluate to true, the result of the || operator also evaluates to true; if both expressions are false, the || operator evaluates to false. A Boolean expression may consist of a comparison expression (using any of the many comparison operators) or a variety of other values. See the discussion of the AND operator for a summary of the most common data types, values, and their Boolean value equivalent.

You can create compound conditions with the help of the || operator. For example, if you want to see if either or both of two conditions are true, you would create a condition such as the following:

```
var userEntry1 = document.forms[0].entry1.value;
var userEntry2 = document.forms[0].entry2.value;
if (userEntry1 || userEntry2) {
    ...
}
```

In the compound condition, the || operator wants to know if either or both operands is true before it evaluates to true. If the user entered text into the first field, the condition short-circuits because a true value of either operand yields a true result. If text were entered only in the second field, the second operand is evaluated. Because it evaluates to true (a nonempty string), the condition evaluates to true. Only when both operands evaluate to false does the compound condition evaluate to false.

### Example

```
if (a <= b || b >= c) {
    ...
}
```

**-**

The subtraction operator subtracts the number to the right of the operator from the number on the left. Both operands must be numbers. An expression with this operator evaluates to a number.

### Example

```
var myDifference = number1 - number2;
```

# delete

The delete operator removes a property from an object (e.g., a prototype property from an instance of an object to whose static object your script added the prototype earlier) or an item from a script-generated array. Removing an array entry does not alter the array's length or the numerical indexes of existing items. Instead, the value of the deleted item is simply undefined. The delete operator is not a memory management tool.

**Example**        delete myString.author;

# in

The in operator lets scripts quickly uncover whether an object has a particular property or method implemented for it. The left operand is a string containing the name of the property or method (method name without parentheses), while the right operand is a reference to the object. If your exploration requires DOM references entailing "dots," put them in the object reference side of the expression. In other words, instead of trying "style.filter" in document.body, use "filter" in document.body.style. Were it not that so few browsers implement this future ECMA operator, it would be a useful tool in object detection.

**Example**
```
if ("createDocument" in document.implementation) {
    // go ahead and use document.implementation.createDocument()
}
```

# instanceof

The instanceof operator lets scripts determine if an object (the left operand) is an instance of a known object (or inherited from the known object). In some ways, this operator is like the typeof operator, but rather than returning a broad object type, an expression with the instanceof operator returns a Boolean value against your test for a more specific object type. In fact, you can query an object against custom objects and, in Netscape 6, W3C DOM tree object prototypes. Whereas the typeof operator on an array returns object, you can find out if an object was instantiated specifically as an array:

```
myVar instanceof Array
```

Note, however, that if the above expression evaluates to true, so does:

```
myVar instanceof Object
```

An array is a descendant of the root Object object, and is thus an instance of that root object, as well.

In Netscape 6, either or both operands can also be references to DOM prototype objects. Therefore, the following expression is legal and operational in Netscape 6:

```
document.getElementById("widget") instanceof HTMLDivElement
```

**Example**
```
if (theVal instanceof Array) {
    // go ahead and treat theVal as an array
}
```

# new

The new operator creates instances of the following ECMA standard static objects:

```
Array
Boolean
Date
Function
Number
Object
RegExp
String
```

An expression with this operator evaluates to an instance of the object. In other words, invoking this operator makes JavaScript look for a constructor function with the same name. Thus, the new operator also works with custom objects that are formed via custom constructor functions. It also works in IE for Windows for creating instances of proprietary objects, such as ActiveX and VBArray objects.

Syntax rules allow naming the static object, the static object with empty parentheses, and the static object with parameters in parentheses:

```
var myArray = new Array;
var myArray = new Array();
var myArray = new Array("Larry", "Moe", "Curly");
```

Only the last two examples are guaranteed to work in all scriptable browser versions. With the exception of the Date object, if you omit assigning parameters during the native object creation, the newly minted instance has only the properties that are assigned to the prototype of the static object.

**Example**        `var now = new Date();`

# this

Refers to the current object. For example, in a form control object event handler, you can pass the object as a parameter to the function:

```
<input type="text" name="ZIP" onchange="validate(this);">
```

Inside a custom object constructor, the keyword refers to the object itself, allowing you to assign values to its properties (even creating the properties at the same time):

```
function CD(label, num, artist) {
    this.label = label;
    this.num = num;
    this.artist = artist;
}
```

Inside a function, the this keyword refers to the function object. However, if the function is assigned as a method of a custom object constructor, this refers to the instance of the object in whose context the function executes.

**Example**        `<input type="text" name="phone" onchange="validate(this.value);">`

# typeof

The typeof operator returns one of six string descriptions of the data type of a value. Those returned types are:

```
boolean
function
number
object
string
undefined
```

The object type includes arrays, but the operator provides no further information about the type of object or array of the value (see the instanceof operator).

**Example**
```
if (typeof someVar == "string") {
    ...
}
```

# void

This unary operator evaluates the expression to its right but returns a value of undefined, even if the expression (such as a function call) evaluates to some value. This operator is commonly used with javascript: pseudo-URLs that invoke functions. If the function returns a value, that value is ignored by the calling expression.

**Example**      `<a href="javascript: void getSound( );" >...</a>`

# Control Statements

# break

Stops execution of the current loop and returns control to the next script statement following the end of the current loop. Note that without a label parameter, the scope of the break statement is its own loop. To break out of a nested loop, assign labels to each nested layer, and use the desired label as a parameter with the break statement. See the label statement (available only starting with Navigator 4 and Internet Explorer 4).

**Syntax**      break [*label*]

**Example**      See the label statement.

# catch

See try.

# continue

Stops execution of the current iteration through the loop and returns to the top of the loop for the next pass (executing the update expression if one is specified in a for loop). If you are using nested loop constructions, assign labels to each nested layer, and use the desired label as a parameter with the continue statement. See the label statement (available only starting with Navigator 4 and Internet Explorer 4).

**Syntax**          continue [*label*]

**Example**

```
outerLoop:
for (var i = 0; i <= maxValue1; i++) {
    for (var j = 0; j <= maxValue2; j++) {
        if (j*i == magic2) {
            continue outerLoop;
        }
    }
}
```

# do/while

Executes statements in a loop while a condition is true. Because the condition is tested at the end of the loop, the statements inside it are always executed at least one time. It is imperative that the expression that makes up the condition have some aspect of its value potentially altered in the statements. Otherwise, an infinite loop occurs.

**Syntax**

```
do {
    statements
} while (condition)
```

**Example**

```
var i = 1;
do {
    window.status = "Loop number " + i++;
} while (i <= 10)
window.status = "";
```

JavaScript Reference

# for

This is a construction that allows repeated execution of statements, usually for a controlled number of times.

## Syntax

```
for ([initExpression]; [condition]; [updateExpression]) {
    statements
}
```

## Example

```
var userEntry = document.forms[0].entry.value;
var oneChar;
for (var i = 0; i < userEntry.length; i++) {
    oneChar = userEntry.charAt(i);
    if (oneChar < "0" || oneChar > "9") {
        alert("The entry must be numerals only.");
    }
}
```

# for/in

This is a variation of the regular for loop that can extract the property names and values of an object. Only properties (and, in Netscape 6, methods) that are set to be enumerable by the browser internals appear in the output of this construction. Opera 6 supports this construction only for custom script-generated objects.

## Syntax

```
for (varName in objectRef) {
    statements
}
```

## Example

```
function showProps( ) {
    objName = "image";
    obj = document.images[0];
    var msg = "";
    for (var i in obj) {
        msg += objName + "." + i + "=" + obj[i] + "\n";
    }
    alert(msg);
}
```

# if

This is a simple conditional statement that provides one alternate execution path.

## Syntax

```
if (condition) {
    statement(s) if true
}
```

## Example

```
if (myDateObj.getMonth( ) == 1) {
    calcMonthLength( );
}
```

# if/else

This is a conditional statement that provides two execution paths depending on the result of the condition. You can nest another if or if/else statement inside either path of the if/else statement.

## Syntax

```
if (condition) {
    statement(s) if true
} else {
    statement(s) if false
}
```

## Example

```
var theMonth = myDateObj.getMonth( );
if (theMonth == 1) {
    monLength = calcLeapMonthLength( );
} else {
    monLength = calcMonthLength(theMonth);
}
```

# label

You can assign a label identifier to any block of executing statements, including control structures. The purpose of the label is to allow break and continue statements within deeply nested control structures to exit to a nested level that may be at levels beyond the scope of the normal break and continue statements.

## Syntax

labelName:

## Example

```
outerLoop:
for (var i = 0; i <= maxValue1; i++) {
    for (var j = 0; j <= maxValue2; j++) {
        if (i == magic1 && j == magic2) {
            break outerLoop;
        }
    }
}
```

# return

Stops execution of the current function. A return statement can be located anywhere within the function, including inside control structures. You can optionally specify a value to be returned to the calling statement. This return value can be any JavaScript data type. If a return statement that returns a value is in a loop or other control structure, there must be a return statement for each branch of the execution tree, including a default return statement if execution should reach the main execution scope near or at the end of the function.

**Syntax**

```
return [value]
```

**Example**

```javascript
function validateNumber(form) {
    var oneChar;
    for (var i = 0; i < userEntry.length; i++) {
        oneChar = form.entry.value.charAt(i);
        if (oneChar < "0" || oneChar > "9") {
            return false;
        }
    }
    return true;
}
```

# switch/case

Provides a shortcut to execution paths for numerous conditions of an expression. The optional break statement at the end of each case block shortcuts execution of the switch statement, and also prevents the inadvertent execution of the default block, if present.

**Syntax**

```
switch (expression) {
    case label1:
        statements
        [break;]
    case label2:
        statements
        [break;]
    ...
    [default:
        statements]
}
```

**Example**

```javascript
var productList = document.forms[0].prodList;
var chosenItem = productList.options[productList.selectedIndex].value;
switch(chosenItem) {
    case "Small Widget":
        document.forms[0].price.value = "44.95";
        break;
    case "Medium Widget":
        document.forms[0].price.value = "54.95";
        break;
```

```
    case "Large Widget":
        document.forms[0].price.value = "64.95";
        break;
    default:
        document.forms[0].price.value = "Nothing Selected";
}
```

# throw

Triggers an exception condition, passing a value along with the exception. Although the value you pass can be a simple string, ideally you should pass an instance of the JavaScript Error object filled with sufficient information for a catch statement to act intelligently on the error. A throw statement must be enclosed in the try portion of a try-catch construction.

**Syntax**        throw *value*;

**Example**

```
function processNumber(inputField) {
    try {
        var inpVal = parseInt(inputField.value, 10);
        if (isNaN(inpVal)) {
            var msg = "Please enter a number only.";
            var err = new Error(msg);
            if (!err.message) {
                err.message = msg;
            }
            throw err;
        }
        // process number
    }
    catch (e) {
        alert(e.message);
        inputField.focus();
        inputField.select();
    }
}
```

# try/catch

This construction provides a nondisruptive way to trap for errors (exceptions) and handle them gracefully. Both parts of this exception-handling construction are required. If an error occurs in the try portion, execution immediately branches to the catch portion, where your scripts can display alert dialogs, modify data, or any other task that keeps the JavaScript interpreter from triggering a disruptive error message. Exceptions that occur naturally (i.e., they are not thrown by a throw statement) pass an instance of the Error object as a parameter to the catch section. Statements inside the catch section can examine properties of the error object to determine how to handle exceptions that land there. Thus, one catch portion can handle errors of various types.

You can use try/catch constructions only in browsers that support them. To protect older browsers from seeing this construction, place all affected code inside a <script> tag that explicitly requires JavaScript 1.5 or later (with the language = "JavaScript1.5" attribute.

### Syntax

```
try {
    statement(s) that could cause error
}
catch (errorInfo) {
    process error(s) gracefully
}
```

### Example

```
function insertOneNode(baseNode, newNode, position) {
    try {
        baseNode.insertBefore(newNode, baseNode.childNodes[position]);
    }
    catch (e) {
        // handle W3C DOM Exception types
        switch (e.name) {
            case "HIERARCHY_REQUEST_ERR" :
                // process bad tree hierarchy reference
                break;
            case "NOT_FOUND_ERR" :
                // process bad refNode reference
                break;
            default :
                // process all other exceptions
        }
    }
    return true;
}
```

# while                                                        NN 2    IE 3    ECMA 1

Executes statements in a loop as long as a condition is true. Because the condition is tested at the beginning of the loop, it is conceivable that under the right conditions, the statements inside the loop do not execute. It is imperative that the expression that makes up the condition have some aspect of its value potentially altered in the statements. Otherwise an infinite loop occurs.

### Syntax

```
while (condition) {
    statements
}
```

### Example

```
var i = 0;
while (!document.forms[0].radioGroup[i].checked) {
    i++;
}
alert("You selected item number " + (i+1) + ".");
```

## with
NN 2    IE 3    ECMA 1

The with statement adds an object to the scope of every statement nested within. This can shorten the code of some statement groups that rely on a particular object reference. Note that with constructions are generally very inefficient. You can achieve better performance by assigning the object reference to a local variable, and using that variable in your function.

### Syntax

```
with (objectRef) {
    statements
}
```

### Example

```
with (document.forms[0]) {
    name1 = firstName.value;
    name2 = lastName.value;
    mail = eMail.value;
}
```

# Miscellaneous Statements

## //, /*...*/
NN 2    IE 3    ECMA 1

These are comment statements that let you enter nonexecuting text in a script. Any text following the // symbol anywhere in a statement line is ignored by the language interpreter. The next line of script, unless it begins with another // symbol, is interpreted by the browser.

For multiline comment blocks, you can begin a block with the /* symbol. Comment blocks may run any number of lines. The block is closed with the */ symbol, after which the interpreter engages subsequent statements.

### Example

```
// convert temp from C to F

/*
many lines
of
comments
*/
```

# @cc_on, @if, @end, @set

**NN** *n/a*    **IE** *4(Win)*    **ECMA** *n/a*

IE for Windows includes a scripting feature called *conditional compilation*. It is a mode that, once turned on via the @cc_on statement, allows JScript statements to run under conditions that are testable within this conditional environment. If you surround conditional compilation statements by JavaScript comments, the conditional statements run only in IE 4 or later for Windows, while not conflicting with other browsers.

The "conditional" part comes from numerous global properties (all preceded with the @ symbol) that reveal environmental properties, such as script engine version, operating system, and CPU type. All of this information is available from the navigator object's properties on a wide range of browsers, so this is not unique information available only to this conditional environment.

To engage conditional compilation, include the following statement in your script:

```
/*@cc_on @*/
```

This is a one-way toggle: once the mode is turned on, it can't be turned off in the current page.

The following fragment shows how the @if and related statements display some environmental information in the window's status bar if the browser is running JScript Version 5.6 or later (IE 6 or later):

```
/*@cc_on @*/
/*@if (@_jscript_version >= 5.6 && @_x86)
    status = "Now running JScript version " + @_jscript_version +
    " with Intel inside.";
  @else @*/
    status = "Have a nice day.";
/*@end @*/
```

The @set statement lets you assign a numeric or Boolean value (no strings) to a variable (a variable with an @ prefix) within a conditional compilation section:

```
@set @isOK = @_win32
```

Once initialized, that variable (including its otherwise unacceptable identifier) can be used in script statements throughout the page. Note that the Visual Basic–inspired syntax of @ statements in conditional compilation statements does not permit semicolons at the end of statements.

On the one hand, conditional compilation could be useful for IE-only deployment to screening older IE versions from new language features that would generate compilation errors (such as try-catch constructions) because such statements compile only under very controllable version situations. In a multibrand browser development shop, however, at most you might find application for IE-only debugging purposes, but probably not for actual application deployment.

**Example**      See the discussion above.


# function

**NN** *2*    **IE** *3*    **ECMA** *1*

The function keyword begins a named function definition. For anonymous functions, see the Function object.

**Example**
```
function myFunc(arg1, arg2) {
    // function statements here
}
```

## var

A keyword that defines the creation of a new variable. Although the keyword is optional for global variables (those not declared or initialized inside a function), it is good form to use this keyword for each new variable. Using the var keyword inside a function makes the variable local to statements inside the function.

You may simply declare one or more variable names, in which case their initial values are null. Or you can also initialize a new variable with a value.

**Example**
```
var a, b, c;
var myName = "Susan";
```

# Special (Escaped) String Characters

## \char

JavaScript provides a mechanism for including common whitespace characters (sometimes called control codes) inside strings, as well as symbols that otherwise conflict with string representation. The key is the backslash character (\), followed immediately by a single character with a special meaning. The following table shows the recognized escaped characters and their meanings.

| Escape sequence | Description |
| --- | --- |
| \b | Backspace |
| \t | Horizontal tab |
| \n | Line feed (new line) |
| \v | Vertical tab |
| \f | Form feed |
| \r | Carriage return |
| \" | Double quote " |
| \' | Single quote ' |
| \\ | Backslash |

JavaScript Reference

These characters come in handy for alert, confirm, and prompt dialog box text. For example, if you want to display multiple paragraphs with a blank line between them in an alert box, you would insert line feed characters:

```
alert("First paragraph.\n\nSecond paragraph.")
```

Note that these characters apply to strings, and do not influence HTML content formatting for carriage returns.

# Cross References

This part of the book, Chapters 13 through 16, provides a different take on the information of Part II. If you have the name of an HTML attribute or an object property, method, or event handler, you can look it up in one of the indices here to find out which elements and/or objects support it.

Chapter 13, *HTML/XHTML Attribute Index*

Chapter 14, *DOM Property Index*

Chapter 15, *DOM Method Index*

Chapter 16, *DOM Event Handlers Index*

# HTML/XHTML Attribute Index

Entries in the following index are arranged alphabetically by HTML attribute. Look up an attribute to find out which HTML elements support it. This listing is a union of attributes defined for elements in Internet Explorer, Navigator, and the latest HTML/XHTML recommendations, including deprecated items. The same attribute name may mean different things for different elements. Be sure to look up the details of the attribute listing in Chapter 8, to find out if the attribute is available for the browser(s) used by your intended audience and whether it does what you want. When you see an attribute with a very long list of elements, the attribute is most likely covered among the shared attributes at the beginning of Chapter 8.

**abbr**   td, th

**above**   ilayer, layer

**accept**   form, input

**accept-charset**   form

**accesskey**   a, acronym, address, applet, area, b, bdo, big, blockquote, body, button, caption, center, cite, custom, dd, del, dfn, dir, div, dl, dt, em, embed, fieldset, font, h1, h2, h3, h4, h5, h6, hr, i, img, input, ins, isindex, kbd, label, legend, li, listing, marquee, menu, object, ol, p, plaintext, pre, q, rt, ruby, s, samp, select, small, span, strike, strong, sub, sup, table, tbody, td, textarea, tfoot, th, thead, tr, tt, u, ul, var, xmp

**action**   form

**align**   applet, caption, col, colgroup, div, embed, fieldset, h1, h2, h3, h4, h5, h6, hr, iframe, img, input, legend, object, p, select, spacer, table, tbody, td, tfoot, th, thead, tr

**alink**   body

**alt**   applet, area, embed, img, input, object

**archive**   applet, object

**autocomplete**   form

**axis**   td, th

**background**   body, ilayer, layer, table, td, th, tr

**balance**   bgsound

**behavior**   marquee

**below**   ilayer, layer

**bgcolor**   body, ilayer, layer, marquee, table, tbody, td, tfoot, th, thead, tr

**bgproperties**   body

**border**   frame, frameset, iframe, img, input, object, table

**bordercolor**   frame, frameset, table, td, th, tr

**bordercolordark**   table, td, th, tr

**bordercolorlight**   table, td, th, tr

**bottommargin**   body

**cellpadding**   table

**cellspacing**   table

**challenge**   keygen

**char**   col, colgroup, tbody, td, tfoot, th, thead, tr

**charoff**   col, colgroup, tbody, td, tfoot, th, thead, tr

**charset** a, link, script

**checked** input

**cite** blockquote, del, ins, q

**class** a, abbr, acronym, address, applet, area, b, basefont, bdo, bgsound, big, blockquote, body, br, button, caption, center, cite, code, col, colgroup, dd, del, dfn, dir, div, dl, dt, em, embed, fieldset, font, form, frame, frameset, h1, h2, h3, h4, h5, h6, head, hr, html, i, iframe, img, input, ins, isindex, kbd, label, legend, li, link, listing, map, marquee, menu, nobr, noframes, noscript, object, ol, optgroup, option, p, plaintext, pre, q, rt, ruby, s, samp, script, select, small, span, strike, strong, sub, sup, table, tbody, td, textarea, tfoot, th, thead, tr, tt, u, ul, var, wbr, xmp

**classid** object

**clear** br

**clip** ilayer, layer

**code** applet, object

**codebase** applet, object

**codetype** object

**color** basefont, font, hr

**cols** frameset, multicol, pre, table, textarea

**colspan** td, th

**compact** dir, dl, menu, ol, ul

**content** meta

**contenteditable** a, acronym, address, b, bdo, big, blockquote, body, button, center, cite, code, custom, dd, del, dfn, dir, div, dl, dt, em, fieldset, font, form, h1, h2, h3, h4, h5, h6, i, input, ins, isindex, kbd, label, legend, li, listing, marquee, menu, nobr, ol, p, plaintext, pre, q, rt, ruby, s, samp, small, span, strike, strong, sub, sup, textarea, tt, u, ul, var, xmp

**coords** a, area

**data** object

**datafld** a, applet, button, div, frame, iframe, img, input, label, marquee, param, select, span, td, textarea, th

**dataformatas** button, div, label, marquee, param, span

**datapagesize** table

**datasrc** a, applet, button, div, frame, iframe, img, input, label, marquee, param, select, span, table, textarea

**datetime** del, ins

**declare** object

**defer** script

**dir** a, abbr, acronym, address, area, b, basefont, bdo, big, blockquote, body, caption, center, cite, code, col, colgroup, dd, del, dfn, dir, div, dl, dt, em, embed, fieldset, font, form, h1, h2, h3, h4, h5, h6, head, html, i, img, input, ins, isindex, kbd, label, legend, li, link, listing, map, marquee, menu, meta, noframes, noscript, object, ol, optgroup, option, p, plaintext, pre, q, rt, ruby, s, samp, select, small, span, strike, strong, style, sub, sup, table, tbody, td, textarea, tfoot, th, thead, title, tr, tt, u, ul, var, xmp

**direction** marquee,

**disabled** a, acronym, address, b, bdo, big, blockquote, body, button, caption, center, cite, code, custom, dd, del, dfn, dir, div, dl, dt, em, fieldset, font, form, h1, h2, h3, h4, h5, h6, i, inpu, ins, isindex, kbd, label, legend, li, listing, marquee, menu, nobr, ol, optgroup, option, p, plaintext, pre, q, rt, ruby, s, samp, select, small, strike, strong, style, sub, sup, textarea, tt, u, ul, var, xmp

**dynsrc** img, input

**enctype** form

**event** script

**face** basefont, font

**for** label, script

**frame** table

**frameborder** frame, frameset, iframe

**framespacing** frameset

**galleryimg** img

**gutter** multicol

**headers** td, th

**height** applet, embed, frame, iframe, ilayer, img, input, layer, marquee, object, spacer, table, td, th

**hidden** embed

**href**   a, area, base, link

**hreflang**   a, link

**hspace**   applet, iframe, img, marquee, object, table

**http-equiv**   meta

**id**   a, abbr, acronym, address, applet, area, b, basefont, bdo, bgsound, big, blockquote, body, br, button, caption, center, cite, code, col, colgroup, dd, del, dfn, dir, div, dl, dt, em, embed, fieldset, font, form, frame, frameset, h1, h2, h3, h4, h5, h6, head, hr, html, i, iframe, img, input, ins, isindex, kbd, label, legend, li, link, listing, map, marquee, menu, nobr, noframes, noscript, object, ol, optgroup, option, p, plaintext, pre, q, rt, ruby, s, samp, script, select, small, span, strike, strong, sub, sup, table, tbody, td, textarea, tfoot, th, thead, tr, tt, u, ul, var, wbr, xmp

**ismap**   img, input

**label**   optgroup, option

**lang**   a, abbr, acronym, address, area, b, basefont, bdo, big, blockquote, body, caption, center, cite, code, col, colgroup, dd, del, dfn, dir, div, dl, dt, em, embed, fieldset, font, form, h1, h2, h3, h4, h5, h6, head, html, i, img, input, ins, isindex, kbd, label, legend, li, link, listing, map, marquee, menu, meta, noframes, noscript, object, ol, optgroup, option, p, plaintext, pre, q, rt, ruby, s, samp, select, small, span, strike, strong, style, sub, sup, table, tbody, td, textarea, tfoot, th, thead, title, tr, tt, u, ul, var, xmp

**language**   a, acronym, address, applet, area, b, bdo, big, blockquote, body, button, caption, center, cite, code, custom, dd, del, dfn, dir, div, dl, dt, em, embed, fieldset, font, form, frame, frameset, h1, h2, h3, h4, h5, h6, hr, i, iframe, img, input, ins, isindex, kbd, label, legend, li, listing, map, marquee, nobr, object, ol, option, p, plaintext, pre, q, rt, ruby, s, samp, script, select, small, span, strike, strong, sub, sup, table, tbody, td, textarea, tfoot, th, thead, tr, tt, u, ul, var, xmp

**left**   ilayer, layer

**leftmargin**   body

**link**   body

**longdesc**   frame, iframe, img

**loop**   bgsound, img, input, marquee

**lowsrc**   img, input

**marginheight**   body, frame, iframe

**marginwidth**   body, frame, iframe

**maxlength**   input

**mayscript**   applet

**media**   link, style

**method**   form

**methods**   a

**multiple**   select

**name**   a, applet, basefont, button, embed, form, frame, iframe, img, input, keygen, map, meta, object, param, select, textarea

**nohref**   area

**noresize**   frame

**noshade**   hr

**nowrap**   body, div, td, th

**pagex**   layer

**pagey**   layer

**pluginspage**   embed

**pluginurl**   embed

**point-size**   font

**profile**   head

**prompt**   isindex

**rbspan**   rt

**readonly**   input, textarea

**rel**   a, link

**rev**   a, link

**rightmargin**   body

**rows**   frameset, textarea

**rowspan**   td, th

**rules**   table

**scheme**   meta

**scope**   td, th

**scroll**   body, html

**scrollamount** marquee

**scrolldelay** marquee

**scrolling** frame, iframe

**security** frame, iframe

**selected** option

**shape** a, area

**size** basefont, font, hr, input, select, spacer

**span** col, colgroup

**src** applet, bgsound, embed, frame, iframe, ilayer, img, input, layer, link, script, xml

**standby** object

**start** img, input, ol

**style** a, abbr, acronym, address, applet, area, b, basefont, bdo, big, blockquote, body, br, button, caption, center, cite, code, col, colgroup, dd, del, dfn, dir, div, dl, dt, em, embed, fieldset, font, form, frame, frameset, h1, h2, h3, h4, h5, h6, hr, i, iframe, img, input, ins, isindex, kbd, label, legend, li, link, listing, map, marquee, menu, nobr, noframes, noscript, object, ol, optgroup, option, p, plaintext, pre, q, s, samp, select, small, span, strike, strong, sub, sup, table, tbody, td, textarea, tfoot, th, thead, tr, tt, u, ul, var, wbr, xmp

**summary** table

**tabindex** a, acronym, address, applet, area, b, bdo, big, blockquote, body, button, caption, center, cite, custom, dd, del, dfn, dir, div, dl, dt, em, fieldset, font, form, frame, frameset, h1, h2, h3, h4, h5, h6, hr, i, iframe, img, input, ins, isindex, kbd, label, legend, li, listing, marquee, menu, object, ol, p, plaintext, pre, q, rt, ruby, s, samp, select, small, span, strike, strong, sub, sup, table, tbody, td, textarea, tfoot, th, thead, tr, tt, u, ul, var, xmp

**target** a, area, base, form, link

**text** body

**title** a, abbr, acronym, address, applet, area, b, basefont, bdo, big, blockquote, body, br, button, caption, center, cite, code, col, colgroup, dd, del, dfn, dir, div, dl, dt, em, embed, fieldset, font, form, frame,

frameset, h1, h2, h3, h4, h5, h6, hr, i, iframe, img, input, ins, isindex, kbd, label, legend, li, link, listing, map, marquee, menu, nobr, noframes, noscript, object, ol, optgroup, option, p, plaintext, pre, q, s, samp, select, small, span, strike, strong, sub, sup, table, tbody, td, textarea, tfoot, th, thead, tr, tt, u, ul, var, wbr, xmp

**top** ilayer, layer

**topmargin** body

**truespeed** marquee

**type** a, button, embed, input, li, link, object, ol, param, script, spacer, style, ul

**units** embed

**unselectable** a, acronym, address, applet, area, b, bdo, big, blockquote, body, button, caption, center, cite, code, custom, dd, del, dfn, dir, div, dl, dt, em, embed, fieldset, font, form, frame, frameset, h1, h2, h3, h4, h5, h6, hr, i, iframe, img, input, ins, isindex, kbd, label, legend, li, listing, marquee, menu, nobr, object, ol, p, plaintext, pre, q, rt, ruby, s, samp, select, small, span, strike, strong, sub, sup, table, tbody, td, textarea, tfoot, thead, tt, u, ul, var, xmp

**urn** a

**usemap** img, input, object

**valign** caption, col, colgroup, tbody, td, tfoot, th, thead, tr

**value** button, input, li, option, param

**valuetype** param

**version** html, script

**visibility** ilayer, layer

**vlink** body

**volume** bgsound

**vspace** applet, iframe, img, marquee, object, table

**weight** font

**width** applet, col, colgroup, embed, frame, hr, iframe, ilayer, img, layer, marquee, multicol, object, pre, spacer, table, td, th

**wrap** pre, textarea

**z-index** ilayer, layer

# DOM Property Index

Entries in the following index are arranged alphabetically by scriptable object properties. Look up a property to find out which objects support it. You need to be aware, however, of what support means within the context of the way that browser makers and the W3C DOM specify the inner workings of their models using object-oriented approaches. For example, the list of objects that "support" the style property includes several nonrendered HTML element objects, such as head and meta. Inside the browsers, many properties are defined for a generic HTML element, and *all* elements, regardless of their purpose, inherit those properties. Clearly, reading or writing style-related properties of nonrendered elements is a waste of time in actual development; but because these element objects expose the style property, they appear in that property's list. Omitting this information here could cause equally serious problems for scripters who write object- and property-detection scripts. It's better to know that a property is defined (that is, its value type isn't undefined) for a particular object than to be misled into thinking that its omission means that the property is undefined for the object.

The listing below is a union of properties defined for document and browser objects in Internet Explorer, Netscape Navigator, and implemented objects from the W3C DOM Level 2. (The exception to this rule is that event handler properties are grouped together in Chapter 16 because of the numerous ways events can be bound to objects.) The same property name may mean different things for different objects. Be sure to look up the details of the property listing in Chapter 9, to find if the property is available for the browser(s) used by your intended audience, and whether it does what you want. If an HTML element object and other scriptable object share the same name, the (element) notation follows its name when referring to the element object. Properties that apply to all input element objects are marked simply input; if only particular input element types apply, the type name follows in parentheses, as in "input (checkbox)". When you see a property with a long list of objects, the property is most likely covered among the shared items at the beginning of Chapter 9.

**abbr**   td, th

**ABORT**   Event

**above**   layer

**accelerator**   currentStyle, runtimeStyle, style

**accept**   input (file)

**acceptCharset**   form

**accessKey**   a, abbr, acronym, address, applet, area, b, base, basefont, bdo, bgsound, big, blockquote, body, br, button, caption, center, cite, code, col, colgroup, comment, dd, del, dfn, dir, div, dl, dt, em, embed, fieldset, font, form, frame, frameset, h1, h2, h3, h4, h5, h6, head, hr, html, i, iframe, img, input, ins, kbd, label, legend, li, link, listing, map, marquee, menu, meta, nobr, noframes, noscript, object, ol, optgroup, option, p, plaintext, pre, q, rt, ruby, s, samp, script, select, small, span, strike, strong, style (element), sub, sup, table, tbody, td, textarea, tfoot, th, thead, title, tr, tt, u, ul, var, wbr, xml, xmp

**action**  form

**activeElement**  document

**align**  applet, caption, col, colgroup, div, embed, fieldset, frame, h1, h2, h3, h4, h5, h6, h2, h3, h4, h5, h6, hr, iframe, img, legend, object, p, table, tbody, td, tfoot, th, thead, tr

**alink**  body

**alinkColor**  document

**all**  a, abbr, acronym, address, applet, area, b, base, basefont, bdo, bgsound, big, blockquote, body, br, button, caption, center, cite, code, col, colgroup, comment, dd, del, dfn, dir, div, dl, dt, em, embed, fieldset, font, form, frame, frameset, h1, h2, h3, h4, h5, h6, head, hr, html, i, iframe, img, input, ins, kbd, label, legend, li, link, listing, map, marquee, menu, meta, nobr, noframes, noscript, object, ol, optgroup, option, p, plaintext, pre, q, rt, ruby, s, samp, script, select, small, span, strike, strong, style (element), sub, sup, table, tbody, td, textarea, tfoot, th, thead, title, tr, tt, u, ul, var, wbr, xml, xmp

**allowTransparency**  frame, iframe

**alt**  applet, area, img, input (image), object

**altHTML**  applet

**altHtml**  object

**altKey**  event

**altLeft**  event

**ALT_MASK**  Event

**anchorNode**  selection

**anchorOffset**  selection

**anchors**  document

**appCodeName**  navigator

**appCore**  window

**applets**  document

**appMinorVersion**  navigator

**appName**  navigator

**appVersion**  navigator

**archive**  applet, object

**areas**  map

**attrChange**  event

**ATTRIBUTE_NODE**  (constant of all W3C DOM nodes and elements)

**attributes**  a, abbr, acronym, address, applet, area, b, base, basefont, bdo, bgsound, big, blockquote, body, br, button, caption, center, cite, code, col, colgroup, comment, dd, del, dfn, dir, div, dl, dt, em, embed, fieldset, font, form, frame, frameset, h1, h2, h3, h4, h5, h6, head, hr, html, i, iframe, img, input, ins, isindex, kbd, label, legend, li, link, listing, map, marquee, menu, meta, nobr, noframes, noscript, object, ol, optgroup, option, p, param, plaintext, pre, q, rt, ruby, s, samp, script, select, small, span, strike, strong, style (element), sub, sup, table, tbody, td, textarea, tfoot, th, thead, title, tr, tt, u, ul, var, wbr, xml, xmp

**availHeight**  screen

**attrName**  event

**availHeight**  screen

**availLeft**  screen

**availTop**  screen

**availWidth**  screen

**axis**  td, th

**BACK**  Event

**background**  body, layer, runtimeStyle, style, table, tags, td, th

**backgroundAttachment**  currentStyle, runtimeStyle, style

**backgroundColor**   currentStyle,   runtimeStyle, style, tags

**backgroundImage**   currentStyle,   runtimeStyle, style, tags

**backgroundPosition**   runtimeStyle, style

**backgroundPositionX**   currentStyle,   runtimeStyle, style

**backgroundPositionY**   currentStyle,   runtimeStyle, style

**backgroundRepeat**   currentStyle,   runtimeStyle, style

**balance**   bgsound

**BaseHref**   object

**baseURI**   a, abbr, acronym, address, applet, area, b, base, basefont, bdo, bgsound, big, blockquote, body, br, button, caption, center, cite, code, col, colgroup, dd, del, dfn, dir, div, dl, dt, em, embed, fieldset, font, form, frame, frameset, h1, h2, h3, h4, h5, h6, head, hr, html, i, iframe, img, input, ins, isindex, kbd, label, legend, li, link, listing, map, menu, meta, nobr, noframes, noscript, object, ol, optgroup, option, p, param, plaintext, pre, q, s, samp, script, select, small, span, strike, strong, style (element), sub, sup, table, tbody, td, textarea, tfoot, th, thead, title, tr, tt, u, ul, var, wbr, xmp

**behavior**   currentStyle, marquee, runtimeStyle, style

**behaviorCookie**   event

**behaviorPart**   event

**behaviorUrns**   a, abbr, acronym, address, applet, area, b, base, basefont, bdo, bgsound, big, blockquote, body, br, button, caption, center, cite, code, col, colgroup, comment, dd, del, dfn, dir, div, dl, dt, em, embed, fieldset, font, form, frame, frameset, h1, h2, h3, h4, h5, h6, head, hr, html, i, iframe, img, input, ins, kbd, label, legend, li, link, listing, map, marquee, menu, meta, nobr, noframes, noscript, object, ol, optgroup, option, p, plaintext, pre, q, rt, ruby, s, samp, script, select, small, span, strike,

strong, style (element), sub, sup, table, tbody, td, textarea, tfoot, th, thead, title, tr, tt, u, ul, var, wbr, xml, xmp

**below**   layer

**bgColor**   body,   document,   layer,   marquee, table, tags, tbody, td, tfoot, th, thead, tr

**bgProperties**   body

**blockDirection**   currentStyle

**blockFormats**   Dialog Helper

**blockquote**   cite

**BLUR**   Event

**body**   document

**bookmarks**   event

**border**   frame, frameset, iframe, img, object, runtimeStyle, style, table

**borderBottom**   runtimeStyle, style

**borderBottomColor**   currentStyle,   runtimeStyle, style

**borderBottomStyle**   currentStyle,   runtimeStyle, style

**borderBottomWidth**   currentStyle,   runtimeStyle, style, tags

**borderCollapse**   currentStyle, runtimeStyle, style

**borderColor**   currentStyle,   frame,   frameset, iframe, runtimeStyle, style, table, tags, td, th, tr

**borderColorDark**   table, td, th, tr

**borderColorLight**   table, td, th, tr

**borderLeft**   runtimeStyle, style

**borderLeftColor**   currentStyle,   runtimeStyle, style

**borderLeftStyle**   currentStyle, runtimeStyle, style

**borderLeftWidth**   currentStyle,   runtimeStyle, style, tags

**borderRight**   runtimeStyle, style

**borderRightColor**   currentStyle, runtimeStyle, style

**borderRightStyle**   currentStyle, runtimeStyle, style

**borderRightWidth**   currentStyle,   runtimeStyle, style, tags

**borderSpacing**  style

**borderStyle**  style, tags

**borderTop**  runtimeStyle, style

**borderTopColor**  currentStyle, runtimeStyle, style

**borderTopStyle**  currentStyle, runtimeStyle, style

**borderTopWidth**  currentStyle,  runtimeStyle, style, tags

**borderWidth**  currentStyle, runtimeStyle, style

**borderWidths( )**  tags

**bottom**  currentStyle,  runtimeStyle,  style, TextRectangle

**bottomMargin**  body

**boundElements**  event

**boundingHeight**  TextRange

**boundingLeft**  TextRange

**boundingTop**  TextRange

**boundingWidth**  TextRange

**browserLanguage**  navigator

**bubbles**  event

**bufferDepth**  screen

**button**  event

**cancelable**  event

**cancelBubble**  event

**canHaveChildren**  a, abbr, acronym, address, applet, area, b, base, basefont, bdo, bgsound, big, blockquote, body, br, button, caption, center, cite, code, col, colgroup, comment, dd, del, dfn, dir, div, dl, dt, em, embed, fieldset, font, form, frame, frameset, h1, h2, h3, h4, h5, h6, head, hr, html, i, iframe, img, input, ins, kbd, label, legend, li, link, listing, map, marquee, menu, meta, nobr, noframes, noscript, object, ol, optgroup, option, p, plaintext, pre, q, rt, ruby, s, samp, script, select, small, span, strike, strong, style (element), sub, sup, table, tbody, td, textarea, tfoot, th, thead, title, tr, tt, u, ul, var, wbr, xml, xmp

**canHaveHTML**  a, abbr, acronym, address, applet, area, b, base, basefont, bdo, bgsound, big, blockquote, body, br, button, caption, center, cite, code, col, colgroup, comment, dd, del, dfn, dir, div, dl, dt, em, embed, fieldset, font, form, frame, frameset, h1, h2, h3, h4, h5, h6, head, hr, html, i, iframe, img, input, ins, kbd, label, legend, li, link, listing, map, marquee, menu, meta, nobr, noframes, noscript, object, ol, optgroup, option, p, plaintext, pre, q, rt, ruby, s, samp, script, select, small, span, strike, strong, style (element), sub, sup, table, tbody, td, textarea, tfoot, th, thead, title, tr, tt, u, ul, var, wbr, xml, xmp

**caption**  table

**captionSide**  style

**CDATA_SECTION_NODE**  (constant of all W3C DOM nodes and elements)

**cellIndex**  td, th

**cellPadding**  table

**cells**  table, tr

**cellSpacing**  table

**ch**  col, colgroup, tbody, td, tfoot, th, thead, tr

**CHANGE**  Event

**characterSet**  document

**charCode**  event

**charset**  a, document, link, meta, script

**checked**  input (checkbox), input (radio)

**childNodes**  a, abbr, acronym, address, applet, area, b, base, basefont, bdo, bgsound, big, blockquote, body, br, button, caption, center, cite, code, col, colgroup, comment, dd, del, dfn, dir, div, dl, dt, em, embed, fieldset, font, form, frame, frameset, h1, h2, h3, h4, h5, h6, head, hr, html, i, iframe, img, input, ins, isindex, kbd, label, legend, li, link, listing, map, marquee, menu, meta, nobr, noframes, noscript, object, ol, optgroup, option, p, param, plaintext, pre, q, rt, ruby, s, samp, script, select, small, span, strike, strong, style (element), sub, sup, table, tbody, td, textarea, tfoot, th, thead, title, tr, tt, u, ul, var, wbr, xml, xmp

**children**  a, abbr, acronym, address, applet, area, b, base, basefont, bdo, bgsound, big, blockquote, body, br, button, caption, center, cite, code, col, colgroup, comment, dd, del, dfn, dir, div, dl, dt, em, embed, fieldset, font, form, frame, frameset, h1, h2, h3, h4, h5, h6, head, hr, html, i, iframe, img, input, ins, kbd, label, legend, li, link, listing, map, marquee, menu, meta, nobr, noframes, noscript, object, ol, optgroup, option, p, plaintext, pre, q, rt, ruby, s, samp, script, select, small, span, strike, strong, style (element), sub, sup, table, tbody, td, textarea, tfoot, th, thead, title, tr, tt, u, ul, var, wbr, xml, xmp

**chOff**  col, colgroup, tbody, td, tfoot, th, thead, tr

**cite**  abbr, acronym, address, b, bdo, big, blockquote, center, cite, code, del, dfn, em, i, ins, kbd, listing, nobr, plaintext, pre, q, rt, ruby, s, samp, small, strike, strong, sub, sup, tt, u, var, xmp

**classid**  object

**className**  a, abbr, acronym, address, applet, area, b, base, basefont, bdo, bgsound, big, blockquote, body, br, button, caption, center, cite, code, col, colgroup, comment, dd, del, dfn, dir, div, dl, dt, em, embed, fieldset, font, form, frame, frameset, h1, h2, h3, h4, h5, h6, head, hr, html, i, iframe, img, input, ins, isindex, kbd, label, legend, li, link, listing, map, marquee, menu, meta, nobr, noframes, noscript, object, ol, optgroup, option, p, param, plaintext, pre, q, rt, ruby, s, samp, script, select, small, span, strike, strong, style (element), sub, sup, table, tbody, td, textarea, tfoot, th, thead, title, tr, tt, u, ul, var, wbr, xml, xmp

**clear**  br, currentStyle, runtimeStyle, style

**CLICK**  Event

**clientHeight**  a, abbr, acronym, address, applet, area, b, base, basefont, bdo, bgsound, big, blockquote, body, br, button, caption, center, cite, code, col, colgroup, com-

ment, dd, del, dfn, dir, div, dl, dt, em, embed, fieldset, font, form, frame, frameset, h1, h2, h3, h4, h5, h6, head, hr, html, i, iframe, img, input, ins, kbd, label, legend, li, link, listing, map, marquee, menu, meta, nobr, noframes, noscript, object, ol, optgroup, option, p, plaintext, pre, q, rt, ruby, s, samp, script, select, small, span, strike, strong, style (element), sub, sup, table, tbody, td, textarea, tfoot, th, thead, title, tr, tt, u, ul, var, wbr, xml, xmp

**clientInformation**  window

**clientLeft**  a, abbr, acronym, address, applet, area, b, base, basefont, bdo, bgsound, big, blockquote, body, br, button, caption, center, cite, code, col, colgroup, comment, dd, del, dfn, dir, div, dl, dt, em, embed, fieldset, font, form, frame, frameset, h1, h2, h3, h4, h5, h6, head, hr, html, i, iframe, img, input, ins, kbd, label, legend, li, link, listing, map, marquee, menu, meta, nobr, noframes, noscript, object, ol, optgroup, option, p, plaintext, pre, q, rt, ruby, s, samp, script, select, small, span, strike, strong, style (element), sub, sup, table, tbody, td, textarea, tfoot, th, thead, title, tr, tt, u, ul, var, wbr, xml, xmp

**clientTop**  a, abbr, acronym, address, applet, area, b, base, basefont, bdo, bgsound, big, blockquote, body, br, button, caption, center, cite, code, col, colgroup, comment, dd, del, dfn, dir, div, dl, dt, em, embed, fieldset, font, form, frame, frameset, h1, h2, h3, h4, h5, h6, head, hr, html, i, iframe, img, input, ins, kbd, label, legend, li, link, listing, map, marquee, menu, meta, nobr, noframes, noscript, object, ol, optgroup, option, p, plaintext, pre, q, rt, ruby, s, samp, script, select, small, span, strike, strong, style (element), sub, sup, table, tbody, td, textarea, tfoot, th, thead, title, tr, tt, u, ul, var, wbr, xml, xmp

**clientWidth**  a, abbr, acronym, address, applet, area, b, base, basefont, bdo, bgsound, big, blockquote, body, br, button, caption, center, cite, code, col, colgroup, comment, dd, del, dfn, dir, div, dl, dt, em, embed, fieldset, font, form, frame, frameset, h1, h2, h3, h4, h5, h6, head, hr, html, i, iframe, img, input, ins, kbd, label, legend, li, link, listing, map, marquee, menu, meta, nobr, noframes, noscript, object, ol, optgroup, option, p, plaintext, pre, q, rt, ruby, s, samp, script, select, small, span, strike, strong, style (element), sub, sup, table, tbody, td, textarea, tfoot, th, thead, title, tr, tt, u, ul, var, wbr, xml, xmp

**clientX**   event

**clientY**   event

**clip**   layer, runtimeStyle, style, tags

**clipboardData**   window

**clipBottom**   currentStyle, style

**clipLeft**   currentStyle, style

**clipRight**   currentStyle, style

**clipTop**   currentStyle, style

**closed**   window

**code**   applet, DOMException, object, RangeException

**codeBase**   applet, object

**codeType**   object

**color**   basefont, currentStyle, font, hr, runtimeStyle, style, tags

**colorDepth**   screen

**cols**   frameset, table, textarea

**colSpan**   td, th

**COMMENT_NODE**   (constant of all W3C DOM nodes and elements)

**commonAncestorContainer**   Range

**compact**   dir, dl, menu, ol, ul

**compatMode**   document

**complete**   img, input (image)

**Components**   window

**content**   meta, style, window

**contentDocument**   frame, iframe

**contentEditable**   a, abbr, acronym, address, applet, area, b, base, basefont, bdo, bgsound, big, blockquote, body, br, button, caption, center, cite, code, col, colgroup, comment, dd, del, dfn, dir, div, dl, dt, em, embed, fieldset, font, form, frame, frameset, h1, h2, h3, h4, h5, h6, head, hr, html, i, iframe, img, input, ins, kbd, label, legend, li, link, listing, map, marquee, menu, meta, nobr, noframes, noscript, object, ol, optgroup, option, p, plaintext, pre, q, rt, ruby, s, samp, script, select, small, span, strike, strong, style (element), sub, sup, table, tbody, td, textarea, tfoot, th, thead, title, tr, tt, u, ul, var, wbr, xml, xmp

**contentOverflow**   event

**contentWindow**   frame, iframe

**CONTROL_MASK**   Event

**controllers**   window

**cookie**   document

**cookieEnabled**   navigator

**coords**   a, area

**counterIncrement**   style

**counterReset**   style

**cpuClass**   navigator

**crypto**   window

**cssFloat**   style

**cssRules**   cssRule, rule, styleSheet

**cssText**   cssRule, rule, runtimeStyle, style, styleSheet

**ctrlKey**   event

**ctrlLeft**   event

**cue**   style

**cueAfter**   style

**cueBefore**   style

**current**   history

**currentStyle**   a, abbr, acronym, address, applet, area, b, base, basefont, bdo, bgsound, big, blockquote, body, br, button, caption, center, cite, code, col, colgroup, comment, dd, del, dfn, dir, div, dl, dt, em, embed, fieldset, font, form, frame, frameset, h1, h2, h3, h4, h5, h6, head, hr, html, i, iframe, img, input, ins, kbd, label, legend, li, link, listing, map, marquee, menu, meta, nobr, noframes, noscript, object, ol, optgroup, option, p, plaintext, pre, q, rt, ruby, s, samp, script, select, small, span, strike, strong, style (element), sub, sup, table, tbody, td, textarea, tfoot, th, thead, title, tr, tt, u, ul, var, wbr, xml, xmp

**currentTarget**   event

**cursor**   currentStyle, runtimeStyle, style

**data**   comment, event, object, Text

**dataFld**   a, applet, button, div, event, frame, iframe, img, input (button), input (checkbox), input (hidden), input (password), input (radio), input (text), label, marquee, object, select, textarea

**dataFormatAs**   a, button, div, img, label, marquee

**dataPageSize**   table

**dataSrc**   a, applet, button, div, frame, iframe, img, input (button), input (checkbox), input (hidden), input (password), input (radio), input (text), label, marquee, object, select, textarea

**dateTime**   abbr, acronym, b, bdo, big, cite, code, del, dfn, em, i, ins, kbd, noBR, q, rt, ruby, s, samp, small, strike, strong, sub, sup, tt, u, var

**DBLCLICK**   Event

**declare**   object

**defaultCharset**   document

**defaultChecked**   input (checkbox), input (radio)

**defaultSelected**   option

**defaultStatus**   window

**defaultValue**   input (file), input (hidden), input (password), input (text), textarea

**defaultView**   document

**defer**   script

**description**   mimeType, plugin

**detail**   event

**deviceXDPI**   screen

**deviceYDPI**   screen

**dialogArguments**   window

**dialogHeight**   window

**dialogLeft**   window

**dialogTop**   window

**dialogWidth**   window

**dir**   a, abbr, acronym, address, applet, area, b, base, basefont, bdo, bgsound, big, blockquote, body, br, button, caption, center, cite, code, col, colgroup, comment, dd, del, dfn, dir, div, dl, dt, em, embed, fieldset, font, form, frame, frameset, h1, h2, h3, h4, h5, h6, head, hr, html, i, iframe, img, input, ins, isindex, kbd, label, legend, li, link, listing, map, marquee, menu, meta, nobr, noframes, noscript, object, ol, optgroup, option, p, param, plaintext, pre, q, rt, ruby, s, samp, script, select, small, span, strike, strong, style (element), sub, sup, table, tbody, td, textarea, tfoot, th, thead, title, tr, tt, u, ul, var, wbr, xml, xmp

**direction**   currentStyle, marquee, runtimeStyle, style

**directories**   window

**disabled**   a, abbr, acronym, address, applet, area, b, base, basefont, bdo, bgsound, big, blockquote, body, br, button, caption, center, cite, code, col, colgroup, comment, dd, del, dfn, dir, div, dl, dt, em, embed, fieldset, font, form, frame, frameset, h1, h2, h3, h4, h5, h6, head, hr, html, i, iframe, img, input, ins, kbd, label, legend, li, link, listing, map, marquee, menu, meta, nobr, noframes, noscript, object, ol, optgroup, option, p, plaintext, pre, q, rt, ruby, s, samp, script, select, small, span, strike, strong, style, style (element), styleSheet, sub, sup, table, tbody, td, textarea, tfoot, th, thead, title, tr, tt, u, ul, var, wbr, xml, xmp

**display** currentStyle, runtimeStyle, style, tags

**doctype** document

**document** a, abbr, acronym, address, applet, area, b, base, basefont, bdo, bgsound, big, blockquote, body, br, button, caption, center, cite, code, col, colgroup, comment, dd, del, dfn, dir, div, dl, dt, em, embed, fieldset, font, form, frame, frameset, h1, h2, h3, h4, h5, h6, head, hr, html, i, iframe, img, input, ins, kbd, label, legend, li, link, listing, map, marquee, menu, meta, nobr, noframes, noscript, object, ol, optgroup, option, p, plaintext, popup, pre, q, rt, ruby, s, samp, script, select, small, span, strike, strong, style (element), sub, sup, table, tbody, td, textarea, tfoot, th, thead, title, tr, tt, u, ul, var, wbr, window, xml, xmp

**DOCUMENT_FRAGMENT_NODE** (constant of all W3C DOM nodes and elements)

**DOCUMENT_NODE** (constant of all W3C DOM nodes and elements)

**DOCUMENT_TYPE_NODE** (constant of all W3C DOM nodes and elements)

**documentElement** document

**domain** document

**DRAGDROP** Event

**dropEffect** clipboardData, dataTransfer

**dynsrc** img, input (image)

**effectAllowed** clipboardData, dataTransfer

**ELEMENT_NODE** (constant of all W3C DOM nodes and elements)

**elements** form

**elevation** style

**embeds** document

**emptyCells** style

**enabledPlugin** mimeType

**encoding** cssRule, rule, form

**enctype** form

**endContainer** Range

**endOffset** Range

**entities** DocumentType

**ENTITY_NODE** (constant of all W3C DOM nodes and elements)

**ENTITY_REFERENCE_NODE** (constant of all W3C DOM nodes and elements)

**ERROR** Event

**event** script, window

**eventPhase** event

**expando** attribute, document

**external** window

**face** basefont, font

**fgColor** document

**fileCreatedDate** document, img

**fileModifiedDate** document, img

**filename** plugin

**fileSize** document.img

**fileUpdatedDate** document, img

**filter** currentStyle, runtimeStyle, style

**filters** a, abbr, acronym, address, applet, area, b, base, basefont, bdo, bgsound, big, blockquote, body, br, button, caption, center, cite, code, col, colgroup, comment, dd, del, dfn, dir, div, dl, dt, em, embed, fieldset, font, form, frame, frameset, h1, h2, h3, h4, h5, h6, head, hr, html, i, iframe, img, input, ins, kbd, label, legend, li, link, listing, map, marquee, menu, meta, nobr, noframes, noscript, object, ol, optgroup, option, p, plaintext, pre, q, rt, ruby, s, samp, script, select, small, span, strike, strong, style (element), sub, sup, table, tbody, td, textarea, tfoot, th, thead, title, tr, tt, u, ul, var, wbr, xml, xmp

**firstChild** a, abbr, acronym, address, applet, area, b, base, basefont, bdo, bgsound, big, blockquote, body, br, button, caption, center, cite, code, col, colgroup, comment, dd, del, dfn, dir, div, dl, dt, em, embed, fieldset, font, form, frame, frameset, h1, h2, h3, h4, h5, h6, head, hr, html, i, iframe, img, input, ins, isindex, kbd, label, legend, li, link, listing, map, marquee, menu, meta, nobr, noframes, noscript, object, ol, optgroup, option, p, param, plaintext, pre, q, rt, ruby, s, samp, script, select, small, span, strike, strong, style (element), sub, sup, table, tbody, td, textarea, tfoot, th, thead, title, tr, tt, u, ul, var, wbr, xml, xmp

**FOCUS** Event

**focusNode** selection

**focusOffset** selection

**font** runtimeStyle, style

**fontFamily** currentStyle, runtimeStyle, style, tags

**fonts** Dialog Helper

**fontSize** currentStyle, runtimeStyle, style, tags

**fontSizeAdjust** style

**fontSmoothingEnabled** screen

**fontStretch** style

**fontStyle** currentStyle, runtimeStyle, style, tags

**fontVariant** runtimeStyle, style

**fontWeight** currentStyle, runtimeStyle, style, tags

**form** button, fieldset, input (button), input (checkbox), input (file), input (hidden), input (image), input (password), input (radio), input (reset), input (submit), input (text), label, legend, object, option, select, textarea

**forms** document

**FORWARD** Event

**frame** table

**frameBorder** frame, frameset, iframe

**frameElement** window

**frames** document, window

**frameSpacing** frame, frameset, iframe

**fromElement** event

**hash** a, area, location

**hasLayout** currentStyle

**headers** td, th

**height** applet, currentStyle, document, embed, frame, iframe, img, input (image), marquee, object, runtimeStyle, screen, style, table, td, th, tr

**HELP** Event

**hidden** embed, layer

**hideFocus** a, abbr, acronym, address, applet, area, b, base, basefont, bdo, bgsound, big, blockquote, body, br, button, caption, center, cite, code, col, colgroup, comment, dd, del, dfn, dir, div, dl, dt, em, embed, fieldset, font, form, frame, frameset, h1, h2, h3, h4, h5, h6, head, hr, html, i, iframe, img, input, ins, kbd, label, legend, li, link, listing, map, marquee, menu, meta, nobr, noframes, noscript, object, ol, optgroup, option, p, plaintext, pre, q, rt, ruby, s, samp, script, select, small, span, strike, strong, style (element), sub, sup, table, tbody, td, textarea, tfoot, th, thead, title, tr, tt, u, ul, var, wbr, xml, xmp

**history** window

**host** a, area, location

**hostname** a, area, location

**href** a, area, base, cssRule, img, link, location, rule, styleSheet

**hreflang** a, link

**hspace** applet, frame, iframe, img, input (image), marquee, object

**htmlFor** label, script

**htmlText** TextRange

**httpEquiv** meta

**id** a, abbr, acronym, address, applet, area, b, base, basefont, bdo, bgsound, big, blockquote, body, br, button, caption, center, cite, code, col, colgroup, comment, dd, del, dfn, dir, div, dl, dt, em, embed, fieldset, font, form, frame, frameset, h1, h2, h3, h4, h5, h6, head, hr, html, i, iframe, img, input, ins, isindex, kbd, label, legend, li, link, listing, map, marquee, menu, meta, nobr, noframes, noscript, object, ol, optgroup, option, p, param, plaintext, pre, q, rt, ruby, s, samp, script, select, small, span, strike, strong, style (element), sub, sup, table, tbody, td, textarea, tfoot, th, thead, title, tr, tt, u, ul, var, wbr, xml, xmp

**ids**   document

**images**   document

**imeMode**   currentStyle, runtimeStyle, style

**implementation**   document

**imports**   styleSheet

**indeterminate**   input (checkbox)

**index**   option

**innerHeight**   window

**innerHTML**   a, abbr, acronym, address, applet, area, b, base, basefont, bdo, bgsound, big, blockquote, body, br, button, caption, center, cite, code, col, colgroup, comment, dd, del, dfn, dir, div, dl, dt, em, embed, fieldset, font, form, frame, frameset, h1, h2, h3, h4, h5, h6, head, hr, html, i, iframe, img, input, ins, isindex, kbd, label, legend, li, link, listing, map, marquee, menu, meta, nobr, noframes, noscript, object, ol, optgroup, option, p, param, plaintext, pre, q, rt, ruby, s, samp, script, select, small, span, strike, strong, style (element), sub, sup, table, tbody, td, textarea, tfoot, th, thead, title, tr, tt, u, ul, var, wbr, xml, xmp

**innerText**   a, abbr, acronym, address, applet, area, b, base, basefont, bdo, bgsound, big, blockquote, body, br, button, caption, center, cite, code, col, colgroup, comment, dd, del, dfn, dir, div, dl, dt, em, embed, fieldset, font, form, frame, frameset, h1, h2, h3, h4, h5, h6, head, hr, html, i, iframe, img, input, ins, kbd, label, legend, li, link, listing, map, marquee, menu, meta, nobr, noframes, noscript, object, ol, optgroup, option, p, plaintext, pre, q, rt, ruby, s, samp, script, select, small, span, strike, strong, style (element), sub, sup, table, tbody, td, textarea, tfoot, th, thead, title, tr, tt, u, ul, var, wbr, xml, xmp

**innerWidth**   window

**internalSubset**   DocumentType

**isChar**   event

**isCollapsed**   selection

**isContentEditable**   a, abbr, acronym, address, applet, area, b, base, basefont, bdo, bgsound, big, blockquote, body, br, button, caption, center, cite, code, col, colgroup, comment, dd, del, dfn, dir, div, dl, dt, em, embed, fieldset, font, form, frame, frameset, h1, h2, h3, h4, h5, h6, head, hr, html, i, iframe, img, input, ins, kbd, label, legend, li, link, listing, map, marquee, menu, meta, nobr, noframes, noscript, object, ol, optgroup, option, p, plaintext, pre, q, rt, ruby, s, samp, script, select, small, span, strike, strong, style (element), sub, sup, table, tbody, td, textarea, tfoot, th, thead, title, tr, tt, u, ul, var, wbr, xml, xmp

**isDisabled**   a, abbr, acronym, address, applet, area, b, base, basefont, bdo, bgsound, big, blockquote, body, br, button, caption, center, cite, code, col, colgroup, comment, dd, del, dfn, dir, div, dl, dt, em, embed, fieldset, font, form, frame, frameset, h1, h2, h3, h4, h5, h6, head, hr, html, i, iframe, img, input, ins, kbd, label, legend, li, link, listing, map, marquee, menu, meta, nobr, noframes, noscript, object, ol, optgroup, option, p, plaintext, pre, q, rt, ruby, s, samp, script, select, small, span, strike, strong, style (element), sub, sup, table, tbody, td, textarea, tfoot, th, thead, title, tr, tt, u, ul, var, wbr, xml, xmp

**isMap**   img

**isMultiLine**   a, abbr, acronym, address, applet, area, b, base, basefont, bdo, bgsound, big, blockquote, body, br, button, caption, center, cite, code, col, colgroup, comment, dd, del, dfn, dir, div, dl, dt, em, embed, fieldset, font, form, frame, frameset, h1, h2, h3, h4, h5, h6, head, hr, html, i, iframe, img, input, ins, kbd, label, legend, li, link, listing, map, marquee, menu, meta, nobr, noframes, noscript, object, ol, optgroup, option, p, plaintext, pre, q, rt, ruby, s, samp, script, select, small, span, strike, strong, style (element), sub, sup, table, tbody, td, textarea, tfoot, th, thead, title, tr, tt, u, ul, var, wbr, xml, xmp

**isOpen**  popup

**isTextEdit**  a, abbr, acronym, address, applet, area, b, base, basefont, bdo, bgsound, big, blockquote, body, br, button, caption, center, cite, code, col, colgroup, comment, dd, del, dfn, dir, div, dl, dt, em, embed, fieldset, font, form, frame, frameset, h1, h2, h3, h4, h5, h6, head, hr, html, i, iframe, img, input, ins, kbd, label, legend, li, link, listing, map, marquee, menu, meta, nobr, noframes, noscript, object, ol, optgroup, option, p, plaintext, pre, q, rt, ruby, s, samp, script, select, small, span, strike, strong, style (element), sub, sup, table, tbody, td, textarea, tfoot, th, thead, title, tr, tt, u, ul, var, wbr, xml, xmp

**keyCode**  event

**KEYDOWN**  Event

**KEYPRESS**  Event

**KEYUP**  Event

**label**  optgroup, option

**lang**  a, abbr, acronym, address, applet, area, b, base, basefont, bdo, bgsound, big, blockquote, body, br, button, caption, center, cite, code, col, colgroup, comment, dd, del, dfn, dir, div, dl, dt, em, embed, fieldset, font, form, frame, frameset, h1, h2, h3, h4, h5, h6, head, hr, html, i, iframe, img, input, ins, isindex, kbd, label, legend, li, link, listing, map, marquee, menu, meta, nobr, noframes, noscript, object, ol, optgroup, option, p, param, plaintext, pre, q, rt, ruby, s, samp, script, select, small, span, strike, strong, style (element), sub, sup, table, tbody, td, textarea, tfoot, th, thead, title, tr, tt, u, ul, var, wbr, xml, xmp

**language**  a, abbr, acronym, address, applet, area, b, base, basefont, bdo, bgsound, big, blockquote, body, br, button, caption, center, cite, code, col, colgroup, comment, dd, del, dfn, dir, div, dl, dt, em, embed, fieldset, font, form, frame, frameset, h1, h2, h3, h4, h5, h6, head, hr, html, i, iframe, img, input, ins, kbd, label, legend, li, link, listing, map, marquee, menu, meta, navigator, nobr, noframes, noscript, object, ol, optgroup, option, p, plaintext, pre, q, rt, ruby, s, samp, script, select, small, span, strike, strong, style (element), sub, sup, table, tbody, td, textarea, tfoot, th, thead, title, tr, tt, u, ul, var, wbr, xml, xmp

**lastChild**  a, abbr, acronym, address, applet, area, b, base, basefont, bdo, bgsound, big, blockquote, body, br, button, caption, center, cite, code, col, colgroup, comment, dd, del, dfn, dir, div, dl, dt, em, embed, fieldset, font, form, frame, frameset, h1, h2, h3, h4, h5, h6, head, hr, html, i, iframe, img, input, ins, isindex, kbd, label, legend, li, link, listing, map, marquee, menu, meta, nobr, noframes, noscript, object, ol, optgroup, option, p, param, plaintext, pre, q, rt, ruby, s, samp, script, select, small, span, strike, strong, style (element), sub, sup, table, tbody, td, textarea, tfoot, th, thead, title, tr, tt, u, ul, var, wbr, xml, xmp

**lastModified**  document

**layers**  document

**layerX**  event

**layerY**  event

**layoutFlow**  currentStyle, runtimeStyle, style

**layoutGrid**  runtimeStyle, style

**layoutGridChar**  currentStyle, runtimeStyle, style

**layoutGridLine**  currentStyle, runtimeStyle, style

**layoutGridMode**  currentStyle, runtimeStyle, style

**layoutGridType**  currentStyle, runtimeStyle, style

**left**  currentStyle, layer, runtimeStyle, style, tags, TextRectangle

leftMargin   body

length   all, anchors, applets, areas, attributes, cells, childNodes, children, comment, css-Rules, elements, embeds, filters, form, forms, frames, history, HTMLCollection, images, imports, links, MediaList, NamedNodeMap, NodeList, options, pages, plugin, plugins, rows, scripts, select, styleSheets, tBodies, Text, window

letterSpacing   currentStyle, runtimeStyle, style

lineBreak   currentStyle, runtimeStyle, style

lineHeight   currentStyle, runtimeStyle, style

link   body

linkColor   document

links   document

listStyle   runtimeStyle, style

listStyleImage   currentStyle, runtimeStyle, style

listStylePosition   currentStyle, runtimeStyle, style

listStyleType   currentStyle, runtimeStyle, style, tags

LOAD   Event

localName   a, abbr, acronym, address, applet, area, b, base, basefont, bdo, bgsound, big, blockquote, body, br, button, caption, center, cite, code, col, colgroup, dd, del, dfn, dir, div, dl, dt, em, embed, fieldset, font, form, frame, frameset, h1, h2, h3, h4, h5, h6, head, hr, html, i, iframe, img, input, ins, isindex, kbd, label, legend, li, link, listing, map, menu, meta, nobr, nof-rames, noscript, object, ol, optgroup, option, p, param, plaintext, pre, q, s, samp, script, select, small, span, strike, strong, style (element), sub, sup, table, tbody, td, textarea, tfoot, th, thead, title, tr, tt, u, ul, var, wbr, xmp

LOCATE   Event

location   document, window

locationbar   window

logicalXDPI   screen

logicalYDPI   screen

longDesc   frame, iframe, img

loop   bgsound, img, input (image), marquee

lowsrc   img, input (image)

margin   currentStyle, fieldset, runtimeStyle, style

marginBottom   currentStyle, runtimeStyle, style, tags

marginHeight   frame, iframe

marginLeft   currentStyle, runtimeStyle, style, tags

marginRight   currentStyle, runtimeStyle, style, tags

margins( )   tags

marginTop   currentStyle, runtimeStyle, style, tags

marginWidth   frame, iframe

markerOffset   style

marks   style

maxHeight   style

maxLength   input (password), input (text)

maxWidth   style

media   cssRule, document, link, rule, style (element), styleSheet

mediaText   MediaList

menubar   window

META_MASK   Event

metaKey   event

method   form

Methods   a

mimeType   a, document, img

mimeTypes   navigator

minHeight   currentStyle, runtimeStyle, style

minWidth   style

modifiers   event

MOUSEDOWN   Event

MOUSEDRAG   Event

MOUSEMOVE   Event

MOUSEOUT   Event

MOUSEOVER   Event

MOUSEUP   Event

MOVE   Event

MozBinding   style

MozOpacity   style

multiple   select

name   a, applet, attribute, button, Document-Type, embed, form, frame, iframe, img, input (button), input (checkbox), input (file), input (hidden), input (image), input (password), input (radio), input (reset), input (submit), input (text), layer, map, meta, object, param, plugin, select, textarea, window

nameProp   a, document, img

namespaces   document

namespaceURI   a, abbr, acronym, address, applet, area, b, base, basefont, bdo, bgsound, big, blockquote, body, br, button, caption, center, cite, code, col, colgroup, dd, del, dfn, dir, div, dl, dt, em, embed, fieldset, font, form, frame, frameset, h1, h2, h3, h4, h5, h6, head, hr, html, i, iframe, img, input, ins, isindex, kbd, label, legend, li, link, listing, map, menu, meta, nobr, noframes, noscript, object, ol, optgroup, option, p, param, plaintext, pre, q, s, samp, script, select, small, span, strike, strong, style (element), sub, sup, table, tbody, td, textarea, tfoot, th, thead, title, tr, tt, u, ul, var, wbr, xml, xmp

naturalHeight   img

naturalWidth   img

navigator   window

newValue   event

next   history

nextPage   event

nextSibling   a, abbr, acronym, address, applet, area, b, base, basefont, bdo, bgsound, big, blockquote, body, br, button, caption, center, cite, code, col, colgroup, comment, dd, del, dfn, dir, div, dl, dt, em, embed, fieldset, font, form, frame,

frameset, h1, h2, h3, h4, h5, h6, head, hr, html, i, iframe, img, input, ins, isindex, kbd, label, legend, li, link, listing, map, marquee, menu, meta, nobr, noframes, noscript, object, ol, optgroup, option, p, param, plaintext, pre, q, rt, ruby, s, samp, script, select, small, span, strike, strong, style (element), sub, sup, table, tbody, td, textarea, tfoot, th, thead, title, tr, tt, u, ul, var, wbr, xml, xmp

nodeType   a, abbr, acronym, address, applet, area, b, base, basefont, bdo, bgsound, big, blockquote, body, br, button, caption, center, cite, code, col, colgroup, comment, dd, del, dfn, dir, div, dl, dt, em, embed, fieldset, font, form, frame, frameset, h1, h2, h3, h4, h5, h6, head, hr, html, i, iframe, img, input, ins, isindex, kbd, label, legend, li, link, listing, map, marquee, menu, meta, nobr, noframes, noscript, object, ol, optgroup, option, p, param, plaintext, pre, q, rt, ruby, s, samp, script, select, small, span, strike, strong, style (element), sub, sup, table, tbody, td, textarea, tfoot, th, thead, title, tr, tt, u, ul, var, wbr, xml, xmp

nodeName   a, abbr, acronym, address, applet, area, b, base, basefont, bdo, bgsound, big, blockquote, body, br, button, caption, center, cite, code, col, colgroup, comment, dd, del, dfn, dir, div, dl, dt, em, embed, fieldset, font, form, frame, frameset, h1, h2, h3, h4, h5, h6, head, hr, html, i, iframe, img, input, ins, isindex, kbd, label, legend, li, link, listing, map, marquee, menu, meta, nobr, noframes, noscript, object, ol, optgroup, option, p, param, plaintext, pre, q, rt, ruby, s, samp, script, select, small, span, strike, strong, style (element), sub, sup, table, tbody, td, textarea, tfoot, th, thead, title, tr, tt, u, ul, var, wbr, xml, xmp

nodeVale   a, abbr, acronym, address, applet, area, b, base, basefont, bdo, bgsound, big, blockquote, body, br, button, caption, center, cite, code, col, colgroup, comment, dd, del, dfn, dir, div, dl, dt, em, embed, fieldset, font, form, frame, frameset, h1, h2, h3, h4, h5, h6, head, hr, html, i, iframe, img, input, ins, isindex, kbd, label, legend, li, link, listing, map, marquee, menu, meta, nobr, noframes, noscript, object, ol, optgroup, option, p, param, plaintext, pre, q, rt, ruby, s, samp, script, select, small, span, strike, strong, style (element), sub, sup, table, tbody, td, textarea, tfoot, th, thead, title, tr, tt, u, ul, var, wbr, xml, xmp

**noHref**   area

**noResize**   frame, iframe

**noShade**   hr

**NOTATION_NODE**   (constant of all W3C DOM nodes and elements)

**notations**   DocumentType

**noWrap**   body, dd, div, dt, td, th

**object**   applet, object

**offscreenBuffering**   window

**offsetHeight**   a, abbr, acronym, address, applet, area, b, base, basefont, bdo, bgsound, big, blockquote, body, br, button, caption, center, cite, code, col, colgroup, comment, dd, del, dfn, dir, div, dl, dt, em, embed, fieldset, font, form, frame, frameset, h1, h2, h3, h4, h5, h6, head, hr, html, i, iframe, img, input, ins, isindex, kbd, label, legend, li, link, listing, map, marquee, menu, meta, nobr, noframes, noscript, object, ol, optgroup, option, p, param, plaintext, pre, q, rt, ruby, s, samp, script, select, small, span, strike, strong, style (element), sub, sup, table, tbody, td, textarea, tfoot, th, thead, title, tr, tt, u, ul, var, wbr, xml, xmp

**offsetLeft**   a, abbr, acronym, address, applet, area, b, base, basefont, bdo, bgsound, big, blockquote, body, br, button, caption, center, cite, code, col, colgroup, comment, dd, del, dfn, dir, div, dl, dt, em, embed, fieldset, font, form, frame, frameset, h1, h2, h3, h4, h5, h6, head, hr, html, i, iframe, img, input, ins, isindex, kbd, label, legend, li, link, listing, map, marquee, menu, meta, nobr, noframes,

noscript, object, ol, optgroup, option, p, param, plaintext, pre, q, rt, ruby, s, samp, script, select, small, span, strike, strong, style (element), sub, sup, table, tbody, td, textarea, tfoot, th, thead, title, tr, tt, u, ul, var, wbr, xml, xmp

**offsetParent**   a, abbr, acronym, address, applet, area, b, base, basefont, bdo, bgsound, big, blockquote, body, br, button, caption, center, cite, code, col, colgroup, comment, dd, del, dfn, dir, div, dl, dt, em, embed, fieldset, font, form, frame, frameset, h1, h2, h3, h4, h5, h6, head, hr, html, i, iframe, img, input, ins, isindex, kbd, label, legend, li, link, listing, map, marquee, menu, meta, nobr, noframes, noscript, object, ol, optgroup, option, p, param, plaintext, pre, q, rt, ruby, s, samp, script, select, small, span, strike, strong, style (element), sub, sup, table, tbody, td, textarea, tfoot, th, thead, title, tr, tt, u, ul, var, wbr, xml, xmp

**offsetTop**   a, abbr, acronym, address, applet, area, b, base, basefont, bdo, bgsound, big, blockquote, body, br, button, caption, center, cite, code, col, colgroup, comment, dd, del, dfn, dir, div, dl, dt, em, embed, fieldset, font, form, frame, frameset, h1, h2, h3, h4, h5, h6, head, hr, html, i, iframe, img, input, ins, isindex, kbd, label, legend, li, link, listing, map, marquee, menu, meta, nobr, noframes, noscript, object, ol, optgroup, option, p, param, plaintext, pre, q, rt, ruby, s, samp, script, select, small, span, strike, strong, style (element), sub, sup, table, tbody, td, textarea, tfoot, th, thead, title, tr, tt, u, ul, var, wbr, xml, xmp

**offsetWidth**   a, abbr, acronym, address, applet, area, b, base, basefont, bdo, bgsound, big, blockquote, body, br, button, caption, center, cite, code, col, colgroup, comment, dd, del, dfn, dir, div, dl, dt, em, embed, fieldset, font, form, frame, frameset, h1, h2, h3, h4, h5, h6, head, hr, html, i, iframe, img, input, ins, isindex, kbd, label, legend, li, link, listing, map, marquee, menu, meta, nobr, noframes, noscript, object, ol, optgroup, option, p, param, plaintext, pre, q, rt, ruby, s, samp, script, select, small, span, strike, strong, style (element), sub, sup, table, tbody, td, textarea, tfoot, th, thead, title, tr, tt, u, ul, var, wbr, xml, xmp

**offsetX**  event

**offsetY**  event

**onLine**  navigator

**opener**  window

**options**  select

**originalTarget**  event

**orphans**  style

**oscpu**  navigator

**outerHeight**  window

**outerHTML**  a, abbr, acronym, address, applet, area, b, base, basefont, bdo, bgsound, big, blockquote, body, br, button, caption, center, cite, code, col, colgroup, comment, dd, del, dfn, dir, div, dl, dt, em, embed, fieldset, font, form, frame, frameset, h1, h2, h3, h4, h5, h6, head, hr, html, i, iframe, img, input, ins, kbd, label, legend, li, link, listing, map, marquee, menu, meta, nobr, noframes, noscript, object, ol, optgroup, option, p, plaintext, pre, q, rt, ruby, s, samp, script, select, small, span, strike, strong, style (element), sub, sup, table, tbody, td, textarea, tfoot, th, thead, title, tr, tt, u, ul, var, wbr, xml, xmp

**outerText**  a, abbr, acronym, address, applet, area, b, base, basefont, bdo, bgsound, big, blockquote, body, br, button, caption, center, cite, code, col, colgroup, comment, dd, del, dfn, dir, div, dl, dt, em, embed, fieldset, font, form, frame, frameset, h1, h2, h3, h4, h5, h6, head, hr, html, i, iframe, img, input, ins, kbd, label, legend, li, link, listing, map, marquee, menu, meta, nobr, noframes, noscript, object, ol, optgroup, option, p, plaintext, pre, q, rt, ruby, s, samp, script, select, small, span, strike, strong, style (element), sub, sup, table, tbody, td, tex-

tarea, tfoot, th, thead, title, tr, tt, u, ul, var, wbr, xml, xmp

**outerWidth**  window

**outline**  style

**outlineColor**  style

**outlineStyle**  style

**outlineWidth**  style

**overflow**  currentStyle, runtimeStyle, style

**overflowX**  currentStyle, runtimeStyle, style

**overflowY**  currentStyle, runtimeStyle, style

**ownerDocument**  a, abbr, acronym, address, applet, area, b, base, basefont, bdo, bgsound, big, blockquote, body, br, button, caption, center, cite, code, col, colgroup, comment, dd, del, dfn, dir, div, dl, dt, em, embed, fieldset, font, form, frame, frameset, h1, h2, h3, h4, h5, h6, head, hr, html, i, iframe, img, input, ins, isindex, kbd, label, legend, li, link, listing, map, marquee, menu, meta, nobr, noframes, noscript, object, ol, optgroup, option, p, param, plaintext, pre, q, rt, ruby, s, samp, script, select, small, span, strike, strong, style (element), sub, sup, table, tbody, td, textarea, tfoot, th, thead, title, tr, tt, u, ul, var, wbr, xml, xmp

**ownerElement**  attribute

**ownerNode**  styleSheet

**ownerRule**  styleSheet

**owningElement**  styleSheet

**padding**  currentStyle, runtimeStyle, style

**paddingBottom**  currentStyle, runtimeStyle, style, tags

**paddingLeft**  currentStyle, runtimeStyle, style, tags

**paddingRight**  currentStyle, runtimeStyle, style, tags

**paddings**  tags

**paddingTop**  currentStyle, runtimeStyle, style, tags

**page**  style

**pageBreakAfter**  currentStyle, runtimeStyle, style

**pageBreakBefore**  currentStyle, runtimeStyle, style

**pageBreakInside**  style

**pages**  styleSheet

**pageX**  event, layer

**pageXOffset**  window

**pageY**  event, layer

**pageYOffset**  window

**palette**  embed

**parent**  window

**parentElement**  a, abbr, acronym, address, applet, area, b, base, basefont, bdo, bgsound, big, blockquote, body, br, button, caption, center, cite, code, col, colgroup, comment, dd, del, dfn, dir, div, dl, dt, em, embed, fieldset, font, form, frame, frameset, h1, h2, h3, h4, h5, h6, head, hr, html, i, iframe, img, input, ins, kbd, label, legend, li, link, listing, map, marquee, menu, meta, nobr, noframes, noscript, object, ol, optgroup, option, p, plaintext, pre, q, rt, ruby, s, samp, script, select, small, span, strike, strong, style (element), sub, sup, table, tbody, td, textarea, tfoot, th, thead, title, tr, tt, u, ul, var, wbr, xml, xmp

**parentLayer**  layer

**parentNode**  a, abbr, acronym, address, applet, area, b, base, basefont, bdo, bgsound, big, blockquote, body, br, button, caption, center, cite, code, col, colgroup, comment, dd, del, dfn, dir, div, dl, dt, em, embed, fieldset, font, form, frame, frameset, h1, h2, h3, h4, h5, h6, head, hr, html, i, iframe, img, input, ins, isindex, kbd, label, legend, li, link, listing, map, marquee, menu, meta, nobr, noframes, noscript, object, ol, optgroup, option, p, param, plaintext, pre, q, rt, ruby, s, samp, script, select, small, span, strike, strong, style (element), sub, sup, table, tbody, td, textarea, tfoot, th, thead, title, tr, tt, u, ul, var, wbr, xml, xmp

**parentRule**  cssRule, rule

**parentStyleSheet**  cssRule, rule, styleSheet

**parentTextEdit**  a, abbr, acronym, address, applet, area, b, base, basefont, bdo, bgsound, big, blockquote, body, br, button, caption, center, cite, code, col, colgroup, comment, dd, del, dfn, dir, div, dl, dt, em, embed, fieldset, font, form, frame, frameset, h1, h2, h3, h4, h5, h6, head, hr, html, i, iframe, img, input, ins, kbd, label, legend, li, link, listing, map, marquee, menu, meta, nobr, noframes, noscript, object, ol, optgroup, option, p, plaintext, pre, q, rt, ruby, s, samp, script, select, small, span, strike, strong, style (element), sub, sup, table, tbody, td, textarea, tfoot, th, thead, title, tr, tt, u, ul, var, wbr, xml, xmp

**parentWindow**  document

**pathname**  a, area, location

**pause**  style

**pauseAfter**  style

**pauseBefore**  style

**personalbar**  window

**pitch**  style

**pitchRange**  style

**pixelBottom**  style

**pixelDepth**  screen

**pixelHeight**  style

**pixelLeft**  style

**pixelRight**  style

**pixelTop**  style

**pixelWidth**  style

**pkcs11**  window

**platform**  navigator

**playDuring**  style

**plugins**  document, navigator

**pluginspage**  embed

**port**  a, area, location

**posBottom**  runtimeStyle, style

**posHeight**  runtimeStyle, style

**position** currentStyle, runtimeStyle, style

**posLeft** runtimeStyle, style

**posRight** runtimeStyle, style

**posTop** runtimeStyle, style

**posWidth** runtimeStyle, style

**prefix** a, abbr, acronym, address, applet, area, b, base, basefont, bdo, bgsound, big, blockquote, body, br, button, caption, center, cite, code, col, colgroup, dd, del, dfn, dir, div, dl, dt, em, embed, fieldset, font, form, frame, frameset, h1, h2, h3, h4, h5, h6, head, hr, html, i, iframe, img, input, ins, isindex, kbd, label, legend, li, link, listing, map, menu, meta, nobr, noframes, noscript, object, ol, optgroup, option, p, param, plaintext, pre, q, s, samp, script, select, small, span, strike, strong, style (element), sub, sup, table, tbody, td, textarea, tfoot, th, thead, title, tr, tt, u, ul, var, wbr, xml, xmp

**previous** history

**previousSibling** a, abbr, acronym, address, applet, area, b, base, basefont, bdo, bgsound, big, blockquote, body, br, button, caption, center, cite, code, col, colgroup, comment, dd, del, dfn, dir, div, dl, dt, em, embed, fieldset, font, form, frame, frameset, h1, h2, h3, h4, h5, h6, head, hr, html, i, iframe, img, input, ins, isindex, kbd, label, legend, li, link, listing, map, marquee, menu, meta, nobr, noframes, noscript, object, ol, optgroup, option, p, param, plaintext, pre, q, rt, ruby, s, samp, script, select, small, span, strike, strong, style (element), sub, sup, table, tbody, td, textarea, tfoot, th, thead, title, tr, tt, u, ul, var, wbr, xml, xmp

**prevValue** event

**PROCESSING_INSTRUCTION_NODE** (constant of all W3C DOM nodes and elements)

**product** navigator

**productSub** navigator

**profile** head

**prompt** isindex

**prompter** window

**propertyName** event

**protocol** a, area, document, img, location

**protocolLong** a

**prototype** img

**pseudoClass** page

**publicID** DocumentType

**qualifier** event

**quotes** style

**rangeCount** selection

**rangeOffset** event

**rangeParent** event

**readOnly** cssRule, input (password), input (text), rule, stylesheet, textarea

**readyState** a, abbr, acronym, address, applet, area, b, base, basefont, bdo, bgsound, big, blockquote, body, br, button, caption, center, cite, code, col, colgroup, comment, dd, del, dfn, dir, div, dl, document, dt, em, embed, fieldset, font, form, frame, frameset, h1, h2, h3, h4, h5, h6, head, hr, html, i, iframe, img, input, ins, kbd, label, legend, li, link, listing, map, marquee, menu, meta, nobr, noframes, noscript, object, ol, optgroup, option, p, plaintext, pre, q, rt, ruby, s, samp, script, select, small, span, strike, strong, style (element), sub, sup, table, tbody, td, textarea, tfoot, th, thead, title, tr, tt, u, ul, var, wbr, xml, xmp

**reason** event

**recordNumber** a, abbr, acronym, address, applet, area, b, base, basefont, bdo, bgsound, big, blockquote, body, br, button, caption, center, cite, code, col, colgroup, comment, dd, del, dfn, dir, div, dl, dt, em, embed, fieldset, font, form, frame, frameset, h1, h2, h3, h4, h5, h6, head, hr, html, i, iframe, img, input, ins, kbd, label, legend, li, link, listing, map, marquee, menu, meta, nobr, noframes, noscript, object, ol, optgroup, option, p, plaintext, pre, q, rt, ruby, s, samp, script, select, small, span, strike, strong, style (element), sub, sup, table, tbody, td, textarea, tfoot, th, thead, title, tr, tt, u, ul, var, wbr, xml, xmp

**recordset** event

**referrer** document

**rel** a, link

**relatedNode** event

**relatedTarget** event

**repeat** event

**RESET** Event

**RESIZE** Event

**returnValue** event, window

**rev** a, link

**richness** style

**right** currentStyle, runtimeStyle, style, TextRectangle

**rightMargin** body

**rowIndex** tr

**rows** frameset, table, tbody, textarea, tfoot, thead

**rowSpan** td, th

**rubyAlign** currentStyle, runtimeStyle, style

**rubyOverhang** currentStyle, runtimeStyle, style

**rubyPosition** currentStyle, runtimeStyle, style

**rules** styleSheet, table

**runtimeStyle** a, abbr, acronym, address, applet, area, b, base, basefont, bdo, bgsound, big, blockquote, body, br, button, caption, center, cite, code, col, colgroup, comment, dd, del, dfn, dir, div, dl, dt, em, embed, fieldset, font, form, frame, frameset, h1, h2, h3, h4, h5, h6, head, hr, html, i, iframe, img, input, ins, kbd, label, legend, li, link, listing, map, marquee, menu, meta, nobr, noframes, noscript, object, ol, optgroup, option, p, plaintext, pre, q, rt, ruby, s, samp, script, select, small, span, strike, strong, style (element), sub, sup, table, tbody, td, textarea, tfoot, th, thead, title, tr, tt, u, ul, var, wbr, xml, xmp

**scheme** meta

**scopy** td, th

**scopeName** a, abbr, acronym, address, applet, area, b, base, basefont, bdo, bgsound, big, blockquote, body, br, button, caption, center, cite, code, col, colgroup, comment, dd, del, dfn, dir, div, dl, dt, em, embed, fieldset, font, form, frame, frameset, h1, h2, h3, h4, h5, h6, head, hr, html, i, iframe, img, input, ins, kbd, label, legend, li, link, listing, map, marquee, menu, meta, nobr, noframes, noscript, object, ol, optgroup, option, p, plaintext, pre, q, rt, ruby, s, samp, script, select, small, span, strike, strong, style (element), sub, sup, table, tbody, td, textarea, tfoot, th, thead, title, tr, tt, u, ul, var, wbr, xml, xmp

**screen** window

**screenLeft** window

**screenTop** window

**screenX** event, window

**screenY** event, window

**scripts** document

**scroll** body

**SCROLL** Event

**scrollAmount** marquee

**scrollbar3dLightColor** currentStyle, runtimeStyle, style

**scrollbarArrowColor** currentStyle, runtimeStyle, style

**scrollbarBaseColor** currentStyle, runtimeStyle, style

**scrollbarDarkShadowColor** currentStyle, runtimeStyle, style

**scrollbarFaceColor** currentStyle, runtimeStyle, style

**scrollbarHighlightColor** currentStyle, runtimeStyle, style

**scrollbars** window

**scrollbarShadowColor**  currentStyle, runtimeStyle, style

**scrollbarTrackColor**  currentStyle, runtimeStyle, style

**scrollDelay**  marquee

**scrollHeight**  a, abbr, acronym, address, applet, area, b, base, basefont, bdo, bgsound, big, blockquote, body, br, button, caption, center, cite, code, col, colgroup, comment, dd, del, dfn, dir, div, dl, dt, em, embed, fieldset, font, form, frame, frameset, h1, h2, h3, h4, h5, h6, head, hr, html, i, iframe, img, input, ins, kbd, label, legend, li, link, listing, map, marquee, menu, meta, nobr, noframes, noscript, object, ol, optgroup, option, p, plaintext, pre, q, rt, ruby, s, samp, script, select, small, span, strike, strong, style (element), sub, sup, table, tbody, td, textarea, tfoot, th, thead, title, tr, tt, u, ul, var, wbr, xml, xmp

**scrolling**  frame, iframe

**scrollLeft**  a, abbr, acronym, address, applet, area, b, base, basefont, bdo, bgsound, big, blockquote, body, br, button, caption, center, cite, code, col, colgroup, comment, dd, del, dfn, dir, div, dl, dt, em, embed, fieldset, font, form, frame, frameset, h1, h2, h3, h4, h5, h6, head, hr, html, i, iframe, img, input, ins, kbd, label, legend, li, link, listing, map, marquee, menu, meta, nobr, noframes, noscript, object, ol, optgroup, option, p, plaintext, pre, q, rt, ruby, s, samp, script, select, small, span, strike, strong, style (element), sub, sup, table, tbody, td, textarea, tfoot, th, thead, title, tr, tt, u, ul, var, wbr, xml, xmp

**scrollTop**  a, abbr, acronym, address, applet, area, b, base, basefont, bdo, bgsound, big, blockquote, body, br, button, caption, center, cite, code, col, colgroup, comment, dd, del, dfn, dir, div, dl, dt, em, embed, fieldset, font, form, frame, frameset, h1, h2, h3, h4, h5, h6, head, hr, html, i, iframe, img, input, ins, kbd, label, legend, li, link, listing, map, marquee,

menu, meta, nobr, noframes, noscript, object, ol, optgroup, option, p, plaintext, pre, q, rt, ruby, s, samp, script, select, small, span, strike, strong, style (element), sub, sup, table, tbody, td, textarea, tfoot, th, thead, title, tr, tt, u, ul, var, wbr, xml, xmp

**scrollWidth**  a, abbr, acronym, address, applet, area, b, base, basefont, bdo, bgsound, big, blockquote, body, br, button, caption, center, cite, code, col, colgroup, comment, dd, del, dfn, dir, div, dl, dt, em, embed, fieldset, font, form, frame, frameset, h1, h2, h3, h4, h5, h6, head, hr, html, i, iframe, img, input, ins, kbd, label, legend, li, link, listing, map, marquee, menu, meta, nobr, noframes, noscript, object, ol, optgroup, option, p, plaintext, pre, q, rt, ruby, s, samp, script, select, small, span, strike, strong, style (element), sub, sup, table, tbody, td, textarea, tfoot, th, thead, title, tr, tt, u, ul, var, wbr, xml, xmp

**scrollX**  window

**scrollY**  window

**search**  a, area, location

**sectionRowIndex**  tr

**security**  document

**securityPolicy**  navigator

**SELECT**  Event

**selected**  option

**selectedIndex**  select

**selection**  document

**selectionEnd**  input (password)

**selectionStart**  input (password)

**selectorText**  cssRule, page, rule

**self**  window

**shape**  a, area

**sheet**  link, LinkStyle, style (element)

**shiftKey**  event

**shiftLeft**  event

**SHIFT_MASK**  Event

**siblingAbove** layer

**siblingBelow** layer

**sidebar** window

**size** basefont, font, hr, input (file), input (password), input (text), select, style

**sourceIndex** a, abbr, acronym, address, applet, area, b, base, basefont, bdo, bgsound, big, blockquote, body, br, button, caption, center, cite, code, col, colgroup, comment, dd, del, dfn, dir, div, dl, dt, em, embed, fieldset, font, form, frame, frameset, h1, h2, h3, h4, h5, h6, head, hr, html, i, iframe, img, input, ins, kbd, label, legend, li, link, listing, map, marquee, menu, meta, nobr, noframes, noscript, object, ol, optgroup, option, p, plaintext, pre, q, rt, ruby, s, samp, script, select, small, span, strike, strong, style (element), sub, sup, table, tbody, td, textarea, tfoot, th, thead, title, tr, tt, u, ul, var, wbr, xml, xmp

**span** col, colgroup

**speak** style

**speakHeader** style

**speakNumeral** style

**speakPunctuation** style

**specified** attribute

**speechRate** style

**src** applet, bgsound, embed, frame, iframe, img, layer, input (image), script, xml

**srcElement** event

**srcFilter** event

**srcUrn** event

**standby** object

**start** img, input (image), ol

**startContainer** Range

**startOffset** Range

**status** button, input (checkbox), input (radio), textarea, window

**statusbar** window

**stress** style

**style** a, abbr, acronym, address, applet, b, base, basefont, bdo, bgsound, big, blockquote, body, br, button, caption, center, cite, code, col, colgroup, comment, cssRule, dd, del, dfn, dir, div, dl, dt, em, embed, fieldset, font, form, frame, frameset, h1, h2, h3, h4, h5, h6, head, hr, html, i, iframe, img, input, ins, isindex, kbd, label, legend, li, link, listing, map, marquee, menu, meta, nobr, noframes, noscript, object, ol, optgroup, option, p, page, param, plaintext, pre, q, rt, ruby, rule, s, samp, script, select, small, span, strike, strong, style (element), sub, sup, table, tbody, td, textarea, tfoot, th, thead, title, tr, tt, u, ul, var, wbr, xml, xmp

**styleFloat** currentStyle, runtimeStyle, style

**styleSheet** cssRule, link, rule, style (element)

**styleSheets** document

**SUBMIT** Event

**suffixes** mimeType

**summary** table

**systemId** DocumentType

**systemLanguage** navigator

**tabIndex** a, abbr, acronym, address, applet, area, b, base, basefont, bdo, bgsound, big, blockquote, body, br, button, caption, center, cite, code, col, colgroup, comment, dd, del, dfn, dir, div, dl, dt, em, embed, fieldset, font, form, frame, frameset, h1, h2, h3, h4, h5, h6, head, hr, html, i, iframe, img, input, ins, kbd, label, legend, li, link, listing, map, marquee, menu, meta, nobr, noframes, noscript, object, ol, optgroup, option, p, plaintext, pre, q, rt, ruby, s, samp, script, select, small, span, strike, strong, style (element), sub, sup, table, tbody, td, textarea, tfoot, th, thead, title, tr, tt, u, ul, var, wbr, xml, xmp

**tableLayout** currentStyle, runtimeStyle, style

**tagName** a, abbr, acronym, address, applet, area, b, base, basefont, bdo, bgsound, big, blockquote, body, br, button, caption, center, cite, code, col, colgroup, comment, dd, del, dfn, dir, div, dl, dt, em, embed, field-set, font, form, frame, frameset, h1, h2, h3, h4, h5, h6, head, hr, html, i, iframe, img, input, ins, isindex, kbd, label, legend, li, link, listing, map, marquee, menu, meta, nobr, noframes, noscript, object, ol, optgroup, option, p, param, plaintext, pre, q, rt, ruby, s, samp, script, select, small, span, strike, strong, style (element), sub, sup, table, tbody, td, textarea, tfoot, th, thead, title, tr, tt, u, ul, var, wbr, xml, xmp

**tags**  document

**tagUrn**  a, abbr, acronym, address, applet, area, b, base, basefont, bdo, bgsound, big, blockquote, body, br, button, caption, center, cite, code, col, colgroup, comment, dd, del, dfn, dir, div, dl, dt, em, embed, fieldset, font, form, frame, frameset, h1, h2, h3, h4, h5, h6, head, hr, html, i, iframe, img, input, ins, kbd, label, legend, li, link, listing, map, marquee, menu, meta, nobr, noframes, noscript, object, ol, optgroup, option, p, plaintext, pre, q, rt, ruby, s, samp, script, select, small, span, strike, strong, style (element), sub, sup, table, tbody, td, textarea, tfoot, th, thead, title, tr, tt, u, ul, var, wbr, xml, xmp

**target**  a, area, base, event, form, link

**tbodies**  table

**text**  a, body, comment, option, script, TextRange, title

**textAlign**  currentStyle, runtimeStyle, style, tags

**textAlignLast**  currentStyle, runtimeStyle, style

**textAutospace**  currentStyle, runtimeStyle, style

**textDecoration**  currentStyle, runtimeStyle, style, tags

**textDecorationBlink**  runtimeStyle, style

**textDecorationLineThrough**  runtimeStyle, style

**textDecorationNone**  runtimeStyle, style

**textDecorationOverline**  runtimeStyle, style

**textDecorationUnderline**  runtimeStyle, style

**textIndent**  currentStyle, runtimeStyle, style

**textJustify**  currentStyle, runtimeStyle, style

**textKashida**  currentStyle, runtimeStyle, style

**textKashidaSpace**  currentStyle, runtimeStyle, style

**textLength**  input (password)

**TEXT_NODE**  (constant of all W3C DOM nodes and elements)

**textOverflow**  currentStyle, runtimeStyle, style

**textShadow**  style

**textTransform**  currentStyle, runtimeStyle, style, tags

**textUnderlinePosition**  currentStyle, runtimeStyle, style

**tFoot**  table

**tHead**  table

**timeStamp**  event

**title**  a, abbr, acronym, address, applet, area, b, base, basefont, bdo, bgsound, big, blockquote, body, br, button, caption, center, cite, code, col, colgroup, comment, dd, del, dfn, dir, div, dl, document, dt, em, embed, fieldset, font, form, frame, frameset, h1, h2, h3, h4, h5, h6, head, hr, html, i, iframe, img, input, ins, isindex, kbd, label, legend, li, link, listing, map, marquee, menu, meta, nobr, noframes, noscript, object, ol, optgroup, option, p, param, plaintext, pre, q, rt, ruby, s, samp, script, select, small, span, strike, strong, style, stylesheet, sub, sup, table, tbody, td, textarea, tfoot, th, thead, title, tr, tt, u, ul, var, wbr, window, xml, xmp

**toElement**  event

**toolbar**  window

**top**  currentStyle, layer, runtimeStyle, style, tags, TextRectangle, window

**topMargin**  body

**trueSpeed**  marquee

**type**  a, button, cssRule, embed, event, input (button), input, li, link, menu, mimeType, object, ol, param, rule, script, select, selection, style (element), styleSheet, textarea, ul

typeDetail selection

unicodeBidi currentStyle, runtimeStyle, style

uniqueID a, abbr, acronym, address, applet, area, b, base, basefont, bdo, bgsound, big, blockquote, body, br, button, caption, center, cite, code, col, colgroup, comment, dd, del, dfn, dir, div, dl, dt, em, embed, fieldset, font, form, frame, frameset, h1, h2, h3, h4, h5, h6, head, hr, html, i, iframe, img, input, ins, kbd, label, legend, li, link, listing, map, marquee, menu, meta, nobr, noframes, noscript, object, ol, optgroup, option, p, plaintext, pre, q, rt, ruby, s, samp, script, select, small, span, strike, strong, style (element), sub, sup, table, tbody, td, textarea, tfoot, th, thead, title, tr, tt, u, ul, var, wbr, xml, xmp

units embed

UNLOAD Event

updateInterval screen

URL document

url meta

URLUnencoded document

urn a

useMap img, input (image), object

userAgent navigator

userLanguage navigator

userProfile navigator

vAlign caption, col, colgroup, tbody, td, tfoot, th, thead, tr

value attribute, button, input, li, option, param, select, textarea

valueType param

vendor navigator

vendorSub navigator

version html

verticalAlign currentStyle, runtimeStyle, style, tags

view event

visibility currentStyle, layer, runtimeStyle, style, tags

visible locationbar, menubar, personalbar, scrollbars, statusbar, toolbar

vLink body

vlinkColor document

voiceFamily style

volume bgsound, style

vspace applet, frame, iframe, img, input (image), marquee, object

wheelData style

which event

whiteSpace currentStyle, runtimeStyle, style, tags

widows style

width applet, col, colgroup, currentStyle, document, embed, frame, hr, iframe, img, input (image), marquee, object, pre, runtimeStyle, screen, style, table, td, th

window window

wordBreak currentStyle, runtimeStyle, style

wordSpacing currentStyle, runtimeStyle, style

wordWrap currentStyle, runtimeStyle, style

wrap textarea

writingMode currentStyle, runtimeStyle, style

x event, img

XFER_DONE Event

XMLDocument xml

y event, img

zIndex currentStyle, layer, runtimeStyle, style, tags

zoom currentStyle, runtimeStyle, style

# DOM Method Index

Entries in the following index are arranged alphabetically by scriptable object methods. Look up a method to find out which document objects support it. You need to be aware, however, of what support means within the context of the way that browser makers and the W3C DOM specify the inner workings of their models using object-oriented approaches. For example, the list of objects that "support" the user-interface–oriented focus( ) method includes several nonrendered HTML element objects, such as head and meta. Inside the browsers, many methods are defined for a generic HTML element, and *all* elements, regardless of their purpose, inherit those methods. Clearly, attempting to set focus to nonrendered elements is a waste of time in actual development; but because these element objects expose the focus( ) method, they appear in that method's list.

Omitting this information here could cause equally serious problems for scripters who write object- and method-detection scripts. It's better to know that a method is defined (that is, its value type is not undefined) for a particular object than to be misled into thinking that its omission means that the method is undefined for the object.

This listing is a union of methods defined for objects in Internet Explorer, Navigator, and implemented objects from the W3C DOM Level 2. The same method name may mean different things for different objects. Be sure to look up the details of the method listing in Chapter 9, to find if the method is available for the browser(s) used by your intended audience and whether it does what you want. If an HTML element object and other scriptable object share the same name, the (element) notation follows its name when referring to the element object. Properties that apply to all input element objects are marked simply input; if only particular input element types apply, the type name follows in parentheses, as in "input (checkbox)". When you see a method with a long list of objects, the method is most likely covered among the shared items at the beginning of Chapter 9.

add( )   options,select

addBehavior( )   a, abbr, acronym, address, applet, area, b, base, basefont, bdo, bgsound, big, blockquote, body, br, button, caption, center, cite, code, col, colgroup, comment, dd, del, dfn, dir, div, dl, dt, em, embed, fieldset, font, form, frame, frameset, h1, h2, h3, h4, h5, h6, head, hr, html, i, iframe, img, input, ins, kbd, label, legend, li, link, listing, map, marquee, menu, meta, nobr, noframes, noscript, object, ol, optgroup, option, p, plaintext, pre, q, rt, ruby, s, samp, script, select, small, span, strike, strong, style (element), sub, sup, table, tbody, td, textarea, tfoot, th, thead, title, tr, tt, u, ul, var, wbr, xml, xmp

**addBinding( )** styleSheet

**addEventListener( )** a, abbr, acronym, address, applet, area, b, base, basefont, bdo, bgsound, big, blockquote, body, br, button, caption, center, cite, code, col, colgroup, dd, del, dfn, dir, div, dl, dt, em, embed, fieldset, font, form, frame, frameset, h1, h2, h3, h4, h5, h6, head, hr, html, i, iframe, img, input, ins, isindex, kbd, label, legend, li, link, listing, map, menu, meta, nobr, noframes, noscript, object, ol, optgroup, option, p, param, plaintext, pre, q, s, samp, script, select, small, span, strike, strong, style (element), sub, sup, table, tbody, td, textarea, tfoot, th, thead, title, tr, tt, u, ul, var, wbr, window, xmp

**addImport( )** styleSheet

**addRange( )** selection

**addReadRequest( )** userProfile

**addRule( )** styleSheet

**alert( )** window

**appendChild( )** a, abbr, acronym, address, applet, area, b, base, basefont, bdo, bgsound, big, blockquote, body, br, button, caption, center, cite, code, col, colgroup, comment, dd, del, dfn, dir, div, dl, dt, em, embed, fieldset, font, form, frame, frameset, h1, h2, h3, h4, h5, h6, head, hr, html, i, iframe, img, input, ins, isindex, kbd, label, legend, li, link, listing, map, marquee, menu, meta, nobr, noframes, noscript, object, ol, optgroup, option, p, param, plaintext, pre, q, rt, ruby, s, samp, script, select, small, span, strike, strong, style (element), sub, sup, table, tbody, td, textarea, tfoot, th, thead, title, tr, tt, u, ul, var, wbr, xml, xmp

**appendData( )** comment, Text

**appendMedium( )** MediaList

**applyElement( )** a, abbr, acronym, address, applet, area, b, base, basefont, bdo, bgsound, big, blockquote, body, br, button, caption, center, cite, code, col, colgroup, comment, dd, del, dfn, dir, div,

dl, dt, em, embed, fieldset, font, form, frame, frameset, h1, h2, h3, h4, h5, h6, head, hr, html, i, iframe, img, input, ins, kbd, label, legend, li, link, listing, map, marquee, menu, meta, nobr, noframes, noscript, object, ol, optgroup, option, p, plaintext, pre, q, rt, ruby, s, samp, script, select, small, span, strike, strong, style (element), sub, sup, table, tbody, td, textarea, tfoot, th, thead, title, tr, tt, u, ul, var, wbr, xml, xmp

**assign( )** location

**attachEvent( )** a, abbr, acronym, address, applet, area, b, base, basefont, bdo, bgsound, big, blockquote, body, br, button, caption, center, cite, code, col, colgroup, comment, dd, del, dfn, dir, div, dl, dt, em, embed, fieldset, font, form, frame, frameset, h1, h2, h3, h4, h5, h6, head, hr, html, i, iframe, img, input, ins, kbd, label, legend, li, link, listing, map, marquee, menu, meta, nobr, noframes, noscript, object, ol, optgroup, option, p, plaintext, pre, q, rt, ruby, s, samp, script, select, small, span, strike, strong, style (element), sub, sup, table, tbody, td, textarea, tfoot, th, thead, title, tr, tt, u, ul, var, wbr, window, xml, xmp

**back( )** history, window

**blur( )** a, abbr, acronym, address, applet, area, b, base, basefont, bdo, bgsound, big, blockquote, body, br, button, caption, center, cite, code, col, colgroup, comment, dd, del, dfn, dir, div, dl, dt, em, embed, fieldset, font, form, frame, frameset, h1, h2, h3, h4, h5, h6, head, hr, html, i, iframe, img, input, ins, kbd, label, legend, li, link, listing, map, marquee, menu, meta, nobr, noframes, noscript, object, ol, optgroup, option, p, plaintext, pre, q, rt, ruby, s, samp, script, select, small, span, strike, strong, style (element), sub, sup, table, tbody, td, textarea, tfoot, th, thead, title, tr, tt, u, ul, var, wbr, window, xml, xmp

**captureEvents( )** document, layer, window

**ChooseColorDlg( )** Dialog Helper

**clear( )**   document, selection

**clearAttributes( )**   a, abbr, acronym, address, applet, area, b, base, basefont, bdo, bgsound, big, blockquote, body, br, button, caption, center, cite, code, col, colgroup, comment, dd, del, dfn, dir, div, dl, dt, em, embed, fieldset, font, form, frame, frameset, h1, h2, h3, h4, h5, h6, head, hr, html, i, iframe, img, input, ins, kbd, label, legend, li, link, listing, map, marquee, menu, meta, nobr, noframes, noscript, object, ol, optgroup, option, p, plaintext, pre, q, rt, ruby, s, samp, script, select, small, span, strike, strong, style (element), sub, sup, table, tbody, td, textarea, tfoot, th, thead, title, tr, tt, u, ul, var, wbr, xml, xmp

**clearData( )**   clipboardData, dataTransfer

**clearInterval( )**   window

**clearRequest( )**   userProfile

**clearTimeout( )**   window

**click( )**   a, abbr, acronym, address, applet, area, b, base, basefont, bdo, bgsound, big, blockquote, body, br, button, caption, center, cite, code, col, colgroup, comment, dd, del, dfn, dir, div, dl, dt, em, embed, fieldset, font, form, frame, frameset, h1, h2, h3, h4, h5, h6, head, hr, html, i, iframe, img, input, ins, kbd, label, legend, li, link, listing, map, marquee, menu, meta, nobr, noframes, noscript, object, ol, optgroup, option, p, plaintext, pre, q, rt, ruby, s, samp, script, select, small, span, strike, strong, style (element), sub, sup, table, tbody, td, textarea, tfoot, th, thead, title, tr, tt, u, ul, var, wbr, xml, xmp

**cloneContents( )**   Range

**cloneNode( )**   a, abbr, acronym, address, applet, area, b, base, basefont, bdo, bgsound, big, blockquote, body, br, button, caption, center, cite, code, col, colgroup, comment, dd, del, dfn, dir, div, dl, dt, em, embed, fieldset, font, form, frame, frameset, h1, h2, h3, h4, h5, h6, head, hr, html, i, iframe, img, input, ins, isindex,

kbd, label, legend, li, link, listing, map, marquee, menu, meta, nobr, noframes, noscript, object, ol, optgroup, option, p, param, plaintext, pre, q, rt, ruby, s, samp, script, select, small, span, strike, strong, style (element), sub, sup, table, tbody, td, textarea, tfoot, th, thead, title, tr, tt, u, ul, var, wbr, xml, xmp

**cloneRange( )**   Range

**close( )**   document, window

**collapse( )**   Range, selection, TextRange

**collapseToEnd( )**   selection

**collapseToStart( )**   selection

**compareBoundaryPoints( )**   Range

**compareEndPoints( )**   TextRange

**compareNode( )**   Range

**comparePoint( )**   Range

**componentFromPoint( )**   a, abbr, acronym, address, applet, area, b, base, basefont, bdo, bgsound, big, blockquote, body, br, button, caption, center, cite, code, col, colgroup, comment, dd, del, dfn, dir, div, dl, dt, em, embed, fieldset, font, form, frame, frameset, h1, h2, h3, h4, h5, h6, head, hr, html, i, iframe, img, input, ins, kbd, label, legend, li, link, listing, map, marquee, menu, meta, nobr, noframes, noscript, object, ol, optgroup, option, p, plaintext, pre, q, rt, ruby, s, samp, script, select, small, span, strike, strong, style (element), sub, sup, table, tbody, td, textarea, tfoot, th, thead, title, tr, tt, u, ul, var, wbr, xml, xmp

**confirm( )**   window

**contains( )**   a, abbr, acronym, address, applet, area, b, base, basefont, bdo, bgsound, big, blockquote, body, br, button, caption, center, cite, code, col, colgroup, comment, dd, del, dfn, dir, div, dl, dt, em, embed, fieldset, font, form, frame, frameset, h1, h2, h3, h4, h5, h6, head, hr, html, i, iframe, img, input, ins, kbd, label, legend, li, link, listing, map, marquee, menu, meta, nobr, noframes, noscript, object, ol, optgroup, option, p, plaintext, pre, q, rt, ruby, s, samp, script, select, small, span, strike, strong, style (element), sub, sup, table, tbody, td, textarea, tfoot, th, thead, title, tr, tt, u, ul, var, wbr, xml, xmp

**containsNode( )**  selection

**createAttribute( )**  document

**createAttributeNS( )**  document

**createCaption( )**  table

**createCDATASection( )**  document

**createComment( )**  document

**createContextualFragment( )**  document

**createControlRange( )**  a, abbr, acronym, address, applet, area, b, base, basefont, bdo, bgsound, big, blockquote, body, br, button, caption, center, cite, code, col, colgroup, comment, dd, del, dfn, dir, div, dl, dt, em, embed, fieldset, font, form, frame, frameset, h1, h2, h3, h4, h5, h6, head, hr, html, i, iframe, img, input, ins, kbd, label, legend, li, link, listing, map, marquee, menu, meta, nobr, noframes, noscript, object, ol, optgroup, option, p, plaintext, pre, q, rt, ruby, s, samp, script, select, small, span, strike, strong, style (element), sub, sup, table, tbody, td, textarea, tfoot, th, thead, title, tr, tt, u, ul, var, wbr, xml, xmp

**createDocument( )**  implementation

**createDocumentFragment( )**  document

**createDocumentType( )**  implementation

**createElement( )**  document

**createElementNS( )**  document

**createEntityReference( )**  document

**createEvent( )**  document

**createEventObject( )**  document

**createPopup( )**  window

**createProcessingInstruction( )**  document

**createRange( )**  document, selection

**createRangeCollection( )**  selection

**createStyleSheet( )**  document

**createTextNode( )**  document

**createTextRange( )**  body, button, input (button), input (hidden), input (password), input (reset), input (submit), input (text), textarea

**createTFoot( )**  table

**createTHead( )**  table

**deleteCaption( )**  table

**deleteCell( )**  tr

**deleteContents( )**  Range

**deleteData( )**  comment, Text

**deleteFromDocument( )**  selection

**deleteMedium( )**  MediaList

**deleteRow( )**  table, tbody, tfoot, thead

**deleteRule( )**  cssRule, rule, styleSheet

**deleteTFoot( )**  table

**deleteTHead( )**  table

**detach( )**  Range

**detachEvent( )**  a, abbr, acronym, address, applet, area, b, base, basefont, bdo, bgsound, big, blockquote, body, br, button, caption, center, cite, code, col, colgroup, comment, dd, del, dfn, dir, div, dl, dt, em, embed, fieldset, font, form, frame, frameset, h1, h2, h3, h4, h5, h6, head, hr, html, i, iframe, img, input, ins, kbd, label, legend, li, link, listing, map, marquee, menu, meta, nobr, noframes, noscript, object, ol, optgroup, option, p, plaintext, pre, q, rt, ruby, s, samp, script, select, small, span, strike, strong, style (element), sub, sup, table, tbody, td, textarea, tfoot, th, thead, title, tr, tt, u, ul, var, wbr, window, xml, xmp

**disableExternalCapture( )**  window

**dispatchEvent( )**  a, abbr, acronym, address, applet, area, b, base, basefont, bdo, bgsound, big, blockquote, body, br, button, caption, center, cite, code, col, colgroup, dd, del, dfn, dir, div, dl, dt, em, embed, fieldset, font, form, frame, frameset, h1, h2, h3, h4, h5, h6, head, hr, html, i, iframe, img, input, ins, isindex, kbd, label, legend, li, link, listing, map, menu, meta, nobr, noframes, noscript, object, ol, optgroup, option, p, param, plaintext, pre, q, s, samp, script, select, small, span, strike, strong, style (element), sub, sup, table, tbody, td, textarea, tfoot, th, thead, title, tr, tt, u, ul, var, wbr, window, xmp

**doReadRequest( )**  userProfile

**doScroll( )**  a, abbr, acronym, address, applet, area, b, base, basefont, bdo, bgsound, big, blockquote, body, br, button, caption, center, cite, code, col, colgroup, comment, dd, del, dfn, dir, div, dl, dt, em, embed, fieldset, font, form, frame, frameset, h1, h2, h3, h4, h5, h6, head, hr, html, i, iframe, img, input, ins, kbd, label, legend, li, link, listing, map, marquee, menu, meta, nobr, noframes, noscript, object, ol, optgroup, option, p, plaintext, pre, q, rt, ruby, s, samp, script, select, small, span, strike, strong, style (element), sub, sup, table, tbody, td, textarea, tfoot, th, thead, title, tr, tt, u, ul, var, wbr, xml, xmp

**dragDrop( )**  a, abbr, acronym, address, applet, area, b, base, basefont, bdo, bgsound, big, blockquote, body, br, button, caption, center, cite, code, col, colgroup, comment, dd, del, dfn, dir, div, dl, dt, em, embed, fieldset, font, form, frame, frameset, h1, h2, h3, h4, h5, h6, head, hr, html, i, iframe, img, input, ins, kbd, label, legend, li, link, listing, map, marquee, menu, meta, nobr, noframes, noscript, object, ol, optgroup, option, p, plaintext, pre, q, rt, ruby, s, samp, script, select, small, span, strike, strong, style (element), sub, sup, table, tbody, td, textarea, tfoot, th, thead, title, tr, tt, u, ul, var, wbr, xml, xmp

**duplicate( )**  TextRange

**elementFromPoint( )**  document

**empty( )**  selection

**enableExternalCapture( )**  window

**execCommand( )**  document, TextRange

**execScript( )**  window

**expand( )**  TextRange

**extend( )**  selection

**extractContents( )**  Range

**find( )**  window

**findText( )**  TextRange

**fireEvent( )**  a, abbr, acronym, address, applet, area, b, base, basefont, bdo, bgsound, big, blockquote, body, br, button, caption, center, cite, code, col, colgroup, comment, dd, del, dfn, dir, div, dl, dt, em, embed, fieldset, font, form, frame, frameset, h1, h2, h3, h4, h5, h6, head, hr, html, i, iframe, img, input, ins, kbd, label, legend, li, link, listing, map, marquee, menu, meta, nobr, noframes, noscript, object, ol, optgroup, option, p, plaintext, pre, q, rt, ruby, s, samp, script, select, small, span, strike, strong, style (element), sub, sup, table, tbody, td, textarea, tfoot, th, thead, title, tr, tt, u, ul, var, wbr, xml, xmp

**focus( )**  a, abbr, acronym, address, applet, area, b, base, basefont, bdo, bgsound, big, blockquote, body, br, button, caption, center, cite, code, col, colgroup, comment, dd, del, dfn, dir, div, dl, dt, em, embed, fieldset, font, form, frame, frameset, h1, h2, h3, h4, h5, h6, head, hr, html, i, iframe, img, input, ins, kbd, label, legend, li, link, listing, map, marquee, menu, meta, nobr, noframes, noscript, object, ol, optgroup, option, p, plaintext, pre, q, rt, ruby, s, samp, script, select, small, span, strike, strong, style (element), sub, sup, table, tbody, td, textarea, tfoot, th, thead, title, tr, tt, u, ul, var, wbr, window, xml, xmp

**forward( )**  history, window

**getAdjacentText( )**  a, abbr, acronym, address, applet, area, b, base, basefont, bdo, bgsound, big, blockquote, body, br, button, caption, center, cite, code, col, colgroup, comment, dd, del, dfn, dir, div, dl, dt, em, embed, fieldset, font, form, frame, frameset, h1, h2, h3, h4, h5, h6, head, hr, html, i, iframe, img, input, ins, kbd, label, legend, li, link, listing, map, marquee, menu, meta, nobr, noframes, noscript, object, ol, optgroup, option, p, plaintext, pre, q, rt, ruby, s, samp, script, select, small, span, strike, strong, style (element), sub, sup, table, tbody, td, textarea, tfoot, th, thead, title, tr, tt, u, ul, var, wbr, xml, xmp

**getAnonymousElementByAttribute()**   document

**getAnonymousNodes()**   document

**GetAttention()**   window

**getAttribute()**   a, abbr, acronym, address, applet, area, b, base, basefont, bdo, bgsound, big, blockquote, body, br, button, caption, center, cite, code, col, colgroup, comment, dd, del, dfn, dir, div, dl, dt, em, embed, fieldset, font, form, frame, frameset, h1, h2, h3, h4, h5, h6, head, hr, html, i, iframe, img, input, ins, isindex, kbd, label, legend, li, link, listing, map, marquee, menu, meta, nobr, noframes, noscript, object, ol, optgroup, option, p, param, plaintext, pre, q, rt, ruby, s, samp, script, select, small, span, strike, strong, style (element), sub, sup, table, tbody, td, textarea, tfoot, th, thead, title, tr, tt, u, ul, userprofile, var, wbr, xml, xmp

**getAttributeNode()**   a, abbr, acronym, address, applet, area, b, base, basefont, bdo, bgsound, big, blockquote, body, br, button, caption, center, cite, code, col, colgroup, comment, dd, del, dfn, dir, div, dl, dt, em, embed, fieldset, font, form, frame, frameset, h1, h2, h3, h4, h5, h6, head, hr, html, i, iframe, img, input, ins, isindex, kbd, label, legend, li, link, listing, map, marquee, menu, meta, nobr, noframes, noscript, object, ol, optgroup, option, p, param, plaintext, pre, q, rt, ruby, s, samp, script, select, small, span, strike, strong, style (element), sub, sup, table, tbody, td, textarea, tfoot, th, thead, title, tr, tt, u, ul, var, wbr, xml, xmp

**getAttributeNodeNS()**   a, abbr, acronym, address, applet, area, b, base, basefont, bdo, bgsound, big, blockquote, body, br, but-

ton, caption, center, cite, code, col, colgroup, dd, del, dfn, dir, div, dl, dt, em, embed, fieldset, font, form, frame, frameset, h1, h2, h3, h4, h5, h6, head, hr, html, i, iframe, img, input, ins, isindex, kbd, label, legend, li, link, listing, map, menu, meta, nobr, noframes, noscript, object, ol, optgroup, option, p, param, plaintext, pre, q, s, samp, script, select, small, span, strike, strong, style (element), sub, sup, table, tbody, td, textarea, tfoot, th, thead, title, tr, tt, u, ul, var, wbr, xmp

**getAttributeNS()**   a, abbr, acronym, address, applet, area, b, base, basefont, bdo, bgsound, big, blockquote, body, br, button, caption, center, cite, code, col, colgroup, dd, del, dfn, dir, div, dl, dt, em, embed, fieldset, font, form, frame, frameset, h1, h2, h3, h4, h5, h6, head, hr, html, i, iframe, img, input, ins, isindex, kbd, label, legend, li, link, listing, map, menu, meta, nobr, noframes, noscript, object, ol, optgroup, option, p, param, plaintext, pre, q, s, samp, script, select, small, span, strike, strong, style (element), sub, sup, table, tbody, td, textarea, tfoot, th, thead, title, tr, tt, u, ul, var, wbr, xmp

**getBindingParent()**   document

**getBookmark()**   TextRange

**getBoundingClientRect()**   a, abbr, acronym, address, applet, area, b, base, basefont, bdo, bgsound, big, blockquote, body, br, button, caption, center, cite, code, col, colgroup, comment, dd, del, dfn, dir, div, dl, dt, em, embed, fieldset, font, form, frame, frameset, h1, h2, h3, h4, h5, h6, head, hr, html, i, iframe, img, input, ins, kbd, label, legend, li, link, listing, map, marquee, menu, meta, nobr, noframes, noscript, object, ol, optgroup, option, p, plaintext, pre, q, rt, ruby, s, samp, script, select, small, span, strike, strong, style (element), sub, sup, table, tbody, td, textarea, tfoot, th, thead, title, tr, tt, u, ul, var, wbr, xml, xmp

**getCharset()**   Dialog Helper

getClientRects( ) a, abbr, acronym, address, applet, area, b, base, basefont, bdo, bgsound, big, blockquote, body, br, button, caption, center, cite, code, col, colgroup, comment, dd, del, dfn, dir, div, dl, dt, em, embed, fieldset, font, form, frame, frameset, h1, h2, h3, h4, h5, h6, head, hr, html, i, iframe, img, input, ins, kbd, label, legend, li, link, listing, map, marquee, menu, meta, nobr, noframes, noscript, object, ol, optgroup, option, p, plaintext, pre, q, rt, ruby, s, samp, script, select, small, span, strike, strong, style (element), sub, sup, table, tbody, td, textarea, tfoot, th, thead, title, tr, tt, u, ul, var, wbr, xml, xmp

getComputedStyle( ) window

getData( ) clipboardData, dataTransfer

getElementById( ) document

getElementsByName( ) document

getElementsByTagName( ) a, abbr, acronym, address, applet, area, b, base, basefont, bdo, bgsound, big, blockquote, body, br, button, caption, center, cite, code, col, colgroup, comment, dd, del, dfn, dir, div, dl, Document, dt, em, embed, fieldset, font, form, frame, frameset, h1, h2, h3, h4, h5, h6, head, hr, html, i, iframe, img, input, ins, isindex, kbd, label, legend, li, link, listing, map, marquee, menu, meta, nobr, noframes, noscript, object, ol, optgroup, option, p, param, plaintext, pre, q, rt, ruby, s, samp, script, select, small, span, strike, strong, style (element), sub, sup, table, tbody, td, textarea, tfoot, th, thead, title, tr, tt, u, ul, var, wbr, xml, xmp

getElementsByTagNameNS( ) a, abbr, acronym, address, applet, area, b, base, basefont, bdo, bgsound, big, blockquote, body, br, button, caption, center, cite, code, col, colgroup, dd, del, dfn, dir, div, dl, Document, dt, em, embed, fieldset, font, form, frame, frameset, h1, h2, h3, h4, h5, h6, head, hr, html, i, iframe, img, input, ins, isindex, kbd, label, legend, li, link, listing, map, menu, meta, nobr, noframes,

noscript, object, ol, optgroup, option, p, param, plaintext, pre, q, s, samp, script, select, small, span, strike, strong, style (element), sub, sup, table, tbody, td, textarea, tfoot, th, thead, title, tr, tt, u, ul, var, wbr, xmp

getExpression( ) a, abbr, acronym, address, applet, area, b, base, basefont, bdo, bgsound, big, blockquote, body, br, button, caption, center, cite, code, col, colgroup, comment, dd, del, dfn, dir, div, dl, dt, em, embed, fieldset, font, form, frame, frameset, h1, h2, h3, h4, h5, h6, head, hr, html, i, iframe, img, input, ins, kbd, label, legend, li, link, listing, map, marquee, menu, meta, nobr, noframes, noscript, object, ol, optgroup, option, p, plaintext, pre, q, rt, ruby, s, samp, script, select, small, span, strike, strong, style (element), sub, sup, table, tbody, td, textarea, tfoot, th, thead, title, tr, tt, u, ul, var, wbr, xml, xmp

getNamedItem( ) attributes, NamedNodeMap

getNamedItemNS( ) attributes, NamedNodeMap

getPreventDefault( ) event

getPropertyCSSValue( ) style

getPropertyPriority( ) style

getPropertyValue( ) style

getRangeAt( ) selection

getSelection( ) document, window

go( ) history

handleEvent( ) document, form, input (button), input (checkbox), input (file), input (image), input (password), input (radio), input (reset), input (submit), input (text), layer, textarea, window

hasAttribute( ) a, abbr, acronym, address, applet, area, b, base, basefont, bdo, bgsound, big, blockquote, body, br, button, caption, center, cite, code, col, colgroup, dd, del, dfn, dir, div, dl, dt, em, embed, fieldset, font, form, frame, frameset, h1, h2, h3, h4, h5, h6, head, hr, html, i, iframe, img, input, ins, isindex, kbd, label, legend, li, link, listing, map, menu, meta, nobr, noframes, noscript, object, ol, optgroup, option, p, param, plaintext, pre, q, s, samp, script, select, small, span, strike, strong, style (element), sub, sup, table, tbody, td, textarea, tfoot, th, thead, title, tr, tt, u, ul, var, wbr, xmp

**hasAttributeNS()** a, abbr, acronym, address, applet, area, b, base, basefont, bdo, bgsound, big, blockquote, body, br, button, caption, center, cite, code, col, colgroup, dd, del, dfn, dir, div, dl, dt, em, embed, fieldset, font, form, frame, frameset, h1, h2, h3, h4, h5, h6, head, hr, html, i, iframe, img, input, ins, isindex, kbd, label, legend, li, link, listing, map, menu, meta, nobr, noframes, noscript, object, ol, optgroup, option, p, param, plaintext, pre, q, s, samp, script, select, small, span, strike, strong, style (element), sub, sup, table, tbody, td, textarea, tfoot, th, thead, title, tr, tt, u, ul, var, wbr, xmp

**hasAttributes()** a, abbr, acronym, address, applet, area, b, base, basefont, bdo, bgsound, big, blockquote, body, br, button, caption, center, cite, code, col, colgroup, dd, del, dfn, dir, div, dl, dt, em, embed, fieldset, font, form, frame, frameset, h1, h2, h3, h4, h5, h6, head, hr, html, i, iframe, img, input, ins, isindex, kbd, label, legend, li, link, listing, map, menu, meta, nobr, noframes, noscript, object, ol, optgroup, option, p, param, plaintext, pre, q, s, samp, script, select, small, span, strike, strong, style (element), sub, sup, table, tbody, td, textarea, tfoot, th, thead, title, tr, tt, u, ul, var, wbr, xmp

**hasChildNodes()** a, abbr, acronym, address, applet, area, b, base, basefont, bdo, bgsound, big, blockquote, body, br, button, caption, center, cite, code, col, colgroup, comment, dd, del, dfn, dir, div, dl, dt, em, embed, fieldset, font, form, frame, frameset, h1, h2, h3, h4, h5, h6, head, hr, html, i, iframe, img, input, ins, isindex, kbd, label, legend, li, link, listing, map, marquee, menu, meta, nobr, noframes, noscript, object, ol, optgroup, option, p,

param, plaintext, pre, q, rt, ruby, s, samp, script, select, small, span, strike, strong, style (element), sub, sup, table, tbody, td, textarea, tfoot, th, thead, title, tr, tt, u, ul, var, wbr, xml, xmp

**hasFeature()** implementation

**hasFocus()** document

**hide()** popup

**home()** window

**importNode()** document

**initEvent()** event

**initKeyEvent()** event

**initMouseEvent()** event

**initMutationEvent()** event

**initUIEvent()** event

**inRange()** TextRange

**insertAdjacentElement()** a, abbr, acronym, address, applet, area, b, base, basefont, bdo, bgsound, big, blockquote, body, br, button, caption, center, cite, code, col, colgroup, comment, dd, del, dfn, dir, div, dl, dt, em, embed, fieldset, font, form, frame, frameset, h1, h2, h3, h4, h5, h6, head, hr, html, i, iframe, img, input, ins, kbd, label, legend, li, link, listing, map, marquee, menu, meta, nobr, noframes, noscript, object, ol, optgroup, option, p, plaintext, pre, q, rt, ruby, s, samp, script, select, small, span, strike, strong, style (element), sub, sup, table, tbody, td, textarea, tfoot, th, thead, title, tr, tt, u, ul, var, wbr, xml, xmp

**insertAdjacentHTML()** a, abbr, acronym, address, applet, area, b, base, basefont, bdo, bgsound, big, blockquote, body, br, button, caption, center, cite, code, col, colgroup, comment, dd, del, dfn, dir, div, dl, dt, em, embed, fieldset, font, form, frame, frameset, h1, h2, h3, h4, h5, h6, head, hr, html, i, iframe, img, input, ins, kbd, label, legend, li, link, listing, map, marquee, menu, meta, nobr, noframes, noscript, object, ol, optgroup, option, p, plaintext, pre, q, rt, ruby, s, samp, script, select, small, span, strike, strong, style (element), sub, sup, table, tbody, td, textarea, tfoot, th, thead, title, tr, tt, u, ul, var, wbr, xml, xmp

**insertAdjacentText( )**   a, abbr, acronym, address, applet, area, b, base, basefont, bdo, bgsound, big, blockquote, body, br, button, caption, center, cite, code, col, colgroup, comment, dd, del, dfn, dir, div, dl, dt, em, embed, fieldset, font, form, frame, frameset, h1, h2, h3, h4, h5, h6, head, hr, html, i, iframe, img, input, ins, kbd, label, legend, li, link, listing, map, marquee, menu, meta, nobr, noframes, noscript, object, ol, optgroup, option, p, plaintext, pre, q, rt, ruby, s, samp, script, select, small, span, strike, strong, style (element), sub, sup, table, tbody, td, textarea, tfoot, th, thead, title, tr, tt, u, ul, var, wbr, xml, xmp

**insertBefore( )**   a, abbr, acronym, address, applet, area, b, base, basefont, bdo, bgsound, big, blockquote, body, br, button, caption, center, cite, code, col, colgroup, comment, dd, del, dfn, dir, div, dl, dt, em, embed, fieldset, font, form, frame, frameset, h1, h2, h3, h4, h5, h6, head, hr, html, i, iframe, img, input, ins, isindex, kbd, label, legend, li, link, listing, map, marquee, menu, meta, nobr, noframes, noscript, object, ol, optgroup, option, p, param, plaintext, pre, q, rt, ruby, s, samp, script, select, small, span, strike, strong, style (element), sub, sup, table, tbody, td, textarea, tfoot, th, thead, title, tr, tt, u, ul, var, wbr, xml, xmp

**insertCell( )**   tr

**insertData( )**   comment, Text

**insertNode( )**   Range

**insertRow( )**   table, tbody, tfoot, thead

**insertRule( )**   cssRule, rule, styleSheet

**intersectsNode( )**   Range

**isEqual( )**   TextRange

**isPointInRange( )**   Range

**isSupported( )**   a, abbr, acronym, address, applet, area, b, base, basefont, bdo, bgsound, big, blockquote, body, br, but-

ton, caption, center, cite, code, col, colgroup, dd, del, dfn, dir, div, dl, dt, em, embed, fieldset, font, form, frame, frameset, h1, h2, h3, h4, h5, h6, head, hr, html, i, iframe, img, input, ins, isindex, kbd, label, legend, li, link, listing, map, menu, meta, nobr, noframes, noscript, object, ol, optgroup, option, p, param, plaintext, pre, q, s, samp, script, select, small, span, strike, strong, style (element), sub, sup, table, tbody, td, textarea, tfoot, th, thead, title, tr, tt, u, ul, var, wbr, xmp

**item( )**   all, anchors, applets, areas, attributes, cells, childNodes, children, cssRules, filters, forms, frames, history, HTMLCollection, images, imports, links, MediaList, NamedNodeMap, NodeList, options, pages, plugins, rows, scripts, select, style, styleSheets, tBodies

**javaEnabled( )**   navigator

**lastPage( )**   table

**load( )**   Document, layer

**loadBindingDocument( )**   document

**mergeAttributes( )**   a, abbr, acronym, address, applet, area, b, base, basefont, bdo, bgsound, big, blockquote, body, br, button, caption, center, cite, code, col, colgroup, comment, dd, del, dfn, dir, div, dl, dt, em, embed, fieldset, font, form, frame, frameset, h1, h2, h3, h4, h5, h6, head, hr, html, i, iframe, img, input, ins, kbd, label, legend, li, link, listing, map, marquee, menu, meta, nobr, noframes, noscript, object, ol, optgroup, option, p, plaintext, pre, q, rt, ruby, s, samp, script, select, small, span, strike, strong, style (element), sub, sup, table, tbody, td, textarea, tfoot, th, thead, title, tr, tt, u, ul, var, wbr, xml, xmp

**move( )**   TextRange

**moveAbove( )**   layer

**moveBelow( )**   layer

**moveBy( )**   layer, window

**moveEnd( )**   TextRange

moveRow( )   table, tbody, tfoot, thead

moveStart( )   TextRange

moveTo( )   layer, window

moveToAbsolute( )   layer

moveToBookmark( )   TextRange

moveToElementText( )   TextRange

moveToPoint( )   TextRange

namedItem( )   all, anchors, applets, areas, cells, children, filters, forms, frames, HTMLCollection, images, links, options, plugins, rows, scripts, select, tBodies

navigate( )   window

nextPage( )   table

normalize( )   a, abbr, acronym, address, applet, area, b, base, basefont, bdo, bgsound, big, blockquote, body, br, button, caption, center, cite, code, col, colgroup, comment, dd, del, dfn, dir, div, dl, dt, em, embed, fieldset, font, form, frame, frameset, h1, h2, h3, h4, h5, h6, head, hr, html, i, iframe, img, input, ins, isindex, kbd, label, legend, li, link, listing, map, marquee, menu, meta, nobr, noframes, noscript, object, ol, optgroup, option, p, param, plaintext, pre, q, rt, ruby, s, samp, script, select, small, span, strike, strong, style (element), sub, sup, table, tbody, td, textarea, tfoot, th, thead, title, tr, tt, u, ul, var, wbr, xml, xmp

open( )   document, window

parentElement( )   TextRange

pasteHTML( )   TextRange

preference( )   navigator

preventDefault( )   event

previousPage( )   table

print( )   window

prompt( )   window

queryCommandEnabled( )   document, TextRange

queryCommandIndeterm( )   document, TextRange

queryCommandState( )   document, TextRange

queryCommandSupported( )   document, TextRange

queryCommandText( )   TextRange

queryCommandValue( )   document, TextRange

recalc( )   document

refresh( )   plugin, table

releaseCapture( )   a, abbr, acronym, address, applet, area, b, base, basefont, bdo, bgsound, big, blockquote, body, br, button, caption, center, cite, code, col, colgroup, comment, dd, del, dfn, dir, div, dl, dt, em, embed, fieldset, font, form, frame, frameset, h1, h2, h3, h4, h5, h6, head, hr, html, i, iframe, img, input, ins, kbd, label, legend, li, link, listing, map, marquee, menu, meta, nobr, noframes, noscript, object, ol, optgroup, option, p, plaintext, pre, q, rt, ruby, s, samp, script, select, small, span, strike, strong, style (element), sub, sup, table, tbody, td, textarea, tfoot, th, thead, title, tr, tt, u, ul, var, wbr, xml, xmp

releaseEvents( )   document, layer, window

reload( )   location

remove( )   options, selection

removeAllRanges( )   selection

removeAttribute( )   a, abbr, acronym, address, applet, area, b, base, basefont, bdo, bgsound, big, blockquote, body, br, button, caption, center, cite, code, col, colgroup, comment, dd, del, dfn, dir, div, dl, dt, em, embed, fieldset, font, form, frame, frameset, h1, h2, h3, h4, h5, h6, head, hr, html, i, iframe, img, input, ins, isindex, kbd, label, legend, li, link, listing, map, marquee, menu, meta, nobr, noframes, noscript, object, ol, optgroup, option, p, param, plaintext, pre, q, rt, ruby, s, samp, script, select, small, span, strike, strong, style (element), sub, sup, table, tbody, td, textarea, tfoot, th, thead, title, tr, tt, u, ul, var, wbr, xml, xmp

removeAttributeNode( )   a, abbr, acronym, address, applet, area, b, base, basefont, bdo, bgsound, big, blockquote, body, br, button, caption, center, cite, code, col, colgroup, comment, dd, del, dfn, dir, div, dl, dt, em, embed, fieldset, font, form, frame, frameset, h1, h2, h3, h4, h5, h6, head, hr, html, i, iframe, img, input, ins, isindex, kbd, label, legend, li, link, listing, map, marquee, menu, meta, nobr, noframes, noscript, object, ol, optgroup, option, p, param, plaintext, pre, q, rt, ruby, s, samp, script, select, small, span, strike, strong, style (element), sub, sup, table, tbody, td, textarea, tfoot, th, thead, title, tr, tt, u, ul, var, wbr, xml, xmp

**removeAttributeNS( )**  a, abbr, acronym, address, applet, area, b, base, basefont, bdo, bgsound, big, blockquote, body, br, button, caption, center, cite, code, col, colgroup, dd, del, dfn, dir, div, dl, dt, em, embed, fieldset, font, form, frame, frameset, h1, h2, h3, h4, h5, h6, head, hr, html, i, iframe, img, input, ins, isindex, kbd, label, legend, li, link, listing, map, menu, meta, nobr, noframes, noscript, object, ol, optgroup, option, p, param, plaintext, pre, q, s, samp, script, select, small, span, strike, strong, style (element), sub, sup, table, tbody, td, textarea, tfoot, th, thead, title, tr, tt, u, ul, var, wbr, xmp

**removeBehavior( )**  a, abbr, acronym, address, applet, area, b, base, basefont, bdo, bgsound, big, blockquote, body, br, button, caption, center, cite, code, col, colgroup, comment, dd, del, dfn, dir, div, dl, dt, em, embed, fieldset, font, form, frame, frameset, h1, h2, h3, h4, h5, h6, head, hr, html, i, iframe, img, input, ins, kbd, label, legend, li, link, listing, map, marquee, menu, meta, nobr, noframes, noscript, object, ol, optgroup, option, p, plaintext, pre, q, rt, ruby, s, samp, script, select, small, span, strike, strong, style (element), sub, sup, table, tbody, td, textarea, tfoot, th, thead, title, tr, tt, u, ul, var, wbr, xml, xmp

**removeBinding( )**  document

**removeChild( )**  a, abbr, acronym, address, applet, area, b, base, basefont, bdo, bgsound, big, blockquote, body, br, button, caption, center, cite, code, col, col-

group, comment, dd, del, dfn, dir, div, dl, dt, em, embed, fieldset, font, form, frame, frameset, h1, h2, h3, h4, h5, h6, head, hr, html, i, iframe, img, input, ins, isindex, kbd, label, legend, li, link, listing, map, marquee, menu, meta, nobr, noframes, noscript, object, ol, optgroup, option, p, param, plaintext, pre, q, rt, ruby, s, samp, script, select, small, span, strike, strong, style (element), sub, sup, table, tbody, td, textarea, tfoot, th, thead, title, tr, tt, u, ul, var, wbr, xml, xmp

**removeEventListener( )**  a, abbr, acronym, address, applet, area, b, base, basefont, bdo, bgsound, big, blockquote, body, br, button, caption, center, cite, code, col, colgroup, dd, del, dfn, dir, div, dl, dt, em, embed, fieldset, font, form, frame, frameset, h1, h2, h3, h4, h5, h6, head, hr, html, i, iframe, img, input, ins, isindex, kbd, label, legend, li, link, listing, map, menu, meta, nobr, noframes, noscript, object, ol, optgroup, option, p, param, plaintext, pre, q, s, samp, script, select, small, span, strike, strong, style (element), sub, sup, table, tbody, td, textarea, tfoot, th, thead, title, tr, tt, u, ul, var, wbr, window, xmp

**removeExpression( )**  a, abbr, acronym, address, applet, area, b, base, basefont, bdo, bgsound, big, blockquote, body, br, button, caption, center, cite, code, col, colgroup, comment, dd, del, dfn, dir, div, dl, dt, em, embed, fieldset, font, form, frame, frameset, h1, h2, h3, h4, h5, h6, head, hr, html, i, iframe, img, input, ins, kbd, label, legend, li, link, listing, map, marquee, menu, meta, nobr, noframes, noscript, object, ol, optgroup, option, p, plaintext, pre, q, rt, ruby, s, samp, script, select, small, span, strike, strong, style (element), sub, sup, table, tbody, td, textarea, tfoot, th, thead, title, tr, tt, u, ul, var, wbr, xml, xmp

**removeNamedItem( )**  attributes, NamedNodeMap

**removeNamedItemNS( )**  attributes, NamedNodeMap

**removeNode( )** a, abbr, acronym, address, applet, area, b, base, basefont, bdo, bgsound, big, blockquote, body, br, button, caption, center, cite, code, col, colgroup, comment, dd, del, dfn, dir, div, dl, dt, em, embed, fieldset, font, form, frame, frameset, h1, h2, h3, h4, h5, h6, head, hr, html, i, iframe, img, input, ins, kbd, label, legend, li, link, listing, map, marquee, menu, meta, nobr, noframes, noscript, object, ol, optgroup, option, p, plaintext, pre, q, rt, ruby, s, samp, script, select, small, span, strike, strong, style (element), sub, sup, table, tbody, td, textarea, tfoot, th, thead, title, tr, tt, u, ul, var, wbr, xml, xmp

**removeProperty( )** style

**removeRange( )** selection

**removeRule( )** styleSheet

**replace( )** location

**replaceAdjacentText( )** a, abbr, acronym, address, applet, area, b, base, basefont, bdo, bgsound, big, blockquote, body, br, button, caption, center, cite, code, col, colgroup, comment, dd, del, dfn, dir, div, dl, dt, em, embed, fieldset, font, form, frame, frameset, h1, h2, h3, h4, h5, h6, head, hr, html, i, iframe, img, input, ins, kbd, label, legend, li, link, listing, map, marquee, menu, meta, nobr, noframes, noscript, object, ol, optgroup, option, p, plaintext, pre, q, rt, ruby, s, samp, script, select, small, span, strike, strong, style (element), sub, sup, table, tbody, td, textarea, tfoot, th, thead, title, tr, tt, u, ul, var, wbr, xml, xmp

**replaceChild( )** a, abbr, acronym, address, applet, area, b, base, basefont, bdo, bgsound, big, blockquote, body, br, button, caption, center, cite, code, col, colgroup, comment, dd, del, dfn, dir, div, dl, dt, em, embed, fieldset, font, form, frame, frameset, h1, h2, h3, h4, h5, h6, head, hr, html, i, iframe, img, input, ins, isindex, kbd, label, legend, li, link, listing, map, marquee, menu, meta, nobr, noframes, noscript, object, ol, optgroup, option, p,

param, plaintext, pre, q, rt, ruby, s, samp, script, select, small, span, strike, strong, style (element), sub, sup, table, tbody, td, textarea, tfoot, th, thead, title, tr, tt, u, ul, var, wbr, xml, xmp

**replaceData( )** comment, Text

**replaceNode( )** a, abbr, acronym, address, applet, area, b, base, basefont, bdo, bgsound, big, blockquote, body, br, button, caption, center, cite, code, col, colgroup, comment, dd, del, dfn, dir, div, dl, dt, em, embed, fieldset, font, form, frame, frameset, h1, h2, h3, h4, h5, h6, head, hr, html, i, iframe, img, input, ins, kbd, label, legend, li, link, listing, map, marquee, menu, meta, nobr, noframes, noscript, object, ol, optgroup, option, p, plaintext, pre, q, rt, ruby, s, samp, script, select, small, span, strike, strong, style (element), sub, sup, table, tbody, td, textarea, tfoot, th, thead, title, tr, tt, u, ul, var, wbr, xml, xmp

**reset( )** form

**resizeBy( )** layer, window

**resizeTo( )** layer, window

**routeEvent( )** document, layer, window

**scroll( )** window

**scrollBy( )** window

**scrollByLines( )** window

**scrollByPages( )** window

**scrollIntoView( )** a, abbr, acronym, address, applet, area, b, base, basefont, bdo, bgsound, big, blockquote, body, br, button, caption, center, cite, code, col, colgroup, comment, dd, del, dfn, dir, div, dl, dt, em, embed, fieldset, font, form, frame, frameset, h1, h2, h3, h4, h5, h6, head, hr, html, i, iframe, img, input, ins, kbd, label, legend, li, link, listing, map, marquee, menu, meta, nobr, noframes, noscript, object, ol, optgroup, option, p, plaintext, pre, q, rt, ruby, s, samp, script, select, small, span, strike, strong, style (element), sub, sup, table, tbody, td, textarea, tfoot, th, thead, title, tr, tt, u, ul, var, wbr, xml, xmp

**scrollTo( )** window

**select( )** input (file), input (password), input (text), textarea, TextRange

**selectAllChildren( )** selection

**selectionLanguageChange( )** selection

**selectNode( )** Range

**selectNodeContents( )** Range

**setActive( )** a, abbr, acronym, address, applet, area, b, base, basefont, bdo, bgsound, big, blockquote, body, br, button, caption, center, cite, code, col, colgroup, comment, dd, del, dfn, dir, div, dl, dt, em, embed, fieldset, font, form, frame, frameset, h1, h2, h3, h4, h5, h6, head, hr, html, i, iframe, img, input, ins, kbd, label, legend, li, link, listing, map, marquee, menu, meta, nobr, noframes, noscript, object, ol, optgroup, option, p, plaintext, pre, q, rt, ruby, s, samp, script, select, small, span, strike, strong, style (element), sub, sup, table, tbody, td, textarea, tfoot, th, thead, title, tr, tt, u, ul, var, wbr, xml, xmp

**setAttribute( )** a, abbr, acronym, address, applet, area, b, base, basefont, bdo, bgsound, big, blockquote, body, br, button, caption, center, cite, code, col, colgroup, comment, dd, del, dfn, dir, div, dl, dt, em, embed, fieldset, font, form, frame, frameset, h1, h2, h3, h4, h5, h6, head, hr, html, i, iframe, img, input, ins, isindex, kbd, label, legend, li, link, listing, map, marquee, menu, meta, nobr, noframes, noscript, object, ol, optgroup, option, p, param, plaintext, pre, q, rt, ruby, s, samp, script, select, small, span, strike, strong, style (element), sub, sup, table, tbody, td, textarea, tfoot, th, thead, title, tr, tt, u, ul, var, wbr, xml, xmp

**setAttributeNode( )** a, abbr, acronym, address, applet, area, b, base, basefont, bdo, bgsound, big, blockquote, body, br, button, caption, center, cite, code, col, colgroup, comment, dd, del, dfn, dir, div, dl,

dt, em, embed, fieldset, font, form, frame, frameset, h1, h2, h3, h4, h5, h6, head, hr, html, i, iframe, img, input, ins, isindex, kbd, label, legend, li, link, listing, map, marquee, menu, meta, nobr, noframes, noscript, object, ol, optgroup, option, p, param, plaintext, pre, q, rt, ruby, s, samp, script, select, small, span, strike, strong, style (element), sub, sup, table, tbody, td, textarea, tfoot, th, thead, title, tr, tt, u, ul, var, wbr, xml, xmp

**setAttributeNodeNS( )** a, abbr, acronym, address, applet, area, b, base, basefont, bdo, bgsound, big, blockquote, body, br, button, caption, center, cite, code, col, colgroup, dd, del, dfn, dir, div, dl, dt, em, embed, fieldset, font, form, frame, frameset, h1, h2, h3, h4, h5, h6, head, hr, html, i, iframe, img, input, ins, isindex, kbd, label, legend, li, link, listing, map, menu, meta, nobr, noframes, noscript, object, ol, optgroup, option, p, param, plaintext, pre, q, s, samp, script, select, small, span, strike, strong, style (element), sub, sup, table, tbody, td, textarea, tfoot, th, thead, title, tr, tt, u, ul, var, wbr, xmp

**setAttributeNS( )** a, abbr, acronym, address, applet, area, b, base, basefont, bdo, bgsound, big, blockquote, body, br, button, caption, center, cite, code, col, colgroup, dd, del, dfn, dir, div, dl, dt, em, embed, fieldset, font, form, frame, frameset, h1, h2, h3, h4, h5, h6, head, hr, html, i, iframe, img, input, ins, isindex, kbd, label, legend, li, link, listing, map, menu, meta, nobr, noframes, noscript, object, ol, optgroup, option, p, param, plaintext, pre, q, s, samp, script, select, small, span, strike, strong, style (element), sub, sup, table, tbody, td, textarea, tfoot, th, thead, title, tr, tt, u, ul, var, wbr, xmp

**setCapture( )** a, abbr, acronym, address, applet, area, b, base, basefont, bdo, bgsound, big, blockquote, body, br, button, caption, center, cite, code, col, colgroup, comment, dd, del, dfn, dir, div, dl, dt, em, embed, fieldset, font, form, frame, frameset, h1, h2, h3, h4, h5, h6, head, hr, html, i, iframe, img, input, ins, kbd, label, legend, li, link, listing, map, marquee, menu, meta, nobr, noframes, noscript, object, ol, optgroup, option, p, plaintext, pre, q, rt, ruby, s, samp, script, select, small, span, strike, strong, style (element), sub, sup, table, tbody, td, textarea, tfoot, th, thead, title, tr, tt, u, ul, var, wbr, xml, xmp

**setCursor( )**   window

**setData( )**   clipboardData, dataTransfer

**setEnd( )**   Range

**setEndAfter( )**   Range

**setEndBefore( )**   Range

**setEndPoint( )**   TextRange

**setExpression( )**   a, abbr, acronym, address, applet, area, b, base, basefont, bdo, bgsound, big, blockquote, body, br, button, caption, center, cite, code, col, colgroup, comment, dd, del, dfn, dir, div, dl, dt, em, embed, fieldset, font, form, frame, frameset, h1, h2, h3, h4, h5, h6, head, hr, html, i, iframe, img, input, ins, kbd, label, legend, li, link, listing, map, marquee, menu, meta, nobr, noframes, noscript, object, ol, optgroup, option, p, plaintext, pre, q, rt, ruby, s, samp, script, select, small, span, strike, strong, style (element), sub, sup, table, tbody, td, textarea, tfoot, th, thead, title, tr, tt, u, ul, var, wbr, xml, xmp

**setInterval( )**   window

**setNamedItem( )**   attributes, NamedNodeMap

**setNamedItemNS( )**   attributes, NamedNodeMap

**setProperty( )**   style

**setStart( )**   Range

**setStartAfter( )**   Range

**setStartBefore( )**   Range

**setTimeout( )**   window

**show( )**   popup

**showHelp( )**   window

**showModalDialog( )**   window

**showModelessDialog( )**   window

**sizeToContent( )**   window

**splitText( )**   Text

**start( )**   marquee

**stop( )**   marquee, window

**stopPropagation( )**   event

**submit( )**   form

**substringData( )**   comment, Text

**surroundContents( )**   Range

**swapNode( )**   a, abbr, acronym, address, applet, area, b, base, basefont, bdo, bgsound, big, blockquote, body, br, button, caption, center, cite, code, col, colgroup, comment, dd, del, dfn, dir, div, dl, dt, em, embed, fieldset, font, form, frame, frameset, h1, h2, h3, h4, h5, h6, head, hr, html, i, iframe, img, input, ins, kbd, label, legend, li, link, listing, map, marquee, menu, meta, nobr, noframes, noscript, object, ol, optgroup, option, p, plaintext, pre, q, rt, ruby, s, samp, script, select, small, span, strike, strong, style (element), sub, sup, table, tbody, td, textarea, tfoot, th, thead, title, tr, tt, u, ul, var, wbr, xml, xmp

**tags( )**   all, anchors, areas, cells, children, forms, images, links, options, rows, scripts, tBodies

**taintEnabled( )**   navigator

**toString( )**   Range, selection

**urns( )**   all, anchors, areas, cells, childNodes, children, forms, images, links, NodeList, options, rows, scripts, tBodies

**write( )**   document

**writeln( )**   document

# DOM Event Handlers Index

Entries in the following index are arranged alphabetically by scriptable object event handlers. Look up an event handler to find out which document objects and HTML elements support it. This listing is a union of event handlers defined for objects in Internet Explorer, Navigator, and the W3C DOM Level 2. The same event handler name may mean different things for different objects. Be sure to look up the details of the event handler listing in Chapter 9, to find if the event handler is available for the browser(s) used by your intended audience and whether it does what you want. Details of the events themselves are in Chapter 10. All event handlers are listed here in all lowercase, as they are in the rest of this book. You may use any case combination you like when specifying the event handler as an HTML element attribute, but you must use the all-lowercase form in scripts for cross-browser compatibility and as HTML attributes if you wish to validate HTML code against strict DTDs.

**DOMActivate**  a, abbr, acronym, address, applet, area, b, bdo, big, blockquote, body, button, caption, center, cite, code, dd, dfn, dir, div, dl, document, dt, em, embed, fieldset, font, form, h1, h2, h3, h4, h5, h6, hr, i, img, input (except hidden), kbd, label, legend, li, listing, map, marquee, menu, nobr, object, ol, p, plaintext, pre, rt, ruby, s, samp, select, small, span, strike, strong, sub, sup, table, tbody, td, textNode, textarea, tfoot, th, thead, tr, tt, u, ul, var, xmp

**DOMAttrModified**  a, abbr, acronym, address, applet, area, b, bdo, big, blockquote, body, button, caption, center, cite, code, dd, dfn, dir, div, dl, document, dt, em, embed, fieldset, font, form, h1, h2, h3, h4, h5, h6, hr, i, img, input (except hidden), kbd, label, legend, li, listing, map, marquee, menu, nobr, object, ol, p, plaintext, pre, rt, ruby, s, samp, select, small, span, strike, strong, sub, sup, table, tbody, td, textNode, textarea, tfoot, th, thead, tr, tt, u, ul, var, xmp

**DOMCharacterDataModified**  characterDataNode

**DOMFocusIn**  a, abbr, acronym, address, applet, area, b, bdo, big, blockquote, body, button, caption, center, cite, code, dd, dfn, dir, div, dl, document, dt, em, embed, fieldset, font, form, h1, h2, h3, h4, h5, h6, hr, i, img, input (except hidden), kbd, label, legend, li, listing, map, marquee, menu, nobr, object, ol, p, plaintext, pre, rt, ruby, s, samp, select, small, span, strike, strong, sub, sup, table, tbody, td, textNode, textarea, tfoot, th, thead, tr, tt, u, ul, var, xmp

**DOMFocusOut**  a, abbr, acronym, address, applet, area, b, bdo, big, blockquote, body, button, caption, center, cite, code, dd, dfn, dir, div, dl, document, dt, em, embed, fieldset, font, form, h1, h2, h3, h4, h5, h6, hr, i, img, input (except hidden), kbd, label, legend, li, listing, map, marquee, menu, nobr, object, ol, p, plaintext, pre, rt, ruby, s, samp, select, small, span, strike, strong, sub, sup, table, tbody, td, textNode, textarea, tfoot, th, thead, tr, tt, u, ul, var, xmp

**DOMNodeInserted**  a, abbr, acronym, address, applet, area, b, bdo, big, blockquote, body, button, caption, center, cite, code, dd, dfn, dir, div, dl, document, dt, em, embed, fieldset, font, form, h1, h2, h3, h4, h5, h6, hr, i, img, input (except hidden), kbd, label, legend, li, listing, map, marquee, menu, nobr, object, ol, p, plaintext, pre, rt, ruby, s, samp, select, small, span, strike, strong, sub, sup, table, tbody, td, textNode, textarea, tfoot, th, thead, tr, tt, u, ul, var, xmp

**DOMNodeInsertedIntoDocument**  a, abbr, acronym, address, applet, area, b, bdo, big, blockquote, body, button, caption, center, cite, code, dd, dfn, dir, div, dl, document, dt, em, embed, fieldset, font, form, h1, h2, h3, h4, h5, h6, hr, i, img, input (except hidden), kbd, label, legend, li, listing, map, marquee, menu, nobr, object, ol, p, plaintext, pre, rt, ruby, s, samp, select, small, span, strike, strong, sub, sup, table, tbody, td, textNode, textarea, tfoot, th, thead, tr, tt, u, ul, var, xmp

**DOMNodeRemoved**  a, abbr, acronym, address, applet, area, b, bdo, big, blockquote, body, button, caption, center, cite, code, dd, dfn, dir, div, dl, document, dt, em, embed, fieldset, font, form, h1, h2, h3, h4, h5, h6, hr, i, img, input (except hidden), kbd, label, legend, li, listing, map, marquee, menu, nobr, object, ol, p, plaintext, pre, rt, ruby, s, samp, select, small, span, strike, strong, sub, sup, table, tbody, td, textNode, textarea, tfoot, th, thead, tr, tt, u, ul, var, xmp

**DOMNodeRemovedFromDocument**  a, abbr, acronym, address, applet, area, b, bdo, big, blockquote, body, button, caption, cen-

ter, cite, code, dd, dfn, dir, div, dl, document, dt, em, embed, fieldset, font, form, h1, h2, h3, h4, h5, h6, hr, i, img, input (except hidden), kbd, label, legend, li, listing, map, marquee, menu, nobr, object, ol, p, plaintext, pre, rt, ruby, s, samp, select, small, span, strike, strong, sub, sup, table, tbody, td, textNode, textarea, tfoot, th, thead, tr, tt, u, ul, var, xmp

**DOMSubtreeModified**  a, abbr, acronym, address, applet, area, b, bdo, big, blockquote, body, button, caption, center, cite, code, dd, dfn, dir, div, dl, document, dt, em, embed, fieldset, font, form, h1, h2, h3, h4, h5, h6, hr, i, img, input (except hidden), kbd, label, legend, li, listing, map, marquee, menu, nobr, object, ol, p, plaintext, pre, rt, ruby, s, samp, select, small, span, strike, strong, sub, sup, table, tbody, td, textNode, textarea, tfoot, th, thead, tr, tt, u, ul, var, xmp

**onabort**  img

**onactivate**  a, abbr, acronym, address, applet, area, b, bdo, big, blockquote, body, button, caption, center, cite, dd, dfn, dir, div, dl, document, dt, em, embed, fieldset, font, form, frame, frameset, h1, h2, h3, h4, h5, h6, hr, i, iframe, img, input, ins, isindex, kbd, label, legend, li, listing, marquee, menu, object, ol, p, plaintext, pre, q, rt, ruby, s, samp, select, small, span, strike, strong, sub, sup, table, tbody, td, textarea, tfoot, th, thead, tr, tt, u, ul, var, window, xmp

**onafterprint**  body, frameset, window

**onafterupdate**  a, bdo, button, div, frame, iframe, img, input (checkbox), input (hidden), input (password), input (radio), input (text), label, legend, marquee, rt, ruby, select, span, textarea

**onbeforeactivate**  a, abbr, acronym, address, applet, area, b, bdo, big, blockquote, body, button, caption, center, cite, code, dd, dfn, dir, div, dl, document, dt, em, embed, fieldset, font, form, h1, h2, h3, h4, h5, h6, hr, i, img, input, kbd, label, legend, li, listing, map, marquee, menu, nobr, ol, p, plaintext, pre, rt, ruby, s, samp, select, small, span, strike, strong, sub, sup, table, tbody, td, textarea, tfoot, th, thead, tr, tt, u, ul, var, xmp

**onbeforecopy** a, abbr, acronym, address, area, b, bdo, big, blockquote, caption, center, cite, code, dd, dfn, dir, div, dl, dt, em, fieldset, form, h1, h2, h3, h4, h5, h6, i, img, label, legend, li, listing, menu, nobr, ol, p, plaintext, pre, s, samp, small, span, strike, strong, sub, sup, td, textarea, th, tr, tt, u, ul

**onbeforecut** a, abbr, acronym, address, applet, area, b, bdo, big, blockquote, body, button, caption, center, cite, code, dd, dfn, dir, div, dl, document, dt, em, embed, fieldset, font, form, h1, h2, h3, h4, h5, h6, hr, i, img, input, kbd, label, legend, li, listing, map, marquee, menu, nobr, ol, p, plaintext, pre, rt, ruby, s, samp, select, small, span, strike, strong, sub, sup, table, tbody, td, textarea, tfoot, th, thead, tr, tt, u, ul, var, xmp

**onbeforedeactivate** a, abbr, acronym, address, applet, area, b, bdo, big, blockquote, body, button, caption, center, cite, dd, dfn, dir, div, dl, document, dt, em, embed, fieldset, font, form, frame, frameset, h1, h2, h3, h4, h5, h6, hr, i, iframe, img, input, ins, isindex, kbd, label, legend, li, listing, marquee, menu, object, ol, p, plaintext, pre, q, rt, ruby, s, samp, select, small, span, strike, strong, sub, sup, table, tbody, td, textarea, tfoot, th, thead, tr, tt, u, ul, var, window, xmp

**onbeforeeditfocus** a, abbr, acronym, address, applet, area, b, bdo, big, blockquote, body, button, caption, center, cite, code, dd, del, dfn, dir, div, dl, document, dt, em, fieldset, font, form, h1, h2, h3, h4, h5, h6, i, input (except hidden), ins, isindex, kbd, label, legend, li, listing, marquee, menu, nobr, object, ol, p, plaintext, pre, q, rt, ruby, s, samp, select, small, span, strike, strong, sub, sup, table, td, textarea, tr, tt, u, ul, var, xmp

**onbeforepaste** a, abbr, acronym, address, applet, area, b, bdo, big, blockquote, body, button, caption, center, cite, code, dd, dfn, dir, div, dl, document, dt, em, embed, fieldset, font, form, h1, h2, h3, h4, h5, h6, hr, i, img, input, kbd, label, legend, li, listing, map, marquee, menu, nobr, ol, p, plaintext, pre, rt, ruby, s, samp, select, small, span, strike, strong, sub, sup, table, tbody, td, textarea, tfoot, th, thead, tr, tt, u, ul, var, xmp

**onbeforeprint** body, frameset, window

**onbeforeunload** body, frameset, window

**onbeforeupdate** a, button, div, frame, iframe, img, input (checkbox), input (hidden), input (password), input (radio), input (text), textarea, label, legend, marquee, select, span, bdo, rt, ruby

**onblur** a, abbr, acronym, address, applet, area, b, bdo, big, blockquote, button, caption, center, cite, dd, del, dfn, dir, div, dl, dt, em, embed, fieldset, font, form, frame, frameset, h1, h2, h3, h4, h5, h6, hr, i, iframe, img, input (except hidden), ins, isindex, kbd, label, layer, legend, li, listing, marquee, menu, object, ol, p, plaintext, pre, q, rt, ruby, s, samp, select, small, span, strike, strong, sub, sup, table, tbody, td, textarea, tfoot, th, thead, tr, tt, u, ul, var, window, xmp

**onbounce** marquee

**oncellchange** applet, object

**onchange** input (text), select, textarea

**onclick** a, abbr, acronym, address, applet, area, b, bdo, big, blockquote, body, button, caption, center, cite, code, dd, dfn, dir, div, dl, document, dt, em, embed, fieldset, font, form, h1, h2, h3, h4, h5, h6, hr, i, img, input (except hidden), kbd, label, legend, li, listing, map, marquee, menu, nobr, object, ol, p, plaintext, pre, rt, ruby, s, samp, select, small, span, strike, strong, sub, sup, table, tbody, td, textNode, textarea, tfoot, th, thead, tr, tt, u, ul, var, xmp

**oncontextmenu** a, abbr, acronym, address, applet, area, b, bdo, big, blockquote, body, button, caption, center, cite, code, dd, dfn, dir, div, dl, document, dt, em, embed, fieldset, font, form, h1, h2, h3, h4, h5, h6, hr, i, img, input (except hidden), kbd, label, legend, li, listing, marquee, menu, nobr, ol, p, plaintext, pre, rt, ruby, s, samp, select, small, span, strike, strong, sub, sup, table, tbody, td, textarea, tfoot, th, thead, tr, tt, u, ul, var, xmp

**oncontrolselect** a, abbr, acronym, address, applet, area, b, bdo, big, blockquote, body, button, caption, center, cite, dd, dfn, dir, div, dl, document, dt, em, embed, fieldset, font, form, frame, frameset, h1, h2, h3, h4, h5, h6, hr, i, iframe, img, input, ins, isindex, kbd, label, legend, li, listing, marquee, menu, object, ol, p, plaintext, pre, q, rt, ruby, s, samp, select, small, span, strike, strong, sub, sup, table, tbody, td, textarea, tfoot, th, thead, tr, tt, u, ul, var, window, xmp

**oncopy** a, abbr, acronym, address, area, b, bdo, big, blockquote, caption, center, cite, code, dd, dfn, dir, div, dl, dt, em, fieldset, form, h1, h2, h3, h4, h5, h6, hr, i, img, legend, li, listing, menu, nobr, ol, p, plaintext, pre, s, samp, small, span, strike, strong, sub, sup, td, th, tr, tt, u, ul

**oncut** a, abbr, acronym, address, applet, area, b, bdo, big, blockquote, body, button, caption, center, cite, code, dd, dfn, dir, div, dl, document, dt, em, embed, fieldset, font, form, h1, h2, h3, h4, h5, h6, hr, i, img, input (except hidden), kbd, label, legend, li, listing, map, marquee, menu, nobr, ol, p, plaintext, pre, rt, ruby, s, samp, select, small, span, strike, strong, sub, sup, table, tbody, td, textarea, tfoot, th, thead, tr, tt, u, ul, var, xmp

**ondataavailable** applet, object, xml

**ondatasetchanged** applet, object, xml

**ondatasetcomplete** applet, object, xml

**ondblclick** a, abbr, acronym, address, applet, area, b, bdo, big, blockquote, body,

button, caption, center, cite, code, dd, dfn, dir, div, dl, document, dt, em, embed, fieldset, font, form, h1, h2, h3, h4, h5, h6, hr, i, img, input (except hidden), kbd, label, legend, li, listing, map, marquee, menu, nobr, object, ol, p, plaintext, pre, rt, ruby, s, samp, select, small, span, strike, strong, sub, sup, table, tbody, td, textarea, tfoot, th, thead, tr, tt, u, ul, var, xmp

**ondeactivate** a, abbr, acronym, address, applet, area, b, bdo, big, blockquote, body, button, caption, center, cite, dd, dfn, dir, div, dl, document, dt, em, embed, fieldset, font, form, frame, frameset, h1, h2, h3, h4, h5, h6, hr, i, iframe, img, input, ins, isindex, kbd, label, legend, li, listing, marquee, menu, object, ol, p, plaintext, pre, q, rt, ruby, s, samp, select, small, span, strike, strong, sub, sup, table, tbody, td, textarea, tfoot, th, thead, tr, tt, u, ul, var, window, xmp

**ondrag** a, abbr, acronym, address, area, b, bdo, big, blockquote, body, caption, center, cite, code, dd, del, dfn, dir, div, dl, document, dt, em, fieldset, font, form, h1, h2, h3, h4, h5, h6, hr, i, img, input (except hidden), kbd, label, li, listing, map, marquee, menu, nobr, object, ol, p, plaintext, pre, q, s, samp, small, span, strike, strong, sub, sup, table, tbody, td, textarea, tr, tt, u, ul, var, xmp

**ondragdrop** window

**ondragend** a, abbr, acronym, address, area, b, bdo, big, blockquote, body, caption, center, cite, code, dd, del, dfn, dir, div, dl, document, dt, em, fieldset, font, form, h1, h2, h3, h4, h5, h6, hr, i, img, input (except hidden), kbd, label, li, listing, map, marquee, menu, nobr, object, ol, p, plaintext, pre, q, s, samp, small, span, strike, strong, sub, sup, table, tbody, td, textarea, tr, tt, u, ul, var, xmp

**ondragenter** a, abbr, acronym, address, area, b, bdo, big, blockquote, body, button, caption, center, cite, code, dd, del, dfn, dir, div, dl, document, dt, em, fieldset, font, form, h1, h2, h3, h4, h5, h6, hr, i, img, input (except hidden), kbd, label, li, listing, map, marquee, menu, nobr, object, ol, p, plaintext, pre, q, s, samp, select, small, span, strike, strong, sub, sup, table, tbody, td, textarea, tfoot, th, thead, tr, tt, u, ul, var, xmp

**ondragleave**  a, abbr, acronym, address, area, b, bdo, big, blockquote, body, button, caption, center, cite, code, dd, del, dfn, dir, div, dl, document, dt, em, fieldset, font, form, h1, h2, h3, h4, h5, h6, hr, i, img, input (except hidden), kbd, label, li, listing, map, marquee, menu, nobr, object, ol, p, plaintext, pre, q, s, samp, select, small, span, strike, strong, sub, sup, table, tbody, td, textarea, tfoot, th, thead, tr, tt, u, ul, var, xmp

**ondragover**  a, abbr, acronym, address, area, b, bdo, big, blockquote, body, button, caption, center, cite, code, dd, del, dfn, dir, div, dl, document, dt, em, fieldset, font, form, h1, h2, h3, h4, h5, h6, hr, i, img, input (except hidden), kbd, label, li, listing, map, marquee, menu, nobr, object, ol, p, plaintext, pre, q, s, samp, select, small, span, strike, strong, sub, sup, table, tbody, td, textarea, tfoot, th, thead, tr, tt, u, ul, var, xmp

**ondragstart**  a, abbr, acronym, address, area, b, bdo, big, blockquote, body, caption, center, cite, code, dd, del, dfn, dir, div, dl, document, dt, em, fieldset, font, form, h1, h2, h3, h4, h5, h6, hr, i, img, input (except hidden), kbd, label, li, listing, map, marquee, menu, nobr, object, ol, p, plaintext, pre, q, s, samp, small, span, strike, strong, sub, sup, table, tbody, td, textarea, tr, tt, u, ul, var, xmp

**ondrop**  a, abbr, acronym, address, area, b, bdo, big, blockquote, body, button, caption, center, cite, code, dd, del, dfn, dir, div, dl, document, dt, em, fieldset, font, form, h1, h2, h3, h4, h5, h6, hr, i, img, input (except hidden), kbd, label, li, listing, map, marquee, menu, nobr, object, ol, p, plaintext, pre, q, s, samp, select,

small, span, strike, strong, sub, sup, table, tbody, td, textarea, tr, tt, u, ul, var, xmp

**onerror**  body, frameset, img, object, style, window

**onerrorupdate**  a, button, div, frame, iframe, img, input (checkbox), input (hidden), input (password), input (radio), input (text), textarea, label, legend, marquee, select, span, bdo, rt, ruby

**onfilterchange**  bdo, body, button, div, fieldset, img, input (except hidden), marquee, rt, ruby, span, table, td, textarea, th, tb

**onfinish**  marquee

**onfocus**  a, abbr, acronym, address, applet, area, b, bdo, big, blockquote, button, caption, center, cite, dd, del, dfn, dir, div, dl, dt, em, embed, fieldset, font, form, frame, frameset, h1, h2, h3, h4, h5, h6, hr, i, iframe, img, input, ins, isindex, kbd, label, layer, legend, li, listing, marquee, menu, object, ol, p, plaintext, pre, q, rt, ruby, s, samp, select, small, span, strike, strong, sub, sup, table, tbody, td, textarea, tfoot, th, thead, tr, tt, u, ul, var, window, xmp

**onfocusin**  a, abbr, acronym, address, applet, area, b, bdo, big, blockquote, body, button, caption, center, cite, code, dd, dfn, dir, div, dl, document, dt, em, embed, fieldset, font, form, h1, h2, h3, h4, h5, h6, hr, i, img, input (except hidden), kbd, label, legend, li, listing, map, marquee, menu, nobr, ol, p, plaintext, pre, rt, ruby, s, samp, select, small, span, strike, strong, sub, sup, table, tbody, td, textarea, tfoot, th, thead, tr, tt, u, ul, var, xmp

**onfocusout**  a, abbr, acronym, address, applet, area, b, bdo, big, blockquote, body, button, caption, center, cite, code, dd, dfn, dir, div, dl, document, dt, em, embed, fieldset, font, form, h1, h2, h3, h4, h5, h6, hr, i, img, input (except hidden), kbd, label, legend, li, listing, map, marquee, menu, nobr, ol, p, plaintext, pre, rt, ruby, s, samp, select, small, span, strike, strong, sub, sup, table, tbody, td, textarea, tfoot, th, thead, tr, tt, u, ul, var, xmp

**onhelp** a, abbr, acronym, address, applet, area, b, bdo, big, blockquote, button, caption, center, cite, code, dd, dfn, dir, div, dl, document, dt, em, embed, fieldset, font, form, h1, h2, h3, h4, h5, h6, hr, i, img, input (except hidden), kbd, label, legend, li, listing, map, marquee, menu, nobr, ol, p, plaintext, pre, rt, ruby, s, samp, select, small, span, strike, strong, sub, sup, table, tbody, td, textarea, tfoot, th, thead, tr, tt, u, ul, var, window, xmp

**onkeydown** a, abbr, acronym, address, applet, area, b, bdo, big, blockquote, body, button, caption, center, cite, code, dd, del, dfn, dir, div, document, dt, em, fieldset, font, form, h1, h2, h3, h4, h5, h6, hr, i, input (except hidden), kbd, label, legend, li, listing, map, marquee, menu, nobr, object, ol, p, plaintext, pre, q, rt, ruby, s, samp, select, small, span, strike, strong, sub, sup, table, tbody, td, textarea, tfoot, th, thead, tr, tt, u, ul, var, window, xmp

**onkeypress** a, abbr, acronym, address, applet, area, b, bdo, big, blockquote, body, button, caption, center, cite, code, dd, del, dfn, dir, div, document, dt, em, fieldset, font, form, h1, h2, h3, h4, h5, h6, hr, i, input (except hidden), kbd, label, legend, li, listing, map, marquee, menu, nobr, object, ol, p, plaintext, pre, q, rt, ruby, s, samp, select, small, span, strike, strong, sub, sup, table, tbody, td, textarea, tfoot, th, thead, tr, tt, u, ul, var, window, xmp

**onkeyup** a, abbr, acronym, address, applet, area, b, bdo, big, blockquote, body, button, caption, center, cite, code, dd, del, dfn, dir, div, document, dt, em, fieldset, font, form, h1, h2, h3, h4, h5, h6, hr, i, input (except hidden), kbd, label, legend, li, listing, map, marquee, menu, nobr, object, ol, p, plaintext, pre, q, rt, ruby, s, samp, select, small, span, strike, strong, sub, sup, table, tbody, td, textarea, tfoot, th, thead, tr, tt, u, ul, var, window, xmp

**onlayoutcomplete** LayoutRect

**onload** applet, body, embed, frame, frameset, iframe, img, link, object, script, window

**onlosecapture** a, abbr, acronym, address, applet, area, b, bdo, big, blockquote, body, br, button, caption, center, cite, code, dd, dfn, dir, div, dl, dt, em, embed, fieldset, font, form, h1, h2, h3, h4, h5, h6, hr, i, img, input, kbd, label, legend, li, listing, map, marquee, menu, nobr, object, ol, option, p, plaintext, pre, s, samp, select, small, span, strike, strong, sub, sup, table, tbody, td, textarea, tfoot, th, thead, tr, tt, u, ul, var, xmp

**onmousedown** a, abbr, acronym, address, applet, area, b, bdo, big, blockquote, body, button, caption, center, cite, code, dd, dfn, dir, div, dl, document, dt, em, embed, fieldset, font, form, h1, h2, h3, h4, h5, h6, hr, i, img, input (except hidden), kbd, label, legend, li, listing, map, marquee, menu, ol, p, plaintext, pre, rt, ruby, s, samp, select, small, span, strike, strong, sub, sup, table, tbody, td, textarea, textNode, tfoot, th, thead, tr, tt, u, ul, var, xmp

**onmouseenter** a, abbr, acronym, address, applet, area, b, bdo, big, blockquote, body, button, caption, center, cite, code, dd, dfn, dir, div, dl, document, dt, em, embed, fieldset, font, form, h1, h2, h3, h4, h5, h6, hr, i, img, input (except hidden), kbd, label, legend, li, listing, map, marquee, menu, ol, p, plaintext, pre, rt, ruby, s, samp, select, small, span, strike, strong, sub, sup, table, tbody, td, textarea, tfoot, th, thead, tr, tt, u, ul, var, xmp

**onmouseleave** a, abbr, acronym, address, applet, area, b, bdo, big, blockquote, body, button, caption, center, cite, code, dd, dfn, dir, div, dl, document, dt, em, embed, fieldset, font, form, h1, h2, h3, h4, h5, h6, hr, i, img, input (except hidden), kbd, label, legend, li, listing, map, marquee, menu, ol, p, plaintext, pre, rt, ruby, s, samp, select, small, span, strike, strong, sub, sup, table, tbody, td, textarea, tfoot, th, thead, tr, tt, u, ul, var, xmp

**onmousemove** a, abbr, acronym, address, applet, area, b, bdo, big, blockquote, body, button, caption, center, cite, code, dd, dfn, dir, div, dl, document, dt, em, embed, fieldset, font, form, h1, h2, h3, h4, h5, h6, hr, i, img, input (except hidden), kbd, label, legend, li, listing, map, marquee, menu, ol, p, plaintext, pre, rt, ruby, s, samp, select, small, span, strike, strong, sub, sup, table, tbody, td, textarea, textNode, tfoot, th, thead, tr, tt, u, ul, var, xmp

**onmouseout**  a, abbr, acronym, address, applet, area, b, bdo, big, blockquote, body, button, caption, center, cite, code, dd, dfn, dir, div, dl, document, dt, em, embed, fieldset, font, form, h1, h2, h3, h4, h5, h6, hr, i, img, input (except hidden), kbd, label, legend, li, listing, map, marquee, menu, ol, p, plaintext, pre, rt, ruby, s, samp, select, small, span, strike, strong, sub, sup, table, tbody, td, textarea, textNode, tfoot, th, thead, tr, tt, u, ul, var, xmp

**onmouseover**  a, abbr, acronym, address, applet, area, b, bdo, big, blockquote, body, button, caption, center, cite, code, dd, dfn, dir, div, dl, document, dt, em, embed, fieldset, font, form, h1, h2, h3, h4, h5, h6, hr, i, img, input (except hidden), kbd, label, legend, li, listing, map, marquee, menu, ol, p, plaintext, pre, rt, ruby, s, samp, select, small, span, strike, strong, sub, sup, table, tbody, td, textarea, textNode, tfoot, th, thead, tr, tt, u, ul, var, xmp

**onmouseup**  a, abbr, acronym, address, applet, area, b, bdo, big, blockquote, body, button, caption, center, cite, code, dd, dfn, dir, div, dl, document, dt, em, embed, fieldset, font, form, h1, h2, h3, h4, h5, h6, hr, i, img, input (except hidden), kbd, label, legend, li, listing, map, marquee, menu, ol, p, plaintext, pre, rt, ruby, s, samp, select, small, span, strike, strong, sub, sup, table, tbody, td, textarea, textNode, tfoot, th, thead, tr, tt, u, ul, var, xmp

**onmousewheel**  a, abbr, acronym, address, applet, area, b, bdo, big, blockquote, body, button, caption, center, cite, code, dd, dfn, dir, div, dl, document, dt, em, embed, fieldset, font, form, h1, h2, h3, h4,

h5, h6, hr, i, img, input (except hidden), kbd, label, legend, li, listing, map, marquee, menu, ol, p, plaintext, pre, rt, ruby, s, samp, select, small, span, strike, strong, sub, sup, table, tbody, td, textarea, tfoot, th, thead, tr, tt, u, ul, var, xmp

**onmove**  a, abbr, acronym, address, applet, area, b, bdo, big, blockquote, body, button, caption, center, cite, dd, dfn, dir, div, dl, document, dt, em, embed, fieldset, font, form, frame, frameset, h1, h2, h3, h4, h5, h6, hr, i, iframe, img, input, ins, isindex, kbd, label, legend, li, listing, marquee, menu, object, ol, p, plaintext, pre, q, rt, ruby, s, samp, select, small, span, strike, strong, sub, sup, table, tbody, td, textarea, tfoot, th, thead, tr, tt, u, ul, var, window, xmp

**onmoveend**  a, abbr, acronym, address, applet, area, b, bdo, big, blockquote, body, button, caption, center, cite, dd, dfn, dir, div, dl, document, dt, em, embed, fieldset, font, form, frame, frameset, h1, h2, h3, h4, h5, h6, hr, i, iframe, img, input, ins, isindex, kbd, label, legend, li, listing, marquee, menu, object, ol, p, plaintext, pre, q, rt, ruby, s, samp, select, small, span, strike, strong, sub, sup, table, tbody, td, textarea, tfoot, th, thead, tr, tt, u, ul, var, window, xmp

**onmovestart**  a, abbr, acronym, address, applet, area, b, bdo, big, blockquote, body, button, caption, center, cite, dd, dfn, dir, div, dl, document, dt, em, embed, fieldset, font, form, frame, frameset, h1, h2, h3, h4, h5, h6, hr, i, iframe, img, input, ins, isindex, kbd, label, legend, li, listing, marquee, menu, object, ol, p, plaintext, pre, q, rt, ruby, s, samp, select, small, span, strike, strong, sub, sup, table, tbody, td, textarea, tfoot, th, thead, tr, tt, u, ul, var, window, xmp

**onpaste**  a, abbr, acronym, address, applet, area, b, bdo, big, blockquote, body, button, caption, center, cite, code, dd, dfn, dir, div, dl, document, dt, em, embed, fieldset, font, form, h1, h2, h3, h4, h5, h6, hr, i, img, input (except hidden), kbd, label, legend, li, listing, map, marquee, menu, nobr, ol, p, plaintext, pre, rt, ruby, s, samp, select, small, span, strike, strong, sub, sup, table, tbody, td, textarea, tfoot, th, thead, tr, tt, u, ul, var, xmp

**onpropertychange** a, abbr, acronym, address, applet, area, b, bdo, big, blockquote, body, button, caption, center, cite, code, comment, dd, dfn, dir, div, dl, document, dt, em, embed, fieldset, font, form, h1, h2, h3, h4, h5, h6, hr, i, img, input, kbd, label, legend, li, listing, map, marquee, menu, nobr, object, ol, option, p, plaintext, pre, s, samp, script, select, small, span, strike, strong, sub, sup, table, tbody, td, textarea, tfoot, th, thead, tr, tt, u, ul, var, xmp

**onreadystatechange** a, abbr, acronym, address, applet, area, b, base, basefont, bdo, bgsound, big, blockquote, body, br, button, caption, center, cite, code, col, colgroup, comment, dd, del, dfn, dir, div, dl, document, dt, em, embed, fieldset, font, form, head, h1, h2, h3, h4, h5, h6, hr, html, i, iframe, img, input, ins, isindex, kbd, label, legend, li, link, listing, map, marquee, menu, namespace, nobr, noframes, noscript, object, ol, option, p, plaintext, pre, q, rt, ruby, s, samp, script, select, small, span, strike, strong, style, sub, sup, table, tbody, td, textarea, tfoot, th, thead, title, tr, tt, u, ul, var, xml, xmp

**onreset** form

**onresize** a, abbr, acronym, address, applet, b, big, blockquote, button, center, cite, code, dd, dfn, dir, div, dl, dt, em, embed, fieldset, form, frame, h1, h2, h3, h4, h5, h6, hr, i, img, input (except hidden), isindex, kbd, label, legend, li, listing, marquee, menu, object, ol, p, pre, s, samp, select, small, span, strike, strong, sub, sup, table, textarea, tt, u, ul, var, window, xmp

**onresizeend** a, abbr, acronym, address, applet, area, b, bdo, big, blockquote, body, button, caption, center, cite, dd, dfn, dir, div, dl, document, dt, em, embed, fieldset, font, form, frame, frameset, h1, h2, h3, h4, h5, h6, hr, i, iframe, img, input, ins, isindex, kbd, label, legend, li, listing, marquee, menu, object, ol, p, plaintext, pre, q, rt, ruby, s, samp, select, small, span, strike, strong, sub, sup, table, tbody, td, textarea, tfoot, th, thead, tr, tt, u, ul, var, window, xmp

**onresizestart** a, abbr, acronym, address, applet, area, b, bdo, big, blockquote, body, button, caption, center, cite, dd, dfn, dir, div, dl, document, dt, em, embed, fieldset, font, form, frame, frameset, h1, h2, h3, h4, h5, h6, hr, i, iframe, img, input, ins, isindex, kbd, label, legend, li, listing, marquee, menu, object, ol, p, plaintext, pre, q, rt, ruby, s, samp, select, small, span, strike, strong, sub, sup, table, tbody, td, textarea, tfoot, th, thead, tr, tt, u, ul, var, window, xmp

**onrowenter** applet, object, xml

**onrowexit** applet, object, xml

**onrowsdelete** applet, object, xml

**onrowsinserted** applet, object, xml

**onscroll** applet, bdo, body, div, embed, map, marquee, object, table, textarea, window

**onselect** body, input (text), textarea

**onselectionchange** document

**onselectstart** a, abbr, acronym, address, area, b, bdo, big, blockquote, body, button, caption, center, cite, code, dd, del, dfn, dir, div, dl, dt, em, fieldset, font, form, h1, h2, h3, h4, h5, h6, hr, i, img, input (except hidden), kbd, label, li, listing, map, marquee, menu, nobr, object, ol, option, p, plaintext, pre, q, rt, ruby, s, samp, select, small, span, strike, strong, sub, sup, table, tbody, td, textarea, tfoot, th, thead, tr, tt, u, ul, var, xmp

**onstart** marquee

**onstart** document

**onsubmit** form

**onunload** body, frameset, window

# Appendixes

This part provides quick access to useful HTML authoring and scripting information. The glossary offers quick explanations of some of the new and potentially confusing terminology of DHTML.

Appendix A, *Color Names and RGB Values*

Appendix B, *HTML Character Entities*

Appendix C, *Keyboard Event Character Values*

Appendix D, *Internet Explorer Commands*

Appendix E, *HTML/XHTML DTD Support*

Glossary

# Color Names and RGB Values

Netscape was the first to develop a library of color names that could be used as attribute and scripted object property color values in place of hexadecimal triplet values. Virtually all modern browsers support the use of these values. Color names in both tag attributes and scripts are case insensitive. Typically, if you set a color attribute or property to one of the named colors, the object property is reflected in scripts as the hexadecimal triplet value for that color. For additional convenience, the table below also shows the decimal equivalents of the RGB value in case you use these color values in style sheet rules. Be aware that some colors in this collection require 16- or 24-bit color to achieve the proper hue.

| Color name | Red | Green | Blue | Red | Green | Blue |
|---|---|---|---|---|---|---|
| aliceblue | F0 | F8 | FF | 240 | 248 | 255 |
| antiquewhite | FA | EB | D7 | 250 | 235 | 215 |
| aqua | 00 | FF | FF | 0 | 255 | 255 |
| aquamarine | 7F | FF | D4 | 127 | 255 | 212 |
| azure | F0 | FF | FF | 240 | 255 | 255 |
| beige | F5 | F5 | DC | 245 | 245 | 220 |
| bisque | FF | E4 | C4 | 255 | 228 | 196 |
| black | 00 | 00 | 00 | 0 | 0 | 0 |
| blanchedalmond | FF | EB | CD | 255 | 235 | 205 |
| blue | 00 | 00 | FF | 0 | 0 | 255 |
| blueviolet | 8A | 2B | E2 | 138 | 43 | 226 |
| brown | A5 | 2A | 2A | 165 | 42 | 42 |
| burlywood | DE | B8 | 87 | 222 | 184 | 135 |
| cadetblue | 5F | 9E | A0 | 95 | 158 | 160 |
| chartreuse | 7F | FF | 00 | 127 | 255 | 0 |
| chocolate | D2 | 69 | 1E | 210 | 105 | 30 |
| coral | FF | 7F | 50 | 255 | 127 | 80 |
| cornflowerblue | 64 | 95 | ED | 100 | 149 | 237 |
| cornsilk | FF | F8 | DC | 255 | 248 | 220 |

| Color name | Red | Green | Blue | Red | Green | Blue |
|---|---|---|---|---|---|---|
| crimson | DC | 14 | 3C | 220 | 20 | 60 |
| cyan | 00 | FF | FF | 0 | 255 | 255 |
| darkblue | 00 | 00 | 8B | 0 | 0 | 139 |
| darkcyan | 00 | 8B | 8B | 0 | 139 | 139 |
| darkgoldenrod | B8 | 86 | 0B | 184 | 134 | 11 |
| darkgray | A9 | A9 | A9 | 169 | 169 | 169 |
| darkgreen | 00 | 64 | 00 | 0 | 100 | 0 |
| darkgrey | A9 | A9 | A9 | 169 | 169 | 169 |
| darkkhaki | BD | B7 | 6B | 189 | 183 | 107 |
| darkmagenta | 8B | 00 | 8B | 139 | 0 | 139 |
| darkolivegreen | 55 | 6B | 2F | 85 | 107 | 47 |
| darkorange | FF | 8C | 00 | 255 | 140 | 0 |
| darkorchid | 99 | 32 | CC | 153 | 50 | 204 |
| darkred | 8B | 00 | 00 | 139 | 0 | 0 |
| darksalmon | E9 | 96 | 7A | 233 | 150 | 122 |
| darkseagreen | 8F | BC | 8F | 143 | 188 | 143 |
| darkslateblue | 48 | 3D | 8B | 72 | 61 | 139 |
| darkslategray | 2F | 4F | 4F | 47 | 79 | 79 |
| darkslategrey | 2F | 4F | 4F | 47 | 79 | 79 |
| darkturquoise | 00 | CE | D1 | 0 | 206 | 209 |
| darkviolet | 94 | 00 | D3 | 148 | 0 | 211 |
| deeppink | FF | 14 | 93 | 255 | 20 | 147 |
| deepskyblue | 00 | BF | FF | 0 | 191 | 255 |
| dimgray | 69 | 69 | 69 | 105 | 105 | 105 |
| dimgrey | 69 | 69 | 69 | 105 | 105 | 105 |
| dodgerblue | 1E | 90 | FF | 30 | 144 | 255 |
| firebrick | B2 | 22 | 22 | 178 | 34 | 34 |
| floralwhite | FF | FA | F0 | 255 | 250 | 240 |
| forestgreen | 22 | 8B | 22 | 34 | 139 | 34 |
| fuchsia | FF | 00 | FF | 255 | 0 | 255 |
| gainsboro | DC | DC | DC | 220 | 220 | 220 |
| ghostwhite | F8 | F8 | FF | 248 | 248 | 255 |
| gold | FF | D7 | 00 | 255 | 215 | 0 |
| goldenrod | DA | A5 | 20 | 218 | 165 | 32 |
| gray | 80 | 80 | 80 | 128 | 128 | 128 |
| grey | 80 | 80 | 80 | 128 | 128 | 128 |
| green | 00 | 80 | 00 | 0 | 128 | 0 |
| greenyellow | AD | FF | 2F | 173 | 255 | 47 |
| honeydew | F0 | FF | F0 | 240 | 255 | 240 |
| hotpink | FF | 69 | B4 | 255 | 105 | 180 |
| indianred | CD | 5C | 5C | 205 | 92 | 92 |

| Color name | Red | Green | Blue | Red | Green | Blue |
|------------|-----|-------|------|-----|-------|------|
| indigo | 4B | 00 | 82 | 75 | 0 | 130 |
| ivory | FF | FF | F0 | 255 | 255 | 240 |
| khaki | F0 | E6 | 8C | 240 | 230 | 140 |
| lavender | E6 | E6 | FA | 230 | 230 | 250 |
| lavenderblush | FF | F0 | F5 | 255 | 240 | 245 |
| lawngreen | 7C | FC | 00 | 124 | 252 | 0 |
| lemonchiffon | FF | FA | CD | 255 | 250 | 205 |
| lightblue | AD | D8 | E6 | 173 | 216 | 230 |
| lightcoral | F0 | 80 | 80 | 240 | 128 | 128 |
| lightcyan | E0 | FF | FF | 224 | 255 | 255 |
| lightgoldenrodyellow | FA | FA | D2 | 250 | 250 | 210 |
| lightgray | D3 | D3 | D3 | 211 | 211 | 211 |
| lightgreen | 90 | EE | 90 | 144 | 238 | 144 |
| lightgrey | D3 | D3 | D3 | 211 | 211 | 211 |
| lightpink | FF | B6 | C1 | 255 | 182 | 193 |
| lightsalmon | FF | A0 | 7A | 255 | 160 | 122 |
| lightseagreen | 20 | B2 | AA | 32 | 178 | 170 |
| lightskyblue | 87 | CE | FA | 135 | 206 | 250 |
| lightslategray | 77 | 88 | 99 | 119 | 136 | 153 |
| lightslategrey | 77 | 88 | 99 | 119 | 136 | 153 |
| lightsteelblue | B0 | C4 | DE | 176 | 196 | 222 |
| lightyellow | FF | FF | E0 | 255 | 255 | 224 |
| lime | 00 | FF | 00 | 0 | 255 | 0 |
| limegreen | 32 | CD | 32 | 50 | 205 | 50 |
| linen | FA | F0 | E6 | 250 | 240 | 230 |
| magenta | FF | 00 | FF | 255 | 0 | 255 |
| maroon | 80 | 00 | 00 | 128 | 0 | 0 |
| mediumaquamarine | 66 | CD | AA | 102 | 205 | 170 |
| mediumblue | 00 | 00 | CD | 0 | 0 | 205 |
| mediumorchid | BA | 55 | D3 | 186 | 85 | 211 |
| mediumpurple | 93 | 70 | DB | 147 | 112 | 219 |
| mediumseagreen | 3C | B3 | 71 | 60 | 179 | 113 |
| mediumslateblue | 7B | 68 | EE | 123 | 104 | 238 |
| mediumspringgreen | 00 | FA | 9A | 0 | 250 | 154 |
| mediumturquoise | 48 | D1 | CC | 72 | 209 | 204 |
| mediumvioletred | C7 | 15 | 85 | 199 | 21 | 133 |
| midnightblue | 19 | 19 | 70 | 25 | 25 | 112 |
| mintcream | F5 | FF | FA | 245 | 255 | 250 |
| mistyrose | FF | E4 | E1 | 255 | 228 | 225 |
| moccasin | FF | E4 | B5 | 255 | 228 | 181 |
| navajowhite | FF | DE | AD | 255 | 222 | 173 |

| Color name | Red | Green | Blue | Red | Green | Blue |
|---|---|---|---|---|---|---|
| navy | 00 | 00 | 80 | 0 | 0 | 128 |
| oldlace | FD | F5 | E6 | 253 | 245 | 230 |
| olive | 80 | 80 | 00 | 128 | 128 | 0 |
| olivedrab | 6B | 8E | 23 | 107 | 142 | 35 |
| orange | FF | A5 | 00 | 255 | 165 | 0 |
| orangered | FF | 45 | 00 | 255 | 69 | 0 |
| orchid | DA | 70 | D6 | 218 | 112 | 214 |
| palegoldenrod | EE | E8 | AA | 238 | 232 | 170 |
| palegreen | 98 | FB | 98 | 152 | 251 | 152 |
| paleturquoise | AF | EE | EE | 175 | 238 | 238 |
| palevioletred | DB | 70 | 93 | 219 | 112 | 147 |
| papayawhip | FF | EF | D5 | 255 | 239 | 213 |
| peachpuff | FF | DA | B9 | 255 | 218 | 185 |
| peru | CD | 85 | 3F | 205 | 133 | 63 |
| pink | FF | C0 | CB | 255 | 192 | 203 |
| plum | DD | A0 | DD | 221 | 160 | 221 |
| powderblue | B0 | E0 | E6 | 176 | 224 | 230 |
| purple | 80 | 00 | 80 | 128 | 0 | 128 |
| red | FF | 00 | 00 | 255 | 0 | 0 |
| rosybrown | BC | 8F | 8F | 188 | 143 | 143 |
| royalblue | 41 | 69 | E1 | 65 | 105 | 225 |
| saddlebrown | 8B | 45 | 13 | 139 | 69 | 19 |
| salmon | FA | 80 | 72 | 250 | 128 | 114 |
| sandybrown | F4 | A4 | 60 | 244 | 164 | 96 |
| seagreen | 2E | 8B | 57 | 46 | 139 | 87 |
| seashell | FF | F5 | EE | 255 | 245 | 238 |
| sienna | A0 | 52 | 2D | 160 | 82 | 45 |
| silver | C0 | C0 | C0 | 192 | 192 | 192 |
| skyblue | 87 | CE | EB | 135 | 206 | 235 |
| slateblue | 6A | 5A | CD | 106 | 90 | 205 |
| slategray | 70 | 80 | 90 | 112 | 128 | 144 |
| slategrey | 70 | 80 | 90 | 112 | 128 | 144 |
| snow | FF | FA | FA | 255 | 250 | 250 |
| springgreen | 00 | FF | 7F | 0 | 255 | 127 |
| steelblue | 46 | 82 | B4 | 70 | 130 | 180 |
| tan | D2 | B4 | 8C | 210 | 180 | 140 |
| teal | 00 | 80 | 80 | 0 | 128 | 128 |
| thistle | D8 | BF | D8 | 216 | 191 | 216 |
| tomato | FF | 63 | 47 | 255 | 99 | 71 |
| turquoise | 40 | E0 | D0 | 64 | 224 | 208 |
| violet | EE | 82 | EE | 238 | 130 | 238 |

| Color name | Red | Green | Blue | Red | Green | Blue |
|---|---|---|---|---|---|---|
| wheat | F5 | DE | B3 | 245 | 222 | 179 |
| white | FF | FF | FF | 255 | 255 | 255 |
| whitesmoke | F5 | F5 | F5 | 245 | 245 | 245 |
| yellow | FF | FF | 00 | 255 | 255 | 0 |
| yellowgreen | 9A | CD | 32 | 154 | 205 | 50 |

# HTML Character Entities

To display symbols and characters beyond the collection of common ASCII alphanumeric values (0–127), browsers recognize a special coding that lets you insert such characters into HTML document content. These *entity* characters start with an ampersand symbol (&) and end with a semicolon (;). Between those symbols goes a representation of the desired character in your choice of letters or numbers. For example, the numeric entity value for a copyright symbol is 169. An HTML statement using that symbol looks as follows:

```
<p style="text-align: center">&#169;2002 MegaCorp, Inc. All Rights Reserved.</p>
```

Because the numbering system is not easy to remember, entities also have case-sensitive word or abbreviation equivalents for their values. For the copyright symbol, for example, the entity is &copy;. This makes the code more readable, as in the following:

```
<p style="text-align: center">&copy;2002 MegaCorp, Inc. All Rights Reserved.</p>
```

This table lists every entity defined in the HTML 4 specification in alphabetical order. Recent browsers support the vast majority of these characters, but the user's operating system version and its internal character set also factors influence support.

| Alpha entity | Numeric entity | Description |
| --- | --- | --- |
| &Aacute; | &#193; | Capital letter A with acute |
| &aacute; | &#225; | Small letter a with acute |
| &Acirc; | &#194; | Capital letter A with circumflex |
| &acirc; | &#226; | Small letter a with circumflex |
| &acute; | &#180; | Acute accent |
| &AElig; | &#198; | Capital ligature AE |
| &aelig; | &#230; | Small ligature ae |
| &Agrave; | &#192; | Capital letter A with grave |
| &agrave; | &#224; | Small letter a with grave |
| &alefsym; | &#8501; | Alef symbol |
| &Alpha; | &#913; | Capital letter alpha |
| &alpha; | &#945; | Small letter alpha |
| &amp; | &#38; | Ampersand |

| Alpha entity | Numeric entity | Description |
|---|---|---|
| &and; | &#8743; | Logical and |
| &ang; | &#8736; | Angle |
| &Aring; | &#197; | Capital letter A with ring above |
| &aring; | &#229; | Small letter a with ring above |
| &asymp; | &#8776; | Almost equal to |
| &Atilde; | &#195; | Capital letter A with tilde |
| &atilde; | &#227; | Small letter a with tilde |
| &Auml; | &#196; | Capital letter A with diaeresis |
| &auml; | &#228; | Small letter a with diaeresis |
| &bdquo; | &#8222; | Double low-9 quotation mark |
| &Beta; | &#914; | Capital letter beta |
| &beta; | &#946; | Small letter beta |
| &brvbar; | &#166; | Broken vertical bar |
| &bull; | &#8226; | Bullet |
| &cap; | &#8745; | Intersection |
| &Ccedil; | &#199; | Capital letter C with cedilla |
| &ccedil; | &#231; | Small letter c with cedilla |
| &cedil; | &#184; | Cedilla |
| &cent; | &#162; | Cent sign |
| &Chi; | &#935; | Capital letter chi |
| &chi; | &#967; | Small letter chi |
| &circ; | &#710; | Modifier letter circumflex accent |
| &clubs; | &#9827; | Black club suit (shamrock) |
| &cong; | &#8773; | Approximately equal to |
| &copy; | &#169; | Copyright sign |
| &crarr; | &#8629; | Downwards arrow with corner leftwards (carriage return) |
| &cup; | &#8746; | Union |
| &curren; | &#164; | Currency sign |
| &dagger; | &#8224; | Dagger |
| &Dagger; | &#8225; | Double dagger |
| &darr; | &#8595; | Downwards arrow |
| &dArr; | &#8659; | Downwards double arrow |
| &deg; | &#176; | Degree sign |
| &Delta; | &#916; | Capital letter delta |
| &delta; | &#948; | Small letter delta |
| &diams; | &#9830; | Black diamond suit |
| &divide; | &#247; | Division sign |
| &Eacute; | &#201; | Capital letter E with acute |
| &eacute; | &#233; | Small letter e with acute |
| &Ecirc; | &#202; | Capital letter E with circumflex |
| &ecirc; | &#234; | Small letter e with circumflex |

| Alpha entity | Numeric entity | Description |
| --- | --- | --- |
| &Egrave; | &#200; | Capital letter E with grave |
| &egrave; | &#232; | Small letter e with grave |
| &empty; | &#8709; | Empty set/null set/diameter |
|   |   | Em space |
|   |   | En space |
| &Epsilon; | &#917; | Capital letter epsilon |
| &epsilon; | &#949; | Small letter epsilon |
| &equiv; | &#8801; | Identical to |
| &Eta; | &#919; | Capital letter eta |
| &eta; | &#951; | Small letter eta |
| &ETH; | &#208; | Capital letter ETH |
| &eth; | &#240; | Small letter eth |
| &Euml; | &#203; | Capital letter E with diaeresis |
| &euml; | &#235; | Small letter e with diaeresis |
| &euro; | &#128;[a] | Euro sign |
| &exist; | &#8707; | There exists |
| &fnof; | &#402; | Small f with hook |
| &forall; | &#8704; | For all |
| &frac12; | &#189; | Fraction one-half |
| &frac14; | &#188; | Fraction one-quarter |
| &frac34; | &#190; | Fraction three-quarters |
| &frasl; | &#8260; | Fraction slash |
| &Gamma; | &#915; | Capital letter gamma |
| &gamma; | &#947; | Small letter gamma |
| &ge; | &#8805; | Greater-than or equal to |
| &gt; | &#62; | Greater-than sign |
| &harr; | &#8596; | Left right arrow |
| &hArr; | &#8660; | Left right double arrow |
| &hearts; | &#9829; | Black heart suit |
| &hellip; | &#8230; | Horizontal ellipsis |
| &Iacute; | &#205; | Capital letter I with acute |
| &iacute; | &#237; | Small letter i with acute |
| &Icirc; | &#206; | Capital letter I with circumflex |
| &icirc; | &#238; | Small letter i with circumflex |
| &iexcl; | &#161; | Inverted exclamation mark |
| &Igrave; | &#204; | Capital letter I with grave |
| &igrave; | &#236; | Small letter i with grave |
| &image; | &#8465; | Blackletter capital I |
| &infin; | &#8734; | Infinity |
| &int; | &#8747; | Integral |
| &Iota; | &#921; | Capital letter iota |

| Alpha entity | Numeric entity | Description |
| --- | --- | --- |
| &iota; | &#953; | Small letter iota |
| &iquest; | &#191; | Inverted question mark |
| &isin; | &#8712; | Element of |
| &Iuml; | &#207; | Capital letter I with diaeresis |
| &iuml; | &#239; | Small letter i with diaeresis |
| &Kappa; | &#922; | Capital letter kappa |
| &kappa; | &#954; | Small letter kappa |
| &Lambda; | &#923; | Capital letter lambda |
| &lambda; | &#955; | Small letter lambda |
| &lang; | &#9001; | Left-pointing angle bracket (bra) |
| &laquo; | &#171; | Left-pointing double angle quotation mark (guillemet) |
| &larr; | &#8592; | Leftwards arrow |
| &lArr; | &#8656; | Leftwards double arrow |
| &lceil; | &#8968; | Left ceiling |
| &ldquo; | &#8220; | Left double quotation mark |
| &le; | &#8804; | Less-than or equal to |
| &lfloor; | &#8970; | Left floor |
| &lowast; | &#8727; | Asterisk operator |
| &loz; | &#9674; | Lozenge |
| &lrm; | &#8206; | Left-to-right mark |
| &lsaquo; | &#8249; | Single left-pointing angle quotation mark |
| &lsquo; | &#8216; | Left single quotation mark |
| &lt; | &#60; | Less-than sign |
| &macr; | &#175; | Macron (overline) |
| &mdash; | &#8212; | Em dash |
| &micro; | &#181; | Micro sign |
| &middot; | &#183; | Georgian comma |
| &minus; | &#8722; | Minus sign |
| &Mu; | &#924; | Capital letter mu |
| &mu; | &#956; | Small letter mu |
| &nabla; | &#8711; | Nabla |
|   |   | Nonbreaking space |
| &ndash; | &#8211; | En dash |
| &ne; | &#8800; | Not equal to |
| &ni; | &#8715; | Contains as member |
| &not; | &#172; | Not sign (discretionary hyphen) |
| &notin; | &#8713; | Not an element of |
| &nsub; | &#8836; | Not a subset of |
| &Ntilde; | &#209; | Capital letter N with tilde |
| &ntilde; | &#241; | Small letter n with tilde |
| &Nu; | &#925; | Capital letter nu |

| Alpha entity | Numeric entity | Description |
| --- | --- | --- |
| &nu; | &#957; | Small letter nu |
| &Oacute; | &#211; | Capital letter O with acute |
| &oacute; | &#243; | Small letter o with acute |
| &Ocirc; | &#212; | Capital letter O with circumflex |
| &ocirc; | &#244; | Small letter o with circumflex |
| &OElig; | &#338; | Capital ligature OE |
| &oelig; | &#339; | Small ligature oe |
| &Ograve; | &#210; | Capital letter O with grave |
| &ograve; | &#242; | Small letter o with grave |
| &oline; | &#8254; | Overline |
| &Omega; | &#937; | Capital letter omega |
| &omega; | &#969; | Small letter omega |
| &Omicron; | &#927; | Capital letter omicron |
| &omicron; | &#959; | Small letter omicron |
| &oplus; | &#8853; | Circled plus |
| &or; | &#8744; | Logical or |
| &ordf; | &#170; | Feminine ordinal indicator |
| &ordm; | &#186; | Masculine ordinal indicator |
| &Oslash; | &#216; | Capital letter O with stroke |
| &oslash; | &#248; | Small letter o with stroke |
| &Otilde; | &#213; | Capital letter O with tilde |
| &otilde; | &#245; | Small letter o with tilde |
| &otimes; | &#8855; | Circled times |
| &Ouml; | &#214; | Capital letter O with diaeresis |
| &ouml; | &#246; | Small letter o with diaeresis |
| &para; | &#182; | Paragraph (pilcrow) sign |
| &part; | &#8706; | Partial differential |
| &permil; | &#8240; | Per mille sign |
| &perp; | &#8869; | Up tack/orthogonal to/perpendicular |
| &Phi; | &#934; | Capital letter phi |
| &phi; | &#966; | Small letter phi |
| &Pi; | &#928; | Capital letter pi |
| &pi; | &#960; | Small letter pi |
| &piv; | &#982; | symbol |
| &plusmn; | &#177; | Plus-or-minus sign |
| &pound; | &#163; | Pound sign |
| &prime; | &#8242; | Prime/minutes/feet |
| &Prime; | &#8243; | Double prime/seconds/inches |
| &prod; | &#8719; | N-ary product (product sign) |
| &prop; | &#8733; | Proportional to |
| &Psi; | &#936; | Capital letter psi |

| Alpha entity | Numeric entity | Description |
|---|---|---|
| &psi; | &#968; | Small letter psi |
| &quot; | &#34; | Quotation mark |
| &radic; | &#8730; | Square root |
| &rang; | &#9002; | Right-pointing angle bracket (ket) |
| &raquo; | &#187; | Right-pointing double angle quotation mark (guillemet) |
| &rarr; | &#8594; | Rightwards arrow |
| &rArr; | &#8658; | Rightwards double arrow |
| &rceil; | &#8969; | Right ceiling |
| &rdquo; | &#8221; | Right double quotation mark |
| &real; | &#8476; | Blackletter capital R |
| &reg; | &#174; | Registered trademark sign |
| &rfloor; | &#8971; | Right floor |
| &Rho; | &#929; | Capital letter rho |
| &rho; | &#961; | Small letter rho |
| &rlm; | &#8207; | Right-to-left mark |
| &rsaquo; | &#8250; | Single right-pointing angle quotation mark |
| &rsquo; | &#8217; | Right single quotation mark |
| &sbquo; | &#8218; | Single low-9 quotation mark |
| &Scaron; | &#352; | Capital letter S with caron |
| &scaron; | &#353; | Small letter s with caron |
| &sdot; | &#8901; | Dot operator |
| &sect; | &#167; | Section sign |
| &shy; | &#173; | Soft hyphen (discretionary hyphen) |
| &Sigma; | &#931; | Capital letter sigma |
| &sigma; | &#963; | Small letter sigma |
| &sigmaf; | &#962; | Small letter final sigma |
| &sim; | &#8764; | Tilde operator |
| &spades; | &#9824; | Black spade suit |
| &sub; | &#8834; | Subset of |
| &sube; | &#8838; | Subset of or equal to |
| &sum; | &#8721; | N-ary sumation |
| &sup; | &#8835; | Superset of |
| &sup1; | &#185; | Superscript digit one |
| &sup2; | &#178; | Superscript digit two (squared) |
| &sup3; | &#179; | Superscript digit three (cubed) |
| &supe; | &#8839; | Superset of or equal to |
| &szlig; | &#223; | Small letter sharp s (ess-zed) |
| &Tau; | &#932; | Capital letter tau |
| &tau; | &#964; | Small letter tau |
| &there4; | &#8756; | Therefore |
| &Theta; | &#920; | Capital letter theta |

Appendixes

| Alpha entity | Numeric entity | Description |
|---|---|---|
| &theta; | &#952; | Small letter theta |
| &thetasym; | &#977; | Small letter theta symbol |
|   |   | Thin space |
| &THORN; | &#222; | Capital letter thorn |
| &thorn; | &#254; | Small letter thorn |
| &tilde; | &#732; | Small tilde |
| &times; | &#215; | Multiplication sign |
| &trade; | &#8482; | Trademark sign |
| &Uacute; | &#218; | Capital letter U with acute |
| &uacute; | &#250; | Small letter u with acute |
| &uarr; | &#8593; | Upwards arrow |
| &uArr; | &#8657; | Upwards double arrow |
| &Ucirc; | &#219; | Capital letter U with circumflex |
| &ucirc; | &#251; | Small letter u with circumflex |
| &Ugrave; | &#217; | Capital letter U with grave |
| &ugrave; | &#249; | Small letter u with grave |
| &uml; | &#168; | Diaeresis |
| &upsih; | &#978; | Upsilon with hook symbol |
| &Upsilon; | &#933; | Capital letter upsilon |
| &upsilon; | &#965; | Small letter upsilon |
| &Uuml; | &#220; | Capital letter U with diaeresis |
| &uuml; | &#252; | Small letter u with diaeresis |
| &weierp; | &#8472; | Script capital P |
| &Xi; | &#926; | Capital letter xi |
| &xi; | &#958; | Small letter xi |
| &Yacute; | &#221; | Capital letter Y with acute |
| &yacute; | &#253; | Small letter y with acute |
| &yen; | &#165; | Yen/yuan sign |
| &Yuml; | &#376; | Capital letter Y with diaeresis |
| &yuml; | &#255; | Small letter y with diaeresis |
| &Zeta; | &#918; | Capital letter zeta |
| &zeta; | &#950; | Small letter zeta |
| &zwj; | &#8205; | Zero width joiner |
| &zwnj; | &#8204; | Zero width nonjoiner |

[a] This character's numeric entity does not render in IE 5 for Macintosh.

# Keyboard Event Character Values

Keyboard events in recent browsers provide information about the keys and, where applicable, characters corresponding to the keys. Character values may be read from the onkeypress event, while the key values, including navigation and function keys, are available from onkeydown and onkeyup events. The event object properties you use to read these values varies with the event object model. See Chapter 6 for cross-browser implementation details.

The following table reveals the codes for characters in the lower ASCII character set. Some of the codes are for action keys (such as **Backspace** and **Tab**), which have character values that are also in this range. Read these values from an onkeypress event object.

| Character | Character Value | Character | Character Value |
|---|---|---|---|
| **Backspace** | 8 | - | 45 |
| **Tab** | 9 | . | 46 |
| **Enter (Return** on Mac) | 13 | / | 47 |
| **Space** | 32 | 0 | 48 |
| ! | 33 | 1 | 49 |
| " | 34 | 2 | 50 |
| # | 35 | 3 | 51 |
| $ | 36 | 4 | 52 |
| % | 37 | 5 | 53 |
| & | 38 | 6 | 54 |
| ' | 39 | 7 | 55 |
| ( | 40 | 8 | 56 |
| ) | 41 | 9 | 57 |
| * | 42 | : | 58 |
| + | 43 | ; | 59 |
| , | 44 | < | 60 |

| Character | Character Value | Character | Character Value |
|---|---|---|---|
| = | 61 | _ | 95 |
| > | 62 | ` | 96 |
| ? | 63 | a | 97 |
| @ | 64 | b | 98 |
| A | 65 | c | 99 |
| B | 66 | d | 100 |
| C | 67 | e | 101 |
| D | 68 | f | 102 |
| E | 69 | g | 103 |
| F | 70 | h | 104 |
| G | 71 | i | 105 |
| H | 72 | j | 106 |
| I | 73 | k | 107 |
| J | 74 | l | 108 |
| K | 75 | m | 109 |
| L | 76 | n | 110 |
| M | 77 | o | 111 |
| N | 78 | p | 112 |
| O | 79 | q | 113 |
| P | 80 | r | 114 |
| Q | 81 | s | 115 |
| R | 82 | t | 116 |
| S | 83 | u | 117 |
| T | 84 | v | 118 |
| U | 85 | w | 119 |
| V | 86 | x | 120 |
| W | 87 | y | 121 |
| X | 88 | z | 122 |
| Y | 89 | { | 123 |
| Z | 90 | \| | 124 |
| [ | 91 | } | 125 |
| \ | 92 | ~ | 126 |
| ] | 93 | **Delete** | 127 |
| ^ | 94 | | |

The following table lists all keys on a typical U. S. English keyboard and their corresponding key codes. Read these codes from an onkeydown or onkeyup event object:

| Key | Key Value | Key | Key Value |
|-----|-----------|-----|-----------|
| Alt | 18 | (NumPad) 2 | 98 |
| Arrow Down | 40 | (NumPad) 3 | 99 |
| Arrow Left | 37 | (NumPad) 4 | 100 |
| Arrow Right | 39 | (NumPad) 5 | 101 |
| Arrow Up | 38 | (NumPad) 6 | 102 |
| Backspace | 8 | (NumPad) 7 | 103 |
| Caps Lock | 20 | (NumPad) 8 | 104 |
| Ctrl | 17 | (NumPad) 9 | 105 |
| Delete | 46 | Page Down | 34 |
| End | 35 | Page Up | 33 |
| Enter | 13 | Pause | 19 |
| Esc | 27 | Print Scrn | 44 |
| F1 | 112 | Scroll Lock | 145 |
| F2 | 113 | Shift | 16 |
| F3 | 114 | Spacebar | 32 |
| F4 | 115 | Tab | 9 |
| F5 | 116 | A | 65 |
| F6 | 117 | B | 66 |
| F7 | 118 | C | 67 |
| F8 | 119 | D | 68 |
| F9 | 120 | E | 69 |
| F10 | 121 | F | 70 |
| F11 | 122 | G | 71 |
| F12 | 123 | H | 72 |
| Home | 36 | I | 73 |
| Insert | 45 | J | 74 |
| Num Lock | 144 | K | 75 |
| (NumPad) - | 109 | L | 76 |
| (NumPad) * | 106 | M | 77 |
| (NumPad) . | 110 | N | 78 |
| (NumPad) / | 111 | O | 79 |
| (NumPad) + | 107 | P | 80 |
| (NumPad) 0 | 96 | Q | 81 |
| (NumPad) 1 | 97 | R | 82 |

| Key | Key Value | Key | Key Value |
|---|---|---|---|
| S | 83 | 8 | 56 |
| T | 84 | 9 | 57 |
| U | 85 | 0 | 48 |
| V | 86 | ' | 222 |
| W | 87 | - | 189 |
| X | 88 | , | 188 |
| Y | 89 | . | 190 |
| Z | 90 | / | 191 |
| 1 | 49 | ; | 186 |
| 2 | 50 | [ | 219 |
| 3 | 51 | \ | 220 |
| 4 | 52 | ] | 221 |
| 5 | 53 | ` | 192 |
| 6 | 54 | = | 187 |
| 7 | 55 | | |

# Internet Explorer Commands

Internet Explorer includes a set of commands that work directly with the document and (Win32 only) TextRange objects. In many cases, these commands mimic the functionality available through setting properties or invoking methods of the objects. Some of the newer commands operate within the context of the MSHTML Edit Mode. All of these commands exist outside of the primary document object model and are therefore treated separately in this appendix.

Access to these commands is through a set of document and TextRange object methods that are described in Chapter 9. These commands and syntax are:

```
execCommand("commandName"[, UIFlag[, value]])
queryCommandEnabled("commandName")
queryCommandIndeterm("commandName")
queryCommandState("commandName")
queryCommandSupported("commandName")
queryCommandText("commandName")
```

This appendix focuses on the commands and values that may be applied to the execCommand( ) method (the commands may also be applied to the other methods).

Some commands work on the current selection in a document, which means that the selection must be made manually by the user or via a script and the TextRange object. For example, the following function locates every instance of a string passed as a parameter and turns its text color to red:

```
function redden(txt) {
    var rng = document.body.createTextRange( );
    for (var i = 0; rng.findText(txt) != false; i++) {
        rng.select( );
        document.execCommand("ForeColor","false","red") ;
        rng.collapse(false);
        rng.select( );
    }
}
```

The process is iterative. After creating a text range for the entire document body, the function repeatedly looks for a match of the string. Whenever there is a match, the matched word is selected, and the execCommand( ) method invokes the ForeColor command, passing the value red as the color. To continue searching through the range, the range is collapsed after the previously found item, and the selection is removed (by selecting a range of zero length).

In general, I recommend using a regular object model method or property setting when one exists for the action you wish to take. Because these commands tend to work only with IE on Win32 operating systems, you may be forced to avoid them if your audience has a wider browser base.

| Command | Description | Parameter |
| --- | --- | --- |
| 2D-Position | Makes absolute-positioned element inherently draggable (IE 5.5 or later) | Boolean to enable (true) or disable (false) dragging |
| AbsolutePosition | Sets style.position property to absolute (IE 5.5 or later) | Boolean to enable (true) or disable (false) setting |
| BackColor | Sets background color of current selection | Color value (name or hex triplet) |
| Bold | Wraps a <b> tag around the range | None |
| Copy | Copies the range to the Clipboard | None |
| CreateBookmark | Wraps an <a name=> tag around the range or modifies an existing <a> tag | A string of the anchor name; tag is removed if value is omitted |
| CreateLink | Wraps an <a href=...> tag around the current selection | A string of a complete or relative URL |
| Cut | Copies the range to the Clipboard, then deletes range | None |
| Delete | Deletes the range | None |
| FontName | Sets the font of current selection | A string of the face attribute |
| FontSize | Sets the font size of current selection | A string of the font size |
| ForeColor | Sets the foreground (text) color of current selection | Color value (name or hex triplet) |
| FormatBlock | Wraps a block tag around the current object | Unknown |
| Indent | Indents current selection | None |
| InsertButton | Inserts a <button> tag at current insertion point | A string for the element ID |
| InsertFieldset | Inserts a <fieldset> tag at current insertion point | A string for the element ID |
| InsertHorizontalRule | Inserts <hr> at current insertion point | A string of the rule size (not working) |
| InsertIFrame | Inserts an <iframe> tag at current insertion point | A string of a URL for the *src* property |
| InsertImage | Inserts an <img> tag at current text selection (IE 5 or later) | A string of a URL for the *src* property |
| InsertInputButton | Inserts an <input type="button"> tag at current insertion point | A string for the element ID |
| InsertInputCheckbox | Inserts an <input type="checkbox"> tag at the current insertion point | A string for the element ID |
| InsertInputFileUpload | Inserts an <input type="file"> tag at the current insertion point | A string for the element ID |

| Command | Description | Parameter |
|---------|-------------|-----------|
| InsertInputHidden | Inserts an `<input type="hidden">` tag at current insertion point | A string for the element ID |
| InsertInputImage | Inserts an `<input type="image">` tag at current insertion point | A string for the element ID |
| InsertInputPassword | Inserts an `<input type="password">` tag at current insertion point | A string for the element ID |
| InsertInputRadio | Inserts an `<input type="radio">` tag at current insertion point | A string for the element ID |
| InsertInputReset | Inserts an `<input type="reset">` tag at current insertion point | A string for the element ID |
| InsertInputSubmit | Inserts an `<input type="submit">` tag at current insertion point | A string for the element ID |
| InsertInputText | Inserts an `<input type="text">` tag at current insertion point | A string for the element ID |
| InsertMarquee | Inserts a `<marquee>` tag at current insertion point | A string for the element ID |
| InsertOrderedList | Inserts an `<ol>` tag at current insertion point | A string for the element ID |
| InsertParagraph | Inserts a `<p>` tag at current insertion point | A string for the element ID |
| InsertSelectDropdown | Inserts a `<select>` tag whose type is `select-one` at current insertion point | A string for the element ID |
| InsertSelectListbox | Inserts a `<select>` tag whose type is `select-multiple` at current insertion point | A string for the element ID |
| InsertTextArea | Inserts a `<textarea>` tag at current insertion point | A string for the element ID |
| InsertUnorderedList | Inserts a `<ul>` tag at current insertion point | A string for the element ID |
| Italic | Wraps an `<i>` tag around the range | None |
| JustifyCenter | Full justifies the current selection | None |
| JustifyLeft | Left justifies the current selection | None |
| JustifyRight | Right justifies the current selection | None |
| LiveResize | Dynamically refresh element resizing in edit mode (IE 5.5 or later) | Boolean to enable (`true`) or disable (`false`) setting |
| MultipleSelection | Allow multiple element selections in edit mode (IE 5.5 or later) | Boolean to enable (`true`) or disable (`false`) setting |
| Outdent | Outdents the current selection | None |
| OverWrite | Sets the input-typing mode to overwrite or insert | Boolean (`true` if mode is overwrite) |
| Paste | Pastes contents of the Clipboard at current insertion point or over the current selection | None |
| Print | Displays Print dialog box (IE 5.5 or later) | None |
| Refresh | Reloads the current document | None |
| RemoveFormat | Removes formatting from current selection | None |
| SaveAs | Saves the page as a local file (optional file dialog) | A string of a URL for the path |
| SelectAll | Selects entire text of the document | None |

Appendixes

| Command | Description | Parameter |
|---------|-------------|-----------|
| UnBookmark | Removes anchor tags from the selection or text range | None |
| Underline | Wraps a `<u>` tag around the range | None |
| Unlink | Removes a link from the selection or text range | None |
| Unselect | Clears a selection from the document | None |

# HTML/XHTML DTD Support

With so many flavors of HTML 4 and XHTML specified by the W3C, it's not always easy to remember which elements and attributes are safe (i.e., validate without error) for a particular Document Type Definition that you specify in the `<!DOCTYPE>` header of your file. The large table in this appendix lists a union of all elements and attributes for the most common HTML 4.01 and XHTML 1.0 DTDs from the W3C. If an attribute is required for validation, it is marked "req'd".

The five DTDs referenced in the table can be specified at the top of your documents as follows:

*HTML 4.01 Transitional*

```
<!DOCTYPE HTML PUBLIC "-//W3C//DTD HTML 4.01 Transitional//EN"
    "http://www.w3.org/TR/html4/loose.dtd">
```

*HTML 4.01 Strict*

```
<!DOCTYPE HTML PUBLIC "-//W3C//DTD HTML 4.01//EN"
    "http://www.w3.org/TR/html4/strict.dtd">
```

*XHTML 1.0 Transitional*

```
<!DOCTYPE html PUBLIC "-//W3C//DTD XHTML 1.0 Transitional//EN"
    "http://www.w3.org/TR/xhtml1/DTD/xhtml1-transitional.dtd">
```

*XHTML 1.0 Frameset*

```
<!DOCTYPE html PUBLIC "-//W3C//DTD XHTML 1.0 Frameset//EN"
    "http://www.w3.org/TR/xhtml1/DTD/xhtml1-frameset.dtd">
```

*XHTML 1.0 Strict*

```
<!DOCTYPE html PUBLIC "-//W3C//DTD XHTML 1.0 Strict//EN"
    "http://www.w3.org/TR/xhtml1/DTD/xhtml1-strict.dtd">
```

See the discussion of the `<!DOCTYPE>` element in Chapter 8 about the implications of DTD specifications in the most recent browsers.

| Element/Attributes | HTML 4.01 Transitional | HTML 4.01 Strict | XHTML 1.0 Transitional | XHTML 1.0 Frameset | XHTML 1.0 Strict |
|---|---|---|---|---|---|
| a | yes | yes | yes | yes | yes |
| accesskey | yes | yes | yes | yes | yes |
| charset | yes | yes | yes | yes | yes |

| Element/Attributes | HTML 4.01 Transitional | HTML 4.01 Strict | XHTML 1.0 Transitional | XHTML 1.0 Frameset | XHTML 1.0 Strict |
|---|---|---|---|---|---|
| class | yes | yes | yes | yes | yes |
| coords | yes | yes | yes | yes | yes |
| dir | yes | yes | yes | yes | yes |
| href | yes | yes | yes | yes | yes |
| hreflang | yes | yes | yes | yes | yes |
| id | yes | yes | yes | yes | yes |
| lang | yes | yes | yes | yes | yes |
| name | yes | yes | yes | yes | yes |
| onblur | yes | yes | yes | yes | yes |
| onclick | yes | yes | yes | yes | yes |
| ondblclick | yes | yes | yes | yes | yes |
| onfocus | yes | yes | yes | yes | yes |
| onkeydown | yes | yes | yes | yes | yes |
| onkeypress | yes | yes | yes | yes | yes |
| onkeyup | yes | yes | yes | yes | yes |
| onmousedown | yes | yes | yes | yes | yes |
| onmousemove | yes | yes | yes | yes | yes |
| onmouseout | yes | yes | yes | yes | yes |
| onmouseover | yes | yes | yes | yes | yes |
| onmouseup | yes | yes | yes | yes | yes |
| rel | yes | yes | yes | yes | yes |
| rev | yes | yes | yes | yes | yes |
| shape | yes | yes | yes | yes | yes |
| style | yes | yes | yes | yes | yes |
| tabindex | yes | yes | yes | yes | yes |
| target | yes | no | yes | yes | no |
| title | yes | yes | yes | yes | yes |
| type | yes | yes | yes | yes | yes |
| xml:lang | no | no | yes | yes | yes |
| abbr | yes | yes | yes | yes | yes |
| class | yes | yes | yes | yes | yes |
| dir | yes | yes | yes | yes | yes |
| id | yes | yes | yes | yes | yes |
| lang | yes | yes | yes | yes | yes |
| onclick | yes | yes | yes | yes | yes |
| ondblclick | yes | yes | yes | yes | yes |

| Element/Attributes | HTML 4.01 Transitional | HTML 4.01 Strict | XHTML 1.0 Transitional | XHTML 1.0 Frameset | XHTML 1.0 Strict |
|---|---|---|---|---|---|
| onkeydown | yes | yes | yes | yes | yes |
| onkeypress | yes | yes | yes | yes | yes |
| onkeyup | yes | yes | yes | yes | yes |
| onmousedown | yes | yes | yes | yes | yes |
| onmousemove | yes | yes | yes | yes | yes |
| onmouseout | yes | yes | yes | yes | yes |
| onmouseover | yes | yes | yes | yes | yes |
| onmouseup | yes | yes | yes | yes | yes |
| style | yes | yes | yes | yes | yes |
| title | yes | yes | yes | yes | yes |
| xml:lang | no | no | yes | yes | yes |
| acronym | yes | yes | yes | yes | yes |
| class | yes | yes | yes | yes | yes |
| dir | yes | yes | yes | yes | yes |
| id | yes | yes | yes | yes | yes |
| lang | yes | yes | yes | yes | yes |
| onclick | yes | yes | yes | yes | yes |
| ondblclick | yes | yes | yes | yes | yes |
| onkeydown | yes | yes | yes | yes | yes |
| onkeypress | yes | yes | yes | yes | yes |
| onkeyup | yes | yes | yes | yes | yes |
| onmousedown | yes | yes | yes | yes | yes |
| onmousemove | yes | yes | yes | yes | yes |
| onmouseout | yes | yes | yes | yes | yes |
| onmouseover | yes | yes | yes | yes | yes |
| onmouseup | yes | yes | yes | yes | yes |
| style | yes | yes | yes | yes | yes |
| title | yes | yes | yes | yes | yes |
| xml:lang | no | no | yes | yes | yes |
| address | yes | yes | yes | yes | yes |
| class | yes | yes | yes | yes | yes |
| dir | yes | yes | yes | yes | yes |
| id | yes | yes | yes | yes | yes |
| lang | yes | yes | yes | yes | yes |
| onclick | yes | yes | yes | yes | yes |
| ondblclick | yes | yes | yes | yes | yes |

| Element/Attributes | HTML 4.01 Transitional | HTML 4.01 Strict | XHTML 1.0 Transitional | XHTML 1.0 Frameset | XHTML 1.0 Strict |
|---|---|---|---|---|---|
| onkeydown | yes | yes | yes | yes | yes |
| onkeypress | yes | yes | yes | yes | yes |
| onkeyup | yes | yes | yes | yes | yes |
| onmousedown | yes | yes | yes | yes | yes |
| onmousemove | yes | yes | yes | yes | yes |
| onmouseout | yes | yes | yes | yes | yes |
| onmouseover | yes | yes | yes | yes | yes |
| onmouseup | yes | yes | yes | yes | yes |
| style | yes | yes | yes | yes | yes |
| title | yes | yes | yes | yes | yes |
| xml:lang | no | no | yes | yes | yes |
| applet | yes | no | yes | yes | no |
| align | yes | no | yes | yes | no |
| alt | yes | no | yes | yes | no |
| archive | yes | no | yes | yes | no |
| class | yes | no | yes | yes | no |
| code | yes | no | yes | yes | no |
| codebase | yes | no | yes | yes | no |
| height | req'd | no | req'd | req'd | no |
| hspace | yes | no | yes | yes | no |
| id | yes | no | yes | yes | no |
| name | yes | no | yes | yes | no |
| object | yes | no | yes | yes | no |
| style | yes | no | yes | yes | no |
| title | yes | no | yes | yes | no |
| vspace | yes | no | yes | yes | no |
| width | req'd | no | req'd | req'd | no |
| area | yes | yes | yes | yes | yes |
| accesskey | yes | yes | yes | yes | yes |
| alt | req'd | req'd | req'd | req'd | req'd |
| class | yes | yes | yes | yes | yes |
| coords | yes | yes | yes | yes | yes |
| dir | yes | yes | yes | yes | yes |
| href | yes | yes | yes | yes | yes |
| id | yes | yes | yes | yes | yes |
| lang | yes | yes | yes | yes | yes |

| Element/Attributes | HTML 4.01 Transitional | HTML 4.01 Strict | XHTML 1.0 Transitional | XHTML 1.0 Frameset | XHTML 1.0 Strict |
|---|---|---|---|---|---|
| nohref | yes | yes | yes | yes | yes |
| onblur | yes | yes | yes | yes | yes |
| onclick | yes | yes | yes | yes | yes |
| ondblclick | yes | yes | yes | yes | yes |
| onfocus | yes | yes | yes | yes | yes |
| onkeydown | yes | yes | yes | yes | yes |
| onkeypress | yes | yes | yes | yes | yes |
| onkeyup | yes | yes | yes | yes | yes |
| onmousedown | yes | yes | yes | yes | yes |
| onmousemove | yes | yes | yes | yes | yes |
| onmouseout | yes | yes | yes | yes | yes |
| onmouseover | yes | yes | yes | yes | yes |
| onmouseup | yes | yes | yes | yes | yes |
| shape | yes | yes | yes | yes | yes |
| style | yes | yes | yes | yes | yes |
| tabindex | yes | yes | yes | yes | yes |
| target | yes | no | yes | yes | no |
| title | yes | yes | yes | yes | yes |
| xml:lang | no | no | yes | yes | yes |
| b | yes | yes | yes | yes | yes |
| class | yes | yes | yes | yes | yes |
| dir | yes | yes | yes | yes | yes |
| id | yes | yes | yes | yes | yes |
| lang | yes | yes | yes | yes | yes |
| onclick | yes | yes | yes | yes | yes |
| ondblclick | yes | yes | yes | yes | yes |
| onkeydown | yes | yes | yes | yes | yes |
| onkeypress | yes | yes | yes | yes | yes |
| onkeyup | yes | yes | yes | yes | yes |
| onmousedown | yes | yes | yes | yes | yes |
| onmousemove | yes | yes | yes | yes | yes |
| onmouseout | yes | yes | yes | yes | yes |
| onmouseover | yes | yes | yes | yes | yes |
| onmouseup | yes | yes | yes | yes | yes |
| style | yes | yes | yes | yes | yes |
| title | yes | yes | yes | yes | yes |
| xml:lang | no | no | yes | yes | yes |

| Element/Attributes | HTML 4.01 Transitional | HTML 4.01 Strict | XHTML 1.0 Transitional | XHTML 1.0 Frameset | XHTML 1.0 Strict |
|---|---|---|---|---|---|
| base | yes | yes | yes | yes | yes |
| href | yes | req'd | yes | yes | yes |
| target | yes | no | yes | yes | no |
| basefont | yes | no | yes | yes | no |
| color | yes | no | yes | yes | no |
| face | yes | no | yes | yes | no |
| id | yes | no | yes | yes | no |
| size | req'd | no | req'd | req'd | no |
| bdo | yes | yes | yes | yes | yes |
| class | yes | yes | yes | yes | yes |
| dir | req'd | req'd | req'd | req'd | req'd |
| id | yes | yes | yes | yes | yes |
| lang | yes | yes | yes | yes | yes |
| onclick | no | no | yes | yes | yes |
| ondblclick | no | no | yes | yes | yes |
| onkeydown | no | no | yes | yes | yes |
| onkeypress | no | no | yes | yes | yes |
| onkeyup | no | no | yes | yes | yes |
| onmousedown | no | no | yes | yes | yes |
| onmousemove | no | no | yes | yes | yes |
| onmouseout | no | no | yes | yes | yes |
| onmouseover | no | no | yes | yes | yes |
| onmouseup | no | no | yes | yes | yes |
| style | yes | yes | yes | yes | yes |
| title | yes | yes | yes | yes | yes |
| xml:lang | no | no | yes | yes | yes |
| big | yes | yes | yes | yes | yes |
| class | yes | yes | yes | yes | yes |
| dir | yes | yes | yes | yes | yes |
| id | yes | yes | yes | yes | yes |
| lang | yes | yes | yes | yes | yes |
| onclick | yes | yes | yes | yes | yes |
| ondblclick | yes | yes | yes | yes | yes |
| onkeydown | yes | yes | yes | yes | yes |
| onkeypress | yes | yes | yes | yes | yes |
| onkeyup | yes | yes | yes | yes | yes |

| Element/Attributes | HTML 4.01 Transitional | HTML 4.01 Strict | XHTML 1.0 Transitional | XHTML 1.0 Frameset | XHTML 1.0 Strict |
|---|---|---|---|---|---|
| onmousedown | yes | yes | yes | yes | yes |
| onmousemove | yes | yes | yes | yes | yes |
| onmouseout | yes | yes | yes | yes | yes |
| onmouseover | yes | yes | yes | yes | yes |
| onmouseup | yes | yes | yes | yes | yes |
| style | yes | yes | yes | yes | yes |
| title | yes | yes | yes | yes | yes |
| xml:lang | no | no | yes | yes | yes |
| blockquote | yes | yes | yes | yes | yes |
| cite | yes | yes | yes | yes | yes |
| class | yes | yes | yes | yes | yes |
| dir | yes | yes | yes | yes | yes |
| id | yes | yes | yes | yes | yes |
| lang | yes | yes | yes | yes | yes |
| onclick | yes | yes | yes | yes | yes |
| ondblclick | yes | yes | yes | yes | yes |
| onkeydown | yes | yes | yes | yes | yes |
| onkeypress | yes | yes | yes | yes | yes |
| onkeyup | yes | yes | yes | yes | yes |
| onmousedown | yes | yes | yes | yes | yes |
| onmousemove | yes | yes | yes | yes | yes |
| onmouseout | yes | yes | yes | yes | yes |
| onmouseover | yes | yes | yes | yes | yes |
| onmouseup | yes | yes | yes | yes | yes |
| style | yes | yes | yes | yes | yes |
| title | yes | yes | yes | yes | yes |
| xml:lang | no | no | yes | yes | yes |
| body | yes | yes | yes | yes | yes |
| alink | yes | no | yes | yes | no |
| background | yes | no | yes | yes | no |
| bgcolor | yes | no | yes | yes | no |
| class | yes | yes | yes | yes | yes |
| dir | yes | yes | yes | yes | yes |
| id | yes | yes | yes | yes | yes |
| lang | yes | yes | yes | yes | yes |
| link | yes | no | yes | yes | no |

| Element/Attributes | HTML 4.01 Transitional | HTML 4.01 Strict | XHTML 1.0 Transitional | XHTML 1.0 Frameset | XHTML 1.0 Strict |
|---|---|---|---|---|---|
| onclick | yes | yes | yes | yes | yes |
| ondblclick | yes | yes | yes | yes | yes |
| onkeydown | yes | yes | yes | yes | yes |
| onkeypress | yes | yes | yes | yes | yes |
| onkeyup | yes | yes | yes | yes | yes |
| onload | yes | yes | yes | yes | yes |
| onmousedown | yes | yes | yes | yes | yes |
| onmousemove | yes | yes | yes | yes | yes |
| onmouseout | yes | yes | yes | yes | yes |
| onmouseover | yes | yes | yes | yes | yes |
| onmouseup | yes | yes | yes | yes | yes |
| onunload | yes | yes | yes | yes | yes |
| style | yes | yes | yes | yes | yes |
| text | yes | no | yes | yes | no |
| title | yes | yes | yes | yes | yes |
| vlink | yes | no | yes | yes | no |
| xml:lang | no | no | yes | yes | yes |
| br | yes | yes | yes | yes | yes |
| class | yes | yes | yes | yes | yes |
| clear | yes | no | yes | yes | no |
| id | yes | yes | yes | yes | yes |
| style | yes | yes | yes | yes | yes |
| title | yes | yes | yes | yes | yes |
| button | yes | yes | yes | yes | yes |
| accesskey | yes | yes | yes | yes | yes |
| class | yes | yes | yes | yes | yes |
| datafld | yes | yes | no | no | no |
| dataformatas | yes | yes | no | no | no |
| datasrc | yes | yes | no | no | no |
| dir | yes | yes | yes | yes | yes |
| disabled | yes | yes | yes | yes | yes |
| id | yes | yes | yes | yes | yes |
| lang | yes | yes | yes | yes | yes |
| name | yes | yes | yes | yes | yes |
| onblur | yes | yes | yes | yes | yes |
| onclick | yes | yes | yes | yes | yes |

| Element/Attributes | HTML 4.01 Transitional | HTML 4.01 Strict | XHTML 1.0 Transitional | XHTML 1.0 Frameset | XHTML 1.0 Strict |
|---|---|---|---|---|---|
| ondblclick | yes | yes | yes | yes | yes |
| onfocus | yes | yes | yes | yes | yes |
| onkeydown | yes | yes | yes | yes | yes |
| onkeypress | yes | yes | yes | yes | yes |
| onkeyup | yes | yes | yes | yes | yes |
| onmousedown | yes | yes | yes | yes | yes |
| onmousemove | yes | yes | yes | yes | yes |
| onmouseout | yes | yes | yes | yes | yes |
| onmouseover | yes | yes | yes | yes | yes |
| onmouseup | yes | yes | yes | yes | yes |
| style | yes | yes | yes | yes | yes |
| tabindex | yes | yes | yes | yes | yes |
| title | yes | yes | yes | yes | yes |
| type | yes | yes | yes | yes | yes |
| value | yes | yes | yes | yes | yes |
| xml:lang | no | no | yes | yes | yes |
| caption | yes | yes | yes | yes | yes |
| align | yes | no | yes | yes | no |
| class | yes | yes | yes | yes | yes |
| dir | yes | yes | yes | yes | yes |
| id | yes | yes | yes | yes | yes |
| lang | yes | yes | yes | yes | yes |
| onclick | yes | yes | yes | yes | yes |
| ondblclick | yes | yes | yes | yes | yes |
| onkeydown | yes | yes | yes | yes | yes |
| onkeypress | yes | yes | yes | yes | yes |
| onkeyup | yes | yes | yes | yes | yes |
| onmousedown | yes | yes | yes | yes | yes |
| onmousemove | yes | yes | yes | yes | yes |
| onmouseout | yes | yes | yes | yes | yes |
| onmouseover | yes | yes | yes | yes | yes |
| onmouseup | yes | yes | yes | yes | yes |
| style | yes | yes | yes | yes | yes |
| title | yes | yes | yes | yes | yes |
| xml:lang | no | no | yes | yes | yes |

Appendixes

| Element/Attributes | HTML 4.01 Transitional | HTML 4.01 Strict | XHTML 1.0 Transitional | XHTML 1.0 Frameset | XHTML 1.0 Strict |
|---|---|---|---|---|---|
| center | yes | no | yes | yes | no |
| class | yes | no | yes | yes | no |
| dir | yes | no | yes | yes | no |
| id | yes | no | yes | yes | no |
| lang | yes | no | yes | yes | no |
| onclick | yes | no | yes | yes | no |
| ondblclick | yes | no | yes | yes | no |
| onkeydown | yes | no | yes | yes | no |
| onkeypress | yes | no | yes | yes | no |
| onkeyup | yes | no | yes | yes | no |
| onmousedown | yes | no | yes | yes | no |
| onmousemove | yes | no | yes | yes | no |
| onmouseout | yes | no | yes | yes | no |
| onmouseover | yes | no | yes | yes | no |
| onmouseup | yes | no | yes | yes | no |
| style | yes | no | yes | yes | no |
| title | yes | no | yes | yes | no |
| xml:lang | no | no | yes | yes | no |
| cite | yes | yes | yes | yes | yes |
| class | yes | yes | yes | yes | yes |
| dir | yes | yes | yes | yes | yes |
| id | yes | yes | yes | yes | yes |
| lang | yes | yes | yes | yes | yes |
| onclick | yes | yes | yes | yes | yes |
| ondblclick | yes | yes | yes | yes | yes |
| onkeydown | yes | yes | yes | yes | yes |
| onkeypress | yes | yes | yes | yes | yes |
| onkeyup | yes | yes | yes | yes | yes |
| onmousedown | yes | yes | yes | yes | yes |
| onmousemove | yes | yes | yes | yes | yes |
| onmouseout | yes | yes | yes | yes | yes |
| onmouseover | yes | yes | yes | yes | yes |
| onmouseup | yes | yes | yes | yes | yes |
| style | yes | yes | yes | yes | yes |
| title | yes | yes | yes | yes | yes |
| xml:lang | no | no | yes | yes | yes |

| Element/Attributes | HTML 4.01 Transitional | HTML 4.01 Strict | XHTML 1.0 Transitional | XHTML 1.0 Frameset | XHTML 1.0 Strict |
|---|---|---|---|---|---|
| code | yes | yes | yes | yes | yes |
|   class | yes | yes | yes | yes | yes |
|   dir | yes | yes | yes | yes | yes |
|   id | yes | yes | yes | yes | yes |
|   lang | yes | yes | yes | yes | yes |
|   onclick | yes | yes | yes | yes | yes |
|   ondblclick | yes | yes | yes | yes | yes |
|   onkeydown | yes | yes | yes | yes | yes |
|   onkeypress | yes | yes | yes | yes | yes |
|   onkeyup | yes | yes | yes | yes | yes |
|   onmousedown | yes | yes | yes | yes | yes |
|   onmousemove | yes | yes | yes | yes | yes |
|   onmouseout | yes | yes | yes | yes | yes |
|   onmouseover | yes | yes | yes | yes | yes |
|   onmouseup | yes | yes | yes | yes | yes |
|   style | yes | yes | yes | yes | yes |
|   title | yes | yes | yes | yes | yes |
|   xml:lang | no | no | yes | yes | yes |
| col | yes | yes | yes | yes | yes |
|   align | yes | yes | yes | yes | yes |
|   char | yes | yes | yes | yes | yes |
|   charoff | yes | yes | yes | yes | yes |
|   class | yes | yes | yes | yes | yes |
|   dir | yes | yes | yes | yes | yes |
|   id | yes | yes | yes | yes | yes |
|   lang | yes | yes | yes | yes | yes |
|   onclick | yes | yes | yes | yes | yes |
|   ondblclick | yes | yes | yes | yes | yes |
|   onkeydown | yes | yes | yes | yes | yes |
|   onkeypress | yes | yes | yes | yes | yes |
|   onkeyup | yes | yes | yes | yes | yes |
|   onmousedown | yes | yes | yes | yes | yes |
|   onmousemove | yes | yes | yes | yes | yes |
|   onmouseout | yes | yes | yes | yes | yes |
|   onmouseover | yes | yes | yes | yes | yes |
|   onmouseup | yes | yes | yes | yes | yes |

| Element/Attributes | HTML 4.01 Transitional | HTML 4.01 Strict | XHTML 1.0 Transitional | XHTML 1.0 Frameset | XHTML 1.0 Strict |
|---|---|---|---|---|---|
| span | yes | yes | yes | yes | yes |
| style | yes | yes | yes | yes | yes |
| title | yes | yes | yes | yes | yes |
| valign | yes | yes | yes | yes | yes |
| width | yes | yes | yes | yes | yes |
| xml:lang | no | no | yes | yes | yes |
| colgroup | yes | yes | yes | yes | yes |
| align | yes | yes | yes | yes | yes |
| char | yes | yes | yes | yes | yes |
| charoff | yes | yes | yes | yes | yes |
| class | yes | yes | yes | yes | yes |
| dir | yes | yes | yes | yes | yes |
| id | yes | yes | yes | yes | yes |
| lang | yes | yes | yes | yes | yes |
| onclick | yes | yes | yes | yes | yes |
| ondblclick | yes | yes | yes | yes | yes |
| onkeydown | yes | yes | yes | yes | yes |
| onkeypress | yes | yes | yes | yes | yes |
| onkeyup | yes | yes | yes | yes | yes |
| onmousedown | yes | yes | yes | yes | yes |
| onmousemove | yes | yes | yes | yes | yes |
| onmouseout | yes | yes | yes | yes | yes |
| onmouseover | yes | yes | yes | yes | yes |
| onmouseup | yes | yes | yes | yes | yes |
| span | yes | yes | yes | yes | yes |
| style | yes | yes | yes | yes | yes |
| title | yes | yes | yes | yes | yes |
| valign | yes | yes | yes | yes | yes |
| width | yes | yes | yes | yes | yes |
| xml:lang | no | no | yes | yes | yes |
| dd | yes | yes | yes | yes | yes |
| class | yes | yes | yes | yes | yes |
| dir | yes | yes | yes | yes | yes |
| id | yes | yes | yes | yes | yes |
| lang | yes | yes | yes | yes | yes |
| onclick | yes | yes | yes | yes | yes |

| Element/Attributes | HTML 4.01 Transitional | HTML 4.01 Strict | XHTML 1.0 Transitional | XHTML 1.0 Frameset | XHTML 1.0 Strict |
|---|---|---|---|---|---|
| ondblclick | yes | yes | yes | yes | yes |
| onkeydown | yes | yes | yes | yes | yes |
| onkeypress | yes | yes | yes | yes | yes |
| onkeyup | yes | yes | yes | yes | yes |
| onmousedown | yes | yes | yes | yes | yes |
| onmousemove | yes | yes | yes | yes | yes |
| onmouseout | yes | yes | yes | yes | yes |
| onmouseover | yes | yes | yes | yes | yes |
| onmouseup | yes | yes | yes | yes | yes |
| style | yes | yes | yes | yes | yes |
| title | yes | yes | yes | yes | yes |
| xml:lang | no | no | yes | yes | yes |
| del | yes | yes | yes | yes | yes |
| cite | yes | yes | yes | yes | yes |
| class | yes | yes | yes | yes | yes |
| datetime | yes | yes | yes | yes | yes |
| dir | yes | yes | yes | yes | yes |
| id | yes | yes | yes | yes | yes |
| lang | yes | yes | yes | yes | yes |
| onclick | yes | yes | yes | yes | yes |
| ondblclick | yes | yes | yes | yes | yes |
| onkeydown | yes | yes | yes | yes | yes |
| onkeypress | yes | yes | yes | yes | yes |
| onkeyup | yes | yes | yes | yes | yes |
| onmousedown | yes | yes | yes | yes | yes |
| onmousemove | yes | yes | yes | yes | yes |
| onmouseout | yes | yes | yes | yes | yes |
| onmouseover | yes | yes | yes | yes | yes |
| onmouseup | yes | yes | yes | yes | yes |
| style | yes | yes | yes | yes | yes |
| title | yes | yes | yes | yes | yes |
| xml:lang | no | no | yes | yes | yes |
| dfn | yes | yes | yes | yes | yes |
| class | yes | yes | yes | yes | yes |
| dir | yes | yes | yes | yes | yes |
| id | yes | yes | yes | yes | yes |

| Element/Attributes | HTML 4.01 Transitional | HTML 4.01 Strict | XHTML 1.0 Transitional | XHTML 1.0 Frameset | XHTML 1.0 Strict |
|---|---|---|---|---|---|
| lang | yes | yes | yes | yes | yes |
| onclick | yes | yes | yes | yes | yes |
| ondblclick | yes | yes | yes | yes | yes |
| onkeydown | yes | yes | yes | yes | yes |
| onkeypress | yes | yes | yes | yes | yes |
| onkeyup | yes | yes | yes | yes | yes |
| onmousedown | yes | yes | yes | yes | yes |
| onmousemove | yes | yes | yes | yes | yes |
| onmouseout | yes | yes | yes | yes | yes |
| onmouseover | yes | yes | yes | yes | yes |
| onmouseup | yes | yes | yes | yes | yes |
| style | yes | yes | yes | yes | yes |
| title | yes | yes | yes | yes | yes |
| xml:lang | no | no | yes | yes | yes |
| dir | yes | no | yes | no | no |
| class | yes | no | yes | no | no |
| compact | yes | no | yes | no | no |
| dir | yes | no | yes | no | no |
| id | yes | no | yes | no | no |
| lang | yes | no | yes | no | no |
| onclick | yes | no | yes | no | no |
| ondblclick | yes | no | yes | no | no |
| onkeydown | yes | no | yes | no | no |
| onkeypress | yes | no | yes | no | no |
| onkeyup | yes | no | yes | no | no |
| onmousedown | yes | no | yes | no | no |
| onmousemove | yes | no | yes | no | no |
| onmouseout | yes | no | yes | no | no |
| onmouseover | yes | no | yes | no | no |
| onmouseup | yes | no | yes | no | no |
| style | yes | no | yes | no | no |
| title | yes | no | yes | no | no |
| xml:lang | no | no | yes | no | no |
| div | yes | yes | yes | yes | yes |
| align | yes | no | yes | yes | no |
| class | yes | yes | yes | yes | yes |

| Element/Attributes | HTML 4.01 Transitional | HTML 4.01 Strict | XHTML 1.0 Transitional | XHTML 1.0 Frameset | XHTML 1.0 Strict |
|---|---|---|---|---|---|
| datafld | yes | yes | no | no | no |
| dataformatas | yes | yes | no | no | no |
| datasrc | yes | yes | no | no | no |
| dir | yes | yes | yes | yes | yes |
| id | yes | yes | yes | yes | yes |
| lang | yes | yes | yes | yes | yes |
| onclick | yes | yes | yes | yes | yes |
| ondblclick | yes | yes | yes | yes | yes |
| onkeydown | yes | yes | yes | yes | yes |
| onkeypress | yes | yes | yes | yes | yes |
| onkeyup | yes | yes | yes | yes | yes |
| onmousedown | yes | yes | yes | yes | yes |
| onmousemove | yes | yes | yes | yes | yes |
| onmouseout | yes | yes | yes | yes | yes |
| onmouseover | yes | yes | yes | yes | yes |
| onmouseup | yes | yes | yes | yes | yes |
| style | yes | yes | yes | yes | yes |
| title | yes | yes | yes | yes | yes |
| xml:lang | no | no | yes | yes | yes |
| dl | yes | yes | yes | yes | yes |
| class | yes | yes | yes | yes | yes |
| compact | yes | no | yes | yes | no |
| dir | yes | yes | yes | yes | yes |
| id | yes | yes | yes | yes | yes |
| lang | yes | yes | yes | yes | yes |
| onclick | yes | yes | yes | yes | yes |
| ondblclick | yes | yes | yes | yes | yes |
| onkeydown | yes | yes | yes | yes | yes |
| onkeypress | yes | yes | yes | yes | yes |
| onkeyup | yes | yes | yes | yes | yes |
| onmousedown | yes | yes | yes | yes | yes |
| onmousemove | yes | yes | yes | yes | yes |
| onmouseout | yes | yes | yes | yes | yes |
| onmouseover | yes | yes | yes | yes | yes |
| onmouseup | yes | yes | yes | yes | yes |
| style | yes | yes | yes | yes | yes |

| Element/Attributes | HTML 4.01 Transitional | HTML 4.01 Strict | XHTML 1.0 Transitional | XHTML 1.0 Frameset | XHTML 1.0 Strict |
|---|---|---|---|---|---|
| title | yes | yes | yes | yes | yes |
| xml:lang | no | no | yes | yes | yes |
| dt | yes | yes | yes | yes | yes |
| class | yes | yes | yes | yes | yes |
| dir | yes | yes | yes | yes | yes |
| id | yes | yes | yes | yes | yes |
| lang | yes | yes | yes | yes | yes |
| onclick | yes | yes | yes | yes | yes |
| ondblclick | yes | yes | yes | yes | yes |
| onkeydown | yes | yes | yes | yes | yes |
| onkeypress | yes | yes | yes | yes | yes |
| onkeyup | yes | yes | yes | yes | yes |
| onmousedown | yes | yes | yes | yes | yes |
| onmousemove | yes | yes | yes | yes | yes |
| onmouseout | yes | yes | yes | yes | yes |
| onmouseover | yes | yes | yes | yes | yes |
| onmouseup | yes | yes | yes | yes | yes |
| style | yes | yes | yes | yes | yes |
| title | yes | yes | yes | yes | yes |
| xml:lang | no | no | yes | yes | yes |
| em | yes | yes | yes | yes | yes |
| class | yes | yes | yes | yes | yes |
| dir | yes | yes | yes | yes | yes |
| id | yes | yes | yes | yes | yes |
| lang | yes | yes | yes | yes | yes |
| onclick | yes | yes | yes | yes | yes |
| ondblclick | yes | yes | yes | yes | yes |
| onkeydown | yes | yes | yes | yes | yes |
| onkeypress | yes | yes | yes | yes | yes |
| onkeyup | yes | yes | yes | yes | yes |
| onmousedown | yes | yes | yes | yes | yes |
| onmousemove | yes | yes | yes | yes | yes |
| onmouseout | yes | yes | yes | yes | yes |
| onmouseover | yes | yes | yes | yes | yes |
| onmouseup | yes | yes | yes | yes | yes |
| style | yes | yes | yes | yes | yes |

| Element/Attributes | HTML 4.01 Transitional | HTML 4.01 Strict | XHTML 1.0 Transitional | XHTML 1.0 Frameset | XHTML 1.0 Strict |
|---|---|---|---|---|---|
| title | yes | yes | yes | yes | yes |
| xml:lang | no | no | yes | yes | yes |
| fieldset | yes | yes | yes | yes | yes |
| class | yes | yes | yes | yes | yes |
| dir | yes | yes | yes | yes | yes |
| id | yes | yes | yes | yes | yes |
| lang | yes | yes | yes | yes | yes |
| onclick | yes | yes | yes | yes | yes |
| ondblclick | yes | yes | yes | yes | yes |
| onkeydown | yes | yes | yes | yes | yes |
| onkeypress | yes | yes | yes | yes | yes |
| onkeyup | yes | yes | yes | yes | yes |
| onmousedown | yes | yes | yes | yes | yes |
| onmousemove | yes | yes | yes | yes | yes |
| onmouseout | yes | yes | yes | yes | yes |
| onmouseover | yes | yes | yes | yes | yes |
| onmouseup | yes | yes | yes | yes | yes |
| style | yes | yes | yes | yes | yes |
| title | yes | yes | yes | yes | yes |
| xml:lang | no | no | yes | yes | yes |
| font | yes | no | yes | yes | no |
| class | yes | no | yes | yes | no |
| color | yes | no | yes | yes | no |
| dir | yes | no | yes | yes | no |
| face | yes | no | yes | yes | no |
| id | yes | no | yes | yes | no |
| lang | yes | no | yes | yes | no |
| size | yes | no | yes | yes | no |
| style | yes | no | yes | yes | no |
| title | yes | no | yes | yes | no |
| xml:lang | no | no | yes | yes | no |
| form | yes | yes | yes | yes | yes |
| accept | yes | yes | yes | yes | yes |
| accept-charset | yes | yes | yes | yes | yes |
| action | req'd | req'd | req'd | req'd | req'd |
| class | yes | yes | yes | yes | yes |

| Element/Attributes | HTML 4.01 Transitional | HTML 4.01 Strict | XHTML 1.0 Transitional | XHTML 1.0 Frameset | XHTML 1.0 Strict |
|---|---|---|---|---|---|
| dir | yes | yes | yes | yes | yes |
| enctype | yes | yes | yes | yes | yes |
| id | yes | yes | yes | yes | yes |
| lang | yes | yes | yes | yes | yes |
| method | yes | yes | yes | yes | yes |
| name | yes | yes | yes | yes | no |
| onclick | yes | yes | yes | yes | yes |
| ondblclick | yes | yes | yes | yes | yes |
| onkeydown | yes | yes | yes | yes | yes |
| onkeypress | yes | yes | yes | yes | yes |
| onkeyup | yes | yes | yes | yes | yes |
| onmousedown | yes | yes | yes | yes | yes |
| onmousemove | yes | yes | yes | yes | yes |
| onmouseout | yes | yes | yes | yes | yes |
| onmouseover | yes | yes | yes | yes | yes |
| onmouseup | yes | yes | yes | yes | yes |
| onreset | yes | yes | yes | yes | yes |
| onsubmit | yes | yes | yes | yes | yes |
| style | yes | yes | yes | yes | yes |
| target | yes | no | yes | yes | no |
| title | yes | yes | yes | yes | yes |
| xml:lang | no | no | yes | yes | yes |
| frame | yes | no | no | yes | no |
| class | yes | no | no | yes | no |
| frameborder | yes | no | no | yes | no |
| id | yes | no | no | yes | no |
| longdesc | yes | no | no | yes | no |
| marginheight | yes | no | no | yes | no |
| marginwidth | yes | no | no | yes | no |
| name | yes | no | no | yes | no |
| noresize | yes | no | no | yes | no |
| scrolling | yes | no | no | yes | no |
| src | yes | no | no | yes | no |
| style | yes | no | no | yes | no |
| title | yes | no | no | yes | no |

| Element/Attributes | HTML 4.01 Transitional | HTML 4.01 Strict | XHTML 1.0 Transitional | XHTML 1.0 Frameset | XHTML 1.0 Strict |
|---|---|---|---|---|---|
| frameset | yes | no | no | yes | no |
| class | yes | no | no | yes | no |
| cols | yes | no | no | yes | no |
| id | yes | no | no | yes | no |
| onload | yes | no | no | yes | no |
| onunload | yes | no | no | yes | no |
| rows | yes | no | no | yes | no |
| style | yes | no | no | yes | no |
| title | yes | no | no | yes | no |
| h1 | yes | yes | yes | yes | yes |
| align | yes | no | yes | yes | no |
| class | yes | yes | yes | yes | yes |
| dir | yes | yes | yes | yes | yes |
| id | yes | yes | yes | yes | yes |
| lang | yes | yes | yes | yes | yes |
| onclick | yes | yes | yes | yes | yes |
| ondblclick | yes | yes | yes | yes | yes |
| onkeydown | yes | yes | yes | yes | yes |
| onkeypress | yes | yes | yes | yes | yes |
| onkeyup | yes | yes | yes | yes | yes |
| onmousedown | yes | yes | yes | yes | yes |
| onmousemove | yes | yes | yes | yes | yes |
| onmouseout | yes | yes | yes | yes | yes |
| onmouseover | yes | yes | yes | yes | yes |
| onmouseup | yes | yes | yes | yes | yes |
| style | yes | yes | yes | yes | yes |
| title | yes | yes | yes | yes | yes |
| xml:lang | no | no | yes | yes | yes |
| h2 | yes | yes | yes | yes | yes |
| align | yes | no | yes | yes | no |
| class | yes | yes | yes | yes | yes |
| dir | yes | yes | yes | yes | yes |
| id | yes | yes | yes | yes | yes |
| lang | yes | yes | yes | yes | yes |
| onclick | yes | yes | yes | yes | yes |
| ondblclick | yes | yes | yes | yes | yes |

| Element/Attributes | HTML 4.01 Transitional | HTML 4.01 Strict | XHTML 1.0 Transitional | XHTML 1.0 Frameset | XHTML 1.0 Strict |
|---|---|---|---|---|---|
| onkeydown | yes | yes | yes | yes | yes |
| onkeypress | yes | yes | yes | yes | yes |
| onkeyup | yes | yes | yes | yes | yes |
| onmousedown | yes | yes | yes | yes | yes |
| onmousemove | yes | yes | yes | yes | yes |
| onmouseout | yes | yes | yes | yes | yes |
| onmouseover | yes | yes | yes | yes | yes |
| onmouseup | yes | yes | yes | yes | yes |
| style | yes | yes | yes | yes | yes |
| title | yes | yes | yes | yes | yes |
| xml:lang | no | no | yes | yes | yes |
| h3 | yes | yes | yes | yes | yes |
| align | yes | no | yes | yes | no |
| class | yes | yes | yes | yes | yes |
| dir | yes | yes | yes | yes | yes |
| id | yes | yes | yes | yes | yes |
| lang | yes | yes | yes | yes | yes |
| onclick | yes | yes | yes | yes | yes |
| ondblclick | yes | yes | yes | yes | yes |
| onkeydown | yes | yes | yes | yes | yes |
| onkeypress | yes | yes | yes | yes | yes |
| onkeyup | yes | yes | yes | yes | yes |
| onmousedown | yes | yes | yes | yes | yes |
| onmousemove | yes | yes | yes | yes | yes |
| onmouseout | yes | yes | yes | yes | yes |
| onmouseover | yes | yes | yes | yes | yes |
| onmouseup | yes | yes | yes | yes | yes |
| style | yes | yes | yes | yes | yes |
| title | yes | yes | yes | yes | yes |
| xml:lang | no | no | yes | yes | yes |
| h4 | yes | yes | yes | yes | yes |
| align | yes | no | yes | yes | no |
| class | yes | yes | yes | yes | yes |
| dir | yes | yes | yes | yes | yes |
| id | yes | yes | yes | yes | yes |
| lang | yes | yes | yes | yes | yes |

| Element/Attributes | HTML 4.01 Transitional | HTML 4.01 Strict | XHTML 1.0 Transitional | XHTML 1.0 Frameset | XHTML 1.0 Strict |
|---|---|---|---|---|---|
| onclick | yes | yes | yes | yes | yes |
| ondblclick | yes | yes | yes | yes | yes |
| onkeydown | yes | yes | yes | yes | yes |
| onkeypress | yes | yes | yes | yes | yes |
| onkeyup | yes | yes | yes | yes | yes |
| onmousedown | yes | yes | yes | yes | yes |
| onmousemove | yes | yes | yes | yes | yes |
| onmouseout | yes | yes | yes | yes | yes |
| onmouseover | yes | yes | yes | yes | yes |
| onmouseup | yes | yes | yes | yes | yes |
| style | yes | yes | yes | yes | yes |
| title | yes | yes | yes | yes | yes |
| xml:lang | no | no | yes | yes | yes |
| h5 | yes | yes | yes | yes | yes |
| align | yes | no | yes | yes | no |
| class | yes | yes | yes | yes | yes |
| dir | yes | yes | yes | yes | yes |
| id | yes | yes | yes | yes | yes |
| lang | yes | yes | yes | yes | yes |
| onclick | yes | yes | yes | yes | yes |
| ondblclick | yes | yes | yes | yes | yes |
| onkeydown | yes | yes | yes | yes | yes |
| onkeypress | yes | yes | yes | yes | yes |
| onkeyup | yes | yes | yes | yes | yes |
| onmousedown | yes | yes | yes | yes | yes |
| onmousemove | yes | yes | yes | yes | yes |
| onmouseout | yes | yes | yes | yes | yes |
| onmouseover | yes | yes | yes | yes | yes |
| onmouseup | yes | yes | yes | yes | yes |
| style | yes | yes | yes | yes | yes |
| title | yes | yes | yes | yes | yes |
| xml:lang | no | no | yes | yes | yes |
| h6 | yes | yes | yes | yes | yes |
| align | yes | no | yes | yes | no |
| class | yes | yes | yes | yes | yes |
| dir | yes | yes | yes | yes | yes |

| Element/Attributes | HTML 4.01 Transitional | HTML 4.01 Strict | XHTML 1.0 Transitional | XHTML 1.0 Frameset | XHTML 1.0 Strict |
|---|---|---|---|---|---|
| id | yes | yes | yes | yes | yes |
| lang | yes | yes | yes | yes | yes |
| onclick | yes | yes | yes | yes | yes |
| ondblclick | yes | yes | yes | yes | yes |
| onkeydown | yes | yes | yes | yes | yes |
| onkeypress | yes | yes | yes | yes | yes |
| onkeyup | yes | yes | yes | yes | yes |
| onmousedown | yes | yes | yes | yes | yes |
| onmousemove | yes | yes | yes | yes | yes |
| onmouseout | yes | yes | yes | yes | yes |
| onmouseover | yes | yes | yes | yes | yes |
| onmouseup | yes | yes | yes | yes | yes |
| style | yes | yes | yes | yes | yes |
| title | yes | yes | yes | yes | yes |
| xml:lang | no | no | yes | yes | yes |
| head | yes | yes | yes | yes | yes |
| dir | yes | yes | yes | yes | yes |
| lang | yes | yes | yes | yes | yes |
| profile | yes | yes | yes | yes | yes |
| xml:lang | no | no | yes | yes | yes |
| hr | yes | yes | yes | yes | yes |
| align | yes | no | yes | yes | no |
| class | yes | yes | yes | yes | yes |
| dir | yes | yes | yes | yes | yes |
| id | yes | yes | yes | yes | yes |
| lang | yes | yes | yes | yes | yes |
| noshade | yes | no | yes | yes | no |
| onclick | yes | yes | yes | yes | yes |
| ondblclick | yes | yes | yes | yes | yes |
| onkeydown | yes | yes | yes | yes | yes |
| onkeypress | yes | yes | yes | yes | yes |
| onkeyup | yes | yes | yes | yes | yes |
| onmousedown | yes | yes | yes | yes | yes |
| onmousemove | yes | yes | yes | yes | yes |
| onmouseout | yes | yes | yes | yes | yes |
| onmouseover | yes | yes | yes | yes | yes |

| Element/Attributes | HTML 4.01 Transitional | HTML 4.01 Strict | XHTML 1.0 Transitional | XHTML 1.0 Frameset | XHTML 1.0 Strict |
|---|---|---|---|---|---|
| onmouseup | yes | yes | yes | yes | yes |
| size | yes | no | yes | yes | no |
| style | yes | yes | yes | yes | yes |
| title | yes | yes | yes | yes | yes |
| width | yes | no | yes | yes | no |
| xml:lang | no | no | yes | yes | yes |
| html | yes | yes | yes | yes | yes |
| dir | yes | yes | yes | yes | yes |
| lang | yes | yes | yes | yes | yes |
| version | yes | no | no | no | no |
| xml:lang | no | no | yes | yes | yes |
| xmlns | no | no | yes | yes | yes |
| i | yes | yes | yes | yes | yes |
| class | yes | yes | yes | yes | yes |
| dir | yes | yes | yes | yes | yes |
| id | yes | yes | yes | yes | yes |
| lang | yes | yes | yes | yes | yes |
| onclick | yes | yes | yes | yes | yes |
| ondblclick | yes | yes | yes | yes | yes |
| onkeydown | yes | yes | yes | yes | yes |
| onkeypress | yes | yes | yes | yes | yes |
| onkeyup | yes | yes | yes | yes | yes |
| onmousedown | yes | yes | yes | yes | yes |
| onmousemove | yes | yes | yes | yes | yes |
| onmouseout | yes | yes | yes | yes | yes |
| onmouseover | yes | yes | yes | yes | yes |
| onmouseup | yes | yes | yes | yes | yes |
| style | yes | yes | yes | yes | yes |
| title | yes | yes | yes | yes | yes |
| xml:lang | no | no | yes | yes | yes |
| iframe | yes | no | yes | yes | no |
| align | yes | no | yes | yes | no |
| class | yes | no | yes | yes | no |
| frameborder | yes | no | yes | yes | no |
| height | yes | no | yes | yes | no |
| id | yes | no | yes | yes | no |

| Element/Attributes | HTML 4.01 Transitional | HTML 4.01 Strict | XHTML 1.0 Transitional | XHTML 1.0 Frameset | XHTML 1.0 Strict |
|---|---|---|---|---|---|
| longdesc | yes | no | yes | yes | no |
| marginheight | yes | no | yes | yes | no |
| marginwidth | yes | no | yes | yes | no |
| name | yes | no | yes | yes | no |
| scrolling | yes | no | yes | yes | no |
| src | yes | no | yes | yes | no |
| style | yes | no | yes | yes | no |
| title | yes | no | yes | yes | no |
| width | yes | no | yes | yes | no |
| img | yes | yes | yes | yes | yes |
| align | yes | yes | yes | yes | yes |
| alt | req'd | req'd | req'd | req'd | req'd |
| border | yes | no | yes | yes | no |
| class | yes | yes | yes | yes | yes |
| dir | yes | yes | yes | yes | yes |
| height | yes | yes | yes | yes | yes |
| hspace | yes | no | yes | yes | no |
| id | yes | yes | yes | yes | yes |
| ismap | yes | yes | yes | yes | yes |
| lang | yes | yes | yes | yes | yes |
| longdesc | yes | yes | yes | yes | yes |
| name | yes | yes | yes | yes | no |
| onclick | yes | yes | yes | yes | yes |
| ondblclick | yes | yes | yes | yes | yes |
| onkeydown | yes | yes | yes | yes | yes |
| onkeypress | yes | yes | yes | yes | yes |
| onkeyup | yes | yes | yes | yes | yes |
| onmousedown | yes | yes | yes | yes | yes |
| onmousemove | yes | yes | yes | yes | yes |
| onmouseout | yes | yes | yes | yes | yes |
| onmouseover | yes | yes | yes | yes | yes |
| onmouseup | yes | yes | yes | yes | yes |
| src | req'd | req'd | req'd | req'd | req'd |
| style | yes | yes | yes | yes | yes |
| title | yes | yes | yes | yes | yes |
| usemap | yes | yes | yes | yes | yes |

| Element/Attributes | HTML 4.01 Transitional | HTML 4.01 Strict | XHTML 1.0 Transitional | XHTML 1.0 Frameset | XHTML 1.0 Strict |
|---|---|---|---|---|---|
| vspace | yes | no | yes | yes | no |
| width | yes | yes | yes | yes | yes |
| xml:lang | no | no | yes | yes | yes |
| input | yes | yes | yes | yes | yes |
| accept | yes | yes | yes | yes | yes |
| accesskey | yes | yes | yes | yes | yes |
| align | yes | yes | yes | yes | yes |
| alt | yes | yes | yes | yes | yes |
| checked | yes | yes | yes | yes | yes |
| class | yes | yes | yes | yes | yes |
| datafld | yes | yes | no | no | no |
| dataformatas | yes | yes | no | no | no |
| datasrc | yes | yes | no | no | no |
| dir | yes | yes | yes | yes | yes |
| disabled | yes | yes | yes | yes | yes |
| id | yes | yes | yes | yes | yes |
| ismap | yes | yes | yes | yes | yes |
| lang | yes | yes | yes | yes | yes |
| maxlength | yes | yes | yes | yes | yes |
| name | yes | yes | yes | yes | yes |
| onblur | yes | yes | yes | yes | yes |
| onchange | yes | yes | yes | yes | yes |
| onclick | yes | yes | yes | yes | yes |
| ondblclick | yes | yes | yes | yes | yes |
| onfocus | yes | yes | yes | yes | yes |
| onkeydown | yes | yes | yes | yes | yes |
| onkeypress | yes | yes | yes | yes | yes |
| onkeyup | yes | yes | yes | yes | yes |
| onmousedown | yes | yes | yes | yes | yes |
| onmousemove | yes | yes | yes | yes | yes |
| onmouseout | yes | yes | yes | yes | yes |
| onmouseover | yes | yes | yes | yes | yes |
| onmouseup | yes | yes | yes | yes | yes |
| onselect | yes | yes | yes | yes | yes |
| readonly | yes | yes | yes | yes | yes |
| size | yes | yes | yes | yes | yes |

| Element/Attributes | HTML 4.01 Transitional | HTML 4.01 Strict | XHTML 1.0 Transitional | XHTML 1.0 Frameset | XHTML 1.0 Strict |
|---|---|---|---|---|---|
| src | yes | yes | yes | yes | yes |
| style | yes | yes | yes | yes | yes |
| tabindex | yes | yes | yes | yes | yes |
| title | yes | yes | yes | yes | yes |
| type | yes | yes | yes | yes | yes |
| usemap | yes | yes | yes | yes | yes |
| value | yes | yes | yes | yes | yes |
| xml:lang | no | no | yes | yes | yes |
| ins | yes | yes | yes | yes | yes |
| cite | yes | yes | yes | yes | yes |
| class | yes | yes | yes | yes | yes |
| datetime | yes | yes | yes | yes | yes |
| dir | yes | yes | yes | yes | yes |
| id | yes | yes | yes | yes | yes |
| lang | yes | yes | yes | yes | yes |
| onclick | yes | yes | yes | yes | yes |
| ondblclick | yes | yes | yes | yes | yes |
| onkeydown | yes | yes | yes | yes | yes |
| onkeypress | yes | yes | yes | yes | yes |
| onkeyup | yes | yes | yes | yes | yes |
| onmousedown | yes | yes | yes | yes | yes |
| onmousemove | yes | yes | yes | yes | yes |
| onmouseout | yes | yes | yes | yes | yes |
| onmouseover | yes | yes | yes | yes | yes |
| onmouseup | yes | yes | yes | yes | yes |
| style | yes | yes | yes | yes | yes |
| title | yes | yes | yes | yes | yes |
| xml:lang | no | no | yes | yes | yes |
| isindex | yes | no | yes | yes | no |
| class | yes | no | yes | yes | no |
| dir | yes | no | yes | yes | no |
| id | yes | no | yes | yes | no |
| lang | yes | no | yes | yes | no |
| prompt | yes | no | yes | yes | no |
| style | yes | no | yes | yes | no |
| title | yes | no | yes | yes | no |
| xml:lang | no | no | yes | yes | no |

| Element/Attributes | HTML 4.01 Transitional | HTML 4.01 Strict | XHTML 1.0 Transitional | XHTML 1.0 Frameset | XHTML 1.0 Strict |
|---|---|---|---|---|---|
| kbd | yes | yes | yes | yes | yes |
| class | yes | yes | yes | yes | yes |
| dir | yes | yes | yes | yes | yes |
| id | yes | yes | yes | yes | yes |
| lang | yes | yes | yes | yes | yes |
| onclick | yes | yes | yes | yes | yes |
| ondblclick | yes | yes | yes | yes | yes |
| onkeydown | yes | yes | yes | yes | yes |
| onkeypress | yes | yes | yes | yes | yes |
| onkeyup | yes | yes | yes | yes | yes |
| onmousedown | yes | yes | yes | yes | yes |
| onmousemove | yes | yes | yes | yes | yes |
| onmouseout | yes | yes | yes | yes | yes |
| onmouseover | yes | yes | yes | yes | yes |
| onmouseup | yes | yes | yes | yes | yes |
| style | yes | yes | yes | yes | yes |
| title | yes | yes | yes | yes | yes |
| xml:lang | no | no | yes | yes | yes |
| label | yes | yes | yes | yes | yes |
| accesskey | yes | yes | yes | yes | yes |
| class | yes | yes | yes | yes | yes |
| dir | yes | yes | yes | yes | yes |
| for | yes | yes | yes | yes | yes |
| id | yes | yes | yes | yes | yes |
| lang | yes | yes | yes | yes | yes |
| onblur | yes | yes | yes | yes | yes |
| onclick | yes | yes | yes | yes | yes |
| ondblclick | yes | yes | yes | yes | yes |
| onfocus | yes | yes | yes | yes | yes |
| onkeydown | yes | yes | yes | yes | yes |
| onkeypress | yes | yes | yes | yes | yes |
| onkeyup | yes | yes | yes | yes | yes |
| onmousedown | yes | yes | yes | yes | yes |
| onmousemove | yes | yes | yes | yes | yes |
| onmouseout | yes | yes | yes | yes | yes |

| Element/Attributes | HTML 4.01 Transitional | HTML 4.01 Strict | XHTML 1.0 Transitional | XHTML 1.0 Frameset | XHTML 1.0 Strict |
|---|---|---|---|---|---|
| onmouseover | yes | yes | yes | yes | yes |
| onmouseup | yes | yes | yes | yes | yes |
| style | yes | yes | yes | yes | yes |
| title | yes | yes | yes | yes | yes |
| xml:lang | no | no | yes | yes | yes |
| legend | yes | yes | yes | yes | yes |
| accesskey | yes | yes | yes | yes | yes |
| align | yes | no | yes | yes | no |
| class | yes | yes | yes | yes | yes |
| dir | yes | yes | yes | yes | yes |
| id | yes | yes | yes | yes | yes |
| lang | yes | yes | yes | yes | yes |
| onclick | yes | yes | yes | yes | yes |
| ondblclick | yes | yes | yes | yes | yes |
| onkeydown | yes | yes | yes | yes | yes |
| onkeypress | yes | yes | yes | yes | yes |
| onkeyup | yes | yes | yes | yes | yes |
| onmousedown | yes | yes | yes | yes | yes |
| onmousemove | yes | yes | yes | yes | yes |
| onmouseout | yes | yes | yes | yes | yes |
| onmouseover | yes | yes | yes | yes | yes |
| onmouseup | yes | yes | yes | yes | yes |
| style | yes | yes | yes | yes | yes |
| title | yes | yes | yes | yes | yes |
| xml:lang | no | no | yes | yes | yes |
| li | yes | yes | yes | yes | yes |
| class | yes | yes | yes | yes | yes |
| dir | yes | yes | yes | yes | yes |
| id | yes | yes | yes | yes | yes |
| lang | yes | yes | yes | yes | yes |
| onclick | yes | yes | yes | yes | yes |
| ondblclick | yes | yes | yes | yes | yes |
| onkeydown | yes | yes | yes | yes | yes |
| onkeypress | yes | yes | yes | yes | yes |
| onkeyup | yes | yes | yes | yes | yes |
| onmousedown | yes | yes | yes | yes | yes |

| Element/Attributes | HTML 4.01 Transitional | HTML 4.01 Strict | XHTML 1.0 Transitional | XHTML 1.0 Frameset | XHTML 1.0 Strict |
|---|---|---|---|---|---|
| onmousemove | yes | yes | yes | yes | yes |
| onmouseout | yes | yes | yes | yes | yes |
| onmouseover | yes | yes | yes | yes | yes |
| onmouseup | yes | yes | yes | yes | yes |
| style | yes | yes | yes | yes | yes |
| title | yes | yes | yes | yes | yes |
| type | yes | no | yes | yes | no |
| value | yes | no | yes | yes | no |
| xml:lang | no | no | yes | yes | yes |
| link | yes | yes | yes | yes | yes |
| charset | yes | yes | yes | yes | yes |
| class | yes | yes | yes | yes | yes |
| dir | yes | yes | yes | yes | yes |
| href | yes | yes | yes | yes | yes |
| hreflang | yes | yes | yes | yes | yes |
| id | yes | yes | yes | yes | yes |
| lang | yes | yes | yes | yes | yes |
| media | yes | yes | yes | yes | yes |
| onclick | yes | yes | yes | yes | yes |
| ondblclick | yes | yes | yes | yes | yes |
| onkeydown | yes | yes | yes | yes | yes |
| onkeypress | yes | yes | yes | yes | yes |
| onkeyup | yes | yes | yes | yes | yes |
| onmousedown | yes | yes | yes | yes | yes |
| onmousemove | yes | yes | yes | yes | yes |
| onmouseout | yes | yes | yes | yes | yes |
| onmouseover | yes | yes | yes | yes | yes |
| onmouseup | yes | yes | yes | yes | yes |
| rel | yes | yes | yes | yes | yes |
| rev | yes | yes | yes | yes | yes |
| style | yes | yes | yes | yes | yes |
| target | yes | no | yes | yes | no |
| title | yes | yes | yes | yes | yes |
| type | yes | yes | yes | yes | yes |
| xml:lang | no | no | yes | yes | yes |

| Element/Attributes | HTML 4.01 Transitional | HTML 4.01 Strict | XHTML 1.0 Transitional | XHTML 1.0 Frameset | XHTML 1.0 Strict |
|---|---|---|---|---|---|
| map | yes | yes | yes | yes | yes |
| class | yes | yes | yes | yes | yes |
| dir | yes | yes | yes | yes | yes |
| id | yes | yes | req'd | req'd | req'd |
| lang | yes | yes | yes | yes | yes |
| name | req'd | req'd | yes | yes | yes |
| onclick | yes | yes | yes | yes | yes |
| ondblclick | yes | yes | yes | yes | yes |
| onkeydown | yes | yes | yes | yes | yes |
| onkeypress | yes | yes | yes | yes | yes |
| onkeyup | yes | yes | yes | yes | yes |
| onmousedown | yes | yes | yes | yes | yes |
| onmousemove | yes | yes | yes | yes | yes |
| onmouseout | yes | yes | yes | yes | yes |
| onmouseover | yes | yes | yes | yes | yes |
| onmouseup | yes | yes | yes | yes | yes |
| style | yes | yes | yes | yes | yes |
| title | yes | yes | yes | yes | yes |
| xml:lang | no | no | yes | yes | yes |
| menu | yes | no | yes | no | no |
| class | yes | no | yes | no | no |
| compact | yes | no | yes | no | no |
| dir | yes | no | yes | no | no |
| id | yes | no | yes | no | no |
| lang | yes | no | yes | no | no |
| onclick | yes | no | yes | no | no |
| ondblclick | yes | no | yes | no | no |
| onkeydown | yes | no | yes | no | no |
| onkeypress | yes | no | yes | no | no |
| onkeyup | yes | no | yes | no | no |
| onmousedown | yes | no | yes | no | no |
| onmousemove | yes | no | yes | no | no |
| onmouseout | yes | no | yes | no | no |
| onmouseover | yes | no | yes | no | no |
| onmouseup | yes | no | yes | no | no |
| style | yes | no | yes | no | no |

| Element/Attributes | HTML 4.01 Transitional | HTML 4.01 Strict | XHTML 1.0 Transitional | XHTML 1.0 Frameset | XHTML 1.0 Strict |
|---|---|---|---|---|---|
| title | yes | no | yes | no | no |
| xml:lang | no | no | yes | no | no |
| meta | yes | yes | yes | yes | yes |
| content | req'd | req'd | req'd | req'd | req'd |
| dir | yes | yes | yes | yes | yes |
| http-equiv | yes | yes | yes | yes | yes |
| lang | yes | yes | yes | yes | yes |
| name | yes | yes | yes | yes | yes |
| scheme | yes | yes | yes | yes | yes |
| xml:lang | no | no | yes | yes | yes |
| noframes | yes | no | yes | yes | no |
| class | yes | no | yes | yes | no |
| dir | yes | no | yes | yes | no |
| id | yes | no | yes | yes | no |
| lang | yes | no | yes | yes | no |
| onclick | yes | no | yes | yes | no |
| ondblclick | yes | no | yes | yes | no |
| onkeydown | yes | no | yes | yes | no |
| onkeypress | yes | no | yes | yes | no |
| onkeyup | yes | no | yes | yes | no |
| onmousedown | yes | no | yes | yes | no |
| onmousemove | yes | no | yes | yes | no |
| onmouseout | yes | no | yes | yes | no |
| onmouseover | yes | no | yes | yes | no |
| onmouseup | yes | no | yes | yes | no |
| style | yes | no | yes | yes | no |
| title | yes | no | yes | yes | no |
| xml:lang | no | no | yes | yes | no |
| noscript | yes | yes | yes | yes | yes |
| class | yes | yes | yes | yes | yes |
| dir | yes | yes | yes | yes | yes |
| id | yes | yes | yes | yes | yes |
| lang | yes | yes | yes | yes | yes |
| onclick | yes | yes | yes | yes | yes |
| ondblclick | yes | yes | yes | yes | yes |
| onkeydown | yes | yes | yes | yes | yes |

| Element/Attributes | HTML 4.01 Transitional | HTML 4.01 Strict | XHTML 1.0 Transitional | XHTML 1.0 Frameset | XHTML 1.0 Strict |
|---|---|---|---|---|---|
| onkeypress | yes | yes | yes | yes | yes |
| onkeyup | yes | yes | yes | yes | yes |
| onmousedown | yes | yes | yes | yes | yes |
| onmousemove | yes | yes | yes | yes | yes |
| onmouseout | yes | yes | yes | yes | yes |
| onmouseover | yes | yes | yes | yes | yes |
| onmouseup | yes | yes | yes | yes | yes |
| style | yes | yes | yes | yes | yes |
| title | yes | yes | yes | yes | yes |
| xml:lang | no | no | yes | yes | yes |
| object | yes | yes | yes | yes | yes |
| align | yes | no | yes | yes | no |
| archive | yes | yes | yes | yes | yes |
| border | yes | no | yes | yes | no |
| class | yes | yes | yes | yes | yes |
| classid | yes | yes | yes | yes | yes |
| codebase | yes | yes | yes | yes | yes |
| codetype | yes | yes | yes | yes | yes |
| data | yes | yes | yes | yes | yes |
| datafld | yes | yes | no | no | no |
| dataformatas | yes | yes | no | no | no |
| datasrc | yes | yes | no | no | no |
| declare | yes | yes | yes | yes | yes |
| dir | yes | yes | yes | yes | yes |
| height | yes | yes | yes | yes | yes |
| hspace | yes | no | yes | yes | no |
| id | yes | yes | yes | yes | yes |
| lang | yes | yes | yes | yes | yes |
| name | yes | yes | yes | yes | yes |
| onclick | yes | yes | yes | yes | yes |
| ondblclick | yes | yes | yes | yes | yes |
| onkeydown | yes | yes | yes | yes | yes |
| onkeypress | yes | yes | yes | yes | yes |
| onkeyup | yes | yes | yes | yes | yes |
| onmousedown | yes | yes | yes | yes | yes |
| onmousemove | yes | yes | yes | yes | yes |

| Element/Attributes | HTML 4.01 Transitional | HTML 4.01 Strict | XHTML 1.0 Transitional | XHTML 1.0 Frameset | XHTML 1.0 Strict |
|---|---|---|---|---|---|
| onmouseout | yes | yes | yes | yes | yes |
| onmouseover | yes | yes | yes | yes | yes |
| onmouseup | yes | yes | yes | yes | yes |
| standby | yes | yes | yes | yes | yes |
| style | yes | yes | yes | yes | yes |
| tabindex | yes | yes | yes | yes | yes |
| title | yes | yes | yes | yes | yes |
| type | yes | yes | yes | yes | yes |
| usemap | yes | yes | yes | yes | yes |
| vspace | yes | no | yes | yes | no |
| width | yes | yes | yes | yes | yes |
| xml:lang | no | no | yes | yes | yes |
| ol | yes | yes | yes | yes | yes |
| class | yes | yes | yes | yes | yes |
| compact | yes | no | yes | yes | no |
| dir | yes | yes | yes | yes | yes |
| id | yes | yes | yes | yes | yes |
| lang | yes | yes | yes | yes | yes |
| onclick | yes | yes | yes | yes | yes |
| ondblclick | yes | yes | yes | yes | yes |
| onkeydown | yes | yes | yes | yes | yes |
| onkeypress | yes | yes | yes | yes | yes |
| onkeyup | yes | yes | yes | yes | yes |
| onmousedown | yes | yes | yes | yes | yes |
| onmousemove | yes | yes | yes | yes | yes |
| onmouseout | yes | yes | yes | yes | yes |
| onmouseover | yes | yes | yes | yes | yes |
| onmouseup | yes | yes | yes | yes | yes |
| start | yes | no | yes | yes | no |
| style | yes | yes | yes | yes | yes |
| title | yes | yes | yes | yes | yes |
| type | yes | no | yes | yes | no |
| xml:lang | no | no | yes | yes | yes |
| optgroup | yes | yes | yes | yes | yes |
| class | yes | yes | yes | yes | yes |
| dir | yes | yes | yes | yes | yes |

| Element/Attributes | HTML 4.01 Transitional | HTML 4.01 Strict | XHTML 1.0 Transitional | XHTML 1.0 Frameset | XHTML 1.0 Strict |
|---|---|---|---|---|---|
| disabled | yes | yes | yes | yes | yes |
| id | yes | yes | yes | yes | yes |
| label | req'd | req'd | req'd | req'd | req'd |
| lang | yes | yes | yes | yes | yes |
| onclick | yes | yes | yes | yes | yes |
| ondblclick | yes | yes | yes | yes | yes |
| onkeydown | yes | yes | yes | yes | yes |
| onkeypress | yes | yes | yes | yes | yes |
| onkeyup | yes | yes | yes | yes | yes |
| onmousedown | yes | yes | yes | yes | yes |
| onmousemove | yes | yes | yes | yes | yes |
| onmouseout | yes | yes | yes | yes | yes |
| onmouseover | yes | yes | yes | yes | yes |
| onmouseup | yes | yes | yes | yes | yes |
| style | yes | yes | yes | yes | yes |
| title | yes | yes | yes | yes | yes |
| xml:lang | no | no | yes | yes | yes |
| option | yes | yes | yes | yes | yes |
| class | yes | yes | yes | yes | yes |
| dir | yes | yes | yes | yes | yes |
| disabled | yes | yes | yes | yes | yes |
| id | yes | yes | yes | yes | yes |
| label | yes | yes | yes | yes | yes |
| lang | yes | yes | yes | yes | yes |
| onclick | yes | yes | yes | yes | yes |
| ondblclick | yes | yes | yes | yes | yes |
| onkeydown | yes | yes | yes | yes | yes |
| onkeypress | yes | yes | yes | yes | yes |
| onkeyup | yes | yes | yes | yes | yes |
| onmousedown | yes | yes | yes | yes | yes |
| onmousemove | yes | yes | yes | yes | yes |
| onmouseout | yes | yes | yes | yes | yes |
| onmouseover | yes | yes | yes | yes | yes |
| onmouseup | yes | yes | yes | yes | yes |
| selected | yes | yes | yes | yes | yes |
| style | yes | yes | yes | yes | yes |

| Element/Attributes | HTML 4.01 Transitional | HTML 4.01 Strict | XHTML 1.0 Transitional | XHTML 1.0 Frameset | XHTML 1.0 Strict |
|---|---|---|---|---|---|
| title | yes | yes | yes | yes | yes |
| value | yes | yes | yes | yes | yes |
| xml:lang | no | no | yes | yes | yes |
| p | yes | yes | yes | yes | yes |
| align | yes | no | yes | yes | no |
| class | yes | yes | yes | yes | yes |
| dir | yes | yes | yes | yes | yes |
| id | yes | yes | yes | yes | yes |
| lang | yes | yes | yes | yes | yes |
| onclick | yes | yes | yes | yes | yes |
| ondblclick | yes | yes | yes | yes | yes |
| onkeydown | yes | yes | yes | yes | yes |
| onkeypress | yes | yes | yes | yes | yes |
| onkeyup | yes | yes | yes | yes | yes |
| onmousedown | yes | yes | yes | yes | yes |
| onmousemove | yes | yes | yes | yes | yes |
| onmouseout | yes | yes | yes | yes | yes |
| onmouseover | yes | yes | yes | yes | yes |
| onmouseup | yes | yes | yes | yes | yes |
| style | yes | yes | yes | yes | yes |
| title | yes | yes | yes | yes | yes |
| xml:lang | no | no | yes | yes | yes |
| param | yes | yes | yes | yes | yes |
| id | yes | yes | yes | yes | yes |
| name | req'd | req'd | req'd | req'd | yes |
| type | yes | yes | yes | yes | yes |
| value | yes | yes | yes | yes | yes |
| valuetype | yes | yes | yes | yes | yes |
| pre | yes | yes | yes | yes | yes |
| class | yes | yes | yes | yes | yes |
| dir | yes | yes | yes | yes | yes |
| id | yes | yes | yes | yes | yes |
| lang | yes | yes | yes | yes | yes |
| onclick | yes | yes | yes | yes | yes |
| ondblclick | yes | yes | yes | yes | yes |
| onkeydown | yes | yes | yes | yes | yes |

| Element/Attributes | HTML 4.01 Transitional | HTML 4.01 Strict | XHTML 1.0 Transitional | XHTML 1.0 Frameset | XHTML 1.0 Strict |
|---|---|---|---|---|---|
| onkeypress | yes | yes | yes | yes | yes |
| onkeyup | yes | yes | yes | yes | yes |
| onmousedown | yes | yes | yes | yes | yes |
| onmousemove | yes | yes | yes | yes | yes |
| onmouseout | yes | yes | yes | yes | yes |
| onmouseover | yes | yes | yes | yes | yes |
| onmouseup | yes | yes | yes | yes | yes |
| style | yes | yes | yes | yes | yes |
| title | yes | yes | yes | yes | yes |
| width | yes | no | yes | yes | no |
| xml:lang | no | no | yes | yes | yes |
| xml:space | no | no | yes | yes | yes |
| q | yes | yes | yes | yes | yes |
| cite | yes | yes | yes | yes | yes |
| class | yes | yes | yes | yes | yes |
| dir | yes | yes | yes | yes | yes |
| id | yes | yes | yes | yes | yes |
| lang | yes | yes | yes | yes | yes |
| onclick | yes | yes | yes | yes | yes |
| ondblclick | yes | yes | yes | yes | yes |
| onkeydown | yes | yes | yes | yes | yes |
| onkeypress | yes | yes | yes | yes | yes |
| onkeyup | yes | yes | yes | yes | yes |
| onmousedown | yes | yes | yes | yes | yes |
| onmousemove | yes | yes | yes | yes | yes |
| onmouseout | yes | yes | yes | yes | yes |
| onmouseover | yes | yes | yes | yes | yes |
| onmouseup | yes | yes | yes | yes | yes |
| style | yes | yes | yes | yes | yes |
| title | yes | yes | yes | yes | yes |
| xml:lang | no | no | yes | yes | yes |
| s | yes | no | yes | yes | no |
| class | yes | no | yes | yes | no |
| dir | yes | no | yes | yes | no |
| id | yes | no | yes | yes | no |
| lang | yes | no | yes | yes | no |

| Element/Attributes | HTML 4.01 Transitional | HTML 4.01 Strict | XHTML 1.0 Transitional | XHTML 1.0 Frameset | XHTML 1.0 Strict |
|---|---|---|---|---|---|
| onclick | yes | no | yes | yes | no |
| ondblclick | yes | no | yes | yes | no |
| onkeydown | yes | no | yes | yes | no |
| onkeypress | yes | no | yes | yes | no |
| onkeyup | yes | no | yes | yes | no |
| onmousedown | yes | no | yes | yes | no |
| onmousemove | yes | no | yes | yes | no |
| onmouseout | yes | no | yes | yes | no |
| onmouseover | yes | no | yes | yes | no |
| onmouseup | yes | no | yes | yes | no |
| style | yes | no | yes | yes | no |
| title | yes | no | yes | yes | no |
| xml:lang | no | no | yes | yes | no |
| samp | yes | yes | yes | yes | yes |
| class | yes | yes | yes | yes | yes |
| dir | yes | yes | yes | yes | yes |
| id | yes | yes | yes | yes | yes |
| lang | yes | yes | yes | yes | yes |
| onclick | yes | yes | yes | yes | yes |
| ondblclick | yes | yes | yes | yes | yes |
| onkeydown | yes | yes | yes | yes | yes |
| onkeypress | yes | yes | yes | yes | yes |
| onkeyup | yes | yes | yes | yes | yes |
| onmousedown | yes | yes | yes | yes | yes |
| onmousemove | yes | yes | yes | yes | yes |
| onmouseout | yes | yes | yes | yes | yes |
| onmouseover | yes | yes | yes | yes | yes |
| onmouseup | yes | yes | yes | yes | yes |
| style | yes | yes | yes | yes | yes |
| title | yes | yes | yes | yes | yes |
| xml:lang | no | no | yes | yes | yes |
| script | yes | yes | yes | yes | yes |
| charset | yes | yes | yes | yes | yes |
| defer | yes | yes | no | no | no |
| event | yes | yes | no | no | no |
| for | yes | yes | no | no | no |

| Element/Attributes | HTML 4.01 Transitional | HTML 4.01 Strict | XHTML 1.0 Transitional | XHTML 1.0 Frameset | XHTML 1.0 Strict |
|---|---|---|---|---|---|
| language | yes | no | yes | yes | no |
| src | yes | yes | yes | yes | yes |
| type | req'd | req'd | req'd | req'd | req'd |
| xml:space | no | no | yes | yes | yes |
| select | yes | yes | yes | yes | yes |
| class | yes | yes | yes | yes | yes |
| datafld | yes | yes | yes | yes | yes |
| dataformatas | yes | yes | yes | yes | yes |
| datasrc | yes | yes | yes | yes | yes |
| dir | yes | yes | yes | yes | yes |
| disabled | yes | yes | yes | yes | yes |
| id | yes | yes | yes | yes | yes |
| lang | yes | yes | yes | yes | yes |
| multiple | yes | yes | yes | yes | yes |
| name | yes | yes | yes | yes | yes |
| onblur | yes | yes | yes | yes | yes |
| onchange | yes | yes | yes | yes | yes |
| onclick | yes | yes | yes | yes | yes |
| ondblclick | yes | yes | yes | yes | yes |
| onfocus | yes | yes | yes | yes | yes |
| onkeydown | yes | yes | yes | yes | yes |
| onkeypress | yes | yes | yes | yes | yes |
| onkeyup | yes | yes | yes | yes | yes |
| onmousedown | yes | yes | yes | yes | yes |
| onmousemove | yes | yes | yes | yes | yes |
| onmouseout | yes | yes | yes | yes | yes |
| onmouseover | yes | yes | yes | yes | yes |
| onmouseup | yes | yes | yes | yes | yes |
| size | yes | yes | yes | yes | yes |
| style | yes | yes | yes | yes | yes |
| tabindex | yes | yes | yes | yes | yes |
| title | yes | yes | yes | yes | yes |
| xml:lang | no | no | yes | yes | yes |
| small | yes | yes | yes | yes | yes |
| class | yes | yes | yes | yes | yes |
| dir | yes | yes | yes | yes | yes |

| Element/Attributes | HTML 4.01 Transitional | HTML 4.01 Strict | XHTML 1.0 Transitional | XHTML 1.0 Frameset | XHTML 1.0 Strict |
|---|---|---|---|---|---|
| id | yes | yes | yes | yes | yes |
| lang | yes | yes | yes | yes | yes |
| onclick | yes | yes | yes | yes | yes |
| ondblclick | yes | yes | yes | yes | yes |
| onkeydown | yes | yes | yes | yes | yes |
| onkeypress | yes | yes | yes | yes | yes |
| onkeyup | yes | yes | yes | yes | yes |
| onmousedown | yes | yes | yes | yes | yes |
| onmousemove | yes | yes | yes | yes | yes |
| onmouseout | yes | yes | yes | yes | yes |
| onmouseover | yes | yes | yes | yes | yes |
| onmouseup | yes | yes | yes | yes | yes |
| style | yes | yes | yes | yes | yes |
| title | yes | yes | yes | yes | yes |
| xml:lang | no | no | yes | yes | yes |
| span | yes | yes | yes | yes | yes |
| class | yes | yes | yes | yes | yes |
| datafld | yes | yes | no | no | no |
| dataformatas | yes | yes | no | no | no |
| datasrc | yes | yes | no | no | no |
| dir | yes | yes | yes | yes | yes |
| id | yes | yes | yes | yes | yes |
| lang | yes | yes | yes | yes | yes |
| onclick | yes | yes | yes | yes | yes |
| ondblclick | yes | yes | yes | yes | yes |
| onkeydown | yes | yes | yes | yes | yes |
| onkeypress | yes | yes | yes | yes | yes |
| onkeyup | yes | yes | yes | yes | yes |
| onmousedown | yes | yes | yes | yes | yes |
| onmousemove | yes | yes | yes | yes | yes |
| onmouseout | yes | yes | yes | yes | yes |
| onmouseover | yes | yes | yes | yes | yes |
| onmouseup | yes | yes | yes | yes | yes |
| style | yes | yes | yes | yes | yes |
| title | yes | yes | yes | yes | yes |
| xml:lang | no | no | yes | yes | yes |

| Element/Attributes | HTML 4.01 Transitional | HTML 4.01 Strict | XHTML 1.0 Transitional | XHTML 1.0 Frameset | XHTML 1.0 Strict |
|---|---|---|---|---|---|
| strike | yes | no | yes | yes | no |
| class | yes | no | yes | yes | no |
| dir | yes | no | yes | yes | no |
| id | yes | no | yes | yes | no |
| lang | yes | no | yes | yes | no |
| onclick | yes | no | yes | yes | no |
| ondblclick | yes | no | yes | yes | no |
| onkeydown | yes | no | yes | yes | no |
| onkeypress | yes | no | yes | yes | no |
| onkeyup | yes | no | yes | yes | no |
| onmousedown | yes | no | yes | yes | no |
| onmousemove | yes | no | yes | yes | no |
| onmouseout | yes | no | yes | yes | no |
| onmouseover | yes | no | yes | yes | no |
| onmouseup | yes | no | yes | yes | no |
| style | yes | no | yes | yes | no |
| title | yes | no | yes | yes | no |
| xml:lang | no | no | yes | yes | no |
| strong | yes | yes | yes | yes | yes |
| class | yes | yes | yes | yes | yes |
| dir | yes | yes | yes | yes | yes |
| id | yes | yes | yes | yes | yes |
| lang | yes | yes | yes | yes | yes |
| onclick | yes | yes | yes | yes | yes |
| ondblclick | yes | yes | yes | yes | yes |
| onkeydown | yes | yes | yes | yes | yes |
| onkeypress | yes | yes | yes | yes | yes |
| onkeyup | yes | yes | yes | yes | yes |
| onmousedown | yes | yes | yes | yes | yes |
| onmousemove | yes | yes | yes | yes | yes |
| onmouseout | yes | yes | yes | yes | yes |
| onmouseover | yes | yes | yes | yes | yes |
| onmouseup | yes | yes | yes | yes | yes |
| style | yes | yes | yes | yes | yes |
| title | yes | yes | yes | yes | yes |
| xml:lang | no | no | yes | yes | yes |

| Element/Attributes | HTML 4.01 Transitional | HTML 4.01 Strict | XHTML 1.0 Transitional | XHTML 1.0 Frameset | XHTML 1.0 Strict |
|---|---|---|---|---|---|
| style | yes | yes | yes | yes | yes |
| dir | yes | yes | yes | yes | yes |
| lang | yes | yes | yes | yes | yes |
| media | yes | yes | yes | yes | yes |
| title | yes | yes | yes | yes | yes |
| type | req'd | req'd | req'd | req'd | req'd |
| xml:lang | no | no | yes | yes | yes |
| xml:space | no | no | yes | yes | yes |
| sub | yes | yes | yes | yes | yes |
| class | yes | yes | yes | yes | yes |
| dir | yes | yes | yes | yes | yes |
| id | yes | yes | yes | yes | yes |
| lang | yes | yes | yes | yes | yes |
| onclick | yes | yes | yes | yes | yes |
| ondblclick | yes | yes | yes | yes | yes |
| onkeydown | yes | yes | yes | yes | yes |
| onkeypress | yes | yes | yes | yes | yes |
| onkeyup | yes | yes | yes | yes | yes |
| onmousedown | yes | yes | yes | yes | yes |
| onmousemove | yes | yes | yes | yes | yes |
| onmouseout | yes | yes | yes | yes | yes |
| onmouseover | yes | yes | yes | yes | yes |
| onmouseup | yes | yes | yes | yes | yes |
| style | yes | yes | yes | yes | yes |
| title | yes | yes | yes | yes | yes |
| xml:lang | no | no | yes | yes | yes |
| sup | yes | yes | yes | yes | yes |
| class | yes | yes | yes | yes | yes |
| dir | yes | yes | yes | yes | yes |
| id | yes | yes | yes | yes | yes |
| lang | yes | yes | yes | yes | yes |
| onclick | yes | yes | yes | yes | yes |
| ondblclick | yes | yes | yes | yes | yes |
| onkeydown | yes | yes | yes | yes | yes |
| onkeypress | yes | yes | yes | yes | yes |
| onkeyup | yes | yes | yes | yes | yes |

| Element/Attributes | HTML 4.01 Transitional | HTML 4.01 Strict | XHTML 1.0 Transitional | XHTML 1.0 Frameset | XHTML 1.0 Strict |
|---|---|---|---|---|---|
| onmousedown | yes | yes | yes | yes | yes |
| onmousemove | yes | yes | yes | yes | yes |
| onmouseout | yes | yes | yes | yes | yes |
| onmouseover | yes | yes | yes | yes | yes |
| onmouseup | yes | yes | yes | yes | yes |
| style | yes | yes | yes | yes | yes |
| title | yes | yes | yes | yes | yes |
| xml:lang | no | no | yes | yes | yes |
| table | yes | yes | yes | yes | yes |
| align | yes | yes | yes | yes | no |
| bgcolor | yes | yes | yes | yes | no |
| border | yes | yes | yes | yes | yes |
| cellpadding | yes | yes | yes | yes | yes |
| cellspacing | yes | yes | yes | yes | yes |
| class | yes | yes | yes | yes | yes |
| datafld | yes | yes | no | no | no |
| dataformatas | yes | yes | no | no | no |
| datapagesize | yes | yes | no | no | no |
| datasrc | yes | yes | no | no | no |
| dir | yes | yes | yes | yes | yes |
| frame | yes | yes | yes | yes | yes |
| id | yes | yes | yes | yes | yes |
| lang | yes | yes | yes | yes | yes |
| onclick | yes | yes | yes | yes | yes |
| ondblclick | yes | yes | yes | yes | yes |
| onkeydown | yes | yes | yes | yes | yes |
| onkeypress | yes | yes | yes | yes | yes |
| onkeyup | yes | yes | yes | yes | yes |
| onmousedown | yes | yes | yes | yes | yes |
| onmousemove | yes | yes | yes | yes | yes |
| onmouseout | yes | yes | yes | yes | yes |
| onmouseover | yes | yes | yes | yes | yes |
| onmouseup | yes | yes | yes | yes | yes |
| rules | yes | yes | yes | yes | yes |
| style | yes | yes | yes | yes | yes |
| summary | yes | yes | yes | yes | yes |

| Element/Attributes | HTML 4.01 Transitional | HTML 4.01 Strict | XHTML 1.0 Transitional | XHTML 1.0 Frameset | XHTML 1.0 Strict |
|---|---|---|---|---|---|
| title | yes | yes | yes | yes | yes |
| width | yes | yes | yes | yes | yes |
| xml:lang | no | no | yes | yes | yes |
| tbody | yes | yes | yes | yes | yes |
| align | yes | yes | yes | yes | yes |
| char | yes | yes | yes | yes | yes |
| charoff | yes | yes | yes | yes | yes |
| class | yes | yes | yes | yes | yes |
| dir | yes | yes | yes | yes | yes |
| id | yes | yes | yes | yes | yes |
| lang | yes | yes | yes | yes | yes |
| onclick | yes | yes | yes | yes | yes |
| ondblclick | yes | yes | yes | yes | yes |
| onkeydown | yes | yes | yes | yes | yes |
| onkeypress | yes | yes | yes | yes | yes |
| onkeyup | yes | yes | yes | yes | yes |
| onmousedown | yes | yes | yes | yes | yes |
| onmousemove | yes | yes | yes | yes | yes |
| onmouseout | yes | yes | yes | yes | yes |
| onmouseover | yes | yes | yes | yes | yes |
| onmouseup | yes | yes | yes | yes | yes |
| style | yes | yes | yes | yes | yes |
| title | yes | yes | yes | yes | yes |
| valign | yes | yes | yes | yes | yes |
| xml:lang | no | no | yes | yes | yes |
| td | yes | yes | yes | yes | yes |
| abbr | yes | yes | yes | yes | yes |
| align | yes | yes | yes | yes | yes |
| axis | yes | yes | yes | yes | yes |
| bgcolor | yes | no | yes | yes | no |
| char | yes | yes | yes | yes | yes |
| charoff | yes | yes | yes | yes | yes |
| class | yes | yes | yes | yes | yes |
| colspan | yes | yes | yes | yes | yes |
| dir | yes | yes | yes | yes | yes |
| headers | yes | yes | yes | yes | yes |

| Element/Attributes | HTML 4.01 Transitional | HTML 4.01 Strict | XHTML 1.0 Transitional | XHTML 1.0 Frameset | XHTML 1.0 Strict |
|---|---|---|---|---|---|
| height | yes | no | yes | yes | no |
| id | yes | yes | yes | yes | yes |
| lang | yes | yes | yes | yes | yes |
| nowrap | yes | no | yes | yes | no |
| onclick | yes | yes | yes | yes | yes |
| ondblclick | yes | yes | yes | yes | yes |
| onkeydown | yes | yes | yes | yes | yes |
| onkeypress | yes | yes | yes | yes | yes |
| onkeyup | yes | yes | yes | yes | yes |
| onmousedown | yes | yes | yes | yes | yes |
| onmousemove | yes | yes | yes | yes | yes |
| onmouseout | yes | yes | yes | yes | yes |
| onmouseover | yes | yes | yes | yes | yes |
| onmouseup | yes | yes | yes | yes | yes |
| rowspan | yes | yes | yes | yes | yes |
| scope | yes | yes | yes | yes | yes |
| style | yes | yes | yes | yes | yes |
| title | yes | yes | yes | yes | yes |
| valign | yes | yes | yes | yes | yes |
| width | yes | no | yes | yes | no |
| xml:lang | no | no | yes | yes | yes |
| textarea | yes | yes | yes | yes | yes |
| accesskey | yes | yes | yes | yes | yes |
| class | yes | yes | yes | yes | yes |
| cols | req'd | req'd | req'd | req'd | req'd |
| datafld | yes | yes | no | no | no |
| dataformatas | yes | yes | no | no | no |
| datasrc | yes | yes | no | no | no |
| dir | yes | yes | yes | yes | yes |
| disabled | yes | yes | yes | yes | yes |
| id | yes | yes | yes | yes | yes |
| lang | yes | yes | yes | yes | yes |
| name | yes | yes | yes | yes | yes |
| onblur | yes | yes | yes | yes | yes |
| onchange | yes | yes | yes | yes | yes |
| onclick | yes | yes | yes | yes | yes |

| Element/Attributes | HTML 4.01 Transitional | HTML 4.01 Strict | XHTML 1.0 Transitional | XHTML 1.0 Frameset | XHTML 1.0 Strict |
|---|---|---|---|---|---|
| ondblclick | yes | yes | yes | yes | yes |
| onfocus | yes | yes | yes | yes | yes |
| onkeydown | yes | yes | yes | yes | yes |
| onkeypress | yes | yes | yes | yes | yes |
| onkeyup | yes | yes | yes | yes | yes |
| onmousedown | yes | yes | yes | yes | yes |
| onmousemove | yes | yes | yes | yes | yes |
| onmouseout | yes | yes | yes | yes | yes |
| onmouseover | yes | yes | yes | yes | yes |
| onmouseup | yes | yes | yes | yes | yes |
| onselect | yes | yes | yes | yes | yes |
| readonly | yes | yes | yes | yes | yes |
| rows | req'd | req'd | req'd | req'd | req'd |
| style | yes | yes | yes | yes | yes |
| tabindex | yes | yes | yes | yes | yes |
| title | yes | yes | yes | yes | yes |
| xml:lang | no | no | yes | yes | yes |
| tfoot | yes | yes | yes | yes | yes |
| align | yes | yes | yes | yes | yes |
| char | yes | yes | yes | yes | yes |
| charoff | yes | yes | yes | yes | yes |
| class | yes | yes | yes | yes | yes |
| dir | yes | yes | yes | yes | yes |
| id | yes | yes | yes | yes | yes |
| lang | yes | yes | yes | yes | yes |
| onclick | yes | yes | yes | yes | yes |
| ondblclick | yes | yes | yes | yes | yes |
| onkeydown | yes | yes | yes | yes | yes |
| onkeypress | yes | yes | yes | yes | yes |
| onkeyup | yes | yes | yes | yes | yes |
| onmousedown | yes | yes | yes | yes | yes |
| onmousemove | yes | yes | yes | yes | yes |
| onmouseout | yes | yes | yes | yes | yes |
| onmouseover | yes | yes | yes | yes | yes |
| onmouseup | yes | yes | yes | yes | yes |
| style | yes | yes | yes | yes | yes |

| Element/Attributes | HTML 4.01 Transitional | HTML 4.01 Strict | XHTML 1.0 Transitional | XHTML 1.0 Frameset | XHTML 1.0 Strict |
|---|---|---|---|---|---|
| title | yes | yes | yes | yes | yes |
| valign | yes | yes | yes | yes | yes |
| xml:lang | no | no | yes | yes | yes |
| th | yes | yes | yes | yes | yes |
| abbr | yes | yes | yes | yes | yes |
| align | yes | yes | yes | yes | yes |
| axis | yes | yes | yes | yes | yes |
| bgcolor | yes | no | yes | yes | no |
| char | yes | yes | yes | yes | yes |
| charoff | yes | yes | yes | yes | yes |
| class | yes | yes | yes | yes | yes |
| colspan | yes | yes | yes | yes | yes |
| dir | yes | yes | yes | yes | yes |
| headers | yes | yes | yes | yes | yes |
| height | yes | no | yes | yes | no |
| id | yes | yes | yes | yes | yes |
| lang | yes | yes | yes | yes | yes |
| nowrap | yes | no | yes | yes | no |
| onclick | yes | yes | yes | yes | yes |
| ondblclick | yes | yes | yes | yes | yes |
| onkeydown | yes | yes | yes | yes | yes |
| onkeypress | yes | yes | yes | yes | yes |
| onkeyup | yes | yes | yes | yes | yes |
| onmousedown | yes | yes | yes | yes | yes |
| onmousemove | yes | yes | yes | yes | yes |
| onmouseout | yes | yes | yes | yes | yes |
| onmouseover | yes | yes | yes | yes | yes |
| onmouseup | yes | yes | yes | yes | yes |
| rowspan | yes | yes | yes | yes | yes |
| scope | yes | yes | yes | yes | yes |
| style | yes | yes | yes | yes | yes |
| title | yes | yes | yes | yes | yes |
| valign | yes | yes | yes | yes | yes |
| width | yes | no | yes | yes | no |
| xml:lang | no | no | yes | yes | yes |

| Element/Attributes | HTML 4.01 Transitional | HTML 4.01 Strict | XHTML 1.0 Transitional | XHTML 1.0 Frameset | XHTML 1.0 Strict |
|---|---|---|---|---|---|
| thead | yes | yes | yes | yes | yes |
| align | yes | yes | yes | yes | yes |
| char | yes | yes | yes | yes | yes |
| charoff | yes | yes | yes | yes | yes |
| class | yes | yes | yes | yes | yes |
| dir | yes | yes | yes | yes | yes |
| id | yes | yes | yes | yes | yes |
| lang | yes | yes | yes | yes | yes |
| onclick | yes | yes | yes | yes | yes |
| ondblclick | yes | yes | yes | yes | yes |
| onkeydown | yes | yes | yes | yes | yes |
| onkeypress | yes | yes | yes | yes | yes |
| onkeyup | yes | yes | yes | yes | yes |
| onmousedown | yes | yes | yes | yes | yes |
| onmousemove | yes | yes | yes | yes | yes |
| onmouseout | yes | yes | yes | yes | yes |
| onmouseover | yes | yes | yes | yes | yes |
| onmouseup | yes | yes | yes | yes | yes |
| style | yes | yes | yes | yes | yes |
| title | yes | yes | yes | yes | yes |
| valign | yes | yes | yes | yes | yes |
| xml:lang | no | no | yes | yes | yes |
| title | yes | yes | yes | yes | yes |
| dir | yes | yes | yes | yes | yes |
| lang | yes | yes | yes | yes | yes |
| xml:lang | no | no | yes | yes | yes |
| tr | yes | yes | yes | yes | yes |
| align | yes | yes | yes | yes | yes |
| bgcolor | yes | no | yes | yes | no |
| char | yes | yes | yes | yes | yes |
| charoff | yes | yes | yes | yes | yes |
| class | yes | yes | yes | yes | yes |
| dir | yes | yes | yes | yes | yes |
| id | yes | yes | yes | yes | yes |
| lang | yes | yes | yes | yes | yes |
| onclick | yes | yes | yes | yes | yes |

| Element/Attributes | HTML 4.01 Transitional | HTML 4.01 Strict | XHTML 1.0 Transitional | XHTML 1.0 Frameset | XHTML 1.0 Strict |
|---|---|---|---|---|---|
| ondblclick | yes | yes | yes | yes | yes |
| onkeydown | yes | yes | yes | yes | yes |
| onkeypress | yes | yes | yes | yes | yes |
| onkeyup | yes | yes | yes | yes | yes |
| onmousedown | yes | yes | yes | yes | yes |
| onmousemove | yes | yes | yes | yes | yes |
| onmouseout | yes | yes | yes | yes | yes |
| onmouseover | yes | yes | yes | yes | yes |
| onmouseup | yes | yes | yes | yes | yes |
| style | yes | yes | yes | yes | yes |
| title | yes | yes | yes | yes | yes |
| valign | yes | yes | yes | yes | yes |
| xml:lang | no | no | yes | yes | yes |
| tt | yes | yes | yes | yes | yes |
| class | yes | yes | yes | yes | yes |
| dir | yes | yes | yes | yes | yes |
| id | yes | yes | yes | yes | yes |
| lang | yes | yes | yes | yes | yes |
| onclick | yes | yes | yes | yes | yes |
| ondblclick | yes | yes | yes | yes | yes |
| onkeydown | yes | yes | yes | yes | yes |
| onkeypress | yes | yes | yes | yes | yes |
| onkeyup | yes | yes | yes | yes | yes |
| onmousedown | yes | yes | yes | yes | yes |
| onmousemove | yes | yes | yes | yes | yes |
| onmouseout | yes | yes | yes | yes | yes |
| onmouseover | yes | yes | yes | yes | yes |
| onmouseup | yes | yes | yes | yes | yes |
| style | yes | yes | yes | yes | yes |
| title | yes | yes | yes | yes | yes |
| xml:lang | no | no | yes | yes | yes |
| u | yes | no | yes | yes | no |
| class | yes | no | yes | yes | no |
| dir | yes | no | yes | yes | no |
| id | yes | no | yes | yes | no |
| lang | yes | no | yes | yes | no |

| Element/Attributes | HTML 4.01 Transitional | HTML 4.01 Strict | XHTML 1.0 Transitional | XHTML 1.0 Frameset | XHTML 1.0 Strict |
|---|---|---|---|---|---|
| onclick | yes | no | yes | yes | no |
| ondblclick | yes | no | yes | yes | no |
| onkeydown | yes | no | yes | yes | no |
| onkeypress | yes | no | yes | yes | no |
| onkeyup | yes | no | yes | yes | no |
| onmousedown | yes | no | yes | yes | no |
| onmousemove | yes | no | yes | yes | no |
| onmouseout | yes | no | yes | yes | no |
| onmouseover | yes | no | yes | yes | no |
| onmouseup | yes | no | yes | yes | no |
| style | yes | no | yes | yes | no |
| title | yes | no | yes | yes | no |
| xml:lang | no | no | yes | yes | no |
| ul | yes | yes | yes | yes | yes |
| class | yes | yes | yes | yes | yes |
| compact | yes | no | yes | yes | no |
| dir | yes | yes | yes | yes | yes |
| id | yes | yes | yes | yes | yes |
| lang | yes | yes | yes | yes | yes |
| onclick | yes | yes | yes | yes | yes |
| ondblclick | yes | yes | yes | yes | yes |
| onkeydown | yes | yes | yes | yes | yes |
| onkeypress | yes | yes | yes | yes | yes |
| onkeyup | yes | yes | yes | yes | yes |
| onmousedown | yes | yes | yes | yes | yes |
| onmousemove | yes | yes | yes | yes | yes |
| onmouseout | yes | yes | yes | yes | yes |
| onmouseover | yes | yes | yes | yes | yes |
| onmouseup | yes | yes | yes | yes | yes |
| style | yes | yes | yes | yes | yes |
| title | yes | yes | yes | yes | yes |
| type | yes | no | yes | yes | no |
| xml:lang | no | no | yes | yes | yes |
| var | yes | yes | yes | yes | yes |
| class | yes | yes | yes | yes | yes |
| dir | yes | yes | yes | yes | yes |

| Element/Attributes | HTML 4.01 Transitional | HTML 4.01 Strict | XHTML 1.0 Transitional | XHTML 1.0 Frameset | XHTML 1.0 Strict |
|---|---|---|---|---|---|
| id | yes | yes | yes | yes | yes |
| lang | yes | yes | yes | yes | yes |
| onclick | yes | yes | yes | yes | yes |
| ondblclick | yes | yes | yes | yes | yes |
| onkeydown | yes | yes | yes | yes | yes |
| onkeypress | yes | yes | yes | yes | yes |
| onkeyup | yes | yes | yes | yes | yes |
| onmousedown | yes | yes | yes | yes | yes |
| onmousemove | yes | yes | yes | yes | yes |
| onmouseout | yes | yes | yes | yes | yes |
| onmouseover | yes | yes | yes | yes | yes |
| onmouseup | yes | yes | yes | yes | yes |
| style | yes | yes | yes | yes | yes |
| title | yes | yes | yes | yes | yes |
| xml:lang | no | no | yes | yes | yes |

# Glossary

**absolute positioning**

Setting the precise location of an element within the coordinate system of the next outermost container. An absolute-positioned element exists in its own transparent layer; it is removed from the flow of content that surrounds it in the HTML source code.

**abstract object**

A specification for the characteristics of other, real objects with which scripts come into contact. Modern document object model designers frequently blend the characteristics of multiple abstract objects into a single scriptable object. For example, the properties, methods, and event handlers for a specific HTML p element object in a document loaded into Netscape 6 are derived from many W3C DOM specification abstract objects: the `Node`, `Element`, `HTMLElement`, `HTMLParagraphElement`, `ElementCSSInlineStyle`, and `EventTarget` objects.

**accessibility**

The design concern for allowing users with physical disabilities to make as full a use of web content as possible. For example, aural style sheets provide increased web accessibility to users who have vision impairments. See also *WAI*.

**API**

Application Programming Interface, which is usually a collection of methods and properties that operate as a convenient layer between programmers and more complex internal computer activity. In Dynamic HTML, it is common to use or create a custom API to act as a buffer between the browser-specific implementations of element positioning and the programmer's desire to use a single coding scheme regardless of browser.

**at-rule**

A type of CSS command used inside a style sheet definition. Typical at-rule commands import external style sheets or download font specifications. An at-rule statement begins with the @ symbol.

**attribute**

A property of an HTML (and XHTML) element or CSS style sheet. Attributes are usually assigned values by way of operators (the = symbol for HTML; the : symbol for CSS). In HTML, sometimes the presence of the attribute name is enough to turn on a feature associated with that attribute (regardless of the value assigned), but XHTML requires that all attributes have values assigned to them. HTML attribute names are case-insensitive; XHTML and CSS attribute names are case-sensitive.

**block-level element**

An HTML element that automatically forces a new line before and after the element, assuring that no other element appears in the same horizontal band of the page (unless another element is absolute-positioned on top of it). An example of a block-level element is the h1 element.

## border

In CSS, a region that exists outside of the content and padding area of a block-level element. The border is always present, even if its thickness is zero, and it can't be seen. A border is sandwiched between the *margin* and *padding*.

## browser sniffing

A script technique (usually involving properties of the navigator object) that sets global variables signifying the current browser's brand, version, operating system, and other environment capabilities. Scripts use the variables to branch code execution to accommodate browser-specific syntax for operations to work across multiple, incompatible browsers. The technique is gradually being displaced by *object detection*.

## cascading rule

One of the sequence of decisions that a CSS-equipped browser uses to determine which one of several possible overlapping style sheet rules applies to a given element. Each cascading rule assigns a value to a specificity rating that helps determine which style sheet rule (and attributes within that rule) applies to the element.

## class

In CSS, a collection of one or more elements (of the same or different tag type) that are grouped together for the purpose of assigning the same style sheet rule throughout the document. Assigning a class identifier to elements via the class attribute (and using that class selector in a style sheet rule) lets authors create element groupings that cannot be created only out of tag names or IDs.

## collection

A group of scriptable objects of the same type. Scripts may reference individual members of the collection via standard numeric array index syntax (*collectionName*[*index*]), aided by the collection's length property for iterative access inside for loops, if desired. In recent browsers, methods allow access via numeric index (*collectionName*.item(*index*)) or, if the objects have names associated with them, their names

(*collectionName*.namedItem("*name*")). Internet Explorer also allows references through its own collection notation (*collectionName*(*index*)). Many DOM properties and methods return values in the form of a collection.

## container

Any element that holds other elements of any type. Tags for contained elements appear between the container's start and end tags.

## contextual selector

In CSS, a way of specifying under what containment circumstances a particular type of element should have a style sheet rule applied to it. The containment hierarchy is denoted in the selector by a space-delimited list. Thus, the rule p em {color: red} applies the red text color to all em elements that are contained by p elements; an em element inside an li element is unaffected by this style sheet rule.

## CSS

Acronym for Cascading Style Sheets, a recommended standard created under the auspices of the World Wide Web Consortium (W3C). The acronym is commonly followed by a number designating the version number of the standard. Level 2 of CSS is known as CSS2.

## CSS-P

Acronym for Cascading Style Sheets-Positioning. Initially undertaken as an effort separate from the CSS work, the two standards come together in CSS2, and the CSS-P terminology is no longer needed.

## data binding

A facility in Microsoft Internet Explorer that allows web page content to be dynamically linked to a data source, such as a server database. For example, a marquee element can grab the latest headlines from a database field as the page loads into the client and display those headlines as a scrolling tickertape. Windows versions have two-way access to many data source types, but IE for Macintosh's data binding works only with static tab- or comma-delimited text file sources.

### declaration

In CSS, the combination of an attribute name, colon operator, and value assigned to the attribute. Multiple declarations in a single style sheet rule are separated by semicolons.

### deprecated

A web standard or language feature (commonly an HTML element or attribute and corresponding DOM equivalent) that is still supported in a standards release version, the use of which is discouraged in documents that support the version. A term that is deprecated in one version release is usually removed in the following release. Browser support for deprecated items usually continues for many generations for backward compatibility with existing documents that use the element or attribute.

### DHTML

Acronym for Dynamic Hypertext Markup Language. DHTML is an amalgam of several standards, including HTML (and XHTML), CSS, and DOM.

### DOM

Acronym for the Document Object Model standards effort headed by the W3C. The term in all uppercase letters is commonly, but perhaps inappropriately, applied to a specific implementation of a document object model in a particular browser.

### DTD

Acronym for the Document Type Definition, a document that defines in excruciating detail the types of elements, attributes, and attribute values that are permissible in an SGML (and thus HTML or XML) document. Users never see DTD documents, but they are commonly referenced within the <!DOCTYPE> element at the top of a document to define the markup rules followed by the document's content. Anyone may create a custom DTD for their documents, but most HTML documents adhere to one of the W3C-published DTDs.

### dynamic content

Any HTML content that changes after the document has loaded. Content that does not require a reflow of the page can be accommodated in Navigator 3 and onward and Internet Explorer 4 and onward. The replaced img element is an example. IE 4 or later and Netscape 6 also allow body content to be changed after the document loads by automatically reflowing the page after the content changes.

### ECMA

A Switzerland-based standards body formerly known as the European Computer Manufacturers Association.

### ECMAScript

The common name for the JavaScript-based scripting language standard ECMA-262. The standard defines a core scripting language, without any specific references to web-based content. The functionality of the first edition of ECMA-262 is roughly equivalent to JavaScript 1.1 as deployed in Navigator 3. The second edition corrected errors of the first, while the third edition adds new features common to JavaScript 1.5.

### element

Refers to a portion of a document that has a specific context within the document defined by an angle-bracketed tag or tag pair (start and end tag set). For example, the <body> tag creates a body element in the document.

### event binding

A technique of instructing an object to process a particular event type when the event fires on that object.

### event bubbling

The Internet Explorer 4 or later and Netscape 6 event model mechanism that propagates events from the target element upward through the HTML element hierarchy. After the event is processed (at the scripter's option) by the target element, event handlers higher up the hierarchy may perform further processing on the event. Event propagation can be halted at any point via the cancelBubble property or, in Netscape 6, the stopPropagation() method.

### event handler

A script-oriented keyword that intercepts an event action (such as a mouse click) and initiates the execution of one or more script statements. An event handler can be specified as an attribute of an HTML element, assigned as a property of the scriptable object version of the element, or associated with the object through event model-specific methods (attachEvent( ) or addEventListener( )). Each element responds to a specific set of events.

### event propagation

The process of event information coursing its way through the element or object hierarchy of a document. In recent browsers, an event propagates from the window, document, or body element (depending on the event type) inward toward the target element. At that point the event propagation performs a U-turn, and bubbles upward through the same container path. For an object to process an event as it passes toward the target element, the object must be set up to capture the event. Event bubbling is automatic for most event types.

### filter

A rendering feature of Internet Explorer 4 or later (for the Windows platform) that adds typographic effects to text content and animated transitions between views. A filter is assigned to an element by way of CSS syntax.

### HTML

Acronym for Hypertext Markup Language, a simplified version of SGML tailored for content that is published across a network via the Hypertext Transfer Protocol (HTTP). Version 4 of the HTML standard (under the auspices of the W3C) extends the notion of separating content from form by letting HTML elements define the context of content, rather than its specific look. HTML is the foundation of *XHTML*.

### ID

An identifier for an element that should be unique among all elements within a single document. The ID of an element is assigned by the id attribute supported by every HTML 4 tag. An ID is used for many purposes, including associating a CSS style sheet rule with a single element among all elements of a document and simplifying script references to a specific element.

### identifier

A name assigned to an id, class, or name attribute of an element, as well as names for objects and variables in a scripting language. The names can begin with any uppercase or lowercase letter of the English alphabet, but subsequent characters may include letters, numerals, or the underscore character.

### inline element

An HTML element that is rendered as part of the same text line as its surrounding HTML content. An em element that signifies an emphasized portion of a paragraph is an inline element because its content does not disturb the regular linear flow of the content. The opposite of an inline element is a *block-level element*.

### intrinsic events

Event handlers defined by the HTML 4 standard as belonging to virtually every element that is rendered on the page. These events are primarily the common mouse and keyboard events.

### JavaScript

A programming language devised by Brendan Eich at Netscape for simplified server and client programming. Originally developed under the name LiveScript, the name changed (under license from Sun Microsystems) before the first commercial release of a scriptable browser, Navigator 2. JavaScript became the basis for ECMAScript. Microsoft's name for its implementation of JavaScript is JScript.

### JavaScript Style Sheets

A Navigator 4-only syntax for defining style sheet rules.

### JScript

Microsoft's formal name for the JavaScript-based scripting language built into Internet Explorer 3 and later. Compatible with ECMAScript and JavaScript.

### layer

Derived from Navigator 4's now-abandoned model for a positionable element, the term is currently a generic reference to any element with a CSS position attribute assigned a value such as absolute, relative, or fixed. Each positioned element exists in its own transparent layer above the main document body.

### margin

In CSS, a region that extends outside of an element's *border*. Every element has a margin, even if its thickness is zero.

### media

In CSS, a reference to the type of output for which the rule is to be applied. Mainstream browsers commonly support the screen and print media, but the other possible media include projection, audio, and small screen displays of portable devices.

### method

A scriptable object's action that can be initiated by any script statement. A reference to a JavaScript-syntax method is easily recognizable by the set of parentheses that follows the method name. Zero or more parameters may be included inside the parentheses. A method may return a value depending on what it has been programmed to do, but it isn't a requirement.

### modifier key

A keyboard key that is usually pressed in concert with a character key or mouse action to initiate a special action. Modifier keys common to all operating system platforms include the **Shift**, **Control**, and **Alt** keys. Modern Microsoft keyboards also have the **Windows** key; Macintosh keyboards have the **Command** key. Keyboard and mouse events can be examined for which (if any) modifier keys were being held down at the time of the character key's event.

### modularization

A tendency in recent W3C standards tracks to divide large standards into multiple modules, each of which has a specific focus, such as the Events module of the W3C DOM recommendation.

### node

In a document object model, an object that can be referenced within the document's hierarchical structure. Some node types act as containers of additional, nested nodes, while other types contain nothing but document text content.

### object

A representation of an HTML element or other programmable item in a scripting language, such as JavaScript. An object may have properties and methods that define the behavior and/or appearance of the object. Scripts typically read or modify object properties or invoke object methods to affect some change of value or appearance of the object. Objects in a browser's document object model reflect HTML elements defined by the document source code. For example, in recent browser versions, if a script assigns a new URL to the value of the src property of an img object, the new graphic replaces the old within the rectangular space occupied by the img element on the page. Other types of objects, such as dates and strings, do not appear on the screen directly but are used in script execution.

### object detection

A scripting technique that verifies whether a browser supports a particular object, property, or method before attempting to execute a statement with that term in it. This technique is gaining favor over *browser sniffing*.

### padding

In CSS, a region that extends between the element's content and the border. Padding provides some breathing space between the content and a border (if one is specified). Every element has padding, even if its thickness is zero. Navigator 4 automatically adds visible padding to all positioned elements.

### parent

For HTML elements, the next outermost element in source code order (the tr element that surrounds a td element, for example). For positioned elements, the parent element determines the coordinate plane for an element's positioning. For scriptable window objects, a frame's parent is the frameset document that defines the frame holding the current document.

**platform**

A software or hardware system that forms the basis for further product development. For web browsers, the term may apply to a browser brand (Netscape Navigator, Microsoft Internet Explorer, etc.) or the operating system on which a browser brand operates (Windows XP, Mac OS X, Solaris, etc.). In this book, *platform* usually applies to the browser brand.

**positioning**

Specifying the precise location of an element on the page. An element may be absolute-, relative-, or (in some browsers) fixed-positioned.

**property**

A single characteristic of an object, such as its ID or value, which can be retrieved (and sometimes set) with the help of scripting. Style sheet attributes are also sometimes referred to as properties because they can be scripted as properties of the style object.

**pseudo-class**

A style sheet selector that points to a particular state or behavior of an HTML element, such as an a element set up as a link that has been visited recently by the user (a:visited).

**pseudo-element**

A style sheet selector that points to a very specific piece of an element, such as the first letter of a paragraph (p:first-letter).

**quirks (mode)**

Reference to a mode whereby modern browsers emulate the nonstandard behaviors of their earlier versions for the sake of backward compatibility with existing HTML and CSS code. The operational mode (quirks versus standards-compatible modes) is controlled by settings in the <!DOCTYPE> tag for browsers such as IE 6 and Netscape 6.

**relative positioning**

Setting the precise location of an element within the coordinate system established by the location where the element would normally appear if it were not positioned. Documents preserve the blank space originally designated for a relative-positioned element so that surrounding content does not cinch up around the place left vacant by a positioned element.

**replaced element**

An inline or block-level element that can have its content replaced without requiring any adjustment of the document. An img element, for example, can have its content replaced by a script after the page has loaded.

**RGB**

An acronym for red-green-blue, the three base colors (in that order) for a popular color specification system, including those used for HTML and CSS color-related attributes. Values for each color are in the range between 0–255 (none to maximum saturation), in decimal or hexadecimal notation.

**rule**

In CSS, a set of style declarations that are associated with one selector. A rule can also be embedded within an element as the value assigned to the style attribute of the element's tag.

**selector**

In CSS, the name of the element(s), ID(s), class(es), or other permissible element groupings to which a style declaration is bound. The combination of a selector and declaration creates a style sheet rule.

**style sheet**

In CSS, one or more rules that define how a particular segment of document content should be rendered by the browser. A style sheet may be defined in an external document, in the style element, or assigned to an element via its style attribute.

**transition**

In Internet Explorer for Windows, a visual effect for hiding and showing elements. Transitions are controlled via filters.

**validation**

Passing source code through a program that compares the code against a standards-based measuring stick for syntactic accuracy, structural integrity, and adherence to standards requirements.

**VBScript**

A scripting language alternate to JScript in Internet Explorer for Windows. You can combine script blocks in VBScript and JScript in the same document, and statements in each block may reference variables and objects in the other.

**W3C**

An acronym for the World Wide Web Consortium (*http://www.w3.org*).

**WAI**

An acronym for the Web Accessibility Initiative activity of the W3C; their goal is to promote web resources for users with disabilities (*http://www.w3.org/WAI*).

**XHTML**

An acronym for the Extensible Hypertext Markup Language recommendation of the W3C. This branch of the HTML activity is a version of HTML implemented as an XML application (*http://www.w3.org/MarkUp*).

**XML**

An acronym for the Extensible Markup Language recommendation of the W3C, which provides the basis for structuring data in a way that facilitates its storage and transfer around the Web (*http://www.w3.org/XML*).

# Index

## Symbols

& (ampersand)
  & (bitwise AND) operator, 183, 1194
  && (AND) operator, 1192
* (asterisk)
  * (multiplication) operator, 1200
  as wildcard character, 65
! (bang)
  ! (NOT) operator, 1201
  != (inequality) operator, 1199
  !== (nonidentity) operator, 1200
  ranking declarations with, 67
{ } (braces), 52, 54, 56
^ (caret), exclusive OR operator, 1195
, (comma)
  , (comma) operator, 1195
  as delimiter, 62
= (equal sign)
  = (assignment) operator, 118, 158, 1193
  == (equality) operator, 1197
  === (identity) operator, 1198
- (hyphen)
  - (negation) operator, 1200
  - (subtraction) operator, 1201
  -- (decrement) operator, 1196
< (left angle bracket)
  < (less-than) operator, 1199
  << (left-shift) operator, 1194
  <= (less-than-or-equal) operator, 1199
% (percent sign)
  % (modulus) operator, 1200

+ (plus sign)
  += (add-by-value) operator, 1192
  + (addition) operator, 1191
  ++ (increment) operator, 1198
# (pound sign), 60
? (question mark)
  ?: (conditional) operator, 1195
" (quotation marks), 8, 51, 54
> (right angle bracket)
  > (greater-than) operator, 1197
  >> (right-shift) operator, 1194
  >>> (zero-fill right-shift) operator, 1195
  >= (greater-than-or-equal) operator, 1198
; (semicolon), 53, 157
/ (slash), 8, 42
  / (division) operator, 1196
  /*...*/ comment statement, 1211
  // comment statement, 1211
  //--> JavaScript comment symbol, 52
~ (tilde)
  ~ (bitwise NOT) operator, 1194
_ (underscore), 161
| (vertical bar)
  | (bitwise OR) operator, 1194
  || (OR) operator, 1201

## Numbers

0,0 coordinate, 72, 95
$1, ..., $9 property
  RegExp objects, 1177

We'd like to hear your suggestions for improving our indexes. Send email to *index@oreilly.com*.

# A

a elements, 55, 64, 109, 204
a objects, 532
abbr elements, 210
abbr property
    td objects, 947
    th objects, 947
above attribute
    ilayer elements, 312
    layer elements, 348
above property
    layer objects, 767
abs() method
    Math object, 1164
absolute positioning, 35, 72–76, 143
absolute value (position attribute), 72
abstract objects, 13, 28, 108
AbstractView objects, 541
accelerator property
    CSSStyleDeclaration objects, 880
    style objects, 880
accept attribute
    form elements, 280
    input elements, 328
accept property
    input (type="file") objects, 735
accept() method
    NodeFilter objects, 809
accept-charset attribute
    form elements, 280
acceptcharset attribute
    form elements, 280
acceptCharset property
    form objects, 684
accessibility
    cross-platform strategies, 32–41
    dynamic content and, 148
    WAI, 17
accesskey attribute, 196
    input elements, 328
    label elements, 346
    legend elements, 355
    select elements, 407
accessKey property, 482
acos() method
    Math object, 1164
Acrobat Forms, 18
acronym elements, 211
acronym objects, 542
action attribute
    form elements, 280

action property
    form objects, 684
actions (see events)
:active pseudo-class, 64, 1042
activeElement property
    document objects, 610
ActiveX
    data binding, 27
    IE for Windows as, 28
    script access to document tree, 136
ActiveXObject objects, 1126
add() method
    options objects, 824
    select objects, 866
addBehavior() method, 504
addBinding() method
    document objects, 625
add-by-value operator (+=), 1192
addEventListener() method, 161, 162, 168, 505
    window objects, 997
addImport() method
    styleSheet objects, 928
addition operator (+), 1191
addRange() method
    selection objects, 871
addReadRequest() method
    userProfile objects, 980
address elements, 212
address objects, 542
addRule() method
    styleSheet objects, 929
adjacent nodes, 121
adjacent sibling selectors, 66
Adobe Systems, 18
:after element, 63, 1041
AfterBegin value, insertAdjacentText()
    method, 119
AfterEnd value, insertAdjacentText()
    method, 119
alert() method
    window objects, 997
align attribute
    applet elements, 213
    caption elements, 244
    col elements, 249
    colgroup elements, 253
    div elements, 261
    embed elements, 270
    fieldset elements, 275
    h1, h2, h3, h4, h5, h6 elements, 298
    hr elements, 301

iframe elements, 306
img elements, 318
input elements, 329
legend elements, 355
object elements, 378
p elements, 391
select elements, 408
spacer elements, 412
align property
   applet objects, 547
   caption objects, 578
   col objects, 586
   colgroup objects, 586
   div objects, 606
   embed objects, 649
   fieldset objects, 680
   h1, h2, h3, h4, h5, h6 objects, 699
   hr objects, 702
   iframe objects, 707
   img objects, 714
   legend objects, 774
   object objects, 812
   p objects, 827
   table objects, 933
   tbody objects, 944
   td objects, 948
   tfoot objects, 944
   th objects, 948
   thead objects, 944
   tr objects, 972
alignment, 9, 10
   centering objects, 94
   constants for, 191–194
alink attribute
   body elements, 234
aLink property
   body objects, 570
alinkColor property
   document objects, 610
all objects, 543
all property, 483
allowtransparency attribute
   frame elements, 285
allowTransparency property
   frame objects, 690
   iframe objects, 707
alt attribute
   applet elements, 214
   area elements, 220
   embed elements, 271
   img elements, 319
   input elements, 329

alt property
   applet objects, 547
   area objects, 552
   img objects, 715
   input (type="image") objects, 741
   object objects, 813
altHTML property
   applet objects, 547
altHtml property
   object objects, 813
altKey property, 170
   event objects, 655
altLeft property
   event objects, 656
anchor( ) method
   String objects, 1182
anchorNode property
   selection objects, 869
anchorOffset property
   selection objects, 869
anchors, 204
anchors objects, 545
anchors property
   document objects, 610
AND operator (&&), 1192
animation, 96–100
API (application programming interface)
   branching code and, 86
   browser accommodations, 39
   dragging example, 176
   positionable elements, 88–94
appCodeName property
   navigator object, 800
appCore property
   window objects, 985
appendChild( ) method, 123, 127, 506
appendData( ) method
   Comment objects, 589
   comment objects, 589
   Text objects, 953
appendMedium( ) method
   MediaList objects, 794
appendNode( ) method, 149
applet elements, 212
applet objects, 546
applets objects, 550
applets property
   document objects, 611
apply( ) method
   function objects, 1154
applyElement( ) method, 506

appMinorVersion property
  navigator object, 800
appName property
  navigator object, 801
appVersion property
  navigator object, 801
archive attribute
  applet elements, 214
  object elements, 379
archive property
  applet objects, 548
  object objects, 813
area elements, 219
area objects, 552
areas objects, 556
areas property
  map objects, 788
arguments objects, 1127
arguments property
  function objects, 1152
arity property
  function objects, 1153
Array objects, 1128
arrays
  custom newsletter example, 144
  document.styleSheets array, 116
  image states and, 108
  storing colors, 114
  table data source, 129
  weight property, 144
asin() method
  Math object, 1164
assign() method
  location objects, 786
assignment operator (=), 118, 158, 1193
assignment statement, 158, 159
atan() method
  Math object, 1165
atan2() method
  Math object, 1165
atEnd() method
  Enumerator objects, 1147
atob() method
  Global objects, 1157
at-rules, 55, 67, 78, 1042
attachEvent() method, 161, 507
  window objects, 997
Attr objects, 558
attrChange property
  event objects, 656
attribute nodes, 14
attribute objects, 558

ATTRIBUTE_NODE property, 481
attributes
  assigning values, 30, 50
  case-sensitivity, 8
  changing via scripting, 82–85
  class attribute, 9, 64
  className property, 114
  common, 45
  Core module and, 12
  CSS value types, 1037–1040
  CSS-P, 72
  event handlers as, 157–158
  for HTML tags, 1217–1220
  HTML validation and, 6
  HTML value types, 190–195
  iframe element, 134
  populating, 30
  positioning, 11, 25, 77–82
  style attributes, 49, 113
  tag values, 111, 112
  XML support, 7
attributes objects, 560
attributes property, 121, 483
attribute/value pairs, 53, 64
attrName property
  event objects, 656
authoring (see web content development)
autocomplete attribute
  form elements, 281
availHeight property
  screen object, 853
availLeft property
  screen object, 854
availTop property
  screen object, 854
availWidth property
  screen object, 853
axis property
  td objects, 948
  th objects, 948
azimuth attribute (CSS), 1044
azimuth property
  CSSStyleDeclaration objects, 881
  style objects, 881

## B

b elements, 224
b objects, 564
back() method
  history objects, 701
  window objects, 997
BackColor command, 1284

background attribute
  body elements, 234
  ilayer elements, 312
  layer elements, 349
background attribute (CSS), 1045
background property
  body objects, 571
  CSSStyleDeclaration objects, 881
  layer objects, 767
  style objects, 881
  table objects, 933
  td objects, 948
  th objects, 948
background-attachment attribute
    (CSS), 1045
backgroundAttachment property
  CSSStyleDeclaration objects, 882
  style objects, 882
background-color attribute (CSS), 1046
backgroundColor property
  CSSStyleDeclaration objects, 882
  style objects, 882
background-image attribute (CSS), 1046
backgroundImage property
  CSSStyleDeclaration objects, 882
  style objects, 882
background-position attribute (CSS), 1047
backgroundPosition property
  CSSStyleDeclaration objects, 882
  style objects, 882
background-position-x attribute (CSS), 1048
backgroundPositionX property
  CSSStyleDeclaration objects, 883
  style objects, 883
background-position-y attribute (CSS), 1048
backgroundPositionY property
  CSSStyleDeclaration objects, 883
  style objects, 883
background-repeat attribute (CSS), 1048
backgroundRepeat property
  CSSStyleDeclaration objects, 884
  style objects, 884
backward compatibility
  "ancient" baggage and, 179
  browsers and, 5
  DOM Level 2 and, 13
  dynamic content and, 101
  event handlers, 157
  Level 0 syntax and, 25
  page branching example, 37
  positioning elements, 72
  recommendations, 8

  syntax and, 41
  this keyword, 157
balance attribute
  bgsound elements, 230
balance property
  bgsound objects, 567
bandwidth, download considerations, 148
base elements, 225
base objects, 564
basefont elements, 227
basefont objects, 565
BaseHref property
  object objects, 813
baseURI property, 484
basic events, 150
bdo elements, 229
bdo objects, 567
:before element, 63, 1041
BeforeBegin value, insertAdjacentText( )
    method, 119
BeforeEnd value, insertAdjacentText( )
    method, 119
behavior attribute
  marquee elements, 364
behavior attribute (CSS), 1049
behavior property
  CSSStyleDeclaration objects, 884
  marquee objects, 789
  style objects, 884
behaviorCookie property
  event objects, 657
behaviorPart property
  event objects, 657
behaviors, 161
behaviorUrns property, 484
below attribute
  ilayer elements, 312
  layer elements, 349
below property
  layer objects, 767
beta versions, 4
bgcolor attribute
  body elements, 235
  ilayer elements, 313
  layer elements, 350
  marquee elements, 364
bgColor property
  body objects, 571
  document objects, 611
  layer objects, 767
  marquee objects, 789
  table objects, 933

bgColor property *(continued)*
  tbody objects, 944
  td objects, 948
  tfoot objects, 944
  th objects, 948
  thead objects, 944
  tr objects, 972
bgproperties attribute
  body elements, 235
bgProperties property
  body objects, 571
bgsound elements, 229
bgsound objects, 567
big elements, 231
big objects, 564, 568
big() method
  String objects, 1182
binding
  class identifiers, 57
  CSS style sheets, 51
  event handlers, 156–162
bitwise AND operator (&), 183, 1194
bitwise NOT operator (~), 1194
bitwise OR operator (|), 1194
blink elements, 232
blink() method
  String objects, 1183
blockDirection property
  CSSStyleDeclaration objects, 885
  style objects, 885
blockFormats property
  Dialog Helper objects, 602
block-level elements
  characteristics, 45–47
  horizontal alignment
    center value, 194
    justify value, 194
    left value, 194
    right value, 194
  iframe element flow and, 134
  as positionable elements, 71
blockquote elements, 232
blockquote objects, 569
blur() method, 507
  window objects, 997
body elements, 233
  browser support flagging, 87
  characteristics, 51
  creating collapsed text range, 141
  custom newsletter example, 144
  document content and, 126

event bubbling and, 166
  iframe resizing example, 135
  inheritance example, 58
  node structure, 126
body objects, 569
body property
  document objects, 611
Bold command, 1284
bold() method
  String objects, 1183
bookmarks, overlaying, 37
bookmarks property
  event objects, 657
Boolean objects, 1134
border attribute
  frameset elements, 293
  img elements, 320
  input elements, 329
  object elements, 379
border attribute (CSS), 1049
border property
  CSSStyleDeclaration objects, 885
  frameset objects, 696
  iframe objects, 708
  img objects, 715
  object objects, 814
  style objects, 885
  table objects, 933
border-bottom attribute (CSS), 1050
borderBottom property
  CSSStyleDeclaration objects, 885
  style objects, 885
border-bottom-color attribute (CSS), 1050
borderBottomColor property
  style objects, 886
border-bottom-style attribute (CSS), 1051
borderBottomStyle property
  CSSSDeclaration objects, 886
  style objects, 886
border-bottom-width attribute (CSS), 1053
borderBottomWidth property
  CSSStyleDeclaration objects, 887
  style objects, 887
border-collapse attribute (CSS), 1053
borderCollapse property
  CSSStyleDeclaration objects, 887
  style objects, 887
bordercolor attribute
  frame elements, 285
  frameset elements, 294
border-color attribute (CSS), 1054

borderColor property
  CSSStyleDeclaration objects, 887
  frame objects, 690
  frameset objects, 697
  iframe objects, 708
  style objects, 887
  table objects, 934
  td objects, 949
  th objects, 949
  tr objects, 973
borderColorDark property
  table objects, 934
  td, th objects, 949
  tr objects, 973
borderColorLight property
  table objects, 934
  td, th objects, 949
  tr objects, 973
border-left attribute (CSS), 1050
borderLeft property
  CSSStyleDeclaration objects, 885, 886
  style objects, 885
border-left-color attribute (CSS), 1050
borderLeftColor property
  style objects, 886
borderLeftStyle
  CSSSDeclaration objects, 886
border-left-style attribute (CSS), 1051
borderLeftStyle property
  style objects, 886
border-left-width attribute (CSS), 1053
borderLeftWidth property
  CSSStyleDeclaration objects, 887
  style objects, 887
border-right attribute (CSS), 1050
borderRight property
  CSSStyleDeclaration objects, 885, 886
  style objects, 885
border-right-color attribute (CSS), 1050
borderRightColor property
  style objects, 886
borderRightStyle
  CSSSDeclaration objects, 886
border-right-style attribute (CSS), 1051
borderRightStyle property
  style objects, 886
border-right-width attribute (CSS), 1053
borderRightWidth property
  CSSStyleDeclaration objects, 887
  style objects, 887
borders
  edge measurement attributes and, 78

element rules, 9
:first-letter element, 63
iframe element, 134
img element, 109
opaque space, 46
span element, 115
as widely-used attribute, 45
border-spacing attribute (CSS), 1055
borderSpacing property
  CSSStyleDeclaration objects, 888
  style objects, 888
border-style attribute (CSS), 1055
borderStyle property
  CSSStyleDeclaration objects, 888
  style objects, 888
border-top attribute (CSS), 1050
borderTop property
  CSSStyleDeclaration objects, 885
  style objects, 885
border-top-color attribute (CSS), 1050
borderTopColor property
  style objects, 886
borderTopStyle
  CSSSSDeclaration objects, 886
border-top-style attribute (CSS), 1051
borderTopStyle property
  style objects, 886
border-top-width attribute (CSS), 1053
borderTopWidth property
  style objects, 887
borderTopwidth propety
  CSSStyleDeclaration objects, 887
border-width attribute (CSS), 1056
borderWidth property
  CSSStyleDeclaration objects, 889
  style objects, 889
bottom attribute, 78, 84
bottom attribute (CSS), 1057
bottom property, 84
  CSSStyleDeclaration objects, 889
  style objects, 889
  TextRectangle objects, 970
bottommargin attribute
  body elements, 235
bottomMargin property
  body objects, 571
boundElements property
  event objects, 657
boundingHeight property
  TextRange objects, 961
boundingLeft property
  TextRange objects, 961

boundingTop property
  TextRange objects, 961
boundingWidth property
  TextRange objects, 961
br elements, 42, 239
br objects, 574
branches, 14
branching
  binding event handlers and, 158
  code branching, 32, 33
  custom APIs and, 86
  explicit branching, 87
  internal branching, 38, 39
  page branching, 35–37
break statement, 1204
browser sniffing, 33–35, 39
browserLanguage property
  navigator object, 801
browsers
  ActiveX and, 28
  adjusting iframe size, 133
  custom newsletter example, 142–149
  decision paths for rendering, 66
  DOM support, 12, 13, 16
  DTHML versions, 32
  event handlers listed, 151–152
  external style sheets and, 54
  fragmentation, 179
  functionality of, 22
  HTML and, 3, 43, 133
  IE caching issues, 111
  ignoring attributes, 25
  image swapping, 108
  important declarations, 68
  intrinsic events, 150
  JavaScript compatibility, 18
  loading dynamic content, 101
  nodeValue property support, 123
  overflow attribute, 80
  position attribute and, 77
  positioning and, 78
  proprietary style attributes and, 113
  pseudo-elements and, 63
  quirks, 10, 11
  recommendations, 5
  script tag support, 160
  scroll value support, 80
  standardization, 10, 19, 117
  style example, 52
  text ranges and, 141
  version releases, 4

web protocols, 21
  (see also backward compatibility;
    platforms)
btoa() method
  Global objects, 1157
bubbles property, 168
  event objects, 657
bubbling phase, 165, 168
bufferDepth property
  screen object, 854
bugs
  browser sniffing and, 35
  Bugzilla tracking system, 69
  prelease versions, 4
Bugzilla, 69
button elements, 240
button objects, 575
button property
  event objects, 657
by-value operators, 84

C

caching, 108, 109, 111
call() method
  function objects, 1155
callee property
  arguments objects, 1127
caller property
  function objects, 1153
cancelable property
  event objects, 658
cancelBubble property, 167, 168
  event objects, 658
canHaveChildren property, 484
canHaveHTML property, 485
caption elements, 243
caption objects, 578
caption property
  table objects, 934
caption-side attribute (CSS), 1058
captionSide property
  CSSStyleDeclaration objects, 890
  style objects, 890
capture phase, 165, 168
captureEvents() method
  document objects, 174, 625
  layer objects, 771
  window objects, 998
Cascading Style Sheets (see CSS)
Cascading Style Sheets-Positioning (see CSS,
    CSS-P)

case-sensitivity
    event handlers, 151, 158
    HTML tags and attributes, 8
    selectors, 52, 57
    tag attributes, 157
catch statement, 1205
@cc_on statement, 1212
CDATA section, 183
CDATA_SECTION_NODE property, 481
ceil( ) method
    Math object, 1165
cellIndex property
    td objects, 949
    th objects, 949
cellPadding property
    table objects, 935
cells objects, 578
cells property
    table objects, 935
    tr objects, 973
cellSpacing property
    table objects, 935
center elements, 245
center objects, 580
centimeter units, 78
CGI programs, 36, 148
ch property
    col objects, 586
    colgroup objects, 586
    tbody objects, 945
    td objects, 950
    tfoot objects, 945
    th objects, 950
    thead objects, 945
    tr objects, 974
challenge attribute
    keygen elements, 344
char attribute
    col elements, 249
    colgroup elements, 254
character codes, keyboard, 1279–1282
character entities, 1272–1278
character escape sequences, 1213
CharacterData objects, 581
characterSet property
    document objects, 612
charAt( ) method
    String objects, 1183
charCode property, 170
    event objects, 658
charCodeAt( ) method
    String objects, 1183

charoff attribute
    col elements, 250
    colgroup elements, 254
charset attribute
    a elements, 205
    link elements, 358
    script elements, 403
charset property
    a objects, 533
    document objects, 611
    link objects, 777
    meta objects, 795
    script objects, 857
@charset rule, 1043
checkbox objects, 581
checked attribute
    input elements, 330
checked property
    input (type="checkbox") objects, 730
    input (type="radio") objects, 750
child nodes, 16, 121, 122
child selectors, 65
childNode property, 121
childNodes objects, 581
childNodes property, 485
children objects, 582
children property, 485
choff attribute
    col elements, 250
chOff property
    col objects, 586
    colgroup objects, 586
    tbody objects, 945
    td objects, 950
    tfoot objects, 945
    th objects, 950
    thead objects, 945
    tr objects, 974
ChooseColorDlg( ) method
    Dialog Helper objects, 603
cite attribute
    blockquote elements, 232
    del elements, 258
    ins elements, 341
    q elements, 397
cite elements, 246
cite objects, 542, 583
cite property, 486
    blockquote objects, 569
    del objects, 601
    ins objects, 763
class attribute, 9, 64, 196

class identifiers, 57
class selectors
  as attribute selector, 64
  characteristics, 57–59
  element styles, 114
  pseudo-element/class, 64
classes
  abstract model, 18
  pseudo-classes, 64
classid attribute
  object elements, 379
classid property
  object objects, 814
classification properties, 50
className property, 486
  custom newsletter example, 144
  dragging example, 175
  features, 114–116
  recommendations, 117
clear attribute
  br elements, 240
clear attribute (CSS), 1058
clear property
  br objects, 575
  CSSStyleDeclaration objects, 890
  style objects, 890
clear( ) method
  document objects, 103, 626
  selection objects, 871
clearAttributes( ) method, 508
clearData( ) method
  clipboardData objects, 584
  dataTransfer objects, 599
clearInterval( ) method
  window objects, 998
clearRequest( ) method
  userProfile objects, 980
clearTimeout( ) method
  window objects, 998
click event, 27, 151
click( ) method, 508
clientHeight property, 472–476, 486
clientInformation objects, 583
clientInformation property
  window objects, 985
clientLeft property, 472–476, 487
client-side scripting
  ECMAScript, 18
  form validation, 13
  HTML 4, 6
  Internet Explorer and, 18

  page branching via, 36
  window object and, 154
clientTop property, 472–476, 487
clientWidth property, 472–476, 486
clientX property
  event objects, 659
clientY property
  event objects, 659
clip attribute, 79, 84
  ilayer elements, 313
  layer elements, 350
clip attribute (CSS), 1059
clip property, 84
  CSSStyleDeclaration objects, 890
  layer objects, 767
  style objects, 890
clipboardData objects, 584
clipboardData property
  window objects, 985
clipBottom property
  CSSStyleDeclaration objects, 891
  style objects, 891
clipLeft property
  CSSStyleDeclaration objects, 891
  style objects, 891
clipping region, 79
clipRight property
  CSSStyleDeclaration objects, 891
  style objects, 891
clipTop property
  CSSStyleDeclaration objects, 891
  style objects, 891
cloneContents( ) method
  Range objects, 841
cloneNode( ) method, 123, 149, 508
cloneRange( ) method
  Range objects, 841
close( ) method
  document objects, 103, 106, 626
  window objects, 998
closed property
  window objects, 986
code attribute
  applet elements, 215
  object elements, 380
code branching, 32, 33
code elements, 246
code objects, 542, 585
code property
  applet objects, 548
  DOMException objects, 645

object objects, 814
    RangeException objects, 849
codebase attribute
    applet elements, 215
    object elements, 380
codeBase property
    applet objects, 548
    object objects, 815
codetype attribute
    object elements, 381
codeType property
    object objects, 815
col elements, 247
col objects, 585
colgroup elements, 252
colgroup objects, 585
collapse( ) method
    Range objects, 841
    selection objects, 871
    TextRange objects, 962
collapsed property
    Range objects, 839
collapsed state, 141
collapseToEnd( ) method
    selection objects, 872
collapseToStart( ) method
    selection objects, 872
colon operator, 50, 53
color attribute
    basefont elements, 227
    font elements, 276
    hr elements, 301
color attribute (CSS), 1059
color property
    basefont objects, 566
    CSSStyleDeclaration objects, 891
    font objects, 682
    hr objects, 703
    span element, 113, 115
    style objects, 891
color values, 1267–1271
colorDepth property
    screen object, 854
colors
    borders and, 46
    element rules, 9
    :first-letter element, 63
    style attributes, 50, 113
    values, 194, 472, 1039
cols attribute
    frameset elements, 294
    multicol elements, 373
    pre elements, 396

cols property
    frameset objects, 697
    table objects, 935
    textarea objects, 956
colSpan property
    td objects, 950
    th objects, 950
comma operator (,)
    as delimiter, 62
comment elements, 256
comment nodes, 14
Comment objects, 587
comment objects, 587
comment statements (// and /*...*/), 1211
COMMENT_NODE property, 481
common denominator, 39
commonAncestorContainer property
    Range objects, 839
compact attribute
    dir elements, 261
    dl elements, 264
    menu elements, 370
    ol elements, 385
    ul elements, 465
compact property
    dir objects, 604
    dl objects, 608
    menu objects, 794
    ol objects, 819
    ul objects, 979
compareBoundaryPoints( ) method
    Range objects, 842
compareEndPoints( ) method
    TextRange objects, 963
compareNode( ) method
    Range objects, 842
comparePoint( ) method
    Range objects, 843
compatibility
    among browsers, 22
    applying class selectors, 57
    browser identification and, 33
    browsers across operating systems, 19
    considerations, 56
    HTML and, 7, 8
    JavaScript variations, 18
    object detection and, 35
    recommendations versus, 39
    (see also backward compatibility)
compatMode property
    document objects, 612
compile( ) method
    regular expression objects, 1179

complete property
    img objects, 715
    input (type="image") objects, 741
componentFromPoint( ) method, 509
Components property
    window objects, 985, 986
computed style, 29, 85
concat( ) method
    Array objects, 1130
    String objects, 1183
conditional operator (?:), 1195
confirm( ) method
    window objects, 999
conformance, 186
Connection preference (Opera 4), 24
constants
    color values, 1267–1271
constructor property
    Array objects, 1129
    Boolean objects, 1134
    Date objects, 1136
    Error objects, 1148
    function objects, 1153
    Number objects, 1169
    Object objects, 1172
    regular expression objects, 1178
    String objects, 1181
containers
    content distinguished from, 47
    document objects as, 13
    dragging elements, 174
    elements and, 43
    loading XML data into, 136
    manipulating text nodes, 123
    nodes as, 14
    placing new text, 118
    style sheet orientation, 42
    W3C event propagation, 165
containment
    descendant selectors and, 61
    element containment, 48, 65
    impact on inheritance, 45
    relationships, 44
contains( ) method, 120, 510
containsNode( ) method
    selection objects, 872
content
    accessing, 16
    adding value considerations, 32
    assigning with font tag, 27
    block-level elements and, 45
    distinguished from, 47

edge measurement attributes and, 78
element positioning and, 11
iframe element, 133
iframe rendering of, 136
manipulation methods, 120
modifying, 30, 128
rendering literally, 119
scrollbars and overflow, 134
separating design from, 56
static content, 23
style definitions and, 6
style sheet links and, 9
XHTML and, 7
(see also dynamic content)
content attribute
    meta elements, 371
content attribute (CSS), 1060
content authors (see web content
        development)
content property
    CSSStyleDeclaration objects, 891
    meta objects, 796
    style objects, 891
    window objects, 985, 986
contentDocument property
    frame objects, 690
    iframe objects, 708
    object objects, 815
contenteditable attribute, 197
contentEditable property, 487
contentOverflow property
    event objects, 659
contentType value, 55
contentWindow property
    frame objects, 691
    iframe objects, 708
contextual selectors (see descendant
        selectors)
continue statement, 1205
controllers property
    window objects, 985, 986
cookie property
    document objects, 612
cookieEnabled property
    navigator object, 802
coords attribute
    a elements, 205
    area elements, 221
coords property
    a objects, 533
    area objects, 553
Copy command, 1284

Core module, 12, 16, 18, 184
cos( ) method
    Math object, 1165
counter-increment attribute (CSS), 1061
counterIncrement property
    style, CSSStyleDeclaration objects, 892
counter-reset attribute (CSS), 1061
counterReset property
    style, CSSStyleDeclaration objects, 892
cpuClass property
    navigator object, 802
createAttribute( ) method
    document objects, 626
createAttributeNS( ) method
    document objects, 626
CreateBookmark command, 1284
createCaption( ) method
    table objects, 939
createCDATASection( ) method
    document objects, 627
createComment( ) method
    document objects, 627
createContextualFragment( ) method
    Range objects, 844
createControlRange( ) method, 510
createDocument( ) method
    implementation objects, 723
createDocumentFragment( ) method
    document objects, 627
createDocumentType( ) method
    implementation objects, 724
createElement( ) method
    document objects, 30, 126, 628
createElementNS( ) method
    document objects, 628
createEntityReference( ) method
    document objects, 628
createEvent( ) method
    document objects, 629
createEventObject( ) method
    document objects, 629
CreateLink command, 1284
createNodeIterator( ) method
    document objects, 630
createPopup( ) method
    window objects, 999
createProcessingInstruction( ) method
    document objects, 631
createRange( ) method
    document objects, 631
    selection objects, 872

createRangeCollection( ) method
    selection objects, 872
createStyleSheet( ) method
    document objects, 631
createTextNode( ) method
    Document objects, 30, 127
    document objects, 632
createTextRange( ) method
    body objects, 574
    button objects, 577
    input (type="button") objects, 729
    input (type="hidden") objects, 740
    input (type="password") objects, 749
    input (type="reset") objects, 756
    input (type="submit") objects, 758
    input (type="text") objects, 762
    textarea objects, 960
createTFoot( ) method
    table objects, 939
createTHead( ) method
    table objects, 939
createTreeWalker( ) method
    document objects, 632
cross-platform
    position scripting, 85
    scripting, 85–94
    strategies, 32–41
    style differences, 69
    techniques, 164
crypto property
    window objects, 986
CSS (Cascading Style Sheets)
    attribute assignment syntax, 50
    cascading precedence rule, 68
    characteristics, 48
    as common denominator, 39
    CSS1
        as common denominator, 39
        cross-platform style differences, 69
        IE 4 support, 25
        Netscape 6, 29
        pseudo-elements/classes, 63
    CSS2
        browser support, 10
        class selector guidelines, 57
        common denominator and, 39
        link element and, 55
        @media rule, 78
        Netscape 6, 29
        overview, 9
        pseudo-elements/classes, 63, 64
    CSS3, 9, 183–184

CSS (Cascading Style Sheets) *(continued)*
  CSS-P (Cascading Style
    Sheets-Positioning)
    absolute positioning, 76
    attributes, 72
    capabilities, 10
    as common denominator, 39
    element positioning, 9
    element positioning origin, 70
    layering and, 25
    overflow attribute, 80
    style sheet rule attributes, 77
  element containment and, 47
  Netscape 6, 29
  overlaying to different pages, 37
  style rules and, 9
  (see also style sheets)
.css extension, 54, 56
CSS2Properties collection, 113
CSSDeclaration object, 85
cssFloat property
  CSSStyleDeclaration objects, 892
  style objects, 892
CSSImportRule objects, 589
CSSMediaRule objects, 589
CSSPageRule objects, 589
cssRule object, 116
CSSRule objects, 589
cssRule objects, 589
CSSRuleList objects, 595
cssRules objects, 595
cssRules property, 116
  CSSRule objects, 590
  cssRule objects, 590
  rule objects, 590
  styleSheet objects, 924
CSSStyleDeclaration objects, 113, 116, 596,
    878
CSSStyleSheet objects, 596
cssText property, 116
  CSSRule objects, 590
  cssRule objects, 590
  CSSStyleDeclaration objects, 892
  rule objects, 590
  style objects, 892
  styleSheet objects, 925
ctrlKey property, 170
  event objects, 660
ctrlLeft property
  event objects, 660
cue attribute (CSS), 1061

cue property
  CSSStyleDeclaration objects, 881, 893
  style objects, 881, 893
cue-after attribute (CSS), 1061
cueAfter property
  CSSStyleDeclaration objects, 881, 893
  style objects, 881, 893
cue-before attribute (CSS), 1061
cueBefore property
  CSSStyleDeclaration objects, 881, 893
  style objects, 881, 893
current property
  history objects, 700
currentNode property
  TreeWalker objects, 977
currentStyle objects, 596
currentStyle property, 25, 84, 487
currentTarget property, 168
  event objects, 660
cursor attribute (CSS), 1062
cursor property
  CSSStyleDeclaration objects, 893
  style objects, 893
custom objects, 596
Cut command, 1284

## D

data attribute
  object elements, 381
data binding, 28, 129
data, embedding for XML, 136–140
data property
  Comment objects, 588
  comment objects, 588
  event objects, 660
  object objects, 815
  Text objects, 953
datafld attribute
  a elements, 205
  applet elements, 216
  button elements, 241
  div elements, 262
  frame elements, 286
  iframe elements, 306
  img elements, 320
  input elements, 330
  label elements, 346
  marquee elements, 365
  param elements, 392
  select elements, 408
  span elements, 414

dataFld property, 129
  a objects, 534
  applet objects, 549
  button objects, 575
  div objects, 606
  event objects, 661
  frame objects, 691
  iframe objects, 709
  img objects, 715
  input (type="button") objects, 727
  input (type="checkbox") objects, 731
  input (type="hidden") objects, 738
  input (type="password") objects, 745
  input (type="radio") objects, 751
  input (type="text") objects, 759
  label objects, 765
  marquee objects, 790
  object objects, 816
  select objects, 862
  textarea objects, 956
dataformatas attribute
  button elements, 241
  div elements, 262
  label elements, 346
  marquee elements, 365
  param elements, 392
  span elements, 414
dataFormatAs property
  a objects, 534
  button objects, 576
  div objects, 606
  img objects, 716
  label objects, 765
  marquee objects, 790
dataPageSize property
  table objects, 936
datasrc attribute
  a elements, 205
  applet elements, 216
  button elements, 242
  div elements, 263
  frame elements, 286
  iframe elements, 307
  img elements, 320
  input elements, 331
  label elements, 347
  marquee elements, 366
  param elements, 392
  select elements, 409
  span elements, 415
dataSrc property
  a objects, 534
  applet objects, 549

button objects, 576
div objects, 607
frame objects, 691
iframe objects, 709
img objects, 716
input (type="button") objects, 727
input (type="checkbox") objects, 731
input (type="hidden") objects, 738
input (type="password") objects, 745
input (type="radio") objects, 751
input (type="text") objects, 760
label objects, 765
marquee objects, 790
object objects, 816
select objects, 862
textarea objects, 957
dataTransfer objects, 597
dataTransfer property
  event objects, 661
Date objects, 1135
datetime attribute
  del elements, 258
  ins elements, 341
dateTime property, 488
  del objects, 601
  ins objects, 763
dd elements, 256
dd objects, 600
declaration block, 52
declarations
  assignment shortcuts, 53
  components of, 50
  important declaration, 67
  precedence rules, 67
  selector, 51
declare attribute
  object elements, 381
declare property
  object objects, 816
decodeURI( ) method
  Global objects, 1157
decodeURIComponent( ) method
  Global objects, 1157
decrement operator (--), 1196
defaultCharset property
  document objects, 613
defaultChecked property
  input (type="checkbox") objects, 731
  input (type="radio") objects, 751
defaultSelected property
  option objects, 822
defaultStatus property
  window objects, 986

defaultValue property
   input (type="file") objects, 735
   input (type="hidden") objects, 739
   input (type="password") objects, 745
   input (type="text") objects, 760
   textarea objects, 957
defaultView property
   document objects, 85, 614
defer attribute
   script elements, 403
defer property
   script objects, 858
del elements, 257
del objects, 601
delays, inserting, 105
Delete command, 1284
delete operator, 1202
deleteCaption() method
   table objects, 939
deleteCell() method
   tr objects, 975
deleteContents() method
   Range objects, 844
deleteData() method
   comment, Comment objects, 589
   Text objects, 954
deleteFromDocument() method
   selection objects, 873
deleteMedium() method
   MediaList objects, 794
deleteRow() method
   table objects, 939
   tbody objects, 946
   tfoot objects, 946
   thead objects, 946
deleteRule() method
   CSSRule objects, 594
   cssRule objects, 594
   rule objects, 594
   styleSheet objects, 929
deleteTFoot() method
   table objects, 939
deleteTHead() method
   table objects, 939
delimiters
   commas, 62
   dot syntax, 47
   spaces, 61
deprecated
   attributes and elements, 8
   IE 5 model, 24
   XHTML, 7

descendant selectors
   characteristics, 61–63
   child selector similarity, 65
   creating subgroups, 57
description property
   Error objects, 1149
   mimeType objects, 798
   plugin objects, 832
detach() method
   NodeIterator objects, 810
   Range objects, 844
detachEvent() method, 161, 510
   window objects, 999
detail property
   event objects, 661
deviceXDPI property
   screen object, 855
deviceYDPI property
   screen object, 855
dfn elements, 259
dfn objects, 542, 601
Dialog Helper objects, 601
dialogArguments property
   window objects, 986
dialogHeight property
   window objects, 987
dialogLeft property
   window objects, 987
dialogTop property
   window objects, 987
dialogWidth property
   window objects, 987
dimensions
   block-level elements and, 45
   iframe elements, 134
   layering as, 70
dimensions() method
   VBArray objects, 1191
dir attribute, 197
dir elements, 260
dir objects, 604
dir property, 488
direction attribute
   marquee elements, 366
direction attribute (CSS), 1064
direction property
   CSSStyleDeclaration objects, 894
   marquee objects, 790
   style objects, 894
directories objects, 604
directories property
   window objects, 987

disability (see accessibility)
disabled attribute, 197
  input elements, 331
  optgroup elements, 387
  option elements, 389
  select elements, 409
  style elements, 417
disabled property, 116, 488
  style (element) objects, 876
disableExternalCapture() method
  window objects, 999
dispatchEvent() method, 511
  window objects, 1000
display attribute, 81
display attribute (CSS), 1064
display property
  CSSStyleDeclaration objects, 894
  style objects, 894
display style property, 144
div elements, 261
  as block-level element, 45
  characteristics, 43
  custom newsletter example, 143, 144
  DHTML browsers and, 43
  dragging elements example, 174
  element containment and, 44
  free-range class rule example, 59
  interleaving example, 82
  internal branching example, 38
  positioning example, 73, 74
  referencing elements example, 83
div objects, 605
division operator (/), 1196
dl elements, 263
dl objects, 607
!DOCTYPE elements, 10, 45, 72, 126, 265
doctype property
  document objects, 614
document node, 14, 126
Document Object Model (see DOM)
Document objects, 640
  captureEvents() method, 174
  clear() method, 103
  close() method, 103, 106
  createElement() method, 30, 126
  createTextNode() method, 30, 127
  defaultView property, 85
  images array, 33
  open() method, 103
  styleSheets array, 116
  write() method, 38, 101–103, 106
  writeln() method, 102
  (see also getElementById method())

document objects, 608
  IE commands for (list), 1283–1286
Document property, 136
document property, 489
  popup objects, 835
  window objects, 988
document trees
  node hierarchy, 126
  removing range content, 142
  script access to, 136
Document Type Definition (DTD), 7
document.all
  custom APIs, 41
  element referencing scheme, 111
  elements and, 24
  object detection example, 34
  reconciling syntax, 82
documentElement property
  document objects, 614
DocumentEvent objects, 641
DocumentFragment objects, 128, 641
DOCUMENT_FRAGMENT_NODE
    property, 481
DOCUMENT_NODE property, 481
DocumentRange objects, 641
documents
  changing structure, 123–129
  collapsed state, 141
  Core module and, 12
  creating for current window, 102
  external documents, 133, 161
  importance of uniqueness, 60
  key W3C node types, 121
DocumentStyle objects, 642
DocumentTraversal objects, 642
DocumentType objects, 642
DOCUMENT_TYPE_NODE property, 481
DocumentView objects, 644
DOM (Document Object Model)
  applied style values, 112
  convenience features, 117
  dynamic content and, 101
  ease of use, 129
  element objects, 118–120
  event handlers, list of, 1257–1264
  event object properties, 155
  image swapping, 108
  methods, list of, 1243–1256
  modularization, 184, 186
  node referencing, 137
  object containment and, 47
  overview, 11–16
  propagation model, 165

DOM (Document Object Model) *(continued)*
  properties, list of, 1221–1242
  reading attribute values, 111
  styleSheet object properties, 116
  text range implementation, 140
  (see also Internet Explorer, IE 4 DOM;
     W3C DOM)
DOMActivate event, 1016
domain property
  document objects, 615
DOMAttrModified event, 1016
DOMCharacterDataModified event, 1016
DOMException objects, 644
DOMFocusIn event, 1016
DOMFocusOut event, 1016
DOMImplementation objects, 184, 646
DOMNodeInserted event, 1017
DOMNodeInsertedIntoDocument
    event, 1017
DOMNodeRemoved event, 1017
DOMNodeRemovedFromDocument
    event, 1017
DOMSubtreeModified event, 1018
doReadRequest( ) method
  userProfile objects, 981
doScroll( ) method, 511
do/while statement, 1205
downloading, 148
dragDrop( ) method, 512
dragging elements, 173–178
drop caps, 63, 64
dropEffect property
  clipboardData objects, 584
  dataTransfer objects, 599
dt elements, 267
dt objects, 646
DTD (Document Type Definition), 7
duplicate( ) method
  TextRange objects, 963
dynamic content
  applied style values, 112–117
  changing, 117–129
  client-side includes, 133–140
  cross-platform expectations and, 41
  custom newsletter example, 142–149
  data binding and, 27
  defined, 3
  dynamic tables, 129–133
  IE DHTML, 23
  image swapping, 108–111
  links to multiple frames, 107
  Mozilla browser and, 28

Netscape 6, 30
  overlaying to different pages, 38
  page rendering and, 26
  text ranges, 140–142
  writing, 101–106
  XHTML 1.1 and, 181
dynamic positioning
  cross-platform scripting, 85–94
  Netscape 6, 29
  positionable elements, 71–77
  positioning attributes, 77–82
  scripting and, 82–85
dynamic tables, 129–133
dynsrc attribute
  img elements, 321
  input elements, 332
dynsrc property
  img objects, 716
  input (type="image") objects, 741

**E**

E property
  Math object, 1163
ECMA, 18, 28
ECMA-262, 18
ECMAScript, 18–19, 111
effectAllowed property
  clipboardData objects, 584
  dataTransfer objects, 599
elem element, 127
element containment, 47, 48, 65
element nodes, 14, 127
Element objects, 647
element objects
  references to, 29
  style property, 56, 84
  text content as properties, 118
element positioning, 11, 70
element text
  changing, 118–123
  Core module and, 12
  encompassing, 142
element types, 57
ElementCSSInlineStyle objects, 647
elementFromPoint( ) method
  document objects, 633
ELEMENT_NODE property, 481
elements
  abstract model and, 18
  altering, 118
  binding to event handlers, 156–162
  changing, 123–129

controlling properties, 11
currentStyle property, 84
custom APIs and, 88
deprecated, 8
div tag containment, 44
document.all collection, 24
dragging, 173–178
dynamic content, 30
event processing and, 153
head element, 53, 126
id attribute, 15
inserting, 142
inserting text, 16
instant access, 14
manipulating via scripts, 150
overlapping versus wrapping, 76
preventing default actions, 162
property example, 112
pseudo-classes and, 64
pseudo-elements, 63
referencing, 13, 24, 82
rules and, 9
as scriptable objects, 23
selector and, 51
style declarations and, 52
unique id identifiers and, 60
XML support, 7, 126
(see also block-level elements; empty
    elements; positioning)
elements objects, 648
elements property
    form objects, 684
elevation attribute (CSS), 1065
elevation property
    CSSStyleDeclaration objects, 881, 895
    style objects, 881, 895
em elements, 48, 121, 125, 268
em objects, 542, 648
em units, 10
embed elements, 269
embed objects, 648
embedding
    event handlers, 157
    external documents, 133
    style sheets, 51–56
    XML data, 136–140
embeds objects, 651
embeds property
    document objects, 615
empty elements
    creating element example, 30
    forward slash and, 42

generating elements example, 126
    requirements, 8
empty strings, 35
empty( ) method
    selection objects, 873
empty-cells attribute (CSS), 1066
emptyCells property
    CSSStyleDeclaration objects, 895
    style objects, 895
enabledPlugin property
    mimeType objects, 798
enableExternalCapture( ) method
    window objects, 999
encodeURI( ) method
    Global objects, 1158
encodeURIComponent( ) method
    Global objects, 1158
encoding property
    CSSRule objects, 590
    cssRule objects, 590
    form objects, 684
    rule objects, 590
enctype attribute
    form elements, 282
enctype property
    form objects, 685
@end statement, 1212
end tags, 8, 42
endContainer property
    Range objects, 839
endOffset property
    Range objects, 840
entities for characters, 1272–1278
entities property
    DocumentType objects, 642
Entity objects, 652
ENTITY_NODE property, 481
EntityReference objects, 652
ENTITY_REFERENCE_NODE
        property, 481
Enumerator objects, 1147
equal sign operator, 50, 53
equality operator (==), 1197
Error objects, 1148
escape sequences, 1213
escape( ) method
    Global objects, 1158
eval( ) method, 110
    Global objects, 1159
event attribute, 160, 181
    script elements, 403
event binding, 156–162

event bubbling
  click event example, 27
  defined, 26
  dragging elements and, 173
  flexibility of, 166
  Netscape 6, 31
  propagation and, 166–168
event capture, 31, 169
event handlers, 476
  binding to objects, 158
  browsers, 31, 151–152
  HTML 4, 6
  list of, 1257–1264
  scripting for actions, 26
  wrapping inside links, 109
event listener function, 162, 164
event listeners
  event capture and, 168
  event objects and, 31
  features, 161
  text nodes as, 167
Event objects, 678
event objects, 652
  characteristics, 153–156
  event model component, 26
  keyboard events and, 170
  Netscape 6, 31
  pageX/pageY properties, 175
  propagation properties, 168
  returnValue property, 163
event parameter, attachEvent( ) method, 161
event propagation
  addEventListener( ) method, 162
  event model component, 26
  features, 165–169
  Netscape 6, 31
event property
  script objects, 858
  window objects, 988
event queues, 153
event types, 31, 150–152
EventListener objects, 678
eventPhase property, 168
  event objects, 662
events
  attaching, 161
  event handlers versus, 151
  future considerations, 178
  keyboard character codes, 1279–1282
  keyboard events, 169–173
  Microsoft syntax and, 24

nodes as targets, 18
  preventing default actions, 162–165
Events module, 27, 161, 169
EventTarget objects, 679
exclusive OR operator (^), 1195
exec( ) method
  regular expression objects, 1180
execCommand( ) method
  commands for (list), 1283–1286
  document objects, 633
  TextRange objects, 963
execScript( ) method
  window objects, 1000
exp( ) method
  Math object, 1165
expand( ) method
  TextRange objects, 964
expandEntityReference property
  NodeIterator objects, 810
  TreeWalker objects, 977
expando property
  Attr objects, 558
  attribute objects, 558
  document objects, 615
explicit branching, 87
extend( ) method
  selection objects, 873
Extensible Markup Language (see XML)
external objects, 679
external property
  window objects, 988
extractContents( ) method
  Range objects, 845

F

face attribute
  basefont elements, 228
  font elements, 277
face property
  basefont objects, 566
  font objects, 682
fgColor property
  document objects, 616
fieldset elements, 275
fieldset objects, 679
fileCreatedDate property
  document objects, 616
  img objects, 716
fileModifiedDate property
  document objects, 616
  img objects, 717

fileName property
    Error objects, 1149
filename property
    plugin objects, 832
files
    font definition files, 27
    importing style sheets, 54–56
fileSize property
    document objects, 616
    img objects, 717
fileUpdatedDate property
    document objects, 617
    img objects, 717
fileUpload objects, 680
filter (new style) attribute (CSS), 1069
filter (old style) attribute (CSS), 1067
filter property
    CSSStyleDeclaration objects, 895
    NodeIterator objects, 810
    style objects, 895
    TreeWalker objects, 977
filter style attribute, 27
filters, 28, 142
filters objects, 680
filters property, 489
find( ) method
    window objects, 1000
findText( ) method, 144
    TextRange objects, 964
fireEvent( ) method, 512
:first pseudo-class, 1042
firstChild property, 121, 489
:first-child pseudo-class, 64, 1042
firstChild( ) method
    TreeWalker objects, 977
:first-letter element, 63, 1041
:first-line element, 63, 1041
fixed value (position attribute), 72, 77
fixed( ) method
    String objects, 1184
flags
    browser support, 86, 87
    global flags, 87, 111
float attribute, 77
float attribute (CSS), 77, 1071
floor( ) method
    Math object, 1166
flying objects, 96–100
:focus pseudo-class, 64, 1042
focus( ) method, 513
    window objects, 1001

focusNode property
    selection objects, 869
focusOffset property
    selection objects, 869
font attribute (CSS), 1072
font definition files, 27
font element, 27
font elements, 276
font objects, 681
font property
    CSSStyleDeclaration objects, 896
    style objects, 896
fontcolor( ) method
    String objects, 1184
@font-face rule, 1043
font-family attribute (CSS), 1073
fontFamily property
    CSSStyleDeclaration objects, 896
    style objects, 896
FontName command, 1284
fonts
    characteristics, 10
    downloadable fonts, 27
    :first-letter element, 63
fonts objects, 683
fonts property
    Dialog Helper objects, 602
font-size attribute (CSS), 1074
FontSize command, 1284
fontSize property
    CSSStyleDeclaration objects, 897
    style objects, 897
fontsize( ) method
    String objects, 1184
font-size-adjust attribute (CSS), 1076
fontSizeAdjust property
    CSSStyleDeclaration objects, 897
    style objects, 897
fontSmoothingEnabled property
    screen object, 855
font-stretch attribute (CSS), 1076
fontStretch property
    CSSStyleDeclaration objects, 898
    style objects, 898
font-style attribute (CSS), 1076
fontStyle property
    CSSStyleDeclaration objects, 898
    style objects, 898
font-variant attribute (CSS), 1077
fontVariant property
    CSSStyleDeclaration objects, 898
    style objects, 898

font-weight attribute (CSS), 1077
fontWeight property
  CSSStyleDeclaration objects, 899
  style objects, 899
fontWeight style property, 34
for attribute
  label elements, 347
  script elements, 160, 404
for statement, 1206
ForeColor command, 1284
for/in statement, 1206
form controls
  backward compatibility, 8
  common elements, 47
  referencing, 13
  z-index attribute and, 81
form elements, 278
  backward compatibility, 8
  onsubmit event and, 162
  this keyword, 157
form objects, 683
form property, 157
  button objects, 576
  fieldset objects, 680
  input (type="button") objects, 728
  input (type="checkbox") objects, 732
  input (type="file") objects, 735
  input (type="hidden") objects, 739
  input (type="image") objects, 742
  input (type="password") objects, 746
  input (type="radio") objects, 751
  input (type="reset") objects, 754
  input (type="submit") objects, 757
  input (type="text") objects, 760
  label objects, 765
  legend objects, 775
  object objects, 816
  option objects, 822
  select objects, 863
  textarea objects, 957
FormatBlock command, 1284
forms objects, 687
forms property
  document objects, 617
forward( ) method
  history objects, 701
  window objects, 1001
fragmentation, 19, 179
frame elements, 103, 284
frame objects, 689
frame property
  table objects, 936

frameborder attribute
  frame elements, 286
  frameset elements, 295
  iframe elements, 307
frameBorder property
  frame objects, 692
  frameset objects, 697
  iframe objects, 709
frameElement property
  window objects, 989
frames, 103–107
  linking multiple, 107
  sending content to, 103
frames objects, 694
frames property
  document objects, 617
  window objects, 989
Frameset doctype, 133
frameset elements, 290
frameset objects, 695
framesets, 103–107
framespacing attribute
  frameset elements, 296
frameSpacing property
  frameset objects, 698
  iframe objects, 709
free-range class rule, 59
fromCharCode( ) method
  String objects, 1184
fromElement property
  event objects, 662
function objects, 1151
function statement, 1212

**G**

galleryimg attribute
  img elements, 321
getAdjacentText( ) method, 120, 513
getAnonymousElementByAttribute( ) method
  document objects, 625, 634
getAnonymousNodes( ) method
  document objects, 625, 634
GetAttention( ) method
  window objects, 1001
getAttribute( ) method, 111, 112, 514
  userProfile objects, 982
getAttributeNode( ) method, 514
getAttributeNodeNS( ) method, 515
getAttributeNS( ) method, 515
getBindingParent( ) method
  document objects, 625, 634

getBookmark( ) method
TextRange objects, 965
getBoundingClientRect( ) method, 516
getCharset( ) method
Dialog Helper objects, 603
getClientRects( ) method, 516
getComputedStyle( ) method, 85
window objects, 1001
getData( ) method
clipboardData objects, 585
dataTransfer objects, 599
getDate( ) method
Date objects, 1136
getDay( ) method
Date objects, 1137
getElementById( ) method, 634
custom APIs and, 41
element references, 112
element referencing scheme, 111
Netscape 6, 29
object detection example, 34
Opera 6 support, 32
overlaying to different pages, 38
page branching example, 36
reconciling syntax, 82
searching document, 15
W3C DOM syntax, 24
getElementsByName( ) method
document objects, 634
getElementsByTagName( ) method, 516
getElementsByTagNameNS( ) method, 517
getExpression( ) method, 517
getFullYear( ) method
Date objects, 1137
getHours( ) method
Date objects, 1137
getItem( ) method
VBArray objects, 1191
getMilliseconds( ) method
Date objects, 1137
getMinutes( ) method
Date objects, 1137
getMonth( ) method
Date objects, 1137
getNamedItem( ) method
attributes objects, 561
NamedNodeMap objects, 561
getNamedItemNS( ) method
attributes objects, 561
NamedNodeMap objects, 561
GetObject( ) method
Global objects, 1159

getPreventDefault( ) method
event objects, 673
getPropertyCSSValue( ) method
CSSStyleDeclaration objects, 922
style objects, 922
getPropertyPriority( ) method
CSSStyleDeclaration objects, 922
style objects, 922
getPropertyValue( ) method, 85
CSSStyleDeclaration objects, 922
style objects, 922
getRangeAt( ) method
selection objects, 873
getSeconds( ) method
Date objects, 1138
getSelection( ) method
document objects, 635
window objects, 1002
getTime( ) method
Date objects, 1138
getTimezoneOffset( ) method
Date objects, 1138
getUTCDate( ) method
Date objects, 1138
getUTCDay( ) method
Date objects, 1138
getUTCFullYear( ) method
Date objects, 1139
getUTCHours( ) method
Date objects, 1139
getUTCMilliseconds( ) method
Date objects, 1139
getUTCMinutes( ) method
Date objects, 1139
getUTCMonth( ) method
Date objects, 1139
getUTCSeconds( ) method
Date objects, 1140
getVarDate( ) method
Date objects, 1140
getYear( ) method
Date objects, 1140
global flags, 87, 111
Global objects, 1155
global property
regular expression objects, 1179
global variables
custom APIs, 94
custom newsletter example, 144
dragging elements, 174, 175
iframe resizing example, 135
multiple browser classes and, 86

global variables *(continued)*
    storing colors, 114
    storing references, 105
go( ) method
    history objects, 701
granularity, 36
greater-than operator (>), 65, 1197
greater-than-or-equal operator (>=), 1198
GUI (graphical user interface)
    activity monitoring, 150
    HTML 4 improvements, 6
    operating systems and, 31
    standards and, 180
gutter attribute
    multicol elements, 374

# H

h1, h2, h3, h4, h5, h6 elements, 45, 297
h1, h2, h3, h4, h5, h6 objects, 698
handleEvent( ) method
    document objects, 635
    form objects, 686
    input (type="button") objects, 729
    input (type="checkbox") objects, 734
    input (type="file") objects, 737
    input (type="image") objects, 744
    input (type="password") objects, 749
    input (type="radio") objects, 753
    input (type="reset") objects, 756
    input (type="submit") objects, 758
    input (type="text") objects, 763
    layer objects, 771
    textarea objects, 960
hasAttribute( ) method, 517
hasAttributeNS( ) method, 518
hasAttributes( ) method, 518
hasChildNodes( ) method, 123, 518
hasFeature( ) method, 184
    implementation objects, 724
hasFocus( ) method
    document objects, 635
hash property
    a objects, 535
    area objects, 553
    location objects, 784
hasOwnProperty( ) method
    Object objects, 1173
head elements, 126, 299
head objects, 699
head section, 51
headers property
    td and th objects, 950

headings, 45
height attribute
    applet elements, 216
    embed elements, 271
    frame elements, 287
    iframe elements, 307
    ilayer elements, 314
    img elements, 322
    input elements, 332
    layer elements, 351
    marquee elements, 366
    object elements, 382
    spacer elements, 412
height attribute (CSS), 1078
height property
    applet objects, 549
    CSSStyleDeclaration objects, 899
    document objects, 617
    embed objects, 649
    frame objects, 692
    iframe objects, 709
    img objects, 718
    input (type="image") objects, 742
    marquee objects, 791
    object objects, 817
    screen object, 856
    style objects, 899
    table objects, 937
    td, th objects, 951
    tr objects, 974
hidden attribute
    embed elements, 272
hidden objects, 700
hidden property
    embed objects, 650
    layer objects, 768
hidden value
    overflow attribute, 80
    visibility attribute, 81
hide( ) method
    popup objects, 836
hidefocus attribute, 198
hideFocus property, 489
history objects, 700
history property
    window objects, 989
home( ) method
    window objects, 1002
host property
    a objects, 535
    area objects, 553
    location objects, 784

hostname property
  a objects, 535
  area objects, 553
  location objects, 784
:hover pseudo-class, 64, 1042
hr elements, 301
hr objects, 702
href attribute, 107
  a elements, 206
  area elements, 221
  base elements, 226
  link elements, 358
href property, 116
  a objects, 536
  area objects, 554
  base objects, 565
  CSSRule objects, 591
  cssRule objects, 591
  img objects, 718
  link objects, 777
  location objects, 785
  rule objects, 591
  styleSheet objects, 925
hreflang attribute
  a elements, 206
  link elements, 359
hreflang property
  a objects, 536
  link objects, 777
hspace attribute
  applet elements, 217
  iframe elements, 308
  img elements, 322
  input elements, 333
  marquee elements, 367
  object elements, 382
hspace property
  applet objects, 549
  iframe objects, 710
  img objects, 718
  input (type="image") objects, 742
  marquee objects, 791
  object objects, 817
HTML attributes
  list of, 1217–1220
html elements, 47, 303
.html extension, 56
HTML (Hypertext Markup Language)
  browser interpretation, 3
  combining sources, 133
  element text and, 118

  elements and, 123–125
  equal sign operator, 50
  link element and, 55
  standards and implementation, 5–7
  style sheets and, 42–45
  swapping images, 109
html objects, 703
HTMLCollection objects, 704
HTMLDocument objects, 705
HTMLDOMImplementation objects, 706
HTMLElement objects, 706
htmlFor property
  label objects, 766
  script objects, 858
htmlText property
  TextRange objects, 962
HTMLUnknownElement objects, 596
HTTP 1.1, 111
http-equiv attribute
  meta elements, 371
httpEquiv property
  meta objects, 796

**I**

i elements, 304
I objects, 706
i objects, 564
ID
  custom newsletter example, 143
  element object references, 24
  instant access, 14
  referencing models and, 111
id attribute, 198
  applet elements, 217
  event handlers, 161
  getElementById( ) method, 15
  HTML requirements, 160
  ilayer elements, 314
  img element, 108
  layer elements, 351
  linking, 64
  name attribute and, 8
  positioning elements, 71
  style sheet links and, 9
id property, 490
ID selectors
  as attribute selector, 64
  characteristics, 60–61
  creating subgroups, 57
  positioning elements, 71
  pseudo-element/class, 64

identifiers
    backward compatibility, 8
    class identifiers, 57
    as index values, 108
    linking style sheets and content, 9
    syntax, 60
    values, 191, 471
identity operator (===), 1198
ids property
    document objects, 618
if conditions, 34
@if statement, 1212
if statement, 1206
if/else statement, 1207
iframe elements, 37, 38, 133–136, 305
iframe objects, 706
ignoreCase property
    regular expression objects, 1179
ilayer elements, 311
ilayer objects, 712
Image object, src property, 108, 109
images
    object detection and, 33
    as scriptable objects, 12
images array (Document object), 33
images objects, 712
images property
    document objects, 618
ime-mode attribute (CSS), 1079
imeMode property
    CSSStyleDeclaration objects, 900
    style objects, 900
img elements, 108, 109, 317
    containment example, 47
    dragging elements example, 174
    event bubbling and, 166
    identifiers and, 108
    mouse events, 109
    as positionable element, 71
    src property, 110
img objects, 714
implementation objects, 723
implementation property
    document objects, 618
@import rule, 55, 67, 1043
!important attribute (CSS), 1079
important declaration, 67
importNode() method
    document objects, 635
imports objects, 725
imports property
    styleSheet objects, 925

in operator, 1202
inch units, 78
incompatibility between platforms, 19, 21
increment operator (++), 1198
Indent command, 1284
indeterminate property
    input (type="checkbox") objects, 732
index property
    option objects, 823
    RegExp objects, 1175
indexOf() method
    String objects, 1185
inequality operator (!=), 1199
Infinity property
    Global objects, 1156
inherit value
    position attribute, 72
    visibility attribute, 81
inheritance
    descendant selectors and, 61
    free-range class rule example, 59
    from parent to child, 18
    p.narrow rule example, 58
    style attributes and, 48
    style sheets and, 47
initEvent() method
    event objects, 673
initKeyEvent() method
    event objects, 674
initMouseEvent() method
    event objects, 675
initMutationEvent() method
    event objects, 676
initUIEvent() method
    event objects, 677
inline elements, 71
innerHeight property
    window objects, 990
innerHTML property, 490
    adding, 16
    altering elements, 118
    cross-platforms and, 26
    dynamic tables, 133
    features, 123
    instant rendering, 14
    interpreting tags, 119
    Mozilla support, 30
    popularity of, 125
    script access, 126
    success of, 129
    text node manipulation, 123

innerText property, 490
  adding, 16
  assigning strings, 14
  features, 123
  IE DOM element objects, 118
  rendering content literally, 119
innerWidth property
  window objects, 990
input elements, 327
input objects, 726
input property
  RegExp objects, 1175
input (type="button") objects, 726
input (type="checkbox") objects, 729
input (type="file") objects, 734
input (type="hidden") objects, 737
input (type="image") objects, 740
input (type="password") objects, 744
input (type="radio") objects, 749
input (type="reset") objects, 754
input (type="submit") objects, 756
input (type="text") objects, 759
inRange() method
  TextRange objects, 965
ins elements, 340
ins objects, 763
insertAdjacentElement() method, 120, 518
insertAdjacentHTML() method, 120, 519
insertAdjacentText() method, 119, 120, 519
insertBefore() method, 123, 127, 520
InsertButton command, 1284
insertCell() method
  tr objects, 975
insertData() method
  comment, Comment objects, 589
  Text objects, 954
InsertFieldset command, 1284
InsertHorizontalRule command, 1284
InsertIFrame command, 1284
InsertInputButton command, 1284
InsertInputCheckbox command, 1284
InsertInputFileUpload command, 1284
InsertInputHidden command, 1285
InsertInputImage command, 1285
InsertInputPassword command, 1285
InsertInputRadio command, 1285
InsertInputReset command, 1285
InsertInputSubmit command, 1285
InsertInputText command, 1285
InsertMarquee command, 1285
insertNode() method, 141
  Range objects, 845

InsertOrderedList command, 1285
InsertParagraph command, 1285
insertRow() method, 133
  table objects, 940
  tbody objects, 946
  tfoot objects, 946
  thead objects, 946
insertRule() method
  CSSRule objects, 594
  cssRule objects, 594
  rule objects, 594
  styleSheet objects, 930
InsertSelectDropdown command, 1285
InsertSelectListbox command, 1285
InsertTextArea command, 1285
InsertUnorderedList command, 1285
instanceof operator, 1202
internal branching, 38, 39
internalSubset property
  DocumentType objects, 643
Internet Explorer (IE)
  advanced selector support, 63
  caching issues, 111
  changing text, 118–120
  commands, list of, 1283–1286
  cross-platform style differences, 69
  CSS1 support, 10
  currentStyle property, 84
  DHTML and, 4
  DHTML version, 23–28
  DocumentFragment object, 128
  ECMAScript, 18
  HTML 4 implementation, 7
  IE 4 DOM
    changing tag attribute values, 111
    dynamic content, 26
    event objects, 154
    overview, 14
    relationships and, 15
  IE DHTML
    CSS, 25
    downloaded fonts, 27
    dynamic content, 26
    dynamic page reflow, 23
    element object references, 24, 25
    Macintosh versions, 28
    transitions and filters, 27
    Windows-only features, 28
  iframe element support, 133
  internal roadmaps, 12
  JScript versions, 1123
  measurement properties supported, 84

Internet Explorer (IE) *(continued)*
  positioning attributes, 70
  proprietary style attributes, 113
  scripted positioning, 11
  scroll value support, 80
  style object as property, 82
  W3C DOM, 16
intersectsNode( ) method
  Range objects, 845
isChar property
  event objects, 662
isCollapsed property
  selection objects, 870
isContentEditable property, 491
isDisabled property, 491
isEqual( ) method
  TextRange objects, 965
isFinite( ) method
  Global objects, 1160
isindex elements, 342
isindex objects, 764
ismap attribute
  img elements, 323
  input elements, 333
isMap property
  img objects, 718
isMultiLine property, 491
isNaN( ) method
  Global objects, 1160
isOpen property
  popup objects, 836
isPointInRange( ) method
  Range objects, 845
isPrototypeOf( ) method
  Object objects, 1173
isSupported( ) method, 520
isTextEdit property, 492
Italic command, 1285
italics( ) method
  String objects, 1185
item( ) method
  all objects, 543
  anchors objects, 545
  applets objects, 551
  areas objects, 557
  attributes objects, 562
  cells objects, 579
  childNodes objects, 581
  children objects, 582
  CSSRuleList objects, 595
  cssRules objects, 595
  CSSStyleDeclaration objects, 923

  Enumerator objects, 1148
  filters objects, 681
  forms objects, 688
  frames objects, 695
  history objects, 702
  HTMLCollection objects, 705
  images objects, 712
  imports objects, 726
  links objects, 781
  MediaList objects, 794
  NamedNodeMap objects, 562
  NodeList objects, 581
  options objects, 825
  pages objects, 829
  plugins objects, 834
  rows objects, 850
  rules objects, 595
  scripts objects, 860
  select objects, 867
  style objects, 923
  StyleSheetList objects, 931
  styleSheets objects, 931
  tBodies objects, 942

## J

javaEnabled( ) method
  navigator object, 807
javascript: pseudo-URL, 107, 110
JavaScript scripting language
  browser compatibility, 18
  by-value operators, 84
  case-sensitivity, 151
  comment symbols, 52
  common symbols, 183
  delimiting objects, 47
  development of, 18
  DHTML, 22, 23, 150
  event queues and, 153
  high-level scripting, 129
  internal branching example, 38
  linking to multiple frames, 107
  loading script functions, 40
  meta tag and, 37
  one-dot evaluation rule, 34
  page branching and, 36
  referencing elements, 13
  repopulating tables, 30
  sorting facilities, 140
join( ) method
  Array objects, 1130
.jpg extension, 167
.js extension, 40, 56, 94, 173

JScript, 18, 1123
JustifyCenter command, 1285
JustifyLeft command, 1285
JustifyRight command, 1285

## K

kbd elements, 343
kbd objects, 542, 764
keyboard
    character codes, 1279
    event handlers for (list), 1262
    events, 169–173
keyCode property, 170
    event objects, 663
keydown event, 151
keygen elements, 343
keytype attribute
    keygen elements, 344
keywords, 142, 144

## L

label attribute
    optgroup elements, 387
    option elements, 389
label elements, 345
label objects, 764
label property
    optgroup objects, 821
    option objects, 823
label statement, 1207
lang attribute, 199
lang property, 492
:lang pseudo-class, 64, 1042
language attribute, 199
    script elements, 404
language codes, 191, 472
language property, 492
    navigator object, 802
lastChild property, 121, 489, 493
lastChild() method
    TreeWalker objects, 977
lastIndex property
    RegExp objects, 1175
    regular expression objects, 1179
lastIndexOf() method
    String objects, 1185
lastMatch property
    RegExp objects, 1175
lastModified property
    document objects, 618

lastPage() method
    table objects, 940
lastParen property
    RegExp objects, 1176
latency, network, 135
layer elements, 347
    content positioning and, 12
    internal branching example, 38
    Navigator 4 and, 11, 22
    Netscape 6, 29
layer objects, 766
layer-background-color attribute (CSS), 1082
layer-background-image attribute
        (CSS), 1082
layering, 25, 70
layers property
    document objects, 619
layerX property
    event objects, 663
layerY property
    event objects, 663
layout-flow attribute (CSS), 1080
layoutFlow property
    CSSStyleDeclaration objects, 900
    style objects, 900
layout-grid attribute (CSS), 1080
layoutGrid property
    CSSStyleDeclaration objects, 900
    style objects, 900
layout-grid-char attribute (CSS), 1080
layoutGridChar property
    CSSStyleDeclaration objects, 900
    style objects, 900
layout-grid-line attribute (CSS), 1081
layoutGridLine property
    CSSStyleDeclaration objects, 901
    style objects, 901
layout-grid-mode attribute (CSS), 1081
layoutGridMode property
    CSSStyleDeclaration objects, 901
    style objects, 901
layout-grid-type attribute (CSS), 1081
layoutGridType property
    CSSStyleDeclaration objects, 901
    style objects, 901
lbound() method
    VBArray objects, 1191
leaves, 14
left attribute, 89
    CSS, 1082
    CSS-P, 72

left attribute *(continued)*
    description, 84
    ilayer elements, 315
    layer elements, 352
    positioning, 72, 74, 75
    values, 78
left property, 84
    CSSStyleDeclaration objects, 901
    layer objects, 768
    style objects, 901
    TextRectangle objects, 970
:left pseudo-class, 1042
leftContext property
    RegExp objects, 1176
leftmargin attribute
    body elements, 236
leftMargin property
    body objects, 572
left-shift operator (<<), 1194
legend elements, 354
legend objects, 774
length property
    all objects, 543
    anchors objects, 545
    applets objects, 551
    areas objects, 556
    arguments objects, 1127
    Array objects, 1129
    attributes objects, 561
    cells objects, 579
    childNodes objects, 581
    children objects, 582
    Comment objects, 588
    comment objects, 588
    CSSRuleList objects, 595
    cssRules objects, 595
    elements objects, 648
    embeds objects, 651
    filters objects, 681
    form objects, 685
    forms objects, 687
    frames objects, 694
    function objects, 1153
    history objects, 701
    HTMLCollection objects, 705
    images objects, 712
    imports objects, 725
    links objects, 780
    MediaList objects, 793
    NamedNodeMap objects, 561
    NodeList objects, 581
    options objects, 824
    pages objects, 829

plugin objects, 832
    plugins objects, 833
    rows objects, 850
    rules objects, 595
    scripts objects, 860
    select objects, 863
    String objects, 1182
    StyleSheetList objects, 931
    styleSheets objects, 931
    tBodies objects, 942
    Text objects, 953
    window objects, 990
length values, 190, 471, 1037
less-than operator (<), 183, 1199
less-than-or-equal operator (<=), 1199
letter-spacing attribute, 63, 1083
letterSpacing property
    CSSStyleDeclaration objects, 902
    style objects, 902
li elements, 45, 355
li objects, 775
line-break attribute (CSS), 1083
lineBreak property
    CSSStyleDeclaration objects, 902
    style objects, 902
line-height attribute, 63, 1083
lineHeight property
    CSSStyleDeclaration objects, 902
    style objects, 902
lineNumber property
    Error objects, 1149
link attribute
    body elements, 236
link elements, 55, 116, 357
link objects, 776
link property
    body objects, 572
:link pseudo-class, 1042
link( ) method
    String objects, 1186
linkColor property
    document objects, 619
linking
    custom APIs, 94
    DTDs, 7
    selector and attributes, 64
    style declarations and elements, 52
    style sheets and content, 9
    to multiple frames, 107
links objects, 780
LinkStyle objects, 782
listing elements, 362
listing objects, 783

list-style attribute (CSS), 1084
listStyle property
    CSSStyleDeclaration objects, 902
    style objects, 902
list-style-image attribute (CSS), 1085
listStyleImage property
    CSSStyleDeclaration objects, 903
    style objects, 903
list-style-position attribute (CSS), 1085
listStylePosition property
    CSSStyleDeclaration objects, 903
    style objects, 903
list-style-type attribute (CSS), 1086
listStyleType property
    CSSStyleDeclaration objects, 903
    style objects, 903
LiveScript, 18
LN10 property
    Math object, 1163
LN2 property
    Math object, 1163
load event, 151
load() method, 136
    Document objects, 640
    layer objects, 771
loadBindingDocument() method
    document objects, 625, 636
local variables, 155
localeCompare() method
    String objects, 1186
localName property, 493
location objects, 783
location property
    document objects, 619
    window objects, 990
locationbar objects, 604, 787
locationbar property
    window objects, 987, 990
log() method
    Math object, 1166
LOG2E property
    Math object, 1163
LOG10E property
    Math object, 1163
logicalXDPI property
    screen object, 855, 856
logicalYDPI property
    screen object, 855, 856
longdesc attribute
    frame elements, 287
    iframe elements, 308
    img elements, 323

longDesc property
    frame objects, 692
    iframe objects, 710
    img objects, 719
loop attribute
    bgsound elements, 230
    img elements, 324
    input elements, 334
    marquee elements, 367
loop property
    bgsound objects, 568
    img objects, 719
    input (type="image") objects, 742
    marquee objects, 791
lowsrc attribute
    img elements, 324
    input elements, 334
lowsrc property
    img objects, 719
    input (type="image") objects, 742

**M**

Macintosh, 28, 38
map elements, 107, 362
map objects, 787
margin attribute (CSS), 1087
margin property
    CSSStyleDeclaration objects, 904
    fieldset objects, 680
    style objects, 904
margin-bottom attribute, 1087
marginBottom property
    CSSStyleDeclaration objects, 905
    style objects, 905
marginheight attribute
    body elements, 237
    frame elements, 287
    iframe elements, 309
marginHeight property
    frame objects, 692
    iframe objects, 710
margin-left attribute, 67, 1087
marginLeft property
    CSSStyleDeclaration objects, 905
    style objects, 905
margin-right attribute, 1087
marginRight property
    CSSStyleDeclaration objects, 905
    style objects, 905
margins
    assigning settings example, 57
    block-level elements and, 45

margins (*continued*)
 edge measurement attributes and, 78
 element rules, 9
 :first-letter element, 63
 float attribute and, 77
 overlaying to different pages, 38
 transparent space, 46
margin-top attribute, 1087
marginTop property
 CSSStyleDeclaration objects, 905
 style objects, 905
marginwidth attribute
 body elements, 237
 frame elements, 287
 iframe elements, 309
marginWidth property
 frame objects, 692
 iframe objects, 710
marker-offset attribute (CSS), 1088
markerOffset property
 CSSStyleDeclaration objects, 905
 style objects, 905
marks attribute (CSS), 1088
marks property
 CSSStyleDeclaration objects, 905
 style objects, 905
marquee elements, 363
marquee objects, 788
match() method
 String objects, 1186
Math object, 1162
max() method
 Math object, 1166
max-height attribute (CSS), 1089
maxHeight property
 CSSStyleDeclaration objects, 905
 style objects, 905
maxlength attribute
 input elements, 334
maxLength property
 input (type="password") objects, 746
 input (type="text") objects, 760
MAX_VALUE property
 Number objects, 1169
max-width attribute (CSS), 1090
maxWidth property
 CSSStyleDeclaration objects, 905
 style objects, 905
mayscript attribute
 applet elements, 218
media attribute
 link elements, 359
 style elements, 417

media property
 CSSRule objects, 591
 cssRule objects, 591
 document objects, 620
 link objects, 778
 rule objects, 591
 style (element) objects, 877
 styleSheet objects, 925
@media rule, 78, 1043
MediaList objects, 793
mediaText property
 MediaList objects, 793
menu elements, 369
menu objects, 794
menubar objects, 604, 795
menubar property
 window objects, 987, 991
mergeAttributes() method, 521
message property
 Error objects, 1149
meta elements, 37, 111, 370
meta objects, 795
metaKey property
 event objects, 663
method attribute
 form elements, 282
method property
 form objects, 685
methods
 Core DOM module and, 12
 element content manipulation, 120
 elements sharing, 18
 object detection and, 33
 W3C DOM node objects, 123
methods attribute
 a elements, 206
methods, list of, 1243–1256
Methods property
 a objects, 536
Microsoft, 18, 24
 IE 4 DOM (see Internet Explorer, IE 4
  DOM)
 Internet Explorer (see Internet Explorer)
 Windows, 10, 26, 28
millimeter units, 78
mimeType objects, 797
mimeType property
 a objects, 536
 document objects, 620
 img objects, 720
mimeTypes property
 navigator object, 803

min( ) method
  Math object, 1166
min-height attribute (CSS), 1089
minHeight property
  CSSStyleDeclaration objects, 905
  style objects, 905
MIN_VALUE property
  Number objects, 1169
min-width attribute (CSS), 1090
minWidth property
  CSSStyleDeclaration objects, 905
  style objects, 905
modifiers property
  event objects, 664
modularization
  CSS, 9, 25
  CSS3, 183–184
  DOM, 184, 186
  opportunities with, 16
  W3C, 180, 181
  XHTML, 7, 181–183
modulus operator (%), 1200
mouse
  event handlers for (list), 1262
MouseEvent objects, 799
move( ) method
  TextRange objects, 966
moveAbove( ) method
  layer objects, 772
moveBelow( ) method
  layer objects, 772
moveBy( ) method
  layer objects, 772
  window objects, 1002
moveEnd( ) method
  TextRange objects, 966
moveFirst( ) method
  Enumerator objects, 1148
moveNext( ) method
  Enumerator objects, 1148
moveRow( ) method
  table objects, 940
  tbody objects, 946
  tfoot objects, 946
  thead objects, 946
moveStart( ) method
  TextRange objects, 966
moveTo( ) method
  layer objects, 772
  window objects, 1002
moveToAbsolute( ) method
  layer objects, 772

moveToBookmark( ) method
  TextRange objects, 965, 966
moveToElementText( ) method
  TextRange objects, 967
moveToPoint( ) method
  TextRange objects, 967
moving objects, 96–100
MozBinding property
  CSSStyleDeclaration objects, 906
  style objects, 906
-moz-border-radius attribute (CSS), 1090
-moz-border-radius-bottomleft attribute
        (CSS), 1091
-moz-border-radius-bottomright attribute
        (CSS), 1091
-moz-border-radius-topleft attribute
        (CSS), 1091
-moz-border-radius-topright attribute
        (CSS), 1091
Mozilla (see Netscape 6)
mozOpacity attribute, 113
-moz-opacity attribute (CSS), 1091
MozOpacity property
  CSSStyleDeclaration objects, 906
  style objects, 906
multicol elements, 373
multiline property
  RegExp objects, 1176
multiple attribute
  select elements, 410
multiple property
  select objects, 863
multiplication operator (*), 1200
MutationEvent objects, 799

**N**

name attribute, 8, 108, 160
  a elements, 207
  applet elements, 218
  basefont elements, 228
  button elements, 242
  embed elements, 272
  form elements, 283
  frame elements, 288
  iframe elements, 309
  ilayer elements, 315
  img elements, 325
  input elements, 335
  keygen elements, 344
  map elements, 363
  meta elements, 372
  object elements, 383

name attribute *(continued)*
  param elements, 393
  select elements, 410
name property
  a objects, 537
  applet objects, 550
  Attr objects, 559
  attribute objects, 559
  button objects, 576
  DocumentType objects, 643
  embed objects, 650
  Error objects, 1150
  form objects, 686
  frame objects, 693
  iframe objects, 710
  img objects, 720
  input (type="button") objects, 728
  input (type="checkbox") objects, 732
  input (type="file") objects, 736
  input (type="hidden") objects, 739
  input (type="image") objects, 742
  input (type="password") objects, 746
  input (type="radio") objects, 752
  input (type="reset") objects, 755
  input (type="submit") objects, 757
  input (type="text") objects, 761
  layer objects, 768
  map objects, 788
  meta objects, 796
  object objects, 817
  param objects, 830
  plugin objects, 832
  select objects, 864
  textarea objects, 957
  window objects, 991
namedItem( ) method
  all objects, 544
  anchors objects, 546
  applets objects, 551
  areas objects, 557
  cells objects, 580
  children objects, 583
  filters objects, 681
  forms objects, 688
  frames objects, 695
  HTMLCollection objects, 705
  images objects, 713
  links objects, 781
  options objects, 826
  plugins objects, 834
  rows objects, 851
  scripts objects, 861

  select objects, 867
  tBodies objects, 943
NamedNodeMap objects, 560, 799
nameProp property
  a objects, 537
  document objects, 620
  img objects, 720
namespaces property
  document objects, 620
namespaceURI property, 493
naming conventions (see standardization)
naming event handlers, 151
NaN property
  Global objects, 1156
  Number objects, 1169
naturalHeight property
  img objects, 721
naturalWidth property
  img objects, 721
navigate( ) method
  window objects, 1003
navigator object, 799
navigator property
  window objects, 991
negation operator (-), 1200
NEGATIVE_INFINITY property
  Number objects, 1170
nesting
  block-level elements and, 47
  child elements and, 14
  cross-platform style differences, 69
  framesets, 103
  @import rule, 56
  Netscape 6 and, 29
  overflow attribute, 80
  positioning example, 76
  referencing element positions, 83
  tags, 13
Netscape 6 (Mozilla)
  advanced selector support, 63
  backward compatibility, 8
  browser development, 11
  Bugzilla tracking system, 69
  changing tag attribute values, 111
  cross-platform style differences, 69
  CSS2 support, 10
  DHTML, 4, 23, 28–32
  DocumentFragment object, 128
  get methods, 1125
  HTML support, 7
  iframe element support, 133
  innerHTML property, 16, 119, 125

proprietary style attributes, 113
scroll value support, 80
set methods, 1125
standards dilemma, 117
Netscape Navigator
    DHTML, 22
    dropping features, 5
    dynamic content and, 101
    ECMAScript, 18
    HTML 4 implementation, 7
    JavaScript development, 18
    layer tag, 12
    positionable elements, 71
    W3C DOM Level 2 specification, 16
network latency, 135
new operator, 1203
newValue property
    event objects, 664
next property
    history objects, 700
nextid elements, 374
nextNode( ) method
    NodeIterator objects, 810
    TreeWalker objects, 978
nextPage property
    event objects, 664
nextPage( ) method
    table objects, 940
nextSibling property, 121, 493
nextSibling( ) method
    TreeWalker objects, 977
nobr elements, 374
nobr objects, 808
Node objects, 808
NodeFilter objects, 809
NodeIterator objects, 810
NodeList objects, 581, 811
nodeName property, 121, 494
nodes
    abstract model and, 18
    accessing nested nodes, 16
    document node, 14, 126
    document object types, 120
    hierarchy, 15
    iframe element and, 133
    key W3C types, 121
    referencing, 137
    sibling nodes, 127
    (see also text nodes)
nodeType property, 120, 121, 494
nodeValue property, 121, 122, 123, 495
noembed elements, 375

noframes elements, 375
noframes objects, 811
nohref attribute
    area elements, 222
noHref property
    area objects, 554
nolayer elements, 376
none value, 81
nonidentity operator (!==), 1200
noresize attribute
    frame elements, 288
noResize property
    frame objects, 693
    iframe objects, 711
normalize( ) method, 521
noscript elements, 6, 377
noscript objects, 811
noshade attribute
    hr elements, 302
noShade property
    hr objects, 703
NOT operator (!), 1201
Notation objects, 812
NOTATION_NODE property, 481
notations property
    DocumentType objects, 643
nowrap attribute
    body elements, 237
    div elements, 263
noWrap property
    body objects, 572
    dd objects, 600
    div objects, 607
    dt objects, 647
    td objects, 951
    th objects, 951
null value, 35, 41
Number objects, 1168
number property
    Error objects, 1150

## O

object attribute
    applet elements, 219
object detection
    browser support flagging, 86
    DHTML DOMs and, 39
    embedding data example, 137
    purpose, 33
object elements, 137, 377
object methods, list of, 1243–1256
Object objects, 1172

object objects, 812
object properties
  list of, 1221–1242
object property
  applet objects, 550
  object objects, 818
objects
  abstract objects, 13, 28, 108
  centering, 94–96
  communication with, 11
  Core DOM module and, 12
  document objects, 47, 120–123
  element objects, 29, 40, 56, 118
  form object components, 47
  moving, 96–100
  object detection and, 33
  text content as, 118
  this keyword, 157
  typeof operator and, 34
  (see also event objects)
offscreenBuffering property
  window objects, 991
offsetHeight property, 472–476, 496
offsetLeft property, 472–476, 496
offsetParent property, 496
offsetTop property, 472–476, 496
offsetWidth property, 472–476, 496
offsetX property
  event objects, 665
offsetY property
  event objects, 665
ol elements, 45, 57, 385
ol objects, 819
onabort event, 151, 1018
onactivate event, 1018
onafterprint event, 1018
onafterupdate event, 1019
onbeforeactivate event, 1019
onbeforecopy event, 152, 1019
onbeforecut event, 152, 1019
onbeforedeactivate event, 1020
onbeforeeditfocus event, 1020
onbeforepaste event, 152, 1020
onbeforeprint event, 1018, 1021
onbeforeprint event handler, 152
onbeforeunload event, 1021
onbeforeupdate event, 1021
onblur event, 1022
onblur event handler, 151
onbounce event, 1022
oncellchange event, 1022
onchange event, 1022

onchange event handler, 151, 157
onclick event, 1023
onclick event handler, 107, 150, 151, 156,
    158
oncontextmenu event, 1023
oncontextmenu event handler, 152, 169
oncontrolselect event, 1024
oncopy event, 1024
oncopy event handler, 152
oncut event, 1024
oncut event handler, 152
ondataavailable event, 1024
ondatasetchanged event, 1024
ondatasetcomplete event, 1024
ondblclick event, 1025
ondblclick event handler, 151
ondeactivate event, 1025
ondrag event, 152, 1025
ondragdrop event, 1026
ondragend event, 152, 1025, 1026
ondragenter event, 152, 1026
ondragleave event, 152, 1026
ondragover event, 152, 1026
ondragstart event, 1025, 1026
ondrop event, 152, 1027
onerror event, 1027
onerror event handler, 152
onerrorupdate event, 1027
onfilterchange event, 1027
onfinish event, 1028
onfocus event, 1028
onfocus event handler, 152
onfocusin event, 152, 1028
onfocusout event, 152, 1028
onhelp event, 152, 1028
onkeydown event, 1029
onkeydown event handler, 152, 153, 170
onkeypress event, 1029
onkeypress event handler, 150, 152, 153,
    163, 165, 170
onkeyup event, 1029
onkeyup event handler, 152, 153, 170
onlayoutcomplete event, 1029
onLine property
  navigator object, 803
onload event, 1029
onload event handler, 87, 134, 137, 144,
    150, 152
onload event listener, 166
onlosecapture event, 1030
onmousedown event, 1030
onmousedown event handler, 152, 167, 174

onmouseenter event, 152, 1030
onmouseleave event, 152, 1030
onmousemove event, 1030
onmousemove event handler, 152, 174
onmouseout event, 1031
onmouseout event handler, 110, 152
onmouseover event, 1031
onmouseover event handler, 110, 111, 150,
    152
onmouseup event, 1030
onmouseup event handler, 152, 174
onmousewheel event, 152, 1031
onmove event, 1032
onmove event handler, 152
onmoveend event, 152, 1032
onmovestart event, 152, 1032
onpaste event, 152, 1033
onpropertychange event, 1034
onreadystatechange event, 1034
onreset event, 1034
onreset event handler, 152
onresize event, 1034
onresize event handler, 152
onresizeend event, 1034
onresizestart event, 1034
onrowenter event, 1035
onrowexit event, 1035
onrowsdelete event, 1035
onrowsinserted event, 1035
onscroll event, 152, 1035
onselect event, 1035
onselect event handler, 152
onselectionchange event, 1035
onselectstart event, 152, 1035
onstart event, 1036
onstop event, 1036
onsubmit event, 1036
onsubmit event handler, 152, 162, 163
onunload event, 1036
onunload event handler, 152
opacity filter attribute, 113
open() method
    Document objects, 103
    document objects, 636
    Window object, 105
    window objects, 1003
opener property
    window objects, 106, 992
Opera browser
    Connection preference, 24
    cross-platform style differences, 69
    DHTML support, 32

element referencing schemes, 111
evaluating tests, 34
identified as IE, 33
overlaying to different pages, 38
operating systems
    browser compatibility, 19
    browser differences, 22
    platforms defined, 21
    UI elements and, 31
operators
    assignment operator, 118, 158
    by-value operators, 84
    colon operator, 50, 53
    equal sign operator, 50, 53
    typeof operator, 34, 37
    void operator, 107
optgroup elements, 386
optgroup objects, 820
option elements, 388
option objects, 821
options objects, 824
options property
    select objects, 864
OR operator (||), 1201
originalTarget property
    event objects, 665
orphans attribute (CSS), 1092
orphans property
    CSSStyleDeclaration objects, 906
    style objects, 906
oscpu property
    navigator object, 803
Outdent command, 1285
outerHeight property
    window objects, 992
outerHTML property, 123, 126, 497
outerText property, 123, 497
outerWidth property
    window objects, 992
outline attribute (CSS), 1092
outline property
    CSSStyleDeclaration objects, 906
    style objects, 906
outline-color attribute (CSS), 1093
outlineColor property
    CSSStyleDeclaration objects, 907
    style objects, 907
outline-style attribute (CSS), 1093
outlineStyle property
    CSSStyleDeclaration objects, 907
    style objects, 907
outline-width attribute (CSS), 1094

outlineWidth property
  CSSStyleDeclaration objects, 907
  style objects, 907
overflow attribute, 80
overflow attribute (CSS), 1094
overflow property
  CSSStyleDeclaration objects, 908
  style objects, 908
overflow-x attribute (CSS), 1095
overflowX property
  CSSStyleDeclaration objects, 908
  style objects, 908
overflow-y attribute (CSS), 1095
overflowY property
  CSSStyleDeclaration objects, 908
  style objects, 908
overlapping
  style rules, 66
  wrapping elements versus, 76
  z-index attribute and, 81
OverWrite command, 1285
ownerDocument property, 121, 498
ownerElement property
  Attr objects, 559
  attribute objects, 559
ownerNode property, 116
  styleSheet objects, 926
ownerRule property
  styleSheet objects, 926
owningElement, 116
owningElement property
  styleSheet objects, 926

**P**

p elements, 42, 43, 390
  as block-level element, 45
  custom newsletter example, 143
  descendant selector example, 61–63
  identifier style rule example, 60
  IE DOM example, 118
  important declaration example, 67
  inheritance example, 48
  p.narrow rule example, 58
  text content, 16
p objects, 827
padding
  block-level elements and, 45
  edge measurement attributes and, 78
  element rules, 9
  :first-letter element, 63
  transparent space, 46
padding attribute (CSS), 1096

padding property
  CSSStyleDeclaration objects, 908
  style objects, 908
padding-bottom attribute (CSS), 1097
paddingBottom property
  CSSStyleDeclaration objects, 909
  style objects, 909
padding-left attribute (CSS), 1097
paddingLeft property
  CSSStyleDeclaration objects, 909
  style objects, 909
padding-right attribute (CSS), 1097
paddingRight property
  CSSStyleDeclaration objects, 909
  style objects, 909
padding-top attribute (CSS), 1097
paddingTop property
  CSSStyleDeclaration objects, 909
  style objects, 909
page attribute (CSS), 1097
page branching, 35–37
page loading, 101, 102, 159
page objects, 827
page property
  CSSStyleDeclaration objects, 909
  style objects, 909
page rendering
  absolute positioning and, 35
  browser decision paths, 66
  differences in, 39
  dynamic content, 26
  HTML 4, 6
  improvements in, 14
  style sheet rules, 10
@page rule, 1043
page-break-after attribute (CSS), 1098
pageBreakAfter property
  CSSStyleDeclaration objects, 909
  style objects, 909
page-break-before attribute (CSS), 1098
pageBreakBefore property
  CSSStyleDeclaration objects, 909
  style objects, 909
page-break-inside attribute (CSS), 1099
pageBreakInside property
  CSSStyleDeclaration objects, 910
  style objects, 910
pages objects, 828
pages property
  styleSheet objects, 927
pagex attribute
  layer elements, 352

pageX property, 175
  event objects, 665
  layer objects, 769
pageXOffset property
  window objects, 992
pagey attribute
  layer elements, 352
pageY property, 175
  event objects, 665
  layer objects, 769
pageYOffset property
  window objects, 992
palette property
  embed objects, 650
param elements, 391
param objects, 829
parent object, 136
parent property
  window objects, 993
parent-child relationship
  descendant selectors and, 63
  element containment and, 47
  elements and, 14
  HTML document example, 15
  nodes and, 18, 121
  positioning context, 74
parentElement property, 498
parentElement( ) method
  TextRange objects, 967
parentLayer property
  layer objects, 769
parentNode property, 121, 128, 175, 498
parentNode( ) method
  TreeWalker objects, 977
parentRule property
  CSSRule objects, 591
  cssRule objects, 591
  rule objects, 591
parentStyleSheet property
  CSSRule objects, 591
  cssRule objects, 591
  rule objects, 591
  styleSheet objects, 927
parentTextEdit property, 499
parentWindow property
  document objects, 621
parse( ) method
  Date objects, 1140
parseFloat( ) method
  Global objects, 1161
parseInt( ) method, 84
  Global objects, 1160
password objects, 831

Paste command, 1285
pasteHTML( ) method (RangeRef
    object), 141
pasteHTML( ) method
  TextRange objects, 967
pathname property
  a objects, 537
  area objects, 554
  location objects, 785
pause attribute (CSS), 1099
pause property
  CSSStyleDeclaration objects, 881, 910
  style objects, 881, 910
pause-after attribute (CSS), 1100
pauseAfter property
  CSSStyleDeclaration objects, 881, 910
  style objects, 881, 910
pause-before attribute (CSS), 1100
pauseBefore property
  CSSStyleDeclaration objects, 881, 910
  style objects, 881, 910
personalbar objects, 604, 831
personalbar property
  window objects, 987, 993
PI property
  Math object, 1163
pica units, 10, 78
pitch attribute (CSS), 1100
pitch property
  CSSStyleDeclaration objects, 881, 910
  style objects, 881, 910
pitch-range attribute (CSS), 1101
pitchRange property
  CSSStyleDeclaration objects, 881, 910
  style objects, 881, 910
pixel units, 78
pixelBottom property
  CSSStyleDeclaration objects, 910
  style objects, 910
pixelDepth property
  screen object, 856
pixelHeight property
  CSSStyleDeclaration objects, 910
  style objects, 910
pixelLeft property
  CSSStyleDeclaration objects, 910
  style objects, 910
pixelRight property
  CSSStyleDeclaration objects, 910
  style objects, 910
pixelTop property, 84
  CSSStyleDeclaration objects, 910
  style objects, 910

pixelWidth property
  CSSStyleDeclaration objects, 910
  style objects, 910
pkcs11 property
  window objects, 986, 993
plaintext elements, 394
plaintext objects, 831
platform property
  navigator object, 804
platforms
  cross-platform strategies, 32–41
  CSS considerations, 49
  defined, 21, 22
  downloadable fonts, 27
  dynamic content, 26
  element object references, 24, 25
  event models, 26
  Navigator 4 DHTML, 22, 23
  Netscape 6 (Mozilla) DHTML, 28–32
  style sheet differences, 69
  (see also browsers)
play-during attribute (CSS), 1101
playDuring property
  CSSStyleDeclaration objects, 881, 911
  style objects, 881, 911
plugin objects, 831
plugins objects, 833
plugins property
  document objects, 621
  navigator object, 804
pluginspage attribute
  embed elements, 272
pluginspage property
  embed objects, 650
pluginurl attribute
  embed elements, 273
point units, 78
point-size attribute
  font elements, 277
pop() method
  Array objects, 1131
popup objects, 834
port property
  a objects, 538
  area objects, 554
  location objects, 785
posBottom property
  style, CSSStyleDeclaration objects, 911
posHeight property
  style, CSSStyleDeclaration objects, 911

position attribute
  fixed value, 77
  positioning context and, 72–76
  positioning elements, 71
position attribute (CSS), 1101
position property
  CSSStyleDeclaration objects, 912
  style objects, 912
positioning
  attributes, 25, 77–82
  box positioning, 46
  common tasks, 94–100
  creating positionable elements, 71–77
  cross-platform scripting, 85–94
  CSS-P and, 9
  element positioning, 11, 70
  graphics rule, 25
  layer elements and, 12
  Netscape 6, 29
  scripting and, 82–85
POSITIVE_INFINITY property
  Number objects, 1170
posLeft property
  style, CSSStyleDeclaration objects, 911
posRight property
  style, CSSStyleDeclaration objects, 911
posTop property, 84
  style, CSSStyleDeclaration objects, 911
posWidth property
  style, CSSStyleDeclaration objects, 911
pow() method
  Math object, 1167
pqg attribute
  keygen elements, 345
pre elements, 395
pre objects, 837
precedence rules, 66–69
preference() method
  navigator object, 807
prefix property, 493, 499
preventDefault() method, 164
  event objects, 677
previous property
  history objects, 700
previousNode() method
  NodeIterator objects, 810
  TreeWalker objects, 978
previousPage() method
  table objects, 940
previousSibling property, 121, 493, 499
previousSibling() method
  TreeWalker objects, 977

prevValue property
  event objects, 664, 666
print( ) method
  window objects, 1005
ProcessingInstruction objects, 837
PROCESSING_INSTRUCTION_NODE
      property, 481
product property
  navigator object, 804
productSub property
  navigator object, 804
profile attribute
  head elements, 300
profile property
  head objects, 699
prompt attribute
  isindex elements, 343
prompt property
  isindex objects, 764
prompt( ) method
  window objects, 1005
prompter property
  window objects, 985, 993
properties
  accessing, 14, 25, 112
  background properties, 50
  client-side activities, 101
  controlling, 11
  Core DOM module and, 12
  data types of, 113
  default values, 476
  elements sharing, 18
  event handlers as, 158, 160
  event objects, 26, 155–156
  list of, 1221–1242
  nodes and, 16, 121
  object detection and, 33
  populating, 30
  positionable elements, 83, 84
  positioning attributes as, 82
  rule objects, 116
  style sheet rules and, 10
  styleSheet objects, 116
  text content as, 118
  typeof operator and, 34
  value types, 471
  (see also style properties)
propertyIsEnumerable( ) method
  Object objects, 1173
propertyName property
  event objects, 666

propertyName property (Event object), 154
protocol property
  a objects, 538
  area objects, 555
  document objects, 621
  img objects, 721
  location objects, 786
protocolLong property
  a objects, 538
prototype property
  Array objects, 1129
  Boolean objects, 1134
  Date objects, 1136
  Error objects, 1150
  function objects, 1154
  img objects, 721
  Number objects, 1170
  Object objects, 1173
  RegExp objects, 1176
  String objects, 1182
pseudoClass property
  page objects, 828
pseudo-classes, 1041
pseudo-elements, 1040
publicId property
  DocumentType objects, 643
push( ) method
  Array objects, 1131

Q

q elements, 397
q objects, 837
qualifier property
  event objects, 666
queryCommandEnabled( ) method
  commands for (list), 1283
  document objects, 636
  TextRange objects, 968
queryCommandIndeterm( ) method
  commands for (list), 1283
  document objects, 637
  TextRange objects, 968
queryCommandState( ) method
  commands for (list), 1283
  document objects, 637
  TextRange objects, 968
queryCommandSupported( ) method
  commands for (list), 1283
  document objects, 637
  TextRange objects, 968

queryCommandText( ) method
   commands for (list), 1283
   document objects, 637
   TextRange objects, 969
queryCommandValue( ) method
   document objects, 638
   TextRange objects, 969
querying, CGI programs and, 148
queues, event, 153
quirks, 10, 11
quotes attribute (CSS), 1102
quotes property
   CSSStyleDeclaration objects, 912
   style objects, 912

# R

radio objects, 838
random( ) method
   Math object, 1167
Range objects, 141, 838
rangeCount property
   selection objects, 870
RangeException objects, 849
rangeOffset property
   event objects, 666
rangeParent property
   event objects, 667
RangeRef object, 141
rb elements, 397
rb objects, 852
rbc elements, 398
rbspan attribute
   rt elements, 400
readonly attribute
   input elements, 336
readOnly property
   CSSRule objects, 592
   cssRule objects, 592
   input (type="password") objects, 747
   input (type="text") objects, 761
   rule objects, 592
   styleSheet objects, 927
   textarea objects, 958
readyState property, 499
   document objects, 621
reason property
   event objects, 667
recalc( ) method
   document objects, 638
recordNumber property, 500
recordset property
   event objects, 667

referrer property
   document objects, 622
Refresh command, 1285
refresh( ) method
   plugin objects, 833
   table objects, 941
RegExp objects, 1174
regular expression objects, 1177
rel attribute
   a elements, 207
   link elements, 359
rel property
   a objects, 539
   link objects, 778
relatedNode property
   event objects, 668
relatedTarget property
   event objects, 668
relationships (see parent-child relationship)
relative positioning, 72–76
relative value (position attribute), 72
releaseCapture( ) method, 169, 522
releaseEvents( ) method
   document objects, 638
   layer objects, 773
   window objects, 1006
reload( ) method
   location objects, 787
remove( ) method
   options objects, 826
   select objects, 867
removeAllRanges( ) method
   selection objects, 874
removeAttribute( ) method, 522
removeAttributeNode( ) method, 522
removeAttributeNS( ) method, 523
removeBehavior( ) method, 523
removeBinding( ) method
   document objects, 625, 638
removeChild( ) method, 123, 524
removeEventListener( ) method, 161, 168,
   524
   window objects, 1006
removeExpression( ) method, 525
RemoveFormat command, 1285
removeNamedItem( ) method
   attributes objects, 562
   NamedNodeMap objects, 562
removeNamedItemNS( ) method
   attributes objects, 562
   NamedNodeMap objects, 562
removeNode( ) method, 120, 525

removeProperty() method
    CSSStyleDeclaration objects, 923
    style objects, 923
removeRange() method
    selection objects, 874
removeRule() method
    styleSheet objects, 930
rendering (see page rendering)
repeat property
    event objects, 668
replace() method
    location objects, 787
    String objects, 1187
replaceAdjacentText() method, 120, 525
replaceChild() method, 122, 123, 128, 526
replaceData() method
    Comment objects, 589
    comment objects, 589
    Text objects, 954
replaceNode() method, 120, 527
reset objects, 850
reset() method
    form objects, 687
resizeBy() method
    layer objects, 773
    window objects, 1006
resizeTo() method
    layer objects, 773
    window objects, 1007
return statements, 163, 164, 1208
return value, 162
returnValue property
    event objects, 669
    window objects, 993
returnValue property (Event object), 163
rev attribute
    a elements, 208
    link elements, 360
rev property
    a objects, 539
    link objects, 778
reverse() method
    Array objects, 1131
RGB values, 1267
richness attribute (CSS), 1103
richness property
    CSSStyleDeclaration objects, 881, 912
    style objects, 881, 912
right attribute, 78, 84
right attribute (CSS), 1103
right property, 84
    CSSStyleDeclaration objects, 912
    style objects, 912

TextRectangle objects, 970
:right pseudo-class, 1042
rightContext property
    RegExp objects, 1176
rightmargin attribute
    body elements, 237
rightMargin property
    body objects, 573
right-shift operator (>>), 1194
root node, 126
root property
    NodeIterator objects, 810
    TreeWalker objects, 977
round() method
    Math object, 1167
routeEvent() method
    document objects, 639
    layer objects, 774
    window objects, 1007
rowIndex property
    tr objects, 974
rows attribute
    frameset elements, 296
rows objects, 850
rows property
    frameset objects, 698
    table objects, 937
    tbody objects, 945
    textarea objects, 958
    tfoot objects, 945
    thead objects, 945
rowSpan property
    td objects, 951
    th objects, 951
rp elements, 399
rt elements, 399
rt objects, 852
rtc elements, 398
ruby elements, 400
ruby objects, 852
ruby-align attribute (CSS), 1104
rubyAlign property
    CSSStyleDeclaration objects, 913
    style objects, 913
ruby-overhang attribute (CSS), 1104
rubyOverhang property
    CSSStyleDeclaration objects, 913
    style objects, 913
ruby-position attribute (CSS), 1104
rubyPosition property
    CSSStyleDeclaration objects, 913
    style objects, 913

rule objects, 116, 589, 852
rule sets, 52, 53, 54
rules
   at-rule, 55
   attribute selectors, 65
   cascade precedence rules, 66–69
   CSS recommendation and, 9
   CSS-P attributes, 77
   curly braces, 52
   free-range class rule, 59
   HTML 4 end tags, 8
   ID selector and, 60
   @media rule, 78
   modifying styleSheet objects, 117
   one-dot evaluation rule, 34
   overlaying to different pages, 38
   p.narrow rule, 58, 62
   positioning graphics, 25
   style sheets, 10, 49
   styleSheet objects and, 116
   two-type selector rules, 61
   visual properties, 10
   (see also style rules)
rules objects, 595, 852
rules property, 116
   styleSheet objects, 927
   table objects, 937
runtimeStyle objects, 852
runtimeStyle property, 85, 500

## S

s elements, 401
s objects, 564, 853
samp elements, 401
samp objects, 542, 853
scheme attribute
   meta elements, 372
scheme property
   meta objects, 797
scope property
   td objects, 951
   th objects, 951
scopeName property, 501
screen object, 853
screen property
   window objects, 994
screenLeft property
   window objects, 994
screenTop property
   window objects, 994

screenX property
   event objects, 669
   window objects, 994
screenY property
   event objects, 669
   window objects, 994
script elements, 6, 160, 183, 402
script objects, 857
ScriptEngine( ) method
   Global objects, 1161
ScriptEngineBuildVersion( ) method
   Global objects, 1161
ScriptEngineMajorVersion( ) method
   Global objects, 1161
ScriptEngineMinorVersion( ) method
   Global objects, 1161
scripting
   client-side includes, 133–140
   cross-platforms, 85–94
   dynamic changing attribute vales, 82–85
   dynamic content, 101
   event handlers, 26, 158
   linking to multiple frames, 107
   modifying style sheet contents, 116
   positioning and, 11
   reconciling idiosyncrasies, 39
   (see also client-side scripting)
scripts
   access to nodes, 126
   manipulating elements, 150
   modifying content, 16
   style rules and, 10
   validating in XHTML, 183
scripts objects, 860
scripts property
   document objects, 622
scroll attribute
   body elements, 238
   html elements, 303
scroll property
   body objects, 573
scroll value (overflow attribute), 80
scroll( ) method
   window objects, 1007
scrollamount attribute
   marquee elements, 368
scrollAmount property
   marquee objects, 792
scrollbar-3dlight-color attribute (CSS), 1105
scrollbar3dLightColor property
   style, CSSStyleDeclaration objects, 913

scrollbar-arrow-color attribute (CSS), 1105
scrollbarArrowColor property
  style, CSSStyleDeclaration objects, 913
scrollbar-base-color attribute (CSS), 1105
scrollbarBaseColor property
  style, CSSStyleDeclaration objects, 913
scrollbar-darkShadow-color attribute
    (CSS), 1105
scrollbarDarkShadowColor property
  style, CSSStyleDeclaration objects, 913
scrollbar-face-color attribute (CSS), 1105
scrollbarFaceColor property
  style, CSSStyleDeclaration objects, 913
scrollbar-highlight-color attribute
    (CSS), 1105
scrollbarHighlightColor property
  style, CSSStyleDeclaration objects, 913
scrollbars, 38, 134
  in clipping regions, 80
scrollbars objects, 604, 861
scrollbars property
  window objects, 987, 995
scrollbar-shadow-color attribute (CSS), 1105
scrollbarShadowColor property
  style, CSSStyleDeclaration objects, 913
scrollbar-track-color attribute (CSS), 1105
scrollbarTrackColor property
  style, CSSStyleDeclaration objects, 913
scrollBy() method
  window objects, 1008
scrollByLines() method
  window objects, 1008
scrollByPages() method
  window objects, 1008
scrolldelay attribute
  marquee elements, 368
scrollDelay property
  marquee objects, 792
scrollHeight property, 501
scrolling attribute
  frame elements, 289
  iframe elements, 309
scrolling property
  frame objects, 693
  iframe objects, 711
scrollIntoView() method, 527
scrollLeft property, 502
scrollTo() method
  window objects, 1008
scrollTop property, 502
scrollWidth property, 96, 501
scrollX property
  window objects, 995

scrollY property
  window objects, 995
search engines, 32, 38
search property
  a objects, 539
  area objects, 555
  location objects, 786
search() method
  String objects, 1187
secondary windows, 105–106
sectionRowIndex property
  tr objects, 975
security attribute
  frame elements, 289
  iframe elements, 310
security property
  document objects, 623
securityPolicy property
  navigator object, 805
select elements, 407
select objects, 861
select() method
  input (type="file") objects, 737
  input (type="password") objects, 749
  input (type="text") objects, 763
  textarea objects, 960
  TextRange objects, 969
SelectAll command, 1285
selectAllChildren() method
  selection objects, 874
selected attribute
  option elements, 389
selected property
  option objects, 823
selectedIndex property
  select objects, 864
selection objects, 868
selection property
  document objects, 623
selectionEnd property
  input (type="password") objects, 747
selectionLanguageChange() method
  selection objects, 875
selectionStart property
  input (type="password") objects, 747
selectNode() method
  Range objects, 846
selectNodeContents() method
  Range objects, 846
selectors
  advanced subgroup, 63–66
  assignment shortcuts, 53
  common subgroup, 56–63

selectors *(continued)*
  determining specificity, 68
  lowercase recommendation, 52
  precedence rules, 67
  purpose, 51
selectorText property, 116
  CSSRule objects, 592
  cssRule objects, 592
  page objects, 828
  rule objects, 592
self property
  window objects, 995
@set statement, 1212
setActive() method, 527
setAttribute() method, 30, 111, 112, 133,
    527
setAttributeNode() method, 528
setAttributeNodeNS() method, 529
setAttributeNS() method, 529
setCapture() method, 169, 530
setCursor() method
  window objects, 1009
setData() method
  clipboardData objects, 585
  dataTransfer objects, 600
setDate() method
  Date objects, 1141
setEnd() method
  Range objects, 847
setEndAfter() method
  Range objects, 848
setEndBefore() method
  Range objects, 848
setEndPoint() method
  TextRange objects, 969
setExpression() method, 531
setFullYear() method
  Date objects, 1141
setHours() method
  Date objects, 1141
setInterval() method, 98, 113
  window objects, 1009
setMilliseconds() method
  Date objects, 1141
setMinutes() method
  Date objects, 1142
setMonth() method
  Date objects, 1142
setNamedItem() method
  attributes objects, 563
  NamedNodeMap objects, 563

setNamedItemNS() method
  attributes objects, 563
  NamedNodeMap objects, 563
setProperty() method
  CSSStyleDeclaration objects, 923
  style objects, 923
setSeconds() method
  Date objects, 1142
setStart() method
  Range objects, 847
setStartAfter() method
  Range objects, 848
setStartBefore() method
  Range objects, 848
setTime() method
  Date objects, 1142
setTimeout() method
  window objects, 1010
setUTCDate() method
  Date objects, 1143
setUTCFullYear() method
  Date objects, 1143
setUTCHours() method
  Date objects, 1143
setUTCMilliseconds() method
  Date objects, 1143
setUTCMinutes() method
  Date objects, 1144
setUTCMonth() method
  Date objects, 1144
setUTCSeconds() method
  Date objects, 1144
setYear() method
  Date objects, 1144
shape attribute
  a elements, 208
  area elements, 222
shape property
  a objects, 540
  area objects, 555
sheet property
  link objects, 779
  LinkStyle objects, 782
  style (element) objects, 877
shift() method
  Array objects, 1131
shiftKey property, 170
  event objects, 669
shiftLeft property
  event objects, 670

shortcuts
    applying values to edges, 46
    assigning declarations, 53
    by-value operators and, 84
show() method
    popup objects, 836
showHelp() method
    window objects, 1011
showModalDialog() method
    window objects, 1011
showModelessDialog() method
    window objects, 1012
sibling nodes, 127
siblingAbove property
    layer objects, 769
siblingBelow property
    layer objects, 769
sidebar property
    window objects, 985, 995
sin() method
    Math object, 1168
size attribute
    basefont elements, 228
    font elements, 277
    hr elements, 302
    input elements, 336
    select elements, 411
    spacer elements, 413
size attribute (CSS), 1106
size property
    basefont objects, 566
    CSSStyleDeclaration objects, 914
    font objects, 682
    hr objects, 703
    input (type="file") objects, 736
    input (type="password") objects, 747
    input (type="text") objects, 761
    select objects, 865
    style objects, 914
sizeToContent() method
    window objects, 1013
slice() method
    Array objects, 1131
    String objects, 1187
small elements, 411
small objects, 564, 875
small() method
    String objects, 1188
sort() method
    Array objects, 1132
source code
    adding style sheets in, 51
    default stacking order, 81

proprietary attributes and, 8
    XHTML validation, 7
source property
    regular expression objects, 1179
sourceIndex property, 502
spacer elements, 412
span attribute
    col elements, 250
    colgroup elements, 255
span elements, 43, 74, 75, 413
    characteristics, 43
    className property, 115
    color property, 113
    content modification example, 128
    dragging elements example, 174
    element text and, 118
    generating elements example, 127
    HTML property example, 125
    positioning example, 71, 73, 74
    referencing elements example, 83
span objects, 875
span property
    col objects, 587
    colgroup objects, 587
speak attribute (CSS), 1106
speak property
    CSSStyleDeclaration objects, 881, 914
    style objects, 881, 914
speak-header attribute (CSS), 1107
speakHeader property
    CSSStyleDeclaration objects, 881, 914
    style objects, 881, 914
speakNumeral
    CSSStyleDeclaration objects, 914
speak-numeral attribute (CSS), 1107
speakNumeral property
    CSSStyleDeclaration objects, 881
    style objects, 881, 914
speak-punctuation attribute (CSS), 1107
speakPunctuation property
    CSSStyleDeclaration objects, 881, 914
    style objects, 881, 914
specificity of selectors, 68
specified property
    Attr objects, 559
    attribute objects, 559
speech-rate attribute (CSS), 1108
speechRate property
    CSSStyleDeclaration objects, 881, 914
    style objects, 881, 914
splice() method
    Array objects, 1132

split( ) method
    String objects, 1188
splitText( ) method
    Text objects, 955
sqrt( ) method
    Math object, 1168
SQRT1_2 property
    Math object, 1164
SQRT2 property
    Math object, 1164
src attribute
    applet elements, 219
    bgsound elements, 230
    embed elements, 273
    frame elements, 290
    iframe elements, 310
    ilayer elements, 315
    img elements, 325
    input elements, 337
    layer elements, 353
    link elements, 360
    script elements, 405
    xml elements, 467
src property
    applet objects, 550
    bgsound objects, 568
    embed objects, 650
    event bubbling, 166
    frame objects, 694
    iframe objects, 711
    image objects, 108, 109
    img element, 110
    img objects, 721
    input (type="image") objects, 743
    layer objects, 769
    script objects, 859
    xml objects, 1013
srcElement element, 156
srcElement property
    event objects, 670
srcFilter property
    event objects, 670
srcUrn property
    event objects, 670
stacking order, 81, 175
standardization
    browsers and, 19, 21, 117
    common denominator, 39
    coordinating with version releases, 4
    CSS modularization, 183–184
    CSS-P origin, 70
    DOM and, 12, 184, 186

HTML implementation, 5–7
IE DHTML and, 23
illegal characters, 111
lowercase tag selectors, 52
Mozilla browser and, 28, 29
W3C modularization, 180, 181
XHTML, 7–9, 181–183
standby attribute
    object elements, 383
standby property
    object objects, 818
start attribute
    img elements, 325
    input elements, 337
    ol elements, 386
start property
    img objects, 722
    input (type="image") objects, 743
    ol objects, 820
start( ) method
    marquee objects, 792
startContainer property
    Range objects, 840
startOffset property
    Range objects, 841
statements
    assignment statement, 158, 159
    inline statements, 157
    referencing elements, 24
    return statements, 163, 164
static objects, 1124
static value (position attribute), 72, 77
status property
    button objects, 577
    input (type="checkbox") objects, 733
    input (type="radio") objects, 752
    textarea objects, 958
    window objects, 995
statusbar objects, 604, 876
statusbar property
    window objects, 987, 996
stop( ) method
    marquee objects, 793
    window objects, 1013
stopPropagation( ) method, 168
    event objects, 677
stress attribute (CSS), 1108
stress property
    CSSStyleDeclaration objects, 881, 914
    style objects, 881, 914
Strict validation, 8
strike elements, 415

strike objects, 564, 876
strike( ) method
   String objects, 1188
String objects, 1181
strings
   CSS2Properties collection, 113
   empty strings, 35
   getElementById( ) method, 41
   innerText property, 14
   referencing elements, 24
   typeof operator, 35
strong elements, 416
strong objects, 542, 876
style attributes, 199
   cross-platform style differences, 69
   filtering, 27
   iframe element, 134
   inheritance and, 48
   number limits, 53
   proprietary, 113
   pseudo-element example, 63
   selecting style sheet style, 56
   specifics, 49
   style rules and, 66
   value types, 1037–1040
style definition, 6, 9
style (element) objects, 876
style elements, 416
   accessing styleSheet objects, 116
   embedding style sheets, 51–54
   positioning elements example, 71
   separating content, 56
   type attribute, 49
style objects, 878
style properties, 503
   components, 25
   CSSRule objects, 592
   cssRule objects, 592
   element objects, 56, 84
   features, 113
   Netscape 6 and, 29
   object detection example, 34
   page objects, 828
   recommendations, 117
   rule objects, 592
   W3C DOM specification, 29
style rules, 49, 60, 71, 143
style sheets
   accessing properties, 25
   advanced subgroup selectors, 63–66
   at-rules, 55, 67, 78, 1042
   block-level elements, 45–47

   browser variance in rendering, 39
   cascade precedence rules, 66–69
   common subgroup selectors, 56–63
   embedding, 51–56
   HTML structures, 42–45
   modifying through scripts, 116
   overlaying to different pages, 38
   overview, 9
   pseudo-classes, 64, 1041
   pseudo-elements, 63, 1040
   setting rules with, 10
   style attributes, 49
   types of containment, 47–48
   XHTML and, 7, 181
styleFloat property
   CSSStyleDeclaration objects, 914
   style objects, 914
styleSheet objects, 84, 116, 117, 924
styleSheet property
   CSSRule objects, 593
   cssRule objects, 593
   link objects, 779
   rule objects, 593
   style (element) objects, 877
StyleSheetList objects, 930
styleSheets array (Document object), 116
styleSheets objects, 930
styleSheets property
   document objects, 623
sub elements, 418
sub objects, 931
sub( ) method
   String objects, 1188
submit objects, 932
submit( ) method
   form objects, 687
substr( ) method
   String objects, 1189
substring( ) method
   String objects, 1189
substringData( ) method
   Comment objects, 589
   comment objects, 589
   Text objects, 955
subtraction operator (-), 1201
suffixes property
   mimeType objects, 798
summary property
   table objects, 938
Sun Microsystems, 18
sup elements, 418
sup objects, 931, 932

sup( ) method
    String objects, 1189
supports( ) method, 123
suppress attribute
    img elements, 326
surroundContents( ) method
    Range objects, 848
swapNode( ) method, 120, 532
swapping images, 108–111
switch/case statement, 1208
systemId property
    DocumentType objects, 644
systemLanguage property
    navigator object, 805

# T

tabindex attribute, 200
    select elements, 411
tabIndex property, 503
table objects, 932
table-layout attribute (CSS), 1109
tableLayout property
    CSSStyleDeclaration objects, 914
    style objects, 914
tables, 30, 129–133
tag attributes, 157–158, 164
tagName property, 503
tags
    case-sensitivity, 8
    changing attribute values, 111, 112
    client-side scripting, 6
    element nodes and, 14
    embedding vent handlers, 157
    end tags, 8, 42
    innerHTML property, 119
    names as links, 9
    nesting, 13
tags objects, 941
tags property
    document objects, 623
tags( ) method
    all objects, 544
    anchors objects, 546
    areas objects, 557
    cells objects, 580
    children objects, 583
    forms objects, 688
    images objects, 713
    links objects, 781
    options objects, 826
    rows objects, 851

scripts objects, 861
    tBodies objects, 943
tagUrn property, 501, 504
taintEnabled( ) method
    navigator object, 807
tan( ) method
    Math object, 1168
target attribute, 8, 107
    a elements, 209
    area elements, 223
    base elements, 226
    form elements, 283
    link elements, 361
target element
    event bubbling, 167
    event capture and, 168
    event objects, 156
    processing events, 165
    this keyword, 157
target property
    a objects, 540
    area objects, 556
    base objects, 565
    event objects, 671
    form objects, 686
    link objects, 779
tBodies objects, 942
tBodies property
    table objects, 938
tbody element object, 129, 133
tbody objects, 943
td element
    containment example, 47
    creation process example, 127
    dynamic content, 129
    element text and, 118
    generating elements example, 127
    HTML property example, 125
td objects, 947
test( ) method
    regular expression objects, 1180
testing
    evaluation tests, 34
    importance of, 39
    prelease versions, 4
text
    appending, 118, 127
    element text, 12, 118–123, 142
    pseudo-elements and inserting, 63
    working with ranges, 140–142

text alignment
  inside the box
    bottom value, 193
    center value, 193
    left value, 193
    right value, 193
    top value, 193
  outside the box
    absbottom value, 192
    absmiddle value, 192
    baseline value, 192
    bottom value, 192
    left value, 192
    middle value, 192
    right value, 193
    texttop value, 193
    top value, 193
  vertical inside element
    baseline value, 194
    bottom value, 194
    middle value, 194
    top value, 194
text attribute
  body elements, 238
text nodes
  creation process, 127
  defined, 14
  document tree structure, 126
  as event listeners, 167
  implementation considerations, 123
  replacing text, 122
  text in elements as, 30
  W3C node example, 121
  whitespace and, 137
Text objects, 952
text objects, 952
text property
  a objects, 541
  body objects, 573
  Comment objects, 588
  comment objects, 588
  option objects, 823
  script objects, 859
  TextRange objects, 962
  title objects, 971
text ranges, 140–142
text-align attribute (CSS), 1109
textAlign property
  CSSStyleDeclaration objects, 915
  style objects, 915
text-align-last attribute (CSS), 1110

textAlignLast property
  CSSStyleDeclaration objects, 915
  style objects, 915
textarea objects, 955
text-autospace attribute (CSS), 1110
textAutospace property
  CSSStyleDeclaration objects, 915
  style objects, 915
text-decoration attribute, 63
text-decoration attribute (CSS), 1110
textDecoration property
  CSSStyleDeclaration objects, 916
  style objects, 916
textDecorationBlink property
  style, CSSStyleDeclaration objects, 916
textDecorationLineThrough property
  style, CSSStyleDeclaration objects, 916
textDecorationNone property
  style, CSSStyleDeclaration objects, 916
textDecorationOverline property
  style, CSSStyleDeclaration objects, 916
textDecorationUnderline property
  style, CSSStyleDeclaration objects, 916
text-indent attribute (CSS), 1111
textIndent property
  CSSStyleDeclaration objects, 916
  style objects, 916
text-justify attribute (CSS), 1112
textJustify property
  CSSStyleDeclaration objects, 917
  style objects, 917
text-kashida-space attribute (CSS), 1112
textKashidaSpace property
  CSSStyleDeclaration objects, 917
  style objects, 917
textLength property
  input (type="password") objects, 748
TextNode objects, 960
TEXT_NODE property, 481
text-overflow attribute (CSS), 1113
textOverflow property
  CSSStyleDeclaration objects, 917
  style objects, 917
TextRange objects, 141, 149, 960
  IE commands for (list), 1283
TextRectangle objects, 970
text-shadow attribute (CSS), 1113
textShadow property
  CSSStyleDeclaration objects, 918
  style objects, 918
text-transform attribute (CSS), 1114

textTransform property
   CSSStyleDeclaration objects, 918
   style objects, 918
text-underline-position attribute (CSS), 1114
textUnderlinePosition property
   CSSStyleDeclaration objects, 918
   style objects, 918
tfoot elements, 133
tfoot objects, 943, 971
tFoot property
   table objects, 938
th objects, 947, 971
thead elements, 133
thead objects, 943, 971
tHead property
   table objects, 938
this keyword, 157
this operator, 1203
throw statement, 1209
timeStamp property
   event objects, 671
title attribute, 201
title objects, 971
title property, 504
   document objects, 624
   styleSheet objects, 928
toArray() method
   VBArray objects, 1191
toDateString() method
   Date objects, 1145
toElement property
   event objects, 671
toExponential() method
   Number objects, 1170
toFixed() method
   Number objects, 1170
toGMTString() method
   Date objects, 1145
toLocaleDateString() method
   Date objects, 1145
toLocaleLowerCase() method
   String objects, 1190
toLocaleString() method
   Array objects, 1133
   Date objects, 1145
   Number objects, 1171
   Object objects, 1174
toLocaleTimeString() method
   Date objects, 1146
toLocaleUpperCase() method
   String objects, 1190

toLowerCase() method
   String objects, 1190
toolbar objects, 604, 972
toolbar property
   window objects, 987, 996
top attribute, 89
   CSS-P, 72
   ilayer elements, 315, 316
   layer elements, 352, 353
   positioning, 72, 74, 75
   positioning property, 84
   relative positioning and, 75
   values, 78
top attribute (CSS), 1115
top property, 84
   CSSStyleDeclaration objects, 919
   layer objects, 770
   style objects, 919
   TextRectangle objects, 970
   window objects, 996
topmargin attribute
   body elements, 238
topMargin property
   body objects, 573
toPrecision() method
   Number objects, 1171
toString() method
   Array objects, 1133
   Boolean objects, 1134
   Date objects, 1146
   Error objects, 1150
   function objects, 1155
   Number objects, 1171
   Object objects, 1174
   Range objects, 849
   selection objects, 875
   String objects, 1190
toTimeString() method
   Date objects, 1146
toUpperCase() method
   String objects, 1190
toUTCString() method
   Date objects, 1146
tr element, 129
tr objects, 972
Transitional doctype, 133
TreeWalker objects, 976
truespeed attribute
   marquee elements, 369
trueSpeed property
   marquee objects, 792
try/catch statement, 1209

tt objects, 564, 978
type attribute
  a elements, 210
  button elements, 243
  embed elements, 274
  input elements, 338
  li elements, 356
  link elements, 361
  object elements, 384
  ol elements, 386
  param elements, 393
  script elements, 406
  spacer elements, 413
  style elements, 417
  ul elements, 465
type attribute (style element), 52
type property
  a objects, 541
  button objects, 577
  CSSRule objects, 593
  cssRule objects, 593
  embed objects, 651
  event objects, 671
  input (type="button") objects, 728
  input (type="checkbox") objects, 733
  input (type="file") objects, 736
  input (type="hidden") objects, 740
  input (type="image") objects, 743
  input (type="password") objects, 748
  input (type="radio") objects, 753
  input (type="reset") objects, 755
  input (type="submit") objects, 757
  input (type="text") objects, 762
  li objects, 775
  link objects, 780
  menu objects, 795
  mimeType objects, 798
  object objects, 818
  ol objects, 820
  param objects, 830
  rule objects, 593
  script objects, 859
  select objects, 865
  selection objects, 870
  style (element) objects, 877
  styleSheet objects, 928
  textarea objects, 959
  ul objects, 979
type selector, 52
typeDetail property
  selection objects, 870
typeof operator, 34, 37, 1204

**U**

u elements, 464
u objects, 564, 978
ubound( ) method
  VBArray objects, 1191
UIEvent objects, 978
ul elements, 45, 464
ul objects, 978
UnBookmark command, 1286
undefined property
  Global objects, 1156
Underline command, 1286
unescape( ) method
  Global objects, 1161
unicode-bidi attribute (CSS), 1115
unicodeBidi property
  CSSStyleDeclaration objects, 919
  style objects, 919
uniqueID property, 504
units attribute
  embed elements, 274
units, edge measurement attributes, 78
units property
  embed objects, 651
Unlink command, 1286
Unselect command, 1286
unselectable attribute, 201
unshift( ) method
  Array objects, 1133
unwatch( ) method
  Global objects, 1162
updateInterval property
  screen object, 856
URIs (Universal Resource Identifiers), 191,
    471, 1038
URL property
  document objects, 624
url property
  meta objects, 797
URLs (Uniform Resource Locators)
  iframe elements, 133, 135
  image swapping, 108
  javascript: pseudo-URL, 107
  navigating to hardcoded, 163
  values, 191, 471, 1038
URLUnencoded property
  document objects, 624
urn attribute
  a elements, 210
urn property
  a objects, 541

urns( ) method
   all objects, 544
   anchors objects, 546
   areas objects, 558
   cells objects, 580
   childNodes objects, 582
   children objects, 583
   forms objects, 689
   images objects, 713
   links objects, 782
   NodeList objects, 582
   options objects, 826
   rows objects, 851
   scripts objects, 861
   tBodies objects, 943
usemap attribute
   img elements, 326
   input elements, 339
   object elements, 384
useMap property
   img objects, 722
   input (type="image") objects, 743
   object objects, 818
USER_AGENT environment variable, 36
userAgent property
   navigator object, 805
userLanguage property
   navigator object, 806
userProfile objects, 979
userProfile property
   navigator object, 806
UTC( ) method
   Date objects, 1147

## V

validation
   documents and, 7
   event binding and, 157, 159
   Strict validation, 8
   XHTML, 151, 157, 159, 183
valign attribute
   caption elements, 245
   col elements, 250
   colgroup elements, 255
vAlign property
   caption objects, 578
   col objects, 587
   colgroup objects, 587
   tbody objects, 945
   td objects, 952
   tfoot objects, 945
   th objects, 952

thead objects, 945
   tr objects, 975
value attribute
   button elements, 243
   input elements, 339
   li elements, 357
   option elements, 390
   param elements, 393
value property, 47
   Attr objects, 560
   attribute objects, 560
   button objects, 577
   input (type="button") objects, 729
   input (type="checkbox") objects, 733
   input (type="file") objects, 737
   input (type="hidden") objects, 740
   input (type="password") objects, 748
   input (type="radio") objects, 753
   input (type="reset") objects, 755
   input (type="submit") objects, 758
   input (type="text") objects, 762
   li objects, 776
   option objects, 824
   param objects, 830
   select objects, 866
   textarea objects, 959
valueOf( ) method
   Boolean objects, 1135
   Date objects, 1147
   function objects, 1155
   Number objects, 1171
   Object objects, 1174
   String objects, 1190
values
   assigning to attributes, 50
   attribute values, 8, 111
   changing for attributes, 82–85, 111, 112
   changing for styles, 112–117
   clip attribute, 79
   edge measurement attributes, 78
   identifiers as index values, 108
   none value, 81
   return false, 162
valuetype attribute
   param elements, 394
valueType property
   param objects, 830
var elements, 466
var objects, 542, 982
var statement, 1213
variable content (see dynamic content)

variables
  environment variable, 36
  global variables, 86
  local variables, 155
VBArray objects, 1190
VBScript scripting language, 18, 150, 161
vendor property
  navigator object, 806
vendorSub property
  navigator object, 806
version attribute
  html elements, 304
  script elements, 406
version property
  html objects, 704
versions, 4, 19
vertical-align attribute (CSS), 1116
verticalAlign property
  CSSStyleDeclaration objects, 919
  style objects, 919
view property
  event objects, 672
ViewCSS objects, 982
virtual documents, 133
visibility attribute, 81, 84
  ilayer elements, 316
  layer elements, 353
visibility attribute (CSS), 1116
visibility property, 84
  CSSStyleDeclaration objects, 919
  layer objects, 770
  style objects, 919
visible property
  directories objects, 605
  locationbar objects, 605
  menubar objects, 605
  personalbar objects, 605
  scrollbars objects, 605
  statusbar objects, 605
  toolbar objects, 605
visible value
  overflow attribute, 80
  visibility attribute, 81
:visited pseudo-class, 1042
vlink attribute
  body elements, 239
vLink property
  body objects, 574
vlinkColor property
  document objects, 625
voiceFamily
  CSSStyleDeclaration objects, 881

voice-family attribute (CSS), 1117
voiceFamily property
  CSSStyleDeclaration objects, 920
  style objects, 881, 920
void operator, 107, 1204
volume attribute
  bgsound elements, 231
volume attribute (CSS), 1117
volume property
  bgsound objects, 568
  CSSStyleDeclaration objects, 881, 920
  style objects, 881, 920
vspace attribute
  applet elements, 217, 219
  iframe elements, 308, 311
  img elements, 322, 327
  input elements, 333, 340
  marquee elements, 367, 369
  object elements, 382, 385
vspace property
  applet objects, 549, 550
  iframe objects, 710, 711
  img objects, 718, 722
  input (type="image") objects, 742, 744
  marquee objects, 791, 792
  object objects, 817, 819

## W

W3C DOM
  abstract model and, 18
  applied style values, 112
  architecture, 14–16
  changing element text, 120–123
  changing elements, 126–129
  computed style, 29
  creating element example, 30
  custom newsletter example, 144
  dynamic content, 26, 101
  element containment and, 47
  event objects, 154
  event propagation, 165
  Events module, 27
  getComputedStyles( ) method, 85
  IE 4 model and, 23
  measurement properties supported, 84
  modularization, 180, 181
  page branching example, 36
  positioning attributes, 70
  reading attribute values, 111
  reference syntax, 25, 83
  script access to document tree, 136
  style objects, 82, 113

W3C DOM (continued)
   styleSheet object properties, 116
   text content, 118
   text range, 140
   XML and, 117
W3C DOM Working Group, 7, 14, 178
W3C (World Wide Consortium), 5
WAI (Web Accessibility Initiative), 17
watch( ) method
   Global objects, 1162
wbr elements, 466
wbr objects, 982
web browsers (see browsers)
web content development
   cross-platform strategies, 32–41, 86
   custom APIs, 88–94
   custom newsletter example, 142–149
   fragmentation, 19
   impact of containment, 45
   platform considerations, 22
   prerelease versions and, 4
   separating design from content, 56
   standardization and, 179
   striking balance, 180
   WAI and, 17
web pages
   beta versions and, 4, 5
   GUI improvements, 6
   need for accessibility, 32
   overlaying to different pages, 37
WEFT tool, 27
weight attribute
   font elements, 278
weight property, 144
whatToShow property
   NodeIterator objects, 810
   TreeWalker objects, 977
wheelDelta property
   event objects, 672
which property
   event objects, 672
while statement, 1210
whitespace
   attribute/value pairs and, 53
   overflow content and, 134
   text nodes and, 123
   XML documents and, 137
white-space attribute (CSS), 1118
whiteSpace property
   CSSStyleDeclaration objects, 920
   style objects, 920
widows attribute (CSS), 1118

widows property
   CSSStyleDeclaration objects, 906, 920
   style objects, 906, 920
width attribute
   applet elements, 216, 219
   col elements, 251
   colgroup elements, 256
   embed elements, 271, 274
   frame elements, 287, 290
   hr elements, 302
   iframe elements, 307, 311
   ilayer elements, 314, 316
   img elements, 322, 327
   input elements, 332, 340
   layer elements, 351, 354
   marquee elements, 366, 369
   multicol elements, 374
   object elements, 382, 385
   pre elements, 396
   spacer elements, 412, 413
width attribute (CSS), 1119
width property
   applet objects, 549, 550
   col objects, 587
   colgroup objects, 587
   CSSStyleDeclaration objects, 899, 920
   document objects, 617, 625
   embed objects, 649, 651
   frame objects, 692, 694
   hr objects, 703
   iframe objects, 709, 711
   img objects, 718, 722
   input (type="image") objects, 742, 744
   marquee objects, 791, 792
   object objects, 817, 819
   pre objects, 837
   screen object, 856, 857
   style objects, 899, 920
   table objects, 937, 939
   td objects, 952
   td, th objects, 951
   th objects, 952
wildcards, 65
Window object, 87, 105
window objects, 983
window property
   window objects, 996
windows
   creating new documents, 102
   iframe element as, 133
   writing to, 103–106
Windows Media Player, 28

with statement, 1211
word-break attribute (CSS), 1119
wordBreak property
    CSSStyleDeclaration objects, 920
    style objects, 920
word-spacing attribute (CSS), 1120
wordSpacing property
    CSSStyleDeclaration objects, 921
    style objects, 921
word-wrap attribute (CSS), 1120
wordWrap property
    CSSStyleDeclaration objects, 921
    style objects, 921
World Wide Consortium (W3C)
wrap attribute
    pre elements, 396
wrap property
    textarea objects, 959
write( ) method
    Document objects, 38, 101–103, 106
    document objects, 639
writeln( ) method
    Document objects, 102
    document objects, 639
writing-mode attribute (CSS), 1121
writingMode property
    CSSStyleDeclaration objects, 921
    style objects, 921

**X**

x property
    event objects, 673
    img objects, 722
XHTML
    capabilities, 7–9
    HTML name changes, 5
    modularization, 181–183
    validation, 151, 157, 159
XHTML Basic, 181
xml
    lang attribute, 201
    space attribute
        script elements, 406
XML documents
    behaviors, 161
    element requirements, 126

table data sources, 129
    whitespace in, 137
xml elements, 467
XML Events, 160
XML (Extensible Markup Language)
    embedding data, 136–140
    external documents and, 133
    HTML 4 standard and, 7
    repopulating tables, 30
    slash technique, 8
    W3C DOM and, 117
xml objects, 1013
XMLDocument property
    xml objects, 1014
xmlns attribute
    html elements, 304
xmp elements, 467
xmp objects, 1014
.xul extension, 31

**Y**

y property
    event objects, 673
    img objects, 722

**Z**

zero values, 35
zero-fill right-shift operator (>>>), 1195
z-index attribute, 81, 84
    CSS, 1121
    ilayer elements, 316
    layer elements, 354
zIndex property, 84
    CSSStyleDeclaration objects, 921
    layer objects, 770
    style objects, 921
z-index value, 88
zoom attribute (CSS), 1122
zoom property
    CSSStyleDeclaration objects, 922
    style objects, 922
z-order, 81

## About the Author

**Danny Goodman** has been writing about personal computers and consumer electronics since the late 1970s. In 2001, he celebrated 20 years as a freelance writer and programmer, having published hundreds of magazine articles, several commercial software products, and three dozen computer books. Through the years, his most popular book titles—on HyperCard, AppleScript, JavaScript, and Dynamic HTML—have covered programming environments that are accessible to nonprofessionals yet powerful enough to engage experts. His *JavaScript Bible* book is now in its fourth edition.

To keep up to date on the needs of web developers for his recent books, Danny is also a programming consultant to some of the industry's top intranet development groups and corporations. His expertise in implementing sensible cross-browser client-side scripting solutions is in high demand and allows him to, in his words, "get code under my fingernails while solving real-world problems."

Danny was born in Chicago, Illinois during the Truman Administration. He earned a B.A. and M.A. in Classical Antiquity from the University of Wisconsin, Madison. He moved to California in 1983 and lives in a small San Francisco–area coastal community, where he alternates views between computer screens and the Pacific Ocean.

## Colophon

Our look is the result of reader comments, our own experimentation, and feedback from distribution channels. Distinctive covers complement our distinctive approach to technical topics, breathing personality and life into potentially dry subjects.

The animal on the cover of *Dynamic HTML: The Definitive Reference*, Second Edition, is a flamingo. Flamingos are easily identifiable by their long legs and neck, turned-down bill, and bright color, which ranges from white to pink to bright red. There are five living species of flamingo, encompassing the family *Phoenicopteridae*. Flamingos are found in Asia, Africa, Europe, South American, and the Caribbean islands. Although wild flamingos are sometimes seen in Florida, they do not naturally nest in the United States.

Flamingos feed on small crustaceans, algae, and other unicellular organisms. Their unusually shaped bills provide flamingos with a unique food-filtering system. A flamingo eats by placing its head upside down below the water surface and sucking in water and small food particles through the serrated edges of its bill. The flamingo then pushes its thick, fleshy tongue forward, forcing the water out but trapping the food particles on lamellae inside the beak.

As a result of this filtration system, flamingos can eat foods few other birds can, and thus can live in otherwise inhospitable salt lakes and brackish waters. The filtration technique varies in the different species of flamingo. As a result of this differentiation, several species can live in the same water source and not disturb each other.

Flamingos are very gregarious birds, and they nest in colonies that sometimes consist of thousands of birds. Males and females together build nests. The nests are composed of mud, stones, and shells, shaped in a cone formation. One, and occasionally two, eggs are laid in a shallow depression at the top of the cone. Both sexes incubate the eggs for 27 to 31 days.

In the wild, flamingos tend to live in remote, difficult-to-reach areas. In the suburbs, however, they stand guard over many a front lawn.

Colleen Gorman was the production editor and copyeditor for *Dynamic HTML: The Definitive Reference*, Second Edition. Sheryl Avruch, Linley Dolby, and Matt Hutchinson provided quality control. Lucie Haskins wrote the index.

Edie Freedman designed the cover of this book. The cover image is a 19th-century engraving from the Dover Pictorial Archive. Emma Colby produced the cover layout with QuarkXPress 4.1 using Adobe's ITC Garamond font.

Melanie Wang designed the interior layout, based on a series design by David Futato. This book was converted to FrameMaker 5.5.6 with a format conversion tool created by Erik Ray, Jason McIntosh, Neil Walls, and Mike Sierra that uses Perl and XML technologies. The text font is Linotype Birka; the heading font is Adobe Myriad Condensed; and the code font is LucasFont's TheSans Mono Condensed. The illustrations that appear in the book were produced by Robert Romano and Jessamyn Read using Macromedia FreeHand 9 and Adobe Photoshop 6. This colophon was written by Clairemarie Fisher O'Leary.

# Other Titles Available from O'Reilly

## Web Programming

### ActionScript for Flash MX: The Definitive Guide, 2nd Edition

*By Colin Moock*
*2nd Edition November 2002 (est.)*
*904 pages (est.), ISBN 0-596-00396-X*

This is the only complete, up-to-date reference available for the latest version of ActionScript, Macromedia's programming language for Flash. The book's language reference alone has nearly doubled from the first edition, with over 250 new classes, objects, methods, and properties! Hundreds of new code examples show new Flash MX techniques in the real world—how to draw circles, save data to disk, convert arrays to onscreen tables, create reusable components, and preload variables, XML and sounds.

### Programming ColdFusion MX, 2nd Edition

*By Rob Brooks-Bilson*
*2nd Edition November 2002 (est.)*
*1000 pages (est.), ISBN 0-596-00380-3*

This exhaustive resource covers everything from ColdFusion basics to advanced topics, so not only is the book ideal for intermediate developers—with topics on sharing application data and accessing databases—*Programming ColdFusion MX* continues to be a one-stop clearinghouse on techniques for the most seasoned ColdFusion developers. Topics include advanced database techniques, working with the Verity search engine, interacting with data sources such as LDAP directories, creating custom tags, integrating ColdFusion with Flash, and calling external objects.

### JavaScript: The Definitive Guide, 4th Edition

*By David Flanagan*
*4th Edition November 2001*
*936 pages, ISBN 0-596-00048-0*

To stay on top of their work, web professionals need the most up-to-date, complete reference available on the core JavaScript language, which is growing more and more essential for effective web design and development. This new edition covers JavaScript 1.5, the latest version of the language. The book's comprehensive reference section documents every object, property, method, event handler, function and constructor used by client-side JavaScript.

### HTTP: The Definitive Guide

*By Brian Totty & David Gourley with Marjorie Sayer, Anshu Aggarwal & Sailu Reddy*
*1st Edition September 2002 (est.)*
*700 (est.) pages, ISBN 1-56592-509-2*

*HTTP: The Definitive Guide* gives a complete and detailed description of the HTTP protocol and how it shapes the landscape of the Web. It doesn't stop at a simple listing of the HTTP methods and headers, but explains HTTP in context of the web technologies that it supports. This is a book that every serious web programmer will need on his or her shelf.

### Building Data-Driven Web Sites with Dreamweaver MX

*By Simon Allardice*
*1st Edition December 2002 (est.)*
*375 pages (est.), ISBN 0-596-00340-4*

The book teaches power users, step by step, how to create web pages with Dreamweaver MX (formerly UltraDev) that access a remote database using ColdFusion, ASP, ASP .Net, JSP, or PHP—without a lot of programming. Readers will benefit from the author's first-hand knowledge and polished teaching style.

### Creating Applications with Mozilla

*By David Boswell, Brian King, Ian Oeschger, Pete Collins & Eric Murphy*
*1st Edition September 2002 (est.)*
*480 pages (est.), ISBN 0-59600052-9*

This book is designed for anyone interested in learning more about what Mozilla really is and how to create applications using Mozilla technologies. Already applications such as Netscape 6, ActiveState's Komodo, Jabberzilla and many others have taken advantage of Mozilla's unique abilities as a development framework. After reading this book you will also be able to take advantage of this framework for your own applications.

# O'REILLY®

To order: *800-998-9938* • *order@oreilly.com* • *www.oreilly.com*
Online editions of most O'Reilly titles are available by subscription at *safari.oreilly.com*
Also available at most retail and online bookstores.

# Web Programming

### Web Services Essentials

*By Ethan Cerami*
*1st Edition February 2002*
*304 pages, ISBN 0-596-00224-6*

This concise book gives programmers both a concrete introduction and handy reference to XML web services. It explains the foundations of this new breed of distributed services, demonstrates quick ways to create services with open-source Java tools, and explores four key emerging technologies: XML-RPC, SOAP, UDDI, and WSDL. If you want to break through the Web Services hype and find useful information on these evolving technologies, look no further.

### PHP Pocket Reference, 2nd Edition

*By Rasmus Lerdorf*
*1st Edition November 2002 (est.)*
*96 pages (est.), ISBN 0-596-00402-8*

Written by the founder of the PHP Project, this valuable little book is both a handy introduction to PHP syntax and structure, and a quick reference to the vast array of functions provided by PHP. Thoroughly updated to include the specifics of PHP 4, the language's latest version, the second edition provides an authoritative overview of PHP packed into a pocket-sized guide that's easy to take anywhere. This handbook acts as a perfect tutorial for learning the basics of developing PHP-based web applications, and is the ideal companion for O'Reilly's *Programming PHP*.

### Web Database Applications with PHP & MySQL

*By Hugh E. Williams & David Lane*
*1st Edition March 2002*
*582 pages, ISBN 0-596-00041-3*

This book offers both theoretical and practical guidance for creating web database applications. The detailed information on designing relational databases and the web application architectures that interact with them will be especially useful to readers who have worked with or built database-backed web sites before. The book implements a sample web application using PHP and MySQL on the Apache platform.

### PHP Cookbook

*By David Sklar & Adam Trachtenberg*
*1st Edition October 2002 (est.)*
*500 pages (est.), ISBN 1-56592-681-1*

This cookbook has a wealth of solutions for problems that PHP programmers face regularly. With topics that range from beginner questions to advanced web programming techniques, the *PHP Cookbook* contains practical examples—or "recipes"—for any programmer or web designer who uses the scripting language to generate dynamic web content. With each recipe, the authors include a discussion that explains the logic and concepts underlying the solution.

### Programming PHP

*By Rasmus Lerdorf & Kevin Tatroe*
*1st Edition March 2002*
*528 pages, ISBN 1-56592-610-2*

*Programming PHP* is a comprehensive guide to PHP, a simple yet powerful language for creating dynamic web content. Filled with the unique knowledge of the creator of PHP, Rasmus Lerdorf, this book is a detailed reference to the language and its applications, including such topics as form processing, sessions, databases, XML, and graphics. Covers PHP 4, the latest version of the language.

## Web Authoring and Design

### HTML & XHTML: The Definitive Guide, 5th Edition

*By Chuck Musciano & Bill Kennedy*
*5th Edition August 2002*
*672 pages, ISBN 0-596-00382-X*

Our new edition offers web developers a better way to become HTML-fluent, by covering the language syntax, semantics, and variations in detail and demonstrating the difference between good and bad usage. Packed with examples, *HTML & XHTML: The Definitive Guide*, 5th Edition covers Netscape Navigator 6, Internet Explorer 6, HTML 4.01, XHTML 1.0, JavaScript 1.5, CSS2, Layers, and all of the features supported by the popular web browsers.

### Cascading Style Sheets: The Definitive Guide

*By Eric A. Meyer*
*1st Edition May 2000*
*470 pages, ISBN 1-56592-622-6*

CSS is the HTML 4.0–approved method for controlling visual presentation on web pages. *Cascading Style Sheets: The Definitive Guide* offers a complete, detailed review of CSS1 properties and other aspects of CSS1. Each property is explored individually in detail with discussion of how each interacts with other properties. There is also information on how to avoid common mistakes in interpretation. This book is the first major title to cover CSS in a way that acknowledges and describes current browser support, instead of simply describing the way things work in theory. It offers both advanced and novice web authors a comprehensive guide to implementation of CSS.

### Learning Web Design

*By Jennifer Niederst*
*1st Edition March 2001*
*418 pages, ISBN 0-596-00036-7*

In *Learning Web Design*, Jennifer Niederst shares the knowledge she's gained from years of experience as both web designer and teacher. She starts from the very beginning—defining the Internet, the Web, browsers, and URLs—assuming no previous knowledge of how the Web works. Jennifer helps you build the solid foundation in HTML, graphics, and design principles that you need for crafting effective web pages.

### Web Design in a Nutshell, 2nd Edition

*By Jennifer Niederst*
*2nd Edition September 2001*
*640 pages, ISBN 0-596-00196-7*

*Web Design in a Nutshell* contains the nitty-gritty on everything you need to know to design web pages. Written by veteran web designer Jennifer Niederst, this book provides quick access to the wide range of technologies and techniques from which web designers and authors must draw. Topics include understanding the web environment, HTML, graphics, multimedia and interactivity, and emerging technologies.

### The Web Design CD Bookshelf

*By O'Reilly & Associates, Inc.*
*1st Edition, November 2001*
*(Includes CD-ROM)*
*640 pages, ISBN 0-596-00271-8*

Six best selling O'Reilly Animal Guides are now available on CD-ROM, easily accessible and searchable with your favorite web browser: *HTML & XHTML: The Definitive Guide*, 4th Edition; *ActionScript: The Definitive Guide*; *Information Architecture for the World Wide Web*; *Designing Web Audio: RealAudio, MP3, Flash, and Beatnik*; *Web Design In a Nutshell*, 2nd Edition; and *Cascading Style Sheets: The Definitive Guide*. As a bonus, you also get the new paperback version of *Web Design in a Nutshell*, 2nd Edition.

### Designing with JavaScript, 2nd Edition

*By Nick Heinle & Bill Pena*
*2nd Edition November 2001*
*240 pages, ISBN 1-56592-360-X*

This major revision to Nick Heinle's best-selling book, is written for the beginning web designers who are the focus of our Web Studio series, teaching core JavaScript with many useful examples and powerful libraries. The second half of the book goes beyond core JavaScript, explaining objects and more powerful event models, and showing how JavaScript can manipulate not only HTML but also XML, CSS (Cascading Style Sheets), and more.

# O'REILLY®

To order: *800-998-9938* • *order@oreilly.com* • *www.oreilly.com*
Online editions of most O'Reilly titles are available by subscription at *safari.oreilly.com*
Also available at most retail and online bookstores.

# How to stay in touch with O'Reilly

## 1. Visit our award-winning web site

*http://www.oreilly.com/*

★ "Top 100 Sites on the Web"—PC Magazine
★ CIO Magazine's Web Business 50 Awards

Our web site contains a library of comprehensive product information (including book excerpts and tables of contents), downloadable software, background articles, interviews with technology leaders, links to relevant sites, book cover art, and more. File us in your bookmarks or favorites!

## 2. Join our email mailing lists

Sign up to get email announcements of new books and conferences, special offers, and O'Reilly Network technology newsletters at:

*http://www.elists.oreilly.com*

It's easy to customize your free elists subscription so you'll get exactly the O'Reilly news you want.

## 3. Get examples from our books

To find example files for a book, go to:

*http://www.oreilly.com/catalog*

select the book, and follow the "Examples" link.

## 4. Work with us

Check out our web site for current employment opportunities:

*http://jobs.oreilly.com/*

## 5. Register your book

Register your book at:

*http://register.oreilly.com*

## 6. Contact us

**O'Reilly & Associates, Inc.**
1005 Gravenstein Hwy North
Sebastopol, CA 95472  USA
TEL:  707-827-7000 or 800-998-9938
     (6am to 5pm PST)
FAX:  707-829-0104

**order@oreilly.com**
For answers to problems regarding your order or our products. To place a book order online visit:

*http://www.oreilly.com/order_new/*

**catalog@oreilly.com**
To request a copy of our latest catalog.

**booktech@oreilly.com**
For book content technical questions or corrections.

**corporate@oreilly.com**
For educational, library, and corporate sales.

**proposals@oreilly.com**
To submit new book proposals to our editors and product managers.

**international@oreilly.com**
For information about our international distributors or translation queries. For a list of our distributors outside of North America check out:

*http://international.oreilly.com/distributors.html*

# O'REILLY®

# Notes

## O'REILLY®

To order: *800-998-9938* • *order@oreilly.com* • *www.oreilly.com*
Online editions of most O'Reilly titles are available by subscription at *safari.oreilly.com*
Also available at most retail and online bookstores.